The Euro

On 1 January 1999 eleven EU Member States adopted a new currency – the euro. The introduction of the euro was a remarkable feat in the history of European monetary, financial, economic and political integration. It was an event of worldwide significance. Despite much criticism and predictions that it would quickly collapse, the first decade of the euro has been a remarkable success. The euro area has now expanded to sixteen members with a combined population of 326 million and contributes 16 per cent of global output. This book is the first to provide a wide-ranging strategic review of the first decade of the euro. Written by an impressive line-up of academic and professional economists, *The Euro: The First Decade* is an invaluable reference for scholars and policy makers who wish to know more about the successes and failures of the euro and the challenges that lie ahead.

MARCO BUTI is Director-General of the Directorate-General for Economic and Financial Affairs at the European Commission.

SERVAAS DEROOSE is Director for the Macroeconomy of the Euro Area and the Union in the Directorate-General of Economic and Financial Affairs at the European Commission.

VÍTOR GASPAR is Acting Director-General of the Bureau of European Policy Advisers at the European Commission.

JOÃO NOGUEIRA MARTINS is an economic adviser to the Director-General of the Directorate-General for Economic and Financial Affairs at the European Commission.

The Euro

The First Decade

Edited by

MARCO BUTI,
SERVAAS DEROOSE,
VÍTOR GASPAR
and
JOÃO NOGUEIRA MARTINS

CAMBRIDGE
UNIVERSITY PRESS

CAMBRIDGE UNIVERSITY PRESS
Cambridge, New York, Melbourne, Madrid, Cape Town, Singapore,
São Paulo, Delhi, Dubai, Tokyo

Cambridge University Press
The Edinburgh Building, Cambridge CB2 8RU, UK

Published in the United States of America by Cambridge University Press, New York

www.cambridge.org
Information on this title: www.cambridge.org/9789279098420

First published 2010

Printed in the United Kingdom at the University Press, Cambridge

A catalogue record for this publication is available from the British Library

ISBN 978-9-279-09842-0 Hardback

To Klaus Regling

Contents

Figures

Comments

Tables

Comments

Boxes

List of contributors

Lourdes Acedo Montoya
CEPS, Brussels

Christopher Allsopp
Oxford Institute of Energy Studies and New College,
University of Oxford

Julian Alworth
Saïd Business School, Oxford University and Econpubblica –
Università Bocconi

Giampaolo Arachi
Università del Salento and Econpubblica – Università Bocconi

Richard Baldwin
Graduate Institute, Geneva

Ray Barrell
National Institute of Economic and Social Research

Iain Begg
European Institute, London School of Economics and Political
Science

Giuseppe Bertola
Università di Torino and CEPR

Michael Bordo
Rutgers University and NBER

Marco Buti
Directorate-General for Economic and Financial Affairs
(European Commission)

Giancarlo Corsetti
European University Institute,
University of Rome III and CEPR

Zsolt Darvas
Bruegel, Brussels, Institute of Economics at the Hungarian Academy of
Sciences and Corvinus University of Budapest

Xavier Debrun
International Monetary Fund

Jörg Decressin
International Monetary Fund

Servaas Deroose
Directorate-General for Economic and Financial
Affairs (European Commission)

Barry Eichengreen
University of California, Berkeley

Carlo Favero
IGIER-Università Bocconi and CEPR

Vítor Gaspar
Bureau of European Policy Advisers (European Commission)

Petra Geraats
University of Cambridge

Stefan Gerlach
Institute for Monetary and Financial Stability,
University of Frankfurt and CEPR

Domenico Giannone
European Central Bank, ECARES and CEPR

Francesco Giavazzi
IGIER-Università Bocconi, MIT, CEPR and NBER

Philipp Hartmann
European Central Bank

Simon Hayes
Barclays Capital

Peter Hoeller
OECD

Mathias Hoffmann
Institute for Empirical Research in Economics,
University of Zurich

Dawn Holland
National Institute of Economic and Social Research

Harold James
Princeton University and European University Institute

Tullio Jappelli
University of Naples Federico II, CSEF and CEPR

Robert Kollmann
ECARES, ECORE, Université Libre de Bruxelles,
Université Paris XII and CEPR

Gert Jan Koopman
Directorate-General for Economic and Financial
Affairs (European Commission)

Martin Larch
Bureau of European Policy Advisers (European Commission)

Michele Lenza
European Central Bank

Iana Liadze
National Institute of Economic and Social Research

Alessandro Maravalle
College of Europe, Bruges

Francesco Paolo Mongelli
European Central Bank

Manfred J. M. Neumann
University of Bonn

João Nogueira Martins
Directorate-General for Economic and Financial
Affairs (European Commission)

Marco Pagano
University of Naples Federico II, CSEF and CEPR

Elias Papaioannou
Dartmouth College and CEPR

Jacques Pelkmans
College of Europe, Bruges, and Vlerick School of Management,
Leuven and Ghent

Lucio Pench
Directorate-General for Economic and Financial Affairs
(European Commission)

Karl Pichelmann
European Commission and IEE, Université Libre de Bruxelles

Jean Pisani-Ferry
Bruegel, Brussels, and Université Paris-Dauphine

Olga Pomerantz
National Institute of Economic and Social Research

Richard Portes
London Business School and CEPR

Lucrezia Reichlin
European Central Bank and CEPR

Gilles Saint-Paul
Toulouse School of Economics and Birkbeck College

André Sapir
Université Libre de Bruxelles, Bruegel and CEPR

Frank Smets
European Central Bank

Emil Stavrev
International Monetary Fund

György Szapáry
Central European University

Niels Thygesen
University of Copenhagen and OECD

Casper van Ewijk
CPB Netherlands Bureau for Economic Policy Analysis,
University of Amsterdam

David Vines
Balliol College, University of Oxford; Australian National
University and CEPR

Jürgen von Hagen
University of Bonn, Indiana University and CEPR

Charles Wyplosz
Graduate Institute of International Studies and CEPR

Foreword

The creation of an Economic and Monetary Union (EMU) in Europe in 1999 was a major and unprecedented event in economic history, and the most tangible step forward in European integration since the Treaty of Rome.

The euro is still a young currency. However, in the short space of a decade, it has accumulated a reputation of solidity and stability, and brought overwhelming benefits to the European economy: both to citizens and to businesses. The contributions collected in this book demonstrate that EMU has been a resounding success. This view is now consensual among economists, although not everything has been perfect. Nevertheless, those who promoted and laid the foundations of EMU have been vindicated; the Cassandras and sceptics who thought the euro was an impossible project or predicted disaster were proven wrong. Testimony to its success is the fact that since its creation, the euro-area membership has been extended from the original eleven to sixteen members, and several other EU countries are lining up to join in future, as soon as they fulfil the convergence criteria of the EU Treaty. The economic advantages of EMU are overwhelming for all its members. In fact, the advantages of belonging to a monetary area with a solid and stable currency increase, and are better perceived by citizens and businesses, in times of hardship.

The European economy – together with the rest of the world – is experiencing testing times. The turmoil that originated in the US sub-prime mortgage market in the summer of 2007 spread into financial markets and impacted economies the world over, in particular after the failure of Lehman Brothers, in September 2008. A squeeze on credit, falls in real estate prices and tumbling stock markets have reinforced a slump in consumer confidence, consumption and investment. Given the global nature and magnitude of the recession, the euro area could not escape unscathed.

I am very much aware of the economic difficulties felt by many European citizens during this crisis, which is the most severe in our lifetime. The Commission, together with the European Central Bank and EU governments have taken every available measure to restore confidence to financial markets and return economic growth.

Clearly, the crisis constitutes a major challenge for the euro-area economy. However, I am profoundly convinced – and there is ample evidence to confirm – that the impact of this global crisis would be disproportionately more severe if each country had to respond to events individually, to worry about the reputation of its national money in foreign exchange markets, to prepare its economy against unexpected depreciation in partners' currencies and sudden changes in competitiveness.

Indeed, the euro is protecting its members from the worst of the economic and financial crisis in several important ways. First, the euro has permanently eliminated the exchange-rate instability and speculative attacks that its members could have expected during the financial turmoil. It suffices to study the foreign exchange crises at the beginning of the nineties to understand how painful disorderly movements in exchange rates can be for highly integrated economic areas. Second, the euro area benefits from an independent central bank whose swift actions to ease liquidity constraints and coordinate monetary policy have helped to avert a financial meltdown. Such rapid, coordinated, steps by sixteen national central banks would have been unthinkable. Moreover, the reputation of the ECB and its strong commitment to price stability were of paramount importance in ensuring that the acceleration in prices in the last months of 2007 and first half of 2008 – because of unexpected and abrupt changes in commodity prices – were transient and did not imply damaging second-round effects. Third, the increase in financial integration over the first decade of the euro has contributed to sharing risks, and a larger financial market contributed to absorbing reverberations in a much more effective way than with segmented domestic markets. Fourth, the EMU's stability-oriented macroeconomic framework has better prepared euro-area countries to deal with a downturn. The fiscal rules of the Stability and Growth Pact helped the euro-area countries to improve fiscal positions and to widen their margins of fiscal manoeuvre, which they can now use to fight the crisis. However, the crisis has also revealed a number of shortcomings and unfinished business for EMU, notably in terms of structural reforms, long-term fiscal sustainability and the external representation of the euro area.

Beyond the current global crisis, I see several clusters of challenges for the euro area. The first concerns the reform of the international financial architecture. This crisis has shaken the foundations of the global economic and financial system. We bear a heavy responsibility in ensuring that such a crisis cannot occur in the future. This requires putting in place a new financial system, one based on transparency, rigorous supervision and vigilant risk management. Although the genesis of the crisis was not in Europe, we have already tabled a number of important legislative proposals to tackle some of the failings that contributed to its propagation. We have taken steps to protect bank depositors, adapt accounting rules, regulate the activities of credit rating agencies and strengthen rules on capital requirements. A priority is to finally resolve the issue of cross-border supervision in Europe. After years of piecemeal advances, we can no longer push this issue to the side.

Before the emergence of the global crisis, in our report 'EMU@10', the Commission had already identified a number of megatrends that would drive the agenda of euro-area reform in the years to come. These trends, namely globalisation, population ageing, climate change and the increasing scarcity of natural resources will, over the next decades, pose challenges for the performance of all advanced economies in terms of growth, macroeconomic stability, the ability to withstand, and adjust to, shocks, and the sustainability of social protection institutions. However, they are even more compelling for the European economy considering its relatively low growth potential and adjustment capacity, and the need to safeguard our European social model. To manage these trends and avoid them running counter to our economic goals, the euro area needs to deepen and broaden macroeconomic surveillance with the aim of identifying and correcting macroeconomic imbalances in a timely fashion; to foster structural reforms and better integrate them in EMU coordination mechanisms; to build an international strategy for the euro area that is commensurate with the international role of our currency, and to adapt accordingly our institutional practices and governance of the euro area.

Making EMU work better in the future will embed stability in Europe in a world of intense transition and fierce competition. It will increase prosperity for citizens of the EU and serve as a tool for alleviating social inequalities. A well-governed, successfully enlarging euro area will deepen integration between Member States and strengthen and extend the EU's sphere of influence. It will give us crucial leverage to influence global dialogue and decision making.

In an increasingly complex world, effective policy makers need to be in permanent discussion with the academic world, learning from new ideas, identifying relevant insights and avoiding the pitfalls revealed by research. The European Commission has a long tradition of inter-acting with academia. This book is one more example of that fruitful cooperation.

All the economists who have contributed to this volume are both distinguished scholars and active participants in the policy debate. Over the years, they have greatly helped policy makers, at the national and EU level, to identify and understand the issues involved in the running of EMU. I have learned a lot from them and am grateful for their con-tribution to this book. I hope that this book will prompt constructive discussion and inspire new analyses both to detect new challenges and to help shape our responses to the current ones.

Joaquín Almunia
Commissioner for Economic and Monetary Affairs

Acknowledgements

This book would not have been possible without the concerted efforts of many people. We would like to thank, first and foremost, all the authors and discussants for their contributions and for coping with our repeated and pressing requests.

Our thanks go also to Klaus Regling, Director-General of Economic and Financial Affairs at the time the preparation of this book started, for his support and encouragement.

We are also grateful to several colleagues of the Directorate-General of Economic and Financial Affairs and of the Bureau of European Policy Advisers, who provided valuable suggestions on the initial versions of each chapter.

We are also indebted to Aurélie Thérace and Christina Jordan for help in preparing the 'manuscript' and the index.

Finally, Chris Harrison and Philip Good guided the publication process at Cambridge University Press.

Marco Buti
Servaas Deroose
Vítor Gaspar
João Nogueira Martins

1 | *The euro: the first decade and beyond*

MARCO BUTI, SERVAAS DEROOSE,
VÍTOR GASPAR AND JOÃO NOGUEIRA MARTINS

1. Introduction

On 1 January 1999 eleven EU Member States adopted a new currency – the euro. The introduction of the euro was a remarkable feat in the history of European monetary, financial, economic and political integration. It was an event of world significance.

Many sceptics had predicted that Economic and Monetary Union (EMU)[1] would never take place or, if it were created, would quickly collapse. In the first years, perceptions about the euro were under the shadow of foreign exchange rate movements as the euro rate plummeted well below parity against the US dollar. Moreover, popular perception suffered as the changeover to the euro banknotes and coins coincided with rising energy and food prices. In many countries the euro was unfairly perceived by public opinion as substantially contributing to the increase in prices.[2]

However, the first decade of the euro area was very successful. It was the result of a coherent framework for stability-oriented policies. At the same time it benefited from favourable supply conditions – associated with fast technological progress and globalisation – justifying accommodative monetary policies all around the world. Moreover the fiscal position in many countries benefited from windfalls associated with booms in real estate and other asset markets. The first decade of the euro area was a period of remarkable macroeconomic stability between two major challenges: the challenge, in the early years, of establishing the credibility of the new regime and, at the end of the first decade and still ongoing, the need to respond to the global economic and financial crisis.

The euro area, with sixteen members[3] in 2009, has a population of 326 million – 5 per cent of world population – and contributes 16 per cent

The views are those of the authors and are not attributable to the European Commission.

1

of global output. The euro area is thus the second economy in the world, after the United States, which generates 21 per cent of global GDP. In spite of disparities across Member States, the euro area as a whole is one of the most prosperous areas of the world, as measured by per capita GDP. Table 1.1 shows a number of main economic indicators for the euro area and compares it with a number of other large economies; Table 1.2 gathers several indicators for the last four decades in the territory that constitutes the euro area and in the USA.

The tenth anniversary of EMU offers an opportunity to revisit the motivations that led to its creation, to document the performance during the first decade, as well as to discuss a number of challenges over several time horizons. This is the aim of this volume and of this overview chapter.[4]

The chapter is organised as follows: Section 2 revisits the political and economic motivations of EMU; Section 3 summarises the main economic achievements of the euro area – which will be discussed in detail in the chapters of this volume. Finally, Section 4 looks into the future, considering the immediate challenges associated with the global crisis, but also some major ones from a longer-term perspective.

2. Motivations for EMU

2.1 Political motivations

The euro and EMU were created for a variety of political and economic reasons. The political reasons were decisive.[5] These were related to the trend initiated in the post-war years, notably with the treaties of Paris and Rome (1951 and 1957), of promoting peace and European unity via economic integration; to the end of the cold war and the need to anchor German reunification in the EU context; as well as to the wish of building a monetary block that could match the USA, and to the perception that a significant share of the American influence on strategic global issues was via the international role of its currency.

The euro is now a tangible symbol of European unity and recognised by citizens as one of the most concrete and successful results of European integration. It is used by millions of people living in sixteen countries, speaking different languages, characterised by different historical memories, traditions, customs, habits, behaviour patterns, cultures and institutions. It is also widely used outside the monetary union borders, in particular in the neighbouring areas.

Table 1.1: *Main indicators for the euro area and other large world economies*

			euro area	EU	US	China	Japan	India	UK	Russia
Population	millions	1	326	496	302	1329	128	1138	61	141
	share (%) of world	2	4.9	7.5	4.6	20.0	1.9	17.2	0.9	2.1
GDP	share (%) of world	3	16.3	22.7	21.2	11.1	6.6	4.6	3.7	3.2
	per capita, % of US	4	71.1	65.2	100	11.9	73.8	5.8	76.3	32.4
	average annual growth rate (1999–2008)	5	2.1	2.3	2.6	9.7	1.4	7.1	2.6	7.0
	idem, per capita	6	1.6	2.0	1.6	9.0	1.3	5.3	2.2	7.5
Industrial structure	% of GDP									
agriculture		7	1.9	1.8	1.2	11.7	1.4	18.1	0.7	4.6
industry		8	26.8	26.6	19.9	49.2	29.1	29.3	23.1	37.4
services		9	71.3	71.6	79.0	39.1	69.5	52.6	76.2	57.9
External accounts	% of world									
exports		10	13.0	16.7	11.4	12.0	7.0	1.5	1.8	3.3
imports		11	13.4	18.0	18.6	8.8	5.7	2.3	2.6	2.2
net borrowing (–) or lending (+)		12	0.3	–0.5	–5.2	10.4	4.7	–	–3.6	5.1

Table 1.1: (*cont.*)

				euro area	EU	US	China	Japan	India	UK	Russia
Inflation rate	average (1999–2008)	13		2.1	2.7	2.9	1.3	–0.3	4.5	1.6	20.5
Government			% of GDP								
total expenditure		14		46.1	45.8	37.4	–	36.0	–	44.4	–
total revenue		15		45.5	44.9	34.6	–	33.8	–	41.6	–
deficit (–) or surplus (+)		16		–0.6	–0.9	–2.8	–1.6	–2.2	–2.8	–2.8	–
gross debt		17		66.1	58.7	63.1	5.4	173.6	–	44.2	–
Labour											
unemployment	% of labour force	18		7.5	7.1	4.6	5.9	3.9	–	5.3	–
employment	% of working age pop.	19		67.4	67.0	73.0	–	76.6	–	72.2	67.4

Notes: Data for 2007, unless otherwise indicated; (2): source of world population: US Census Bureau; (3–4): data are in purchasing power standards (PPS); (5–6): data at constant prices of 2000; (7–9): data for Japan are of 2006; source of data for China: UNSD; (10–11): exports and imports of goods; data for the EU and euro area exclude intra-EU trade; (12): data for China do not include capital transfers; (13) HICP inflation for euro area, EU and UK; national definitions for other economies; (16) source for India: IMF; (18): China: urban population; (19) employment as percentage of working age population.

Sources: Ameco databank, unless indicated otherwise; and own calculations.

Table 1.2: *Economic performance in the euro area and the USA (1970s, 1980s, 1990s and the first decade of EMU)*

		1970–9		1980–9		1990–9		First decade of EMU (1999–2008)	
		euro area	US	euro area	US	euro area	US	euro area	US
GDP (US=100)									
PPS; average	1	90.1	100	86.1	100	82.7	100	77.2	100
PPS; end of period	2	88.9	100	83.1	100	77.6	100	75.7	100
market exchange rates; average	3	78.7	100	74.5	100	89.6	100	77.1	100
GDP per head of population (US=100)									
PPS; average	4	73.7	100	74.8	100	73.3	100	72.5	100
PPS; end of period	5	74.4	100	74.2	100	71.4	100	72.4	100
market exchange rates; average	6	64.5	100	64.7	100	79.3	100	72.5	100
real GDP growth rate per annum (p.a.)	7	3.8	3.3	2.3	3.0	2.1	3.1	2.1	2.6
per head of population	8	3.2	2.2	2.0	2.0	1.8	1.9	1.6	1.6
per person employed	9	3.4	1.3	1.7	1.2	1.9	1.6	1.1	1.7
employment, average growth rate p.a.	10	0.4	2.0	0.5	1.8	0.7	1.2	1.3	1.0
unemployment rate									
average	11	3.8	6.2	8.4	7.3	9.7	5.7	8.3	5.0
end of period	12	5.6	5.8	8.1	5.3	9.2	4.2	7.5	5.7
activity rate	13	63.2	67.5	62.4	73.2	65.5	75.9	69.8	75.5
employment rate	14	63.7	65.2	60.0	69.1	61.4	73.1	65.9	72.9
inflation	15	9.2	7.1	7.5	5.5	2.8	2.7	2.2	2.9
government deficit (–)	16	–2.0	–1.8	–4.4	–3.9	–4.0	–2.6	–1.8	–2.4

Table 1.2: (*cont.*)

		1970–9		1980–9		1990–9		First decade of EMU (1999–2008)	
		euro area	US	euro area	US	euro area	US	euro area	US
government debt; end of period	17	32.9	41.4	55.7	62.0	71.9	61.4	67.2	67.5
external net borrowing (–) / lending (+)	18	0.2	0.2	–0.1	–1.5	0.3	–1.4	0.4	–4.7

Notes: Euro-area data in this table refer to EUR-12 (i.e. excluding Slovenia, Cyprus, Malta and Slovakia). Given the break in series because of German reunification, averages for the 1990s decade for variables (1) to (6) and (11) to (14) have been calculated for the period 1991–9; (11–12): Eurostat definition of unemployment rate; (13): civilian labour force divided by working age population (15–64 years); (14): number of employed persons divided by working age population; (15) average annual increase in the consumer price index; for the euro-area countries: HICP or national indices when the former is not available; (16) government deficit as percentage of GDP; excludes Luxembourg for 1980–9; (17) government consolidated gross debt as percentage of GDP; (18): net lending (+)/borrowing (–) vis-à-vis the rest of the world as percentage of GDP; data for euro area starts in 1971 and exclude Luxembourg for the whole period, Austria and Portugal until 1989 and Greece until 1994.
Source: Ameco databank.

The contribution of EMU to the sense of belonging among Europeans – in particular since the changeover to the euro banknotes and coins in 2002 – should not be neglected, though it may be difficult to measure. One should not ignore either the fact that the prospect of adopting the euro was a powerful magnet for the twelve countries that joined the EU in 2004 and 2007, and for those that are candidates to EU accession. Popular support for the monetary union has remained stable, although EMU has often been used by some political commentators as the scapegoat for inefficiencies and difficulties unrelated to it. In this context, the ongoing global crisis may actually improve the visibility and popularity of the euro in public opinion, since it has demonstrated that monetary union provides insulation against the disruption that the financial crisis could cause on national economies through turbulence in foreign exchange markets. Some small countries neighbouring the euro area have indeed experienced such painful disturbances (e.g. Iceland and Hungary).

However, so far, the monetary union has not been the prelude to a deeper political union that some ambitioned – and several other feared – and does not seem to have whetted the appetite, either of the public opinion, or of political elites, for bolder developments towards political union.[6] In any event the debate on the causes of 'political integration fatigue' seems to have little to do with monetary union.[7]

2.2 *Economic motivations and the optimum currency area (OCA) theory*

As far as economic motivations are concerned, EMU was conceived first and foremost as a complement, not to say a component, of the EU Single Market. Transaction costs and exchange rate risk, associated with different national currencies, constituted barriers to intra-EU trade similar to the physical frontiers and the technical obstacles that the Single European Act (1986) and the single market programme aimed at eliminating.[8] The removal of the physical, technical and monetary barriers was thus expected to boost trade and financial integration among participant countries and to generate a virtuous circle of 'one market–one money–one market'. These trade and financial integration dynamics, together with price transparency and heightened competition, would contribute to a better use of scarce resources, thus increasing productivity and adding to growth.

The traditional OCA theory sees a currency union as a tradeoff between microeconomic efficiency gains, on the one hand, and costs related to inefficient macroeconomic stabilisation, on the other. The costs are related to the fact that, in EMU, monetary policy is decided in a centralised manner, taking into account the macroeconomic conditions of the monetary union as a whole and no longer of each of the participant countries. However, most models – notably those of Lucas (1987 and 2003) – suggest that the costs of inefficient monetary stabilisation are small. Moreover, the benchmark for those costs in the traditional OCA theory is unrealistic, as it assumes that national central banks are always able to pursue country-specific efficient stabilisation, and neglects spillovers on partners. All the more as, in a highly integrated economic area as the EU, exchange rate movements are often a source of disturbances instead of shock absorbers, and that, given the exchange rate mechanism of the EMS, national monetary policies had already lost much of their efficacy as stabilisation tools.

The main economic incentive for most EU countries that decided to participate in EMU was of a macroeconomic nature. This was related to the experience in the seventies and eighties of the costs of an unstable macroeconomic framework with high inflation, high interest rates and unsustainable fiscal policies. EMU eliminated the damaging intra-area exchange rate crises (such as those of 1983, 1987 and 1992–3) that had been recurrent since the collapse of the Bretton Woods regime in 1971, and that the EMS had managed to reduce, but not eliminate. Joining EMU and its unique stability-oriented policy framework – with centralised monetary policy entrusted to an independent central bank and decentralised fiscal policies subject to rules and coordination – was an effective and credible commitment device particularly useful for a number of countries with experience of inflation, budgetary indiscipline and inability to reform. Participation in EMU was thus for most EU countries – with the notable exception of Germany – an opportunity of shifting to a culture of macroeconomic stability, of importing credibility and of reducing disinflation costs.

2.3 *OCA theory revisited*

This volume contains two chapters, by Francesco Mongelli (Chapter 4) and Giancarlo Corsetti (Chapter 5), which revisit the OCA theory and help in understanding the economic motivations for EMU. Mongelli's chapter discusses the interactions and synergies between the OCA theory and the political and economic developments that led to the creation of the euro in 1999. Although the OCA theory and the process of monetary integration in Europe emerged at the same time and developed somehow in parallel, the theory could not deliver operational views or clear guidance at the time crucial decisions were taken. However, he notes that the balance of judgement provided by the theory has progressively shifted in favour of EMU: this is now deemed to generate fewer costs and there is more emphasis on benefits than two decades ago. The endogeneity of OCAs has further strengthened this consideration. Moreover, when looking at the broad governance structure of EMU, Mongelli notes that there may be also an exogeneity of OCA, by reference to a number of institutional developments that help participating countries tackle structural weaknesses and acquire the properties on the basis of which the theory defines an optimum currency area.

The chapter by Corsetti presents a modern reconsideration of the OCA theory in light of recent advances in monetary theory. He elaborates on a microfounded model of the costs of adopting a common currency, relative to an ideal benchmark in which the domestic central bank pursues country-specific efficient stabilisation. The costs of surrendering monetary autonomy and exchange rate flexibility are found to be small. Moreover, in so far as exchange rates do not perform the stabilisation role that is considered by the traditional OCA theory, a single monetary policy can be as efficient as national policies. On this issue, it is worth bearing in mind that supporters of EMU have often been sceptics of the advantages of exchange rate flexibility. The efficiency of the single monetary policy is valid even when shocks are strongly idiosyncratic, provided that the composition of aggregate spending tends to be symmetric at the currency union-wide level. Therefore, the convergence of spending patterns appears as a novel attribute of successful currency areas.

In his comments on Corsetti's and Mongelli's chapters, Peter Hoeller acknowledges a number of structural reforms in the euro area that may have led the euro-area countries to approach the optimality conditions identified by the theory. However, he is not convinced that those reforms were a consequence of EMU and notes that reform intensity may have slowed down since 1999. Moreover, he notes that the conclusion of Corsetti's model – according to which the welfare costs of imperfect stabilisation in a monetary union are small – may be related to the nature of the nominal rigidities considered in the model. If real rigidities and hysteresis are considered, boom-bust cycles may be much more costly.

3. Achievements of the first decade

The establishment of EMU was so smooth, and the macroeconomic stability over the first ten years in monetary union was such that one may be tempted to forget or dismiss the challenges that the euro area was confronted with at the outset. The challenges involved in the creation of the euro area went well beyond the irrevocable fixing of exchange rates.

The euro area is characterised by an unprecedented institutional architecture. The single monetary policy and the European Central

Bank (ECB) interact with a large number of governments, with their own competences in the areas of economic and fiscal policies. The relationship between the single monetary policy and multiple economic and budgetary policies is a novel feature of the euro area. Elements of tension could not be excluded – and did occur. Many other questions loomed large at the beginning. For example, would the transition from national currencies to the euro proceed smoothly? Would the single monetary policy be perceived as credible? Would the fiscal rules – embodied in the Stability and Growth Pact (SGP) – ensure budgetary discipline? Would the institutional architecture of the euro area prove flexible enough to withstand the pressure of unforeseen change? Would a monetary union be sustainable in the absence of a political union? Or even, how would the public react to euro banknotes without national symbols? For a discussion on the challenges of the early years, see Buti and Sapir (1998 and 2002) and Issing *et al.* (2001). On the specific challenge of uncertainty in the conduct of monetary policy in a new economic entity – from data uncertainty given the discontinuity in data series, to parametric and model uncertainty given the regime change ('à la Lucas'), to the uncertain reaction of the transmission mechanism to monetary policy and to the lack of reputation[9] and track record of the new monetary authority – see Issing (1999a) and Gaspar (2003).

3.1 Inflation and monetary policy

The shift to EMU was first and foremost a change in monetary regime. When the monetary union was created, the most obvious question mark and the most serious risk concerned price stability. With the aim of establishing price stability as a permanent feature of EMU, the Maastricht Treaty granted the ECB an independent status and established price stability as the primary objective of the new central bank. However, the credibility of the ECB in fulfilling its mandate was one of the crucial questions economists were asking themselves a decade ago.

The three contributions on monetary policy in this volume, by Petra Geraats, Manfred J. M. Neumann and Frank Smets (Chapters 6 and 7, and Comment 3 respectively), all focus on the performance of the ECB in its primary goal of maintaining price stability and in anchoring inflation expectations. The emphasis is entirely appropriate. Monetary policy, conducted by an independent central bank, has the ability to deliver price stability and to anchor inflation expectations. A credible central bank, following a systematic and well-understood monetary policy strategy, is also able to contribute to macroeconomic stability, which is part of an overall framework fostering growth and development. Not surprisingly, they also all comment on the ECB's communication policy.

The conventional wisdom is that the ECB and the national central banks, constituting the Eurosystem, have been fully successful at establishing the credibility of the single monetary policy from day one. Helped by the 'Great Moderation', the transition to the euro was so smooth that it is easy to overlook the magnitude of the unique and historically unprecedented challenge associated with the conduct of monetary policy for a group of politically sovereign countries. An aspect which is often underestimated is communication in a large geographical area, characterised by diverse traditions, customs, habits and languages.

The importance of credibility and endogenous private sector expectations about inflation was clear from the 'Great Inflation' episode in the seventies and the early eighties. The gains from commitment have been explored in the literature starting with Kydland and Prescott (1977) and Barro and Gordon (1983) and, more recently, using the standard new Keynesian model by Clarida *et al.* (1999), Woodford (2003) and Galí (2008).

The ECB aims at maintaining price stability. The ECB itself has clarified that this means annual price increases, measured by the harmonised index of consumer prices (HICP), of less than (but close to) 2 per cent, over the medium term. Neumann, Geraats and Smets concur that, during the first decade, inflation has been *close* to but *not below* 2 per cent. Specifically, excluding 1999 (on the ground that, given transmission lags, the ECB could not be held responsible for the outcome), inflation averaged 2.2 per cent over the period. However, Smets attributes the deviation to unforeseen and sizeable oil and commodities price developments. Excluding energy and unprocessed food prices – i.e. taking into account the most popular measure of core inflation – the average inflation rate was 1.8 per cent.

The three authors' overall assessment of the ECB's success is, however, different. Geraats concludes: '(…) euro area inflation has been close but mostly above 2 per cent. In addition, the high levels of inflation have had a negative impact on the ECB credibility, and inflation expectations and probabilities from surveys indicate that the private sector no longer believes that the ECB will achieve price stability over the medium term.' In contrast, Neumann writes: 'After ten years of operation the ECB has reached the status of an international leading central bank that serves the citizens of the euro area well by providing and safeguarding an internationally demanded stable currency.' He further finds that the ECB compares favourably with other successful central banks during the period. Specifically he considers the euro area, the USA, the UK, Canada and Sweden. Finally, Smets concludes: 'Overall, it appears that over the past 10-years, long-term inflation expectations have remained solidly anchored, which is remarkable considering the series of adverse economic disturbances that have hit the euro area since its inception.'

Geraats and Smets both emphasise the importance of private sector expectations about the ECB's ability to deliver medium-term price stability. They both review the available evidence based on financial market information and surveys. Drawing on earlier research (Geraats *et al.*, 2008) Geraats uses the ECB's own *Survey of Professional Forecasters* (SPF) to compute a measure of credibility. She focuses on the likelihood of inflation staying in the range 0 to 2 per cent, in two to five years. She interprets the measure as a quantitative measure of ECB's credibility and explains: '(…) according to the professional forecasters polled by the ECB it has become increasingly unlikely for the ECB to achieve price stability in the euro area in the medium to long term.' Geraats carefully investigates the relation between the ECB's credibility and its track record. She concludes: '(…) high inflation in the euro area appears to have a persistent negative effect on ECB credibility.'

Smets presents evidence for a much more benign interpretation. He shows that five-year ahead inflation forecasts, according to the SPF and the *Consensus* have been mostly close to and below 2 per cent. Geraats is well aware of this evidence. The explanation of the difference in views derives from differences in their preferred definition of the medium term. Geraats argues for a horizon of eighteen months to two years, while Smets emphasises a horizon of five years and beyond.

Neumann reports on the performance of the ECB's staff projections in comparison with those of the European Commission, the *Consensus* forecasts and the ECB's SPF. It turns out that the ECB's staff forecasts for real GDP growth compare well with other forecasts. However, for HICP inflation, the ECB staff has systematically underestimated inflation going forward. During the period Neumann finds that the forecasts by the Commission services have displayed smaller and less volatile errors.

Neumann also looks at the systematic conduct of monetary policy over time. He asks whether the outcome of the review of the ECB's monetary policy strategy, in 2003, led to a change in behaviour. He questions the evolution of the role of monetary analysis over time. He concludes that monetary analysis has certainly been important in the more recent period. Interestingly, Smets shows that a simple first-difference rule performs very well.

One such rule is of the form: $\Delta i = 0.5(E_t\pi_{t+m} - \bar{\pi}) + 0.5(E_t\Delta y - \Delta \bar{y})$, where i denotes the interest rate, π the inflation rate and y potential output; the sub-script denotes time and Δ the difference operator. The rule has been proposed by Orphanides (2003) as a robust rule. Orphanides (2006) has also applied it to the euro area. The rule is robust in the sense that it performs well even when there is substantial uncertainty concerning the measurement of the levels of potential output and of the natural interest rate. It is also the case that optimal monetary policy under commitment has a first-difference form. Also interestingly Beyer *et al.* (2008) have shown that a rule of this form can be derived as an implication from monetary targeting and that it tracks well the systematic behaviour of the Bundesbank in the period 1975–98. Orphanides proposed weights of 0.5 both on the inflation gap and on the output growth gap. Smets confirms the accuracy of Orphanides's approach since he finds estimated coefficients that do not differ significantly from 0.5.

Smets goes on to use the same approach to comment on the role of monetary analysis. He finds no significant additional influence from monetary factors in the policy rule. Both monetary analysis indicators he uses become significant once the inflation forecast is omitted. He interprets the finding as showing a high degree of consistency between economic analysis and monetary analysis, as conducted by the ECB, since its inception in 1999. Neumann, in turn, finds that references to monetary analysis in the ECB President's introductory statement to the press conference after the Governing Council's monthly monetary policy meeting, have increased after the review of the monetary policy strategy in 2003.

Geraats argues that the erosion in the ECB's credibility could be solved by embracing stronger transparency. Specifically, she asks for further precision in the formulation of the price stability objective, release of more detailed macroeconomic projections (include the projected policy path) and the release of minutes and voting patterns. Furthermore, added transparency would, for Geraats, also help solve the time-inconsistency problem, associated with the forward-looking approach to monetary policy pursued by the ECB. Neumann also emphasises the importance of transparency, especially in the case of an international central bank such as the ECB. He acknowledges that the 'bank does a lot by publishing detailed annual reports, monthly bulletins, press releases and press conferences after sessions of the Governing Council, by explaining regularly its monetary policy to the Committee of Economic and Monetary Affairs of the European Parliament and by providing public access to a large and well-kept data bank.' Nevertheless, he also stresses the desirability of more transparency and recommends the publication of non-attributed votes on monetary policy proposals. Smets does concur with the importance of communication, and agrees that there is always room for improvement. Nevertheless, with Neumann, he stresses the quantity and quality of the information already made available by the ECB. He asserts that many of the proposals by Geraats come from the practice of inflation targeting central banks which is different from the ECB's stability-oriented monetary policy strategy. Moreover, he argues against the publication of voting records – on this dimension the debate is reminiscent of the early exchange between Buiter (1999) and Issing (1999b).

3.2 *Financial integration*

EMU has been a powerful catalyst for financial integration. This has been not only the result of the disappearance of exchange rate risks and the reduction in cross-border transaction costs, but also from a number of EMU-related institutional changes, such as the removal of capital controls, harmonised rules for banking and financial services and issuance of public debt, as well as from improvements in financial market infrastructures. The euro has become a major global currency in all segments of the international financial markets and in relation to all international roles of currencies. Financial issues, including the international role of the euro are analysed by Carlo Favero and Francesco Giavazzi (Chapter 8), Tullio Jappelli and Marco Pagano (Chapter 9), and Elias Papaioannou and Richard Portes (Chapter 10).

Favero and Giavazzi's chapter is an investigation into the factors that determine long-term interest rates in the euro area. Their interest is in understanding whether the establishment of the euro has affected co-movements of US and EU yields. Since long rates incorporate long-term inflation expectations, it provides an assessment of the central bank's inflation objective. They start from the observation that despite the low correlation between policy rates in the USA and in the euro area over the past decades, long-term interest rates in the two regions have been highly correlated. Moreover, since the early 1990s their levels have been closer. They find that this convergence reflects the similarity in economic structures between the USA and the euro area. As far as the response to shocks is concerned, since the start of EMU, euro-area long rates have become more responsive to local non-monetary shocks: in the long run, however, they converge to the same level as US rates because expected inflation and expected monetary policy also converge to similar levels. Policy rates in the euro area have also become more responsive to local non-monetary shocks. Moreover, they show that, since the start of EMU, a monetary tightening by the ECB raises long rates, contrary to what used to happen in the 1990s when the Bundesbank was running monetary policy. In their comments, Domenico Giannone, Michele Lenza and Lucrezia Reichlin show that, when the dynamics of the euro area and the USA are jointly modelled, long and short rates in the euro area are mostly explained by shocks that are common with the USA. This raises doubts about Favero and Giavazzi's finding on rates responding aggressively to shocks that are specific to the euro area. Moreover they find it difficult to reconcile the analysis of central bank credibility with evidence on convergence of nominal rates in the euro area and on inflation expectations.

Jappelli and Pagano provide an account of how the process of financial integration has promoted financial development in the euro area. They start by defining financial integration and how to measure it. Then they analyse the barriers that can prevent it and the effects of their removal on financial markets, and assess whether the euro area has actually become more integrated. Their chapter then explores the extent to which these changes in financial markets have influenced the performance of the euro-area economy in terms of growth and investment, as well as its ability to adjust to shocks and to allow risk sharing. Their contribution also discusses further steps – from prudential regulation and banking supervision to deposit guarantee schemes and contract enforcement issues – that would contribute to consolidation of financial integration and enhance the future stability of financial markets. In his comments, Simon Hayes notes that the integration of EU financial markets during the first decade of EMU continues longer and broader trends that are largely independent from the creation of the euro. It might even be tempting to view the euro as one among many drivers leading to financial market integration. He believes, however, that such a perspective underestimates the effect that the euro has had on markets. Moreover, he argues that the role of the euro as a reserve currency will continue to foster the depth and the liquidity of euro-denominated financial assets.

Papaioannou and Portes survey the evidence on the international role of the euro. Prior to the creation of EMU, while sceptics had raised concerns that the single currency would lead to political disintegration and economic divergence, some argued that the euro could become a major international currency within a relatively short time. In fact, the international use of the euro is rising incrementally among a number of dimensions, and a 'middle-euro scenario' is emerging. The share of the euro in foreign exchange reserves is rising, as is its usage in international trade. An increasing number of countries use the euro to anchor their currencies and issue their debt. The global economic configuration of rising US inflation, a depreciating dollar, and American trade and fiscal deficits reinforce the 'middle-euro scenario', in which the dollar and the euro share central roles in international markets. Yet, the adjustment is likely to occur gradually, rather than abruptly and only if European policy makers continue financial market reforms and the ECB maintains low inflation expectations. In his comments, André Sapir disputes the response – 'perhaps yes' – given by Papaioannou and Portes to the question whether the euro will match or overcome the US dollar as a leading international currency and offers instead a negative reply. To his mind, the relative positions of international currencies are shaped by both economic and political factors. Economic considerations play in favour and against the euro. However, a reason for scepticism about the euro surpassing the US dollar is related to the stateless nature of the euro. In his view, ultimately, it is finance ministries, not central bankers, who determine the place of a currency in the international monetary system.

3.3 *Budgetary discipline and stabilisation*

The interplay between the single monetary policy and decentralised fiscal policies has always been identified as one of the acid tests for the macroeconomic architecture of the EMU. To minimise negative spillovers on the monetary union partners and in the conduct of monetary policy, as well as to provide leeway for the normal functioning of automatic stabilisers, fiscal autonomy of Member States is subject to the incentives and constraints of the SGP.[10]

Member States have the obligation of gearing their fiscal policies towards a medium-term objective (MTO) of 'close to balance or in surplus'; and a complex procedure exists to prevent and correct gross fiscal errors. While the fiscal convergence criterion in the Maastricht Treaty had been very effective in reducing fiscal imbalances in the run-up to EMU, it was not clear whether the removal of the 'carrot' of euro-area entry would lead to opportunistic fiscal policies especially in traditionally undisciplined countries. Or, would the implementation of the Pact imply a suboptimal degree of fiscal stabilisation?

Neither fear was realised. Government deficits in the euro area as a whole fell to a record low of 0.6 per cent of GDP in 2007 – this was the lowest deficit ratio recorded by the same group of countries since 1973[11] – and compares well with averages of close to or above 4 per cent of GDP in the 1980s and 1990s. Moreover, as a number of studies have shown, the quality of fiscal stabilisation has improved.[12] Fiscal policy is more clearly countercyclical – or less procyclical – and it is more readily used to restore competitiveness than to attempt to boost demand when competitiveness is eroded.

However, the assessment of fiscal policy in EMU fiscal framework is mixed. While in the run-up to the euro there was a marked improvement in fiscal positions in all countries, progress in the immediate aftermath of its launch was much less uniform. A number of Member States did reach their MTOs of fiscal situations close to deficit or in surplus, but several others repeatedly failed to fulfil their fiscal commitments, in spite of favourable macroeconomic conditions. Expenditure and deficit slippages were frequent, the SGP ceiling for government deficit was breached by several countries and reductions in debts were slow. There were doubts about the durability of the deficit reductions of a few countries given the frequency of one-off deficit-decreasing operations, as well as about the veracity of statistics.

The difficulties in applying the SGP procedures to the largest EU countries culminated in a temporary suspension, and then reform, of the Pact. While the SGP reform of 2005 has arguably improved the economic rationale of a number of procedures and strengthened the political ownership of EMU's budgetary rules, it was first and foremost

motivated by a lack of political commitment in applying agreed procedures in 2003 to the two largest Member States.

This book contains four chapters on fiscal policy by Jürgen von
Hagen and Charles Wyplosz (Chapter 11), Xavier Debrun, Jean
Pisani-Ferry and André Sapir (Chapter 12), Christopher Allsopp and
David Vines (Chapter 13), and Julian Alworth and Giampaolo Arachi
(Chapter 14).

The chapter by von Hagen and Wyplosz reviews the macroeconomic
use of national fiscal policy in EMU and examines the rationale and
scope for a collective insurance system which would redistribute income
in response to asymmetric shocks. They find evidence that the quality of
fiscal stabilisation has improved since the Maastricht Treaty. A pertinent question is whether the fiscal policy role can be augmented with a
collective insurance system. This would be one alternative to external
borrowing and lending and therefore one way to deal with the concerns
that led to the adoption of the SGP. While a collective insurance system
based on tax revenue sharing appears more promising than a collective
unemployment insurance it would generate moral hazard and raise a
number of practical implementation difficulties. In their comments,
Lucio Pench and Martin Larch note that the empirical tests by von
Hagen and Wyplosz are broadly in line with previous studies for what
concerns the use of discretionary fiscal policy over the cycle. However,
they believe it would also be useful to study further the interaction
between discretionary policy and the operation of the built-in mechanisms. As far as the collective insurance mechanism is concerned, they
believe the authors place excessive faith in the ability of econometric
models to correctly identify the nature of shocks, and share the authors'
reservations about the feasibility of a common insurance scheme.

Prior to the launch of the euro, there were concerns as to whether the
loss of the monetary policy instrument would deprive countries of a
vital tool to respond to country-specific economic shocks. Hence it was
hoped that improved fiscal policy could partly compensate for the loss
of monetary policy in stabilising national macroeconomic conditions.
In this context, Debrun, Pisani-Ferry and Sapir discuss the effectiveness
of fiscal automatic stabilisation in the EU and ask whether participation
in the euro area calls for enhanced automatic stabilisation through
bigger government. They find a negative answer. First, because government expenditure is already large in the euro area, beyond the point
at which government size no longer has a meaningful benefit on

stabilisation; second, because any potential gain in stabilisation would be at the cost of efficiency. In his comments, Gilles Saint-Paul suggests that government size is no longer stabilising, once it has passed a certain threshold, because of non-Keynesian effects. Beyond a given level of government expenditure, economic agents will expect painful adjustment in the future given the increase in government debt. This effect, which is well known from the expansionary fiscal contraction, would be valid both in the presence of discretionary policy, but also of automatic stabilisation.

Allsopp and Vines acknowledge that the first decade of EMU was successful. However, while some Member States enjoyed participation in the euro area and experienced high growth rates, others have gone through protracted periods of low growth. This may be related to the difficulty of ensuring adjustment in the face of asymmetric shocks in EMU with the possibility that real exchange rates overshoot. They argue that fiscal policy could contribute to improving macroeconomic performance in a monetary union. Therefore, the authors recommend using fiscal policy to stabilise inflation and target the real exchange rate rather than the government deficits or debt. Such a policy would require a more active use of fiscal policy than prescribed by the SGP. In his comments, Robert Kollmann notes that the Allsopp-Vines policy proposal would require reliable estimates of the response of the terms of trade to government spending shocks. However, there is much controversy in the empirical literature regarding that response. While the Allsopp and Vines model predicts that a rise in government purchases improves a country's terms of trade, results of the empirical research are ambiguous.

Alworth and Arachi examine whether and how EMU changed the impact of taxes on the economy or influenced tax policy. They survey a number of channels through which tax policy and exchange rate regimes are interrelated, such as capital mobility, strategic tax setting and trade policy. Though there is no strong empirical evidence of major, unique changes in the impact or determination of tax policy following the introduction of the euro – the internal market has had by far a greater impact – they highlight certain aspects that deserve specific attention. The most important concerns the use of tax policy to improve competitiveness by changing the tax mix and thereby achieving an internal devaluation. A second issue concerns tax competition in the area of corporate taxes. They provide some tentative evidence that capital movements to and from euro-area countries have become more responsive to corporate taxation. In his comments Casper van Ewijk takes the view that there are no convincing arguments for strong tax policy coordination among EMU members. Notably, some competition in capital income taxation may put a healthy restraint on overexpansive governments. Moreover, he argues that the scope for using taxes in a competitive process of internal devaluations is very limited, notably because those strategies raise opposition from domestic interest groups. However, he acknowledges that coordination could be considered for corporate taxes, as countries compete over multinational profits.

3.4 Growth, employment, trade and volatility

During the first decade of EMU, economic growth in the euro area was, on average, 2.1 per cent per annum (see Table 1.2). This result was virtually identical to the previous decade, but significantly below the outcome in the USA (2.6 per cent). When growth is related to demography, euro-area performance relative to the USA is more favourable. Data indicate that the average annual growth per capita – which is a better measure of developments in economic prosperity – were identical in the euro area and the USA (1.6 per cent). Yet, given the differences in the levels of GDP per capita, a growth rate per capita that is identical to the USA is not particularly outstanding, as it simply perpetuates the existing gap.

The reduction in unemployment and growth in employment was much more impressive. From 1998 to 2008, unemployment fell from 10 to 7.5 per cent of active population. Employment grew at an annual rate of 1.4 per cent on average, that is, 18 million jobs for the whole decade.[13] This is three times more than in the previous decade, and significantly more than in the USA despite the differences in demography.

The growth and jobs outcome during the first decade of the euro has resulted from a countless number of underlying trends, policy measures and other shocks, including many that predate the monetary union – only a subset of those growth drivers can be directly assigned to the new monetary regime. Therefore, it would be inappropriate to fully credit the favourable employment performance to the establishment of EMU. However, the favourable unemployment and employment developments in several euro-area countries in recent years owe a lot to wage moderation – which was possible thanks to low inflation expectations – and to labour market reforms in the run-up to the euro and in the EMU years. Though labour market reforms were decided autonomously by each of the participating countries outside the institutional architecture of EMU, they were often politically and economically related to the monetary union. In particular, as shown by Buti *et al.* (2007), the fiscal convergence criterion of the Maastricht Treaty and the adoption of the SGP boosted the incentives to adopt labour market reforms by electorally motivated governments.

Economists are not able to measure with precision the impact that a monetary regime – such as EMU – has on economic activity in participating countries. However, some elements of response and attempts to estimate the impact of EMU on economic growth, volatility and trade can be found in the contributions by Ray Barrell, Dawn Holland, Iana Liadze and Olga Pomerantz (Chapter 15), as well as by Stefan Gerlach and Matthias Hoffmann (Chapter 16), and Richard Baldwin (Chapter 17).

The aim of the chapter by Barrell and co-authors is to evaluate the impact of the monetary union on economic growth. In their view, real GDP growth in the euro area has been weak and somehow disappointing during the first decade since the formation of EMU, notably weaker than in the UK, Denmark and Sweden. Is this a consequence of the new monetary and exchange rate arrangements? To reply to the question, they undertake a growth accounting exercise and an econometric investigation of the determinants of output in EU and the USA. They conclude that, actually, EMU has had a direct positive effect on growth of the core euro-area economies of around 2 per cent. This is smaller than the impact of the Single Market programme in the late 1980s and early 1990s, and like those effects it builds up slowly. A corollary of the growth accounting exercises by Barrell and co-authors is that, without the monetary union, growth performance in the euro-area economies would have been particularly disappointing. Their analysis also shows that the differences in growth across the euro-area economies, and in relation to the USA and UK is in the underlying hourly productivity per person, which is mainly related to the accumulation of skills and labour input growth. In their comments, Jörg Decressin and Emil Stavrev raise a number of issues concerning the econometric setup of Barrell and co-authors. Notably, cross-sectional variation might be insufficient to provide reliable estimates; findings may also be distorted by cyclical effects. Moreover, there is no conclusive answer to what lies behind the positive estimate for the EMU dividend, and why growth has been lower than in the USA. Another question that is left without response is how to reconcile poor productivity growth with a favourable employment performance. Anyhow, the discussants agree that EMU cannot be blamed for a slowdown in the euro-area productivity.

The fact that the growth effect of EMU is smaller than the estimated impact of the single market programme in the late 1980s and early 1990s is not entirely surprising: international economists have long believed that physical and technical barriers were more detrimental to economic growth than currency differences. Furthermore, the estimated impact of the euro on economic activity may not fully reflect the impact of monetary union on welfare. The reduction in macroeconomic volatility that has resulted from EMU, in particular the reduction in consumption volatility, should have had a direct and significant impact on households' welfare. This is the issue considered by Gerlach and Hoffmann. They show that the volatilities of inflation and nominal interest rates have declined. More importantly, the volatility of real consumption growth has also fallen. Since global volatility has fallen for reasons unrelated to EMU (the 'Great Moderation'), they focus on the volatilities of bilateral differences in growth rates (or changes). Pairs of EMU countries have experienced the greatest fall in consumption volatility, followed by pairs in which one country is an EMU member. They demonstrate that these findings are closely linked to changes in consumption risk sharing, and conclude that, overall, EMU has made a difference in terms of macroeconomic stability. In his commentary on Gerlach and Hoffmann's analysis, Philipp Hartmann raises issues that could question the authors' conclusions. He discusses a number of points of an econometric and statistical nature which are relevant in distinguishing between the declines in volatility because of global developments and those that are EMU-related. Moreover, he compares evidence of consumption smoothing with other results in the literature that come to different conclusions. Finally, he wonders whether the favourable risk-sharing patterns are durable, since major international shocks could have lasting effects on inflation and inflation variability.

After the publication of Rose (2000), many researchers have considered whether, how much, and how, a currency union increases trade among its members. Empirical estimates of the boost to trade because of the euro vary widely. Based on the most comprehensive study to date

(Baldwin *et al.* (2008)), Baldwin revisits the issue in Chapter 17. After a careful separation of the euro's impact from other effects, notably the Single Market programme, he concludes that the aggregate impact on trade of the euro is significant, but small: around 2 per cent; this is one of the smallest estimates available in the literature. As far as the channels through which the currency union increased trade, he argues that the impact of transaction costs has not been of first-order importance, since the euro has not led to trade diversion. However, the euro did have a pro-competitive effect on prices: there is evidence of exporters moving towards pricing-to-market strategies, suggesting that they view the euro area as a single market. Empirical evidence on foreign direct investment (FDI) is much less rich than on trade. However, Baldwin concludes that both Single Market integration and euro-area membership have had pro-FDI effects, and this has been much larger in manufacturing than in services given barriers to entry in the service sector. In his comments Karl Pichelmann focuses on the measurement of the 'Rose number'. He believes that the downward correction of the 'number' by Baldwin may have gone too far, reaching figures that are no longer plausible. In particular, he suggests that any attempt to distinguish the Single Market from EMU effects is somewhat artificial, as they interact in a complex dynamic way and one cannot really have one without the other.

3.5 Structural reforms

The flipside of the favourable employment developments in the euro area during the 1999–2008 decade can be found in productivity which slowed down from 1.5 per cent to 0.75 of a percentage point per annum, on average. The causes of the productivity slowdown have been studied extensively. Notably the European Commission (2007c) shows that the productivity differential between the euro area and the USA is related to the low level of private ICT and R&D expenditure and by regulatory issues, as well as by the urgency of structural reforms in the product and labour markets, in spite of progress over the last decade. Labour and product market reform issues feature in two chapters, by Giuseppe Bertola (Chapter 18) and by Jacques Pelkmans, Lourdes Acedo Montoya and Alessandro Maravalle (Chapter 19).

The chapter by Bertola reviews theoretical and empirical aspects of the interaction between the establishment and working of EMU and labour market developments. Since policies designed to increase and stabilise labour incomes also tend to reduce employment and productivity, theory suggests that the latter effects should be sharper and more relevant within an integrated market area. This would make it harder for national policy makers to address the consequences of financial and other market imperfections. Empirical patterns of policy and outcome indicators in member and non-member countries of EMU are consistent with that theoretical mechanism. In the data, tighter economic integration is associated with better employment performance, substantial deregulation, sharper disemployment effects of remaining regulatory differences and somewhat higher inequality and larger private financial market volume.

After elaborating on what product market reforms are, as well as the main measurement issues, Pelkmans and co-authors discuss how such reforms lubricate adjustment processes in EMU, in particular via the competitiveness channel. They address two main questions: how likely is it for euro-area countries to experience an asymmetric shock, and what empirical evidence can one deduce about the euro-area countries' capacities to adjust to those shocks? The approach is disaggregated and highlights the sectors with relatively greater adjustment problems in each country. They show that, although substantial reforms have been undertaken in the euro area, market reforms in services would have to be intensified; these reforms would augment the single currency benefits. They also discuss complementarities with reforms in labour and financial markets and the design of reforms in the specific context of EMU.

In his comments on the chapters by Bertola, and Pelkmans and co-authors, Gert Jan Koopman suggests that euro-area membership has played a broadly positive role in promoting structural reforms. However, these are still insufficient to increase the potential rate of growth in the euro area and to avoid the emergence of significant macroeconomic imbalances. Remedying this reform deficit is one of the main challenges for the coming years. Aligning the policy recommendations under the Lisbon Strategy and the SGP in combination with a stronger role of the Eurogroup should greatly assist a more forceful implementation of the structural reform agenda in the euro area.

3.6 Governance and euro-area enlargement

The euro area is a dynamic entity and its process of enlargement is ongoing. After its creation in 1999, the monetary union extended its border on four occasions: first to encompass Greece in 2001, and then to take in four of the new EU Member States – Slovenia in 2007, Cyprus and Malta in 2008 and Slovakia in 2009. Each of the four enlargements of the euro area so far has been very successful; the changeover from a national currency to the euro was smooth both from a national and EMU perspective. The EU treaties provide a clear institutional path for euro adoption and each of the twelve Member States of the fifth and sixth EU enlargements (of 2004 and 2007) is expected and willing to adopt the euro as their national currency. Most likely, the euro-area membership will approach or exceed twenty-five by the end of the second decade, and the monetary union borders will be progressively indistinct from those of the EU.[14]

Part VIII of this book discusses issues on the governance of EMU and its enlargement; it includes two chapters, by Zsolt Darvas and György Szapáry, and Iain Begg. Over the next decade, the euro area is expected to continue expanding and encompassing a progressively large share of the EU. In this context, Darvas and Szapáry discuss the risks and challenges faced by the new EU members on the road to the euro and the strategies for, and timing of, euro adoption. They investigate the real-nominal convergence nexus from the perspective of euro-area entry and argue that the initial level of economic development and the speed of real convergence are relevant for both strategy and timing. The authors argue that inflation targeting with floating rates is better suited than hard pegs to manage the price level catching-up process. Moreover, they suggest a modification in the Maastricht inflation criterion.

Iain Begg's chapter looks at the governance of EMU and how it may need to evolve as the euro area progressively enlarges. The author discusses the meaning of economic governance and puts forward a conceptual model embracing different facets of governance, highlighting the significance of policy coordination, then assesses how well EMU fares on these aspects of governance. He also discusses how the institutional structures for managing EMU are evolving and need to keep evolving. Specific attention is given to the Eurogroup, which in spite of its informal nature, has become progressively the most influential political forum for the governance of the euro area. The need for greater politicisation of economic decision making and for new approaches to policy coordination – especially to integrate the supply side more effectively – is stressed as a likely way forward if EMU is to deal with emerging demands on policy making.

Enlargement will make the euro area more diverse. However, EMU was not designed to include countries whose development levels differ widely. Thus, in his discussion of these two chapters, Jean Pisani-Ferry identifies the ability of the EMU to adapt to a new context and to change as a major issue for the second decade of the monetary union. In his view, the required change will have to overcome both intellectual and institutional constraints.

3.7 Success but no ultimate assessment

During its first decade, the euro was very successful. However, a decade is not sufficient to provide an ultimate assessment of monetary unification in Europe and to present definitive evidence that the representative euro-area citizen will, over the long term, be better off than (s)he would be if EMU had not happened. First, ten years is a relatively short time-span in the life of nations, institutions, currencies and even in the life of persons. Just to illustrate the point, the national currencies that the Member States gave up to adopt the euro existed for several decades, in some cases centuries; the same for the national central banks that were previously in charge of domestic monetary policies. Second, the establishment of a monetary union constitutes such a major change in economies that one cannot expect its achievements or costs to fully materialise in ten years; some commentators have suggested that the effects of EMU will take a generation or more before materialising fully.[15] Third, the challenges that the euro-area economy will have to overcome over several time horizons are considerable. Although most economists used to see the test of the early years as of first-order magnitude, the unfolding of events – and the removal of favourable exogenous conditions over the first ten years – suggests that harsher tests and defining moments are still ahead. Finally, because EMU is such an unprecedented endeavour, our ability to learn from historical experiences is limited as shown in Chapters 2 and 3 by Michael Bordo and Harold James, and Barry Eichengreen, respectively.

The chapter by Bordo and James assesses the first ten years of the euro in historical perspective. The origins, characteristics and problems encountered by earlier monetary arrangements constitute the back-ground for the evaluation of the euro performance. When looking to the future, the authors warn of bumpy areas. In particular, low growth in some regions may produce challenges to the management of EMU and calls for a politically driven monetary policy. Financial instability, as well as globalisation-related disturbances, may also be sources of difficulty. However, if those hurdles are overcome, the euro may be as successful as the US dollar and the German Deutschmark.

Eichengreen stresses that there is no historic precedent to European monetary unification. The historical experiences are no more than imperfect analogies that may mislead. However, history is useful in identifying what is distinctive in EMU. His chapter focuses on financial integration and financial stability, noting the differences between EMU and the US financial unification at the beginning of the twentieth century. Eichengreen also discusses the break-up of monetary unions, illustrating it with the dissolution of the Austro-Hungarian Empire and of the respective currency, and the more recent experience of Argentina. He concludes that it is unlikely that any country participating in the euro area will defect.[16] The process of exiting a monetary union would be very disruptive and costly.

In his comments, Niels Thygesen acknowledges that the challenges highlighted in Chapters 2 and 3 are real. However, he agrees that the tensions internal to EMU are unlikely to escalate to the level where exit would be an option. The institutional developments in the EU, including the emergence of the Eurogroup and the pragmatic cooperation at the political level[17] should suffice to remedy potential conflicts.

4. Beyond the first decade

4.1 The global crisis

The benign macroeconomic outcomes that prevailed for most of the first decade of EMU were interrupted by the global economic and financial crisis. The crisis, which erupted in 2007–8, plunged the world economy into a severe recession, leading to lower employment, higher unemployment and ballooning fiscal deficits.

Many factors contributed to the global financial crisis. Although it was triggered by US-specific developments – the rise in delinquencies in the subprime segment of the mortgage market – several other factors were at the root of the crisis. These included mispricing of risk in a context of dynamic financial innovation, the change of the finance model from 'originate-to-hold' to 'originate-to-distribute', failed risk management and governance structures in global institutions, flaws in the rating agencies' business model, compensation schemes that provided inappropriate incentives to bank managers, inadequate regulatory supervisory and surveillance frameworks, housing bubbles, inflated financial assets and long-standing unsustainable external imbalances.

Clearly the genesis of the global crisis is not to be found in EMU. However, the crisis exposed a number of unsustainable imbalances that accumulated over the first decade of monetary union. In some countries, easy access to foreign capital led to misallocation of resources. As suggested by the European Commission (2008a), these imbalances show that the euro area needs to broaden its surveillance to address macroeconomic imbalances beyond its remit on fiscal issues.

The crisis has revealed, as no other episode before, the extent of interlinkages and spillover effects. Therefore crisis management required unprecedented international cooperation. In the monetary field, the major world central banks – notably the ECB, the Fed and the Bank of England – took joint action, on a number of occasions, aimed at ensuring orderly provision of market liquidity at the global level. It is doubtful whether these coordinated actions would have been possible if monetary authority in the euro area was divided among the national central banks concerned with foreign exchange turbulences, as in critical episodes before EMU.

In the euro-area context, the Eurosystem's operational framework has proved remarkably resilient under stress conditions. The Eurosystem's liquidity provision aims at ensuring orderly market conditions and at contributing to the reduction of risks to financial stability. Gaspar (2006) argues that, in the context of a corridor system for monetary policy implementation, the classical lender of last resort function – as conceived in the writings of W. Bagehot and H. Thornton – is best understood as subsumed in the operational framework for monetary policy. The recent experience did prove the crucial role of central banks in limiting spillover effects to broader financial markets and economic activity.

The EMU economic policy framework relies on monetary policy to offset symmetric demand shocks. Fiscal policy was geared towards the achievement of fiscal positions close to balance or in surplus. At the same time such an approach allows automatic stabilisers to play and absorb disturbances that are specific to each country and improve the sustainability of government accounts. However, given the magnitude of the financial crisis – the most serious downturn for seventy years – and its nature – with dysfunctional financial markets, thus impairing the monetary policy transmission mechanism – discretionary fiscal policy clearly has a role to play. Thus, while the letter of the SGP only allows fiscal expansions under very strict conditions, the euro area (and the EU) policy makers have shown flexibility and agreed on discretionary fiscal expansion.[18] However, fiscal expansion is only successful if it is perceived by the markets and public opinion to be of short duration, that is, if the deterioration in government deficits and increase in debts are temporary and do not enter into conflict with long-term sustainability. This is all the more the case as, given the projected demographic developments for the coming decades, fiscal sustainability is a pressing issue in several euro-area and other EU economies. Otherwise, that is, if economic agents expect a durable fiscal deterioration that is substantially detrimental to the fiscal sustainability indicators in each country, fiscal expansions are ineffective – if not counterproductive – given the Ricardian reactions from consumers cutting demand, and financial markets increasing the interest rate on the government debts.

The crisis provides an opportunity for changes in the euro-area governance. The sense of urgency to respond to the crisis made clear the need for enhanced cooperation in other areas within the EU and beyond. The foremost example is cooperation between authorities responsible for the supervision of large cross-border institutions with systemic implications and the need to ensure a convergent and consistent application of the existing regulations.

The immediate post-crisis period raises several policy issues. First, support measures have to be withdrawn in an orderly and coordinated manner, as soon as the financial system and the economies show signs of a return to normality. Liquidity has to be absorbed to avoid a rise in inflationary pressures; the toxic assets bought by governments or government-established special purpose entities have to be liquidated in a manner that minimises the overall cost borne by – or maximises potential gains for – taxpayers. Deposit guarantees should return to normal levels, and guarantees to interbank lending should be discontinued, to avoid inefficiencies and moral hazard. In a more medium-term perspective, the weight of the public sector in the economies has to return to normal by privatising the banks that had to be nationalised or those in which the government acquired major stakes. These 'exit strategies' have to be carefully coordinated to avoid conflicts and to ensure fair competition in the single market. This is no single task, all the more as the sense of emergency and of need of cooperation, which prevailed when the coordinated support measures were adopted, may no longer be felt by policy makers.

The reform of the global financial system is a major task post-crisis. The reform should increase the ability of the global financial system – which includes frameworks of official oversight – to prevent the build-up of the kind of imbalances that could again threaten global financial systemic stability and the global economy in the future. Equally importantly, supervisors and regulators need to monitor systemic risk and to act early in order to prevent it. It is also important to consider reforms that significantly strengthen market discipline, provide incentives for finance and financial innovations that produce intertemporal efficiencies as opposed to short-term gains that are more than offset by losses and system-wide problems later on. Success in these areas will require greater global cooperation and coordination at least among the major international financial centres.

4.2 Beyond the crisis: longer-term challenges

While the financial crisis has made stabilisation of the economy the first priority, it is important not to overlook a number of longer-term challenges. The concrete evolution of the EU economy over the coming decades – say until 2025 or further to 2050 – cannot be predicted with much rigour. However, the policy making challenges and main drivers of economic evolutions in the coming decades can be identified, as they are the same that have shaped economic developments and the relative influence of global powers for centuries: demography,[19] technology, globalisation and access to natural resources. The way the EU[20] manages these challenges will define its competitiveness and ability to adjust to changing global macroeconomic conditions.

In 2009, the EU amounts to 7.5 per cent of the world population and its economy to 22 per cent of world GDP. According to Eurostat and UN projections, the share of the EU in the world population will fall to 6.25 per cent in 2030 and 5.5 per cent in 2050. There are no reliable long-term GDP projections. However, the reduction in the share of the EU GDP in the world economy will be, in all likelihood, faster.

The fall in the weight of the EU population and GDP in world totals is neither a symptom of failure nor a new phenomenon. The share in the world of EU population and in GDP has been falling since the beginning of the twentieth century, only partially disturbed by the First and Second World War.[21] The same phenomenon happens with the USA and other Western countries. It is the result of the 'escape from hunger and premature death' because of the diffusion of technology around the world and globalisation of economies. The policy implication is that the way the EU influences world issues needs to be more and more through the reform of global governance structures that reflect the relative powers of economies. In this context, the reforms of the international financial architecture and of the global governance institutions do offer an opportunity not to be missed.

Notes

1. According to the language in the Maastricht Treaty, the economic and monetary union (EMU) covers the whole EU. The EU Member States that keep their own national currencies are said to 'have a derogation'. Moreover, according to the Treaty language, the economic and monetary union evolved in stages: the first stage started in July 1990, the second in January 1994 and the third in January 1999. The monetary union became a currency union in January 2002 when the euro banknotes and coins started circulating. However, in daily parlance, in this chapter and in several other chapters of this volume, EMU means the euro area created on 1 January 1999.
2. According to Eurostat, the changeover to the euro banknotes and coins may have increased the consumer price level by up to 0.3 per cent.
3. The founding members of the monetary union were Belgium, Germany, Ireland, Spain, France, Italy, Luxembourg, the Netherlands, Austria, Portugal and Finland. Greece joined in 2001, while Slovenia; Cyprus and Malta; and Slovakia followed suit in 2007, 2008 and 2009, respectively.
4. The tenth anniversary of EMU has led to a mushrooming of publications that celebrate the euro area, assess its performance and/or consider future challenges. Besides this volume, the interested reader may also refer notably to European Commission (2008a), ECB (2008c and 2009), Issing (2008a), Dyson (2008), Alesina and Giavazzi (2010).
5. The famous Jacques Rueff saying, quoted by Gros and Thygesen (1992: 3), according to which 'l'Europe se fera par la monnaie ou elle ne se fera pas' presumably indicates that the monetary unification is not an end in itself but an indispensable stage in the establishment of a political Europe.
6. Since the Maastricht Treaty (1992), that is, during the years just before the establishment of the euro and since, the European political union has not taken more than a few timid and painful steps forward. The ambitions of

the Amsterdam Treaty (1997) were limited in spite of the creation of the high representative for the common foreign and security policy; the ratification of the Treaty of Nice (2001) was not without difficulties; the Constitutional Treaty (2004) had to be abandoned. The ratification of the Treaty of Lisbon (2007) has just been completed.

7. Issing (2008b) has warned against overburdening expectations of the single currency with a political 'mission'. He argues, however, that while political union cannot be attained through the back door of EMU, undermining the stability of the euro would 'spell the end to hope of achieving political union'.

8. In its classic study 'One Market, One Money', the European Commission had estimated that the single currency would eliminate costs associated with converting currencies of about 0.4 per cent of GDP (European Commission (1990).

9. The crucial importance of reputation and credibility was one of the important lessons from the experience of the Great Inflation. See Beyer *et al.* (2008).

10. On the genesis of the Pact, its rationale and working in practice see the several contributions to Brunila *et al.* (2001). On the SGP reform of 2005, see i. a. Buti *et al.* (2003 and 2008), Buti (2006), Morris *et al.* (2006), European Commission (2005: 75–100 and 2006b: 76–90) and Fischer *et al.* (2007).

11. According to the available series, in 2000, the initial EUR-11 group of countries recorded a small surplus of 0.1 per cent of GDP; this result owing mainly to the very large non-recurrent receipts in relation to the sale of mobile telephony licences.

12. See for example Deroose *et al.* (2008).

13. Note however a significant difference between the increase in the number of employed persons and the total number of hours worked. The latter indicator grew annually by 1 per cent, on average, over the whole decade.

14. The EU is also itself a dynamic entity and may be enlarged again over the next years. Currently, there are three official candidates to EU accession: Croatia, FYROM and Turkey. At the end of 2008, Iceland's prime minister announced the setup of a Committee on Europe to investigate joining the EU.

15. Glick and Rose (2002) suggest that two-thirds of the trade effect of a change in monetary regime will take three decades to be reached.

16. For a different view, see Feldstein (2009).

17. See for example the meeting of the heads of state and government of the euro area in October 2008, which devised a collective response to the financial crisis.

18. In the context of the financial crisis, the EU has also shown flexibility with a pragmatic way of implementing the single market state aid rules in relation to the recapitalisation of banks, granting of guarantees to bank lending to restore the functioning of interbank markets, and granting of deposit guarantees.
19. Specifically an ageing population and its implications on potential growth and fiscal sustainability.
20. The dynamic nature of the euro area implies that longer-term issues should be discussed at the EU scale, rather than in relation to the sixteen countries that currently share the euro as their national currency.
21. See for example the very long time series for GDP compiled by Maddison (2006).

PART I

Historical perspective

2 | *A long-term perspective on the euro*

MICHAEL BORDO AND HAROLD JAMES

European economic and monetary union (EMU) and the euro, the single currency of its members, are ten years old. Monetary unions as currency arrangements have been implemented for a few centuries, but the European experiment of embarking on one without an accompanying full political union is bold and unprecedented. Monetary union has run ahead of the process of fiscal integration. EMU has helped to develop an integrated capital market, as well as providing many obvious consumer benefits in convenience and price transparency for an increasingly mobile European population. However, the novelty of the single currency while accompanied by divided sovereignty raises a number of problems and potential threats, some of which were anticipated at the time of the institutional preparations for monetary union, while others were not.

This chapter will evaluate the experience of the first decade of EMU and the euro in historical perspective. It will ground the establishment of EMU and the euro in the context of the history of international monetary cooperation and of monetary unions. A discussion of the origins, key operating characteristics and problems encountered by earlier monetary arrangements will serve as a backdrop for an evaluation of the euro's performance and challenges in future decades. The chapter will develop and expand upon the following three themes: 1. Lessons from the evolution of past monetary unions for EMU; 2. Fiscal policy arrangements for EMU in historical perspective; 3. Challenges facing EMU. The first two take an historical perspective. The third looks to the future.

1. Lessons from the evolution of past monetary unions for EMU

A monetary union, defined as a common currency and set of monetary arrangements (including cooperation among central banks and a common central bank) for a group of member states is a form of international monetary cooperation. In the past, international monetary regimes evolved to facilitate international commerce. The earliest regime, the international specie standard, in its most well-known variety, the gold standard, emerged de facto because participating countries defined (pegged) their currencies in terms of a common precious metal. This led to a fixed exchange rate arrangement which in the late nineteenth century encouraged international trade and capital movements. The limitations on government fiscal and monetary action implied by the gold standard enhanced policy credibility, and consequently reduced the cost of borrowing for both governments and private actors (Bordo and Rockoff 1996). Central banks, by following the rule of gold convertibility, implicitly cooperated with each other. In some cases direct cooperation was arranged. In the twentieth century, more explicit forms of monetary cooperation evolved, first with the Gold Exchange Standard in the 1920s, then the Tripartite agreement in the 1930s and then with the Bretton Woods Articles of Agreement in 1944, which required all members to adhere to a set parity and to other rules.

Monetary unions of the past were set up under two circumstances: as international arrangements between countries using similar specie currencies, to harmonize interstate transactions and as part of the creation of a nation state from a number of smaller political units. In the latter case monetary unification was part of the process of nation building which was combined with the creation of a fiscal union. A common currency was seen as a way to avoid the costs of currency competition and currency instability among the member states.

International monetary unions of the past were successful as long as the international environment was stable. Large shocks such as wars led to their dissolution. National monetary unions were also successful as long as the nation was politically cohesive. It took the historical national monetary unions decades to establish the necessary integration of goods and factor markets and the creation of well-functioning central banks. The greater success of some monetary unions over others reflected their patterns of economic development and evolution of sound financial institutions and sound monetary and fiscal policies.

1.1 The history of monetary unions[1]

A monetary union or a unified currency area is the extreme version of a fixed exchange rate regime. The essence of a monetary union is that all the member states adopt the same currency as a unit of account, medium of exchange and store of value. This implies that the monetary union has one exchange rate towards the rest of the world.

The history of monetary unions is best understood if we make a distinction between national and multinational monetary unions. By a national monetary union we mean that political and monetary sovereignty go hand in hand. Roughly speaking, the borders of the nation state are the borders of the monetary area. A national monetary union has as a rule one single monetary authority, commonly a central bank.

By a multinational monetary union we mean an international monetary arrangement between independent countries based on permanently fixed exchange rates between their currencies. Multinational monetary unions occur when independent nation states link their monies together through a perfectly fixed exchange rate so that one member's money is perfectly exchangeable for another member's at a fixed price. An extreme example of this would be that all member states use the same currency.

A second important distinction is between the monetary union per se and the type of monetary policy pursued within the union. Adoption of a common money by a number of states can be consistent with alternative sets of institutional arrangements governing monetary policy, ranging from complete laissez faire to monolithic central banking. As we demonstrate below, monetary unions, once created, differed substantially depending on the evolution of monetary institutions. The currencies could be unified without specifying any particular rule for governing monetary policy as will be seen from the examples of the US, German and Italian monetary unions and two multinational monetary unions, the Latin Monetary Union (LMU) and the Scandinavian Monetary Union (SMU).

1.2 National monetary unions

1.2.1 The United States monetary union

The US monetary union was created with the signing of the Constitution in 1789. The Constitution gave the Congress the sole power to "coin money" and "regulate the value thereof." Moreover, the Coinage Act of 1792 defined the US dollar in terms of fixed weights of gold and silver coins, placing the country on a bimetallic standard. Finally, establishment of a national mint in Philadelphia in 1792 secured the foundations of an effective currency area.

In the preceding two centuries, the colonial experience was chequered with examples of excessive issue of paper money, "the bills of credit," leading to high inflation as well as competing seigniorage between the colonies. This experience was repeated after independence during the Confederation period from 1783 to 1789. The Constitution of 1789 was designed expressly to avoid giving the states the power to issue paper money and to preserve the control of the currency for the Congress.

While the Congress was given the exclusive power to coin money, the states were allowed to charter commercial banks and to regulate their note-issuing activity. All bank notes had to be convertible into specie. In the early decades of the nineteenth century, bank note issue varied considerably and various state bank notes circulated at a discount. Moreover there is evidence that the price level may have been higher in the west than the east.

The movement towards a complete currency union with a more uniform nationwide price level was aided by the practices of the First Bank of the United States (1791–1811) and the Second Bank of the United States (1816–36). Neither bank was designed as a central bank but as a public one. Both banks were sufficiently well capitalized to be able to provide the government with medium-term bridge loans to finance shortfalls in government tax receipts. Both were also intended to provide loans to the private sector to spur economic development. Finally, it was deemed imperative that they hold sufficient specie reserves to always maintain convertibility of their notes. One of the practices of both banks was to enforce the convertibility of state bank note issues and to transfer specie between regions.

After the demise of the Second Bank of the United States in 1836, the United States did not have any form of a central bank until the establishment of the Federal Reserve System in 1914. However, the US Treasury served as a monetary authority and maintained specie convertibility. Although the nineteenth century was characterized by considerable banking instability, the currency union remained intact, with the exception of the Civil War period when the Confederate States issued their own fiat currency. In the face of great difficulties in raising tax revenues and in selling debt both at home and abroad, the Confederate government expanded its money issues at an ever increasing rate. By the end of the Civil War a hyperinflation vastly reduced the value of Confederate notes.

Upon Union victory in April 1865, Confederate notes were declared illegal in the United States. The National Banking system, established in 1865, finally created a uniform national bank note system. Several different types of high-powered money: gold coins, silver coins, gold and silver certificates, and US notes (greenbacks) circulated at par for the next half century until the creation of the Federal Reserve system in 1914, which issued Federal Reserve notes. Although bank notes now circulated across the country at par, demand deposits did not; charges for check clearing varied depending on the distance from the East coast money centers. The Fed instituted par checking for the member banks, but not for non-members, eliminating the final hurdle to par acceptance of all forms of money.

The Federal Reserve System consisted of twelve regional Reserve Banks coordinated by the Board of Governors in Washington DC. As described by Eichengreen (1997a, 1997b) and Wheelock (2000), the Reserve Banks initially had some monetary independence within their respective regions with the power to set discount rates. Regional conflicts over the conduct of monetary policy occurred throughout the 1920s and 1930s, and many scholars believe that those conflicts were an important part of the paralysis in decision making that helped create the Great Depression (Friedman and Schwartz 1963 and Meltzer 2003). It was only with the Banking Act of 1935 that full power to implement monetary policy was given to the Board of Governors. Thus monetary unification of the United States was not finalized until long after political unification.

1.2.2 The Italian monetary union

The main reason for the establishment of a currency union on the Appenine peninsula in the 1860s was political unification under the leadership of the Kingdom of Sardinia. The Kingdom of Italy was proclaimed in 1861, and completed in stages in 1866 and 1871. Prior to unification as many as ninety different metallic currencies were legal tender in the many small Italian states. In addition, major banks in the small states issued bank notes that served as legal tender. The variety of different currencies was commonly regarded as a barrier to trade. In order to achieve more than a *de jure* unified Italy, measures were taken to turn the country into a monetary union as well.

The issue of coins was resolved quickly. During a brief transition period, four currencies were accepted while all other old currencies were exchanged into these. Finally, in 1862, a new, unified coinage was introduced based on the lira of Sardinia. All pre-unification coins and paper monies were abolished and exchanged for coins denominated in the new lira, equal in value to the French franc. A bimetallic currency standard was preferred, primarily to conform to the monetary system of Italy's major trading partners and to accommodate the dominance of silver coins in southern Italy. The currency ratio between silver and gold was set at the French ratio of 15.5 to 1.

Although Italy had unified its coinage in 1862, it had considerable difficulty in remaining on the specie standard in which its currency was defined. In 1862, Italy adopted the bimetallic standard, although de facto the standard was gold. In 1865 Italy joined the Latin Monetary Union (see Section 1.3.1 below). Fiscal improvidence and the war of unification against Austria in 1866, however, ended convertibility (with a new regime known as the *Corso Forzoso*). Fiscal and monetary discipline was achieved by 1874, and exchange rate parity was restored. The government announced on March 1, 1883, that it would restore convertibility on April 12, 1884, but convertibility only took place in silver because it was overvalued at the mint. Public finances then deteriorated and unlawful bank note issues indicated an absence of monetary discipline. By 1894 Italy was back on a paper standard, and floating exchange rates. Inconvertibility lasted until 1927.

It took Italy thirty years to establish a central bank. No immediate action was taken to establish a single monetary authority. Several regional banks were issuing notes as well as performing central bank functions. The Banca Nazionale del Regno d'Italia (BNR), which was formed by the previous national bank of Sardinia, absorbing some other state banks in the process, held a leading position among banks, however, partly by being the largest bank in operation and partly by being the bank of the state that led the political unification process.

In the following decades a number of competing banks of issue coexisted. By 1884 the number had declined to six. There has been considerable debate on whether the existence of multiple banks of issue was per se inflationary or whether the lack of fiscal difference and intermittent departures from specie were the causes of the inflationary episodes (Fratianni and Spinelli 1997). An enquiry into the state of the banking system led to a major restructuring in 1893. The Banca d'Italia was formed as an amalgamation between the BNR and the two remaining Tuscan banks. The three remaining note-issuing banks were put under direct state supervision. In sum, the formation of the Italian monetary union, as was the case with the US, took place after political unification and it was a time-consuming process.

1.2.3 The German monetary union

The German monetary- as well as political-unification process proceeded stepwise. Prior to monetary unification, each principality and free town issued its own coins and a multiplicity of issue banks gave out paper money. In addition, large numbers of foreign coins circulated. The diversity of coins was perceived as a great nuisance. Merchants and industrialists, often with a liberal orientation, became the main proponent of unified economic and monetary conditions to reduce transactions costs emanating from monetary disarray, while the governments of the principalities resisted, safeguarding their seigniorage gains.

In 1834, under the Zollverein, all internal customs barriers were removed. The 1838 Dresden Coinage Convention brought some simplification, with southern states adopting the gulden and northern states the thaler. Both the thaler and the gulden were explicitly linked to silver, with one thaler being valued at 1.75 gulden. The Vienna Coinage Treaty of 1857 constituted a further step towards monetary unification. The Treaty incorporated Austria into the Dresden arrangement by fixing the exchange rate of 1 thaler to 1.5 Austrian gulden and to 1.75 south German gulden. In addition, the amount of petty coins that each state could issue was regulated. The circulation of gold coins, previously left to the discretion of each state, now became subject to stringent rules. No gold coins other than special *Vereinshandelsgoldmünze* designed for foreign trade were minted. The exchange of gold coins into silver at a fixed parity was forbidden as well, avoiding the risk of turning the currency standard into a bimetallic one. Secondly, the treaty dealt with paper money, the first international monetary arrangement to do so, by prohibiting the granting of legal tender status to inconvertible paper money.

The establishment of the new unified German empire following Germany's war of unification (the Franco-Prussian war) induced further steps. The coinage acts of 1871 and 1873 unified coinage throughout the empire and introduced the mark as the unit of account, based on the decimal system. Individual states continued to have their own coinage, with images of their rulers on the heads of their now standardized coins. In order to link the German currency to the British pound, at the time the leading currency, the gold standard was adopted with silver being reduced to use in coins of small denominations with less metal content than their face value. In 1875 a new banking act created a new central bank, the Reichsbank, and forced most of the other issue banks to restrict themselves to ordinary banking business. The Reichsbank was to serve as the central bank for the new Germany.

From the 1870s to the outbreak of World War I, Germany was part of the international gold standard. German monetary conditions were determined by international ones. Political unification epitomized by the creation of the German Reich was followed by three major changes in the German monetary system: the conversion of the currency standard from silver to gold; the replacement of the thaler with the mark as the unit of account and the formation of a single central bank that in practice monopolized the issuing of paper money. These changes meant that Germany after a lengthy process was a fully fledged monetary union. Again monetary unification followed political unification, with concessions being made in the form of coinage design to people who still clung to the old states that made up the new federally organized empire (James 1997).

1.3 Multinational monetary unions

We consider two multinational monetary unions, the Latin and Scandinavian monetary unions. Both were based on a common coinage but where each member country retained its central bank.

1.3.1 The Latin Monetary Union

The Latin Monetary Union (LMU) was created in 1865 by France, Belgium, Switzerland and Italy. Prior to its establishment these countries had a history of recognizing each other's currencies as means of payment based on the French bimetallic system, in operation since 1803. The French system stipulated that the fineness of each coin, regardless of whether it was a gold or silver coin, was to be 90 percent and fixed the value between gold and silver to 15.5. (Redish 2000).

In the 1850s, a fall in the price of gold relative to silver made gold coins overvalued at the mint. Consequently it became profitable to melt silver coins and sell silver for gold at the market rate. As the price of gold continued to fall, even worn coins with low silver content started to disappear. The process left the countries virtually with a gold standard currency since gold was the only medium of exchange that remained in circulation. However, the shortage of silver coins meant a lack of small denomination monies for use in minor transactions.

Switzerland was the first country to enact a feasible solution by reducing the silver content to 80 percent of all coins except the five franc one, thus ensuring that it was no longer profitable to export the newly reduced value silver coins. Italy, upon unification, decided to lower the silver content of every coin smaller than one franc to 83.5 percent. The result of these Italian and Swiss actions was that France and Belgium were flooded by debased silver coins from their neighbors, creating seigniorage gains for the issuers. France reacted in 1864 by reducing the silver content in each silver coin, except the five franc one, to Italy's 83.5 percent and by suspending the acceptance of Swiss coins by its customs offices (Einaudi 2001).

Thus there was an apparent need for coordination. The acute shortage of small denomination coins constituted a hindrance to trade both within and between countries and forced them into action to remedy the problem. The unilateral response by each country of creating token coins of varying fineness created an additional problem in the form of one country reaping seigniorage benefits at the expense of the others. To deal with this situation, Belgium proposed a joint monetary conference, held at the end of 1865, that created the LMU.

The main issues at the conference in 1865 were to secure and standardize the supply of subsidiary coinage for smaller transactions and the formal adoption of gold as the currency standard. The first issue was unanimously resolved by deciding that all silver coins less in value than the five franc coin were to be token coins with 83.5 percent silver fineness which the state treasuries had to accept as payment up to one hundred francs regardless of the country of origin. Each state treasury was then obliged to exchange the other state treasury's holdings of its token coins into gold or silver five franc coins at par. The total value of token coins that each country was permitted to mint was restricted to six francs per capita. The adoption of a gold standard was rejected in favor of retaining the bimetallic standard.

The existing currencies continued to be in use virtually unchanged as parallel currencies. Each state treasury remained ultimately responsible for the redemption of its own coins. Apart from solving the problem of scarcity of small denomination coins, the purpose of the standardization of the dimension and metal content of the coins was to eliminate the possibility of seigniorage gains through the minting of debased coins. While aiming to restrict the amount of money in circulation, the conference failed to consider restrictions preventing the member countries from issuing other forms of money – a failure that was to be exploited by the issue of paper notes. Consequently the members still had considerable monetary independence.

Initially, the union achieved what it had set out to achieve. However, two problems soon emerged. After the inauguration of the union, the price of gold started to rise again, and led to silver five franc coins returning to circulation and gold coins being exported or melted. At the same time, France and Italy began to issue inconvertible paper money. In the case of France, it was a temporary measure due to the Franco-Prussian war in 1870–1. Italy's chronic government deficit preserved inconvertibility of the lira until 1881 and then introduced it again in 1894. The increased money supply in Italy led to a depreciation of the lira. Consequently, Italian silver coins were exported to the other member countries where they were legal tender. Obviously, this enabled the Italian government to finance part of its deficits with seigniorage, the costs of which were shared between all four countries.

In response to the problems facing the union, a conference by the members in 1874 decided to maintain the bimetallic standard but restrict the minting of silver five franc coins. In 1878 the members agreed to cease issuing five franc silver coins, although those still in circulation were to remain legal tender, and the silver coins remained as in effect token coinage. This arrangement established the "limping gold standard."

As the relative price of gold continued to rise, the union in 1885 considered full adoption of the gold standard and thus withdrawing the five franc silver coins. The main problem was once again the cost of redeeming silver in circulation, since its intrinsic value was now far below its face value. In the end, this proved too great an obstacle to overcome and a new agreement was signed stipulating that any party leaving the union would have to exchange the others' holdings of its silver coins into gold.

World War I led to the break-up of the LMU. The sharp increase in military expenditures left the members with no choice but to issue paper money. The large quantities of fiat issued during the war remained in circulation after hostilities ended. As paper money was not recognized as legal tender in any country other than the issuing one, the union was in effect put out of business. During the war, silver coins were melted or exported. The remaining coins constituted a small share of the total money supply. Belgium was the first country to act accordingly, declaring in 1925 that it would leave the union at the start of 1927. The other countries followed and the LMU was dissolved.

1.3.2 The Scandinavian Monetary Union

Prior to the formation of the Scandinavian Monetary Union (SMU) in 1873, the three Scandinavian countries had a long history of similar units of account and exchange of notes and coins between them (Bergman *et al.* 1993). They were all on the silver standard and they all used the riksdaler as the unit of account. One Norwegian specie rigsdaler was roughly equal to two Danish rigsdaler which in turn was roughly equal to four Swedish riksdaler. In consequence, a considerable fraction of the coin circulation in either of the three countries consisted of coins minted in the other two. The difference in value separating these exchange rates from those based on the currencies' values in silver was small enough in the case of the Danish and Norwegian currencies for any profits that could have arisen from arbitrage to be negligible. This was not the case for the Swedish currency, whose value exceeded 0.5 Danish or 0.25 Norwegian riksdaler by an amount sufficiently large to produce an inflow of Danish and Norwegian coins into Sweden to be perceived as a nuisance.

In addition to this currency flow there were other reasons for aiming at a unified coinage. There was a lively debate across Scandinavia over which metal – gold or silver – would be most suitable for the monetary standard. There was also discussion regarding the merits of basing the unit of account on the decimal system. The intellectual climate favored the decimal system on the grounds of rationality and adherence to the gold standard – the standard followed by the leading commercial nations Britain and Germany. In addition the nationalistic movement called Scandinavism fostered social and political willingness to bring the Nordic countries closer together. All of these factors contributed to the three countries creating a common currency in 1873. Norway did not formally sign the agreement until 1875, but in practice altered her monetary standard in 1873.

The formation of the SMU in 1873 replaced the old unit of account, the riksdaler, with a new one, the krona, which was specified in terms of gold and was to be equal in all three countries. Subsidiary coins were to be minted in silver and copper with a fineness of 80 percent and no restrictions were placed on the amount of subsidiary coins minted. All coins were given legal tender status throughout the union. The state treasuries accepted unlimited amounts of coins irrespective of their country of origin. The only restrictions were a maximum amount stipulated for the settlement of private debts.

Notes were used widely in Sweden because of the larger denominations of the gold coins. Intercountry circulation consisted of notes and subsidiary coins. This caused some dissatisfaction since notes were not covered by the union agreement and thus did not always circulate at par.

In 1885 the three central banks decided to establish intercountry drawing rights. Transactions between the central banks were made free of interest and other charges. Then in 1894 Sweden and Norway further extended the scope of the union by accepting each other's notes at par without restrictions. The Danish central bank joined the agreement in 1901.

The SMU worked smoothly in the years before World War I. The gold standard, by requiring convertibility into gold, ensured stability in the money supply. All three countries avoided issuing excessive amounts of subsidiary coins. The money supply in the member countries expanded in line with economic growth. Inflation rates and interest rates exhibited identical patterns in Scandinavia during the union.

Like the LMU, the SMU's collapse was induced by World War I. At the outbreak of the war, Scandinavian notes were declared inconvertible into gold. At the same time, in order to prevent an outflow of gold, the export of gold was prohibited. Money growth ceased to be tied to the supply of gold and the basis for the exchange of Scandinavian notes at par was eliminated. Monetary policy was more expansive in Denmark and Norway than in Sweden. In 1915, the official exchange rates changed accordingly, with one Swedish krona buying more than one Danish or Norwegian krona.

Since the legal tender status of Scandinavian coins in all Scandinavian countries was still in force, Danish and Norwegian gold coins were exported to Sweden. The governments in Denmark and Norway often granted exemptions from the prohibition of export of gold coins. The Swedish central bank objected to the inflow of gold coins. Negotiations were opened in order to achieve the suspension of the legal tender arrangement. Neither Denmark nor Norway wished to terminate it, however, and the outcome in 1917 was instead a strict enforcement of the prohibition of gold exports.

At the end of the war, the three Scandinavian currencies were no longer traded at par. Gold coins could not circulate across borders because of the ban on gold exports. In virtually all respects the SMU had been rendered ineffective by the war. The only remaining parts of the original agreement were the legal tender and equal value status and unrestricted minting and flow of subsidiary coins. Because the Swedish coins were more valuable than Danish and Norwegian ones, subsidiary coins flowed into Sweden. To come to terms with this situation, a supplementary agreement was put into force in 1924 which stated that, without regard to the coinage treaty of 1873, each country could only issue new subsidiary coins that were legal tender in the issuing country, thus phasing out the common subsidiary coins in circulation. The union was effectively terminated by the decision.

1.4 Lessons from the historical record

The past monetary unions we have described were demarcated into the categories of national and multinational. The evolution of the former set of arrangements was tied up closely with the creation of nascent national states in the three countries we examined. The economic case for monetary unification in each of them was clear: to reduce transactions costs of multiple currencies and thereby facilitate commerce; to reduce exchange rate volatility; and to prevent wasteful competition for seigniorage. The multinational monetary unions were set up for basically similar economic reasons but there was no underlying political imperative to create a nation state. The two international unions we examined were part of a more general international monetary standard based on specie, and although the members had central banks, the scope for following monetary policies inconsistent with the rules of the gold standard regime were limited. This made coordination between the monetary authorities relatively easy.

This key distinction between the two types of arrangements was reflected in their durability. The national monetary unions we describe have endured for two centuries, reflecting the cohesion of their underlying nation states. The record was not without serious strains produced by political forces; witness the American Civil War and the post-war division between West and East Germany. There have been prominent dissolutions in the twentieth century of national monetary unions which reflected the break-up of their underlying polities, for instance Austria-Hungary, the USSR, Czechoslovakia and Yugoslavia. But the key element in the survival of these unions has always been political.

In the case of the international monetary unions we have covered, dissolution occurred when faced with the large exogenous shock of World War I. The exigencies of war put the various member states on divergent paths of monetary and fiscal rectitude. The underlying common nominal anchor, gold convertibility, became inconsistent with pressing national goals. Moreover both the LMU and SMU were part of a broader international monetary system which, because of its common basis of adherence to specie, also implicitly fostered monetary cooperation (although not as clearly demarcated as by the monetary unions). Like the two regional subarrangements, it collapsed with the strains of the war. In the post-war period the gold exchange standard and Bretton Woods were arrangements which combined the discipline of gold adherence with the flexibility of allowing domestic financial authorities to pursue domestic stability goals. In both cases the regimes collapsed ultimately because of the incompatibility between the two goals.

An additional lesson is the role of the monetary authority in the two types of arrangements. The national monetary unions all developed central banks as part of the process of monetary unification. It took a long time in each of the three examples for this process to reach fruition and for the central banks to provide monetary stability. The path was far from smooth, as seen in the US case in the destruction of the two Banks of the United States in the early nineteenth century and the Federal Reserve's massive failure in the 1930s; in Germany in hyperinflations after the two world wars; and in Italy in monetary instability for most of the Banca d'Italia's existence. The multinational monetary unions we examine kept separate monetary authorities. Cooperation between them was focused primarily on the limited goals of maintaining compatible coinages and in the case of the SMU the international clearing of bank notes. They did not engage in policy coordination in the modern sense in part because given the common adherence to the gold standard it was not necessary.

EMU is different from the earlier experiences with monetary unification that we have described. It has created a single currency, the euro, and a common monetary authority, the ECB, as in the case of the national monetary unions, but the member states have kept a substantial part of their political sovereignty and, as will be discussed in Section 2, their fiscal sovereignty. Also, like the historic gold standard, EMU has a common nominal anchor, the commitment by the ECB to price stability, albeit in a fiat regime. A key potential problem as in the case of the earlier international monetary arrangements and the multinational monetary unions is conflict between national agendas for growth and full employment, a problem which is related to the incidence and severity of potential asymmetric shocks. Here political will in either driving towards greater political integration or in the creation of cooperative fiscal arrangements will be vital for the underlying durability of EMU.

2. Fiscal policy arrangements for EMU in historical perspective

National monetary unions of the past, like Germany, Italy and the United States, which in some respects served as prototypes for EMU, also evolved as fiscal unions with either a centralized fiscal authority or fiscal federalism with revenue sharing. In this section we consider some theoretical and historical perspectives on fiscal unions.[2]

2.1 Theoretical perspectives: fiscal unions and fiscal federalism

The concept of a fiscal union entails fiscal federalism or some other kind of cooperative arrangement between the members regarding the rules designed to allow the long-run sustainability of fiscal positions. Fiscal federalism defines the roles of the different levels of government and the way in which they relate to one another through different instruments like grants and transfers.

The traditional theory of fiscal federalism contends that the central (federal) government should have the basic responsibility for macroeconomic stabilization and income distribution. It also provides national public goods. According to the theory, decentralized levels of government should provide goods and services whose consumption is linked to their own jurisdictions. The economic argument for providing public goods at the subnational level is based on the Decentralization Theorem, namely that "the level of welfare will always be as high if Pareto-efficient levels of consumption are provided in each jurisdiction than if any single, uniform, level of consumption is maintained across all jurisdictions" (Oates 1972).

The most obvious cost of federalism is the loss of autonomy by the central government. In fact, the advantages of decentralization require that the central government's authority be limited. As a result, in highly decentralized fiscal federations, central governments might find it difficult to implement coordinated policies and provide federation-wide collective goods.

That decentralized governments will provide the efficient level of public goods depends on three assumptions: a) households are freely mobile and generate competition between jurisdictions. If this is not the case, competition among local governments can lead to suboptimal outcomes; b) the lack of interdependencies between jurisdictions. When interdependencies are significant, competition among local governments can generate spillovers; c) a federation should be properly structured and its actions disciplined.

Thus if there are strong interdependencies between subnational jurisdictions, local officials may face incentives to increase their expenditure while externalizing the costs to others. This incentive is higher if the central government cannot fully commit to a no-bailout rule. And the central government's commitment becomes less credible if subcentral governments are heavily dependent on transfers from the central authority.

The interplay between several fiscal and one monetary authority can lead to free-riding. Each individual fiscal authority sees itself as a small player who has little impact on monetary policy. In equilibrium each country free-rides and the outcome is worse than in a cooperative equilibrium. An extensive literature has analyzed the existence of independent fiscal authorities with a single central bank (Dixit and Lambertini 2001, Chari and Kehoe 2004, Uhlig 2002; see also von Hagen and Wyplosz (this volume)). In line with the proposition by Rodden (2004 and 2006), these studies point out that a setup of a single monetary authority and numerous fiscal authorities requires effective fiscal policy constraints to avoid excessive deficits.

2.2 Theoretical perspectives: optimum currency areas

The classical case for a fiscal union accompanying a monetary union is the theory of optimum currency areas (OCAs) pioneered by Mundell (1961), Kenen (1969) and McKinnon (1963). The original OCA approach weighed the benefits of adopting a single currency against the costs of abandoning independent monetary policy. The benefits of adopting a single currency and a single monetary policy are the reduction of transactions costs of using multiple currencies. These benefits would be greater the more open and the more extensive the trade connections are for the economies involved. The costs occur in the face of shocks which hit the members asymmetrically. Adjustment to such shocks can be facilitated by flexible wages and prices and by labor mobility. If these mechanisms do not function well then this approach makes the case for a common fiscal authority or a formal fiscal arrangement (fiscal federalism) to transfer resources from the members facing positive shocks to those facing negative shocks.

Mundell (1973a), referred to as Mundell II in distinction to his 1961 article (McKinnon 2004), argued that in the case of free capital mobility, the exchange rate becomes a target for speculative movements and a source of asymmetric shocks. Hence abandoning a flexible exchange rate is an additional benefit of a currency union. Therefore a country might be interested in joining a currency union even if other adjustment mechanisms are not well developed. More recently it has been argued that financial integration leads to the development of market-based risk-sharing arrangements which will offset the effects of asymmetric shocks and obviate the need for additional fiscal stabilizing instruments.

Two market-based mechanisms can provide private agents insurance against negative idiosyncratic shocks and hence ameliorate the negative consequences of EMU: an internationally diversified portfolio can protect private individuals from a negative idiosyncratic shock to their domestic assets and borrowing and lending can smooth consumption.

Finally Frankel and Rose (1998) have argued that areas which do not qualify *ex ante* as OCAs may actually ex post become OCAs. They present evidence that ex-post integration of goods and capital markets follows monetary unions. In rationalizing production across national boundaries, the asymmetry of real output movements between markets is reduced and hence there is less of a need either for fiscal transfers or for the preservation of independent monetary policies.

2.3 Empirical evidence

An extensive empirical literature since the 1990s has ascertained the extent to which the euro area satisfied the various criteria for an OCA and whether there is a case for a fiscal union or fiscal federalism to supplement the monetary union.

2.3.1 Asymmetric shocks?

The literature assesses the extent to which the euro area is subject to idiosyncratic shocks, defined as different economic disturbances that are either initially different or affect regions in different ways. Eichengreen (1997b) finds that asymmetric disturbances, measured by the real exchange rate, are more variable in Europe than in the USA. Other evidence by Bayoumi and Eichengreen (1993) and von Hagen and Neumann (1994) complement these results. According to Bayoumi and Eichengreen (1993), "These studies uniformly point to the conclusion that adjustment to region-specific shocks, whether by market or by policy, is faster in the USA than in Europe."

2.3.2 Labor mobility

De Grauwe and Vanhaverbeke (1993) report very low migration within the European countries. Eichengreen (1993) finds that interregional mobility is much more sensitive to changes in wage differentials in the USA than in the UK and in Italy. Obstfeld and Peri (1998) find that there is little migration in response to asymmetric shocks within European countries, relative to the USA. The literature suggests that intraregional mobility in the euro area is low. International migration in the euro area will probably be even lower since language and culture add further barriers to labor mobility.

2.3.3 Wage and price flexibility

The empirical evidence indicates that both wages and prices are sticky in the short run, indicating a costly adjustment to negative shocks, involving an increase in unemployment. Dessy (2004) analyses wage dynamics using the European Community Household Panel data for twelve countries, 1994–6. She finds a high degree of nominal wage rigidity for all the countries. Thus wage/price flexibility in the euro area does not seem to be very helpful in accommodating idiosyncratic shocks.

2.3.4 Risk-sharing mechanisms

The early OCA literature emphasized the role of government-based risk-sharing mechanisms consisting of transfers and other discretionary grants. Initial evidence by Sala-i-Martin and Sachs (1992) showed for the USA that a one dollar drop in state income could be compensated by an increase in net transfers of 60 cents, while Eichengreen (1997a, 1997b) calculated that fiscal transfers between the member states of the EU was only a fraction of the US magnitudes. According to Hartland (1949), fiscal federal transfers served to offset much of the interregional losses following the collapse of the US banking system in the 1930s. However, recent work (von Hagen 2000; Obstfeld and Peri 1998; Mélitz and Zumer 2002; Balli and Sørensen 2007) has greatly diminished the size of the offsets estimated by Sala-i-Martin and Sachs and by Eichengreen to between 5 percent and 15 percent.

The recent evidence on risk sharing finds that for the USA, the capital markets provide most of the insurance against idiosyncratic shocks (Asdrubali *et al.* 1996, Mélitz 2004). Europe lags behind the USA in pooling risks through portfolio diversification (Mélitz 2004) but the borrowing channel is almost as well developed in the EU as in the USA (Balli and Sørensen 2007). Increasing financial integration in the EU, although less than the USA, suggests an even stronger contribution of financial markets to risk sharing. Finally, recent evidence (Mélitz 2004, Kalemli-Ozcan *et al.* 2005, Balli and Sørensen 2007) finds that financial and real integration in the EU has increased the symmetry of business cycles. This again may reduce the need for accommodation of idiosyncratic shocks through risk-sharing mechanisms. This is in line with the hypothesis of endogeneity of currency unions advanced by Frankel and Rose (1998) (see also Mongelli (this volume)).

2.4 Monetary and fiscal unions: history and current practice

The argument by Eichengreen (1991) and others that fiscal federalism can offset the effects of asymmetric shocks and improve upon the operation of a monetary union depends on a number of assumptions which may not hold. To isolate the characteristics that make fiscal unions successful we describe the historical experience of several fiscal unions: the United States, Argentina and Germany. The first can be viewed as a successful fiscal union. Canada and Australia have had similar experiences. The second, Argentina can be viewed as a less successful monetary union. Brazil may fit into the same category. Germany is an intermediate case.

2.4.1 The United States
The history of US fiscal federalism goes back to the Constitution of 1789. After the Declaration of Independence in 1776, the Articles of Confederation created a league of sovereign states in which the Congress

did not have the power of taxation, or the power to control trade or the currency. This arrangement was unsuccessful, largely because of: spillover effects of each state's independent monetary and fiscal policy; the impediments to a free market; and the weakness of Congress. The Constitution of 1789 gave the federal government the power to collect taxes and tariffs and to issue currency, and to provide the public goods of defense and international diplomacy. The tenth amendment declared that all powers not expressly delegated to the federal government by the Constitution were preserved for the states. This laid the foundation for the concept of states' rights, limited national government and dual spheres of authority between the state and federal governments.

The period from 1789 to 1901 was the era of dual federalism, characterized by little collaboration between the federal and state governments. In the 1830s many states ran large fiscal deficits to finance infrastructure projects. In the face of a major international financial crisis and fiscal shock in the years 1837 to 1840, many states faced insolvency and demanded a bailout by the Congress. This was refused, leading to widespread defaults in 1840. Thus the federal government sent a costly signal of the limits to its commitments to the states. As a result the states have approximate fiscal sovereignty.

Between 1901 and 1960 cooperation and collaboration between various levels of government increased. The defining moment in US fiscal federalism was the Great Depression (Bordo *et al.*, 1998). In the face of the massive decline in real income, the states were unable to raise the revenue necessary to meet unavoidable expenditure. In 1933, as a major component of the New Deal, President Roosevelt greatly expanded the role of the federal government in the domestic economy. In the 1930s there was a massive shift in expenditure from the local to the state and federal levels. Before 1932 the relative shares of government expenditures were: 50 percent local, 20 percent state and 30 percent federal government. After 1940 the shares were: local 30 percent, state 24 percent and 46 percent federal (Oates and Wallis 1998). Most of the increase in government expenditure came in programs administered at the federal level in cooperation with state and local governments.

Creative federalism from 1960–8 further shifted the power relationship between government levels toward the federal government through the expansion of the grant in aid system and the increasing use of regulations. Since 1970 there has been some devolution of powers back to the states.

2.4.2 Argentina

Argentina is a federal republic with twenty-four provinces. It was born out of the union of colonial regions with differing economic and social characteristics. The establishment of a national government and a constitution took almost four decades, accompanied by violent struggle. The Constitution gave the provinces priority over the nation.

The Great Depression, although milder in impact than in the USA, also led to major changes in the role of government. The key events of the 1930s were the abandonment of a currency board linked to gold and the creation of a central bank (della Paolera and Taylor 1999). The Depression led to the insolvency of many of the provinces. They were bailed out by transfers from the federal government financed by paper money issues by the central bank. The Depression also spawned an increase in both the federal and state government's shares in national income.

In subsequent decades the states kept running large fiscal deficits which were financed by transfers and loans from the federal government and by loans from the provincial banks. These loans were then discounted at the central bank. By the late 1980s Argentina had hyperinflation. It was ended by the 1991 Convertibility Law which established a currency board arrangement ending inflationary central bank financing of public sector deficits at all levels.

By the mid 1990s many provinces again began running large deficits which were funded by national treasury bonds. In 2002, Argentina suffered a serious debt, banking and currency crisis which ended the Convertibility Law. Many commentators have attributed the 2002 crisis to irresponsible behavior by the provinces and the subsequent run-up in the public debt to GDP ratio.

2.4.3 Germany

The Federal Republic of Germany consists of a federal government, sixteen Länder (state) governments and numerous municipal governments. The national unification of Germany in 1871 was based on a strong tradition of regional governments. After unification of the German Reich total government spending increased from 10 percent of GDP in 1881 to 18 percent in 1913 with an increase in the central government's share from 3 percent to 6 percent.

The Weimar Republic was founded as a "decentralized unitary state" after the defeat of World War I, and experienced dramatic shocks in quick succession: the hyperinflation of 1922–3, the stabilization of 1923–4, and the Great Depression. The Nazi regime after 1933 created a unitary state with all power held by the central government while the states were relegated to administrative districts.

After World War II, a federal state was created based on Länder which were conceived as state units. They were given considerable power. The German system is less cooperative and more competitive than federations like the USA, Canada and Switzerland. Although the central government officially follows the no-bailout rule, the commitment is not fully credible and this can create an incentive by the Länder to borrow excessively. This was the case in the 1970s and 1980s when the Länder of Bremen and Saarland received special supplementary transfers from the federal government. Many have argued that the large deficits of the Länder were largely responsible for Germany's breach of the EU's Stability and Growth Pact (SGP).

2.5 Some lessons from history

The brief historical comparison of three fiscal unions has some relevance for the case for a fiscal union for the EU. First, we observe that all of the fiscal unions were preceded by political ones. In each case independent regions decided to found a union because of military insecurity and a consequent need for common defense or the desire to be independent of foreign powers. Second, institutional development in these federations was driven by exceptional events, often economic disasters. The best example is the Great Depression which affected the institutions at all levels of government. In all cases it lent to an increase in government power and its centralization. Third, institutional evolution worked through an "institutional learning by doing" process. Not all the federations learned from their negative experiences of the past. In the presence of moral hazard the federal government has to give a signal of commitment and often a lesson to the subnational authorities, otherwise they do not learn. Thus the US federal government taught the right lesson to the states in 1840 that there would be no bailout of their debt. This was not the case in Argentina or Germany. In the case of Argentina (and Brazil) there is still no credible mechanism to impose fiscal discipline.

3. Future challenges facing EMU

Institutions may be conceived of as continually evolving systems of rules, that depend for their legitimacy on a relatively widely shared consensus that they are not actively dysfunctional. They are not usually transformed without a major crisis. This paper tries to evolve a few lessons that can be learnt about transformative crises in the histories of national currencies and national central banks. In the past, central banks, and the currencies they managed, have been discredited or put under severe strain as a result of:

- severe or endemic fiscal problems creating pressures for the monetization of public debt;
- low economic growth which may produce demands for central banks to pursue more expansionary policies;
- regional strains producing a demand for different monetary policies to adjust to particular regional pressures (such conflicts have played an important part in the near or actual break-up of federations);
- severe crises of the financial system (which discredited the central banks of the interwar era); and
- tensions between the international and the domestic role of a leading currency, which produced conflicts about British monetary policy in the 1920s and about US policy in the 1960s and 1970s.

How far do there exist analogies between the circumstances that produced these historical problems and the likely development of the euro?

3.1 *The fiscal dilemma*

The extreme fiscal strains that destroyed monetary regimes such as that of the French revolutionary regime, or of Russia and the central European states in the first decades of the twentieth century, were the result of prolonged and intense military conflict of a type that is no longer conceivable in contemporary Europe. But in the second half of the twentieth century all industrialized states, including especially those of western Europe, experienced a sustained rise in government expenditure that was historically unique in that it was not an accompaniment of war. While it is often argued that the increase in such expenditure has made the states concerned more socially stable and also more resilient to economic shocks, there is also a limit to that expansion of public sector activity. At some stage, a society reaches the limit of the impositions it can bear.

In a globalized world, there is increasing pressure to reduce rates of taxation, especially corporate taxation. The accession to the EU of new member countries with a low tax regime (notably the flat tax regimes of Estonia and Slovakia) has produced additional tax competition within the EU. On the other hand, the political pressures that result in rising demand for public services are continually increasing. The ageing of the population, and the increased technical availability of expensive medical treatments, add to those pressures.

One way of solving the fiscal dilemma in the past was inflation. In the 1970s and 1980s Europe, and the world, had generally high levels of inflation. But it was also increasingly recognized that such inflation imposed a cost because it distorted incentives; and at higher levels, it provoked considerable political unease. One way of seeing the evolution of an increasingly hard European Monetary System (EMS), and then the EMU, is as a mechanism for the imposition of external discipline. The European framework made it easier for governments to press on with reforms to limit expenditure, that could be presented to hostile parliaments and pressure groups as an unavoidable part of an exercise in integration that promised substantial long-run benefits. Within the EMS, however, some countries still experienced considerable fiscal pressure; and fiscal stimuli translated into increased demand, increased prices and a real exchange rate appreciation that threatened competitiveness. These countries could still in the EMS resort to an exchange rate realignment (as in 1992, where pressure in Italy set off a general realignment). The monetary union obviously prevents such adjustment measures being undertaken by national policy makers. The only (partially effective) substitute left is fiscal measures to compensate firms for real exchange rate appreciation. But such measures have a fiscal cost.

The most obvious threat to the single currency is usually held to arise out of the imperfect control and coordination of national fiscal policies. Some commentators argue as a result that monetary unions produce an inexorable dynamic in the direction of fiscal unions.

The fiscal criteria in the Maastricht Treaty (and later on in the SGP) were the subject of immensely protracted and complicated negotiation, and were intended to address this problem. In the aftermath of the recession of 2000–1, and of Europe's weak growth performance, substantial pressure from the large states led to some loosening of the criteria. When most of the large member states broke the rules, the then President of the Commission, Romano Prodi, referred to the pact as "stupid," and a 2005 summit formally modified the rule so as to make it more flexible in the face of cyclical downturns.

A formalized system of fiscal federalism would however not necessarily deal with the problems of fiscal indiscipline on the part of member states. Indeed, the expectation of institutionalized transfers or bailouts following fiscal problems might well be expected to increase the incentives for bad behavior. Stricter observance of the existing system and its rules, on the other hand, might lead to pressure to reform. Fiscal reforms would in the longer run be expected to raise the rate of growth.

3.2 Growth rates

The growth rate of the economy is a central determinant of the likely long-run success of the euro. For reasons that will be discussed below, low growth, or very different rates of growth in different parts of the euro area, would be likely to raise political questions and produce political tensions around the setting of the monetary policy. Both the ability to comply with the SGP, and the political tolerance of an independent central bank, are highly dependent on the overall rate of economic growth. The revival of growth in Europe since 2005 brought a reduction in the deficits, but they reappeared because of the crisis. In the longer term (as in other rich industrial countries), the additional costs imposed by increased life expectancy, an ageing population structure, and rising health costs are likely to impose a heavy strain. Forecasting long-run developments involves many uncertainties, but almost every contemporary prognosis sees Europe as growing significantly slower than other parts of the world. Fogel (2007) suggested a rate of real GDP growth for the period 2000–40 of 1.2 percent for the industrialized EU15, a slightly higher figure than the 1.1 percent for Japan, but much lower than the 3.8 percent for the United States or 7.1 percent for India or 8.4 percent for China.

The relatively poor growth performance is conventionally explained by inflexible labor markets and by more limited capital markets that make venture capital harder and scarcer. In both areas, the introduction of the single currency has brought greater flexibility, but one other brake on European growth remains widely recognized but poorly counteracted in policy terms. The Lisbon Agenda included an opening-up of services, yet this is the area where the most restrictions still apply, and where national governments are powerfully pressed to resist attempts on an EU-wide basis to introduce greater elements of competition. The services directive was effectively so watered down in 2007 that little remains of the reform initiative. There is, in short, especially at a national level, a critical resistance to important elements of the liberalizing agenda. The blockage is historically disappointing, in that in the early stages of European integration in the 1950s and 1960s, the European authorities enforced a highly competitive market in the dynamic sectors of the time, in manufacturing, while offering compensation to the less dynamic agricultural sector. This highly successful strategy would, if translated into today's circumstances, involve enforcing a high level of competition in the dynamic areas of today, mostly services, while providing safety nets to those affected by the relative decline of Europe's competitive advantage in some areas of manufacturing. But the vision of the EU as providing enhanced competition has not been universal or pervasive, and the consequence has been suboptimal growth.

There is a political economy reason to worry about the effects of low growth on the euro, and to see it as vulnerable politically to backlashes against globalization. In many parts of Europe, globalization is seen widely as a major threat to the social order; and the resentments are used by politicians eager to establish a higher political profile. Workers, especially in manufacturing, are faced with a threat of job losses or radical reductions in income as a consequence of low-wage competition from Asia or from eastern Europe. Workers in manufacturing and in services are worried about the effects of immigration on income levels. Politically, the backlash against globalization is associated with the extremes of left and right, which often take their themes and rhetorical engagement from each other. But since the conventional right and the conventional left compete against each other, and need to mobilize as many votes as possible, they are also likely to take up some of the anti-globalization language in order to maximize their support and prevent a slippage of voters to the extremes. Sometimes they will also experience pressure to transform this rhetoric into policy.

The anti-globalization movement, however, finds it hard to identify concrete targets against which to direct the widespread malaise. In consequence, the single currency has already become a popular whipping boy for anti-globalization sentiment. It is blamed for price increases of some consumer items: in Germany, popular newspapers launched campaigns detailing the effects of the "Teuro" (expensive euro; teuer = expensive). In Italy, some very prominent consumer items, such as pizza or coffee, became much more expensive.[3]

The immediate wave of dissatisfaction surrounding the introduction of the euro quickly ebbed. But it holds an instructive lesson: the episode was used by governments, and governments took at least some part in the mobilization of critical opinion. The German Finance Minister Hans Eichel endorsed the view that the euro had led to price increases, and the Consumer Affairs Minister Renate Künast created an office to marshal complaints from customers. The Greek Socialist government under Costas Simitis encouraged a one-day boycott of shops.

A major feature in anti-globalization sentiment is the belief that some protection against the forces of the world economy is needed. According to this view, the primary obligation of the political system is to steer or cushion the process of globalization: to stop takeovers by predatory investment groups (in German referred to as locusts or *Heuschrecken*); to protect local jobs; and to provide credit to liquidity-lacking businesses. An obvious corollary to this argumentation sees a national currency as a better carapace than a Europeanized currency. The necessity of a common monetary policy requires interest rates that are "too high" in some countries and areas (higher than the rate that would be desirable if a domestic central bank were setting rates).

Consequently, interests that demand a monetary policy more focused on growth are usually critical of the ECB; and in some cases (such as the Italian *Lega Nord*) see a return to national money as an appropriate solution. In the 2007 French presidential election, Nicolas Sarkozy derived considerable mileage from criticism of the ECB, and then repeated the criticism after the election.

At present, the signs of such a use of the euro as a focus of globalization fears are relatively weak. Indeed, the euro is generally quite popular – more so than at its launch as a circulating currency in 2002. Since the Maastricht Treaty, and even more dramatically since the introduction of the euro, public opinion surveys conducted by Eurobarometer have shown increasing degrees of support for the single currency. But these figures also reflected a general increase in satisfaction that accompanies better economic performance and might have reverted at the onset of economic difficulties.

3.3 Regional pressures

Regions with different growth patterns or different political economies are likely to press for different monetary policies, and in a democratic setting the result might be extreme polarization and conflict. Such polarization occurred in many gold standard countries in the late nineteenth century, when farming regions believed that they would benefit from the abandonment of a deflationary gold regime and the adoption of a bimetallic standard. In the United States, the agrarian mid-West and the South were pitted against the North-east; in Germany there was a similar divide between a grain-producing East and the industrial areas of western Germany. Until a general price rise occurred after the discovery of gold in Alaska, Australia and South Africa in the last years of the century, monetary policy was highly politicized. In more extreme settings, federations can even break up. In the last years of the Yugoslav Federation, as democratization began, a gap opened up between the industrially stagnant Serb areas and more dynamic regions in the north, and fuelled the ethnic conflict. For the non-Serbs, the realization that Serbians were imposing an inflation (and using the fiscal proceeds of inflation to finance their own goals) made a break-up of the Federation an urgent political demand for Slovenes, Croats and, tragically, also for Bosnians. Similarly, in post-1918 Germany, the idea that Berlin was promoting an inflationary policy to its own advantage prompted Rhineland, Saxon and Bavarian separatism and a "Los von Berlin" movement.

These may appear to be extreme and problematic precedents. But very different economic experiences undoubtedly promote feelings of regional and sometimes even of ethnic difference. Given Europe's highly troubled twentieth century history, many responsible policy makers are worried about a resurgence of historical divides.

The extension of the euro to new Member States in itself will create new challenges. This issue has already been widely debated with regard to the adoption of the euro by the Baltic states. The new member countries are powerfully growing emerging market economies, which experience and will continue to experience rising inflation as prices for services rise, corresponding to the increased incomes producers of tradeables derive from selling to global markets (the Balassa-Samuelson effect). Correspondingly, the mature markets of the west are likely to experience periodic bouts of anxiety about deflation (and anxiety about excessively tight ECB policy), as competition on markets for tradeable goods and services drives down prices.

In the longer run, there is a different sort of question about growth in the European setting. Will there be unequal growth across the EU, with faster growth in the catch-up economies of central and eastern Europe? At present, the disparity in growth is very apparent, and is causing significant problems for the formulation of an appropriate monetary policy (see below); but in the longer run, these disparities may disappear. The major channel here is migration flows: the inflow of central Europeans to Britain, Ireland and Sweden since 2005 has significantly raised growth rates in those recipient economies.

Conversely, the outflow from eastern and central Europe of the most skilled and active sectors of the labor force is likely to reduce the growth potential in the long run, and create the fiscal problems associated with ageing and with demographic imbalances elsewhere in the EU. By 2025 a fifth to a quarter of the East European population is estimated to be sixty-five or older. The World Bank takes this argument to forecast a sharp reduction in growth in eastern Europe, which it terms "from red to gray" (Chawla *et al.*, 2007). Low growth rates are likely to become a common European destiny.

3.4 Financial stability

In the past, financial sector shocks have played a decisive role in the undermining of monetary regimes and the discrediting of the central banks responsible for their operation. The most dramatic of such episodes occurred in the interwar Great Depression, where banking panics in central Europe and the United States exacerbated the problems of the real economy. Unstable banks withdrew credits from borrowers, forcing firms that would otherwise have been solvent to liquidate stock at depressed prices. The major industrial countries that had significant banking problems fared significantly worse than those economies with no or only limited banking collapses. In particular the United States, with waves of banking panics after the fall of 1930, and Germany, with a meltdown of the banking system in June and July 1931, were very badly hit by the real consequences of the financial storm.

The weakness of the American and German banks in the interwar era was at least in some measure the consequence of political federalism.

1. Federalism encouraged the development of a banking system that was regional in character. In particular in the United States, state banks suffered because their risk was concentrated in particular sectors.
2. Federalism made for inefficiencies in regulating banks. In Germany, a major source of difficulty was the parallel system of savings banks (*Sparkassen*) which were controlled by local authorities, and which responded to local political pressures to lend.
3. Federalism produced a dispute about the appropriate monetary response of the central banking institutions. This may be an especially acute problem in the early life of the federation or the central bank. With regard to the United States, Eichengreen (1992) and Wheelock (2000) showed how the Federal Reserve found it difficult to resolve regional conflicts in the early 1920s. Friedman and Schwartz (1963) famously presented a major cause of the immobilization of the Federal Reserve System after 1930 as lying in tensions between the New York and Chicago banks.

Europe is an integrated capital market with national bank regulators that respond in different ways to incipient problems. Since the 1980s, and especially since the introduction of the single currency, the euro-zone capital market has become partially integrated, but there are still in some countries substantial impediments to cross-national financial ownership (see Jappelli and Pagano, this volume). Nevertheless, financial institutions operate in this single capital market across national boundaries. Big mergers, such as those between Santander and Abbey National in 2004 and Unicredit and Hypervereinsbank (which had previously acquired a dominant share in the Austrian banking industry) in 2005, have started to create Europe-wide superbanks. The problem of a bank getting into difficulties because of engagements in a different country is a widely recognized problem, in theoretical discussions. But a unification of banking regulation is still a long way from being realized.

At the same time as finance has become internationalized, each country preserves its own idiosyncratic system of financial supervision and regulation. Though there has been an extensive discussion of the possibility of shifting supervision to the European level (Prati and Schinasi 1999), there are practical obstacles to making such a shift (apart from inbuilt bureaucratic resistance from existing regulators). In particular, regulation is often linked to implicit or explicit lender of last resort functions. But such activity has a significant fiscal cost, which at present cannot be assumed at a European level but would remain an issue for national governments and parliaments. Much of the previous literature has concentrated in consequence on the issue of how bailouts and rescues should be paid for after a financial crisis, as a result of the reluctance of national authorities (and their tax payers) to bear the financial burden of bailing out depositors or creditors in other states (Goodhart and Schoenmaker 2006). The current institutional framework unambiguously limits socially beneficial post-crisis workouts. But it may also limit the capacity to provide efficient preventative or pre-crisis prudential supervision. The consequent limits on the extent to which national regulators were aware of bank problems became highlighted in the credit crunch of the summer of 2007. The ECB supplied general liquidity to the market, and may have been able to avoid some financial distress.

Additionally, in the event of financial sector difficulty, the monetary policy response would be highly contested. Conventionally, bailout or reorganization is seen as the answer to solvency problems, while liquidity provision is an answer for solvent but temporarily illiquid institutions. In crisis situations, and where information about credit risk is faulty or incomplete, as in the summer of 2007, such a judgement between solvency and liquidity problems is impossible to undertake. In the absence of an ability to deal specifically with the threat posed by individual institutions and to make choices about crisis support or closing the institution, there will be more pressure on the ECB to simply deal with the situation by extending large amounts of liquidity rather than to address the solvency issues which may be concealed.

The difficulty of an effective Europe-wide response to financial sector problems thus reflects a more general problem with respect to the making of monetary policy: there may be a different political economy of money in regions of the eurozone and EU member countries, leading to contradictory pressures on policy.

3.5 The euro as an international currency

Another set of contradictory pressures on policy arises out of the increasingly important international role of the euro. The euro quickly became the second largest reserve currency of the world: the IMF's figures show for December 2006 the euro accounting for 25.8 percent of world declared reserves, with the dollar at 64.7 percent (these figures however only cover around half the world's total reserves, with another quarter held in undeclared currencies, and a further quarter in also generally hidden sovereign wealth funds outside the control of central banks) (ECB 2007a). The euro has also become the second largest currency for the issuance of securities. For short-term international debt issue, in the last quarter of 2006, it had a share of 34 percent (with the USA at 40 percent).

The euro is attractive to some countries and governments because it is not the dollar. While the international role of the dollar is deeply associated with the political and economic pre-eminence of the United States, the euro is not the currency of a superpower or even of a conventional state. For general political strategy reasons it looks more attractive. Russia in particular has made an explicitly political point in progressively raising the weight of the euro in its operational currency basket (from 35 to 40 percent in December 2005 and then again to 45 percent in February 2007).

But there is also an economic rationale in terms of diversification. The euro is not as precariously dependent on continued capital inflows as is the dollar. It may also appear better on more technical policy grounds. As a consequence of the complicated institutional structure guaranteeing the independence of the ECB, it appears to be less vulnerable to political pressure.

Considerations such as greater independence and a healthier eurozone current account may make the euro desirable as an international currency: as a reserve currency, as a store of value and as an invoicing currency. But a potential development of the euro as *the* major international currency poses policy problems analogous to those faced by Britain and the Bank of England in the nineteenth century and by the United States and the Federal Reserve System in the second half of the twentieth century. What are the ECB's global obligations as to the creation of liquidity in the case of emerging market crises? How should the ECB support the US dollar in order to forestall a dollar collapse which would be harmful for Europe in particular as well as the world at large? Would political pressure be stronger or even irresistible in these circumstances?

For both the Bank of England and the Federal Reserve System, there were moments when international considerations seemed to outweigh ones connected with domestic stability. In the most dramatic of such crises in 1931, the Bank of England was largely discredited, and the response to the crisis ended in 1945 with the nationalization of the Bank. One widely accepted interpretation of the collapse of the Bretton Woods fixed exchange rate regime between 1968 and 1973 is that at crisis moments, the United States was unwilling to sacrifice domestic priorities (particularly maintaining fast economic growth) for the sake of maintaining an international regime that was in any case widely criticized.

By contrast with Britain and the United States, Japan and Germany took a very different stance. They did not see themselves as political hegemons, and saw a widespread use of their currencies as reserves as inherently dangerous, because it would make the export economy more vulnerable to exchange rate swings. In consequence, the two fast-growing big industrial economies of the second half of the twentieth century, sought as much as possible to avoid an international role for their currencies (as did Switzerland, whose currency also seemed attractive as a stable measure of value).

The euro is in a quite different position to the yen or the Deutschmark. It has inevitably become the world's second reserve currency. One of the causes of the appreciation of the euro is often supposed to lie in the triangular relation between Asia, the United States and Europe. If for trade reasons many Asian economies, notably China, try to hold their dollar exchange rate stable (in the so-called Bretton Woods II regime), exchange rate movements arising out of large US deficits mean the appreciation of the euro. Even in the largely favorable environment of 2002–7, many European exporters complained about the appreciation of their currency, especially in countries such as Italy which compete quite extensively with the textiles, clothing and leather goods production of Asian economies. In these circumstances, the political debate about the euro can be a reflection of much larger concerns with globalization, and of Europe's perceived vulnerability in the face of the challenges that global markets in goods and services will pose.

It is – projecting into the future – quite conceivable that there will be moments at which massive political pressure, built up by underlying anti-globalization concerns and focused on the technical necessities of dealing with major international crises, leads to a serious onslaught against the ECB and against the euro.

4. Conclusions

The past experience is of monetary unions developing as part of a process of political and consequently fiscal integration. By contrast, EMU is neither purely a national nor purely an international monetary union, but has characteristics of both types, because the transfer of sovereignty is incomplete. This may mean that objections that it is not an optimum currency area (OCA) are misplaced, because the workings of an integration process are likely also to induce moves toward a closer approximation to an OCA. The incomplete transfer of sovereignty on the other hand means that there are substantial political pressures that build up in national areas that are no longer also the area of a single currency that can be adjusted against external currencies. There may be a momentum toward further fiscal integration, and that will be an indication of success in that the monetary union is working as similar unions did in the past, especially in the case of the USA and Germany, and fiscal centralization gradually emerged over a rather lengthy period of time. Analogies with the monetary unions of Germany, Italy and the USA suggest that the process of evolving a fiscal union takes a long time. The EMU has the additional problem that its area will change more dramatically because of the addition of new members, and because of the governance issues raised by the non-coincidence of EMU and the EU.

On that long road to more fiscal integration, however, there may be many bumpy areas. Some of these bumps cannot easily be measured or mapped in advance. In particular, unpleasant fiscal arithmetic for member countries may produce strain in the area as a whole. Such arithmetic is most likely to arise as a consequence of continually depressed rates of growth. One of the benefits that the move to the single currency brought was a reduction of interest rates that might lead to better fiscal performance but also better growth performance. But supposing that this stimulus is not adequate, and the euro area continues to face sluggish growth? In order to reap the benefits of a better growth performance, competitive stimuli as well as a low interest environment are needed, but EU countries have been slow in opening up the potentially fast-growing services sector to competition.

Low growth will also produce direct challenges to the management of the currency, and a demand for a more politically controlled and for a more expansive monetary policy. Such demands might arise in some parts or regions or countries of the euro area, but not in others. They would lead to a politically highly difficult discussion of monetary governance. This discussion will be more difficult if there is a widespread perception that the international role of the euro is at odds with domestic political demands that the currency should be supportive or sustaining of growth. Financial sector instability, with a potential need for bank bailouts, could also be a source of difficulty. Finally, in addition to all these threats, domestic responses to the challenge of globalization in markets for goods and services may also be displaced into a discussion of the euro, with the single currency and the central bank that manages it taking the position of fall guy for radicalized and generalized discontent. On the other hand, if all these bumps are overcome, and a process of gradual transfer of fiscal responsibility toward greater centralization occurs, there is the possibility that the eurozone will match the achievement of other late realizers of monetary unification, such as the United States or Germany.

Notes

1. See Bordo and Jonung (2003).
2. See Bordo *et al.* (2007).
3. See for an academic treatment: Gaiotti and Lippi (2005).

3 | Sui generis *EMU*

BARRY EICHENGREEN

1. Introduction

The thesis of this chapter is that there is no historical precedent for Europe's monetary union. To be sure, it is possible to point to similar historical experiences, the most obvious of which were in the nineteenth century, occurred in Europe, and had "union" as part of their names. But EMU differs from these earlier monetary unions.[1] The closer one looks the more uncomfortable one becomes with the effort to draw parallels on the basis of this, and related, historical experience.

I elaborate these points by reviewing previous efforts to use historical experience to shed light on European monetary union. I argue that these earlier efforts to draw parallels between EMU and monetary unions past are more likely to mislead than to offer useful insights. The important lesson is the need for nuance when drawing lessons from this history.

Where history is useful is not in drawing parallels but in pinpointing differences. It is useful for highlighting what is distinctive about EMU and why, therefore, parallels mislead. I illustrate the point with reference to three issues around which discussion of EMU currently focuses: the relationship between monetary union and financial integration; the connections between monetary union and financial stability; and the probability that the euro area might break up.

2. Imperfect analogies

The leading historical analogies with EMU are the classical gold standard, the Latin and Scandinavian Unions, a number of relatively

Financial support from the European Commission and the Coleman Fung Risk Management Center at the University of California, Berkeley is gratefully acknowledged, as are comments from Lars Jonung and other participants in the Commission workshop.

specialized twentieth century monetary unions, and various national experiences with monetary and political unification.

2.1 The gold standard

A number of authors have sought to use gold standard experience to draw implications for EMU. The idea is that the gold standard constrained national monetary autonomy in the same manner as EMU. Its maintenance therefore required the development of alternative adjustment mechanisms. Evidence from the gold standard permits one to test the notion that wage and price flexibility – and the flexibility of markets generally – is important for the smooth operation of such a regime. It can be used to explore whether adoption of this regime encouraged the development of the relevant flexibility. It can be used to test whether by limiting exchange rate variability the gold standard was conducive to the growth of international trade and to financial integration. It can be used to investigate how much fiscal and macroeconomic policy coordination was needed for the operation of this system.[2]

The problem is that the gold standard was first and foremost a national arrangement. It involved a national decision to peg the national currency to an external numeraire, like Latvia's today, not a decision to abolish the bilateral exchange rate by abolishing the national currency, as the founding members of EMU agreed in 1999. The attractions of adopting the gold standard were not independent of the number of other countries that similarly adopted it.[3] But occasional international conferences on the desirability of harmonizing national monetary arrangements notwithstanding, the decision was taken at the national level and the regime was operated by the national central bank, treasury or equivalent.

Under the gold standard, as in the case of all exchange rate pegs, the central parity was surrounded by a fluctuation band, reflecting transactions costs.[4] Thus the gold standard, unlike a monetary union, did not eliminate exchange rate variability among the participants.[5] Studies of modern experience caution against drawing inferences about the effects of monetary union on, say, the volume of trade from evidence on the effects of reducing exchange rate volatility. They suggest that the trade-promoting effects of reducing exchange rate variability, even to low levels, are less powerful than those of establishing a monetary union. (This is the finding of Rose 2000.) Similarly, in their study of exchange rate regimes and international trade prior to 1913, Lopez-Cordova and

Meissner (2000) find a smaller trade-promoting effect of the gold standard on a pair of gold-standard countries than when two or more countries established a monetary union.

Moreover, because the gold standard was a national arrangement, it was straightforward for the national authorities to suspend or abandon it, as they not infrequently did. They could and did suspend the law or statute requiring the free convertibility of the national currency into gold at a fixed domestic-currency price or even just complicate the operation of convertibility.[6]

It has been argued that suspensions of convertibility in periods of distress, during which the exchange rate was allowed to depreciate, were integral to the operation of this system.[7] In the absence of another adjustment mechanism, this escape clause provided partial insulation from balance-of-payments disturbances. Countries were able to peg under normal circumstances precisely because they could float in periods of exceptional volatility. This escape clause was not destabilizing because it was presumed that convertibility at the previous parity would be restored as soon as the crisis had passed. There is no analogous escape clause in EMU.

This mechanism functioned differently at different times and places. The presumption that, as soon as the period of distress had passed, convertibility would be restored at the previously prevailing price of gold applied more powerfully in some cases than others. The more economically and financially developed a country was the more likely it was that it would adhere to this resumption rule. The assumption that convertibility would be restored at the earlier exchange rate was also more prevalent before World War I than after.[8]

Whatever the other advantages of the escape clause, it created uncertainty. Currency stability today did not guarantee currency stability tomorrow. Especially after 1914 and especially in less developed countries, there was little assurance that the exchange rate would retain its value. Investors in domestic-currency-denominated securities might see their claims devalued. The literature on interest rate spreads suggests that the gold standard made for interest rate convergence, but it does not suggest that the gold standard, unlike EMU, eliminated currency risk.[9]

2.2 Multinational monetary unions

Pre-1913 monetary unions, the Latin Monetary Union and Scandinavian Monetary Union, have also been studied in an effort to shed light on these questions. The Latin Union was established in 1866 by France, Belgium, Italy and Switzerland, joined subsequently by Greece. The union treaty specified standard sizes and fineness for the gold and silver coins of the participating countries, guaranteed the acceptability of each member's coins as legal tender for effecting private and public payments in other member states, and attempted to regulate the emission of subsidiary silver coins (with lower specie content) by each union member.

Flandreau (2000), Einaudi (2001) and Helleiner (2003) discuss the members' motivations. These included the desire to simplify international transactions and foster trade, the desire on the part of France to enhance the position of Paris as a financial center by enlarging the domain over which a franc-like monetary unit circulated, and the effort to reinforce French foreign policy by raising the influence of the franc.[10] But the fundamental problem that the Latin Union was designed to solve had nothing to do with modern arguments for or against monetary unification. The participating countries, led by France, operated a bimetallic system under which they supplemented full-bodied large-denomination coinage with less valuable silver coins and, where necessary, subsidiary coinage whose metallic content was less than its face value. Bimetallism required stabilizing the relative price of silver and gold in the face of fluctuations in world market prices. This could be done if central banks paid out the metal whose price was high in return for the metal whose price was low and allowed the composition of the domestic circulation to change so as to meet changes in the composition of global demand without exhausting the circulation of either metal.[11] While a single bimetallic country, even one as large as France, was too small to exercise this stabilizing influence, doing so might be easier for a collection of countries whose weight relative to world markets was greater. From this flowed the effort to coordinate.

In the event, the Latin Union proved too small to stabilize the world market price of silver. As silver supplies continued to expand, the Latin Union countries were forced to suspend silver convertibility and go onto de facto gold standards. Now the problem shifted to their subsidiary coinage, which they had an incentive to overproduce and circulate in neighboring countries. There followed a series of agreements designed to limit its emission, which proved incompletely effective. The Latin Union treaty was another effort to solve this problem.

In contrast to EMU, then, this was an attempt to create a common monetary circulation without a common monetary authority. There was no central bank at the level of the union. Precisely because policy was not decided by a transnational entity like the European Central Bank, there was more scope than in Europe today for individual member states to control their money supplies. Countries were able to produce their own subsidiary coinage in excess of levels specified in the monetary union treaty so long as they could get away with it. They had an incentive to do so, since increases in the circulation drove up prices not just at home but monetary-union-wide.[12] The requirement that the issuing central bank redeem that subsidiary coinage at par or accept it in payment of taxes and other public obligations provided a check, but an imperfect one insofar as collecting large amounts of small coin and transferring it from, say, Paris to Athens was costly. Greece's partners in the Latin Union sought to solve this problem by requiring that all small Greek coins be produced at the Paris mint, but the provision does not appear to have been effective.[13] No analogous free-rider problem exists under EMU, since the national central banks participating in the eurosystem have no independent control of the money supply.

Nor does membership in the Latin Union appear to have been as difficult to modify as membership in EMU. Within a few months of ratification of the Latin Union treaty, Italy suspended the convertibility of her banknotes into metal coin and injected into circulation large numbers of small denomination banknotes, contravening provisions of the treaty. The result was increased seigniorage for Italy and inflation for its partners, as Italy's small silver coins flowed into the Latin Union countries.[14] Monetary options under this earlier union were thus quite different than under EMU.

The other prominent nineteenth century experiment along these lines, the Scandinavian Monetary Union, was in many respects similar.[15] The motivation for its formation was to standardize on a decimal basis the coinage of the participating states (Denmark and Sweden, joined after two years by Norway), given their extensive economic, financial and political relations – and the intercirculation of national currencies within the region. The union was formed in the 1870s following Germany's adoption of the gold standard and concurrently with the shift of the Latin Union countries to gold. Hence the circulation of the participating countries was based on gold. Gold coins being impractical for small transactions, they were supplemented (in practice dominated) by token coins and notes convertible into gold.[16] From the late 1870s the Bank of Sweden agreed to formally accept Danish and Norwegian notes at par. From 1894 the participating central banks agreed to permit the drawing of drafts on one another at par. From 1901 the Bank of Norway and Bank of Denmark accepted one another's notes at par.[17] The result was a significant narrowing of the gold points.[18]

Again, however, analogies with EMU are strained because there was no central bank at the level of the union. The three members retained their national central banks and the ability, within the constraints of the gold-bullion standard, to regulate their money supplies. There was only limited communication between the participating central banks at the outset. Separate exchange rates continued to be quoted in financial centers like Copenhagen on their respective monies, reflecting the fact that the gold points had been narrowed but not eliminated. All this is quite different from the current European situation.

What deterred the excessive emission of token coins and banknotes during the period when these were accepted at par? In part the answer is the gold standard: partner central banks could demand conversion into gold by the issuing monetary authority; knowledge of this restrained the temptation to overissue.[19] Another part of the answer is mechanisms for detecting attempts to renege on the agreement: to prevent debasement, the union agreement provided for regular examinations of national coins and for sharing of information on minting and issuance practices. A final part of the answer is political. Sweden and Norway maintained a political union from 1814 until 1905. Revealingly, dissolution of that union led the Bank of Sweden to terminate the agreement to accept the notes and drafts of its partners at par, though it continued to accept them at a discount. The outbreak of World War I then led national imperatives to the fore and forced the participating central banks to suspend gold convertibility and subordinate the creation of paper money and token coins to the war effort. Sweden threatened to withdraw from the union unless its partners agreed to embargo gold exports, which they quickly did. Even this did not prevent the agreement to accept one another's gold coins at par from being terminated in 1920.

The Scandinavian Union was more durable than the Latin Union.[20] But exit – either partial as in 1905 or complete as during and after World War I – was relatively easy because the participating countries never stripped their national central banks of the power to create money. Indeed, the Scandinavian Union treaty included an explicit exit clause, which required members terminating their participation only to give one year's notice (Bergman, 1999, p. 365). In this respect as well, the Scandinavian Union was very different from EMU.

2.3 Twentieth-century monetary unions

Previous work has also examined a number of nineteenth century monetary unions. Examples include the Anglo-Irish monetary union that prevailed from the foundation of the Irish Republic until the creation of the European Monetary System in 1979; the CFA franc zone of francophone West and Central Africa (and one former Portuguese overseas province, Guinea-Bissau) that has operated for more than forty-five years; the Belgium-Luxembourg monetary union that prevailed from the early 1920s until the advent of the euro; the Switzerland-Liechtenstein monetary union; the France-Monaco monetary union; the Italy-San Marino-Vatican City monetary union; the US-Liberia monetary union; and the US-Panama monetary union.[21] There have also been attempts to draw lessons for EMU from these experiences. Studies have shown that members of these common-currency groupings trade more extensively with one another than their characteristics otherwise predict.[22] They run lower inflation rates than otherwise comparable countries with national currencies. Their financial markets are unusually integrated. There is little evidence that they exhibit more fiscal discipline than non-members (Fatás and Rose 2001).

The problem is that these arrangements are all quite unlike EMU. Typically they are composed of one large country and a much smaller one rather than of several comparably sized members.[23] Policy is delegated to the large member, giving the small member little say. Belgium determined monetary policy for the Belgium-Luxembourg monetary union.[24] The Swiss National Bank makes policy for the Switzerland-Liechtenstein union. The Federal Reserve Board sets policy without input from the Liberian or Panamanian authorities. Issues of shared governance and of the creation of transnational institutions analogous to the ECB do not arise.

One can reasonably question the generality of inferences drawn from trade, financial and other effects when one country is so small relative to the other. Technically, the problem is that the control group and treatment group are very different.[25] At least this is the problem if one doubts the ability of multivariate regression (where the independent variables include measures of country size) to adequately control for differences in the two groups (Baldwin 2006a).

An unusual case is the CFA franc zone, which includes a number of countries of broadly similar size and where there exist two transnational monetary authorities, one for the West African Currency Union and one for the Central African Currency Union.[26] But countries are restrained from exiting (and their policies are restrained in other ways) by the fact that France provides them with direct assistance and subsidies, partly contingent on their participation in the arrangement. France's ability to do so derives from the fact that its financial system is roughly thirty times the combined size of the financial systems of the CFA franc zone countries; in this sense this system exhibits the same asymmetry as the other monetary unions enumerated above. The relationship between France and the members of the CFA zone is not exactly that of monetary union partners. Indicative of this, the CFA franc has been devalued several times against the French franc, most recently in 1999. France's role in the system means that this case is not particularly useful for drawing analogies with EMU.

2.4 *National monetary unions*

At one level, the most relevant of these imperfect analogies are cases of national monetary unification – how the United States became a monetary union (Rockoff 2003), how Germany became a monetary union (Holtfrerich 1989), how Italy became a monetary union (Toniolo *et al.* 2003). These countries all evolved true monetary unions, with a single currency whose availability was regulated by a single central bank. They were more than quasi-fixed-exchange-rate arrangements like the gold standard, the Latin Union and the Scandinavian Union. They all ended up creating central banks at the level of the union that effectively monopolized control of the money supply.[27] All of them eventually abandoned monetary rules like gold convertibility that had relieved the central bank of responsibility for making policy decisions.[28]

At another level, however, these national cases lack the distinguishing feature of EMU, which is monetary union in the absence of political union. In Europe today there exists a central bank whose domain is wider than that of the national political institutions whose consent was required for its creation and continued existence. The United States and Germany have (or had) a federal government and a central bank at the level of that federation. Europe possesses the central bank but not the federal government.[29]

This is not simply EMU's distinguishing feature but also the source of its most fundamental challenges. How can the ECB be held socially accountable for its decisions in the absence of an equally consequential political counterweight at the level of the monetary union? In the absence of political federation, how can the fiscal policies of the member states be restrained? How can a monetary union work in the absence of a federal government with an economically consequential budget to effect stabilizing transfers across member states?

History offers few useful answers. Some observers argue that monetary union without political union is not viable in the long run, either because the answers to the preceding questions are negative on a priori grounds or because evidence shows that monetary union not accompanied by political union tends to be unstable.[30] My own view is that history does not demonstrate any such incompatibility because the combination has never been tried. History provides no useful evidence one way or the other. Again, the point is that EMU is sui generis.

3. Highlighting differences

I have argued that historical experience with monetary unification is quite different from EMU. Where that history is useful, therefore, is in identifying what is distinctive about Europe's twenty-first century monetary union. I now illustrate the point with reference to three issues concerning the operation of Europe's monetary union: implications for financial integration, provision of the financial stability function, and exit and dissolution. In the first two contexts I contrast EMU with the experience of the United States.[31] In the last one I look at the collapse of the Austro-Hungarian empire, a case that has attracted considerable attention.

3.1 *Financial integration*

I first show that the connections between financial integration and monetary union are different in twenty-first century Europe than in earlier historical cases. I do so with reference to the experience of the United States in the nineteenth century.

The relevance of the US case derives from the fact that, as in Europe today, the task was to build a monetary union and an integrated financial market that were continental in scope. Physical distance posed a challenge for monetary and financial integration (Snowden 1995a), as did cultural and institutional differences between north and south (Wright 1986) not to mention limited labor mobility. Different levels of development (lack of cohesion in EU parlance) – implying excess supplies and demands for capital and therefore large capital flows and current account balances – placed further demands on the financial system.

The Constitution had prohibited the states from issuing paper money and gave Congress the exclusive right to "coin money."[32] The United States thus entered the post-confederation period with a monetary union based on specie. But the convenience of paper money was irresistible. Where the Constitution had prohibited state governments from issuing notes, it did not prevent commercial banks from doing so. This they began doing, especially once the charter of the Bank of the United States was not renewed.[33] Had those notes always been convertible into specie at par, the resulting system would have been no different from a conventional gold-bullion standard in which the circulation of gold coin was supplemented by convertible paper. In practice, however, convertibility of notes was less than assured – the states relaxed restrictions on bank entry, allowing fly-by-night operators to obtain charters and emit inadequately backed notes that traded at a discount (Rockoff (1974) and Rolnick and Weber (1983)). In effect, the USA had two monetary systems: a unified system of coinage based on specie, and a fragmented paper system in which the notes issued by banks in different states traded at variable exchange rates against one another.[34]

Markets and institutions responded with mechanisms for dealing with the information and transactions costs associated with incomplete monetary integration. Banks in New England formed the Suffolk System to clear drafts at par, sharing information and imposing sanctions and rewards to make par clearing incentive compatible.[35] Other banks built reputation by cultivating correspondent banking relationships with institutions in regional financial centers, holding deposits with them in return for par clearing of their notes. Circulars known as "note reporters" listed the discounts at which different banknotes traded in different financial centers, easing the conduct of business.

The severity of the obstacles that all this posed to the integration of US financial markets is the subject of ongoing debate.[36] The key point for present purposes, and on which there is no dispute, is that US financial markets remained much less integrated than European financial markets today – even after residual barriers to full monetary integration dissolved following the Civil War.[37] While there was convergence over time – according to the conventional wisdom, from the 1870s – interregional interest rate differentials on bank funds of 100 basis points and more remained unexceptional. These large and persistent interest rate gaps were an order of magnitude larger than those under EMU.[38]

The explanation lies in a set of factors that were quite different than in the euro area. The risks of banking differed more dramatically across regions than today, and banks had more limited mechanisms for diversifying them away. Default rates were higher in the agricultural west, where knowledge of temperature and precipitation patterns was imperfect and much of the population was transient.[39] Regulation prohibited banks from branching across state borders and lending out of state. Barriers to entry, both regulatory and economic, were significant, rendering some regions underbanked and giving incumbent financial institutions significant market power.[40] There was no efficient, centralized clearing and settlement system. There was no modern interbank market. There was no integrated commercial paper market. Rather than a single, centralized stock market, there were a set of segmented regional markets.

With time, financial innovation, including regulatory innovation, responded to these imperfections. Capital requirements, which were a significant obstacle to entry in small markets in particular, were reduced for country banks.[41] Information accumulated about the determinants of agricultural yields, and financial institutions developed mechanisms (*inter alia*, sending loan officers into the field) to more effectively monitor their clients. There was some diversification of regionally concentrated portfolios, as mortgage companies in the west sold portfolios of mortgages to insurance companies in the east (Snowden (1995a)). Some mortgage companies further spread the risks of lending by issuing mortgage-backed securities.[42] Bill brokers took commercial paper on consignment from wholesale grocers, manufacturers and others, offering it to potential buyers, including out-of-town banks and individual investors. They formed correspondent relationships with brokers in other cities to facilitate the collection and resale of bills. The development of commercial paper houses, which purchased commercial paper outright and then offered it in secondary markets, thus bringing together lenders and borrowers from different regions, played a key role in integrating the market.[43] With the telegraph and the decline in information and communication costs, there was arbitrage among regional stock markets and competition between banks and security markets.[44]

These are the explanations for how it was that regional interest rate differentials showed a tendency toward convergence in the decades leading up to World War I. Historians disagree about when a substantially integrated national money market developed – in the 1870s and 1880s, in the first decade of the twentieth century, in some accounts only following the foundation of the Fed. Still, the striking fact is that these differentials remained substantial for many years following the completion of the country's monetary union. Unlike Europe today, monetary unification did not catalyze an immediate and dramatic increase in financial integration.

On reflection, the explanations for this difference are obvious enough. Suspicion of financial markets and institutions with national scope was an abiding characteristic of the United States in the nineteenth century. This explains Jacksonian opposition to the First and Second Banks of the United States, restrictions on interstate branching, and the absence of a central bank until the twentieth century. Regulation did as much to segment financial markets as to integrate them, and its effects were not easy for market forces, even invigorated by monetary integration, to overcome. There was no attempt to build a centralized clearing and settlement system. There was no lender of last resort to provide liquidity to securities markets and banks. There was no public-policy argument that an integrated financial market was needed to support the monetary union.

In contrast, European policy makers today see financial integration as an achievement in and of itself and a foundation stone of monetary union. Financial integration is not something to be avoided on the grounds that it allows those in the financial centers to exploit their brethren in low-income regions (the complaint of Populists in nineteenth century America). Rather, it is something to be sought as a way of fostering growth and convergence. Financial integration is also seen as buttressing support for monetary integration, insofar as financial integration is conducive to efficiency and growth and as a backlash against EMU is more likely in a low-growth, high-unemployment environment.

Efforts to encourage financial integration go back to the Single European Act, if not before; in other words, they preceded monetary union by fifteen and more years. Among the corollaries was the removal

of restrictions on cross-border branching by existing financial institutions and on cross-border mergers and acquisitions. European policy
makers similarly saw the creation of TARGET, Europe's wholesale
payments system, as an integral corollary of monetary union. Another
integral element of the monetary union was a central bank with a
mandate to contribute to the stability of the payments system by providing emergency liquidity assistance. The fact that the euro area has an
active, liquid interbank market through whose operation the cost of
bank funds is equalized across countries and regions is due in no small
part to the fact that this market is backstopped by the central bank.
Proactive policies in this area continue. The European Commission has
issued a Green Paper detailing measures to promote the integration of
national mortgage markets. The Giovannini Group has recommended
simplifying cross-border securities clearing and settlement so as to
facilitate the emergence of an integrated securities market.

There has been considerable discussion in Europe about how
quickly monetary union will deepen financial integration. The issue
is important, but it is not one on which historical experiences like that
of the United States in the nineteenth century can shed much light,
because the economic, political and regulatory circumstances are all
quite different.

3.2 *The financial stability function*

Next I examine the experience of the United States in the Great
Depression in order to highlight what is different about the financial
stability function in the European System of Central Banks.

The role of the banking crisis in the spread of the Depression and the
failure of the policy response were famously highlighted by Friedman
and Schwartz (1963). That failure had multiple sources, but one was
that the framers of the Federal Reserve Act were ambiguous about the
locus of responsibility.[45] Under the 1913 Act, reserves were held by the
regional reserve banks, which could then provide credit to commercial
banks operating in their region, up to the limit consistent with their
holdings of reserves, via the discount window. Notes injected via the
discount window (or for that matter via open market operations) had to
be backed with 40 percent gold. The remainder of the collateral could
take the form of eligible paper, defined as commercial, agricultural and
industrial paper and bankers' acceptances ("real bills").

But the 1913 Act was ambiguous about the roles of the reserve banks and the Federal Reserve Board in determining the rates charged for discounts and advances.[46] The relevant passage read that: "Every Federal Reserve Bank shall have the power ... to establish from time to time, subject to review and determination of the Federal Reserve Board, rates of discount to be charged by the Federal Reserve Bank for each class of business." In January 1915 Reserve Bank governors formed the Governors Conference to defend their prerogatives against encroachment by the Board. The outcome of their deliberations, predictably, confirmed the right of each regional bank to decide its own operations (Meltzer, 2003: 142).[47]

In 1923, Adolph Miller, an economist on the Board, tabled a proposal to empower it to control the intervention policies of the Reserve Banks. Again the Reserve Banks resisted the recommendation. In response to Miller's proposal, an Open Market Investment Committee of five governors (led by Benjamin Strong of the New York Fed) was created to direct the intervention policies of the system, but individual Reserve Banks retained the right to opt out, as insisted on most vocally by James McDougal of the Chicago Fed.

In March 1930, the Open Market Investment Committee was replaced by the Open Market Policy Conference. All twelve Reserve Bank governors were represented, this reform being designed to reduce what other banks complained was the excessive influence of the New York Fed. But again it was unclear whether the banks were obliged to accept the recommendations of the Conference and execute its instructions. The 1930 resolution creating the Open Market Policy Conference stated that recommendations of the Conference, when approved by the Board, should be submitted to each Reserve Bank "for determination as to whether it will participate in any purchases or sales recommended; any Federal Reserve bank dissenting from the proposed policy shall be expected to acquaint the Federal Reserve Board ... for the reasons for its dissent." "Acquaint" was ambiguous in this context, but evidently individual banks were still entitled to decline to engage in interventions recommended by the Open Market Policy Conference and the Board.

When it came to supervision and regulation, the Board had the power to conduct special examinations of member banks, but for information on where special examinations were required it relied on the Reserve Banks, which were in more regular communication (and were also allowed to examine) member banks in their districts. At the outset, the Office of the

Comptroller of the Currency also conducted twice-yearly examinations of all national and state member banks, but the Comptroller was jealous of his prerogatives and instructed examiners not to provide the Federal Reserve with all the information they collected. Resentment of these actions led the Congress to strip the Comptroller of responsibility for examining state member banks in 1923, but this left the banks subject only to the oversight of state inspectors, the quality of whose supervision was variable (White, 1983, p. 166 and *passim*).

This combination of decentralization and ambiguous responsibility undermined policy coherence. The Reserve Banks in their role as gatherers of intelligence on the local financial system did not provide accurate information in timely fashion to the Board in Washington, DC. (The same could be said of the Office of the Comptroller until the mid-1920s.) This was less a conscious attempt on the part of the Reserve Banks to increase their power by withholding information than a reflection of the view that if intervention was required it should be organized by the Reserve Banks and not the Board. State banking agencies responsible after 1917 for inspecting state member banks were even less efficient at passing information to the Board, given that this had to first be communicated to a Reserve Bank and from there to Washington, DC. The result was that the Board knew too little about the condition of the banking system.

Most importantly, disagreements among Reserve Banks over lender of last resort intervention compounded the difficulty of the system in providing financial assistance to problem banks and liquidity to distressed markets.[48] The New York Fed, attuned to liquidity problems in the New York market, decided on its own to inject $100 million in the wake of the 1929 crash in order to assist banks that had taken stocks as collateral against loans.[49] Although the majority of the Board approved of the intervention, it objected to New York having acted without prior authorization. The New York Fed was threatened with various consequences if, in the future, it did not secure authorization for similar action. Although this did not necessarily prevent Reserve Banks from intervening – they were still permitted to do so with prior authorization and unilaterally in the event that the Board was not available – it created uncertainty about how the system would respond.[50]

A more extreme example was the third banking panic in early 1933. By late February, this had risen to the level of a run on the US banking system. Intervention was essential to prevent the payments system from seizing up. But the New York Fed, which had disproportionately borne the burden of earlier interventions, saw its gold-reserve ratio fall to the statutory minimum of 40 percent on March 4. Providing emergency liquidity now required intervention by other regional reserve banks; equivalently, intervening in the central money market required other Reserve Banks to transfer gold to the New York Fed.[51] But the Chicago Fed, which by this time was the principal repository of the system's gold reserves, was reluctant. Together with the Boston Fed, it emphasized the dangers of moral hazard; the two banks had repeatedly warned that providing emergency liquidity might only encourage another round of stock market speculation leading to an even more devastating crash. On March 1st the Chicago Fed had lent $105 million to its counterpart in New York. But on March 3 it withdrew its cooperation. On March 4 the Board declined to compel the Chicago bank to support New York, and the New York Fed curtailed its intervention in the markets. The situation deteriorated further, leading the Board to reverse its decision three days later. But by this time the damage had been done.

The situation in Europe today is different. The ECB is not constrained in providing emergency liquidity by any remaining vestiges of the gold standard. The closest analogy is with the central bank's commitment to stabilize the general price level.[52] From the start there have been worries that fixation on this mandate might lead the ECB to neglect its other responsibilities.[53] But in fact that mandate is multifaceted: the central bank is also responsible for contributing to the stability of the payments and financial system. It does not have to keep inflation below 2 percent week by week. If emergency liquidity creates inflationary pressure, it can be drained from the financial system subsequently. The knowledge that interventions with inflationary consequences will be reversed out should minimize those inflationary consequences in the first place, assuming the credibility of the ECB's commitment to price stability. Thus, the ECB can be thought of as possessing the stabilizing escape clause that the Fed and other interwar central banks lacked.

The Eurosystem has simulated a variety of crisis scenarios. An April 2006 simulation exercise, for example, involved representatives from all EU banking supervisory authorities, central banks and finance ministries. The results "indicated that the relevant Member State authorities were able and willing to cooperate in managing cross-border systemic financial crises" (ECB, 2006a: 173).

Of course, one can question whether an exercise where the stakes are hypothetical and the participants know that they will be judged on their

cooperation is a useful predictor of how they will act in true crisis
situations. But we now possess evidence on this, courtesy of the subprime crisis. The precipitating event of the crisis was the revelation at
the beginning of August 2007 of large losses at IKB Deutsche
Industriebank, a prominent small-company lender. The German financial regulator Bafin, the German finance ministry, and the Bundesbank
swiftly cobbled together a $5 billion rescue package.[54] While this inter-
vention did not eliminate questions about the adequacy of risk standards at other German banks, it prevented runs.

Then on August 10, in response to evidence of stringency in the
interbank market, the ECB injected €95 billion of liquidity in the first
of a series of special tenders.[55] These took the form of reverse repurchase
agreements under which the ECB lent funds to commercial banks
against eligible collateral.[56] Initially the ECB provided funds at its
policy interest rate of 4 percent without limit. A series of further such
operations followed. On September 27, for example, the ECB granted
a $5.5 billion loan to an unnamed borrower, again through its standing
facility, against collateral, using an overnight reverse-repo transaction.
In December 2007 the ECB agreed to coordinate further liquidity
auctions with the Fed and the Bank of England.

Europe's response to the crisis remains controversial. But while there
were sporadic reports of depositors queueing up at banks (in Spain for
example, and outside the euro area at offices of Northern Rock in
Britain), there were no widespread bank runs. There was no cascade
of defaults. The ECB's response was not obviously delayed by the failure of regulatory authorities to convey information about the delicate
condition of financial institutions and markets.[57] There was no 1933-
style scenario.

If anything, the problem lay not in the ECB's capacity to respond to
the crisis but with the ability of European authorities to anticipate it.[58]
Padoa-Schioppa (2007) criticizes supervisors for failing to see the crisis
developing, for failing to share critical information before it erupted,
and for failing to hold emergency meetings. Supervisors, he argues,
adopted narrowly national perspectives and resisted pooling the information needed to anticipate problems in transnational banks and contagion through interbank markets. Although the EU possesses common
principles for bank supervision, those principals are implemented in
different ways by different national supervisors overseeing local
branches of the same banking group. There is also a race to the bottom

insofar as supervisors have an incentive to apply common standards forgivingly in order to make their market attractive to footloose financial institutions.

But Padoa-Schioppa also suggests that Europe possesses arrangements and understandings capable, if suitably strengthened, of solving these problems. Discussion of these issues dates back to 2000, when the Economic and Financial Committee (or EFC, established by treaty to advise the ECOFIN Council and the Commission) established an ad hoc "Financial Stability Table" comprised of finance ministry and central bank representatives. In April 2000 the EFC recommended measures to strengthen cross-sector cooperation, enhance the exchange of information among responsible authorities, reinforce cooperation between supervisors and central banks, and foster the convergence of regulatory practice. Its conclusions were quickly endorsed by the ECOFIN Council. A second report in April 2001 offered three specific recommendations. Supervisors should adopt measures ensuring their access to accurate information (from large financial groups, in particular) and establish contingency plans. Member states should remove legal and practical obstacles to the exchange of information among supervisors and central banks. And there should be *ex ante* agreement on who would do what in a crisis situation.[59]

These recommendations informed the EU-wide Memorandum of Understanding (MoU) on cooperation in crisis situations adopted under the auspices of the ESCB's Banking Supervision Committee (BSC) in March 2003. This MoU set out procedures for identifying which authorities were responsible for taking the lead in a crisis situation, enumerated the required flows of information between supervisors and central banks, and specified modalities for information sharing.[60] A second MoU in 2004–5 provided a more detailed description of procedures for sharing information and assessments.[61]

None of this is to deny that more needs to be done to strengthen the supervisory function so that nascent threats to financial stability in the monetary union are more effectively anticipated. Padoa-Schioppa (2007) argues against creating a single European supervisor, in parallel to the ECB, suggesting instead that existing arrangements should simply be strengthened. Specifically, there should be more uniformity in the application of EU regulations and more systematic information sharing.[62] Again, the situation ten years after the creation of the euro is very different from the situation in the United States ten years after the creation of the Fed, when there was open hostility among competing supervisors.

3.3 Exit and dissolution

Finally, I discuss the disintegration of the Austro-Hungarian monetary union and how it should make us think about the possible dissolution of EMU.

Elsewhere (Eichengreen, 2007) I have analyzed the barriers to exit facing an incumbent member of the euro area struggling with problems of competitiveness and high unemployment.[63] My argument emphasizes procedural obstacles to exit. There may be economic costs, but it is not clear *ex ante* that these will dominate the benefits. The main such cost is likely to be the increase in debt service if investors anticipate that exit will be followed by chronic deficits. However, countries can minimize and may even be able to eliminate that increase if they take their exit from the euro area as an occasion to strengthen fiscal institutions and procedures. Similarly, there may be political costs – a member state unilaterally abrogating its EMU obligations will not be welcomed at the table where EU policies are made. But it is not clear that such international political considerations dominate domestic political pressures, especially in periods of high unemployment.

In the end, the binding constraints are likely to be procedural. In a democracy, the decision to exit will require discussion. Executing it will require planning. Computers will have to be reprogrammed. Vending machines will have to be modified. Payment machines will have to be serviced to prevent motorists from being trapped in subterranean parking garages. To prevent counterfeiting, high-quality notes and coins will have to be printed, imported, and positioned around the country. One need only recall the elaborate planning that preceded the introduction of the physical euro.

During the transition to the euro there was little reason to expect changes in exchange rates and thus little incentive for currency speculation during the period when discussion and planning were under way. In 1998 the founding members of the euro area agreed to lock their exchange rates at the then-prevailing levels as of the beginning of 1999. This effectively ruled out efforts to manipulate currencies in order to steal a competitive advantage prior to the locking of parities in 1999.

In contrast, during a period when the reintroduction of the national currency is discussed, changes in exchange rates would be viewed as all but certain, since the very motivation for leaving would be to change the parity. Market participants would be aware of this fact. Households and firms anticipating that domestic deposits would be involuntarily converted into, say, lira, which would then depreciate against the euro, would shift their deposits to other euro-area banks. In the worst case a system-wide banking panic would ensue. Investors anticipating that their claims on the Italian government would be redenominated into lira would shift into claims on other euro-area governments, causing a bond-market collapse. Insofar as the precipitating event was a government decision to abandon the lira, the ECB would not be inclined to provide lender-of-last-resort support. And if the government was already in a tenuous fiscal position, it would not be able to borrow to bail out the banks and buy back its debt. This would be the mother of all financial crises.

History, specifically in the form of the dissolution of the Austro-Hungarian empire, is invoked by those who argue that the problem is not so difficult (see e.g. Dornbusch 1992 and Garber and Spencer 1994). Austria, Hungary and the other ethnic regions of the empire all successfully introduced national currencies following World War I. Previously they had operated a formal monetary union, with control of the circulation vested in the Austro-Hungarian bank in Vienna. The component parts of the empire constituted a free-trade zone, and both real and financial integration were extensive. At the same time, like EMU today, constituent states (Austria and Hungary) decided on separate budgets while contributing to some of the expenditures of the union.[64]

Ethnic demands for autonomy boiled up during World War I. Vienna, occupied elsewhere, lost the capacity to assert its control over non-Austrian parts of the empire. Other regions held back food supplies, disrupting the operation of the internal market. With the armistice, the Czechs, Poles and Hungarians declared their political independence and sought to establish and defend their national borders. They also abandoned prior restraints on their fiscal policies, partly owing to postwar exigencies, partly in reflection of the value they now attached to political sovereignty.

Importantly, however, the Austrian crown remained the basis for the monetary circulation throughout the former empire.[65] This was awkward for separate sovereign nations that did not share the seigniorage, experienced asymmetric shocks, and suffered from chronic fiscal and financial imbalances. Starting with Czechoslovakia and the Kingdom of Serbs, Croats and Slovenes (Yugoslavia), one successor state after another left the monetary union and introduced a national currency.

Typically, this involved first announcing that only stamped Austrian banknotes would be acceptable in transactions. Stamping (either over-printing with an ink stamp or adding a physical stamp) had to be conducted carefully, with a high level of uniformity, to discourage forgery. At the same time the currency was stamped, a portion was withheld as a capital levy (as a way of transferring desperately needed resources to the government). In Hungary, for example, 50 percent of tendered notes were withheld as a forced loan. In Czechoslovakia, the 50 percent tax was applied to current accounts and treasury bills when these were redenominated in stamped crowns.

In turn this created an incentive to withhold currency from circula-tion if there were prospects of using it in other countries where stamping had not yet taken place. Thus, there was an incentive for capital flight not unlike that which might afflict an inflation-prone country today that chose to opt out of Europe's monetary union. Stamping was therefore accompanied by physically closing the country's borders and compre-hensive exchange controls. Individuals were prohibited from traveling abroad, and merchandise trade was halted. The capital levy, equivalent to depreciation of the new currency against the old one, could also precipitate a run on the banks, as it did in Czechoslovakia. In Austria, which could observe Czechoslovakia's earlier experience, bank securi-ties and deposits were frozen at the outset of the transition.

One interpretation is that this history demonstrates the feasibility of exiting from a monetary union and (re)introducing a national currency. But in these historical cases, avoiding serious financial dislocations required closing borders, banning foreign travel, halting merchan-dise trade, and imposing draconian exchange controls while the con-version was under way. The feasibility of similar measures today is dubious. Exchange controls would be difficult to enforce in a European country with a highly developed financial system that is the host and home of international banks. Given the development of the single market, suspending foreign trade would be prohibitively expen-sive. Residents would not stand for a ban on foreign travel. And then there are the country's other obligations to the single market. Exit would be relatively attractive if the country exiting the monetary union did not lose the other privileges of EU membership. But that it would have to interrupt the free movement of goods and services suggests that its partners in the single market would not be inclined to look the other way.

All this suggests that circumstances today are quite different than those following World War I. In today's more financially developed economies, freezing bank accounts and halting credit transactions would have higher costs. In long-established democracies, where citizens are accustomed to traveling freely, the acceptability of closing borders is questionable. The costs of disrupting merchandise transactions would be greater than a century ago. Again, this history is useful not as a parallel or precedent but precisely for illustrating what is different about current circumstances.

A more recent historical precedent, with similar implications, is the *corralito* imposed in Argentina when one-to-one peso-dollar parity was abandoned in 2001.[66] The end of "convertibility" was not the same as reintroducing a national currency, since the peso had never been withdrawn from circulation. But discussions of the possibility that the currency might be devalued after a ten-year period in which the one-to-one parity had been treated as sacrosanct, together with the fact that bank deposits and other financial claims were denominated in dollars, created analogous problems for the Argentine authorities.

The Argentine crisis and the policy response have been extensively documented.[67] The authorities first suspended trading in their bonds. On December 1, 2001, in order to stop the hemorrhage of deposits out of the banking system precipitated by the impending devaluation, they froze all bank accounts, initially for 90 days; they permitted only very small withdrawals, initially 250 pesos a week. No withdrawals from accounts denominated in dollars were allowed without agreement to convert the proceeds into pesos. Cross-border transfers were limited to trade-related transactions and international credit card clearing.

In fact, news of the freeze only accelerated the withdrawal of deposits by corporations and individuals able to circumvent its provisions. Depositors filed lawsuits in the effort to access their funds, and in several cases the courts decided in their favor. Protests and demonstrations, some violent, then led to the resignation of President Fernando de la Rua on December 21. A five-day bank holiday ensued. De la Rua's second interim successor, Eduardo Duhalde, announced further bank holidays and hardened the *corralito*, requiring the compulsory exchange of many deposits for bonds denominated in pesos. On January 11, 2002 the government lifted its three-week ban on foreign exchange transactions, but the *corralito* remained in place.

On February 1, the Argentine Supreme Court ruled against the restrictions on deposit withdrawals in response to claims filed by individuals.[68] In response, the government declared another bank holiday. At the end of the holiday the authorities announced a new plan, which entailed the conversion of all debts into pesos at a one-to-one parity; conversion of dollar deposits into pesos at a one-to-four parity; the transfer of government bonds to banks that had suffered balance sheet damage as a result of differential conversion rates on bank deposits and assets; and a 180-day embargo on legal actions against the deposit restrictions. Further adjustments to these measures followed in February and March. The last vestiges of the *corralito* were only eliminated in December 2002, a year after its imposition.

This was an exceptionally messy and costly episode. It disrupted the operation of the payments and financial system for the better part of twelve months. The *corralito* was only one factor in Argentina's economic collapse. And it is possible to suggest that restrictions on deposit withdrawals, the conversion of foreign currency debt into local units, and limits on capital-account transactions could have been applied in a less chaotic manner. But the fact is that as soon as agents get wind of the government's intentions, they will act, requiring the authorities to respond before they are ready. There will be pressure to treat debtors and creditors differently when converting assets and liabilities into local currency. In turn this will require compensating the banks, a decision that will require further deliberation, during which the payments system will remain frozen.

There is no avoiding the conclusion that the process would be costly and disruptive. And, in turn, this makes it unlikely that a disaffected euro-area member would abandon the monetary union.

4. Conclusion

Everyone has a favorite quote about the uses and misuses of history. Mine is "History is the science of what never happens twice."[69] The point is that those drawing parallels should proceed cautiously. The point applies to the search for lessons for EMU from the classical gold standard, multinational monetary unions in the nineteenth and twentieth centuries, and experience with monetary unification at the national level. EMU is different. It is not like the gold standard, which left room for fluctuations in the exchange rates between participating countries and from which members could and did exit at will. It is not like multilateral monetary unions in the nineteenth century under which there was no centralized control of money supplies by a transnational central bank. It is not like the monetary union inherited by the successor states of the Austro-Hungarian empire, from which exit was straightforward because of relatively low levels of financial development and the ease of freezing transactions and sealing borders during the period when national currencies were being (re)introduced. It is not like national experiences with monetary unification, precisely because these were virtually all cases where political unification preceded monetary unification.

Does this mean that our editors erred in commissioning historical chapters for the present book? My defense of our editors is that history is useful precisely for pointing up what is distinctive about EMU. EMU is monetary unification, extending to centralized control of the money supply by a central bank at the level of the union, without political unification. It takes place in an environment of deep financial integration among a group of countries with well-developed capital markets. There is no provision for exiting and reintroducing a national currency. And there is no historical precedent for any of this.

Notes

1. Here I use EMU to refer to European Monetary Union (as opposed to Economic and Monetary Union as tends to be the practice in Brussels). Alas, "sui generis euro area" does not roll off the tongue.
2. Thus, Flandreau *et al.* (1998) inquire into how much fiscal autonomy was retained under the gold standard and attempt to draw out lessons for EMU. Panic (1992) seeks to draw a variety of lessons from the gold standard for Europe's monetary union.
3. Gallarotti (1995) and Meissner (2005) analyze these interdependencies.
4. The edges of the band being the famous gold import and export points, defined by the costs of international gold market arbitrage. Giovannini (1989) generalizes the point, showing that all fixed-rate regimes have in practice involved not just a central parity but a fluctuation band. The point will also be familiar to students of Argentina's recent quasi-currency board and Hong Kong's currency-board regime.

5. Thus, countries that maintained the gold standard but also formed a monetary union where they committed to accepting the obligations of their
   partners at par further narrowed these fluctuation bands. See the discussions
   of the Latin Monetary Union and Scandinavian Monetary Union below.
6. Thus, the authorities might use moral suasion in an effort to discourage
   banks and others from converting domestic currency into coin, or they
   might follow the Banque de France by only accepting requests for conversion at a remote country office of the central bank (for details see
   Bloomfield 1959).
7. See Bordo and Kydland (1995).
8. This is the argument about the decline in the stability of the gold standard
   between the pre-World War I and interwar periods developed in
   Eichengreen (1996).
9. See Bordo and Rockoff (1996) and Ferguson and Schlurarick (2006).
   Similarly, even if adherence to the gold standard enhanced the ability of
   governments to issue long-term, domestic-currency-denominated debt
   securities on international markets, this does not tell us anything about
   how quickly monetary union might solve this problem. See e.g. Flandreau
   and Sussman (2005) and Bordo *et al.* (2005).
10. Some of these ambitions will resonate with historians of the euro.
    Certainly the possibility that the euro would encourage intra-European
    trade figured prominently in discussions of whether to create a single
    currency. There were also those who suggested that the single currency
    would encourage the development of a European financial center to rival
    New York (not that they anticipated that this financial center would
    develop outside the euro area, namely in London). And, in academic
    circles at least, there was also the argument that the single currency
    would encourage political integration.
11. How exactly this worked is the subject of Flandreau (1997).
12. Equivalently, the cost of producing subsidiary coins whose metallic
    content was less than their face value was less than the ability of those
    coins to command goods and services in neighboring countries.
13. See Bailey and Bae (2003).
14. Just why the Latin Union agreement was not more effective and why it
    was not as constraining as the EMU treaty are interesting questions. My
    view is that the LMU treaty was not part of a larger political bargain that
    involved also commitments on other nonmonetary issues that could be
    jeopardized by reneging on its monetary provisions (for more on this, see
    below). Others would say that the LMU treaty was less effective because
    there was nothing to constrain irresponsible fiscal behavior, which led
    countries like Italy to pursue policies that heightened their need for
    seigniorage.

15. For an overview of the history of the Scandinavian Union see Jonung (2007).
16. This, then, was a gold bullion standard, under which notes were backed by the bullion reserves of the respective central banks. This is distinct from a gold coin standard (where only gold coin circulates, obviating the need for the central bank to hold bullion reserves) and a gold-exchange standard, where notes are backed not just with gold bullion but also with convertible foreign exchange.
17. See Bergman *et al.* (1993) and Hendriksen and Kaergard (1995).
18. See Bergman (1999), p. 366 and note 4 above.
19. Although it did not eliminate that tendency, owing to transactions costs. See also the discussion of this question in the subsection on the Latin Union above.
20. This is also the conclusion of de Cecco (1992).
21. Rose (2000) provides a catalog of such arrangements.
22. Although how much more is disputed; see Baldwin (2006a). The same qualitative result as obtained in these cross-country comparisons has been found in time-series studies of countries forming or dissolving a monetary union (as in the case of Ireland in 1979; see for example Dwane *et al.* (2006).
23. Together with some smaller ones.
24. An interesting study of this case is Meade (1956).
25. Unless one limits the latter to country pairs where one member is also very small relative to the other.
26. See Masson and Patillo (2004) for details. Comoros, an island in the Indian Ocean, has its own currency, the Comoros franc, and its own central bank, although it pegs to the CFA franc and participates in other CFA franc zone arrangements.
27. "Effectively" because a number of private banks retained limited note-issuing powers in Italy significantly into the post-unification period.
28. In these respects the analogy with EMU is direct. Hence these are the type of cases on which I focus for much of Section 3 below.
29. This is not to overlook the existence of political institutions like the European Commission, the EU Council and the European Parliament or the emergence of proto-European politics (Hix *et al.* 2007). But the degree of centralized decision making characteristic of true political federation is still far off in the case of Europe.
30. The analytical and historical arguments are advanced by De Grauwe (2006a) and Bordo (2004), respectively.
31. Which I have argued previously is a particularly revealing national case. See Eichengreen (1992).

32. Why is debated. Rockoff (2003) argues that the motivation was to restrain inflationary tendencies in the Western states. Rolnick *et al.* (1993) suggest that it was to encourage trade within the new federation.
33. As Bodenhorn (2000: 169) explains, the Second Bank under Nicholas Biddle possessed a large volume of state bank notes and used them to discipline those banks by threatening to redeem them or actually doing so if a bank showed signs of emitting excessively and allowing its notes to trade at a significant discount. With the expiry of the Second Bank, this mechanism no longer operated.
34. Again, this was not the case in the 1820s, when Biddle oversaw the operations of the Second Bank. Under his direction, the Bank integrated the operation of its branches. Acting as a quasi-central bank, it then used that branch network to purchase and sell inland bills of exchange at a fixed price, effectively pegging interregional exchange rates. See Fraas (1974).
35. Bodenhorn (2002) questions the incentive compatibility of the system.
36. The traditional argument, due to Davis (1965), is that the domestic financial market was fragmented until the very late nineteenth century. Bodenhorn and Rockoff (1992) and Rockoff (2003) are two of the very few studies to look explicitly at ante-bellum data. They argue that financial integration traced out more of a U-shaped pattern over time: reasonably high prior to the Civil War, then low during the Reconstruction period as a result of wartime destruction of financial institutions and relationships, and gradually rising to ante-bellum levels and presumably beyond up to the turn of the century.
37. Following the Civil War, new taxes and restrictions on state bank note issues were imposed, and par clearing of the notes issued by more stringently regulated national banks became the rule.
38. See Lane and Wälti (2007) and Baele *et al.* (2004). ECB (2007b), especially pp. 24–5, provides an analysis of country differences in bank interest rates that is most directly comparable to the historical evidence discussed here.
39. As emphasized by Smiley (1975) and Eichengreen (1984).
40. As emphasized by Sylla (1969).
41. Most notably under the provisions of the Gold Standard Act of 1900.
42. Aficionados of the "subprime crisis" will appreciate knowing that many of these securities then lapsed into default with the rural property downturn of the 1890s. Many of the Western mortgage companies failed in the course of this crisis, not unlike subprime lenders in 2007. On the history of mortgage-backed securities in the United States, see Snowden (1995b).
43. See Davis (1965) and James (1976). This is another context in which the debate over timing arises. Whereas Davis emphasized the development of commercial paper houses in the 1880s, Bodenhorn (2000) emphasizes

that those houses did not simply materialize at that point; rather, they developed out of the network of exchange brokers that was already active before the Civil War (see above). His amendment to the conventional wisdom only reinforces the present point, namely that financial integration was long in developing.

44. This is the factor emphasized by Sushka and Barrett (1984).

45. This changed with the passage of the 1935 Banking Act, which definitively consolidated authority with the Board, but that episode is beyond the parameters of the present book.

46. Even more ambiguously, nothing was said about responsibility for the conduct of open market operations, since their importance was not anticipated by the framers.

47. It was also agreed to execute those operations in the central money market, New York.

48. In reviewing these ideological disagreements about the desirable extent of liquidity provision, one is reminded about differences between the ECB and the Bank of England in August 2007 – when the Bank of England took a harder line, at least initially, about the danger of moral hazard and was therefore more reluctant to intervene. The difference then was that no one was constrained in intervening by the availability of gold reserves. The ECB could therefore proceed unilaterally, and problem banks in the UK could turn to it, as those with euro-area branches in fact did.

49. And which therefore experienced withdrawals from correspondent banks in the interior of the country that had placed deposits with them.

50. Friedman and Schwartz (1963) and Meltzer (2003) disagree on the nature of the conflict and its consequences. Friedman and Schwartz argue that the New York Fed curtailed its operations due to criticism from the Board that these would aggravate moral hazard – together with the threat of consequences if New York officials failed to comply. Meltzer argues that there was no real difference between the New York Fed and the Board over appropriate policies but that the Board was concerned to establish its prerogatives.

51. Alternatively, it would have been possible to suspend the statutory gold backing provision or take a variety of other exceptional measures, but this was not something that officials were yet prepared to broach.

52. As opposed to a specific component of that price level, namely gold.

53. In fact, even before the start: such warnings go back to Folkerts-Landau and Garber (1992).

54. With the participation of private banks as well as public Landesbanken and Sparkassen. One reason for involving private banks was to minimize the likelihood that the rescue would be found to conflict with the EU's competition laws. In the event, the Commission quickly announced that it

would examine the rescue's compliance with those regulations. Note that the decision to aid a bank that lacks the collateral needed to tap the ECB's standard facility (the ECB's equivalent of the Fed's discount window) resides with the national central bank (NCB) of the relevant jurisdiction. That national central bank is required to inform the other members of the Eurosystem of its actions so that, *inter alia*, the ECB can adjust the provision of liquidity to limit the potential impact on monetary policy. One can imagine an NCB ideologically opposed to the provision of emergency assistance might refuse to aid a bank in its jurisdiction even when the ECB and other NCBs were concerned about the implications for systemic stability. One can imagine that, even in the absence of ideological considerations, emergency liquidity assistance might be underprovided if the adverse effects of that bank's failures were felt in other jurisdictions. But one can also argue that there is nothing unique to EMU about these problems: cross-border banking is widespread in the twenty-first century; such structures and therefore the associated externalities are not limited to Europe. That said, the fact that the EU has gone further in promoting the development of an integrated financial market suggests that, qualitative similarities notwithstanding, the problem is probably more pervasive in Europe.

55. This was its first emergency injection of liquidity since September 12 and 13, 2001, when the ECB had injected €100 billion of liquidity in the aftermath of terrorist attacks in New York and Washington, DC.

56. Which was then repurchased the next day, at the agreed price, by the counterparty.

57. This is not to deny that inadequate information was a problem for crisis management. But the problem was that all of the relevant regulators were incompletely informed about, *inter alia*, the position of conduits and structured investment vehicles (SIVs) to which commercial banks had off-balance-sheet exposures. A unified regulator at the level of the monetary union would have been little different in this regard.

58. The ECB's June 2007 *Financial Stability Review* had in fact anticipated at least some of the problems that followed.

59. In addition, there was a fourth recommendation: competition authorities were called on to "maintain timely and robust procedures" for considering the competitive implications of crisis-management efforts. The issue here was whether public credit or a public takeover of a distressed institution might violate anti-subsidy provisions of the single market.

60. Including a list of emergency contacts.

61. One could go on. In addition there exist a series of bilateral and regional agreements for managing financial crises arising out of problems in banks with cross-border establishments. Beyond that, there are EU Committees

(the EFC, BSC, Committee of European Banking Supervisors, and Financial Services Committee), all of which include banking supervisors, central bank officials, and/or representatives of finance ministries that provide venues for ad hoc information sharing. A number of these bring together European officials from both inside and outside the monetary union, which is helpful insofar as cross-border establishment and other links do not respect the borders of EMU. Finally, the Eurosystem itself has formed committees of ECB and national central bank officials in order to establish operational procedures for dealing with financial disturbances.

62. Charlie McCreevy, the European Commissioner overseeing the operation of financial markets, in January 2008 proposed in addition the establishment of a so-called college of supervisors to more systematically share information, discuss risks, and coordinate supervisory activities. UK Chancellor of the Exchequer Alisdair Darling, for his part, recommended that the International Monetary Fund and the Financial Stability Forum take steps to foster closer cooperation in efforts to anticipate and head off cross-border financial risks. But neither McCreevy's nor Darling's proposals are intended to apply to larger economic entities (the EU and the global financial system, respectively), which is why their recommendations are consigned to this note.

63. The case of a country that abandoned the monetary union over dissatisfaction with excessive inflation is more complicated to think about. This is discussed in the revision to the aforementioned paper (available from the author on request).

64. Flandreau (2006) describes how budgetary autonomy was granted to Hungary in 1867 in order to damp seccessionist pressures.

65. In Poland, rubles and German marks circulated alongside Austrian crowns, while in the Kingdom of Serbs, Croats and Slovenes Serbian dinars, Montenegrin perpers and Bulgarian leva circulated alongside the crown. But these cases were exceptional.

66. "Corralito" being Spanish for little corral.

67. See for example Mussa (2003). On the *corralito* itself, see Lopez (2002).

68. Previously the court had ruled in favor of the restrictions, but justices had been subjected to continuous public demonstrations and threats of impeachment proceedings by the Congress.

69. Due to Paul Valéry. My second favorite is attributed to Mark Twain. "Get your facts first, and then you can distort them as much as you please." Quoted in Kipling (1900: letter 37).

Comment 1: Comment on Chapters 2 and 3

NIELS THYGESEN

Longer-term challenges for EMU

It is a pleasure to read and to be invited to comment on the reflections of three eminent US economists and economic historians on the subject of the many longer-term challenges facing Europe's Economic and Monetary Union (EMU) and its currency, the euro. Their contributions are greatly appreciated, not only because they draw on a rich body of research on the experience of past and existing monetary unions, but also because the authors have, throughout the two decades of preparing for and then implementing EMU, demonstrated both an impressive degree of familiarity with the European integration process and a constructively critical attitude to its ambitions – in contrast to the more dismissive attitudes of some of their US colleagues.

The two chapters draw to some extent on the same literature and both survey the experience of past international monetary unions as well as that of national monetary unifications in large federal countries – the United States, Germany and Italy. This is natural, since EMU has similarities to both an international treaty and to a national system. It is, indeed, the very uncertainty in the classification of EMU that lends particular interest to the analysis of how it operates. EMU is *sui generis* by combining centralisation of monetary policy with decentralised responsibility for fiscal policy as well as for structural policies, so there are, as both chapters recognize, elements of both national policy making and international policy coordination involved. Are these components compatible, or can they be made so? Or is the political tension between them sufficiently important to make a break-up of EMU possible or even likely?

These questions were at the centre of the European debate nearly two decades ago when the main features of EMU were designed in the Delors Report and subsequently in far more detail in the negotiations leading to the Maastricht Treaty. Hence, they have an almost nostalgic quality for someone who was active in that early phase. There were two strongly held views at the time, often rather crudely labelled the 'monetarist' and the 'economist' perspective. The former held that monetary union and a single currency would inevitably trigger major moves towards more political union and, in particular, more centralisation of fiscal and other economic policies. It is remarkable that this so-called monetarist view was held both by European federalists, who were keen to see such a process developing, and by British and other Eurosceptics who saw a single European currency as the main stepping stone to political integration in Europe.[1] The opposing views held that monetary union not underpinned by significant elements of political union would founder. This latter view was most explicitly advanced by policy makers in Germany, and it inspired efforts to advance political union through an Intergovernmental Conference parallel to that for EMU and later to tighten the fiscal rules applied to national governments.

The first decade of EMU does not lend support to either of these two views. EMU and its single currency have not triggered major advances in political integration, but this 'failure' does not appear to have raised serious doubt about the survival of the present framework. Yet, the jury is still out, and careful analysis in the light of historical experiments with the construction of monetary unions is highly valuable.

The two chapters provide such an analysis of particular relevance for an evaluation of the economist perspective, viz that there may well be exits from EMU unless the political underpinnings are reinforced. Very usefully, the authors adopt somewhat different approaches. Eichengreen focuses on financial aspects of European integration in a comparative perspective and, in particular, on the difficulties of exit from EMU. Bordo and James focus on the challenges to EMU that arise from unsatisfactory economic performance of the participants as reflected in some combination of fiscal deficits, slow growth and major divergence among participants – though they also look at tensions arising from financial markets and from the external role of the euro.

Although both chapters offer extensive discussion of the two major examples of international monetary unions – the Latin and Scandinavian Monetary Unions which operated for nearly four decades prior to the eruption of World War I in 1914 – both seem to regard the experiment of national monetary unification as more relevant to the analysis of the prospects for EMU. The main reason is that there were no common institutional underpinnings in either of the two international unions, only the common adherence of the participants to the principles of the gold standard. Commitments were basically unilateral – as was the case with the forms of monetary cooperation with which Europe experimented prior to EMU. Low inflation and relatively rapid economic growth helped to assure the survival of the two unions over a lengthy period, and war among the participants – an event beyond the imagination in EMU – was obviously too dramatic to permit the survival of monetary arrangements and too traumatic to make their later revival politically feasible.

Exit from a national monetary union is a very different matter from the break-up of an international arrangement, although examples can be found also in recent decades in the break-up of the former Soviet Union, of former Yugoslavia and of Czechoslovakia. All of these involved the introduction of national currencies, but circumstances were marked on the one hand by sharp political conflicts, on the other hand by a far lower degree of financial integration than is observable today. Something similar applies to the case study reviewed by Eichengreen in more detail – the disintegration of the Austro-Hungarian monetary union shortly after the end of World War I. Although this particular episode may seem to provide evidence of the feasibility of exiting from a monetary union, such a step required a number of regulatory measures in exchange transactions which are very hard to imagine in today's circumstances. The experience of Argentina in 2001–2 in breaking up the peso-USD link and in redenominating contracts is a vivid reminder of the difficulties. Even though the Argentinian authorities contributed to the messy nature of the episode, the basic lesson is clear: exiting a currency area or a fixed-rate relationship to redefine one's national currency is highly disruptive.

The replacement of national currencies by the euro provides no counterexample to this analysis. Extreme care was taken to assure the continuity of the arrangements under EMU with the past. In particular, there was no basis for any expectation that the euro would be of poorer quality, i.e. have weaker purchasing power than the national currencies it replaced. Introducing the euro could therefore be seen as analogous to national currency reforms in which the monetary unit is modified, e.g. by slashing zeros, but no substantive change is observed. There is a strong asymmetry with the case of preparing for an exit, the purpose of which will be justified by a desire to change policy. It is hard to conceive of circumstances in which preparation of an exit would not trigger expectations of depreciation and more inflation, in addition to intricate legal problems in the relabelling of contracts.

The notion that the introduction of a single currency in a monetary union implies a high degree of irreversibility of joining such a union was clearly expressed in the preparation for EMU.[2] Obviously, the Treaty establishing EMU does not prescribe that participation is irreversible. But the costs of testing the exit option are, as Eichengreen argues, likely to deter any participant from any such temptation.

With the bar against exit raised to a high level the obligation on the EMU participants to make their joint undertaking work as well as possible becomes very strong. And the historical experience of national monetary unions is relevant, even though, as already noted, political unification had preceded monetary union in the three main cases in recent history, the United States, Germany and Italy. Bordo and James list five major possible challenges to EMU, which I take as my point of departure.

Before I take up these points I cannot resist underlining two challenges which EMU (and the Eurosystem) has faced. The first has apparently been met more smoothly than in at least the United States, viz to build up a cohesive central banking system capable of taking decisions in the national interest. Although US political unification preceded the start of the Federal Reserve System by 125 years it took a couple more decades before effective centralisation of decision making occurred in 1935 after rather detrimental failures of governance. In the Eurosystem the six members of the Executive Board and the national central bank governors seem to have been able to cooperate smoothly on the basis of a common analysis of what the average situation in EMU required of monetary policy in the light of the relatively clear mandate of the Eurosystem to achieve price stability in the medium term. This is no mean achievement when compared to the difficulties experienced particularly in the United States in achieving a similarly cohesive structure.[3]

The second challenge is that of finding a place for policy making in EMU outside the area of monetary policy. EMU is *sui generis* not only because it is not part of a political union, but also because great care was taken in the Maastricht Treaty to protect the 'purity' of monetary policy, based on the two principles of medium-term price stability as the primary objective and independence of the central bank from national and EU political authorities. While these principles are hard to question, they were applied with unusual zeal in several directions. The main effort was to protect the Eurosystem's pursuit of its objective against erosion that could weaken its control over the creation of money: direct and indirect monetary financing of public deficits, large-scale interventions in currency markets, and liquidity injections at times of financial turbulence. The Treaty did so by introducing fiscal rules – upper limits and reference values for public sector deficits and debt – by making decisions on currency intervention more complex to arrive at, and by leaving no role beyond a purely consultative one for the Eurosystem in financial supervision.

All these features, combined with the obvious difficulties of modifying them through future revisions in the Treaty, have assured an exceptional degree of independence of the Eurosystem as a monetary authority. But the ambition of purity has had costs as well. Some relate to the amputations of some dimensions of a normal central bank mandate, notably with respect to financial supervision. Others manifest themselves in the evident frustration in the past decade of some national politicians that the Eurosystem appears as the only important actor on the EU economic policy stage. The general heading to this second challenge encompasses all the five more specific ones identified by Bordo and James, to which I will now turn.

1. Fiscal policy and debt

Initial work on the approach to EMU left some doubt as to the relative importance on the one hand of fiscal rules to contain divergent behaviour by individual member states, and on the other hand of coordination of national fiscal policies to achieve a better policy mix between the joint monetary policy and the aggregate of national fiscal policies. Following Kenen (1989), one may label the former purpose that of 'regime preservation'.[4] In the end, EMU works with almost exclusive emphasis on the latter, and the achievement of a good policy mix is expected to emerge as the result of prudent national fiscal policies, oriented towards medium-term objectives and long-term sustainability, in combination with the joint monetary policy oriented towards price stability. This model has considerable support in economic research as being difficult to improve on.

The evolution of the fiscal rules embodied in the Stability and Growth Pact (SGP) has, however, significantly modified the operation of the rules. While the original version emphasised simple and uniform rules for deficits, mainly to be reviewed on a factual basis and subject to sanctions in case of transgressions, the changes agreed in 2005 have underlined a more discretionary approach to the evaluation of national budgets in the ECOFIN Council. In addition to detailed exchanges on the objectives for underlying budget balances over a three-year period and on the appropriate pace of approaching them, the new procedures also include reviews of longer-run developments in public debt in the light of expenditure trends, notably for ageing-related purposes. Although the modification of the SGP was on paper a clear weakening of the fiscal rules, it would appear from the early and still very preliminary experience that the present procedures contribute to improvements in national budgetary approaches while offering increased scope for the involvement of national policy makers in European macroeconomic policy – though still on a country-by-country basis rather than in defining what is an appropriate aggregate fiscal stance.

2. Slow growth

Bordo and James are correct in identifying the relatively unsatisfactory rate of economic growth – at least relative to expectations in the late 1990s – over most of the life of the euro as a longer-term threat to the perception of a successful euro – even if the joint monetary policy cannot be held responsible for the growth performance. Maybe one of the costs of devoting much attention to perfecting the design of EMU was to leave the perception that, after building a very independent central bank and setting fiscal rules, little more sovereignty over economic policy could be pooled. This view has analytical justifications in the observation that structural policy reforms leave the gains in terms of economic growth which they make possible much more inside national borders than is the case with the impact of shorter-term macroeconomic policies, and that decisions in this wide area could safely be left to national policy. Hence reforms in labour and product markets to increase flexibility and intensify competition were left to the so-called open method of coordination. With the gradual tightening of the monitoring of national reform programmes under the Lisbon Strategy, assisted by some common guidelines as regards overall EU objectives and with selective support from EU budgetary resources, the open method of coordination is now evolving more constructively, and with increasing use of benchmarking to facilitate comparisons of economic performance between countries.

One positive factor making this evolution possible is the operation of the Eurogroup, the Ministers of Economics and Finance of the euro-area countries. The efficiency of this less formal and more collegial and confidential forum is hard to evaluate for outsiders, but participants testify to its usefulness also in beginning to address the underlying causes of slow growth as well as the monitoring of the SGP rules.

3. Regional pressures

When EMU was on the drawing board two decades ago many econo-mists saw the occurrence of disturbances affecting individual euro-area participants differentially – so-called asymmetric shocks – as a major threat to the viability of the single currency. A sharp reminder of such a threat was the German unification process and the shorter-term tension in cyclical developments it generated. The authors wisely do not return to this issue, since asymmetric shocks have been less evident than symmetric ones. But more persistent divergences in both growth and inflation performance have become observable and more entrenched than expected, creating tensions both among the old members of the EMU and in relation to several of the countries in Central and Eastern Europe, now in the process of joining the euro area. These divergences weaken the degree of consensus on monetary policy in the former group and delay the entry process for the second group.

The regional tensions that have arisen were to a considerable extent unforeseen at the design stage of EMU and quite different from the longer-term tendencies discussed at the time. Then the fears of the low-inflation countries was that wide participation in EMU would subject them to constant pressure to keep interest rates lower than would be appropriate for them, while the Mediterranean countries had the mirror image of those concerns. But Germany has been a steady advocate of relatively low interest rates while the Mediterranean countries and others with rapidly rising housing and other asset prices have needed interest rates above those required for the average of the euro area. This source of tension may now be in the process of unwinding as some of the strongest housing booms cool off, but the divergence in both economic growth and inflation with the new member states has moved to the centre stage. Here the main issue is how countries which start their adjustment process from a much lower price level than the old members – and where therefore the alignment of prices is largely an equilibrium phenomenon implying either nominal appreciation of the exchange rate, a higher national inflation rate or some combination of both – can meet the criteria for euro entry which require both exchange-rate stability *and* inflation convergence. Since participation in the euro area is seen by the new member states as one of the main attractions of joining the EU, the relatively long delay for entry currently envisaged for several new Member States is a source of tension also politically. While this does not yet affect the performance of the euro area itself, conflicts may well persist beyond the date of entry. But gradually the catching-up phase will taper off, assisted, as Bordo and James point out, by gradual liberation of migration inside the EU, and the economic performance of the new member states will increasingly resemble that of the older participants.

4. Financial stability

It was recognised from the start of the EMU that financial stability offered important challenges in a union where monetary policy was centralised, but financial supervision was to remain a national responsibility. Furthermore, the home country principle for attributing authority was likely to require greatly intensified cooperation among national supervisors in a financial area the deeper integration of which was a key purpose of the euro to contribute to. As Eichengreen reminds us, there was no antagonism in Europe to financial integration of the kind observed in the United States over much of its history. And the EU authorities soon recognised that the existence of a single currency was only a necessary, not a sufficient condition for financial integration, and that a very detailed Financial Services Action Plan was required – which has now largely been implemented. The one potentially serious remaining gap is that cooperation between national supervisors may not be enough at a time of growing cross-border financial transactions and mergers of banks in different European countries. Although the euro-area financial institutions and markets appear to have withstood recent turbulence quite well – and lapses in financial monitoring were more visible in the United States and in the United Kingdom – Eichengreen is very much up to date in expressing surprise that supervision remains subject to intransparent Memoranda of Understanding, apparently not followed up by contacts at the European level during the recent turbulent times.

This may be another cost of the emphasis on the purely monetary policy aspects of EMU. The ECB was carefully constrained to a consultative role in EU financial supervision. Given the ECB's essential role in assuring liquidity in the euro-area money market the ECB needs to be very well informed about institutional weaknesses in the banks in the euro area. A less purist view of its role in at least macroprudential supervision could be seen as a logical development.

5. The external role of the euro

A large external role for the euro was one of the purposes of moving to EMU. Some were attracted by the prospect of issuing a global currency which would provide a more comfortable framework for financing external imbalances. Others were keen on the more political objective of providing a challenge to the US dollar and to the predominant role of US macroeconomic policies in shaping the global economy. Still others – probably a majority – accepted that the euro would necessarily become the world's second reserve currency while hoping that this status would not imply major complications for achieving internal objectives.

The euro area is now at a point which well illustrates the problem of becoming an international reserve currency. The weakness of the US dollar at the end of a long boom and the increasing demand for euro-denominated assets has pushed the euro to unprecedented levels – though so far with limited effects on the current account of the euro area, which remains near balance. The calls for intervention to stem and reverse an appreciation which may have overshot longer-run equilibrium levels are testing the independence of the ECB. Nevertheless, there are signs, in the absence of open disagreements between the monetary and the political authorities, in the recent period that a common position could be defined, as was the case in 2000 when the euro was at its trough.

6. Conclusion

The challenges defined in the Bordo and James chapter and also referred to by Eichengreen are real and will continue to test the authorities of the euro area. My own evaluation based on the challenges identified is that they are unlikely to escalate to the level where exit from EMU becomes a realistic option for any participant, given the very considerable costs and uncertainties involved. The premise for this relative optimism – which is not totally at odds with the conclusions in the two papers – is that there are by now sufficiently promising signs of pragmatic cooperation at the political level in the euro area to gradually remedy the potential dangers from the originally purist and somewhat lopsided emphasis on the monetary aspects of EMU. The emergence of the Eurogroup as a useful interlocutor of the ECB and as a forum for peer reviews over a range of topics that is widening from monitoring of the fiscal rules to the vital area of structural reforms is in this respect promising, since it should enable EMU to face the challenges more efficiently and harmoniously.

Notes

1. This latter group took to heart the dictum by French economist, Jacques Rueff, 'L'Europe se fera par la monnaie, ou elle ne se fera pas' (Europe will be built by its currency – or it will not be built).
2. See Delors Report (Committee for the Study of Economic and Monetary Union, 1989: para. 23).
3. Eichengreen provides a rich narrative on the early decades of the Fed, but limits his comparison of central bank behaviour to the respective responses to recent financial turbulence; though highly relevant, he may not give enough credit to the way in which the Eurosystem has overcome the teething problems of a new central bank.
4. A terminology usefully recalled by Pisani-Ferry *et al.* (2008).

PART II

OCA *theory revisited*

4 | The OCA theory and the path to EMU

FRANCESCO PAOLO MONGELLI

1. Introduction

The establishment of the European Central Bank (ECB) in June 1998 and the launch of the euro in January 1999 brought to completion the process of European monetary integration. This process started back in the early 1960s when the six members of the then European Economic Community (EEC) began to cooperate in monetary affairs. This chapter examines the synergies between the process of monetary integration and the optimum currency area (OCA) theory, which also emerged in the early 1960s. The OCA theory is a grouping of analytical apparatuses examining a variety of economic characteristics – called the OCA properties – which are desirable for economies wanting to integrate monetarily (i.e. share a single currency).

This chapter is organised as follows. Section 2 briefly surveys the OCA theory and the various OCA properties supporting the launch of a single currency. Section 3 reviews the path to European monetary integration and the role played by OCA theory. Section 4 provides some final remarks on OCA theory and its links with Economic and Monetary Union (EMU). Since it emerged, OCA theory has witnessed several ups and downs, but undeniably it has greatly contributed to the debate on the underpinnings of a successful monetary union.

I would like to thank Ivo Maes, João Nogueira Martins, Peter Hoeller, Hedwig Ongena and several participants in the Commission workshop 'EMU@10: Achievements and Challenges' (Brussels on 26–7 November 2007) for their various comments and suggestions, and Juliette Cuvry for her assistance. An earlier and longer version of this chapter was circulated in Mongelli (2008). The views expressed are mine and do not necessarily reflect those of the ECB.

2. The evolving optimum currency area theory

2.1 Various OCA properties

An optimum currency area can be defined as the optimal geographical area for a single currency, or several currencies, whose exchange rates are irrevocably pegged. The single currency, or the pegged currencies, fluctuate jointly vis-à-vis other currencies. The borders of an OCA are defined by the countries or regions choosing to participate in the currency area. Optimality is defined in terms of the following OCA properties:[1]

a. Mobility of factors of production including labour.
   High-factor market integration within a group of partner countries can reduce the need to alter real factor prices and the nominal exchange rate between countries in response to disturbances (Mundell, 1961). Trade theory established long ago that the mobility of factors of production enhances both efficiency and welfare. Such mobility is likely to be modest in the very short run and could display its effect over time. The mobility of factors of production is limited by the pace at which direct investment can be generated by one country and absorbed by another. Similarly, labour mobility is likely to be low in the short run, due to significant costs, such as those for migration and retraining. Mobility, however, may increase in the medium and long run, easing the adjustment to permanent shocks.

b. Price and wage flexibility.
   When nominal prices and wages are flexible between and within countries contemplating a single currency, the transition towards adjustment following a shock is less likely to be associated with sustained unemployment in one country and/or inflation in another. This will in turn diminish the need for nominal exchange rate adjustments (Friedman, 1953). Alternatively, if nominal prices and wages are rigid downwards, some measure of real flexibility could be achieved by means of exchange rate adjustments. In this case, the loss of direct control over the nominal exchange rate instrument represents a cost.

c. Financial integration.
   Ingram (1962) noted that financial integration can reduce the need for exchange rate adjustments. It may cushion temporary adverse

disturbances through capital inflows – e.g. by borrowing from surplus areas or by a decumulation of net foreign assets, which can be reversed when the shock is over. With a high degree of financial integration, even modest changes in interest rates would elicit equilibrating capital movements across partner countries. This would reduce differences in long-term interest rates, easing the financing of external imbalances but also fostering an efficient allocation of resources. Financial integration is not a substitute for a permanent adjustment when necessary: in this case, it can only smooth this process. Mundell (1973a) discusses the importance of cross-country asset holding for international risk sharing. Countries sharing a single currency can mitigate the effects of asymmetric shocks by diversifying their income sources. This can operate through income insurance when a country's residents hold claims to dividends, interest and rental income from other countries. Such ex-ante insurance allows the smoothing of both temporary and permanent shocks as long as output is imperfectly correlated. Countries' residents can also adjust their wealth portfolio – e.g. in response to income fluctuations – by buying and selling assets and borrowing and lending on international credit markets (i.e. an ex-post adjustment).[2]

d. Degree of economic openness.

The higher the degree of openness, the more changes in international prices of tradeables are likely to be transmitted to the domestic cost of living. This would in turn reduce the potential for money and/or exchange rate illusion by wage earners (McKinnon, 1963). Also, a devaluation would be more rapidly transmitted to the prices of tradeables and the cost of living, negating its intended effects. Hence the nominal exchange rate would be less useful as an adjustment instrument.

e. Diversification in production and consumption.

High diversification in production and consumption, such as the 'portfolio of jobs', and correspondingly in imports and exports, dilutes the possible impact of shocks specific to any particular sector. Therefore, diversification reduces the need for changes in the terms of trade via the nominal exchange rate and provides 'insulation' against a variety of disturbances (Kenen, 1969). Highly diversified partner countries are more likely to incur reduced costs as a result of forsaking nominal exchange rate changes between them and to find a single currency beneficial.

f. Similarity of inflation rates.

External imbalances can also arise from persistent differences in national inflation rates resulting from differences in structural developments, labour markets, economic policies and social preferences (e.g. inflation aversion). Fleming (1971) notes that when inflation rates between countries are low and similar over time, terms of trade will also remain fairly stable. This will foster more equilibrated current account transactions and trade, reducing the need for nominal exchange rate adjustments.

g. Fiscal integration.

Countries sharing a supranational fiscal transfer system to redistribute funds to a member country affected by an adverse asymmetric shock would also be facilitated in the adjustment to such shocks and might require less nominal exchange rate adjustments (Kenen, 1969). However, this would require an advanced degree of political integration and willingness to undertake such risk sharing.

h. Political integration.

The political will to integrate is regarded by some as among the most important conditions for sharing a single currency (Mintz, 1970). Political will fosters compliance with joint commitments, sustains cooperation on various economic policies and encourages more institutional linkages. Haberler (1970) stresses that a similarity of policy attitudes among partner countries is relevant in turning a group of countries into a successful currency area. Tower and Willett (1976) add that for a successful OCA, policy makers need to trade off between objectives.

2.2 Weaknesses and limitations of the OCA theory

After the OCA theory had been completely mapped out, several weaknesses and limitations started emerging. Others emerged over time and are decades apart. They are listed here for presentational convenience. These weaknesses and limitations hampered the normative appeal of OCA theory.

a. Robson (1987) notes how several OCA properties are difficult to measure unambiguously. They are also difficult to evaluate against each other, i.e. OCA theory as a whole lacked a unifying framework. One could still end up drawing different borders for a currency area by referring to different OCA properties. Tavlas (1994) calls this the 'problem of inconclusiveness', as OCA properties may point in different directions: for example, a country might be quite open in terms of reciprocal trade with a group of partner countries, indicating that a fixed exchange rate regime is preferable, or even monetary integration, with its main trading partners. However, the same country might display a low mobility of factors of production, including labour, vis-à-vis these trading partners, suggesting instead that a flexible exchange rate arrangement might be desirable.

b. Tavlas (1994) also observes that there can be a 'problem of inconsistency'. For example, small economies, which are generally more open, should preferably adopt a fixed exchange rate, or even integrate monetarily, with their main partners following the openness property. However, the same small economies are more likely to be less differentiated in production than larger ones. In this case, they would be better candidates for flexible exchange rates according to the diversification in production property. Conversely, McKinnon (1963) notes that more differentiated economies are generally larger and have smaller trade sectors.

c. Studies investigating OCA properties are by necessity backward looking. They cannot reflect a change in policy preferences, or a switch in policy regime such as monetary unification. Instead, in the second half of the 1990s, several authors started raising the issue of the endogenous effects of monetary integration, i.e. whether sharing a single currency may set in motion forces bringing countries closer together (which is discussed later in this chapter).

d. The subject of the benefits and costs of sharing a single currency remains incomplete at best, and arbitrary and partial at worst. This subject, with ill-defined contours and boundaries, is perplexing given that, after all, countries choose to share a single currency – i.e. proceed to monetary union – in expectation of positive net benefits.

e. With hindsight the early OCA theory could not have predicted the growing importance of services in post-industrialised economies. The services sector is by its nature more diversified, diffuse and fragmented. This renders European economies more similar than if one were to just look at their manufacturing sectors.

f. Perhaps the most important weakness of the OCA theory was the crumbling of its conceptual framework: all its main tenets were called into question by new theoretical and empirical advancements. The

early OCA theory was embedded in a Keynesian stabilisation framework and based on the belief that, at least in the short run, monetary
policy is an effective policy instrument which could facilitate the
adjustment of relative wages and prices in the wake of some types
of idiosyncratic shocks, i.e. it could help to undertake business cycle
stabilisation. This would provide a less costly adjustment than having
to endure higher rates of unemployment to facilitate a real adjustment. Buiter (1999) calls the argument that monetary and also fiscal
policy could successfully manipulate aggregate demand to offset
private sector shocks the 'fine-tuning fallacy'. The rational expectations revolution of the 1970s, the monetarist critique, and the literature on the inflation bias postulating the long-run ineffectiveness of
monetary policy, helped change this perception.

A few other weaknesses and limitations are listed later in the chapter. In
any case, Tavlas (1993) notes that from the mid-1970s until the mid-
1980s 'the subject [OCA theory] was for years consigned to intellectual
limbo'. Economists and policy makers looking at the OCA theory could
not find clear answers to the questions of whether Europe should proceed
towards complete monetary integration, and which countries would be fit
to join. Interest in the OCA theory re-emerged only in the mid-1980s with
the advancements in monetary integration discussed in the next section.

2.3 Operationalising the OCA theory and some 'meta' OCA properties

When interest in European monetary integration resurfaced, there were
also advancements in econometric techniques to sustain empirical studies of the diverse OCA properties. These studies sought to assess why
specific groups of countries may form an OCA by analysing and comparing a variety of OCA properties utilising several econometric techniques. Thus they aimed to operationalise the OCA theory.[3] Therefore,
the assessment of OCA properties has now become more articulated.

Some *'meta' OCA properties* were put forward in the 1990s. The
similarity of shocks and of policy responses to those shocks is almost a
'catch all' OCA property capturing the interaction between several
properties. The intuition is that if the incidence of supply and demand
shocks and the speed with which the economy adjusts – taking into
consideration also the policy responses – are similar across partner

countries, then the cost of losing direct control over domestic monetary policy and the nominal exchange rate falls.[4] Hence, countries exhibiting significant co-movements of outputs and prices exhibit the lowest costs of abandoning monetary independence vis-à-vis their partners.

Another important meta OCA property is provided by studies looking at the monetary transmission mechanism that can tell us something about the similarity of financial structures. In recent years, several new studies have emerged (see Angeloni *et al.*, 2003). Such studies analyse and compare, *inter alia*, the financial structures of countries. They show that European countries display significant differences in terms of interest sensitivity of spending, the maturity structure of debt, the net worth of corporate and household sectors, the legal structure, contract enforcement costs, the bank lending channel and the alternatives to bank financing. Such differences are likely to diminish over time. Angeloni and Ehrmann (2003) argue that the pass-through of changes in money market rates is not only faster and more complete, but also increasingly homogeneous across the euro area. Bank retail spreads have also fallen sharply.

2.4 From the endogeneity of OCA to endogeneities of OCA

The hypothesis of an 'endogeneity of OCA' permitted a leap forward for the OCA theory. By studying the effects of several monetary unions that occurred in the past, Jeffrey Frankel and Andrew Rose (see Frankel and Rose (1998 and 2001) and Rose (2000 and 2004)) showed that monetary integration leads to a very significant deepening of reciprocal trade. The implication for EMU is that the euro area may turn into an OCA after the launch of monetary union even if it were not an OCA before. As Frankel and Rose (1998) put it: 'countries which join EMU, no matter what their motivation may be, may satisfy OCA properties ex post even if they do not *ex ante*!' Consequently, the borders of new currency unions could be drawn larger in the expectation that trade integration and income correlation will increase once a currency union is created. This has been termed the 'endogeneity of OCA' and it completely turned around the perspective on the OCA theory.[5]

What might be so special about monetary unions? With a single currency some pecuniary costs disappear or decline. For example, the euro is helping, *inter alia*, to reduce trading costs both directly and indirectly, e.g. by removing exchange rate risks and the cost of currency hedging. Information costs will be reduced as well. The euro is also expected to have a catalysing role for the Single Market Programme (SMP) by enhancing price transparency and discouraging price discrimination. This should help reduce market segmentation and foster competition. A single currency is more efficient than multiple currencies in performing the roles of medium of exchange and unit of account. It can also promote convergence in social conventions with potentially far-reaching legal, contractual and accounting implications. These are principally market-based forces.

Furthermore, a common currency among partner countries is seen as 'a much more serious and durable commitment' (McCallum, 1995). It precludes future competitive devaluations, facilitates foreign direct investment and the building of long-term relationships, and might over time encourage forms of political integration. This will promote reciprocal trade (productivity shocks might also spill over via trade) and economic and financial integration, and may even foster business cycle synchronisation among the countries sharing a single currency. It also reveals the willingness to commit over time to even broader economic integration 'on issues of property rights, non-tariff trade barriers, labour policy, etc.' (Engel and Rogers, 2004). This might in turn boost progress in several OCA properties.

Additional sources of 'endogeneities of OCA' may be present as well. Several authors have in fact put forward concepts similar to the above hypothesis of 'endogeneity of OCA' but in areas other than trade. De Grauwe and Mongelli (2005) examine three other sources of endogeneities of OCA and review some similar concepts:

- the endogeneity of financial integration or equivalently of insurance schemes provided by capital markets (see Baele *et al.* (2004) and Adjaouté and Danthine (2003)). For example, Kalemli-Ozcan *et al.* (2001) and other authors have discussed the effects of sharing a single currency on financially based insurance schemes;
- the endogeneity of symmetry of shocks and (similarly) synchronisation of outputs (see Artis (2003), Mélitz (2004) and Fidrmuc (2005)); and
- the endogeneity of product and labour market flexibility (see Bertola and Boeri, 2004). For example, Blanchard and Wolfers (2000), Bentolila and Saint-Paul (2001) and Saint-Paul (2004) discuss the endogeneity of labour market institutions.

A common thread among these sources of endogeneities of OCA is that monetary integration represents a removal of 'borders', very broadly intended to include also national currencies. This in turn contributes to the shortening of distances and a change in the incentive structure of agents. In any case, this analysis is still relatively new and therefore still evolving.

3. Monetary integration in Europe

3.1 From Bretton Woods to the end of the EMS

The first formal steps of European monetary integration go almost as far back in time as the OCA theory.[6] In October 1962 the Commission issued a memorandum (Commission, 1962), known as the Marjolin Memorandum, that represented an important initiative to foster monetary integration in Europe. The memorandum kicked off the discussion of a common currency and prompted several measures in the field of monetary cooperation. The exchange rates of the members of the EEC were never directly fixed, although they were all pegged to the US dollar (the anchor currency). In fact, at the time exchange rate stability was still secured by the Bretton Woods arrangement, and there was no immediate need for separate exchange rate arrangements among European currencies. By the end of the 1960s, the international environment had changed due to the persistent current account deficits of the USA and the emergence of widespread inflationary pressures that were then exacerbated by the first oil shock. The Bretton Woods system collapsed in August 1971 and the members of the EEC pursued different economic policies that in turn led to exchange rate tensions among them and even threatened to disrupt the customs union and the common agricultural policy (CAP).

In 1969 the heads of state or government requested a plan for the realisation of an economic and monetary union. The result was the Werner Report published in 1970, which proposed to achieve economic and monetary union in several stages by 1980.[7] The final goal of monetary union was never achieved, as the report turned out to be too advanced for the level of economic and financial integration prevailing at the time – i.e. the prospective members posted very low scores under several OCA properties[8] – but some of its elements could still be implemented. Instead, in 1972, after the demise of the Bretton Woods system, the 'currency snake', an exchange rate arrangement for European countries, was created.[9]

In March 1979 the process of monetary integration was revamped with the founding of the European Monetary System (EMS). The principal aim of the EMS was to reduce the disruptive impact of sizeable exchange rate devaluations and regulate changes in parities. The basic elements of the EMS were: the definition of the European Currency Unit (or ECU) as a basket of currencies; and an Exchange Rate Mechanism (ERM) based on the concept of fixed currency exchange rate margins, but with variable exchange rates within those margins (see De Grauwe (2005), and Baldwin and Wyplosz (2006)).[10]

These elements had important implications in relation to the OCA theory. Internal and external monetary stability became important goals. Domestic economic policies were instrumental in achieving exchange rate stability. Countries with relatively high inflation found it easier to pursue disinflation policies. This fostered a downward convergence of inflation rates, reduced excessive exchange rate volatility, and promoted trade and an improvement in overall economic performance. Capital controls were gradually relaxed. However, the lack of fiscal convergence remained a source of tension as some countries ran persistently large budget deficits. The EMS lasted from 1979 until the launch of the euro in 1999. During these two decades it went through four main phases and several periods of turbulence.

The first phase of the EMS spanned from 1979 to 1985. Some countries, including Italy, still maintained capital controls in place and exhibited significant inflation differentials. With fixed nominal exchange rates, this resulted in continued misalignments that required frequent adjustment of the official parities. Nominal convergence had not yet been established.[11]

The second phase lasted from 1986 to September 1992. Several EMS members, but not all, managed to bring down their inflation rates towards German ones. In this phase the EMS is described by many as a 'Deutschmark area' as the monetary policies of all members (except Germany) were de facto surrendered, i.e. the Deutschmark was effectively the anchor of the EMS. Between early 1986 and January 1987 there were three more adjustments, and then until September 1992 there were no realignments (with the exception of an adjustment of the central parity of the Italian lira). During this period the nature of monetary cooperation in Europe switched to mild forms of coordination of monetary policies. Capital controls were being dismantled and were officially banned as of July 1990. All central banks participating in the ERM had de facto renounced an independent monetary policy. This was known as the 'impossible trinity proposition' or the 'inconsistent quartet' (Padoa-Schioppa, 1982). This second phase of the EMS bore several fruits from the standpoint of various OCA properties, as integration deepened in several areas.

An opportunity for setting a course towards economic and monetary union arose after the adoption of the Single European Act in 1986 (which introduced the Single Market as a further objective of the Community). Jacques Delors, then President of the Commission, set up a committee to study the feasibility of a monetary union. The resulting report of the Delors Committee was approved in Madrid in 1989. The completion of the Delors Report was accelerated at the time of the break-up of the former Soviet Union and the looming German reunification, i.e. a unique window of opportunity had just opened up. It laid out the blueprint of the Maastricht Treaty that was signed in February 1992. A three-stage process leading to the single currency and designing the corresponding institutions was completely mapped out at the end of the decade (see Box 4.1. on the three stages of EMU).

In 1990 a group of economists led by Michael Emerson finalised 'One Market, One Money: An Evaluation of the Potential Benefits and Costs of Forming an Economic and Monetary Union' (European Commission, 1990, and Emerson *et al.*, 1992). This evaluation had been commissioned in 1988 as an input for the Delors Report.

Box 4.1: **Three stages of EMU and the launch of the euro**

The Delors Report provided the blueprint for the Maastricht Treaty which in turn envisaged a three-stage path to EMU. The **first stage of EMU** coincided with the complete liberalisation of capital movements in Europe, and several other steps (see Figure 4.1 for a list of the measures and principles marking each of the three stages). It was also postulated that Member States could only participate in the forthcoming monetary union if they could show a high degree of lasting convergence confirmed by the fulfilment of four main economic criteria (inflation, long-term interest rates, fiscal debt and deficit, and exchange rates). The Delors Report also advocated an independent central bank with the primary objective of price stability.

The establishment of the European Monetary Institute (EMI) in early 1994 as a transitional institution marked the start of the **second stage of EMU**. Responsibility for the conduct of monetary policy in the EU remained the preserve of the national authorities. The two main tasks of the EMI were (a) to strengthen central bank cooperation and monetary policy coordination (including the assessment of progress in the fields of economic and legal convergence); and (b) to make the preparations required for the establishment of the European System of Central Banks, for the conduct of the single monetary policy and for the creation of a single currency in the third stage. On 1 January 1999 the **third and final stage of EMU** started with the introduction of the euro in eleven EU Member States, the establishment of the Eurosystem, and the transfer of responsibility for the conduct of monetary policy to the ECB. At the same time, the intra-EU exchange rate mechanism for some Member States not participating in the euro (ERM II) and the Stability and Growth Pact (SGP) came into force.

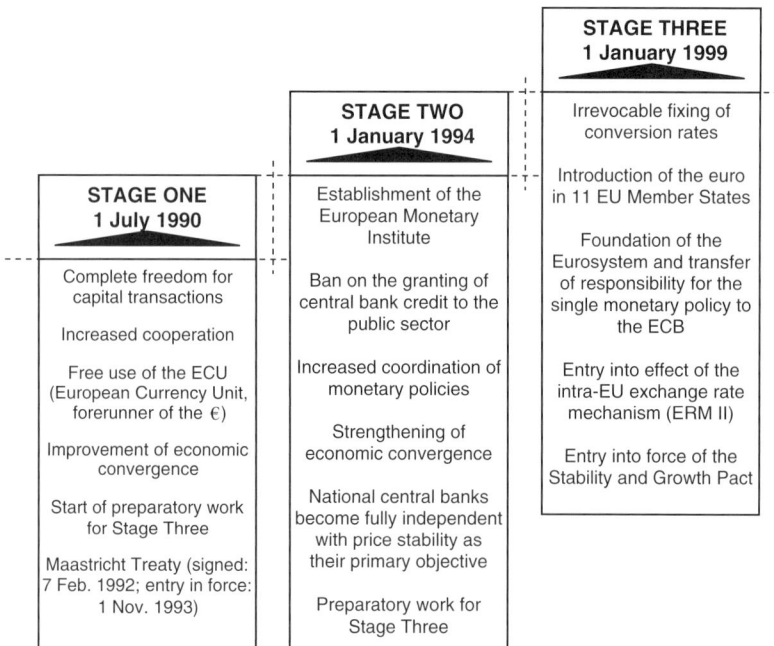

		STAGE THREE **1 January 1999**
	STAGE TWO **1 January 1994**	Irrevocable fixing of conversion rates
STAGE ONE **1 July 1990**	Establishment of the European Monetary Institute	Introduction of the euro in 11 EU Member States
Complete freedom for capital transactions	Ban on the granting of central bank credit to the public sector	Foundation of the Eurosystem and transfer of responsibility for the single monetary policy to the ECB
Increased cooperation		
Free use of the ECU (European Currency Unit, forerunner of the €)	Increased coordination of monetary policies	Entry into effect of the intra-EU exchange rate mechanism (ERM II)
Improvement of economic convergence	Strengthening of economic convergence	Entry into force of the Stability and Growth Pact
Start of preparatory work for Stage Three	National central banks become fully independent with price stability as their primary objective	
Maastricht Treaty (signed: 7 Feb. 1992; entry in force: 1 Nov. 1993)	Preparatory work for Stage Three	

Figure 4.1: The three stages of Economic and Monetary Union
Source: Adapted from the ECB website.

The evaluation points out that 'there is no ready-to-use theory for assessing the costs and benefits of economic and monetary union'. The OCA theory, in their view, has provided important early insights, but offers only a narrow and outdated analytical framework to define the optimum economic and monetary competencies of a given 'area' such as the EU, i.e. it is unable to tell which countries should share a single currency. The latter EMU question is more complex than the OCA question. Later on, Wyplosz (2006) observed that while 'One Market, One Money' was completed too late to provide an academic input into the blueprint of the Maastricht Treaty, it drew researchers back into the study of monetary integration and opened the way for a spectacular comeback of the OCA theory.

The third phase of the EMS, from September 1992 until March 1993, was marked by the most severe crisis of the whole EMS arrangement. There were several concurring adverse events. Misalignments kept growing, albeit at a slower pace, because inflation differentials, despite their decline, were still significant for some countries. The tight monetary policy pursued by the Bundesbank following reunification and the shock of the Danish electorate voting against the Maastricht Treaty in referendum (2 June 1992) alarmed the foreign exchange markets and prompted speculative attacks on the overvalued currencies.[12]

The fourth phase ran until the launch of the euro, allowing the principle of fixed exchange rates, although much weakened, to be kept alive. The EMS ceased to function in its original form when eleven EU countries irrevocably fixed their exchange rates in preparation for the adoption of the euro. The successor of the original arrangement was ERM II, launched on 1 January 1999. In it, the ECU basket was discarded and the euro became an anchor for other participating currencies.

Two decades with the EMS (and the ERM therein) taught us that keeping separate currencies with fixed exchange rates among them and full capital mobility is always open to financial tensions and vulnerabilities: in particular, nominal pegs can become unsustainable if the goals pursued by national governments conflict. Even tightly pegged exchange rates cannot impose sufficient discipline on 'domestic economic policies'. Even a strengthened ERM would not be sufficient. Consequently, the Delors Report presented the path to monetary union as a natural follow-up of the Single European Act. Hence, the Delors Report was grounded on the assumption that a 'corner solution', such as monetary union, can solve the dilemma and remove the pains of periodical exchange rate realignments.

3.2 What influence did OCA theory have on the design of EMU?

As just noted, the Delors Report and subsequently the Maastricht Treaty, set out to reduce the risk from destabilising exchange rate volatilities and misalignments. There was a defensive intent as exchange rate volatility and misalignment were deemed costly. Furthermore, there was also a widely held view that the Single Market was not expected to be able to deliver its full potential without a single currency.[13] Several commentators noted that this argument had no direct links, or very tenuous links at best, with the OCA theory (Baldwin and Wyplosz, 2006), i.e. the OCA properties did not figure prominently in the Delors Report. For example, the 'One Market, One Money' evaluation held a critical view of the 'early' OCA theory. Admittedly, a rigorous application of all OCA properties at the time would have provided some mixed results. Wyplosz (2006) noted that this was not a very attractive proposition from a political standpoint when pushing for monetary union.

Hence, the OCA theory was sidelined at this crucial juncture, or as Wyplosz (2006) aptly put it: 'With little experience to rely upon and limited theoretical backing, economists and policy makers had to invent practically everything in little time. Policy makers rushed to negotiate a detailed agreement [i.e. the 1992 Maastricht Treaty], having no time for detailed economic analysis'. In this lies a paradox as, at the same time, the 'One Market, One Money' evaluation greatly contributed to revitalising interest in the debate on OCA theory, brought together many strands of theoretical and empirical literature (directly or indirectly related to OCA theory), and spurred a vast amount of new research. Another merit of the evaluation was to discuss several desirable features and possible implications of EMU. Gaspar and Mongelli (2003) note that in retrospect it is interesting that 'One Market, One Money' did not place much emphasis on the impact of monetary unification on economic integration, i.e. no forward-looking provisions for some endogenous effects ('Rose effects') were postulated.[14]

In the end, the 'One Market, One Money' evaluation came out in clear favour of proceeding towards complete monetary integration in Europe for several EU members. Emerson *et al.* (1992) argue that the many shortcomings of the 'old' OCA theory were likely to bias downwards the expected net benefits from monetary integration: EMU is likely to be more beneficial than what can be presumed on the basis of the application of the OCA properties alone. For example, although labour mobility is low in Europe, the mobility of capital is instead quite high and rising. This provides an alternative adjustment channel. In the meantime, the 'new OCA theory' was slowly emerging. The hypothesis of the endogeneity of the OCA did the rest in terms of revitalising the debate on OCAs and played an important role in the policy debate during the 1990s.

3.3 Convergence criteria instead of OCA properties?

If we recall the juxtaposition between those advocating a long convergence process to favour an alignment of monetary policies (i.e. the 'economists' camp) and those for whom full nominal convergence was not indispensable prior to EMU (i.e. the 'monetarists' camp), the economists secured the following set of convergence criteria that were laid down in the Maastricht Treaty, while the monetarists obtained a final date by which Stage Three would start (i.e. 1 January 1999):

- the price stability criterion, implying that the inflation rate of any country could not exceed a reference value calculated as the unweighted arithmetic average of the rate of inflation in the three countries with the lowest inflation plus 1.5 percentage points;
- sustainable fiscal policies, requiring that the government budget deficit cannot exceed 3 per cent of GDP in normal circumstances, and the government public debt should not exceed 60 per cent of GDP or, when above this threshold, should steadily move in that direction;
- exchange rate stability and ERM membership for two years prior to the adoption of the single currency without devaluation; and
- long-term interest rates should not exceed the average interest rate in the three lowest inflation countries by more than 2 percentage points.

A lot of emphasis has been given to all the convergence criteria. What is the link between these convergence criteria and OCA theory?

The price stability criterion bears a clear resemblance to the OCA property indicating the desirability of similarity in inflation rates among countries contemplating monetary union. The criterion that has been subject to most discussion has been that about the sustainability of fiscal policy and avoidance of excessive deficits.[15] Although the EU does not have a supranational fiscal transfer system (like the USA), fiscal discipline permits the unobstructed working of fiscal stabilisers and grants some room for manoeuvre to national governments: hence it enhances the dynamic adjustment of the members of the monetary union, which in turn reduces the risk of persistent differentials and dissimilar shocks. The exchange rate stability criterion and similarity of long-term interest rates would reflect several OCA properties including a high degree of financial integration, economic openness and similarity of inflation rates.

A noteworthy aspect should be mentioned here. While OCA theory is primarily concerned with diverse economic and financial characteristics, success of a currency union (i.e. in some sense the optimality of a currency area) rests a lot on its implementation and management. Institution-building and institutional settings play a big role. Building a new supranational central banking system made it necessary to agree upon its (future) working arrangements. With the launch of the euro in January 1999, responsibility for the single monetary policy in the euro area was transferred to a supranational central banking system: the Eurosystem. The latter comprises the ECB and the national central banks of those countries that have adopted the euro.[16]

3.4 'Eurosclerosis' and the role of institutions and structural rigidities

EMU and the launch of the euro created laboratory conditions for examining whether the countries joining in the euro formed an optimum currency area. What would an 'OCA scientist' have found by looking at some crucial OCA properties for the functioning of the soon-to-be-born EMU? She or he would have had to report some encouraging aspects such as a high degree of openness and diversification in production and consumption, similar (low) inflation rates, and the acceptance of a joint governance structure. However, price and wage flexibility was modest overall, and labour mobility low. Financial market integration was also low, but rising.[17] All in all, European countries might not have scored very highly on various OCA properties.

Actually, some concerns arose. In the early 1980s a debate on the causes of high and persistent unemployment took root in the UK (see Layard *et al.* 2005). A few years later, when economic performance deteriorated in continental Europe as well, this debate became main-stream in the policy debates, and on academic agendas. The term 'eurosclerosis' was coined to describe a pattern of high unemployment, slow job creation, low participation in the labour force and weakening overall economic growth during the 1980s and most of the 1990s (see Bentolila and Saint-Paul, 2001). Eurosclerosis contrasted with the more dynamic experience of the United States where economic expansion was accompanied by high job growth.

What is remarkable is that over the last two decades, academics, applied researchers and several international organisations (with a leading role played by the OECD) made tremendous progress in under-standing the root causes of the dismal performance. A rich literature ensued, illustrating the role of labour market institutions, product market regulations, social preferences and conventions, and other economic features.[18] The normative implications for EMU were cautionary. It also became clear that a poor performance under these OCA properties would have hampered the dynamic adjustment of euro-area economies vis-à-vis economic shocks. Ceteris paribus, the costs of sharing a single currency would have been higher. In order to promote some remedies, the nature and depth of such product, labour and financial market rigidities had to be addressed by means of policy initiatives. The diagnosis of the causes of structural rigidities in product and labour markets and low financial integration was intimidating. Some of the main points are discussed briefly below.

Among the main labour market institutions that are recognised as having an impact on the functioning of the labour market are the influence of wage bargaining systems, trade unions, unemployment benefits (and social security in general), employment protection legislation, the mismatch between job seekers and vacancies, the minimum wage, taxes on labour, and other factors driving a wedge between the wage paid by employers and the wage received by employees.[19] The importance of active labour market measures aimed at improving the search effectiveness of the unemployed and hence increasing their downward pressure on wage formation has also come to the fore (see Calmfors, 2001a). Blanchard and Wolfers (2000) have clearly illustrated how rigid labour market institutions, when the economy is hit by adverse shocks, generate a 'ratcheting effect' on unemployment. This helps to explain the persistence of European unemployment and the high share of long-term unemployment.[20]

The need for structural reforms, as well as the difficulty of under-taking them, have become quite apparent. Duval and Elmeskov (2006) argue that reforms are not Pareto improving and those whose rents or benefits are reduced by reforms oppose them strenuously. Bertola (2000) argues that institutions serve purposes that were clear at the time of their creation, for example protecting labour market partici-pants. Removing the various sources of labour market rigidity may be neither easy nor rational if completed in a piecemeal fashion (see also European Commission, 2004a). Work on labour market reforms has been very high on the European policy agenda since the mid-1990s, and led to the Lisbon Agenda.

Product market regulations were also examined. Price flexibility is hampered, albeit to different degrees across the euro area, by the slow implementation of the Single Market Programme and by a slow dis-mantling of some non-tariff internal and external trade barriers (see European Commission, 2004a). For example, there is relatively low market competition and monopolistic tendencies in sectors with a high concentration of state-owned enterprises or of previous state monopolies, i.e. 'network industries' (such as public utilities and energy companies). The work on a set of product and labour market indica-tors – first pioneered by the OECD (see OECD Jobs Study (1994) and several other OECD publications) – provided a remarkable impulse to these studies. All of the above factors hampering product and labour market flexibility, i.e. weakening these OCA properties, could then be examined in detail.

Concerning financial market integration, or the lack thereof, there was also a flourishing of studies and analyses. Emerson *et al.* (1992) and the Giovannini Group identified various inefficiencies in EU financial markets and proposed practical solutions to foster financial market integration in its four reports concerning: the impact of the introduction of the euro on capital markets (1997); EU repo markets (1999); the coordinated issuance of public debt in the euro area (2000); and EU cross-border clearing and settlement arrangements (2002).

What these comprehensive and articulate studies concerning product, labour and financial markets show is that these OCA properties can now be discussed in great detail. Countries exhibit, or do not exhibit, price and wage flexibility, labour mobility and financial integration due to a variety of factors. If we were to 'wear an OCA theory hat', our task would become more challenging: we would then have to find out with some precision to what extent and why certain OCA properties are shared, or are not shared, by partner countries.

The fact that we can tell which countries underperform under some OCA properties, and why, opens up a whole new perspective: that countries performing modestly under *some* OCA properties (but not all) could share efforts to improve their performance. This would be equivalent to an 'OCA theory in reverse'. The various international studies, comparisons and benchmarking would chart the route for the countries needing to reform. The context of EMU and the need to gain flexibility and adaptability should provide an added incentive for structural reforms.

3.5 Institutional forces fostering OCA properties: the 'exogeneity of OCA'

The rich literature on the endogeneity of OCA that was pioneered by Frankel and Rose (1998) argues that there is something special about monetary unions. Sharing a single currency is associated with more reciprocal trade. We argued in Section 2.5 that a new single currency might also improve the *OCA rating* of the euro area through other channels, e.g. by fostering financial integration and greater business cycle synchronisation. Hence, from our standpoint we will want to see evidence of diverse market-based forces bringing euro-area countries closer together.

But there are also *institutional forces* at play. Initiatives to promote structural reforms have been at the centre of policy making in the EU over the last decade. This is true for all the areas in which the 'OCA theory in reverse' holds. The execution of the three stages of EMU – and in particular the run-up to the launch of the euro – intensified ongoing structural reforms, such as those fostered and monitored by the European Commission, the OECD and other organisations.

All of these forces and institutional processes might be generating an 'exogeneity of OCA'; for example, countries that score below others (or below a certain benchmark) for some OCA criteria could experience more pressure to undertake structural reforms in order to improve their performance. Such pressure would come from the European Commission, the ECB and the OECD, as well as the governance framework of economic policy coordination in the EU, including reviews by the ECOFIN Council and the Eurogroup.

The previous discussion in Section 3.3 and the concise summary of the links between institutional integration and economic integration are an illustration of such a causality at work: institutional integration 'causes' trade deepening, while at the same time trade deepening also 'causes' institutional integration (but with a lower intensity).

Institutional arrangements and exogenous commitments are only part of the story, however. There are two other aspects to consider. The first aspect is that there is now a broadly shared analytical apparatus – based on the various established indicators and academic research previously mentioned – that fosters an understanding of the adverse effects of not reforming, and the favourable effects of sharing best practices. Hence, member countries are aware that reforms are needed. The second aspect is that there are more incentives for peer pressure because countries that are more integrated have a bigger stake in the well-being of the others.

Concerning product and labour market reforms, recent initiatives have been the Single Market Programme, the 1994 OECD Jobs Strategy, the 2000 Lisbon Agenda (and its review in 2005), and other institutional initiatives and processes.

In the late 1980s the OECD launched a study of the factors underlying the high and persistent unemployment and poorly functioning product and labour markets in many OECD countries. This study was published in 1994 as the OECD Jobs Strategy and proposed a wide-ranging set of policy recommendations for its constituency. These recommendations covered several policy areas, including macroeconomic policy, creation and diffusion of innovation, entrepreneurial climate, labour force skills, competences and education, as well as various other aspects concerning labour market policies and institutions. In 1995 the recommendations were expanded to also cover policies related to product market competition (see OECD (1999), Brandt *et al.* (2005) and Duval and Elmeskov (2006)). The strength of the Jobs Strategy lies in a careful compilation of harmonised product and labour market indicators across its constituency. There is also a collection of data on past policies and efforts at reform. This wealth of information makes it possible, among other things, to rank countries according to their product and labour market conditions and performance, review and compare their past reform efforts, and recommend some benchmarking concerning the reform gap of each OECD member. A host of studies and analyses on what works and what does not work have been rendered possible by the OECD Jobs Strategy.

The Lisbon Agenda is one of the clearest examples of the exogeneity of OCA. It was first adopted by the European Council in Lisbon in March 2000, and sets out a strategy which aims at addressing the issues of low productivity and stagnation of economic growth in the EU over a ten-year period. The purpose of the Agenda was to make the EU the world's most dynamic and competitive economy by 2010, a goal that was to be achieved by transforming Europe into the world's largest knowledge-based economy. The initiatives in the Agenda were organised under three pillars: economic, social and environmental. This postulates that enhancing knowledge generates direct and indirect benefits. The belief is that various high-technology businesses, especially computer software, telecommunications and virtual services, as well as educational and research institutions and other aspects of an 'information society', can contribute to boosting creativity and innovation, enhancing productivity and propping up the economy.

In March 2005 the European Council completed the mid-term review of the Lisbon Agenda, based on an independent review by a High Level Group headed by Wim Kok and on the Spring Report by the European Commission. The review illustrated that little/modest progress had been made over the first five years of implementation, and recommended refocusing the Agenda on the economic pillar, and particularly on growth and employment. Both reports also proposed an overhaul of the governance of the strategy and underlined the need for real ownership by the Member States in which the reforms were necessary. Four areas were identified as fundamental for relaunching the Lisbon Agenda: 1. improving knowledge and innovation; 2. making the EU an attractive area in which to invest and work; 3. fostering growth and employment, thereby also contributing to social cohesion; and 4. promoting sustainable development and human capital. The various original targets were toned down (though not abandoned). The European Council also endorsed a new governance framework streamlining the open method of coordination and preparing an EU Annual Progress Report with a set of Integrated Guidelines, a package including the Broad Economic Policy Guidelines (BEPGs) and the Employment Guidelines (EGs). Member States prepare National Reform Programmes (NRPs) that have a three-year span but are updated annually. There is a 'Partnership for Growth and Jobs', which is supported by an action plan at European Union level, and the NRPs allow the implementation of both of these to be monitored. Member States and social partners were also encouraged to take ownership of the reform process and bring it into national political debates.

These various reports and guidelines are provided as part of an annual coordination cycle. Early in the year, the ECOFIN Council provides input for the Guidelines, and the Spring European Council takes note of the EU Annual Progress Report and endorses the Integrated Guidelines. Around May, the European Parliament provides a resolution on the BEPGs and opinions on EGs. After the Council adopts the Integrated Guidelines package, the European Commission holds bilateral meetings with Member States to discuss the respective NRPs, which are then officially submitted in the autumn. Towards the end of the year, the European Commission reviews the implementation of NRPs and the Council conducts multilateral surveillance and provides reactions to NRPs.

Concerning financial market integration, significant reports include the Financial Services Action Plan (FSAP); the Lamfalussy Report and its follow-ups; the Giovannini Report and its follow-ups; as well as other initiatives listed in the Commission's Scoreboard.

4. Some final remarks ...

4.1 ... on the OCA theory

About fifty years have passed since the founding of the OCA theory. Its basic pioneering intuitions were remarkably strong. In fact, all OCA properties are still relevant. However, over these five decades OCA theory has witnessed several ups and downs. Between the early-1960s and mid-1970s, the early OCA theory was completely mapped out. Several weaknesses and limitations of the analytical framework behind the OCA theory then started to emerge and the theory fell into neglect from the mid-1970s to the mid-1980s. It was difficult to find clear normative implications for the European countries considering monetary unification. Furthermore, the stabilisation framework underlying the OCA theory started crumbling.

In the second half of the 1980s, OCA theory missed an important appointment. When monetary integration made the formidable leap forwards that ultimately led to the 1989 Delors Report and the 1992 Maastricht Treaty, OCA theory could not deliver a clear view. In the event, plans for EMU including the launch of the euro went ahead, but OCA theory had a limited direct input.

In subsequent years, several of the weaknesses and limitations of OCA theory were addressed. Some significant advances in econometrics made it possible to 'operationalise' various OCA properties. Studies of each OCA property – and also of the similarities between the transmission of shocks and the monetary transmission mechanism – have become comprehensive and well articulated. We now discuss the institutional environment in which economic agents operate and can better address to what extent and why certain OCA properties are shared or not shared. A new OCA theory has emerged over the last two decades.

The literature on the endogeneity of the OCA reinvigorated the debate on OCA theory. There is, by now, compelling empirical evidence that sharing a single currency is a powerful magnet for deeper economic and financial integration. Such endogenous effects could stem from deeper financial integration and greater risk sharing, increased symmetry of shocks and output synchronisation, and a faster pace of product and labour market reforms to enhance flexibility. Correspondingly, the borders of new currency unions could be drawn larger in the expectation that trade integration and income correlation will increase once a currency union is created.[21]

Notwithstanding its weaknesses and limitations, OCA theory has shown great merits as an organising device and as a catalyst for analysis over all these years. Without OCA theory there may not have been such a systematic scrutiny of so many diverse economic features, which are after all the building blocks of monetary unions. Such scrutiny will continue well into the future.

4.2 … on monetary integration

Monetary unification among European countries was first tackled as a concrete project at the time of the 1970 Werner Report. Although the implementation of the plan was abandoned at a relatively early stage, some of its elements resurfaced later and were useful for drawing up the blueprint for EMU. A coherent and viable plan for full monetary union emerged with the Delors Report of 1989, which in turn led to the Maastricht Treaty in 1992.

On the surface OCA theory played only a modest role in the preparation of the Delors Report and then the Maastricht Treaty. At the time, the main concern was to remove the risks of destabilising exchange rate volatilities and misalignments that had disrupted the European Monetary System on several occasions. A 'corner solution' such as monetary union is seen as a way of combating these risks. Hence, EMU has a defensive purpose. This reflects several lessons from the two decades with the EMS, when it was clearly seen that keeping separate currencies with fixed exchange rates between them and with full capital mobility can lead to tensions. The path to monetary union is therefore a natural follow-up to the Single European Act and supports the implementation of the Single Market Programme. The view became widely held that the Single Market could not be expected to exploit its full potential without a single currency.

While the debate on EMU was taking place, a pattern of high unemployment, slow job creation, low participation in the labour force and weakening overall economic growth emerged. These malaises are grouped together under the term 'eurosclerosis'. A wide range of literature ensued, illustrating the role of labour market institutions, product market regulations, social preferences and conventions, and other economic features. The normative implications for EMU were cautionary. Initiatives to promote structural reforms have been at the centre of policy making in the EU over the last ten to fifteen years. The Lisbon Agenda is an example that we have already discussed in depth.

This illustrates that, beneath the surface, OCA theory was being heeded. European countries were de facto tackling their structural weaknesses. We can talk of an OCA theory in reverse in the area of (tight) product market regulations, labour market rigidities, and modest financial integration. Frankel and Rose (1998 and 2001) have argued that there is something special about monetary unions, and pioneered a rich literature on the 'endogeneity of OCA'. Perhaps, at the broad governance of EMU, there may also be an exogeneity of OCA.

A relevant question for the future may be: even if OCA theory is neglected, will this theory and its various properties be condemned to oblivion? Our feeling is that monetary unions have to reckon with all OCA properties at some point in the future. The balance between the benefits and costs of EMU hinges on the ability of each country to enhance its dynamic adjustment. This aspect is still poorly researched and explained to the general public. The role of financial integration and risk sharing is also critical for the success of EMU. These aspects should figure prominently in any future research agenda.

4.3 ... on the links between OCA and EMU

The OCA theory and the process leading to EMU started at almost the same time in the early 1960s. Since then, a new OCA theory has gradually evolved. However, it is still complex to measure and compare the various OCA properties, and there is still no simple OCA test with a clear-cut scorecard. Therefore, using OCA theory has not become any simpler.

Over the last two decades the balance of judgements has shifted in favour of monetary unions. Similarity of shocks is not a strict prerequisite for sharing a single currency if all members of the currency area are financially integrated and hold claims on each other's output. In this case they would 'insure' one another through private financial markets. This explains the emphasis on the need to strengthen financial integration in EMU. Association to a currency union is now deemed to generate fewer costs in terms of the loss of autonomy in domestic macroeconomic policies. There is also a greater understanding of the benefits of monetary unions. The 'endogeneity of OCA' has further strengthened this consideration.

While plans for EMU were advancing, it became apparent that several EU countries – prospective members of the euro area – were still faring poorly under some OCA properties, and concerns about eurosclerosis emerged. The implications for EMU were cautionary. Initiatives to promote structural reforms have been at the centre of policy making in the EU over the last fifteen to twenty years. The Lisbon Agenda and the OECD Jobs Strategy are clear examples. Hence, beneath the surface, OCA theory was being heeded and European countries were tackling their structural weaknesses. We can almost talk of an OCA theory in reverse. If we look at the broad governance structure of EMU, there may in fact be an 'exogeneity of OCA'.

EMU might have been quite different without the OCA theory, while the OCA theory found several motivations and challenges in the process of European integration. However, the launch of the euro marked the beginning of a new process with new challenges and rewards. Over time, the effects of the endogeneities and exogeneities of OCA should become apparent.

Notes

1. Sharing these OCA properties reduces the usefulness of nominal exchange rate adjustments within the currency area by lessening the impact of some

types of shocks or facilitating their adjustment thereafter. Countries forming a currency area expect benefits to exceed costs.

2. A corollary of this argument is that similarity of shocks is not a strict
prerequisite for sharing a single currency if all members of the currency
area are financially integrated and hold claims on each other's output. In
many ways, some speak of a Mundell I versus a Mundell II. Unfortunately
this crucial argument was neglected until the rediscovery of Mundell II by
McKinnon (2004).

3. A common denominator across these empirical studies is that their analyses go deep into the features of the economy, as well as the institutions of
each country and the preferences of economic agents (see Mongelli, 2005).

4. See Bayoumi and Eichengreen (1997), Masson and Taylor (1993), Alesina
et al. (2002) and Demertzis *et al.* (2000). These studies also drew some
criticism: for example, Tavlas (1994) notes that their results are ambiguous
and the theoretical underpinnings of the tests are often conflicting.

5. The endogeneity emerges from two main channels. The first is that the
degree of openness – i.e. reciprocal trade between the members of the
currency area – is likely to increase after a single currency is launched.
This insight is widely accepted. The second channel postulates a positive
link between trade integration and income correlation. On this insight
diverging views exist, i.e. some think that monetary unification would
instead spur specialisation and asymmetry of shocks (see Bayoumi and
Eichengreen, 1997). Mongelli (2005) illustrates the implications of both
views. For a 'meta-analysis' of the effects of monetary unions on trade, see
Rose and Stanley (2005).

6. Monetary integration in Europe has always been part of a broader process
of economic integration which started already in the 1950s. These three
aspects of integration – i.e. economic, financial and monetary integration –
overlap and complement each other.

7. The Werner Report prescribed three main elements for monetary union:
1. 'Within the area of a monetary union, currencies must be fully and
irreversibly convertible, fluctuation margins around exchange rates must
be eliminated, par values irrevocably fixed, and capital movements completely free.' 2. 'It is of primary importance that the main decisions regarding monetary policy be centralized, whether such decisions concern
liquidity, interest rates, intervention on the exchange markets, management of reserves, or the fixing of currency parities vis-à-vis the rest of the
world.' and 3. 'Under such a system, national currencies could be maintained, or a single Community currency could be created.'

8. Early on, the mobility of factors of production was still low, the degree of
economic openness was growing fast (but was still modest), financial
integration was fairly low, inflation rates were too dissimilar (and diverged

even more significantly in the wake of the twin oil shocks) and, in particular, political integration was still incipient. EEC countries would have failed any OCA test.

9. Several EEC countries agreed to prevent exchange rate fluctuations of more than 2.25 per cent. De facto in the late 1970s only the Deutschmark, the Benelux currencies and the Danish krona were still members of the snake. The pound sterling, the Irish pound, the French franc and the Italian lira all entered and exited after shorter time periods.

10. Officially no currency was designated as an anchor. However, the Deutschmark and the Bundesbank were unquestionably the centre of the EMS. The critical role of an anchor currency in the process of monetary integration is not addressed by the OCA theory.

11. Differentials in budget deficits and public debt were also substantial. The adjustment of official parities often occurred in the wake of financial market turmoil, which periodically brought up questions about the sustainability of the ERM. During this phase, there were nine adjustments involving several currencies (see Baldwin and Wyplosz, 2006).

12. Such attacks were in fact one-way bets: the speculations could either win (if the parities were indefensible) or lose very little. Speculative attacks almost destroyed the EMS in the period between September 1992 and March 1993. The UK and Italy were forced to leave the ERM (Italy then rejoined in 1996) and the fluctuation margins were widened to +/–15 per cent in March 1993, which marked the end of the tight ERM.

13. Over time, a single currency would, amongst other things, bring about greater price transparency for consumers and investors, eliminate exchange rate risks, reduce transaction costs and, as a result, significantly increase economic welfare.

14. The empirical studies surveyed did not show strong effects of exchange rate volatility on either trade or international investment flows. This, in turn, justifies that monetary unification was seen as a limiting case of reduction of exchange rate volatility leading to the elimination of exchange rate uncertainty and to reductions in transaction costs and hedging costs.

15. The Stability and Growth Pact was then added in 1997 to clarify the functioning of the excessive deficit procedure in the Maastricht Treaty and laid down the procedures for multilateral surveillance (see Brunila *et al.*, 2001).

16. There is a vast literature describing the monetary policy framework of the ECB and the workings of the Eurosystem. See, amongst others, Issing *et al.* (2001), Baldwin and Wyplosz (2006), Gerdesmeier *et al.* (2007), ECB (2004a), and Moutot *et al.* (2007).

17. The Giovannini Report remarked that European financial markets were still a juxtaposition of national markets. Money markets were still

separate, reflecting the existence of national currencies and still fragmented payment systems. The repo segment, where market participants
exchange short-run liquidity against collateral, was even less well integrated (Berg *et al.*, 2005). Bond markets were also fragmented into
national currencies. Equity risk premia were still substantial and displayed different country risks which had an impact on the domestic
cost of capital. The average European investor was not very financially
diversified. Risk sharing through cross-country ownership of assets was
still negligible, indicating a 'home bias' in portfolio holdings.

18. It is impossible to do justice to such a vast body of literature. The
following contributions are listed as a general source of reference:
Duval and Elmeskov (2006), Fagan *et al.* (2003), Baldwin and Wyplosz
(2006), Elmeskov *et al.* (1998), Nickell (1997), Bertola (2000) and
Blanchard and Wolfers (2000).

19. Such a wedge is composed of two parts: the terms of trade and indirect
tax effect (the GDP deflator divided by the consumption deflator) and the
direct tax wedge. The first effect takes into account the fact that workers
are likely to have an objective for the real wage in terms of consumer
prices, while the output deflator is more relevant for firms. The two
deflators may exhibit divergent evolutions when an exogenous shock –
for instance an oil price shock – hits the economy (see Fagan *et al.*, 2003).

20. There is also a debate on collective policy choices and social models that
has acquired great prominence in recent years. Early on there were
references to a European social model, and later a qualification was
made among four main models: the Continental model, the Nordic
model, the Anglo-Saxon model and the Southern European model.

21. However, could any group of countries form a monetary union and wait
for deeper integration to occur automatically and thereby inevitably reap
net benefits from a single currency? Could there instead be a critical
threshold in the mix of OCA properties beyond which the 'endogeneity
of OCA' types of effects could manifest themselves? Ultimately these are
empirical questions.

5 | A modern reconsideration of the OCA theory

GIANCARLO CORSETTI

1. Introduction

Economic heterogeneity across regions and countries is, in many ways, a vital sign of growing and healthy economies. By the same token, differences in institutions and policies may reflect diversity in preferences and political orientations across communities in a currency area, consistent with the democratic nature of our societies. Nonetheless, the literature on Optimal Currency Areas (henceforth OCAs) has long emphasized that some elements of economic heterogeneity increase the likelihood of asynchronous business cycle fluctuations at regional level, which interfere with the efficient conduct of stabilization policy in a currency area, and in principle may prevent a single monetary authority from achieving successfully its goals.

The traditional debate pointed out that the likelihood of asymmetric shocks is higher in the presence of national differences in product specialization, and/or sectoral composition of output. Over the years, the list of relevant asymmetries has grown to include also structural differences which may affect the way a common shock is transmitted

I thank the discussant and the participants in the Commission workshop 'EMU@10', Brussels, November 26–7 2007 for comments. An earlier related paper circulated with the title 'A Microfounded Reconsideration of the Theory of Optimal Currency Area.' I also thank the participants in the conferences 'Monetary Policy Implications of Heterogeneity in a Currency Area', organized by the ECB; '40 anni di attività dell'Ente Einaudi (1965–2005)' organized by Ente Einaudi in 2005, as well as participants in the International Workshop of the EUIJ Tokyo Consortium at the Hitotsubashi University, and the 2007 Meetings of the European Economic Association in Budapest, for comments, in particular Luca Dedola, Phil Lane and Etsuro Shioji. Karel Mertens and Francesca Viani provided excellent research assistance, Lucia Vigna invaluable help with the text. Financial support by the European Commission is gratefully acknowledged. This chapter is part of my activities in the framework of the Pierre Werner Chair Programme on Monetary Union at the European University Institute, generously supported by the Luxembourg government.

across regions – such as different degrees of nominal rigidities and frictions across sectors and regions (arguably reflecting differences in the pace of deregulation and liberalization), or differences in financial structures and labour (and goods) market institutions. Policy makers are obviously interested in understanding the extent to which they should worry about these specific dimensions of heterogeneity, beyond monitoring their role in macroeconomic developments, i.e. in determining the output gap and (core) inflation.[1] The European Central Bank (ECB) is by no means the only central bank facing this issue – but national differences and the lack of political integration make it more pressing in the euro area than elsewhere.

In this chapter, I take a step back from the current debate, and reconsider the very foundations of the theory of OCAs, drawing on recent contributions to stabilization theory in closed and open economies (see for instance Woodford 2003, Galí 2008 and especially the vast body of contributions to the so-called New Open Economy Macroeconomics after Obstfeld and Rogoff (1995, 1996), as surveyed by Corsetti (2008)). The objective is to shed light on what we can (and did) learn about OCAs adopting a new, modern approach to macrostabilization, relative to the body of knowledge already accumulated on the foundations laid out by the classical OCA contributions, and the many later developments.

Relative to the traditional literature, the approach pursued in this chapter is different in at least two important respects. First, all the arguments in the text are derived from a stylized 'microfounded' model in which households maximize expected utility, firms maximize expected profits and monetary authorities maximize national welfare, indexed by the representative household's utility. As in the traditional literature, however, because of frictions in the goods market (which are not modelled explicitly), prices are assumed to be sticky – for simplicity, firms are assumed to preset nominal prices for one production period. Second, the analysis is developed under the assumption that policy makers can credibly commit to policy rules in either exchange rate regimes (currency union, or flexible rates), with the objective of maximizing an average of the consumers' expected utility. Optimal stabilization policy is therefore characterized as optimal rules, rather than discretionary reactions to shocks – the distinction is not treated explicitly in the original OCA theory. I emphasize two main results.

First, as is well understood, in a monetary union inefficient stabilization of national economies is due to (a) insufficient stabilization of domestic marginal costs/output gap, *and* (b) monetary movements unrelated to the fundamentals of a country – in a currency union the common monetary stance can be a source of demand noise for some members of the union, depending on the degree of symmetry of cyclical shocks across countries. An important advantage of a microfounded framework consists of making it clear that, from the vantage point of the representative national household, the combined welfare cost of insufficient stabilization and monetary shocks unrelated to a country's fundamentals are essentially of the same order of magnitude of the costs of the business cycle. It follows that if one is sceptical about these costs, he/she must also be sceptical about the costs of monetary unification.

This consideration emphasizes an important open issue in OCA theory. According to the stylized model employed in the text, the welfare gap between a monetary union and independent monetary policies is consistent with the assessment of the costs of the business cycle by Lucas (1987, 2003). Many feel that Lucas's calculation severely underestimates the welfare effects of cyclical fluctuations. Yet the literature has so far fallen short of providing a paradigm which radically differs from Lucas's benchmark calculations: much richer models than the one employed in the text end up predicting costs that are only marginally higher. Moreover, by no means a sceptical view of the stabilization costs after monetary unification is a prerogative of the new microfounded literature: Buiter (2000) expresses essentially the same view drawing on the IS-LM framework.

A second result sheds new light on an old debate in OCA theory, concerning the extent to which asymmetries in national economic structures and shocks magnify the costs of a single monetary policy. To appreciate this result, recall that arguments in favour of monetary unions typically build on some criticism of the benefits from exchange rate movements as envisioned by the traditional OCA theory. Traditional arguments view currency markets as a source of noise and financial instability. Recent literature instead points out that nominal rigidities in local currency prevent import prices from falling with currency depreciation (see Devereux and Engel, 2003, among others): if import prices remain stable in local currency, exchange rate movements cannot foster relative price adjustment. Building on this view, it is indeed possible to produce examples in which a common monetary policy is as efficient as national differentiated policies, irrespective of specialization in production, and independently of the correlation between country-specific shocks.

The conditions under which such 'equivalence result' holds bear an important lesson for OCA. Namely, what reduces the gap between monetary policy in a common currency area and independent monetary policies is the degree of symmetry in the composition of national consumption. One can show that, if there were only tradeable goods, and consumption baskets were identical across countries, monetary unification would not affect the monetary policy stance at national level at all. In light of this consideration, convergence in consumption (and spending) patterns emerges as a candidate novel attribute of countries participating in an efficient currency area.

Before proceeding, it is appropriate to clarify what this chapter deals and does not deal with. Its main goal is to analyze the difference at national level between participating in a monetary union and retaining the national currency, treating the two regimes on a level playing field. Consistent with this goal, the costs of a single monetary policy will be assessed relatively to an ideal benchmark of efficient domestic stabilization at country level, and not relative to any historical benchmark. In this respect, the analysis abstracts from a wide variety of inefficiencies and sources of instability – including some which have arguably played a prominent role in the historical process towards the euro, but are not essentially related with the adoption of a common currency. For instance, as shown in Section 4.3, the analysis does lend support to the view that gains from joining a monetary union are potentially sizeable, when participating in the union allows a country to benefit from a better (more disciplined) macroeconomic policy framework. However, the text does not offer an explicit model of the reasons why countries may be unable to adopt a good policy framework on their own. Instead, the exercise provides an assessment of the potential gains from activating (non-monetary) instruments of business cycle stabilization at national or union-wide level, including fiscal policy (see e.g. the discussion in Adão *et al.*, 2006).

Second, the analysis de facto assumes that consumption risk is perfectly diversified, corresponding to the case of perfect and frictionless financial markets: therefore, the text will not discuss the sensitivity of the welfare gap across regimes to different degrees of financial market integration and development (on this issue, see Sutherland 2004). Financial issues, together with fiscal issues, are briefly touched upon in a final section, while factor mobility is ignored altogether. By no means do I regard these issues as secondary in OCA theory. If anything, they define core chapters of a research agenda which has motivated this chapter in the first place, and hopefully will attract more research in the near future.

The chapter is organized as follows. Section 2 briefly summarizes the findings of traditional OCA theory. Section 3 lays out a stylized model of a closed economy to present the foundations of stabilization theory. Section 4 uses this model to assess the national welfare costs of losing monetary autonomy, and being exposed to monetary policy decisions responding to average fundamentals in the union. Section 5 introduces a two-country model, analyzing the international transmission mechanism and setting the stage for welfare analysis. Section 6 studies optimal stabilization policy under different policy regimes, revisiting the roots of the aversion to monetary union by classical authors. Section 7 revisits the OCA theory in light of nontraditional views of the international transmission of fundamental and policy shocks. Section 8 reconsiders the role of symmetry in economic structures in undermining the viability of currency unions. Section 9 discusses some extensions of the analysis, including fiscal policy and the policy mix. Section 10 concludes.

2. From the original OCA theory to microfounded analyses of the costs and benefits of monetary unification

The seminal contributions to the so-called OCA theory, including Mundell (1961), McKinnon (1963), Kenen (1969) and Ingram (1973), analyze the costs of adopting a common currency in the presence of asymmetric, country-specific temporary shocks and (by logical extension) asymmetric short-run response to common temporary and permanent shocks. The well-known argument is that these asymmetries weaken the case for a common currency, as members of monetary union lose the benefits from:

i. monetary autonomy;
ii. stabilizing movements of the exchange rate.

The same literature then stresses that the benefits from i. and ii. above are low if at least one of the following is true:

a. prices and wages are sufficiently flexible;
b. fiscal policy effectively stabilizes national economies;
c. consumption risk is sufficiently diversified across borders (or international financial markets work smoothly, so that agents can easily smooth consumption);

d. factors are sufficiently mobile also in the short run, at low private
   and social costs;
e. there are little asymmetries in shocks and in macroeconomic
   transmission.

The original contributions to this theory abstract from other potentially sizeable benefits of a monetary union, e.g. benefits from policy
delegation, gains from political integration (reflecting the opinion that
this is more likely in the presence of monetary union), saving on
transaction costs (possibly increasing trade), and so on. These arguments – sometimes included in modern textbooks as extensions of OCA
beyond its original theoretical boundaries – have arguably played an
important role in the debate on EMU. For instance, it is well understood
that they can explain why some small European countries, whose
specific cyclical conditions have a very limited weight in the ECB's
decisions, have nonetheless been eager to adopt the euro. However,
following the original contributions to the OCA literature, I will
abstract from these issues altogether.

In my discussion, I will revisit OCA theory in the framework of a
stylized choice theoretical model of currency union. The model in the
background of the analysis is specified in Corsetti and Pesenti (2005a,
2005b) and Corsetti (2006) – in this text, I will only use a minimal set of
analytical expressions referring the reader to these references for details
and a formal derivation. As is well known, the advantage of this model
is that it can be solved in closed form. Relative to its original formulation, I augment the model with a nontradeable good sector (as in
Obstfeld and Rogoff 2002), and allow for home bias in consumption
of tradeables (as in Corsetti 2006).[2]

The main arguments are developed in two steps. The next section
introduces the main ideas by using a simplified version of the model,
whereas the countries in a monetary union are treated as if they were
closed economies, i.e. without trade among them. Thanks to this simplification, the analysis will focus sharply on the costs of losing monetary autonomy, that is, the costs of giving up the possibility of
implementing monetary stabilization policies specifically tailored to
the need of the domestic economy. The following sections develop a
full model of monetary unions with trade and financial links among
countries, and complete the analysis contrasting different views on the
benefits from exchange rate flexibility.

3. Monetary stabilization: basic ideas from a choice-theoretic model

This section sketches the main principle of macroeconomic stabilization based on a stylized model of an individual country in a monetary union, abstracting from trade in goods and assets. For later reference, the country on which I focus the analysis will be called the Home country; when appropriate Home variables are denoted with the subscript H.

3.1 A stylized closed-economy setup

Consider a closed economy populated by many identical households, which derive utility from consumption of goods, and leisure, i.e. their utility is decreasing in labour effort. In the analysis, the expected utility of the national representative household provides a natural index of national welfare.

In the tradition of macroeconomic models, the demand and the supply side of the economy are discussed in turn. Consider the demand side first. The dynamic of aggregate demand is governed by the optimal consumption-saving and investment decisions by households and firms. For simplicity, as in many modern contributions to monetary theory, posit that the aggregate demand coincides with consumption expenditure, i.e. abstract from investment and government spending. Let C denote domestic aggregate consumption and P its price (or CPI). Nominal aggregate demand is thus given by PC, and real domestic output Y_H coincides with real consumption expenditure, i.e. $C = Y_H$.

For the purpose of this chapter, it is convenient to relate nominal aggregate demand PC to a variable μ, which indexes the stance of monetary policy: a higher μ means that monetary authorities pursue expansionary policies, raising aggregate demand and thus nominal consumption. Provided that there are no asset market frictions, the dynamic of aggregate demand (in nominal terms) reflecting optimal consumption and saving decisions by households can be written as follows

$$\mu_t = \frac{1}{\beta(1+i)} \frac{1}{E\left(\frac{1}{\mu_{t+1}}\right)} \tag{1}$$

where β is the discount factor reflecting consumers' impatience, E denotes expectations of future variables, indexed by the subscript +1.

The above equation makes it clear that, for given expectations of future prices and future real demand, current spending (corresponding to the current monetary stance) μ is decreasing in the nominal interest rate.

As regards the supply side of the model, output is produced in many varieties by (a continuum of) small firms, each of them with monopoly power on a specific good variety. Production can be written as $Y_H = Z_H \ell$, where Z_H denotes the level of productivity, identical across firms; ℓ denotes employment. Labour productivity Z_H is assumed to vary randomly at business cycle frequency.

Each firm faces a product-specific demand for its output with a constant price elasticity. Taking into account this demand, firms set their monopolistic prices subject to nominal rigidities. Assume for simplicity that firms preset their product prices in nominal terms, and keep them fixed for one production period only (say, one quarter), adjusting the scale of production to meet demand. The general principle is that firms will optimally choose the preset product price which maximizes their market value. Under the assumptions underlying our reference model (utility from consumption is logarithmic, disutility from labour effort is linear), this leads to a very simple and intuitive expression: the optimal preset price results from charging the equilibrium markup over *expected* marginal costs, i.e.

$$P_H = mkp \cdot E[MC_H] = mkp \cdot E\left[\frac{wage}{Z_H}\right] \tag{2}$$

where the marginal costs MC_H are given by wage costs per unit of output (i.e. the nominal wage divided by productivity); and, by standard results in micro theory, the equilibrium markup mkp is a decreasing function of the elasticity of substitution across domestically produced varieties of the Home goods. As this price is fixed over the production period, the (ex-post) realized markup will obviously vary (inversely) with marginal costs.

To keep the analysis as straightforward as possible, I do not model policy tradeoffs stemming from the coexistence of price and wage rigidities (as in e.g. Erceg *et al.* 2000; see also Galí 2008, chapter 6). I therefore posit that the labour market is competitive, so that the nominal wage rate moves proportionally with nominal consumption, hence with the monetary stance μ. The marginal costs can then be rewritten by linking them directly to our index of monetary stance:

$$MC_H = \left(\frac{wage}{Z_H}\right) = \overbrace{\underbrace{\left(\frac{\mu}{Z_H}\right)}_{\text{productivity}}}^{\text{monetary policy stance}} \tag{3}$$

a property that will become central to our discussion of stabilization below.

The description of the model is completed with the characterization of the natural rate of employment (or output), that is, the employment (output) rate if all prices were flexible. In the absence of nominal rigidities, each firm would maximize current profits by charging the equilibrium markup over current marginal costs:

$$P_H^{flex} = mkp \cdot MC_H = mkp \cdot \frac{\mu}{Z_H}. \tag{4}$$

This expression differs from the case of nominal rigidities because all fluctuations of nominal marginal costs affect prices ex-post. Substituting the definition of μ, the production function $Y_H = Z_H \ell$, and rearranging, yields the result that the natural level of employment, ℓ^{nr}, is constant:

$$\ell^{nr} = \frac{1}{mkp} \tag{5}$$

In the long run, ℓ^{nr} is decreasing in the degree of monopoly power of domestic firms. As goods become better substitutes, or regulation and competition policy reduces average markups in the economy, the natural rate of employment and output rise. At business cycle frequencies, the natural rate of output obviously fluctuates with productivity, i.e. $Y_H^{nr} = Z_H \ell^{nr}$.

3.2 Efficient monetary stabilization

The above expressions provide the key elements to analyze, in a stylized way, the macroeconomic implications of random fluctuations in current and future productivity, and the optimal policy response to stabilize the economy. Consider how current productivity shocks are transmitted to the economy (demand shocks will be discussed below). Holding monetary stance μ (hence nominal wages) fixed, a positive productivity shock (an increase in Z_H) lowers marginal costs ex post. But, if prices are preset, firms cannot take advantage of the higher productivity to lower prices and raise output: a fixed μ implies that aggregate demand is also fixed in nominal and real terms. As a result, firms satisfy the current demand using less productive inputs. The positive productivity shock opens a positive *output gap*: employment and output fall short of their natural rate, i.e. their equilibrium value in a flexible price allocation.

In response to an unexpected increase in productivity, however, monetary authorities *can* improve welfare by expanding aggregate demand, up to the level of output if prices were flexible. In other words, at given prices, a sufficiently large monetary expansion can close the output gap described above, preventing any fall in employment relative to the flex-price equilibrium. Observe that, by raising the monetary stance in response to a positive productivity shock (and contracting it in response to a negative shock, as to rule out overheating and excessive employment), a country's monetary authorities can completely stabilize marginal costs in nominal terms. Provided that they have enough information on current productivity, they can do so by setting monetary policy such that nominal marginal costs are constant during the period:

$$MC = \frac{\mu}{Z_H} = \Gamma \tag{6}$$

If the above holds, i.e. if private agents expect the central bank to credibly pursue rules such that $\mu = Z_H\Gamma$, optimal prices would remain constant in nominal terms also in the absence of nominal rigidities, as there would be no difference between the expressions (4) and (2). By pursuing monetary rules satisfying the above condition, the monetary authorities make nominal rigidities inconsequential as regards the equilibrium allocation, in the sense that in each period the sticky price allocation coincides with the flex-price allocation. The economy operates at the natural rate.

Observe that (6) requires a central bank to commit to (a) align aggregate demand with productivity, responding within each period to current productivity fluctuations; and (b) keep the price level along a predetermined path, indexed by Γ. By way of example: a credible inflation target of 2 per cent would translate into a growth rate of prices at the constant rate $\frac{\Gamma_{+1}}{\Gamma} = 1.02$ (see Adão *et al.* 2005 for an analysis of determinacy).

For the simple economy specified above, it is easy to show that policies implementing the flex-price allocation also maximize welfare, i.e. the expected utility of the representative agent. While this result does not hold in more general models, the literature has nonetheless produced several examples of economies where a natural-rate policy would not produce appreciable losses relative to the optimal policy.

3.3 Interest rates and demand stabilization

In the language of traditional models of stabilization, the optimal policy condition characterized above prescribes central banks to 'lean against the wind of excess demand (opening output gaps)'. This section elaborates on this point. Specifically, after substituting the optimal policy condition (6) into the dynamic demand equation, that is,

$$\frac{1}{\Gamma Z_H} = \beta(1+i)E\left(\frac{1}{\Gamma_{+1}Z_{H,+1}}\right), \tag{7}$$

one can derive the interest rate corresponding to the implementation of the optimal stabilization policy[3]

$$i = -\ln\beta + \ln\frac{\Gamma_{+1}}{\Gamma} + E\ln Z_{H,+1} - \ln Z_H + \frac{1}{2}Var\ln Z_{H,+1} \tag{8}$$

This expression suggests a different way to state the main conclusion of the analysis in the previous subsection. Namely, given the path of price levels Γ to which the central bank commits when it defines inflation targets at different horizons, and holding expectation of future productivity constant, the natural rate of interest falls with current productivity gains – which, in the absence of a contingent optimal reaction by monetary authorities, would open a positive output gap. It raises with anticipated productivity growth.

It is important to understand that condition (6) prescribes monetary authorities to respond efficiently not only to current productivity shocks, but also to current aggregate demand disturbances. To see this point most clearly, suppose that in some periods private agents become more optimistic, or pessimistic, about the future state of the economy. Specifically, they receive an informative signal about the level of productivity one period ahead, which can be expected to be either high or low. This is a type of expectations shock which is reminiscent of traditional Keynesian theory, where movements in the so-called autonomous components of spending for consumption and investment are driving forces of business cycle fluctuations.

For a given path of prices (the Γ's) and interest rates over time, the expressions (1) and (7) make it apparent that fluctuations in expectations of future productivity translate into fluctuations in future incomes and consumption demand C_{+1}; in turn (holding current interest rates fixed) this moves current real aggregate demand C away from the natural rate. For instance, given Γ_{+1} and i, optimistic expectations raise demand above natural output, opening a positive output gap.

A central bank implementing optimal rules ($\mu = \Gamma Z_H$) however would systematically and completely stem any excess demand on current resources, including those driven by anticipation of future growth. Under the optimal monetary regime, the nominal rate indeed rises with $E \ln Z_{H,+1}$, causing households to postpone optimally the spending plans they would have pursued in response to optimistic expectations, had the nominal rate been left constant. Without investment and international borrowing, whether or not private expectations turn out to be correct ex post is utterly inconsequential for the evolution of the economy. Given the optimal rule, in the next period the policy stance will be such that households again consume the efficient level of output.[4]

Note that, in addition to signals about future average productivity, current demand would also fluctuate inefficiently with uncertainty about future productivity, i.e. with changes in the variance term in (8). Monetary authorities are obviously required to stabilize fluctuations in demand also when these are driven by perceived uncertainty.

An observation on the so-called zero bound problem is in order before closing this section. As is well known, according to (8) the implementation of optimal stabilization policy may at times require that nominal interest rate be negative, if the economy is hit by a sufficiently large negative shock to, say, expected productivity growth. In such circumstances, the implementation of optimal stabilization rules would be constrained by the fact that nominal rates cannot fall below zero. Holding the price level target constant, monetary authorities would not be able to keep efficient control of aggregate demand.

4. The costs of losing monetary autonomy

It is well understood that a welfare-optimizing central bank in a monetary union should react to the average cyclical conditions of the common currency area. While there could be different views on the weighting scheme used in building area-wide averages, a single (optimal) monetary policy will not be able to stabilize fully output gaps and producers' marginal costs at national level – as crudely captured by the slogan 'one size cannot fit all'. To the extent that it translates into insufficient stabilization, the costs of monetary union are clearly akin to the costs of the business cycle.

Since insufficient stabilization of national cycles is a dimension of the cost from monetary unification which has received a very large share of attention in the debate, it is useful to start our analysis by focusing sharply on it, before moving to other dimensions.

4.1 Heterogeneous monetary union and the welfare costs of the business cycle

The main inefficiencies from insufficient stabilization can be characterized in terms of relative price distortions, translating into a suboptimal level of output and consumption. According to the model discussed above, if the central bank does not stabilize marginal costs completely, at national level demand does not fall optimally when productivity is low: with preset prices, these turn out to be too high relative to factor costs, and firms supply too much relative to the flex-price level of output. Conversely, when productivity is high, demand does not rise enough: product prices are too low relative to factor costs, and firms supply too little relative to the flex-price allocation. It follows that, with insufficient stabilization, average output will fall short of its flex-price counterpart.

To derive these results formally, set for simplicity $\Gamma = 1$ and

$$\mu = Z_H^\xi, \qquad 0 \leq \xi \leq 1 \tag{9}$$

When $\xi < 1$, stabilization is incomplete: demand varies too little relative to productivity, translating into positive or negative output gaps. Under this parameterization, it is easy to verify that the expected value of marginal costs will be larger than in the case of complete stabilization[5]

$$E\left[\frac{\mu_{(\xi<1)}}{Z_H}\right] = \Gamma E\left[Z_H^{\xi-1}\right] < \Gamma. \tag{10}$$

For any given average monetary stance, the lower the extent of stabilization, the higher the preset product prices. Now consider the limiting case $\xi = 0$, when monetary policy is not contingent on the state of the economy at all – this would be the case if money grows at some predetermined rate between periods. Holding μ constant, it is easy to see that higher prices translate into a lower constant level of consumption and output as $C_H = Y_H = \mu/P_H$ (see also the discussion in Section 9 on related results when price setting is staggered).

The property of recent monetary models just discussed should be properly emphasized: with nominal rigidities, incomplete stabilization affects average prices, consumption and output in equilibrium. For standard parameterization, average prices will be too high, average output and consumption of Home goods (as well as average wages) will be too low relative to the flex-price benchmark. Observe, however, that the growth rate of the economy is not affected: in the long run the economy will expand at the same rate of productivity growth, independently of the monetary regime. Yet, there will be a gap between potential and current output on average, depending on the monetary regime.[6]

What is the cost of inefficient stabilization in terms of welfare? As already mentioned, this will simply coincide with the cost of inefficient business cycle movements. To see this most clearly, assume that Z_H is lognormally distributed. In our model, with utility from consumption being in log form, i.e. $\ln C = \ln \frac{\mu}{p}$, the loss in expected log consumption due to incomplete stabilization – denoted ΔW – can be written as follows:[7]

$$\Delta W = \frac{1}{2}(1 - \xi)^2 \, Var \ln Z_H \tag{11}$$

When $\xi = 1$ the economy is fully stabilized: the variance of the shock does not affect expected utility from consumption, and the above expression is identically equal to zero. If $\xi < 1$, instead, expected utility will be decreasing in the variance of the shock.

Not surprisingly, expression (11) is very close to the formula expressing the costs of business cycles in the seminal contributions by Lucas (1987, 2003).[8] Indeed, many models currently used in the design and assessment of monetary stabilization policy share this very feature. As in Lucas, back-of-the-envelope calculations of the order of magnitude of the welfare costs of insufficient stabilization lead to very small estimates. To wit: let the standard deviation of productivity be 1 per cent per period. Moving from no stabilization $\xi = 0$ to full stabilization $\xi = 1$ is worth approximately one half of a hundredth of a per cent of consumption per quarter.[9] Adding some preference shocks to the model may marginally raise this estimate, but not substantially so.

Not only are these numbers are strikingly low: remarkably, the above estimates actually provide an upper bound to the welfare losses due to insufficient stabilization in a common currency, derived for the case in which domestic productivity shocks have no common component across countries, i.e. they are purely idiosyncratic.[10] The parameter ξ above can be interpreted as the weight assigned by a common central bank to the stabilization of the output gap in country H.

Sure enough, the issue of assessing the (welfare) costs of the business cycle is far from being settled. The literature provides examples of frictions and inefficiencies which can raise their assessment relative to Lucas's estimates. In addition, low aggregate welfare losses may correspond to large losses for some groups in the society. Yet, the main message of this section is apparent.

The analysis suggests a close link between the magnitude of welfare gains from stabilizing the business cycle, and the magnitude of welfare costs due to a single monetary policy. If one is sceptical about the former, he/she must be sceptical about the latter.[11] It is worth noting, here, that similarly sceptical views of the welfare costs of monetary union had been expressed early on by critics of the OCA theory using the same theoretical model underlying the original contributions to this theory, most notably by Willem Buiter (see for instance Buiter (2000)).

4.2 Country-specific monetary 'noise'

So far, we have discussed the implications of a single monetary policy in terms of insufficient domestic stabilization. However, from the vantage point of a country whose business cycle is not synchronized with the rest of the union, a common monetary policy also generates destabilizing 'monetary noise'.

For this reason, a common currency could potentially be more consequential for national welfare than suggested above. Accounting for monetary noise, rewrite expression (9) as follows

$$\mu = \Gamma Z_H^{\xi} \Omega_H$$

where Ω_H indexes changes in the union-wide monetary stance which are unrelated to the Home country's fundamental Z_H. This new variable captures policy decisions by the common central bank, in response to average fundamentals in the currency union. If Z_H and Ω_H are independently lognormally distributed, the welfare costs of joining a monetary union become:[12]

$$\Delta W = 0.5. \left[Var \ln \Omega_H + (1 - \xi)^2 Var \ln Z_H \right] \tag{12}$$

Welfare losses are obviously higher than (11). However, to the extent that monetary authorities follow optimal rules, Ω_H reflects some weighted average of country-specific domestic productivity shocks in the union as a whole. Thus, in the expression above, the magnitude of the two terms in square brackets cannot be very different. It follows that 'monetary noise' due to lack of business cycle synchronization in a monetary union can hardly raise the order of country-specific welfare losses, relative to our assessment of the costs from incomplete stabilization.

4.3 Monetary instability and the advantages of joining a disciplined monetary union

An important observation suggested by expression (12) is that a highly unstable monetary policy could potentially produce large welfare losses, up to dwarfing the costs of insufficient stabilization. The point is that the variance of Ω_H can rise substantially in the presence of noisy behaviour by central bankers, and/or monetary instability due to fiscal or financial instability – in more general specification of the model, the size of welfare losses will be sensitive to the degree of risk aversion of the representative agents, which magnifies the effects of non-fundamental nominal volatility.[13]

The strong welfare implications of an unstable monetary policy back a well-known argument which, historically, has played an important role in the political process towards the creation of the European monetary union. Namely, countries that are unable to adopt a stable monetary framework (for a variety of reasons) are bound to gain the most from joining a union that guarantees monetary and fiscal discipline.

As monetary instability plausibly reflects a weak macroeconomic and/or political framework, however, assessing these gains requires a careful specification of what prevents national monetary authorities from following optimal rules consistent with the analysis in Section 3 – a task beyond the goal of this text.

5. Adding the costs of giving up exchange rate flexibility

Having clarified some basic ideas about the costs of losing monetary autonomy, the next step consists of reconsidering the second element of OCA theory – the consequences of giving up exchange rate flexibility – using a fully fledged model of international macroeconomic interdependence. What follows will briefly describe the main elements of a general equilibrium, two-country, choice-theoretic stochastic model with nominal rigidities and imperfect competition in production.

5.1 A model with trade and international interdependence

Consider a model of macroeconomic interdependence consisting of two countries, Home and Foreign, denoted by *H* and *F*, each perfectly specialized in the production of a tradeable good (in many varieties), and a nontradeable good (also in many varieties). The Home representative household combines these goods in a consumption basket, which may take the following form:

$$C = C[C_H, C_F, C_N] = \left[C_H^\alpha C_F^{1-\alpha} \right]^\gamma C_N^{1-\gamma} \tag{13}$$

where C_H, C_F and C_N denote consumption of Home tradeables, Foreign tradeables and Home nontradeables, respectively. Note that, in the model I use to develop my arguments, tradeable and nontradeable goods have unit elasticity of substitution in consumption, i.e. the consumption aggregator is Cobb-Douglas. The weight of nontraded goods is $1 - \gamma$, so that γ is the weight of the basket of traded goods. Within this basket, also Home and Foreign traded goods have unit elasticity, with weights α and $1 - \alpha$. Foreign consumption is similarly defined

$$C^* = C^* \left[C_H^*, C_F^*, C_N^* \right] = \left[\left(C_H^* \right)^{1-\alpha} \left(C_F^* \right)^\alpha \right]^\gamma \left(C_N^* \right)^{1-\gamma} \tag{14}$$

where an asterisk denotes foreign variables. Comparing the two expressions above shows that preferences over tradeable goods are assumed to be asymmetric across countries: national representative consumers assign the same weight α to the goods produced in the country where they live. If $\alpha > 1/2$, preferences for tradeables have a 'home bias'. Preferences for consumption are in log form and additive separable in labour – the disutility from labour effort ℓ is linear (as in the previous section). I again abstract from investment and government consumption.

In the economy, labour is employed in the production of tradeables and nontradeables. We therefore have four measures of labour productivity, each subject to shocks that are country- as well as sector-specific: Z_H, Z_N, Z_F, Z_N^* denoting productivity in the Home tradeable sector, the Home nontradeable sector, the Foreign tradeable sector, the Foreign nontradeable sector, respectively. Labour is immobile across borders.

Let P_N, P_H and P_F denote the Home prices of nontraded goods, Home-produced traded goods, and Foreign-produced traded goods; P_N^*, P_H^* and P_F^* are the corresponding prices in foreign currency. The welfare-based consumer price indexes P (in Home currency for the Home country) and P^* (in Foreign currency for the Foreign country) combine the prices of domestic goods and imports

$$P = P[P_H, P_F, P_N] \qquad P^* = P\left[P_H^*, P_F^*, P_N^*\right] \tag{15}$$

Let ε denote the nominal exchange rate between the Home and the Foreign currency (measured in units of Home currency per unit of Foreign currency). For the sake of analytical tractability, I assume that households can perfectly insure consumption risks across countries.[14] As mentioned above, this means that the model leaves no room for improvements in welfare through the development of financial markets – an issue often discussed in reference to OCAs.

With efficient consumption risk sharing, exchange rate determination is straightforward. As is well known, perfect consumption insurance implies that the growth rates of marginal utilities are equalized across countries in purchasing power parity (PPP) terms. As our two countries are perfectly symmetric *ex ante*, in the stylized model I am using in this paper this condition means that wealth and consumption are always equalized in nominal terms across countries:

$$PC = \varepsilon P^* C^*. \tag{16}$$

As explained above, it is convenient to define nominal demand as a synthetic indicator of domestic monetary stance – whatever the instruments used by the central bank. Abstracting from government spending and investment, nominal demand coincides with nominal consumption

$$\mu = PC, \qquad\qquad \mu^* = P^* C^*$$

An increase in μ (μ^*) corresponds to Home (Foreign) monetary policy expansion. Using the definition of μ and μ^*, it follows that the exchange rate depends on Home and Foreign monetary stances

$$\varepsilon_t = \frac{\mu}{\mu^*} \tag{17}$$

If the two countries adopt a fixed exchange rate regime, then $\mu = \mu^*$.

5.2 Nominal rigidities and the local currency price stability of imports

In our stylized model, domestic firms selling in the domestic market optimally preset prices by charging a constant markup over expected marginal costs, according to (2). This will be true both in the Home and in the Foreign country. However, modelling nominal rigidities in the export markets requires additional assumptions about the elasticity of prices to exchange rate movements. The literature has emphasized that the macroeconomic allocation will depend crucially on this elasticity (e.g. see Corsetti and Pesenti 2005a).

Several contributions have emphasized the radically different macro-economic implications of two alternative hypotheses, 'producer currency pricing' (PCP) versus 'local currency pricing' (LCP). According to the former hypothesis, foreign firms preset prices in their own currency, and let the Home currency price of their goods move one-to-one with the exchange rate. The prices that maximize the value of the firm under PCP are:

$$P_F^* = mkp \cdot E\left(MC_F^*\right)$$
$$P_F = P_F^* \cdot \varepsilon \tag{18}$$

where MC_F^* denotes foreign marginal costs (in foreign currency). In this case, the exchange rate passthrough into Home import prices is clearly 100 per cent. Nominal rigidities do not prevent flexibility of import prices, in response to shocks which appreciate or depreciate the currency. Observe that the law of one price holds exactly, because of the assumption that demand elasticities are identical in the two national markets.

LCP instead corresponds to the case in which export prices are preset in the currency of the destination markets. Foreign firms thus preset two prices, one in the local market, one in their exports' market. These two prices are:

$$P_F^* = mkp \cdot E(MC_F^*)$$
$$P_F = mkp \cdot E(MC_F^* \cdot \varepsilon)$$
(19)

As Foreign goods prices are preset in local currency, exchange rate passthrough is zero. Exchange rate movements translate into deviations from the law of one price, since in general $P_F \neq \varepsilon P_F^*$.[15]

The macroeconomic effects of a given monetary policy rule vastly differ depending on export pricing behaviour. To see this most clearly, rewrite the prices of Foreign goods in the Home market expressing marginal costs in terms of the two indicators of monetary stance μ and μ^*, and productivity. In the case of PCP, we have:

$$\frac{P_F}{\varepsilon} = mkp \cdot E[MC^*] = mkp \cdot E\left[\frac{\mu^*}{Z^*}\right].$$
(20)

In each period, Home import prices in the Home currency vary one-to-one with movements in the exchange rate induced by Home monetary policy. A domestic monetary expansion results in a higher nominal price of Foreign goods in the Home market (and a correspondingly lower nominal price of Home goods in the Foreign market). These price movements redirect global demand towards Home goods, and away from Foreign goods: exchange rate movements have 'expenditure switching effects'. Yet, as apparent from the above expression, when expressed in *Foreign* currency Foreign prices are totally independent of Home monetary policy. Indeed, under PCP, perfect passthrough implies that Foreign firms' unit revenue and marginal costs are completely insulated from the Home monetary stance.

Policy tradeoffs are potentially different in the LCP model. In this case, a Home nominal depreciation following a Home monetary expansion has no expenditure switching effects: relative prices faced by consumers are preset. It does however lower the revenues Foreign firms earn on each unit of goods sold in the Home market: a Home currency depreciation worsens the Foreign country's terms of trade. Thus, it is not surprising that preset import prices in Home currency do depend on Home monetary policy.

$$P_F = mkp \cdot E[MC_F^* \cdot \varepsilon] = mkp \cdot E\left[\frac{\mu}{Z^*}\right]$$
(21)

In other words, the policy pursued by Home monetary authorities directly affects optimal export pricing by Foreign firms. For the very reason studied in the previous section, exchange rate volatility that is unrelated to Foreign productivity fluctuations will translate into higher import prices in the Home country.

5.3 From macroeconomic analysis to policy assessment and design

One of the most appealing features of the model is its tractability for welfare analysis. Thanks to well-educated assumption on preferences and technology, in a rational expectations equilibrium the expected utility in any given period can be approximated by looking at expected log consumption only:

$$W = E \ln[C] \tag{22}$$

This is clearly not general. However, the model captures essential policy tradeoffs at the core of the stabilization debate, as well as the focus of this contribution. Now, recall that consumption can be written as the ratio between the monetary stance for the economy μ (i.e. the level of aggregate nominal spending) and the price level. Hence we can also write:

$$\begin{aligned} W &= E\{\ln \mu - \ln P\} \\ &= E\{\ln \mu - (1-\gamma)\ln P_N - \gamma\alpha \ln P_H - \gamma(1-\alpha)\ln P_F\} + \text{t.i.p.} \end{aligned} \tag{23}$$

where t.i.p. stands for 'terms independent of policy'. The corresponding expression for the Foreign country is:

$$\begin{aligned} W^* &= E\ln[C^*] = E\{\ln \mu^* - \ln P^*\} \\ &= E\{\ln \mu^* - (1-\gamma)\ln P_N^* - \gamma(1-\alpha)\ln P_H^* - \gamma\alpha \ln P_F^*\} + t.i.p.^* \end{aligned} \tag{24}$$

Observe that all we need to know to characterize optimal policies is the equilibrium expression for the optimal preset prices (shown in the previous subsection).[16]

Optimal stabilization policies are fully characterized by solving the problem of two national monetary authorities whose objective is to maximize domestic welfare, assuming that these authorities can commit to policy rules and these are perfectly credible. I comment on these conditions below. As the optimal policy varies depending on the international arrangements between the two authorities, I consider three regimes. The first is the *Nash equilibrium*: the two authorities act independently of each other, each setting the domestic monetary stance taking the monetary stance abroad as given; the second is *international policy coordination*: the two authorities maximize a joint welfare function; the third is *monetary union*, which is different from coordination in that there is only one monetary instrument, so that $\mu = \mu^*$.[17] To characterize optimal policies, I will study which monetary stance μ and μ^* maximizes the objective function given by (23) and (24).

6. At the root of the aversion to currency unions

A first set of results from our analysis sheds light on the root of the aversion to currency unions expressed by economists who share the classical view of international transmission – as exemplified by Friedman (1953). According to such a view, exchange rate movements are efficient substitutes for international relative price adjustment, when nominal rigidities prevent price flexibility in domestic currency. If exchange rates regulate international relative prices, giving up flexibility is obviously costly.

To revisit this fundamental critique of monetary unification, consider the model under the PCP assumption where P_F^* is sticky, but the price of imports in Home currency P_F moves one-to-one with the exchange rate: $P_F = \varepsilon P_F^*$. In this case, the objective functions of monetary authorities are obtained by substituting (18) into the price index (15).

Nash equilibrium
Consider first the case of two national authorities acting independently (the case of a Nash equilibrium). In this economy, each of them will find it optimal to stabilize a weighted average of marginal costs in the two production sectors of the economy (nontradeable and tradeable). As we have seen above that, with PCP, average import prices do not depend on domestic monetary policy, the optimal stabilization policy rules under commitment in the Home and Foreign country will take the form[18]

$$\mu_{PCP,Nash} = \mu[Z_H, Z_N] \qquad \mu^*_{PCP,Nash} = \mu^*[Z_F, Z_N^*]. \qquad (25)$$

This states that the optimal monetary policy is a function of domestic shocks only. Home monetary authorities optimally choose an expansionary stance (raising μ) in response to positive productivity shocks in either sector of the domestic economy (either Z_N or Z_H). National central banks are only concerned with domestic policy tradeoffs (Home monetary authorities do not respond to Z_N^* or Z_F): there is no 'international dimension' in monetary policy making. The reason why with PCP policy makers are not concerned with foreign shocks is that, once optimal monetary rules are in place, the implied exchange rates fluctuations automatically move relative prices in the right direction, at no cost. For instance, any positive supply shock to tradeables in the Foreign economy is matched by a Foreign expansion, appreciating the Home currency. The exchange rate response lowers the relative price of Foreign tradeables in the global economy, switching domestic and world demand towards Foreign output. This is exactly what would happen in a flex-price (efficient) equilibrium.

A common currency ($\mu = \mu^*$) cannot be optimal in this environment. To see this, combine the expressions above, as to derive the equilibrium exchange rate conditional on implementing optimal monetary rules:

$$\frac{\mu_{PCP,Nash}}{\mu_{PCP,Nash}^*} = \varepsilon = \frac{\mu[Z_H, Z_N]}{\mu^*[Z_F, Z_N^*]}. \tag{26}$$

In general, there is no solution for $\mu = \mu^*$. The exception is the (obviously implausible) case of two identical economies where shocks are also perfectly symmetric both *across countries* and *across sectors*. Clearly, adopting fixed exchange rates has a cost in terms of stabilization: in a monetary union the central bank cannot stabilize four marginal costs with a single instrument. These costs are arguably falling in the correlation among shocks.

Observe that, because of sectoral asymmetries, similar considerations also apply to domestic stabilization. Unless the sectoral shocks are perfectly correlated at domestic level, the central bank will not be able to stabilize both aggregate demand and the relative demand for the tradeables and nontradeables with a single instrument. Benevolent policy makers will maximize over the resulting policy tradeoffs, reacting more to shocks hitting the largest sector, and de facto placing more weight on the sector with the highest variance of shocks.

Coordination

If policy rules are jointly determined to maximize the sum of welfare in the two countries, the fact that import prices in a country do not depend on the monetary stance in that country implies that monetary authorities are still completely inward looking, in the sense that they only stabilize the marginal costs in the two sectors of the domestic economy. Yet optimal monetary policies will generally differ from the case of the Nash equilibrium, implying that there are gains from international policy coordination. Indeed, it can be shown that, in comparison with the non-coordinated case, monetary authorities react relatively more to shocks in the nontraded-good sector. This is because, according to the classical view of the international transmission mechanisms, a monetary expansion in one country worsens the country's terms of trade, thus favouring consumers abroad: hence, the international spillovers from monetary policy are positive. In the Nash equilibrium, the Home monetary authorities ignore these spillovers when solving the policy problem: they react too little to shocks to nontradeables. For this reason, it follows that, in general, gains from coordination do not provide an argument in favour of limiting exchange rate flexibility.

Monetary union

As discussed in Section 4, a common currency imposes losses in national welfare, due to both insufficient domestic stabilization, and destabilizing monetary shocks. The fully fledged model provides a better analytical characterization of 'monetary noise'. Consider a common central bank interested in maximizing an equally weighted average of Home and Foreign welfare. With a common currency the optimal monetary policy rule becomes a function of all shocks in the area:

$$
\mu_{MU} = \mu\left[Z_H, Z_N, Z_F, Z_N^*\right] = \mu \begin{bmatrix} \overbrace{Z_H, Z_N,}^{\substack{\text{Home output–gap} \\ \text{stabilization}}} & \overbrace{Z_F, Z_N^*,}^{\substack{\text{Monetary noise} \\ \text{in the Home country}}} \\ \underbrace{}_{\substack{\text{Monetary noise} \\ \text{in the Foreign country}}} & \underbrace{}_{\substack{\text{Home output–gap} \\ \text{stabilization}}} \end{bmatrix}
$$

(27)

From the vantage point of the Home country, the common monetary policy stabilizes domestic output and marginal costs only to the extent that it is driven by the first two terms on the right-hand side of this expression. Systematic policy responses to the last two terms translate into monetary noise – as already anticipated discussing (12). The opposite is true from the vantage point of the Foreign country.

7. Are there benefits from monetary autonomy when exchange rate movements do not stabilize international prices?

In the previous section, we have seen that at the root of the classical aversion to monetary union is a positive view of exchange rate movements, according to which exchange rate adjustment is driven by changes in economic fundamentals (in the model above, exchange rates move with relative productivity shocks), and regulates the global demand for a country's products (inducing expenditure switching effects).

However, the traditional view of international transmission has been strongly questioned by authors who cast doubts on the stabilization properties of the exchange rate. Namely, an important strand of the literature stresses the empirical evidence on the local currency price stability of imports, i.e. on the fact that the price in domestic currency of Foreign goods tends to move very little with the exchange rate (see Corsetti 2008 for a survey). The observed local currency price stability of imports arguably reflects both real factors and nominal rigidities.[19] But to the extent that this is due to nominal rigidities, we have seen above that exchange rate movements do not help correcting international relative prices (they have no 'expenditure switching effect'). Actually, they tend to make the international transmission of monetary policy harmful ex post: a Home depreciation worsens the Foreign terms of trade, raising equilibrium foreign labour for every level of Foreign consumption.

Nash equilibrium and coordination

When both domestic and import prices are sticky (and preset in local currency), expected utility should be evaluated using import prices given by expression (20). As apparent from this expression, under LCP import prices depend on the domestic monetary regime. The behaviour of domestic monetary authorities influences expected marginal costs, thus average prices, charged by foreign exporters in the local market. It follows that the optimal domestic monetary policy will react also to productivity shocks abroad, in addition to domestic shocks, with an intensity that is increasing in the weight of imports in the national consumption basket:[20]

$$\mu_{LCP,Nash} = \mu[Z_H, Z_F, Z_N] \qquad \mu^*_{LCP,Nash} = \mu^*[Z_H, Z_F, Z^*_N] \qquad (28)$$

Relative to the PCP case, optimal monetary policies are no longer 'inward-looking'. In this sense, as discussed in previous work with

Pesenti (Corsetti and Pesenti 2005b), nominal frictions in local currency provide an argument in favour of an 'international dimension' in the optimal design of monetary policy rules. Also, relative to the PCP case, the fact that optimal policies now depend on shocks abroad make national monetary stances more symmetric. Symmetry in monetary stance in turn implies a lower volatility of the nominal exchange rate. This result is hardly surprising, given that with LCP exchange rate movements do not have any desirable effects on international relative prices, i.e. they are not associated with the 'expenditure switching effects' described in the previous section.

An important example

As an extreme example, the literature has long noted that the policy reaction functions (28) actually become identical, if tradeables are the only goods delivering utility (i.e. $\gamma \rightarrow 1$), *and* national consumers demand an equally weighted basket of domestic and foreign-produced goods, i.e. $\alpha = 1/2$ (see Devereux and Engel 2003 and Corsetti and Pesenti 2005a). Under these conditions, it can be shown that optimal stabilization implies no movement in exchange rates ($\mu = \mu^*$) for *any* distribution of the shocks, and irrespective of international policy coordination:

$$\lim_{\gamma \rightarrow 1, \alpha \rightarrow 1/2} \varepsilon = \frac{\mu_{LCP,Nash}}{\mu^*_{LCP,Nash}} = \frac{\mu[Z_H, Z_F]}{\mu[Z_H, Z_F]} = 1 \qquad (29)$$

In other words, under the conditions spelled out above, a fixed exchange rate is by no means an impediment to optimal stabilization. Whether or not the two monetary authorities act independently, monetary stances are symmetric, ruling out exchange rate variability altogether.

The main lesson to draw from the above example is that the stability of import prices in local currency in the form of LCP generally causes monetary authorities to dampen exchange rate volatility in equilibrium. Since exchange rate movements are not useful to correct relative prices, one can even build examples of economies in which these movements can be shut down altogether at no cost.

Conversely, a lesson which should *not* be drawn from the above example is that LCP pricing (and the implied absence of expenditure switching effects from exchange rate movements) provides a case against monetary autonomy and exchange rate flexibility. The stability of import prices in local currency per se does not imply that national central banks would find it optimal to stabilize the same weighted average of Home and Foreign marginal costs (thus prices), so to make optimal monetary policies symmetric.

First, stabilizing domestic and foreign costs in the tradeable sector is not the only relevant policy tradeoff faced by monetary authorities: a large share of domestic output consists of nontradeables. Even if the consumption baskets of tradeables were identical cross-border ($\alpha = 1/2$), shocks to the nontradeable sector will break the symmetry in optimal policy – this is the essence of the critique of Devereux and Engel (2003) by Duarte and Obstfeld (2008).[21]

Second, and perhaps more fundamentally, many empirical contributions taking a microeconomic perspective on exporters' behaviour emphasize price discrimination and distribution as key reasons for the observed low elasticity of retail prices to the exchange rate (this point is spelled out in detail by Corsetti and Dedola, 2005). If low exchange rate passthrough cannot be attributed to nominal rigidities, the above results do not apply. Whether or not consumption baskets are identical, a fixed exchange rate would imply an undue constraint on the optimal conduct of stabilization policy.

8. A new perspective on an old debate: asymmetric shocks and the relative efficiency of a common monetary policy

In the literature on OCA, some authors (most notably, Krugman 1993a) have argued that the scope and likelihood of asymmetric shocks are linked to the degree of production specialization across areas. With specialization – the argument goes – any industry-specific shock will also be region-specific, raising the stabilization costs of monetary unification. If the economic structure is instead symmetric across countries, industry-specific shocks will affect all regions in the union in the same way, reducing the strain on the central bank (see the text after expression (26) above).

Now, the previous section has presented an admittedly extreme example at odds with Krugman's argument, that complete specialization raises the costs of monetary unification because of its implications for the scope and likelihood of asymmetric shocks. If (a) all goods are tradeable, (b) tradeable goods have the same weight in the consumption basket in the union and (c) before monetary unification import prices are sticky in local currency, the exchange rate remains optimally fixed, even if countries are perfectly specialized and shocks are asymmetric. This is so, because Home and the Foreign monetary authority react to the same average of domestic and foreign shocks: optimal monetary policy in the union will do no worse than independent monetary policy at national level. In this sense, there is no cost in renouncing national currencies.

Which symmetry matters?

On logical ground, these considerations show that production specialization and asymmetries in economic structures are not necessarily inconsistent with the comparative efficiency of a common currency. Observe that without nontradeables and with symmetry in tradeable consumption ($\gamma \to 1$ and $\alpha = 1/2$), the share of consumption expenditure on each national good is identical to the share of each good in the total value added produced by the two countries. By way of example, setting the *value* of the union GDP equal to 1, each country produces half of it. Symmetry between consumption and the (endogenous) value of production is essential for the strong result of optimality of fixed exchange rates derived in the previous section. Under LCP, it is the breaking-down of *this* symmetry that makes exchange rate flexibility an essential prerequisite for optimal stabilization policy.

Implications for endogenous OCA

On empirical and historical ground, however, the above considerations also provide a new perspective on OCA, built on the maintained hypothesis of LCP pricing. The idea is that, holding such a hypothesis, the relative performance of a currency union may improve with the emergence of similar consumption patterns across countries joining the union.

In a well-known contribution, Frankel and Rose (1998) build a case for 'endogenous currency areas', stressing that, even if countries joining a monetary union do not satisfy the conditions for an OCA, they may do so over time, as economic integration fosters intra-industry over inter-industry trade, reducing the extent of specialization in production. Taking the logic of the argument above a step further, one could build a totally different argument. Namely, countries joining a common currency lose nothing in terms of stabilization efficiency relative to a regime with independent monetary policies, even if a common currency leads to specialization in production and inter-industry trade. The key point is that economic monetary and economic integration must foster convergence in consumption patterns of households in the countries of the union.

Observe that this argument could shed some light on a long-lasting question in European monetary study, regarding the reasons why European policy leaders have traditionally shown a preference for fixed exchange rates at regional level. Based on the results above, a possible answer lies in a sceptical view about the role of exchange rates in adjusting relative prices among relatively open European countries, coupled with the observation that production and consumption patterns for Europe as a whole tend to be relatively symmetric.

9. Extensions of the analysis and directions for future research

To conclude this chapter, it is appropriate to discuss briefly the implications for our analysis of different assumptions about nominal price rigidities, fiscal and monetary policy interactions, and the degree of development of financial markets.

9.1 Policy tradeoffs when price adjustment is staggered

In the baseline model adopted in this text, prices are assumed to be predetermined and fixed during each production period, and simultaneously updated between periods. In models with partial price adjustment, incomplete stabilization of output gaps generates inflation variability and inflation dispersion. Differences in inflation rates across countries (or sectors) may reflect desirable adjustment in international relative prices – and therefore be welfare-enhancing. However, to the extent that price adjustment is staggered, a correction of international relative prices can only materialize over time, resulting in price dispersion, which is well known to have important negative implications on efficiency. With staggered adjustment, positive inflation means that the market price of ex-ante symmetric goods in preferences and production is not necessarily symmetric. Hence, the design of optimal monetary policy in a currency union must address the tradeoff between the benefit of fostering relative price adjustment *across types of goods*, and its costs in terms of relative price distortions *within categories of goods* (see Corsetti *et al.* 2007).

Elaborating on this tradeoff, recent contributions have presented applications of the principle that central banks should target inflation in those sectors/countries that have the highest degree of nominal rigidities. The reason is straightforward. Suppose some fundamental shock creates the need for adjustment in relative prices across different types of goods, or across countries. In response to these shocks, it is highly inefficient to place the burden of price adjustment on sectors/countries that have high and persistent nominal rigidities. If policy makers try to do so, adjustment will take time, and it will be costly due to distortions in relative prices of similar goods – since some firms will happen to adjust prices early on, others will happen to adjust prices at a later time. Conversely, it is efficient to pursue policies that target desired relative price adjustment via nominal price changes in the most flexible sectors or countries of the union. Clearly, adjustment will be faster and less costly.[22]

The implementation of this principle is, however, more controversial than appears. Suppose that one can provide empirical evidence that the degree of nominal price or wage rigidity is higher in a particular country. Unless there are fundamental reasons to expect these rigidities to persist over time and be extremely costly to remove, increasing the weight of this country in union-wide policy making would possibly contribute to delay any reform or structural change that could in principle bring this economy in line with the rest of the union.

9.2 Fiscal and monetary policy interactions

An important policy conclusion from the traditional OCA theory is that monetary union challenges domestic policy makers to find alternative instruments of business cycle stabilization, or implement reforms that reduce the magnitude of frictions and distortions creating a stabilization problem. These conclusions are still valid in the above analysis – it is indeed desirable to use additional policy instruments, such as fiscal policy.

In general, the stabilization properties of fiscal policy will depend on the fiscal instruments available to the government, the distortionary nature of taxation, and financial and nominal frictions affecting the transmission of demand and tax shocks. The macro literature has moved some steps towards more realistic and articulated models of fiscal stabilization, accounting for distortionary taxes and spending on useful public goods, and/or introducing liquidity-constrained agents in general equilibrium models.

A key contribution to OCA theory in this respect is provided by Adão *et al.* (2006), a paper which, to a large extent, can be interpreted as a microfounded reconsideration of the OCA literature, focusing on fiscal instruments. This paper shows that, if the government has enough tax instruments, including income and consumption taxes, there exists a fiscal regime with state-contingent tax rates which support a flexible-price equilibrium independently of nominal rigidities and the exchange rate (monetary policy) regime. Intuitively, with enough instruments to affect all the relevant margins, fiscal policy can ensure that relative prices across countries and sectors, and the level of aggregate demand, are the same as in the (Pareto-efficient) allocation.[23] These results provide a useful benchmark for other studies, which proceed by (realistically) constraining the set of fiscal instruments available to the policy makers.

In the rest of this section, I briefly sketch an analysis of fiscal policy in a monetary union without state-contingent instruments, as an extension of the framework adopted in this text (see Galí and Monacelli, 2008). Suppose that taxes are lump sum and government spending falls on useful public goods which provide utility to the representative national consumers. In a Pareto-efficient allocation, government spending should be higher in states of nature where productivity is high, since it is efficient to produce more (private and public) goods in these states of nature. To characterize an equilibrium allocation with an optimal policy mix, recall the main result of the previous section: with nominal rigidities, monetary policy should be expansionary when productivity is high. These considerations suggest that monetary policy and fiscal policy should both be expansionary in response to a positive productivity shock.

In a monetary union, however, it is reasonable to expect that the correlation between these two policies might be lower than in a regime of flexible exchange rates. Specifically, consider the optimal single monetary response to a positive productivity shock in the Home country. As this shock raises average productivity in the union as a whole, monetary policy will be expansionary, raising both domestic and foreign private consumption. But since by assumption productivity has not changed in the Foreign country, the single monetary policy will move output gaps in different directions: output will be too low in the Home country (since the shock is not fully stabilized); it will be too high in the Foreign country. What about fiscal policy? Clearly, it will be optimal to expand government spending on public goods in the Home country, where productivity is high. It will not be optimal to raise public spending in the Foreign country, where productivity has not changed. Actually, welfare could be improved by reducing, at the margin, public activity, to compensate (at least partially) for the high employment rates driven by monetary policy.

In a monetary union, therefore, the optimal policy mix differs at national level, requiring fiscal policy to be anti-cyclical depending on domestic conditions. In the countries experiencing positive productivity shocks, fiscal and monetary policy will both be expansionary. In the countries not experiencing these shocks, fiscal policy should be used to cool down the national economy response to a monetary shock motivated by cyclical conditions elsewhere in the union. This is clearly not optimal, relative to the benchmark case of complete stabilization and efficient provision of public goods.

9.3 Financial issues

The analysis of fiscal policy sketched above is based on a model which abstracts from liquidity and/or borrowing constraints. In their presence, Ricardian equivalence no longer holds: spending and taxation policy can also have a direct effect on private consumption through disposable income. The analysis also abstracts from issues related to fiscal solvency and loss of seigniorage revenue, as well as from noisy behaviour in financial markets. Including these elements in a formal model would clearly enhance our understanding of the macroeconomic policy trade-offs in a currency union.

However, in focusing on fiscal and monetary interactions, it is important to keep in mind that increasing participation in financial markets and market development has arguably relaxed the frictions underlying the traditional output multiplier process, stressed by the conventional analysis of fiscal policy. Deregulation and liberalization of financial markets may be expected to undermine the effectiveness of budget policy as a stabilization tool (see e.g. Perotti 2005 for empirical evidence). The unwelcome implication is that, to the extent that monetary union enhances financial integration and development, fiscal stabilization correspondingly becomes less appealing as a substitute for monetary policy from an aggregate perspective[24] – while of course it may still be quite powerful in correcting market distortions, or providing insurance for specific groups of agents with limited or no access to financial markets.[25]

In light of these considerations, a research agenda on the role of financial market development in monetary unions appears the most promising – and high-priority – area where to concentrate theoretical and empirical analyses on OCA. By eliminating currency risk and reducing transaction costs within the euro area, the introduction of the new European currency has arguably boosted European financial market integration. A core question is the extent to which enhanced opportunities to borrow and share risk through portfolio diversification achievable in a currency union can contribute to reduce the welfare consequences of the stabilization deficits (see e.g. Kalemli-Ozcan *et al.* 2005). A second related core question is the extent to which monetary and financial authorities in a common currency area can foster financial stability. The answer to these questions is particularly intriguing, as it is well understood that the transmission of shocks across countries and sectors can be fundamentally different across economies with different structures of financial markets (see Sutherland 2004). Appropriately developed, these are chapters of the OCA theory which could provide substantial contributions to institutional and policy design.

10. Conclusions

The adoption of a common currency has fostered European economic integration and given many European countries the benefits of low inflation and financial stability. It is well understood, however, that a single monetary policy cannot deliver efficient business cycle stabilization at national level, relative to an ideal benchmark in which region-specific monetary policy stabilizes domestic output gaps and marginal costs.

The analysis in this paper reconsidered the foundations of traditional OCA theory in light of recent advances in monetary theory. The exercise sheds new light on two fundamental propositions underlying the conventional wisdom. First, aggregate welfare losses from monetary unification are found to be small – arguably smaller than the benefits from joining a disciplined currency area for countries without a stable and efficient macroeconomic policy framework. Current and future advances in the literature may of course refine our understanding of the transmission of shocks causing cyclical fluctuations, perhaps challenging the current conventional wisdom on welfare losses from lack of stabilization. Even so, it will still be necessary to verify the extent to which stabilization issues can outweigh other benefits from monetary unification.

Second, specialization in production and asymmetric cyclical shocks do not necessarily make a common monetary policy less efficient than nationally differentiated policies. This is so for two reasons. First, exchange rate movements do not necessarily perform the stabilizing role envisioned by the traditional theory – as is the case when import prices are preset in local currency. In this respect, it is worth stressing that, historically, supporters of a European currency union have often shared a high degree of scepticism on the benefits from exchange rate flexibility. Second, and most importantly, monetary unification may foster processes of convergence in the composition of spending at national level. Convergence in spending patterns tends to make the policy stance which is optimal at regional level more symmetric across different regions in the union, even if regional shocks are uncorrelated and local production is specialized. Convergence of spending patterns emerges as a potential novel attribute of successful monetary unions.

Notes

1. Recent literature has already provided important insights into this question, for instance by developing the standard closed-economy monetary models (e.g. Woodford (2003)), as to encompass asymmetry in nominal or financial frictions across sectors or regions (see Benigno (2004) among others).
2. The full specification of the model and its solution are available at www. eui.eu/Personal/corsetti/
3. Taking logs of the expression in the text and rearranging, yields the nominal interest rate implicitly defined by the optimal policy condition:

$$i = -\ln\beta + \ln\frac{\Gamma_{+1}}{\Gamma} + \ln\frac{1}{Z_H} - \ln E\left(\frac{1}{Z_{H,+1}}\right).$$

   The expression in the text follows from assuming that shocks are lognormally distributed.
4. The presence of capital as productive input and investment shocks do not necessarily modify this conclusion – see for instance Bergin and Corsetti (2005).
5. Technically, the inequality above follows as a straightforward implication of Jensen's inequality.

6. In joint work with Bergin, I show that models including both firms' entry and nominal price rigidities confirm the main result of this section, namely, lack of stabilization raises the price level (Bergin and Corsetti 2005). In addition, the model suggests that insufficient stabilization at national level reduces the number of firms created in equilibrium, depressing the level of investment relative to the flex-price allocation benchmark.

7. Define welfare with flexible prices (or in a fully stabilized economy) W^{flex} as

$$W^{flex} = E \ln \mu - E \ln P^{flex}$$
$$= E \ln \mu - E \ln \frac{\mu}{Z_H} + \text{constant} = E \ln Z_H + \text{constant}.$$

Consider now the case of sticky prices under the assumption $\mu = Z_H^\xi$

$$W^{sticky} = E \ln Z_H^\xi - E \ln E \left(\frac{Z_H^\xi}{Z_H} \right)$$
$$= \xi E \ln Z_H - (\xi - 1) E \ln Z_H - (\xi - 1)^2 * 0.5 * Var \ln Z_H$$
$$= E \ln Z_H - (\xi - 1)^2 * 0.5 * Var \ln Z_H$$

The expression in the text is the difference between the two.

8. In standard monetary models, the goal of stabilization is not to eliminate consumption variability around a smooth trend. Rather, it is to reduce the gap between consumption and its efficient level – which may well be time varying depending on the state of the economy. In the model underlying the calculations above, full stabilization completely closes the output gap, ensures that employment is at its flex-price rate, and lets consumption fluctuate optimally with the state of the economy. Conversely, a constant μ (or μ growing at a deterministic rate) will imply that consumption is constant, but at a lower average relative to a perfectly stabilized economy. Somewhat paradoxically, it is incomplete stabilization which makes consumption 'smoother' relative to a flex-price economy, but suboptimally so. At the same time, it induces excessive volatility of employment.

9. In Bergin and Corsetti (2005), we also allow for product diversification and love for variety. In such a model, business fluctuations reduce product variety available to consumers. The cost of insufficient stabilization is higher, depending on preferences for variety (see Ghironi and Melitz 2005, Corsetti *et al.* 2005, among others).

10. Obviously, the cost of a single currency will be decreasing in the degree of symmetry of productivity shocks hitting the different regions of the monetary union. Similarly, it is well understood that the cost of joining a

currency area will not be symmetric. For instance, ceteris paribus, it will be higher for smaller countries, i.e. countries whose macroeconomic conditions have a small weight in the union-wide aggregates used by the central bank to assess the macroeconomic conditions of the area as a whole.

11. In the discussion of this chapter during the Commission workshop, many voiced the widespread opinion according to which the cost of the business cycle is larger than predicted by most standard models – a concern that has motivated quite a bit of theoretical and empirical work. Unfortunately, none of the contributions mentioned in the discussion succeeds in accounting for more than a marginal upward revision of the standard calculation. The literature may eventually provide convincing models predicting large average welfare losses from the business cycle. It is worth stressing that, in this case, it would still be important to verify that the welfare gap between monetary union and national currencies is correspondingly large.

12. To wit:

$$
\begin{aligned}
W^{sticky} &= E \ln \mu - E \ln E\left(\frac{\mu}{Z_H}\right) \\
&= E \ln \Omega_H + \xi \ln Z_H - E \ln\left(\Omega_H Z_H^{\xi-1}\right) - 0.5 \cdot Var(\ln \Omega_H + (\xi - 1)\ln Z_H) \\
&= E \ln \Omega_H + \xi \ln Z_H - E \ln \Omega_H - (\xi - 1)E \ln Z_H \\
&\quad - 0.5 \cdot \left[Var \ln \Omega_H + (\xi - 1)^2 Var \ln Z_H\right] \\
&= E \ln Z_H - 0.5 \cdot \left[Var \ln \Omega_H + (\xi - 1)^2 Var \ln Z_H\right]
\end{aligned}
$$

13. It is worth noting here that the assumptions underlying the baseline model above actually rule out costs of monetary shocks via mispricing of goods and services: optimally preset prices do not depend on the variance of monetary policy. For more general specifications of preferences and technology, however, a noisy conduct of monetary policy would also affect average prices.

14. In the Corsetti-Pesenti model (as in Cole and Obstfeld 1991) equilibrium terms of trade movements are such that, independently of whether asset markets are complete (but provided there is no outstanding net debt), cross-border consumption risk sharing is efficient. So the solution in the text would also characterize financial autarky.

15. Note the difference in the currency denomination of the marginal costs in the above expressions. In the case of $P_{F,t}$, the Foreign marginal costs are expressed in Home currency.

16. It should be stressed here that, for simplicity, the analysis ignores utility or other gains from liquidity services. The analysis thus abstracts from considerations that could make it optimal to follow the Friedman rule (see Adão *et al.* 2003).

17. In a Nash equilibrium, the Home policy maker problem is

    $$Max_\mu EW$$

    taking μ^* as given. The corresponding problem for the Foreign policy maker is

    $$Max_{\mu^*} EW^*$$

    taking μ as given. With international policy coordination, the joint problem is

    $$Max_{\mu,\mu^*}[EW + EW^*].$$

    In a monetary union, the problem is the same as above, subject to the constraint $\mu = \mu^*$.

18. Optimal policy stances satisfy:

$$1 = \frac{1-\gamma}{1-\gamma(1-\alpha)} \frac{\frac{\mu_{PCP,Nash}}{Z_N}}{E_{t-1}\left(\frac{\mu_{PCP,Nash}}{Z_N}\right)} + \frac{\gamma\alpha}{1-\gamma(1-\alpha)} \frac{\frac{\mu_{PCP,Nash}}{Z_H}}{E_{t-1}\left(\frac{\mu_{PCP,Nash}}{Z_H}\right)}$$

$$1 = \frac{1-\gamma}{1-\gamma(1-\alpha)} \frac{\frac{\mu^*_{PCP,Nash}}{Z^*_N}}{E_{t-1}\left(\frac{\mu^*_{PCP,Nash}}{Z^*_N}\right)} + \frac{\gamma\alpha}{1-\gamma(1-\alpha)} \frac{\frac{\mu^*_{PCP,Nash}}{Z_F}}{E_{t-1}\left(\frac{\mu^*_{PCP,Nash}}{Z_F}\right)}$$

19. Real factors include distributive trade, difference in preferences generating differences in elasticities across markets, vertical and horizontal interactions in noncompetitive markets, or other factors creating scope for optimal price discrimination.

20. To wit, optimal policy stances satisfy

$$1 = (1-\gamma)\frac{\frac{\mu_{LCP,Nash}}{Z_N}}{E_{t-1}\left(\frac{\mu_{LCP,Nash}}{Z_N}\right)} + \gamma\left[\alpha\frac{\frac{\mu_{LCP,Nash}}{Z_H}}{E_{t-1}\left(\frac{\mu_{LCP,Nash}}{Z_H}\right)} + (1-\alpha)\frac{\frac{\mu_{LCP,Nash}}{Z_F}}{E_{t-1}\left(\frac{\mu_{LCP,Nash}}{Z_F}\right)}\right]$$

$$1 = (1-\gamma)\frac{\frac{\mu^*_{LCP,Nash}}{Z^*_N}}{E_{t-1}\left(\frac{\mu^*_{LCP,Nash}}{Z^*_N}\right)} + \gamma\left[(1-\alpha)\frac{\frac{\mu^*_{LCP,Nash}}{Z_H}}{E_{t-1}\left(\frac{\mu^*_{LCP,Nash}}{Z_H}\right)} + \alpha\frac{\frac{\mu^*_{LCP,Nash}}{Z_F}}{E_{t-1}\left(\frac{\mu^*_{LCP,Nash}}{Z_F}\right)}\right]$$

21. By the same token, in models with capital accumulation symmetry breaks down when shocks generate nation-specific investment dynamics.

22. Observe that the analysis of the Nash equilibrium in Section 6 (where import prices are flexible in local currency) and Section 7 (where import prices are sticky in local currency) can be interpreted as an application of the same principle.

23. Interestingly, Adão *et al.* (2006) build an economy where lack of labour mobility across the border is by no means an impediment to optimal stabilization. Rather, it is a prerequisite to it, since optimal labour income and consumption taxes are not efficient if workers can arbitrage net wages across markets.

24. As a caveat, even with integrated financial markets, financial turmoil and liquidity crises could cause temporary exacerbations of borrowing constraints, arguably requalifying fiscal policy as an effective instrument of output stabilization. The social value of spending and taxation measures rises when cyclical fluctuations are rooted in financial stress which interferes with the normal functioning of credit markets.

25. Another reason for scepticism on the role of fiscal policy is that countries have become much more open to trade, and monetary union is expected to foster trade integration even above global trends – a point amply debated in the empirically controversy after Rose (2000), but also discussed above in relation to the convergence of consumption patterns. According to the received wisdom, increasing openness raises the magnitude of international spillovers from fiscal policy, while reducing its impact on the demand for domestic output.

Comment 2: Comment on Chapters 4 and 5

PETER HOELLER

Mongelli provides an excellent overview of the old and new optimum currency area (OCA) theories as well as the wide range of policies and processes underpinning the monetary union. He emphasises that the balance of judgement has shifted in favour of monetary union. Nowadays, monetary union is thought to generate fewer costs, while the benefits loom larger. But he also stresses that OCA theory is still not operational and that it did not deliver much in terms of policy guidance for those countries entering monetary union. At the same time, the insights of OCA theory were heeded: the single market has been improved further over the last ten years, most importantly perhaps in the financial area and more recently with tackling lacunae in the non-financial services sectors. At the same time, the Lisbon Strategy has provided impetus for reforms at the national level. Mongelli dubs this tackling of structural weaknesses prior to monetary union and since the creation of the euro 'OCA theory in reverse'. I agree with Mongelli that OCA theory, whether old or new, is still central in the debate on the merits of a monetary union. But I am somewhat sceptical about the benefits becoming larger and the costs smaller.

Corsetti applies a new tool, a DSGE (dynamic stochastic general equilibrium) model, to one aspect of traditional OCA theory, namely the issue of the size of welfare costs from not being able to stabilise the cycle at the country level in a monetary union. He finds that they are small and Mongelli indeed shows that cyclical cross-country developments are close to that of states in federations, but deviations are more persistent. Corsetti, moreover, finds that the costs of monetary union are low, if consumption patterns converge, in spite of specialisation of production.

1.1 The growth context

In Europe, policy tends to rest on two pillars. So let me put my comments into a growth and stability context. Since 1999, euro-area growth per capita was close to but below 2 per cent (Figure C2.1). At 1.7 per cent, per capita growth was just the same as in the period between 1990 and 1999, which Mongelli sees as being afflicted by eurosclerosis. It could come as a consolation that growth in the United States was not any better than in the euro area since 1999. In this comparison, Europe could be seen as playing in the growth champions league. But this would be misleading. The income level in the United States is considerably above that in the euro area. This implies that at the same growth rates, the difference in income levels has widened further and the euro area has quite some catching up to do.

It is also clear that the outs (Denmark, Sweden and the United Kingdom) did not suffer from being out. The difference in growth performance between Sweden, the United Kingdom and the euro area is actually quite wide, while the difference for Denmark, which shadows euro-area monetary policy, is much narrower. A striking feature is the dismal growth performance of the three largest euro-area countries, while the smaller ones have flourished.

Inflation has been much lower since 1999 than it was in the decade before. Since January 1999, it has been 2.1 per cent and thus extremely close to the monetary policy objective of being close to, but below 2 per cent. Also inflation volatility has come down and, measured by the standard deviation, was only 0.3 per cent. These patterns have also been observed in other countries. What stands out, however, is the success of the European Central Bank in controlling inflation as well as in

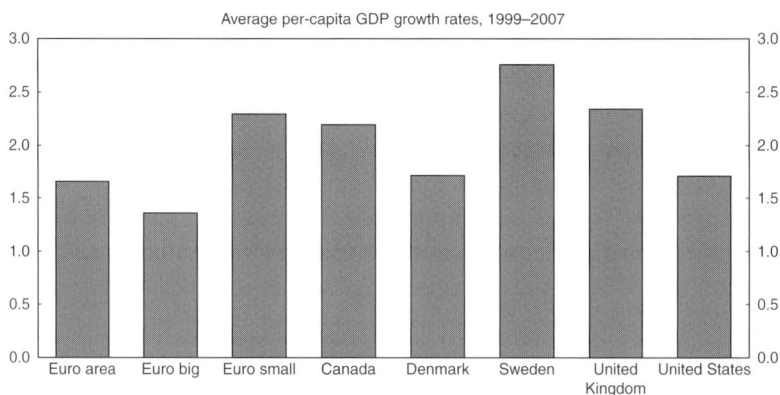

Figure C2.1: The growth context
Source: OECD Economic Outlook 81 database.

restraining its volatility. The European Commission (2007a), for instance, shows that inflation was closer to target in the euro area than in the United States, the United Kingdom and Sweden, and inflation volatility about half. Whatever comments have been made about the ECB's performance in various respects, the outcomes in terms of hitting the inflation target and inflation volatility are excellent.

1.2 Why do the smaller countries fare better?

A major conclusion by Mongelli is that currency unions are now deemed to generate fewer costs and that there are more benefits. Given the growth record this is hard to swallow, or one would have to conclude that the net benefits from monetary union came on top of deepening eurosclerosis. In this context it is important to understand why the smaller countries have consistently outperformed the largest euro-area countries. There are, of course, many explanations for their better performance and it is difficult to disentangle them: some, but not all of them were favoured by a sharp reduction in real interest rates in the run-up to monetary union and again some, but not all, are still in an economic catch-up phase. But it is probably also because the old OCA criteria are better fulfilled: trade as well as financial market integration with the rest of the union is tighter and most have opened their borders to inward migration for the countries that acceded the European Union in 2004. They could thus raise the speed limit of their economies, though migration is more a boost to GDP growth than growth in terms of GDP per capita.

The smaller countries also seem to do better on another OCA criterion: their wage formation process seems to internalise competitiveness issues much better than in the large countries. As their export and import shares are large, they will be punished harshly even for small changes in competitiveness, while there is much more domestic production consumed internally in the largest countries, so that competitiveness problems will not become an issue quickly. Mongelli, for instance, cites the Netherlands as an example of rapid wage adjustment. The country overshot the euro-area cycle considerably in the late 1990s and early 2000s with high wage inflation and a heavy loss in competitiveness. But wages were then frozen for several years, competitiveness was recouped and the economy started to grow strongly again. Wage growth was also subdued in Germany for many years. That has improved competitiveness slowly but surely, but has at the same time

Cumulative change from 1999 to 2005

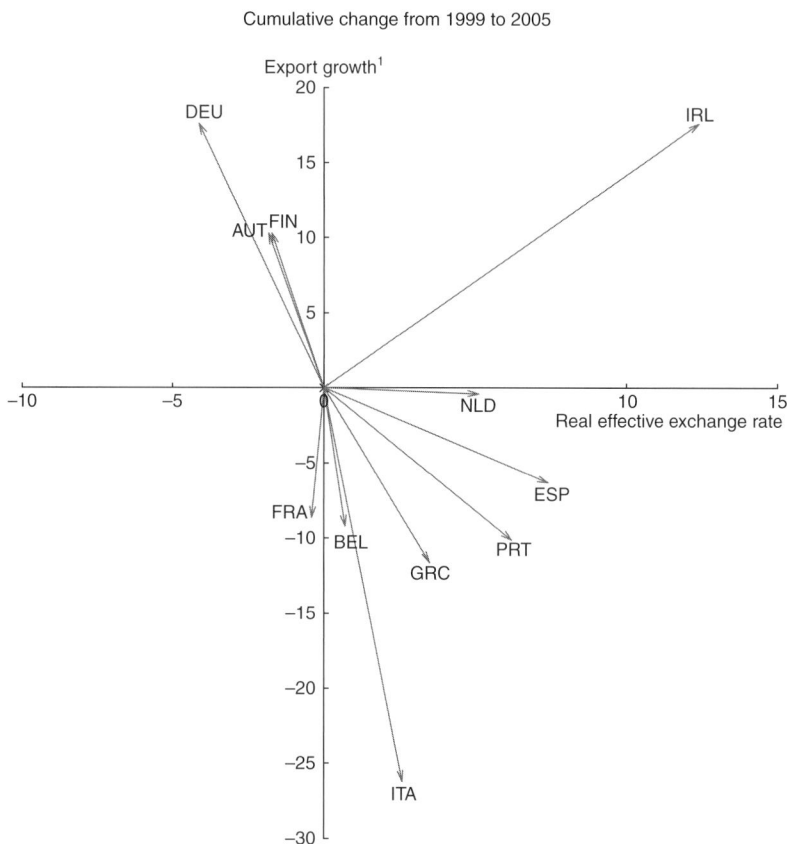

Figure C2.2: Real effective exchange rate and gross exports
[1] Excess over euro area average.
Source: Eurostat and OECD, Economic Outlook database.

restrained domestic demand, while the low inflation rate has pushed up the real interest rate.

The adjustment in the largest countries seems to be much slower, because i) the competitiveness channel is weaker due to their lower trade openness and ii) wage formation is not flexible enough to underpin a swift adjustment. In this respect, Italy is in a league of its own. Despite very low growth, labour costs have risen faster than the euro-area average. This has cumulated to a sizeable increase in the real effective exchange rate and a loss in competitiveness (Figure C2.2). The large euro-area countries tend to have sectoral wage agreements that cover many enterprises. This implies that wage and productivity developments could get out of line for many of them. The persistent problems of large areas in these two countries (East Germany and the Mezzogiorno) are testimony that this way of setting wages is likely to set them at the wrong level. The situation in Germany has changed, though, in recent years, with many enterprises taking advantage of the possibility of opting out of the sectoral agreements. There should still be a stronger shift away from sectoral to enterprise bargaining as it would help firms to deal with shocks by adjusting wages rather than employment. It would also insulate exporters from developments in other sectors and would increase the incentives for the workforce to boost productivity because they could share in the gains.

1.3 The perils of slow growth and adjustment

Corsetti's model suggests that the welfare effects of the business cycle are minor and this is in line with much earlier work by Lucas, which demonstrated that the welfare effects of raising growth just a bit in the long term has much greater welfare effects than abolishing the cycle. But Corsetti's model only includes nominal rigidities, while the welfare effects of the cycle would probably be larger if real rigidities were also included. Moreover, slow adjustment in the euro area could lead to persistence in growth differentials. There may be self-reinforcing mechanisms at play so that what starts out as a temporary downturn ends up with protracted or permanent effects. Hysteresis channels in the labour market are well understood, although they tend to affect the level rather than the growth rate of employment and output. They include a ratcheting-up of structural unemployment due to insider-outsider dynamics, a loss of morale and skills by the unemployed, stigmatisation of the jobless which reduces their subsequent employment prospects, and a reduction in regional labour mobility, especially if house prices are flat or falling. Most of these effects should wane in the long term, although labour market withdrawal by older workers is effectively permanent if they leave the workforce through early retirement or disability schemes. Once on a disability benefit, almost nobody goes back to work.

There may also be product market hysteresis effects that could have a persistent impact on potential growth by affecting the drivers of innovation and productivity growth. For example:

- Cash-strapped firms may reduce spending on R&D due to borrowing constraints in a downturn (Aghion and Howitt, 2006).
- Similarly, government expenditure in growth-enhancing areas such as education, public R&D support and infrastructure investment may be crowded out by increased transfer spending.
- When there are sunk costs to investment, investing in a growing economy is less risky because it is easier to expand capacity than to cut it. A prolonged slump may therefore reduce investment through the uncertainty channel over and above the normal output and cash-flow channels.
- Entrepreneurship and innovation may fall for a similar reason. People may be less willing to gamble on starting a new company. Less firm turnover leads to lower productivity growth through the creative destruction process (OECD, 2001a).
- Workers may also become more risk averse, lowering employment turnover. New blood and fresh ideas are important drivers of innovation at the firm level.
- Firms can hoard labour for a short while, but in a long slump employees with firm-specific skills will have to be laid off. If firms know that recessions tend to be drawn out, they will have less incentive to invest in the human capital of their workforce.
- Governments may put off growth-enhancing reforms and fiscal consolidation until better times.

Self-reinforcing mechanisms can also work in a positive direction. For example, strong growth in Ireland and Spain has boosted government revenues. In the case of Ireland, government spending in real terms has gone up by 60 per cent since 2000, while in Spain it has risen by nearly 30 per cent (Figure C2.3). It has enabled the Spanish and Irish government to spend considerably more on education, R&D and infrastructure, while still allowing a reduction in government debt as a per cent of GDP. In Germany and Italy, on the other hand, government spending has been nearly flat. Immigration, which has been very strong in Ireland and Spain, is another factor that has reinforced growth.

Hysteresis effects could thus drive up the cost of persistent cyclical divergence for the sluggish economies. These issues are not the topic of much research, but they may have contributed to raising the costs of joining monetary union.

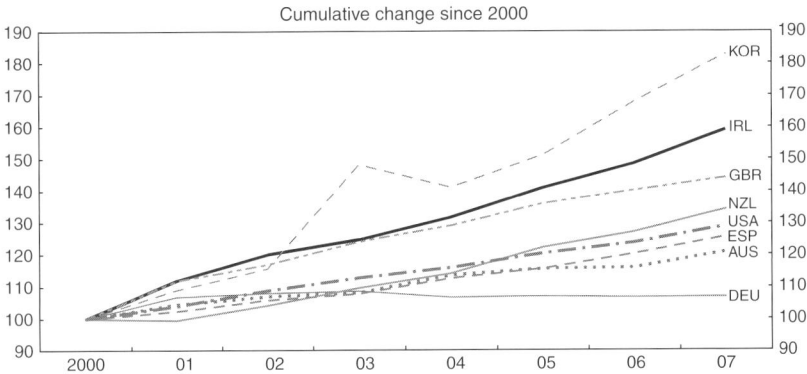

Figure C2.3: **Real government spending**
Source: OECD (2008), Economic Outlook 83 database.

1.4 The perils of booming ahead

Both chapters neglect another important issue: the probability of boom-bust cycles in monetary union and how to deal with costly busts. Due to inflation differentials real interest rates have differed a lot across the euro-area countries. In some countries, and especially so in Ireland and Spain, the boost from low real interest rates was compounded by a steep rise in housing prices. Housing markets are important in the transmission of monetary policy and a high interest rate sensitivity is beneficial as monetary policy is more powerful in damping cyclical fluctuations in the euro area as a whole. But the characteristics of housing and mortgage markets still differ widely across the euro area, leading to asymmetric behaviour of individual countries. These concern mainly differences in home-ownership rates, financial markets, taxation and supply constraints. Supply constraints and tax incentives to stimulate house ownership can exacerbate volatility in house prices and cyclical divergence. In both Ireland and Spain, housing benefits from a generous tax treatment and there is a strong cross-country correlation between this generosity and the variability of house prices. Supply, on the other hand, has reacted swiftly in both countries, but it has also meant that housing investment as a per cent of GDP has risen to peaks of 10 per cent or even more as compared to a euro-area average of about 5 per cent. In both countries housing investment has plummeted now. Housing busts seldom end up in a soft landing, especially in countries with a fixed exchange rate.

In monetary union, it is important to have a tax system in place that does not favour housing so as not to exacerbate cyclical differences. Higher taxation of residential property would also help in dampening house price cycles. However, the property tax take tends to be low in the euro-area countries at typically well below 1 per cent of GDP. This is because tax rates are low and in many countries property values are updated with a considerable lag. Taxation of residential property is close to 3 per cent of GDP in Canada, the United Kingdom and the United States.

Housing bubbles can be very costly. In Finland, the bursting of the housing bubble in the early 1990s led to a decline of GDP of more than 10 per cent and in Sweden of nearly 5 per cent, even though they eased monetary policy a lot and fiscal policy absorbed part of the shock. In the absence of a monetary policy at the national level and with fiscal policy constrained, this leaves a heavy responsibility for the institutions that supervise the financial system. While regulators, as central banks, may not be in a good position to recognise bubbles, they can put a regulatory system in place that makes the financial system resilient in the face of asset market bubbles. Strong consumer protection, for instance, can avoid problems related to predatory lending, risk weightings can be changed, while Spain has put in place a unique system of dynamic bank provisioning. The current financial market turmoil provides a live stress test on whether current arrangements are sufficiently robust at the country level. Prudential supervision across the area has become better coordinated but the major responsibility remains at the country level. The current arrangements may provide a coherent and flexible strategy for safeguarding financial stability. However, the current fragmentation – together with the information and incentive problems that come with it – may raise systemic risks, the costs of financial instability and hinder the speedy resolution of failed banks.

1.5 Should fiscal policy be activist?

Corsetti suggests that fiscal policy should be used to ensure the right level of aggregate demand following productivity shocks that differ across countries. It is clear that fiscal policy is the only macro stabilisation tool left at the country level. On the other hand, fiscal multipliers are small in the smaller euro-area countries and large swings in tax rates or spending programmes would be needed to stabilise incomes. As these changes would only be temporary, people may not react much to fiscal stimulus or contraction. And as Mongelli points out, the fiscal stance in the euro area has been mildly procyclical, rather than anti-cyclical, and some countries are still not close to the Stability and Growth Pact objective of moving from sizeable government deficits to close to balance or into surplus. In this context, I think Solow's (2002) observations on fiscal policy in the United States also apply to Europe: 'Maybe prolonged imbalances between aggregate supply and demand so occur in market economies, and maybe appropriately tuned fiscal policy could help to relieve them. But maybe also democratic politics is simply incapable of making the appropriate fiscal-policy adjustments in time to do much good. (…) Whenever discretionary fiscal policy rises to the top of the political agenda, special interests come out of the woodwork. Every tax change, every increase or decrease in public spending is caught over by the potential winners and losers, their lobbyists and elected representatives. The final outcome may often be distributionally and allocationally, and even macroeconomically, perverse. (…) Note that this is not some kind of minor flaw in the system; it is the system.'

1.6 Has monetary union spurred structural reforms?

Mongelli argues that the run-up to monetary union and monetary union itself has spurred efforts to reform labour, product and financial market policies. There are good arguments in favour of this hypothesis, but there are also arguments against. Ultimately this is an empirical issue. The euro-area countries have undertaken more comprehensive and far-reaching reforms than the other OECD countries since the early 1990s. This may reflect a greater need for reform rather than the effects of monetary union per se. Indeed, the evidence suggests that reform intensity has fallen since the implementation of the single currency in 1999, while there has been little slowdown elsewhere. This is in line with evidence in Duval and Elmeskov (2006) that a lack of monetary autonomy tends to reduce the probability of structural reform on average. The evidence on this point is not strong, though, and any effects of monetary union are likely to be marginal as compared to the larger political barriers to reform.

1.7 Conclusion

I am a great fan of the monetary union. I travel a lot and price comparisons are much easier now, while I do not have to change currencies all the time. I also like the ECB's firm stance on inflation.

On the other hand, one should not underestimate the strictures imposed by monetary union. The euro-area countries should be more flexible than the others and there is still a long way to go. The Lisbon Strategy is starting to deliver results and the future could bring stronger growth, while stability is being maintained. But I want to see it, before I believe it.

PART III

Monetary policy

6 ECB credibility and transparency

PETRA GERAATS

1. Introduction

The European Central Bank (ECB) was established on 1 June 1998 as the head of the European System of Central Banks (ESCB) and has been responsible for monetary policy in the euro area since 1 January 1999. During its first decade, the ECB has been successful in many respects. Highlights include the formation of a monetary union on 1 January 1999, which gradually expanded from eleven to sixteen European countries. At the same time, a new single currency, the euro, was created as an electronic means of payment. This was followed by the introduction of euro banknotes and coins on 1 January 2002. Furthermore, the euro-area economy has performed remarkably well during its first decade: inflation has been low at an average level of 2.0 per cent, while average real GDP growth has been robust at 2.2 per cent.[1]

The ECB's achievements so far have defied the pessimistic views of some critics, who sometimes gave the impression that the European monetary union was a grand economic experiment that was doomed to fail. On the other hand, the ECB's successes have not met the optimistic hopes of some supporters, who seemed to consider it a panacea for a European economy beset by structural shortcomings. Moreover, the ECB has fallen short of meeting its primary objective, gauged by its own criteria.

The primary objective of the ECB is to maintain price stability. This is enshrined in article 105(1) of the Treaty establishing the European Community, as amended by the 1992 'Maastricht' Treaty on European Union, but it leaves open how to interpret 'price stability'. To mitigate this ambiguity, the ECB has defined price stability as 'a year-on-year increase

I thank Chris Crowe, Vítor Gaspar and Frank Smets for useful comments. In addition, this paper has benefited from discussions I had with Francesco Giavazzi, Charles Wyplosz and a few ECB Executive Board members during the preparation of the 2008 MECB report. Needless to say, all views expressed in this paper are my own.

193

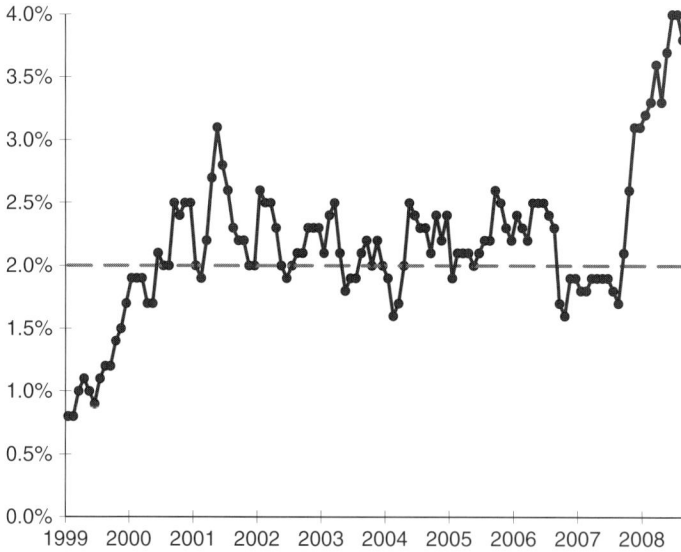

Figure 6.1: Euro-area HICP inflation (year-on-year)
Sample: 1999M1–2008M8. Source: Eurostat.

in the Harmonized Index of Consumer Prices (HICP) for the euro area of below 2 per cent' and decided that 'price stability is to be maintained over the medium term' (ECB 1998b). Using the ECB's quantitative definition, the euro area failed to exhibit price stability most of the time. Figure 6.1 shows that euro-area inflation has often been above the 2 per cent ceiling during the last decade. To be precise, year-on-year HICP inflation in the euro area exceeded 2 per cent for 58 per cent of the months from January 1999 to August 2008.

Using annual data, the verdict is even more damning. Figure 6.2 reveals that average HICP inflation in the euro area has been above 2 per cent for eight out of nine years from 1999 to 2007. The only year for which average inflation stayed below 2 per cent was 1999, but monetary policy transmission lags make it hard to attribute 1999 inflation to the ECB's actions. Excluding 1999, average euro-area HICP inflation has been 2.2 per cent using annual data.

The picture looks different when we use an alternative annual measure of inflation, namely the increase in euro-area HICP per annum. To capture the increase in HICP during year t, we take the (geometric) average of the HICP index for December in year t and January in year

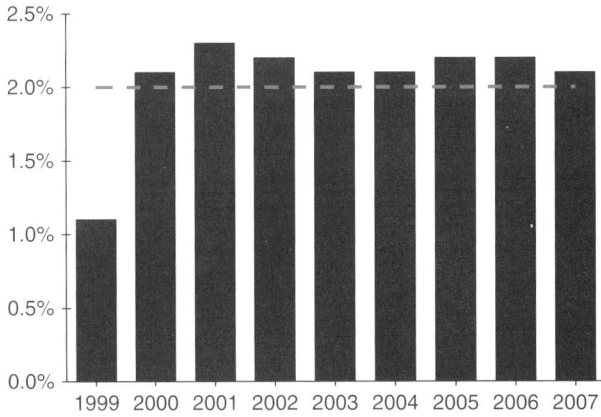

Figure 6.2: Euro-area HICP inflation (annual average)
Source: Eurostat.

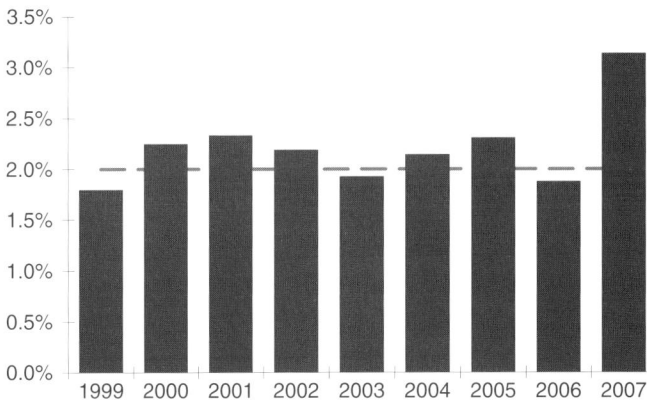

Figure 6.3: Increase in euro-area HICP (per annum)
Source: Eurostat and author's calculations (see note 2).

$t + 1$ to approximate the HICP index at the end of year t, and compare this to the HICP index at the end of year $t - 1$.[2] Figure 6.3 shows that by this measure, the increase in euro-area HICP has been above 2 per cent in six out of nine years. Price stability, according to the ECB's quantitative definition, was achieved in 1999, 2003 and 2006. But on average, the increase in euro-area HICP was 2.2 per cent per year from 1999 to 2007. In 2007 it even reached 3.14 per cent. So, no matter which measure is used, the overall conclusion remains the same. Based on its

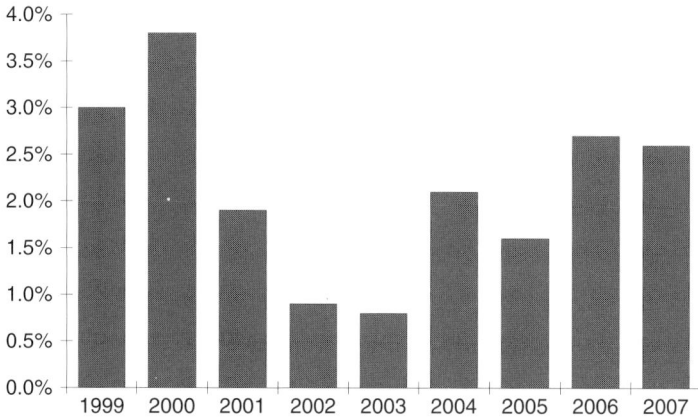

Figure 6.4: Euro-area real GDP growth (annual average)
Source: Eurostat.

own quantitative definition, the ECB has failed to maintain price stability over the medium term.

While average inflation has been higher than the ECB's objective, economic activity has been in line with the ECB's assumption of a medium-term trend growth rate for real GDP of 2 per cent to 2.5 per cent (ECB 1998a). Figure 6.4 shows that real GDP growth in the euro area has been quite healthy and only dipped below 1.5 per cent in 2002 and 2003. This economic slowdown reduced the yearly increase in euro-area HICP from 2.3 per cent in 2001 to 1.9 per cent in 2003 (see Figure 6.3). In the meantime, the ECB had embarked on a monetary easing that lowered its main refinancing (or 'refi') rate from 4.75 per cent in April 2001 to 2 per cent in June 2003, as is shown in Figure 6.5. While the refi rate was maintained at 2 per cent for over two years, inflation per annum rose again above the 2 per cent ceiling. As a result, monetary policy was very expansionary and short-term real interest rates, as measured by real three-month Euribor, even turned negative. The highly accommodative monetary policy stance was gradually removed as the ECB steadily increased the refi rate from 2 per cent in December 2005 to 4 per cent in June 2007 (and then to 4.25 per cent in July 2008). But this did not prevent inflation per annum from soaring to 3.1 per cent in 2007, partly as a result of sharply rising food and oil prices.

Unanticipated adverse shocks may also explain why the ECB has not managed to maintain price stability (according to its own

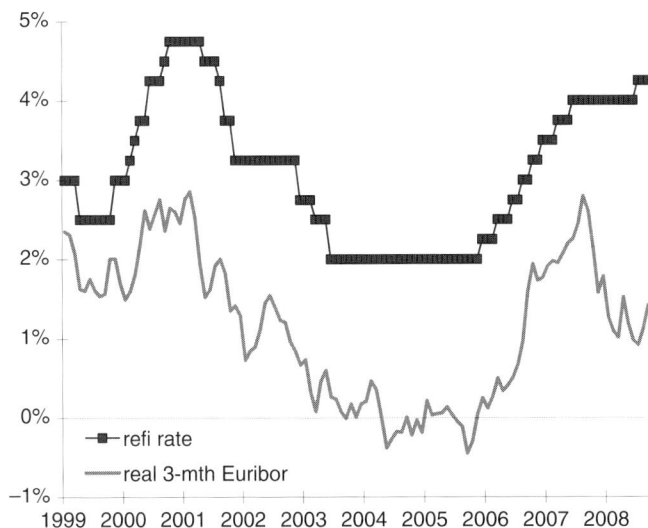

Figure 6.5: ECB main refinancing rate and real three-month Euribor
Note: The refi is the end of month fixed tender rate (before June 2000) or
minimum bid rate (from June 2000) for ECB main refinancing operations.
Real three-month Euribor is a monthly average. Sample: 1999M1–2008M9.
Source: ECB Statistical Data Warehouse.

quantitative definition) during its first decade. Since unforeseeable
shocks make an evaluation based on ex-post performance problematic, it is better to assess the ECB's success by checking whether the
private sector expects the ECB to deliver price stability in the medium
term. In other words, how credible is it that the ECB achieves its
primary objective? Section 2 analyses ECB credibility and finds that
it has steadily eroded over time as (average) euro-area inflation has
been creeping up. The private sector now appears to doubt the ECB's
ability to secure price stability in the medium term. Presuming the ECB
maintains an unwavering commitment to meeting its primary objective, this suggests that it has not been successful in persuading the
public of its intentions. So, there appears to be a compelling case to
improve ECB transparency. Section 3 analyses to what extent the ECB
discloses information that is pertinent to understanding monetary
policy making, and it identifies areas in which there is scope for
improvement.[3] The findings are further discussed in Section 4, which
considers the role of transmission uncertainty and the possibility of

time-inconsistency in the ECB's medium-term-oriented monetary policy strategy. Section 5 concludes that the ECB could greatly benefit from adopting a higher degree of transparency to overcome the decline in its credibility and succeed during its second decade.

2. ECB credibility

To assess how credible the private sector considers the ECB's objective to deliver price stability over the medium term, two types of measures are discussed. Section 2.1 considers euro-area inflation expectations, including market measures extracted from financial asset prices and estimates based on surveys. Section 2.2 analyses an alternative measure of ECB credibility that is specifically catered to its price stability objective. For a nice overview and discussion of (market and survey) measures of euro-area inflation expectations, see ECB (2006b).

2.1 Inflation expectations

The ECB considers it very important that medium- to long-term inflation expectations in the euro area remain solidly anchored at levels consistent with price stability.[4] A popular measure of market expectations is the 'breakeven' inflation rate that is the difference in the yield on nominal and inflation-indexed government bonds. This measure has the advantage that it is available in real time and based on financial market transactions. On the other hand, breakeven inflation reflects not only inflation expectations, but also inflation risk premia and (differences in) liquidity and term premia (between nominal and inflation-indexed government bonds).[5] So, the level of breakeven inflation is only an imperfect proxy for inflation expectations.

Figure 6.6 shows long-term breakeven inflation rates computed from seasonally adjusted estimates of the zero coupon yield curves for nominal and inflation-indexed government bonds in the euro area.[6] Although the ten-year spot rate and five-year forward rate five years ahead for euro-area breakeven inflation have been very volatile, they clearly declined from over 2.4 per cent in mid-2004 to around 2.15 per cent in mid-2005, and have shown an upward trend since early 2007. The recent increase in the ten-year spot rate for breakeven inflation, which measures the average from zero to ten years into the future, could be due to a sharp short-run rise in inflation that is unavoidable due to

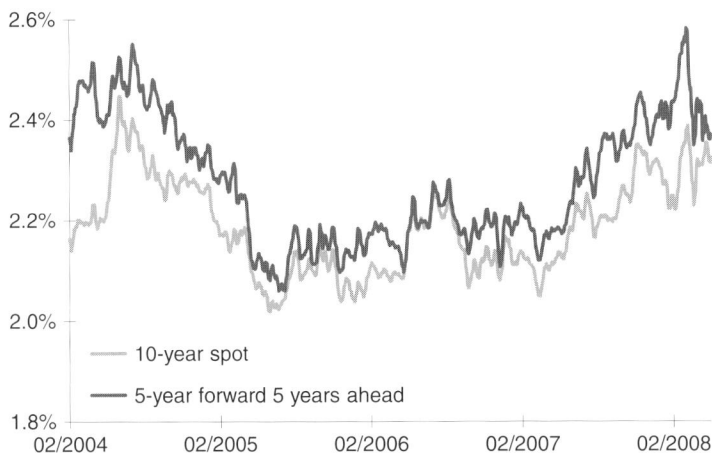

Figure 6.6: Long-term euro-area breakeven inflation
Note: Five-day moving average of seasonally adjusted zero coupon breakeven
inflation. Sample: 6 February 2004–6 May 2008.
Source: ECB Statistics.

food and energy price developments. For instance, an expected one-year
increase in inflation from 2 per cent to 3 per cent would increase average
ten-year inflation expectations by ten basis points. However, there has
also been a large increase in the five-year forward rate for breakeven
inflation five years ahead, which measures the average from five to ten
years into the future and is therefore not directly affected by (unavoidable) short-run inflation fluctuations. This makes the five-year forward
breakeven inflation rate five years ahead a better measure of long-term
inflation expectations. Nevertheless, changes in breakeven inflation
may not be due to movements in inflation expectations but to shifts in
risk premia. So, it is difficult to interpret the recent rise in long-term
breakeven inflation in the euro area, especially in the aftermath of the
financial market turmoil of August 2007.

The problems associated with market expectations of inflation
implied by nominal and real bond yields can be overcome by using
surveys that directly ask about inflation expectations. Such survey
measures have the drawback that they are not available at high frequency or in real time. In addition, in contrast to financial market
transactions which often put large sums at stake, survey participants
have no incentive to provide high-quality estimates. However, surveys

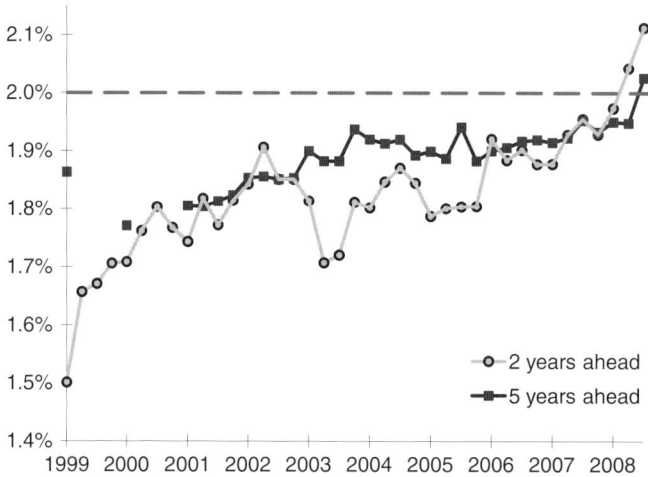

Figure 6.7: Euro-area inflation expectations
Note: Average two- and five-year ahead point estimates for euro-area HICP inflation. Sample: 1999Q1–2008Q3 for two years ahead; 1999Q1, 2000Q1 and 2001Q1–2008Q3 five years ahead.
Source: ECB Survey of Professional Forecasters.

are likely to provide a more accurate measure of the level of inflation expectations than breakeven inflation rates distorted by risk premia.

The ECB conducts a Survey of Professional Forecasters (SPF) that asks a panel of approximately seventy-five European professional forecasters once a quarter about their euro-area macroeconomic forecasts at horizons of about one, two and five years ahead.[7] Figure 6.7 shows the mean of the SPF estimates for euro-area HICP inflation in two and five years. Five-year ahead inflation expectations have gradually risen from around 1.8 per cent in 2000 to 2.03 per cent in 2008, inching above the 2 per cent limit that the ECB deems consistent with price stability. Medium-term inflation expectations have mostly been lower but more volatile than longer-term inflation expectations, with an average of 1.83 per cent and 1.89 per cent, and a mean absolute change of 0.041 and 0.019 per quarter (since 2001), for two-year and five-year ahead inflation estimates, respectively. Nevertheless, two-year ahead euro-area inflation expectations have also clearly exhibited an upward trend during the last decade. These medium-term inflation forecasts breached the 2 per cent ceiling in the second quarter of 2008 and rose

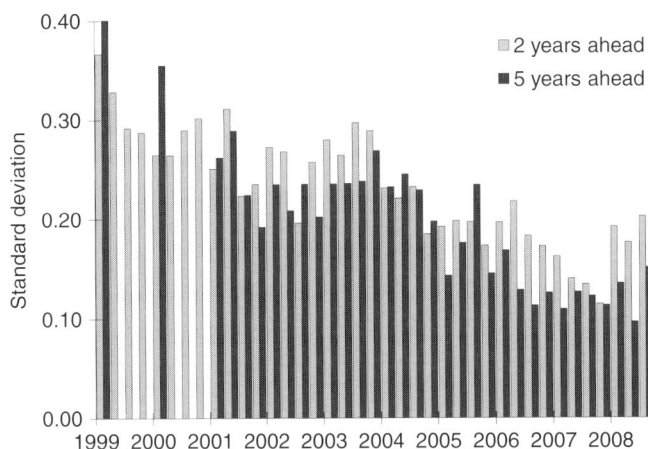

Figure 6.8: Dispersion of euro-area inflation expectations
Note: Standard deviation of two- and five-year ahead point estimates for euro-area HICP inflation, excluding one outlier in 2003Q2 for two-year ahead inflation. Sample: 1999Q1–2008Q3 for two years ahead; 1999Q1, 2000Q1 and 2001Q1–2008Q3 for five years ahead.
Source: ECB Survey of Professional Forecasters.

to 2.11 per cent in the following quarter, so they are no longer consistent with the ECB's objective of price stability.

The high level of longer-term HICP inflation expectations for the euro area is confirmed by other surveys. The euro area Barometer estimate for 2012 and the Consensus Economics forecast for 2014–18 were both 2.0 per cent mid-2008.[8] So, longer-term expectations for euro-area HICP inflation have now reached the upper limit of the ECB's quantitative definition of price stability.

In addition to the mean it is useful to consider the standard deviation of the individual SPF forecast estimates, which measures the dispersion or disagreement among the forecasters. Figure 6.8 shows that the standard deviation of the SPF inflation estimates has declined over time from around 0.3 to 0.15.[9] Forecast dispersion tends to be a bit higher for two-year than for five-year ahead inflation estimates, with an average of 0.23 and 0.20, respectively, which is in line with the greater volatility of the former. The reduction in dispersion over time indicates a stronger consensus among professional forecasters, while their medium- and long-term inflation expectations for the euro area have been reaching ever higher levels.

Regarding the dispersion of long-term SPF inflation estimates, the lower quartile of the five-year ahead forecasts has gradually increased from 1.6 per cent to 1.9 per cent, while the upper quartile has stayed at 2.0 per cent (see Bowles *et al.* 2007). So, the fraction of SPF respondents that expect long-term inflation in the euro area to be at or above 2 per cent has been 25 per cent. In other words, a quarter of SPF participants believe that the ECB will fail to achieve its objective of price stability in the long-term.

Bowles *et al.* (2007) report some additional interesting findings based on individual SPF forecasts. They find that there is no significant correlation between changes in one-year and five-year ahead SPF inflation forecasts, which suggests that short-term fluctuations are generally not expected to have a persistent effect on long-term inflation. Nevertheless, individual SPF respondents frequently update their long-term inflation expectations and the fraction that change their five-year ahead inflation forecasts compared to the previous quarter has remained approximately 30 per cent since 2002. This suggests that professional forecasters continue to face considerable uncertainty about the long-term inflation prospects for the euro area.

2.2 Uncertainty and credibility

An interesting feature of the ECB Survey of Professional Forecasters is that participants are asked not only to provide a point estimate of inflation but also to assign probabilities to ranges of inflation outcomes. Thus, quantitative measures of forecast uncertainty can be constructed. In particular, the standard deviation of the individual and aggregate SPF forecast distributions could be used as a measure of individual and aggregate forecast uncertainty, respectively. Although the dispersion of five-year ahead SPF inflation estimates has declined from 0.3 to 0.1 (as shown in Figure 6.8), Bowles *et al.* (2007) find that individual forecast uncertainty has increased mildly, while aggregate forecast uncertainty has remained roughly stable at 0.6.[10]

Moreover, the aggregate SPF probability distribution for inflation allows us to compute the likelihood that the SPF respondents collectively attach to a realisation of euro-area HICP inflation of at least 0 per cent and less than 2 per cent, consistent with the ECB's quantitative definition of price stability. Following Geraats *et al.* (2008), the SPF probability of euro-area HICP inflation in the 0–2 per cent range in two

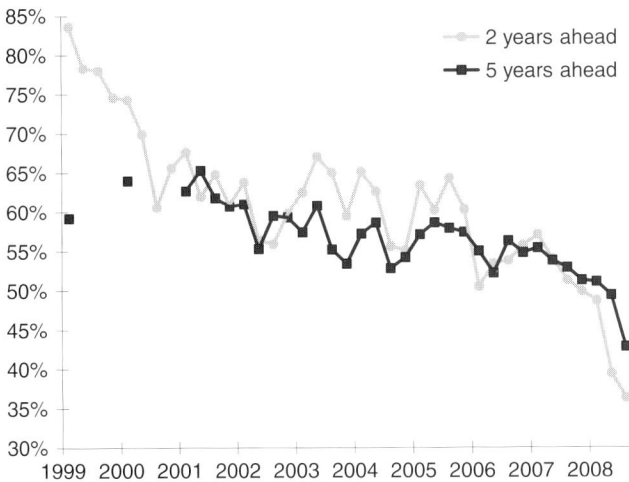

Figure 6.9: ECB credibility
Note: SPF probability of euro-area HICP inflation of at least 0 per cent and less than 2.0 per cent. Sample: 1999Q1–2008Q3 for two years ahead; 1999Q1, 2000Q1 and 2001Q1–2008Q3 for five years ahead.
Source: ECB Survey of Professional Forecasters and author's calculations.

to five years can be interpreted as a quantitative measure of the credibility of the ECB in meeting its primary objective in the medium to long term.[11] This measure has the advantage that it depends on both the mean and standard deviation of the SPF forecast density. So, it captures not only the expected level of future inflation but also inflation uncertainty. For instance, suppose that private sector forecasters believe that the ECB aims for an average level of 1.8 per cent inflation, but that they start doubting the ECB's commitment to keeping inflation stable. Then, their point estimate for inflation may not be affected, but the probability they assign to an inflation outcome of 0–2 per cent is bound to drop, reflecting their doubts. Thus, the probability measure of credibility provides valuable information in addition to the level of inflation expectations.[12]

Figure 6.9 shows that ECB credibility has gradually declined during the last decade. The SPF probability of euro-area HICP inflation in the 0–2 per cent range in five years has dropped from a respectable level of over 60 per cent in 1999 to a paltry 42.8 per cent in the third quarter of 2008. This means that based on the collective judgement of SPF respondents, there is a less than even chance of the ECB delivering price stability in the long run. At a two-year horizon, ECB credibility has fallen even further from more than 80 per cent at the start of 1999 to 36.3 per cent in the third quarter of 2008. This shows that according to the professional forecasters polled by the ECB it has become increasingly unlikely for the ECB to achieve price stability in the euro area in the medium to long term.

Similarly, one could construct a more narrow measure of ECB credibility that uses the SPF probability that HICP inflation in the euro area will be between 1.5 per cent and 2 per cent in two to five years' time.[13] This measure is motivated by the clarification in May 2003 that the ECB aims to maintain euro-area HICP inflation below but close to 2 per cent over the medium term (which is further discussed in Section 3.1). Gauged by this narrow measure, ECB credibility has been more stable, but at an average level of 40 per cent and 38 per cent for a two-year and five-year horizon, respectively. Nevertheless, the narrow credibility measures have also declined recently and for a two-year horizon it sunk to an unprecedented low of 24.8 per cent in the third quarter of 2008. So, in the opinion of the SPF forecasters it has become quite unlikely that euro-area inflation will be below but close to 2 per cent in the medium term. In fact, it is more likely to be between 2 per cent and 2.5 per cent, with a two-year ahead SPF probability of 38.5 per cent in the third quarter of 2008. At the same time, the SPF probability of at least 2.5 per cent inflation reached 25.1 per cent two years ahead and 20.2 per cent five years ahead. These results indicate that ECB credibility is at risk.

Not surprisingly, the (broad) SPF measure for ECB credibility is (strongly) negatively correlated with the SPF inflation expectations at the corresponding horizon.[14] But more interesting is whether these survey measures are correlated with market measures of inflation expectations.

Table 6.1 shows (Pearson) correlation coefficients between the SPF measures and breakeven inflation. Since the SPF survey is conducted in the second half of the first month of each quarter, breakeven inflation is computed as the average over the same half-month period using the seasonally adjusted data shown in Figure 6.6. As expected, there is a positive relation between SPF inflation expectations two to five years ahead and long-term breakeven inflation, although this is not statistically significant. The correlations between the SPF probabilities and

Table 6.1: *Correlation between breakeven inflation and SPF measures*

| | Breakeven inflation 5-year forward rate | |
Correlation	10-year spot rate	5 years ahead
SPF inflation expectations		
– two years ahead	0.404	0.348
– five years ahead	0.363	0.330
SPF probability of 0–2 per cent inflation		
– two years ahead	–0.441*	–0.317
– five years ahead	–0.527**	–0.435*
SPF probability of 1.5–2 per cent inflation		
– two years ahead	–0.571**	–0.462*
– five years ahead	–0.547**	–0.591**

Notes: Pearson correlation coefficients. SPF measures are for euro-area HICP inflation. Breakeven inflation is average seasonally adjusted euro-area zero-coupon breakeven inflation in the second half of the first month of the quarter. Asterisks indicate correlation significant at * 10 per cent and ** 5 per cent. Sample: 2004Q2–2008Q2. Source: ECB Statistics and Survey of Professional Forecasters, and author's calculations.

breakeven inflation are negative and mostly significant. The relation is weakest for the SPF probability two years ahead and the five-year forward breakeven inflation rate five years ahead, which is not surprising since their horizons do not overlap. For all four cases, the narrow credibility measure exhibits the strongest correlation with breakeven inflation. Compared to the broad credibility measure this suggests that the SPF probability in the range of 0–1.5 per cent inflation provides little value added. All in all, the results in Table 6.1 indicate that ECB credibility is more important for financial markets than the level of inflation expectations. This is not surprising since the credibility measures also take into account uncertainty about inflation, which affects inflation risk premia.[15]

The decline in ECB credibility raises the question whether it may be due to its disappointing inflation performance in comparison to its own criteria. To investigate this, Table 6.2 shows the correlation between the SPF measures and euro-area HICP inflation. Since the SPF survey is conducted every quarter immediately after the release of HICP inflation for the last month of the previous quarter, the

Table 6.2: *Correlation between SPF measures and past inflation*

	Euro-area HICP inflation	
Correlation	Previous quarter	History
SPF inflation expectations		
– two years ahead	0.735***	0.695***
– five years ahead	0.345**	0.597***
SPF probability of 0–2 per cent inflation		
– two years ahead	−0.779***	−0.776***
– five years ahead	−0.477***	−0.614***
SPF probability of 1.5–2 per cent inflation		
– two years ahead	−0.528***	−0.611***
– five years ahead	−0.185	−0.315*

Notes: Pearson correlation coefficients. SPF measures are for euro-area HICP inflation. Inflation π_q is average year-on-year inflation over the previous quarter. Inflation history satisfies $H_q = \pi_q - 2\ per\ cent + 0.75 H_{q-1}$, where $H_0 = 0$. Asterisks indicate correlation coefficients significant at * 10 per cent, ** 5 per cent and *** 1 per cent. Sample: 1999Q1–2008Q3 for two-year ahead SPF measures, and 1999Q1, 2000Q1 and 2001Q1–2008Q3 for five-year ahead measures.
Source: ECB Survey of Professional Forecasters, Eurostat and author's calculations.

average of year-on-year euro-area HICP inflation over the previous quarter is used. This is positively related with SPF inflation expectations and negatively with all the SPF inflation range probabilities. The level of inflation during the previous quarter is strongly and significantly correlated with the SPF measures for the two-year horizon, but the results for the five-year horizon are noticeably weaker. This suggests that past inflation mostly affects medium- rather than longer-term inflation prospects. However, this presumes that the inflation experience before the previous quarter is immaterial.

To analyse whether the inflation history matters, a measure is constructed that depends on the extent to which past inflation has deviated from the 2 per cent ceiling of the ECB's price stability objective. In particular, inflation history is defined as a geometrically declining weighted average of the inflation differential for past quarters.[16] This means that a deviation from 2 per cent inflation in the past is not completely 'forgotten'. In particular, when inflation has been in excess of 2 per cent, the measure of inflation history will still be positive even if inflation equalled 2 per cent in the previous quarter. Similarly, inflation outcomes below 2 per cent lead to a persistent reduction in the inflation history measure, although the effect diminishes over time as past inflation experiences are gradually discounted. Thus, the measure for euro-area inflation history is inversely related to the 'reputation' that the ECB has built up through its inflation performance over time.

The results in Table 6.2 show the relation between the SPF measures and inflation history for a conservative persistence or 'retention' coefficient of 0.75, which implies that a fraction of only 0.32 and 0.10 of excess inflation is 'remembered' after one and two years, respectively. The two-year ahead SPF measures continue to exhibit a highly significant correlation with inflation history. In addition, both recent inflation and inflation history appear to have a larger effect on two-year than on five-year ahead SPF measures, which helps to explain the greater volatility of the former. Furthermore, compared to inflation in the previous quarter, the five-year ahead SPF measures show a considerably stronger correlation with inflation history. Similar results hold for other plausible values of the retention coefficient. These findings suggests that the memory of past inflation raises long-term inflation expectations and reduces ECB credibility.[17]

The correlation with inflation history is weakest for the narrow credibility measure five years ahead. This suggests that the longer-term credibility of the ECB has not been affected as much by the experience of high inflation in the euro area. However, this conclusion is incorrect because the broad credibility measure has sharply dropped at the same time. In particular, a relatively stable probability of 1.5–2 per cent inflation together with a decline in the probability of 0–2 per cent inflation implies that the mode of the forecast density remains within the 1.5–2 per cent range while the probability mass shifts to the right to inflation levels exceeding 2 per cent.[18] This makes the forecast density more skewed to the right, reflecting a rise in perceived inflation risks. So, when inflation estimates are below but close to 2 per cent, the broad probability measure provides a more robust indication of ECB credibility since it also captures changes in perception about the balance of inflation risks.

Combining the results in Table 6.2 for all the SPF measures suggests that for the medium term, a high inflation history tends to shift the forecast density to the right, thereby raising inflation expectations and reducing the inflation probabilities. But for the long term, high inflation in the past does not tend to affect the mode of the forecast density, although it appears to make the forecast density more skewed to the right, thereby increasing inflation expectations and reducing the 0–2 per cent inflation probability. As a result, high inflation in the euro area appears to have a persistent negative effect on ECB credibility.

This helps to explain the upward trend in two- and five-year ahead SPF inflation expectations (illustrated in Figure 6.7) and the decline in the two- and five-year ahead SPF probabilities of 0–2 per cent inflation (shown in Figure 6.9). Although the ECB has repeatedly stressed the importance of ensuring that medium- and long-term inflation expectations remain firmly anchored in line with price stability, the analysis in this section reveals that during its first decade, ECB credibility has steadily drifted down.

It is useful to compare the performance of the ECB in this respect to another major central bank with an explicit inflation objective, the Bank of England. In contrast to the ECB, the Bank of England has a point target, equal to 2 per cent HICP inflation (since 2004). Interestingly, it has not suffered from a marked increase in medium-term inflation expectations, as measured by its survey of external forecasters.[19] In fact, two-year ahead expectations for HICP inflation in the United Kingdom have remained remarkably stable at between 1.9 per cent and 2.0 per cent since 2004, while they rose from 1.8 per cent to 2.1 per cent in the euro area.

The Bank of England survey of external forecasters also provides inflation probabilities. Since the Bank of England is required to write an open letter to the Chancellor of the Exchequer if HICP inflation deviates more than one percentage point from its target, it is natural to use the two-year ahead probability of HICP inflation between 1 per cent and 3 per cent as a measure of credibility for the Bank of England. This measure has slightly declined from around 90 per cent to 85 per cent since 2004, while ECB credibility two years ahead has dropped from around 65 per cent to nearly 35 per cent.[20] Although both credibility measures span an inflation range of two percentage points, the much lower probability for the ECB reflects the asymmetry in its inflation objective, which aims for a level close to its 2 per cent upper bound for price stability, whereas the Bank of England has a symmetric point target. Nevertheless, the strong decline in the ECB credibility measure together with the increase in euro-area inflation expectations above 2 per cent indicate that unlike the Bank of

England, the ECB has experienced a loss of confidence in its ability to achieve its primary objective over the medium term.

3. ECB transparency

The decline in credibility suggests that the ECB could have benefited from communicating its intentions more effectively by embracing greater transparency, which refers to a reduction in asymmetric information about monetary policy making. The disclosure of monetary policy information has the advantage that it reduces private sector uncertainty and enhances the predictability of monetary policy actions and macroeconomic outcomes (e.g. Swanson 2006; Crowe and Meade 2008). In addition, it directly affects expectations in financial markets and the labour market, which are critical to monetary policy outcomes. In particular, greater transparency makes it easier for economic agents to understand monetary policy and align their expectations with the central bank's intentions, thereby greatly enhancing the effectiveness of monetary policy. Furthermore, transparency allows the private sector to infer the central bank's intentions from monetary policy actions and outcomes, which gives the central bank a powerful incentive to deliver price stability. After all, any attempt to pursue inflationary policy would quickly be detected and penalised by financial markets (through higher long-term nominal interest rates) and by unions (through higher wage demands). Thus, transparency effectively allows the private sector to hold the central bank accountable.[21]

During its first decade, the ECB has accomplished significant transparency improvements. In an international comparison of one hundred central banks by Dincer and Eichengreen (2007) using the transparency index by Eijffinger and Geraats (2006), the ECB even ranks in the top 10. Nevertheless, it still falls short in comparison with the top three central banks, which are the Swedish Riksbank, the Reserve Bank of New Zealand and the Bank of England. The Eijffinger and Geraats (2006) index, which covers the political, economic, procedural, policy and operational aspects of monetary policy making, indicates that the ECB has made most progress in economic transparency, which refers to the economic information that is used for policy decisions, but still performs poorly on procedural transparency, which pertains to the way monetary policy decisions are taken.

Sections 3.1, 3.2 and 3.3 analyse ECB transparency about its monetary policy objectives, macroeconomic forecasts and policy rate decisions, respectively.[22] A more extensive, recent review of ECB transparency is provided by Geraats *et al.* (2008). For an interesting early exchange, see Buiter (1999) and Issing (1999b).

3.1 Policy objectives

The objectives of the ESCB are stipulated by article 105(1) of the Treaty establishing the European Community, as amended by the 1992 'Maastricht' Treaty on European Union. The primary objective is to maintain price stability, which the ECB has defined as 'a year-on-year increase in the Harmonized Index of Consumer Prices (HICP) for the euro area of below 2 per cent' together with the clarification that 'price stability is to be maintained over the medium term' (ECB 1998b). In addition, article 105(1) of the Treaty specifies that 'without prejudice to the objective of price stability, the ESCB shall support the general economic policies in the Community with a view to contributing to the achievement of the objectives of the Community as laid down in Article 2.' These include 'a harmonious and balanced development of economic activities, sustainable and non-inflationary growth respecting the environment, a high degree of convergence of economic performance, a high level of employment and of social protection, the raising of the standard of living and quality of life, and economic and social cohesion and solidarity among Member States.'

In the pursuit of its objectives, the ECB enjoys a high degree of independence, which is also enshrined in the Treaty (in particular article 107). In fact, the ECB is one of the most independent central banks in the world.[23] So, it is protected from political pressures in the pursuit of its primary objective of price stability.

The ECB deserves to be commended for clarifying some of the woolly words of the Treaty. Nevertheless, the specification of the ECB's objectives remains rather opaque. First of all, its quantitative objective of price stability implies a range of 0–2 per cent for euro-area HICP inflation, without indicating any preferred or focal point. For instance, the ECB may be pretty much indifferent between inflation outcomes within the range, or perhaps aim for the midpoint of 1 per cent. However, using the quantitative reference value for monetary growth (ECB 1998a) that is part of the ECB's monetary policy strategy (see Section 3.3), it is possible to narrow down the inflation range to 1–2 per cent.[24]

Furthermore, the ECB's preference for the upper part of the 0–2 per cent range was made explicit in May 2003 when it formally announced that 'in the pursuit of price stability it will aim to maintain inflation rates close to 2 per cent over the medium term' (ECB 2003a). What this entails was suggested by ECB chief economist Otmar Issing: 'This "close to 2 per cent" is not a change, it is a clarification of what we have done so far, what we have achieved – namely inflation expectations remaining in a narrow range of between roughly 1.7 per cent and 1.9 per cent – and what we intend to do in our forward-looking monetary policy.'[25] However, these intentions have not been realised – long-term euro-area inflation expectations as measured by the ECB SPF have mostly drifted above 1.9 per cent since 2004 (as shown in Figure 6.7). Moreover, medium-term SPF inflation expectations have been well above 1.9 per cent since the second quarter of 2007, reaching as high as 2.04 per cent in the second quarter of 2008. In the same quarter, the SPF probability of 1.5–1.9 per cent inflation in two years fell to an all-time low of 28.5 per cent. So, using Issing's criterion of inflation expectations around 1.7 per cent to 1.9 per cent, the ECB has failed to maintain price stability over the medium term.

A second respect in which the ECB's objectives are ambiguous is the relevant horizon of the 'medium term'. This horizon determines how quickly the ECB aims to bring inflation back to below but close to 2 per cent after an unanticipated shock. In economics, the medium term often refers to a period of between two to five years. It is only recently that ECB President Trichet clarified that 'medium term' means eighteen months to two years.[26] So, the two-year ahead SPF measures are the most appropriate for evaluating whether inflation expectations remain firmly anchored at levels consistent with price stability for the medium term. However, these expectations have trended upward during the last decade and recently breached the 2 per cent ceiling.

Furthermore, two-year ahead SPF inflation expectations have been quite volatile (see Figure 6.7) and two-year ahead SPF measures are significantly correlated with recent inflation (see Table 6.2), which is in contrast to the five-year horizon. This suggests that the professional forecasters in the SPF panel do not believe that the ECB can or will stabilise inflation in two years. The reason could be that monetary policy transmission lags prevent the ECB from completely offsetting shocks over this horizon, or that the ECB actually prefers to accommodate shocks to some extent. In either case, the ECB has not been effective in stabilising inflation expectations over Trichet's medium term.

A third respect in which the ECB's objectives are opaque is the nature of its secondary goals according to article 105(1) of the Treaty. Supporting the general economic policies of the European Union to contribute to its economic objectives could legitimise a role for economic growth considerations. However, President Trichet has repeatedly responded to questions about this at the ECB press conferences that the Governing Council has only 'one needle in its compass' when setting interest rates for the euro area, and that is price stability.[27] Prospects for economic growth only matter to the extent that they are relevant for price stability.[28] In addition, the ECB argues that it contributes to economic growth and job creation by (being credible in) maintaining price stability in the medium and long run.

In any case, the role of secondary objectives is intrinsically related to the horizon of the primary objective. There is only scope for tending to other goals if the price stability horizon is longer than the monetary policy transmission lag, which is not the case for Trichet's notion of the medium term.

Notwithstanding the focus on its primary objective, the ECB has recently shown a deep concern for the smooth functioning of money markets. Its swift liquidity interventions during the summer and fall of 2007 prevented money markets from seizing up. However, the ECB has emphasised that such liquidity operations are conducted to preserve the proper functioning of money markets, which is important for the effective implementation of monetary policy, and they do not influence the determination of the monetary policy stance, which is solely based on the objective of price stability.[29] The E(S)CB Statutes (article 12) also clearly separate these two tasks: the ECB Governing Council is responsible for formulating monetary policy, the Executive Board for implementing it. So, the Governing Council decides the refi rate and the Executive Board directs liquidity operations to ensure this interest rate prevails in money markets. As a result, liquidity interventions are conducted to support the ECB's primary objective.

To conclude, the ECB's primary objective is to maintain euro-area HICP inflation below but close to 2 per cent over the medium term. Using Issing's criterion and Trichet's medium term, this entails maintaining inflation expectations between 1.7 per cent to 1.9 per cent for a horizon of 1.5 to 2 years ahead. However, two-year ahead inflation expectations have been far from stable and have even moved above 2 per cent. Although five-year ahead inflation expectations have been less volatile, they have also drifted up and have stayed above 1.9 per cent for over two years. So, medium- and long-term inflation expectations suggest that the ECB's aim for inflation is actually very close to 2 per cent and that its horizon exceeds two years. This suggests that the ECB would benefit from clarifying its price stability objective by providing a firmer anchor for inflation expectations than the fuzzy 'below but close to 2 per cent' and by specifying a horizon that is more realistic. This would also yield more specific performance criteria for the evaluation of monetary policy and thereby improve ECB accountability.

3.2 Macroeconomic forecasts

The formulation of ECB monetary policy relies on an extensive amount of economic information, which is communicated in the ECB's Monthly Bulletin. This voluminous document is published one week after the monthly monetary policy meeting and provides a detailed description of macroeconomic and financial developments. In addition, it includes informative boxes and articles on interesting topics, and once a quarter, the E(S)CB macroeconomic projections. Potential risks to financial stability in the euro area are elaborately examined in the Financial Stability Review, which the ECB has published twice a year since December 2004.

Since changes in the policy rate have their main impact on inflation in about two years, macroeconomic forecasts are crucial for the determination of the monetary policy stance. The ECB started to publish macroeconomic projections for the euro area in December 2000, at the urging of the Committee on Economic and Monetary Affairs of the European Parliament.[30] The projections, which are based on a euro area-wide macroeconometric model (Fagan *et al.* 2001), were initially issued semi-annually and constructed in a collaborative effort by Eurosystem staff. Updated projections produced by ECB staff have been released in the intervening quarters since September 2004, so that the ECB now provides quarterly projections by E(S)CB staff in March, June, September and December. This means that a new E(S)CB forecast is available for every quarterly release of national accounts data, which enhances transparency. In addition, the E(S)CB staff projections have gained greater prominence since June 2004, when the ECB started to publish them on the day of the monetary policy meeting and discuss them in the Introductory Statement of the press conference.

The quarterly staff projections are available for euro-area HICP inflation and real GDP growth, including its main expenditure components, for the current and next (two) calendar years (in December). The projections for each calendar year are presented as a range that equals twice the average absolute value of past forecast errors, but they provide no indication of the central tendency, its quarterly dynamics, anticipated changes in uncertainty or the balance of risks surrounding the projections. These are significant shortcomings, especially because uncertainty and asymmetry are important features of macroeconomic probability estimates by professional forecasters (García and Manzanares 2007b). The ECB would benefit from following the practice first introduced by the Bank of England to present forecasts in 'fan charts' for at least two years ahead, showing the dynamics and (possibly asymmetric) risks throughout the medium term.[31]

Initially, the E(S)CB projections were based on the technical assumption that short-term interest rates, measured by three-month Euribor, remain constant over the projection horizon, while the projected path for long-term interest rates, measured by euro-area ten-year nominal government bond yields, is in line with market expectations extracted from the yield curve. But this leads to an internal inconsistency in the projections since financial markets seldom anticipate short-term rates to stay the same for so long. This problem has been overcome in the staff projections since June 2006 by assuming that the path of short-term interest rates is in line with forward rates derived from the yield curve. Oil and non-energy commodity prices are also assumed to develop in line with market expectations (derived from futures prices), while bilateral exchange rates, which are notoriously hard to predict, are assumed to remain constant over the projection horizon. Finally, fiscal policy assumptions are based on national budget plans in the euro area.

Besides these key assumptions, which are explicit stated, the macroeconomic projections also incorporate the professional judgement of E(S)CB staff, but this does not necessarily correspond to the views of the Governing Council. In fact, the ECB has consistently emphasised that the Governing Council does not underwrite the staff projections.[32] But to understand the policy rate decisions, it is important to know the macroeconomic outlook of the Governing Council. Since December 2005, the discussion of the staff projections in the Introductory Statement has included an explicit statement of the Governing Council's views on the 'balance of risks' to the projections or outlook. However, it is hard to interpret this balance of risks since the staff projections are only presented as a range without a central tendency. This could be remedied by publishing fan charts of macroeconomic projections endorsed by the Governing Council, similar to the established practice at the Bank of England.

In addition, the E(S)CB projections are based on market expectations for interest rates that may not be in line with the policy intentions of the Governing Council.[33] This means that the macroeconomic projections are not unconditional forecasts and the Governing Council may expect to achieve different outcomes for inflation and output growth based on its intended policy. So, transparency could be further improved by releasing macroeconomic forecasts by the Governing Council that are based on its projected policy path, just like the Swedish Riksbank.

Although the quarterly E(S)CB staff projections are not endorsed by the Governing Council, it pays 'great attention' to them and considers them an 'important input'.[34] Their role in the policy making process has been summarised as follows by ECB President Trichet: 'We take these Eurosystem staff projections as an important information, we consider it, then we make our own judgement and we take our decision.'[35]

However, as pointed out by Geraats *et al.* (2008), it can be hard to understand the policy decisions based on the staff projections, even when combined with the Governing Council's balance of risk. For instance, the ECB staff projections for euro-area HICP inflation that were released on 31 August 2006 were 2.3–2.5 per cent for 2006 and 1.9–2.9 per cent for 2007. The midpoints of these inflation projections were unprecedentedly high and well above the 2 per cent ceiling deemed consistent with price stability. In addition, the Governing Council considered the risks to this inflation outlook to be on the upside. This suggested an urgent need for a policy tightening beyond market expectations, which showed an increase in average three-month Euribor from 3.1 per cent in 2006 to 3.9 per cent in 2007. Nevertheless, the Governing Council decided to maintain the refi rate at 3 per cent for another month.[36] This is puzzling, especially since it had raised the refi rate to 2.75 per cent in June 2006 when staff projections for inflation and output based on the same average Euribor path were slightly lower. Clearly, it would be useful to have better information about the

Governing Council's medium-term macroeconomic outlook to better understand its monetary policy decisions.

Medium-term macroeconomic projections are useful since they are informative about shocks that are anticipated by the ECB and reflected in its monetary policy actions. Thus, they help the private sector to infer the ECB's intentions from its interest rate decisions.[37] But short-term macroeconomic forecasts are also valuable, because they provide information about unforeseen sudden shocks that affect monetary policy outcomes. So, an explanation of unanticipated short-term fluctuations could help the private sector to better infer the ECB's policy intentions from euro-area inflation outcomes. Using the terminology of Geraats (2002), these two different roles of medium- and short-term macroeconomic forecasts refer to economic and operational transparency, respectively. Empirical evidence suggests that the publication of forecasts is indeed beneficial as it helps to reduce inflation and lower the sacrifice ratio (Chortareas *et al.* 2002, 2003). In addition, greater transparency tends to make private sector inflation expectations less sensitive to past inflation outcomes (van der Cruijsen and Demertzis 2007).

The experience of summer 2006 mentioned above makes clear that the ECB could use some improvement in economic transparency, in particular by communicating the judgement of the Governing Council to the extent that this is not reflected in the staff projections but relevant for its monetary policy decisions. Furthermore, the analysis in Section 2 has shown that medium- and longer-term inflation expectations and 0–2 per cent inflation probabilities are strongly correlated with past inflation outcomes. This suggests that the ECB would benefit from enhancing operational transparency to help prevent the private sector from mistaking unforeseen inflation shocks for shifts in policy intentions.

Operational transparency could be enhanced by the explanation of revisions to macroeconomic projections, the discussion of past forecast errors and a regular evaluation of monetary policy. The Swedish Riksbank provides a leading example.[38] It routinely explains revisions to its macroeconomic projections, discussing all relevant and even counteracting factors. In addition, it evaluates the performance of its forecasts every year. Furthermore, it performs an annual monetary policy assessment that carefully accounts for any deviations of macroeconomic outcomes from its objectives and rigorously identifies the main driving forces behind them. Such thorough reviews could help the ECB to mitigate the effect of high inflation on its credibility.

3.3 Interest rate decisions

The way in which the ECB uses its economic information to reach its policy objectives is in principle described by its monetary policy strategy. The ECB decided to adopt a two-pillar strategy (ECB 1998b) that is characterised by (i) a prominent role for money that centres on a quantitative reference value for monetary growth, and (ii) a broadly based assessment of the outlook for price developments and the risks to price stability in the euro area. This hybrid of monetary and inflation targeting lead to confusion. First, monetary aggregates are notoriously noisy, so it is hard to gauge whether the monetary pillar, which uses only a point target for money (M3) growth, actually signals a risk to price stability. Second, in case of conflicting signals, the strategy failed to specify which pillar prevails. The latter problem has been partly overcome by the clarification that 'the monetary analysis mainly serves as a means of cross-checking, from a medium to long-term perspective, the short to medium-term indications coming from economic analysis' (ECB 2003a). Nevertheless, the two-pillar strategy leaves the ECB with a wide degree of discretion and is inadequate to fully understand its monetary policy decisions. So, it is essential to provide sufficient information to allow the private sector to learn the ECB's monetary policy reaction over time.

In this respect, the minutes of monetary policy meetings are an invaluable source, since they detail policy makers' assessments of the current macroeconomic situation and outlook, and their discussion of the policy options. However, the ECB has not published the minutes of the Governing Council's monetary policy meetings.[39] In principle, the ECB could make up for this by resorting to other communication tools, such as the Monthly Bulletin and the Introductory Statement at the ECB press conference following the monthly monetary policy meeting.[40]

Although the Monthly Bulletin presents the economic information used by the Governing Council, it does not reveal the Governing Council's interpretation of it (with the exception of the editorial, which is essentially the same as the Introductory Statement). In fact, the Introductory Statement provides the only formal account that sheds some light on the considerations of the Governing Council, mainly in the form of a brief discussion of risks to (the outlook for) price stability and economic growth, summarised as a 'balance of risks'. But the Introductory Statement, which under the first ECB President was sometimes jokingly dubbed 'Duisenberg minutes', contains no information about (the diversity of opinions during) the actual policy deliberations. Journalists sometimes manage to extract precious nuggets from an often evasive President Trichet during the question and answer session of the ECB press conference, for instance which policy options were considered and whether the policy decision was unanimous.[41] Financial markets react significantly to such answers involving the Governing Council's policy rate discussions (Ehrmann and Fratzscher 2007b).

Nevertheless, the information about the monetary policy deliberations that is provided by the ECB Introductory Statement and press conference pales in comparison to the minutes of the US Federal Reserve, the Bank of England and the Swedish Riksbank. Instead of identifying the key variables that the monetary policy makers considered decisive for the interest rate decision, and documenting the reservations of any dissenters, the ECB resorts to its mantra that the Governing Council is monitoring all developments very closely and made its decision by consensus. This deprives the private sector of a priceless opportunity to better understand the ECB's monetary policy reaction, which is important for ECB credibility and predictability over the medium term.

The ECB's opacity extends to its decision procedure. Although article 10(2) of the E(S)CB Statutes requires that the Governing Council decides about monetary policy 'by a simple majority of the members having a voting right', the Governing Council does not vote about its interest rate decisions.[42] Instead, its monetary policy actions are decided 'by consensus'. Although consensus need not mean unanimity, it suggests the absence of strong disagreements. However, evidence from other central banks shows that disagreements about monetary policy decisions are actually very common. In particular, Geraats *et al.* (2008) analysed eight central banks that publish their voting patterns and found that the rate of unanimity about monetary policy actions ranges from 85 per cent to only 42 per cent, with a median of 60 per cent. So, if the ECB Governing Council only decides to adjust the refi rate if there is no (strong) disagreement, it is likely to be much more inertial than a central bank acting by a simple majority. Perhaps this helps to explain why the ECB left the refi rate at 2 per cent for over two years (from June

2003 to December 2005) before it started removing this highly accommodative policy stance; or why the Governing Council did not decide to raise the refi rate at the end of August 2006 despite unprecedentedly high E(S)CB inflation projections.[43]

Another reason for publishing the voting patterns of the Governing Council is that they help to improve the public's understanding of monetary policy. In particular, the direction of dissents against a particular decision provides information about the policy inclination or bias. In addition, the number of dissents indicates the likelihood of a policy move in that direction. Furthermore, it provides an indication of the ambiguity of the macroeconomic signals (presuming all members share the same objectives), which allows the public to exploit the degree of unanimity to more efficiently learn the monetary policy reaction. As a result, the publication of voting patterns enhances both short- and medium-term predictability of monetary policy. Empirical evidence has confirmed that the publication of voting records makes monetary policy more predictable (Gerlach-Kristen 2004).

The desirability of the publication of the ECB's voting patterns does not extend to individual voting records. Although knowing the identity of the voters, especially of dissenters, is likely to be useful for predicting monetary policy actions as well as enabling individual accountability, it could negatively affect voting behaviour in the Governing Council because it could subject national central bank governors to greater political pressures from their governments.[44] Considering the continued sensitivity of national sentiments in the eurozone, it is therefore prudent to only publish the voting patterns (or 'balance of votes') of the Governing Council but to refrain from releasing individual voting records.

Once the Governing Council has made its decision about the policy rate, it is promptly communicated and briefly explained in the Introductory Statement. But this does not provide a complete description of the policy stance. The reason is that the policy rate is adjusted in discrete steps of typically 25 basis points, so the policy decision (say, to maintain a rate of 4 per cent) may differ from the desired policy rate (e.g. 4.1 per cent). Clearly, it would be useful to convey this information, for example through a policy 'tilt', 'bias' or 'inclination' that provides a qualitative indication of the policy stance relative to the policy decision.[45]

Although a policy inclination could be used to convey the current policy stance, it may be desirable to provide guidance over a longer horizon. For instance, Geraats *et al.* (2008) find that financial markets failed to foresee the steady removal of the prolonged accommodative policy stance, even after the first rate hike in December 2005. They argue that monetary policy would have been less expansionary if financial markets had anticipated the ECB's path of rate rises, which would have contributed to lower inflation.

In general, the publication of a projected interest rate path provides an important tool for central banks to influence market expectations and thereby enhance the effectiveness of monetary policy. In fact, the effect of a change in the policy rate depends critically on how prolonged it is (anticipated to be). As a result, for a forward-looking central bank, the projected policy path is an integral part of the monetary policy stance. Of course, this projection is subject to considerable uncertainty and would therefore most suitably be presented in the form of a fan chart, as is done by Norges Bank and the Swedish Riksbank. Both central banks also use scenarios to explain how monetary policy would be affected by specific circumstances (e.g. high oil prices or wage growth). This makes it much easier for the private sector to understand monetary policy reactions. In addition, it illustrates the conditionality of the interest rate projections and underscores that the interest rate path is not a commitment but is adjusted in response to macroeconomic circumstances. Using short-term interest rates (e.g. three-month Euribor) instead of the policy rate would also help to prevent the interest rate path from being perceived as a commitment.

The interest rate path could also be used for the macroeconomic projections, so that they actually reflect the outcomes anticipated by the policy makers. But macroeconomic forecasts based on the interest rate path (and therefore the optimal policy path itself) require assumptions about how financial markets will react when the interest rate path differs from their expectations. This issue does not arise when market expectations are used for interest rates since they are already consistent with other asset prices. But for an interest rate path, the projections need to incorporate the financial market reactions to deviations from market expectations, to ensure internal consistency. Since such financial market reactions tend to be highly uncertain, they add additional noise to the forecast when compared to projections based on market interest rates.

This suggests that it may not always be worthwhile to publish (forecasts based on) a projected interest rate path. In fact, if the signal provided by the interest rate path is noisy compared to private signals of agents, publication of the path could even be detrimental as markets rely on it to coordinate their actions, thereby inducing greater economic volatility (Morris and Shin 2002). In addition, the focus of markets on the projected interest rate path would reduce the informativeness of market signals (Morris and Shin 2005). Nevertheless, whenever market expectations differ significantly from policy intentions, the central bank could greatly benefit from publishing the projected interest rate path to facilitate the alignment of expectations and increase the effectiveness of monetary policy. Moreover, focusing on the policy path helps to avoid a potential pitfall of the ECB's forward-looking monetary policy strategy, which is discussed in the next section, and may explain the difficulty the ECB has experienced in achieving price stability.

4. Discussion

As shown in Section 1, euro-area inflation has been above 2 per cent for most of the ECB's first decade. One reasonable explanation for this is that sudden surges of adverse shocks disturbed the monetary policy transmission process and led to outcomes different from the ECB's intentions. In addition, greater volatility of commodity, energy and food prices and, more recently, turbulence in financial markets, could have led to more inflation uncertainty and thereby explain the decline in the credibility measures shown in Section 2.2. In particular, the anticipation of a prolonged period of larger transmission disturbances would lead to a drop in the SPF inflation probabilities for two and five years ahead.

This underscores the importance of a careful interpretation of the measure for credibility (like any other statistic). To be precise, the credibility measure equals the probability, according to the collective judgement of the SPF respondents, that the outcome for euro-area HICP inflation is consistent with the ECB's objective of price stability. This means that it captures not only the willingness (commitment) and skill (competence) of the ECB, but also luck (good fortune) in the form of facing no sudden shocks to the monetary policy transmission process. As a result, it would be inappropriate to interpret the credibility measure as an indication of the ECB's commitment to price stability. Instead, it captures the ECB's ability to achieve price stability in the euro area, which relies on its commitment, competence as well as good fortune.

The ECB has only limited control over inflation. It sets the refi rate and conducts open market operations to try to ensure that this rate prevails in money markets. The resulting short-term interest rates have their effect on longer-term interest rates through market expectations. These longer-term interest rates affect aggregate demand and thereby inflation, which is also determined by the expectations of price and wage setters. Although private sector expectations could be influenced by ECB communication policy to bring them in line with its intentions, there are often many shocks completely beyond the ECB's control that disturb the transmission of its monetary policy.

So, perhaps (part of) the drop in the credibility measures is due to transmission uncertainty. But it is harder to explain the persistent decline during the last decade in this way. In addition, it is difficult to invoke transmission uncertainty to account for the upward trend in medium-term inflation expectations shown in Section 2.1. Furthermore, there is no reason why the level of long-term inflation expectations would be affected by any transmission disturbances. So, the relentless rise in five-year ahead inflation expectations in the euro area is an unmistakable indication of the erosion of ECB credibility.

The high average level of euro-area inflation during the last decade and the increase in medium- to long-term inflation expectations give rise to the question whether there may be some structural weaknesses in the ECB's monetary policy framework. As Section 3 has shown, the ECB suffers from some significant transparency deficiencies. Providing greater clarity about its objectives, macroeconomic forecasts and, especially, its decision making, would help the private sector to better understand ECB monetary policy, which is likely to bolster its credibility.

It could be argued that the ECB has no need for greater transparency because financial markets have largely been able to predict its next policy decision. However, this is undoubtedly attributable to the ECB's traffic-light system of code-word communication, which signals an imminent rate change by including 'strong vigilance' in the Introductory Statement (see Geraats *et al.* (2008, box 6)). So, financial markets have managed to predict the ECB's next policy move without really understanding its monetary policy making. But by delaying policy decisions to avoid market surprises, it becomes harder for the public to understand the ECB's monetary policy reaction. As a result, the ECB's focus on short-term predictability could actually undermine its transparency and thereby its predictability (and credibility) in the medium and long run.

However, there is also a major vulnerability in the ECB's forward-looking monetary policy strategy. The ECB aims to maintain price

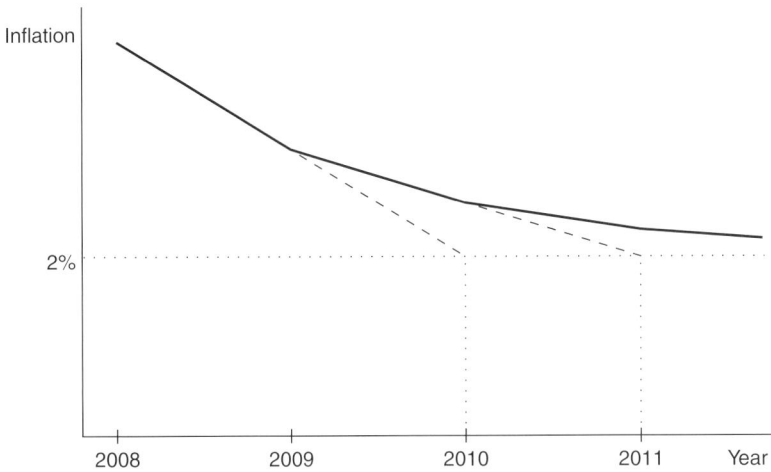

Figure 6.10: Time-inconsistency of medium-term-oriented strategy
Note: Intended inflation path (dashed line) and actual inflation path (solid line) when monetary policy is set each year to achieve price stability (2 per cent) in the medium term (two years ahead).

stability over the medium term, which amounts to achieving (slightly below) 2 per cent inflation in about two years (using Trichet's definition). So, if there is an adverse shock in 2008 that drives two-year ahead inflation projections to say 3 per cent, then the ECB decides to raise the refi rate to bring inflation back to (slightly below) 2 per cent in 2010. But when the ECB reviews the refi rate in 2009 and has a fresh look at the forecasts, it finds that (presuming no further shocks) there is leeway to loosen monetary policy to achieve price stability over the medium term, so it reduces the refi rate (relative to the policy path that was optimal in 2008) to reach (slightly below) 2 per cent in 2011. Clearly, the ECB's medium-term-oriented monetary policy strategy is prone to time-inconsistency.[46] The problem is that the 'medium term' is a moving horizon, that is always two years ahead and never actually reached.

The effect of time-inconsistency, which is illustrated in Figure 6.10, is that the ECB's primary objective of price stability is achieved too slowly. As a result, once inflation is above the 2 per cent ceiling for price stability, it is likely to take longer than two years before it is brought back to 2 per cent, which makes it rational for two-year ahead inflation expectations to exceed 2 per cent (as happened in 2008). Another symptom of time-inconsistency is that inflation expectations two years ahead are likely to depend significantly on recent inflation, while the effect on inflation expectations five years ahead is much smaller, which is consistent with the findings in Table 6.2.

The time-inconsistency problem of the medium-term-oriented strategy can be prevented by focusing on the policy path and only updating it in response to new information.[47] Furthermore, by publishing the projected interest rate path and carefully explaining whenever it is revised, the ECB could persuade the private sector that it is not succumbing to time-inconsistency. In this way, the ECB would be better able to anchor medium-term inflation expectations and secure price stability.

5. Conclusions

Despite all the challenges of managing monetary policy in a continent-wide currency area with a new single currency, the euro-area economy has performed remarkably well during its first decade: on average, inflation has been low while economic growth has remained robust. Although the ECB's performance has definitely been better than the fears expressed by its fiercest critics, it has also fallen short of the high hopes cherished by some of its strongest supporters. Moreover, with respect to its primary objective of price stability, the ECB has failed to meet the high standard it set itself, namely euro-area HICP inflation below but close to 2 per cent over the medium term.

Although the higher level of inflation may be attributed to unantici-pated adverse circumstances, the analysis in this chapter points to some structural shortcomings. First of all, there has been an upward trend in euro-area inflation expectations for the medium and long term. Two-year ahead inflation expectations have even breached the 2 per cent ceiling for price stability. So, medium- and long-run inflation expecta-tions are far from solidly anchored.

Furthermore, the credibility of the ECB achieving price stability in the medium term has gradually eroded to critically low levels. The prob-ability that professional forecasters (polled by the ECB) attach to euro-area inflation within 0–2 per cent in two to five years has steadily declined to less than 50 per cent. This means that they consider it more likely than not that the ECB will fail to achieve price stability in the medium term.

Another worrisome sign is that medium- and long-term inflation expectations and forecast probabilities for 0–2 per cent inflation are significantly correlated with the inflation history of the euro area. So, high levels of euro-area inflation are not forgotten but have a persistent negative effect on ECB credibility. This suggests that the ECB's credibility problems could aggravate due to the high levels of inflation in 2008.

However, this chapter argues that the loss of ECB credibility could be overcome by embracing greater transparency. In particular, it is recommended to further clarify the ECB's objectives, since the fuzzy 'below but close to 2 per cent' provides a flimsy anchor. In addition, the ECB would benefit from presenting more detailed macroeconomic projections and shedding more light on its policy deliberations by releasing minutes and voting patterns, so that the public is able to better understand monetary policy actions and outcomes. It is also pointed out that by always diligently aiming for inflation below but close to 2 per cent two years ahead, the ECB is prone to suffering from time-inconsistency that prevents it from achieving price stability over the medium term. This potential pitfall of its medium-term-oriented monetary policy strategy can be prevented by focusing on the projected policy path and only updating it in response to new information.

In a speech on the experience with the European Monetary Union so far, ECB President Trichet declared:[48]

As a result, over the past ten years, the inflation rate in the euro area has remained on average in a tight vicinity of 2 per cent, although it has occasionally risen above levels that the ECB considers consistent with conditions of price stability. It is remarkable that even amidst such adverse and potentially unsettling disturbances, financial markets and the public at large have not lost faith that, in line with our strategy, we would reaffirm price stability over the medium term.

However, this chapter shows that euro-area inflation has been close, but mostly above 2 per cent. In addition, the high levels of inflation have had a negative impact on ECB credibility, and inflation expectations and probabilities from surveys indicate that the private sector no longer believes that the ECB will achieve price stability in the medium term. So, the experience of the ECB's first decade has not been as favourable as suggested by President Trichet.

For the ECB to succeed in its next decade, it should exert greater efforts to explain its monetary policy actions and outcomes so that the public is able to verify that they are consistent with the ECB's stated objectives. Thus, a higher degree of ECB transparency can overcome the problem of its low credibility.

Notes

1. These averages are based on 1999–2007 annual data from Eurostat using the contemporaneous composition of the euro area (i.e. ranging from eleven countries in 1999 to thirteen in 2007).
2. Formally, the per cent increase in HICP per annum is calculated as $\pi_t = (HICP_t/HICP_{t-1} - 1) \ast 100$ per cent, where $HICP_t \equiv \sqrt{HICP_{12,t}HICP_{1,t+1}}$ and $HICP_{m,t}$ denotes the HICP index in month m of year t. In contrast, the inflation measure based on annual data equals $\bar{\pi}_t = (\overline{HICP_t}/\overline{HICP_{t-1}} - 1) \ast 100$ per cent, where $\overline{HICP_t}$ denotes the average HICP index for year t. Thus, $\bar{\pi}_t$ is effectively an average of year-on-year inflation during year t, which is distorted by price developments in year $t-1$ (so-called 'base' effects).
3. Some of the material in this section has been drawn from Geraats *et al.* (2008).
4. This has been repeatedly stressed in the Introductory Statement of the monthly ECB press conference since October 2005.
5. In addition, euro-area inflation-indexed bonds have an indexation lag of three months, so breakeven inflation also captures inflation realised in the past quarter. Another issue is that the bonds are linked to euro-area HICP excluding tobacco. As a result, the inflation-indexed bonds do not completely compensate for euro-area HICP inflation.
6. The estimation of a seasonally adjusted term structure of zero coupon breakeven inflation is described by Ejsing *et al.* (2007).
7. For a detailed description and evaluation of the ECB SPF, see García (2003) and Bowles *et al.* (2007). Note that in 1999 and 2000 the SPF only asked about the five-year horizon in the first quarter.
8. See *ECB Monthly Bulletin*, August 2008, Box 5.
9. Note that one outlying observation for two-year ahead inflation has been excluded in 2003Q2, which significantly reduces the standard deviation from 0.5 to 0.3, but has little effect on the mean.
10. Note that these measures are related. To be precise, the variance of the aggregate forecast distribution (aggregate uncertainty) equals the average

variance of the individual forecast distributions (average individual uncertainty) plus the variance of the individual point estimates (forecast dispersion).

11. To be precise, the credibility measure captures the range of [0 per cent, 1.95 per cent) as it adds the probability mass for the ranges 0.0–0.4 per cent, 0.5–0.9 per cent, 1.0–1.4 per cent and 1.5–1.9 per cent from the aggregate SPF probability distributions available at www.ecb.int/stats/prices/indic/forecast/html/index.en.html.

12. The interpretation of the credibility measure is further discussed in Section 4.

13. To be precise, this measure captures the range of [1.45 per cent, 1.95 per cent) as it equals the probability mass for the 1.5–1.9 per cent range of the aggregate SPF probability distribution.

14. To be precise, the correlation between SPF inflation expectations and ECB credibility at a two-year and five-year horizon is –0.96 and –0.88 for the broad measure, and –0.48 and –0.44 for the narrow measure.

15. In fact, a measure of 'inflation risk' could be constructed by taking the SPF probability that inflation is at least 2 per cent. This measure of inflation risk is the (near) complement of the broad credibility measure (in case of some deflation risk).

16. To be precise, the inflation history for quarter q is defined as $H_q \equiv \sum_{i=0}^{q-1} \rho^i (\pi_{q-i} - 2)$ for $q = 1, 2, \ldots$, where π_q is average year-on-year inflation (in per cent) in quarter $q-1$ (which is not observed until quarter q), $q = 1$ corresponds to 1999Q1, and ρ is the persistence coefficient ($0 < \rho < 1$). Note that $H_q = \rho H_{q-1} + \pi_q - 2$, where $H_0 = 0$. For $\rho = 0$, H_q would yield the same correlations as π_q in the first column of Table 6.2.

17. It would be interesting to investigate this further and perform more formal econometric analysis, but the small sample (with only thirty-one continuous observations for the five-year ahead SPF measures) makes it hard to get reliable regression results.

18. This presumes that the probability of inflation below 0 per cent (i.e. deflation) remains negligibly small, which is a reasonable assumption for the medium to long term, especially when inflation has been high.

19. This quarterly survey of approximately twenty external forecasters is reported in the Bank of England *Inflation Report*.

20. Regarding longer horizons, the Bank of England survey of external forecasters only has three-year ahead expectations and probabilities since 2006, but these show a similar pattern as those for two years ahead.

21. For a further explanation of the effects of transparency, see for instance Geraats (2002, 2006).

22. In terms of the five aspects distinguished by Geraats (2002), Section 3.1 pertains to political transparency, 3.2 to economic and operational transparency and 3.3 to procedural and policy transparency. This structure is more natural in light of the ECB's main communication instruments.

23. Arnone *et al.* (2007) find that the ECB has the highest degree of (political and economic) central bank autonomy, together with Latvia, in a sample of 163 central banks.

24. The ECB set a reference value for M3 growth $(\hat{M})$ of 4.5 per cent based on the assumption of a medium-term trend growth of real GDP $(\hat{Y})$ and of M3 income velocity $(\hat{V})$ in the range of 2 per cent to 2.5 per cent and –1 per cent to –0.5 per cent, respectively. Thus, the quantity equation $(\hat{M} + \hat{V} = \pi + \hat{Y})$ implies a range for inflation (π) of 1–2 per cent.

25. Statement in response to a question at the press seminar on the evaluation of the ECB's monetary policy strategy, 8 May 2003.

26. See the question and answer session of the hearing at the Economic and Monetary Affairs Committee of the European Parliament in Brussels on 26 March 2008, and of the ECB press conference on 5 June 2008.

27. See for instance the question and answer session of the ECB press conference on 3 June 2004, 6 September 2007 and 6 December 2007.

28. This suggests that the ECB comes close to being a strict inflation targeter (or 'inflation nutter'), whose monetary policy objective function only depends on inflation stabilization.

29. ECB President Trichet in the introductory speech at the hearing at the Economic and Monetary Affairs Committee of the European Parliament in Brussels on 26 March 2008.

30. See European Parliament Resolutions A5-0035/1999 and A5-0169/2000.

31. In the Introductory Statement of the ECB press conference on 5 June 2008, it was even pointed out that the latest projections of annual growth rates misleadingly mask quarterly dynamics.

32. This has been repeatedly mentioned in the ECB press conferences at which the staff projections are discussed.

33. This has been regularly stressed in the Introductory Statements that discuss the projections.

34. See for instance the answers by President Trichet at the ECB press conference of 31 August 2006, 8 February 2007 and 8 March 2007.

35. See the question and answer session of the ECB press conference of 7 December 2006.

36. Similarly, in June 2008 the staff projections for inflation were 3.2–3.6 per cent for 2008 and 1.8–3.0 per cent for 2009, based on an average three-month Euribor of 4.9 per cent in 2008 and 4.3 per cent in 2009, with

upside risks to the inflation outlook according to the Governing Council, yet it decided to keep the refi rate at 4 per cent.

37. See Geraats (2005) for a formal analysis.

38. See the Riksbank's *Monetary Policy Report* and its annual review entitled *Material for Assessing Monetary Policy*.

39. Note that article 10(4) of the E(S)CB Statutes states that: 'The proceedings of the meetings shall be confidential. The Governing Council may decide to make the outcome of its deliberations public.' But the latter leaves the ECB sufficient flexibility to release (unattributed, non-verbatim) minutes.

40. Ehrmann and Fratzscher (2007a) argue that the different communication strategies of the ECB, Bank of England and US Federal Reserve are similarly effective based on short-term predictability and financial market responses.

41. For instance, see the ECB press conference of 6 December 2007.

42. During the question and answer session of the ECB press conference of 10 January 2008, President Trichet declared: 'As you know, we do not vote and have never voted in the past.'

43. It is plausible that the inertia caused by consensus decision making is stronger for rate hikes, which would lead to an inflationary bias.

44. This argument is formalised by Gersbach and Hahn (2005).

45. The voting patterns could reveal a policy bias, but they will fail to correctly signal the policy inclination if the distribution of desired policy rates across policy makers is quite narrow (e.g. 4.0–4.1 per cent) or skewed (e.g. all 4.1 per cent, except for one outlier of 3.8 per cent).

46. This issue was first discussed by Leitemo (2003), who analysed it for inflation-forecast targeting with constant-interest projections.

47. See Bjørnland *et al.* (2004, chapter 3) for a further discussion.

48. ECB President Trichet in the speech 'Toward the First Decade of Economic and Monetary Union: Experiences and Perspectives', Vienna, 28 April 2008.

7 | Some observations on the ECB's monetary policy

MANFRED J. M. NEUMANN

1. Introduction

The European Central Bank (ECB) was founded in 1998 and started to run monetary policy for the euro area at the turn of the year 1998–9. During the ten years since, the Bank has established itself as the leading central bank besides the Federal Reserve System. The main achievement is to be seen in the successful establishment of the euro as an accepted stable currency that makes headway in the world's financial markets. This is certainly the result of an all in all successful conduct of monetary policy but foremost it is the result of the remarkable independent status of the ECB and the national member banks of the Eurosystem. The first two presidents of the ECB, Willem F. Duisenberg and Jean-Claude Trichet, have made prudent use of this independence from politics by reminding European governments repeatedly of the limits that are set by the European Treaty.

In this chapter I will take a critical look at the ECB's monetary policy performance. I begin by examining the developments of inflation and real growth in the euro area and by taking a comparative look at other economies (Section 2). The policy strategy chosen by the ECB in 1998 and its revision in 2003 are examined in Section 3. A major question is whether the revision reflected a fundamental change of policy behavior or just a change in the communication of policy. This is investigated in Section 4, first by estimating Taylor equations and then by studying the introductory statements to press conferences by the ECB president. A major conclusion is that the Governing Council has returned to taking the monetary analysis seriously if indeed it had ever stopped doing so. In Section 5 a closer look is taken at the ECB's published projections of inflation and real growth. Concluding remarks follow in Section 6.

230

2. Output and inflation: how has the ECB fared in comparison?

Monetary policy is able to control the evolution of the price level over the medium to long term and to impact on aggregate economic activity in the short to medium term. A successful monetary policy is one that achieves anchoring the rate of inflation at a desired low level and stabilizing the economy.

A straightforward test of the relative success of the ECB's monetary policy is examining the developments of prices and gross domestic product in the euro area and comparing them with those of other major economies. In Table 7.1 I focus on GDP growth and CPI inflation and add the overnight money rate as an indicator of monetary policy. The overnight money rate can be understood to represent the supply price of base, or central bank, money as it is perfectly controllable by the central bank. The economies selected for comparison here include the United States and three countries whose central banks

Table 7.1: *Comparative economic performance, mean (standard deviation)*

	Euro area	Canada	Sweden	United Kingdom	United States
GDP growth					
2000–3	2.3 (1.63)	2.9 (1.56)	2.4 (1.61)	2.7 (0.77)	2.1 (1.34)
2004–7	2.5 (0.49)	2.8 (0.59)	3.5 (1.06)	2.7 (0.65)	2.9 (0.66)
2000–7	2.4 (1.18)	2.9 (1.16)	2.9 (1.44)	2.7 (0.70)	2.5 (1.11)
Overnight money rate					
2000–3	3.53 (0.92)	3.76 (1.34)	3.84 (0.44)	4.58 (1.05)	3.23 (2.15)
2004–7	2.71 (0.77)	3.32 (0.93)	2.29 (0.29)	4.86 (0.61)	3.64 (1.58)
2000–7	3.12 (0.94)	3.54 (1.17)	3.55 (0.74)	4.72 (0.86)	3.43 (1.89)
CPI inflation					
2000–3	2.2 (0.27)	2.6 (0.90)	1.8 (0.75)	RPIX 2.3 (0.76)	2.5 (0.81)
2004–7	2.2 (0.30)	2.1 (0.44)	1.1 (0.85)	HICP 2.0 (0.50)	3.0 (0.70)
2000–7	2.2 (0.29)	2.3 (0.75)	1.5 (0.88)		2.8 (0.80)

Sources: Eurostat; IFS Statistics.

Note: GDP and inflation data are quarterly, overnight money data are monthly. In the UK, the inflation targeting was based on the retail price index RPIX until the end of 2003, on the harmonized index of consumer prices since then.

apply the strategy of inflation targeting (Canada, Sweden, and the United Kingdom) since the 1990s. The table presents data for the period 2000–7 as well as two subperiods of equal length 2000–3 and 2004–7. The first year of the ECB's regime, i.e. 1999, is not taken into consideration on the grounds that it hardly had a chance to affect the 1999 level of inflation in the euro area given that the transmission lag of monetary policy is generally assumed to be a year at least. The measures provided in the table are period averages and standard deviations.

As a first observation from Table 7.1 I note that the volatility of GDP growth, as measured by the standard deviation, has been much lower in all five economies considered during the more recent period 2004–7. The observation reflects the general fact that cyclicality has become less pronounced over recent years in industrial countries. The decline in output volatility has been the strongest in the euro area, in Canada, and in the United States where the volatility measures have more than halved. A question is whether this change to more stable output growth can be attributed at least in part to progress made by the respective central banks as regards the design and implementation of monetary policy. As a second and fitting observation in this respect I note from Table 7.1 that all central banks have reduced the volatility of their main policy instrument, the overnight money rate. Policy behavior has become more stable everywhere. This very fact permits me to conclude that in all likelihood the central banks indeed have effectively contributed to moderating the cyclicality of their economies.[1]

As a third observation I note that in none of the five economies considered has the average level of GDP growth been significantly lower in the more recent period compared to earlier. In three of them, namely in the euro area, the United States, and Sweden, growth has even come out higher in the second subperiod. This again supports the conclusion that monetary policies have become more stabilizing during the more recent years 2004–7.

How have the five central banks fared with respect to their mandate of maintaining price stability? Given that it is common to equate price stability with a state of low and stable inflation, the following conclusions can be drawn: first, as regards the average level of inflation the Bank of Sweden has delivered the lowest result with a record low of 1.5 percent for the total period 2000–7 and of only 1.1 percent for the more recent subperiod. But note that the Swedish inflation target is 2 percent.

The ECB and the Bank of Canada, in contrast, have not secured an inflation level below 2 percent, but they have almost matched their medium-term inflation objective, the magic two, from above with 2.2 and 2.3 percent, respectively, on average over the total period. Similarly, the Bank of England came close to the retail-price inflation target of 2.5 percent during the early period 2000–3 and has matched its revised (harmonized price index) target of 2 percent thereafter. Not unexpectedly, the Fed was last in the competition with an average rate of 2.8 percent for the total period.

A final aspect to consider is the degree of inflation volatility. Low volatility of inflation is a value in itself because – as Milton Friedman (1977) once put it in his Nobel lecture – the signals about relative prices are "jammed by the noise coming from the inflation broadcast." It is noteworthy in this respect that the inflation-targeting central banks have apparently not been overly cautious as regards inflation volatility but permitted the rate to wander in a tolerance range of about plus/minus one percentage point around target. As a matter of fact, such tolerance ranges belong to the defining characteristics of inflation targeting.

The ECB, for contrast, appears to have been more diligent. Suppose one did not know which of the five central banks was following the strategy of inflation targeting. In that case one would be entitled to conclude that it must have been the ECB given that this central bank has managed to hold the volatility of inflation to a minimum, way below what the other central banks have achieved. Of course, the ECB's record would also suggest that the Bank apparently equates price stability with an HICP rate of inflation of 2.2 percent, a message that the ECB would hardly want to endorse. I will come back to this in Section 3 below.

Summing up, the evidence permits the conclusion that the ECB has presented an impressive start. The Bank has been able to stabilize the inflation in the euro area at a low level and this way has been able to collect the credibility of a central bank that takes the mandate of maintaining price stability seriously. It is to be acknowledged that of the four central banks considered for comparison, one, the Swedish central bank, has provided a much lower rate of inflation, 1.5 percent on average over the period 2000–7. However, it is not clear whether this was not by accident given that the respective inflation target was 2 percent.

3. The ECB's monetary policy strategy

The strategy or concept of the ECB for the internal formulation of
monetary policy and its communication to the outside was negotiated
within the Governing Council during the second half of 1998. Two
years before he was appointed Chief Economist of the ECB, Otmar
Issing (1996) had put forward a cautious plea for choosing an intermediate target strategy which he considered "a self-commitment vis-à-
vis the general public" and his conjecture was that should a regime of
intermediate targeting be agreed upon, it would scarcely be possible to
avoid the adoption of a variant of monetary targeting. However, neither
a variant of Bundesbank-style policy making nor of British inflation
targeting was appealing to a majority in the Governing Council. It will
probably take another two decades until the 1998 files of the Governing
Council's deliberations will be accessible in order to learn who proposed what at the time and how the final compromise concept was
achieved.

In this next section I will recall the main bones of the ECB's strategy as
it was laid down in 1998, and review the restructuring of the strategy
in 2002–3. A guiding question is why the restructuring may have
happened.

3.1 *The strategy of 1999–2002*

Based on a press release, President Willem Duisenberg presented in a
press conference on 13 October 1998 the three main "elements" of the
ECB's new monetary policy strategy – the quantitative definition of
price stability, a prominent role for money, and a broadly based assessment of the outlook for future price developments.

The decision to provide an official quantitative definition of the
objective of price stability was a very intelligent answer to the question
of what could be done to gain as quickly as possible the trust of the
inhabitants of the euro area that the newly established central bank
would provide stable money. Offering a precise, easy to grasp, and easy
to monitor target could be understood as a longing for a high reputation
based on solid control.

However, the definition given – "Price stability shall be defined as a
year-on-year increase … of below 2 percent" – was not without problems. First, a case can be made that monetary policy should avoid

validating inflation but not try fighting one-off shifts in the price level, resulting from tax increases or shocks in world markets to the relative prices of raw materials (von Hagen and Neumann, 1996). In this respect, a fixed numerical target may be prejudicial. Second, the ECB's definition set an upper limit but appeared to avoid a floor. In fact, that was not the case because it was out of the question to assume that the ECB would equate deflation with price stability.[2] Nevertheless, the lack of a lower bound as part of the definition was an unnecessary drawback.

The second element of the strategy was assigning "a prominent role" to money. When at the press conference on October 13, 1998 an inventive journalist asked Duisenberg whether the "... dual pillars of the strategy, the monetary element and the inflation forecast," would carry equal weight, Duisenberg answered: "... it is not a coincidence that I have used the words that money will play a prominent role. So if you call it the two pillars, one pillar is thicker than the other is, or stronger than the other, but how much I couldn't tell you." This little event shows how quick Duisenberg was in grasping the colorful expression "pillar" and also that it was clear, at least to him, that the monetary pillar was chosen to be the stronger one. It fits that the monetary analysis was ranked before the economic analysis.

"To signal the prominent role" of money, a reference value for the growth rate of the broadly defined money stock M3, was announced and set at 4.5 percent. It was supposed to serve as a yardstick of that level of M3 growth that was considered to be consistent with the aim of maintaining price stability over the medium term. The reference value was another feature that helped the ECB to quickly gain credibility, if only in Germany and Austria. But note that Duisenberg made it clear from the outset that the reference value was not a monetary target: "... the concept of a reference value does not imply a commitment ... to mechanistically correct deviations of monetary growth ... over the short term" (ECB 1998b).

As regards the third element of the strategy, the "broadly based assessment of the outlook for price developments," later called economic pillar or economic analysis, not much was said initially, except that "all information available" or "a wide range of indicators" would be analyzed "regarding the prospects for, and the risks to, price stability" and that it would be useful to "evaluate the full range of inflation forecasts" (ECB 1998b).

While it was easy to understand that the information collected under both pillars was complementary, the ECB avoided explaining how the two separate types of analysis would be brought together. Issing (2000) admitted this – "it is hard to find a satisfactory way to integrate money into traditional macro-economic analysis" – and considered the two-pillar strategy a matter of openness and honesty. But this did not help the outsider. The question remained what would the ECB do if the information about inflation risks that flowed from the two pillars pointed in opposite directions.

3.2 *The strategy since 2003*

In May 2003 the Governing Council declared that it had reviewed the monetary policy strategy. The following changes were introduced:

First, the price stability definition was changed from a year-on-year increase "of below 2 percent" to "of below but close to 2 percent." Second, the annual review of the reference value for money growth was ended. Third, the introductory statement of the President was restructured, to start with economic analysis instead of monetary analysis.

The announced change of the "definition" of price stability implied for all practical purposes a readjustment upwards of the inflation rate aimed at, from 1.5 to 2 percent. While the old inflation objective of 1.5 percent was never confirmed by the ECB, it was an open secret. Given that the reference value of money had been set by the ECB at 4.5 percent, while the trend growth rate for GDP was assumed to lie in the range of 2 to 2.5 percent and the trend rate of decline in the velocity of circulation of M3 in the range of 0.5 to 1 percent, the arithmetic of the quantity equation of money did not allow any other inflation number than 1.5 percent. But note that in a special seminar for the press both Issing and Papademos said on May 8, 2003 that an inflation rate close to 2 percent was what they always had had in mind and actually had pursued.[3] If this was so, then it follows that the reference value for money growth had been set too low from the beginning of European Monetary Union (EMU). In any case, the official upward revision of the inflation objective was defended by pointing to the remote possibility of a deflation. These days the ECB calls its definition of price stability a "sufficient hedge against the risks of both very low inflation and deflation."

The decision to put the reference value into the asides by ending the rule of reviewing it annually signifies the reasoning that was behind the restructuring of the strategy. A rising number of governors felt that they were hindered by the prominent role given to money growth to lower more sharply interest rates in support of the weak economy. And Lucas Papademos (2003), the Vice President of the ECB, gave them a voice when speaking in March 2003 at a symposium of the Banque de France about "Economic Cycles and Monetary Policy." Papademos recommended for the ECB a strategy of "constrained discretion" that Governor Bernanke (2003) had praised a few weeks before as "the best operating framework for monetary policy."[4] In fact, the strategy contained nothing new but the well-known idea that a central bank that has established credibility can trade on it in support of the real economy. The advertisement of "constrained discretion" just served to justify another large cut of the ECB's interest rates.

It is to be acknowledged that the criticism of the "prominent role for money" was also nourished by the non-obvious link between observed money growth and headline inflation and by the puzzling practice of letting the Governing Council confirm year after year that the reference value did not need to be adjusted in the light of new information.[5] This practice contrasted starkly with the great efforts that had been reported in 1998/9 as regards determining empirically by studies of money demand the chosen value of 4.5 percent. In this respect, it almost read like a joke when the ECB in 2003 rationalized the abandonment of the annual reviewing by stating that this was decided to "underscore the longer-term nature of the reference value for money growth as a benchmark for the assessment of monetary developments …" In any case, the Governing Council has achieved the fact that the reference value has become forgotten.

Finally, it is worth mentioning that the restructuring of the President's introduction has brought a great and lasting improvement to the exposition. Indeed, it makes a much better reading of the analysis to start with an evaluation of the recent developments of the economy and a short-term inflation outlook and thereafter to shift to the supplementary analysis of money, financial markets, and long-term expectations as regards the inflation trend.

4. The change of concept – a change in policy behavior?

In this section we will investigate whether the change in the ECB's concept has induced the Bank in recent years to run a policy quite different from the pattern used during the first four years of EMU. To this end we estimate variants of a forward-looking Taylor equation in Section 4.1. Normative aspects aside, the Taylor equation provides a flexible form for describing monetary policy behavior. The estimates will be used to check by means of simulations whether the ECB's interest rate policy was systematically changed after 2002. Since this appears to have been the case, we will discuss in Section 4.2 the standard statements made by the Governing Council on the justification of policy action and inaction during the period 2003–5. Finally, we will briefly discuss whether there is evidence that the council may have returned to taking monetary analysis seriously.

4.1 Evidence from Taylor estimates

The Taylor equation starts from the assumption that the central bank desires to set its short-term interest rate in equilibrium equal to the equilibrium real rate of interest plus the target rate of inflation, both denoted by a star, but will outside equilibrium respond in a stabilizing fashion to deviations of inflation from target and to temporary output gaps. We assume that the ECB is forward looking, hence bases its interest rate decision in period t on expectations about the rate of inflation in period t+m and of the output gap in t+n. We assume that m > n because the Bank will wish to consider that the transmission of policy action to consumer prices takes longer than to output, hence the gap. This gives

$$i_t^* = (r^* + \pi^*) + \alpha_\pi (E_t \pi_{t+m} - \pi^*) + \alpha_{gap} E_t gap_{t+n} \tag{1}$$

It is well known that the ECB, like other central banks, does some interest rate smoothing. Modelling this as a partial adjustment process with smoothing parameter ρ

$$i_t = [i_t^*](1 - \rho) + \rho i_{t-1} + \varepsilon_t \tag{2}$$

and using (1) yields the full-blown Taylor equation

$$i_t = [\alpha_\pi (E_t \pi_{t+m} - \pi^*) + \alpha_{gap} E_t gap_{t+n} + (r^* + \pi^*)] (1 - \rho) + \rho i_{t-1} + \varepsilon_t \tag{3}$$

For monetary policy to be stabilizing, the parameters α_π and α_{gap} should be positive; moreover the parameter α_π should exceed 1.

Equation (3) will be estimated. It is to be noted, however, that Taylor estimates for the ECB covering the past nine years are likely to lack stability and will hardly provide reliable estimates of the ECB's response to undesired movements of the inflation rate. For example, Gortler *et al.* (2007), using the sample 1997–2006, come up with estimates of the ECB's reaction to inflation between –0.4 and +1.7.[6] The reason for this variety of parameter values is to be seen in the remarkably high degree of inflation persistence or inflation stickiness in the euro area. Clarida *et al.* (2000) had already pointed to the need for sufficient variation in the inflation rate relative to the sample mean to receive reliable estimates. Since mid-2003 the monthly deviations of inflation from the ECB's target rate have not exceeded 0.15 percentage points on average, one third of what they had been during the years 1999–2002. Similarly, the volatility of the monthly deviations as measured by the standard deviation has almost halved, from 0.56 to 0.32. This makes it difficult to receive a reliable estimate of the parameter multiplying expected inflation.

To avoid this problem, we chose the research strategy of estimating variants of (3) for monthly data from the early sample period 1999–2002. The results of those will then be used to compute dynamic simulations of the interest rate for the period 2003–7. Thus the idea is to check which path the interest rate would have followed if the ECB had not changed its strategy and to compare the simulated to the historical path.

The data used for the following estimates are monthly data. The rate of inflation is the year-over-year HICP rate of inflation; the gap is measured as the difference between the log-level of industrial production excluding construction and the respective Hodrick-Prescott trend expressed in percentage points. The interest rate is the annualized overnight rate EONIA.

Table 7.2 presents four forward-looking Taylor regressions. As regards the gap we assume that the ECB sets in period t the interest rate with regard to the gap expected for period t+1. While it is true that as a rule the ECB, like any other central bank, does not have precise knowledge even about the current gap of period t, it would not make much sense to assume that the ECB responds to a state that cannot be affected any more. As regards the rate of inflation, in contrast, we assume with Sauer and Sturm (2007) that the ECB responds to the inflation level expected for period t+3. While the assumption that the Bank looks three months ahead instead of, say, six is an arbitrary one, it serves to underline the fact that the time-horizon chosen as regards the rate of inflation should be longer than the one chosen as regards the

Table 7.2: *Forward-looking Taylor estimates, January 1999 – December 2002*

$$i_t = [\alpha_\pi(E_t \pi_{t+3} - \pi^*) + \alpha_{gap} E_t gap_{t+1} + \alpha_0](1 - \rho) + \rho i_{t-1} + \varepsilon_t$$

| | OLS estimates employing estimated expectations of the inflation rate and the gap | | GMM estimates | |
	(1)	(2)	(3)	(4)
α_π	1.04 (4.36)	0.45 (0.83)	0.85 (16.53)	1.01 (9.09)
α_{gap}	0.40 (5.61)	0.69 (4.11)	0.36 (22.75)	0.45 (17.88)
α_0	2.91 (20.60)	3.24 (3.69)	3.02 (10.10)	2.98 (14.66)
ρ		0.81 (14.39)		0.75 (45.37)
R^2 adj.	0.74	0.96	0.61	0.96
DW	0.92	1.89	0.56	2.11
Q_3	0.00	0.93	0.00	0.39
Q_6	0.00	0.27	0.00	0.21
Wald: $\alpha_\pi = 1$	0.87	0.23	0.01	0.93

Note: t-values in brackets. OLS regressions (1) and (2) employ the Newey-West estimator; similarly the GMM regressions (3) and (4) use the Newey-West bandwidth (3). Q_3 and Q_6 provide the p-values of the Ljung-Box Qstatistics at lags 3 and 6. Wald gives the p-value for accepting the restriction.

gap.[7] To try in estimation a longer time-horizon would be of interest but is not done here because of the relative shortness of the sample period.

The regressions (1) and (2) in Table 7.2 are OLS estimates that employ explicit estimates of the rate of inflation expected for period t+3 and of the gap expected for period t+1. The underlying inflation estimate uses lag 4 of the rate of inflation, lag 5 of the growth rate of money stock M3 and lags 5 to 7 of the gap. Thus the rate of inflation to be expected in period t for period t+3 can be computed from the information provided by lag 1 of the inflation rate, lag 2 of the money growth rate and lags 2 to 5 of the gap. The estimated gap regression employs the gap's own lags 3 and 4 as well as lags 3 and 4 of the rate of inflation. This implies that lags 2 and 3 of both variables serve to compute the gap expected to prevail in period t+1. For both variables constructed the lag distribution was determined using the Schwartz criterion. Regressions (3) and (4) in Table 7.2 are the results of direct GMM estimates. We require orthogonality between the parameters and a larger set of instrumental variables. The set chosen includes, apart from a constant, six lags for each of the following variables: rate of inflation, industrial production gap, growth of money stock M3, and overnight rate.

The estimates may appear not to look so different at first glance. For example, regressions (1) and (3), where interest rate smoothing is ignored, suggest roughly the same reaction to a change in the expected gap, with a parameter estimate α_{gap} of 0.36 to 0.40. Also, the estimates of the constant α_0, representing the sum of the equilibrium real rate of interest and the target rate of inflation, are rather close with 2.9 to 3.0. However, the estimated responses to inflation are significantly different. The Wald test indicates that the estimate of 1.04 for α_π in regression (1) is not significantly different from 1 while the competing estimate of 0.85 in regression (3) is significantly below 1. The latter estimate would imply that the ECB's interest rate policy had been destabilizing. This is unlikely.

In regressions (2) and (4) interest rate smoothing is added. We now find that the parameter α_π is positive though not significant in regression (2). The technical reason for this econometric result is that the expectations variable employed to model $E_t \pi_{t+3}$ turns out to be equally strongly correlated to the current interest rate as well as its first lag with a correlation coefficient of 0.75. This high multicollinearity precludes identifying the separate contributions of the two r.h.s. variables. The GMM regression (4), in contrast, provides a parameter estimate of 1.01 which is not significantly different from 1 as is indicated by the high p-value of the Wald test. The result implies that the ECB's interest rate policy was neither stabilizing nor destabilizing.[8]

We use regressions (2) and (4) to compute dynamic simulations of the ECB's overnight rate for the period 2003–7 under the counterfactual assumption of unchanged policy behavior. Figure 7.1 shows the alternative paths. We note first that the simulated path based on GMM estimate (4) runs below the path suggested by the OLS estimate (2) and that the largest discrepancy between the two series is to be observed for the period mid-2006 to mid-2007. The latter observation reflects the characteristic that the GMM estimate of the interest rate is dominated by the actual rate of inflation which fell temporarily below the "target rate" of 2 percent during 2006/7. The OLS model, in contrast, employs an estimate of the future inflation rate that is dominated by lagged money growth and, therefore, provides a simulation that is much less affected by the actual course of headline inflation.[9]

As a second result we find that both simulated paths of the interest rate approach the historic path towards the end – the OLS-based

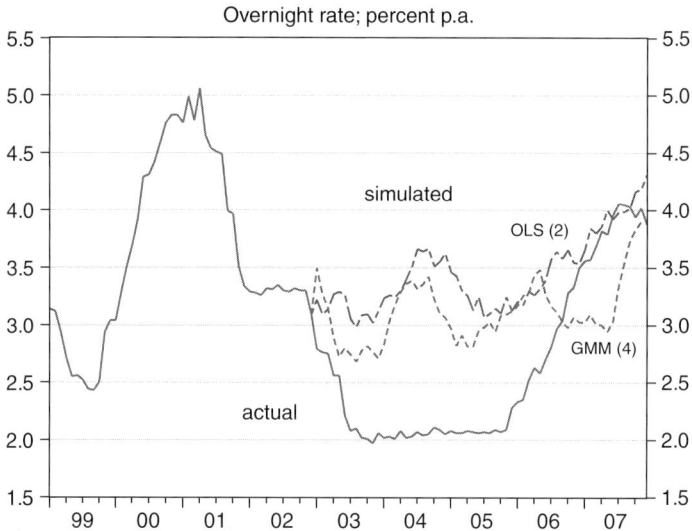

Figure 7.1: ECB's interest rate policy
Source: ECB and author's calculations.

simulation meets it already by late-2006, the GMM-based simulation a year later. This suggests that the ECB has finally returned to the less expansionary policy making of the early years.

The most important result of the simulation exercise is that the two paths simulated both lie way above the actual historic path of the ECB's overnight rate during 2003–5. If we focus on the subperiod of the lowest interest rate level – 2003 (July) to 2005 (November) – we find that the EONIA was kept during this period at 2.06 percent p.a. on average. The simulations, in contrast, signal that the policy rate would have been set much higher if the Governing Council had not changed its policy behavior. The GMM simulation suggests a level of 3.02 percent, and the OLS simulation even of 3.24 percent.

4.2 The Governing Council's explanation of action and inaction 2003–5

The ECB started into the year 2003 with a main refinancing rate of 2.75 percent at a time when the Fed fund rate had already been lowered to 1.25 percent. Half a year later the Fed had brought its rate down to the floor of 1 percent and the ECB had reached its floor of 2 percent. Both central banks kept their record lows for quite some time, the Fed for a year until mid-2004, the ECB for two and a half years, i.e. until the end of 2005.

Why did the ECB hold its interest rate at such a historically unique low level for so long? Was there a gradual shift in the preferences of the Governing Council away from the mandate of maintaining price stability toward the secondary objective of contributing to the stabilization of the economy? There is no easy answer to this question. In search for evidence one might examine the annual reports and monthly bulletins of the ECB and/or read the speeches of all the Council members. But how is one to aggregate this probably diverse information?

There are several studies that focus on transforming qualitative information about monetary policy intentions into quantitative indicators that can be used in regression analysis. For example, Gerlach (2004) read the long Editorials in the ECB's monthly bulletins in order to construct variables that were supposed to measure the perceived degree of the risk to price stability stemming from observed developments in economic activity, inflation, and money growth. Similarly, Berger *et al.* (2006) exploited their detailed reading to again construct indicators of policy intentions. Rosa and Verga (2005), in contrast, were interested in studying by this way the impact of the information provided by the ECB on market expectations, and Heinemann and Ullrich (2007) even tried to develop a scale reflecting the hawkishness of the rhetorics.

In what follows I will not try to construct subjective indicators of specific policy intentions. Instead I wish to study whether a subtle shift in the Council's preferences away from the aim of maintaining price stability was to be observed during the years 2003–5. To this end I chose a simple approach of checking the Council's opinion by reading just the opening passage of the President's introductory statements to the press conferences after the monthly meetings of the Governing Council.[10] The advantage of using those texts is threefold: first, these statements condense the essence as they are kept short; second, they are the most reliable mirrors of Council opinion as they are drafted immediately after each session; third, they can be considered an authoritative aggregation of the Council members' preferences because any member can intervene if he or she feels the text was misleading.

In the Appendix I provide an account of the main statements that were offered in the opening passage of the introductory statement to explain or rationalize the policy actions of the Governing Council or, more accurately, its inaction over the period July 2003 to December 2005. What reasoning was offered with respect to the state of the economy and the prospects of price development?

First, as regards its preferences for supporting the economy, the messages of the Governing Council were straightforward. By November 2003 the council reported "signs of a gradual economic recovery" and by December "economic recovery has started." Thereafter the Council sent each month the message that "low interest rates are supporting the economic recovery" or a variant of this. Starting March 2005 the message was subtly changed to "interest rates ... are making an important contribution to the economic recovery" or "... considerable support to economic activity."

Second, as regards the ECB's mandate of maintaining price stability the information offered was less simple because the medium-term perspective was often supplemented by information about an adverse short-term outlook.

As regards the medium-term perspective of inflation the standard message during the period July 2003 through to June 2004 was that the outlook for price stability over the medium term was "favorable." Subtle changes followed in July "the outlook still remains ..." and in September and October "the overall outlook remains ..." In November 2004 the Council switched to the more alarming statement "upside risks to price stability over the medium term" and repeated it month after month through April 2005. In addition, the apparently loved term "vigilant" that had been used since June 2004 in a gradually more dramatizing fashion over time – "we will remain vigilant," "strong vigilance is warranted," "continued vigilance is of the essence" – was connected with a perceived inflation risk to read "continued vigilance with regard to upside risks to price stability is warranted" (May 2005). This statement was repeated in June and again in September, October, and November. But it was not before December that the Council took action, raising the ECB's interest rates by 25 basis points.

In contrast to the medium-term perspective the short-term inflation outlook was rarely mentioned in the opening passage of the President's introductory statement. But in December 2003 for the first time it was said "While inflation rates are likely to fluctuate around 2%, a gradual and limited decline should take place later." Only half a year later the Council showed more concern, pointing in June 2004 to "stronger inflationary pressures over the short-term" and in July to "somewhat stronger inflationary pressure." By November 2004 it was admitted that "inflation is likely to remain significantly above 2%." But note that the statement of November was quickly discarded a month later by concluding "no significant evidence that stronger underlying domestic inflationary pressures are building up." This pacifying statement was then repeated each month until mid-2005 and again in September 2005.

Summing up, the review of the messages sent by the Governing Council in the opening statements leads me to draw the following conclusion:

There can be no doubt that the Governing Council decided to hold interest rates down in the interest of promoting stronger economic growth in the euro area during the period 2003–5. To convince the public that monetary policy was kept on the right track, it was necessary to assure that price stability over the medium term was not endangered and that any undesired rise of headline inflation was just a temporary phenomenon. The Governing Council has clearly followed this rationale.

The reported statements about the economy reflect the Council's concern about the recovery lacking strength during 2004 and a grain of proud satisfaction about the results during 2005. In the course of 2004 the Council apparently began to worry about the implications of its expansionary policy for price stability. It admitted that inflation had moved above the critical level of 2 percent since spring of 2004 but it did not want to raise the ECB's interest rates even a little. Consequently the Council played the observation down, time and again, by claiming that significant evidence of a build-up of inflationary pressure was missing. The rise of asset prices was ignored.

This was a very risky strategy because the longer it was played down, the higher became the risk that agents' inflation expectations might no longer remain anchored but suddenly rise and spill over into wages. The Council was clearly aware of that danger and therefore went to great pains to defend its passiveness. It took defensive recourse to perpetual reassurances that it was ready to act should that become necessary if not unavoidable. All the emphasis that was put on formulations about central bankers' vigilance, which Council members have become so used to, is a telling indication of the Council's fear of losing its grip on inflation expectations.

Finally, note that the Governing Council's turnaround from inaction to action in December 2005 happened in a somewhat hasty fashion, apparently mainly in response to a spurt in headline inflation. After its meeting of September the public was still lulled by being told "the monetary policy stance remains appropriate, given the current outlook for inflation rates over the medium term" and "although upside risks to price stability exist, we continue to see no significant evidence of a build-up in underlying inflation pressures." This was continued after the Council's meeting of October 6 with "the monetary policy stance still remains appropriate" and "strong vigilance with regard to upside risks to price stability is warranted" and an exact repetition of these two sentences after the meeting of November 3. It is tempting to speculate that the co-existence of both messages reflected a split in the Council. From hindsight the jump in the rate of inflation from 2.2 to 2.6 percent in September and the still high rate in October (2.5 percent) are likely to have been decisive for gaining a majority in favor of ending the long period of inaction.

4.3 Does money matter to the Council?

Svensson (2003) and Svensson and Woodford (2005) applauded the rearrangement of the pillars that the ECB had decided on in 2003, on the grounds that it appeared to imply that the monetary analysis was finally being placed on the sidelines. As Woodford (2006) holds, the monetary pillar was very useful during the first years of the ECB as it made it easier for it to gain credibility as a sign of "the new institution's fidelity to principles stressed earlier by the Bundesbank, which had in turn played a critical role as the anchor of the previous European Monetary System." But the monetary pillar was not needed otherwise, because in Woodford's view, any refinement of the ECB's policy is likely to require deeper study of the role of inflation expectations in shaping wage and price setting instead of studying money demand and supply.

The question whether the majority in the Governing Council, which had enforced the change of concept, was of the same belief that money did not matter, has been investigated. Gerlach (2004) finds, from estimating probit models for the sample period 1999 to mid-2004, that money growth probably mattered for interest rate decisions but the result might reflect the relations that existed before the change of concept. Berger *et al.* (2006), studying indicators constructed for the period 1999–2004, conclude that the ECB's decision was barely influenced by money-based policy intentions and in any case only during the early years of the sample period. Apart from the fact that those studies do not reach beyond 2004 they employ subjective indicator variables that are debatable.

Recalling the evidence derived above from the Taylor estimates and from the review of the major policy statements after sessions of the Governing Council during the period mid-2003 through to end of 2005, I can draw the conclusion that during this period the Governing Council indeed disregarded the monetary analysis in the sense that it did not believe that the rising growth of money and credit, notably of the money stock M3, was of much relevance with respect to interest rate decisions.

But from hindsight this was not the end of the story. Figure 7.2 brings together the number of standardized lines that are devoted in the President's introductory statement to a summary of the monetary pillar and the growth rate of money stock M3. It is no surprise that the number of lines written about monetary analysis has fluctuated over time. Until the end of 2005 about ten to eleven lines were written on average. Since then the number of lines has soared, in parallel with money growth, although steeper to about thirty to thirty-five lines.

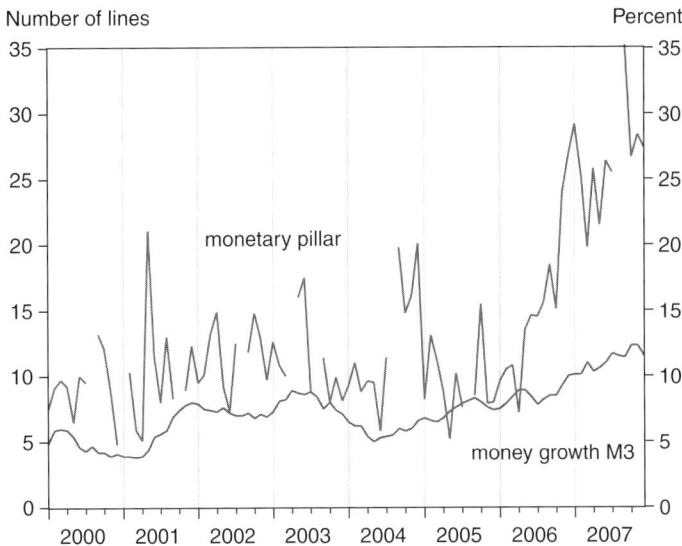

Figure 7.2: Monetary pillar and money growth
Source: ECB and author's calculations.

This is telling of a new twist in the Governing Council's reasoning about the risks to price stability.

But there is more evidence still that money matters to the Governing Council. Since late 2005 the opening passage of the President's introductory statement to the press conferences have contained words that have a money interpretation. For example, in the first time in years *ample liquidity* was acknowledged in the opening passage in October, followed by the conclusion of a *very accommodative stance of monetary policy* in November, and the verdict in December that served to explain the decision to raise the ECB interest rates read: "*taking into account the risks to price stability that we have identified in our economic analysis, cross-checked by our monetary analysis, our policy remains accommodative.*"

Since then the President has become used to declaring after each Council session that the ECB's monetary policy stance remains accommodative and, moreover, starting in July 2006 the new formula was added that *a progressive withdrawal of monetary accommodation is warranted.*

5. The staff economic projections

Monetary policy cannot do without projections or forecasts of a host of economic variables, among which real growth and inflation figure prominently. At the start of EMU the ECB was hardly in a position to produce macroeconomic forecasts on its own. There were forecasts available from public institutions like the OECD and the IMF, or private institutions such as Consensus. Nevertheless, the ECB started an expectations survey for selected macroeconomic variables, the Survey of Professional Forecasters (SPF) in 1999. While all available forecast, were used internally, the ECB was careful not to put emphasis on any of them in public for fear of being identified with any particular inflation forecast.

When asked by a journalist why the ECB did not want to put forward an inflation forecast with a time horizon of two years, President Duisenberg emphasized that the ECB would use forecasts but not publish them "because of the danger that they would become self-fulfilling prophecies."[11] It is open to doubt that Duisenberg believed what he said because if he did he might have considered adopting the practice of the Bank of England of publishing a fan chart that always shows inflation returning to the desired target rate within two years' time.

It took two years until the end of 2000 when the ECB felt ready to publish its internal "projections" for real GDP growth and its expenditure counterparts as well as for HICP inflation.[12] Initially, the projections were published twice a year, in June and in December. Since 2004 they have been updated each quarter. Naturally, the projections are based on econometric models, such as the area-wide model, and on a host of technical assumptions that have been changed and refined over time. A crucial assumption concerns the future monetary policy course which enters the projections via assumptions about interest rates while money supply developments are neglected. When the economic analysis team of the ECB's staff started out, the rather rigid practice was to assume that short-term interest rates would remain unchanged over a projection horizon of up to 24 months. Later on, this rather demanding approach was replaced by the more convincing procedure of utilizing market expectations about future monetary policy derived from forward rates as input.

An interesting aspect of the projections is that their implications for monetary policy decision making have been downplayed from the beginning. They have "... an important but limited role in the discussions of the Governing Council. The Governing Council only uses the projections as an input into its deliberations and does not assume responsibility for the projections."[13] The Council stresses the point that the projections are those of the staff and as such are only one piece of information from a broader range of analyses to be looked at. A problem with this characterization is that one wonders why the ECB publishes them at all, moreover, on what grounds it may be sensible to assume the Council really knows better than the staff. A puzzling aspect in this respect is the assertion that "... the Governing Council's own best prediction for price developments over the medium term must always be consistent with its quantitative definition of price stability."[14] This suggests that either as a principle the prediction should always be set at 2 percent, in which case it is useless due to lack of content, or that the Council believes in always being able to display the perfect policy.

The demonstrative downplaying if not negligence of the published staff projections probably reflects the Council's averseness to the concept of explicit inflation targeting and its central feature, the targeting of an inflation forecast. It fits that Otmar Issing, in a hearing of the Committee on Economic and Monetary Affairs of the European Parliament, advised parliament and public to "... evaluate the published projections for what they are and not for what some observers might wish them to be in the context of different approaches to monetary policy making."[15]

It is worthwhile inspecting the ECB staff's projections of GDP growth and inflation and comparing the performance to that of the predictions by other institutions. I chose three institutions the ECB regularly reports on: the European Commission, Consensus Economics, and the ECB's Survey of Professional Forecasters (SPF). As regards the prediction horizon I focus on 24 and 12 months. The respective data are published in the Monthly Bulletin of December each year. As regards its own predictions, the ECB's practise is not to publish point predictions but prediction ranges. For comparability I compute the midpoint predictions. Tables 7.3 and 7.4 show the annual average realizations for GDP growth rates and inflation rates and the computed prediction errors of the competing institutions for the two forecasting horizons of 24 and 12 months. Prediction errors are defined as the difference between the realizations and the predictions. Consequently, a negative sign indicates an overprediction, a positive one an underprediction.

According to Table 7.3, the staff has overpredicted GDP growth in a row, over the 24-month horizon for the years 2002–5 and over the 12-month horizon for the years 2001–3 and again for 2005. The period of overprediction was one of slow growth well below potential, averaging 1.2 percent. It fits that the staff switched to underprediction for the period 2006–7 when real growth more than doubled, rising to 2.8 percent. This remarkable pattern in forecast errors is similar for all the competing forecasts considered here and for both time-horizons. While the ECB staff's prediction errors are sizeable, ranging between − 2.1 and +0.7 percentage points for the 24-month horizon and between − 1.6 and +1.0 percentage points for the shorter horizon, it is to be noted that the ECB's staff performed well in comparison. At least as regards the 12-month horizon it committed the smallest over- and underpredictions while with the 24-month horizon the performance is mixed.

In contrast to the experience with GDP predictions, one does not find a single overprediction of HICP inflation; see Table 7.4. All prediction errors are positive, indicating a downward bias. The staff has continuously underpredicted inflation. On average the prediction errors are close to 0.5 percentage points for the 24-month horizon and close to 0.3 percentage points for the 12-month horizon. This is a remarkably unsatisfactory performance. If one takes as a benchmark the naïve

Table 7.3: *Forecasts of GDP growth (percent p.a.)*

Year	Actual	Forecast errors (actual – forecast) 24 months ahead				Forecast errors (actual – forecast) 12 months ahead			
		ECB	Consensus	SPF	Europ. Com.	ECB	Consensus	SPF	Europ. Com.
2001	1.5	na	na	na	na	-1.6	-1.6	-1.6	-1.7
2002	0.9	-2.1	na	-1.9	-2.1	-0.3	-0.6	-0.6	-0.4
2003	0.5	-2.0	na	-2.0	-2.4	-1.1	-1.2	-1.3	-1.3
2004	1.8	-0.6	na	-0.7	-0.8	0.2	0.1	0.1	0
2005	1.5	-0.9	na	-0.8	-0.8	-0.4	-0.4	-0.5	-0.5
2006	2.9	0.7	na	0.7	0.7	1.0	1.2	1.2	1.0
2007	2.6	0.7	na	0.6	0.5	0.4	0.7	0.6	0.5
Average 2001–05	1.2	-1.40		-1.35	-1.53	-0.64	-0.74	-0.78	-0.78
2006–07	2.8	0.70		0.65	0.60	0.70	0.95	0.90	0.75
2001–07	1.7	-0.70		-0.68	-0.82	-0.26	-0.26	-0.30	-0.34
St. dev. 2001–07	0.86	1.23		1.17	1.28	0.89	1.00	1.00	0.95

Source: ECB Monthly Bulletin, December issues. Real time data.

Table 7.4: *Forecasts of inflation (percent p.a.)*

Year	Actual	Forecast errors (actual – forecast) 24 months ahead					Forecast errors (actual – forecast) 12 months ahead				
		naïve	ECB	Consensus	SPF	Europ. Com.	naïve	ECB	Consensus	SPF	Europ. Com.
2001	2.5		na	na	na	na		0.2	0.5	0.5	0.3
2002	2.3	-0.4	0.4	na	0.5	0.4	-0.2	0.7	0.6	0.6	0.5
2003	2.1	-0.2	0.6	na	0.3	0.3	-0.2	0.3	0.2	0.3	0.1
2004	2.1	0.1	0.5	na	0.2	0.3	0.0	0.3	0.5	0.5	0.1
2005	2.2	0.1	0.6	na	0.4	0.5	0.1	0.2	0.3	0.3	0.3
2006	2.2	-0.1	0.6	na	0.3	0.5	0.0	0.1	0.3	0.2	0
2007	2.1		0.1	na	0.3	0.3	-0.1	0.1	0	0	0
Average		-0.1	0.47		0.33	0.38	-0.1	0.27	0.34	0.34	0.18
St. dev.		0.21	0.20		0.10	0.10	0.12	0.21	0.21	0.21	0.19

Source for the data: ECB Monthly Bulletin, December issues. Real time data. For example, due to statistical revision of the harmonized index of consumer prices, the rate of inflation for 2001 was later revised downward to 2.3 percent.

prediction of no change against the previous year, one receives a much smaller average error of no more than – 0.1 percentage points for both time-horizons. This exercise is certainly not to suggest that the ECB should not have invested resources into the production of inflation forecasts of its own. It serves to highlight the fact that more needs to be done for improvement. While it may be consoling that the competing inflation forecasts of several public and private institutions have been biased downwards, too, it is a fact that the staff of the European Commission has been able to produce a better record. Table 7.4 reveals that for the two time-horizons inspected the inflation forecast errors of the Commission's staff have been smaller and less volatile.

Summing up, we find that the ECB staff's projections are biased. The staff has tended to overpredict real growth for the early years of slow growth and vice versa. More importantly, the staff has underpredicted inflation year after year. This is a bit puzzling. García and Manzanares (2007a) have recently analyzed reporting biases in the ECB's Survey of Professional Forecasters (SFP). They conclude that the features of over-predicting growth and underpredicting inflation are intrinsic features of the reporting practises of survey participants. If correct, it explains the patterns found in the prediction errors of SPF and of Consensus as well, given that Consensus Economics, too, aggregates predictions of survey respondents. However, the observation does not answer the question why the staff of the ECB would tend to systematically produce too low inflation predictions. Projections or forecasts are the result of technical inputs, such as econometric models, data and reports, and of judgement. Technical inputs are under continual scrutiny by the staff and are improved over time. It is unlikely, therefore, that the prediction bias results from some undetected technical defect even though it cannot be ruled out that the models used in the context of the ECB's economic pillar do not adequately mirror the transmission of monetary policy action.

A more tempting conjecture is that strategic bias might be involved. The staff requires the consent of the chief economist if not of the whole executive board to publish its projections. Given that the ECB, as a newcomer among central banks, needed to gain credibility as quickly as possible in order to achieve anchoring of longer-term inflation expectations, it is conceivable that any planned action and publication of the staff received scrupulous scrutiny beforehand in order to make sure that it would not run counter to the ECB's overriding aim. Hence, the proposal to publish an inflation projection above the critical value of 2 percent would certainly have raised unpleasant discussion within the ECB as well as the member banks of the Eurosystem.[16] If taken into account, this should have provided an incentive to bias the projections downward, if only a little.

6. Concluding remarks

After almost ten years of operation the ECB has reached the status of an internationally leading central bank that serves the citizens of the euro area well by providing and safeguarding an internationally demanded stable currency. The trust that is put by the inhabitants of the euro area into the ECB is promoted in addition by the relatively high degree of transparency. In fact, in the case of the ECB the requirement of high transparency is all the more important as this bank serves a large number of nations. The Bank does a lot for transparency by publishing detailed annual reports, monthly bulletins, and press releases, by holding press conferences after sessions of the Governing Council, by explaining regularly its monetary policy to the Committee of Economic and Monetary Affairs of the European Parliament, and by providing public access to a large and well-kept data bank.

Still, the ECB should and could do more to raise transparency regarding policy intentions. In this chapter we have documented somewhat the Governing Council's practise of explaining its expectations by means of coded sentences. The underlying idea seems to be to provide information about intentions but not to commit to this. We believe that this practise is problematic as it may foster misunderstanding. There is a more fruitful avenue to be considered and that is to begin with publishing non-attributed voting as regards interest rate decisions. The Governing Council had started out by applying a "consensus principle" regarding decision making. This appears to have served well during the first years when the governors from different nations had to become used to another, but this is no longer necessary as the institution and the rules of conduct are established. The members of the Governing Council should have learned meanwhile that they cannot have their way all the time and that losing a vote is neither a personal nor a national tragedy.

Appendix: messages from the opening passage of the President's introductory statement

2003

July
- current monetary policy stance is appropriate
- favorable outlook for price stability over the medium term
- safeguard against downside risks to economic growth

September
- current level of ECB interest rates remains appropriate
- medium-term outlook for price stability continues to be favorable

October
- historically low level of ECB interest rates remains appropriate
- medium-term outlook for price stability continues to be favorable
- ongoing support to economic activity

November
- current stance of monetary policy appropriate
- medium-term outlook for price stability remains favorable
- signs of a gradual economic recovery

December
- monetary policy stance remains appropriate
- annual inflation rates likely to fluctuate around 2%, a gradual and limited decline should take place later
- economic recovery has started

2004

January
- current stance of monetary policy appropriate
- ongoing economic recovery

February
- no fundamental changes to the medium-term outlook for price stability
- inflationary risks should be contained by more favorable import price development
- economic recovery in line with our expectations

March
- current stance of monetary policy remains appropriate
- favorable outlook for price stability ... over the medium term
- support to the economic recovery

April
- current stance of monetary policy remains in line with the maintenance of price stability over the medium term
- ongoing support to the economic recovery

May
- we did not change our assessment of the monetary policy stance
- price stability will be maintained over the medium term
- low interest rates ... supporting the economic recovery

June
- we will remain vigilant
- the medium-term outlook remains in line with price stability

	– we … have witnessed stronger inflationary pressures over the short term
	– low level of interest rates continues to support the economic recovery
July	– Governing Council … will remain vigilant
	– outlook still remains in line with price stability over the medium term
	– somewhat stronger inflationary pressure over the short term
	– interest rates … lending support to economic activity
September	– we will remain vigilant
	– overall prospects remain in line with price stability over the medium term
	– some upside risks to price stability exist
	– interest rates … lending support to economic activity
October	– strong vigilance is warranted
	– overall outlook remains consistent with price stability over the medium term
	– as regards economic growth … uncertainty concerning strengthening of activity
November	– strong vigilance is warranted
	– upside risks to price stability over the medium term
	– inflation is likely to remain significantly above 2%
	– ongoing moderate real GDP growth
December	– continued vigilance is of the essence
	– upside risks to price stability over the medium term
	– no significant evidence that stronger underlying domestic inflationary pressures are building up

2005

January	– continued vigilance is of the essence
	– upside risks to price stability over the medium term remain
	– no significant evidence that stronger underlying domestic inflationary pressures are building up
February	– continued vigilance is of the essence
	– upside risks to price stability over the medium term remain
	– no significant evidence that stronger underlying domestic inflationary pressures are building up
March	– continued vigilance required
	– upside risks to price stability over the medium term remain
	– no significant evidence of underlying domestic inflationary pressures building up
	– important contribution to the economic recovery

April	– continued vigilance is of the essence
	– upside risks to price stability over the medium term remain
	– no significant evidence of underlying domestic inflationary pressures building up
	– important contribution to the economic recovery
May	– continued vigilance with regard to upside risks to price stability is warranted
	– no significant evidence of a build-up of underlying domestic inflationary pressures
	– considerable support to economic activity
June	– we will remain vigilant with regard to upside risks to price stability
	– underlying inflationary pressures ... remain contained in the medium term
	– considerable support to economic activity
July	– the Governing Council remains vigilant
	– monetary policy stance is appropriate given the current outlook
	– ongoing support to economic activity
September	– particular vigilance ... is warranted
	– monetary policy stance remains appropriate given the current outlook
	– no significant evidence of a build-up in underlying domestic inflationary pressures
	– considerable support to economic activity
October	– strong vigilance with regard to the upside risks to price stability is warranted
	– monetary policy stance still remains appropriate
	– strong vigilance is also called for in the light of ample liquidity
	– ongoing support to economic activity
November	– strong vigilance with regard to upside risks to price stability is warranted
	– monetary policy stance still remains appropriate
	– current very accommodative stance of monetary policy lends considerable support
December	– we have decided to increase the key ECB interest rates by 25 basis points
	– so as to adjust our accommodative monetary policy stance
	– taking into account the risks to price stability that we have identified in our economic analysis, cross-checked by our monetary analysis
	– our policy remains accommodative

Notes

1. The conclusion is admissible even though it might not hold for each of the countries considered because, say, some unidentified third source of shocks might have dominated the observed output stabilization while the country's central bank may have continued experimenting in a desta-bilizing fashion though on a reduced scale.
2. See ECB (1999), p. 46.
3. See ECB (2003a), Press seminar on the evaluation of the ECB's monetary policy strategy.
4. By the way, Papademos pointed out that inflation expectations had consistently remained "below but close to 2 percent," a formulation that later entered the revised monetary policy strategy.
5. It is well known that estimates of money demand for the euro area indicate a serious break in 2001. An example is Neumann and Greiber (2004).
6. Note that Gerdesmeier *et al.* (2007) estimate an inflation reaction of 1.5. Their sample period, however, extends backward to 1993, hence cannot be considered to produce an adequate picture of the ECB's policy reactions.
7. Note that Sauer and Sturm (2007) assume the time-horizon of three months forward for both expected inflation and expected gap.
8. Sauer and Sturm (2007) using the sample January 1999 – March 2003 present a GMM estimate for the inflation parameter of 0.88.
9. Recall that the underlying inflation estimate uses lag 5 of the growth rate of money stock M3, lag 4 of the inflation rate, and lags 5 to 7 of the gap.
10. Note that the Editorials of the monthly bulletins are slightly polished versions of the President's introductory statements.
11. ECB Press conference, October 13, 1998.
12. ECB Monthly Bulletin, December 2000, p. 49.
13. ECB Annual Report 2000, p. 11.
14. ECB Annual Report 2000, p. 12.
15. Hearing, Committee on Economic and Monetary Affairs, European Parliament, Brussels, January 24, 2001.
16. We acknowledge that the staff has projected inflation to rise in 2008 to 2.5 percent on average but a return to 1.8 percent for 2009.

Comment 3: Comment on Chapters 6 and 7

FRANK SMETS

1. Introduction

The establishment of the European Central Bank (ECB) and the single monetary policy in the euro area almost a decade ago was a historical step in the process of completing the single market in the European Union. In this contribution, I comment on the two chapters in this volume, by Petra Geraats and Manfred J. M. Neumann respectively, that investigate the performance of the ECB's monetary policy during its first decade. In their analysis, both Geraats and Neumann examine whether the ECB has achieved its primary objective of maintaining price stability as mandated by the Treaty and whether in the process it has built up and established credibility for achieving this objective. This focus is, of course, entirely appropriate. Both the negative experience with the Great Inflation in the 1970s and its aftermath and the advances in monetary theory starting with Friedman, Lucas and Kydland and Prescott have contributed to a consensus amongst central bankers and monetary economists that the credibility of a central bank for maintaining price stability is by far its most important asset. High credibility ensures that medium- and long-term inflation expectations remain anchored when the economy is buffeted by shocks, which in turn helps stabilise inflation and economic activity in response to those shocks. Although the debate continues about the sources of the greater real and nominal economic stability that has characterised much of the world economy since the late 1980s, it is unlikely to be a coincidence that it has coincided with a strengthening of monetary policy frameworks in many countries, based on the three pillars of a clear price

I would like to thank Vítor Gaspar, Huw Pill, Massimo Rostagno, Jean-Claude Trichet and Oreste Tristani and Jean-Pierre Vidal for insightful discussions. The views expressed are my own and not necessarily those of the European Central Bank.

stability objective, central bank independence and greatly improved transparency and communication.

The Treaty's emphasis on price stability as the primary objective of the ECB is also borne out by the importance the general public in the euro area attaches to the goal of price stability. Towards the end of 2005, the European Commission asked citizens across the euro area to pick the most important goal for the next ten or fifteen years among four options: maintaining order in the country; giving people more say in important government decisions; fighting rising prices; protecting freedom of speech. The largest share (one third) of the respondents chose fighting rising prices as the most important goal, followed by 30 per cent for maintaining order and 26 per cent for giving people more say. More recently in the context of rising oil, food and commodity prices, the goal of price stability was considered to be the most important policy goal among thirteen alternative options including reducing unemployment.[1]

The overall conclusions regarding the ECB's performance that Geraats and Neumann reach in their respective chapters are somewhat different. Neumann concludes: 'Summing up, the evidence permits the conclusion that the ECB has presented an impressive start. The Bank has been able to stabilise inflation in the euro area at a low level and in this way been able to collect the credibility of a central bank that takes the mandate of maintaining price stability seriously.' Geraats, in contrast, emphasises: 'Although the ECB's performance has definitely been better than the fears expressed by its fiercest critics, it has fallen short of the high hopes cherished by some of its strongest supporters. … the ECB has failed to meet the high standard it set itself. … Furthermore, the credibility of the ECB achieving price stability in the medium term has gradually eroded to critically low levels.' In the first section of this comment, I will briefly review the ECB's performance with respect to achieving price stability, echoing some of the analysis in Geraats and Neumann. I will comment on the various measures of credibility and on whether the ECB's credibility is at stake. One important issue in this respect is the horizon over which performance and credibility should be assessed. In response to Geraats's assertion that insufficient transparency is at the root of the ECB's credibility problems, I will argue that the ECB's transparency and communication regime must be seen in the context of its multinational and multilingual environment.

At the start of EMU, many observers feared that the new institution in charge of the single monetary policy, the ECB, would have to be relatively tough on inflation to establish its reputation, leading to slower growth and an overly strong euro exchange rate. The design of the ECB's monetary policy strategy was geared towards making this transition period as smooth as possible by borrowing elements of continuity from the best performing predecessor central banks.[2] In the second section, I will review some of the elements of the ECB's monetary policy strategy, in particular its two-pillar structure and the role of economic and monetary analysis and analyse how this has contributed to the setting of policy-controlled short-term interest rates using a simple benchmark policy rule proposed by Orphanides (2003).

2. Maintaining price stability: facts and perceptions

The Maastricht Treaty identifies price stability as the primary objective of monetary policy. To provide a clear yardstick against which the public can hold the ECB accountable and with a view to anchoring medium- to long-term inflation expectations, the Governing Council adopted a quantitative definition of price stability in 1998. This definition reads: 'Price stability shall be defined as a year-on-year increase in the Harmonised Index of Consumer Prices (HICP) for the euro area of below 2 per cent. Price stability is to be maintained over the medium term.' Following a thorough evaluation of the monetary policy strategy in 2003, the Governing Council clarified that, within this definition, it aims to keep HICP inflation 'below, but close to, 2 per cent'.

As illustrated by the analysis of Geraats and Neumann, the clear definition in terms of year-on-year inflation allows economic agents and observers to assess the ECB's performance at any time and over any horizon. It thereby enhances the ECB's accountability by forcing the central bank to explain why inflation has at times deviated from its definition. At the same time, it is important to emphasise the medium-term orientation of the ECB's strategy. Since monetary policy can affect price developments only with significant and variable time lags, and only to an extent that is uncertain, it is impossible to maintain a specific predefined inflation rate at all times or to bring it back to a desired level within a very short period of time. Consequently, monetary policy needs to act in a forward-looking manner and focus on the medium term. This helps to avoid excessive activism and the introduction of unnecessary volatility into the real economy. Also this needs to be taken into account when evaluating the ECB's performance.

The medium-term orientation of the ECB's policy strategy was confirmed at the time of the clarification of the strategy in 2003.[3] Three aspects are worth mentioning in this respect. First, the ECB has always emphasised that there is no fixed time-horizon over which price stability has to be re-established, as monetary policy should react differently to different sources of economic shocks (e.g. demand versus supply shocks).[4] Secondly, the medium-term orientation implies a lengthening of the monetary policy horizon beyond the usual two years associated with inflation forecasts and the lags in monetary policy transmission. Or, as stated by Trichet (2003), 'Monetary policy needs to focus on the period covering the whole transmission process, bearing in mind that this may sometimes span a protracted period of time.' In the context of a discussion on the relationship between asset price booms and monetary policy, Trichet (2004) writes: 'Incidentally, ... adopting a flexible medium-term orientation in the pursuit of price stability has the effect of lengthening the monetary policy horizon beyond the two years within which meaningful inflation forecasts are usually constructed, depending on the prevailing circumstances.'[5] Thirdly, in the light of the robust longer-term relationship between money growth and inflation, the monetary analysis in the two-pillar strategy serves to underpin the ECB's medium-term orientation. Importantly, the monetary analysis complements the economic analysis which focuses on the short- to medium-term risks to price stability with a central role for the macro-economic projections.

The ECB's preferred horizon for evaluating the credibility of the central bank is five years and beyond, as in this case the effects of shocks the central bank cannot control should clearly wash out.[6] To be sure, this is not to say that inflation expectations at shorter horizons are not important indicators. On the contrary, as I will discuss in the next section, short-term inflation forecasts have been an important input in setting the monetary policy stance in the context of the ECB's economic analysis. However, they are imperfect indicators for assessing the credibility of the central bank given their dependence on the current state of the economy and the central bank's inability to keep inflation in line with the objective at all times.

Figure C3.1 updates the graph that was also presented and discussed in the 2003 Monthly Bulletin article on the clarification of the monetary policy strategy in order to illustrate the anchoring of inflation expectations. It shows actual annual HICP inflation and HICP inflation

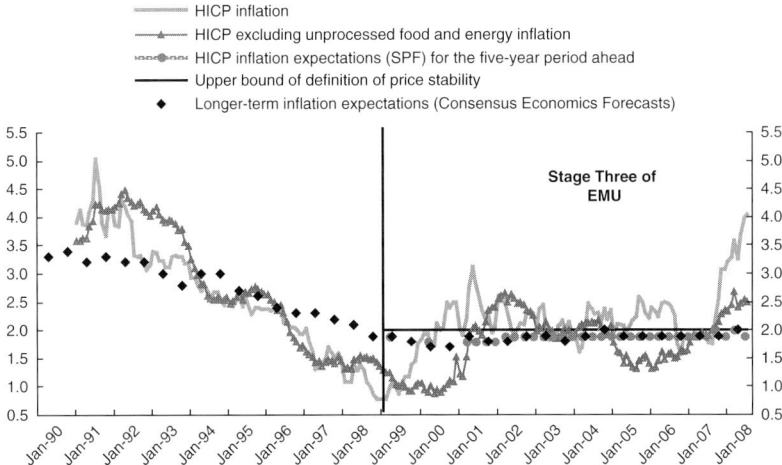

Figure C3.1: Inflation rates and longer-term inflation expectations in the euro area
Source: Eurostat and ECB.

excluding unprocessed food and energy inflation, as well as two measures of longer-term inflation expectations based on surveys. The first one is based on the Survey of Professional Forecasters conducted by the ECB as of 1999; the second one is based on responses collected by Consensus Economics. A few observations can be made. First, as highlighted by Geraats and Neumann, at 2.1 per cent the average HICP inflation rate over the EMU period has been somewhat above the definition of price stability. From an ex-post point of view, there is therefore no doubt that at any reasonable medium-term horizon the ECB has not fully fulfilled its objective of keeping HICP inflation close to, but *below* 2 per cent, although it came close. The main reason has been the historically very big and mostly unexpected increase in energy and commodity prices over the EMU period. In real terms, until recently oil prices have since 1999 increased by as much as the two big oil price increases in the 1970s and early 1980s together. Moreover, consistent with futures prices, these persistent increases were largely unexpected. At the same time, the behaviour of inflation has been very different in both periods. While average inflation excluding energy and unprocessed food over the EMU period stands at 1.8 per cent, it was much higher in the 1970s and the 1980s.

While an average inflation rate of 2.1 per cent is above the 2 per cent threshold, it is worth mentioning that it is as good as the best performers amongst the predecessor central banks in the decade before. Amongst those countries, Belgium and France had the lowest average inflation rate of 2.1 per cent over the period 1990–8, and Germany and the Netherlands had an average inflation rate of 2.2 per cent. This performance is also better than the 2.9 per cent that Germany and the Netherlands obtained in the period 1980–9, a period characterised by a significant fall in oil prices.[7]

Second, as argued by Geraats, 'it is better to assess the ECB's success by checking whether the private sector expects the ECB to deliver price stability in the medium term'. Figure C3.1 shows two such measures. The longer time series is from Consensus Economics and shows how long-term inflation expectations in the euro area converged towards a level slightly below 2 per cent in 1999 and have remained there with a few exceptions at the end of 2004 and most recently. Figure C3.1 also depicts the five-year-ahead inflation expectations from the ECB's Survey of Professional Forecasters. This measure has also been continuously below 2 per cent with the exception of some of the most recent observations which put it at 2 per cent. Based on this graph, it appears somewhat stretched to conclude like Geraats that 'ECB credibility has steadily drifted down'. Part of the difference in assessment comes from the fact that Geraats focus on two-year-ahead inflation forecasts. Geraats interprets President Trichet's recent responses to questions about the policy horizon as a clarification that the 'medium term' means 18 months to 2 years and concludes that therefore the two-year-ahead SPF measure is the most appropriate for evaluating whether inflation expectations remain firmly anchored at levels consistent with price stability in the medium term. A time-lag of 18 to 24 months is usually associated with the typical lags in the effects of monetary policy on inflation. President Trichet's precision regarding the policy horizon must be seen in the context of high headline inflation and rising short-to medium-term inflation expectations. As this puts the credibility of the ECB at stake, a short policy horizon is important to ensure a continued anchoring of medium-term inflation expectations and to avoid second-round effects from high headline inflation.[8] The importance of responding more aggressively to inflation when inflation expectations risk becoming unanchored is clearly born out in the analysis of Gaspar *et al.* (2006) and Orphanides and Williams (2005). Gaspar *et al.* (2006) show how the response to cost-push shocks needs to be stronger when the degree of inflation persistence perceived by the private sector is higher. There is an intertemporal tradeoff between the cost of anchoring inflation expectations now by raising interest rates by more and the cost of higher inflation and output volatility in the future when inflation expectations are unanchored. Such a shorter policy horizon in the current context does not imply, however, that the principles behind the medium-term orientation discussed above have changed. In particular, it remains the case that inflation expectations over a horizon of two years are likely to be affected by shocks to inflation that cannot be controlled without unnecessary volatility in economic activity and interest rates. They may therefore not capture very well the credibility of the central bank for anchoring inflation expectations over the medium term.

To further examine the credibility of the ECB, it is also worth looking at alternative credibility measures. As mentioned by Geraats, one is breakeven inflation rates embedded in index-linked bonds. One problem with those measures is that, like all financial asset prices, they will be affected by potentially time-varying risk premia. Figure C3.2 plots the unadjusted five-year five-year-forward breakeven inflation rate together with the corresponding inflation forecast from Consensus Economics and two inflation-risk-premium-adjusted measures based on two distinct term structure models. Both models lead to a downward

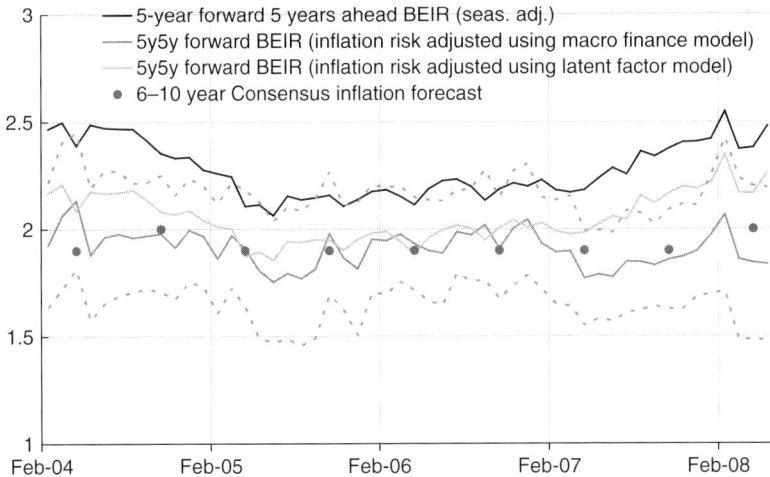

Figure C3.2: Five-year five-year-forward breakeven inflation rates in the euro area

Source: ECB.

adjustment of the estimated five-year five-year-forward inflation rate. The latent factor model gives rise to a relatively constant risk premium of between 20 and 30 basis points. The macrofinance model of Hordahl *et al.* (2006) leads to a more variable inflation risk premium and implies a medium-term inflation forecast that is closer to the Consensus one. The uncertainty around those estimates is, however, quite large.[9] Overall, the estimates based on index-linked bonds are consistent with the six-to-ten-year Consensus inflation forecast.

The measures depicted in Figures C3.1 and C3.2 both focus on central tendency measures of inflation expectations. As emphasised by Geraats, an alternative approach is to look at the cross-sectional distribution of private sector forecasts. Figure C3.3, taken from Orphanides and Williams (2008), shows the standard deviation of one-year and five-year-ahead inflation forecasts across respondents in the Survey of Professional Forecasters. It shows that the disagreement among professional forecasters about the medium- to long-term inflation objective of the ECB, as captured by the standard deviation, has

Per cent

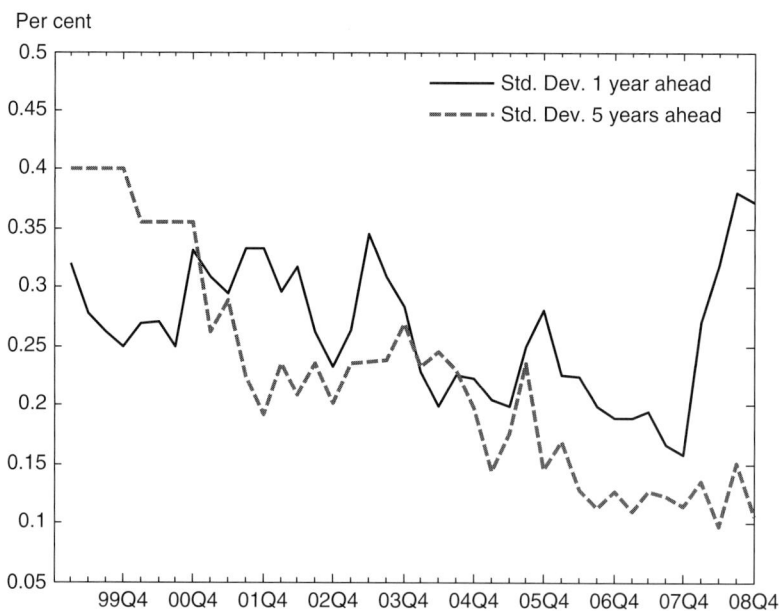

Figure C3.3: Disagreement about inflation expectations
Source: Survey of Professional Forecasters; Orphanides and Williams (2008).

fallen significantly from 0.4 per cent in 1999 to around 0.1 per cent most recently. Moreover, this measure of disagreement is currently quite a bit lower than in a similar survey for the United States. In contrast, disagreement on the forecast of one-year-ahead inflation has fallen by much less and has recently increased considerably as uncertainty regarding the persistence of recent increases in oil, commodity and food prices and regarding the likelihood of future shocks has increased. This underlines again that a better measure for central bank credibility refers to a longer horizon.

Tsenova (2008) argues that a more robust measure of disagreement is to look at the interquantile range rather than standard deviations. Figure C3.4, which is based on Tsenova (2008), shows the quantile plot of the cross-sectional distribution of point estimates of five-year ahead inflation expectations from the ECB's Survey of Professional Forecasters. It confirms that disagreement has narrowed over time. Moreover, with the exception of the most recent observation, more than 75 per cent of the respondents expect long-term inflation to be at

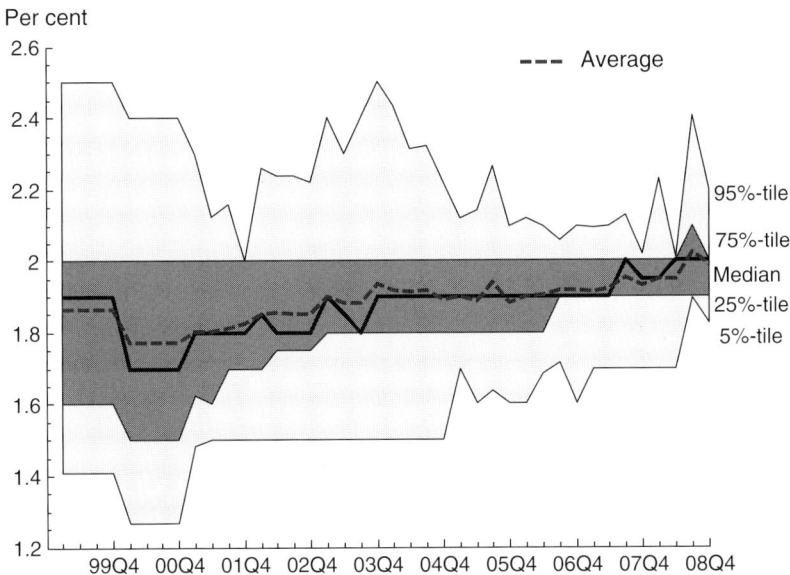

Figure C3.4: Cross-section distribution of five-year-ahead inflation expectations (SPF)
Source: Tsenova (2008).

or below 2 per cent. However, consistent with some of the discussion in Geraats (Table 6.2), it also reveals some sensitivity of the median five-year-ahead inflation expectation to persistent inflation developments. In particular, while long-term inflation expectations moved somewhat below 1.9 per cent in the beginning of the EMU period as actual head-line inflation was historically low, since the second half of 2007 they have moved towards 2 per cent as headline inflation has been quite a bit higher than 2 per cent.

Tsenova (2008) analyses to what extent various moments of the cross-sectional distribution of long-term inflation expectations respond to revisions in the short-term inflation outlook. Overall, the results are not very robust and depend on details of how the moments are calculated, but in line with the results emphasised by Geraats there is some evidence that long-term inflation expectations have been sensitive to the inflation history, although the effects are small.

Finally, the credibility of a central bank can also be assessed by investigating how bond markets and, in particular, the inflation compensation embedded in long-term bond yields respond to current inflation and other news. Recent empirical evidence has shown that long forward rates do not respond to short-run inflation news, suggesting again that credibility is indeed well maintained. Ehrmann *et al.* (2007) and Beechey *et al.* (2007) both show that long-term inflation expectations seem to react to news in the USA, but not so in inflation-targeting countries and in the euro area, again suggesting that long-term inflation expectations have been well anchored. These studies do, however, not include the most recent period of high inflation.

Overall, it appears that over the past ten years, long-term inflation expectations have remained solidly anchored, which is remarkable considering the series of adverse economic disturbances that have hit the euro area since its inception. However, the recent rise in headline HICP inflation has been accompanied by a slight deterioration of longer-term inflation expectations. One question which is worth addressing is to what extent central banks should let bygones be bygones and solely concentrate on the future. As Geraats discusses towards the end of her contribution, a purely forward-looking central bank may suffer from a time-inconsistency problem in the sense that it never reaches its projected inflation path. One way of ensuring time-consistency is to aim for price level path stability and not let bygones be bygones. As Beyer *et al.* (2008) have recently argued, monitoring underlying money growth may also induce some history dependence as shown by the experience of the Bundesbank in the post Bretton Woods period. Whether central banks should go one step further and focus on the stability of the price level path is a question of current debate. Gaspar *et al.* (2007) review some of the pros and cons. It is clear, however, that if persistent overshooting of the central bank's inflation objective risks leading to a deterioration of the bank's credibility, prompt action to prevent such an erosion is necessary to avoid higher volatility in the future.

Before moving to the next section, which will look more in detail at the actual interest rate setting by the ECB, it is worth making two comments about Section 3 of Geraats in which a number of recommendations for greater ECB transparency are made. First, in this section Geraats suggests that greater transparency could have avoided the deterioration of inflation expectations towards the end of the sample. While it is difficult to assess such a counterfactual, I have my doubts. The ECB makes a lot of effort in explaining its monetary policy decisions through the monthly introductory statement and Q&A session, the hearings before the European Parliament, the many speeches by executive board members and the Monthly Bulletin. While one can always improve the quality and quantity of information, I feel it is unlikely that by itself this would have helped much in better anchoring long-term expectations. In the end, it is the track record that prevails.

Second, many of the suggestions by Geraats regarding improvements in transparency refer to the practice of inflation-targeting central banks in countries where communication is relatively easy and decision making is relatively simple because often there is a single decision maker or a small-sized MPC. While many of these suggestions are sensible, often they ignore and/or underestimate the constraints coming from pursuing monetary policy in a multinational, multilingual monetary union. The ECB has adjusted its communication and transparency policy over time, but a number of features of the ECB's communication and transparency regime are driven by this institutional environment which is unlikely to change soon. As argued by Blinder *et al.* (2008), different communication regimes may work equally well in different environments. First, the ECB's single-voice policy is an important element of efficient communication in a multinational and multilingual environment. It partly explains why the ECB has opted for giving real-time explanations of its policy decisions, through the introductory statement and the Q&A

session during the press conference immediately after the first Governing Council meeting on monetary policy during the month. Having to wait for two or more weeks for the release of the minutes risks creating confusion as Governing Council members return to their countries and need to explain the Governing Council's policy decisions against different backgrounds. Second, the fact that the projections are owned by the staff and not the Governing Council is partly due to the fact that it would be very difficult to come up with Governing Council-agreed projections given that it currently consists of twenty-two members, most of whom are not located in Frankfurt. Similar arguments can be used for why it would be difficult for the Governing Council to agree on an interest rate path. At the same time, having such a large Governing Council helps efficient information sharing and solidifies the legitimacy of the single monetary policy in a multicountry monetary union. Third, the attribution of different votes to national central bank governors risks complicating communication. While in principle one can have non-attributed votes the practice shows that it will not take long for observers to find out who was on what position. This would risk having a discussion which focuses on national developments rather than on the outlook for the euro area as a whole. In contrast, with the current setup the Governing Council can still bring in all the evidence from various regions. At the same time, it can give an aggregate assessment of the risks to price stability and economic activity and thereby convey a measure of uncertainty.

3. The ECB's monetary policy strategy in practice

In order to maintain price stability, the Governing Council of the ECB sets the main refinancing rate using all available information relevant for assessing the outlook for price stability. The ECB's monetary policy strategy provides a framework to structure the information relevant for policy. One of its innovative features is the two-pillar structure. Following the clarification of the strategy in 2003, those pillars are denoted economic analysis and monetary analysis respectively. The economic analysis, of which the quarterly macroeconomic projections are an important part, helps to identify the risks to price stability in the short to medium term. The monetary analysis aims at identifying risks to price stability at medium to longer horizons and thereby helps in maintaining an appropriate medium-term orientation. The monetary

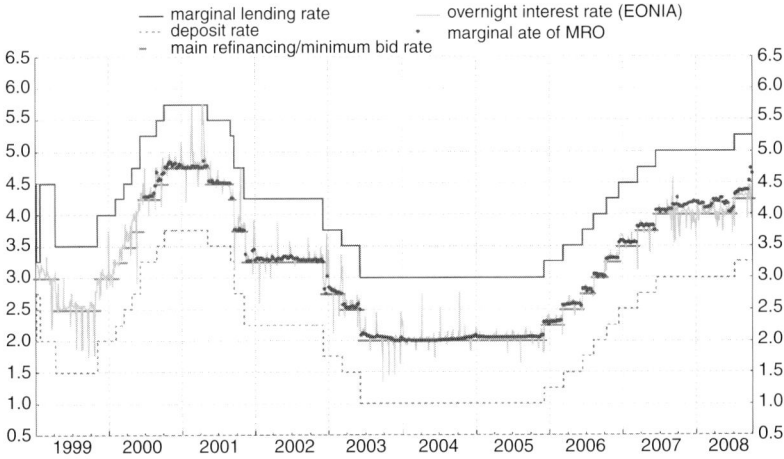

Figure markers:
— marginal lending rate
···· deposit rate
– main refinancing/minimum bid rate
— overnight interest rate (EONIA)
• marginal ate of MRO

Figure C3.5: Main policy rates of the ECB
Source: ECB.

(1) Excludes outright operations and the issuance of debt certificates by NCBs in Stage Two and outstanding over the period considered in the table. These items are included in 'Other factors (net)'.

(2) Due to rounding, components may not add up to the totals reported.

(3) Calculated as the sum of the deposit facility (the liquidity-absorbing component of the standing facilities). Banknotes in circulation and credit institutions' holdings on current accounts with the Eurosystem.

analysis is used to cross-check the findings coming from the economic analysis from this longer-term perspective.

Figure C3.5 depicts the development of the main policy rates since the start of EMU. With the exception of the initial weeks and the more recent narrowing of the corridor to 100 basis points, the overnight interest rate has fluctuated inside a 200 basis point corridor given by the marginal lending rate and the deposit rate. The main objective of the ECB's operational framework is to steer very short-term interest rates in line with the decisions of the Governing Council. Until very recently the main policy rate was the minimum bid rate (MBR) in the ECB's weekly main refinancing operations (MROs). These are liquidity-providing repo operations conducted as variable rate tenders, subject to the minimum bid rate, in which the ECB determines the total amount that is allotted to counterparties, while banks submit bid schedules expressing the price they are willing to pay for liquidity in these operations.[10]

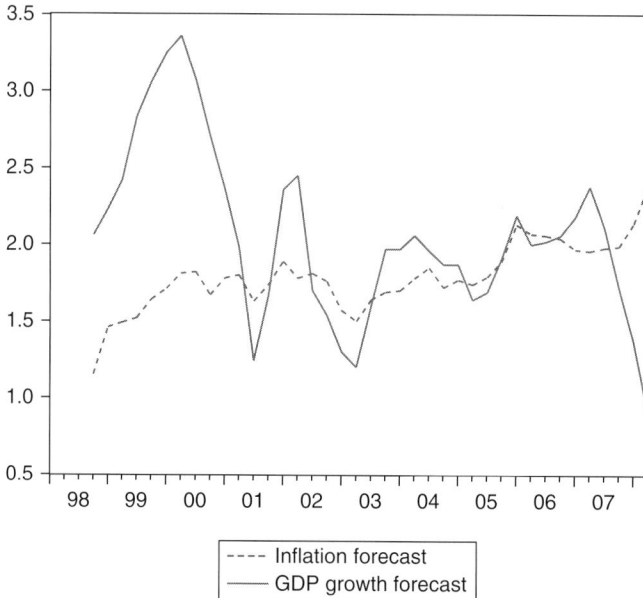

Figure C3.6: Short-term inflation and growth forecasts in the euro area
Source: Survey of Professional Forecasters.

Figure C3.5 also summarises some of the refinements that have been made to the ECB's operational framework over the past decade.[11] One change was the transition from a fixed-rate tender to a variable-rate tender with a minimum bid rate in June 2000. Another notable change is the reduced end-of-maintenance period volatility of the overnight interest rate starting in November 2004 with a better alignment of the schedule of repo operations with that of monetary policy decisions. Finally, also the tensions in the euro-area money market with the outbreak of the financial turmoil in August 2007 are visible in Figure C3.6, as the spread between the marginal rate of the MROs and the minimum bid rate, as well as the volatility of the overnight interest rate increases.[12]

During the first decade the main refinancing/minimum bid rate has fluctuated between 2 and 4.75 per cent. The amplitude of the policy interest rate cycle in the euro area is less than that in the United States, where it was more than 4 percentage points over the same period. This has led some observers to conclude that the ECB's monetary policy is less activist than that of the Federal Reserve Board. A number of studies have examined whether this different behaviour is due to differences in the objectives of the central bank, to differences in the economic structure and monetary policy transmission mechanism or to differences in the shocks affecting both economies. Using different versions of DSGE models for the US and euro-area economy, Sahuc and Smets (2007), Christiano *et al.* (2008) and Uhlig (2008) point out that most of the differences are due to differences in the underlying shocks. In addition, the euro-area economy is also characterised by a stronger stickiness (e.g. in price setting) which may explain a more gradual approach in interest rate setting.

Neumann analyses the interest rate setting of the ECB and asks whether the clarification of the strategy has led to a change in ECB behaviour. In this section, I will use a simple benchmark policy rule to interpret the ECB's response to changes in the outlook for inflation and economic activity. In addition, I will briefly review the impact of monetary analysis as a cross-check.

As mentioned above, the economic analysis is geared at identifying the short- to medium-term risks to price stability. It consists of a full analysis of economic activity in goods and labour markets and its implications for inflation as well as of a detailed analysis of the HICP and various price, wage and profit indicators on the nominal side. It also includes a variety of other indicators including asset prices, survey expectations and economic forecasts of other institutions. While only one element in the overall input coming from the economic analysis, the macroeconomic projections of the ECB and the Eurosystem provide an important staff summary of the economic analysis on a quarterly basis. In the following, we analyse the influence of the economic analysis on the interest rate setting of the ECB through the lens of a simple, but robust policy rule proposed by Orphanides (2003), a simple first-difference policy rule.[13] This rule links the change in the main refinancing rate (the minimum bid rate) of the ECB to deviations of expected inflation from the ECB's inflation objective and deviations of expected real GDP growth from potential output growth

$$\Delta i = 0.5(E\pi - \bar{\pi}) + 0.5(E\Delta y - \Delta \bar{y}) \tag{1}$$

As discussed by Orphanides (2006), the advantages of this simple rule, which can also be derived from the combination of the quantity theory of money and a money demand function, is that it avoids having to rely on unobservable concepts such as the output gap and the natural rate of interest. Moreover, the first-difference rule has been shown to be robust in a variety of models, reflecting a wide range of uncertainty.[14] At the same time, it can be implemented on the basis of short-term forecasts, which facilitates the communication of policy regarding the outlook for inflation and GDP growth.

In order to implement the policy benchmark, I will use the short-term inflation and GDP growth forecasts from the SPF as depicted in Figure C3.6. The published ECB/Eurosystem projections are more difficult to use because they refer to calendar years. The correlation between the SPF forecasts and the corresponding ECB projections is, however, very high, so that similar findings are obtained. A few observations are worth making. First, one-year ahead inflation forecasts from the SPF have been below 2 per cent during most of the EMU period. Only since the beginning of 2006 have they exceeded the 2 per cent threshold. Second, one-year-ahead GDP growth forecasts have been quite volatile, ranging between almost 3.4 per cent in 2000 and 0.9 per cent (and lower) most recently.

Figure C3.7 uses the SPF forecasts to calculate the benchmark quarterly change in the policy rate and compares it with actual changes in the ECB's minimum bid rate. In order to calculate the benchmark, I use 1.8 per cent as the ECB inflation objective (very similar pictures can be

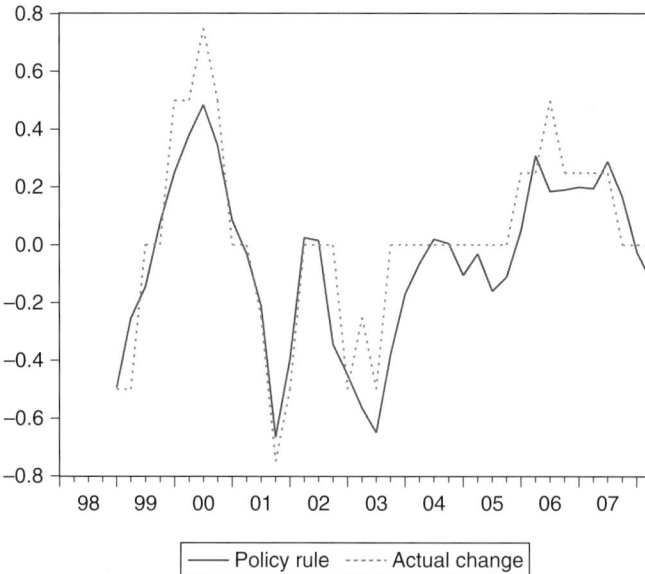

Figure C3.7: Actual and benchmark changes in the policy rate

obtained using inflation objectives between 1.5 and 2 per cent) and the IMF's real-time estimates of potential output growth as in Orphanides (2006). Figure C3.7 shows that changes in the ECB's policy rate can be captured quite well by the benchmark rule. The increase in rates in 1999 and 2000 and the subsequent fall, the pause in 2000 and the subsequent fall and the rise starting in 2006 are all captured fairly well by a simple response to deviations of the inflation forecast from the objective and the deviation of the growth forecast from estimated potential output growth. As this rule has also been shown to capture US monetary policy quite well, there is therefore very little evidence that the response of the ECB to the short-term outlook for economic activity and inflation is very different. The correlation between the actual and the benchmark policy rate change is almost 80 per cent. Interestingly, this correlation drops if ex-post estimates of potential output growth are used (not shown).

These findings are confirmed by a formal regression analysis in which I regress the policy rate on its own lag and on the deviation of the inflation forecast from 1.8 per cent and the growth forecast from potential growth (Eq(1) in Table C3.1). The estimation results show that the coefficients on both of the latter regressors are not significantly different from 0.5, the coefficients postulated by Orphanides (2003) for an analysis of US monetary policy. Moreover, the coefficient on the lagged policy rate is close to one although significantly different from one. The R^2 is 96 per cent.

Figure C3.8 plots the actual and the fitted policy rate as well as the residuals of the estimated policy rule.

Table C3.1: *Estimation of a simple policy rule*

	Eq(1)	Eq(2)	Eq(3)	Eq(4)	Eq(5)
Constant	0.37* (0.10)	0.28 (0.19)	0.04 (0.22)	0.11 (0.14)	0.03 (0.17)
θ_i	0.89* (0.03)	0.90* (0.03)	0.96* (0.04)	0.91* (0.03)	0.97* (0.03)
θ_π	0.47* (0.14)	0.33 (0.25)	0.11 (0.22)	-	-
$\theta_{\Delta y}$	0.48* (0.05)	0.49* (0.06)	0.45* (0.06)	0.50* (0.06)	0.45* (0.06)
$\theta_{\Delta m3c}$	-	0.01 (0.02)	-	0.03* (0.01)	-
θ_{QMA}	-	-	0.10 (0.06)	-	0.12* (0.05)
R^2	0.96	0.96	0.97	0.96	0.97

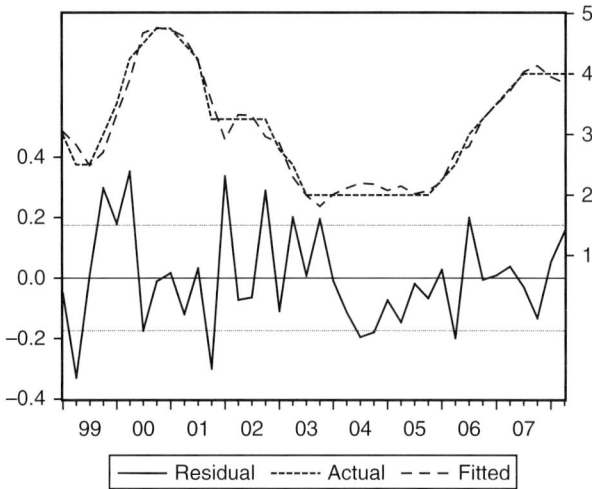

Figure C3.8: Actual and fitted policy rate

This simple analysis shows, first, that the ECB did respond to the outlook for both inflation and output. Moreover, these estimates are very similar to those estimated by Orphanides (2003) for the Fed using survey forecasts over the period 1982Q3–2002Q4. Secondly, there is no evidence of a break in 2003. Chow breakpoint tests reject the hypothesis that the policy rule has changed around the middle of the sample.

What about the monetary analysis? Fischer *et al.* (2008) investigate the practice of monetary analysis at the ECB from 1999 until 2006 and illustrate the usefulness of cross-checking the economic analysis with the monetary analysis. They use a qualitative indicator of the language used in the introductory statement to assess the relative importance of the monetary analysis compared with the economic analysis. They derive two conclusions. First, there is a high collinearity between the communication regarding the monetary and economic analyses, which reflects the common thrust of the analyses themselves. This makes identifying the independent effect of monetary analysis – at least insofar as it is captured in the official communication – difficult to assess. They identify two broad periods in which the economic analysis and monetary analysis point to different actions. In the 2001–3 period the economic analysis saw risks to the downside, leading to successive cuts of interest rates. In the 2005 period instead, monetary analysis saw upward risks to price stability, whereas economic analysis suggested a more balanced outlook.

Eventually, interest rates were progressively increased when the economic analysis also started signalling upward risks.

Given the robust link between trend developments in money and inflation, the primary role of the ECB's monetary analysis is to help look through the transient impact of the many temporary shocks that buffet the economy. This helps the ECB to act in a consistent manner over time and to maintain a focus on the medium-term horizon. The monetary analysis is therefore mostly geared at retrieving the underlying or trend component of money growth that is relevant for the assessment of risks to price stability. The prominent role assigned to money also provides a nominal anchor which helps to cement the credibility of the ECB's commitment to price stability.

The identification of the policy-relevant signal in money contained in its lower frequency developments involves 'filtering' the monetary data in order to quantify and remove short-term noise. This filtering process entails an encompassing and detailed examination of bank balance sheet data and is complemented by an analysis of the balance sheet of households, non-financial corporations and other financial institutions.

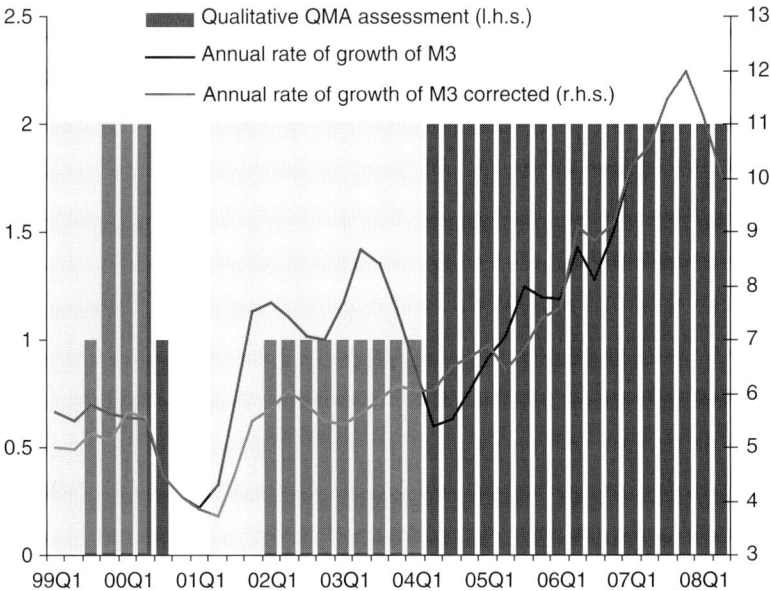

Figure C3.9: Summary indicators of monetary analysis at the ECB
Source: Fischer *et al.* (2008).

Figure C3.9 reproduces a graph from Fischer *et al.* (2008) that shows the development of annual M3 growth and M3 growth corrected for real-time estimates of portfolio shifts, as well as a quantitative indicator that signals the risks from price stability coming from the monetary analysis based on a reading of the quarterly monetary analysis.

It shows that with the exception of a short period in 2001, money growth has been above the reference value of 4.5 per cent. Moreover, during the full decade the monetary analysis has indicated balanced or upward risks to price stability.

In order to see whether the monetary analysis has had an impact on the interest rate setting, we introduce either the lagged money growth corrected for portfolio shifts or the Quarterly Monetary Assessment indicator in the policy reaction function estimated above (Eqs. (2) and (3) in Table C3.1). Neither of the two enters with a significant coefficient. Moreover, the significance of the inflation forecast also disappears, suggesting that there is a multicollinearity problem. Indeed, if we exclude the inflation forecast from the regression analysis, both monetary analysis indicators become significant, confirming that during most of the period the general thrust of the economic and monetary analysis with respect to the outlook for price stability went in the same direction. Recently, Stark (2008b) has reviewed the role of monetary analysis in the context of the current credit market turmoil. He illustrates the usefulness of the analysis of money and credit developments for assessing not only longer-term nominal trends, but also the cyclical situation, in particular in times of financial stress.

Notes

1. See http://ec.europa.eu/public_opinion/archives/eb/eb69/eb_69_first_en.pdf.
2. See Issing *et al.* (2001).
3. See ECB (2003b), Monthly Bulletin, June 2003, pp. 79–92.
4. See Trichet (2003), Section 2.2, The medium-term orientation of monetary policy.
5. Arguably the ECB was a front runner in this respect as a number of inflation-targeting central banks made their policy horizon more flexible and longer following their initial experience with a fixed, relatively short policy horizon.
6. See ECB (2003b).
7. See ECB (2008c), Monthly Bulletin on the occasion of the tenth anniversary of the ECB, Table 7, p. 78.
8. See Trichet (2008a).

9. García and Werner (2008) estimate a macrofinance model that includes inflation expectations from the SPF as an observable variable in the estimation procedure and come to similar conclusions.

10. In the context of the financial crisis, fixed rate tenders were again introduced in October 2008.

11. For an early description of the operational framework see Chapter 8 in Issing *et al.* (2001).

12. As argued in Cassola *et al.* (2008), five features of the operational framework of the Eurosystem seem to have been crucial in managing the liquidity crisis amongst banks in the money market: (i) the large number of counterparties that have access to intraday credit; (ii) the characteristics of the minimum reserve requirement with the monthly averaging period; (iii) the wide collateral framework; (iv) the availability of an automatic lending facility with no significant stigma; (v) the flexibility allowed by the design of its open market operations framework, including the use of fine-tuning operations and longer-term repo operations.

13. Orphanides (2003) calls this type of rule a natural-growth targeting rule. See also Orphanides (2006) for an application to the euro area.

14. See, for example, Orphanides and Williams (2008). Beyer *et al.* (2008) show that this type of rule also explains the historical behaviour of the Bundesbank in the period after the breakdown of Bretton Woods.

PART IV

Financial markets

8 | *The ECB and the bond market*

CARLO FAVERO AND FRANCESCO GIAVAZZI

1. The convergence of US and euro-area long rates

This chapter is an investigation into the factors that determine long-term interest rates in the euro area. We measure these rates with the yield on ten-year German benchmark government bonds: we thus abstract from credit and liquidity spreads that vary both among euro bonds issued by different governments and between corporate and sovereign bonds. We are interested in understanding to what extent – if at all – and through which channels the transition to a monetary union has affected European long rates. In particular we are interested in understanding whether it has affected the comovement of US and European yields. Why is this relevant? Because long rates incorporate long-term inflation expectations and expectations on future monetary policy: they thus provide a direct assessment of the credibility of a central bank's inflation target.

Our data on long rates (the frequency is monthly and the source is Datastream) are shown in Figure 8.1. The sample extends over three decades: we divide it into three subsamples (the 1980s, the 1990s, and the years following the start of EMU), which correspond to distinct periods in the euro area: the EMS, its crisis in the early nineties, followed by the transition to EMU, and the years since the creation of EMU. Along with European rates Figure 8.1 also shows the evolution of US long rates: the ten-year benchmark US Treasury. We note two facts: (i) the correlation between European and US yields has always been high (*rho* in Figure 8.1 indicates the coefficient of correlation between the two series), but the levels of the two yields, which were different in the 1980s, have converged to the same unconditional mean since the early 1990s; (ii) the high positive correlation between US and European long-term rates is not a feature shared by monetary policy rates (shown in Figure 8.2) in any of

Prepared for EMU@10 Workshop. Brussels November 26–27, 2007. We thank participants in the workshop and especially Vítor Gaspar for useful comments.

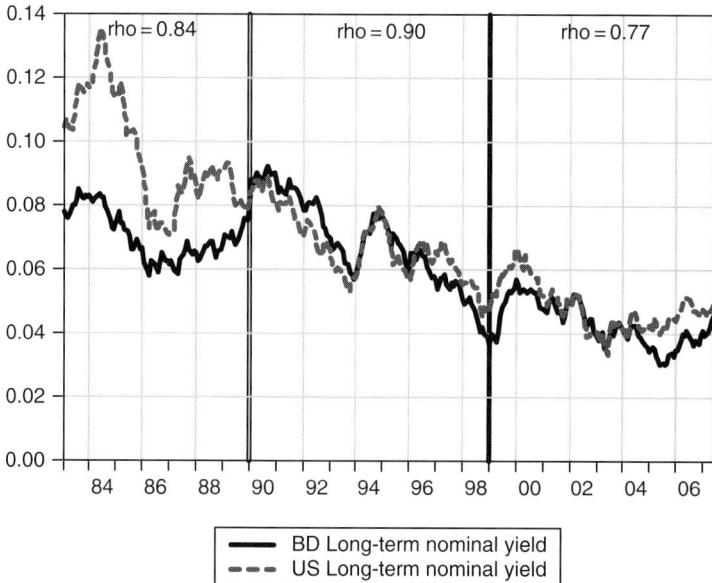

Figure 8.1: Yields to maturity of US and German ten-year benchmark bonds
Source: Datastream.

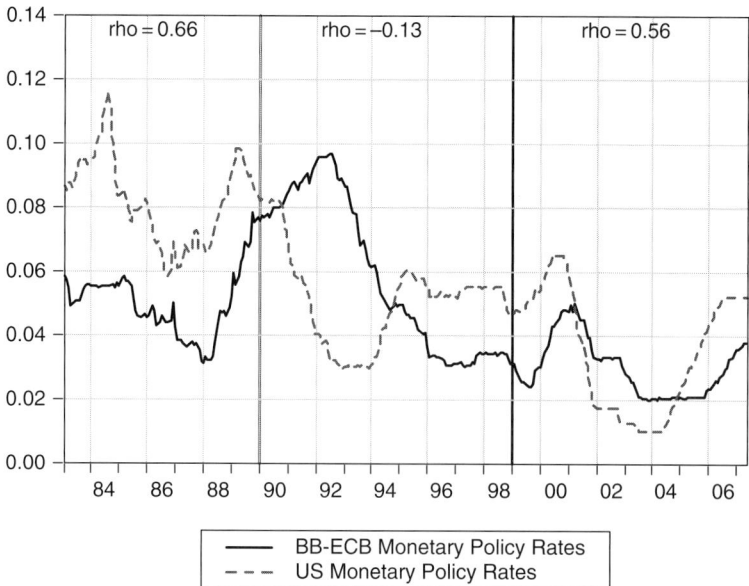

Figure 8.2: US and Bundesbank-ECB monetary policy rates

the periods we have considered. This suggests that there are factors beyond monetary policy that explain the correlation between euro-area and US long rates.

To understand which factors these might be it is useful to start by decomposing ten-year yields in two different ways:

- first, we split the nominal yield on a T-year bond, $i_{t,T}$, in the weighted sequence of expected future policy rates – which we denoted with $i^*_{t,T}$ – and a term pre-mium, $TP_{t,T}$, as shown in equation (1);
- alternatively, in equation (2), we split the nominal yield in the expected inflation over the remaining life of the bond, $\pi^*_{t,T}$, and the sum of the inflation risk premium, $IP_{t,T}$ and the real rate, $rr_{t,T}$ both also measured over the remaining life of the bond:

$$
\begin{aligned}
i_{t,T} &= i^*_{t,T} + TP_{t,T} \\
&= \frac{1-\gamma}{1-\gamma^{T-t}} \sum_{j=1}^{T} \gamma^{j-1} E_t i_{t+j-1,t+j} + TP_{t,T}
\end{aligned}
\tag{1}
$$

$$
\begin{aligned}
i_{t,T} &= \pi^*_{t,T} + (rr_{t,T} + IP_{t,T}) \\
&= \frac{1-\gamma}{1-\gamma^{T-t}} \sum_{j=1}^{T} \gamma^{j-1} E_t \pi_{t+j-1,t+j} + (rr_{t,T} + IP_{t,T})
\end{aligned}
\tag{2}
$$

Equation (1) applies the linearized expectations model of Shiller (1979). It is derived from a no-arbitrage condition: expected one-period returns from holding a long-term bond must be equal to the one-period risk-free interest rate, plus a one-period term premium. For long-term bonds bearing a coupon C, the one-period holding-return is a non-linear function of the yield to maturity $i_{t,T}$. Shiller (1979) proposes a linearization in the neighborhood of $i_{t,T} = i_{t+1,T} = \overline{R} = C$, in which case we have:

$$
E[h_{t,T}|I_t] = E\left[\frac{i_{t,T} - \gamma_T i_{t+1,T}}{1-\gamma_T}|I_t\right] = i_{t,t+1} + \phi_{t,T}
\tag{3}
$$

where $h_{t,T}$ is the one-period holding return of a bond with maturity date T, I_t is the information set available to agents at time t, $i_{t,t+1}$ is the short-term (one-period) risk-free interest rate, γ_T is a constant of linearization which depends on the maturity of the bond. (For a long-term bond such a constant can be approximated by $1/(1+\overline{R})$, since $\lim_{T\to\infty} \gamma_T = \gamma = 1/(1+\overline{R})$). $\phi_{t,T}$ is a term premium – defined over a one-period horizon – for holding for one period a bond with residual maturity $T - t$. Solving equation (3) forward we obtain (1), where $TP_{t,T}$ is the term premium over the entire residual life of the bond.

Equation (2) decomposes the nominal long-term yield to maturity into an expected inflation component, a real long-term interest rate and an inflation risk premium (see for instance Blanchard and Summers, 1984 and Ang *et al.* 2007).

To carry out these decompositions we need forecasts of future policy rates and future inflation. We construct them by estimating the following VAR:

$$\mathbf{y}_t = \mathbf{A}_t(L)\mathbf{y}_{t-1} + \mathbf{u}_t$$

where

$$\mathbf{y}_t = [\mathbf{y}_t^{US} \quad \boldsymbol{\pi}_t^{US} \quad i_{t,t+1}^{US} \quad i_{t,t+120}^{US} \quad \mathbf{y}_t^{EU-GER} \quad \boldsymbol{\pi}_t^{EU-GER} \quad i_{t,t+1}^{GER} \quad i_{t,t+120}^{GER}]'$$

$$\mathbf{A} = \begin{bmatrix} \mathbf{A}_{11} & \mathbf{0} \\ \mathbf{A}_{21} & \mathbf{A}_{22} \end{bmatrix}$$

- $\mathbf{y}_t^{US}$ and $\mathbf{y}_t^{EU-GER}$ are measures of the output gap computed by applying the Hodrick-Prescott filter to the log of industrial production. The filter is one-sided and it is computed recursively in real time, that is, the output gap at time t uses only information available at time t. $\mathbf{y}_t^{EU-GER}$ is obtained using German industrial production up to 1998:12 and euro-area industrial production from 1999:1 onward;
- $\boldsymbol{\pi}_t^{US}$ and $\boldsymbol{\pi}_t^{EU-GER}$ are annual inflation rates (based on consumers' prices). $\boldsymbol{\pi}_t^{EU-GER}$ is obtained by considering German data up to 1998:12 and the euro-area HICP index from 1999:1 onward;
- the short-term rates $i_{t,t+1}^{US}, i_{t,t+1}^{GER}$ are the policy rates: the Federal Funds rate for the US, the German policy rate up to 1999:1, and the euro-area overnight rates thereafter;
- the long-term rates $i_{t,t+120}^{US}, i_{t,t+120}^{GER}$ are the yields to maturity on ten-year bench-mark government bonds.

To construct forecasts of future policy rates and future inflation, we estimate a sequence of VARs by rolling least squares using a window of ten years of observations. The lag length of each estimated VAR is decided on the basis of standard optimal lag-length selection criteria. The restriction $\mathbf{A}_{12} = 0$ saves degrees of freedom by applying the standard assumption that US variables do not respond to euro-area variables.

Denoting with $\mathbf{Z}_t = \mathbf{A}_t\mathbf{Z}_{t-1} + \mathbf{u}_t$ the stacked representation of the sequence of estimated VARs, we construct $i_{t,T}^{*,US}, i_{t,T}^{*,GER}, \pi_{t,T}^{*,US}$ and $\pi_{t,T}^{*,EU-GER}$ as follows:

$$i_{t,T}^{*,US} = \frac{1-\gamma_{US}}{1-\gamma_{US}^{T-t}}\sum_{j=1}^{T}\gamma_{US}^{j-1}e_3'\mathbf{A}_t^{j-1}\mathbf{Z}_t$$

$$i_{t,T}^{*,GER} = \frac{1-\gamma_{GER}}{1-\gamma_{GER}^{T-t}}\sum_{j=1}^{T}\gamma_{GER}^{j-1}e_7'\mathbf{A}_t^{j-1}\mathbf{Z}_t$$

$$\pi_{t,T}^{*,US} = \frac{1-\gamma_{US}}{1-\gamma_{US}^{T-t}}\sum_{j=1}^{T}\gamma_{US}^{j-1}e_2'\mathbf{A}_t^{j-1}\mathbf{Z}_t$$

$$\pi_{t,T}^{*,EU-GER} = \frac{1-\gamma_{GER}}{1-\gamma_{GER}^{T-t}}\sum_{j=1}^{T}\gamma_{GER}^{j-1}e_6'\mathbf{A}_t^{j-1}\mathbf{Z}_t$$

$$T = t + 120$$

where γ_{US} and γ_{GER} are computed using average long-term rates over the previous 120 observations and the $e_k'\,(k=2,3,6,7)$ are column selection vectors with elements equal to 1 in the kth position, and equal to 0 anywhere else.

Figures 8.3 and 8.4, and 8.5 and 8.6 show the results of our two decompositions. We are unable to identify separately the long real rate $rr_{t,T}$ from the inflation premium $IP_{t,T}$ in equation (2), since we can only project future values of observed variables: thus, in Figure 4, we report the sum of the two.

Before analyzing the various components we check the reliability of our VAR-based decompositions comparing $\pi_{t,T}^{*,US}$ and $\pi_{t,T}^{*,EU-GER}$ with the breakeven inflation rates implicit in the yield on inflation-indexed bonds: ten-year US TIPs and the French ten-year OATi (indexed to the French CPI) for the euro area. The comparison – over the available sample – is reported in Figures 8.7 and 8.8. In both series expected inflation is the average expected inflation over a ten-year period computed using the same weights used to build long rates from a sequence of expected short rates. Breakeven inflation rates built from indexed bonds include, however, an inflation risk premium that is not present in the series we construct. As Figure 8.7 and 8.8 shows the measures of expected inflation constructed using our VAR are close to breakeven inflation.

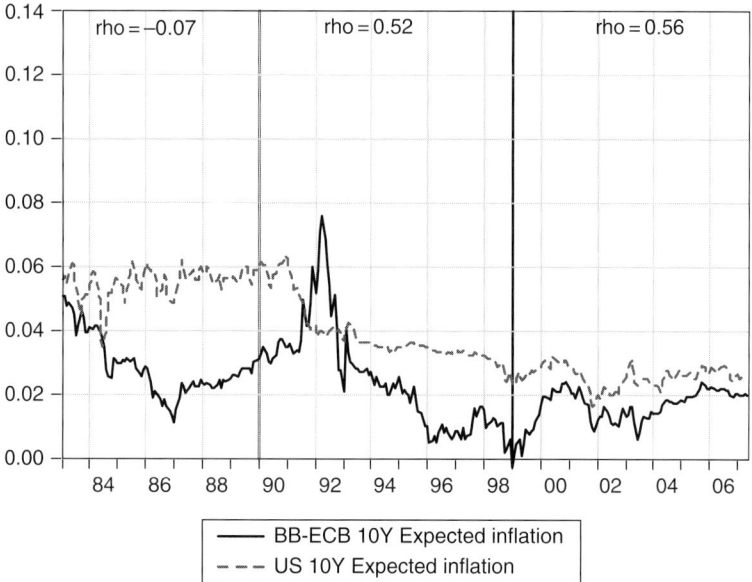

Figure 8.3: Ten-year expected inflation

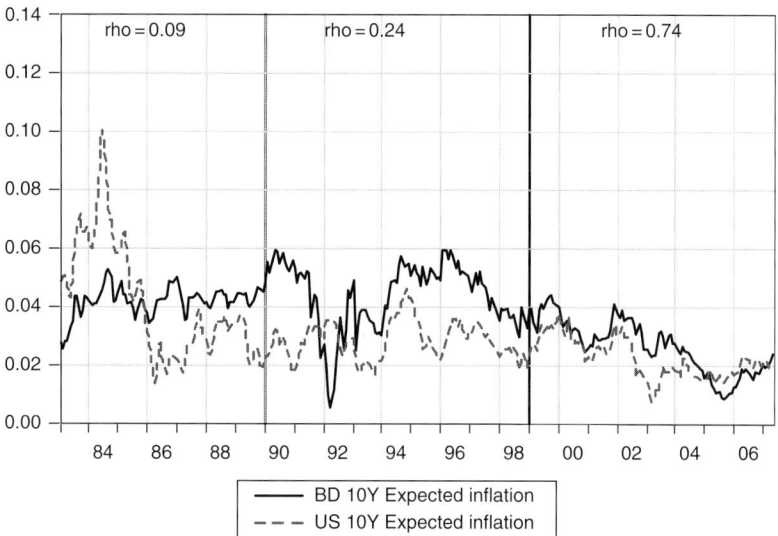

Figure 8.4: Ten-year yields – ten-year expected inflation

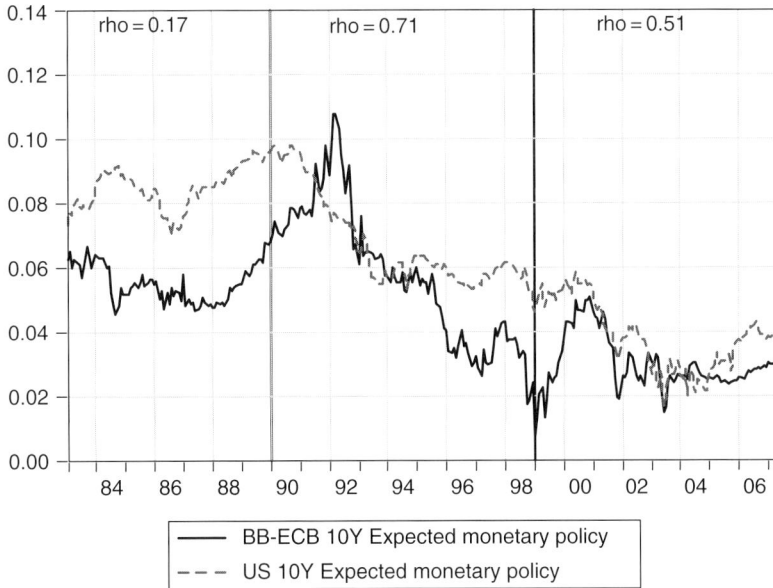

Figure 8.5: Ten-year expected monetary policy

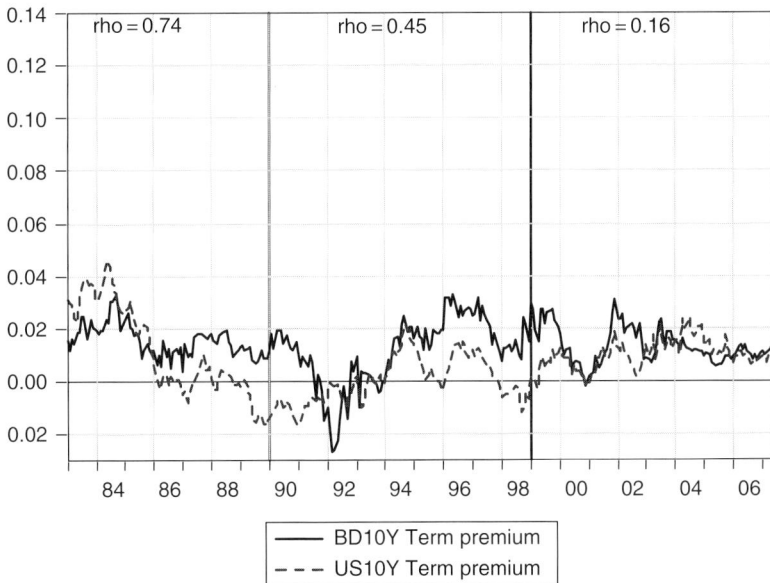

Figure 8.6: Ten-year term premia

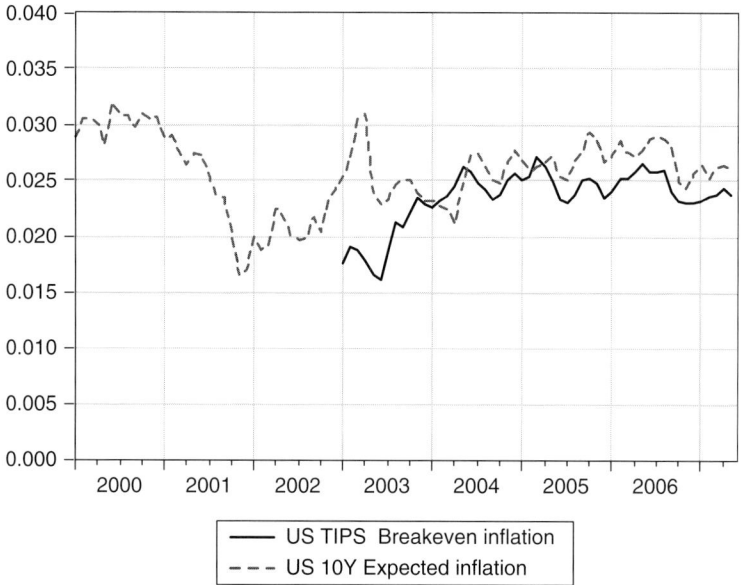

Figure 8.7: US VAR-based ten-year expected inflation and breakeven inflation in US ten-year TIPS

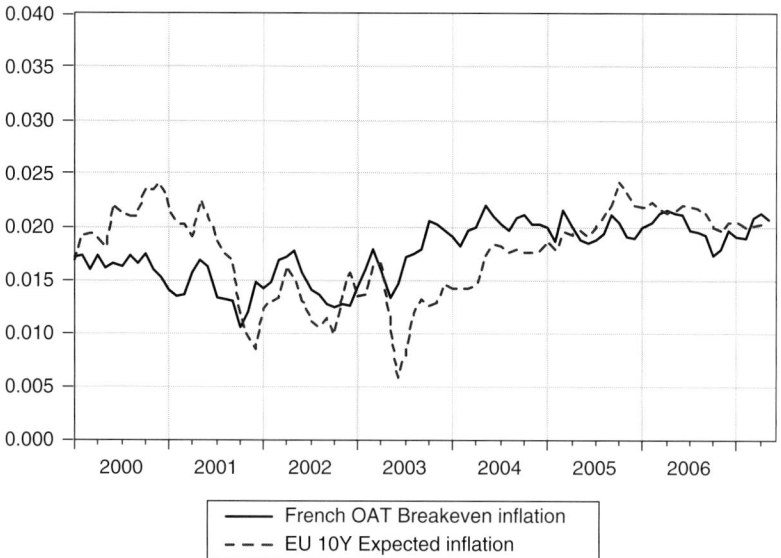

Figure 8.8: VAR-based ten-year euro-area expected inflation and breakeven inflation in ten-year French OATi

We now return to Figures 8.3 through 8.6. The main message from these figures is that the convergence in the levels of euro-area and US long rates, documented in Figure 8.1, is mainly due to the convergence in expected inflation and in expected monetary policy. More specifically:

- convergence in the levels of nominal yields is mainly due to the convergence in the levels of expected monetary policy in the two areas (Figure 8.5): the convergence in levels is paired with a clear increase in the correlation between the two series that rises from a value of 0.17 in the first decade to values of 0.71 and 0.51 in the second and third decades;
- parallel to the convergence in expected monetary policy there has been a sharp (though not complete) convergence in long-term expected inflation – though expected inflation remains slightly higher in the US relative to the euro area (Figure 8.3);
- term premia fall, from the first to third decade, in both the US and in the euro area (Figure 8.6). Their correlation across the two regions also becomes smaller (from 0.74 in the first decade to 0.16 in the most recent one). A lower level of term premia and a lower correlation of term premia across regions – while the correlation between long rates remains high – suggests that the importance of term premia in explaining fluctuations in US and German yields has declined over time;
- finally, convergence of nominal yields, but higher expected inflation in the US than in the euro area means that the sum of real long-term yields plus the inflation risk premium has become higher in the euro area compared with the USA.

An alternative way to investigate what determines the convergence of long rates in the two regions is to analyze the steady state solutions of the VARs we have estimated. These are reported in Figure 8.9 and show the long-run equilibrium values of long rates and their components. (For each of the samples we dynamically simulate the three estimated VARs starting from the initial conditions for all observable variables at the beginning of the sample.) The results suggest that the convergence in the levels of long-term rates is explained by the fact that the equilibrium values of all components have become more similar: real rates (plus the inflation risk premium), term premia, expected monetary policy, and expected inflation all appear to converge.

An interesting fact emerges from the lower panel of Figure 8.9: the convergence between euro-area and US expected monetary policy and

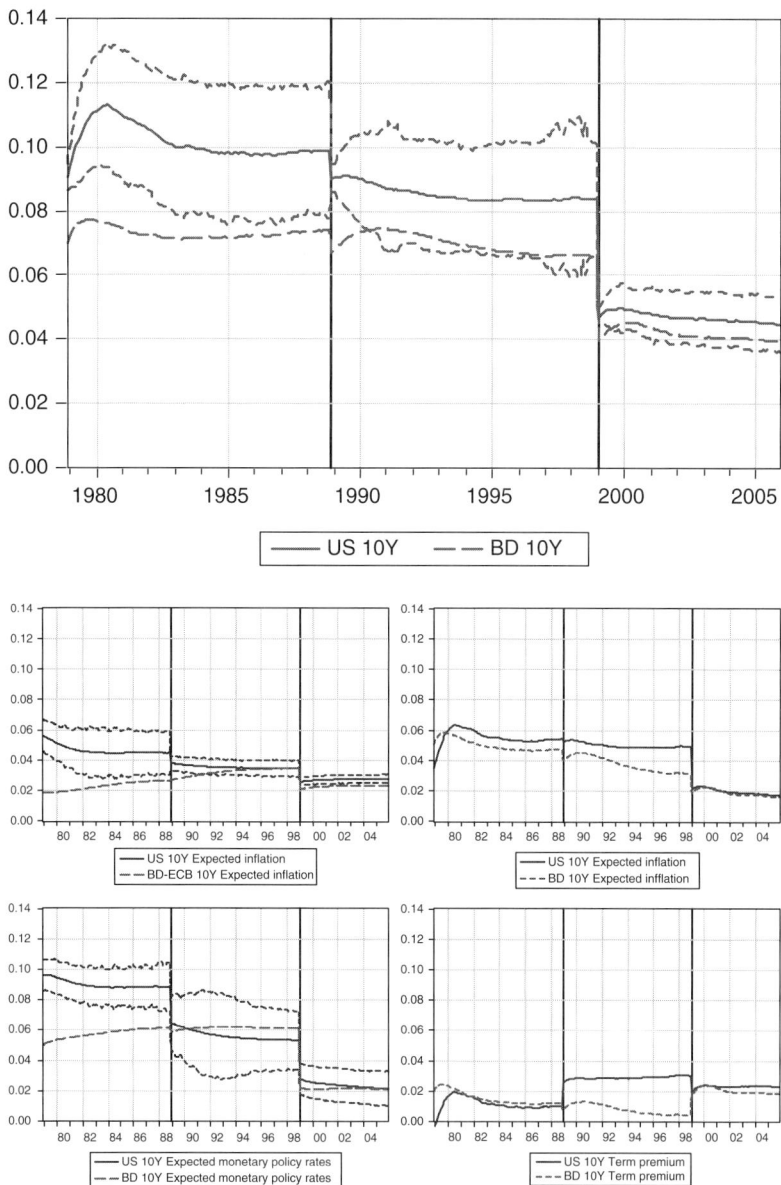

Figure 8.9: Dynamic simulations of VARs estimated over three different decades

expected inflation was already achieved in the early nineties; there is no difference between the second and third decades of our sample. This is not the case for term premia and real rates (plus the inflation risk premium) for which convergence happens only in the EMU decade. Thus, to the extent that one can detect a difference between the last decade of the 1990s and the most recent one, this seems to depend on factors that are not directly related to monetary policy.

2. Shocks or structure?

Long rates have converged because expected monetary policy (and thus expected inflation) has converged. But why did expected monetary policy converge? One possibility is that the shocks that hit the two regions are increasingly correlated: if this were the case it would not be surprising that expected monetary policies also converge. An alternative is that the shocks keep being different (as the low correlation of policy rates suggests) but long rates have converged because the structures of the two economies, including importantly the objectives of the two central banks, have become more similar.

To provide evidence on the relative importance of shocks and changes in economic structure – the systematic components of the VARs – in determining the convergence in the levels of long-term rates we run the following simple experiment.

- We first construct counterfactual long rates post-1990. We do this by simulating (dynamically) a model constructed by augmenting the systematic part – the VAR estimated over the post-1990 sample – with residuals drawn from their empirical distribution estimated on the pre-1990 sample;
- We then run the reverse exercise. We construct counterfactual pre-1990 rates by (dynamically) simulating a model constructed by augmenting the systematic part – the VAR estimated over the pre-1990 sample – with residuals drawn from their empirical distribution estimated on the post-1990 sample. (Note that this exercise uses the reduced form residuals: it is thus independent of any assumption needed to identify structural shocks, except for the restriction $A_{12} = 0$.)

These counterfactual simulations are shown in Figure 8.10. The results strengthen the evidence in favour of the hypothesis that the level of yields converged because the structure of the US and euro-area

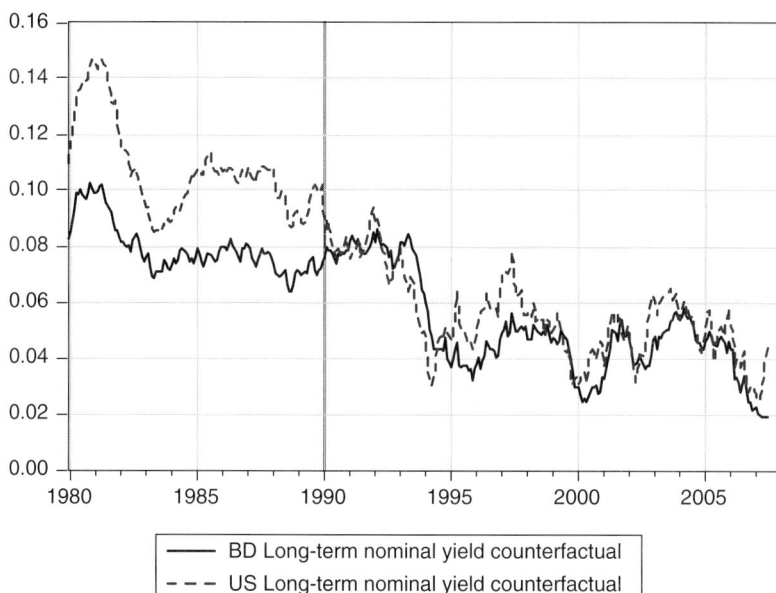

Figure 8.10: Counterfactual simulations: pre-1990 structure with post-1990 shocks, and post-1990 structure with pre-1990 shocks

economies converged, rather than the shocks which hit them.[1] In the pre-1990 counterfactual, the levels of European and US yields – generated using the pre-1990 structure and the post-1990 shocks – remain different. On the contrary, in the post-1990 sample, the counterfactual of the level of yields – constructed using post-1990 structure and pre-1990 shocks – remain close to each other.

2.1 Which elements of the "economic structure" have converged?

To address this question (remembering that "economic structure" includes the objectives of central banks) we study how the two long rates respond to monetary, to macroeconomic, and to term premia shocks and whether these responses have changed over time.

To do this we need first to identify such shocks: this requires additional identifying assumptions beyond $A_{21} = 0$. We identify four financial shocks: two monetary policy and two non-monetary policy shocks, respectively in the US and in the euro area. Monetary policy shocks are deviations from the systematic response of the two central banks to macroeconomic variables.

Non-monetary shocks – as we shall learn from impulse responses – are shocks to term premia: thus from now on we shall refer to them as "term premia shocks." We do not identify the shocks to the two macro variables, inflation and the output gap: we just consider them as macro shocks.

We make the following identifying assumption on the contemporaneous relations among the variables in the VAR: all macro variables react with at least a one-month lag to financial variables. Financial variables react simultaneously to macroeconomic developments. Monetary policy does not react to financial shocks in the month they happen. The recursive structure between the US and the euro area ($A_{21} = 0$) is assumed to hold also for the simultaneous relation among shocks.

Imposing these identification assumptions on the relation $C \epsilon = B\mathbf{u}$ between the eight VAR residuals $\mathbf{u}$ and the structural shocks

$$\epsilon = \left[\epsilon_t^{US,MP} \quad \epsilon_t^{US,TP} \quad \epsilon_t^{US,macro} \quad \epsilon_t^{US,macro} \quad \epsilon_t^{EU,MP} \quad \epsilon_t^{EU,TP} \quad \epsilon_t^{EU,macro} \quad \epsilon_t^{EU,macro}\right]'$$

means restricting B to be a diagonal matrix (i.e. standardizing the shocks) and imposing upon C the following restrictions:[2]

$$C = \begin{bmatrix} 1 & 0 & 0 & 0 & 0 & 0 & 0 & 0 \\ c_{21} & 1 & 0 & 0 & 0 & 0 & 0 & 0 \\ c_{31} & c_{32} & 1 & 0 & 0 & 0 & 0 & 0 \\ c_{41} & c_{42} & c_{43} & 1 & 0 & 0 & 0 & 0 \\ c_{51} & c_{52} & 0 & 0 & 1 & 0 & 0 & 0 \\ c_{61} & c_{62} & 0 & 0 & c_{65} & 1 & 0 & 0 \\ c_{71} & c_{72} & c_{73} & c_{74} & c_{75} & c_{76} & 1 & 0 \\ c_{81} & c_{82} & c_{83} & c_{84} & c_{85} & c_{86} & c_{87} & 0 \end{bmatrix}$$

Table 8.1 summarizes the effects of the structural shocks on euro-area long rates. The entries in the table are the forecasting errors when we use our VAR to predict long rates in the future. Our identification assumptions allow us to decompose the variance of these forecasting errors in six orthogonal components: monetary policy, term premia, and macro shocks (a combination of shocks to inflation and output gaps) in the US and in the euro area. We compute the variance of the forecasting errors at two different horizons: one month ahead and 120 months (ten years) ahead. The exercise is repeated for three subsamples.

Two findings emerge from Table 8.1:

- the one-month ahead forecasting error is always almost totally explained by a combination of US and euro-area term premia shocks; the forecasting variance of long rates attributable to monetary policy

Table 8.1: *Variance decomposition of European ten-year rates*

sample		US shocks			Euro-area shocks		
		macro	MP	TP	macro	MP	TP
79–89	1-step	0.09	0.06	0.21	0.02	0.01	0.62
	120-step	0.35	0.11	0.24	0.11	0.05	0.14
90–98	1-step	0.03	0.01	0.11	0.04	0.01	0.80
	120-step	0.27	0.01	0.25	0.33	0.01	0.12
99–07	1-step	0.01	0.01	0.38	0.05	0.01	0.57
	120-step	0.12	0.06	0.18	0.30	0.04	0.30

shocks is small, both at the short and long (ten-year) horizon. This is as true in EMU as it was in the two previous decades;

- since the start of EMU the share of the forecasting variance (at the ten-year horizon) attributable to euro-area idiosyncratic macro and term premia shocks has increased. In the 1999–2007 sample 60 percent (0.30+0.30) of the variance of the forecasting error at a ten-year horizon is attributable to local non-monetary policy shocks; this share was 45 percent in the previous decade (0.33+0.12). Thus, when euro-area long rates deviate from their systematic component $(\mathbf{A}_t(L)\mathbf{y}_{t-1})$ this is mainly because of shocks to the local and US term premia and to local macro variables.

To better understand the effects of financial shocks on long rates in Figures 8.11–8.14 we analyze impulse responses. We report the responses of long-term rates and of their components as generated by the two decompositions proposed in the first section of the paper.

- The impact of US monetary policy shocks is shown in Figures 8.11.1–8.11.2. The response of euro area long-term rates changed significantly since the start of EMU. Now a US monetary tightening induces a fall in long rates in the euro area: this was not the case in the two preceding decades. As far as US variables are concerned our evidence confirms recent results by Roush (2007) who finds that the expectations theory works well to explain the behavior of the US term structure, conditionally upon monetary policy shocks.

- The effect of US non-monetary policy financial shocks is analyzed in Figures 8.12.1–8.12.2. The impulse responses show that these are

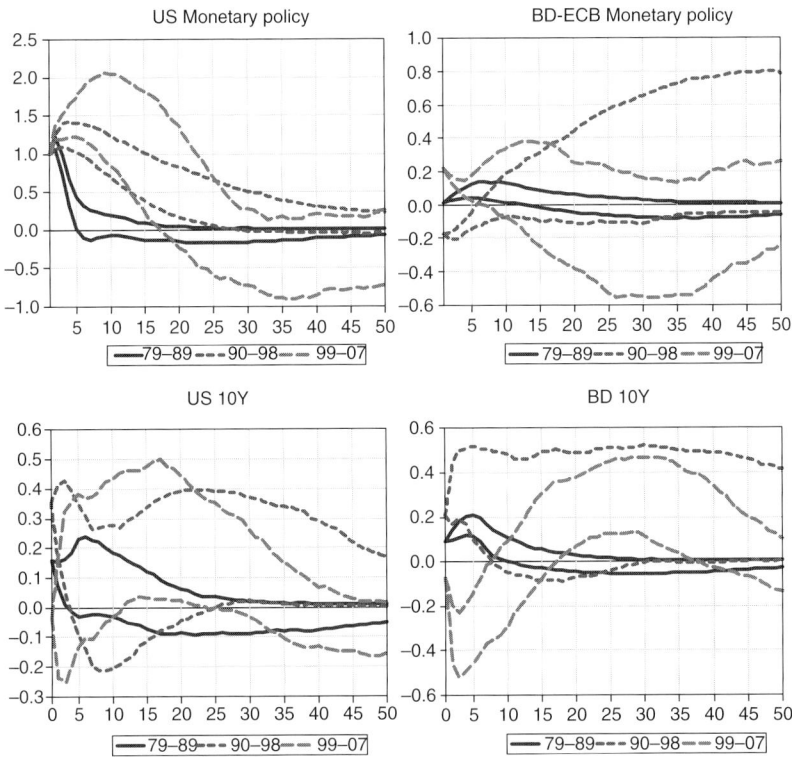

Figure 8.11.1: Impulse responses to US monetary policy shocks

shocks to US term premia and real ten-year rates (plus an inflation term premium). These shocks have a much stronger impact than US monetary policy shocks on European long rates. They generate a significant response in all subsamples, but the response is consistently much stronger in the post-1990 period than in the pre-1990 period. The response of European monetary policy to these shocks was much stronger in the 1990–8 period than it is the post-1999 period. As a consequence, in the 1990–8 period, the non-monetary policy-related components of long rates react less to US term premia shocks. This is consistent with decoupling of term premia in the period 1990–8 reported in the dynamic simulation shown in Figure 8.9.

- The effect of euro-area (Germany prior to 1999) monetary policy shocks is shown in Figure 8.13. Here we note immediately that in the

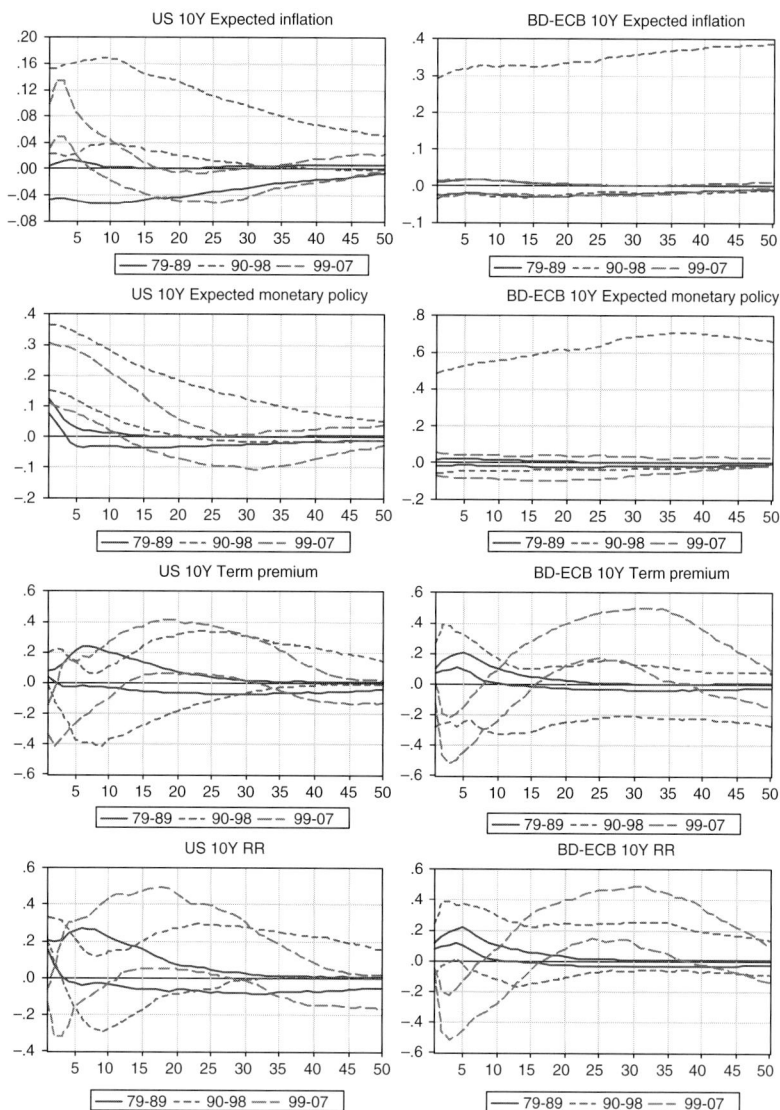

Figure 8.11.2: Impulse responses to US monetary policy shocks

period 1990–8, when the Bundesbank was conducting monetary policy, what we found in the US case – namely the evidence in favour of the expectations theory conditional upon monetary policy shocks – is not replicated in Europe (Germany): monetary policy shocks

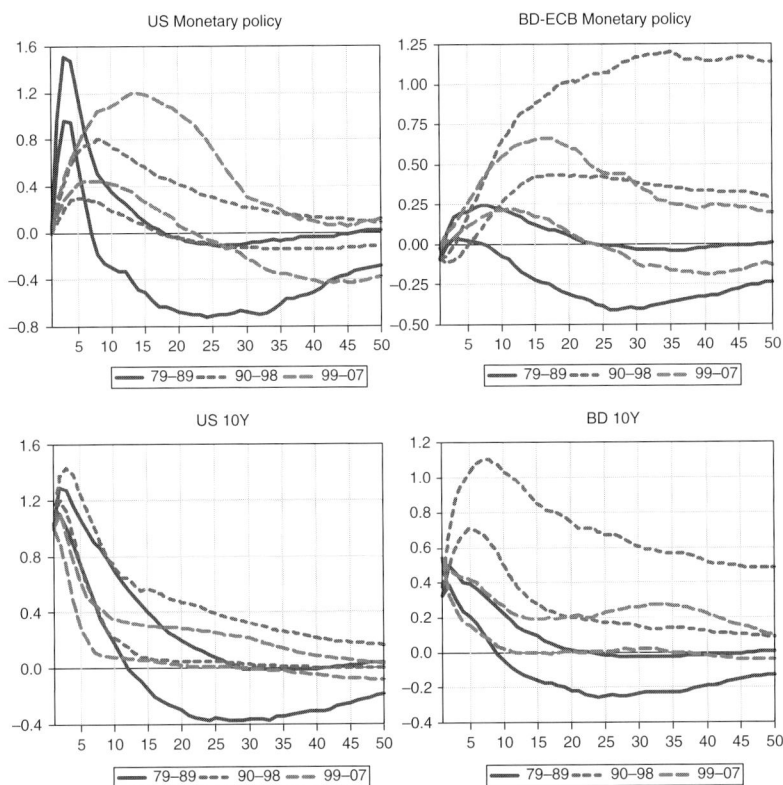

Figure 8.12.1: Impulse responses to US term premia shocks

have a significant negative effect on term premia. Interestingly, a contractionary monetary policy shock over the 1990–8 period induces a negative response in nominal long-term rates, as the reduction in risk premia more than compensates for the increase in expected monetary policy rates. Real and nominal long-term rates move in different directions. Such a response is completely overturned in the 1999–2007 period where a surprise monetary tightening moves the longrate upwards, as term premia, expected monetary policy, and the real long-term rates all move in the same direction.

- Finally, Figure 8.14 considers responses to euro-area financial, non-monetary policy shocks. Once again, these shocks can be interpreted as shocks to term premia and real rates, and are always paired with

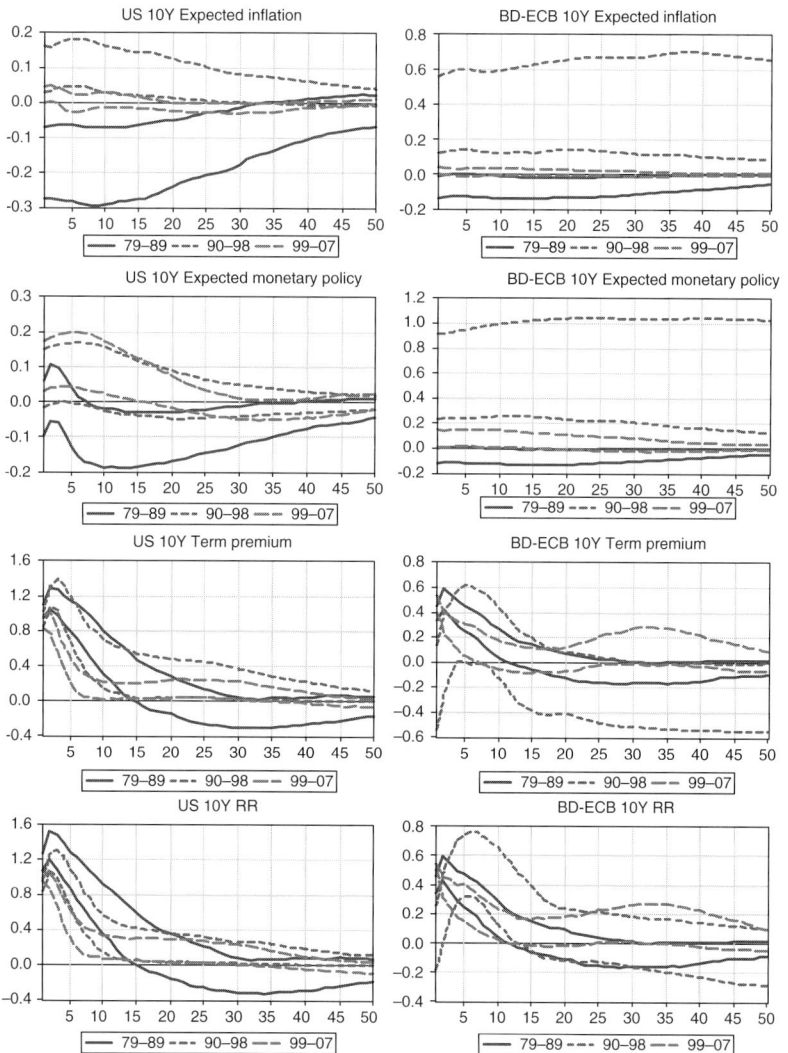

Figure 8.12.2: Impulse responses to US term premia shocks

a vigorous response of monetary policy, with the ECB being more aggressive than the Bundesbank. This evidence, along with the finding commented on above on the response to US term premia shocks, suggests that the ECB has responded to local financial shocks more than the Bundesbank used to.

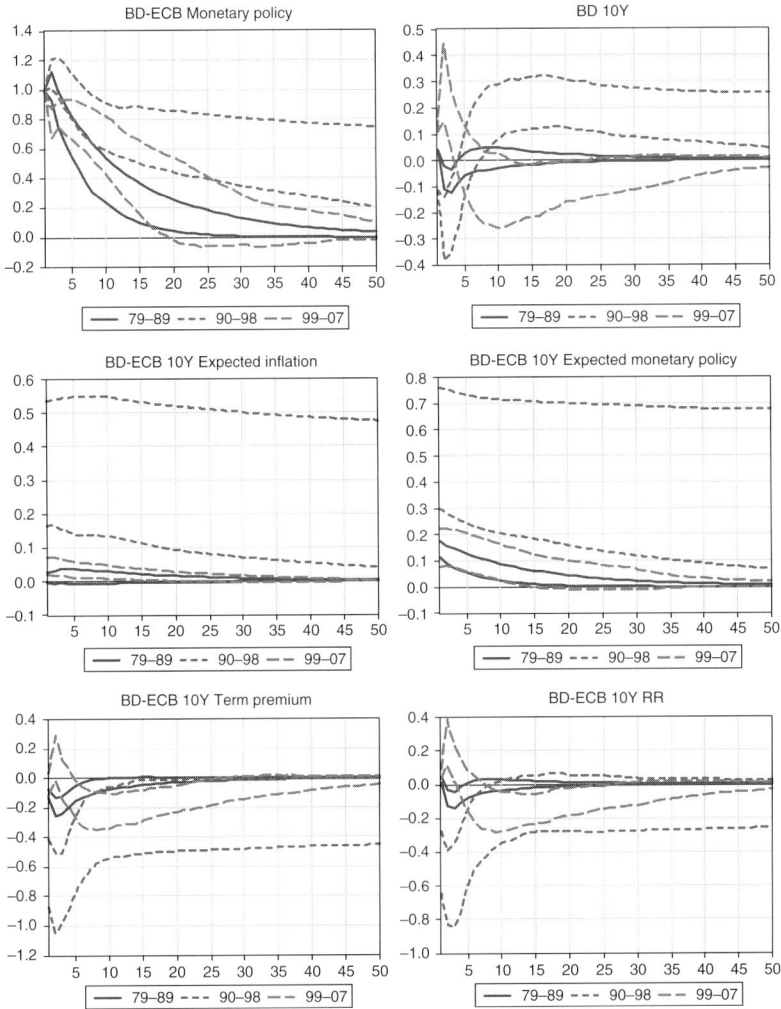

Figure 8.13: Impulse responses to Bundesbank-ECB monetary policy shocks

3. Conclusions

We have concentrated on two important facts emerging from the evolution of long rates in the euro area and in the USA over the past three decades:

- the correlation between euro-area and US yields has always been high, but the levels of the two yields, which were different in the 1980s, have converged to the same unconditional mean since the early 1990s;

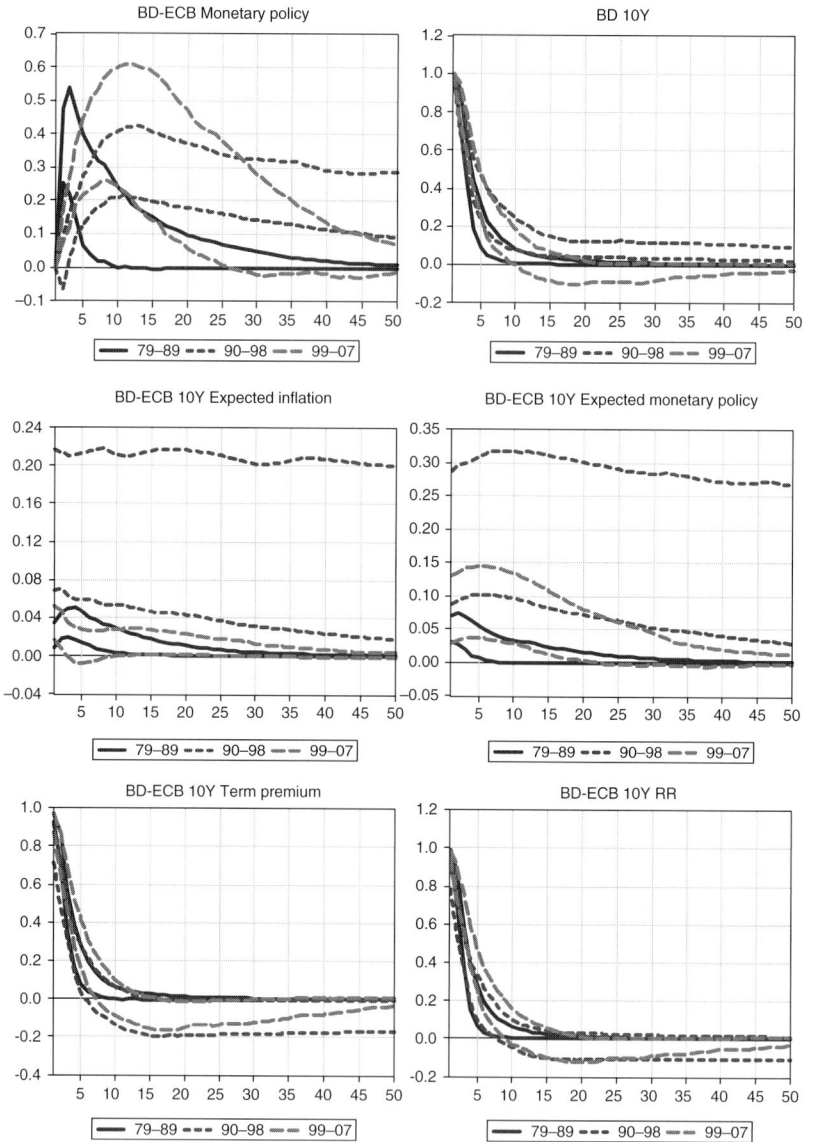

Figure 8.14: Impulse responses to German-Euro term premia shocks

- the high positive correlation between US and euro-area long-term rates is not a feature shared by monetary policy rates in any of the periods we have considered.

Decomposing long rates in their underlying factors – real rates (plus an inflation risk premium), term premia, expected monetary policy, and expected inflation – we find that the convergence of long rates reflects more similar economic structures in the USA and in the euro area, rather than a change in the distribution of shocks that hit the two regions.

As far as the response to shocks is concerned, since the start of EMU euro-area long rates have become more responsive to local non-monetary shocks: in the long run, however, they converge to the same level of US long rates because expected inflation and expected monetary policy also converge to similar levels. Policy rates in the euro area have also become more responsive to local non-monetary shocks.

Finally, since the start of EMU, a monetary tightening by the ECB raises long rates, contrary to what used to happen in the 1990s when the Bundesbank was running monetary policy. Interestingly, long rates in the euro area fall following a monetary tightening in the USA

Our evidence calls for a close study of the relative importance of monetary policy and international asset price fluctuations in determining euro-area macroeconomic variables. If macro fluctuations in the euro area depend more on asset price fluctuations than on shifts in the monetary policy rate, then the impact of policy on macro fluctuations is likely to be limited. Our results thus suggest that the models used for the design of euro-area monetary policy should consider explicitly the effects of asset price fluctuations and of their international comovements. This feature is currently absent from the main DSGE models used at the ECB – for example Smets and Wouters (2004).

Notes

1. Our exercise is similar to what Stock and Watson (2003) and Ahmed *et al.* (2004) have done to evaluate the "good policy" against "good luck" explanations of the Great Moderation. Benati and Surico (2008) argue that the evidence that switching shocks across subperiods inverts the final outcome is not decisive: the volatility of estimated shocks could be affected by the structure of the economy. However, our result – namely that

switching shocks does not invert the final outcome – cannot be explained by the Benati and Surico (2007) argument.

2. These assumptions are often used to identify US monetary policy shocks (see, for example, Christiano *et al.* 1999) and shocks to US long-term rates (see Evans and Marshall, 1998 and Edelberg and Marshall, 1996). The restrictions they imply satisfy the rank and order conditions for identification discussed in Amisano and Giannini (1997).

Comment 4: Comment on Chapter 8

DOMENICO GIANNONE, MICHELE LENZA AND
LUCREZIA REICHLIN

1. The chapter and its implications

Has the establishment of the European Monetary Union (EMU) affected European long-term interest rates and their comovement with those in the USA? What do you learn about European Central Bank (ECB) credibility and the transmission mechanism of monetary policy by answering this question? Favero and Giavazzi (FG)'s chapter is organized around these questions.

They start from the observation that long-term interest rates have been converging since the early nineties, before the establishment of the ECB. Their analysis attributes this process to convergence of expected monetary policy. The further narrowing of the gap between US and euro-area rates achieved in the last decade, on the other hand, is attributed to term premia and real rates, causes which have nothing to do with monetary policy. FG therefore seem to conclude that the EMU has not affected the dynamics of long rates. This is their answer to the first question.

To answer the second question the authors present two exercises: a counterfactual simulation which aims at identifying the causes of convergence in expected monetary policy and Vector Auto Regression (VAR) estimates of the joint dynamics of euro-area and US interest rates over different subsamples.

The first exercise tells us that convergence in expected monetary policy is due to convergence in the structure of the US and the German (1990–8) euro-area (1999–2007) economy rather than to similar exogenous shocks.

The second exercise produces several empirical results, two of which are key for understanding ECB monetary policy and its credibility with respect to that of the Bundesbank. One result is that, during ECB years, long rates have reacted positively to an unanticipated monetary policy contraction in contrast to the negative reaction during Bundesbank years. This suggests that the Bundesbank enjoyed more credibility than the ECB. Another result is that policy rates in the ECB sample respond more forcefully to non-monetary shocks specific to the euro area than in the Bundesbank years, suggesting that the ECB, insofar as this response is a deviation from systematic policy, has been inducing volatility in the market. This result, according to the authors, explains why short rates in the last decade have not been synchronized across the USA and euro area even if long rates have.

In our discussion we will focus on the two main points of the paper, credibility and policy response to idiosyncratic shocks. We will then extend the analysis of the bond market by proposing a unified explanation of the different degree of cross-country correlation of short and long rates. Finally, we will show that the cross-country synchronization of long rates over the last ten years is attributed to common global forces.

2. Credibility and the EMU

A standard way to assess the credibility of the EMU is to analyze inflation expectations and verify whether they have been well anchored around the ECB target. Below we provide some evidence to serve as background information for interpreting FG's results.

Figure C4.1 shows inflation rates in France, Germany, Italy, and the euro area as a whole from 1970 to 2006. Clearly, since the mid-nineties inflation rates have decreased drastically in Italy and France converging to those of Germany and stabilizing around the target of the ECB.

Convergence of inflation rates in countries of the euro area other than Germany is an important effect of the process leading to the monetary union and an aspect of ECB credibility not discussed by FG's chapter.

To examine inflation expectations during the ECB years, we report below the (quarterly) Survey of Professional Forecasters (SPF) for inflation in the euro area in the sample 1999Q1–2008Q2. Figure C4.2 plots the median, the mean, and the 25th and 75th percentiles of the distribution of the SPF's responses.[1]

Clearly, expectations have been well anchored in the period 1999Q1–2008Q2.

Beyond these data on professional forecasters, the ability of the ECB to anchor inflation expectations has been analyzed in depth by Ehrmann *et al.* (2007). Those authors study the effects of news on macroeconomic announcements and find that with the inception of

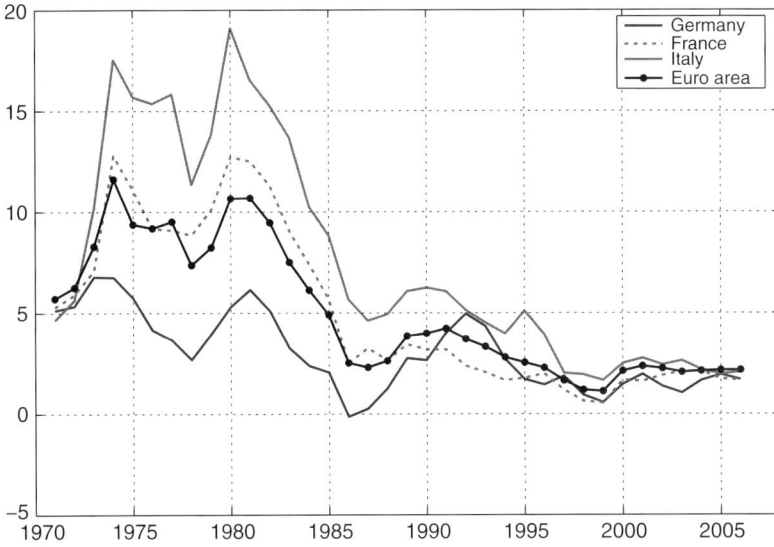

Figure C4.1: Inflation rates
Source: Eurostat.

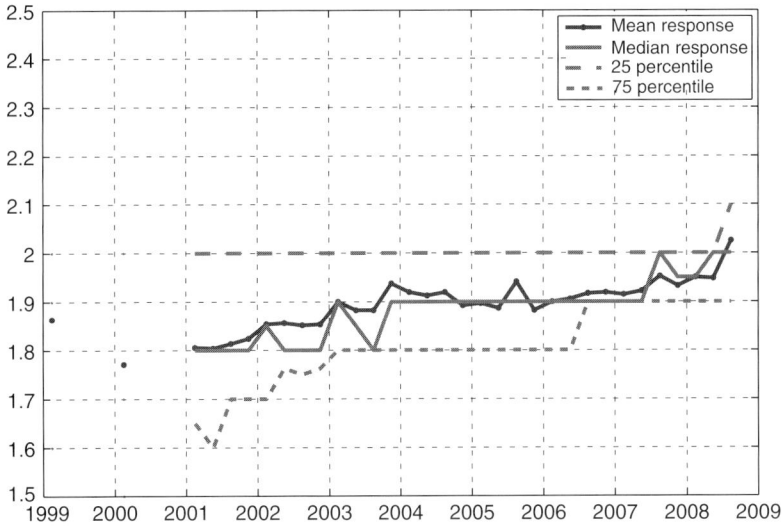

Figure C4.2: Long-run inflation expectations from the SPF
Source: ECB.

the EMU the long end of the yield curve (in particular, they look at very far ahead forward interest rates) has become less reactive to macroeconomic announcements that move the short end of the yield curve. This is true not only for countries that had a less credible monetary policy like Italy and France, but also for Germany.

FG propose an exercise which is similar in spirit to that of Ehrmann *et al.* (2007). However, instead of relying on observable measures of news, they use monetary policy shocks identified from their estimated VAR. Their results lead to a very different conclusion.

There are two reasons which may explain why results differ. First, FG's measure of news depends on their identification assumption and may not be robust to different identifying restrictions. Notice that, beside the assumptions implicit in the Choleski representation, the authors also assume that the USA is exogenous with respect to Germany (and, then, the euro area). Second, the VAR analysis is based on a very short sample of nine years of data and results are likely to be unstable.

Given the evidence on inflation expectations presented above and what is found in the literature on the effect of macro announcements, FG's result remains puzzling.

3. Response to idiosyncratic euro area shocks

One of the key results of the chapter is that both long and short rates in the euro area are mainly affected by idiosyncratic (euro-area specific) sources of fluctuations.

The result on the long rate is surprising since, as the authors themselves argue, US and euro-area rates have been very synchronized over the last fifteen years. The result on short-term rates is not as surprising, but needs further investigation.

To this aim, and to cross-check FG's result, we conduct a counter-factual experiment. Precisely, we estimate a VAR on the levels of real GDP, the GDP deflator, short and long rates for the USA and the euro area using quarterly data from 1970 to 2006[2] and we compute the most likely path of euro-area variables conditional only on the history of the US variables.

Let us collect US variables in the vector X_t^{US} and euro-area variables in X_t^{EA}. Defining $X_t = \begin{bmatrix} X_t^{US} & X_t^{EA} \end{bmatrix}$, the estimated model is:

$$X_t = A(L)X_{t-1} + e_t.$$

Then, on the basis of VAR estimates, we can compute the conditional expectation:[3]

$$\hat{E}\left(X_t^{EA}\middle|X_{t0}^{US}\dots X_T^{US}\right).$$

Clearly, if it were true that the two economies faced large idiosyncratic shocks, the conditional expectation would be very different from the observed euro-area variables. We report results for short (Figure C4.3) and long interest rates (Figure C4.4).

Clearly, the fit is very good for both rates: the simulated long rate is always within the bands and so is the short rate, with the exception of a couple of years in the early nineties. This implies that idiosyncratic European shocks play a very limited role in explaining not only fluctuations in the long rates in the euro-area economy, but also fluctuations in the policy rate.

As an additional cross-check we compute the percentage of the variance of euro-area interest rates accounted for by idiosyncratic sources of fluctuations. For the generic euro-area variable x_t, this is defined as:

$$V = \frac{Var\left(x_t - E\left(x_t\middle|X_{t0}^{US}..X_t^{US}..X_T^{US}\right)\right)}{Var(x_t)}.$$

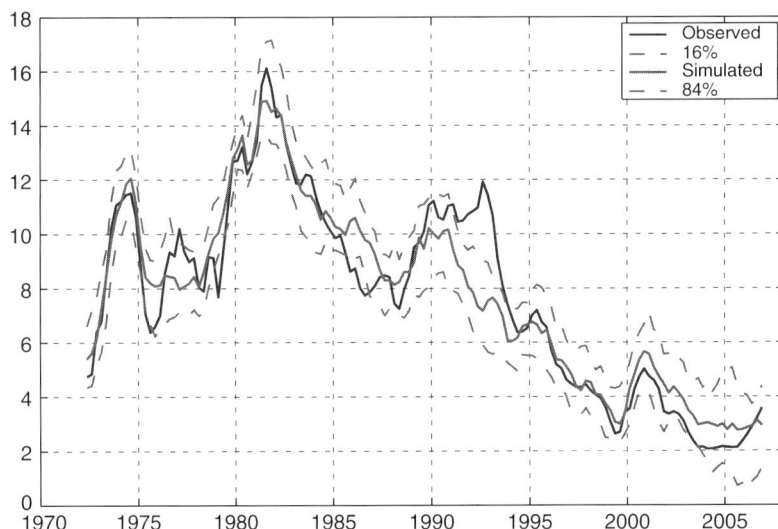

Figure C4.3: Short-term interest rates in the euro area
Source: ECB and authors' calculations.

Table C4.1: *Percentage of variance of interest rates
accounted for by idiosyncratic sources of fluctuation*

	Short rates	Long rates
Idiosyncratic variance	9.7%	4.6%

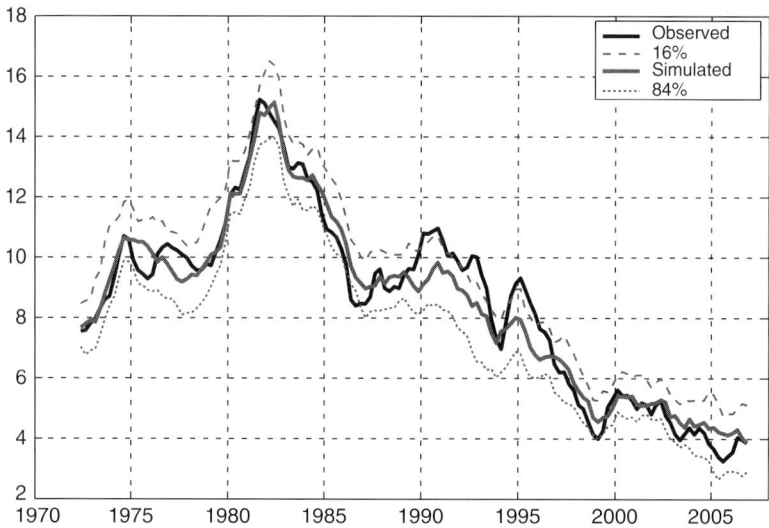

Figure C4.4: Long-term interest rates in the euro area
Source: ECB and authors' calculations.

Results are reported in Table C4.1.

Results confirm what was found for the conditional expectations. Global shocks explain a very high share of the variance of euro-area interest rates.

These findings are difficult to reconcile with FG's results which point to a large response of short and long rates to idiosyncratic euro-area specific shocks.

4. US-euro area business cycle and the policy rates

How do we reconcile the result from the previous section on the relation between US and the euro-area short rates and the observed lack of synchronization of these rates?

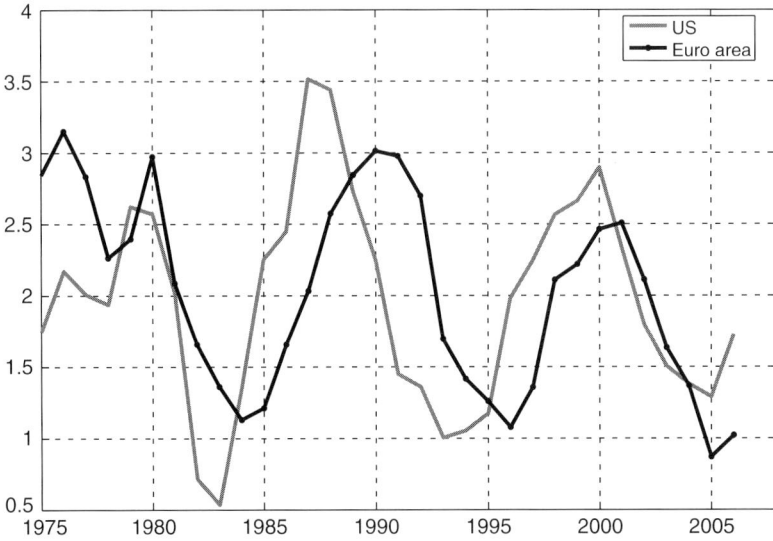

Figure C4.5: Five years (annualized) moving average of per capita real GDP growth rates
Source: Eurostat and authors' calculations.

Here we explore the conjecture that their lack of synchronization reflects the lead-lag relation among the US and euro-area business cycles and not idiosyncratic causes of variations.

We report the five-year moving average of output per capita GDP growth in the euro area and the USA (Figure C4.5) and the corresponding levels (Figure C4.6) (see Giannone and Reichlin, 2006b).

These figures suggest the hypothesis that real long rates have been similar since 1970 because long-run real economic activity has been the same in Europe and in the USA (the trend in GDP growth is the same), while differences in short-run rates reflect temporary non-synchronous output gaps. This explanation would be compatible with all the evidence we have shown so far.

5. World factors in long-term interest rates

The last decade has been a period of global financial integration which has affected the bond market and the relation between the short- and long-run rates worldwide. It is therefore difficult to analyze

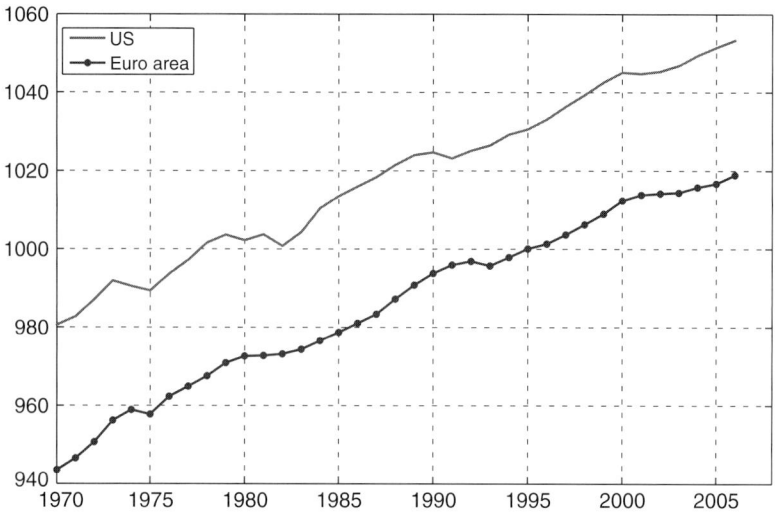

Figure C4.6: Levels of per capita real GDP
Source: Eurostat.

the credibility of the ECB on the basis of the changes in the transmission of policy rates to long rates since global forces have affected this relation.

Below we consider a wider panel of countries than we have done so far, and examine the relation between short and long rates in different subsamples.

Precisely, we consider a panel regression of the nominal long-term interest rate ($i_{i,t}^L$) on the nominal short-term interest rate ($i_{i,t}^S$) for all OECD countries[4] as a baseline:

Baseline

$$i_{i,t}^L = a_{i,b} + \beta_b i_{i,t}^S + e_{i,t}$$

where b stands for baseline and i for country (we include all the countries).

In order to control for the world interest rate we also consider the alternative "global" specification:

Global

$$i_{i,t}^L = a_{i,b} + \beta_g i_{i,t}^S + \gamma i_{W,t}^L + u_{i,t}$$

Table C4.2: *Estimated beta coefficients:*
panel regression results

Sample	Baseline	Global
1974–2004	0.8 (0.02)	0.5 (0.02)
1974–83	0.6 (0.04)	0.5 (0.05)
1984–93	0.6 (0.03)	0.5 (0.03)
1994–2004	0.8 (0.04)	0.2 (0.03)

where $i^L_{W,t}$ is the global interest rate measured as a weighted average of the countries' interest rates. The weights for the country-specific interest rates in the aggregate are those of the first principal component.

We consider different subsamples: 1974–2004, 1974–83, 1984–93, 1994–2004 and report the estimated β_b and β_g with standard error in parenthesis.[5]

Results are illustrated in Table C4.2. They indicate that, since the last decade and once we control for the world interest rate, the sensitivity of the long interest rates to the policy rates declines quite substantially.

The implications of these results for our discussion is that, as conjectured, the differences in interest rate dynamics between the period 1994–2004 and the previous decades (the Bundesbank versus the ECB) are difficult to interpret in terms of relative credibility of the central bank. In the last decade, world factors have become a more important component of interest rate dynamics everywhere, changing the transmission of monetary policy to long-term interest rates worldwide.

In fact, the authors are well aware of the importance of global factors for the bond market and indeed the interaction between the world and the euro area is central in their empirical exercise. However, they fail to see the implications of this point when comparing the last decade and the previous period.

6. Conclusions

The world indeed matters for the bond market, as argued by FG's chapter. The world also matters for explaining both short and long interest rates. We have shown that, when the dynamics of the euro area and the USA are jointly modelled, long and short rates in the euro area are mostly explained by shocks common with the USA. This result, obtained with a different methodology than that proposed in the chapter, sheds doubts on

FG's finding on long and short rates responding aggressively to idiosyncratic euro-area shocks.

Evidence from the bond market in countries other than Germany and the analysis of long rates' response to macro announcements (see Ehrmann *et al.*, 2007) suggest that ECB matters for the bond market for having contributed with other central banks to a low inflation credible environment. The expectation of the EMU triggered the convergence of the nominal rates in those countries of the euro area whose central banks did not enjoy the Bundesbank's credibility. Moreover, since 1999, evidence from the Survey of Professional Forecasters points to anchored inflationary expectations. This evidence is difficult to reconcile with the analysis of credibility offered by the paper. FG's analysis of ECB credibility is ingenious, but seems to miss the big picture. Should we conclude that the ECB has lost credibility with respect to the Bundesbank by just looking at Germany? Should we trust results of impulse response functions estimated on the basis of less than ten years of data which do not appear to be robust to alternative model specifications? Finally, in interpreting term structure facts over the last ten years we must be aware of changes which have affected financial markets globally. These are the points we have developed in our discussion.

Notes

1. Notice that the SPF has been quarterly since 2001, while for both 1999 and 2000 there is only one observation.
2. The short-term interest rates for the USA are the three-month T-bill rate and the ten-year bond rate. The interest rates and the macroeconomic data for the USA are taken from the IMF International Financial Statistics database. As for the euro area, data are taken from the Area Wide Model database.
3. The VAR is estimated by Bayesian techniques using Litterman/Random Walk priors. The tightness of the prior for the degree of shrinkage is set using ideas developed in Bańbura *et al.* (2008). Precisely, since a bivariate VAR with the GDP of the USA and the euro area provides a very accurate description of the fluctuations in European economic activity (see Giannone and Reichlin, 2006b; Giannone *et al.*, 2008b), we set the tightness parameter such that the eight variables VAR fits the euro-area GDP as well as the bivariate VAR. The algorithm used to compute the conditional expectation is the same as in Giannone and Lenza (2008).
4. The data for the interest rates come from the OECD Economic Outlook and refer to the following countries: Australia, Austria, Belgium, Canada, Finland, France, Germany, Italy, Japan, the Netherlands, New Zealand, Portugal, Switzerland, the United Kingdom, and the United States.
5. Results are reported from Reichlin (2006).

9 | Financial market integration under EMU

TULLIO JAPPELLI AND MARCO PAGANO

1. Introduction

The single most important policy-induced innovation in the international financial system since the collapse of the Bretton-Woods regime is the institution of the European economic and monetary union (EMU). It has opened up the possibility of a fully integrated continental financial market comparable to that of the United States. By eliminating exchange rate risk, EMU has taken away a crucial obstacle to financial integration. Before EMU, otherwise identical financial claims denominated in different euro-area currencies were imperfect substitutes and traded at different prices. EMU has put an end to this source of market segmentation.

Yet if a single currency is a necessary condition for the emergence of pan-European capital markets, it is not a sufficient one. Other frictions may still impede full integration: even after the removal of exchange rate risk, persistent differences in the regulations applying to financial intermediaries, tax treatment, standard contractual clauses and business conventions, issuance policy, security trading systems, settlement systems, availability of information, and judicial enforcement may still segment markets along national lines. In the process that preceded and accompanied the introduction of the euro, however, monetary unification also triggered a sequence of policy actions and private sector responses that swept many of these other regulatory barriers aside.

To what extent has this process of regulatory reform led to actual financial integration? And if European financial markets have actually become more integrated, to what extent have these changes spurred – or

We thank John Berrigan, Marie Donnay, Christine Gerstberger (European Commission), and Simon Hayes (Barclays Capital) for their helpful remarks and suggestions. We also acknowledge useful comments from Michael Bordo, Richard Portes, and other participants to the Commission's EMU@10 Workshop, 26–7 November 2007.

can be expected to spur – growth and investment in Europe? Will financial integration also affect the ability of households to shoulder risks, or the ability of European economies to adjust to macroeconomic shocks? This chapter seeks to answer these questions in the broader context of the burgeoning literature on the complex links between regulation, finance, and real economic activity.

To put matters in perspective, Figure 9.1 provides a road map to the main links, underscoring that legal norms and their enforcement can spur financial development. For instance, cross-border liberalization can sharpen banking competition and thereby expand the credit industry. It is at this juncture that financial reform designed to integrate national capital markets can have an impact on financial development.

Why is the development of financial markets important? As the figure shows, improved access to bank lending and to securities markets is associated with increased investment and economic activity. The vast literature on the role of financial markets in spurring growth has identified a number of channels through which financial development affects investment and growth. First, by narrowing the wedge between the cost of capital to firms and the return paid to households, a more efficient financial industry should raise the level of investment. Second, it should improve the allocation of investment across alternative projects, with

Road map

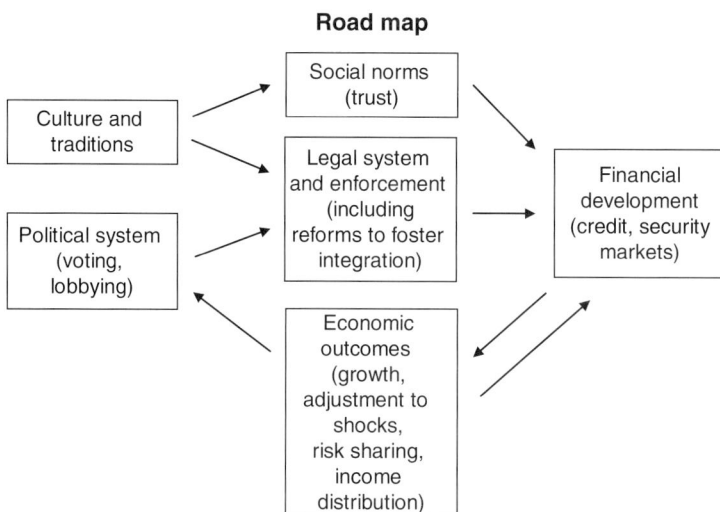

Figure 9.1: Road map

the funding of higher-return and riskier ventures, thanks to enhanced risk sharing.[1]

To evaluate the effects of financial development on investment and growth empirically, one must control for reverse causality: real economic activity may have a feedback effect on financial development, insofar as greater investment means a greater demand for external finance – an effect that Figure 9.1 captures in the arrow from economic outcomes to financial development. Indeed, empirical researchers in this area have been busy sorting out whether it is finance that facilitates investment and growth or the other way around.

The possible effects of financial development on the real economy go beyond the growth rate, however. Developed financial markets change the way the economy responds to shocks, insofar as they enable firms to use international capital markets to fund domestic investment, and households to invest savings abroad. More generally, financial development enhances the ability of households and financial institutions to diversify risks. It can also affect the distribution of income between social groups and industries by favoring the expansion of groups and industries with strong growth opportunities but low current resources.

Figure 9.1 also illustrates that regulatory change does not take place in a vacuum: it requires political support and an appropriate cultural climate. Identical formal rules can have vastly different effects depending, for instance, on prevailing social norms, as is shown by the literature on the role of trust in economic interactions.[2] Indeed, social norms can even have a direct impact on the development of capital markets. Franks *et al.* (2003) show that in the early twentieth century British firms could rely on a dispersed shareholder base, due more to informal relations of trust than to formal regulation.

The politics of financial regulation are important for the future of European financial integration: to command continued political support, the reforms designed to create an integrated financial market must be perceived as beneficial by a sufficiently large constituency. This of course underscores the key question: whether the degree of financial integration triggered by monetary unification has paid – or can be expected to pay – a "growth dividend." This explains why Figure 9.1 also shows a feedback effect from the real effects of financial development to the political forces that determine regulation.

With these questions in mind, in this chapter we define financial integration and consider how to measure it, analyze the barriers to it and how their removal should affect financial markets, and assess whether the euro area has actually become more integrated (Section 2). Then we inquire how far these changes in financial markets have affected the performance of the real economy, that is, growth and investment (Section 3), as well as the ability of the entire economy to adjust to shocks (Section 4) and that of European households to share risks (Section 5). We conclude with some policy implications for the future of European financial markets (Section 6).

2. Financial integration and financial development

Financial markets are integrated when the law of one price holds; that is, when securities with identical cash flows command the same price. In other words, if a firm issues bonds in two countries or regions, it must pay the same interest rate to both sets of bondholders. Similarly, if it raises equity, it must pay the same for capital in both markets. This notion also extends to credit markets: when they are integrated, a firm or household should be able to borrow on the same terms irrespective of the location of its bank.

This definition immediately implies that to measure the degree of financial integration of a region one needs to compare prices – or rates of return – for comparable securities issued in different areas within it. This generates price-based or return-based measures, such as interest rates differentials, and calls for the analysis of interest rate convergence. But since the definition also implies the ability to access external finance on the same terms both domestically and internationally, one can also look at the cross-border provision of credit and equity financing, and especially how it has changed in the wake of financial market reforms. This produces another set of indicators, i.e. quantity-based measures of financial integration.[3]

2.1 Barriers to financial integration

What can stand in the way of the law of one price? First, if two jurisdictions have different currencies, exchange rate fluctuations create additional risk, and investors will require a risk premium to hold a security denominated in a foreign currency. And even if there are no exchange rate fluctuations, transaction costs for currency conversion will induce a deviation from international arbitrage. A second barrier to integration stems from differential taxes and subsidies, which drive a wedge between the after-tax cost of capital in different countries.

Next, differences in regulation and enforcement can prevent financial intermediaries from competing across borders on equal footing. For instance, regulation can create stiffer entry barriers for foreign inter- mediaries; similarly, judicial efficiency can differ across countries, requiring intermediaries to charge higher interest rates in inefficient jurisdictions to compensate for expected recovery costs in case of default.

Finally, entry barriers may arise not from regulatory constraints but from asymmetric information between potential foreign entrants and domestic incumbents. This is particularly relevant in credit markets, where the opacity of firms and households combines with local knowl- edge to give local lenders an informational advantage.

The introduction of the euro has eliminated exchange rate risk and the costs of exchange rate transactions within the eurozone, directly removing one of the main barriers to financial integration. In addition, the process leading to monetary unification triggered a sequence of policy actions and private sector responses that swept aside many other regulatory barriers to financial integration. For instance, controls on capital flows were removed, banking and financial service directives created a level playing field in the credit and securities markets, and the rules governing the issuance of public debt were harmonized. These effects are captured in Miniane's index of legal restrictions on cross- border capital flows, which dropped sharply for most euro-area coun- tries in the 1990s (Miniane, 2004).

By eliminating some barriers to financial integration, these policy actions boosted efficiency in the financial intermediaries and markets of the euro-area countries where the financial system was more back- ward and more heavily regulated. To the extent that greater efficiency stimulates the demand for funds and for financial services, this also fostered the growth of domestic financial markets or improved access to foreign markets and intermediaries.

2.2 The effect of integration on financial development

The main channel through which the removal of barriers to integration can spur domestic financial development is increased competition with more sophisticated or lower-cost foreign intermediaries. This competitive pressure drives down the cost of financial services for the firms and households of countries with less developed financial systems, and thus expands local financial markets. In some cases, the foreign entrants themselves may supply the additional financial services. Direct penetration by foreign banks and cross-border acquisitions of intermediaries are likely to erode local banks' rents. If mergers bring banks closer to their efficient scale, the process will also be associated with a decreasing cost of intermediation. Sharper competition, possibly coupled with cost cutting, translates into more abundant credit and/or lower interest rates.

A second channel is through harmonization in national regulations (accounting standards, security laws, bank supervision, corporate governance), which the process of integration requires. To the extent that regulatory harmonization promotes convergence to the best international standards, it will also enhance domestic financial development and the entry of foreign financial intermediaries in more backward countries.

On both accounts, therefore, the removal of barriers to financial integration can bring about an improvement in the supply of finance in less developed markets and an increase in their depth as measured by size-based gauges of financial development, such as domestic stock market capitalization and the volume of bank lending relative to GDP. Insofar as financial integration induces this "catching-up effect," one should observe some convergence in the indicators of domestic financial development. Figure 9.2 displays the time pattern of the coefficient of variation across the eleven initial euro-area countries for three such indicators: the GDP ratios of stock market capitalization, private bond market capitalization, and private credit, all drawn from the online database of Ross Levine.[4]

International convergence should translate into a lower cross-country dispersion in these indicators between 1990 and 2005. And in fact there is a perceptible, steady decline in the coefficient of variation for the private bond market, from almost 0.7 in 1990 to about 0.5 in 2005. For the credit market the reduction is not as large, though still appreciable (from about 0.4 to 0.3), but this market was already much more uniform across countries in 1990. For stock market capitalization, no clear trend is to be observed possibly because this indicator is dominated by country-specific stock price swings.

It is interesting that, of these three markets, the bond market has taken the largest step towards convergence. As we shall see in the next

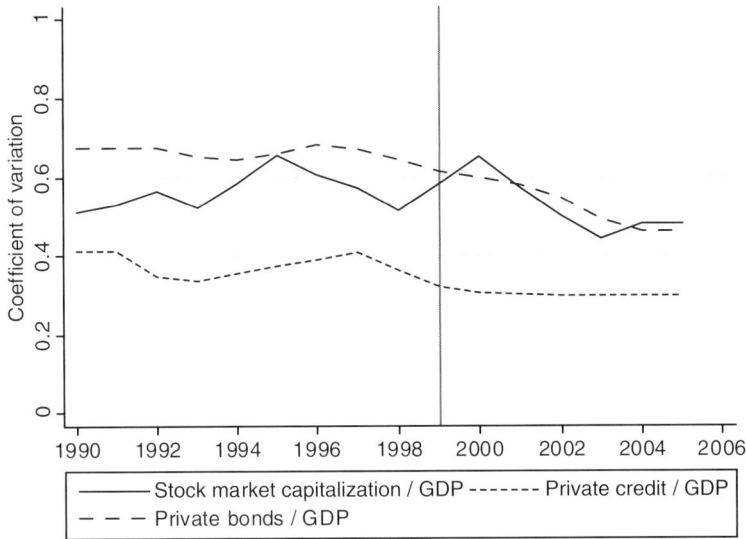

Figure 9.2: Indicators of domestic financial development in the euro area

section, there are also other indicators that the bond market has been the greatest beneficiary of the single currency. As for the credit and the stock markets, Figure 9.2 suggests a less definitive verdict.

However, the convergence in the depth of *domestic* financial markets may give a very incomplete account of the degree of financial integration and of its true effects on the availability of finance to firms and households. Indeed, it may happen that, as financial integration proceeds, the most developed financial systems increase the provision of services to firms and households located in less developed markets. The economies of scale and the external economies involved in financial intermediation can be a powerful force for the expansion of the established intermediaries of already developed markets. The banks of the more developed countries can lend cross-border to firms in less advanced countries, in which case the additional credit will not show up as private domestic credit in those countries. Similarly, financial services provided by foreign intermediaries will not appear in the domestic supply of such services in less financially developed countries. Thus, size-based measures of local financial development alone may not fully reflect the improvement in the availability of credit and financial services.

A similar argument applies to equity markets. As these become more integrated, firms in the less financially developed countries can access major financial centers more easily by listing on foreign stock exchanges. They may want to do so for a variety of reasons: overcoming equity rationing in the domestic market, reducing their cost of capital by turning to a more liquid market, signaling their quality by accepting the scrutiny of more informed investors or the rules of a better corporate governance system (Pagano et al., 2001, 2002; Halling et al., 2008). Whatever the reasons, by listing abroad these firms add to the stock market capitalization and turnover of foreign exchanges rather than their domestic ones, as documented by Claessens et al. (2002a, 2002b). Thus the increase in domestic stock market capitalization may not fully reflect the impact of financial integration on access to equity markets in the less financially developed countries.

The implication is that as financial integration proceeds, the size of a country's financial market may provide a misleading picture of its degree of financial development. Distance, and hence geographical segmentation, become less important in financially integrated markets. Indeed, with full integration what matters is the total size of the market of the entire integrating area. Domestic firms may have the same access as foreign ones, even if the domestic financial sector is smaller. For the same reason, countries that specialize in financial services will have a domestic financial sector that serves domestic as well as foreign firms.

The importance of cross-border provision of debt and equity finance in the process of integration is illustrated in Figure 9.3. The gross international investment position – the sum of the stock of external assets and liabilities of each area vis-à-vis the rest of the world – is shown for the euro area, the United States, and Japan. The figure suggests that euro-area integration accelerated impressively, compared with the United States and Japan, starting in 1996. Most of the advance since 1999 has actually been due to the increase in external assets and liabilities *within* the euro area, as documented by Garcia-Herrero and Wooldridge (2007).

In conclusion, comparing different countries' supply of domestic finance (as measured for instance by the ratio of private credit or stock market capitalization to GDP) may well give an incomplete picture of financial integration. In the next section, accordingly, we assess the degree of financial integration of the euro area by price-based indicators, such as interest rate differentials, and by cross-border flows of credit and equity finance.

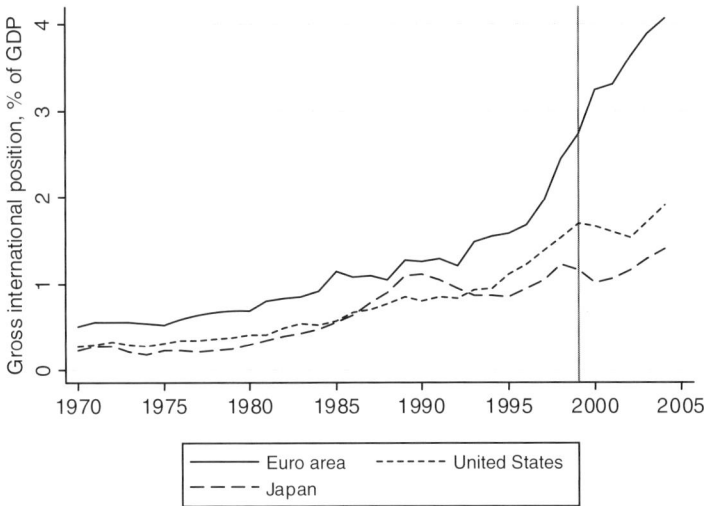

Figure 9.3: Gross international investment position in the euro area, Japan and USA

2.3 How integrated are European financial markets?

Integration and consolidation have proceeded at different paces in different financial markets. In the eurozone, the money and public debt markets integrated almost immediately with the adoption of the single currency. In the equity, repo, corporate bond, and especially credit markets integration has instead proceeded more slowly and is currently still incomplete.

2.3.1 Bond and credit markets

The combination of EMU with the concomitant institutional changes produced a dramatic convergence of the yields on national public debt on the eve of monetary unification (Pagano and von Thadden, 2004). This is illustrated in Figure 9.4 for the ten-year benchmark bonds (and qualitatively similar patterns obtain for other maturities). The figure shows end-of-month yield spreads for euro-area benchmark government bonds relative to the ten-year German Bund from January 1993 to September 2007. The convergence toward zero is dramatic. Considering all initial EMU participants (and thus excluding Greece), the mean yield spread over the German yield fell from 218 basis points

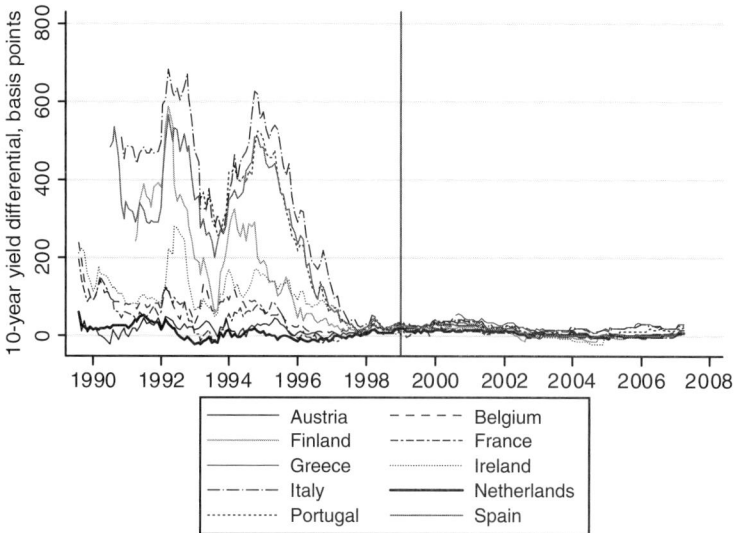

Figure 9.4: Ten-year benchmark bond yield spreads before and after EMU, 1990–2007

Note: Yield differentials are computed relative to the yield on the benchmark German ten-year Bund, based on monthly data (end-of-month observations). Source: Datastream.

in 1995 to 111 in 1996, 39 in 1997, 19 in 1998, and 20 in 1999. It rebounded slightly in 2000–1, before resuming its downward trend.

Most of the action came before the launch of the euro and derived from the convergence of the non-core EMU participants: Finland, Ireland, Italy, Portugal, and Spain, and later Greece, which joined the euro area at the beginning of 2001, while Austria, Belgium, France, and the Netherlands already featured low spreads over German bonds in 1996. This is because before EMU the probability of depreciation relative to the D-Mark was considerable in the first set of countries, but not in the second. For the non-core EU countries, the drastic narrowing of the ten-year yield spreads was due almost entirely to the elimination of this risk.

Baele *et al.* (2004) analyze the degree of integration of the corporate bond market under EMU, taking into account that corporate bonds differ in several key respects other than the country of issue (time-profile of the cash flow, likelihood of default, liquidity). They find that yields are mostly driven by common factors, while the effect of the country of issuance is extremely small (less than 10 basis points). This suggests that the corporate bond market too has achieved a remarkable degree of integration.

The introduction of the euro promoted soaring corporate bond issuance in 1999, when volumes more than doubled from $273 billion to $657 billion. Issue volume in the euro area thus jumped from less than 26 percent of that in the USA in 1998, to over 74 percent in 1999. Rajan and Zingales (2003b) show that the boom of the corporate bond market after 1999 was stronger in the euro area than outside and suggest that the introduction of the euro was a major causal factor in this development.

That the development of an active euro-denominated corporate bond market is the true success story of EMU is confirmed by the great liquidity of the market. As Biais *et al.* (2006) document, euro-area corporate bonds have narrower bid-ask spreads than comparable sterling- and dollar-denominated bonds, even after the introduction of the TRACE system, which increased post-trade transparency in the USA. The authors attribute this finding precisely to the integration of the European corporate bond market since the advent of the euro, which allowed investors from all European countries to trade in the same market, thus attracting a large pool of professional intermediaries to compete in providing liquidity. This mutually reinforcing process between liquidity demand and supply has driven bid-ask spreads down below those in the USA (p. 41).

Has the convergence of euro-area government bond yields continued since the institution of EMU, so differentials should soon be a thing of the past? The distinct trend reduction in yield differentials from the Bund shown in Figure 9.4 might seem to suggest so, but this is only apparent. Most yield differentials have been trending downward because the Bund yield has been rising relative to most other euro-area public debt, as the German budget position has weakened. But yield differentials have not declined in absolute value since 1999, much less disappeared; euro-area sovereign bonds, that is, are still not perfect substitutes.

This can be seen in Figure 9.5, which is based on the same data except that it covers only the period of EMU. Even after 1999, yield differentials vary considerably across countries, from a few basis points for French, Irish or Dutch debt to a maximum of 20 points for Portuguese

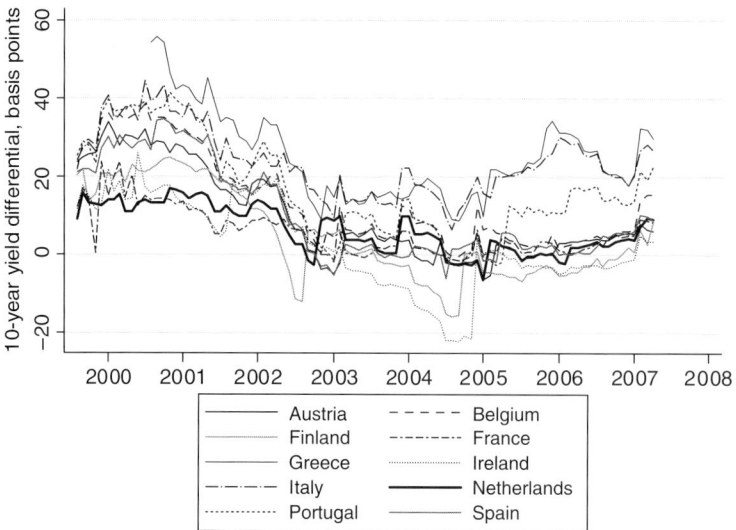

Figure 9.5: Ten-year benchmark bond yield spreads under EMU
Note: Yield differentials are computed relative to the yield on the benchmark German ten-year Bund, based on monthly data (end-of-month observations). Source: Datastream.

debt and 30 points for Italian or Greek bonds after 2005. Yield differentials also vary considerably over time for some countries, notably Ireland, Italy, Greece, and Portugal. The differentials have a tendency to move together (Codogno *et al.*, 2003; and Geyer *et al.*, 2004), which implies that yield spread risk cannot be fully hedged by holding a diversified portfolio of euro-area bonds, so that their risk is to be taken into account and priced by investors.

Figure 9.5 also suggests that convergence of interest rates on public debt may have reversed slightly after 2005. This visual impression is confirmed by Figure 9.6, which shows the cross-sectional standard deviation of the yields from 1990 to 2007: this measure of convergence bottomed out in 2005 after a long decline and has risen slightly since. It remains to be seen whether this residual difference between public debt yields will be a persistent characteristic of the euro area for years to come.

Credit markets have integrated much more slowly than bond markets, presumably because of the heterogeneity of borrowers and the local nature of the information that lenders need. Legally, the rules on

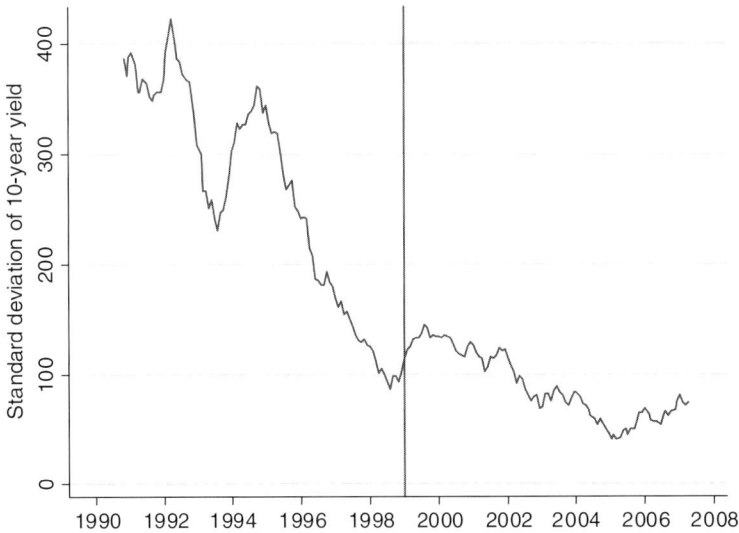

Figure 9.6: Standard deviation of the ten-year benchmark bond yield spreads
Note: The standard deviation is computed excluding Greece.

euro-area banking markets are quite homogeneous, but interest rate differentials remain wider than in the bond market, as documented by Adam *et al.* (2002) and Baele *et al.* (2004). In particular, there are persistent differentials in the medium- and long-term corporate loan market and in the consumer credit segment. Furthermore, retail cross-border lending within the area is still limited; it only increased from 3 percent in 1999 to 4 percent in 2003. Credit market integration is now gaining momentum, especially because cross-border banking mergers and acquisitions have become more common, although much of the cross-border integration and restructuring has yet to take place. The near future is likely to witness much more sweeping changes than have occurred so far.

2.3.2 Stock markets
Assessing whether European stock markets have become more integrated since the introduction of the euro is more difficult than for bond markets. The most common approach posits that when segmented markets start to integrate, stock market returns, like interest rates,

should become more closely correlated. The evidence does show that European stock returns have increasingly been driven by common European shocks since the early 1980s (Baele, 2005), but these changes in the covariance of ex-post returns do not necessarily reflect integration. Market returns may exhibit common patterns simply because markets are increasingly hit by the same shocks (oil prices, say, or monetary policy). This point is particularly relevant for the EU, where the integration of goods and labor markets is likely to have increased the common component of real shocks across countries, and where by definition monetary policy has now become common.

As a consequence some researchers, in search of the possible effects of financial integration, have turned to analyzing the ex-ante returns in European markets. Estimating and comparing expected returns is tantamount to gauging the risk premium required by investors and thus calls for the specification of an asset pricing model. According to the capital asset pricing model (CAPM), with fully integrated stock markets only covariance risk with the world portfolio is priced in ex-ante returns, while diversifiable country-specific risk commands no return. As Stulz (1999) points out, if the country-specific risk exceeds the world covariance risk, financial integration should be accompanied in equilibrium by a decrease in the risk premium required by investors, hence in the expected return on equity and the cost of capital.

Possible tests of capital market integration then involve estimating whether the evolution of the risk premium of domestic stocks is sensitive to the country-specific risk in relation to the covariance with an EU-wide portfolio. This is the approach of Hardouvelis *et al.* (2006), who inquire whether the convergence of European economies towards monetary union led to increased integration of European stock markets. They estimate a conditional asset pricing model, allowing for a time-varying degree of integration that measures the importance of EU-wide risk relative to country-specific risk. The results indicate that the degree of integration is closely related to forward interest rate differentials vis-à-vis Germany, i.e. to the probability of a country joining the EMU. Integration increased substantially over time, especially since 1995, when these differentials began shrinking, and by mid-1998, six months before the official launch of EMU, stock markets appear to have been almost fully integrated. An alternative measurement approach was proposed by Chen and Knez (1995), based on the law of one price and the absence of arbitrage opportunities. Using this approach, Ayuso and Blanco (2001) find that financial market integration between stock markets increased during the nineties.

Different tests of stock market integration rely on quantity indicators, such as the volume of capital flows or the composition of financial portfolios. There is abundant evidence for the "home equity bias," i.e. investors' failure to diversify sufficiently into foreign stocks (see for instance Tesar and Werner, 1995, and Lewis, 1999). If households hold portfolios that are not enough internationally diversified, their consumption growth will disproportionately reflect domestic shocks. In the same vein, Ayuso and Blanco (2001) study how foreign direct and portfolio investment evolved in selected countries. They find that the fraction of wealth held in foreign assets increased significantly in the last few years considered. This is also reflected in the behavior of institutional investors: Adam *et al.* (2002) and Baele *et al.* (2004) show that the home bias of euro-area investment funds decreased gradually after the introduction of the euro, while that of pension funds dropped more abruptly after 1999. Belgian and Dutch pension funds, in fact, increased the fraction of non-domestic assets from 60 percent in 1998 to more than 80 percent in 2000. Large increases also took place in Ireland, Spain, and France.

For equity markets too, then, both return-based evidence and quantity measures of home bias indicate increasing integration. However, significant institutional barriers to integration remain, notably the considerable costs for cross-border trades arising from the fragmentation of the clearing and settlement system (Giovannini Group, 2002) – a point to which we shall return in Section 6.

3. Effects on growth

The evidence surveyed in the previous section indicates that the introduction of the single currency has been accompanied by a process of financial market integration, and that this has resulted both in financial deepening – as witnessed for instance by the creation of a continental corporate bond market – and by the increasing access of households and firms to financial markets and intermediaries located beyond their national borders.

The natural question is whether this has been a purely financial phenomenon or whether it has also had effects on investment and growth. To put it simply, is there a "growth dividend" from the euro?

In answering, let us first recall the channels through which financial market reforms (such as those spurred by integration) may affect growth:

i. They may increase competition between intermediaries, by removing entry barriers, or enhance the protection of creditors and shareholders, encouraging them to provide more abundant and cheaper finance. As a result, the costs of intermediation will fall and the savings channeled to investment will increase.

ii. Deeper and competitive financial markets can also contribute to growth by allocating capital more efficiently. First, by facilitating the trading, hedging, and pooling of risks, a more highly developed financial sector allows investors to fund profitable but risky investment opportunities that would otherwise be forgone. Second, to the extent that more sophisticated intermediaries can distinguish good projects from bad, funds will go to the more profitable projects and the productivity of the economy will increase.

A significant issue is whether financial development mainly has "level effects" – that is, allows countries to raise long-run per capita output – or rather affects steady-state growth. In principle, both outcomes are possible, depending on the nature of the growth process. In endogenous growth models, financial development permanently raises the national growth rate. In traditional models with exogenous technological progress, financial development – by allowing more investment – can cause a transitory (but possibly quite protracted) increase in the growth rate and a permanent increase in per capita GDP. If it stimulates financial development in more backward countries, integration allows them to converge on the growth rate of the more technologically advanced and capital-rich countries (Aghion *et al.*, 2005). These authors also show that countries that do not take part in this process and remain below a critical level of financial development are trapped in a low-growth equilibrium. So financial integration should produce income convergence within the integrating area, which becomes a "convergence club," where faster growth in the more backward countries may be fuelled not only by domestic saving but also by resources generated in the more advanced economies. In fact, financial liberalization should be accompanied by capital flows from developed economies to developing ones.

The thesis that finance matters for growth has been tested empirically in many studies, and it has been found that countries with better financial markets grow faster. Already in 1969 Goldsmith stated that "a rough parallelism can be observed between economic and financial development if periods of several decades are considered" (p. 48). However, the correlation between finance and growth does not establish that finance actually causes growth. To identify this causal link, researchers have used econometric techniques and identification strategies that can control for possible feedback of economic growth on financial development – that is, for the fact that faster growth tends to elicit an increased supply of financial services. The work designed to disentangle this causality issue has relied on three types of data: country-level, industry-level, and firm-level.

3.1 Cross-country studies

King and Levine (1993a, 1993b) attack the reverse causality issue by relating economic growth rates to measures of lagged financial development in a cross-section of eighty countries. Their main finding is that all the indicators of economic performance are positively associated with the predetermined component of financial development, as measured by the size of financial sector at the beginning of the sample period. Levine and Zervos (1998) explore the relation further, looking at the relative importance of banks and securities markets. Interestingly, the size of the stock market appears not to have any impact on subsequent growth, while its liquidity and the development of the banking system are important.

However, the use of predetermined variables to measure financial development can overcome endogeneity problems only in part. Rajan and Zingales (2003a) point out that an omitted common variable – say, the household saving rate – could still drive both long-run growth and the initial level of financial development, generating a spurious correlation. Moreover, precedence in time does not logically imply causality: the econometrician may find in the data that financial development predicts economic growth only because financial markets anticipate future economic opportunities. For instance, stock market valuations may reflect changes in future growth opportunities, and banks may lend more in anticipation of high increasing sales by their customers. In other words, financial development could be only a leading indicator, and not a cause, of growth.

In order to effectively overcome the reverse causality problem, one must find instruments that are unquestionably exogenous, i.e. variables that affect financial development but are not correlated with economic performance. When using aggregate data, this is difficult indeed. Some scholars have identified such an instrument in the type of legal system. La Porta *et al.* (1998) show that the size of a country's financial market is related to the original nature of its legal system, and hypothesize that this is because common-law countries offer better investor protection than civil-law countries. The legal origin of a country can be considered exogenous to economic growth, because the English, French, and German legal systems were all created centuries ago and spread mainly through occupation and colonialism. Hence Beck *et al.* (2000a) use the legal origin of the financial system as an instrument for financial development. With this technique, they again find that the size of the financial sector has a positive and robust correlation both with the rate of growth of both per-capita GDP and total factor productivity. Beck *et al.* (2000b) use a wider range of instruments and show that accounting standards and the level of contract enforcement are also important instruments of financial development.

The conclusions of these studies on aggregate cross-country data are brought together by Demirgüç-Kunt and Levine (2001), who examine how indicators of financial market efficiency and size correlate with long-run growth. According to their estimates, both the development of financial markets and that of intermediaries correlate with long-run growth, when they are instrumented by indicators of the quality of the legal system, such as measures of investor rights protection and of the quality of enforcement.[5] Aghion *et al.* (2005) emphasize the implications of financial development for income convergence, and present evidence that is consistent with a "convergence clubs" model, in which membership in the high-growth club depends on a sufficiently high degree of financial development. It is only within this group that income convergence is observed.

Other strong empirical evidence on the nexus between finance and growth comes from Jayaratne and Strahan (1996), who rely on data on US states. They exploit the effects of intrastate branch deregulation and the attendant increase in competition, which came at different times in different states, and find that the states that removed restrictions on branching achieved faster economic growth than the others. Since bank lending did not grow, the authors attribute this effect to increased banking efficiency. This study provides quasi-experimental evidence on the causal nexus between finance and growth, because deregulation could hardly have occurred in anticipation of future business cycle expansions.

Important insights into the relation between financial integration, financial development, and growth are also offered by the literature on capital account liberalization and its effects on real variables, such as investment, productivity, and growth. In the standard neoclassical framework, internationally open capital markets generate capital flows from capital-abundant developed countries, where the return to capital is low, to capital-scarce developing countries, where it is high. The latter should therefore experience a foreign-financed increase in investment and growth. But skeptics argue that the opening of capital markets triggers speculation and the recurrence of market crises. Rodrik (1998b), using cross-sectional data, finds no correlation between the international openness of countries' capital markets and the amount that they invest or the rate at which they grow. In a careful review of the empirical evidence, Henry (2007) criticizes empirical studies based on purely cross-sectional data, suggesting that time-series data are needed to determine whether countries invest and grow more in the aftermath of a change in their capital movement policy. Using this policy-experiment approach, he shows that in countries that liberalize capital flows, the cost of capital falls and investment does increase, along with the growth rate of per capita GDP. However, the effect of liberalization is often of limited magnitude, a likely reflection of capital market imperfections, asymmetric information, poor investment protection, weak institutions, and government regulations distorting economic decisions.

Bonfiglioli (2007) has sought to distinguish the different effects of financial integration on productivity and investment using a panel of seventy countries from 1975 to 1999 and several indicators of capital flow liberalization. Her results suggest that financial integration does have a positive effect on productivity but not on capital accumulation, even controlling for financial market development. This study also cautions against the syllogism that since (i) capital market liberalization tends to further financial development, and (ii) financial development tends to increase investment and its efficient allocation, then capital market liberalization is necessarily associated with higher investment and productivity. In the words of Henry (2007), "without a convincing body of time series evidence that the quality of a country's capital allocation improves as its level of financial development rises, no basis exists for concluding that liberalization indirectly improves the efficiency of domestic capital allocation through its impact on financial development" (p. 917).

Since EU countries' capital flows were already completely liberalized before the introduction of the euro, the literature on the real effects of capital market liberalization is not directly relevant for an evaluation of the real effects of EMU, but it has an important methodological bearing on the evaluation of EMU itself, in that it cautions against the dangers of using cross-sectional data to gauge the effects of policy regime changes.

3.2 Industry-level studies

Another strand of empirical work relies on industry-level data to study the issue of causality. Financial market development should disproportionately benefit firms or industries that are highly dependent on external finance. The testable hypothesis of this approach is the prediction that these firms and industries will grow faster where financial markets are more highly developed. The approach was applied by Rajan and Zingales (1998) on industry-level data for a large sample of countries in the 1980s. They construct their test by first identifying each industry's need for external finance from firm-level data for the USA, on the assumption that the US financial system is the most highly developed. Then they interact this industry-level "external dependence" variable with a country-level proxy for the degree of financial development (obtaining a variable that measures how severely financial development constrains the growth of each industry in each country). Then they use that variable in a regression for industry-level growth.

One strength of this approach is that it can sort out the effect of financial development from that of other country and sector characteristics. This is a major advance, because many variables that might affect growth are typically left out in cross-country studies, creating potential biases in the estimated relationship between financial development and growth. Rajan and Zingales find that various measures of financial development (total stock market capitalization, domestic credit to the private sector, accounting standards) do disproportionately affect real economic growth in the externally dependent industries.

This approach can assess the differential impact of financial integration, identifying the countries and sectors that are most likely to benefit. Clearly, the countries bound to gain more are those with backward financial markets that specialize in sectors that rely heavily on external finance. At the other end of the spectrum, countries that have already developed financial markets and that specialize in financially self-sufficient sectors are likely to gain little. Guiso *et al.* (2004) conduct an exercise assuming that financial integration in the EU will eventually produce the same level of financial development as the United States. They consider the USA as an upper bound – a highly developed continent-wide financial market, not dissimilar from what a fully integrated European financial market would presumably look like. Averaging over all countries and sectors, the estimated impact of financial integration on the growth of manufacturing value added in the EU works out at 0.72 percentage points per year, and for manufacturing output growth 0.89 points. Considering that manufacturing accounts for about one quarter of EU total value added, this would mean incremental GDP growth of about 0.2 percentage points, assuming that financial integration has no impact on non-manufacturing growth.

This average, however, conceals quite considerable diversity by country and sector, reflecting both the degree of financial development (the more backward countries gain more) and sectoral specialization (countries that specialize in financially dependent sectors gain more). Figure 9.7 reports the increment to value added and output growth country-by-country. In one group, growth increases substantially, by well over 1 percentage point a year: Belgium, Denmark, Germany, Greece, Italy, Portugal, and Spain. In a second group, there is an increment of 1 point or almost that much: Austria, Finland, France, and Ireland. Predictably, the third group – the countries that gain just half a point or less – are the most financially developed countries: the Netherlands, Sweden, and the UK.[6]

Figure 9.8 plots the effect on the ten industries that are expected to contribute most to total European growth. Again there is some similarity between the impact of financial integration on output and value-added growth. In all the sectors considered, growth increases by over 1 percentage point. And in the most financially dependent industries – notably pharmaceuticals and plastic – the yearly increment exceeds 3 percent. In conclusion, the potential growth benefits of financial integration are considerable but unevenly distributed among countries and sectors.

Recognizing industry heterogeneity has proven to be important not only to study the effect of financial development on growth but also to

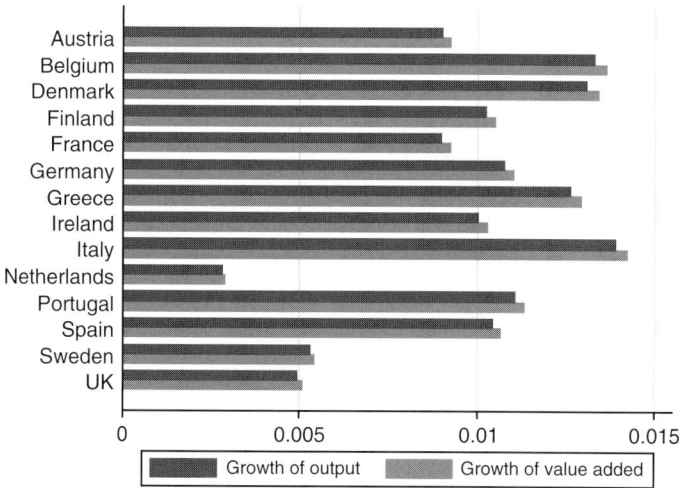

Figure 9.7: Potential growth of value added and output in manufacturing industry by country: raising financial development to the US standard
Source: Guiso *et al.* (2004).

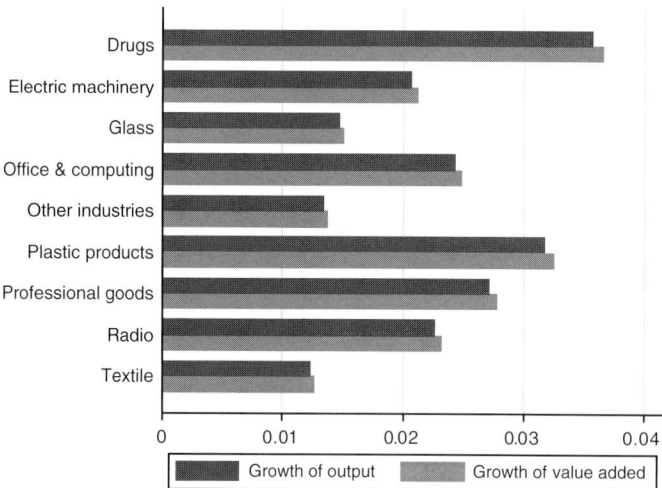

Figure 9.8: Potential growth of value added and output in manufacturing industry by sector: raising financial development to the US standard
Source: Guiso *et al.* (2004).

understand the specific channels through which these effects are attained. Carlin and Mayer (2003) use the Rajan-Zingales approach to probe further into the relationships between industrial activity, financial systems, and legal arrangements, concluding that in OECD countries market-based finance and legal protection of investors are correlated with the growth of equity-financed and skill-intensive industries, and particularly with R&D investment. In contrast, market-based finance and accounting standards are not important for tangible capital accumulation.

These findings indirectly support the claim of Allen and Gale (2000) that markets and intermediaries are complementary and favor growth of technologies with different characteristics. Intermediaries are most useful when a substantial amount of capital has to be raised by firms in traditional sectors, whereas new technologies in high-risk sectors are favored by the concurrent funding of diverse investors who receive different, complementary signals on a project's prospects, which allows pooling several pieces of independent information.

3.3 Firm-level studies

Further evidence on the nexus between finance and growth is offered by work using firm-level data. One advantage is that this permits considering the structure of the financial system as exogenous to individual firm performance, especially for small and medium-sized firms. Firm-level data also make it possible to address issues that are impermeable using country or sector data: for instance, whether financial integration disproportionately affects some groups of firms.

Guiso *et al.* (2004) apply the Rajan-Zingales approach also to microeconomic data for companies incorporated in the EU and in Central and Eastern Europe. Their firm-level estimates prove to be consistent with the estimates produced by studies based on industry-level data. In addition, the use of firm-level data allows them to investigate whether the effect of financial development differs by firm size, so that the projected effects of financial integration can also be expected to differ. Their results indicate that smaller businesses stand to be the main beneficiary of integration, which for them means access to a larger and more developed financial market than their national one. This is consistent with a study based on Italian firm-level data by Guiso *et al.* (2004), who show that local financial development helps the growth of small firms more than that of large firms.

Firm-level data can also be used to detect the impact of financial development on the entry of new firms and on the expansion of successful new businesses. Aghion *et al.* (2007) apply the Rajan-Zingales approach to harmonized firm-level data in sixteen industrialized and emerging economies and find that financial development has either no effect or a negative effect on entry by large firms but that access to finance is very relevant to the entry of small firms in the sectors that are most dependent on external finance, and also helps new firms expand. Their data is drawn mostly from business registers available in the pre-EMU years and do not directly assess the impact of the euro on firms' access to finance. But all in all the results suggest that in many countries, including those of Continental Europe, efficient financial markets play a major role in ensuring that the process of industrial restructuring typical of market economies will bring the entry and then the expansion of new (especially small) firms.

These findings are consistent with other recent studies. For European firms, Klapper *et al.* (2006) document that financial development favors entry in the sectors that are relatively dependent on external finance. Moreover, they find that entry regulations are associated with lower entry rates and larger entry size in sectors with higher natural turnover rates. This evidence parallels that described by Bertrand *et al.* (2007) in their analysis of the firm-level effects of deregulation in the French Banking Act of 1985: banks became less willing to bail out poorly performing firms, while firms in bank-dependent sectors became more likely to restructure. At industry level, they document an improvement in allocative efficiency across firms, and a decline in concentration.

Recent microeconomic evidence also sheds light on the possible role of international financial integration in improving the allocation of capital across firms, and – most interestingly – on the specific role of domestic financial development in the process. Galindo *et al.* (2007) use firm-level panel data from twelve Latin American countries to investigate whether capital flow liberalization has increased the share of investment going to firms with a higher marginal return to capital. They develop an indicator of investment allocation efficiency, and find that in most cases financial liberalization has increased allocation efficiency. Since the study spans pre- and post-reform periods, it is one of the few capable of demonstrating that this improvement is actually traceable to financial development in the wake of liberalization. In the case of liberalizations, the entry of new firms also appears to be an important element at work: using cross-sectional data for approximately 24 million firms in nearly a hundred countries for 1999 and 2004, Alfaro and Charlton (2007) show that easing restrictions on international capital flows enhances firm entry and other measures of entrepreneurship. They document that this effect of capital flows works both through foreign direct investment (creating new domestic firms) and through financial development, as entrepreneurship in more financially dependent industries is more sensitive to restrictions on capital mobility and more strongly affected by increased flows of finance.

Two recent studies based on firm-level data are directly relevant to evaluating the growth effects of financial integration in the EU. Bris *et al.* (2006) use data from the original eleven countries that adopted the euro and a control sample of five European countries and find that the euro boosted investment by financially constrained firms. Giannetti and Ongena (2007) instead investigate the effects of foreign bank entry on the performance of Eastern European firms. For a panel of 60,000 firm-year observations on listed and unlisted companies in Eastern Europe, they find that foreign lending stimulates growth in sales, assets, and use of financial debt, particularly for young firms. By contrast, firms connected with domestic banks or the government suffer, which highlights another possible benefit of financial liberalization: foreign bank entry may correct credit market distortions due to political connections and government intervention.

4. Effects on macroeconomic adjustment to shocks

Beside its beneficial effects on long-run growth, the increased capital mobility brought about by integration should have increased the ability of each country to draw on the area's common pool of savings. For instance, a country that experiences a drop in national saving due to an increase in the public deficit can more easily draw on foreign saving to maintain the level of national investment. Or an economy with sharply increasing growth opportunities can fund additional investment even if domestic households do not increase their saving correspondingly.

To test for this effect of financial integration, Feldstein and Horioka (1980) suggested studying the correlation between domestic saving and domestic investment. They argued that under perfect capital mobility and unchanged investment opportunities, an increase in a country's saving rate would be associated with an increase in investment in all countries. Therefore, a low correlation between domestic saving and investment would indicate strong integration. The Feldstein-Horioka premise has been qualified many times since, but it is still considered a useful basis to gauge the macroeconomic effects of capital market integration. Armstrong *et al.* (1996), in an analogous study for Europe, found low correlations between savings and investment. More recently, Blanchard and Giavazzi (2002) documented a reduced correlation between saving and investment in the euro area.

To show how financial integration has affected the saving-investment correlation, we have estimated it for each year between 1980 and 2005 for the fifteen countries that belonged to the European Union when the euro was introduced. We define the investment rate as gross capital formation over GDP and the saving rate as gross saving over GDP. The data are drawn from the OECD National Accounts and the results are reported in Figure 9.9.

The correlation declines almost monotonically from values around 0.5 in the 1980s to nil in the later part of the sample. Moreover, at first the coefficient is statistically different from zero at the 5 percent confidence level, but after 1993 the confidence bounds of the correlation bracket the zero line. Therefore, in the EU domestic investment rates are no longer significantly correlated with saving rates. In the interpretation proposed by Feldstein and Horioka, the integration of European capital

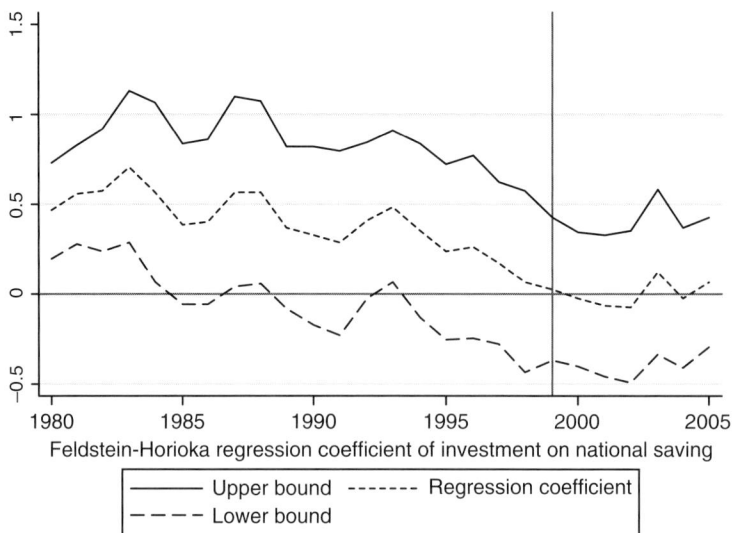

Feldstein-Horioka regression coefficient of investment on national saving

——— Upper bound   ------- Regression coefficient
– – – – Lower bound

Figure 9.9: Correlations between saving and investment for EU countries

markets has decoupled domestic investment from domestic saving. The question is whether this is due to EMU, to the general process of European integration or to the increasing integration of world capital markets, even beyond Europe. To this end we have re-estimated the Feldstein-Horioka correlations also for the broader group of OECD countries.[7] The pattern of the estimated coefficients, shown in Figure 9.10, is similar to that of Figure 9.9: the coefficients are initially positive and statistically different from zero, and towards the end of the sample decline to near zero. However, in the larger OECD sample the correlation remains significantly positive until 1998, whereas in Europe it vanishes as early as 1993.

This evidence suggests that the decoupling of saving and investment in Europe is part of a more general, OECD-wide trend. In this sense, the introduction of the euro can be seen as one aspect of this broader pattern. Figures 9.9 and 9.10 also show that integration has proceeded faster in Europe than in the rest of the developed world. This is confirmed – and indeed amplified – by the studies that also cover the eight new EU member states in Central and Eastern Europe. Abiad *et al.* (2007) show that they have benefited from a steady inflow of capital

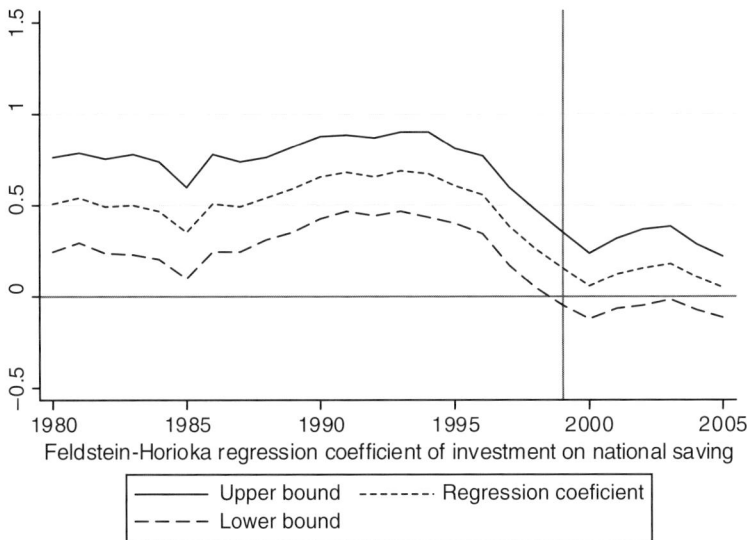

Figure 9.10: Correlations between saving and investment for OECD countries

from the more mature and capital-rich EU15, which has fuelled income convergence. This is precisely the outcome that one would expect in the process of integration. As Caselli and Tenreyro (2006) put it, Europe has proved to be "the quintessential convergence club."

Yet it should be noticed that European income convergence has been an exception, not the rule. In the last decade East Asian countries have been running large balance-of-payment surpluses, and the same is true of many other developing countries since 2002 (Abiad *et al.*, 2007). Therefore, despite (slowly) increasing financial integration, the savings of poorer countries have been flowing towards the richer ones. At the same time, for the world as a whole, income divergence rather than convergence has been pervasive (Pritchett, 1997).

5. Effects on risk sharing

Economic theory predicts that financial integration should have a third effect, in addition to those on growth and adjustment to macroeconomic shocks, namely facilitating risk sharing. It allows households to hold more diversified equity portfolios, and in particular to diversify the portion of risk that arises from country-specific shocks. Similarly, it allows banks to diversify their loan portfolios internationally. This diversification should help euro-area households to buffer country-specific income shocks, so that shocks to domestic income should not affect domestic consumption, but be diversified away by borrowing or investing abroad.

Accordingly, a whole line of research studies the covariance of consumption across regions or countries to test whether financial markets afford full risk sharing to consumers in different jurisdictions. Conditional on consumers exploiting all risk-sharing opportunities, the growth of consumption in all areas should be perfectly correlated when financial markets are integrated and thus depend only on common (non-diversifiable) shocks. This key point was recognized and applied to microeconomic data by Cochrane (1991) and Mace (1991), and later brought to bear on macroeconomic data by Obstfeld (1994), van Wincoop (1994), and Townsend (1994), among others.[8]

Unlike Feldstein-Horioka, the risk-sharing approach can distinguish the contributions of different financial markets and public tax-transfer mechanisms, as is shown by Asdrubali, *et al.* (1996) and Sørensen and Yosha (1998). Using US data for 1963–90, Asdrubali and co-authors develop an accounting framework to break down the cross-sectional variance of individual states' gross output into components, capturing the different sources of income smoothing. They find that 39 percent of a shock to gross state product is smoothed by corporate savings, 13 percent by the federal government, and 23 percent by credit markets (the remaining 25 percent is not smoothed). Sørensen and Yosha, applying the same approach to the EU and the OECD for 1966–90, find that the unsmoothed residual is much larger, around 60 percent. They also find that half of what income risk smoothing there is comes through national government budget deficits and the other half through corporate savings.

To test whether the advent of the euro has been associated with improved risk sharing among households, one could take indicators based on the microeconomic work of Cochrane (1991) and Mace (1991). The idea is that under perfect risk sharing individual consumption growth should not depend on idiosyncratic shocks (such as a fall in income or health problems). If instead consumption growth is affected by such shocks, this is evidence of incomplete risk sharing. These tests were designed to be applied with panel data on households. In principle, they can also be applied to a sample of countries, assuming that each country is populated by identical consumers. Sørensen *et al.* (2007) have done so for OECD countries, and report that risk sharing increased between 1993 and 2003; the increase was correlated with a concomitant reduction in home-country bias, especially for equities, but this finding is much weaker for EU countries. But these results are subject to considerable caution: for aggregate data, the tests require highly unrealistic assumptions – essentially, the heterogeneity of the population within each country is assumed away. Hopefully, future microeconometric research will use household panel data to assess how the response to shocks in EU countries has changed with the introduction of the euro.

Before concluding, it should be mentioned that some recent literature has highlighted a potential cost of financial integration, countering the benefits from improved risk sharing. In a world with imperfect capital markets, integration can make a country more vulnerable to external macroeconomic shocks and financial crises. Contagion effects, possibly amplified by "fickleness" and herding behavior of financial institutions, may actually increase output and consumption volatility, instead of lowering them as the risk-sharing thesis holds. The evidence is inconclusive (Rogoff *et al.*, 2006).

Most likely, the potential dangers of greater contagion due to financial integration are not as relevant to the euro area as to developing countries. This is because countries with relatively well-developed financial systems, such as the euro area, are less vulnerable to financial crises (Lane and Milesi-Ferretti, 2006). In particular, the most vulnerable appear to be countries that liberalize their financial systems without strong institutions and sound macroeconomic policies (Demirgüç-Kunt and Detragiache, 1999).

At the same time, it cannot be denied that there are ways in which integration may heighten the vulnerability of the European financial system, unless the implied increase in contagion risk is appropriately offset by regulatory convergence (as is explained in Section 6.2.4 below). First, by fostering banking concentration both within and across national boundaries, integration is creating a few pan-European banks, whose solvency is increasingly crucial to the stability of the entire credit system. Second, the large European financial institutions' exposure to systemic risk has not been attenuated since the early 1990s, but has actually increased considerably in most countries (De Nicolò and Tieman, 2006). This is at least partly due to the fact that bond and stock returns in Europe are increasingly driven by common factors (see Section 2.3). Next we discuss the policy implications of this concern.

6. Policy implications

Financial integration has proceeded at a remarkably rapid pace within Europe in the past two decades, especially following the introduction of the euro. The process has affected not only the working of financial markets but also the real economy. But financial integration is far from complete, especially in the credit market, which is still central to the financing of small and medium-sized enterprises in much of the EU. So it is natural to ask whether the process should be expected to continue spontaneously and smoothly, or whether further regulatory intervention is required (i) to remove remaining obstacles and (ii) to cope with some of the undesired effects of financial integration, such as the danger for financial stability discussed above. In other words, can financial integration be safely entrusted to market participants alone from now onwards? Arguably, the answer will differ depending on which market is involved, in keeping with the uneven pace of integration in security markets and bank lending.

6.1 Future securities market integration

In securities markets, most of the legal obstacles to integration were removed by the 1999 Financial Services Action Plan, and since 2005 all listed EU companies have been required to prepare their consolidated accounts using International Financial Reporting Standards (IFRS). The number doing so thus rose from some 350 to 7,000. By making the accounting information available to analysts and investors more easily comparable, this is likely to provide further impetus to the integration of stock and corporate bond markets.

The four main remaining obstacles to the integration of euro-area securities markets are (i) the segmentation of the clearing and settlement system; (ii) the fragmentation of the trading infrastructure among too many stock exchanges; (iii) the fragmented issuance of government bond markets; and (iv) the poor post-trade transparency in corporate bond markets.

6.1.1 Clearing and settlement

The segmentation of the clearing and settlement system entails improperly high costs for cross-border trades. Segmentation depends partly on the persistent fragmentation of stock trading platforms. Some exchanges, such as Deutsche Börse, in fact, are vertically integrated, with both a platform to provide trading services and a proprietary clearing and settlement system for the corresponding post-trading services ("silo structure"). This limits the competition from other trading platforms, since new entrants' customers would still have to use the incumbent's post-trade clearing and settlement system.

Entry foreclosure generates rents for incumbent exchanges, and overcoming this problem is likely to require regulatory action at the EU level. This is recognized both by the European Commission (whose competition and internal market departments conducted studies on the role of competition policy in securities trading and post-trading in 2006) and by the ECB, which announced in July 2006 that it was considering the desirability of going into the settlement business itself, with a system called "Target 2 Securities" (T2S). The ECB would not be the first public institution to provide central clearing and settlement services. In the United States, the Federal Reserve Board runs a bond settlement business, and both clearing and settlement are the product of the Depository Trust and Clearing Corporation, a user-owned service company that was created as a direct result of government pressure.

6.1.2 Stock trading infrastructure

Unlike clearing and settlement, the trading infrastructure of European stock markets – once organized on a national basis – is already being restructured along transnational lines at the initiative of exchanges and financial intermediaries, although fragmentation is not necessarily being reduced. For one thing, existing exchanges have pushed for consolidation: the Paris, Amsterdam, Brussels, and Lisbon stock exchanges merged into Euronext; Stockholm's OMX AB has acquired and now operates exchanges in Sweden, Finland, Denmark, Iceland, Estonia, Lithuania, and Latvia; and in 2007 the London Stock Exchange acquired Borsa Italiana. Meanwhile, the EU's Markets in Financial Instruments Directive (MiFID) has opened the door to the creation of new trading platforms operated by intermediaries, and a consortium of seven investment banks (Citi, Crédit Suisse, Deutsche Bank, Goldman Sachs, Merrill Lynch, Morgan Stanley, and UBS) has already launched a new pan-European equities trading platform called "Project Turquoise." All clearing, settlement and risk management services for "Turquoise" will be provided by a single company (European Central Counterparty Ltd), while Citi's global transaction services unit will serve as settlement agent. So, as existing platforms are consolidated, new ones are being instituted; in both cases the tendency is towards pan-European, not national trading platforms.

6.1.3 Government bond issuance

There is room for further progress towards integration in euro-area government bond markets as well. Dunne *et al.* (2006) show that in the MTS platform for euro-area bonds, trading costs (median effective bid-ask spreads) are significantly higher than in the US Treasury market. They attribute this persistent liquidity gap to greater fragmentation, with many issuers and smaller issue size than in the USA (pp. 44–5). Fragmented issuance is also at the root of investors' often imperfect hedging strategies in the euro-area market. To hedge positions in bonds issued by small countries, investors often have to use German futures contracts or the liquid Italian spot market. To overcome this hurdle, however, euro-area governments should tackle the politically thorny problem of joint debt issuance, with the attendant implications for further fiscal policy coordination. Some progress might be made by limiting joint issuance to just a few maturities, at least initially, so as to test the potential magnitude of the liquidity gains and debt servicing savings from joint bond issuance.

6.1.4 Transparency in the corporate bond market

As in the USA, in the euro-area corporate bond markets are mainly organized as an OTC dealer market, where trading is decentralized and dealers satisfy customers' sell and buy orders at their bid and ask quotes. Although electronic trading platforms are now starting to emerge, most orders are still routed to brokers and dealers by telephone. For investors, in such a decentralized market information on prices of the trades effected becomes an essential sign of "where the market is going" and guide to trading strategy. Absent such "post-trade transparency," investors hesitate to place orders, and the new information about fundamentals that their orders could convey is embodied in prices much more slowly.

Biais *et al.* (2006) note that "currently there is no systematic post-trade transparency in the European corporate bond market" (p. 5), especially for retail investors and small institutions. As a result, price discovery is very slow: it often takes more than a day for the information content of a trade to be fully reflected in market prices. Increasing post-trade transparency is likely to speed up the price discovery process and to increase the liquidity of the market, although this prediction is not unambiguous, since greater transparency would also reduce dealers' profits and might lead some to leave the market. Biais and co-authors do suggest that on balance "it would be reasonable to introduce some limited post-trade transparency," by requiring "anonymous reporting of transaction yields, after a delay of one hour, for trades below one million, and anonymous reporting of transaction yields after a delay of one day for larger trades," but not exact reporting of the trade size, only its range (p. 69).

6.2 *Future credit market integration*

That the credit market has been the laggard in the process of European financial integration is probably due to the intrinsic nature of lending, which depends on local and customer-specific information and on the enforceability of contracts in national jurisdictions. These obstacles to the entry of foreign lenders and to cross-border credit will not disappear soon, even though the lack of information about local customers can be attenuated by foreign banks taking over local banks and making them subsidiaries – a process that is now getting under way.

However, some changes in regulation and enforcement may help to dismantle the remaining national barriers to entry in the EU credit market and to reduce the risks of cross-border integration. Credit market integration would benefit from further EU regulatory intervention on at least four distinct fronts.

6.2.1 Loan contract enforcement

A burgeoning literature suggests that speedy and effective contract enforcement is essential to the development of the credit market, since the efficiency and honesty of the judiciary determines the real degree of creditor protection. La Porta *et al.* (1997) document a positive cross-country correlation between the ratio of private debt to GDP and the "rule of law." That there are dramatic cross-country differences in enforcemcnty efficiency – even within the euro area – is demonstrated by Djankov *et al.* (2003). For example, a dispute over cashing of a cheque takes as long as 645 days in Italy, 434 in Portugal and 420 in Austria, and as little as 39 days in the Netherlands and 11 in Ireland; France and Germany are in the middle, at 181 and 154 days respectively.

Such enormous differences in the length (and cost) of enforcement are a barrier to credit access for firms in the most inefficient jurisdictions. Of course, bringing judicial enforcement in the more backward jurisdictions up to the best EU standards is a huge task for national legislators. The magnitude of the problem goes far beyond credit market integration, and its solution is not something that we can expect to happen swiftly.

6.2.2 Information sharing systems

Recent research has shown that information sharing arrangements or "credit reporting" systems between banks play an important role in credit markets. Based on a survey of credit reporting in forty-three countries, Jappelli and Pagano (2002) show that bank lending to the private sector is greater and default rates are lower where information sharing is broader and more solidly established. Djankov *et al.* (2007) confirm that the ratio of private sector credit to GDP is positively correlated with information sharing in 129 countries for the period 1978–2003.

For credit markets to integrate cross-border, information on loan applicants must become available on a comparable basis to banks in different countries. Unless data on would-be borrowers' characteristics, repayment record, and current debt exposure are available to potential foreign lenders just as they are to domestic ones, the national credit markets of the euro area will not be integrated. Consolidation of customer debt records on a supranational basis is also necessary for banks to be able to estimate default risk accurately and so lend safely, in a situation where cross-border lending may become increasingly common.

Unfortunately, the information-sharing arrangements in the euro area are still predominantly national. Today's credit registers and credit bureaus were created to serve domestic banks (and sometimes at these banks' own initiative) and reflect a range of national regulations and privacy laws. On this front, concerted action by the agencies that manage public credit registries in Europe to harmonize and interlink their databases could produce substantial benefits for credit market integration.

6.2.3 Deposit guarantee schemes

Another often overlooked difference in EU national regulations that heightens the segmentation of banking markets involves deposit guarantee schemes.[9] The problem does not involve cross-border retail deposits, which are still small-scale, but banks that compete cross-border, though subject to differing rules on deposit insurance.

Deposit insurance differs from country to country both in coverage and in funding. Since larger depositors are more likely to be sophisticated and able to exert some market discipline on banks, the high-coverage countries may have less incentives for banks to protect their depositors. Deposit insurance schemes also differ in funding structure. Some are pre-funded (the amounts due in case of a bank failure are prepaid into a fund), while others are funded ex post, once a bank actually fails; still others combine the two mechanisms. Moreover, in the pre-funded schemes the premium structure also differs: some use flat rates in proportion to deposits, others make rates contingent on measures of bank risk. Due to the implied differences across the EU in "coverage ratios" (the available funds divided by the volume of deposits covered), deposit insurance generates different incentives and costs for banks in different countries and can thus affect competition.

The problem is aggravated by the fact that banks with foreign subsidiaries must comply with the deposit insurance scheme in each country where they are present. This deters banks from transforming foreign subsidiaries into branches, which would streamline their groups, because when a subsidiary is part of a national scheme, it is often impossible to recover the funds it has already paid. Again, this may impede progress towards further credit market integration.

A certain degree of convergence between deposit insurance schemes would not only remove this regulatory obstacle to financial integration but also help to deal with threats to the stability of the European banking system. This leads us to the fourth – and certainly the most important – concern for financial regulators in Europe today, namely prudential supervision.

6.2.4 Prudential regulation and banking supervision

Securing the stability of the European banking system is the key to reaping the benefits of financial integration while avoiding such unwelcome effects as the risk of financial contagion discussed in Section 5. If it were needed, the financial turmoil of 2007–8 provides a good case in point, a further pressing reminder of the need to address the interrelated issues of prudential regulation, surveillance and crisis resolution in the euro area.

The crisis has vividly highlighted the shortcomings of the current fragmented EU banking supervisory system. "Even with signs of a clear risk of contagion, no common analysis of the situation, no sharing of confidential information, no coordinated communication and no emergency meetings appear to have taken place among EU supervisors. Even the ECB, unlike the Federal Reserve, lacked the information on the soundness of counterparties normally available to national central banks" (Padoa-Schioppa, 2007).

The problem is that despite the emergence of a few pan-European banks, prudential regulation and supervision are still mainly organized along national lines, which entails considerable risk for the stability of the credit market. For instance, if a pan-European bank were to have solvency problems at home or at one of its foreign subsidiaries, the rules for crisis management and burden sharing are unclear. Uncoordinated actions by the various national supervisory agencies could actually exacerbate the crisis, when instead swift, coordinated action would be essential.

Admittedly, major regulatory progress has been made. The European Commission has largely harmonized financial regulations with the Financial Services Action Plan of 1999; and in 2004 it established a common advisory body grouping all European banking supervisory agencies, the Committee of European Banking Supervisors (CEBS). These agencies have reached a whole series of bilateral "memorandums of understanding" to strengthen coordination in the event of banking crises involving joint responsibilities. However, the EU prudential regulation is still removed from the uniform framework and enforcement structure that would be needed to reduce the likelihood of crises involving pan-European banks and to mitigate their effects: the CEBS has a purely monitoring role, with no direct responsibility for banking stability, and the memorandums are non-binding. These concerns are particularly serious considering that, as mentioned in Section 5, banking concentration and the lending and portfolio policies of large European financial institutions have increased their exposure to systemic risk in recent years.

Of course, this is not a call to halt or even slow down these market processes, which are part and parcel of integration. Quite the contrary; we intend to emphasize the need to accompany integration with the appropriate institutional framework to ensure the stability of credit markets, and particularly of the few EU banking groups with extensive cross-border operations.

6.3 Political sustainability

Are these further steps to consolidate financial integration and enhance the stability of financial markets likely to be taken anytime soon? Much depends on the political support that regulators will be able to build in favor of such reforms. It is important to realize that the reforms will generate losers as well as winners, and the former will try to obstruct them. For instance, some financial intermediaries and marketplaces stand to lose from the consolidation of cross-border clearing and settlement. And much more seriously, national central banks are most likely to oppose any attempt to institute centralized supranational prudential regulation and crisis management quite fiercely. For euro-area central banks, this would strip them of the last serious justification for their power; the conduct of monetary policy having already been surrendered to the ECB. It is quite likely that they will be able to mobilize support from their national politicians, especially at a time when political opinion in Europe has become less friendly towards EU institutions.

To some extent, however, these political difficulties may be mitigated by the proviso that if an integrated EU-level banking supervision were introduced, its powers would not have to extend beyond the few major banks whose operations stretch substantially beyond national boundaries, while the supervision of the thousands of purely national and sub-national banks in Europe would best be left with current regulators. This proposal, recently advanced by Padoa-Schioppa (2007), would not only be easier for national authorities to accept, but would also be efficient. That is, it would preserve the accumulated know-how of national regulators and supervisors for the vast majority of banks and – in keeping with the principle of subsidiarity – it would deploy the new central regulator only where it is strictly necessary.

True, even with this restricted jurisdiction, the proposal for a single EU banking regulator is still likely to face fierce opposition. But the consequences of stopping halfway in the process of financial integration can be quite serious indeed: a failure to reform prudential regulation might precipitate another major banking crisis, which would be devastating to the economy and would thus threaten to dramatically undercut the political support for the financial market reforms already enacted, and even for the ECB and the single currency itself.

Even apart from the danger of a banking crisis, a deep and integrated capital market in the euro area is important to the sustainability of the single currency and the conduct of monetary policy by the ECB. This is best exemplified by the euro area's monetary reaction to the recent financial market turmoil. One wonders whether the scale of the ECB reaction to liquidity problems in August 2007 might not have been motivated by the fact that several key financial markets in the euro area remain segmented. The ECB may have felt the need to overreact to any potential systemic risk because it lacked confidence in the capacity of today's fragmented supervisory framework to manage a systemic crisis. Similar concerns could constrain the ECB's reaction to inflationary pressures, when these arise.

Finally, furthering financial integration may diminish the role of fiscal policy in countries with initially less developed financial markets. As Bertola (2007c) argues, financial development may lower their need for government-provided insurance, insofar as the markets will be able to provide the risk-sharing services that people would otherwise expect from the social security system and the welfare state. This would allow these countries to focus their social welfare systems more closely on its redistributive role, and away from risk sharing.

Notes

1. See Pagano (1993) for a survey of theoretical work on the channels through which financial markets may affect the level and growth rate of income.
2. See Guiso *et al.* (2006).
3. It should be noticed, however, that financial integration may not necessarily be accompanied by an increase in international capital flows. Hnatkovska and Evans (2007), in a theoretical examination of how world financial market integration affects international capital flows, point out that these should be large and very volatile during the early stages of financial integration, when international asset trading is concentrated in bonds, and that as integration progresses and households gain access to world equity markets, the size and volatility of international bond flows should fall but continue to exceed the size and volatility of equity flows.
4. The database is available at www.econ.brown.edu/fac/Ross_Levine/Publications.htm.
5. There is no definite evidence, however, on the relative importance of banking versus securities markets: only aggregate measures of financial development appear to matter.
6. The results implied by this scenario are similar to those of a slightly less optimistic scenario where the level of financial development of all EU countries is raised to that of the UK or the Netherlands. The rankings of the simulated impacts would not be affected by considering British or Dutch rather than American standards.
7. The results for the subset of EMU countries are similar to those shown in Figure 9.9.
8. Obstfeld's (1994) model shows that financial development can affect growth by creating more risk-sharing opportunities, since individuals invest in high-profit, high-risk sectors only if they can share business risk. The reference to financial integration is direct, since access to foreign assets – promoted by integration – improves portfolio diversification. The model shows that finance can influence growth also by affecting industry specialization. Recently, Svaleryd and Vlachos (2005) have tested these predictions, using the methodology of Rajan and Zingales (1998) to study the relation between financial market development and specialization. They conclude that countries with efficient financial institutions tend to specialize in sectors that use financial services more intensively. The comparative advantage seems to derive primarily from stock markets, since only the indicators of stock market development and efficiency are significant in explaining specialization in more finance-intensive industries.
9. On this important point we draw largely on the insightful remarks of Trichet (2008b).

Comment 5: Comment on Chapter 9

SIMON HAYES

1. Was EMU a staging post or a watershed?

The pursuit of ever-closer financial integration within the euro area is a laudable goal, one that has the potential to generate enormous economic benefits through the improved allocation of capital and more optimal risk sharing. From the perspective of economic efficiency, history bequeathed a financial market setup that was far from ideal, with a hotchpotch of currencies, security structures and regulatory regimes. As Jappelli and Pagano note, the elimination of exchange rate risk that was brought about by the introduction of the euro removed a key obstacle to financial integration.

Jappelli and Pagano consider a broad range of important questions relating to European financial market integration. What is the empirical evidence that financial markets in the euro area have indeed become more integrated? Has increased financial integration generated higher levels of investment and higher rates of growth? Does increased financial integration mean that European economies are better able to adjust to macroeconomic shocks? Are European households better placed to share risks?

The empirical evidence for increased integration is found to be especially strong in the bond market, which Jappelli and Pagano describe as 'the true success story of EMU'. Since the introduction of the euro, issuance volumes have ballooned and bid-ask spreads have tightened, so that the latter are now lower than their sterling and US dollar counterparts. There is some evidence of increased integration of equity markets, with a decline in home bias, although some important institutional barriers remain. Credit markets, by contrast, have integrated at a much slower pace, reflecting in large part the informational advantage enjoyed by local lenders.

A 'growth dividend' from financial market integration is apparent in some countries (particularly those that began the process at a lower level of financial development) and in some sectors (particularly those reliant on external financing). This benefit is, however, likely to take some time to

354

accrue fully, as the evidence suggests that improved efficiency in financial markets may be particularly powerful in aiding the process of industrial restructuring by facilitating the entry of new (especially small) firms. This highlights the potential macrolevel benefits of microlevel developments, but also implies that further progress towards credit market integration may be necessary if the full benefits of integration are to be felt.

Regarding the ability of European economies to adjust to economic shocks, the evidence suggests that this has indeed improved over time, but as part of a more general trend among developed economies. Also, the substantive improvements pre-date the introduction of the euro by some way. In particular, the de-coupling of savings and investment in Europe appears to have occurred in the early 1990s.

Evidence on improved risk sharing is less encouraging: although the robustness of the extant studies could be questioned, the evidence to date suggests that the increase in risk sharing in European countries has actually been less than that seen elsewhere in the developed world. Also, Jappelli and Pagano highlight the fact that increased financial integration might actually increase the vulnerability of the European financial system if it is not appropriately counterbalanced by regulatory convergence.

Jappelli and Pagano devote less attention to the specific question of just how much effect the introduction of the euro itself has had in generating increased financial market integration. On one level this question is perhaps not so interesting, boiling down as it does to the somewhat technical question of the marginal effect of currency risk on expected rates of return. However, there is also the question of the extent to which the development of a substantial currency bloc may generate a 'critical mass' of international investment flows such that the scope of financial instruments available for issuance and purchase is broad, and liquidity premia are driven to a minimum.

This question is important because it marks the line between the introduction of the euro being seen simply as the elimination of one source of inefficiency, and therefore as one of potentially many staging posts on the way to full financial integration, and the introduction of the single currency being the catalyst for a surge in European financial intermediation – potentially a watershed for financial and economic development. Suppose, for example, that a bloc of countries was considering adopting a single currency, and was looking to the euro area as a guide to the potential benefits of such a move. If the direct benefits of

EMU were limited to the elimination of foreign exchange risk premia then the euro area would arguably be an appropriate benchmark for any such change, regardless of the size and international importance of the prospective currency bloc. However, if, as seems plausible, the benefits, in terms of financial development, from EMU have been enhanced by the new currency's international standing, there is a risk that the potential benefits in other cases of a similar move would be overestimated.

This issue is pertinent now because of the confluence of two unrelated developments. The first is the growth of the euro as an international reserve currency. The second is the pronounced escalation in foreign exchange reserve accumulation by some economies, particularly in Asia and the Middle East. 'Excess' reserves accumulation – i.e. the building-up of reserves over and above the level needed to ward off speculative attacks on currency pegs and/or to cover potential short-term foreign exchange liabilities in the event of a liquidity crisis – has recently led some countries to expand the range of instruments in which they are willing to invest beyond the traditional safe sovereign bonds. It is possible to make a *prima facie* case that, together, these developments have the potential to improve further the depth and liquidity of markets in euro-denominated financial instruments, if that has not happened already. More research would, however, be needed to establish the quantitative importance of these effects.

That the euro should have become a major international reserve currency seems unsurprising now. However, as Papaioannou *et al.* (2006) point out, this was not always the case. At its inception, doubts were expressed about the degree to which the euro area could be considered an optimal currency area, and there was a view that political tensions within the currency bloc (partly relating to the operation of a 'one-size-fits-all' monetary policy, partly reflecting more ingrained differences in cultural and political outlooks) would impede international investors' willingness to hold the currency in size. Many were sceptical that the introduction of the euro would cause much of a ripple in world financial markets.[1]

The euro's share in (identified) official holdings of foreign exchange has, however, grown steadily. In 1998, the Deutschmark accounted for 13.8 per cent of foreign exchange reserve holdings, with other euro legacy currencies making up perhaps a further 3 per cent. By 2006 the euro accounted for 25.8 per cent of official foreign exchange holdings. Given the usual snail-like pace with which the composition of official reserves tends to shift over time, this has been a healthy pace of growth, even if it does leave the euro still some way behind the 64.7 per cent share enjoyed by the US dollar (down from 69.4 per cent in 1998). Growth in the euro share has been skewed towards developing countries, which have seen a near 10 percentage point rise in the fraction of reserves held in euros (from 19.9 per cent in 1999 to 29.6 per cent in 2006).

Interestingly, Papaioannou and co-authors find that the actual share of the euro in global foreign exchange reserves exceeds that predicted by their model of the optimal currency composition for a representative central bank. They interpret this finding as indicating that the euro has attained an enhanced role as an international reserve currency, and is, in their words, 'punching above its weight'.

There are many reasons why the euro has been embraced so quickly by the international financial system. The European Central Bank has been effective in anchoring inflation expectations through the pursuit of the focused objective of inflation control. The occasional political call for the emphasis of monetary policy to be switched to other, more 'growth friendly' objectives, has been consistently met by the mantra that the best contribution the ECB can make to growth in the long run is to keep inflation in check. The credibility of the ECB, and by extension the euro, has been enhanced as a result.

Empirically, the composition of monetary authorities' reserve holdings tends to mimic the currency composition of their economy's international trade. As such, the rise in economic activity in Asia, and associated acceleration in trade flows (and therefore export opportunities for euro-area firms), has also contributed to growth in euro-denominated reserve holdings. Similarly, as governments and firms have increased their issuance of euro-denominated securities, so monetary authorities have increased their holdings of euro reserves. Partly reflecting these developments, the euro has become increasingly popular as a reference currency in currency pegs. Perhaps more fortuitously, the euro has also benefited from concerns about the medium-term outlook for the US dollar, with the euro-area's current account surplus standing in marked contrast to the USA's large and chronic deficit.

Arguably, however, just as important as the growth in the *share* of foreign exchange reserves held as euros has been the rapid growth in the *stock* of reserves worldwide, and the concomitant changes in monetary authorities' approach to reserves management. According to the IMF, the stock of international foreign exchange reserves stood at some SDR3.9 trillion in March 2007, twice the level seen in 2001. Eighty per cent of the rise in global reserves over this period was accounted for by developing countries.

The reasons behind this rapid reserves growth are well known. In the aftermath of the emerging market crises in 1997–8 and 2001 many emerging markets chose to 'self-insure' against future crises by boosting their Guidotti ratios (the ratio of a country's foreign exchange reserves to its total external short-term debt). A focus on export-led growth motivated the development of more-or-less hard currency pegs. Initially these were supported by sizable foreign exchange reserves in the standard way, but then arguably became the cause of rapid foreign exchange accumulation as the perception grew that currencies were being held at fundamentally undervalued levels, generating strong capital inflows. At the same time, an excess of domestic savings over investment (the so-called 'savings glut') led to sizable purchases of foreign assets.

These developments, which have been most apparent in emerging Asia, have been given further impetus by the rapid rise in commodity – particularly oil – prices in recent years. Commodity exporters have seen a marked improvement in their current account balances. And although there are increasing signs that import demand from such countries is rising, a large fraction of the funds has been recycled through the international financial system. Indeed, we estimate that the combined current account surpluses of just seven countries (China/Hong Kong, Japan, Norway, Russia, Saudi Arabia, Singapore and Taiwan) was approaching $1 trillion in 2007, equivalent to 1.75 per cent of annual global GDP – a figure we expect to see repeated over the next few years.

The rapid accumulation of official reserves has spawned the development of the so-called sovereign wealth fund – a catch-all term for government investment vehicles that manage foreign assets with a higher risk tolerance than is traditionally associated with reserves management. To be sure, such funds are not new – the first, the Kuwait Investment Office, was set up in 1953, and the 1970s and 1980s saw the establishment of a number of funds by oil exporters seeking to spread the benefits of their valuable natural resource across future generations. However, as several large emerging markets have shifted from being debtors to creditors in recent years more and more sovereign wealth funds have been set up.

Although there are no definitive figures for the size of sovereign wealth funds, their assets are thought to total around $2–3 trillion,

(Gieve, 2008). The IMF estimates that this could grow to $6–10 trillion within the next five years. From the perspective of financial market development, the attractive feature of sovereign wealth funds is that they tend to have long investment horizons and, in contrast to hedge funds, are not leveraged. This means not only that investment flows from sovereign wealth funds are likely to be more stable than other sources of funds, but that these funds may be inclined to 'lean against' prevailing shorter-term investor trends and help stabilise market movements. More generally, however, the existence of such large quantities of funds searching for attractive investment opportunities, in currencies that enjoy reserve status, would seem to provide the euro area with a valuable opportunity to increase further the depth and liquidity of its securities markets. Sovereign wealth funds' appetite for equity investment, as opposed to the more traditional bond ones, may add impetus to the ongoing move, noted by Jappelli and Pagano, to develop pan-European equity trading platforms.

There is clear evidence that European financial markets have become increasingly integrated over the past ten years. In many respects this marks the continuation of longer-term and/or broader trends that are largely independent of the introduction of the euro. From this perspective it may be tempting to view the introduction of the euro as one of a series of measures designed to do away with particular financial market frictions. We think, however, that this underplays the effect that the single currency has had – and is likely to have – on the development of financial markets in Europe. Arguably, the establishment of the euro as a credible international reserve currency has fostered, and will continue to foster, improvements in the depth and liquidity in euro-denominated financial assets. An interesting question for future research is to attempt to quantify how much of the improvement in financial development in the euro area has stemmed from this source, as opposed simply to the elimination of foreign exchange risk.

Note

1. See also the next chapter by E. Papaioannou and R. Portes and the respective discussion by A. Sapir.

10 | *The international role of the euro: a status report*

ELIAS PAPAIOANNOU AND RICHARD PORTES

1. Issues

1.1 Introduction

The euro has been in the global markets for a decade. The introduction of the euro has coincided with a surge in globalisation. Trade has continued to grow, and cross-border capital flows have risen much faster. There has been widespread financial liberalisation, while companies have out-sourced many operations abroad. Turnover in securities and foreign exchange markets has risen dramatically, as have cross-border asset holdings. The past decade has also been marked by growing current account imbalances that have led to a massive accumulation of foreign exchange reserves. The single European currency came to fruition in a very interesting period in international markets. It is now time to make a first detailed assessment of its international role. This chapter combines data from various sources and recent research that examines various aspects of the euro's rising internationalisation. We aim to provide a synthetic assessment of the international status of the single European currency, ten years since its birth.

Reserve accumulation, the expansion of capital and trade flows, the prolonged US current account deficit and the trade surpluses in many developing economies are closely linked. Thus, understanding the driving factors and consequences of the euro's role in international markets may shed light on some of the most controversial issues in international economics. For example, portfolio shifts from dollar-denominated

This chapter has been prepared for the EMU@10 workshop, organised by the European Commission on 26 and 27 November 2007. It was thus written before the recent financial crisis. We thank Matteo Bobba for superb research assistance, and Moreno Bertoldi, Antonio de Lecea, Heliodoro Temprano, Joachim Wadefjord and João Nogueira Martins for helpful comments and discussions, André Sapir for his discussion, and Hélène Rey for comments on a draft.

assets to those denominated in the euro and other main currencies could result in sharp dollar depreciation. Indeed, remarks by Chinese officials that the People's Bank of China will 'favour stronger currencies over weaker ones, and will readjust accordingly' appear to have contributed to the decline of the dollar.[1] A major portfolio shift would significantly affect exchange rates and the status of the dollar as the dominant international currency. Conversely, continued dollar depreciation could also reduce the attraction of the dollar as an international currency. This could have far-reaching consequences in the international financial system.

A portfolio shift could come from private investors, central banks, or both. The consequences would go beyond exchange rates. For example, if the dollar were to lose part of its international status, this would reduce the 'exorbitant privilege' of the United States, which has been able to finance large and prolonged current account deficits in its own currency and to maintain higher returns on its foreign-currency assets than foreigners achieve on their dollar assets (Gourinchas and Rey, 2007a). In addition, both economists and international relations scholars have argued that the international dominance of the dollar is a key foundation for American foreign policy and geopolitical as well as economic dominance.[2] The converse, that US geopolitical strength underpins the international role of the dollar, is also widely believed.

1.2 Globalisation fact I: increase in trade and financial openness

International currencies are used in the trade of goods, services and financial assets. Traded goods and services are usually denominated in the currency of the exporter or the importer. Yet when one or the other of the two counterparties has a volatile and risky currency, then often one of the major international currencies is used for trade invoicing. A similar pattern applies in asset trade. For example, most emerging market economies tend to borrow from the international capital markets in foreign currency, because the interest rate will be lower. Thus, the global stock of financial assets is overwhelmingly denominated in those same international currencies. Cross-border trade and asset transactions generate customer-dealer transactions in the foreign exchange markets. Those in turn give rise to large volumes of inter-dealer transactions in the foreign exchange markets. So the accelerating globalisation over the past two decades, the strong rise in trade and financial integration, has affected the functioning of currencies in the international markets.

International trade has expanded over the past decades globally. The USA, Japan and the UK have seen only moderate increases in the importance of international trade relative to GDP since the early 1990s, while the euro area, other industrial countries and developing countries have experienced a fairly rapid growth of trade. International financial flows have grown at a remarkable pace in the past fifteen years, and for industrial countries as a whole, much faster than trade in goods and services. For example, external bank assets and liabilities have grown more than fourfold since 1990.

The foreign exchange markets have also expanded dramatically. Total turnover in April 2007 was US $3.2 trillion/day, up 270 per cent since 2001 (which was somewhat smaller than 1998, partly because the euro eliminated intra-EMU forex trading). The increased turnover in forex markets has been accompanied by increased international use of derivatives and other structured products.

The message from these developments is clear: the international role of currencies today must be more closely related to financial flows than to trade flows, relative to even fifteen years ago. And if we go back further, it is only in the period 1870–1913 that international financial flows had the same importance relative to trade that they did in the mid-1990s. Now, the dominance of financial flows and the importance of cross-border financial asset holdings have no precedent. And the international financial integration underlying these flows is unlikely to be reversed – the forces behind it are too strong: technical progress in information and communications technology; financial deregulation and liberalisation; increased efforts to protect investors (hedging); a significant fall in transaction costs; and the recognition by investors that 'home bias' meant sacrificing better risk-return combinations (Ferguson *et al.*, 2007: chapter 6).

1.3 Globalisation fact II: global imbalances

The expansion of international financial markets has permitted countries to run current account deficits at levels that were not possible in the Bretton Woods period, when capital flows were heavily restricted. That is true regardless of whether current account deficits and surpluses 'cause' the capital flows, or the reverse. These large current account deficits and corresponding surpluses are often called 'global imbalances'. The euro area has shown small surpluses and deficits, but the United States has run a very large current account deficit since the late 1990s.

There are of course other countries that have run large and persistent deficits (e.g. Australia, New Zealand, Hungary, Turkey, Iceland), with corresponding surpluses elsewhere (China, Japan, oil exporters, etc.). It is again unprecedented, however, that the main international currency is that of a country in substantial, continuing deficit, with a large negative net international investment position.[3] When sterling was the dominant international currency, in the period prior to 1914, the UK borrowed short and lent long, as the USA does now. But it ran a large current account surplus, because its investment income was high, and it was a substantial net creditor.

The US current account deficit generates foreign reserve accumulation in dollars. Foreign central banks must then decide how to invest those reserves, insofar as the private flow of capital to the USA does not absorb them. Two questions arise: how far is the deficit sustainable, and what will be the allocation across currencies of the foreign surpluses.

The consensus view among international macroeconomists is that the US deficit is not sustainable, and a correction will be required, with an associated adjustment of exchange rates (e.g. Eichengreen, 2005, although see the discussion of alternative views below). The dollar will have to depreciate further (Obstfeld and Rogoff, 2005), whether the depreciation is gradual (Blanchard *et al.*, 2005) or possibly abrupt (Krugman, 2007). The dollar's depreciation may be moderated by the valuation effect that gives the US a net capital gain with depreciation, because its assets are denominated primarily in other currencies and its liabilities in dollars (Gourinchas and Rey, 2007b). While a dollar depreciation will help close the large trade deficit and mitigate global imbalances, a substantial depreciation could, however, threaten the dollar's international status (Chinn and Frankel, 2007, 2008, discussed below). Conversely, a major portfolio switch out of dollars by foreign exchange reserve holders or private investors would accelerate the depreciation. And the US Federal Reserve might not be able to prevent the dollar's depreciation, as its reserve holdings are small compared to the dollar assets held in the international markets.

1.4 Globalisation fact III: reserve accumulation

There has been a remarkable accumulation of foreign exchange reserves in recent years. At the end of 2006 the stock of reported international foreign exchange reserves was $5 trillion. Total reserve holdings are even higher, since an increasing amount is held outside central banks and official monetary authorities in so-called 'sovereign wealth funds' that aim to invest in nontraditional reserve assets (see Section 2.1.2 below). Market estimates of reserves in such funds are around $2 trillion, suggesting that the current stock of total international reserves is reaching $7 trillion.

Official foreign reserve holdings doubled over the four years from end-2002 to end-2006 (from $2.4 trillion to $5.03 trillion), while they have increased fourfold since the introduction of the euro in January 1999. This increase is driven by the emerging and underdeveloped world (the increase in industrial countries is almost exclusively attributable to Japan, which has tripled its reserves since the introduction of the euro). While in the 1990s, industrial and developing countries were holding roughly equal amounts of reserve assets, at the end of 2006 developing economies held roughly 70 per cent of the total. This illustrates the strong interlinkages between industrial and developing countries, since the latter tend to hold a sizable portion of the assets that the former issue.

The demand for low-risk foreign reserve assets has been driven mainly by large emerging economies, such as China, Brazil and India, and oil-exporting countries, such as Russia, Mexico and the Gulf states. Among the ten countries with the largest reserve holdings (by the end of 2006 and early 2007), only Japan and the combined euro area are from the industrial world. The People's Bank of China holds more than $1.3 trillion of foreign exchange reserves, while the Bank of Japan manages $900 billion of foreign assets. The third-largest country in reserve holdings is Russia, which has tripled its foreign assets over the past two years (from $120 billion in December 2004 to $360 billion in March 2007). The rest of the top-ten list includes mainly East Asian countries (namely Taiwan, South Korea, India, Singapore and Hong Kong) and Brazil.

There are several reasons behind the vast reserve accumulation. On the demand side, following the financial and currency crises of the 1990s in East Asia and Latin America, many developing countries have accumulated foreign assets as a precaution against future speculative attacks, sudden stops and massive capital outflows (Feldstein, 1999).[4]

Second, some East Asian countries pursue export-led growth policies, which may involve maintaining undervalued currencies and accumulating reserves (Dooley *et al.*, 2003, 2005).

Third, the recent increase in oil (and some other primary commodity) prices has accelerated the accumulation of reserves in the Gulf States, Russia and the other oil-producing countries. For example, foreign reserve holdings in Libya and Algeria have increased tenfold since the introduction of the euro.

Fourth, financial underdevelopment and other institutional frictions (such as low levels of investor protection or weak property rights) in developing countries hamper the channelling of savings to domestic investment. The excess savings go to the countries with developed financial markets (Caballero, 2006; Caballero *et al.*, 2008).

From the supply side, the main factor is the US current account deficit. If the current account deficit stems from low US savings and rising US demand for foreign goods (Blanchard *et al.*, 2005; Blanchard, 2007) the exchange rate will eventually have to adjust. According to Caballero *et al.* (2008) and Mendoza *et al.* (2007), however, this need not be the case, since the high sophistication of US financial intermediaries enables the USA (and to a lesser extent the UK and some other industrial countries) to finance large current account deficits, because of their ability to offer appealing financial assets to global investors.[5] This argument is less plausible now that the financial turmoil since August 2007 has revealed the weaknesses of many of these assets and the financial engineering behind them. Moreover, the developing world might in any case prefer investing in assets of other industrial countries that offer superior returns and have appealing diversification (hedging) properties. The recent slide of the dollar has clearly illustrated that the cost of investing in only one currency does carry some risk, no matter how strong the underlying economy.

1.5 Financial history

The dollar did not figure at all as an international currency before 1914, although the US weight in world output and trade would have justified parity with the UK and precedence over France and Germany. The reason carries an important lesson for the role of the euro a century later. The key obstacle to the rise of the dollar in the *international* financial system was the absence of broad, deep and liquid *domestic* financial markets.

Paul Warburg and others perceived that there were benefits ('denomination rents')[6] that accrued to the banking centre of the issuer of an international currency. He linked financial reform – in the guise of the Federal Reserve Act of 1913 – to promotion of the dollar in competition with sterling and other international currencies. With the promise of gains for the New York money centre banks, he enlisted their financial and other support for the major lobbying effort which was necessary to overcome populist opposition to institutional changes that were widely seen to favour Wall Street over Main Street.[7] That opposition accounts for the highly decentralised structure of Federal Reserve System governance that may indeed have hindered effective response to the monetary disturbances beginning in 1929. Federal Reserve monetary policy decision making has since become much more centralised in the Federal Open Market Committee, and some argue that this has implications for European Central Bank (ECB) governance today.[8]

1.6 Intellectual history

Following the design of the European monetary union plans in the early nineties (and even earlier) there was a lively debate on whether the euro would challenge the dollar as the main international currency. Some argued that the euro could become a major international currency (Alogoskoufis and Portes, 1991, 1992, 1997; Portes and Rey, 1998; Bergsten, 1997). The dominant view, however, held that the euro's international impact would be small, maybe somewhat larger than that of the Deutschmark, but by no means a threat to the dominance of the dollar (e.g. Frankel, 1995; Eichengreen, 1998). Others argued that the euro's emergence in the international financial system would be very slow (Hartmann, 1998a, 1998b), and some even expressed scepticism regarding whether EMU would be sustainable (e.g. Feldstein, 1997a).

Portes and Rey (1998) shifted the emphasis of the discussion from goods markets to financial markets. ('The internationalisation of the euro will depend mainly on the liquidity of the euro financial markets', p. 315.) Their analysis set out several scenarios, which formally were multiple equilibria in a calibrated three-region model that identified feasible configurations in the light of transaction costs in securities and forex markets. The key roles for the international currency were that of the vehicle currency in foreign exchange markets and the dominant currency in financial market transactions. The two scenarios they found most plausible were *quasi status quo*, in which the euro replaces the dollar in Europe-Asia securities transactions; and the 'medium euro', in which the euro also takes the dominant role in financial market exchanges between Europe and the USA. The 'big euro', in which the euro takes over the vehicle currency role, might also be feasible, but appeared unlikely. They concluded that 'the most likely outcome is that the dollar will have to share the number-one position ... depend[ing] on policy decisions and on the beliefs of market participants' (pp. 308, 310). Structural reforms (in particular, in financial markets) would be necessary to move beyond the *quasi status quo*, and 'the willingness of the ECB not to hinder internationalisation ... [as well as] UK participation' would be critically important. Their time frame for all this was 'five to ten years'.

The early analysis of Alogoskoufis and Portes correctly identified the issues, but with inadequate emphasis on financial markets, and foresaw a major role for the euro as an international currency, although they believed that inertia was likely to maintain dollar dominance. Feldstein overstated by far the political and economic vulnerabilities of EMU. Bergsten believed wrongly that a massive portfolio shift towards the euro was likely in the fairly short run, and Portes and Rey also thought this was a serious possibility. Hartmann was right to believe that the euro would not soon challenge the dollar's dominance as vehicle currency in the forex markets, but he underestimated the speed of financial development accompanying EMU and the EU Financial Services Action Plan (which was not introduced until after he wrote). Frankel has changed his view since 1995, in the light of changes in the data (see Chinn and Frankel, 2007, 2008, who now suggest that the euro could pass the dollar in central bank reserves by 2015).

Regarding the conditions set by Portes and Rey, financial market reforms have been extensive, though so far weak in regard to some aspects of cross-border transactions (especially clearing and settlement); the UK has not joined EMU; and the ECB has been less than enthusiastic about internationalisation of the euro. Nevertheless, the euro's status as the second reserve currency is confirmed (and has expanded), and the euro has progressed fairly steadily in the other dimensions of international currency status, especially in the financial markets. We see the 'medium euro' scenario as now the most likely development over the next few years, although a major shock could result in the 'big euro' configuration (see Section 5 below).

Table 10.1: *Functions of an international currency*

Function of money	Government	Private agents
Store of value	International reserves	Investment currency (incl. currency substitution)
Medium of exchange	Vehicle currency for foreign exchange intervention	Invoicing (vehicle) currency for trade in goods and assets
Unit of account	Anchor for currency peg	Quotation currency for trade in goods and assets

1.7 The functions of an international currency

Table 10.1 from Kenen (1983) is the standard summary of the functions of an international currency. It is based on the idea that money is used by governments, firms and individuals, as a store of value (in investment, for example), as a medium of exchange (e.g. in international trade) and as a unit of account (e.g. quoting commodity prices). Thus for analytical purposes we will use it to structure our discussion below. Yet it should be stressed from the outset that there are strong links among these functions, so they cannot be understood in isolation.

For example, the choice of international *reserve* currency is now thought to depend on currency stability (inflation rate, exchange rate – see Chinn and Frankel, 2007) as well as the size of the economy and the country's role in world trade (Eichengreen and Mathieson, 2000; Dooley *et al.* 1989). Portes and Rey (1998) argue that the use of the vehicle currency for intervention plays a major role in determining the composition of reserves. In the choice of vehicle currency, they stress the underlying *financial market determinants*: the size, depth and liquidity of the issuing country's financial markets, the latter being measured by transactions costs in foreign currency and bond markets, as represented by bid-ask spreads. And these are of course important in the choice of investment currency – this is the interaction of asset and vehicle currency roles referred to above (see also Dwyer and Lothian, 2003 and Tavlas, 1998).

Others stress the medium of exchange and unit of account functions for private users of the international currency. The literature on invoicing is scant, primarily because the data are limited (see, however,

Goldberg, 2005, as well as Kamps, 2006). Another aspect of firms' behaviour, almost totally ignored by the existing international currency literature, is hedging. Here we have an important paper by Campbell *et al.* (2007), which relates also to the central bank optimising behaviour studied by Papaioannou *et al.* (2006, 2008). These studies offer some evidence that the importance of the euro in mean-variance portfolios is increasing. Some analysts believe that the currency of invoicing of raw materials, especially oil, plays a major role in international currency status (Toloui, 2007, also discussed by Hartmann, 1998b).

1.8 The determinants of currency internationalisation

The dollar has been the main international currency during the post-war period. The Bretton Woods agreement established its 'key currency' role in the fixed exchange rate system. Most international trade transactions were held in dollars; the dollar was used even when neither the importing nor the exporting party was a US resident. The dollar was the dominant currency in international foreign exchange reserves and the main forex market intervention currency, and even after the breakdown of the Bretton Woods exchange rate system, most countries outside Europe were explicitly or implicitly pegging their currencies to the dollar.

The continuing dominance of the dollar was usually explained with theories of 'network externalities' that arise from the use of a single currency in the international financial system (Rey, 2001; Zhou, 1997; and Matsuyama *et al.*, 1993). An economic agent (individual, corporation or government) is more likely to use a particular currency in the goods or asset markets if others are also using this money. Dollar dominance was strengthened since the USA was by far the largest economy, and the Deutsche Bundesbank was unwilling to see a rising international role of the Deutschmark. In addition, inertia might arise from legal and administrative restrictions in the operations of the central banks or big banks (Truman and Wong, 2006). On the other hand, the introduction of the euro offers an alternative to the dollar. Its use (at least as a pegging or 'anchor' currency) by other countries may create new network externalities that partly counterbalance those associated with the dollar.[9]

Network externalities give a strong argument favouring the use of a single currency in the international financial system; yet there is an inherent tradeoff between holding assets in just one currency and *diversifying risk* among other monies. Although the literature has recognised this tradeoff, the argument was that market size and liquidity were too low and transaction costs too high in other currencies. While this was indeed the case throughout the post-war period, it is no longer so. There is now a viable alternative to the dollar as an international currency: the euro. The literature suggests the following main determinants of international currency status:

- Economic size – GDP and trade
- Economic strength – growth rates
- Financial stability – low inflation, exchange-rate stability
- Broad, deep and efficient financial markets
- Political stability and geopolitical strength

Today the euro area is comparable with the American economy in terms of GDP and trade openness; it may become even larger, as and when the big non-eurozone EU members join. Euro-area real *per capita* GDP grew almost as fast as the USA in 1989–98 and has actually grown slightly faster since.[10] Posen (2007a) claims a supposed US growth superiority as a key reason why the euro cannot challenge the dollar; Cohen (2008) takes the same view and attributes the eurozone's poor performance to an ECB 'anti-growth bias'. The data do not support these assertions.

The ECB has kept inflation expectations low, minimising fears that it might abandon the anti-inflationary tradition of the 'core' countries. Meanwhile, the dollar has depreciated substantially against the euro over the past six years. Trading costs in the euro forex markets are almost zero. Furthermore, transaction trading costs in the currencies and short-term notes of several other economies have fallen drastically, making diversification cheaper and thus more attractive.[11] The integration and development of euro-area financial markets since 1999 has been substantial. The US deficits raise fears of a 'hard landing' and thus make diversification to other currencies even more appealing. We cover these issues in detail below.

The euro area is still a group of independent nation states, however much they are tied together in the European Union (EU) and EMU. That is unlikely to change in the foreseeable future. But many academics and politicians argue that US geopolitical strength has declined significantly since the turn of the century. There may be no President of the euro area, but the US President is an unlikely and enfeebled defender of a strong and internationally dominant dollar.

While we take into account the interconnections among the various international currency roles discussed in Section 1.7, our analysis follows the simple taxonomy there. In the next section we analyse government use of the euro, mainly in international reserves and as an anchor currency. In Section 3 we turn to the private sector use of the euro, covering the impact of the single European currency in international trade, security issuance and invoicing. In Section 4 we turn to political economy considerations. Section 5 concludes.

2. Government use

2.1 *International reserves*

2.1.1 Trends in reserve management

Around two-thirds of global central bank foreign exchange reserves are in US dollar assets, mainly in short-term Treasury bills and highly rated agency debt. About one-quarter is in euro-denominated securities, while the yen, the pound sterling and the Swiss franc play a considerably smaller role. Table 10.2 illustrates this. The table reports the shares of the main international currencies in international allocated reserve holdings, as communicated by the IMF in its Annual Report. A limitation of the IMF data is that the currency composition does not cover all of the official reserve holdings, since most East Asian central banks (including China) do not report this information to the IMF. In addition, the data do not cover assets held in sovereign investment funds (to the order of $2 trillion).

The share of the dollar in international reserves increased over the 1990s, partly reflecting the initial uncertainty regarding the EMU project and the reserve accumulation of emerging economies after the crises of the nineties. Yet central banks face an increasing 'concentration risk' (in the terminology of Greenspan, 2004) and may wish to diversify away from the dollar to other currencies. The recent slide of the dollar illustrates this risk. But some (for example former US Treasury Secretary John Snow, 2006) argue that diversification away from the dollar is unlikely or will be moderate and slow. The high inertia illustrated in Table 10.2 hints that this might be the case.

Table 10.2: *Share of main currencies in total identified official holdings of foreign exchange*

	1995	1996	1997	1998	1999	2000	2001	2002	2003	2004	2005	2006
US dollar	59.02%	62.07%	65.16%	69.30%	70.98%	71.10%	71.48%	67.04%	65.90%	65.81%	66.75%	64.75%
UK pound sterling	2.12%	2.69%	2.58%	2.66%	2.89%	2.76%	2.71%	2.82%	2.77%	3.38%	3.62%	4.43%
Deutschmark	15.77%	14.69%	14.49%	13.80%	–	–	–	–	–	–	–	–
French francs	2.36%	1.85%	1.44%	1.62%	–	–	–	–	–	–	–	–
Japanese yen	6.78%	6.72%	5.78%	6.24%	6.38%	6.07%	5.05%	4.36%	3.95%	3.85%	3.61%	3.19%
Swiss francs	0.33%	0.30%	0.35%	0.33%	0.23%	0.27%	0.28%	0.41%	0.23%	0.17%	0.15%	0.18%
Netherlands guilder	0.32%	0.24%	0.35%	0.27%	–	–	–	–	–	–	–	–
ECUs	8.54%	7.09%	6.08%	1.30%	–	–	–	–	–	–	–	–
euro	–	–	–	–	17.91%	18.31%	19.21%	23.82%	25.18%	24.91%	24.21%	25.80%
Other	4.78%	4.34%	3.76%	4.47%	1.61%	1.50%	1.28%	1.56%	1.97%	1.88%	1.67%	1.65%

Notes: Country coverage changes every year, especially before 1997 (so the observations are not fully comparable across years). ECU reserves held by the monetary authorities existed in the form of claims on both the private sector and the European Monetary Institute (EMI), which issued official ECUs to European Union central banks through revolving swaps against the contribution of 20 per cent of their gross gold holdings and US dollar reserves. On 31 December 1998, the official ECUs were unwound into gold and US dollars; hence, the share of ECUs at the end of 1998 was sharply lower than a year earlier. The remaining ECU holdings reported for 1998 consisted of ECUs issued by the private sector, usually in the form of ECU deposits and bonds. On 1 January 1999, these holdings were automatically converted into euro. All shares are estimated at the end of year.
Source: IMF.

Theories of network externalities usually feature multiple equilibria, however, suggesting that there might be an abrupt switch between equilibria if expectations change, in particular if there are high elasticities of substitution between assets denominated in the different major currencies. Those who foresee a moderate and gradual adjustment contend that most central banks with large reserve holdings, especially those in East Asia, wish to maintain exchange rate stability relative to the dollar (Bretton Woods II, see Dooley *et al.*, 2005). That in turn supposedly implies accumulating dollar-denominated reserves.[12]

The Bretton Woods II story runs in parallel with Caballero's (2006) 'global asset shortage' argument, noted above, according to which both central banks and the private sector outside the United States have no alternative but to put their excess savings into dollar-denominated assets. This is because emerging economies do not have efficient financial intermediaries to transform savings into investment. The argument further maintains that the USA has a comparative advantage in transforming fixed assets into securities, i.e. in issuing tradeable claims, and the US capital markets are significantly more attractive than elsewhere (Rajan 2005 and Mendoza *et al.* 2007 take similar views – see the discussion in Ferguson *et al.*, 2007, Chapter 3.3).

It is not clear, however, even on the Bretton Woods II hypothesis, why the central banks should buy only dollar-denominated assets. The euro area is nowadays a trading partner comparable to the US market for China, India and other emerging economies with large reserve holdings. And the relative depth and liquidity of euro-denominated asset markets is increasing, as we discuss below. Moreover, there are various shocks that could reverse the pattern modelled by Caballero *et al.* (2008): an acceleration of growth in Europe and Japan, with a deceleration in the USA; accelerated financial development in Asia, and a shift in Asia's appetite for its own financial assets; a credit-risk concern with growing US liabilities; a fall in Asian savings (see Ferguson, *et al.*, 2007, Chapter 3.4.2).

Traditionally foreign exchange reserves were held in highly liquid (mainly short-term) US assets. The primary consideration of central banks is wealth preservation and liquidity in turmoil periods; in addition, during the period 1945–71, reserves were mainly used for intervention purposes. Yet the massive accumulation of foreign reserves is exerting pressure on central banks to seek alternative investment assets and to diversify. There are two main issues. First, should the central banks move away from government securities and invest in riskier assets? Second, should central banks diversify away from the dollar and invest in securities of other industrial countries?

2.1.2 Diversification across asset classes and currencies

The historically low yields in US and in other industrial countries' government securities are pushing central banks to consider investing in alternative assets, such as corporate bonds, hedge fund composites, derivative products, even equity. For example, it has become clear that some central banks invested heavily in US mortgage-backed securities. In addition, central banks are steadily increasing the duration of their portfolio, moving away from short-term money market instruments and T-bills to medium- and long-term government securities.

In recent years, many countries, such as Norway, Singapore, South Korea and Russia, have transferred a sizable portion of their reserves to investment funds ('sovereign wealth funds') that explicitly aim to pursue active asset management strategies in an effort to increase returns.[13] The China Investment Corporation began in summer 2007 with $200 billion and a clear mandate to invest in a range of securities, including illiquid non-voting shares. In addition, an increasing number of central banks now consult asset managers in an effort to increase the return-risk profile of their investment (see for example Gmuer and Cavegn, 2003). Royal Bank of Scotland's recent survey (RBS, 2007) suggests that reserve managers have recently started investing in riskier and longer-maturity securities. For example, more than half of respondents believe that they should be able to invest in equities, although in many countries this is not permitted. Furthermore, many central bank managers also believe that they should be able to invest in commodities other than gold. The massive reserve holdings and the nice return-volatility characteristics of some alternatives push central banks further away from traditional instruments. Indeed, almost all respondents in the RBS survey argued that diversification across assets will most likely continue in future.

The issue that has received most attention is whether central banks will shift away from the dollar, allocating an increasing amount of their reserves to the euro and possibly some other industrial countries' currencies. The main message of Table 10.2 is the high inertia in the currency composition of global reserves; yet there are some noteworthy dynamic patterns. First, the share of the dollar has fallen somewhat from 70 per cent (in 1998–2002) to 65 per cent (at end-2006). While this is partly driven by the recent weakening of the dollar, it suggests that central banks may be willing to reduce their exposure to the US currency (by passive reserve diversification).[14]

The Chinese authorities do not disclose the composition of their reserves, but market estimates suggest that the share of the dollar is currently between 65 and 75 per cent. In recent work, Brad Setser (2008) argues that China raised the share of the dollar from around 65 per cent to around 80 per cent after the euro was introduced, then cut back and by 2006 held 72–5 per cent of its reserves in dollars.

Returning to the IMF global data, we see that following the initial period since its introduction in 1999, the share of the euro has increased to 25 per cent (in 2002–3) and since then has remained relatively stable.[15] The importance of the yen has fallen from 6 per cent (in 2000) to roughly 3 per cent (the share of the yen had reached 10 per cent in the early nineties), most likely reflecting the structural problems of the Japanese economy and its financial sector and the low returns of yen short-term fixed-income assets. The share of the pound sterling has increased, probably due to the higher yields that UK money market instruments and government bonds offer to global investors.

The academic literature has used various approaches to explain the determinants of the currency composition of foreign exchange reserves.[16] Historical analyses (e.g. Eichengreen, 2005), surveys (RBS, 2003, 2005, 2006, 2007), case studies (ECB, 2005), regression-based work (e.g. Eichengreen and Mathieson, 2000; Chinn and Frankel, 2007), and other applied studies (e.g. Papaioannou *et al.*, 2006) all tend to suggest that besides inertia, the following factors are key: the country's dominant invoicing currency in international trade, the currency of its foreign debt, the anchor currency (if the exchange rate is pegged or otherwise managed), as well as the diversification strategy of the central bank. In addition, although hard to measure, the development of the financial sector and political issues also appear to be important. For example, the US dollar played no international role until institutional changes created the basis of a modern financial system (Section 1.5 above). The pound sterling established its position as the main international reserve currency during the Industrial Revolution, when the UK became the dominant imperial power. Likewise the pound weakened after the First and especially the Second World War, when the UK lost its political dominance to the USA (see Eichengreen, 2005, for a historical overview).

Data limitations, the unwillingness of central banks to give information on their practices and the high inertia observed in aggregate data make it extremely hard to quantify the importance of each of these underlying factors.[17] The literature is also inconclusive on whether the international financial system will be dominated by a single currency or whether a multipolar system with two (or more) currencies of similar importance is a likely scenario. While in most periods there was just a single dominant international currency, in some periods two currencies were of equal importance in the global financial system (the pound sterling and the dollar in the interwar period, the pound and the Dutch guilder before the Industrial Revolution). We return to this issue in Section 4 below. In addition, since the decisions on the anchor currency or the currency of international debt and the share in international reserves are jointly determined, it is hard to establish causal mechanisms.

There is a high persistence in the currency composition of international reserve holdings. For example, the dollar has been the dominant currency over the past fifty years, while the pound sterling was the dominant currency throughout the nineteenth century. This is clearly illustrated in Table 10.3. High inertia in the usage of currencies is also present in asset trade, the invoicing of international trade and transactions in the foreign exchange market (see Hartmann (1998a) for a general discussion). Econometric studies that regress the aggregate shares of each currency on various characteristics of the economy of the main international currencies – such as inflation, exchange rate volatility, financial depth, GDP, etc. – formally demonstrate the high persistence. Thus Chinn and Frankel (2007) report an autoregressive coefficient of 0.85–0.95 when they examine the determinants of the currency composition of global international reserves in the period 1973–98 (they find similar results when they distinguish between industrial and developing countries).[18] While some other factors, such as size and exchange rate volatility, are also significant factors, the bulk of the explanatory power comes from high inertia. The RBS surveys (RBS, 2003, 2005, 2007) also show that, while respondents say that they have increased their exposure to the euro (and expect a further increase in the upcoming years), they believe that this change will occur gradually rather than abruptly.

Table 10.3: *Currency breakdown of the total foreign exchange reserves of selected countries (in percentages)*

	Month-Year	Euro	Dollar	Yen	Other
Australia (inc. SDR & gold)	Dec 06	22	55	19	4
Canada	Dec 06	51	47	1	0
United Kingdom	Sept 06	58	33	9	0
United States	Dec 06	61	0	39	0
Bulgaria	Dec 06	100	0	0	0
Latvia	Dec 06	46	44	10	0
Lithuania	June 05	100	0	0	0
Romania	Nov 06	68	28	0	4
Slovakia	Dec 06	69	26	0	5
Algeria	Dec 06	60	40	0	0
Croatia	Dec 06	85	15	0	0
Iceland	June 05	40	40	5	15
Norway	June 05	54	38	0	5
Switzerland	Dec 06	47	33	5	15
Chile	June 06	26	67	n.a.	7
Colombia	March 06	12	85	n.a.	3
Peru	Dec 05	n.a.	79.1	n.a.	n.a.
Uruguay	Dec 06	1	99	0	0

Source: ECB (2007a); based on various primary sources.

Some empirical studies employ confidential (from the IMF COFER database) country-specific data on the shares of major international currencies in reserve holdings (e.g. Dooley *et al.*, 1989; Eichengreen and Mathieson, 2000). In contrast to work that uses global (reported) shares, these studies are able to identify which country characteristics correlate with the currency shares in reserve holdings. While there are non-trivial data issues, these studies formally show that the currency of the peg, the direction of international trade and the currency of foreign debt are significant correlates of the currency shares of foreign exchange reserve holdings. These results appear very stable across periods and are very robust to various model permutations. This evidence also formalises the strong regionalism in international reserve holdings. As trade and financial flows exhibit strong regional patterns and are quite sensitive to distance and information asymmetries (e.g. Portes and Rey, 2005; Lane, 2006b; Aviat and Coeurdacier, 2007; Papaioannou, 2005), this yields a similar pattern in international reserve holdings. In Table 10.3 above we report the currency composition of reserves for some central banks that reveal this information. The euro is dominant in non-euro-area EU countries, such as the Baltic states and the Balkans (Bulgaria and Romania), while its share in Latin America is minimal. The share of the euro is also high in countries that have strong trade and financial linkages with the euro area, such as Algeria, Norway and Switzerland, and countries to the east and southeast of the EU. Similarly, the dollar is dominant in Latin America and Australia.

Papaioannou, *et al.* (2006) quantify the potential gains from diversification across currencies, employing a finance-based approach. They develop a dynamic mean-variance currency portfolio optimiser with rebalancing costs to obtain the optimal global currency composition of a global central bank during the years surrounding the introduction of the euro (Fisher and Lie (2004) employ a similar though static and somewhat *ad hoc* approach; see also Codirla *et al.* (2006) and Dellas and Yoo (1991)). The authors study the five main international currencies, namely the US dollar, the euro, the Swiss franc, the British pound sterling and the Japanese yen, to assess how the 'optimal' share of the euro altered after 1999, compared to the optimal pre-1999 allocation to the three main euro predecessor currencies, the French franc, the Deutschmark and Dutch guilder. In the optimisation they allow for various forms of dynamic correlations and serial dependence in the variance-covariance matrix of returns and make various assumptions (scenarios) about currency returns.

Papaioannou and co-authors start by performing the analysis for a global 'representative central bank' and compare the estimated optimal currency shares with the reported aggregate shares. This enables them to construct a measure of currency internationalisation, defined as the difference between the optimal and the actual allocations. Then they perform simulations for optimal currency allocations for four large emerging market countries: Brazil, Russia, India and China (the BRICs), incorporating into the optimisation framework constraints capturing central banks' interest in holding a sizable portion of their portfolios in the currencies of the peg, the foreign debt and international trade.

The analysis reveals some noteworthy results. First, as already documented in the finance literature, the mean-variance optimisation yields unstable results. Small changes in the variance-covariance matrix or minimal perturbations alter the optimal allocations noticeably. In addition, the optimal allocations change considerably across years; since the actual allocations do not, this suggests high rebalancing costs. The results also change depending on the various assumptions about expected currency returns. In addition, if the central banks could take short positions, the optimal allocation implies that they should apply 'carry strategies' (i.e. shorting low yield currencies, such as the yen and the Swiss franc, and investing heavily in the pound sterling that has the highest return).[19] This result may explain the high inertia in reserves and shows that, while diversification is a theoretically plausible counterargument to network externalities, it is quite hard to implement. Second, the currency optimiser can match the high allocation of the dollar in reserve holdings (about 65 per cent) when the US currency is used as the base-reference currency (risk-free asset). Thus the high share of the dollar should not come as a surprise, since most central banks (even in industrial currencies) express their returns in dollar terms. Third, the optimiser yields roughly equal allocations of about 10 per cent to each of the four non-dollar currencies (the pound sterling, the Japanese yen, the euro and the Swiss franc). Since the actual share of euro-denominated assets in global foreign exchange reserves is significantly higher (around 25 per cent), this may be interpreted as tentative evidence of an increasing international role of the euro as a reserve currency. Fourth, the constraints reflecting the currency of external debt and international trade have a small effect compared to the reference currency in explaining the currency composition of reserves.[20]

2.2 Vehicle currency for foreign exchange intervention

A main reason behind the prominent role of the dollar in international reserves was its use for foreign exchange market intervention. Until the break-up of the Bretton Woods (I) exchange rate system, most countries were anchoring their monetary policies to that of the USA, employing exchange rate arrangements that were targeting the level of the exchange rate, usually at a small band with the dollar. To minimise exchange rate fluctuations and keep the official exchange rate within the pre-announced band, the central bank had to hold adequate dollar reserves to be able to intervene in the forex market if there was pressure on the currency to depreciate. The potential need for forex market intervention also required central banks to hold most of their reserves in highly liquid, mainly short-term, assets and money market instruments.

In recent years there has been a gradual shift of monetary policy from targeting the level of the exchange rate to targeting inflation (e.g. Mishkin (2007)). Rose (2006) concludes that inflation targeting appears more stable, and thus more appealing for both industrial and developing countries, than fixed exchange rate regimes. The increased tendency of many countries to shift their monetary policy to inflation rather than exchange rate targeting and to let their currencies float makes foreign exchange market intervention less important in the conduct of monetary policy. Thus, while central banks will likely allocate a portion of their reserves for market interventions in turmoil or crisis periods, this fundamental policy change leads monetary authorities to consider alternative instruments and currencies to maximise the risk-adjusted returns of their portfolio.

2.3 Anchor currency

As discussed above, mean-variance (or the risk/variance minimisation) approaches do not yield very stable results; yet the analysis in Papaioannou *et al.* (2006) illustrates that among the various factors that determine global currency allocation, the choice of the reference currency is quantitatively the most important factor. The intuition is simple. Since currency and bond returns among developed countries do not differ considerably, the optimal allocations are mainly driven by the variability of returns. The variance of bond returns across the main developed countries, however, is quite similar, and bond returns tend to be positively correlated among Europe, the USA, UK and Japan. Therefore, if a central bank pegs its currency vis-à-vis the dollar (or expresses its balance sheet in dollars) then returns in dollar-denominated assets (of any kind) will exhibit significantly lower variability than returns in other currencies (just because returns in non-dollar assets will also incorporate exchange rate variability). Thus the optimiser will naturally put a very high weight on dollar-denominated assets.[21]

To forecast the dynamics of currency shares in global central bank portfolios, therefore, one has to forecast whether countries in the developing world will switch from dollar pegs to either euro-based pegs or anchor to a basket of currencies (such as the SDR), where the euro is a significant part. Currently the dollar is still the main anchor currency. But the importance of the euro is steadily increasing. While pegging to the euro is mainly observed in the new EU member states and

EU-neighbouring regions (ECB, 2007a), countries with sizable reserve holdings outside the European sphere of influence, like Russia and Libya, are using the euro in their basket pegs (or basket reference value, like China). It now seems likely that some of the Gulf Cooperation Council (GCC) countries, like the UAE and Qatar, will shift from their dollar pegs to basket pegs that include the euro. Dollar depreciation has generated inflationary pressures in countries pegged to the dollar, and the domestic monetary strains of maintaining the peg are greater for countries running large balance of payments surpluses (GCC, China, Russia).

In several steps, Russia rapidly raised the share of the euro in its basket peg from 10 per cent in February 2005 to 45 per cent from February 2007 (with the dollar at 55 per cent). On the other hand, Frankel and Wei (2007) estimate that although China switched from a dollar peg to a basket peg in 2005, the implicit weight of the dollar is still high (87 per cent), with little or no weight on the euro and the yen; rather, the other currencies with a significant role in the basket appear to be the Malaysian ringgit, the Thai baht and the Korean won. Yet their estimates imply that the importance of the dollar (which in 2005 was the sole currency in the peg) will most likely fall.

Cobham (2007) constructs indicators of de facto anchoring to the dollar and the euro using monthly exchange rate data for the period 1994–2006. A very strong peg is identified when the percentage change in the exchange rate vis-à-vis either of the two currencies is less than 0.5 per cent. A strong peg is defined when the percentage change in the exchange rate is greater than 0.5 per cent but less than 2 per cent, while a weak alignment (weak peg) is defined when the percentage change is between 2 per cent and 5 per cent. Table 10.4 reproduces his tentative results. In 2001–6, 23–34 countries anchored strongly or very strongly to the dollar and 25–9 to the euro. While this difference is not big, a significantly larger number of countries loosely align their exchange rates with the dollar rather than the euro. Most importantly, most countries with large reserves (such as China, Hong Kong and Malaysia) peg to the dollar, while none of the top-twenty countries in reserve holdings pegs to the euro. Yet the number of countries that align their currencies to the euro (or its predecessors) in a strong and very strong peg is higher in 2005–6 than in 1994–8. In addition, the group of countries whose currencies are more closely aligned to the euro than to the dollar includes some big economies with significant reserves (such as Norway, Switzerland and the UK). In addition, Cobham documents

Table 10.4: *De facto dollar and euro pegs (Cobham classification)*

Number of countries	1994–8	1999–2000	2001–4	2005–6
$$$ – Very strong dollar peg	18	20	20	28
$$ – Strong dollar peg	3	4	3	6
$ – Aligned to the dollar	6	17	60	17
0 – No dollar or no euro peg	94	48	22	52
€ – Aligned to the euro	39	35	20	7
€€ – Strong euro peg	0	7	4	8
€€€ – Very strong euro peg	0	21	21	21
euro member countries	0	11	12	12

Source: Cobham (2007).

that many countries that formerly anchored their currencies to the dollar now take a neutral position between the two currencies. This is also in line with the results of Frankel and Wei (2007) that to a small extent the Chinese central bank is in fact relaxing its alignment with the dollar. This result is also in line with the increasing tendency of many countries to adopt baskets of currencies (such as the SDR or their own trade-weighted baskets) to anchor their exchange rates.

3. Private use

3.1 Invoicing in international goods and asset trade

A key aspect of a currency's international role is its use in international trade. While data on international trade invoicing are scant, most studies illustrate the primary role of the dollar throughout the past fifty years. Yet there are some indications that the euro's importance is modestly increasing. Thus the euro share in British imports and exports is around 21 per cent and 27 per cent, respectively, not far from the dollar's share of 27 per cent and 37 per cent (ECB, 2007a). But the importance of the euro has mainly increased in transactions in which one of the two counterparties is an EU member country. This is, for example, illustrated by the recently released data from the Japanese Ministry of Finance on the invoicing patterns of Japanese firms (summarised in Table 10.5). Roughly 4 per cent and 8 per cent of all Japanese imports and exports respectively are invoiced in euro. The share of the

Table 10.5: *International trade invoicing patterns in Japan*

	From Asia				From the US				From the EU			
	Euro	JPY	USD	Pound	Euro	JPY	USD	Pound	Euro	JPY	USD	Pound
Panel A: Imports												
2001	0	24.2	74.5	0	0.2	20.5	78.8	0	12.3	48.1	16.9	4.3
	0	24.2	74.5	0	0.2	19	80.3	0	16.9	49.7	14.8	4.4
2002	0	25.5	73.2	0	0.2	19.4	80	0.1	28.7	49.3	15	3.9
	0	27.5	71.2	0	0.2	19.8	79.7	0	31	50.5	13.4	3.7
2003	0	27.8	71	0	0.2	19.3	80.2	0.1	32	49.4	13.2	3.7
	0.2	28.1	70.6	0	0.8	19.1	79.9	0	32.3	50.9	12	3.5
2004	0.2	28.4	70.2	0	0.4	21.6	77.8	0	32.4	51.3	11.8	3
	0.3	27.2	71.4	0	0.6	20.7	78.5	0	34.1	49.5	11.7	3.2
2005	0.2	28.2	70.4	0	0.4	21.9	77.5	0	33.9	50.2	11.4	3.2
	0.2	26.7	71.9	0	0.4	22.8	76.6	0	32.4	50.7	12.4	3.2
2006	0.3	25.9	72.6	0	0.5	21.8	77.6	0	32.5	50	13.2	3.1
	0.3	26	72.4	0	0.7	23.6	75.6	0	34	49	12.5	3.2
2007	0.4	28.6	71.8	0	0.7	22.2	76.9	0.1	34.6	47.7	13.6	3

Table 10.5: (cont.)

	To Asia				To the US				To the EU			
	Euro	JPY	USD	Pound	Euro	JPY	USD	Pound	Euro	JPY	USD	Pound
Panel B: Exports												
2001	0	49	48.9	0	0	12.5	87.4	0	42.6	30.4	12.8	6.9
	0.3	50.1	47.9	0	0.1	12.2	87.7	0	45	31.3	12.8	7.3
2002	0.4	49.4	48.6	0	0.1	11.8	88	0	52.2	28.4	11.7	7.1
	0.5	51.3	46.6	0	0.1	12	87.9	0	53.5	28.5	10.4	7
2003	0.5	53.3	44.7	0	0.1	13.4	86.4	0	54.4	27.4	11.2	6.6
	0.4	53	44.9	0	0.1	12.5	87.3	0	54.1	27.3	11.4	6.6
2004	0.4	53.4	44.6	0	0.1	13.3	86.5	0.1	54.8	27.5	11	6.3
	0.4	52.8	45.5	0	0.1	12.9	86.9	0	53.9	29.3	10.3	6
2005	0.2	51.6	46.6	0	0.1	13	86.9	0	53.6	29.3	10.2	6.6
	0	49.5	48.8	0	0.1	12.3	87.6	0	52.2	29.3	11.9	6.3
2006	0	50.7	47.5	0	0.1	11.9	88	0	51.5	28.5	13.8	5.9
	0	48.8	49.5	0	0.1	10.8	89.1	0	54	26.6	13.4	5.6
2007	0	49.9	48.4	0	0.2	11.5	88.3	0	54.6	26.4	13.6	5.7

Source: Ministry of Finance, Japan.

euro in Japanese exports to Europe has risen from roughly 40 per cent to almost 60 per cent since 2001. Similarly, the share of the euro in Japanese imports from the EU is around 35 per cent, significantly higher than that of the dollar, at 10–15 per cent. Yet the importance of the euro in international trade in Asia and the USA is low.

The dollar has enjoyed a prominent role in international trade for three main reasons. First, before the creation of the euro area, the USA was by far the largest market in the world. Thus most imports to the USA as well as exports from US firms were settled in dollars. Yet nowadays the euro-area economy equals the size of the US economy. In addition, the euro area is a market equally important to the USA for most big emerging economies (such as China and India). The GCC's exports of oil increasingly go to Asia, and its imports come from Asia and Europe. More broadly, financial flows (in particular, reserve currency accumulation) no longer correspond well to trade flows. This suggests that a rising number of international trade transactions that involve the euro area will be settled in euro. The euro has clearly more than replaced the legacy currencies in European imports and exports. Kamps (2006) studies a large number of countries and shows that the prospect of joining the single currency also raises use of the euro, both with existing euro-area countries and also with third parties. The role of the euro in international trade is also high in countries that peg their monetary policy to that of the euro area.

Second, trade invoicing is affected positively by low exchange rate risk, low volatility of inflation (menu costs), developed capital markets, absence of capital controls and no black market. Kamps (2006) provides cross-country empirical evidence, while Donnenfeld and Haug (2003), Wilander (2004) and Silva (2004) study the trading invoicing patterns in Canada, Sweden and the Netherlands, respectively. Traditionally, the USA offered a stable currency with low inflation and risk. (Tavlas (1991) shows that the importance of the Deutschmark in international goods markets rose considerably in the 1970s and 1980s, when US inflation was high.) Yet the euro is nowadays offering an attractive alternative. The ECB has kept inflation low; the euro exchange rate volatility is not higher than that of the dollar, and the euro area has developed sophisticated capital markets. Wilander (2004) presents evidence that the euro has increased its status in Swedish exports. Yet the increased share of the euro compared to the legacy currencies comes at the expense of the Swedish krona rather than the dollar.

Third, the major factor behind the dollar's dominance in international trade arises from its use in reference-priced and organised-exchange traded goods. For example, most commodities, including oil, are settled in international markets in dollars. Indeed McKinnon (1980) and Krugman (1980) have argued that when a currency has established itself in a particular market, then a small price-taking firm always finds it optimal to follow, because if it were to choose another invoicing currency this would yield more volatile sales. The key insight is that once a currency has acquired a dominant role due to historically low costs, then it will continue to enjoy this status, even if alternative currencies offer similar (or even smaller) costs.

Recent theoretical work by Bacchetta and van Wincoop (2005) and Goldberg and Tille (2008) stresses the effects of the structure of demand and production on invoicing (see also McKinnon (1980) and Swoboda (1968) for early contributions). These models yield a herding effect, implying that the exporter has an incentive to follow its competitors and use the same currency, because this limits output volatility. The main empirical prediction of this theoretical work is that reference-based pricing is more likely in homogeneous goods, such as oil, gold and basic commodities. The intuition is simple. If a firm produces and sells differentiated goods, then it faces (the usual) downward-sloping demand curve and thus can choose to index sales in the currency of the exporter. When the good is homogeneous, the producer is typically a price taker and thus will use the currency that the good is settled in to minimise loss of sales and profits arising from exchange rate fluctuations. Goldberg and Tille (2008) assemble invoicing data from twenty-four countries and show that the dollar's importance in international transactions is mainly driven by its predominant role in reference-priced goods, usually traded on organised exchanges.[22] Kamps (2006) reaches similar results, showing that the dollar is still the dominant vehicle currency, mainly because of its role in settling commodities and oil transactions. Theories of network externalities suggest that it is unlikely that these markets will switch to another currency, unless transaction costs (broadly defined to include exchange rate volatility, inflation and other risk considerations) in the dollar increase significantly. Yet the euro might still play some role in newly established markets (as for example natural gas, discussed below).

3.2 Investment currency – transaction costs and financial development

Theory and empirical studies have stressed the importance of financial development and transaction costs in securities and foreign exchange markets as determinants of the international role of a currency in those markets (e.g. Portes and Rey, 1998). During the Bretton Woods period and the 1970s and 1980s, the US capital markets were significantly larger and more liquid than the segmented European markets. The USA offered liquid markets with low transaction costs as well as a variety of alternative instruments, such as agency debt, highly rated commercial paper and low-risk equity. The US markets had sound investor protection and were relatively transparent, with a reassuring political risk environment. All these factors translated into low transaction costs, as measured by bid-ask spreads.

Yet after the initial period of euro introduction in 1999, bid-ask spreads in euro-denominated corporate bond markets are nowadays actually below those for corresponding dollar-denominated bonds (Biais *et al.*, 2006), while spreads in the euro-denominated government bond markets are not much higher than those for US Treasuries (Dunne *et al.*, 2006). Transaction costs (bid-ask spreads) for euro transactions in the foreign exchange markets have fallen to equality with dollar transactions (both now close to zero). In addition, foreign exchange traders now look as closely at 'euro crosses' as they do at 'dollar crosses' to interpret exchange rate movements.

While transaction costs have fallen in other industrial countries' markets as well, the evidence suggests that investing in euro-denominated securities is not more expensive than investing in similar US assets. Coeurdacier and Martin (2007) find that the transaction costs of buying assets from the eurozone are substantially lower than they would be without the single currency.[23] In the same spirit, Hartmann *et al.* (2007) show that the euro area has improved its performance across a variety of proxy measures of financial development. While there are still non-negligible differences in financial market sophistication and efficiency across euro-area countries, at the aggregate level the euro area's financial development is comparable to that of the USA and the UK, and probably superior to Japan.

Moreover, the euro-area equity markets and both government and corporate bond markets show very considerable evidence of integration since the late 1990s (Jappelli and Pagano, this volume; Lane, 2006b; Lane and Wälti, 2007). The comovement of asset returns across euro-area countries has risen significantly. Countries' common membership of the euro area raises their bilateral bondholdings and portfolio equity holdings very substantially.

There are, however, still yield differentials across euro government bonds issued by the various euro-area countries. This will continue until and unless there is joint issuance and liability. This limitation on government bond market integration is a significant disadvantage in the competition with the US Treasuries market. On the other hand, there is a single hedging instrument for the entire euro-denominated government bond market: the ten-year German bond (Bund). This is the highest-volume futures contract in the world.

The fall of transaction costs, financial development and financial integration, and the enlargement of the euro area have all increased the attractiveness of euro-area securities. As the euro area enlarges, it offers foreign and domestic investors a larger variety of financial claims (in imperfectly correlated assets) and thus makes the euro area more attractive for diversifying risk (Martin and Rey, 2005). But the euro-area bond market is overall only a little more than half the size of that in the USA (the corporate bond market, in particular, is much smaller), and euro-area equity market capitalisation is also half that of the USA (data from end-2006, ECB, 2008d). UK adoption of the euro would bring about a substantial increase in the size of the euro-area securities markets.

Global investors also take into account the hedging properties of international stocks, bonds and currencies. Campbell *et al.* (2007) consider the optimal currency hedging allocation of a global equity and (alternatively) bond investor over the past thirty years, with a portfolio in the currency, bond and equity markets of the USA, the UK, the eurozone, Canada, Australia, Japan and Switzerland. They build their empirical (regression-based) analysis on an international capital asset pricing model (CAPM) that stresses the benefits of diversification in hedging. Given the unpredictability of currency returns, they just examine the variance-covariance properties of currency returns with the equity and (separately) with the bond markets.

They identify the currencies with good hedging properties in periods of bond and equity market turmoil. In this framework, global investors want to hold long positions in currencies that have low (or even negative) correlation with bond or equity returns. Their analysis yields interesting results on the international role of the euro and the dollar as hedging instruments in global portfolios. First, the risk-minimisation problem of global bond investors (particularly relevant for central banks) leads to long positions in the dollar, which has desirable hedging properties: while currency and bond returns are only weakly correlated, the dollar appreciates when global bond prices fall (especially in the short run). The optimal currency hedging strategies of equity investors, however, are to go long in the euro, the dollar and the Swiss franc and hold short positions in the other currencies. This is because the euro, the Swiss franc and the dollar are all negatively correlated with global equity returns, while the Australian dollar, the Japanese yen and the Canadian dollar are positively correlated.

The dollar has in the past been viewed as a 'safe haven' currency. Geopolitical, financial and economic disturbances supposedly prompt investors to switch into the dollar because of its dominant international role and the political and economic stability of the USA. Behaviour since the beginning of global financial turmoil in early August 2007 does not support this hypothesis. There was a very brief upward movement of the dollar exchange rate in mid-August, but the currency has followed a downward trend since, in particular against the euro (and the Swiss franc). This may be because the markets see the disturbances as emanating from the USA – but that too would suggest lack of confidence in the currency.

Currency (notes and coins) is also a store of value, and private agents hold dollars outside the United States and euro outside the euro area. The value of euro bank notes in circulation globally (both inside and outside the euro area) was close to the value of dollar bank notes in circulation in 2006. But the US Treasury estimates (data of 2006) that around $450 billion in bank notes circulate outside the USA (about 60 per cent of the total outstanding), whereas the ECB (2007a) estimates that only €60–100 billion in bank notes were in circulation outside the euro area in late 2006. Even the upper estimate for the euro is somewhat less than one-third the value of the dollar estimate. But there is a high share of euro-denominated bank deposits in new EU member states not yet in EMU, as well as in the UK (22.5 per cent of total deposits!); even Sweden (10 per cent) and Switzerland (9 per cent) have significant shares of euro-denominated deposits (ECB, 2007a).

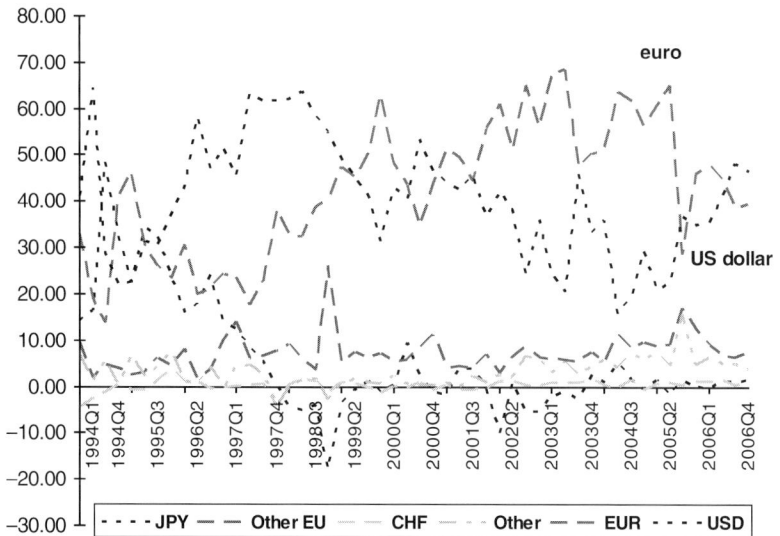

Figure 10.1: Net issues of international debt securities (bonds, notes and money market instruments) including home currency issuance ('broad' measure)
Source: BIS.

3.3 Quotation currency

The euro has increased its status as a unit of account in international markets. As Figure 10.1 illustrates, since 1999, the euro has come to surpass the dollar as an issuing currency in international debt markets.[24] While in the initial years following the euro's introduction its share in international debt markets was about half of that of the dollar (the share of euro-denominated international debt securities was around 25 per cent, while that of the dollar around 45–50 per cent), nowadays the amounts outstanding in euro- and dollar-denominated international debt securities (bonds and notes) are roughly the same; if anything the share of the euro is slightly higher (Figure 10.2 and Figure 10.3). The share of total claims of BIS reporting banks denominated in euro rose from 34 per cent to 41 per cent during 1999–2003, but has since fallen back to 39 per cent (losing ground to sterling).[25]

Bobba *et al.* (2007) formally examine the impact of the euro in international debt markets in an event study framework. Using BIS data on debt issuance for sixty-four developing countries and forty-two developed countries and the five major currencies, namely the

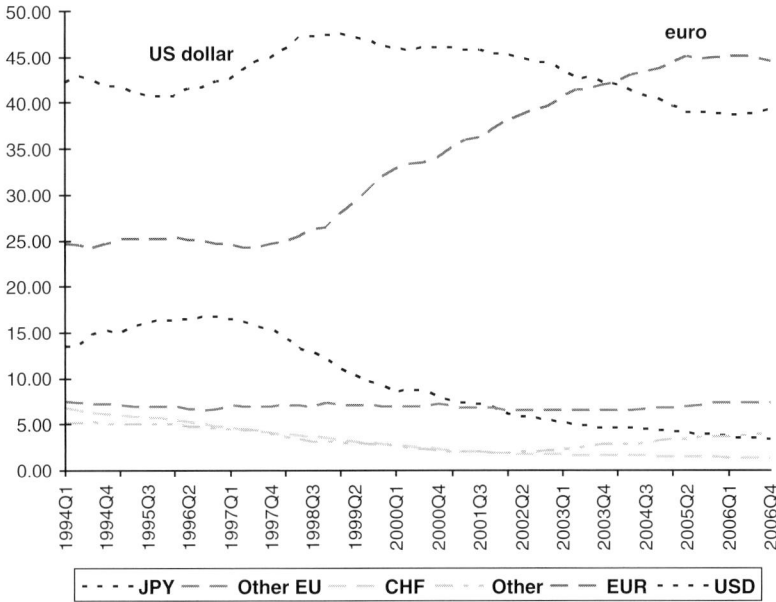

Figure 10.2: Amounts outstanding international debt securities (bonds, notes and money market instruments) including home currency issuances ('broad' measure)
Source: BIS.

US dollar, the euro, the yen, the pound sterling and the Swiss franc, the authors examine the liquidity effects of the euro.[26] To test for these effects, the authors include individual currency dummies, taking the value of one from 1999 onwards for each currency to pick up liquidity effects throughout the sample period. Their regressions show that conditional on various other factors and unobservable country characteristics, the euro has brought a significant increase in the liquidity of international debt markets. In addition an increased number of countries 'tipped' or suddenly switched to issuing euro-denominated securities.

In spite of the euro's rising role in international debt markets, the dollar is still the dominant international currency as a unit of account in private transactions, since most commodities are traded in dollars. The key example is of course oil, but almost all of the main commodities are currently indexed and invoiced in dollars. Theories of network externalities and trade invoicing suggest that

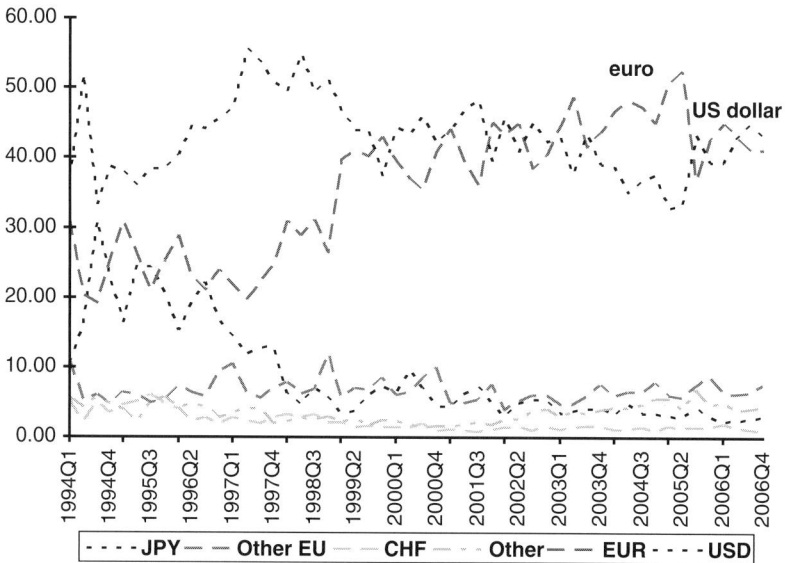

Figure 10.3: Amounts outstanding international long-term debt securities (bonds and notes) including home currency issuances ('broad' measure) Source: BIS.

the dollar's dominance will most likely continue in highly homogeneous goods (such as oil). Yet the euro might still play a role, mainly in differentiated goods. The euro's status as a unit of account in international markets will be affected significantly by whether the currently developing natural gas market will use the euro.[27] The euro area is geographically well positioned in realising this opportunity, as it is almost in the middle of the Russian and North African natural gas reserves; and it is the largest importer of Russian natural gas.

3.4 Vehicle currency in foreign exchange markets

The latest BIS Triennial Survey (2007) shows little change in the dominance of the dollar in the foreign exchange markets. 86.3 per cent of all transactions had the dollar on one side (down slightly from 88.7 per cent in 2004). The corresponding figure for the euro was 37.0 per cent

(37.2 per cent in 2004). Dominguez (2006, p. 68) says, 'the euro is less widely used than the combination of European currencies that it replaced'. She gives no data, but she must be comparing the BIS forex market surveys for 1998 and 2004; as we have shown, there is no other domain in which this could be true. But it is not true here, either, because these data do not adjust for the disappearance of trading between the pre-euro EMU currencies. The forex market role of the euro exceeds that of the 'legacy currencies' when those trades are netted out.

The dollar also takes precedence in the market for OTC foreign exchange derivatives, with $233 billion traded daily as opposed to $119 billion in euro FX derivatives ($110 billion and $61 billion, respectively, in 2004). On the other hand, the euro exceeds the dollar in the market for OTC interest rate derivatives, where $656 billion were traded daily in euro-denominated trades and $552 billion in dollar-denominated interest rate derivatives. There is an interesting analogy here with the markets for government bonds in the USA and the euro area. The US Treasuries market is dominated by cash transactions – the cash market is about twice the size of the combined futures and interest rate swaps market. In the euro area, the position is reversed: the derivatives markets are twice the size of the cash market, and price discovery takes place primarily in the interest rate swaps market (Dunne *et al.*, 2006).

3.5 Creeping 'euroisation' in asset markets – the case of Iceland[28]

An interesting example illustrating the euro's increased international status is Iceland's recent move towards 'euroisation'.[29] Iceland has the fifth highest per capita income (PPP-adjusted) in the OECD. Its financial sector is highly developed and exceptionally large relative to the economy. Bank lending in foreign currency is already 63 per cent of total domestic bank lending to businesses (end-August 2007). It is sensible for firms that derive a substantial part of their income from exports to finance themselves in foreign currency – the loans are then naturally hedged. But many firms that do not have substantial foreign currency income also borrow in foreign currency, because of Iceland's high interest rates. This has not appeared risky to them, since the real exchange rate has appreciated over the past several years (though it has fallen substantially since December 2007).

Firms listed on the stock exchange – all of which have a substantial share of foreign income – increasingly keep their accounts in foreign currency in order to avoid the adverse effects of volatility of the Icelandic krona (ISK). Several are moving to list their shares on OMX ICE in foreign currency.

Icelandic households have increasingly begun to borrow in foreign currency, in particular to finance their homes and cars. The share of banks' foreign currency-linked loans to households is still low, at 14 per cent, but 42 per cent of the increase in loans to households over the year to 31 August 2007 were foreign currency linked. Again, this is a response to the high domestic interest rate. Foreign borrowing creates a risk for most households, since generally their income is in ISK.[30] Households will therefore wish to hedge that risk by taking some of their wages in foreign currency. Some firms with a substantial foreign currency income already offer this as an option for their employees.

Policy makers in Iceland will therefore have to consider explicitly the option of formally adopting the euro (Portes, 2008). Euroisation[31] – using a stable currency issued by a monetary authority outside the country, whose domestic supply is limited to that earned through balance of payments surpluses – would be feasible for Iceland. At the end of October 2007, foreign exchange reserves were ISK157.6 billion, much more than enough to cover base money of ISK91 billion.

The ECB and the European Commission oppose formal euroisation, at least for countries that are members of or might accede to the EU (and thus to EMU, in due course). The ECOFIN Council opinion of 7 November 2000 asserts that 'before finally adopting the euro', the candidate countries must fulfil the Maastricht criteria: 'any unilateral adoption of the single currency by means of "euroisation" would run counter to the underlying economic reasoning of EMU in the Treaty. [It would] be a way to circumvent the stages foreseen by the Treaty for the adoption of the euro.'[32]

Iceland is in the unusual position of being a member of the European Economic Area but not yet, at least, a candidate for EU membership. Thus in principle, it should not encounter the Commission-ECB opposition suggested above, and indeed there are countries that use the euro and are not EU members or (yet) 'accession countries' (Kosovo, Montenegro).

There is an untidy alternative: international companies (and their employees) could shift to using the euro, while the rest of the economy stays on the ISK. But this degree of domestic liability euroisation would be an emerging market response, not appropriate for Iceland. Moreover, the dynamics of partial euroisation could be unstable: if exchange rate adjustment is needed, a diminishing local currency base would have to support the required change, which could make people switch even more aggressively out of the currency. And if it were believed that this was a prelude to adoption of the euro, that could provoke major, destabilising capital inflows. How to respond to creeping euroisation will henceforth be at the heart of Iceland's political debate.

Authors' note: This was written in early 2008. Unfortunately, Iceland did not choose to replace its domestic currency with the euro. The sequel is well known.

4. Political economy and institutions

4.1 Historical evidence and the 'hegemonic stability' theory

Charles Kindleberger (1973) argued that the instability of the world economy between the wars reflected the absence of a dominant power willing and able to stabilise the international system. But both theoretical and historical analyses indicate that the relationship between the power of the leading economy and the stability of the international monetary system is considerably more complex than suggested by simple variants of hegemonic stability theory. Economic theory can in fact explain the 'manias, panics and crashes' of financial markets with rational agents that exhibit behaviour adapting to that of other market participants (i.e. rational herding), which in turn provokes self-fulfilling crises and the financial instabilities of the type emphasised by Kindleberger, as well as the more recent episodes of financial turmoil.

Indeed, there seems to be little causal relation between periods of financial instability and the degree of market power in the world economy. From the second half of the twentieth century onwards, the global economy has been unambiguously dominated by the United States. During this period of 'hegemonic stability', we have witnessed a historically high frequency and severity of financial crises. According to Bordo (2007), crises appear to be growing more frequent in the recent era than ever before. Crisis frequency since 1973 exceeds even the unstable interwar period and is three times as great as in the pre-1914 earlier era of globalisation in which Britain was the international hegemonic power.

Economic leadership goes hand in hand with monetary leadership. The currency of a country that has a large share in international output, trade and finance has a big natural advantage. The US economy is still the world's largest in terms of output and trade, and the dollar has been the dominant currency since the middle of the twentieth century.

There is of course an important historical precedent. The pound sterling was the premier international currency of the gold standard period. That Britain was an imperial power reinforced sterling's role. From the early eighteenth century, a conscious effort was made to encourage the use of the pound throughout the empire as a way of simplifying and regularising transactions. British financial institutions established branches in the colonies, and colonial banks opened offices in London. These banks maintained assets and liabilities in London and issued bank notes for the colonies, maintaining a fixed exchange rate between those notes and sterling. Historians estimate, for example, that 60–90 per cent of the world's trade was invoiced in sterling in the nineteenth century.

In order to explain the remarkable phenomenon that usually only a few currencies dominate the international scene, economists have suggested that transaction costs act as an invisible hand, leading decentralised agents to coordinate on the cheapest currency or currencies. This general agreement covers two alternative emphases. One treats transaction costs as essentially exogenous and relates them to intrinsic properties of the candidate currencies. According to this view of currency competition, monetary instability increases transaction costs, so agents use those currencies with the best prospects of holding their value. The other emphasises that transaction costs are determined by size. An international currency is valuable because a lot of other people are using it. This creates room for strategic complementarities and externalities, in the sense that the unit transaction cost is a decreasing function of the volume of transactions, and this can lead to the conclusion that there is scope in the market for only one international currency. While this argument carries some weight in the choice of currency for invoicing trade or denominating foreign debt securities, and indeed for financial markets more generally, it is less obviously valid for the currency of denomination of reserves, in which market liquidity is not all that matters and the benefits of diversification may play a role

(Eichengreen, 2005). In addition, the diversification and hedging properties of currencies are of primary importance for private agents, such as investment banks, pension funds, corporations, etc. Moreover, the formal models with network externalities (including a calibrated version like that of Portes and Rey 1998) and the search models both typically yield multiple equilibria. While a major event is needed to shift expectations, this possibility, even if it is remote, should push governments and private agents to hedge this risk.

In fact, if we focus on the store of value role of an international currency, historical evidence suggests that there need not be a single dominant currency. At the end of 1913, at the peak of Britain's world economic leadership, sterling balances accounted for less than half of the total official foreign exchange holdings whose currency denomination is known, while French francs accounted for perhaps a third and German marks a sixth. Over the preceding quarter century, sterling's share had in fact been falling, not rising, mainly in consequence of the growing share of the French franc. In Europe itself, sterling was a distant third as a form in which to hold official reserves behind both the franc and the mark (Eichengreen (2005), Lindert (1969)). Flandreau and Jobst (2005) show that sterling was not that far ahead of the franc and the mark in terms of the number of currencies quoted against each of these in the foreign exchange markets (the *vehicle currency* role). The historical survey of Dwyer and Lothian (2003) reinforces these observations.

The conventional wisdom that one currency denominates *reserve holdings* worldwide thus derives mainly from the second half of the twentieth century alone, when the dollar accounted for as much as 85 per cent of global foreign exchange reserves. The post-World War II reign of the dollar was institutionalised at Bretton Woods and subsequently reflected the exceptional dominance by the United States of global trade and payments, in a period when Europe and Japan had not yet fully recovered from the war and modern economic growth had yet to spread to what we now refer to as emerging markets. In addition, it reflected the efforts of the governments of other potential reserve centres to discourage international use of their currencies. Germany saw the internationalisation of the Deutschmark as a threat to its control of domestic monetary conditions and of inflation (a view that continues to have weight in the ECB). Japan saw the internationalisation of its currency as incompatible with its system of directed credit.

France had seen more than once how allowing private foreign funds to move in also allowed them to move out if investors concluded that the government's macroeconomic policy aspirations were incompatible with its putative commitment to currency stability. These and other considerations led the countries whose currencies were potential alternatives to the dollar to maintain significant capital controls well into the post-World War II period, in some cases until the end of the 1980s. Controls limited the liquidity of their securities markets. Thus, it is not simply the unusually large size of the US in the world economy or the admirable liquidity of US financial markets but also the maintenance of controls by other potential reserve centres that explains why the dollar was so dominant in reserves for so long after World War II.

There is no reason why in future, two or three reserve currencies could not share the market, not unlike the situation before 1914. The two obvious candidates are the euro and the dollar, although the yen (and maybe the pound sterling) cannot be excluded. The US and euro-zone economies are likely to be of equal size, to engage in similar levels of external trade and financial transactions, and to have comparably liquid securities markets. The advent of the euro has done much to increase the liquidity of European bond markets, which considerably enhances the attractiveness of the euro as a reserve currency. A key question is whether sound macroeconomic policies will be maintained in the United States or whether the dollar's reserve currency status could be impaired by an extended bout of inflation or a very substantial depreciation. Recall that the analysis of Triffin (1960) suggested that currency dominance itself can generate forces that lead to currency decline.

4.2 *Is the euro area capable of managing an international currency?*

There are institutional features of EMU that may be seen as constraints on the development of the euro's international role. The following seem particularly important:

- Ambiguity in the Maastricht Treaty regarding authority over exchange rate policy
- A related potential weakness in euro-area representation in international fora (IMF, G3, G7 ...) and bilateral discussions

- Fragmentation of financial supervision and regulation and unclear lender of last resort (LLR) authority
- ECB monetary policies
- ECB attitudes towards the euro as an international currency

Each has given rise to an extensive literature, but we can treat them only briefly here.

Article 111 of the Maastricht Treaty gives finance ministers (now the 'Eurogroup') power to prescribe 'general orientations' for euro exchange rate policy. Any currency market intervention is conducted by the ECB, however, whose price stability objective takes priority (for a discussion of exchange rate policy, see Alesina *et al.*, 2001). This ambiguity, or indeed conflict, may have inhibited intervention as the euro depreciated from $1.16 to $0.83 in the period January 1999 to September 2000 (one of the authors of this chapter publicly advocated intervention at the time). Intervention did finally come, and although the scale and duration were limited, it did have some effect. The underlying conflict has recently resurfaced as the euro has risen against the dollar (to over $1.55 in March 2008), with some senior politicians calling on the ECB to intervene or relax monetary policy in order to stop or even reverse the appreciation. This makes good headlines in the press, while academics and officials can argue at length about the effectiveness of sterilised intervention. If the divided authority does inhibit intervention, and if intervention could help to stabilise the currency's value, then resolving the ambiguity might indeed enhance the euro's international attractiveness in the various roles we have discussed. But neither premise is fully established. And a member of the ECB Executive Board has argued that the divided authority is indeed 'efficient', because both the central bank and finance ministries should be involved in policy formulation (Bini-Smaghi, 2007).

On the broader question of euro-area international representation, it is hard to deny that there are structural weaknesses. As long as euro-area countries cannot even agree to take a single seat (and quota) in the IMF Executive Board, they cannot exert their due influence over international financial affairs. This does limit their ability to exploit the advantages of the growing international role of the euro, but it does not clearly constrain that role.[33]

Financial supervision and regulation are indeed national responsibilities in EMU, although there are EU-level committees composed of the national regulators (for banks, securities markets and insurance). Many observers have argued that the growing cross-border activities of banks and cross-border integration of financial markets require more unified supervision and regulation. Posen (2007a, 2007b) and Cohen (2008) see the fragmentation as a major obstacle to the euro's development as an international currency.

There are clear dangers in the current structure (for an early critique, see Begg *et al.*, 1998). Committees without executive authority are not well suited to discover or deal with solvency or even liquidity problems arising for a large complex financial institution (LCFI) present throughout the euro area. Yet there is an ECB responsibility for financial stability, and in particular for the payments system. And the unfavourable comparison with the USA has less weight in view of recent events, which have exposed deep weaknesses in American financial supervision and regulation.[34] Indeed, there too we find fragmentation and lack of coordination, starting with the division of authority among the Federal Reserve, Office of the Currency Controller, Securities and Exchange Commission, Office of Thrift Supervision, Federal Deposit Insurance Corporation and fifty state-level insurance regulators. It is likely that we shall see some rationalisation, unification and strengthening of financial supervision and regulation on both sides of the Atlantic.[35]

Equally problematic and potentially serious is the ill-defined locus of lender of last resort responsibility for eurozone financial institutions. The ECB is clearly the sole guarantor of financial market liquidity, and it appears to have exercised that authority rather better than either the US Federal Reserve or the Bank of England since 7 August 2007.[36] But if an LCFI were in difficulty, who would decide whether and how to provide assistance, and whose taxpayers would be liable if illiquidity turned into insolvency? EU ministers and the ECB have resolutely opposed any *ex ante* rules for 'burden sharing', on the (indefensible) ground that they would create moral hazard. On this count, the US structures are clearly superior. Again, however, financial turmoil may motivate some improvement.

Criticism of the ECB's monetary policies has stressed its supposedly restrictive bias or alternatively its inability to meet its inflation target (for the latter, see Galí *et al.*, 2004); its slow responses to changing data, which some regard however as desirable stability; the muddle of its 'two-pillar strategy'; its governance (too many Council members, supposedly acting by consensus); and its lack of transparency (Geraats *et al.*, 2008 and Geraats, this volume), which makes it hard to assess whether any of these criticisms is justified. On the whole, however, the actual policies followed by the ECB seem to have been fairly successful, and the comparison with US monetary policy since 1999 does not seem unfavourable to the ECB.

Despite the lack of transparency, there are evidently strong voices within the ECB seeking to limit the euro's international role. There are counterweights too, and the result is the oft-repeated mantra, 'The Eurosystem neither promotes nor hinders the development of the euro as an international currency.' But the ECB has never published an analysis of the costs and benefits of internationalisation of the euro, so one cannot know whether its 'neutrality' reflects an explicit judgement that there is no clear positive or negative balance.

5. Conclusions

Although we still have insufficient data to quantify precisely the implications of the euro's introduction in international markets and the global economy, the evidence suggests a steady rise in the euro's status as an international currency. Early fears that the euro might destabilise the European economy and cause political disintegration (e.g. Feldstein, 1997a, 1999), seem unwarranted today. Subsequent scenarios in which a crisis-stricken eurozone country gives up the euro[37] are equally unjustified, if only because the economic and political costs of doing so are likely to exceed by far any possible benefits (Eichengreen, 2007 and this volume). The euro has not so far achieved the dollar's status as an international currency, although its international role has notably increased since 1999. The euro's first decade has been marked by incremental, yet noticeable, steps towards becoming an equal to the dollar as an international currency.

Some fairly clear conclusions emerge from the discussion above.

- Even ignoring the geopolitical implications, international currency status is important. It affects exchange rates and the distribution of the benefits and costs associated with the international currency or currencies.
- 'Global imbalances' threaten the dollar's status as the major international currency – the 'exorbitant privilege' now appears in foreign central banks financing the US current account deficit (net private capital inflows into the US have been negative).

- An international currency performs multiple roles, and these are interconnected – in particular, the reserve currency role, though most studied, is closely related to choice of vehicle currency, investment currency and invoicing.
- Perhaps the most underrated determinant and measure of international currency status, however, is the 'anchor currency' (peg) function.
- The dollar is still the dominant reserve currency, but the share of the euro in central bank reserves appears to be significantly higher than that which mean-variance portfolio optimisation would yield.
- The data indicate a narrowing of spreads and enhanced liquidity of the euro, a rising share of the euro area in trade, an increasing number of non-EU governments and firms issuing euro-denominated assets, some shift away from the dollar towards the euro in the anchor currency role, and little change in their relative importance in the foreign exchange markets.
- The euro has displaced the dollar as the reserve currency of (non-euro-area) Europe, including non-EU countries, as well as some countries in the geographical hinterland of Europe.
- The data also suggest increasing private-sector substitution of the euro for the dollar in various functions, as the level of financial development of the euro area has risen and transaction costs in euro-denominated markets have fallen.

Looking forward is difficult. The dollar has the advantage of incumbency, but diversification motives favour the euro as an asset currency. A sufficiently strong shock could move the international financial system to a new equilibrium. This would likely be parity between the euro and the dollar (a version of the 'middle euro' scenario of Portes and Rey, 1998). Plausible shocks could be a shift to the euro in invoicing of oil and perhaps other commodities; a massive portfolio shift into euro-denominated assets; a substantial rise in US inflation; a major loss of confidence in the US economy and financial system.

Chinn and Frankel (2008) run simulations in which the euro's share of international reserves exceeds that of the dollar by 2015, without any such shocks. The shift is due primarily to an assumed continuing dollar depreciation and the rising financial depth of the euro area, because of London's growth as a financial centre and its key role in euro-area finance.[38] As we have stressed, however, reserve currency status is only one dimension of the international role of a currency.

At the time of writing, the euro appears to have an overall advantage on the criteria of financial stability (inflation, exchange rate). Its institutional framework now seems less inferior to the US financial sector and regulatory system than was previously thought. The US current account deficit makes the dollar vulnerable.

Another important factor may be the progressive elimination of the existing asymmetry between global trade and global finance. The BRICs and other emerging markets are global in trade but not in finance. They will catch up. They are perhaps just as likely to go for euro-denominated as for dollar-denominated financial instruments.[39] But all this is conjectural.

The major disadvantage of the euro is clear: it is the currency of a group of nation states rather than of a single country. The euro area is much less a unitary actor than the USA. That must have some negative effect – that we believe unjustified – on confidence in the euro's stability over the very long term, as it does on the euro area's weight in international monetary affairs – that we believe is fully justified. But these effects must be balanced against the growing strains on the dollar and indeed on American geopolitical and economic dominance.

Notes

1. See for example the recent Bloomberg report, 'Dollar Slumps to Record Low on China's Plans to Diversify Reserves', 7 November 2007 (Agnes Lovasz and Stanley White). See also the *Economist*, 9 November 2007.
2. See for example David Hale in the *Financial Times* 23 November 2007: 'The great irony is that Washington's effort to slow the rise of China threatens to undermine one of the foundations of US economic power – the dollar's reserve currency status.' The dollar is also seen as a major element in American 'soft power' (the term is from Joseph Nye 1990, 2004).
3. Both the euro area and the United Kingdom also have negative net international investment positions (NIIP), but of a much smaller magnitude than that of the United States.

4. Reserve accumulation in East Asia is linked to sovereign risk concerns, which increase in periods of huge financial flow volatility (Aizenman and Marion, 2003; Aizenman and Lee, 2007). In addition, theory suggests that developing countries accumulate reserves due to their inability to collect taxes and because they are unwilling to reduce (mainly short-term) foreign borrowing.

5. An additional factor, but of lesser importance, is the decision of many industrial countries (e.g. the Netherlands, the United Kingdom, Switzerland) to substitute interest-bearing assets for reserves held in gold. Furthermore, there might be some country-specific reasons for reserve accumulation. For example, it is argued that the Chinese government is accumulating foreign capital as a hedge to its fragile government controlled banking system (the Chinese central bank injected $60 billion of its reserves to recapitalise state-owned banks).

6. Swoboda (1968); see also Tavlas (1991), Cohen (1971), Frankel (1995).

7. This explicit recognition a century ago of the private benefits of running an international currency is well documented by Broz (1999).

8. See Faust (1996) and the application to EMU in Dornbusch *et al.* (1998).

9. Bobba *et al.* (2007) interpret their results in this way. Note that they find a significant euro anchor currency effect on securities issuance only for developing countries – this may be related to the observation that developing country reserves have shifted towards euro more rapidly than those of developed countries.

10. IMF (2007b), Table B1.

11. See Detken and Hartmann (2000, 2002), Hau *et al.* (2002a, 2002b), and Papaioannou *et al.* (2006) for details on the evolution of bid-ask spreads in forex markets following the introduction of the euro. After a brief period of contradictory movements in the euro markets, these spreads have fallen dramatically over the past six years.

12. Eichengreen (2005) and Roubini (2007) argue that Bretton Woods II is unstable and will break up sooner rather than later. In contrast, Rose (2006) argues that the Bretton Woods II system is inherently more stable than the original Bretton Woods system.

13. Norway and Singapore were among the first countries to set up sovereign wealth funds over a decade ago. Several countries have since followed this example, setting up investment companies separate from the central bank to manage part of their reserve holdings actively. South Korea, for example, established in 2005 the Korean Investment Corporation (KIC) with an initial capital of $20 billion (mainly transferred from the central bank) having a clear mandate to increase returns. See Portes (2007) on sovereign wealth funds.

14. The share of the dollar in the eighties and the early nineties was around 50 per cent (down from 70 per cent in the early seventies).

15. Truman and Wong (2006) gather data from countries that release information on the currency composition of their reserves, and they document a gradual shift towards the euro in the period 2000–4, mainly at the expense of the dollar and the yen.

16. See Lim (2006) for an overview.

17. In Table 10.2 we report the composition of foreign exchange reserves from selected countries that disclose this information.

18. Bobba *et al.* (2007) also show high inertia in international debt issuance. They document autoregressive coefficients in the range of 0.75–0.85.

19. For details on the profitability of 'carry trades', see Burnside *et al.* (2007), and Burnside, *et al.* (2006), as well as Ferguson *et al.* (2007).

20. In ongoing work (Papaioannou *et al.*, 2008) we explore currency diversification, disaggregating across various assets within each country (currency).

21. The importance of the anchor currency in explaining the composition of foreign exchange reserves has also been shown by studies that use confidential IMF data (e.g. Eichengreen and Mathieson, 2000).

22. A critical assumption of these models is that actions are taken by small firms/individuals, who are price takers. Yet in many commodities, like oil, a small number of countries control most of global supply. There might be big changes if a large player decides to switch to an alternative currency.

23. The fall in transaction costs for non-eurozone investors is estimated at 17 per cent for equities and 14 per cent for bonds (it is roughly twice as large for cross-country investments within the eurozone). Coeurdacier and Martin point out that the impact on cross-border holdings is much greater for bonds than for equities, because bonds are much closer substitutes.

24. In the judgement of Bertuch-Samuels and Ramlogan (2007), 'The euro has experienced phenomenal growth as a currency of issue for international bonds and notes.'

25. McGuire and Tarashev (2007).

26. The authors have aggregated all the data on the currencies of the pre-euro period that came to form the euro and aggregated the economic data on the countries, so that the eurozone is considered as one country.

27. The recent decline of the dollar is putting pressure on oil-producing countries to index oil in alternative currencies. According to the *Financial Times* (19 November 2007), some OPEC member countries are considering quoting oil in other currencies.

28. The material in this section is adapted from Portes and Baldursson (2007), which discusses the internationalisation of Iceland's financial sector in detail.

29. Some East European EU member states, as well as some Balkan countries that are not EU members, exhibit a similar pattern, although none of these is anywhere near Iceland's level of economic and financial development.

30. This is similar to the position of many East Asian economies in the 1990s, when most of household and banking sector liabilities were denominated in dollars, while their assets and income were in domestic currency. Such a mismatch might lead to a currency banking crisis (if positions are not hedged), since currency movements can trigger margin calls and massive capital outflows (see Caballero and Krishnamurthy, 2004, 2006, for formal models).

31. The extensive literature on this issue normally speaks of 'dollarisation', but in the Icelandic context it would clearly mean a move to the euro rather than the dollar. The weight of the euro in the 2006 'narrow' trade-weighted effective exchange rate basket was 44.8 per cent, with the pound sterling at 12.8 per cent and the US dollar at 9.8 per cent (www.sedlabanki.is/lisalib/getfile.aspx?itemid=4863). A recent, comprehensive paper on dollarisation is Levy-Yeyati (2006).

32. See Stark (2008a) for a recent statement of the ECB's postion. Portes (2002) argues that this position is inappropriate for some countries already in the EU, such as Estonia (which has had since 1992 a currency board peg to the Deutschmark, then to the euro). Moreover, he maintains, it is only once a country enters the EU that its exchange rate policies become legally a matter of common concern – but not before. And *using* the euro in no way prejudices or impinges on the accession process or the subsequent process of entering into monetary union. It cannot run counter to any legal provision of the Treaties. *Using* the euro is *not* equivalent to participating in EMU, nor 'unfairly' getting a 'head start', nor does it implicate the ECB in any significant way, except insofar as the euroising country is providing seigniorage to the ECB. Unilateral euroisation cannot affect the credibility of the euro, since the euroising country cannot participate in the economic institutions of EMU.

33. 'As long as no "single voice" has the political authority to speak on behalf of the euro area … the pre-eminence of the US in international monetary matters … is likely to remain unchallenged.' (McNamara and Meunier, 2002, p. 850).

34. Cf. Cohen (2008): 'The euro area is remarkably unprepared to cope with any major disruption in banking or financial markets.' No worse prepared than the USA, it would seem.

35. For example: 'In Congress, Democrats are drafting bills that would create a powerful new regulator – or simply confer new powers on the Federal Reserve – to oversee practices across the entire array of commercial

banks, Wall Street firms, hedge funds and nonbank financial companies. The Treasury Department is rushing to complete its own blueprint for overhauling what is now an alphabet soup of federal and state regulators that often compete against each other and protect their particular slices of the industry as if they were constituents.' *Wall Street Journal*, 23 March 2008.

36. Another comment which could not be published today: 'The US Federal Reserve has proved itself able to calm financial markets ... even in the face of dramatic financial market turbulence ... It is less clear what role the European Central Bank would play ...' Dominguez (2006, p. 86). That is clearer now.

37. These stories typically come from UK and US authors, it has to be said – see Tilford (2006) and Dominguez (2006). The latter says, 'Leaders of a number of eurozone countries including Germany, France and Italy have ... hinted that an exit strategy might be needed under certain economic conditions ... [this] leaves ... a nagging sense of doubt about the longevity of euroland' (p. 86). No specific 'leaders' are named.

38. The UK is on all measures the most important international banking centre (von Peter, 2007).

39. Some have suggested that the Chinese yuan could become a third major international currency. But it will take several decades to remedy the underdevelopment of the Chinese financial sector.

Comment 6: Comment on Chapter 10

ANDRÉ SAPIR

Since the launch of Economic and Monetary Union (EMU) in the early 1990s, Richard Portes, together with several co-authors, has consistently argued that the euro will become a major international currency, possibly on par with, or even surpassing, the dollar. With few exceptions, most economists generally regarded this view as extreme, considering instead that the euro is bound to remain an international currency far less important than the dollar.

The early weakness of the euro vis-à-vis the dollar, after it was launched in 1999, seemed for a while to confirm the view that the 'dollar is king' and will remain so. However, the subsequent reversal of the euro, and especially its sharp appreciation against the dollar in 2007 and 2008, has unleashed a wave of 'dollar pessimism' that sees the euro rapidly gaining the upper hand. Perhaps the most striking reversal comes from Jeffrey Frankel who had argued early on that the euro would pose no threat to the dominance of the dollar (Frankel, 1995). By 2005, he and Menzie Chinn were arguing that the euro may 'eventually surpass the dollar as leading international reserve currency' (Chinn and Frankel, 2005). By February 2008, their prediction had become that 'the euro may *over the next 15 years* surpass the dollar as leading international currency' (Chinn and Frankel, 2008, emphasis added). And by March 2008, Frankel was even claiming that 'the euro could surpass the dollar *within ten years*' (Frankel, 2008, emphasis added).

The contribution by Papaionnou and Portes (PP) is a welcome addition to the debate. Their paper does two things. First, it presents a balanced and up-to-date review of the arguments for and against the emergence of the euro as a leading international currency. Second, it offers a well-documented and lucid account of where the euro actually stands in the international arena after ten years of existence.

The facts are fairly straightforward. The international standing of the euro has steadily increased since 1999. The euro now accounts for roughly 25 per cent of worldwide official reserve holdings (compared

408

to less than 20 per cent in 1999), 45 per cent of outstanding international debt securities (compared to around 30 per cent in 1999), and 20 per cent of foreign exchange transactions. These are impressive figures given that the euro has been in existence for only ten years. The euro is now ahead of the dollar for outstanding international debt securities (the share of the dollar has fallen to 40 per cent), but remains far behind for official reserves (the share of the dollar is still 65 per cent) and for forex transactions (where the dollar still has a share of 45 per cent). In other areas, such as the pricing of commodities or the invoicing of international trade, the euro continues to trail far behind the dollar.

Do its first ten years of existence point to the euro equalling or even overcoming the dollar within the next ten years as the leading international currency?

The answer given by PP is a cautious 'perhaps yes'. Mine is a less cautious 'no'.

There are essentially two types of factors that shape the relative positions of the euro and the dollar as international currencies: economic and political ones.

The economic determinants of currency internationalisation include economic and financial size of the issuing countries, and history. Size favours an increasing role of the euro. After all the euro area is already three-quarters the economic size of the United States and would become as large as the USA if the rest of the European Union adopted the euro. At the same time, rapid financial integration among the EU countries and the growth of London as a financial centre – key in euro-area finance even if it remains outside the euro area – suggest that Europe is closing in on US financial supremacy.

History works both for and against the dollar. As PP rightly point out, the dollar has the advantage of incumbency, but diversification motives favour the euro as an asset currency. This is consistent with the finding that the international role of the dollar remains very strong as medium of exchange (vehicle currency for foreign exchange intervention and invoicing currency for trade in goods and assets) and as unit of account (anchor for currency peg and quotation currency for trade in goods and assets), but that the euro is progressing rapidly as store of value, although much more for private agents (as an investment currency) than for public ones (as currency for international reserves).

This suggests, therefore, perhaps an international division between the euro and the dollar. The dollar might retain its supremacy in functions that involve substantial network externalities, due to its incumbent status, whereas the euro might become as important as the dollar when diversification matters. Such a scenario that would see the euro and the dollar play different roles for different functions of an international currency – store of value, medium of exchange and unit of account – is more realistic in my eyes than a scenario involving the euro and the dollar sharing equal weight – let alone the euro replacing the dollar altogether – for all the three functions.

My main reason for being sceptical about predictions that the euro will be one day on par with, or even surpass, the dollar is simple: the euro is 'a currency without a state', as Tommaso Padoa-Schioppa was first to point out. As I argued elsewhere (see Sapir, 2006), ultimately it is finance ministries and treasuries, not central banks, that decide the place of an international currency in the international monetary system. Just remember the roles played by Harry Dexter White, the Deputy Secretary of the US Treasury, and John Maynard Keynes, the envoy of the British Treasury, during the Bretton Woods negotiations. By contrast, history has forgotten the names of the Fed President or the Bank of England Governor, or of their envoys, at Bretton Woods. In Europe today, the opposite situation prevails. Everyone knows the name of Jean-Claude Trichet, the President of the European Central Bank (ECB), but few know the name, or even the function, of the Eurogroup President, Jean-Claude Juncker, who is well known, however, as Prime Minister of Luxembourg.

There is no prospect that the euro area will become one day an entity like a state with a single treasury. However, this may not actually be necessary for the euro to take on a leading international role. What would be essential, though, would be to set up a delegation system where euro-area member states entrust a common institution with their external representation and give it negotiating authority. Two models of delegation typically prevail in the EU: an unconditional model in which the member states fully and unconditionally delegate responsibility, and a supervised delegation model in which the member states retain control rights. Either model would do, so far as the external side of the euro is concerned, but the latter is more realistic (or, at least, more conceivable) in a domain that lies at the core of national economic sovereignties.

Precisely because of sensitivities about sovereignty, member states are unlikely to want to delegate responsibility to the Commission, even partially by retaining control rights. A more realistic option would be to entrust external representation and negotiation authority to the Eurogroup, the currently informal group of euro-area Finance Ministers. Under the new Lisbon Treaty, the Eurogroup is set to become a formal body. 'In order to enhance the euro's place in the international monetary system', euro-area countries will be able to decide – voting among themselves – on financial relations with the outside world. More specifically, they will be allowed to vote to decide 'common positions on matters of particular interest for economic and monetary union within the competent international financial institutions and conferences'. Euro-area countries will also be able to vote on 'measures to ensure unified representation within the international financial institutions', e.g. a single seat at organisations like the Bretton Woods institutions.

The Lisbon Treaty, therefore, provides an embryo that might allow the Eurogroup and its President not only to effectively represent the euro area on the international scene but also to gradually negotiate on its behalf. If ratified, the new treaty would probably pave the way towards a single voice at the IMF and in the G-7.

Another option for the external representation of the euro would be to follow the model of the High Representative of the Union for Foreign Affairs and Security Policy envisaged by the new Lisbon Treaty (see Sapir, 2007). The High Representative will wear two hats: he/she will be appointed by the European Council, with the agreement of the President of the European Commission, and will be one of the Vice-Presidents of the Commission. A similar template could be used for economic and monetary affairs, with the President of the Eurogroup being jointly appointed by the members of the European Council belonging to the euro area and the President of the European Commission. Like the High Representative for Foreign Affairs, the President of the Euro Group and High Representative for Economic and Financial Affairs would there-fore be a member of both the Council and the Commission, which would greatly facilitate the external representation of the euro.

PP recognise that because the euro area is much less a unitary actor than the USA, its weight in international monetary affairs is much less than its economic and financial size would otherwise suggest. Yet, they remain bullish on the international role of the euro because ultimately they attribute more weight to the current economic weakness of the dollar than to the structural political weakness of the euro area. On the contrary, I tend to think that the status of the euro as an international currency cannot grow much further in the absence of progress on the political front. Perhaps after a first decade full of economic and financial success the euro will witness a second decade equally successful on the political front. If so, I would concur with PP that we might observe parity between the euro and the dollar as international currencies if the US economy and financial system suffer heavy losses.

PART V

Fiscal policy

11 | *EMU's decentralized system of fiscal policy*

JÜRGEN VON HAGEN AND CHARLES WYPLOSZ

1. Introduction

Ten years after the adoption of the single currency, the status of national fiscal policies remains an unresolved and controversial issue. On the one hand, fiscal policy is not a shared competence. On the other hand, the excessive deficit procedure (EDP) rests on the principle that national budget outcomes are an area of common interest. As implemented by the Stability and Growth Pact (SGP), it envisages situations where a national government is requested to make explicit quantitative commitments, which can be specified by the Council, following recommendations from the Commission. More broadly, within the stability programs, each euro-area country must present each year its intended budget balance to be reached over the following three years, with the explicit aim of achieving budgets close to balance or in surplus. These programs must gain Council approval when they are presented and cannot be subsequently changed unless specific conditions are deemed acceptable. A country found in violation of its commitments, with a deficit ratio in excess of 3 per cent of GDP, is bound to face increasingly tight requests, with the possibility of being imposed a fine.

Thus, national fiscal policies belong to a grey zone of potentially constrained sovereignty. Governments remain fully sovereign in setting the level and detailed composition of their spending and revenues[1] and they can run smaller deficits or larger surpluses than they committed themselves to. The SGP only deals with the balance and is geared towards limiting deficits, both absolutely by setting a maximum deficit of 3 per cent of GDP and by aiming at budgets close to balance or in surplus, and relatively by banning larger deficits or smaller surpluses than those initially approved.

Paper presented at the Commision workshop on EMU@10: Achievements and Challenges, held in Brussels on 26–7 November 2007. We are grateful to Lucio Pench, Martin Larch, our discussants, and the conference participants for very useful comments.

This grey zone aspect raises important constitutional issues, as was amply illustrated by the November 2003 Council decision to put the EDP procedures against Germany and France "in abeyance" and by the subsequent deliberation of the European Court of Justice. The new SGP, adopted in June 2005, has not addressed this particular issue, which, consequently, remains open. The revision instead introduced some implementation flexibility, with the aim of preventing economically inefficient consequences.[2]

This paper starts with the macroeconomics of fiscal policy to evaluate various institutional arrangements. It argues that limits to budget balance sovereignty need to be carefully justified. The usual argument in favor of the EDP and the SGP is that fiscal indiscipline by one or more euro-area members constitutes a negative externality that threatens price stability. The basis of this argument can be found in the theory of fiscal dominance, which is reviewed in Section 2. Whether this argument is strong enough to justify the EDP remains an unresolved issue. At any rate, even if it is justified, there remains the need to examine how it can be implemented without excessive economic costs.

In section 3, we evaluate the empirical performance of national fiscal policies under EMU so far. We are particularly interested in whether and how much monetary union has constrained the national governments' ability to conduct countercyclical policies. The more this is the case, the stronger would be the argument that, to be sustainable, restraints to the countercyclical use of national fiscal policy must be compensated for by an adequate collective insurance system. This idea has a long legacy. The desirability of a collective insurance system in a European Monetary Union was mentioned early on in the MacDougall Report (European Commission 1977a, 1977b) and the Delors Report (Delors, 1989) and presented as an extension of the Optimum Currency Area theory (see, e.g. Wyplosz, 1991). It has given rise to a significant literature, both theoretical (van Wincoop, 1995; Sørensen and Yosha, 1997; Persson and Tabellini, 1996b; Fatás, 1998; Kletzer and von Hagen, 2001) and empirical (Sala-i-Martin and Sachs, 1992; von Hagen, 1992; Pisani-Ferry *et al.*, 1993; Bayoumi and Masson, 1995; Hammond and von Hagen, 1998; Mélitz and Zumer, 1999).

In section 4, we review the theory behind this discussion and develop some pertinent considerations of political economy. On this basis, we examine, in section 4.3, a number of proposals that have surfaced in the

European discussion. Section 5 considers the institutional requirements of a fiscal insurance system in EMU. Section 6 concludes.

2. The fiscal dominance case for the SGP

There are a number of justifications for the SGP. Two of them are unconvincing. It is argued that one country's deficit stands to raise the euro-area interest rate and thus impose a cost externality on all other countries. This view seems rooted in an IS-LM view of the world. Even then, since Europe is financially integrated in world markets, its interest rate is essentially exogenous, especially as each member country is "small." A more elaborate version allows for interest rate parity and argues that a deficit raises the interest rate through expected depreciation. The theory behind this assertion is at best weak and, importantly, there is no evidence linking budget balances to the exchange and interest rates. The only evidence is that investors discriminate among borrowers, which means that there is no externality.[3]

Another argument in favor of the SGP is that it is a form of coordination among national fiscal authorities. Here again, the need for coordination must rest on some substantial externality that is demonstrated. Moreover, even if such an externality were to exist, it would remain to establish that the SGP-induced coordination is optimal. There is no theoretical or empirical evidence that this is the case.[4]

The fundamental argument in favor of the SGP is that fiscal indiscipline can become the source of inflation. It is based on solid empirical evidence. Indeed, it is well known since (at least) the hyperinflation episodes of the 1920s that fiscal indiscipline can lead to inflation. The theoretical interpretation has been elaborated by Sargent and Wallace (1981), Canzoneri *et al.* (2001) and Woodford (2001) among others. It can be briefly summarized with the government budget constraint:

$$B_{t+1} - B_t = i_t B_t - (1 + i_t)[S_t + (M_{t+1} - M_t)], \tag{1}$$

where S_t is the primary budget surplus in period t, i_t the interest rate and B_t and M_t are the beginning of period stocks of public debt and base money, all expressed in nominal terms. Dividing by the nominal GDP $P_t Y_t$ and denoting the total public sector debt as $D_t = B_t + M_t$, (1) can be rewritten as:

$$\frac{D_t}{P_t Y_t} = \left(\frac{S_t}{P_t Y_t} + \frac{i_t}{1 + i_t} \frac{M_{t+1}}{P_t Y_t} \right) + \rho_t \frac{D_{t+1}}{P_{t+1} Y_{t+1}} \tag{2}$$

where $\rho_t = \left(\dfrac{1 + i_t}{\frac{P_{t+1}}{P_t}\frac{Y_{t+1}}{Y_t}}\right)^{-1}$ is the growth-adjusted real interest rate factor.

Public sector solvency requires that the transversality condition $\lim_{T \to \infty} \left(\prod_{s=t}^{T-1} \rho_s\right) \dfrac{D_T}{P_T Y_T} = 0$ be satisfied. When this is the case, iterating (2) forward, we get:

$$\frac{D_t}{P_t Y_t} = \sum_{i=0}^{\infty} \left(\prod_t^{t+i-1} \rho_k\right) s_{t+i} \tag{3}$$

where $s_t = \left(\dfrac{S_t}{P_t Y_t} + \dfrac{i_t}{1 + i_t}\dfrac{M_{t+1}}{P_t Y_t}\right)$ is the budget surplus inclusive of seigniorage as a ratio to GDP.

The solvency condition can be satisfied in many ways. First, budget discipline may ensure that future budget surpluses S_{t+i} are such that they match the actual public sector debt. Second, fiscal discipline can be weak and recourse to seigniorage is needed to deliver the needed sequence of $\{s_{t+i}\}$. This is the channel through which, historically, fiscal indiscipline has repeatedly delivered inflationary episodes. This is why the Maastricht Treaty explicitly rules out any financing of budgets through seigniorage, both on a routine basis and in an emergency situation, the latter case being dealt with through the no-bailout clause. This is also why the independence of the ECB is guaranteed by the treaty.

The third case is the relevant one. If the sequence of $\{s_{t+i}\}$ violates the solvency condition, it is the price level P_t on the left-hand side of (3) that becomes the variable of adjustment. This is the case of fiscal dominance where the budgetary authorities can impose their will and carry out unsustainable budget deficits. Monetary dominance is the opposite case, when neither seigniorage nor the price level are made to be endogenous in (3) so that the variable of adjustment is the disciplined sequence of $\{s_{t+i}\}$. The task of the SGP can be seen as imposing monetary dominance so that control of the price level is not lost and without having to call upon seigniorage as mandated by the treaty.

3. What do national governments do with their fiscal policies?

3.1 Policy effects

Unsurprisingly, the question of the usefulness of fiscal policy as a macroeconomic tool is highly controversial. At the theoretical level, the debate pits (neo)Classical against (neo)Keynesian macroeconomists. The former asserts that, one way or another, consumers and firms view public debts as their own liability; accordingly, they reduce their expenditures whenever the debt increases or diminishes less than previously expected. The latter relies on price stickiness, borrowing constraints and/or other market imperfections to find that fiscal policy can affect output.[5] In view of such conflicting theoretical results, the verdict should come from empirical studies.

Empirically, too, the issue is controversial. Some authors find that fiscal policy affects output, even though the multipliers are small and have possibly declined in recent years (Blanchard and Perotti, 2002; Perotti, 2005, 2007; Favero and Giavazzi, 2007; Romer and Romer, 2007). Others find that consumption moves in an offsetting direction, although the offset effect is partial, which leaves a small output effect (Ramey, 2006).

Why do different authors reach different results? All the above papers use VAR estimates to pinpoint the relationship between output and fiscal policy. All of them also use the cyclically adjusted balance as a measure of the fiscal policy stance.[6] They differ in the way they identify the VARs. Those who find a positive effect of fiscal shocks on consumption, and therefore output, typically use quarterly variables and make the assumption that there is no contemporaneous effect from cyclical conditions to discretionary policy actions. Working with US data, Edelberg *et al.* (1999) and Burnside *et al.* (2004), Ramey (2006) and Romer and Romer (2007) adopt the event study approach and identify discretionary actions by studying contemporaneous press reports, focusing on war-related military spending or on tax changes not related to cyclical conditions.

The first approach suffers from two main limitations: first, the use of quarterly data sits uncomfortably with the typical annual frequency of budgetary exercises; second, discrete fiscal policy actions are usually prepared over a significant period of time, which opens up the possibility that output responds to expectations of fiscal shocks, not just to the shocks themselves. The second approach suffers from some arbitrariness in identifying the relevant policy episodes, which are large by nature, possibly overlooking other, smaller episodes, which may have different effects.

These controversies are unlikely to be resolved in the near future. We note that there is no empirical evidence in favor of the assumption that fiscal policy has no effect. The debate is about the consumption impact of fiscal policies and on the size of the overall output effect, which is mostly found to be in the Keynesian direction.[7] Skeptics may argue that fiscal policy is not very powerful, but they do not claim that it is wholly impotent.

3.2 Policy motivation: the euro effect

That fiscal policy can be used as a macroeconomic policy tool does not mean that governments do so in an appropriate way. A long tradition has identified a number of lags – recognition, decision, implementation – which could result in badly timed effects. An equally long tradition has pointed out that governments may be more motivated by political gains rather than by economic management concerns. If fiscal policy actions are not driven by a macroeconomic stabilization motive, it may not be systematically countercyclical.

The question, then, is whether euro-area membership affects policy makers' incentives and, if so, how. A first place to look at is the SGP. On one hand, it can help governments to resist pressure from interest groups and therefore improve the quality of fiscal policy. On the other hand, it reduces the room for maneuver and leads to procyclical policies.

Another consideration is the fact that the exchange rate is no longer available to boost external competitiveness, with two opposite potential effects on the conduct of fiscal policy. First, governments may be tempted to use fiscal policy instead of monetary policy to counteract a temporary competitiveness loss when a euro appreciation reduces domestic demand. A different case concerns a loss of external competitiveness due to domestic inflation or to a relative productivity decline. In a monetary union, external competitiveness can only be restored the hard way, through sustained cost and price moderation or enhanced productivity gains. Fiscal policy is no longer a substitute to monetary policy.[8] Its only possible macroeconomic contribution is to encourage cost and price moderation, possibly by restricting demand in goods and labor markets. This would make fiscal policy countercyclical during upswings and acyclical during downswings as long as the exchange rate is overvalued. A case in point is Germany over 2000–6.

All in all, the impact of the adoption of the euro on the macroeconomic use of fiscal policy is ambiguous. We expect more countercyclical action as fiscal policy substitutes for the lost monetary policy instrument, less use of this instrument in downswings as a result of the SGP, especially in countries where the budget deficit is not far enough from its 3 per cent ceiling, and an asymmetric use for countries with an external competitiveness shortfall.

3.3 The evidence

Some of these presumptions have been tested. Looking at euro-area countries, Galí and Perotti (2003), Fatás and Mihov (2001b, 2003), and Wyplosz (2005) have found that in most cases fiscal policy has been acyclical, sometimes even procyclical. They also report that the constraints imposed by the monetary union, the convergence criteria of the "Maastricht years" 1992–8 and the SGP since 1999, have led to somewhat less policy activism and, as a consequence, to less procyclical policies. Fatás and Mihov (2001b, 2003) further document that the SGP constraints seem to have mitigated the various influences that are believed to distort the use of the fiscal policy instrument.

These estimates are based on the early experience of monetary union. We revisit them with data that extend to 2006 (see the appendix on data sources). We adopt the formulation proposed by Galí and Perotti (2003):

$$d_t = c + \beta^b E_{t-1} y_t + \beta^a E_{t-1} y_t + \gamma b_{t-1} + \rho d_{t-1} + u_t \tag{4}$$

where d_t is the annual budget deficit, $E_{t-1} y_t$ is the expected output gap and b_t is the public debt (d_t and b_t are expressed as per cent of GDP). The coefficients β^b and β^a correspond to the period before and after 1992 onward; the break is introduced to test whether the restrictions adopted in the Maastricht treaty have affected the cyclical use of fiscal policy. An alternative is to break the sample in 1999, or even to consider three subperiods, separating out the Maastricht from the monetary union years, but the data support the break as indicated. The expected output gap is estimated as in Galí and Perotti (2003) by replacing $E_{t-1} y_t$ with y_t and instrumenting it with the US and Japanese output gaps and the lagged output gap y_{t-1}. A countercyclical use of fiscal policy implies that $\beta^b < 0$ and $\beta^a < 0$. The assumption that the adoption of the common currency has fostered a substitution of fiscal for monetary policy as the macroeconomic stabilization tool implies that $\beta^b > \beta^a$.

We also use this framework to test the other hypotheses presented above. To test whether the SGP has an asymmetric effect over the cycle, limiting the countercyclical use of fiscal policy in downswings, we replace $\beta^a E_{t-1} y_t$ with $\beta^a E_{t-1} y_t + \beta^{a-} E_{t-1} y_t^-$ where y_t^- is the output gap when it is negative and zero when it is positive. The hypothesis implies that $\beta^{a-} < 0$.

We have also noted that fiscal policy could be used as a substitute for lost monetary policy when dealing with external competitiveness. One hypothesis is that, independently of the cyclical position already captured with $E_{t-1} y_t$, fiscal policy is expansionary when external competitiveness is declining. Another hypothesis is that fiscal policy is instead used to reduce costs and regain competitiveness by being restrictive. We can test which hypothesis is borne out by adding:

$$\theta^b X + \theta^a X$$

where X is a measure of external competitiveness and θ^b and θ^a correspond to before and after 1992. When fiscal policy is used to compress costs when competitiveness is low, we expect to find $\theta^i > 0$. If instead fiscal policy is used to offset the demand effects of poor competitiveness, we should have $\theta^i < 0$. If the Maastricht Treaty and the creation of the euro area have reinforced the use of fiscal policy as a countercyclical tool, we should find $\theta^a > \theta^b \geq 0$. If instead fiscal policy was initially used as a demand management tool before the Maastricht Treaty and then was put in charge of restoring competitiveness because exchange rate realignments are no longer possible, we expect to find $\theta^b < 0$ and $\theta^a > 0$.

Another hypothesis, mentioned above, is that the use of fiscal policy in the face of a deterioration of competitiveness depends on the cyclical position of the economy. For instance, it could be pro-cyclical during upswings and acyclical or countercyclical during downswings. This hypothesis can be tested by adding the following terms:

$$\lambda^{b+} E_{t-1} y_t^+ + \lambda^{b-} E_{t-1} y_t^- + \lambda^{a+} E_{t-1} y_t^+ + \lambda^{a-} E_{t-1} y_t^-$$

where λ^{b+} and λ^{b-} refer to periods before 1992 when external competitiveness is weak and when, respectively, the output gap is positive and negative, with a similar definition for λ^{a+} and λ^{a-}, the coefficients corresponding to the post-1992 period. Since, in our empirical estimations reported below, these terms never turned out to be significant, we do not pursue this argument further.

In the end, therefore, we estimate:

$$d_t = c + \beta^b E_{t-1} y_t + \beta^a E_{t-1} y_t + \beta^{a-} E_{t-1} y_t^- + \theta^b X_t + \theta^a X_t + \gamma b_{t-1} + \rho d_{t-1} + u_t$$

$$(5)$$

To measure competitiveness, we use the real exchange rate, defined as relative unit labor costs, constructed such that an increase represents a fall in external competitiveness. Since some real exchange rates are trended, we use the Hodrick-Prescott filter with a high degree of smoothing to preserve low frequency fluctuations.[9] We instrument X_t with its lag and the real exchange rates of Japan and the USA and their own lags.

Table 11.1 presents our results.[10] The deficit d_t is cyclically adjusted and net of interest payments on the debt. We present first country-by-country estimates and then the results from pooling all euro-area countries together. The country-by-country estimates suffer from the short sample; the longest time series are only available for 1971–2006, and much less so for some countries. The pooled estimates assume that the coefficients are the same for all countries, which may not be the case, but they rely on a larger sample (the panel is unbalanced with a total of 270 observations).

The country-by-country estimates are often imprecise, which partly reflects the short size of the sample. We focus our discussion on the panel estimates, as shown in the columns labeled "Pooled 1." Table 11.2 summarizes the test results. These results confirm previous findings that fiscal policy has become counter-cyclical since 1992. Yet, the finding that $\beta^{a-} > 0$ indicates that this shift occurred during upswings while fiscal policy remains approximately acyclical during downswings. In other words, the SGP is having asymmetrical effects. These results differ from those reported in the European Commission (2006b) which finds that prior to 1992 fiscal policy was procyclical in bad times and acyclical otherwise, while it has become procyclical in good times after the adoption of the euro. To check our results, the column "Pooled 2" shows the results when we break the sample in 1999, so that "before" refers to the period 1970–98 and "after" to the period 1999–2006. The results remain practically unchanged.[11]

Regarding the use of fiscal policy to deal with external competitiveness, we find that the situation has been radically altered following the adoption of the Maastricht Treaty. Up until 1991, our results suggest that governments used fiscal policy to make up for demand shortfall

Table 11.1: *The budget deficit reaction function*

	Austria	Belgium	Finland	France	Germany	Ireland	Italy	Netherlands	Spain	Pooled 1	Pooled 2
$\beta^b E_{t-1} y_t$	0.15	0.08	0.47	0.25	-0.24	0.12	0.55	-0.09	-0.10	-0.11	-0.01
	0.56	0.67	0.27	0.24	0.55	0.62	0.23	0.80	0.68	0.43	0.92
$\beta^a E_{t-1} y_t$	0.80	1.28	-1.37	0.19	0.71	-0.07	1.05	-0.25	-0.03	-1.14	-1.17
	0.26	0.66	0.42	0.76	0.57	0.90	0.09	0.72	0.95	0.07	0.06
$\beta^{a-} E_{t-1} y_t^-$	-1.32	-0.63	0.78	0.11	-1.05	0.26	-0.79	1.36	0.45	1.50	0.57
	0.22	0.82	0.77	0.90	0.64	0.68	0.48	0.23	0.57	0.12	0.28
$\theta^b X$	-0.06	0.01	-0.03	0.07	-0.19	-0.11	0.02	-0.10	-0.13	-0.14	-0.03
	0.05	0.89	0.79	0.26	0.11	0.02	0.88	0.28	0.15	0.04	0.17
$\theta^a X$	-0.11	-0.51	0.21	0.01	0.11	0.05	-0.12	0.01	0.23	0.25	0.28
	0.19	0.41	0.49	0.91	0.35	0.33	0.04	0.95	0.09	0.03	0.09
b_{t-1}	-0.05	-0.04	0.04	-0.01	-0.03	-0.02	-0.10	-0.01	-0.03	-0.01	0.02
	0.01	0.06	0.41	0.63	0.50	0.16	0.00	0.84	0.39	0.46	0.00
d_{t-1}	0.12	0.73	-0.08	0.71	0.59	0.51	0.30	0.44	1.04	0.79	0.73
	0.60	0.00	0.83	0.05	0.00	0.02	0.33	0.06	0.00	0.00	0.00
Sample period	1977–2006	1971–2006	1976–2006	1979–2006	1971–2006	1986–2006	1981–2006	1971–2006	1981–2006	1971–2006	1971–2006

Source: see Appendix.

Notes: p-statistic reported under coefficients; White heteroskedasticity-consistent standard errors. Instruments: y_{t-1} and X_{t-1}, and y_t, y_{t-1}, X_t and X_{t-1} for the USA and Japan, the constant and country fixed-effects not reported. In the case of Italy, the set of available information for $\lambda^b E_{t-1} y_t^+$ and $\lambda^a E_{t-1} y_t^+$ is too small so we do not distinguish between pre- and post-1992 – i.e. we impose $\lambda^b = \lambda^a$. Unbalanced panel.

Table 11.2: *Tests*

Fiscal policy countercyclical until 1991 acyclical	$\beta^b < 0$	No
Fiscal policy countercyclical after 1992	$\beta^a < 0$	Yes
Fiscal policy more countercyclical in Maastricht years	$\beta^a < \beta^b$	Yes
SGP limits countercyclical policy in downswings	$\beta^{a-} > 0$	Yes
Fiscal policy acts on demand to compensate for external competitiveness difficulties until 1991	$\theta^b < 0$	Yes
Fiscal policy acts on demand to compensate for external competitiveness difficulties after 1992	$\theta^a < 0$	No
Fiscal policy acts on costs to deal with external competitiveness until 1991	$\theta^b > 0$	No
Fiscal policy acts on costs to deal with external competitiveness after 1992	$\theta^a > 0$	Yes

when they faced external competitiveness losses, and conversely tightened up fiscal policy when external competitiveness was boosting demand. After 1992, instead, they tightened up fiscal policy in the face of deteriorating competitiveness as if they were using their last remaining macroeconomic instrument to weigh on costs. These results suggest that governments are now willing to suffer short-term demand shortfalls to restore cost competitiveness. Put differently, fiscal policy is not necessarily misused.

The recent literature has emphasized the importance of budgeting institutions, i.e. the rules and norms under which governments plan their budgets, pass them through the legislature and implement them, for achieving fiscal discipline. Empirical research in this area, documented and summarized in Hallerberg *et al.* (2007), supports the view that good budgeting institutions are a precondition for achieving the fiscal discipline desired for EMU. It is, therefore, interesting to see whether budgeting institutions which are strongly conducive to fiscal discipline prevent governments from using fiscal policy effectively for macroeconomic stabilization. Hallerberg and von Hagen (1999) find that governments following the "delegation approach" to budgeting institutions conduct more effective stabilization policies than others.[12] In this view the Stability and Growth Pact can operate as a substitute for weak budgetary institutions.

In order to test whether different qualities of institutions have indeed affected the budget outcomes, we use four indicators developed by Hallerberg *et al.* (2007):

- Good budgeting institutions under either approach make fiscal policy more countercyclical;
- Good budgeting institutions under the contracts approach make fiscal policy more countercyclical;
- Good budgeting institutions under the delegation approach make fiscal policy more countercyclical;
- Stringent fiscal rules make fiscal policy more countercyclical.

We successively augment the panel regression shown in Table 11.1 with each of four dummy variables, coded 1 for the country and period when the corresponding property is found to apply, and 0 otherwise.

The resulting regressions, not shown, fail to detect any significant effect. This may be due to the small size of the sample – data availability limits the sample to only nine euro-area member countries. Alternatively, it may be that these institutional differences have not affected the governments' ability to conduct countercyclical policies. This would indicate that there is, from an institutional design perspective, no trade-off between fiscal discipline and effective macroeconomic stabilization.

4. Mutual insurance via transfers

4.1 Principles of fiscal insurance

All existing federations provide mechanisms to redistribute income among their constituent regions in response to economic developments that affect the latter in different ways (Ingram, 1959). These mechanisms can be explicit, as in the case of Germany's "Finanzausgleich," or the Canadian and Australian systems of fiscal equalization, or implicit, as in the case of the USA, where redistribution works through the federal government budget. They can be organized horizontally, as in Germany and Canada, where state governments pay and receive transfers to and from other state governments, or vertically, as in Australia, where the federal government pays transfers to the individual territories in accordance with their fiscal needs. They can be transfers between governments or the result of transfers to and from private households through a nationwide social insurance system such as unemployment insurance. Such mechanisms are generally based on equity considerations: The aim of protecting the individual against economic hardship is part of the solidarity defining a society. As Delors (1989: 89) put it in his plea for a risk-sharing mechanism among the members of the European Monetary Union (EMU), "… in all federations the different combinations of federal budgetary mechanisms have powerful 'shock-absorber' effects dampening the amplitude either of economic difficulties or of surges in prosperity of individual states. This is both the product of, and the source of the sense of national solidarity which all relevant economic and monetary unions share."

Although they were not designed explicitly for that purpose, transfer mechanisms of this kind can be regarded as an insurance mechanism against asymmetric cyclical fluctuations. Regions in a more favorable cyclical position than the federation on average pay transfers to regions in a less favorable position. This dampens the relative boom in the former and the relative recession in the latter. If each region had its own currency and exchange rates were flexible, exchange rate adjustments would provide a similar stabilizing function, as regions in a relative boom would experience an appreciation of their real exchange rates and a worsening of their current accounts, while regions in a relative recession would experience the opposite.[13] This consideration is the basis for Kenen's (1969) suggestion that fiscal transfers among the member states of a monetary union could replace the adjustment to asymmetric cyclical shocks otherwise provided by the exchange rate.

Empirical research in the 1990s has sought to estimate how important the transfer mechanisms in existing federations and large unitary states are in this regard. This discussion was spurred by Sala-i-Martin and Sachs's (1992) estimates that the US federal budget smoothes around 33–40 per cent of asymmetric shocks to regions in the USA. Subsequent research has shown, however, that, for a number of data and conceptual reasons, these authors grossly overestimate the smoothing function of the federal budget. Estimates of this kind are sensitive to the use of different national accounting concepts (Mélitz and Zumer, 1999) and must distinguish between permanent redistribution among regions and the response to transitory shocks (von Hagen, 1992). The consensus estimate today is that the federal budget smoothes about 10–15 per cent of asymmetric shocks in the USA.[14] Estimates for Canada yield similar results.

One might argue that such a mechanism is not required in the European monetary union (or elsewhere), as markets can fulfill the same function. Free trade and mobility of capital and labor generate opportunities for the citizens of the member states to protect themselves against asymmetric shocks. Indeed, empirical studies for the USA suggest that financial markets smooth 30–50 per cent of state-specific income shocks (Asdrubali *et al.*, 1996; Athanasoulis and van Wincoop, 1998; Mélitz and Zumer, 1999). Mélitz and Zumer report similar results for Canada, suggesting that markets are more important in providing insurance than fiscal mechanisms. But, even if monetary integration promotes financial market integration and, thereby, the scope for protection against asymmetric shocks, one may argue that markets provide less insurance than citizens demand. Thus, the question remains whether EMU needs a fiscal insurance mechanism against asymmetric shocks.

To explore the principles of fiscal insurance, consider a monetary union consisting of $i = 1, ..., n$ states or regions. Each region is endowed in each period with a stochastic per-capita income y_{it} with expected value y in all regions. Let y_t be the average income in the monetary union. There is a fiscal transfer mechanism in the monetary union paying transfers τ_{it} to consumers in region i and period t. Households in each region are risk averse and have linear-quadratic utility functions in consumption, c_{it},

$$U_{it} = c_{it} - \frac{\gamma}{2}\operatorname{var}(c_{it}), \tag{6}$$

where $\gamma > 0$. The households' budget constraint is $c_{it} = y_{it} + \tau_{it} - \theta_i$, where θ_i is a constant tax imposed by the regional government, which means that individuals cannot borrow to smooth consumption in the presence of shocks. For now, assume that $\theta_i = 0$.

The fiscal transfer mechanism can be designed to make consumers in all regions better off by paying transfers that partially offset deviations from expected income. A first, important question is whether or not the fiscal mechanism must be balanced at all times. If budget balance is only required in expectation, the optimal policy is to set consumption equal to expected income each period and eliminate all variance. In this case, the optimal transfers are

$$\tau_{it} = y - y_{it}, \tag{7}$$

where y is potential output. Consumers are fully insured against income shocks. This is so, because it eliminates any variance in consumption over time. Note that each government could achieve the same outcome by taxing its citizens when income is above its expected value and paying transfers when income is below its expected value. In this case, each government would borrow on behalf of its citizens in the international capital market when income is low and pay back when income is high.

A natural question then is, why should there be a fiscal insurance at the level of the monetary union? The answer is twofold. First, small countries in particular may face upward-sloping credit supply curves in the capital market, implying that they pay higher interest rates for borrowing funds when income is low than they receive on funds invested when income is high. Under such circumstances, pooling the individual consumption-smoothing policies will yield a reduction in the aggregate cost of borrowing (see Hammond and von Hagen, 1998). Second, if the monetary union imposes restrictions on public debts and deficits to safeguard the stability of the common currency, as EMU does, a common fiscal insurance mechanism assures that countries are not forced into suboptimal consumption patterns. By creating a common fiscal insurance the member countries delegate their borrowing capacity to the monetary union.

If budget balance is required each period, the transfers are

$$\tau_{it} = \alpha(y_t - y_{it}) + \pi_i, \sum_i \pi_i = 0. \tag{8}$$

They consist of a state-dependent part linked to the deviation of a region's income from average income in the monetary union, and a state-independent part. Using (8) in (6), we obtain

$$U_{it} = \alpha y_t + (1 - \alpha)y_{it} + \pi_i$$
$$- \frac{\gamma}{2}[\alpha^2 \text{var}(y_t) + 2\alpha(1 - \alpha)\text{cov}(y_t, y_{it}) + (1 - \alpha)^2 \text{var}(y_{it})]. \tag{9}$$

Forcing the system to balance at the aggregate level implies that fiscal insurance now smoothes fluctuations of regional income around average income in the monetary union, which itself is a random variable that fluctuates over time. We can use equation (9) to calculate the optimal, utility-maximizing transfer rate α^* from the point of view of households in each region i,

$$\alpha_i^* = \frac{w_i(w_i - \rho_i)}{1 + w_i(w_i - 2\rho_i)}, w_i = \sqrt{\frac{\text{var}(y_{it})}{\text{var}(y_t)}}, \tag{10}$$

where ρ_i is the correlation between income in region i and average income in the monetary union, and w_i indicates how volatile a region's income is compared to average income in the monetary union. Equation (10) shows that, in this case, full insurance will generally not be optimal for all regions. Instead, different regions have different optimal transfer rates and each region's optimal degree of insurance depends on its risk profile compared to the monetary union. Note, first, that $a_i^* = 1$ for all regions, if all individual regional incomes are uncorrelated and identically distributed.[15] Otherwise, the optimal degree of insurance depends on the correlation between regional and average income and on the relative volatility of regional and average income. If all regions have the same variance of regional income, the optimal degree of insurance approaches zero, as the correlation among the incomes approaches one. Thus, the more similar income fluctuations are over time, the less scope there is for insurance. But note that even with positive correlations, regions with relatively large income variances compared to others find insurance attractive, while regions with relatively low income variance would prefer no insurance at all.

The point of this discussion is that, if the fiscal mechanism must be balanced each period, regions with different risk profiles demand different degrees of insurance. Designing a common fiscal insurance then requires finding a compromise among the regions. This can be done using the state-independent transfers π_i to make side payments between the regions. Specifically, relatively high-risk regions can pay a premium to relatively low-risk regions to compensate for providing more insurance than the latter would find optimal. Consider the following example for illustration. Let n=2 and consider a region's expected utility given some transfer rate $\alpha = a$. From equation (9) we have

$$EU_i(a) = y + \pi_i$$
$$- \frac{\gamma}{2}[a^2 \mathrm{var}(y_t) + 2a(1-a)\mathrm{cov}(y_t, y_{it}) + (1-a)^2 \mathrm{var}(y_{it})],$$
$$(11)$$

where $\pi_1 = -\pi_2$. Assume that the two countries use Nash bargaining to establish the state-independent transfers, and that each region's fall-back position is $\alpha = 0$. The equilibrium transfer can be found by maximizing the product $[EU_1(1) - EU_1(0)][EU_2(1) - EU_2(0)]$. This yields the equilibrium state-independent transfer:

$$\pi_1^* = -\pi_2^* = \frac{a\gamma \operatorname{var}(y_t)}{4}[(2-a)(w_2^2 - w_1^2) + 2(1-a)[w_1\rho_1 - w_2\rho_2].$$
(12)

Assume, first, that the relative variances w_i are the same. Then the first term is zero and equation (12) says that the region whose income is more highly correlated with average income receives a transfer from the region whose income is less correlated with average income. Clearly, the former has less interest in fiscal insurance against fluctuations around the average than the latter. The side payment is used to induce it to agree to the insurance mechanism. Next, assume that both correlations are negligible such that the second term disappears. In that case, equation (12) says that the region with the more volatile income pays a state-independent transfer to the region with the less volatile income.

Generally, this discussion shows that a welfare-maximizing fiscal insurance mechanism will combine fixed transfers with state-dependent transfers, if it is required to achieve budget balance each period. Thus, whether or not the fiscal mechanism is allowed to borrow in times when average income in the monetary union is low to pay back when average income is large is an important aspect of the design of fiscal insurance.

Consider now the possibility that regional governments can undertake policies that reduce the variability of regional income, and that doing so requires a fixed tax $\theta_i > 0$ from all households. Such policies might consist of running a *rainy day fund* from which the government can in draw in times of low income, or in investing in projects improving the flexibility of local markets and factors of production. An important question then is, how does the fiscal mechanism at the level of the monetary union interfere with the regional governments' optimal policy at the regional level?

To answer this question, we assume that the variance of regional income and its covariance with average income are functions of θ_i. Each regional government will choose θ_i such that

$$\frac{\partial EU}{\partial \theta_i} = -1 - \frac{\gamma}{2}[(1-a^2)\frac{\partial \operatorname{var}(y_{it})}{\partial \theta_i} + 2a(1-a)\frac{\partial \operatorname{cov}(y_{it}, y_t)}{\partial \theta_i}$$
$$+ a^2 \frac{\partial \operatorname{var}(y_t)}{\partial \theta_i}] = 0.$$
(13)

It is plausible to assume that the derivatives of the two variances with respect to θ_i are negative, since reducing the variance of regional income is likely to result in a reduction in the variance of aggregate income. Whether or not such policies reduce the covariance, however, is uncertain. Using condition (13), we can derive the effect of an increase in the degree of fiscal insurance on the optimal policy of a regional government:

$$\frac{\partial \theta_i^*}{\partial \alpha} = \frac{2(1-\alpha)\dfrac{\partial \mathrm{var}(y_{it})}{\partial \theta_i} - 2(1-2\alpha)\dfrac{\partial \mathrm{cov}(y_{it}, y_t)}{\partial \theta_i} - 2\alpha \dfrac{\partial \mathrm{var}(y_t)}{\partial \theta_i}}{(1-\alpha)^2 \dfrac{\partial^2 \mathrm{var}(y_{it})}{\partial \theta_i^2} + 2\alpha(1-\alpha)\dfrac{\partial^2 \mathrm{cov}(y_{it}, y_t)}{\partial \theta_i^2} + \alpha^2 \dfrac{\partial^2 \mathrm{var}(y_t)}{\partial \theta_i^2}}.$$

(14)

Assume that policies to reduce income risk have declining marginal returns, i.e. the second derivatives are all positive. Equation (14) then says that the effect of fiscal insurance on the optimal regional policy depends crucially on the effect a region's variance has on the variance of average income. If this effect is small, as it would be for small regions, regional policies have small effects only on the covariance of regional and average income and the variance of average income, and (14) is negative. Thus, an expansion of the fiscal insurance mechanism reduces efforts for less income variance at the regional level. The opposite may be true, however, for large regions, whose policies have strong effects on the monetary union's average income variability.

Furthermore, equation (14) shows that the response of regional policies to a small increase in fiscal insurance provided by the monetary union depends on the degree of insurance already in place. Assuming that the changes in the covariances are of smaller magnitude than the changes in the variances, (11) shows that an increase in fiscal insurance reduces local efforts to reduce income variance if α is initially close to zero. The opposite is true, however, if the degree of insurance is already large. In that case, regions have an incentive to engage in policies reducing regional income variance as this contributes to a more stable average income.

This discussion shows that a fiscal insurance mechanism changes the incentives for regional governments to protect their citizens against income fluctuations, a point discussed also by Persson and Tabellini (1996a, 1996b) and Migué (1993). However, it is not clear a priori which way these incentive effects go. One can only conclude that a fiscal insurance mechanism may require additional policies at the level of the monetary union that rectify or amplify the incentive effects on local governments.

Turning from a simple endowment economy to a macroeconomic environment raises additional concerns. In an economy with production, household welfare will depend not only on consumption but also on employment. To offset the effects of asymmetric shocks, a fiscal insurance mechanism should then aim at stabilizing fluctuations in employment and consumption. In the simple, traditional Keynesian framework with fixed prices and Keynesian unemployment considered by Mundell (1961) and Kenen (1969), stabilizing household income through fiscal insurance would still be sufficient. In a more general, dynamic macroeconomic framework, it is not.[16] An important aspect of fiscal insurance then is whether the monetary union pays transfers to the regional governments or the households in the individual regions (Kletzer and von Hagen, 2001). Transfers to regional governments directly affect the demand for goods and services in regional markets. Transfers to households do so only indirectly, as they operate through the households' budget constraint and distort their choices between current and future consumption on the one hand and between consumption and leisure on the other hand. The resulting effects on employment and savings may destabilize regional employment even if they reduce the impact of asymmetric shocks on regional consumption (Evers, 2006).

As it turns out, in a more general macro framework, the optimal design of a fiscal insurance mechanism depends crucially on the type of shock hitting the economies. It is now well understood that, in the context of dynamic general equilibrium models and in the presence of aggregate productivity shocks, output stabilization is not an efficient policy.[17] The reason is that such shocks move the economy's efficient (flexible-price) equilibrium level of output. They should be accommodated, since households want to adjust their levels of consumption and investment accordingly (Rotemberg and Woodford, 1997). Carrying over this insight to asymmetric productivity shocks implies that full insurance against such shocks is undesirable in a monetary union. Pure relative demand shocks of the kind considered by Mundell (1961) can be offset completely by transfers paid between regional governments, provided that the governments use these transfers to finance the purchase of goods and services in the local markets. In the case of productivity shocks, however, neither transfers between regional governments nor transfers between private households alone are sufficient to achieve optimal insurance. A combination of both is required to stabilize consumption and employment (Evers, 2006).

As argued above, the scope for fiscal insurance among the participants of the European monetary union depends on the correlation of income and employment fluctuations among the states and regions of the union. Recent empirical work that has investigated the correlation of business cycles in the EMU sheds some light on this issue. Von Hagen and Traistaru-Siedschlag (2006) find that the correlation between country-specific and the euro-area business cycles is positive for all EMU member countries. Correlation coefficients vary between 0.30 and 0.50. Acedo Montoya and de Haan (2008) consider NUTS-1 regions in the EMU. They find that the average correlation between regional business cycles and the euro-area business cycle is above 0.60 and has been growing over the past decade. This is consistent with earlier results by Artis and Zhang (1997) and Fatás (1998) who find that business cycles became more correlated among the member states of the ERM during the 1980s and 1990s. Overall, this literature suggests that monetary integration has led to more strongly correlated business cycles without eliminating the scope for fiscal insurance altogether. Von Hagen and Traistaru-Siedschlag (2006) show that the business cycle correlations between the new EU member states and the euro area have increased but remain much weaker than the correlations among the EU15 states. Future enlargements of the euro area by Central and East European countries will, therefore, increase the scope and desirability of a fiscal insurance mechanism.

4.2 Political economy considerations

For a fiscal insurance mechanism in the euro area, additional considerations arise (Hammond and von Hagen, 1998). Since the euro area is not fully politically integrated, the political acceptability of a fiscal insurance mechanism is an important constraint on its design. A first point is that the mechanism must be fully automatic and tied to a formula determining the transfers. If the latter were left to the discretion of the governments, they would soon become politicized, e.g. by paying transfers to governments facing re-elections. Since a fiscal transfer mechanism would create opportunities for politicians to spend monies raised from tax payers in other countries, it would set up a classical fiscal commons problem, allowing politicians to spend money without regard to the full cost of taxation. The result would be a tendency to increase the volume of transfers over time. This tendency could be mitigated by requiring unanimity for all decisions over the payment of transfers, but this would make the system too rigid to respond quickly to economic shocks as they arise.

A second point is that such a mechanism must avoid the impression of bureaucratic discretion and that it serves other distributional goals than insurance. This requires transparency and, therefore, a relatively simple transfer formula. Furthermore, the mechanism must clearly address cyclical fluctuations. Hammond and von Hagen (1998) show that these two requirements create a tradeoff. Identifying cyclical shocks properly calls for the use of sophisticated econometric models which result in fairly complicated formulas to calculate the transfers. If, however, transfers are based simply on differences in real growth rates across member states, they generate permanent flows from fast- to slow-growing countries and may even destabilize cyclical movements.

A third point is that, if it aims at offsetting the loss of the exchange rate channel of macroeconomic adjustment, a fiscal insurance mechanism would have to target the national economies of the member states. The different sizes of the national economies then create an obvious problem if the mechanism is required to be balanced every period, i.e. stabilizing a negative, asymmetric shock of one percent of GDP in Luxembourg would require a transfer of small absolute size from the remaining countries, while stabilizing a shock of the same relative size in Germany would require a payment of very large absolute size from the remaining countries. This problem could be overcome by allowing the mechanism to run surpluses and deficits at the aggregate level. In that case, however, one would have to pay close attention to the risk that the national governments abuse it as a new source of permanent borrowing circumventing the strictures of the SGP.

4.3 Assessment of individual proposals

An important message from the discussion above is that the design of a fiscal transfer mechanism for the euro area depends critically on the question whether or not this mechanism would be required to be balanced financially every period. If not, the main issue that remains is to identify the shocks properly; once this is done, full insurance against asymmetric demand shocks and some partial insurance against asymmetric productivity shocks is desirable. A second, important message is that such an insurance mechanism should not be exposed to moral hazard. Proposals for fiscal insurance in the euro area should be evaluated on the basis of these two tenets. We consider two insurance mechanisms frequently found in existing federal systems. The first is the sharing of tax revenues among the government of euro-area member states. The second is a euro-area wide unemployment insurance. The former would pay transfers among the governments, while the latter would pay transfers directly to the households.

4.3.1 Tax revenue sharing

Insurance through tax revenue sharing can be achieved by having all member governments pay a fixed proportion of their tax revenues annually into a common euro-area tax fund, which simultaneously pays out transfers to these governments on a fixed (per capita) basis. Payments into the fund would then vary with the evolution of the tax base over time, while payments out of the fund would not follow any cyclical movements. Thus, countries with temporarily high tax bases would pay more, countries with temporarily low tax bases would pay less than they receive. As governments adjust their spending accordingly, stabilization is provided.

The appropriate tax base for such a mechanism would be VAT rather than income or payroll taxes. The reason is that, first, VAT is closer to demand shocks than income or payroll taxes, and, second, it reacts faster to cyclical movements in the economy than income taxes or payroll taxes which are often declared and paid with delays. To set up such a mechanism, member countries of the euro area could agree to share a portion of their VAT revenues through the common fund. In fact, different countries could participate in such a fund with different shares of their VAT revenues according to national preferences and economic circumstances. For example, governments with more volatile economies could decide to bring a larger share of their revenues into the fund. Implementation of such a mechanism would, therefore, not require raising VAT rates in any member state, an important condition for the acceptability of the proposal.

An advantage of such a mechanism is that it would allow member governments to engage in countercyclical policies addressing asymmetric shocks in a way fully consistent with the rules of the SGP.

States receiving net transfers could increase government spending without violating their commitment to keeping their budgets close to balance or in surplus. Note that the additional spending should have a greater effect on aggregate spending in the country concerned, as households would recognize that it is not connected with an increase in future tax liabilities and, hence, would not cut back private demand as in the case of deficit-financed government spending; a point confirmed empirically by Bayoumi and Masson (1995).

Assume, first, that the mechanism does not have to achieve balance at the aggregate level. Effectively, it would then compensate the restrictions on borrowing at the national level by allowing borrowing at the level of the euro area. A strict control of the mechanism assuring that it does not build up a stock of permanent debt would be required; we return to this issue in the next section. The main moral hazard problem here is that governments would not adjust spending in accordance with the net transfers they pay or receive under the mechanism, and, thus, not provide the desired stabilization. But this problem need not worry the euro area as a whole. It could be left up to the national electorates to make sure that their governments use the resources they have available properly.

Things are more complicated if the mechanism had to be balanced financially, because it would then have to be combined with permanent transfers among the governments compensating for differences in their risk profiles. Negotiating these transfers and adjusting them over time would require a way to reveal the true degree of risk aversion of the national populations and the true volatility of the asymmetric shocks. Both would be difficult to achieve and subject the mechanism to political games. Since governments with less volatile economies would receive permanent transfers under such a scheme, the mechanism would create incentives to implement policies at the national level that reduce the national economies' exposure to asymmetric shocks. Thus, the incentive effects would work in the direction of reducing asymmetric shocks in this case.

4.3.2 Euro-area unemployment insurance

The alternative proposal would be to implement a euro-area wide unemployment insurance. Under such a scheme, households in economies enjoying positive asymmetric shocks would pay rising insurance contributions which would be paid to households suffering from negative asymmetric shocks. This would help stabilize aggregate demand across euro-area countries. Since unemployment insurance would constitute an entitlement for individuals, such a scheme cannot be forced to balance at the aggregate level unless the governments pay additional contributions making good for any shortfalls of revenues over expenditures.[18]

An insurance mechanism of this sort would have to address a variety of problems. First, given that levies on labor income are large in most European countries already, it would have to be implemented in a way that does not increase the cost of labor further. An obvious way to do that would be to replace a part of the existing unemployment insurance schemes at the national level to the euro-area level. Note, however, that Italy today does not have an unemployment insurance system at the national level. Thus, this approach would require the institution of a new branch of social insurance in this country.

Second, many European countries have experienced an increase in nontraditional forms of employment in recent years, which are not included in the existing social insurance schemes. However, these new forms of employment are precisely those that are the most flexible ones in the labor market and, therefore, the most responsive ones to asymmetric shocks. The implementation of a euro-area-wide unemployment insurance would most likely be most efficient, if nontraditional jobs could be integrated into the scheme. But doing so should not destroy their very purpose of providing flexibility to the labor market.

Third, European countries suffer from very different rates of permanent unemployment. The main moral hazard problem of a euro-area-wide insurance is that it creates incentives for national governments to raise (or to not do enough to lower) permanent unemployment in order to receive permanent net transfers through the mechanism. One obvious way of dealing with this problem is to insist on coinsurance. Euro-area-wide unemployment insurance would only be provided for countries that have substantial unemployment insurance at the national level. Given the concern over the high cost of labor in the euro area, this would limit the amount of insurance that can be provided at the aggregate level. An alternative solution would be to limit the duration of the unemployment insurance provided by a euro-area-wide mechanism strictly to periods of six to twelve months.

5. Institutional requirements for a transfer system

The analysis carried out in the previous section suggests that the most promising mutual insurance system rests on tax revenue sharing with a mutual fund that need not be balanced year after year. There are two main moral hazard problems challenging the viability of such a system. The first is that it might create opportunities for cheating by individual countries trying to induce permanent redistribution in favor of individual countries. The second is that it will be abused as a way to circumvent the borrowing restrictions under EMU, leading to permanent indebtedness of the system at the aggregate level. We now take issue with these challenges.

5.1 Moral hazard problems at the country level

The purpose of the fiscal insurance system would be to insure the tax revenues of the participating governments against transitory asymmetric shocks. Such shocks may be correlated over time, but, in order to guarantee that the insurance system does not run permanent surpluses or deficits, only shocks that do not affect the level of taxes permanently can be insured. Since tax revenues in practice are affected by a mixture of permanent and transitory shocks, the viability of a fiscal insurance system requires a method to identify transitory shocks and separate them from permanent shocks. As demonstrated in Hammond and von Hagen (1998), this is possible, if the system can be based on sophisticated econometric models. This, however, is unlikely for a system that results from an agreement among governments of different countries.

Ruling out complicated econometrics, a simple mechanism for calculating the transfers paid within the system must be found. Assuming that tax revenues of government i in period t, T_{it}, are proportional to GDP, Y_{it},

$$T_{it} = \alpha Y_{it} \tag{15}$$

this can be achieved by tying payments into the system to the asymmetric deviation between actual and potential GDP, P_{it},

$$t_{it} = \lambda \alpha[(Y_{it} - P_{it}) - \beta(Y_t - P_t)], \tag{16}$$

where λ determines the degree of insurance chosen by government i, Y_t and P_t, are the actual and the potential level of euro-area GDP, and β is the weight of country i in euro-area potential GDP. Countries enjoying a boom relative to the euro area would pay into the insurance scheme, while countries suffering from a relative recession would receive transfers. By definition, these deviations are transitory, assuring that the system is balanced on average over the business cycle. Note that, as business cycles among the participating countries become more corre-lated, transfer payments into and out of the system will become smaller.

A moral hazard problem arises from the fact that, in each period, a government has an incentive to overstate its potential GDP in order to reduce its payment into the system. To see this, note that $(dt_{it}/dP_{it}) = -\lambda a(1 - \beta^2) < 0$. In other words, faced with formula (16) as a basis for its payments, governments have an incentive to declare that their economy is in a recession. This implies that the computation of potential GDP cannot be left to the governments alone. One approach would be to delegate these computations to a politically independent agency, e.g. the European Commission or an independent research institute.

An alternative solution would be to modify (16) in a way that assures balance over time independently of the way how potential (and actual) output are calculated. Assuming that potential output is constant over time for simplicity, this can be done by using the following formula:

$$t_{it} = \lambda a[(Y_{it} - P_{it}) - \beta(Y_t - P_t)] - \sum_{j=0}^{t-N}(1 + r_t)^{N+j}t_{it-N-j}. \qquad (17)$$

The penalty term reduces any transfers received in period t by a part of the accumulated transfers paid in the past. Letting N be the length of the business cycle assures that this would not interfere with stabilizing cycli-cal movements. Under this approach, any misrepresentation of potential output in period t leads to a reduction in transfers received or an increase in payments made into the system in the future. By applying an appro-priate interest rate r, the incentive to cheat is balanced by the desire to avoid future reductions in transfers received. If potential output is calcu-lated properly, the penalty term converges to zero over time. It is straight-forward to extend this approach to the case of growing potential output.

5.2 Moral hazard problems at the aggregate level

At the aggregate level, the moral hazard problem lies in the possibility for the participating countries to abuse the insurance scheme as a way of circumventing the borrowing constraints under EMU. Governments running budget deficits close to 3 percent of GDP might ask for pay-ments out of the insurance system in order increase its borrowing outside its own budget. Obviously, as long as a penalty as in equation (17) is applied and strictly enforced, these governments will be forced to run budget surpluses in future periods in order to pay back what they borrowed indirectly. If this is true, such indirect borrowing does not increase government debt permanently and does not endanger the sustainability of the common currency. Therefore, there is no problem for the monetary union as a whole.

The moral hazard problem comes from the possibility that the governments agree collectively not to enforce the repayment embedded in the penalty. Note that, as long as each country strictly keeps its own account within the fiscal insurance system and is responsible for the liabilities created by any transfers paid to it, no government must fear becoming financially responsible for the misbehavior of other governments. But this may imply that governments would rather give into the demands of others to borrow indirectly through the insurance mechanism than face an open conflict with them. The experience with the enforcement of the SGP in the years after 2001 suggests that this possibility cannot be ruled out.

Ultimately, this problem is linked to the governance of the insurance mechanism. It could be mitigated by delegating the governance of the system to a politically independent body which has a vital interest in preserving its financial sustainability, either the European Commission or the European Central Bank. These bodies would then have the right to veto the payment of transfers to individual countries and to impose a penalty formula such as the one given in equation (17). For example, a veto might be triggered, if the sum of a government's budget deficit and the transfer payment received from the insurance system exceeds 3 percent of GDP. Even if it is hard to imagine that such an outside body could consistently withstand pressures from the participating governments, delegating such veto power would have the advantage that such pressures are made visible to the public in the countries participating in the monetary union. This would strengthen the democratic accountability of the governments and give the voters an opportunity to penalize financially irresponsible governments.

6. Conclusions

The euro area will likely remain for a long time a one-of-its-kind arrangement with a centralized monetary policy and decentralized fiscal policies. This is, after all, the same arrangement as in most federal states, with two key differences. First, in Europe, the "federal" budget is very small and largely automatic. Second, in contrast with many federations where decentralized budgets are subject to strict imbalance limits while the center carries out fiscal policy, Europe's centralized budget must be balanced while subcentral budgets are in charge of fiscal policies.

Concern with this arrangement has led to the SGP. We have argued that the meaningful concern is the risk of fiscal dominance. We have also examined the record of national fiscal policies before and after the adoption of the Maastricht Treaty and found evidence that the quality of fiscal policies has improved in two ways: they are more clearly countercyclical – or less procyclical – and they are more readily used to restore competitiveness than to attempt to boost demand when competitiveness is eroded.

These observations suggest that fiscal policy remains a useful instrument. One question is whether it can be augmented – or perhaps substituted for – with a collective insurance system. Collective insurance is one alternative to external borrowing and lending and therefore one way to deal with the concerns that the SGP is meant to address. It is no panacea, though. We find that, to be effective and politically acceptable, a collective insurance system must be able not to balance every period. Put differently, an effective system moves (part of) national deficits to the collective level.

We have examined in more detail two collective insurance systems: tax revenue sharing and unemployment insurance sharing. We find that the earlier is more promising and examine in some detail how it could be set up. A nice feature of any sharing system is that it is structurally balanced over time. In other words, it cannot lead to debt accumulation. But is it foolproof? Examining various potential loopholes, we find that, if well structured, such a system has desirable incentives characteristics. Individual countries that attempt to take advantage of the system to achieve short-term political advantage can be discouraged.

There remains the possibility that collectively, euro-area governments may be tempted to use the insurance scheme to raise their debts. Individual governments could be tempted to misrepresent their true economic situation – by providing overblown estimates of their potential GDP – in order to obtain larger transfers. This moral hazard can be dealt with either by delegating the task of assessing potential GDP to an independent body, or by including in the net transfers a penalty, respectively a repayment, that correspond to the accumulated transfers received from, respectively paid into, the insurance scheme. Another risk is that collectively member governments agree to use the insurance mechanism to bypass the SGP. Here again, a solution would be to delegate to an independent body the right to block payments and to impose a penalty scheme. Of course, it is impossible that the independent body will always have the gravitas to overrule a strong coalition of member governments.

In the end, therefore, we face the unavoidable fact that any insurance mechanism entails moral hazard and that moral hazard can, at best, only be mitigated, not eliminated. If the risks are perceived as being too large, then we come back to the traditional view: cyclical fluctuations must be dealt with through individual borrowing and lending, augmented by the national use of fiscal policies. This leaves the task of imagining how to enforce fiscal discipline; the SGP, we argued, has probably improved the situation, but it suffers from a number of weaknesses. How to improve on the existing arrangement is an issue that goes beyond the scope of the present chapter.

Appendix on data sources

Output gap: AMECO (except USA and Japan: OECD Economic Outlook).

Cyclically adjusted primary deficit: AMECO (except Spain, overall cyclically adjusted deficit: OECD Economic Outlook).

Relative unit labour costs (ULC): OECD Economic Outlook (missing countries: Greece and Portugal).

Notes

1. There exist some limits on the size of taxes like VAT.
2. On the accumulation of tensions in, and the reform of, SGP, see Van den Noord *et al.* (2008).
3. For empirical evidence showing that investors indeed discriminate among public borrowers in the euro area see Bernoth *et al.* (2004).
4. Krogstrup and Wyplosz (2006) conclude that the pact is far from optimal.
5. For a brief review of the arguments, see Ramey (2006) and Perotti (2005).
6. A different literature looks at the automatic stabilizers. Buti *et al.* (2003) claim that a heavy tax burden may well reduce the effectiveness of the stabilizers. See also Debrun *et al.* (this volume).

7. Yet another empirical literature examines the possibility of non-Keynesian effects, whereby a fiscal expansion (contraction) has contractionary (expansionary) effects. We ignore this small literature as it seems to concern exceptional events; see Giavazzi and Pagano (1990) and Giavazzi *et al.* (2000).

8. Tax changes, as enacted in Germany in 2007, may partly mimic a depreciation, but this is not a macroeconomic use and it does not require any change in the budget balance.

9. We set the smoothing parameter to 1,000.

10. Due to missing data, Greece, Luxembourg, and Portugal are not included in the sample.

11. They are also unchanged if we compare the periods 1970–91 and 1999–2006, dropping the Maastricht years 1992–8. A possible explanation is that the Commission's results are based on a graphical analysis. Another possibility is that they look at the relationship between changes in the cyclically adjusted budget and in the output gap while we look at levels.

12. Under the delegation approach, budgeting institutions lend significant agenda-setting powers to the finance minister. In contrast, the "contracts approach" builds on binding numerical targets negotiated among all actors in the budget process at the beginning of the process. See Hallerberg *et al.* (2007).

13. See Stockman (1998) for a broad review of the theoretical and empirical research on the stabilizing function of the real exchange rate.

14. See von Hagen (2007) for a review of the empirical literature.

15. To see this, note that $w_i = \sqrt{n}$ and $1/\sqrt{n}$ for all i in this case.

16. For recent analysis of these issues in the framework of a new-Keynesian dynamic general equilibrium model see Evers (2006).

17. See Canzoneri (2007) for a summary of the relevant discussion.

18. This system would differ from European regional policies since these policies involve transfers based on income levels, not cyclical fluctuations.

Comment 7: Comment on Chapter 11

MARTIN LARCH AND LUCIO PENCH

1. Introduction

The advent of the single European currency has fundamentally changed the macroeconomic policy assignments in the countries participating in the Economic and Monetary Union (EMU). Prior to the
introduction of the euro, the task of stabilizing country-specific cyclical
fluctuations of output was spread across two pairs of shoulders:
national monetary and national fiscal policy makers. In 1998, when
the exchange rates of, at the time, eleven countries very irrevocably
fixed vis-à-vis the euro, the design of EMU required monetary policy
makers to eventually turn their backs on strictly national fortunes and
to henceforth look after the common currency. The until then shared
objective of stabilizing idiosyncratic shocks was left with national
fiscal policy.

Ten years after this major change in macroeconomic governance, the
chapter by von Hagen and Wyplosz looks back and addresses two
crucial questions. Firstly, how did the decentralized system of fiscal
policy making in the participating countries cope with the task of
smoothing country-specific swings of aggregate output? Secondly,
does EMU need a common stabilization tool to compensate for the
evacuation of national monetary policy to the EU level?

These basic and straightforward interrogations have inspired von
Hagen and Wyplosz to a thorough and comprehensive assessment of
the experience with national fiscal policy making in the EMU accumulated over the past ten years. The analysis laid out in the chapter is
rigorous and broadly balanced. It provides an excellent account of (i)
what fiscal policy can do and has done in EMU coupled with (ii) an
original and insightful discussion of whether a collective insurance
mechanism against idiosyncratic shocks would improve the track
record of fiscal stabilization in the countries adopting the single
currency.

Our discussion follows the road map of the chapter. We first touch upon the authors' views of the fiscal policy arrangement in the EMU, move on to the question of whether fiscal policy has an impact on aggregate demand of national economies and beyond, and eventually discuss the authors' analysis and conclusions concerning the scope for a collective insurance mechanism.

2. Fiscal policy in EMU: what it should do, can do and actually does

For those who have followed von Hagen's and Wyplosz's work on the Stability and Growth Pact (SGP) over the years, it will not come as a complete surprise that their assessment of the theoretical underpinnings of the EU fiscal surveillance framework is lukewarm. One of the authors' main arguments challenging the rationale of the SGP is that in their view national fiscal policy making does not produce sufficiently strong spillovers to the rest of the currency area to justify the tight bodice of rules of the Pact.

While there are no ultimate empirical findings about the exact size of fiscal policy spillovers, simulations with state-of-the-art econometric models such as the Commission's QUEST model suggest that national fiscal policies can produce sizable effects on the rest of the euro area and hence complicate monetary policy making (see Larch and Turrini, 2007). Specifically, a temporary fiscal expansion by a large Member State such as Germany, France or Italy of the order of 1 percent of GDP, is estimated to gradually increase the rate of inflation in the rest of the euro area by around half a percentage point, i.e. a non-negligible magnitude.

In the part of the chapter dealing with preliminaries, von Hagen and Wyplosz also touch upon the question of whether and by how much fiscal policy impacts on aggregate economic activity. Their discussion of the issue is standard but complete. It covers the conceptual antipodes of the Keynesian and Ricardian paradigm and describes the range of available empirical estimates. The way the evidence is presented and assessed is very impartial, maybe too impartial. The section of the chapter ends on a very agnostic note about the actual effects of discretionary fiscal policy making on aggregate output. Confronted with such a degree of impartiality, the reader is actually tempted to ask her- or himself the question of why one should actually carry on with an assessment of fiscal policy making if one cannot be sure whether fiscal policy has an effect or not; any further discussion risks being very hypothetical.

The empirical test presented in the chapter of how national fiscal policies actually performed before and within EMU follows the by now established approach whereby a measure of the budget balance is modeled as a function of economic and fiscal conditions. While the framework is in line with the established approach in the literature – it tracks the prominent precedent of Galí and Perotti (2003) and others – the empirical test carried out by von Hagen and Wyplosz includes specific elements that deserve more attention. On top of the commonly used indicators gauging fiscal and economic conditions, notably the output gap and the lagged deficit and debt ratio, von Hagen and Wyplosz also include variables capturing the degree of external competitiveness. The conjecture underlying the inclusion of such a variable is that fiscal policy may be used to address changes in competitiveness:[1] turning expansionary (contractionary) when relative costs increase (decrease) vis-à-vis the rest of the world.

On the whole, the results of the empirical test are broadly in line with previous studies for what concerns the use of discretionary fiscal policy over the cycle, i.e. the tendency towards procyclical policies has declined after 1992, the year in which the Maastricht Treaty, the road map towards the euro, was signed. Although these results seem to be robust from an econometric point of view, they tend to overlook specific and serious episodes of procyclical fiscal policies in the recent past, notably at the end of the 1990s and the early 2000s. In those years, fiscal policy turned procyclical in a number of large euro-area countries (Germany, France, Italy, and the Netherlands) which in econometric tests carry the same weight as smaller countries but have a larger impact on the euro-area aggregate and hence on the policy mix of the single currency area. Concretely, sizeable revenue windfalls led policy makers to believe that underlying budget balances had improved considerably and that part if not all of the extra revenue could be spent. The decision to loosen the fiscal stance came at a moment when the respective economies were operating above potential.

The assessment of fiscal policy making carried out by von Hagen and Wyplosz remains silent about the role played by automatic stabilizers. It could be interesting to know whether and to what extent discretionary fiscal policy was aligned with the operation of the build-in mechanisms (i.e. progressive taxation, unemployment benefits and, most importantly, the inertia of non-cyclical spending with respect to GDP) or whether it has offset them in part or completely.

As regards external competitiveness, von Hagen and Wyplosz's results seem to suggest that fiscal policy was used to counter variations in relative costs before 1992 and has been used to restore cost competitiveness thereafter. While this constitutes an interesting finding it would be worth checking in greater detail how cost competitiveness behaves vis-à-vis the cycle. It may be the case that the two variables co-move in some way.

Finally, von Hagen and Wyplosz also examine the link between institutions and fiscal performance, assuming that some arrangements of fiscal governance may be more conducive to fiscal stabilization than others. The indicators used to capture institutions are those developed by Hallerberg *et al.* (2007) and are relatively limited in terms of their availability across countries and time. Not least because of this, the empirical results are not conclusive. In the recent past, a number of more detailed and comprehensive set of indicators measuring fiscal governance have become available (see in particular European Commission, 2006b). They are likely to be more useful for the type of regression run by the authors.

3. The mutual insurance via transfers

After the assessment of fiscal policy in EMU, von Hagen and Wyplosz address the issue of a possible supranational insurance mechanism complementing fiscal policies conducted by euro-area members at national level. As indicated by the authors, the issue is not new. It had already been discussed at the time of the adoption of the Maastricht Treaty (see for instance Sala-i-Martin and Sachs, 1992, or Pisani-Ferry *et al.*, 1993) reflecting the concern that national discretionary fiscal policy might be overburdened with the stabilization of idiosyncratic shocks. However, what is new in von Hagen and Wyplosz's paper is the effective way to model the issue. It is likely to set a benchmark for future research in the area.

The starting point is that, unlike in national systems, where transfer mechanisms are typically justified on equity considerations with the insurance properties as a by-product, the arrangement at euro-area level examined by von Hagen and Wyplosz, by which credit-constrained consumers can be made better off in the presence of stochastic shocks, is based on strict insurance principles, that is, not allowing for permanent transfers. This leaves two basic operational options: either the mechanism is required to be balanced in each period or to balance only in expectation, that is, over time. As von Hagen and Wyplosz make clear, the options have stark implications for the design and functioning of the common insurance.

If the transfer mechanism must be balanced in each period and countries have different risk profiles, as defined by the correlation of national income with the euro-area income *and* the volatility of national income relative to that of euro-area income, then the attractiveness of the insurance mechanism will differ across countries. Achieving balance will be possible only through a system of side payments related to each country's risk profile. In some way, this insight mirrors the more general finding of the insurance literature according to which setting one price means that individuals with lower risk tend to go uninsured, i.e. there is the risk of adverse selection. The difficulties in devising a system of side payments are enough to make the mechanism unviable even before considering the issue of cross-country differences in size.

If, by contrast, the transfer mechanism can run temporary deficits, then von Hagen and Wyplosz point out that in principle national governments could obtain the same stabilization objectives by borrowing on behalf of their own citizens in "bad" times and running surplus in "good" times. What the transfer mechanism would effectively achieve is a (further) delegation of borrowing capacity, from the governments to the euro-area level. Apart from second-order benefits linked to the functioning of capital markets, the main justification for introducing such a mechanism, according to the authors, could only be that the EU fiscal rules, and specifically the 3 percent of GDP deficit threshold, place excessive constraints on fiscal stabilization conducted at national level.

On balance, von Hagen and Wyplosz believe that there might be a case for a collective insurance system to augment national fiscal policies, which is consistent with their critical assessment of the rationale of the SGP. At the same time they draw attention to an often overlooked potential drawback of common insurance mechanisms, namely, that cross-country transfers in the wake of supply shocks is likely to be counterproductive by seeking to stabilize output at the "wrong" level. While they seem to place excessive faith in the ability of "sophisticated econometric models" to correctly identify the nature of the shocks, they readily admit that a real-world insurance mechanism would have to be based on a relatively simple formula. They find a tax revenue-sharing scheme more attractive than a common unemployment insurance scheme, for the greater automaticity it affords. Accordingly, they sketch out possible ways to meet the institutional requirements for such a scheme, essentially the need to avoid moral hazard leading to permanent accumulation of debt either at national or EU level. One variant they discuss, whereby countries would pay an appropriate interest on the accumulated transfers received, effectively comes close to a *rainy day fund* run at European level. Compared to previous work on common insurance schemes, the detailed discussion of the political economy aspects provided by von Hagen and Wyplosz constitutes a clear step forward. The dispassionate nature and width of their analysis also sets them apart from more recent studies on the same subject, such as by Dullien (2007), who argues for a common unemployment insurance by focusing on the normative aspects of the mechanism and turning a blind eye on the operational or political economy dimensions. While both proponents and critics of a common insurance mechanism may find ammunition in this chapter to confirm their deeply held preferences, the former may have a hard time to push aside von Hagen and Wyplosz's reservations about the feasibility of a common insurance scheme.

Note

1. See also Allsopp and Vines (this volume).

12 | Government size and output volatility: should we forsake automatic stabilization?

XAVIER DEBRUN, JEAN PISANI-FERRY AND
ANDRÉ SAPIR

1. Introduction

Prior to the launch of the euro, academics and policy makers were equally concerned that the loss of the monetary policy instrument would deprive participating countries of a vital tool to respond to country-specific economic shocks. This concern was rooted in the generally accepted proposition that market-based adjustment channels – i.e. labour mobility and capital flows – tended to be weaker among euro-area countries than among regions of existing monetary unions such as the United States.

   Those arguing that the Economic and Monetary Union (EMU) would nonetheless be capable of coping with idiosyncratic shocks (Emerson *et al.*, 1992 or Buti and Sapir, 1998) built their case on two main arguments. First, they claimed that EMU would actually reduce the occurrence of country-specific shocks, not only because it would decrease country specialization, but also because it would limit the possibility of policy-induced shocks. There would, by definition, be no more policy-related disturbances emanating from national monetary authorities, whereas EMU fiscal rules would limit the scope for major fiscal slippages (including procyclical impulses) by national governments. Second, it was claimed that the new macroeconomic policy framework, and in particular the fiscal rules, would enable automatic stabilizers to operate more effectively as fears of persistent deteriorations in fiscal positions following bad times would dissipate.

The title of this chapter is inspired by Franco Modigliani's 1977 address to the American Economic Association "The Monetarist Controversy, or Should We Forsake Stabilization Policies?" *American Economic Review*, 67: 1–19. We are very grateful to Jérémie Cohen-Setton and Salvatore Dell'Erba for superb research assistance as well as to Gilles Saint-Paul, Carlos Martinez-Mongay, and the participants in the EMU@10 workshop for their comments. The views expressed in this chapter do not necessarily reflect those of the IMF, or IMF policies.

Automatic stabilizers had long been regarded as playing a key role in macroeconomic stabilization, mainly because they are not subject to the typical lags (information, decision, and implementation) undermining the effectiveness of discretionary stabilization measures. In particular, they were generally considered as having contributed significantly to the decrease of output volatility witnessed in Europe and in the United States after World War II, when the size of governments increased substantially on both sides of the Atlantic. Hence it was hoped that improved national fiscal policy could partly make up for the loss of monetary policy in stabilizing national macroeconomic conditions.

That said, of the three traditional goals of public finances enunciated by Musgrave (1959), macroeconomic stabilization is arguably "residual," in the sense that it is only a by-product of choices regarding the size, the structure, and the financing of government spending that are dictated by either efficiency or distributive considerations. This led to concerns that euro-area countries would actually be torn between the need to ensure adequate macroeconomic stabilization and the reduction in the size of governments that often accompanied efforts to boost market efficiency and promote long-term growth. EMU countries would thus be facing a difficult tradeoff between maintaining large governments to ensure sufficient automatic fiscal stabilization and leaner ones to ensure efficiency and growth: in EU jargon, there could be a tension between the "Maastricht" and the "Lisbon" goals (Buti *et al.*, 2003). Such a tradeoff would be particularly unfavourable in countries where growth performance was deemed dismal and the perceived need for reforms correspondingly large.

The aim of the chapter is to discuss this issue in the light of recent experience. It is divided into five substantive sections. In section 2, we briefly discuss the economic benefits of macroeconomic stability and the rationale for government policies playing an active role in delivering it. Section 3 reviews the economic literature on the determinants of output volatility and its link with government size. Two separate strands of the literature are surveyed: cross-country studies focusing on OECD members and time-series studies of a single country, typically the United States. The cross-section studies confirm that countries with large governments tend to enjoy less output volatility, but also that there may be a threshold level beyond which the negative relationship disappears or even reverses. The studies that focus on the United States show, however, that the country has recently experienced an important reduction in output volatility, despite probably lying below this threshold and having witnessed a less pronounced increase in government size than most OECD countries. This suggests that something else than automatic stabilization has been at work: either an exogenous fall in volatility, an increase in market-based stabilization, or an improvement in monetary policy.

Section 4 shows descriptive evidence on the size of government, macroeconomic volatility, and the role of fiscal stabilization policies in supporting consumption smoothing in the OECD countries, including eleven euro-area members. The evidence confirms the contrast between time-series and cross-sectional studies. The main finding, however, is that the negative correlation between government size and output volatility, which is a major finding of the literature, seems to vanish for more recent cross-country data. In the traditionally volatile, small government countries, volatility has decreased substantially while government size has grown less than elsewhere.

Section 5 builds on these stylized facts to present new econometric estimates of the relationship between government size and output volatility using both time-series and cross-country information. We first confirm that the traditional link between government size and macroeconomic volatility disappeared during the 1990s. We then explore possible reasons for this breakdown, focusing on the role of improvements in the quality of monetary policy and on progress in financial development. The evidence suggests that monetary policy and financial development can both be substitutes for government size as a stabilizing force, and that once this substitutability is taken into account, the relationship between government size and macroeconomic stability remains strong, although non-linear: the marginal effect of an increase in government size on output volatility is found to be negligible for public expenditure levels above 40 percent of GDP. Conclusions and policy implications are given in Section 6.

2. Does volatility matter? Does government matter?

The Musgravian perspective of the 1960s took for granted that more stabilization is always better and that delivering it belongs to governments. Each of those two assumptions deserves discussion.

The Keynesian paradigm of the times assumed that the private economy is inherently unstable and that output volatility involves significant economic costs. A bigger government could perhaps imply microeconomic inefficiencies but it would be regarded as a macroeconomic blessing because it contributes to stability. As James Tobin reportedly said, "it takes a lot of Harberger triangles to fill an Okun gap."

A completely different perspective was offered by the literature of the 1980s. The real business cycle models first emphasized that fluctuations could be originating on the supply side rather than the demand side, thereby questioning the wisdom of containing them – a view later reinforced by the Schumpeterian approach to growth. Second, Lucas (1987) proposed a microfounded evaluation of the welfare cost of US post-war macroeconomic fluctuations in a model with infinitely lived representative agents, and found that the utility gain from eliminating fluctuations in consumption was equivalent to the gain from a permanent increase in the consumption level by 0.1 percent only. This led him to conclude that "economic instability of the level [the USA had] experienced since the Second World War [was] a minor problem."

The Lucas result has been challenged by a number of papers pointing out that it is not robust to changes in several restrictive assumptions, including the absence of unemployment, perfect financial markets, and the functional form of preferences and risk aversion (see for example Otrok, 2001, for a survey). The empirical literature on the relationship between volatility and growth has also suggested that volatility may have detrimental effects on long-term growth (Ramey and Ramey, 1995), at least for countries where financial markets are not fully developed (Aghion *et al.*, 2006).

The purpose of the present chapter is more modest than assessing the welfare consequences of economic fluctuations. We only seek to examine the impact of government size on economic fluctuations. However, keeping in mind that what matters ultimately is the welfare consequence of government intervention on economic fluctuations, we retain from the Lucas argument the need to assess volatility of consumption, not output. We will therefore look at both and confirm that they are highly correlated.

Turning to the second assumption, that bigger governments are needed to deliver macroeconomic stability, we note that it rests on two further hypotheses: that there are no available substitutes to government-induced stabilization; and that the demand for stabilization remains constant over time, regardless of changes in the structure of the economy.

Both are questionable. The reason why public budgets provide automatic stabilization function is that governments face no liquidity constraint and can therefore behave as infinitely lived agents engaged in intertemporal optimization. It is not their governmental character that matters but the fact that, barring exceptional situations, they enjoy unrestricted access to the capital market and can therefore borrow to smooth out fluctuations in income.

In this role, however, there can be various alternatives to a big government: monetary policy may take up the role devoted to fiscal policy by the traditional literature; financial liberalization may allow more households to have access to financial intermediation and "self-insure" against the impact of economic fluctuations; private insurance institutions that substitute for government insurance may manage their budget constraint in an intertemporal manner. Moreover, structural changes can reduce the magnitude of shocks or help in absorbing them: lean management techniques may reduce the procyclical behavior of inventories; firms may make use of financial deepening and invest countercyclically; openness to trade and capital flows may reduce the multiplier effects of domestic shocks.

This discussion suggests that the relationship between government size and the cyclical behavior of the economy is unlikely to be constant over time because it probably adjusts to a host of structural changes. This is what we intend to explore in the remainder of the chapter.

3. Automatic stabilizers and the Great Moderation

The cyclical pattern of Western economies underwent a profound transformation during the twentieth century. As carefully documented by Romer (1999) or Blanchard and Simon (2001) for the United States, recessions have become less frequent and business expansions have tended to last longer since the 1950s. In addition, the variance of output growth has declined substantially. Similar trends have been observed in some European countries, most clearly in the case of Germany and the UK (Stock and Watson, 2003); although output volatility in the early post-World War II decades was generally even lower than in the United States (Sapir *et al.*, 2004).

Researchers have explored the links between economic structures, economic policy, and volatility. Two different, unrelated approaches emerged in the literature. Adopting a cross-country perspective, the first

focused on the link between government size and macroeconomic stability. The second approach is longitudinal and has aimed at explaining
the steady decline in the volatility of US output.

While we are primarily concerned with the first question, we cannot
ignore the second one. Automatic stabilizers are deemed important
because economies are subject to shocks and prone to volatility. If
volatility vanishes, so does the importance of automatic stabilizers. In
what follows, we review the two strands of the literature, starting with
the relationship between the size of government and macroeconomic
stability.

3.1 Do bigger governments deliver greater macroeconomic stability?

In line with the Keynesian tradition, economists have long argued that
the growing size of governments after World War II contributed to
greater macroeconomic stability because of the near proportionality
between the magnitude of automatic fiscal stabilizers and the size of
government expenditure (Blinder and Solow, 1974).[1] The basic idea of
this literature is that, by lessening the effects of the liquidity constraints
faced by households, automatic stabilizers – including the income-based
tax system and unemployment insurance benefits – alleviate the impact
of aggregate income fluctuations on current consumption and output.

3.1.1 A negative relationship between government size and volatility …

The paper by Galí (1994) is a seminal contribution to both empirical
and theoretical research on the link between government size and
macroeconomic stability. Empirically, it seems to have been the first to
systematically investigate the relationship between fiscal aggregates and
output volatility for a cross-section of countries. More specifically, the
paper examines the role of income taxes and government purchases as
automatic stabilizers in twenty-two OECD countries over the period
1960–90.[2] The basic finding is that government size is negatively associated with output volatility: economies with large governments (such
as the Netherlands, Norway, and Sweden) experience milder economic
fluctuations than economies with small governments (such as Japan,
Portugal, and Spain). This finding appears to be robust to the use of
alternative measures of government size and output variability.

The theoretical contribution of the paper is an attempt to build a non-Keynesian model capable of generating predictions that fit the results of the cross-country regressions. Galí's idea is to introduce the concept of automatic stabilizers in a basic real business cycle (RBC) model. In particular, he examines whether income taxes and government spending respond in a stabilizing way to technology shocks in a model with perfect markets. The canonical RBC model fails to match the empirical results.[3] There are, obviously, two possible conclusions from the exercise undertaken by Galí (1994). One is that the empirical findings of the paper were flawed. The other is that RBC models are ill-designed to account for the available evidence, pointing to the importance of introducing market imperfections and other frictions in these models. The recent literature has pursued both avenues.

One potential problem with Galí's empirical approach is that it fails to account for a possible simultaneity bias in ordinary least squares (OLS) estimates of the relationship between government size and macroeconomic stability. One reason for that is provided by Rodrik (1998a) who argues that, precisely because governments tend to stabilize output, one should expect the size of government to be relatively larger in more open economies, which are also more volatile because of their specialization and their exposure to international shocks. Ignoring such reverse causality may result in a downward bias of the estimated impact of government size on macroeconomic stability.

Several recent studies have explicitly attempted to address the simultaneity issue. In a widely cited study, Fatás and Mihov (2001a) replicate Galí's exercise on a cross-section sample of twenty OECD countries over the period 1960–97, using regressions with instrumental variables to solve the possible simultaneity problem. Government size is measured as the (logarithm of the) average ratio of government spending to GDP for the period, while volatility is measured as the standard deviation of the growth rate of real GDP for the same period. Their main finding is that the negative effect of government size on output volatility becomes larger in absolute value and more precisely estimated when the simultaneity bias is corrected. This result is robust to various measures of output volatility and government size.

Kim and Lee (2007) use a Keynesian framework to estimate the impact of government size (measured by the share of total government expenditure in GDP) on economic uncertainty (measured by intersectoral income fluctuation). Their estimates, based on a cross-section sample of fifteen OECD countries over the period 1981–98 and on estimation techniques taking into account the simultaneity argument, confirm that a larger government reduces economic uncertainty.

Having validated (and amplified) Galí's (1994) empirical finding, we now turn to its theoretical puzzle, namely the absence of a clear connection – or even, under some reasonable assumptions, a positive correlation – between government size and volatility in the context of a standard RBC model.

The failure of RBC models to predict basic stylized facts of the relationship between fiscal policy and private behavior has led researchers to incorporate realistic frictions, including market imperfections, nominal rigidities, and non-Ricardian behaviors. For instance, Andrés *et al.* (2007) show that adding nominal rigidities and costs of capital adjustment to a standard RBC model can generate a negative correlation between government size and output volatility. However, in their augmented model, the stabilizing effect of government is only present because of a "composition effect." In fact, increasing the share of government spending in GDP produces two effects in opposite directions. On the one hand, it increases the share of the non-volatile component of GDP; on the other, it increases the volatility of consumption (and investment) in contrast with the empirical findings cited above.

To address this oddity of their model, Andrés and co-authors further introduce credit-constrained (or "rule-of-thumb") consumers, who cannot borrow and lend in financial markets and are therefore constrained to optimize on a period-by-period basis. They find that the modified model is capable of generating a fall in output and consumption volatility when the size of government rises, provided that the rigidities and the proportion of rule-of-thumb consumers are both sufficiently large. This leads them to conclude that models with Keynesian and non-Ricardian features can better replicate the empirical evidence about the effects of fiscal policy on the volatility of output fluctuations than pure RBC models.

3.1.2 ... but the relationship is likely to be a complex one

The basic relationship between government size and output volatility has been extended in several directions. Several researchers have examined the role of the composition of taxes and government expenditure. An important step in this direction is the paper by Buti *et al.* (2003), which argues that automatic stabilizers operate not only on the demand side through their (positive) impact on disposable income, but also on the supply side through the (negative) impact of taxes on production. Distortionary taxes tend to increase the level of equilibrium unemployment and lower potential output. What is more important, however, in the present context is that distortionary taxes also affect the economy's supply response to economic shocks: the more progressive the tax system, the less responsive the supply, because workers demand higher wages to compensate for higher taxes and to maintain their net wages.

Incorporating the supply-side channel of automatic stabilizers in the standard AD/AS model leads to interesting results. Although automatic stabilizers continue to stabilize output in the event of demand shocks, it turns out that they may in fact be destabilizing in the event of supply shocks. Whether or not this is the case depends on the level of taxes: if taxes are above a critical level, a further increase due to the working of automatic stabilizers may result in perverse stabilization effects. Buti and his co-authors find that the critical tax level depends primarily on the size of the economy: the larger the economy, the larger the demand impact of automatic stabilizers relative to the supply impact, and therefore the higher the tax threshold.

Martinez-Mongay and Sekkat (2005) attempt to test the potentially destabilizing effect of taxes on output. They begin by estimating the same equation as Fatás and Mihov (2001a), using total tax revenues as a percentage of GDP to measure government size and the standard deviation of the output gap as a percentage of trend GDP to measure volatility. After corroborating the negative relationship between government size and output volatility, they examine whether the tax mix affects this relationship. In particular, they are interested in testing whether countries with high distortionary taxes display destabilization effects. Since they are focusing on supply effects, they use the effective tax rate on labor to measure the importance of distortionary taxes. They find weak evidence in support of their hypothesis.

The traditional macroeconomic literature on automatic stabilizers tends to focus on taxes and to dismiss the relevance of government spending other than unemployment benefits. Yet the studies reviewed here indicate that researchers who econometrically analyze the link between government size and macroeconomic stabilization use indiscriminately taxes and government spending as measures of government size.

Darby and Mélitz (2007) systematically evaluate the contribution of individual tax and government spending items on automatic stabilization for a cross-country sample of twenty OECD countries for the period 1980–2001. Their data allow a distinction between four revenue[4] and seven expenditure[5] items. The degree of stabilization provided by each tax and spending item is measured by the coefficient of the output gap in regressions of (first differences in) individual budgetary items on a number of macroeconomic variables, including (first differences in) the output gap. The regressions are estimated by instrumental variable techniques in order to account for the potential simultaneity problem between (non-discretionary) fiscal policy and the business cycle. Seemingly unrelated techniques are also used to correct the potential correlation between residuals across individual budgetary items.

Darby and Mélitz estimate two sets of equations: one with budgetary items in levels (constant prices), the other with items in ratios to GDP. The results they obtain differ substantially between the two specifications. When working with levels, they assign most of the stabilization to taxes; when working with ratios, they find that all the contribution to stabilization comes from the spending side. This is clearly an effect of the choice of specification. Because ratios fully reflect GDP fluctuations (through the denominator), public expenditure – which is tied to budget commitments in nominal terms – will *mechanically* exhibit a rising GDP ratio in bad times and a declining one in good times. By contrast, *nominal* revenues automatically decrease in bad times and increase in good times, giving a more stable ratio to GDP. The correct measure of *stabilization* (i.e. the proportion of output shocks effectively *absorbed* by government) is clearly the second one.[6] Looking at their nominal evidence, they find aggregate automatic stabilization in the OECD of around 68 percent: a positive output gap of one euro produces 50 cents more tax revenue and 18 cents less expenditure. Household direct taxes (which constitute 28 percent of total government revenue) alone produce nearly half the total stabilization effect. The authors also present results for the subsample of EU15 countries, which broadly agree with those for the full OECD sample.

Silgoner *et al.* (2003), attempt, like Martinez-Mongay and Sekkat (2005), to test for the presence of a nonlinear threshold effect in the relationship between government size and output stabilization. The authors start by estimating the same (linear) equation as Fatás and Mihov (2001a), but with a number of modifications. First, they remove discretionary fiscal measures from government spending, their measure of government size. Second, they introduce additional instrumental variables to deal with possible reverse causation. Third, their sample covers twelve EU countries for the period 1970–99. Finally, they use five-year averages for the dependent and explanatory variables, instead of averages for the entire period, and do pooled estimation in order to obtain sufficient observations. Their regression results are somewhat surprising. While they obtain OLS estimates for the coefficient of government size that are very similar in size and level of significance to those of Fatás and Mihov (2001a), their instrumental variable estimates are very different. They turn out to be smaller than the OLS estimates – which runs counter to the expectation that OLS produces a downward bias when there are simultaneity problems – and not statistically significant.

Silgoner and her co-authors interpret their results as supportive of the fact that the relationship between government size and output volatility may not be linear. They re-estimate, therefore, a nonlinear model of output variability, where the ratio of government spending (net of discretionary measures) to GDP enters as an explanatory variable in both linear and quadratic forms. They obtain highly significant coefficients for both the linear and the quadratic variables, thereby confirming the existence of nonlinearities. Their results imply a threshold level for government expenditures of about 38 percent of GDP. For government sizes below this threshold there is a significant negative relationship between the government expenditure ratio and GDP growth volatility. Beyond this level, however, the relationship turns positive: an increase in public spending will, ceteris paribus, raise the variability of output growth. Since the median value of the government spending to GDP ratio in the study sample is almost 41 percent, the possibility of destabilizing nondiscretionary public expenditure in Europe seems real.

3.2 Fiscal stabilization is not a free lunch

It is generally recognized that large government size may have detrimental effects on economic efficiency and growth. Most of the related arguments developed in the literature focus on the potential disincentive effects of high taxation and the perverse effects of inappropriate stabilization. There is a longstanding theoretical (e.g. Barro, 1990) and empirical (e.g. de la Fuente, 1997) literature showing that high levels of taxation tend to impair the allocation of resources, mainly by depressing incentives to work, to invest, and/or to save.

There is also some literature arguing that large governments may impinge on efficiency and growth through the working of automatic stabilizers. In particular, van den Noord (2002) sees two potential pitfalls associated with automatic stabilizers. First, there is a risk that automatic stabilizers operate more during slowdowns than booms, which may result in adverse debt dynamics leading eventually to higher taxation and long-term interest rates. Second, large automatic stabilizers may delay necessary adjustment to structural changes if they are associated with public spending and revenue that tend to reduce the flexibility of markets, especially the labor market.

Afonso *et al.* (2005) review the extensive empirical literature on government size and growth in the OECD countries. The authors conclude that: "The evidence on size effects of fiscal variables supports the case for quantitative consolidation with a view to reducing total spending, thus in turn enabling reductions of deficits and lower levels of taxation" (p. 24). At the same time, they insist that: "The review of empirical findings on growth effects of the composition of government activities clarifies that not all kinds of government spending should be treated alike when consolidating public finances" (pp. 24–5). In other words, provided it targets wasteful spending, the reduction in the size of government is likely to raise economic efficiency and growth (see also Tanzi and Schuknecht, 2000).

The debate on the need to reduce the size of government for efficiency reasons has been particularly lively in Europe, where large public spending combined with a rapidly ageing population has often led to unsustainable fiscal positions. The fiscal retrenchment was politically facilitated during the 1990s by the willingness of most EU member states to accept and fulfill the Maastricht criteria in order to qualify for EMU membership. After the introduction of the euro, the consolidation of public finances has continued, although generally less vigorously than before as the Stability and Growth Pact (SGP) has proved to be a softer constraint than the Maastricht entry criteria.

The question raised by Buti *et al.* (2003) is whether there is a potential conflict between efficiency and stabilization in EMU. The question is pertinent because efforts to reduce the size of government by EMU members risk jeopardizing their automatic stabilizers, precisely when they are most needed to compensate for the loss of national monetary policy.

As already alluded to, Buti and co-authors find that this tradeoff may not always be relevant because there may be a critical level of the tax burden beyond which a reduction in taxation may increase the effectiveness of automatic stabilizers. This leads them to conclude that, under certain circumstances, a reduction in the tax burden may in fact result in a "double dividend": gains in efficiency and better automatic stabilizers. The empirical studies by Martinez-Mongay and Sekkat (2005) and Silgoner *et al.* (2003) lend some tentative evidence in support of Buti *et al.*'s conclusion.

3.3 The Great Moderation: why has output volatility declined?

A widely reported stylized fact of the early post-war period was the higher volatility of the US economy in comparison to the European economies – a fact that was often attributed to lower government spending. Yet starting in the mid-1980s, there was a significant decline in US output volatility – what has been dubbed the *Great Moderation* (Bernanke, 2004). Since the late 1990s, the causes of this decline have been discussed in a series of papers, most of which exclusively address developments in the USA. More recently, similar analyses have been conducted in a cross-country perspective.

3.3.1 A large decline in volatility

Basic facts are not a matter for discussion. It is generally recognized that US output volatility has declined by about one-half in comparison to the 1960s and the 1970s (and by about two-thirds in comparison to the 1950s); that the break occurred around 1984 (Kim and Nelson, 1999; McConnell and Perez-Quiros, 2000); that popular explanations such as the increasing share of services in the economy are of little relevance; and that the main proximate causes of the decline in aggregate volatility have been a lower variance of consumption and residential investment, as well as a lower covariance between them (Blanchard and Simon, 2001; Stock and Watson, 2003; IMF, 2007a). Figure 12.1, which updates and complements a figure from Blanchard and Simon, illustrates the magnitude of the decline in the historical volatility of US GDP. It shows that consumption volatility followed a roughly similar evolution (the correlation between the rolling standard deviation of output growth and that of consumption growth is 0.8) and that volatility remains at a historically low level in the 2000s.

Historical volatility
(Five-years standard deviation of growth rates)

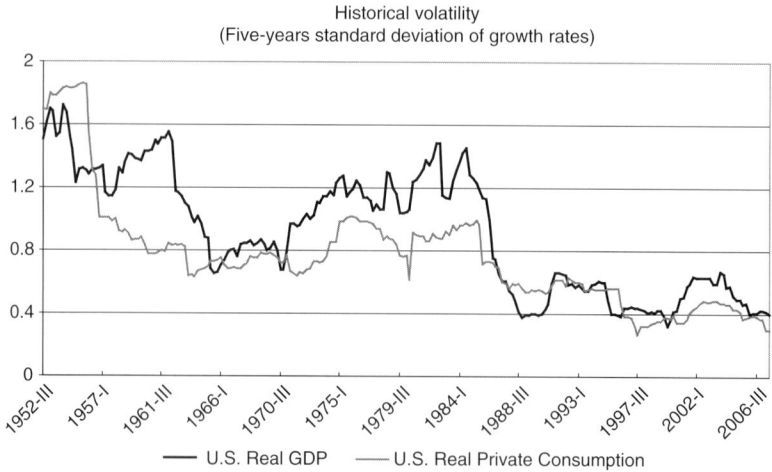

— U.S. Real GDP   —— U.S. Real Private Consumption

Figure 12.1: Historical volatility of US GDP and consumption
Source: BGA.

There is also consensus on the framework best suited to analyzing the reasons for the decline. Stock and Watson (2003), Bernanke (2004), and IMF (2007a) all rely on a "Taylor curve" that corresponds to monetary policy's efficiency frontier (see Figure 12.2). The downward-sloping curve represents the combinations of output and inflation volatility attainable for a given distribution of shocks and a given structure of the economy. The distance between an observation, say point A, and the efficiency frontier characterizes the quality of macroeconomic stabilization. There can also be different combinations such as B and C of output and inflation volatility along the efficiency frontier, which therefore depicts a tradeoff.

3.3.2 Possible explanations
Where there is disagreement is on the causes of the decline in output volatility. Three main categories of explanations have been put forward:

a. an improvement in the performance of macroeconomic (especially monetary) stabilization in comparison to the volatility-generating policy mistakes of the 1970s;
b. structural changes in the economy, resulting for example from a relaxation of the liquidity constraints that affect consumer spending or from leaner inventory management; and

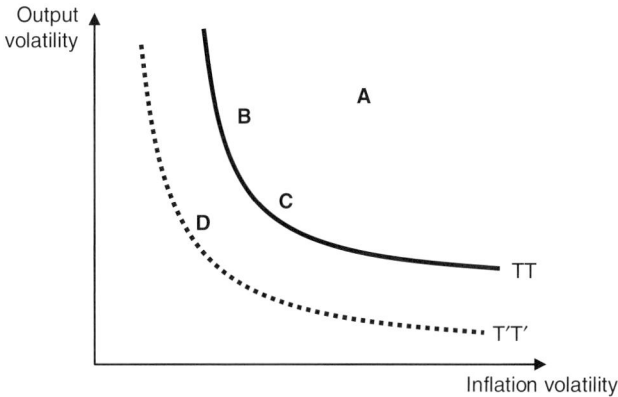

Figure 12.2: The Taylor curve and the inflation-output volatility tradeoff

c. a temporary reduction in the magnitude of shocks, at least in comparison to the oil shocks period of the 1970s, which is generally referred to as the "good luck" factor.

Those three categories of explanation are not mutually exclusive, as indicated by Figure 12.2: better macroeconomic stabilization can result in a move closer to the efficiency frontier (for example from A to B or from A to C), but at the same time there can be an inward shift of that frontier (from TT to T'T'), either as a permanent consequence of a permanent change in the economic structure or as a result of temporary luck.

Research has not reached agreement on the main factors behind the observed reduction in US output volatility. Each of the three main views has supporters: good policies (Bernanke, 2004), structural change (Blanchard and Simon, 2001), and good luck (Stock and Watson, 2003); there are also more eclectic views that attribute the change in output volatility to a combination of good policies and structural changes (IMF, 2007a).

3.3.3 Why there is disagreement

Why has consensus not been reached on what is after all an essentially empirical matter? There are two reasons for that. The first is that policy improvements are hard to isolate from structural and random factors. Figure 12.2 helps to understand why. Let us leave for the moment the discussion on whether the frontier shift is temporary or permanent and assume that the observed combination of output and inflation volatility has moved from A to D. Then policy and structures (or luck) must both be part of the explanation. But decomposing between the two requires determining which combination of inflation and output volatility would have been optimal, had the TT frontier not shifted. Assuming the move has been from A to B and D would lead to ascribing the bulk of the reduction in output volatility to structures (or luck). Assuming it has been from A to C and D would result in ascribing the main role to policy improvements instead. So deciding on what has mattered implies making a judgement on policy optimality, thereby on preferences.

Stock and Watson's (2003) assessment that luck was the main factor behind the reduction in output volatility is not based on a denial of the improvements in monetary policy. On the contrary, they estimate that starting in the mid-1980s the reactions of monetary policy to shocks to output and inflation became more stabilizing (essentially thanks to a rise in the coefficient of inflation in the Taylor rule in comparison with the policy behavior of the 1970s). But they conclude from counterfactual simulations with the policy rules of the 1970s that this change did not play a major role in the observed reduction of aggregate volatility. In other words, they view that reduction as resulting from a move along A-B-D. However, the IMF (2007a) reaches a different conclusion on the basis of a similar, yet more satisfactory, method. Instead of using just one counterfactual policy rule, they construct the efficiency frontier by simulating the outcome of an optimal policy rule for different relative weights of inflation and output volatility. Their conclusion is that improvements in monetary policy account for one-third of the total reduction in output volatility.

The second reason why the empirical analysis does not yield unambiguous results is that structural and random factors are hard to disentangle from each other. Discussion on this issue often tends to rely on an unsystematic reading of the empirical evidence. Exceptions are the IMF (2007a), which assesses changes in the distribution of shocks, and Cecchetti *et al.* (2006), who estimate the share of credit-constrained agents in the economy and the evolution over time in a sample of industrialized countries. The IMF concurs with Stock and Watson (and disagrees with Blanchard and Simon) in concluding that luck dominates structural changes. By contrast, Cecchetti and co-authors concur with Blanchard and Simon in ascribing an important and permanent role in the relaxation of credit constraints. A recent paper by Giannone *et al.* (2008a) brings an additional and interesting dimension to the discussion.

It points out that the typical reliance on small- or medium-scale models leads to overstating the role of "good luck" compared to structural factors because these models tend to omit structural variables.

Summing up, this literature focuses on the time dimension that is generally neglected in cross-countries studies, and hence complements them. Its most relevant conclusion for the issue we investigate in this chapter is that the desirability of automatic stabilization cannot be taken as exogenous. From a macroeconomic standpoint, government size can be substituted by better discretionary policies (either monetary or fiscal), by financial development (better access to credit) and by more resilient structures (leaner inventory management). To the extent that those factors have played a role in the reduction of aggregate macroeconomic volatility, they reduce the benefits of automatic stabilization through bigger governments.

4. Government size, fiscal stabilization and volatility

As our selective review of the literature suggests, the relationship between the magnitude of automatic stabilizers (government size) and macroeconomic volatility remains vexingly elusive. On the one hand, theoretical models rely on ad hoc features to replicate the stylized fact that large governments produce more macroeconomic stability than their leaner counterparts. On the other hand, existing empirical analyses indicate that the relationship between government size and macroeconomic volatility is strong but likely to be complex (non-linear), and that it may have changed over time as time-series evidence appears at odds with cross-sectional regularities.

This section sets the stage for a more formal empirical analysis by providing descriptive evidence on the size of government, macroeconomic volatility, and on the role of fiscal stabilization policies in supporting consumption smoothing. We illustrate the contrast between time-series and cross-sectional evidence. For data availability reasons and to ensure comparability with the existing literature, we focus on a sample of twenty OECD countries[7] over the period 1960–2006.

4.1 The end of big government?

Government size in OECD countries, as measured by the ratio of general government expenditure to GDP, has exhibited strikingly

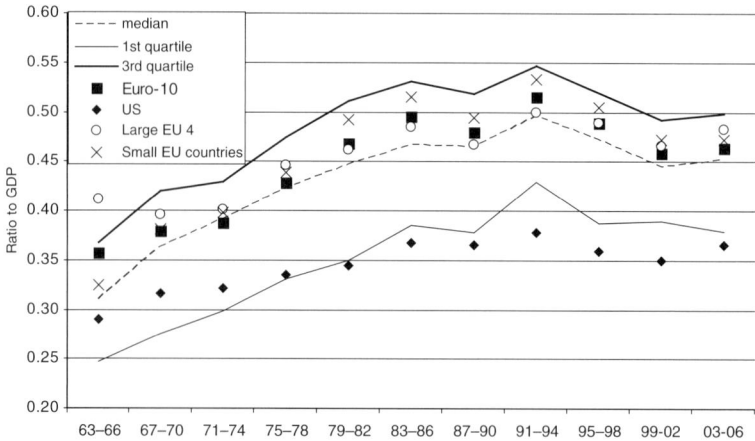

Figure 12.3: Total expenditure to GDP ratio (1963–2006)

similar time trends over the last four decades (Figure 12.3), with a significant increase until the first half of the 1990s followed by a moderate downsizing. Notable exceptions include the USA, where the size of government has remained broadly constant since the mid-1980s, and the UK, where a downward trend began in the mid-1980s before being reversed recently. From a cross-country perspective, European countries, and especially the smaller economies (except Ireland and Greece), consistently remained in the higher end of the distribution, as predicted by Rodrik's (1998a) argument. On average, euro-area members,[8] which make up half of our sample, closely followed the median over the entire period.

Overall, while the cross-country distribution of government size appears to have been fairly stable over time, time trends suggest that "something happened" in the mid-1990s. Why this has taken place is outside the scope of this chapter.

4.1.1 Is social security the determinant of cross-country differences?

Given our focus on the nexus between fiscal stabilization and government size, it seems natural to refine the analysis by distinguishing between expenditure items that are by design part of a public insurance scheme – namely social security (SS) transfers – and those that are not. Social security is stabilization by definition (the very purpose of unemployment insurance, welfare benefits, and old-age insurance is to reduce fluctuations in individual income) and the building of large social insurance systems may reflect a greater preference or need for fiscal stabilization. But it could also be argued that significant portions of social security spending, including the health and pension pillars, are not obviously public by nature and can be placed in private hands without materially affecting their insurance function or the "automatic stabilizer" role of transfers to these schemes (health care premiums, pension payments or social contributions). Under the first hypothesis, the size of SS transfers would be the key to detecting a preference for stability. Under the second, trends in SS spending would simply reflect either changes in the demand for (or relative price of) these insurance products or changes in the relative shares of private and public providers of insurance, not a change in the preference/need for stabilization (or the perceived cost of it). In both cases, it is instructive to compare trends in SS and non-SS expenditures (Figure 12.4).

Broadly similar developments have affected both SS and non-SS spending over the last forty years. However, it appears that the rise in spending from the 1960s to the 1980s was more pronounced for SS spending (median spending increased by a factor of 2.5) and that also the bulk of the recent downsizing took place in non-SS expenditure, whereas SS-related outlays essentially stabilized relative to GDP. Correspondingly, SS spending nowadays typically amounts to one-third of total spending against one-fifth in the early 1960s. If the first hypothesis is correct, this composition shift could have increased the stabilizing character of government spending.

From a cross-country perspective, differences in government size appear to be more driven by differences in non-SS spending than by differences in the size of social security systems. Therefore, neither expenditure trends nor cross-country differences can be explained by variations in the size of social security systems. A natural implication is that the demand for fiscal stabilization cannot be disentangled from the general public's appetite for public goods, income redistribution, and government intervention.

4.1.2 Openness and government size

Looking into possible determinants of these empirical regularities, Rodrik's (1998a) argument that more open economies may find it desirable to have bigger governments seems highly relevant. Cross-sectional evidence shows that the positive relationship between government size and trade openness holds for our sample (Figure 12.5, top

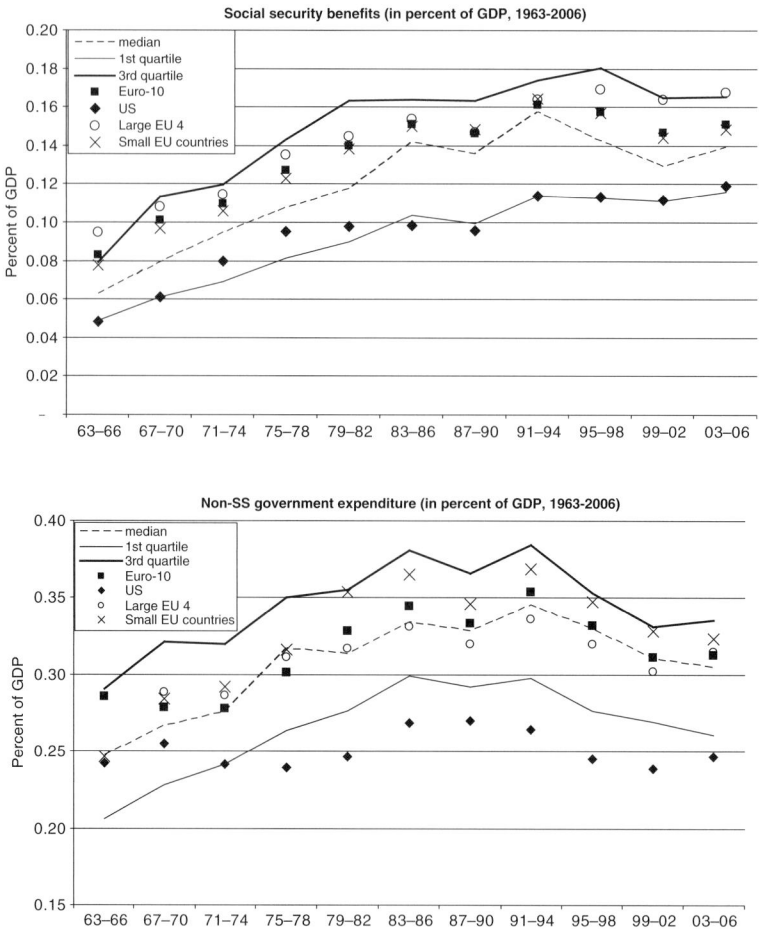

Figure 12.4: Social security vs. non-social security expenditure (ratio to GDP 1963–2006)

panel). Over time, however, the link weakens considerably after the mid-1990s (compare top right and bottom left panels in Figure 12.5) as changes in trade openness are negatively related to changes in government size (Figure 12.5, bottom right panel). Although the latter result is evidently driven by two outliers (Belgium, denoted by a dot, and Ireland, denoted by a triangle), the contrast between time-series and cross-sectional evidence remains striking.

The negative time-series correlation between government size and trade openness (or even the absence thereof) thus suggests qualifying

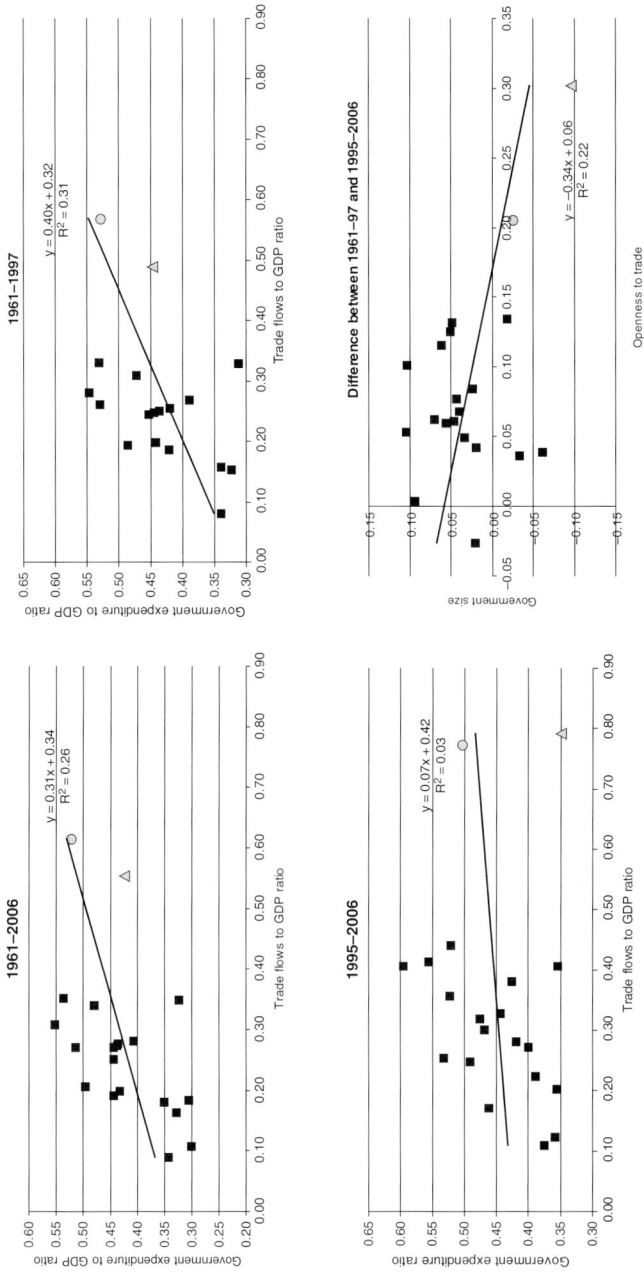

Figure 12.5: Openness to trade and government size

Rodrik's point by accounting for the existence of potential "collateral benefits" to trade openness in terms of stabilization. Specifically, if stronger trade linkages are accompanied by heightened financial integration and a smoother functioning of global and domestic financial intermediation, both the need for fiscal stabilization and the costs of producing it could have changed. On the one hand, an open capital account expands opportunities for smoothing economy-wide consumption and increases pressures for adopting market-friendly reforms, especially in the financial sector (Kose *et al.*, 2006). Greater financial openness coupled with a strengthening of domestic financial market institutions may therefore reduce the need for fiscal stabilization. On the other hand, global competition puts pressure on tax bases, and places a premium on less distortive tax systems and less regulated markets, which increases the marginal cost of "producing" fiscal stabilization. These arguments seem particularly relevant for the euro area where financial integration has been proceeding at a rapid pace (see Decressin *et al.*, 2007).

4.2 The Great Moderation: beyond the USA

We now move to addressing the evolution of volatility and its relationship to the two broad characteristics of countries assessed as relevant by the literature: openness and government size.

4.2.1 Volatility over four decades

We first look at the evolution of output volatility in our sample of countries since the early 1960s. Our preferred measure is the standard deviation of quarterly GDP growth rates over eleven quarters, which allows us to compare results obtained with country characteristics over the same periods.

The decline in output volatility pointed out in US studies is a general trend which started in the 1980s in the USA but took place somewhat later in other countries (Figure 12.6). One interesting observation is that this decline was significantly more pronounced in the more volatile economies, so that the variance diminished dramatically from the 1960s to the 2000s; and, second, that the USA, which was among the volatile economies in the 1970s, has been since the late 1980s among the least volatile ones.

A second observation is that more open economies also experienced a decline in volatility, but seem to remain more vulnerable to shocks and

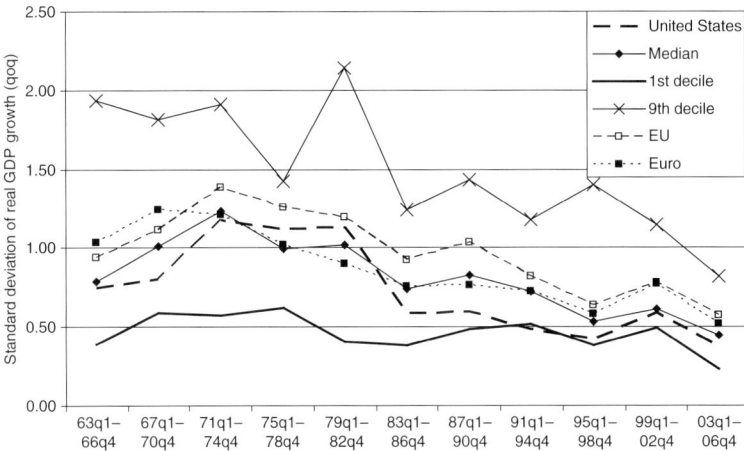

Figure 12.6: The Great Moderation (1963–2006)

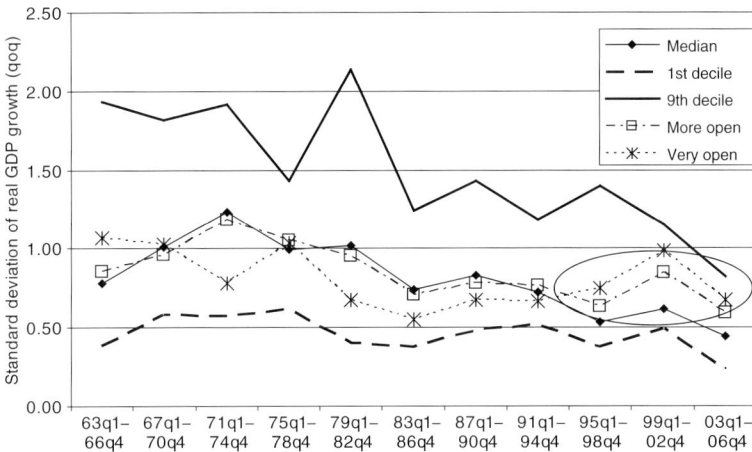

Figure 12.7: The Great Moderation: more open economies (1963–2006)

global downturns (Figure 12.7). In spite of an increased ability to smooth out fluctuations through accessing world capital markets, they have recently exhibited above-average inflation. If anything, the relationship between openness and volatility seems to have strengthened.

4.2.2 Where has volatility declined?
To find out which characteristic matters, we now consider a matrix splitting countries into four categories combining openness and government-size

criteria (cut-off levels for each criterion are the median) and we also consider two subperiods, 1961–97 (the Fatás-Mihov sample) and 1995–2006.

The top and medium panels of Figure 12.8 indicate that, for the whole period as well as in the first subperiod, volatility is greater in countries with smaller governments and that more open economies tend to be more volatile than closed economies despite having larger governments. This reproduces the standard stylized facts pointed out in the literature.

The bottom panel displays the evidence for the last decade 1995–2006. It appears that volatility has decreased much more in relatively closed countries with smaller governments than anywhere else, and that more open economies remain more volatile, especially if their governments are small. So the relationship between volatility and government size only holds for open economies while that between openness and volatility holds across the board.

This leads us to test the implications for a bivariate expression of the Fatás-Mihov-Galí relationship. When re-estimated over the 1995–2006 period, it breaks down entirely (Figure 12.9). We also test for a relationship with government size measured either by social security or non-social security spending. In both cases we find that the relationship held good in the 1961–97 period but has disappeared in more recent times.

The factor behind this breakdown is that the reduction in volatility has been on average weaker in countries with larger governments. This is evidenced in Figure 12.10, which plots the relationship between government size and the decline in volatility.

The reasons why countries with larger governments have failed to fully benefit from the Great Moderation are unclear and call for a more detailed analysis, with a view to identifying which factors do not apply to the countries with big governments (through interaction terms, see Section 5). Is it that the benefits of financial deepening have been higher in small-government countries, because markets have substituted what was previously a (lack of) government-induced stabilization? Is it because shocks have been small over the last decade, which has made automatic stabilizers temporarily less relevant? Or could it be that countries with larger governments (many of them in the euro area) have simply not experienced improved monetary policy management, for instance because of inappropriate exchange rate regimes? Finally, it may be the case that governments contribute little to stabilization after all because the operation of automatic stabilizers has been offset by discretionary actions.

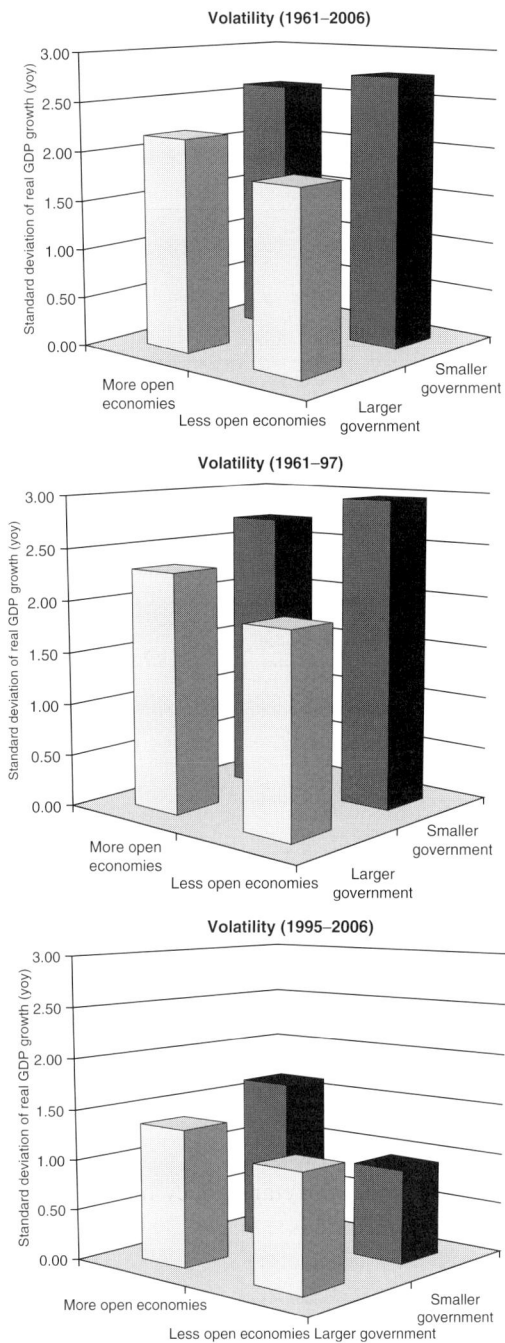

Figure 12.8: Volatility by country groupings: openness and government size

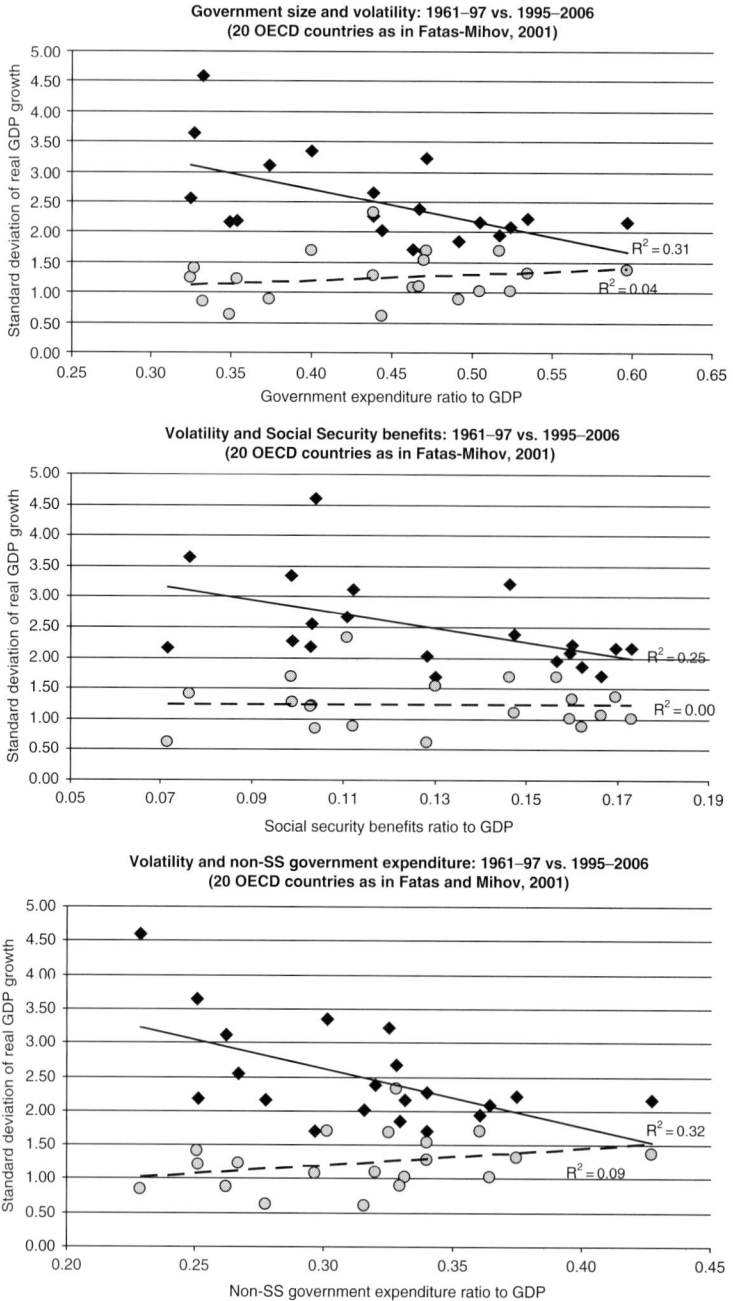

Figure 12.9: The changing relationship between volatility and government size

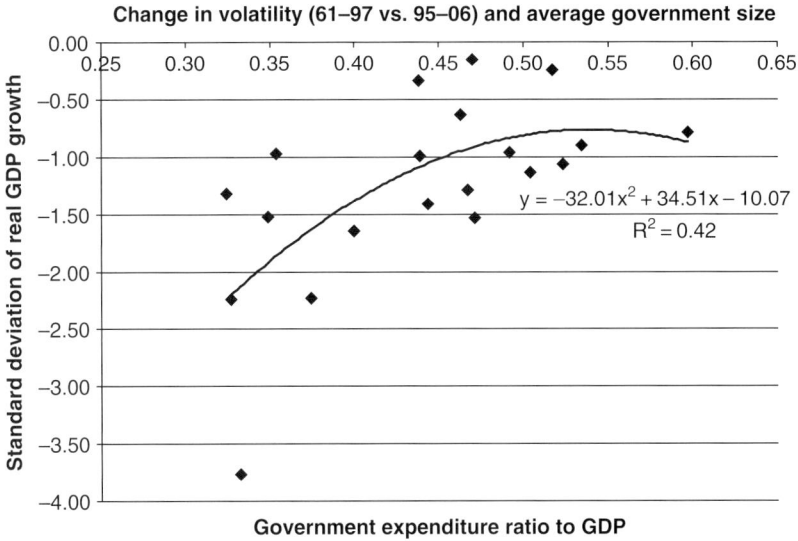

Change in volatility (61–97 vs. 95–06) and average government size

$y = -32.01x^2 + 34.51x - 10.07$

$R^2 = 0.42$

Standard deviation of real GDP growth

Government expenditure ratio to GDP

Figure 12.10: Government size and change in output volatility

4.3 *What stabilizes private consumption?*

As discussed above, consumers able to optimally adjust their savings could maintain a stable consumption profile regardless of transitory income fluctuations. In the extreme case of perfect and complete markets, income disturbances would be irrelevant for welfare as individuals would have unrestricted access to credit and could trade a wide array of contingent claims. It is therefore important to find out what lies behind the volatility of aggregate private consumption, and whether this has changed over time, while volatility in income was steadily declining. Particular attention is paid to the behavior of fiscal variables (income taxes and transfers) and savings. In doing so, we use the period budget identity of a representative consumer (i) to decompose the variance of real household consumption (C_i) into its key components, namely personal primary income (Y_i), direct taxes (T_i), social transfers (B_i), and households' savings (S_i):

$$C_i = Y_i - T_i + B_i - S_i + \varepsilon_i, \tag{1}$$

where ε_i is a residual that includes items not taken into account in primary income such as interest payments (income) on outstanding

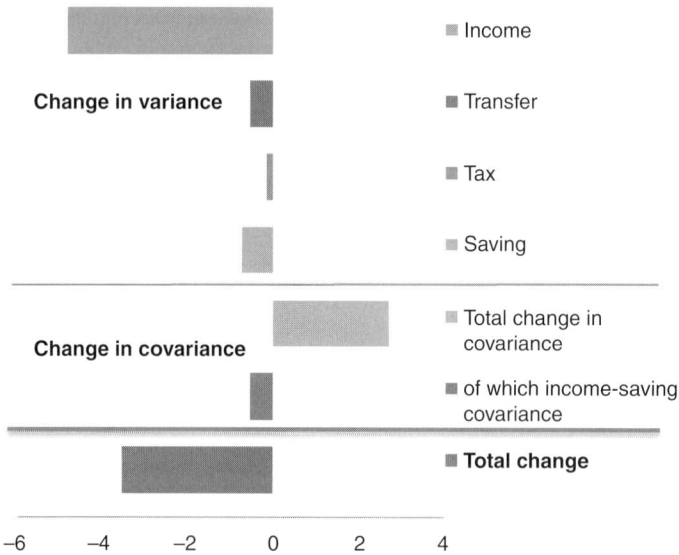

Figure 12.11: Variance decomposition of US household consumption, pre- and post-1984
Sources: OECD and authors' calculations.

liabilities (assets). The variance of C_i can therefore be decomposed as follows:

$$Var(C) = Var(Y) + Var(T) + Var(B) + Var(S) \\ + 2[Cov(Y,T) + Cov(Y,B) + Cov(Y,S) + Z],$$

where Z stands for all other covariance terms.

We compute this decomposition for the USA and major European countries, distinguishing between pre- and post-1984 periods.[9] Figure 12.11 first summarizes the results for the USA. It shows that the decline in the variance of income accounts for the largest fraction of the reduced variance of consumption. A lower variance of savings and a lower (initially positive) covariance between savings and consumption also contribute to reducing consumption fluctuations, but to a significantly lesser degree. Changes in covariances contribute to increasing volatility because of a significantly lower (negative) correlation between income and transfers. There is no meaningful change in the income-tax correlation. Our analysis of US data thus suggests that (i) consumption volatility has declined in line with income volatility; (ii) automatic stabilizers have not contributed to this decline, quite to the contrary:

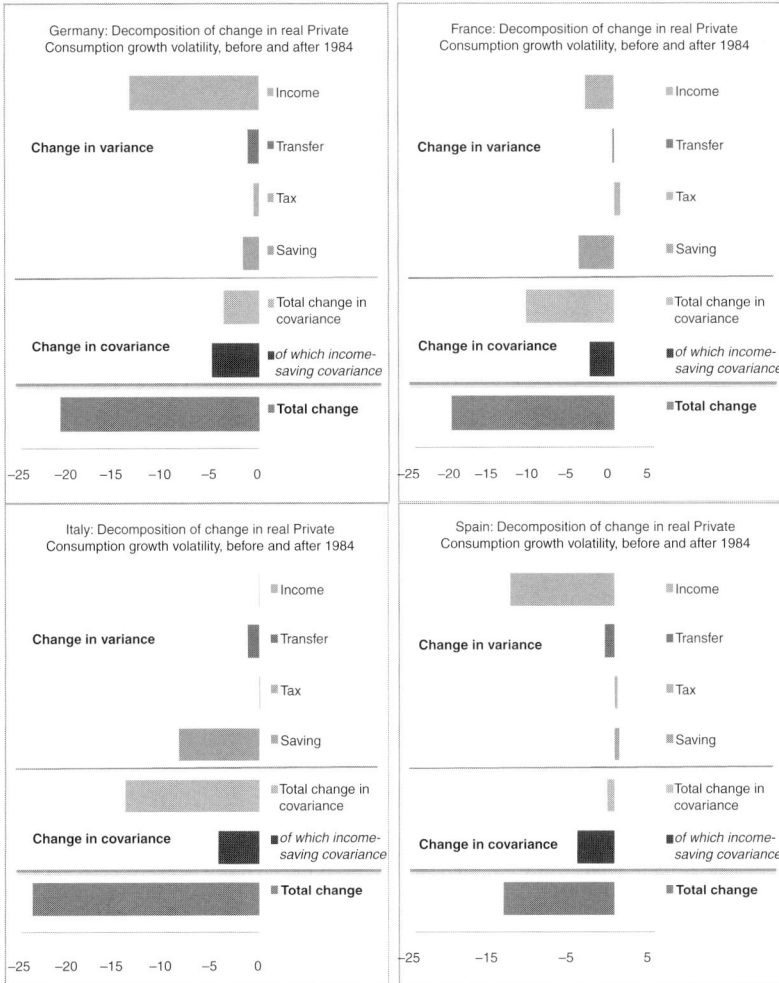

Figure 12.12: Variance decomposition of household consumption in selected euro-area countries, pre- and post-1984
Sources: OECD and authors' calculations.

the insurance role of transfers seems to have declined; and (iii) financial development has played a role – albeit a minor one.

We do the same exercise for the four largest euro-area economies, namely France, Germany, Italy, and Spain (see Figure 12.12). We find that all four experienced a very large decline in the variance of consumption. In Germany, Spain and to a lesser extent France, lower income volatility accounts for the largest fraction of this decline. With the exception of Spain, the decline in the variance of savings is also substantial, and in all four countries there is a reduction in the (initially positive) covariance between savings and income. Household saving behavior seems to be more consistent with buffering income shocks and correspondingly less prone to precautionary saving in bad times. Finally, changes in taxes and transfers seem to have played no meaningful role in the reduction of consumption volatility.

These observations are consistent with the view that the change in government size is unlikely to have contributed to lower consumption volatility, and that the latter has instead been driven by the overall reduction in output volatility and more countercyclical saving behavior (to which financial development may have contributed).

5. A fresh look at the link between government size and volatility

As discussed above, there are two main reasons as to why large governments are expected to contribute more to output stability than small ones. The first is that the magnitude of automatic stabilizers depends primarily on the size of the government sector (Galí, 1994; Girouard and André, 2005); the second results from a composition effect of domestic expenditure. Specifically, if the response of public spending to the business cycle is muted, it mechanically contributes to the stability of aggregate demand (Darby and Mélitz, 2007).

The stylized facts presented in the previous sections fail to provide overwhelming support for the general argument. Looking at time series, it seems clear that volatility is unrelated to government size. And from a cross-country perspective, the well-documented negative relationship between government size and volatility seems to have broken down in the mid-1990s as the general decline in output volatility among OECD countries was less pronounced in those countries with relatively larger governments.

Econometric techniques are now needed to examine more rigorously the conditional correlations among these variables and to establish causality. A natural way to proceed is to merge arguments about the link between government size and volatility with those about the Great Moderation to obtain a more complete picture of the key determinants of output volatility. Indeed, interesting correlations may emerge both from time-series and cross-sectional dimensions of the data, calling for a panel-data analysis. Our panel includes annual data averaged over ten years.[10] In our view, that time span strikes a good balance between the need to have sufficient observations and the desirability to minimize purely cyclical effects – such as mechanical increases (decreases) in expenditure-to-GDP ratios during downturns (upturns).

5.1 Specification and econometric issues

As theory provides limited guidance, if any, on the specification of a growth-volatility model, we focus on a parsimonious set of explanatory variables identified as relevant in the literature. Indeed, our objective is not to uncover a new powerful explanation of recent trends through an exhaustive search process, but to take a hard look at conventional wisdom in the face of these new trends, and suggest policy implications.

Our starting point is the standard analysis of Fatás and Mihov (2001a), which we extend in three directions. First, we reduce concerns about the small size of the sample (twenty OECD countries)[11] by exploiting the time dimension through panel-data analysis. Second, the panel approach allows us to test for two central hypotheses of the Great Moderation debate, namely improvements in the conduct of monetary policy, and greater financial development. While a more credible anchoring of inflationary expectations is expected to facilitate countercyclical actions by monetary authorities, expanded access to credit should result in a smoother aggregate consumption path because more individuals can self-insure against adverse income shocks. These two hypotheses are essential in our investigation because financial markets and monetary policy are two primary substitutes for fiscal stabilization. Specifically, we conjecture that in comparison to an economy with dysfunctional monetary and financial institutions, a financially developed economy with credible monetary authorities would likely (i) have a smaller government; and (ii), for a given size of government, contribute less to fiscal stabilization.[12] We approach the second issue by introducing interaction variables in the model. Interaction terms will also inform us about possible causes of the apparent breakdown in the relationship between government size and volatility in the 1990s, and in particular whether this is related to greater monetary policy credibility and improved access to financial intermediation during that period. The third difference with Fatás and Mihov (2001a) follows from Buti *et al.* (2003), who suggested that the relationship between government size and volatility could be non-linear. We therefore allow for non-constant "returns" of government size in terms of output stability.

The unrestricted form of the estimated equation is as follows:

$$Y_{i,t} = \alpha_0 + \sum_{t=2}^{5} \alpha_t P_t + \theta_1 G_{i,t} + \theta_2 G_{i,t}^2$$

$$+ \sum_{j=1}^{J} \beta_j X_{j,i,t} + \sum_{j=1}^{J} \gamma_j G_{i,t} X_{j,i,t} + \varepsilon_{i,t}, \tag{2}$$

with $i = 1, \ldots, 20$, and $t = 1, \ldots, 5$;

where the dependent variable Y denotes real GDP volatility, G symbolizes government size, X is a vector of other explanatory variables, P_t's are period fixed-effects, and $\varepsilon_{i,t}$ is an error term. Estimates of γ_j's and θ_2 provide direct tests of the interactions and non-linearities discussed above. We also performed so-called "spline" regressions, using the term $\theta_2 D_{i,t}(G_{i,t} - G^*)$ instead of $\theta_2 G_{i,t}^2$, where $D_{i,t}$ is a binary variable equal to 1 when G exceeds a given threshold G^* and equal to 0 otherwise. By allowing for a kink in the relationship between Y and G, the "spline" term can be useful in pinning down threshold effects provided that there exists a G^* for which the overall fit of the model is materially better than for alternative thresholds.

Following Fatás and Mihov (2001a), our preferred measures of government size and output volatility are the logarithm of the general government's expenditure-to-GDP ratio, and the standard deviation of real GDP growth, respectively. While the expenditure ratio is a proxy for the magnitude of automatic stabilizers, the measure of volatility raises two issues. The first is that it captures variations in potential growth (over time and across countries) which, as such, should not trigger a stabilizing response from macroeconomic policies. However, all the results discussed below are robust to the use of an alternative volatility measure not subject to the same problem – the standard deviation of first-differenced output gaps – and to the introduction of average real GDP growth as a control variable (see Table 12.5 in the Appendix). The second concern is that the focus on GDP volatility (as opposed to private consumption volatility) is questionable because the estimated stabilizing effect of government size would also reflect composition effects in addition to private consumption smoothing.

While we do not dispute that private consumption volatility is closer to generally accepted welfare metrics, we have documented above the high positive correlation between these two measures. Moreover, we believe that the eventual composition effect (or the absence thereof) is an integral part of the stabilization debate and should be preserved. One reason is that government spending could also be a source of shocks that would only be imperfectly reflected in private consumption. The opposite argument holds: government expenditure (e.g. public investment) could be used to enact discretionary stabilization packages without immediate effect on private consumption but with an undeniably *stabilizing* impact on the overall economy.

All equations are estimated with ordinary least squares (OLS), adjusting standard errors for the presence of heteroskedasticity. As we introduce only two key determinants of the Great Moderation, our estimates may suffer from bias due to the *omission of variables* explaining variations in output volatility over time. To alleviate this concern, the panel regressions include time fixed-effects, a choice largely supported by the corresponding specification tests. Time fixed-effects also ensure that our estimates are driven by cross-country variations under the assumption that the same model applies to each period. The focus on the cross-sectional dimension of the sample is in line with the existing literature. To reduce concerns about omitted cross-country determinants of output volatility, we test the robustness of our results to the introduction of plausible control variables (see Table 12.6 in the Appendix).[13]

As discussed in Section 3, another source of concern in the absence of strong theoretical priors is that estimates derived from a single-equation approach may be biased by *reverse causation*, that is the possibility that volatility itself affects the delivery of insurance against macroeconomic risk, including through automatic stabilizers, monetary policy, and financial intermediation. In particular, more open economies tend to opt for larger governments *because* of their intrinsically greater exposure to external shocks and a correspondingly greater appetite for fiscal stabilization (Rodrik, 1998a). If sufficiently large, such reverse causality would create an upward bias in the OLS estimates of θ_1, and possibly also in the β's and the γ_j's corresponding to Great Moderation variables. We therefore explicitly tested for possible endogeneity problems and took that into account in our estimation to correct for any bias (see Table 12.7 in Appendix). In general, we found no evidence of a

statistically significant bias related to reverse causality running from
volatility to government size. This is in contrast to Fatás and Mihov
(2001a) and can be explained by the fact that the time-series dimension
of our sample is likely to attenuate that particular reverse causation
problem – more related to a cross-country argument (i.e. the link
between openness and volatility). Only the measure of monetary policy
quality (QMP) used in our regressions – the exponential deviation of
inflation from a 2 percent target, as in IMF (2007a) – fails the exogeneity test at the 10 percent level of significance.[14] Because our results
appeared robust to using an index of central bank independence instead
of QMP (see Tables 12.8 to 12.10 in the Appendix), we kept the latter in
our regression for the sake of comparability with existing analyses.

5.2 Results

The first step in our empirical analysis is to assess the extent to which the
time dimension of our sample is affecting the strong negative cross-
sectional relationship between government size and output volatility
documented in Galí (1994) and Fatás and Mihov (2001a). Table 12.1
displays estimates obtained with a parsimonious version of equation (2)
explaining volatility by the size of government and the degree of openness to trade.[15] For the sake of comparison with previous studies, we
report both cross-country and panel regressions for different time spans
of the sample. First, although trade openness tends to increase volatility,
the effect is in general not statistically significant, and quantitatively
sensitive to time. Second, the negative relationship between government size and volatility weakens dramatically when the sample
includes the post-1990 periods. In fact, when the sample is truncated
to include only the 1991–2007 period, the relationship turns positive,
although it remains statistically non-significant. Similar results hold
when our alternative measure of output volatility is used, and when
additional control variables (GDP per capita at PPP and average real
growth) are introduced (Appendix Tables 12.5 and 12.6). This first
exercise suggests that the Galí (1994) and Fatás-Mihov (2001a)
results may be specific to the small sample used in their study (twenty
observations and time averages heavily influenced by pre-1990 observations). In subsequent regressions, we focus on results obtained
for the full panel (that includes all available data points over 1961–
2007).

Table 12.1: *Government size and volatility: basic results*

	Cross-section OLS				Pooled OLS			
	Dependent variable: standard deviation of real GDP growth							
	1	2	3	4	5	6	7	8
	1961–2000	1961–90	1961–2007	1991–2007	1961–2000	1961–90	1961–2007	1991–2007
Openness	0.76	1.98	0.40	0.60	1.35*	2.20***	0.84	0.54
	(0.66)	(1.49)	(0.48)	(0.87)	(1.67)	(2.79)	(1.56)	(0.79)
Government size	−1.34*	−2.23***	−0.90	0.42	−1.78***	−2.68***	−1.32**	0.61
	(−1.72)	(−2.88)	(−1.37)	(0.58)	(−2.60)	(4.35)	(−2.37)	(0.81)
Constant	0.61	−0.47	0.90	1.57**	−0.36	−1.59*	0.30	1.36
	(0.63)	(−0.46)	(1.16)	(2.25)	(−0.39)	(1.98)	(0.41)	(1.64)
N. obs.	20	19	20	20	71	51	91	40
Time fixed-effects (p-value)	...	...	...	...	0.09	0.00	0.00	0.00
R-squared	0.16	0.36	0.11	0.08	0.24	0.43	0.38	0.31

Notes: Robust t-statistics are reported in parentheses. Panel regressions include time effects. The p-value of the time-effects test is associated with the null hypothesis (F-test) that all period effects are jointly equal to zero.

Although the inclusion of time fixed-effects should prevent any statistical bias related to the omission of determinants of output volatility over time, it is useful to check the extent to which progress in the quality of monetary policy and financial development (FD) – two potential substitutes for fiscal stabilization – plays a significant role in reducing volatility when the size of government is taken into account (table 12.2).[16] Both variables seem to individually contribute to lower volatility over and above the contribution of automatic stabilizers[17] (columns 1 and 2). Interestingly, the estimated effect of government size appears to weaken when QMP is present, while it seems unaffected by the introduction of FD. This may point to a greater substitutability between monetary and fiscal stabilization than between the latter and expanded opportunities for individuals to smooth consumption through financial intermediation. However, when both QMP and FD are simultaneously included, their respective effects are not fully robust to time dummies, especially for FD (columns 3 and 4), which becomes statistically insignificant. This suggests that other related developments (omitted here) may have played a role in the decline of output volatility.

Allowing for the impact of government size to vary over time – one coefficient for the period 1961–90 and another for the period 1991–2007 – confirms the apparent break in the stabilizing role of government size after 1990 (column 5), while leaving the estimated role of FD and QMP largely unchanged. This indicates that the structural break cannot be (entirely) due to the emergence of substitutes to fiscal stabilization. Yet the weak role played by FD and QMP when fiscal stabilization is taken into account contrasts with the conventional Great Moderation literature, where these two variables seem to matter more. The last step in our investigation is therefore to test more directly for the possibility that, for a given size of government, the impact of fiscal stabilization is contingent on the presence of alternative ways for economic agents to insure against macroeconomic risk. It is also important to consider the hypothesis of decreasing returns in terms of fiscal stabilization with larger governments as one possible reason for the structural break of the 1990s, when the size of governments reached a peak in most OECD countries.[18]

Table 12.3 explores the role of two interaction terms – between FD and government size, and between the latter and QMP– and one non-linearity – the square of government size.[19] To help in reading

Table 12.2: *Government size and the Great Moderation (pooled OLS, 1961–2007)*

	Dependent variable: standard deviation of real GDP growth				
	1	2	3	4	5
Openness	0.81	0.77	0.25	0.77	0.95*
	(1.52)	(1.46)	(0.41)	(1.46)	(1.77)
Government size (all	−1.06*	−1.40**	−0.83	−1.15*	...
sample)	(−1.92)	(−2.48)	(−1.58)	(−1.94)	
Government size	...	...	...	...	−1.98***
(1961–90)					(−3.43)
Government size	...	...	...	...	0.45
(1991–2007)					(0.60)
Quality of monetary	−1.36***	...	−1.79***	−1.12*	−0.95*
policy[1]	(−2.51)		(−3.13)	(−1.88)	(−1.67)
Financial	...	−0.40**	−0.41***	−0.27	−0.17
development[2]		(−1.94)	(−2.65)	(−1.21)	(−0.83)
Constant	1.91**	0.37	2.92***	1.68*	0.47
	(2.05)	(0.53)	(4.03)	(1.71)	(0.51)
N. obs.	91	90	90	90	90
Time fixed-effects:					
p-value	0.00	0.00	...	0.00	0.00
included	yes	yes	no	yes	yes
R-squared	0.41	0.40	0.30	0.42	0.49

Notes: Robust t-statistics are reported in parentheses. Panel regressions include time effects. The p-value of the time-effects test is associated with the null hypothesis (F-test) that all period effects are jointly equal to zero.

[1] IMF measure (exponential deviation from a 2 percent inflation target, see September 2007 World Economic Outlook).

[2] Financial development is measured as the total credit by deposit money banks to the private sector in percent of GDP.

Table 12.3: *Government size and volatility: interactions and non-linearities (pooled OLS, 1961–2007)*

	1	2	3	4	5	6	7	8	9	10
	Dependent variable: standard deviation of real GDP growth									
Openness	0.74	0.73	0.70	0.90*	0.20	0.73	0.48	0.13	0.62	0.71
	(1.45)	(1.34)	(1.25)	(1.78)	(0.34)	(1.40)	(1.02)	(0.21)	(1.12)	(1.41)
Government size (GS)	−2.74***	−5.04**	3.34	...	−2.77***	−2.47***	−2.10***	2.16	1.94	...
	(−3.26)	(−2.23)	(1.42)		(−3.94)	(−3.50)	(−2.70)	(0.86)	(0.82)	
Financial development (FD)	1.42*	...	...	...	...	...	...	...	...	...
	(1.83)									
Quality of monetary policy (QMP)	...	3.35	...	...	...	...	...	...	...	...
		(1.32)								
GDP per capita (at PPP)	...	...	...	...	...	...	−0.01	...	...	...
							(−0.59)			
Average real growth	...	...	...	...	...	...	0.09	...	...	...
							(1.19)			
Non-linear terms:										
Interaction GS*FD	1.92**	...	...	...	0.50***	0.38	0.29	0.35**	0.25	0.31
	(2.35)				(2.85)	(1.49)	(1.09)	(2.41)	(1.17)	(1.43)
Interaction GS*QMP	...	4.60*	...	...	1.83***	1.21*	1.31**	2.01***	1.35**	1.41**
		(1.74)			(3.12)	(1.83)	(2.01)	(3.76)	(2.19)	(2.17)
Squared GS	...	...	2.37**	0.76***	...	...	...	2.55**	2.25*	1.35***
			(2.03)	(2.90)				(2.09)	(1.92)	(4.18)
Constant	−0.99	−2.10	2.35*	0.73*	1.02	0.51	0.68	3.34***	2.57*	1.66***
	(−1.06)	(−0.95)	(1.85)	(1.66)	(1.08)	(0.68)	(0.84)	(2.54)	(1.87)	(2.86)

	Marginal effect on volatility of an increase in...[1]									
Financial development if										
government expenditure is 35 percent of GDP	−0.60	...	...	...	−0.52	−0.40	−0.30	−0.37	−0.26	−0.33
government expenditure is 50 percent of GDP	0.09	...	...	...	−0.35	−0.26	−0.20	−0.24	−0.17	−0.21
Quality of monetary policy if										
government expenditure is 35 percent of GDP	...	−1.48	...	...	−1.92	−1.27	−1.38	−2.11	−1.42	−1.48
government expenditure is 50 percent of GDP	...	0.16	...	...	−1.27	−0.84	−0.91	−1.39	−0.94	−0.98
Size of government if										
expenditure is 35 percent of GDP	−1.30	−1.03	−1.65	−1.60	−0.80	−1.13	−0.74	−1.18	−1.42	−1.37
expenditure is 50 percent of GDP	−1.30	−1.03	0.05	−1.05	−0.80	−1.13	−0.74	0.64	0.18	−0.41
N. obs.	90	90	91	91	90	90	90	90	90	90
Time fixed-effects:										
p-value	0.00	0.00	0.00	0.00	...	0.00	0.00	...	0.00	0.00
included	yes	yes	yes	yes	no	yes	yes	no	yes	yes
R-squared	0.44	0.45	0.43	0.41	0.33	0.44	0.46	0.38	0.49	0.48

Notes: Robust t-statistics are reported in parentheses. The F-test is associated with the null hypothesis that all time effects are jointly equal to zero.

[1] Numbers show the value of the estimated derivative function of volatility with respect to the relevant explanatory variable. Bold numbers denote cases where all estimated coefficients used in the calculations are statistically different from zero. The marginal impact of government size is measured at sample mean of FD and QMP.

the results (the reader should bear in mind that the logarithm of government size is always negative), the middle panel of table 12.3 displays the marginal effects of our variables of interest on volatility, with bold numbers identifying effects for which all the estimated coefficients involved in the calculation are statistically different from zero.

A number of novel insights emerge from these results. First, government size plays a statistically significant stabilization role across a wide range of specifications, regardless of the combination of interaction terms, non-linearities, and control variables. This underscores the importance of studying the stabilization function of fiscal policy in relation to the existence of alternative policy instruments (monetary policy) and of ways for individuals to self-insure against aggregate shocks (financial intermediation). This also helps qualify the tempting, and probably simplistic, conclusion that automatic stabilizers abruptly stopped contributing to stabilization in the mid-1990s.

Second, financial development and, even more so, the quality of monetary policy make a greater contribution to the reduction of volatility when the government (automatic fiscal stabilization) is smaller. In the case of monetary policy, this result lends further support to our conjecture that better monetary stabilization partly relieves fiscal policy makers of the "stabilization burden," allowing them to pursue other objectives not necessarily consistent with macroeconomic stabilization. In the case of financial development, our estimates could indicate that the "demand" for self-insurance (and the corresponding contribution of FD to stability) is likely to be greater if automatic fiscal stabilization is limited. Overall, this supports the view that greater FD and QMP over time have mostly contributed to increased stability in countries that had small governments to start with, which is fully consistent with our stylized facts. The same result also supports the idea that wherever government provides considerable automatic stabilization, economic agents may not embrace self-insurance through the financial sector (see smaller contribution of FD) as much as elsewhere. This could point to a "revealed preference" for fiscal stabilization against the alternative. One reason for such preference could be that private lending decisions may turn out to be inconsistent with self-insurance for consumers with limited collateral.

Finally, we find support for the conjecture by Buti *et al.* (2003) of decreasing returns in fiscal stabilization. This non-linearity in the relationship between government size and output volatility points to the fact that larger governments are increasingly inefficient at providing stabilization (at the extremes, when government spending equals either zero or the entire GDP, the contribution to stabilization is nil). That said, the relationship is hard to estimate precisely,[20] and it was not possible to convincingly pin down a specific size threshold beyond which any further expansion of government expenditure would become harmful for stability. However, as shown in Figure 12.13 (using the results in column 3 of Table 12.3), an increase in government size by one percent of GDP is unlikely to yield a reduction in output growth volatility exceeding 0.1 percentage point once the overall size of public expenditure approaches 40 percent of GDP.

One last issue investigated in the size-volatility literature is whether the composition of government revenue and expenditure materially affects the magnitude of automatic stabilizers for a given size. The

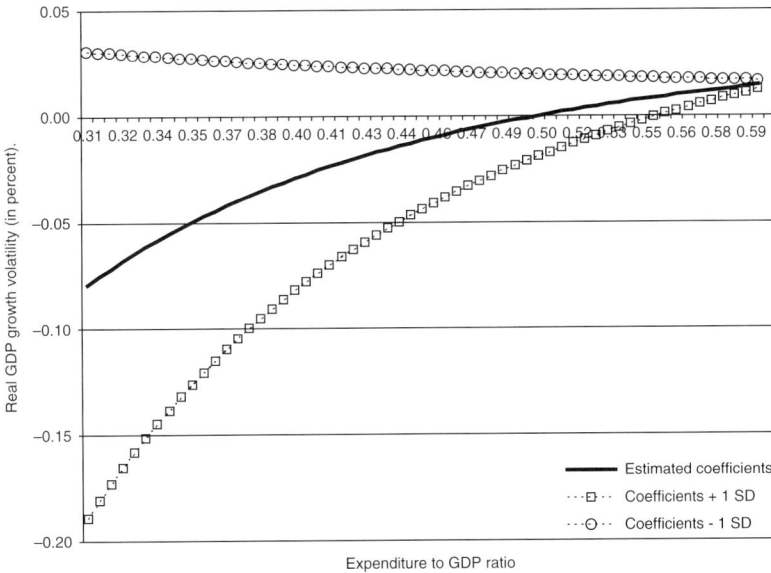

Figure 12.13: Government size and estimated impact on volatility of an increase in government expenditure by 1 percentage point of GDP

most straightforward way to answer this question is to re-estimate one of our equations (in this case, the parsimonious specification of Table 12.1) using a variety of revenue and expenditure categories (or more precisely the logarithms of their ratio to GDP) as the relevant measures of government size. The estimates for θ_1 are displayed in Table 12.4.

In line with Fatás and Mihov (2001a), we do not find consistent and robust evidence of significant composition effects, as all expenditure and revenue categories have the same sign regardless of the timespan. It is nevertheless worth noting that government consumption and social transfers are the only categories retaining a significant stabilizing effect when using the entire timespan 1961–2007. Also, the contribution of indirect taxes generally seems statistically weaker than that of direct taxes, reflecting the lower elasticity

Table 12.4: *Output volatility and alternative measures of government size (pooled OLS)*

	Dependent variable: standard deviation of real GDP growth			
	1	2	3	4
	1961–90	1961–2000	1961–2007	1991–2007
Total expenditure	−2.68***	−1.78***	−1.32**	0.61
	(4.35)	(−2.60)	(−2.37)	(0.81)
Government consumption	−2.03***	−1.34**	−0.98**	0.53
	(−4.09)	(−2.40)	(−2.17)	(0.79)
Government wage consumption	−1.26**	−0.65	−0.42	0.46
	(−2.64)	(−1.34)	(−1.12)	(0.70)
Direct taxes	−0.62**	−0.49**	−0.36	0.48
	(−2.53)	(−2.07)	(−1.58)	(1.64)
Indirect taxes	−0.67*	−0.27	−0.22	0.46
	(−1.89)	(−0.80)	(−0.81)	(1.29)
Social security transfers paid	−0.76**	−0.63*	−0.46*	0.26
	(−2.32)	(−1.80)	(−1.67)	(0.54)

Notes: Robust t-statistics are reported in parentheses. All regressions include time fixed-effects. The baseline specification is that in Table 12.1. Other coefficients and statistics are not reported but are available upon request.

of the former to the business cycle (Girouard and André, 2005). This would suggest that the scope for enhancing automatic fiscal stabilization through a deliberate reshuffling of the structure of government expenditure or revenue may be rather limited. Moreover, it is unclear whether such reshuffling (e.g. a shift in favour of direct taxation) would be advisable in terms of the other objectives of public finances (e.g. efficiency).

6. Conclusions

In the euro area, the loss of monetary policy as an instrument to offset country-specific disturbances naturally places the onus on fiscal policy. While there is little doubt that the anti-inflationary credibility of the ECB leaves ample room for an effective monetary stabilization of common demand shocks, only national fiscal authorities can provide public insurance against country-specific disturbances. A natural question in regard to our analysis is whether participation in the euro area calls for enhanced automatic stabilization through bigger government. The evidence discussed in the previous section points to a negative answer, for several reasons.

First, government expenditure is already large in the euro area, exceeding 45 percent of GDP on average, a range in which any further increase in size does not appear to yield any meaningful benefit in terms of automatic stabilization. Second, while automatic stabilizers can be enhanced through changes in the composition of expenditure and revenue (for instance by increasing social transfers and shifting the tax burden towards direct taxation), it is unclear whether the gains in terms of stabilization would not be offset by efficiency losses. Finally, the apparent substitution between monetary and fiscal stabilization, and between the latter and market-based self-insurance/stabilization, suggests two alternatives to bigger governments. The first is that further financial development could alleviate the need for fiscal stabilization. The second is that governments may be shifting objectives, opting for more stabilization-friendly policies when alternatives do not appear to be available. Widespread evidence of procyclicality in discretionary fiscal policies in the euro area suggests that there is room for more fiscal stabilization without necessarily increasing the overall size of the public sector. In comparison, countries with relatively lean public sectors like Japan and the United States have a consistent record of enacting discretionary fiscal packages explicitly aimed at stabilizing the economy (albeit with variable degrees of success). The challenge is to make sure that such actions are timely – which requires short information, decision and implementation lags – and that they are symmetric over the cycle – i.e. any stimulus should be reversed during the upturn. Reforms of fiscal institutions aimed at enhancing such discretionary stabilization – instead of focusing exclusively on fiscal discipline – are conceivable, and emerge as a fruitful area for further research.

Finally, the econometric evidence pointing to a degree of substitution between fiscal stabilization and other contributions to stability (monetary policy and financial development) arguably reflects fairly recent developments that may owe much to the circumstances of the 1990s and the early 2000s and ultimately turn out to be exceptional by historical standards. In particular, it is unclear how much extra stability could arise from further improvements in monetary policy design. Also, the extent to which financial development can play an effective stabilization role through self-insurance remains debatable in light of the procyclical nature of lending standards. The latter tend to be loose in good times when the expected future value of collateral and income gains reduce credit risk, and tighter in bad times for the opposite reasons. The implication is that the prospect for further stability gains outside improved fiscal policies may well be fairly limited and that it may probably be too early to forsake automatic fiscal stabilization.

Appendix: robustness checks

Table 12.5: *Government size and volatility: basic results with output gap volatility*

	Dependent variable: standard deviation of output gap changes							
	Cross-section OLS				Pooled OLS			
	1	2	3	4	5	6	7	8
	1961–2000	1961–90	1961–2007	1991–2007	1961–2000	1961–90	1961–2007	1991–2007
Openness	0.42	1.51	0.17	0.41	0.82	1.63**	0.62*	0.42
	(0.43)	(1.23)	(0.24)	(0.85)	(1.64)	(2.29)	(1.87)	(1.16)
Government size	−1.10	−1.89**	−0.69	0.44	−1.46***	−2.22***	−1.14**	0.43
	(−1.67)	(−2.65)	(−1.22)	(0.86)	(−2.66)	(2.68)	(−2.54)	(0.93)
Constant	0.67	−0.26	0.95	1.47***	−0.02	−1.08	0.40	1.24**
	(0.82)	(−0.28)	(1.42)	(3.01)	(−0.02)	(−1.39)	(0.70)	(2.56)
N. obs.	20	19	20	20	71	51	91	40
Time fixed-effects (p-value)	...	...	...	...	0.12	0.03	0.00	0.00
R-squared	0.17	0.33	0.10	0.11	0.30	0.39	0.39	0.26

Notes: Robust t-statistics are reported in parentheses. Panel regressions include time effects. The p-value of the time-effects test is associated with the null hypothesis (F-test) that all period effects are jointly equal to zero.

Table 12.6: *Government size and volatility: additional controls*

	Cross-section OLS				Pooled OLS			
Dependent variable: standard deviation of real GDP growth								
	1	2	3	4	5	6	7	8
	1961–2000	1961–90	1961–2007	1991–2007	1961–2000	1961–90	1961–2007	1991–2007
Openness	0.24	2.01*	0.23	-0.02	0.58	1.57*	0.53	0.23
	(0.26)	(1.85)	(0.32)	(-0.03)	(0.72)	(1.75)	(1.16)	(0.46)
Government size	-0.94	-3.87***	-0.46	1.02	-1.11	-2.45***	-0.92	0.90
	(-1.37)	(-4.29)	(-0.73)	(1.31)	(-1.45)	(-2.98)	(-1.61)	(1.25)
GDP per capita (at PPP)	-2.01***	-1.61***	-1.20*	-0.11	1.21***	-0.92*	-0.96***	-0.52
	(-3.02)	(-3.05)	(-2.05)	(-0.14)	(-2.75)	(-1.88)	(-2.66)	(-0.92)
Average real growth	-0.21	-0.70***	0.00	0.22*	0.04	-0.10	0.04	0.13
	(1.18)	(-3.93)	(0.02)	(1.82)	(0.42)	(-0.87)	(0.55)	(1.32)
Constant	7.53***	4.89***	4.73	2.06	3.21*	1.56	2.85	3.15
	(3.04)	(2.37)	(2.10)	(0.85)	(1.70)	(0.77)	(2.18)**	(1.64)
N. obs.	20	19	20	20	71	51	91	40
Time fixed-effects (p-value)	...	...	...	...	0.00	0.00	0.00	0.00
R-squared	0.53	0.72	0.46	0.25	0.33	0.48	0.43	0.35

Notes: Robust t-statistics are reported in parentheses. Panel regressions include time effects. The p-value of the time-effects test is associated with the null hypothesis (F-test) that all period effects are jointly equal to zero.

Table 12.7: *Government size and volatility: instrumental variables (pooled TSLS, period fixed effects, 1961–2007)*

First-stage regression (dependent variable: log of government expenditure to GDP ratio)

	1	2	3	4	5	6
Openness	…	0.39***	0.39***	0.39***	0.39***	0.36***
		(2.97)	(2.84)	(2.86)	(2.90)	(2.65)
Rate of urbanization	0.00**	0.00**	0.00	0.00	0.00*	0.00
	(1.91)	(1.83)	(1.54)	(0.78)	(1.76)	(0.47)
Dependency ratio	0.04***	0.04***	0.04***	0.04***	0.04***	0.04***
	(4.97)	(6.10)	(6.03)	(6.07)	(5.76)	(5.29)
Government fragmentation	0.35***	0.19**	0.19**	0.17**	0.19**	0.17**
	(4.46)	(2.11)	(1.97)	(1.99)	(2.17)	(2.07)
Majoritarian electoral rule (dummy)	−0.58**	−0.45**	−0.46**	−0.48**	−0.46**	−0.50**
	(−2.57)	(−2.20)	(−2.14)	(−2.53)	(−2.22)	(−2.07)
GDP per capita at PPP	…	…	−0.02	…	…	…
			(−0.15)			
Quality of monetary policy	…	…	…	0.31***	…	0.38***
				(2.80)		(3.30)
Financial development	…	…	…	…	−0.03	−0.08
					(−0.70)	(−1.60)
Constant	−1.40***	−1.59**	−1.57***	−1.80***	−1.55***	1.36
	(−7.18)	(1.98)	(−4.05)	(−10.62)	(−7.42)	(1.64)
R-squared	0.57	0.63	0.63	0.66	0.63	0.67
Partial R-squared of excluded instruments	0.50	0.45	0.43	0.44	0.43	0.40
Hansen J-test (p-value)	0.17	0.14	0.29	0.28	0.16	0.22
Weak identification test	19.6**	15.27*	14.51*	14.4*	13.6*	12.17*

Table 12.7: (cont.)

	Dependent variable: standard deviation of real GDP growth rate					
Openness	...	1.06*	0.80	0.97*	1.06*	0.93*
		(1.80)	(1.62)	(1.75)	(1.83)	(1.71)
Government size	-1.22**	-1.61**	-1.19**	-1.18*	-1.84***	-1.27*
	(-2.35)	(2.44)	(-2.01)	(-1.82)	(2.54)	(-1.65)
GDP per capita (at PPP)	...	...	-1.04***	...	...	...
			(-2.66)			
Quality of monetary policy	...	...	...	-1.31**	...	-1.13*
				(-2.32)		(-1.66)
Financial development	...	...	...	...	-0.38*	-0.21
					(-1.72)	(-0.83)
Constant	0.04	-0.70	3.21**	1.00	-0.47	0.98
	(0.08)	(-0.95)	(3.21)	(0.94)	(-0.67)	(0.87)
N. obs.	78	78	78	78	78	78
R-squared	0.35	0.36	0.42	0.41	0.37	0.41
Exogeneity tests:						
- Government size (p-value of Hausman test)	0.27	0.27	0.52	0.35	0.21	0.40
- Quality of monetary policy (p-value of C statistic)	...	...	...	0.07*	...	...
- Financial development (p-value of C statistic)	...	...	...	...	0.74	0.11[1]

Notes: Robust t-statistics are reported in parentheses.
[1] Joint test.

Table 12.8: *Government size and the Great Moderation (pooled OLS, 1961–2007)*

	Dependent variable: standard deviation of real GDP growth				
	1	2	3	4	5
Openness	0.84	0.77	0.38	0.79	0.97
	(1.64)	(1.46)	(0.68)	(1.54)	(1.85)
Government size (all sample)	−1.16**	−1.40**	−0.84*	−1.26**	...
	(−2.26)	(−2.48)	(−1.74)	(−2.35)	
Government size (1961–90)	...	...	...	...	−2.07***
					(−3.91)
Government size (1991–2007)	...	...	...	...	0.35
					(0.48)
Central bank independence	−0.78**	...	−1.25***	−0.67*	−0.56*
	(−2.21)		(−3.62)	(−1.79)	(−1.74)
Financial development[1]	...	−0.40**	−0.41***	−0.32	−0.22
		(−1.94)	(−2.88)	(−1.59)	(−1.12)
Constant	0.81	0.37	1.98***	0.79	−0.28
	(1.14)	(0.53)	(3.51)	(1.14)	(−0.28)
N.obs.	91	90	90	90	90
Time fixed-effects:					
p-value	0.00	0.00	...	0.00	0.00
included	yes	yes	no	yes	yes
R-squared	0.41	0.40	0.30	042	0.49

Notes: Robust t-statistics are reported in parentheses. Panel regressions include time effects. The p-value of the time effects test is associated with the null hypothesis (F-test) that all period effects are jointly equal to zero.

[1] Financial development is measured as the total credit by deposit money banks to the private sector in percentage of GDP.

Table 12.9: *Government size and volatility: instrumental variables (pooled TSLS, period fixed effects, 1961–2007)*

First stage regression (dependent variable: log of government expenditure to GDP ratio)

	1	2	3	4	5	6
Openness	...	0.39***	0.39***	0.38***	0.39***	0.37***
		(2.97)	(2.84)	(2.78)	(2.90)	(2.68)
Rate of urbanization	0.00**	0.00**	0.00	0.00*	0.00*	0.00
	(1.91)	(1.83)	(1.54)	(1.75)	(1.76)	(1.64)
Dependency ratio	0.04***	0.04***	0.04***	0.04***	0.04***	0.04***
	(4.97)	(6.10)	(6.03)	(5.82)	(5.76)	(5.28)
Government fragmentation	0.35***	0.19**	0.19*	0.19**	0.19**	0.19**
	(4.46)	(2.11)	(1.97)	(2.16)	(2.17)	(2.25)
Majoritarian electoral rule (dummy)	−0.58**	−0.45**	−0.46**	−0.53**	−0.46**	−0.55***
	(−2.57)	(−2.20)	(−2.14)	(−2.57)	(−2.22)	(−2.66)
GDP per capita at PPP	...	...	−0.02	...	...	...
			(−0.15)			
Central bank independence	...	...	...	0.12	...	0.14
				(1.48)		(1.64)
Financial development	...	...	...	...	−0.03	−0.05
					(−0.70)	(−1.03)
Constant	−1.40***	−1.59**	−1.57***	−1.63***	−1.55***	−1.36
	(−7.18)	(1.98)	(−4.05)	(−9.05)	(−7.42)	(1.64)
R-squared	0.57	0.63	0.63	0.64	0.63	0.65
Partial R-squared of excluded instruments	0.50	0.45	0.43	0.46	0.43	0.44

			Dependent variable: standard deviation of real GDP growth rate			
Hansen J-test (p-value)	0.17	0.14	0.29	0.18	0.16	0.20
Weak indentification test	19.58**	15.27*	14.51*	15.17*	13.59*	13.20*
Openness	...	1.06*	0.80	1.13**	1.06*	1.11**
		(1.80)	(1.62)	(2.07)	(1.83)	(2.06)
Government size	−1.22	−1.61	−1.19	−1.54	−1.84	−1.71
	(−2.35)	(2.44)	(−2.01)	(−2.45)	(2.54)	(−2.44)
GDP per capita (at PPP)	...	...	−1.04***	...	...	...
			(−2.66)			
Central bank independence	...	...	...	−0.76**	...	−0.66*
				(−2.04)		(−1.63)
Financial development	...	...	...	...	−0.38*	−0.31
					(1.72)	(−1.34)
Constant	0.04	−0.70	3.21**	−0.06	−0.47	0.07
	(0.08)	(−0.95)	(3.21)	(−0.07)	(−0.67)	(0.09)
N. obs.	78	78	78	78	78	78
R-squared	0.35	0.36	0.42	0.39	0.37	0.40
Exageneity tests:						
- Government size (p-value of Hausman test)	0.27	0.27	0.52	0.21	0.21	0.19
- Central bank independence (p-value of C statistic)	...	...	...	0.19	...	0.27[1]
- Financial development (p-value of C statistic)	...	...	...	...	0.74	...

Note: Robust t-statistics are reported in parentheses.

[1] Joint test.

Table 12.10: *Government size and volatility: interactions and non-linearities (pooled OLS, 1961–2007)*

	Dependent variable: standard deviation of real GDP growth							
	1	2	3	4	5	6	7	8
Openness	0.74	0.72	0.70	0.90*	0.75	0.63	0.67	0.74
	(1.45)	(1.37)	(1.25)	(1.78)	(1.50)	(1.38)	(1.25)	(1.54)
Government size (GS)	−2.74***	−2.79***	3.34	...	−1.91***	−1.64**	1.54	...
	(−3.26)	(−3.66)	(1.42)		(−3.37)	(−2.46)	(0.65)	
Financial development (FD)	1.42*	...	...	...	...	...	...	...
	(1.83)							
Central bank independence (CBI)	...	2.73**	...	...	...	...	...	...
		(2.17)						
GDP per capita (at PPP)	...	...	...	...	...	−0.02	...	...
						(−1.12)		
Average real growth	...	...	...	...	...	0.03	...	...
						(0.64)		
Non-linear terms:								
Interaction GS*FD	1.92**	...	...	...	0.39*	0.32	0.34*	0.38*
	(2.35)				(1.78)	(1.29)	(1.66)	(1.82)
Interaction GS*CBI	...	3.83***	...	...	0.88**	0.81*	0.71**	0.79**
		(2.84)			(2.14)	(1.86)	(1.71)	(1.97)
Squared GS	...	...	2.37**	0.76***	...	...	1.72	1.00***
			(2.03)	(2.90)			(1.51)	(4.02)
Constant	−0.99	−0.73	2.35*	0.73*	0.25	0.58	1.72	1.01**
	(−1.06)	(−0.82)	(1.85)	(1.66)	(0.38)	(0.75)	(1.35)	(2.48)

Marginal effect on volatility of an increase in…[1]								
Financial development if								
government expenditure is 35 percent of GDP	**−0.60**	…	…	…	**−0.41**	**−0.34**	−0.36	−0.40
government expenditure is 50 percent of GDP	0.09	…	…	…	−0.27	−0.22	−0.24	−0.26
Central bank independence if								
government expenditure is 35 percent of GDP	…	**−1.29**	…	…	**−0.93**	**−0.85**	**−0.75**	**−0.83**
government expenditure is 50percent of GDP	…	0.08	…	…	**−0.61**	**−0.56**	**−0.49**	**−0.55**
Size of government if								
expenditure is 35 percent of GDP	**−1.30**	**−0.70**	**−1.65**	**−1.60**	**−1.13**	**−0.96**	**−1.43**	**−1.38**
expenditure is 50 percent of GDP	**−1.30**	**−0.70**	0.05	**−1.05**	**−1.13**	**−0.96**	−0.20	−0.67
N. obs.	90	90	91	91	90	90	90	90
Time fixed-effects:								
p-value	0.00	0.00	0.00	0.00	0.00	0.00	0.00	0.00
included	yes	yes	yes	yes	yes	yes	yes	yes
R-squared	0.44	0.46	0.43	0.41	0.45	0.46	0.49	0.48

Notes: Robust t-statistics are reported in parentheses. The F-rest is associated with the null hypothesis that all time effects are jointly equal to zero.
[1] Numbers show the value of the estimated derivative function of volatility with respect to the relevant explanatory variable. Bold numbers denote cases where all estimated coefficients used in the calculations are statistically different from zero. The marginal impact of government size is measured at sample mean of FD and CBI.

Notes

1. This reflects the fact that the elasticity of government revenues to output growth is close to one – Girouard and André (2005) – while expenditure is largely inelastic to growth – because it reflects commitments made during budget preparation. As a result, the revenue-to-GDP ratio is broadly insensitive to the business cycle, whereas the expenditure-to-GDP ratio moves in the opposite direction to GDP. The overall budget balance (in percent of GDP) thus tends to be countercyclical (deteriorating in bad times and improving in good times), with a semi-elasticity to GDP roughly equal to the share of government expenditure in GDP.

2. It uses two indicators of fiscal intervention (the standard deviation of both the tax revenues/GDP and government purchases/GDP ratios) and two measures of output variability (the standard deviation of both linearly de-trended log GDP and GDP growth). The study reports ordinary least squares (OLS) estimates of regressions using the two measures of output variability as the dependent variable and alternative combinations of fiscal intervention as regressors.

3. In all its specifications, the model predicts a positive relationship between the size of income taxes and the degree of output volatility. By contrast the model is capable of replicating the empirical finding of a negative relationship between the size of government expenditure and the degree of macroeconomic instability, but the magnitude of the predicted effect is far smaller than the empirical evidence suggests.

4. Household direct taxes, other direct taxes, social contributions, and indirect taxes.

5. Current spending (besides health), health expenditure, age-related benefits, incapacity-related benefits, unemployment benefits, sick pay benefits, and subsidies.

6. The first one is fundamentally flawed because it *presumes* that only the private sector can be a source of shock in the economy (essentially suppressing the widely documented tendency of governments to behave in a procyclical fashion). Pushing this argument to the limit, if the government sector were to represent 100 percent of the economy, budget ratios would be constant, with no guarantee that the nominal figures would not fluctuate.

7. Australia, Austria, Belgium, Canada, Denmark, Finland, France, Germany, Greece, Ireland, Italy, Japan, the Netherlands, Norway, Sweden, Switzerland, Spain, Portugal, the United Kingdom, and the United States. OECD data were used throughout.

8. To keep the composition of the euro area constant over time, we include the eleven original members minus Luxembourg.

9. The 1984 cut-off date is standard in the US literature on the Great Moderation. This is why we adopted it here, even though it may not be the ideal cut-off for all EU countries.

10. In earlier decades, we have in some cases less than ten yearly observations available. To avoid losing too many degrees of freedom, we included averages for decades in which we had at least 5 consecutive annual data points. We are therefore working with a maximum of 91 data points (out of a possible 100).

11. The countries are Australia, Austria, Belgium, Canada, Denmark, Finland, France, Germany, Greece, Ireland, Italy, Japan, the Netherlands, Norway, Portugal, Spain, Sweden, Switzerland, the United Kingdom, and the United States.

12. This could be because the composition of expenditure and revenues entails smaller stabilizers (e.g. fewer unemployment benefits, greater reliance on indirect taxation), or because discretionary policy may conflict more often with macroeconomic stabilization.

13. Regressions including country-fixed effects (for which estimates reflect time variations under the assumption that all countries follow the same model) did not yield any meaningful result.

14. Such a measure is subject to a reverse causality problem to the extent that real volatility translates into inflation volatility.

15. Openness to trade is measured as the sum of imports and exports divided by twice the GDP.

16. As previously indicated, the quality of monetary policy is measured as the exponential deviation of actual inflation from a 2 percent inflation target (see IMF, 2007a). This captures the idea that a credible inflation anchor helps monetary policy makers to stabilize the economy. The financial development variable is the total credit by deposit money banks to the private sector in percent of GDP.

17. The relevant comparison in Table 12.1 is column 7.

18. Table 12.7 in the Appendix confirms these results using instrumental-variables (IV) techniques. As excluded instruments (i.e. variables that are highly correlated with government size but orthogonal to the error term), we use the rate of urbanization, the dependency ratio, and political indicators, including the average degree of fragmentation of coalition governments (known to increase the size of government due to more pervasive common pool problems), and the existence of majoritarian electoral rule (known to be associated with smaller government for the opposite reason as fragmentation). Exogeneity tests suggest that reverse causality is not a statistical issue in our sample. However, it is interesting to observe that, as in Fatás and Mihov (2001a), the estimated coefficients for government size are higher (in absolute value), and that trade

openness has a stronger and often weakly significant effect, in line with
Rodrik (1998a).

19. The square was preferred to spline coefficients because we could not
    identify a plausible threshold of government size (between 35 and 55
    percent of GDP) that yielded a significantly better fit of the estimated
    model.

20. Figure 12.13 illustrates the extent of the uncertainty arising from errors in
    the estimated coefficients, using the variance-covariance matrix of coeffi-
    cients to calculate the impact of a 1 standard-deviation difference. Notice
    that the correlation of errors is almost equal to 1.

Comment 8: Comment on Chapter 12

GILLES SAINT-PAUL

This chapter starts from the observation that monetary policy is no longer available to countries within the eurozone as a tool of stabilization. It then naturally asks whether fiscal policy can be substituted to monetary policy, and focuses on automatic stabilizers. The conventional view is that the larger the size of government, the stronger these automatic stabilizers. The chapter then proceeds to examine this claim empirically: do we observe that countries with larger governments have less volatile macroeconomic fluctuations?

To answer that question, they perform two exercises. First, they provide an informative survey of the existing literature. Second, they provide new evidence on the link between government size and volatility using both descriptive statistics and econometric techniques.

There are two key messages in the paper. First, while the existing literature has extensively documented a negative effect of government size on volatility, this correlation vanished during the 1990s. Second, as was already hinted by Silgoner *et al.* (2003) and Martinez-Mongay and Sekkat (2005), it seems to disappear or even be inverted if the size of government becomes larger than a certain threshold. The authors conclude that the view that an increase in government size should be allowed for in order to compensate for the impossibility of using a monetary instrument is unwarranted.

The nature of the authors' exercise is to examine the empirical validity of the claim without questioning too much its analytical validity, although there is a brief discussion of it in Section 2. Similarly, the reader is left with not too many conclusive thoughts about why the government size/volatility correlation has disappeared and why it seems to no longer work if the government is too big. I also think there is a little bit of confusion between two issues that are related but substantially different, namely (i) should the government reduce the volatility of GDP vs. (ii) should the government provide consumption insurance to credit-constrained agents.

The first question has to do with the desirability of macroeconomic fluctuations from the point of view of social welfare, which, as recognized by the authors in Section 2, depends crucially on which macroeconomic model is relevant. Keynesian thinking traditionally considers that macroeconomic fluctuations are the by-product and the sign of non-market-clearing phenomena. Macroeconomic stabilization is good because it reduces excess supply in slumps and excess demand in booms. Modern "New Keynesian" macroeconomics provides foundations for this by assuming that nominal prices are sticky and that there are fluctuations in aggregate demand, part of which are actually due to the government: fiscal and monetary mistakes, shocks to public spending, political business cycles, etc. In contrast, the real business cycle view assumes that most shocks are fluctuations in productivity and that a market-clearing economy will naturally fluctuate in response to these shocks, while remaining efficient. Output must obviously fall when the economy is less productive, so will investment to the extent that the marginal product of capital is lower, and employment will also fall if there is some elasticity of labor supply with respect to the real wage. In such a world there is no need for stabilization: it would actually be harmful.

The size of government is a very coarse instrument to use in order to introduce stabilization to the economy. Granted, the associated stabilizers have the merit of being "automatic," so we expect them to kick in more quickly as they are not subject to decision lags. But, even if the evidence of a stabilizing effect of larger governments were undisputable, using such an instrument to achieve such a goal really looks like overkill, especially in light of the Lucas point, mentioned by the authors, that the welfare costs of fluctuations are small. One could instead introduce a fiscal instrument specifically designed for stabilization, which will have no effect on the long-term size of government. This could be, for example, a stabilization fund that would finance tax cuts in slumps and tax increases in booms according to some prespecified contingent rule. It would run a deficit in slumps and a surplus in booms in such a way that its budget would on average be equal to zero. I am not saying that such a device is easy to design but it illustrates how one could in principle entirely decouple stabilization from the size of government. The contingent rule would probably allow the economy to reach a better degree of stabilization than the automatic stabilizers that we have. The latter are a by-product of the designs of the tax and welfare systems which were originally meant to address other objectives than stabilization, while the contingent rule would be specifically designed to achieve stabilization. For example, we know that the greater the progressivity of the income tax, the more it is stabilizing. But its progressivity itself should not be designed as a stabilizer but should essentially depend on how the distortions from taxation are distributed through the economy and on the degree of inequality aversion in society. These are clearly the long-run considerations that are crucial to the design of the tax system, and stabilization only comes as a by-product. The fact that the rule governing the fiscal stabilization fund is prespecified could also mean that it would act quickly on the economy, in fact even more quickly than some automatic stabilizers that act with a substantial lag because of fiscal year effects. In principle, the rule could be set optimally by computing some optimal proactive fiscal stabilization policy taking into account the relative importance of supply and demand shocks and the degree of stabilization already present in the tax system. For example, if society becomes less averse to inequality then it will opt for a less progressive tax system but then this should be compensated by a more proactive rule for the stabilization fund, in order to maintain the degree of stabilization at its optimal level. Similarly the rule will imply fewer interventions when the economy is hit by supply shocks.

The second question is conceptually different: in principle, one may insure without stabilizing, just like one may stabilize without insuring beyond the obvious effect of a reduced variance of shocks. Let us start from the most simple case where there are no aggregate shocks, only individual ones. Then, under perfect financial markets, people can insure against these shocks and achieve the same consumption level. If financial markets are imperfect, institutions like unemployment benefits, progressive income taxes, and so on, can alternatively provide insurance. They do so not as automatic macroeconomic stabilizers but as palliatives for imperfect financial markets. Let us now assume that there are aggregate shocks. If we are in a *closed economy*, it is clearly impossible to insure consumers against these aggregate shocks. Stabilization can then appear as an ersatz for insurance, in the sense that the gains from stabilization, if any, are likely to be larger, the more risk-averse the consumers are. But this will be true regardless of the development of financial markets: financial development helps diversify away whatever risk is diversifiable, not the nondiversifiable component created by aggregate shocks. So we should expect no effect of financial

development on aggregate volatility, and no cross-effect between financial development and the desirability of stabilization. And we also know
that transfers and government expenditures will only work as stabilizers
if the economy is Keynesian – nominal prices are sticky and demand
shocks are dominant – and that they are dominated by more adequate
instruments. The story is yet different if this is an *open economy* with
access to international capital markets. The economy can then insure
against shocks by borrowing and lending abroad. In fact private individuals can do it on their own and if the country is small enough the
aggregate risk can be entirely diversified. Does that mean that stabilization of the aggregate economy is useless? No, but again this has little to
do with insurance: if the economy is Keynesian then aggregate demand
volatility is inefficient. Resources are underutilized in slumps (marginal
costs are too low), and overutilized in booms (marginal costs are too
high). So even though consumption is entirely insured against aggregate
shocks thanks to international capital markets, we still want to stabilize
the economy because sticky prices make volatility productively inefficient. Stabilization yields a productive gain by smoothing the profile of
marginal costs over time. Of course this conclusion is entirely reversed if
the driving force for the economy's fluctuations is the supply shocks as
assumed by the real business cycle approach.

To conclude, let me offer some thoughts about what may explain the
authors' finding that government size is no longer stabilizing once it has
passed a certain threshold. Authors like Giavazzi and Pagano (1990)
have shown that in some cases, fiscal expansions can be contractionary.
These anti-Keynesian effects will be important, for example, if, as a
result of an expansion, public debt reaches such critical levels that
consumers expect painful distortionary adjustments to take place in
the future. Consequently, they will reduce their consumption both to
accumulate savings in anticipation of these adjustments, and as a result
of a sheer precautionary motive. It is this drop of consumption which
generates the contractionary effect of the fiscal expansion. Clearly, the
effect is relevant both for discretionary fiscal policy and economic
stabilizers. If the unemployment benefit system and the general government budget dip into a deficit when the economy slows down, this may
well critically increase future fiscal liabilities so as to have anti-
Keynesian effects. And it is quite reasonable to believe that such a
situation is more likely, the larger the size of the government initially.

13 | *Fiscal policy, intercountry adjustment and the real exchange rate within Europe*

CHRISTOPHER ALLSOPP AND DAVID VINES

1. Introduction

The establishment of the euro has been highly successful. Nevertheless, whilst some Member States have fully enjoyed the benefits of belonging to the currency union, notably by experiencing high growth rates, there have been large divergences in growth rates. One example of these differences in economic performance is the protracted period of slow growth and low inflation in Germany, from 2001 onwards, which contrasts with a prolonged period of high growth and more rapid inflation in Ireland and Spain. Such divergences partly reflect the process of economic catching-up under way in certain euro-area members. But even within the latter group, there have been marked differences over an extended period. Most strikingly, since 1990 Ireland has achieved particularly rapid real convergence, which has led to living standards above the euro-area average since 1997. On the other hand, Portugal experienced a stalling of real convergence after 2000.

Which factors lay behind such inter-EMU divergences? The conventional view is that they relate to long-standing issues about progress in enhancing the flexibility of markets. This leads to the conventional suggestion that to improve performance the emphasis should be on supply-side flexibility – and on the Lisbon agenda.

However, there is another possibility. This is that interactions between competitiveness, prices and fiscal positions within EMU might cause intercountry divergences to cumulate, even in the presence of supply-side flexibility.

Within EMU the adjustment process which brings national conditions back in line with the euro-area average works as follows. Within EMU,

This is a revised version of a paper presented at the EMU@10 Conference in Brussels in November 2007. It builds on joint work which David Vines has done with Tatiana Kirsanova and Simon Wren-Lewis. We are grateful to Tatiana Kirsanova for much assistance in the preparation of the chapter, and to Robert Kollman for very helpful comments on earlier drafts.

there is a single centralised monetary policy. A recession in one nation, caused, say, by competitiveness in that nation being less than in the rest of the union, will not lead to an EMU-wide response in monetary policy, even if the country is small, or if there is a corresponding, offsetting, boom elsewhere. But it will lead to a reduction in inflation in that nation, and to a corresponding gain in competitiveness there, and this will moderate the recession. Similarly the reverse will occur if there is a boom in one nation, caused, say, by a gain in competitiveness there; inflation will rise there and so the competitiveness of that nation will worsen, damping the boom. The former kind of adjustment is what has been happening in Germany throughout the present decade. The conventional view is that this equilibrating process will work satisfactorily, so as to ensure intercountry adjustment within EMU. This conventional view is discussed in detail in the European Commission (2006a).

It has long been believed that this adjustment process will be difficult within a monetary union. The speed of the process will necessarily depend on the *degree of price flexibility*; within a monetary union competitiveness cannot be rapidly adjusted by exchange rate change. If this price flexibility is low then the adjustment process will be prolonged. Hence the conventional beliefs, described above, about the need to promote supply-side flexibility.

In this chapter we explore a new and different argument about the difficulty of adjustment, to do with the dynamics of the adjustment process. We show that difficulty depends not only on the degree of price flexibility but also on the *degree of forward-lookingness* in the economy. We show that in a monetary union in which (i) a sufficient number of price setters follow a backward-looking adjustment process and (ii) a sufficient number of consumers are indebted and credit constrained (and so cannot practice forward-looking consumption smoothing) there can be forces which offset the stabilising forces described above, and which can lead towards cumulative divergence between countries.

1.1 *Analysis of the chapter*

The ECB sets a single nominal interest rate for all eurozone countries. In countries experiencing a loss of competitiveness and so a recession, inflation will begin to fall gradually. (How gradually it falls will depend on the degree of forward-lookingness of price setters.) The opposite is true in countries experiencing a boom. This means that in uncompetitive countries with a recession the real interest rate (the single common nominal rate minus domestic inflation) will begin to rise, and vice-versa in competitive countries experiencing a boom. But as the real interest rate gradually rises in countries with a recession, consumption will gradually fall (at least amongst credit-constrained consumers). As a result there will be further downward pressures on domestic economic activity. This means that the rate of inflation will fall, the real interest rate will rise further, and consumption will fall further. Output may continue to fall, even though the country is becoming more competitive. The opposite is true in the countries with a boom. As a result, while aggregate inflation in the eurozone may be on target, inflation rates across individual countries may not converge; the resulting real interest rate differences may diverge, and outputs may diverge cumulatively. This may happen, even though the relative competitive position of countries changes, in a direction which would promote convergence, in the conventional manner described above. The present chapter analyses this adjustment difficulty using a formal model. The model will be used to examine how the possibility of cumulative divergence depends on the degree of forward-lookingness in both consumption and price setting.

We will show that, within this model, a tendency towards divergence could not arise without *both* kinds of backward-lookingness. First, we will show that the problem of divergence could not arise if all price setting were forward-looking. In this case, the inflation rate would immediately jump down in the uncompetitive economy, and then gradually return to equilibrium in such a way as to return the competitiveness of the economy to its required level. The opposite would happen in the competitive economy. The forward-lookingness of price setters would ensure that the economies did not diverge. Second, we will show that divergence could not arise if all consumers were forward-looking. Even if inflation were entirely backward looking, and only adjusted gradually, forward-looking consumers in the uncompetitive country would immediately jump down their level of consumption, in response to a projected sequence of higher interest rates in the future, and, after this their consumption would gradually rise again. The recession in the economy would be removed over time, along with the economy's gradual improvement in competitiveness. The opposite would happen in the competitive economy. Forward-looking consumers would ensure that the economies did not diverge.[1]

The chapter will also show that forward-lookingness in price setting and in consumption can substitute for each other in avoiding such cumulative divergence. Using a particular calibration of the model, we show that the larger the proportion of consumers who are liquidity constrained, the greater the proportion of forward-looking price setters has to be to avoid the possibility of cumulative divergence. Similarly, the smaller the proportion of price setters who are forward-looking, the greater the proportion of forward-looking consumers needs to be to avoid the possibility of cumulative divergence.

Going on from this, the chapter also shows that, even if this adjustment process is stable, competitiveness can overshoot in this adjustment process, causing cyclical outcomes. Using the particular calibration of the model, we show that in the uncompetitive economy, the adjustment process can cause 'too much' deflation, so that the price level overshoots too far in the downward direction. This is what appears to have been happening in Germany recently.

Finally, the chapter shows that fiscal policy could contribute to this adjustment process, offsetting the way in which real interest rate effects push in the wrong direction. We show that fiscal policy could help to avoid a process of cumulative divergence, given the degree of backward-lookingness of consumption and of price setting in the economy. Further we show that, even if cumulative divergence was avoided, fiscal policy could help to dampen any overshooting of competitiveness and cycles. We also show that tightly controlling debt, as required by the Stability and Growth Pact (SGP), can prevent fiscal policy having either of these effects. Our model thus suggests that, in a world in which there is a considerable degree of backward-lookingness, the SGP does not provide a framework which will facilitate inter-European adjustment. This may be the case, even although the SGP might provide a valuable framework in which the *aggregate* fiscal stability of the euro area as a whole can be managed.

1.2 Plan of the chapter

The chapter is structured as follows. In the next section of the chapter, we present some data which suggest that the difficulties which we have just described may be real difficulties within EMU. In Section 3 we sketch a very simple model which gives an analytical proof of the argument described above.

Then in Sections 4 and 5, we develop our argument using a micro-founded macro model in which the inflation process is partly forward-looking and partly backward-looking, and in which some consumers are forward-looking, and act as if they are infinitely lived, but in which other consumers are credit constrained. We examine a standard calibration of the model, and use it to perform the analysis described above.

Section 6 considers policy implications of this analysis. A final section concludes.

There already exist important papers on the subject of this paper, namely the conduct of fiscal policy in a monetary union in which there are nominal rigidities, in particular those by Galí and Monacelli (2008) and Beetsma and Jensen (2005). The contribution of present paper is to show that the task for fiscal policy is more demanding if (a) the nominal rigidities arise from a partly forward-looking and partly backward-looking inflation process which gives rise to inflation persistence; and (b) not all consumers are forward-looking but there are also credit-constrained consumers. The first of these features is contained in the model in Kirsanova *et al.* (2007), but the model in that paper contains no credit-constrained consumers. Both of these features are present in the model of Kirsanova *et al.* (2006); the model of the present paper is an extension of the model in that paper, obtained by adding a public sector to their model.

2. Intercountry differences

Figures 13.1 to 13.5 display some relevant recent developments in the euro area. These figures show steady divergence.

The German economy entered EMU with high costs, in an uncompetitive position; Figure 13.1 shows a continuing relative gain in competitiveness for Germany since then. Similarly this graph shows a continuing loss of competitiveness for Spain and Portugal; which entered EMU with low costs, in a competitive position. This cumulative gain or loss is repeated, as a long and drawn-out process, in a number of countries including Italy. Wickens (2007) draws attention to this feature.

Figure 13.2 shows that real interest rates have been high, and have remained high, in the country, Germany, which entered EMU in an uncompetitive position, even though competitiveness has been continuing to improve as a result of relatively low inflation. Similarly real interest rates have been low in Spain, even though its competitive position has been continuing to worsen, as a result of relatively high inflation (the same is true for Portugal). This position has been sustained not just for a

1999 = 100, measured as unit labour costs, whole economy

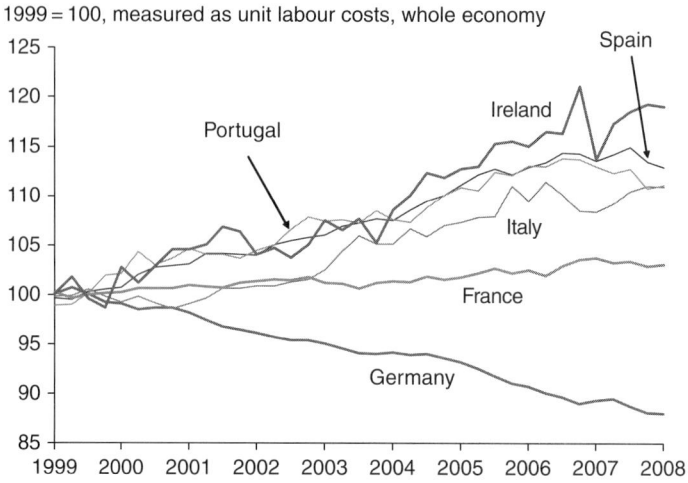

Figure 13.1: Real exchange rate
Source: Oxford Economics/Haver Analytics.

%, deflated with the GDP deflator

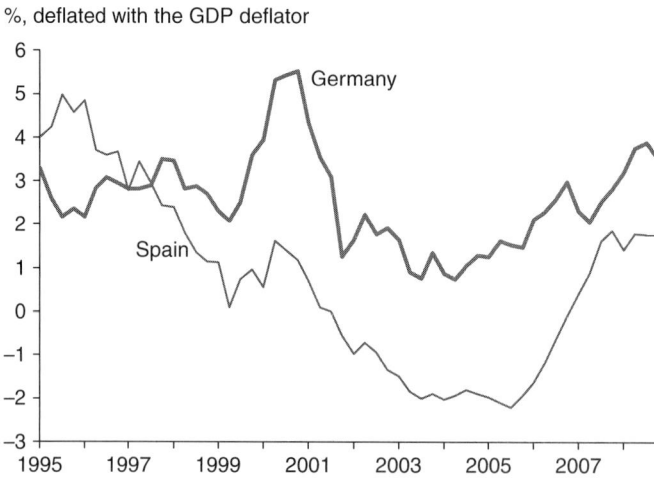

Figure 13.2: Real short-term rate of interest
Source: Oxford Economics.

%, deflated with the GDP deflator

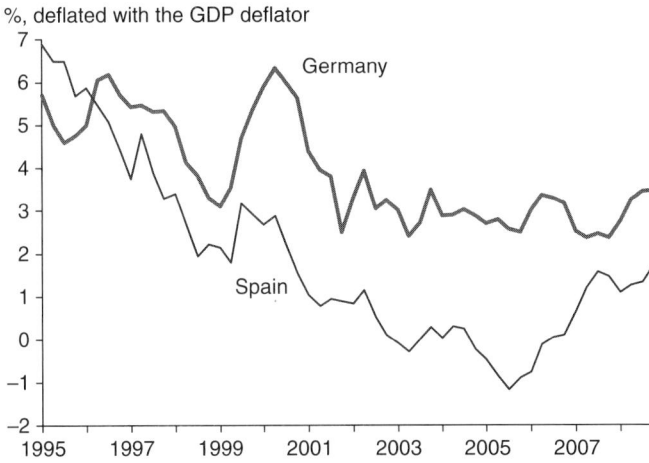

Figure 13.3: Real long-term rate of interest
Source: Oxford Economics.

% of GDP

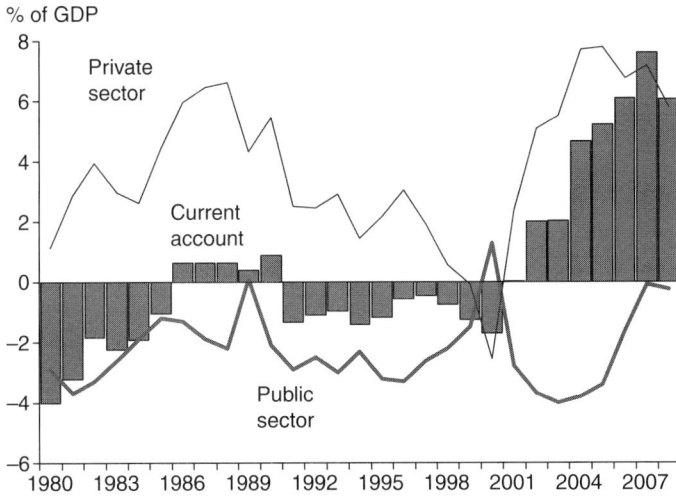

Figure 13.4: Sectoral balances for Germany
Source: Oxford Economics – 2008 estimate.

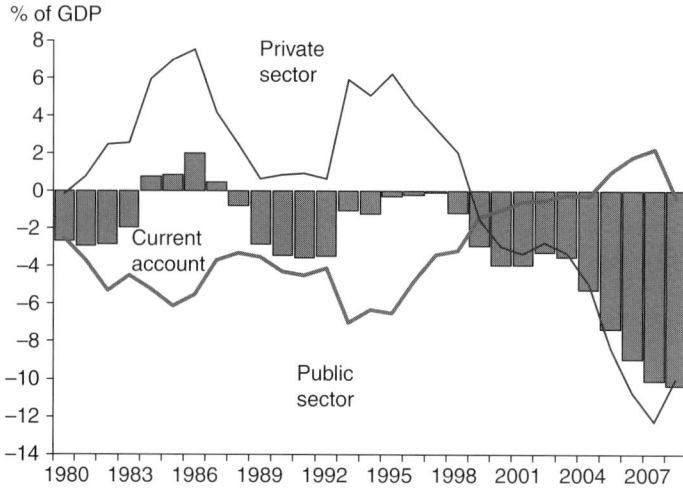

Figure 13.5: Sectoral balances for Spain
Source: Oxford Economics – 2008 estimate.

short period, but over the full period since the creation of EMU, suggesting pronounced overshoot in response to the shock. Figure 13.3 shows that this has been a feature of long rates as well as short rates.

Figures 13.4 and 13.5 describe further aspects of the adjustment process. They show the German current account balance moving into a marked surplus, as the real exchange rate has become more competitive. Figure 13.4 suggests that this adjustment process may have gone far enough by 2004 or 2005, and that the continuing improvement in the German real exchange rate since then may have gone too far. It is apparent that German fiscal policy has not played a part in helping to bring the real exchange rate to a longer-term equilibrium position. (The German fiscal figure for the year 2000 should be discounted because this was when German telephone licences were auctioned.) Such a policy might have required a more contractionary stance early in the period – to help bring the initial adjustment about more quickly – and a more expansive position more recently, to prevent the real exchange rate being driven down too far. The Spanish position also does not show fiscal policy moderating the recent private sector boom, a boom which has been assisted by a low real interest rate. This boom has continued to drive the Spanish real exchange rate in an uncompetitive direction. (In the case of Portugal an uncompetitive position has been sustained for nearly a decade, and the continuing fiscal deficit has not played a part in adjusting this position. Similarly, in Greece fiscal policy does not appear to have played a part in adjusting the external position.)

The models which follow in Sections 3 and 4 are designed to explain such cumulative divergence shown in these Figures.

3. A very simple model of a small member of a monetary union

We first demonstrate analytically that the kind of cumulative instability, discussed in the introduction to the chapter, is possible; and we show how fiscal policy might prevent such instability. We do this assuming that the behaviour of both consumers and price setters is entirely backward-looking. We then show that if either (a) all price setters are forward-looking, or (b) all consumers are forward-looking, then this might be sufficient to remove such a tendency to cumulative instability. We are able to show this using a simple model in continuous time. A fuller model is developed in the next section in discrete time; in that model both consumption and price setting are determined by a mixture of forward-looking and backward-looking behaviour.

In both this section and next we suppose that the country is small enough that developments in it do not influence the interest rate in the union as a whole.

3.1 A fully backward-looking model

We represent output as follows

$$y = c + \sigma s + g, \tag{1}$$

where y is output in the particular country, c is consumption in the country, s competitiveness of the country, where an increase in s denotes a depreciation in the real exchange rate of the country, and g is government spending. We suppose that consumers are credit constrained and indebted, so that a rise in the real interest rate causes a reduction in consumption; for simplicity we model this effect in a static way. (In the full model in the next section consumption expenditure is derived from microfoundations and partly forward-looking and partly backward-looking, and so the relevant expression is more complicated.)

Noting that the real interest rate r is affected negatively by the inflation rate, π, we write

$$c = \varsigma\pi. \tag{2}$$

We can represent fiscal feedback on inflation and on the real exchange rate as

$$g = -\theta\pi + \lambda s. \tag{3}$$

We can thus represent output in the economy by an equation in which the divergence in output in the country depends on inflation and on its real exchange rate relative to the rest of the monetary union

$$y = \delta\pi + \varepsilon s, \tag{4}$$

where $\delta = (\varsigma - \theta)$. The sign of δ depends on fiscal feedback; $\delta > 0$ unless fiscal feedback is sufficiently strong. $\varepsilon = (\sigma + \lambda)$ is necessarily positive because any fiscal feedback from the real exchange rate augments competitiveness effects.

We represent inflation as follows. In continuous time we can write a NAIRU Phillips curve with backward-looking price setters as

$$\dot\pi = \gamma y, \tag{5}$$

where $\gamma > 0$.

Finally, in a monetary union, inflation in the country erodes its competitiveness relative to that in the rest of the union,

$$\dot s = -\pi. \tag{6}$$

We can thus represent the economy by two dynamic equations

$$\begin{bmatrix} \dot\pi \\ \dot s \end{bmatrix} = \begin{bmatrix} \gamma\delta & \gamma\varepsilon \\ -1 & 0 \end{bmatrix} \begin{bmatrix} \pi \\ s \end{bmatrix}.$$

The eigenvalues of the system are $\frac{1}{2}\gamma\delta \pm \frac{1}{2}\sqrt{\gamma^2\delta^2 - 4\gamma\varepsilon}$.

Here inflation is a predetermined variable and, since competitiveness s is also predetermined, we need two negative roots if there is to be stability. But, in the absence of fiscal feedback $\delta = \varsigma < 0$, because of the effect of inflation on the real interest rate and so $\gamma\delta > 0$. Also $\sqrt{\gamma^2\delta^2 - 4\gamma\varepsilon} < \gamma\delta$. As a result both of the roots are positive, and so no stable solution exists. This means that if for some reason, the economy starts out of the steady state, for example it is uncompetitive and so that s is below equilibrium, inflation will fall without limit, consumption will collapse, and competitiveness will improve without limit.

There are two forces at work determining this unstable outcome. Consider a shock which makes the economy uncompetitive.[2] Output falls and so inflation begins to fall, which gradually causes the competitive position to improve, and makes output increase. But the fall in inflation also causes the real interest rate to rise which causes consumption to fall, which makes output decrease. Since, as here, all price setting is backward-looking and so inflation only adjusts gradually, changes in the level of competitiveness are only gradual, and occur as the integral of the changes in inflation. By contrast, changes in the rate of inflation, and in the real interest rate, occur immediately once output falls. This is why these effects dominate, and go on dominating, cumulatively, offsetting the effects of improvements in competitiveness. The danger of this outcome became known as 'Walters' critique', stemming from the opposition of Sir Alan Walters to British membership of the Exchange Rate Mechanism of the European Monetary System (EMS), when he was an advisor to Margaret Thatcher. This idea lies at the heart of the analysis in this chapter.

This potential for instability in fixed exchange rate regimes is raised in Kirsanova *et al.* (2006). Surprisingly it is not discussed in textbook accounts of fixed versus flexible exchange rate regimes, and does not feature in most official discussions of the advantages and disadvantages of monetary unions (European Commission (1990), HM Treasury (2003)).

In the present simple model, such an unstable outcome can only be avoided if fiscal policy is sufficiently strong in its response to inflation, so as to make $\delta = (\varsigma - \theta) < 0$. In that case both roots will be negative and stability obtains. The reduction in inflation will cause both a gradual increase in competitiveness and an immediate increase in domestic expenditure, because – by construction – the positive effects of falling inflation on fiscal expenditure outweigh the negative effects on consumption coming from a rising real interest rate.

If fiscal policy ensures that $\delta = (\varsigma - \theta) < 0$ and so that the roots are negative and the system is stable, cycles in competitiveness may nevertheless occur. This will happen if the eigenvalues of the system are complex. By inspection, this will occur if ε is large enough, which will be the case if the effect of competitiveness on demand is large. To prevent such cycles, the fiscal feedback on inflation would need to be large enough not only to make δ positive but also large enough to ensure that $\gamma^2\delta^2 - 4\gamma\varepsilon$ is positive, and so prevent such cyclical behaviour. Likewise if the fiscal feedback on the real exchange rate is large, so as to make ε larger and therefore speed up the adjustment of competitiveness, then δ would need to be even larger still to prevent cyclical overshoot.

3.2 Forward-looking price setting

We can represent a fully forward-looking, perfect-foresight Phillips curve in continuous time as the limit, as the interval of time shrinks to zero, of an equation of the form $\pi_t = \phi y_t + \pi_{t+1}$. This may be written as

$$\dot{\pi} = \gamma y, \tag{7}$$

where now $\gamma < 0$. With this one change the model remains as before.[3]

Competitiveness is a predetermined variable, but we now suppose that inflation is a jump variable. We thus have one predetermined variable and one jump variable. Suppose that there is *no* fiscal intervention, so that now $\delta = \varsigma < 0$. As a result $\gamma\delta < 0$ and also $\sqrt{\gamma^2\delta^2 - 4\gamma\varepsilon} < \gamma\delta$. This means that there is one negative eigenvalue and one positive eigenvalue. We suppose – in a conventional manner – that forward-looking price setters are capable of jumping the inflation rate so as to eliminate the unstable root and so putting the economy on a stable path. That is, we assume that they behave so as to ensure that the transversality condition – that the economy does not experience explosive behaviour – is satisfied.[4] As a result the model will be saddle-path stable.

Following an initial shock which causes competitiveness to fall below its equilibrium level, there will be no gradual, cumulative fall of inflation. Instead inflation will jump down, and gradually rise back to equilibrium again, during which time the disturbance to competitiveness will gradually be removed; competitiveness will gradually return to equilibrium. As it does this the real interest rate will immediately rise, causing consumption to fall, and so causing output to fall initially for a further reason, in addition to the effects of worsened competitiveness. But after its initial downward jump, inflation will be gradually rising again, and so the real interest rate will be gradually falling, and consumption will gradually be rising, back to equilibrium.

There will be no need for fiscal intervention in this case to ensure stability, since the behaviour of the private sector in jumping the inflation rate will instead ensure this (given that we have assumed that forward-looking inflation will jump in such a way as to cancel out the unstable root in the system.) In such a setup, forward-lookingness can remove the problem of instability.

3.3 Forward-looking consumption

We can represent the behaviour of fully forward-looking, perfect-foresight consumers in continuous time by means of an Euler equation, written as

$$\dot{c} = \varsigma r, \tag{8}$$

which, noting the dependence of the real interest rate on the inflation rate, may be written as

$$\dot{c} = -\varsigma \pi. \tag{9}$$

With this change, and supposing that there is no fiscal intervention, the model may now be written as

$$\begin{bmatrix} \dot{c} \\ \dot{\pi} \\ \dot{s} \end{bmatrix} = \begin{bmatrix} 0 & -\varsigma & 0 \\ \gamma & 0 & \gamma\varepsilon \\ 0 & -1 & 0 \end{bmatrix} \begin{bmatrix} c \\ \pi \\ s \end{bmatrix} \tag{10}$$

As initially, we suppose that inflation is entirely backward-looking, and does not jump. Similarly competitiveness is predetermined. But we suppose that consumption is a jump variable. We thus have two pre-determined variables and one jump variable. The eigenvalues of this system are $\lambda = 0$, and $\lambda = \pm\sqrt{-\gamma(\varepsilon + \varsigma)}$. There is one zero root, and two pure imaginary roots. We suppose – in a conventional manner – that forward-looking consumers are capable of choosing the initial level of consumption so as to put the economy on a stable path. That is, we assume that they behave so as to avoid Ponzi-game outcomes.[5] As a result the model will be saddle-path stable.[6]

This system will not explode, but it will cycle in an undamped manner. Following an initial shock which causes competitiveness to fall below its equilibrium level, there will be a gradual fall of inflation. But at some stage competitiveness will improve enough, and output increase enough, so that inflation begins to rise again. Consumption will initially jump down and then begin to rise in line with the behaviour of the real interest rate which gradually rises as inflation gradually falls. (The Euler equation shows that along the adjustment path consumption will be rising when the real interest rate is high.) This happens until the point where inflation stops falling; at this point consumption will start to fall again. The solution will lead to an undamped cycle in all of inflation, competitiveness and consumption.

It is possible to show that if there is any fiscal feedback on inflation, this will damp the resulting cycle and if fiscal policy is sufficiently strong this will ensure that there is no cycle. Thus, although forward-looking consumption can be sufficient to prevent instability, it will not eliminate a cyclical response. For this some fiscal policy is needed (or, as we shall see in the next section, some forward-lookingness on the part of price setters).

4. A microfounded model of a small member of a monetary union

In this section, we develop a microfounded model in which both inflation and consumption are forward-looking and backward-looking. This model enables us to explore the potential for instability, and the possibility of cycles, in more detail than has been done in the previous section, using a model with proper microfoundations. This model is too complex to allow us to derive analytic results; we will thus examine a standard calibration of it.

The model which we develop is in the 'New Open Economy Macroeconomics' tradition; we take the model developed in Kirsanova *et al.* (2006) and modify it to include effects of fiscal policy. Our analytical framework is close to that of Beetsma and Jensen (2005), a setup which we generalise in three important respects. First, while that paper embodies nominal inertia in the form of Calvo contracts, we also, following Kirsanova *et al.* (2007), allow for some additional backward-looking inflation inertia and so introduce inflation persistence, using a setup outlined in Steinsson (2003). (This is realistic, as suggested by Mankiw (2001) and Benigno and López-Salido (2006) among many others.) Second, following Kirsanova *et al.* (2006), we then allow for some households to be credit constrained and so unable to implement an optimal consumption plan. As a result the consumption of this group is governed by its current budget constraint and so is backward-looking rather than forward-looking. (This is also realistic, as argued by Wright (2004).) Third, we introduce the government solvency constraint into the model. As a result, any short-run stabilisation undertaken by the fiscal authorities is constrained, as it should be, by the long-run need to ensure debt stabilisation.

It is possible to study a monetary union with, say, two countries, each of which is big relative to the other, as in Kirsanova *et al.* (2006). Here the country we study is sufficiently small that developments in it have no effect on the nominal interest rate in the union, and, for simplicity, we abstract from the existence of other countries in the world. In this regard, the model is similar to that in Galí and Monacelli (2008).

We will use this model to study how the dynamic behaviour of the economy is influenced by the proportion of backward-looking and forward-looking behaviour, and by fiscal policy. We will describe the behaviour of the economy in response to a particular shock – a shock to the *level* of competitiveness rather than to the rate of inflation – since the discussion in Section 2 above has suggested that such shocks are important in a monetary union.

4.1 Households

There are two groups of consumers: those that are credit constrained, and those that are not. For both groups the aggregate consumption bundle is defined as

$$C = \frac{C_H^{1-\alpha} C_F^{\alpha}}{(1-\alpha)^{(1-\alpha)} \alpha^{\alpha}}, \tag{11}$$

where we drop time subscripts, since all variables are contemporaneous. C_H is a composite of domestically produced goods given by

$$C_H = \left(\int_0^1 C_H(z)^{\frac{\varepsilon-1}{\varepsilon}} dz \right)^{\frac{\varepsilon}{\varepsilon-1}}, \tag{12}$$

where z denotes the good's type or variety. The aggregate C_F is an aggregate of consumption across all other countries in the union i

$$C_F = \left(\int_0^1 C_i^{\frac{\eta-1}{\eta}} di \right)^{\frac{\eta}{\eta-1}}, \tag{13}$$

where C_i is an aggregate similar to (12). There is a public goods aggregate given by

$$G = \left(\int_0^1 G(z)^{\frac{\varepsilon-1}{\varepsilon}} dz \right)^{\frac{\varepsilon}{\varepsilon-1}}, \tag{14}$$

which implies that public goods are all domestically produced. The elasticity of substitution between varieties $\varepsilon > 1$ is common across countries. The parameter α is (inversely) related to the degree of home bias in preferences, and is a natural measure of openness.

Optimisation of expenditure for any individual good implies the demand functions

$$C_H(z) = \left(\frac{P_H(z)}{P_H} \right)^{-\varepsilon} C_H, \quad C_i(z) = \left(\frac{P_i(z)}{P_i} \right)^{-\varepsilon} C_i, \tag{15}$$

where we have price indices given by

$$P_H = \left(\int_0^1 P_H(z)^{1-\varepsilon} dz \right)^{\frac{1}{1-\varepsilon}}, \quad P_i = \left(\int_0^1 P_i(z)^{1-\varepsilon} dz \right)^{\frac{1}{1-\varepsilon}}. \tag{16}$$

It follows that

$$\int_0^1 P_H(z)C_H(z)dz = P_H C_H, \quad \int_0^1 P_i(z)C_i(z)dz = P_i C_i \tag{17}$$

Optimisation across imported goods by country implies

$$C_i = \left(\frac{P_i}{P_F} \right)^{-n} C_F, \tag{18}$$

where

$$P_F = \left(\int_0^1 P_i^{1-\eta} di \right)^{\frac{1}{1-\eta}}. \tag{19}$$

This allows us to write

$$\int_0^1 P_i C_i di = P_F C_F. \tag{20}$$

Optimisation between imported and domestically produced goods implies

$$P_H C_H = (1-\alpha)PC, \quad P_F C_F = \alpha PC, \tag{21}$$

where

$$P = P_H^{1-\alpha} P_F^{\alpha} \tag{22}$$

is the consumer price index (CPI).

The representative unconstrained consumer household maximises

$$E_0 \sum_{t=0}^{\infty} \beta^t \left(\ln C_t^u + \chi_t \ln G_t - \frac{(N_t^u)^{1+\varphi}}{1+\varphi} \right), \tag{23}$$

where N^u is labour supply for the unconstrained consumer. The budget constraint facing both constrained and unconstrained consumers is

$$\int_0^1 P_{H,t}(z) C_{H,t}(z) dz + \int_0^1 \int_0^1 P_{i,t}(z) C_{i,t}(z) dz di + E_t \{ Q_{t,t+1} A_{t+1} \}$$
$$\leq A_t + (1-\tau)(W_t N_t + \Pi_t), \tag{24}$$

where $P_{i,t}(z)$ is the price of variety z imported from country i expressed in home currency, A_{t+1} is the nominal payoff of the portfolio held at the end of period t, W are wages (the same wage rate is faced by constrained and unconstrained consumers), τ is an income tax rate and Π are profits. $Q_{t,t+1}$ is the stochastic discount factor for one period ahead payoffs. Using the definitions above, the budget constraint for either group of consumers can be rewritten as

$$P_t C_t + E_t \{ Q_{t,t+1} A_{t+1} \} = A_t + (1-\tau)(W_t N_t + \Pi_t). \tag{25}$$

Unconstrained consumers are able to maximise

$$E_t \sum_{v=t}^{\infty} \beta^{v-t} \left(\ln C_v^u + \xi_v \ln G_v - \frac{(N_v^u)^{1-\varphi}}{1+\varphi} \right)$$
$$- \lambda \left(\sum_{v=t}^{\infty} E_t (Q_{t,v} P_v C_v^u) - A_t^u - E_t \sum_{v=t}^{\infty} (Q_{t,v}((1-\tau)(W_v^u N_v^u + \Pi_v^u))) \right),$$

because they face no constraints on their borrowing (or lending). This optimisation produces the standard first-order conditions

$$\frac{\partial}{\partial C_s^u} : \beta^{s-t} \frac{1}{C_s^u} - \lambda Q_{t,s} P_s = 0,$$

$$\frac{\partial}{\partial N_s^u} : -\beta^{s-t}\left(N_s^u\right)^{\varphi}+(1-\tau)\lambda Q_{t,s} W_s^u = 0.$$

It follows that

$$\beta\frac{C_s^u}{C_{s+1}^u}\frac{P_s}{P_{s+1}} = Q_{s,s+1},$$

$$\frac{C_s^u\left(N_s^u\right)^{\varphi}}{(1-\tau)} = \frac{W_s^u}{P_s}.$$

Taking conditional expectations of the first equation and rearranging gives

$$\beta R_t E_t\left\{\frac{C_t^u}{C_{t+1}^u}\frac{P_t}{P_{t+1}}\right\} = 1, \tag{26}$$

where $R_t = \frac{1}{E_t\{Q_{t,t+1}\}}$ is the gross return on a riskless one period bond paying off a unit of domestic currency in $t + 1$.

Credit-constrained households differ from unconstrained households in that they are unable to borrow all they require to implement their optimal consumption plan.[7] The reasons why consumers might face borrowing constraints are well understood: expectations about future labour income depend on knowledge of human capital which in many situations is likely to be imperfect and asymmetric, such that lenders may be unwilling to lend all that agents require to implement their optimal plan. (The classic reference here is Stiglitz and Weiss (1988).)[8] However, it is unlikely that constrained consumers will be unable to borrow anything: we postulate that each member of this group faces an upper limit on their borrowing.[9] As a result, the consumption of this group will be governed by their budget constraint

$$C_t^c = \frac{(1-\tau)\left(W_t^c N_t^c + \Pi_t^c\right)}{P_t} + \bar{D}\frac{E_t(Q_{t,t+1}P_t) - P_{t-1}}{P_t}, \tag{27}$$

where $\bar{D}$ is an upper limit on borrowing $(\bar{D}<0)$.[10] However, it is straightforward to show that the first-order condition for labour supply will still hold for this group i.e.

$$\frac{C_t^c\left(N_t^c\right)^{\varphi}}{(1-\tau)} = \frac{W_t^c}{P_t}.$$

As constrained consumption is below desired levels, then for a given level of the wage these consumers will increase their labour supply in an effort to moderate the impact of the borrowing constraint.

4.2 Identities with PPP

The bilateral terms of trade with respect to country i in the union are the price of country i's goods relative to home goods prices. The effective terms of trade are given by aggregating across countries i

$$S = \frac{P_F}{P_H}. \tag{28}$$

The CPI and domestic price level are related as

$$P = P_H S^\alpha. \tag{29}$$

We also define the nominal relative price EX_i

$$EX_i = \frac{P_{H,i}}{P_H}. \tag{}$$

4.3 Allocation of government spending

The allocation of government spending across goods is determined by minimising total costs. This implies

$$G(z) = \left(\frac{P_H(z)}{P_H}\right)^{-\varepsilon} G. \tag{30}$$

4.4 Firms and price setting

Suppose the production function for firm j is

$$Y_t(j) = AN_t(j). \tag{31}$$

Both types of consumer supply labour of an identical type, so there is a uniform wage. (This assumption is not essential, but simplifies the exposition.)

Note that we can write the following expression for the wage

$$W_t = \frac{P_t C_t^c (N_t^c)^{\varphi}}{(1-\tau)} = \frac{P_t C_t^c (N_t - N_t^u)^{\varphi}}{(1-\tau)} = \frac{P_t C_t^c}{(1-\tau)} \left(N_t - \left(\frac{(1-\tau) W_t}{C_t^u P_t} \right)^{\frac{1}{\varphi}} \right)^{\varphi},$$

from where, using $N_t = \frac{1}{A} Y_t$ we obtain

$$\frac{(1-\tau) W_t}{P_t} = \left(\frac{1}{A} Y_t \right)^{\varphi} \left(\left(C_t^c \right)^{-\frac{1}{\varphi}} + \left(C_t^u \right)^{-\frac{1}{\varphi}} \right)^{-\varphi}.$$

The formula for marginal cost then is

$$MC_t = \frac{W_t}{A_t P_{Ht}} = \frac{P_t}{A_t P_{Ht}} \frac{W_t}{P_t} = \frac{P_t}{A_t (1-\tau) P_{Ht}} \left(\frac{Y_t}{A_t} \right)^{\varphi} \left(\left(C_t^c \right)^{-\frac{1}{\varphi}} + \left(C_t^u \right)^{-\frac{1}{\varphi}} \right)^{-\varphi}$$

$$= \frac{Y_t^{\varphi} S_t^{\alpha}}{A^{\varphi+1} (1-\tau)} \left(\left(C_t^c \right)^{-\frac{1}{\varphi}} + \left(C_t^u \right)^{-\frac{1}{\varphi}} \right)^{-\varphi},$$

and the log-linearised marginal cost is given as

$$mc_t = \varphi y_t + \alpha s_t + \frac{\kappa^{\frac{1}{\varphi}}}{\kappa^{\frac{1}{\varphi}} + (1-\kappa)^{\frac{1}{\varphi}}} c_t^c + \frac{(1-\kappa)^{\frac{1}{\varphi}}}{\kappa^{\frac{1}{\varphi}} + (1-\kappa)^{\frac{1}{\varphi}}} c_t^u, \tag{32}$$

where lower case denotes log deviations from steady state. Here $\kappa = C^c/C$ in steady state, so κ represents the proportion of consumers who are credit constrained.

Price setting is based on an extension to Calvo contracting set out in Steinsson (2003).[11] Each period, agents recalculate their prices with fixed probability $1-\gamma$. If prices are recalculated, then a proportion of agents ω use a backward-looking rule of thumb to reset prices, while the remainder calculate the optimum price. If prices are not recalculated (with probability γ), they rise at the steady state rate of inflation.

We use an asterisk to denote those firms that do reset their price. Their average price set is a weighted average of forward- and backward-looking components: $P_t^* = \left(P_t^F \right)^{1-\omega} \left(P_t^B \right)^{\omega}$. Backward-looking agents set their prices P_t^B according to the rule of thumb:

$$P_t^B = P_{t-1}^* \Pi_{t-1} \left(\frac{Y_{t-1}}{Y_{t-1}^n} \right) \delta, \tag{33}$$

where $\Pi_t = P_t/P_{t-1}$ and Y_t^n is the flexible-price equilibrium level of output (defined later). The forward-looking agents are able to solve the first-order conditions for profit maximisation and obtain an optimal solution P_t^F, see Rotemberg and Woodford (1997). For the rest of the sector the price will rise at the steady state rate of domestic inflation $\bar{\Pi} = 1$ with probability γ, $P_t = \bar{\Pi}P_{t-1}$. For the sector as a whole, the price equation can be written as:

$$P_t = \left[\gamma(\bar{\Pi}P_{t-1})^{1-\varepsilon} + (1-\gamma)(1-\omega)\left(P_t^F\right)^{1-\varepsilon} + (1-\gamma)\omega\left(P_t^B\right)^{1-\varepsilon}\right]^{\frac{1}{1-\varepsilon}}.$$
(34)

All optimising producers reset prices in period t according to the following approximate (log-linear) rule:

$$p_{Ht}^F = (\beta\theta)E_t p_{Ht+1}^F + (1 - \beta\theta)(mc_t + p_{Ht}).$$
(35)

This is formula (B.2) in Steinsson (2003). The derivation is the same in our case, so we do not present it here.

Steinsson (2003) has shown that (formula (A.3))

$$p_{Ht}^B = (1-\omega)\left(p_{Ht-1}^F\right) + \omega\left(p_{Ht-1}^B\right) + \pi_{H,t-1} + \delta y_{t-1},$$
(36)

and average inflation is defined as

$$\pi_{Ht} = \frac{(1-\gamma)}{\gamma}\left((1-\omega)\left(p_{Ht}^F\right) + \omega p_{H,t}^B - p_{Ht}\right).$$
(37)

Manipulations with formulae (35), (36) and (37) (see Steinsson (2003), formulae (A.5), (A.3) and (A. 1)) lead to the following equation

$$\begin{aligned}
\pi_{Ht} = &\frac{\gamma}{(\gamma+\omega(1-\gamma+\beta\gamma))}\beta\pi_{Ht+1} + \frac{\omega}{(\gamma+\omega(1-\gamma+\beta\gamma))}\pi_{Ht-1}\\
&+ \frac{(1-\gamma)\omega\delta}{(\gamma+\omega(1-\gamma+\beta\gamma))}y_{t-1} - \frac{(1-\gamma)\gamma\beta\omega\delta}{(\gamma+\omega(1-\gamma+\beta\gamma))}y_t\\
&+ \frac{(1-\beta\gamma)(1-\gamma)(1-\omega)}{(\gamma+\omega(1-\gamma+\beta\gamma))}mc_t.
\end{aligned}$$
(38)

We can substitute mc_t from formula (32).

4.5 Capital markets

If we assumed that all consumers were unconstrained, and that capital markets were complete such that international risk sharing applied, then our model would be identical to Galí and Monacelli (2005), apart from the addition of inflation inertia and credit-constrained consumers.

However, the assumption of international risk sharing would seem inappropriate for consumers who are rationed in credit markets, so we do not assume international risk sharing here. However, we do assume uncovered interest parity holds, which implies under fixed exchange rates that the domestic nominal interest rate is fixed, and equal to overseas interest rates. As is well known, a consequence of this setup is that the steady state for the economy is not unique, but depends on the initial level of wealth held by unconstrained consumers. (A classic example is Obstfeld and Rogoff (1995).)[12]

4.6 Aggregate demand

Goods market clearing requires

$$Y(j) = C_H(j) + \int_0^1 C^i(j)di + G(j). \tag{39}$$

Symmetrical preferences imply

$$C_H^i(j) = \alpha \left(\frac{P_H(j)}{P_H}\right)^{-\varepsilon} \left(\frac{P_H}{EX_i P^i}\right)^{-1} C^i, \tag{40}$$

which allows us to write

$$Y(j) = \left(\frac{P_H(j)}{P_H}\right)^{-\varepsilon} \left[(1-\alpha)\frac{PC}{P_H} + \alpha \int_0^1 \frac{EX_i P^i C^i}{P_H}di + G\right]. \tag{41}$$

Defining aggregate output as

$$Y = [\int_0^1 Y(j)^{\frac{\varepsilon-1}{\varepsilon}}dj]^{\frac{\varepsilon}{\varepsilon-1}} \tag{42}$$

allows us to write

$$\begin{aligned} Y &= (1-\alpha)\frac{PC}{P_H} + \alpha \int_0^1 \frac{EX_i P^i C^i}{P_H}di + G \\ &= S^\alpha\left[(1-\alpha)C + \alpha \int_0^1 Q_i C_i di\right] + G = CS^\alpha + G. \end{aligned} \tag{43}$$

4.7 Fiscal constraint and simple rules for fiscal policy

The government buys goods (G_t), taxes income (with constant tax rate τ), raises lump-sum taxes, pays an employment subsidy and issues nominal debt β_t. The evolution of the nominal debt stock can be written as:

$$\beta_{t+1} = (1 + i_t)(\beta_t + P_{Ht}G_t - \tau P_{Ht}Y_t - T + \mu^\omega). \tag{44}$$

The employment subsidy (μ^ω) and lump-sum taxes (T) are constant and cannot be used in stabilisation. This equation can be linearised as follows (defining $B_t = \beta_t/P_{t-1}$, denoting the steady state ratio of debt to output as ζ; here and everywhere below, for each variable X_t with steady state value X, we use the notation $x_t = \ln(X_t/X)$).

$$b_{t+1} = i_t + \frac{1}{\beta}\left(b_t - \pi_t + \frac{(1-\theta)}{\zeta}g_t - \frac{\tau}{\zeta}y_t\right). \tag{45}$$

where $\theta = C/Y$ in steady state.

We let government expenditure be the fiscal policy instrument. We postulate that out-of-steady-state government expenditure G_t is related to out-of-steady-state debt, and also to inflation and to the real exchange rate, according to the following simple feedback rule

$$\frac{G_t}{G} = \left(\frac{\Pi_{Ht}}{\Pi_H}\right)^{\phi_\pi}\left(\frac{S_t}{S}\right)^{\phi_s}\left(\frac{B_t}{B}\right)^{-\phi_b}, \tag{46}$$

where $\Pi_{Ht} = (1 + \pi_{Ht})$. Log-linearisation of this rules yields

$$gt = \phi_\pi\pi_{Ht} + \phi_s S_t - \phi_b b_t. \tag{47}$$

In what follows we shall explore the implications of different values of fiscal feedback parameters. In all cases, we assume that there is at least a minimum fiscal feedback on debt, so there are no debt sustainability issues.

4.8 The complete model

Our system consists of equations (26), (25), (27), (43), (28), (38) and (44) and the equation for fiscal policy. Assuming a fixed exchange rate regime, and log-linearising (for each variable X_t with steady state value X, using the notation $x_t = \ln(X_t/X)$), we obtain the following:

$$c_t^u = c_{t+1}^u + (1-\alpha)\pi_{Ht+1} + \alpha\pi_{Ht+1}^*, \tag{48}$$

$$a_{t+1}^u = \frac{1}{\beta}\left(a_t^u - (1-\alpha)\pi_{Ht} - \alpha\pi_{Ht}^* - \frac{(1-\kappa)\theta\bar{Y}}{\bar{A} - \bar{D}}c_t^u \right.$$
$$\left. + \frac{(1-\rho)(1-\tau)\bar{Y}}{\bar{A} - \bar{D}}(y_t - \alpha s_t)\right), \tag{49}$$

$$c_t^c = \frac{(1-\tau)\rho}{\kappa\theta}(y_t - \alpha s_t) - \frac{\bar{D}}{\kappa\theta\bar{Y}}\left((1-\alpha)\pi_{Ht} + \alpha\pi_{Ht}^*\right), \tag{50}$$

$$y_t = \theta(1-\alpha)((1-\kappa)\,c_s^u + \kappa\,c_s^c) + (1-\theta)g_t + 2\theta\eta\alpha(1-\alpha)s_t \\ + \theta\alpha c_t^*, \tag{51}$$

$$s_t = \pi_{Ht}^* - \pi_{Ht} + s_{t-1}, \tag{52}$$

$$\pi_{Ht} = X^f \beta E_t \pi_{Ht+1} + X^b \pi_{Ht-1} + \xi_c(\xi_{cc}c_t^c + \xi_{cu}c_t^u) + \xi_s s_t + \xi_{y0}y_t + \xi_{y1}y_{t-1}, \tag{53}$$

$$b_{t+1} = \frac{1}{\beta}\left(b_t - \pi_t + \frac{(1-\theta)}{\zeta}g_t - \frac{\tau}{\zeta}y_t\right), \tag{54}$$

$$g_t = \phi_\pi \pi_{Ht} + \phi_s s_t - \phi_b b_t, \tag{55}$$

where $\theta = C/Y$ in steady state and ρ is the share of output produced by workers who are borrowing constrained. Bars above variables are added to indicate steady state values. The derived parameters $\xi \chi^f$ and χ^f in the Phillips curve, and the value of ρ, are given in the Appendix.

How does this model compare with the stylised system outlined in Section 3? Equation (53) is a generalisation of the simple Phillips curve considered there, where we allow for a combination of forward and backward price setters. We can get the purely backward-looking, or purely forward-looking Phillips curves as special cases, although in the latter case expected future inflation is discounted. In addition, inflation depends on consumption and on the real exchange rate as well as on output, reflecting the interaction between marginal costs and labour supply.

The 'IS curve' in our microfounded model is clearly much more elaborate. However, in both cases output depends on the level of competitiveness, in this case acting through the terms of trade. The impact of inflation on output varies with the two types of consumer. For unconstrained consumers, inflation (working through real interest rates) influences the (expected) *change* in consumption, and consumption itself is a forward-looking, 'jump' variable. For constrained consumers, inflation influences the *level* of consumption, and the consumption function is static. The stylised model of Section 3 can be thought of as a special case in which all consumers are credit constrained. As we show in the following section, this distinction between forward-looking consumers and backward-looking ones is critical for issues of stability when inflation contains a significant backward-looking element.

5. Calibration

In our simple model in Section 3, we were able to analyse stability analytically. In our more complex model, the algebraic expressions for eigenvalues are intractable, so we need to examine a calibrated model. In this section we describe a standard calibration, with particular discussion of credit-constrained consumers.

Our 'base case' calibration of most of the parameters is taken from Rotemberg and Woodford (1997). One period is taken as equal to one quarter of a year. We set the one period discount factor of the private sector (and policy makers) to $\beta = 0.99$. We calibrate $\varphi = 2.0$. We assume that $\gamma = 0.75$, which corresponds to an average contract length of one year.

Our knowledge regarding inflation persistence is very insecure. All empirical studies are unanimous in concluding that an empirical Phillips curve has a significant backward-looking component. Estimates of the relative importance of backward-looking price setters differ widely. Galí and Gertler (1999) and Benigno and López-Salido (2006) find a predominantly forward-looking specification, while Mehra (2004) finds an extremely backward-looking specification of the Phillips curve. Mankiw (2001) argues that stylised empirical facts are inconsistent with a predominantly forward-looking Phillips curve. A figure of $\omega = 0.75$ corresponds to an equal weight on forward and backward inflation terms suggested by results in Fuhrer and Moore (1995). As a result of this uncertainty, we look at a range of alternative values between the two extreme cases of complete forward- and backward-looking behaviour.

Since the seminal paper by Hall (1978), empirical studies have rejected the simple Euler equation formulation implied by (26). Studies have also shown that consumption tracks income over the life-cycle, which is again inconsistent with our model in which all consumers are unconstrained. One of the most popular explanations for these empirical findings is that at least some consumers face binding credit constraints. A large number of papers have tried to estimate the proportion of consumers who are credit constrained, and many of these are surveyed in Grant (2003). That paper also suggests that 26–31 per cent of US households are credit constrained. We assume a base value of 30 per cent for κ, but we also look at the implications of varying this parameter.

The amount of gross debt as a proportion of annual GDP varies substantially between economies. (It is roughly equal to unity in the

UK and Netherlands, for example; is a little lower for the USA, but substantially lower for Italy.) We adopt a base figure for the constrained debt to annual GDP ratio of 1.0, but we also investigate the implications of alternative values. We assume that unconstrained consumers collectively hold a similar quantity of wealth, so that the net asset position of the country as a whole is zero. We assume a value of $\alpha = 0.3$, $\theta = 0.7$, and our demand curve parameters are $\varepsilon = 5$ and $\eta = 1$ (as assumed in Galí and Monacelli (2005)). However, as we show in Kirsanova *et al.* (2006), our basic result is robust to these and most other parameter values besides those associated with credit-constrained consumers.

6. Analysis

We use this model to study the effects of an initial, unexpected, one-off shock to competitiveness, which causes the economy to begin in an uncompetitive position. This could happen because the underlying competitiveness of the economy changes, so that an initial position, which was initially competitive, ceases to be so. We study the model's behaviour in the absence of active fiscal policy, the only form of fiscal policy consists of a low feedback on debt, $\varphi_b = 0.05$. We show how this behaviour varies with the proportion of forward-looking price setters and with the proportion of forward-looking consumers. In particular, we show that, in the absence of fiscal policy, stability is only assured if there is a sufficiently large proportion of forward-looking prices setters and/or a sufficiently large proportion of forward-looking consumers. We also show that a fiscal policy which responds to the level of inflation lowers the degree of forward-lookingness which is necessary to ensure stability.

We then show how, even if the economy is forward-looking enough to respond to the shock in a stable manner, the competitiveness of the economy can overshoot, and the outcome can be a cyclical process of convergence to equilibrium. Such cycles are bound to impact on social welfare (see, for example, Kirsanova *et al.* (2007)).We also show how fiscal policy can moderate such cyclical behaviour.

It would be valuable to study the response of the economy to stochastic disturbances. We leave this as a study for further work, confining our attention here to analysis of this one shock.

6.1 Instability and the Walters critique

We consider the combinations of credit-constrained consumers κ and backward-looking price setters ω, with no fiscal feedback present, for which stability is possible. See Figure 13.6.

In the special case when we have complete inflation persistence, $\omega = 1$, a negative shock to competitiveness will cause inflation to fall and this will lead real interest rates to rise. This is a violation of the Taylor principle. As in our simple model analysed in Section 3, when all price setters are also backward-looking and there are no forward-looking consumers, so that also $\kappa = 1$, then the outcome will be unstable. That outcome is depicted at the top right-hand corner of Figure 13.6. The country's falling inflation, caused by its lack of competitiveness, would cause its price level to gradually fall relative to that in the other country, and the country's real exchange rate would depreciate. This will cause a rise in net exports, and that would cause a stabilising rise in the demand for output. If also $\kappa = 1$ then, even although inflation is falling and competitiveness is improving, the continuing fall in inflation, and continuing rise in the real interest rate, would provoke a continuing fall in consumption. For reasons explained in Section 3.1, this second effect

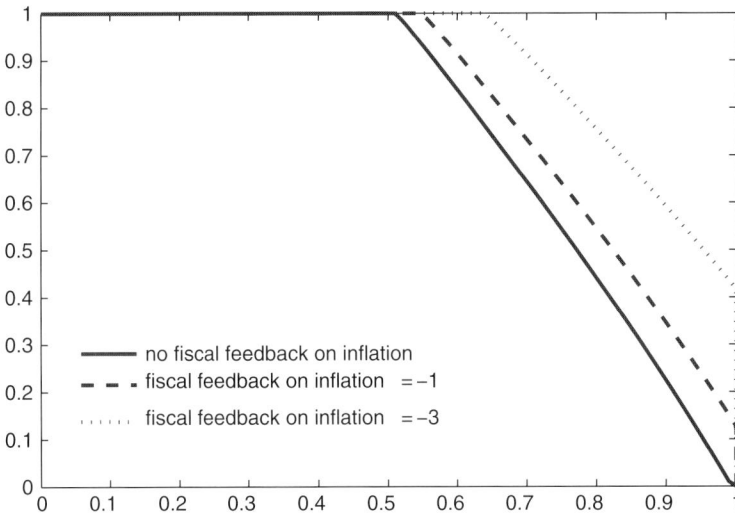

Figure 13.6: Stability boundary as a function of proportion of backward-looking price setters, ω, and proportion of credit-constrained consumers, κ

would dominate, and output would fall cumulatively in an unstable manner. As noted in Section 3, this instability is what was identified in the 'Walters critique' of the EMS.

If all price setters were all forward-looking, but all consumers were backward-looking then we are at the top left-hand corner of Figure 13.6. Assuming that forward-looking price setters are capable of jumping the inflation rate so as to ensure that the transversality conditions hold, they will put the economy on a stable saddle-path, in the Blanchard-Kahn manner. We have discussed in Section 3.2 what happens then. Following the initial downward shock to competitiveness, inflation will jump down, and gradually rise back to equilibrium again, during which time the disturbance to competitiveness will gradually be removed. Along the adjustment path, consumption will fall initially and then gradually rise again.

If all price setters were backward-looking, but all consumers were forward-looking then we are at the bottom right-hand corner of Figure 13.6; numerical analysis of the calibrated model shows this point to be exactly on the stability boundary. Assuming that forward-looking consumers are capable of placing the initial level of unconstrained consumption so as to avoid Ponzi-game outcomes, they will put the economy on a stable path in the Blanchard-Kahn manner. We have described in Section 3.3 what happens then. The system will not explode, but it will cycle in an undamped manner. Following the initial downwards shock to competitiveness, there will be a gradual fall of inflation. Consumption will initially jump down and then begin to rise – in line with an expectation of higher real interest rates in the future. (As noted in Section 3.3 the Euler equation shows that, along the adjustment trajectory, forward-looking consumption must be rising in the presence of a positive real interest rate.) But at some stage inflation will begin to rise again, so that competitiveness begins to worsen again; consumption will begin to fall again at this point. The solution gives rise to an undamped cycle of inflation, competitiveness and consumption.

In the presence of forward-looking consumers and price setters, the system described by our model involves two jump variables: forward-looking consumption and inflation. We suppose that forward-looking price setters and consumers are together capable of ensuring that the economy does not experience explosive behaviour. This requires that they jump the initial level of both unconstrained consumption and the inflation rate so as to place the economy on a stable saddle-path, in the Blanchard-Kahn manner. Such an outcome requires that there be two eigenvalues outside the unit circle.[13] The solid line in Figure 13.6 shows the stability boundary for different proportions of credit-constrained consumers κ and backward-looking price setters ω, with no fiscal feedback present. Saddle-path stability occurs to the south-west of the boundary. The stability boundary shows that stability can be achieved, without fiscal intervention, even if neither consumption nor price setting are entirely forward-looking. For example if $\omega = 0.75$, then stability is ensured if $\kappa < 0.55$. In that case, then, providing that forward-looking consumers and forward-looking price setters are together capable of jumping consumption and the inflation rate so as to ensure that the economy is on a stable Blanchard-Kahn path, stability will be ensured.

The solid line in the first column of Figure 13.7 shows outcomes of this kind, when both price setting and consumption are partly forward-looking and partly backward-looking, in this case when $\omega = 0.75$ and $\kappa = 0.3$. Along these paths, backward-looking price setters gradually adjust inflation after the shock, and forward-looking price setters adjust inflation more rapidly than this. Overall the movement in inflation is gradual, not only because of the weight of 0.75 on backward-looking price setters, but also because, due to this weight, forward-looking price setters expect a gradual downward movement in overall inflation, and so jump forward-looking inflation down by less than they would have done if all price setters had been forward-looking. Overall the movement of inflation is more rapid than it would have been if all price setters had been backward-looking. Similarly backward-looking consumers cut consumption by increasing amounts over the first few periods after the shock, as the rate of inflation falls and so the real rate of interest rises. But, in the light of this rise in the real interest rate, forward-looking consumers initially jump consumption downwards and then, after the first period, cause their consumption to rise again. This continuing rise in forward-looking consumption, along with the improvement in competitiveness caused by falling inflation, comes to stimulate demand and so gradually to arrest the fall in inflation. The resulting turnaround in inflation ensures stability.

The stability boundary shows that forward-looking consumption and forward-looking price setting can substitute for each other in ensuring stability; the figure shows that the larger the proportion of consumers who are liquidity constrained, the smaller the proportion of

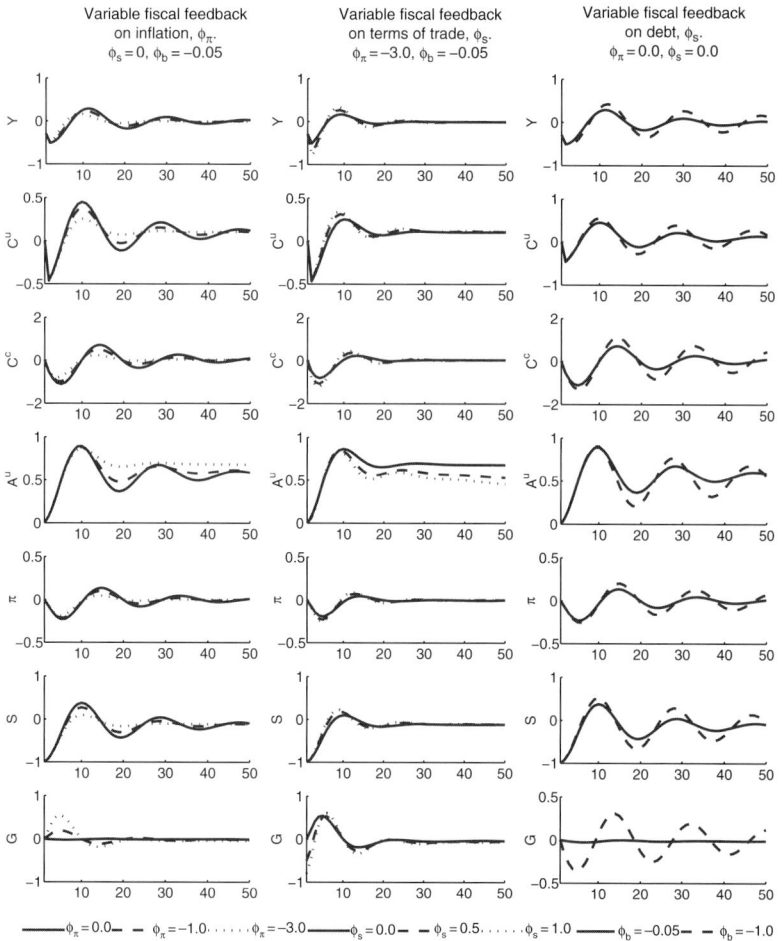

Figure 13.7: Response to a shock of -1 to competitiveness, s
Note: The figures assume that the proportion of backward-looking price setters, ω, is 0.75, and that the proportion of credit-constrained consumers, κ, is 0.3. They show the effects of different fiscal feedback parameters.

backward-looking price setters has to be in order to ensure stability. For example, if κ does not have the value of 0.3 assumed in Figure 13.7 but instead had a value of 1.0, then stability would not be possible if ω remained equal to 0.75, but would only be possible if ω instead had a lower value of 0.5. In this case the proportion of forward-looking price setters would be large enough to ensure that, even if there were no forward-looking consumers to moderate a continuing fall in consumption after an initial shock to competitiveness, the initial downward jump in the price level would be large enough to ensure that improvements in competitiveness were large enough to offset the effects of the continuing fall in consumption.

If the parameters of the economy are such that it lies to the right of the stability boundary in Figure 13.6 then a stable rational expectations equilibrium solution will not exist. For example, if $\omega = 0.75$, but $\kappa > 0.55$ then it would not be possible for forward-looking consumers and price setters to put the economy on a stable saddle-path trajectory. We can see why this is. Suppose that, for these values of ω and κ, forward-looking price setters expected a gradual downward movement of inflation of the kind shown in Figure 13.7, for reasons described above. Then, in the expectation of this, backward-looking consumers would cut their consumption by increasing amounts over the first few periods after the shock, as the rate of inflation fell and so the real rate of interest rose. Stability requires that this effect be counterbalanced by the behaviour of forward-looking consumers, in the way shown in Figure 13.7. But with a low value of κ, this proportion of forward-looking consumers is small. As a result, any hypothetical attempt by them to jump consumption downwards and then, after the first period, to cause consumption to rise again – in the manner described above – would not be sufficient to cause output to begin to rise again. As a result inflation would continue to fall over time, and the real interest rate would continue to rise. That would increase the expectation by forward-looking consumers of higher interest rates in the future, requiring a larger initial downward jump in the value of forward-looking consumption than what has been supposed – a contradiction.

Figure 13.6 shows that fiscal feedback on inflation will raise the value of κ consistent with stability given any value for ω. This is consistent with the analysis for the backward-looking model presented in Section 3.1, but generalises that analysis. It is now the case that for a range of values of κ and ω, stability is possible without any fiscal feedback. But a fiscal feedback on inflation will increase the range of κ and ω for which stability is possible. This is because as inflation falls and the real interest rate rises, expansionary fiscal policy offsets the effects of these higher interest rates in causing backward-looking consumption to fall. This means that there do not need to be as many forward-looking consumers to offset this effect, or forward-looking price setters do not need to cause inflation to fall so fast. Policy makers can thus use fiscal policy to ensure that less forward-lookingness is necessary to ensure stability.

If stability is ensured, there may still be a possibility of overshooting and cycles, to which we now turn.

6.2 *Overshooting of the price level*

The solid line in the first column of Figure 13.7 shows that, even when stable, outcomes without fiscal policy intervention may give rise to overshooting and to cycles. In response to a temporary shock to competitiveness within a monetary union, the real exchange rate s must return to its initial level. The shock causes output – which depends negatively on competitiveness – to fall. This low level of output will cause inflation to become negative, so that competitiveness rises back towards equilibrium, as shown. There will come a time when the price level has fallen enough to remove the reduction in demand which resulted from the initial fall in competitiveness. But, at this point, as Figure 13.7 shows, the persistence of inflation means that the rate of inflation will be negative. Thus when equilibrium has been reached the price level will still be falling and the real exchange rate will still be appreciating; i.e. it will overshoot. If the overshoot is large enough, the behaviour of the real exchange rate will be oscillatory.

Given stability, the oscillatory behaviour will be damped, and the proportion of backward-looking price setters will determine how damped it is. The figure shows that the behaviour of the economy is highly cyclical when $\kappa = 0.3$ and $\omega = 0.75$; oscillations are still marked after more than 50 periods. It can be shown that, when $\omega = 0.5$, the model's dynamic is still cyclical, although the cycles are much reduced in amplitude after 50 periods. If $\omega = 0.15$ cyclical movements are much less apparent, although overshooting still occurs in constrained consumption.

There is a contrast here with inflation-targeting systems. In such systems, if inflation were to rise above its target level, and then be brought down again by monetary policy, the price level will slip away from the level which it would have had if, instead, it had risen at a steady rate without the shock. Such slippages are not normally corrected in inflation-targeting regimes. In this EMU regime, however, such a slippage of the price level is not possible. In this system any rise in the price level causes loss of competitiveness of the kind studied here. Their level of competitiveness must be brought to the level at which full employment of resources can be regained by a high enough level of net exports.

The proportion of unconstrained forward-looking consumers (i.e. those who are not liquidity constrained) helps to contribute to cyclicality (whereas it is the existence of liquidity-constrained consumers which gives rise to the possibility of instability). We can see this from Figure 13.7. Unconstrained consumption initially falls and then begins to rise. The Euler equation shows that it will not stop rising until inflation has risen back to zero (because only then will the real interest rate have risen back to zero). But as the Figure shows, at that point unconstrained consumption is above equilibrium. (This is because it will be falling in the future because, with inflation persistence, inflation will be positive in the future and so the real interest rate will be negative in the future). But this positive consumption will be adding to the demand pressure caused by the real exchange rate, which has over-depreciated at that point. Thus although an increase in the degree of forward-lookingness of consumption makes instability less likely, it does not help eliminate cyclicality. That depends on the forward-lookingness in price setting.

6.3 Fiscal policy rules

If the economy is not forward-looking enough to ensure stability, or to moderate a process of cyclical response, then policy makers may use fiscal policy to ensure that the economy behaves how it would if consumption and price setting were forward-looking. Such fiscal policy will influence how quickly prices, competitiveness and output return to their original levels.

6.3.1 Responding to inflation

If the economy is uncompetitive after a shock then – given stability – inflation begins to fall. Fiscal policy can be expanded as this happens. The first column of Figure 13.7 shows the effects of doing this. Along the adjustment path, fiscal policy could cancel out at least some of the effects on consumption of the higher real interest rates – the consequence of relative disinflation – so that the demand-increasing effects of improved competitiveness can take hold. Kirsanova *et al.* (2007) show that such a policy could significantly improve welfare within EMU. The required policy described in Figure 13.7 would require a negative feed-back from lower inflation, to a higher level of government expenditure – or a positive feedback to the tax rate. This is a fiscal feedback rule of the kind described in Westaway (2003).

In this case fiscal policy must also continue to stabilise debt, to ensure that there is no instability caused by, for example, the loss in tax revenues caused by a loss in output. But the feedback coefficient can be small, and is set equal to 0.05. This value is large enough to ensure that the government's debt stock reaches its steady-state value, but otherwise small enough to give policy the freedom to also help stabilise inflation. The reason why very slow adjustment of debt may be optimal is explored extensively in Kirsanova and Wren-Lewis (2008).

Such a feedback rule would mean that fiscal policy would be com-pensating for the failure of the Taylor principle to hold in a fixed exchange rate system in response to asymmetric shocks, and helping to avoid cycles. And the more that such policy stabilised demand and inflation the less the price level would overshoot.

6.3.2 Responding to the real exchange rate

Adjustment of the real exchange rate in the face of a competitiveness shock will require that the country's nominal prices end up in a lower position, relative to the level of prices in the EMU area as a whole. If competitiveness begins below equilibrium, as studied here, then fiscal policy might take additional corrective action of a contractionary kind to help speed the adjustment process. This form of response is depicted in the second column of Figure 13.7. It can clearly help to speed up the adjustment process. This would be a parallel to the circumstances in which the monetary-policy regime can choose the speed at which infla-tion is controlled in the face of an inflation shock in an inflation-targeting regime. The simple model in Section 3 above has shown that such feedback from the real exchange rate, and higher speed of adjust-ment, would make a cyclical overshoot of the real exchange rate more likely. This too is borne out by the pictures shown in the second column of Figure 13.7. To prevent such a cyclical response, the feedback on the real exchange rate would need to be coupled with a stronger response to inflation. A fiscal response to the level of the real exchange rate, as well as a response to inflation, could bring about more rapid convergence without cycles. Kirsanova *et al.* (2007) show that such more rapid, non-cycling, convergence could lead to a significant improvement in welfare.

6.3.3 Responding to debt: the Stability and Growth Pact

It is clear that this interventionist policy points in the opposite direction to the Stability and Growth Pact (SGP). The response shown in the third column of Figure 13.7 shows the effect of operating a policy more like the SGP, in which there is no fiscal feedback on inflation and in which spending is cut strongly in response to an increase in debt. The Figure shows how such a feedback on debt could lead to more cycles of larger amplitude than those which would occur with the value of the feedback on debt of $\varphi_b = 0.05$. Under the operation of a policy of this kind, a low level of competitiveness would cause output to fall. But this would cause tax receipts to fall, causing an increase in debt. Under this policy, government spending would be cut, augmenting the downturn. That would cause tax revenues to fall, leading to an increase in debt, to a further cut in government spending, further augmenting the downturn. This is why such a policy can worsen cycles. It is possible to show that it can make saddle-path stability impossible, for values of the range of κ and ω which would otherwise make such stability possible.

As already noted above, it is clear that fiscal policy must stabilise debt, to ensure that there is no instability caused by, for example, the loss in tax revenues caused by a loss in output. But as shown in Kirsanova and Wren-Lewis (2008) the optimal feedback coefficient is small, and this avoids the cycles shown in the third column. This is one of the reasons why it is optimal for the stabilisation of debt to be slow: it avoids such cycles. A relaxed version of the SGP would allow that, in each country, fiscal policy fixed tax rates and let the deficit run up, and debt increased, as output fell and tax revenues fell, only gradually reducing so as to bring debt under control.

7. Policy implications

7.1 *Difficulties with the Stability and Growth Pact*

The above analysis suggests that the fiscal rules of the Stability and Growth Pact (SGP) could be unhelpful in EMU in response to asymmetric shocks. They suggest that if the fiscal authorities tightly target fiscal sustainability (aiming, say, for a particular deficit or debt ratio) as in the SGP, this may cause the economy to cycle, or may even make stability difficult to achieve.

If a country were to follow the SGP, when adjusting to a downturn in competitiveness, the fiscal authorities would be unable to allow the in-built stabilisers to operate – i.e. they would need to cut government spending. Further, this would prevent them from intervening so as to compensate for the violation of the Taylor principle. As inflation fell and debt increased, government expenditure would need to fall, causing further falls in inflation. The level of competitiveness would be likely to overshoot, leading to cycles. Secondly, the fall in inflation would, quite possibly, be undesirably rapid, possibly making stability difficult to achieve, as suggested by the Walters critique.

There may thus be interference between the fiscal arrangements of the SGP, and the need to adjust real exchange rates and competitiveness between countries within EMU. It appears that the constraints of the SGP, which – unlike the analysis here may apply asymmetrically to countries facing competitiveness difficulties – do interfere with the fiscal policy responses that may be desirable in such countries. Because of this, such countries may experience unnecessary and costly deflation, or instability, or cycles. Our general prescription is that there should be a greater delegation of fiscal freedom to those countries that are suffering from such sustained negative shocks to competitiveness.

Importantly, such policies, if adopted, must not lead to the postpone-ment of necessary adjustments of the relative real exchange rate. The additional fiscal freedom should be used in such a way as to be con-sistent with the long-run outcome. The analysis here does *not* suggest that there be fiscal expansion to prevent adjustment in these countries. Instead it suggests that fiscal policy could be used to speed adjustment – fiscal expenditures could be cut initially in countries suffering from a low level of competitiveness – as shown in column 2 of Figure 13.7. But fiscal policy would subsequently become expansionary to prevent adjustment going too far.

Our overall conclusion is that, such additional policy freedom is likely to improve the tradeoffs in the country concerned, resulting in better adjustment to competitiveness shocks, without causing addi-tional inflation.

7.2 A proposal

We suggest that, for a good outcome, the choice for fiscal policy might need to involve:

i. only very gradual feedback from the level of debt to the fiscal position;

ii. active fiscal policy feedback which becomes more stimulatory if inflation becomes low, to prevent unstable developments in the price level, and to prevent the price level overshooting; and

iii. active feedback to fiscal policy from the future equilibrium value of the real exchange rate, being cut if the economy is uncompetitive but becoming more expansionary as the real exchange rate depreciates towards its equilibrium level, in order to help prevent the real exchange rate overshooting.

Thus we are suggesting that the fiscal authorities target the longer-term fiscal position in such a way that they steer the real exchange rate towards the appropriate position. Or alternatively, we suggest they might target (i.e. introduce feedback from) an appropriate future real exchange rate, where that target is chosen to give a competitive position which would be consistent with full employment.

This course of action seems desirable because the debt ratio per se does not normally, of itself, have much weight in the authorities' objective function. The fiscal position needs to be sustainable, as we have seen, but otherwise debt should be allowed to act as a shock absorber, and has been discussed above. This point is discussed in detail in Kirsanova *et al.* (2005) and Kirsanova *et al.* (2007).

The appropriate real exchange rate would be that which ensured that, after any worsening of the external competitiveness position which was expected to be sustained, competitiveness was again returned to a position at which demand for domestic resources was restored. At this point the level of capacity utilisation would have returned to a normal position, and tax revenues would have been restored, rather than being low because output was below capacity. At that position the sustainability of the budgetary position would be assured.

The contrast between such a conduct of fiscal policy, and one directed to the control of deficit and debt, is as follows. Initially, once it became clear that the position was one of worsened external competitiveness, fiscal policy would be tightened, with the aim of putting downward pressure on wage and price settlements, so as to help speed the adjustment of the real exchange rate by 'Phillips-curve pressure'. But as the adjustment happened, fiscal policy would become looser again, to ensure that downward pressure on wages and prices did not continue to be exercised even after competitiveness had improved sufficiently relative to other countries within EMU.

What we are suggesting for fiscal policy involves a regime of 'constrained discretion'. The longer-term objective for fiscal policy, or the 'constraint', would remain that of 'sustainability'. This would be an objective just like that in the SGP, specified in accordance with a framework of 'sustainability pacts' (see Coeuré and Pisani-Ferri (2005)). The difference of our approach from that in the SGP lies in the way in which 'discretion' would operate. The policy action which we suggest, in response to indications of 'unsustainability', would be different from what is now meant to happen within the SGP. At present, within the SGP, the required response to such a problem is a programme of budgetary cuts, even if the problem is caused by a loss of competitiveness, as in the thought experiment that we have been carrying out. What we are suggesting instead would be a policy directed towards achieving changes in the real exchange rate over time, towards a long-run target. That target would be the one which was consistent with the sustainability objective. The required move of the economy towards this position would be assisted by fiscal restraint. But that restraint would be devised so as to help avoid cycles, as has been explained.

There is an additional reason that such a policy might be desirable, beyond that shown in our modelling simulations discussed above. That modelling work assumed that those setting prices in a forward-looking way would know by how much competitiveness would need to be improved when bringing down the inflation rate so as to improve competitiveness. In reality it may be difficult for the private sector to determine the degree of adjustment of competitiveness that is required. If fiscal policy were to target the level of competitiveness, in the way discussed here, that might make it easier for the private sector to form the appropriate expectations.

The policy framework which we are outlining is not a simple one. But adjustment of the real exchange rate, in a way consistent with fiscal sustainability in the longer term, is not a simple problem within a monetary union. It is clear that the computation of the appropriate real exchange rate would require significant modelling work. In the same way in which inflation targeting does not operate by the mechanical operation of a Taylor rule, this kind of fiscal policy would need to operate in a non-mechanical way. Such policy might be managed by national fiscal policy committees, in the way advocated by Charles

Wyplosz (Wyplosz (2005)), Jean Pisani-Ferry (2002) and Simon Wren-Lewis (2002).

8. Conclusion

Europe has been underperforming, not only in terms of productivity performance, but also in terms of an apparently unfavourable tradeoff between growth and inflation. The normal diagnosis of this problem has given macroeconomic policy a relatively clean bill of health, and has pointed instead to supply-side issues and the need for supply-side reform.

This chapter presents an alternative argument which focuses on the process of intercountry adjustment, and on the connections between this adjustment process and fiscal policies within the euro area. We argue that fiscal policy and adjustment issues have, within EMU, interacted in unfavourable, and possibly destabilising, ways. Our analysis suggests that these problems arise in particular for countries that are needing to improve their relative international competitiveness, and that are also suffering from downturns in spending resulting from such poor international competitiveness. It is in countries in these circumstances that fiscal rules of the SGP bind most strongly.

In broad terms, this combination of adjustment problems and binding fiscal constraints can be seen as characterising the 'German problem'. We believe that the poor performance in Germany for some years, and some other large countries, has been caused by the problems described in this chapter. We think that this could explain a large part of the euro area's poor performance in aggregate in the first part of this decade. Our argument suggests that restoring greater fiscal sovereignty to national governments could enable better performance to be achieved in countries such as Germany, without engendering inflation, since there is no reason why such policies should be inconsistent with the requirement that fiscal policy be sustainable in the longer run.

Our arguments do not suggest that supply-side problems are not important or that they should not be addressed. It may be that important supply-side reforms and adjustments would be easier to introduce with a better macroeconomic framework, and that greater confidence in the euro area's growth potential would then be realised.

Appendix: Coefficients

Coefficients of the Phillips curve can be written as:

$$X^f = \frac{\gamma}{(\gamma+\omega(1 - \gamma+\beta\gamma))}, \quad X^b = \frac{\omega}{(\gamma+\omega(1 - \gamma+\beta\gamma))},$$

$$\xi_{cc} = \frac{\kappa^{\frac{1}{\varphi}}}{\kappa^{\frac{1}{\varphi}} + (1 - \kappa)^{\frac{1}{\varphi}}}, \quad \xi_{cu} = \frac{(1 - \kappa)^{\frac{1}{\varphi}}}{\kappa^{\frac{1}{\varphi}} + (1 - \kappa)^{\frac{1}{\varphi}}},$$

$$\xi_c = \frac{(1 - \beta\gamma)(1 - \gamma)(1 - \omega)}{(\gamma+\omega(1 - \gamma+\beta\gamma))}, \quad \xi_s = \alpha\xi_c,$$

$$\xi_{y0} = \frac{(1 - \gamma)((1 - \beta\gamma)(1-\omega)\varphi-\gamma\beta\omega\delta)}{(\gamma+\omega(1 - \gamma+\beta\gamma))},$$

$$\xi_{y1} = \frac{(1 - \gamma)\omega\delta}{(\gamma+\omega(1 - \gamma+\beta\gamma))}.$$

From the two steady-state relationships:

$$D = \frac{1}{\beta}(D + \rho(1 - \tau)Y + T) - C^c),$$

$$A^u = \frac{1}{\beta}(A^u + (1 - \rho)((1 - \tau)Y + T) - C^u),$$

we obtain the steady-state share of output produced by workers who are borrowing constrained (ρ):

$$\rho = \frac{\left(\kappa - (1 - \beta)\frac{D}{\theta}\right)}{\left(1 - (1 - \beta)\frac{A^u+D}{\theta}\right)}.$$

Notes

1. We will see that if consumers are forward-looking, but all price setters are backward-looking, the economy will only *just* be stable; it will cycle in an undamped manner. If some price setters are also forward-looking, then the resulting cycles will be damped.
2. We could extend our analysis to a stochastic setting, since linear models are certainty equivalent.
3. In the full model in the next section, we present a partly forward-looking and partly backward-looking Phillips curve; the forward-looking component of that Phillips curve is New Keynesian, and so the Phillips curve in the full model does not have the NAIRU property.
4. The system is solved using the Blanchard-Kahn procedure.

5. The system is solved using the Blanchard-Kahn procedure.

6. Here this involves eliminating any effect of the zero root which would introduce a constant into the solution and prevent the economy returning to equilibrium.

7. Our analysis is similar to that in Wright (2004).

8. Graham and Wright (2007) differentiate between constrained and unconstrained consumers by assuming that the former have a higher discount rate. Here we simply assume that the returns on some forms of human capital are easier to evaluate than others, and that those workers with more uncertain future earnings are credit constrained.

9. The justification for assuming a fixed nominal limit on borrowing, at least over the short term, is discussed in detail in Wright (2004).

10. This constraint on nominal debt is what ensures, in Equation (50) below (which is the linearised equation for constrained consumption), that unconstrained consumption falls if inflation falls, because such a fall would raise the real rate of interest and so cause interest obligations on unconstrained consumers to rise. In the longer term, one would expect such a nominal constraint to be indexed to the price level.

11. Christiano *et al.* (2005) introduce inflation inertia by adapting Calvo in a different way: they assume that those firms that do not calculate the profit-maximising price each period instead index their prices, rather than keeping them fixed as Calvo (1983) assumes. This results in a Phillips curve with inflation inertia that has the NAIRU property. The difference between these two formulations will not be important for the results in this chapter.

12. We would get very similar results to those described below if we assumed interest risk sharing applied only to unconstrained consumers.

13. In addition there is a unit eigenvalue reflecting the unit root process for wealth, a feature not present in our simpler model.

Comment 9: Comment on Chapter 13

ROBERT KOLLMANN

1. General comments

Under EMU, monetary policy is oriented towards union-wide economic conditions, and cannot effectively address country-specific macroeconomic disturbances. Should national *fiscal policy* be used more actively, for stabilizing individual economies, now that exchange rate changes among member countries are no longer possible? Several recent studies answer this important normative question, based on sticky-price (New Keynesian) dynamic stochastic general equilibrium (DSGE) models with rigorous microeconomic foundations – see Galí and Monacelli (2008), Beetsma and Jensen (2005), Adão *et al.* (2006), Kirsanova *et al.* (2007), Ferrero (2007) and Forlati (2007).[1] That research suggests that the adjustment of government purchases and tax rates in response to country-specific disturbances may noticeably improve economic welfare, in a monetary union; constraints on fiscal policy (ceilings on budget deficits or debt levels) can thus lower welfare. The research also shows that welfare-maximizing fiscal policy depends on the economic structure of the member countries, especially on the nature of market frictions and of shocks, and on what fiscal policy instruments can be used (spending or tax rates). However, rigorous analysis of these key issues is still in its infancy – the available studies use very stylized models. Research based on more realistic models is needed to permit reliable operational fiscal policy advice.

The chapter by Christopher Allsopp and David Vines is an interesting contribution to the literature on fiscal policy in a monetary union. Its main merit is the use of a sticky-price DSGE model with a richer, more realistic policy transmission mechanism. A small economy in a monetary union is considered. The country's government levies an income tax, purchases local goods, and issues debt. The tax rate is

I thank Pedro Teles for helpful discussions and advice.

constant. Government purchases are used as a stabilization tool. Government purchases are set as a function (feedback rule) of the country's inflation rate, terms of trade (defined as the domestic price level divided by the foreign price level) and public debt.

2. The main contributions

The methodological contribution is that the authors use a model which incorporates the following two key features (that are not considered by the studies cited above):

i. a fraction of households faces binding nominal *credit constraints*;
ii. *inflation is persistent*, due to a Phillips curve with a backward-looking component.

Credit-constrained households cannot smooth consumption intertemporally. A rise in the price level lowers the real value of their debt, and triggers a rise in consumption. Thus, price level changes have a powerful effect on consumption, and hence on real activity, in the model here (output is demand determined, in the short run). Also, credit-constrained households adjust their consumption one-to-one to changes in their current factor income. By contrast, the related literature on monetary unions discussed above assumes free household borrowing and lending; those models capture less well the empirical fact that consumption tracks disposable income very closely (Campbell and Mankiw (1989)). Galí *et al.* (2007) show that a model in which households cannot smooth consumption captures much better the empirical responses of aggregate demand to government spending shocks. Several recent large macroeconomic models developed by policy making institutions thus allow for credit-constrained households (e.g. Erceg *et al.* (2006), Ratto *et al.* (2008)). Hence, it clearly makes sense to use a model with credit constraints for *normative* fiscal policy analysis.

Inflation persistence is likewise a key feature of the data (e.g. Smets and Wouters (2007)). Previous analyses of fiscal policy in monetary unions have mostly assumed price setting à la Calvo (1983) – which implies that inflation has a purely forward-looking dynamic. By contrast, Allsopp and Vines assume that a fraction of firms index their prices to lagged inflation and output, so that aggregate domestic inflation depends on *lagged* inflation and output (as well as on current output and expected future inflation).[2]

The analytical contribution of the paper is as follows. The authors demonstrate that a model with the two features described above may exhibit boom-bust cycles in response to a persistent shock which lowers the external competitiveness of the country being studied. This happens because backward-looking price setting implies protracted deviations of the terms of trade, output and employment from efficient levels. The presence of credit-constrained households magnifies these effects. Consider a shock that lowers the external competitiveness of the small country studied in the model. The model predicts that the shock triggers a subsequent gradual fall of the country's price level, and thus of its terms of trade; due to inflation inertia, the terms of trade may overshoot their long-run equilibrium level, during the adjustment process. As the union-wide central bank does not change the interest rate, in response to a country-specific disturbance, the gradual fall in the country's price level during the adjustment process is associated with a rise in its real interest rate (in terms of the local good), which dampens local output. The model predicts that, with a sufficiently high proportion of credit-constrained households, and a sufficiently strong backward-looking component of the Phillips curve, the terms of trade and real activity exhibit cyclical oscillations (i.e. boom-bust cycles). Thus, both of these two key features of the model play a role in leading to such an outcome.

The policy prescription of the chapter is that government purchases in the small country should be cut initially, when a sustained adverse shock to competitiveness occurs, in order to speed up the fall of domestic prices, but that government purchases should be increased once the terms of trade approach their long-run post-shock equilibrium level, in order to prevent the competitiveness of the economy from overshooting.

How important is this analysis? The authors provide empirical plots, at the beginning of their paper, that suggest that some countries entered EMU in an uncompetitive position, that others entered in a too-competitive position, and that there has been overshoot in response to this problem. However, there is a need for more systematic empirical work, to test the overshoot hypothesis. Empirical research (using VAR methods) on the effect of fiscal shocks in open economies by Corsetti and Müller (2006), Beetsma *et al.* (2008), Ravn *et al.* (2007), and Kim and Roubini (2007) finds no evidence of boom-bust cycles. But those studies are all based on data for countries with floating exchange rate regimes – whereas the overshoot analyzed by Allsopp and Vines is caused by asymmetric shocks within a monetary union.

3. Suggestions

The chapter focuses on the consequences of an exogenous change in external competitiveness. In future research, the authors should be more explicit about the causes of that disturbance – for example, it may matter a great deal for policy whether a worsening of competitiveness is due to an adverse supply shock (negative technology or labor supply shock), or whether it reflects a "cost-push shock" (an increase in the market power of local monopolistic firms that allows them to charge higher prices). In the former case, the Pareto-efficient output level drops, and fiscal policy should seek to bring output down to the efficient level; in the latter case, by contrast, fiscal policy should stimulate output (as a rise in market power depresses output below its efficient level).

Unfortunately, the paper does not provide stochastic model simulations. Stochastic simulations with the standard set of disturbances considered in macroeconomics (e.g. Smets and Wouters (2007)) would be needed to characterize the welfare-maximizing fiscal policy feedback rule. And such simulations would also allow evaluating how well the model captures the actual behavior of key macro variables within EMU.

As discussed above, a model with credit-constrained households generates a more realistic policy transmission mechanism. However, a fully satisfactory analysis of the transmission mechanism requires physical investment – which is not considered here (and also not in the related literature cited above).

It would also be important to allow for the simultaneous adjustment of government purchases and taxes, in response to shocks (recall that the chapter assumes a constant tax rate). Ferrero (2007) considers a model of a monetary union, in which the *income* tax is used as a policy instrument (while government purchases are exogenous); he shows that this tax is a powerful stabilization tool. Adão *et al.* (2006) consider a model of a monetary union, in which governments can use income taxes and *consumption taxes* as policy instruments. In their setup, the second-best efficient allocation that obtains under flexible prices can also be achieved under sticky prices – irrespective of the exchange rate regime. Essentially, Adão and co-authors show that the adjustment of country-specific consumption taxes can be used as a substitute for exchange rate changes. Thus optimal fiscal policy can fully eliminate the welfare cost of a monetary union. Adão *et al.* conclude hence that, when a sufficiently rich set of tax instruments is available, "every currency area is an optimal currency area!"

Allsopp and Vines's policy proposal clearly requires reliable estimates of the response of the terms of trade to government spending shocks. There is much controversy in the empirical literature, regarding that response. Like standard macro models, the Allsopp-Vines model predicts that a rise in government purchases improves a country's terms of trade. The empirical research on fiscal shocks by Corsetti and Müller (2006) and Beetsma *et al.* (2008) reports estimated responses that are consistent with the standard prediction. However, Ravn *et al.* (2007), and Kim and Roubini (2007) find that a rise in government purchases has the opposite effect (the terms of trade worsen). As mentioned above, these four empirical studies use data for countries with a floating exchange rate. There is thus urgent need for empirical research on the effect of fiscal shocks in a monetary union.

4. Summary

In summary, Allsopp and Vines provide a valuable contribution to the recent literature on fiscal policy in a monetary union. Clearly, much more theoretical and empirical research on this important topic is needed.

Notes

1. For related work on the optimal monetary/fiscal policy mix, in *closed* economies with nominal rigidities, see, among others, Benigno and Woodford (2006), Schmitt-Grohé and Uribe (2006) and Kollmann (2008).
2. Optimal fiscal policy in a model with such a "hybrid" Phillips curve (with backward- and forward-looking components) has recently been studied by Kirsanova *et al.* (2007) – but that paper abstracts from credit constraints.

14 | *Taxation policy in EMU*

JULIAN ALWORTH AND GIAMPAOLO ARACHI

1. Introduction

At least since the Delors report, much attention has been devoted to the implications of the introduction of a common currency for the conduct of budgetary policy and for the appropriate nature of fiscal arrangements between countries. However, tax policy as such has not been seen as raising any specific issue for the coming into existence of a common currency. The euro has not been closely associated with changes in tax policy nor has concern been expressed that the domestic tax systems of euro-area countries are influencing economic activity in the euro area relative to non-euro-area countries.

At the same time, domestic tax policy within EU member states has been increasingly affected by decisions taken at the EU level. Tax competition and the impact of globalisation on the degree of autonomy of tax policy appear to dominate EU-wide tax policy debates. Domestic policy within individual countries also appears to be influenced by decisions taken in other EU countries.

It is somewhat surprising that there has been little discussion of the linkages between the euro and tax policy within the euro area (and possibly in an indirect fashion for other countries) since many of the issues associated with tax policy (for example, 'competitiveness') overlap with broader policy concerns.

This chapter proposes to examine whether and how the introduction of the euro changed the impact of taxes on the economy, or influenced the direction of tax policy. It also seeks to identify any potential problem areas. A two-pronged framework is adopted to provide guidance in

We would like to thank, without implication, Giuseppe Carone, Beata Heimann, Gaëtan Nicodème, Lucio Pench and Paul Van den Noord for helpful comments and suggestions and Carlos Martinez-Mongay for providing us with the data on implicit tax rates on labour and capital. We are grateful to Michele Genghini, Pasquale Merella and Katuscia Anelli for their research assistance.

interpreting the importance and the potential magnitude of the influence of the euro on tax policy (and possibly of tax policy on the euro). The first follows the three traditional functional branches of analysis put forth by Richard Musgrave (1959): 'stabilisation, allocation and distribution'.[1]

The other useful framework is that set forth by Frenkel and Razin (1987) to examine the international transmission channels or spillover effects of domestic tax policy. These consist of focusing on price, wealth and tax-revenue erosion channels. The price channel examines the impact of tax changes on the relative prices of goods and financial assets. The wealth channel analyses how changes in tax policy can redistribute holdings of physical and financial assets across countries, individuals and generations. The tax-revenue erosion channel is a by-product of the former two and examines how tax policy changes may be induced by the erosion of tax revenues and can lead to strategic behaviour on the part of the fiscal authorities.

The question of whether the euro has affected the uses of tax policy for stabilisation purposes has many dimensions. The most obvious dimension is the concern with whether countries that joined the euro adopted more restrictive tax policies in order to comply with the Maastricht criteria than countries that opted to remain outside the euro area, and that in so doing these countries chose to change the composition of tax revenues. There is strong anecdotal evidence that this took place in the build-up to the euro in the cases of Italy and Greece. In this chapter we substantiate the evidence of increased tax pressure and show that the increase in tax pressure did not continue once the euro was adopted. We also examine whether the introduction of the euro resulted in a changing composition of tax revenues. Another dimension concerns whether euro-area countries have been forced to use tax policy to accommodate idiosyncratic shocks which in other circumstances could have been dealt with by exchange rate adjustments. We shall discuss this issue with respect to proposals regarding 'internal devaluations'.

As regards allocation effects, theoretical models strongly suggest that shifts from destination-to origin-based taxes, from income to consumption taxes, and from residence-to source-based taxes can alter equilibrium exchange rates. To be sure, the magnitude of the interaction between taxes and exchange rate regimes is not well understood and there is unfortunately very little (hard) evidence to corroborate some of the implications of theoretical conjectures regarding potential interactions between exchange rate regimes and taxes. At the same time it is important to note that the introduction of the euro led to a dramatic reduction in risk premia and market segmentation. This in turn has made tax differentials a more significant relative factor in investment decisions and created a climate potentially more conducive to tax arbitrage. We discuss these various potential linkages, drawing on various strands of literature that link taxes to trade and to exchange rates.

Capital market integration and tax competition are alleged to limit redistribution because on the one hand it is more difficult for the single country to tax the rich and mobile, and on the other redistributive policies may attract poor individuals from foreign countries. There is evidence to suggest increasing inequality in the euro area at the same time as overall economic performance has improved. This development does not appear to have limited the ability of member states to use the tax lever to redistribute income.

In drawing any conclusions regarding the effects of tax policy in the euro area, it is important to realise that governments are not passive participants in the potential changes in tax incidence which are induced by a move towards fixed exchange rates. Strategic responses cannot be analysed in a simple incidence model since tax-setting behaviour becomes an endogenous decision. It is possible that governments attempt to improve their terms of trade or borrowing and lending on international financial markets by changing the level or composition of taxes or utilising tax policy to attract mobile factors of production to their tax jurisdictions.

The remainder of the chapter is organised as follows. The second section examines the structure of tax revenues in the euro area prior to EMU. In Section 3 we turn to discuss the potential linkages between EMU and tax policy, focusing on financial and real capital mobility, changes in strategic interactions between governments and the potential impact of changes in tax policy on the trade balance. We then examine in Section 4 some empirical evidence regarding tax policy and EMU in three specific areas: the impact of capital market integration on the tax burden of labour and capital; the effects of EMU on progressivity; the relationship between taxes, exchange rates and employment. In the final section we highlight some potential areas that may require changes in tax policy going forward while providing some tentative overall conclusions on how tax policy has changed in the EMU area.

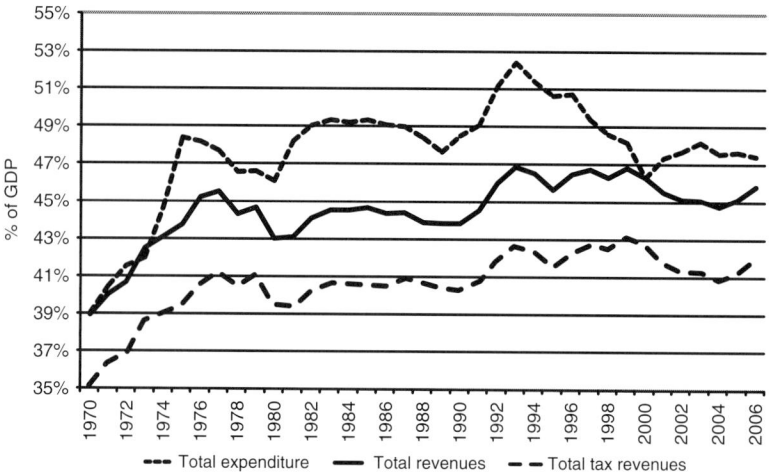

Figure 14.1: Long-term trends in general government total expenditure, total revenue and overall tax ratio in the euro area
Source: Own calculations based on AMECO data.

2. The structure of tax systems in the euro area

2.1 *Main features and trends of tax systems prior to EMU*

The euro area has been a 'high tax' zone at least since the mid-1980s. As can be seen from Figure 14.1 the increase in the overall tax pressure took place in two successive waves. The first and very rapid increase took place between 1970 and the early 1980s, and saw the tax to GDP ratio within the eurozone rise by six percentage points from 35 to 41 per cent. The overall tax burden then stabilised at this higher level for roughly a decade before increasing again by a further three percentage points during the 1990s. Since 2000 the tax burden has stabilised at a rate around 41 per cent.

The rise in total revenue as a share of GDP was driven, with a lagged effect, by the rapid growth of government expenditure that began in the 1960s and continued through to the mid-1990s. While differing in size and composition across countries, the general rise in expenditure was mainly the result of expanding social transfers in the 70s and 80s triggered by changes enacted a decade earlier, as well as the need to confront a sharp slowdown in economic activity and an increasing level of unemployment that followed the first and second oil price shocks. The increase in expenditures was initially largely financed through a persistent and widening budget deficit (European Commission, 2000). By the early 1990s, the period of rising government expenditure came to an end with the ratio of expenditures to GDP peaking in 1993. In the years that followed, however, total tax revenue continued to rise (European Commission, 2000; Carone *et al.*, 2007).

The rise in the ratio of taxes to GDP between 1970 and 1990 was a general feature of the EU area. It is also interesting to note that on average the increase in tax pressure amongst EU countries was far more significant than that of other OECD-area countries during this period. Nevertheless a number of EU countries were able to stabilise their total tax to GDP ratios in the 1970s (Ireland and the UK at around 35 per cent) or in the early 1980s (Germany at around 40 per cent and the Benelux countries at around 45 per cent).

Over this time period, the overall share in total tax revenues of direct and indirect taxes and of social contributions remained fairly stable – at around 30–35 per cent – after allowing for changes associated with the business cycle (Carone *et al.*, 2007; Cnossen, 2002). The only notable change was a mild increase in the relative importance of social contributions and a decrease in indirect taxation (mainly through a reduction in excises). However, this overall stability masked sharp differences in the composition of revenues across countries that have persisted up to this day.

While the overall structure and composition of tax revenues did not change dramatically (for the tax structure in recent years, see Table 14.1), there were profound changes within the broad groups of taxes and in the actual mechanics and workings of individual taxes. As far as consumption taxes are concerned, VAT spread to all countries that acceded to the EU throughout this period. Moreover, the average top VAT rate increased in most countries and there was a general tendency to reduce the number of rate bands. The influence of EU directives also influenced the dispersion of VAT rates across countries[2] reducing it significantly over time. EU directives also aligned the structure of alcohol and tobacco excises more closely.

There were also very significant changes in the functioning of personal and corporate income taxes. In the case of the personal income taxes, most countries reduced the top personal tax rate and reduced the number of rate bands (Messere *et al.* 2003). At the same time, in many countries the tax base was widened; for example, many countries limited the deductibility of interest expenditure and reduced the

Table 14.1: *Tax structure in the euro area*

	EU25			EUR13		
	1995	2000	2005	1995	2000	2005
Consumption	27.9	28.0	28.3	26.5	26.9	26.9
VAT	16.7	17.1	17.3	16.0	16.8	16.6
Excises[1]	11.2	10.8	10.9	10.5	10.1	10.3
Labour	56.0	55.3	56.4	58.6	57.8	58.8
Income tax[2]	21.9	23.8	23.6	20.2	22.5	22.4
Social security contributions	34.2	31.5	32.8	38.4	35.3	36.4
Capital	16.1	17.0	15.5	15.1	15.6	14.5
Corporation tax	7.5	8.0	6.7	7.0	7.7	6.5
Income tax	1.8	2.2	2.0	1.7	1.9	1.7
Property taxes[3]	6.8	6.8	6.9	6.4	6.0	6.2
Total	100.0	100.0	100.0	100.0	100.0	100.0

[1] Taxes on tobacco, alcohol, petrol, motor vehicles and other specific goods and services.
[2] Including taxes on labour income imputed to the self-employed and payroll taxes.
[3] Taxes on net wealth, immovable property and property transfers.
Source: Martinez-Mongay (2000), OECD (2001b), Cnossen (2002) and own calculations based on eurostat (2007).

differential treatment of various types of financial instruments. The 1980s and early 1990s saw the gradual dismantling of exchange controls and in many instances significant changes in inbound and outbound capital movements. These changes were also associated with the growing institutionalisation of savings and of cross-border portfolio capital flows.

With regard to corporation tax, one can observe a number of common trends taking place over time. The first trend was the decline in the statutory tax rate beginning in the mid-1980s (we shall discuss this trend at greater length below). The reduction in statutory rates was accompanied by a widening of the tax base resulting in a reduction of exemptions but most significantly in a cut in the rate of depreciation allowances. Finally, many EU countries in the 1970s introduced some form of imputation system between corporate and personal income taxes. As we shall see below, by the 1990s the enthusiasm for tax integration had waned considerably.

2.2 *Tax revenues and tax structure in EMU countries: are they different and have they changed?*

Given the coincidence of EMU with a number of other developments, it is difficult to carry out a proper analysis of the differentiating features of EMU on tax policy. We use four dummy variables to test whether a wide number of tax ratios have changed following entry into the European Union and the introduction of the euro. The first dummy is equal to one if a country has actually introduced the euro. The second is equal to one when a country is discussing whether to join the euro area. The third is equal to one when a country is a member of the EU. The fourth is equal to one if a country is discussing EU membership. We test the effects of the euro against the OECD countries that were not members of the euro area in the period from 1970 to 2005. The regressions are repeated over four time periods all ending in 2005. The results of these regressions should be merely interpreted as descriptions of the data and suffer from the absence of any adjustment for cyclical factors.

As can be seen from Table 14.2, EU countries have a much higher tax/GDP ratio relative to other OECD countries and the ratio for the EMU-area countries is on average even higher. It appears that this higher rate coincided with the announcement of the euro[3] but not with its actual introduction (1999). This suggests some degree of fiscal adjustment associated with the need to comply with the Maastricht criteria. Breaking down by type of tax it appears that the upward adjustment took place with employer social contributions. VAT revenues were unaffected. The impact of the euro is most visible on individual and corporate income taxes: EMU countries have lower individual income tax revenues and higher revenues from the corporate tax.

3. The links between EMU and tax policy

The link between the advent of EMU and changes in the tax system is not immediate. Firstly, while fiscal rules have been established for EMU they are not specific to taxation. Although tax collections are in many circumstances the easiest policy lever that can be utilised to achieve budgetary objectives there is no specific rule that mandates the use of tax policy. It should also be remembered that with few exceptions tax policy remains an area of national sovereignty among EU member states. Up to now, the 'deeper integration' among EMU countries has

Table 14.2: *Tax structure in EMU and OECD countries*

		85–05	90–05	95–05	00–05
Total tax revenues	OECD average	30.46	30.16	30.18	30.68
		(0.00)	(0.00)	(0.00)	(0.00)
	euro accession	-1.21	-1.22	-1.23	1.51
		(0.23)	(0.21)	(0.25)	(0.80)
	euro discussion	3.28	2.85	-3.64	-8.00
		(0.45)	(0.00)	(0.01)	(0.02)
	EU accession	5.21	4.16	12.88	12.86
		(0.00)	(0.01)	(0.00)	(0.00)
	EU discussion	1.22	3.02	0.78	1.80
		(0.36)	(0.04)	(0.68)	(0.48)
Social contributions (employers)	OECD average	2.81	2.53	2.43	2.49
		(0.00)	(0.00)	(0.00)	(0.00)
	euro accession	0.21	0.36	0.36	1.65
		(0.60)	(0.35)	(0.42)	(0.52)
	euro discussion	2.32	3.58	1.95	0.26
		(0.00)	(0.00)	(0.00)	(0.92)
	EU accession	0.25	-0.77	1.72	1.80
		(0.65)	(0.20)	(0.06)	(0.14)
	EU discussion	1.43	1.33	0.57	0.80
		(0.01)	(0.02)	(0.47)	(0.47)

		85–05	90–05	95–05	00–05
Taxes on individuals	OECD average	9.71	9.54	9.30	9.26
		(0.00)	(0.00)	(0.00)	(0.00)
	euro accession	-2.16	-2.24	-1.68	3.16
		(0.00)	(0.00)	(0.03)	(0.45)
	euro discussion	0.21	-1.29	-5.79	-11.83
		(0.75)	(0.12)	(0.00)	(0.01)
	EU accession	2.80	3.16	9.78	11.49
		(0.00)	(0.00)	(0.00)	(0.00)
	EU discussion	-1.85	-0.46	-2.89	-3.43
		(0.05)	(0.66)	(0.04)	(0.05)
Taxes on property	OECD average	2.24	2.37	2.35	2.31
		(0.00)	(0.00)	(0.00)	(0.00)
	euro accession	0.14	0.09	0.06	-0.43
		(0.31)	(0.49)	(0.72)	(0.65)
	euro discussion	-0.42	-0.80	-0.92	-0.24
		(0.00)	(0.00)	(0.00)	(0.81)
	EU accession	1.09	1.32	1.84	1.57
		(0.00)	(0.00)	(0.00)	(0.00)
	EU discussion	-1.18	-1.10	-1.45	-1.34
		(0.00)	(0.00)	(0.00)	(0.00)

Social contributions (employees)	OECD average	1.56 (0.00)	1.62 (0.00)	1.78 (0.00)	1.88 (0.00)
	euro accession	0.28 (0.28)	0.31 (0.25)	0.37 (0.21)	1.25 (0.08)
	euro discussion	0.64 (0.01)	1.26 (0.00)	1.55 (0.00)	0.83 (0.32)
	EU accession	0.83 (0.02)	0.45 (0.28)	0.14 (0.83)	-0.22 (0.79)
	EU discussion	0.86 (0.01)	0.54 (0.18)	0.33 (0.55)	0.46 (0.53)
Taxes on goods and services	OECD average	9.66 (0.00)	9.45 (0.00)	9.42 (0.00)	9.50 (0.00)
	euro accession	-0.53 (0.20)	-0.51 (0.19)	-0.47 (0.28)	-1.56 (0.51)
	euro discussion	0.40 (0.28)	0.10 (0.83)	-1.22 (0.05)	-0.33 (0.89)
	EU accession	0.66 (0.23)	0.22 (0.72)	0.41 (0.65)	-1.36 (0.22)
	EU discussion	1.47 (0.01)	2.39 (0.00)	3.51 (0.00)	5.39 (0.00)
Taxes on corporate income	OECD average	2.11 (0.00)	2.17 (0.00)	2.34 (0.00)	2.64 (0.00)
	euro accession	0.68 (0.00)	0.64 (0.01)	0.38 (0.20)	-1.11 (0.57)
	euro discussion	-0.10 (0.63)	-0.33 (0.22)	-0.12 (0.78)	1.40 (0.49)
	EU accession	1.12 (0.00)	1.23 (0.00)	0.97 (0.11)	0.78 (0.40)
	EU discussion	-0.36 (0.23)	-0.27 (0.44)	-0.13 (0.80)	-0.28 (0.73)
VAT	OECD average	4.03 (0.00)	4.38 (0.00)	4.58 (0.00)	4.93 (0.00)
	euro accession	-0.03 (0.93)	-0.02 (0.94)	-0.24 (0.51)	-1.80 (0.04)
	euro discussion	0.98 (0.00)	0.53 (0.21)	-0.54 (0.37)	0.59 (0.57)
	EU accession	0.03 (0.94)	-0.23 (0.66)	0.73 (0.38)	0.58 (0.57)
	EU discussion	2.08 (0.00)	2.44 (0.00)	2.56 (0.00)	2.81 (0.00)

P-values in round brackets

not extended to tax policy. Secondly, the internal market programme which preceded EMU by a decade already introduced a number of very significant changes in tax policy whose implications have been fully appreciated only in recent years. Several rulings in tax matters by the European Court of Justice since the beginning of this decade are an example of the internal market implications. Thirdly, it should also be remembered that several countries that are part of EMU were operating under a quasi-fixed exchange rate regime for over a decade prior to the introduction of the euro. Fourthly, it is important to note that the euro-area countries are not a homogeneous group: the potential links between tax policy and EMU may differ by country size, as will the potential size of spillover effects. For example, a major tax change in a large country in the euro area could potentially have an impact on the equilibrium exchange rate and thereby affect the overall trade balance of other euro-area countries. A similar change in a small country would not give rise to such spillover effects. Finally, many exogenous developments that have influenced the process of tax reform in EU member states, such as the high levels of unemployment in the 90s and the globalisation of capital markets have been impinging on *all* EU countries and are independent of the existence of the euro.[4]

Hence, in most respects it is arguable that the influence of the EMU on tax policy – if any – is a question of incremental change or a matter of degree. The remainder of this section reviews factors that may have altered the influences of taxes on economic decisions and the setting of tax policy largely from this standpoint.

3.1 Capital mobility

There are many reasons for believing that the mobility of financial capital and the location and investment decisions of companies have been affected by the introduction of the euro and that this 'deeper' integration influenced certain types of tax change and affected the channels through which tax policy influences economic decisions.[5]

3.1.1 Financial markets

Hardouvelis *et al.* (2006) suggest three potential dimensions specific to the introduction of the euro that may have enhanced capital mobility within the euro area. Firstly, the creation of the eurozone was preceded by a gradual regulatory harmonisation among European financial markets, including the development of a common payment and settlement system, and by the abolition of various restrictions on non-residents, including in some instances the vestiges of capital controls (Licht, 1997). It was also preceded by a concerted effort among EU countries to satisfy the Maastricht criteria for joining the euro area, amongst one of which was the nominal convergence of inflation and long-term interest rates toward German levels.[6]

Secondly, the introduction of the euro improved transparency, standardised pricing in financial markets, and reduced investors' transaction and information costs. Moreover, it removed various legal restrictions within the EU on the foreign currency composition of assets held by institutional investors, like pension funds and life insurance companies. The market expectations before the advent of the monetary union may well be affected by the broadening of investment opportunities across the EMU countries. As a consequence the integration of European stock markets may have increased as the probability of the formation of a monetary union gained strength (Danthine *et al.* 2000).

Finally, the introduction of a single currency, coupled with the nominal and real convergence just outlined, should have led to more homogeneous valuations of equities in EMU countries and a reduction of the home bias by eliminating the intra-European currency risk. To the extent that currency risk was priced, the overall exchange rate exposure of European stocks was reduced.[7]

There are several potential linkages between the heightened mobility of savings in the euro area and the impact of taxes, as well as the setting of tax policy. For example, the presence of a wide range of tax-sensitive foreign investors in domestic financial markets may also change the nature of domestic tax policy formulation, particularly in bond markets. Withholding taxes on interest payments to non-residents have often been revised in the face of heightened capital mobility because of the distortions to which they can give rise. The abolition of withholding tax in the USA was largely triggered by the inability of the US authorities to hinder inflows through tax-favoured channels. In the late 1990s foreign market participants in the Italian government bond market argued strongly for a change in the nature of the withholding tax regime on government bonds on the grounds that reimbursement of tax withheld under the existing double taxation agreements was cumbersome and uncertain. In order to achieve nominal convergence this risk premium should be eliminated. As a result Italy shifted from withholding tax at source (i.e. on individual coupons at the payment date and the pricing of bonds on a net of accrued tax basis) to exemption from withholding for all domestic corporate entities and foreign investors from treaty countries. Domestic and international paying agents were entrusted for withholding accrued tax on all other investors. Violi (2004) argues that in the build-up to the introduction of the euro the tax-exempt status afforded to foreign investment was an important factor in fostering convergence in bond yields across Europe; such status has removed the distortion implied by double taxation on interest income and has contributed substantially to a more level playing field in euro-area financial markets.

As regards stock markets, heightened capital mobility may have resulted in changes in the marginal investor, i.e. the investor affecting the prices of assets in markets. There is considerable evidence suggesting that the behaviour of marginal investors is determined by the institutional characteristics of markets (Allen and Michaely, 2003) and that existing pricing relationships have changed in line with market practices, participation and regulatory restrictions (Lasfer, 2007). Foreign participation in markets is also associated with a greater volume of arbitrage activity on ex-dividend days (Liljeblom and Felixson, 2008). In the case of the euro, a recent study by Simonetta (2007) suggests that the dividend payout behaviour of Euro-area companies changed following the introduction of the euro with companies having higher 'free float' becoming more reactive to the implicit tax rates associated with price changes on ex-dividend dates. He interprets this result as being due to the decline in the risk premium and the greater presence of international price-sensitive investors.

3.1.2 Foreign direct investment (FDI)

Monetary integration may affect FDI through different channels.[8] First, monetary integration reduces macroeconomic uncertainty by removing exchange rate volatility, declining and stabilising inflation, reducing price dispersion across members. It also increases transparency and credibility of rules and policies. These effects are important since the greater the economic and political uncertainty, the more likely the firm will wait before entering the market. Indeed, uncertainty about future returns may deter irreversible investments as there is an 'option value' of waiting (Dixit and Pindick, 1994).

Second, by removing intra-euro-area exchange rate volatility, monetary integration increases the certainty-equivalent value of expected profits of risk-averse firms and should foster overall FDI. Moreover, this removal of volatility reduces trade costs and may favour vertical FDI insofar as firms fragment their production and locate their activities in different countries according to international differences in factor prices. However, if foreign investment is a way to serve foreign markets (horizontal FDI), a removal of exchange rate volatility may decrease FDI and increase trade as a substitute.

Finally, a single currency could promote FDI by easing comparison of international costs and price decisions and by reducing transaction costs, such as currency conversion costs and in-house costs of maintaining separate foreign currency expertise (Blonigen, 2005; Crowley and Lee, 2003; Goldberg and Kolstad, 1995; Jeanneret 2008; Kiyota and Urata, 2004; Pain, 2002).

The literature on the determinants of the interactions between FDI decisions and taxation is wide ranging. There is growing evidence that differences in statutory rates affect the multinationals' decision on where to locate new plants and where to report profits (Gordon and Hines, 2002). However, the focus of this chapter, namely whether changes in exchange rate regimes or the creation of common currency areas affected the impact of tax policy on decision making has not been examined.

Currency stability within the euro area may also have affected intragroup financial policies and specifically profit-shifting behaviour to lower taxed jurisdictions within the euro area. There is much evidence that intracompany profit-shifting increased significantly in the late 1990s. For example, Altshuler and Grubert (2005), Weichenrieder (1996), and Huizinga *et al.* (2008) suggest that many transactions may have been redirected between European countries to take advantage of specific tax provisions to minimise the global burden of multinationals. However, these shifts have been the result of changes in taxation that cannot be associated directly with EMU and in some cases relate to changes in tax provisions of non-EU countries (for example, the treatment of hybrid entities in the United States has facilitated tax planning strategies between related parties).

3.2 Strategic tax setting

The increased mobility of tax bases may have enhanced the interdependence of national tax policies leading to tax competition.

Indeed, there is overwhelming anecdotal evidence that governments' decisions on domestic tax issues are often affected by the choices of foreign countries (Simmons, 2006, reports some examples). However, this type of evidence is not sufficient to answer more specific questions like 'did strategic interdependence increase as a result of higher economic integration?' or 'are countries changing their tax system because policies abroad are more conducive to better resource allocation?'.[9]

In the last decade several studies have tackled this issue, highlighting the difficulty in devising tests that can provide strong statistical evidence of strategic behaviour. Besides specific statistical issues, which are discussed in Brueckner (2003), the main problem every study faces is to find a strategy to disentangle the effects of common movements of exogenous explanatory variables of tax policies from the strategic reactions to the choices made by foreign governments.

An illustrative example is provided by the evolution of statutory tax rates on corporate income. Since the 1980s there has been a clear convergence of statutory tax rates and a reduction in their mean value. The dynamics of the statutory rates are not entirely reflected in the evolution of the marginal tax rate on investments, as the rate cuts have been usually coupled with a widening of the tax base. Therefore, it cannot be taken as *prima facie* evidence of a 'race to the bottom' for attracting investment. The convergence in statutory rates is consistent with the theoretical prediction that increased economic integration of capital stimulates strategic interaction, forcing high tax countries to reduce their rates in order to avoid profit shifting towards low tax countries and to attract new multinational firms.

The problem is to weight this explanation with competing ones. One alternative is suggested by the view that the corporate tax is a backstop to the income tax (Gordon and MacKie-Mason, 1994). When the corporate tax rate is lower than the tax rate on personal income the burden of the income tax could be reduced by retaining earnings within a corporation or by reclassifying labour and interest income as business income. The size of the gain from such strategies depends on a number of factors, such as the effective tax rates on capital gains, the degree of integration between corporate and personal income tax, and the structure and burden of social contributions. In any case, there is empirical evidence which confirms that taxpayers do react to differences in rates (see Weichenrieder, 2005 for a survey). If the corporate tax is a backstop to the income tax, corporate tax rates are related to personal tax rates on labour and capital income and trends in corporate tax rates can be driven by changes in personal taxation.

Further evidence of the link between corporate and individual tax rates is provided by Slemrod (2004) and Clausing (2007). Obviously, simple correlation does not tell us anything about causality. It is possible that higher mobility of profits and firms forced a convergence in statutory tax rates and this caused a similar convergence in individual rates. But causality may well go in the opposite direction. The trend towards flatter income taxes (with smaller tax brackets and lower top rates), was certainly driven, at least in the 1980s, by the growing concern about the negative effect of highly progressive rates on labour supply. Furthermore, as shown by Fuest and Weichenrieder (2002) in many OECD countries the decrease in top personal rates on capital income has been larger than the decrease in corporate rates and is certainly related to a widespread tendency to abandon comprehensive income taxation and to introduce separate schedular taxation for interest and/ or dividend income.

Summing up, to the extent that the corporate tax is a backstop to personal income taxation, the correlation among corporate tax rates of different countries can be the result of common trends in tax rates on personal income.

Another view is that countries are not engaged in tax competition but in yardstick competition. According to this view, countries try to mimic each other's tax policy to seek the votes of informed voters (Besley and Case, 1995). More simply it is also arguable that the lowering and convergence of statutory tax rates across countries merely reflect a convergence in economic structures and/or dominant economic thinking (Slemrod, 2004). According to these positions the reduction in statutory rates accompanied by the widening of the tax base – a widespread phenomenon in the late 1980s and early 1990s following the US tax reforms – was due to the opinion that it was conducive to a more neutral tax environment.

Among European countries, an additional source of correlation in corporate tax rate cuts, which is usually overlooked by the literature, is the general switch from full integration between corporate and personal taxes towards double taxation of dividend income at (usually) reduced rates. The disappearance of the imputation system is related to the more general move towards schedular taxation of capital income. The debate on the dual income tax in the Nordic countries has highlighted several reasons for such a change. Among the most relevant is the increasing awareness that non-linear taxation of capital income is untenable in well-developed capital markets (Alworth 1998). However, the dismissal of the full imputation system was catalysed by the decisions of the European Court of Justice and by the action of the European Commission which developed the view that the imputation system, by discriminating against foreign investors, is not consistent with the EU Treaty. It is likely that the extra revenue from the removal of the tax credit related to imputation has been compensated, at least in part, by a reduction in the corporate tax.[10]

Bearing in mind the previous caveats, it is useful to survey the main results of some papers which provide empirical tests for strategic inter-action in corporate taxes. Altshuler and Goodspeed (2002) investigate the interaction between corporation taxes in per cent of GDP among OECD countries between 1968 and 1999. Devereux *et al.* (2008) test whether OECD countries compete with each other over statutory and effective marginal tax rates (EMTR) using data from 1982 to 1999. Besley *et al.* (2001) analyse the interdependence in setting average rates for five different taxes in the OECD between 1965 and 1997. Finally, Redoano (2007) examines the interaction in statutory corporate tax rates among European countries during the period 1970–99.

All papers find evidence of strategic interaction among countries. In particular, the tests performed by Devereux *et al.* (2008) and Redoano (2007) support the hypothesis that countries compete in statutory rates in order to attract profits, and of strategic interaction in EMTR for attracting investment. However, the evidence on the relationship between economic integration and strategic interaction is somewhat puzzling. Besley *et al.* (2001) find that interdependence is higher the more mobile the tax base is. Further, they find higher interdependence amongst EU countries than between EU and non-EU countries. In contrast, Redoano (2007) shows that competition appears to be higher among non-EU countries; EU members seem to compete mainly among themselves, but with less intensity. Altshuler and Goodspeed (2002) find that interaction among EU countries has become weaker over time. At first, these findings may seem to contrast with the theory which suggests that market integration should enhance strategic interaction in tax policies. Nonetheless, it should be borne in mind that market integration has two different effects. First, it increases capital mobility and makes each government's revenues more dependent on the tax rates of neighbouring countries. Second, it widens the size of the world capital market making each single country relatively small. This reduces the interdependence among fiscal policies.

3.3 Tax policy, exchange rate adjustments and trade balance

Individual EMU countries can no longer rely on nominal exchange rate adjustments. The consequences for domestic tax policies of the change in exchange rate regime can be evaluated from both a positive and normative framework.

In an ideal setting with perfectly competitive markets and flexible prices, the change in regime would have no implications for tax policies as any change in the nominal exchange rate would be offset by a suitable adjustment in the domestic price level, leaving the real exchange rate unaffected. When some prices are rigid or sticky, the short-run impact of tax policy and the adjustment process to the new long-run equilibrium will be in general different under flexible or fixed nominal exchange rate. This is illustrated by the well-known Mundell-Fleming model of a small open economy, where a fiscal expansion increases the equilibrium level of domestic income under fixed exchange rates, while it translates into an exchange rate appreciation with no real consequences on equilibrium income under a flexible exchange rate regime.

The literature has seldom analysed the impact of domestic tax reforms on the nominal exchange rate, the capital account and the ensuing adjustment of the trade balance. One study in this vein is Sinn (1985) who argued that the accelerated tax depreciation regime introduced in 1981 in the United States was the driving force behind the investment boom in that country, high world interest rates, the strength of the US dollar, and the US trade deficit at the beginning of the 1980s. The mechanism envisaged by Sinn was the following. The introduction of the accelerated tax depreciation reduced the effective marginal tax on capital invested in the United States and drove the post-tax return on investment above the pre-tax interest rate. This difference triggered a capital inflow into the United States which in turn brought about an exchange rate appreciation and a current account deficit. Under a fixed exchange rate regime, the cut in the effective marginal tax rate would eventually lead to the same current account deficit. But the mechanism would be different. The increase in net imports would be driven by the increase in domestic income brought about by the capital inflow.

The longer-term consequences of tax policies on exchange rates have also been examined, in a neoclassical monetary growth model by Kimbrough (1984). He shows that a cut in the corporation income tax rate may have almost any impact on the various balance of payments accounts even if, as a practical matter, a cut in the corporation income tax rate is likely to lead to an improvement of the capital account and deterioration of the goods and service account. The trade account may either improve or deteriorate depending on the magnitudes of the rate of growth of the domestic population and the world real interest rate. A reduction in the corporation tax rate results in a one-shot appreciation of the domestic currency even if the steady-state rate of depreciation will be unaffected.

Similar complications to transmission mechanisms were also considered by Meade (1978a and 1978b), who looked at the impact on the structure of interest rates and the trade balance from a unilateral shift from an income tax to an expenditure tax. In particular Meade noted that if one country followed an income tax and the other adopted an expenditure tax, under certain types of expenditure tax regimes, the global interest rate level could be undetermined with potential implications for exchange rates.

From a normative perspective, where the nominal exchange rate is considered as a policy instrument, the introduction of the single currency raises the issue of whether domestic taxes may be used to affect the trade balance. This question has been largely neglected both in the debate which preceded EMU and in the economic literature that has discussed the economic consequences of the euro. This is rather surprising since, as noted by Calmfors (1998), the variations of social contributions paid by employers is one of the most direct substitutes for nominal exchange rate changes. In particular, in the short run with fixed nominal wages, a cut in social contributions paid by employers lowers the labour cost relative to foreign prices measured in domestic currency in the same way as a nominal exchange rate devaluation (Calmfors, 1993). If the government budget is kept balanced by raising the tax burden on workers and households, or by reducing public expenditure, there are no direct effects on aggregate demand and the final outcome is a devaluation of the real exchange rate. The similarity between an external and an internal devaluation is most clear when the reduction in social contributions is financed by an increase in taxes on labour income such as employee contributions, personal income tax or VAT.

Employees will experience in both cases a loss in purchasing power in terms of imports. At the same time, to the extent that lower labour costs are reflected in lower prices for domestically produced commodities, the purchasing power in terms of domestic goods will remain unchanged.

A mechanism similar to the internal depreciation can be found in the so-called 'EMU buffer funds' set up in Finland at the end of the 1990s through an agreement among the central organisations of the social partners – with support from the government. The basic idea of the buffer funds is that during good times, employers and employees pay slightly higher social contributions than necessary – with the result that, during bad times, increases in these contributions can be controlled by using the buffer fund for paying social security costs. In theory the funds could be used to actively stabilise the economy, i.e. lower the social contributions in a recession and raise them again in a boom. The agreement by the social partners on the funds does not mention this possibility but does not exclude it either. A cut in social contribution financed by the buffer funds will produce an expansionary effect larger than a nominal depreciation because of the increase in aggregate demand.

Some additional insights on the impact of domestic taxes on the trade balance are also provided by the literature which has developed from a longstanding controversy on VAT. The debate is rooted in the United States where it is commonly argued that the border tax adjustment for VAT on exports places foreign countries (notably the European countries) at an unfair competitive advantage in world markets relative to the United States, which are more reliant on the corporate income tax.[11]

From a theoretical perspective the literature has reached an almost unanimous consensus on the conclusion that a uniform VAT, whether destination or origin based, is irrelevant to trade behaviour under a number of assumptions (Keen and Syed, 2006). A uniform destination-based VAT taxes all final goods which are consumed domestically at the same effective rate regardless of whether they are produced domestically or abroad. As a consequence VAT does not distort the choice between domestically produced and foreign commodities, and does not affect the intertemporal distribution of production and consumption.

However, the irrelevance of VAT to trade rests on the assumption of uniform rates across all consumption goods. Apart from the case where a discriminatory rate is set on foreign-produced goods there are several cases where rates differ significantly across goods. The first one is given by several (mainly) nontradeable goods and services which are exempted by law (such as financial intermediation, education and transports, or activities which are exempted because their turnover is below a given threshold) or exempted because they operate in the informal economy or taxed at a lower rates (e.g. foodstuffs). In this case, as noted by Krugman and Feldstein (1989) the VAT will tend to decrease the size of the tradeable sector and hence the export intensity of countries.

The second exception occurs when producers do not receive the right refunds for their exports. Refunding of credits is the 'Achilles heel' of the VAT. Several OECD countries have detected significant tax frauds related to the credit refund. This has led some countries to introduce complex administrative measures that may significantly undermine the functioning of the VAT system (Harrison and Krelove 2005). In the absence of a correct refund VAT may work either as an export tax (if the credit is limited) or as an export subsidy (in the case of an undue refund). Finally, tax rates may vary across time. A fully anticipated increase in VAT lowers the real return on savings, leading consumers to anticipate consumption to avoid the higher tax in the future. As a consequence a fully anticipated rise in VAT brings about a deterioration of the trade balance which is financed through an inflow of capital from abroad.

More recently, a few papers have tried to test the theoretical predictions by the empirical analysis of the effect of domestic taxes on trade balance. Desai and Hines (2005) have considered the impact of the VAT on export and trade intensity. Their results are somewhat mixed (at least for high-income countries): in the presence of fixed effects, VAT has no effect on either export or trade intensity. The share of VAT in total tax revenue, however, is significantly and negatively related to both. As regards the trade impact of the corporate tax, Slemrod (2004) finds a significant positive association between corporate tax revenues relative to GDP and trade intensity. In a far more ambitious study, Keen and Syed (2006) partly confirm these results. They find that increased reliance on VAT tends to be associated with a sharp reduction in net exports, which quickly fades. The results also point, however, to powerful and complex effects from the corporate tax. Increases in corporate taxation – whether measured by revenues or the statutory rate – are associated with sharp short-run increases in net exports (consistent with induced capital flows abroad); these are then subsequently and quickly reversed (consistent with increased income from investments abroad), leaving an increase in net exports that converges to zero.

4. The impact of EMU on the main functions of the tax system

To what extent had higher capital mobility, tax competition and the change of the exchange rate regimes triggered a change in the tax systems in the euro area? The discussion of the previous section has highlighted several potential linkages between these factors and the tax policies. In this section we will focus on three issues: a) whether higher capital mobility brought about a shift of the tax burden from capital to labour; b) whether it caused a reduction in tax progressivity and c) whether domestic tax reforms were driven by the aim of achieving an internal devaluation.

The first two issues are relevant as they represent the major concerns on fiscal policy at the time of the introduction of the euro. The fear that the integration of capital markets could lead to a shift of the tax burden from capital to labour was fuelled by a stunning consistency between the theory and the empirical evidence available at that time. Revenues from capital income and statutory rates on corporate income appeared to be on a sharp downward trend in existing member countries and a number of (relatively small) accession countries were proceeding to adopt very low rates of corporate tax.

In contrast, the third issue has been largely neglected but may become a relevant matter in the near future, as some members of the euro area have sought to implement changes in the tax mix which may substitute for devaluations of the nominal exchange rate in an attempt to stimulate the growth without breaching the Stability and Growth Pact (SGP).

4.1 Has capital market integration shifted the tax burden from capital to labour?

A central result in the theory of optimal taxation is that source-based taxes on capital income are inefficient instruments with which to raise revenue in a small open economy. Under perfect capital mobility a small open economy faces a perfectly elastic supply of capital. Any source-based tax on capital will bring about an outflow of capital which drives up the pre-tax return and decreases the marginal productivity of other immobile domestic productive factors. As a result the tax burden is fully borne by the immobile factors, e.g. labour, which must accept a lower compensation. It is clearly more efficient to tax the immobile factors directly, preventing the fall in productivity, rather than indirectly via the

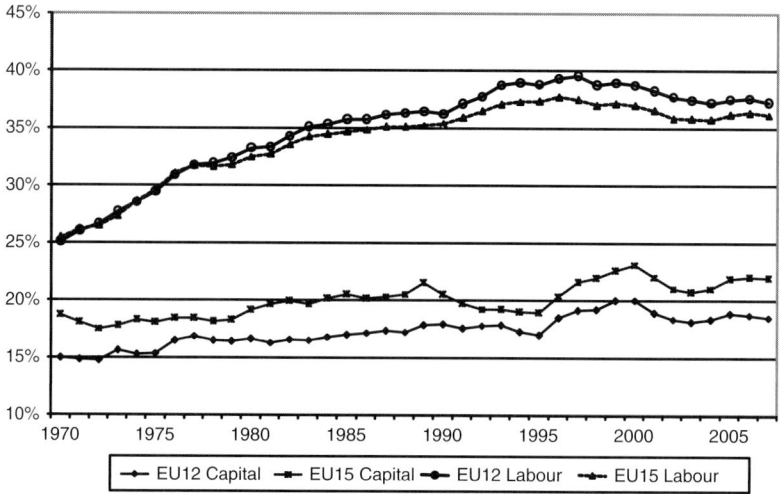

Figure 14.2: Implicit tax rates on labour and capital
Source: Unpublished data by Carlos Martinez-Mongay.

capital tax. Insofar as the voting process allows governments to implement Pareto-efficient tax policies, the theory predicts a gradual decline of capital income taxes, and a parallel increase in taxes on labour, as capital markets integrate.

In fact, these trends were evident in the 1980s and mid-1990s when considering the implicit tax rates on capital and labour for the EU15 and EU12 countries that are reported in Figure 14.2.

However, surprisingly, the same figure shows that these trends were somewhat reversed in the last decade. Why did capital income taxation not decline further as predicted by the theory?

The first possible explanation is that tax competition has brought about a change in the structure of capital income taxation, with a shift from source-based to residence-based taxes. There is no reason for a small open economy to give up residence-based capital taxation provided it has sufficient information to tax foreign investments by its residents. However, there is no clear evidence of such a change in the data. We should observe, for example, a gradual dismissal of the main source-based tax, namely the corporation tax. But despite the sharp decline in statutory tax rates, corporate tax revenues relative to GDP remained stable or even increased in most OECD countries (Sørensen, 2007).[12] Furthermore, as highlighted by Devereux *et al.* (2002) no clear trend can be detected in EMTRs, as the cuts in statutory rates went along with reductions in investment-related deductions.

A number of papers have tried to solve the puzzle of the surviving corporate tax. It is important to distinguish the problem of the stability of revenue from that of the stability of the EMTRs. The first reason is that the EMTRs can be driven down to zero without repealing the corporate tax, by exempting the normal return to capital. This can be achieved either through a cash-flow tax or by allowing the deduction of the opportunity cost of equity (the so-called ACE proposal or allowance for corporate equity) or capital (the so-called BEIT proposal, or business enterprise income tax) invested in the firm. In this case the tax base is given by the pure risk premium on capital invested in the company and by any return in excess of the normal return to capital which may stem from the exploitation of a scarce natural resource or by advantages due to a particular location (low input cost or conglomeration effects) and can certainly be positive. The second reason is that changes in revenue actually collected may be driven not only by tax reforms but also by several factors which affect the tax base.

In order to disentangle the different variables which affect corporate revenue Sørensen (2007) analyses a useful decomposition of the ratio between the corporate tax and GDP:

R/GDP = (R/C)(C/P)(P/GDP)

which shows that an increase in the ratio of corporate taxes (R) to GDP may be due to an increase of the average effective tax burden on corporate sector (R/C), an increase in the share of total profits accruing to the corporate sector (C/P) or, possibly, to an increase in the share of profits (P) in GDP. Sørensen (2007) calculated such decomposition for a number of OECD countries back to the early 1980s. The data show that the changes in revenue over GDP are mainly driven by the first two factors, given that the profit share of GDP is stable over the period. There is no clear tendency of the average effective tax rate to decline over time. As for EMTR this may be the result of the base broadening reforms which had offset the sharp reduction in statutory rates.

For the US, Auerbach (2006) noticed that an additional factor which may have contributed in raising the average effective rate in recent years is an unprecedented increase in profit volatility. Given the asymmetry of the tax system, which does not provide for an immediate compensation or tax credit in case of losses, the average tax rate on net corporate profits had increased substantially simply because a larger proportion of firms were experiencing losses. Unfortunately, there is no evidence on whether this phenomenon is widespread internationally.

However, the most clear and interesting trend is given by the rise in the ratio between profits in the corporate sector and total profits. This may reflect both a growing divergence in profitability between the corporate sector and the rest of the economy or an increasing preference for the corporate organisational form. In part the growing importance of incorporated firms may be due to structural transformation of the economy such as the decline of sectors with a higher intensity of non-corporate firms, e.g. agriculture. But it may also reveal important side effects of tax competition. In closely held corporations, entrepreneurs may usually choose to receive a large part of their compensation as salary or profit. To the extent that the decline in corporate rates has reduced the effective tax burden on profit relative to labour income, there should be a reduction in the personal income tax base and an increase in corporate profits. The growth in corporate profits may also reflect higher incentives to defer taxes on capital income by reducing interest payments (Fuest and Weichenrieder, 2002).

A second type of income shifting occurs through the choice of the legal form of companies. Entrepreneurs face a choice between a (closely held) corporation and other legal forms of doing business, such as the (sole) proprietorship or partnerships. Lower corporate tax rates may have induced them to switch to the corporate form, which then broadens the corporate tax base. Using a panel of European data de Mooij and Nicodème (2008) have found a large and significant effect of lower corporate tax rates on incorporation choices. Their simulations suggest that between 12 and 21 per cent of corporate tax revenue can be attributed to income shifting and that income shifting has raised the corporate tax to GDP ratio by some 0.25 percentage points since the early 1990s. This reconciles, albeit in part, the empirical evidence with theory. As predicted by the theory it seems that tax competition is driving down the tax burden on capital income but, given the optimal response of taxpayers, aimed at reducing the overall tax bill, the revenue loss shows up in personal taxation of business income rather than corporate tax as expected.

Other forms of change in organisational form may also have contributed to the stability of corporation tax and have been apparently neglected by the literature. A share of corporate tax revenue may simply stem from the reallocation of revenue in the public sector. The main example is given by privatisation. In many countries (e.g. the United Kingdom, see Florio, 2004) state-owned enterprises were not responsible for paying company taxes (Mintz *et al.*, 2000). But even in the case where they did pay corporate taxes, the privatisation process usually leads to higher profit and higher tax revenues. Overall, the large scale privatisations of the 1990s may then explain a significant share of corporate tax revenue. Another example of revenue reallocation is given by countries with large natural resources, which may have changed the classification of revenue.[13]

Finally, mention should be made of changes in organisational form associated with 'demutualisation'. This change is most apparent in the case of UK building societies which were largely transformed into companies in the 1990s, but similar phenomena have occurred in Continental companies.

It is more difficult to find consistent explanations for the relative stability of EMTRs. Ex-post changes in the tax bases and taxpayers' behavioural responses cannot account for variations in the EMTRs as the latter are ex-ante measures of the tax burden on investment based on tax provisions rather than company data.

A first reason for the survival of positive source-based EMTRs may be found in the nature of FDI. It is well know that most FDI is in the form of mergers and acquisitions (M&A). Brakman *et al.* (2006) calculate that 78 per cent of all FDI, in value terms, are M&A while greenfield investment account for just 22 per cent of total FDI value. Within M&A, 97 per cent of deals are acquisitions. Further, the share of M&As have risen sharply in the last decades, as shown by Calderón *et al.* (2004). While it is clear that a reduction in EMTR increases the net return on capital and makes the country more attractive for greenfield investment, the effect on the probability of a takeover by a foreign company is less obvious. To the extent that taxes on income are capitalised on the value of the assets, a reduction in EMTR will increase the value of domestic companies, leaving unchanged the net return that a foreign company may have earned through a takeover. This suggests that the existing literature may overstate the case for the inefficiency of source-based capital income taxation by focusing on the case of greenfield investment.[14]

A second reason which may explain why small countries choose to levy a source-based tax on capital income is related to redistribution. The argument against capital taxation in an open economy rests on the assumption that governments can optimally tax the immobile factors which ultimately bear the burden on the capital income tax. Notice that when the governments wish to affect the distribution of income this is equivalent to assuming that they may levy optimal differential lump-sum taxes. In the more sensible framework where the government may only levy a linear or a non-linear tax on labour income, the source-based tax is an efficient tool for redistributing income to the extent that the tax is shifted onto the wages of workers with different abilities in different proportions (Arachi, 2007; Huber, 1999).

4.2 Was there a reduction in tax progression and in the redistribution carried out by the tax system?

Capital market integration and tax competition are alleged to limit redistribution because on the one hand it is more difficult for a single country to tax the rich and mobile, and on the other redistributive policies may attract poor individuals from foreign countries (Feld 2000; Wildasin 2000).

Tax progression may vary for two different reasons: the revenue composition may change, and the progression of each single tax may vary. With reference to the first reason, we have shown that there is no clear evidence that EMU has forced a significant shift among taxes. This leaves us with the question of whether the progression of the personal income tax (PIT) has been affected by the single currency. We have already noticed that there is a general trend among OECD countries towards a reduction of tax brackets and marginal tax rates in the PIT. However, these changes in the tax schedule do not allow us to conclude that the PIT has become less progressive, as the shape of the average tax function depends on tax allowances and credits.

One way to evaluate the overall change in progression is to rely on the average PIT rates on gross labour income calculated by OECD (2007a). The OECD tax database contains data since 2000. We took the difference of average tax rates (excluding social contributions and payroll taxes) between 2000 and 2006 for two different types of single earners without children: one with income equal to 67 per cent of the income of the average worker (AW) and another with income equal to 167 per cent of that of the average worker. The changes in tax rates are depicted in Figure 14.3. The graph shows some general trends. First, most countries in the euro area have decreased the average two rate on low incomes. But at the same time, the majority have decreased the average tax rate on high incomes.

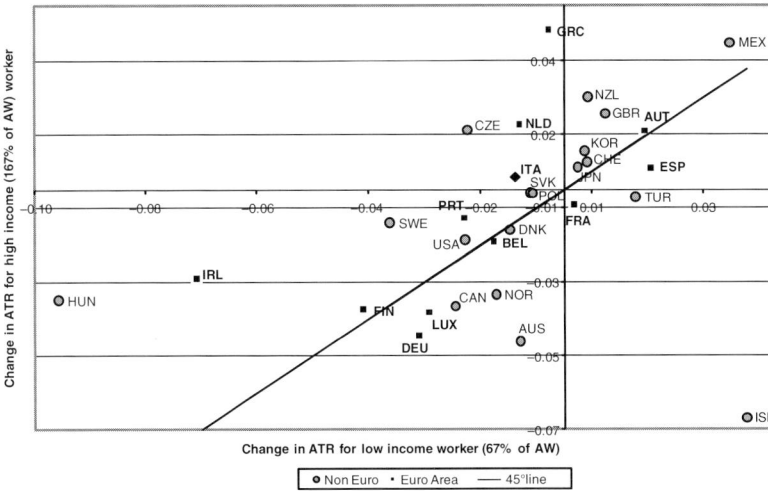

Figure 14.3: Changes in average tax rates (ATR) on labour income 2000–6
Source: OECD (2007a) and authors' own calculations.

The impact on tax progression can be evaluated through Figure 14.4 where tax progression is measured by the ratio between the difference of the average tax rates at 167 per cent of average earnings and at 67 per cent of average earnings. When an observation lies above the 45 degrees line tax progression has increased since 2000. Only three countries (Austria, France and Spain) show a reduction in tax progression, while the remaining nine countries have moved toward higher progression.

However, the most interesting feature of the data is that EMU countries seem to behave differently from the rest of the OECD ones. On average, non-euro countries have reduced the tax progression of the PIT. Albeit preliminary, these findings are suggestive that there may be a relationship between capital market integration and the political demand for higher tax progression. A possible explanation is provided by Arachi and D'Antoni (2004). Higher capital mobility reduces the variance in the return for capital owners while at the same time increasing the wage risk of immobile sector-specific skilled workers. Redistribution among workers plays an insurance role and makes the investment in specific skills more attractive. The insurance effect of redistribution can be stronger than the distortionary effect, so that the optimal progression of the labour income tax can increase when capital markets become more integrated.

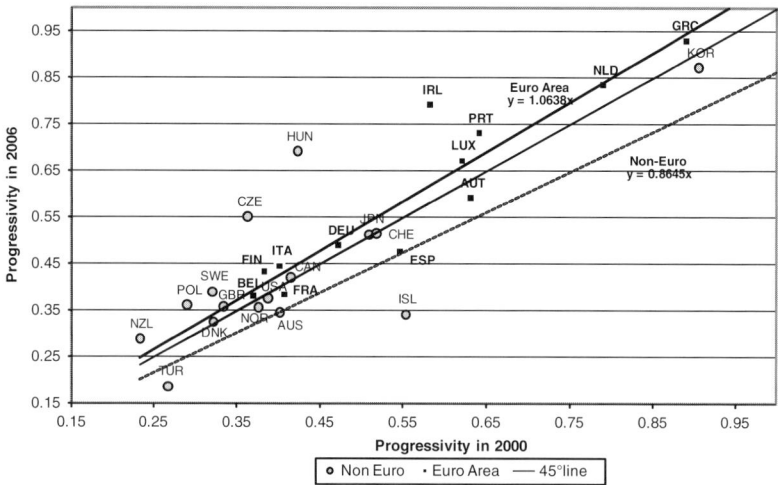

Figure 14.4: Progressivity of income taxes: 2000 and 2006
Note: Mexico (1.75 in 2000, 1.24 in 2006) has been taken out to improve visibility
Source: OECD (2007a) and authors' own calculations.

4.3 Have domestic tax reforms been driven by concerns regarding the relation between taxes, international trade and domestic employment?

To our knowledge there is no empirical study on the impact of domestic taxes on trade in the euro area. The only limited evidence is provided by the simulations performed with the Commission's QUEST model, in European Commission (2002). The study analyses the effects on the main macroeconomic variables of different discretionary fiscal measures for three countries: Germany, Ireland and Greece. The simulations show that a permanent tax shift from labour income taxes to VAT may have sizeable positive long-run effects on GDP for a large country like Germany, while the impact is negligible in the short run and for the small countries, Ireland and Greece. The effects on the trade balance, are in general negligible. Only in the long run (three years after the policy change) does Germany experience a reduction in net exports. It is not clear, however, whether the 'tax swap' considered by the Commission can be strictly interpreted as an internal devaluation, as the reduction in labour income taxes seems to include taxes which are not (at least in the short run) production costs such as those paid by the employees.

We looked for further empirical evidence by conducting a simple analysis on the correlation between the trade balance and current values of domestic taxes on GDP using an unbalanced panel of OECD countries from 1970 to 2005. The results are reported in Table 14.3.[15]

Table 14.3: *Taxes and net exports*

	1	2	3	4
VAT/GDP	0.064	0.182	−0.164	
	(0.147)	(0.178)	(0.144)	
(VAT/GDP)$_{noEA}$				−0.164
				(0.144)
(VAT/GDP)$_{EAanteEuro}$			−0.089	−0.254
			(0.164)	(0.185)
(VAT/GDP)$_{EApostEuro}$			0.047	−0.117
			(0.374)	(0.392)
Social contributions/ GDP		0.111	0.023	
		(0.086)	(0.052)	
(Social contributions/ GDP)$_{noEA}$				0.023
				(0.052)
(Social contributions/ GDP)$_{EAanteEuro}$			−0.086	−0.062
			(0.131)	(0.122)
(Social contributions/ GDP)$_{EApostEuro}$			−0.510*	−0.486*
			(0.274)	(0.275)
CIT/GDP	1.084***	1.212***	0.766***	
	(0.178)	(0.194)	(0.158)	
(CIT/GDP)$_{noEA}$				0.765***
				(0.159)
(CIT/GDP)$_{EAanteEuro}$			0.635**	1.400***
			(0.312)	(0.301)
(CIT/GDP)$_{EApostEuro}$			1.057***	1.823***
			(0.257)	(0.244)
TAX/GDP	−0.059	−0.161***	0.034	0.034
	(0.039)	(0.052)	(0.040)	(0.040)
Obs.	695	656	656	656
R2	0.44	0.44	0.48	0.48

All regressions include countries effects, years effects, per-capita GDP control.

Robust standard errors in parentheses.

* means significant at 10 per cent;

** significant at 5 per cent;

*** significant at 1 per cent.

We considered first a very simple specification where net exports in goods and services on GDP are regressed on VAT, corporate tax and total tax revenue as a percentage of GDP. The estimates (column 1) confirm the main findings of Keen and Syed (2006): export performance is unrelated to reliance on VAT, but positively related to reliance on corporate taxes. However, while Keen and Syed (2006) report a negative correlation between the trade balance and total tax revenues, no significant association can be detected in our sample. Column 2 tests whether employers' social contributions have an impact on the trade balance. The theory on internal devaluation predicts a negative association between these two variables. In contrast, the estimated coefficient is positive and not significant. We further explored whether the sensitivity of trade to domestic taxes has changed with the creation of EMU. To this end column 3 uses two dummies (the first equal to one for EMU countries up to 1998 and the second equal to one for EMU countries for the period 1999–2005) interacted with the tax variables. There is no evidence that the association between trade and VAT is different between EMU and other OECD countries before and after the introduction of the new currency. But, interestingly, there is weak evidence that the single currency has increased the responsiveness of net exports to employers' social contributions. Further, the estimated coefficient for employers' social contributions for EMU countries after the introduction of the euro has a negative sign as predicted by the theory (column 4). A similar pattern can be detected for the corporate income tax. The sensitivity of trade to the corporate tax is significantly higher for EMU members, and further increases after the introduction of the euro.

The previous conclusions are only provisional. A more sophisticated analysis is needed to control for the endogeneity of the tax variables and to detect more complex dynamic effects, especially for VAT and corporate taxation. However, with reference to VAT and corporate taxes, Keen and Syed (2006) have shown that the results of the simple specification in column 1 (no trade effects of VAT, strong short-run effects of corporate tax) are confirmed by a more general dynamic model. Therefore our regression results suggest that the introduction of the euro has increased the responsiveness of trade to domestic taxes, in particular the corporate tax and employers' social contributions. The association between taxes and trade is consistent with the theory of the internal devaluation: a cut in employer tax-related costs has a positive effect on net exports while an increase in VAT is neutral.[16]

In the light of this conclusion it appears somewhat surprising that until recently there was little evidence that tax reforms have been driven by trade concerns given the potential trade effects. Apart from the cases discussed in Section 3.3, in the past decades the main reforms in the field of social contributions have actually resulted in an *increase* in employers' social contributions to finance growing entitlements. To be sure, since the introduction of the euro there has been a number of reductions in social contributions, but these have been, by and large, targeted to specific groups or sectors. A summary analysis of changes in VAT and social contribution revenues as a percentage of GDP did not reveal any significant correlation. Why did euro-area countries not pursue 'internal devaluations' more often? A first set of reasons, highlighted by Calmfors (1998), stems from political economy considerations. The obvious difference between an external and an internal devaluation is that the latter requires an explicit political consensus to vary taxes or expenditures whereas devaluations are at the discretion of governments or the monetary authorities. The quest for a political agreement may find several hurdles in the choice of the tax increases or expenditure cuts needed to finance a reduction in employers' social contribution since each alternative would have different distributional consequences.[17] In the case of tax-financed internal devaluations, a VAT increase is not entirely equivalent to an increase in employee social contributions or to a tax on labour. An increase in VAT has an effect on the consumption of all residents. A fully anticipated increase in VAT lowers the real return on savings, leading consumers to reduce current consumption in order to avoid higher tax in the future and tends to entail a reduction of net exports in the short run.[18] By contrast, a fully anticipated increase in the labour income tax does not lead to an immediate impact on consumption and net exports.

The difficulties related to the political process could be partly overcome if the cut in social contributions is debt financed, as in the case of the Italian reduction of IRAP (*imposta regionale sulle attività produttive*), or through the creation of 'buffer funds' as in the case of Finland. However, these strategies may currently be constrained by the limit set on debt financing by the SGP.

A second set of reasons that may explain why countries have not relied on internal devaluations is that the final effects of such a strategy on unemployment are unclear. Hoon and Phelps (1996) explore the effects of a shift to an increased VAT offset by lighter payroll taxation in a version of the labour-turnover model of unemployment. They find that such a shift decreases the natural rate of unemployment in a closed economy and in a two-country world, while for a small open economy whose interest rate is given by the world rate, the tax shift is neutral for employment. In contrast, Goerke (1999) finds that in an efficiency wage model of employment the shift from social contributions to VAT has uncertain economic consequences which depend on whether VAT is shifted forward into consumer prices and on the nature of the employment compensation system.

Finally, the ambiguity on the employment consequences of an internal devaluation is also consistent with the fact that despite the widespread concerns on the effect of taxes and social contributions on labour cost the theoretical prediction and the empirical evidence are rather mixed (Arpaia and Carone, 2004). From a theoretical perspective, the incidence of social contributions depends on a series of institutional factors such as the relative strength of unions, the centralisation of the wage bargaining process, the structure of product and capital markets, and the interaction of tax with other institutions (e.g. the fiscal treatment of unemployment benefits). Furthermore, the degree of shifting of social contributions on labour may also depend on the link between the tax payment and the future benefit. If this link is strong and correctly perceived by the agents the negative effects of social contributions may be significantly alleviated (Butler, 2002; Disney, 2004). This implies that, when there is a link between social contributions and benefits, the shift from social contributions to VAT taxes increases the tax wedge.[19]

The empirical evidence mirrors the mixed results of the theoretical analysis. Arpaia and Carone (2004) suggest that there is probably some wage resistance in the short term but not in the long term, although the transition to the long term can be very long and therefore the short-term impact and the dynamics of adjustment can be long-lasting. In the short term, an increase in the tax wedge has an impact on the labour cost and thus on employment, although limited. The estimates suggest that a one percentage point increase in the tax wedge leads to a contemporaneous increase in the real labour costs of only 0.1 per cent.

As mentioned above, until recently there has not been much evidence of explicit policies directed at achieving an internal devaluation. However, in 2007 Germany increased its VAT rate by 3 p.p. to 19 per cent and reduced at the same time its social contributions by 2.3 p.p.[20] In 2007, Italy cut the tax wedge on labour by reducing its value-added business tax (IRAP). The cut was financed by reforming the mandatory severance indemnity scheme (*trattamento di fine rapporto* or TFR). The reform turned the existing fully funded scheme run by individual firms into a pay as you go scheme run by the National Social Security Agency (Istituto Nazionale Previdenza Sociale or INPS). The additional revenue came from the first generation effect of the reform. More recently, the proposal of a 'social VAT' has been hotly debated during the French election campaign and resulted in a government report on the feasibility of its introduction (Besson, 2007).

5. Tax systems in the EMU: future developments and prospects for reforms

The survey of theory and evidence above confirms the difficulties of singling out some clear links between the introduction of the common currency and the evolution of the tax system in the euro area. However, there are several interesting conclusions that can be drawn. First, the data show the clear effect of the adjustment to the Maastricht criteria on total tax revenue. Countries joining the euro area were characterised by high fiscal pressure but their total tax to GDP ratio increased more than other EU and OECD countries after 1992.

Second, most of the concerns that were raised during the build-up to monetary union did not materialise. In the 'One Market, One Money' report the European Commission (1990) took the view that the main effect of the euro on the tax system would have operated through the increased mobility of capital. In the middle of the 1990s the Commission voiced the fear that capital mobility was bringing about a shift of the tax burden to the less mobile tax base – labour – causing in turn high employment and hindering redistribution. The empirical literature has confirmed that the euro has increased both the mobility of financial and real capital but there is no clear evidence that this has fostered strategic interaction among EMU countries or a decline of capital income taxes, in particular the corporate income tax. Furthermore, there are no apparent signs that higher capital mobility is jeopardising the progression of personal income taxes.

However, we have highlighted several factors that may have disguised the erosion of capital income taxes: income shifting between the personal and the corporate tax bases; privatisation; revenue reallocation in countries with large natural resources; and changes in organisational form associated with 'demutualisation'. Further, we have shown that the sensitiveness of the trade balance to corporate taxation has increased in the EMU, which may be taken as tentative evidence that capital movements to and from euro-area countries have become more responsive to the levels of corporate taxation. As a consequence, the case for further corporate tax coordination in the euro area should be taken up seriously.

At present one of the main objectives of the European Commission in the tax field is to provide companies with a consolidated corporate tax base for their EU-wide activities, focusing in particular on the common consolidated tax base (CCTB). The Commission's strategy is mainly driven by the aim of removing in a systematic way the tax obstacles which exist for companies operating in more than one Member State in the internal market. From this perspective, the CCTB does not raise any obvious problems or advantages directly related to EMU. In contrast, it may have relevant consequences for tax competition. In the short run such a proposal is likely to increase the sensitivity of FDI to national corporate tax rates and may lead to a further decline in tax rates and revenues. However, the implementation of a CCTB may provide the basis for an effective discipline among EMU countries. Even if the European Commission has stated on several occasions that it has no intention of linking the CCTB with any proposal to harmonise tax rates, it is a fact that the harmonisation of the tax base opens up the possibility of implementing a mutually beneficial minimum level of taxation in the euro area.

Finally, the recent experience of the largest EMU countries (Germany, France and Italy) suggests that members of the euro area are looking for changes in the tax mix which may substitute for devaluations of the nominal exchange rate in an attempt to stimulate growth without breaching the SGP.

The prospect that internal devaluations may proliferate in the euro area raises a number of issues. The first question is whether there is a need to limit national autonomy in this field or to coordinate the choices of single Member States. If the answer is yes, a further question is what kind of coordination could minimise the inefficiency of strategic interaction allowing a sufficient degree of national autonomy into the choice of the tax mix.

The history of the EMS leaves little room for arguing against the need to set a limit to 'beggar-thy-neighbour' devaluations. The real issue is which kind of constraint is needed. From a theoretical perspective, it is quite hard to find a way to prevent countries affecting the real exchange rate through taxes. As explained in the previous section, an internal devaluation may be achieved in several ways, provided that there is a cut in taxes that adds to labour cost. However, in the limited sample of significant attempts to pursue such a strategy, the cut in social contributions paid by employers was financed mainly through an increase in VAT (e.g. the reform implemented in Germany and the debate on social VAT in France). Simple considerations can explain such behaviour. On the one hand, in recent years many euro countries have failed in any attempt to reduce public expenditure. On the other hand, a shift of taxation from employers to employees is likely to face a strong political opposition on the equity ground. The quest for avoiding competitive internal devaluations leads therefore to analysing the need for further coordination of VAT.

This is the field where the Commission exerted a strong effort during the 1990s. The Commission initiatives were driven by the objective of improving the functioning of the internal market. Ever since it adopted its first and second VAT Directives in April 1967, the EU has been committed to introducing a 'definitive system' of taxation which eliminates import taxes and export tax exemptions in trade between the Member States by taxing goods and services in the Member State of origin (Bill, 2004). The abolition of internal border controls and formalities, in 1993, created problems in the working of a destination-based VAT system in intra-EC trade and stimulated several proposals for a definitive origin-based VAT system (Keen *et al.*, 1996). The large literature which rapidly developed on the theme provided clear policy guidelines (Lockwood, 2001). Under the origin principle countries have the incentive to set taxes at a level which is inefficiently low. The inefficiency of tax competition is larger the wider the differences in country size. Small countries undercut large ones and produce the largest tax externalities. The introduction of a minimum tax rate is Pareto improving while the welfare effect of harmonisation of tax rates is in general ambiguous. Following these prescriptions the rules determining the tax base and the procedures for tax collection and administration were harmonised to some extent (even if there remain significant differences among Member States), the range of statutory rates was reduced and minimum statutory rates were set.[21] This has resulted in a convergence of statutory tax rates, though differences persist in the efficiency of tax collection due to national derogations and exemptions and to the different size of the informal economy (Mathis, 2004).

Is this framework adequate to deal with the possibility of a strategic use of VAT to affect the real exchange rate? To answer the question notice first that the transition to the origin principle was never completed and that there are no signs that the 'transitional system' implemented in 1993 is going to be replaced in the near future (Bill, 2004; Cnossen, 2002). In practice, in the 'transitional system' the origin principle is applied to individual cross-border shopping while the destination principle applies to transactions between firms (on a reverse charge basis). Despite the widespread concern that cross-border shopping may rapidly swell due to the change in regime, the more recent evidence suggests that there have been no significant changes in cross-border purchasing patterns, nor any significant distortions of competition or deflections of trade through disparities in VAT rates (Cnossen, 2002). De facto, VAT still adheres to the destination principle both in intra- and extra-EU transactions.

The fact that European VAT is at present mainly destination based is crucial for understanding the incentives countries have to manipulate the tax rates in order to increase competitiveness. Under a destination-based VAT an internal devaluation can be achieved by increasing the VAT rate and cutting employers' social contributions. Under the origin principle an increase in VAT rate would raise the price of domestically produced commodities relative to the price of imports. Therefore in order to achieve a devaluation of the real exchange rate under the origin-based principle, the VAT rate should be cut and the revenue loss should be financed through an increase in taxes on employees.

The predominance of the destination principle both in intra- and extra-EU transactions is also fundamental in identifying the welfare loss due to strategic interaction and possible remedies. To the extent that a country succeeds in achieving a welfare-improving increase in net exports by cutting tax-related labour costs and raising destination-based VAT, it will inflict a welfare loss to its trading partners. This implies that a process of competitive internal devaluation will lead to VAT rates which are inefficiently high, rather than too low as in the case of tax competition under the origin principle. Furthermore, if we focus on the welfare of euro-area countries, the largest damages may be caused by large countries. It is likely that a successful internal devaluation by a small country will have a negligible impact on the nominal exchange rate between the euro and other currencies. As a consequence, the devaluation of the real exchange rate will hurt in the same way trading partners in and outside the eurozone. In contrast, when the same policy is implemented by a large country, there may be an effect on the nominal exchange rate. To the extent that the increase in net exports will trigger an appreciation of the euro respect to the other currencies, euro-area countries will suffer a greater loss of competitiveness.

These simple considerations suggest three solutions which range from weak to strong forms of coordination. The first one is the introduction of a maximum VAT rate. Since its original proposal on VAT rates,[22] the Commission has recommended several times the introduction of a maximum rate of 25 per cent, but the Council only agreed in 1996 to make 'every effort' not to go beyond that level. The problem is that such a limit seems too high to be effective: the largest economies (Germany, France, Italy, Spain) have rates which are still significantly lower, ranging from 16–20 per cent, and many of them (France, Italy and Spain) apply a reduced rate on a substantial share of the tax base. On the other hand, the implementation of an explicit maximum rate at 20 per cent would drastically reduce the national autonomy in this field, leaving a band of 5 percentage points only.

The alternative to the maximum rate could be found in the reform of the EU's own resources. At present, the VAT-based own resource results from the application of a uniform rate of call (around 0.33 per cent in 2007) to a common tax base. This base is a theoretical construct that compensates for the fact that neither the VAT rates nor the list of goods and services covered by VAT are harmonised at EU level. As a consequence the payment of each Member State is not affected by variations in revenue due to changes in its own tax bases and rates. In contrast, a tax-sharing scheme of actual VAT revenues could be a means of internalising the effect of beggar-thy-neighbour strategies, as this would raise the perceived cost of raising revenue through VAT for national governments.

The third solution is given by the transition to the definitive origin-based regime. As explained above, in order to decrease the ratio between domestically produced good and imports, a country should cut VAT and increase taxes on the income of employees. However, on the one hand tax rates cannot be reduced below the minimum levels already set and on the other hand it may be difficult to find the consensus for increasing taxes on labour, given that in many countries the tax wedge on labour is quite high.

It is worthwhile noticing that, even with perfect price flexibility, under the destination principle uncoordinated tax setting brings about inefficient equilibria (Arachi, 2001). The tax rates are too high and a coordinate reduction in rates on imported goods (through a maximum rate) yield a Pareto improvement (Lockwood, 2001). This implies that EMU may act as forerunner for a new coordination strategy in the VAT field that may be later extended to the rest of the EU countries.

6. Conclusions

Tax policy as such has not been generally seen as raising any specific issues for the coming into existence of a common currency. The euro has not been closely associated with changes in tax policy nor has concern been expressed that the domestic tax systems of euro-area countries are influencing economic activity in the euro area relative to non-euro-area countries. At the same time tax policy is very actively discussed within the EU.

This chapter has examined whether and how the introduction of the euro changed the impact of taxes on the economy or influenced the direction of tax policy. It surveyed potential theoretical channels through which tax policy and exchange rate regimes are interrelated (capital mobility, strategic tax setting and trade policy). It is difficult to find strong empirical evidence of major, unique changes in the impact or determination of tax policy following the introduction of the euro. The internal market has had by far a greater impact and it has affected all EU countries.

Nevertheless, we highlighted that, going forward, certain specific aspects deserve attention and call for further tax coordination among EMU and EU countries. The most important concerns the use of tax policy by individual EMU countries to improve competitiveness by changing the mix of taxes and thereby achieving an internal devaluation. A second issue deserving attention concerns tax competition, particularly in the area of corporation tax. We provided some tentative evidence that capital movements to and from euro-area countries have become more responsive to the levels of corporate taxation.

Notes

1. We do not propose to examine the issues associated with 'tax assignment' and deeper integration of euro-area countries relative to the other members of the EU.

2. The efficiency of tax collection of VAT varies significantly across EU countries.

3. We have tested for the announcement of the euro using alternatively the publication date of the Delors report and the signing of the Maastricht Treaty. The results remain largely unchanged.

4. Ultimately the political and legal processes are mainly driven by structural and institutional changes in the underlying economy which have been very significant in all respects. In our view the most important have been: (1) the creation of the internal market and the EMU, which have greatly increased trade between member countries, fostered the development of single financial market and enhanced capital mobility across Europe; (2) globalisation, which has increased competition in goods and factor markets and potentially shifted the nature of exposures to external shocks; (3) ageing, which is putting pressure on social security and health systems and, as a consequence, on the fiscal wedge on labour; (4) the enlargement of the EU.

5. For a thorough analysis of financial integration in EMU, see Jappelli and Pagano (this volume).

6. The effort to satisfy the Maastricht criteria also led to better-balanced fiscal budgets, which may have led to a 'real convergence' of European economies, that is, an increased synchronisation in business cycles across the European economies (Darvas *et al.* (2005)).

7. See e.g. Danthine *et al.* 2001, De Santis and Gérard 2006, Fidora *et al.* 2007, Fratzscher 2002, Galati and Tsatsaronis 2003, Hartmann *et al.* 2003, Lane 2006b, Pagano and von Thadden 2004, and Jappelli and Pagano, this volume.

8. See Baldwin *et al.* (2008) for a thorough analysis of the impact of EMU on FDI.

9. For example, lower tax rates with base broadening may be an attempt to attract foreign investment or create a more level playing field among domestic companies.

10. Germany (2001), Finland (2005), France (2004), Ireland (1999), Italy (2004), Portugal, UK (1999) have all moved from imputation to partial exemption or (modified) classical system. In Germany, Italy and the UK, higher personal taxation of dividend income has been explicitly linked to reductions in corporate income tax rates.

11. In the United States the Domestic International Sales Corporation (DISC) and its successor, the Foreign International Sales Corporation (FISC) were created with the objective of offsetting the adverse competitive effects of corporate tax. These regimes were found contrary to GATT rules.

12. Steward and Webb (2006) analyse the evolution of corporate tax burdens – measured as corporate tax collected on GDP and on total taxes – in the OECD countries between 1950 and 1999. Descriptive analysis of

these time series reveals no evidence of a competitive 'race to the bottom' in corporate taxation and little evidence of even a harmonisation of the tax burden.

13. This occurred for instance in the United Kingdom where corporate income tax has gradually replaced the royalty payment and part of the petroleum revenue tax.

14. For a review of the recent literature and an empirical analysis on the effect of taxes on M&A see Huizinga and Voget (2006).

15. Though not reported, all specifications include country effects, year dummies to control for any unobserved common time-specific effects and per-capita GDP. All standard errors are heteroskedasticity-robust.

16. We also tested additional specifications which include social contributions paid by employees as a percentage of GDP. In the simple regression with no interacted dummies, the estimated coefficient of this variable is negative but not significant. Using interacted dummies the regressions show a significant negative impact on trade for countries outside the euro area, while the coefficients are still not significant for EMU members, both before and after the introduction of EMU, as predicted by the theory of internal devaluation.

17. Besson (2007) argues that the introduction of a social VAT to replace a part of social contributions would not have the degree of widespread social consensus that similar measures had in Denmark in the late 1980s, and that the ideal design from a political standpoint (i.e. reductions in social contributions aimed at lower income groups) would not necessarily be sufficient to offset foreign competitive pressures.

18. An unanticipated increase in VAT decreases the value of existing assets and leads to a decrease in current consumption.

19. This point is acknowledged by the European Commission (2002), which observes that the simulated effects of an internal devaluation on GDP are larger for Germany than for Ireland and Greece, since the indexation of benefits to taxes is lower in Germany and consequently labour income taxes are more distortionary.

20. A similar policy was followed in 1998. In 1987, Denmark introduced a 'social VAT' to calm an overheated economy while reducing the impact of the tax measures on the export sector.

21. There is also a political commitment on a maximum rate of 25 per cent.

22. The Commission's proposal for a Council Directive Supplementing the Common System of Value-Added Tax and Amending Directive 77/ 388/ EEC (COM(87) 321).

Comment 10: Comment on Chapter 14

CASPER VAN EWIJK

How the EMU has influenced tax policy in the Member States is an intriguing, but not easy to answer question. Alworth and Arachi (AA) make an admirable attempt to evaluate the different channels through which the monetary union could affect domestic tax policies, and to gather evidence on their relevance during the ten-year experience of the EMU. This has resulted in an outstanding overview of the state of the art in this field, and a thorough assessment of the policy implications.

In my reading, two channels stand out. First, in so far as the EMU has further enhanced mobility of (financial) capital, Member States can be expected to shift the composition of taxes away from the mobile factor (capital) to less mobile factors (labour, consumption). Second, as EMU members have lost the exchange rate as a policy instrument, the issue arises whether taxes would offer an alternative instrument for accommodating idiosyncratic shocks. In particular, AA discuss the idea that tax policies could be used to achieve real exchange rate adjustments necessary for stabilising the national economy. I will comment on both these channels.

1. Strategic setting of capital income taxation

One of the interesting features in the evolution of tax rates during the past decade – as carefully documented by AA – is that the fears about a race to the bottom in capital income taxation (CIT) were unfounded. On the contrary, CIT revenues recently seem to have stabilised as a percentage of GDP, or even gone up. In many countries, the fall in statutory rates has been compensated by an equivalent broadening of the tax base. Yet, there is still a fear that strategic setting of tax rates will put further pressure on the CIT rates. AA rightly point out that the race to the bottom is by no means an inevitable law of nature, and that there are other factors that may well compensate for the downward tendency. In particular, they mention the role of corporate tax as a backstop to the income tax. Indeed, a tendency can be observed for the (top) rates in income tax to converge with CIT rates, pointing to a concern to avoid tax shifting between domestic sources, viz. income taxes and corporate taxes. This domestic concern may compensate or even dominate possible incentives for strategic competition to attract foreign capital by lowering CIT rates.

There are also further reasons, not discussed in AA, why one would expect CIT rates not to be driven down excessively. First, some tax competition and downward pressure on (capital) income tax rates can be healthy as it helps to restrain the Leviathan tendencies of governments who seek to increase expenditures and accordingly have to raise taxes (Bovenberg *et al.* 2003). From this point of view, the fall in tax rates in the run-up to the EMU can be seen as a wholesome process of restructuring government budgets. Second, the CIT is not only a tax on capital income, which is distortionary, but it also puts a non-distortionary levy on pure profits which may be due to location rents and earnings falling to fixed factors. According to simulations with CPB's Cortax model this is an important factor which effectively limits the downward pressure on CIT rates due to strategic competition (Bettendorf *et al.* 2006). The Cortax model is developed to analyse strategic tax setting among European countries and explicitly takes account of tax spillovers between countries. The model confirms that strategic motives lead to some downward pressure on CIT rates. While for most of the countries Bettendorf *et al.* find welfare effects of multilateral tax reductions to be negative, simulations show that unilateral tax cuts tend to yield positive welfare gains. The reason is that fiscal spillovers within the EU via multinational profit shifting are relatively strong. Individual countries can exploit such spillovers in their favour by reducing statutory corporate tax rates, thereby broadening their corporate tax base. By coordinating such policies, however, the benefits for individual countries are much smaller as coordination mitigates the international spillover effects. This indicates that without coordination countries will choose lower CIT rates than they would have chosen when tax rates were set in a coordinated manner. At the same time actual tax rates are close to the optimal tax rates in a uncoordinated setting. This is illustrated in Figure C10.1 showing that for most countries the strategically optimal rates are below actual rates. The gap between actual and optimal rates is small, however, in general. For Italy, Greece and Sweden optimal rates turn out to be even higher

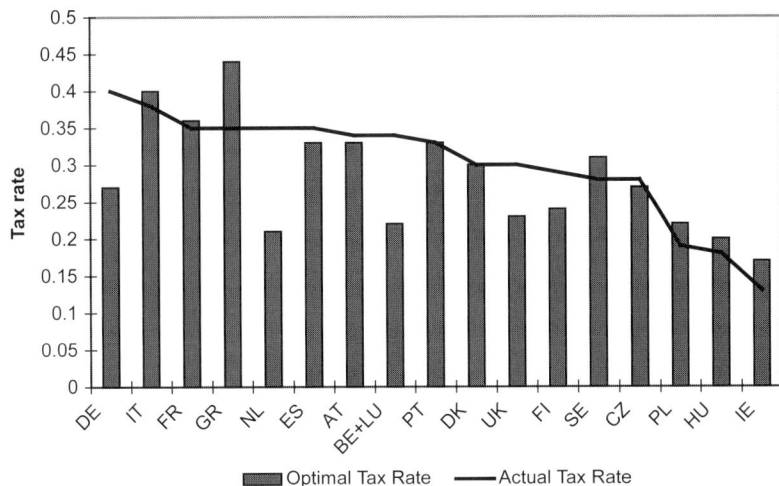

Figure C10.1: Actual and optimal CIT rates in EU countries
Source: Based on Bettendorf *et al.* (2006).

than their actual rates. So there is still some downward pressure according to these simulations, but it is very limited, and it will certainly not
lead to a race to the bottom.

An interesting exercise in the context of the tenth anniversary of EMU
is how these optimal tax rates would change in the presence of highly
integrated capital markets. This is a way to establish how the EMU,
which enhances capital market integration, could have influenced strategic CIT setting among its Member States. Figure C10.2 presents the
welfare gains of a one percentage-point unilateral decrease in CIT rates
for the same selection of EU countries and compares it with the welfare
gains in the baseline case. High capital market integration in this exercise
features a doubling of inward and outward FDI. For all countries, the
increase in capital market integration raises the welfare gain from an
unilateral reduction of the tax rate, indicating that optimal strategic CIT
rates will go down when capital market integration increases.

Whether this has been a major factor in the introduction of the EMU
is hard to tell. The evidence discussed in AA is rather mixed, and it is
difficult to single out the contribution of the EMU relative to other
major changes such as the deepening of the internal market, the widening of international capital markets, and the need for tax reforms
anyway.

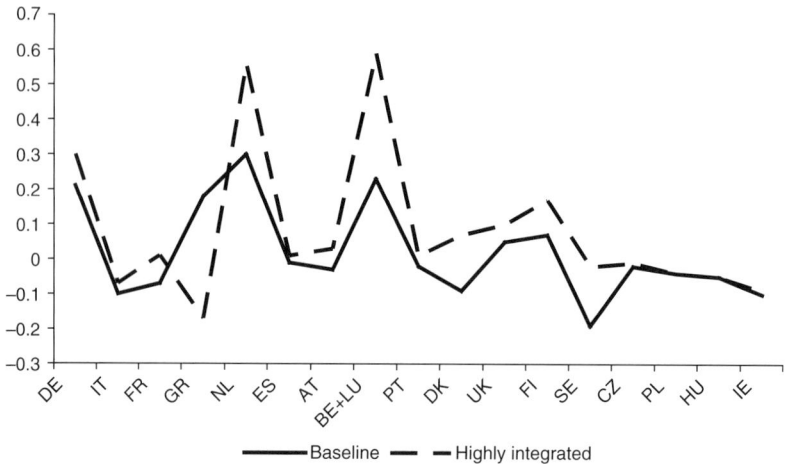

Figure C10.2: Welfare gains (per cent of GDP) of unilateral reduction in CIT by 1 point
Source: Based on Bettendorf *et al.* (2006).

As said, the fact that CIT also puts a levy on pure profits raises some interesting issues. First, it is not entirely certain that the tendency in policy to broaden the tax base and reduce statutory rates will be considered as a beneficial impact, as often thought. Reducing the rate also lowers the tax on pure rents. When the loss of these non-distortionary taxes has to be compensated for by less generous allowances for capital, the cost of capital may increase and investment distortions may be exacerbated. Also raising distortionary taxes on other factors may on balance lead to welfare losses instead of welfare gains. Second, as far as increasing international competition exacerbates income inequality, and leads to higher rents on fixed factors, this might even further reinforce the role of CIT as an effective instrument to reap rents.

2. Internal devaluation

A second channel through which the EMU may affect tax policy arises from the loss of the exchange rate instrument for individual countries. AA raise the interesting question whether tax policy might offer an alternative to the exchange rate instrument in accommodating idiosyncratic shocks. On this point the analysis is a bit confusing. On the one hand there is the traditional argument of the beneficial impact of automatic stabilisers: keeping tax rates constant and running surpluses and deficits when shocks hit the economy can help to smooth the economy. This holds for the government budget, but can also be extended to social insurance funds. This is, in my view, the essential idea of the Finnish EMU buffer funds discussed by AA. The suggestion that these funds could also be used in a more active manner by raising rates in good times and lowering them in bad times seems a bad idea to me. Such activist policies have a bad track record, and trusting this instrument to the social partners, as in the Finnish case, may make it even worse. It will give rise to a serious hold-up problem as the same partners have to decide on wages. The simple economists' truth that in a monetary union wage flexibility is the key mechanism for adjustment remains valid in the Finnish case.

Another argument discussed by AA is that the government may deliberately change the tax mix in order to achieve a real depreciation of the exchange rate. Specifically, raising VAT rates while reducing social contributions, or taxes on labour income, could make domestic products cheaper, and therefore strengthen the competitive position of domestic producers. In this way the tax system could in principle be used to produce an 'internal devaluation'. Here, we should distinguish between the short term and the long term, however. In the short term, reducing social contributions may help to bring about a reduction in real wage costs, especially when nominal wages are rigid. This effect is temporary, though, as wages will return to their equilibrium level again.

More interesting is the issue of whether a change in the tax system could improve the trade balance, and contribute to a nation's welfare in a structural manner. AA provide a very helpful discussion on the significance of tax composition for the trade balance. There is a long-standing debate as to whether a shift from labour taxes to consumption taxes or VAT may help to improve a country's competitive position, and thus can be used in a strategic manner. Indeed, VAT rates seem to have been on the rise in EU countries in recent years. Whether this is the result of a deliberate action aiming at internal devaluation, as suggested by AA, is not evident to me. In practice, other effects play a role as well, which may be at least as important as the real exchange rate channel. First, higher VAT rates – from a short-term perspective – are likely to exert an upward pressure on consumer prices of goods and services, thereby eroding real wages if they are rigid. As pointed out above, this is however only a temporary effect. More important is that increasing the

VAT and lowering labour income taxes is a way to reshuffle the tax burden from workers to other groups. In particular pensioners and people receiving social benefits (if not indexed in real terms) will suffer from such a shift while workers will benefit. Accordingly, raising VAT rates is an effective way of reducing the real value of transfers to the old and others outside the labour process. On balance, such a restructuring of the tax burden alleviates labour market distortions, and thus increases employment and total welfare. As with any tax reform, this reform does not feature a free lunch, however, as the distribution is altered to the detriment of the pensioners and all others depending on non-labour income. Furthermore, there are other drawbacks of a too high VAT rate. First, one should take into account the potential implications for the hidden or black economy. It is well established that high VAT tends to boost activities in the hidden sector. This is because the black economy competes primarily with companies providing consumer goods and services subject to VAT. However, lower labour income taxes are likely to reduce the supply of undeclared labour. On balance, it depends on the country's specific situation whether shifting the tax burden from labour towards VAT will reduce or boost the informal sector. Finally, substantial differences in VAT between countries may encourage cross-border shopping. The effects of this on imports and exports are small, even for the smaller EU member states.

3. Policy implications

To what policy conclusions do these comments lead? Policy coordination may be called for if strategic interaction between EMU or EU members leads to a suboptimal tax system, and *a fortiori* if this interaction degenerates into a race to the bottom in the case of CIT, or into a vicious circle of competitive devaluations in the case of VAT. If there is no such a threat, there is no need for coordination and tax policies can – according to the subsidiarity principle – be left to the discretion of the Member States. Both from a theoretical and a practical perspective there seem to exist no convincing arguments for strong coordination at the level of the EU or EMU. On the theoretical level some tax competition in the CIT may put a healthy restraint on overexpansive national governments. Furthermore, as CIT is an effective instrument for reaping rents due to locational advantages and other fixed factors, governments will take care not to reduce CIT rates too much. Model simulations indicate that actual rates are actually quite close to the optimal rates in a strategic setting. Accordingly, no drastic further reductions are to be expected for the future. Similarly for VAT, the scope for using this instrument in a competitive process of internal devaluations is very limited. First, the effects of such a reshuffle in taxes are modest from a structural point of view. Second, drastic increases in VAT will raise opposition from domestic interest groups, in particular pensioners, who have to pay higher prices due to VAT while they do not benefit from the lower taxes on labour income. This group has a strong voice, and it will grow even more powerful in the future as ageing continues. Third, there are also domestic concerns about not making VAT rates too high as this will boost the informal economy. All these factors imply that domestic policy makers are seriously restrained in their pursuit of strategic gains in international tax competition. This should be kept in mind when thinking of CIT floors, VAT caps and other forms of tax coordination at the European level. If there is no clear evidence of detrimental strategic tax competition, tax policies should be left to the individual Member States according to the subsidiarity principle. The steady decline in corporate tax rates suggests that countries compete primarily over multinational profits. To remedy this form of tax competition, coordination may be considered either in the form of a minimum CIT rate in the EU, or by introducing consolidation and formula apportionment.

PART VI

Growth, trade and volatility

15 | *The impact of EMU on growth in Europe*

RAY BARRELL, DAWN HOLLAND,
IANA LIADZE AND OLGA POMERANTZ

1. Introduction

This chapter addresses and evaluates the impacts of the introduction of
the euro on both actual and potential output in the euro area. There are
several channels through which the euro may have affected growth:
greater transparency and its impact on competitiveness and the effectiveness of the single market; integration of financial markets, which
may raise productivity; and a more stable macroeconomic environment,
which affects risk and investment decisions. We analyse the impact of
each of these channels on the drivers of growth, after controlling for
factors such as workforce skills, research base, openness, demographic
developments and structural reform on the evolution of output.

The central result of our chapter is that EMU affects output growth
directly and the many potential concerns preceding the launch of the
euro seem to have been unfounded. Our work suggests that the effects
of EMU that we observe have been beneficial for economic growth and
employment overall. Our analysis suggests that the direct positive
effects of EMU are likely to be larger in the core countries, despite
their recent slow growth, and that EMU may lead to agglomeration of
activities.

The effects of EMU on output can come through a number of channels. Economists find it useful to describe output as being the result of
inputs such as capital and labour organised for output through a
production function and influenced by efficiency and technology.

We would like to thank Martin Weale and other members of the National Institute
staff and participants at the EFN EUROFRAME conference on EMU @ 10 in Dublin
in June 2008 for their comments on this paper. The research reported here is part of a
larger study undertaken for the European Commission (Barrell *et al*. 2008a). We
would like to thank our co-authors on that report, Ehsan Khoman and Sylvia
Gottschalk, for their input. That paper has a long literature survey and a discussion
of the determinants and effects of volatility.

EMU might influence the stock of capital or the supply of labour. It might also affect the efficiency with which factors are used as it may reduce barriers to competition. The time frame over which these effects may come through will vary; it may be particularly long for capital, and hence it may not be possible to uncover the effects directly. However, the effects on labour markets and on efficiency may be more visible after a decade of EMU.

The structure of the chapter is as follows. Section 2 sets out the issues to be discussed, with a comparison of output, factor input and productivity growth, and the factors behind recent slow productivity growth in the euro area. Section 3 presents a simple approach to modelling productivity and output, within a framework that allows us to test the impact of EMU on growth after allowing for other systemic factors and structural reforms. We then report the results of econometric estimation of this model and discuss the multiple channels through which EMU may impact output and productivity growth.

2. Factors behind the recent slow euro area growth

Since the introduction of the common currency, growth in the euro area has been weak relative to that in the USA and the EU countries outside the euro area – the UK, Denmark and Sweden.[1] Figure 15.1 highlights the average annual growth rate differentials among the USA, the euro area, the UK and Sweden.[2] In the USA and the euro area growth was similar in the two decades to 1991 whilst Swedish and UK growth rates were generally lower than those in the USA and the euro area over the same period. Since the mid-1990s growth in the euro area has lagged behind that of other economies, with the gap widening from 2002. The UK and Sweden, both of whom were in the EU for (much of) the period from 1992, have been performing significantly better than the other members of the EU, while they have stayed outside EMU.

A closer look at the output growth in individual euro-area members reveals a significant degree of variation in rates. Output growth rates, presented in Table 15.1, suggest that the weak performance in the euro area in the early half of the current decade was driven primarily by slow output growth in Germany and Italy, each of which expanded at an average rate of less than 1 per cent per annum over the five-year period from 2002 to 2006. Growth in the Netherlands was also less than the euro-area average over the same period. By contrast, GDP growth in

Table 15.1: *Output growth – country details*

Average annual growth rates

Period	BE	DK	FI	FR	DE	IT	NL	AT	SE	ES	UK	US	EMU
72–76	3.8	2.7	2.4	3.4	2.6	3.8	3.4	4.1	2.6	5.0	2.2	3.1	3.4
77–81	1.5	1.0	3.2	2.7	2.3	2.8	1.7	2.4	1.1	1.1	0.9	3.1	2.4
82–86	1.4	3.6	3.0	2.0	1.6	2.1	1.9	1.9	2.2	2.1	3.1	3.4	1.8
87–91	3.1	0.8	1.5	3.1	4.0	2.8	3.2	3.5	1.6	4.4	2.2	2.5	3.4
92–96	1.9	2.6	1.2	1.2	1.3	1.1	2.3	2.0	1.2	1.2	2.5	3.2	1.4
97–01	2.6	2.4	4.6	3.0	2.1	2.1	3.7	2.6	3.2	4.4	3.1	3.5	2.8
02–06	1.9	1.8	3.1	1.7	0.9	0.7	1.3	1.9	3.0	3.3	2.6	2.9	1.6

Note: BE=Belgium, DK=Denmark, FI=Finland, FR=France, DE=Germany, IT=Italy, NL=Netherlands, AT=Austria, SE=Sweden, ES=Spain.

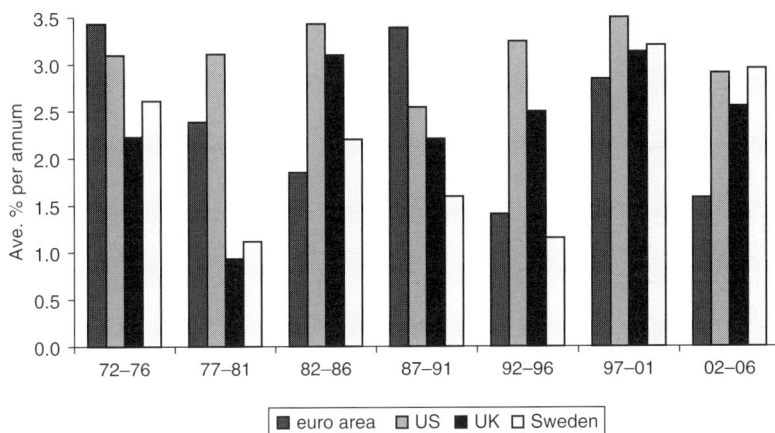

Figure 15.1: Output growth in the euro area, the USA, the UK and Sweden

Finland and in Spain outpaced that recorded in the USA and the non-EMU EU members. Growth picked up noticeably in 2006 and 2007 in much of the area and differentials narrowed. The slowdown in growth in the euro area after the adoption of the common currency has led many to look for the causes coming from the monetary arrangements.

A decomposition of GDP growth into changes in labour input and labour productivity gives some insight into the source of growth differentials observed between the euro-area members and other OECD countries in recent years. Figure 15.2 shows this breakdown, with labour

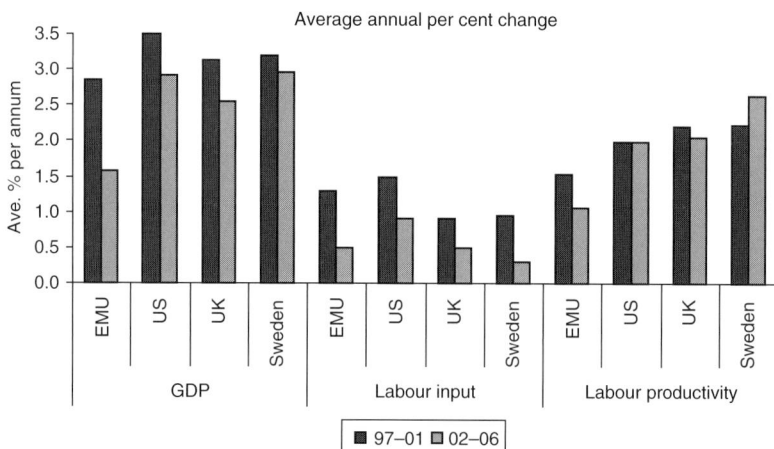

Figure. 15.2: GDP, labour input and labour productivity growth

input measured as total hours worked and labour productivity measured as real GDP per hour worked. This latter measure reflects the impacts of changes in capital per person employed as well as improvements in the efficiency of the use of factors. From 2002 to 2006, labour input in the euro area grew at a similar rate to that in the EU countries outside EMU, but somewhat more slowly than it did in the USA. However, labour productivity grew noticeably more slowly in the euro area over this period, and is largely responsible for the weaker output growth recorded.

Tables 15.2 and 15.3 present labour input and labour productivity growth for individual EU member states and the USA. Over the whole of the period labour input growth was more rapid in the USA than in the euro area, in part because average hours worked per person employed declined by less, but also because the population of working age has been growing more rapidly in the USA, in part due to migration. The labour input growth differential was much lower in the last ten years than previously, and it contributed less to the recent growth differential than in previous periods. Participation and employment rates in Europe have been rising, whilst they have fallen marginally in the USA. Labour input growth in the UK and Sweden was marginally lower than in the euro area in the last decade, and hence this cannot be a major factor behind the relative slowdown in euro-area growth.

The breakdown of labour productivity growth by country reveals significant variation. During the early years of the current decade,

Table 15.2: *Average annual growth of labour input*

Period	BE	DK	FI	FR	DE	IT	NL	AT	SE	ES	UK	US	EMU
72–76	–0.9	–1.5	0.9	–0.3	–1.7	–0.3	–1.9	–0.6	0.1	0.1	0.0	1.8	–0.7
77–81	–1.4	0.1	0.2	–0.9	–0.1	0.1	0.0	–0.9	–0.6	–3.2	–0.9	2.0	–0.6
82–86	–0.8	1.9	–0.1	–1.1	–0.4	–0.4	–0.8	–0.8	0.9	–1.9	0.2	1.9	–0.8
87–91	0.7	–1.4	–1.3	0.5	0.9	0.5	1.2	0.4	0.7	2.9	0.9	1.2	0.9
92–96	–0.6	0.0	–1.9	–0.5	–1.0	–1.5	0.8	0.4	–1.0	–0.5	–0.1	1.7	–0.8
97–01	1.3	1.6	2.0	0.9	0.2	1.0	2.3	0.6	0.9	4.6	0.9	1.5	1.3
02–06	0.3	0.5	0.3	0.0	–0.5	0.6	0.0	0.5	0.3	3.1	0.5	0.9	0.5

Table 15.3: *Average annual growth of labour productivity*

Period	BE	DK	FI	FR	DE	IT	NL	AT	SE	ES	UK	US	EMU
72–76	4.7	4.2	1.5	3.7	4.3	4.1	5.4	4.8	2.5	4.9	2.3	1.3	4.2
77–81	2.9	1.0	3.0	3.6	2.4	2.7	1.7	3.3	1.7	4.4	1.9	1.1	3.0
82–86	2.2	1.6	3.1	3.1	2.1	2.6	2.7	2.7	1.3	4.1	2.9	1.5	2.6
87–91	2.4	2.3	2.8	2.6	3.1	2.4	1.9	3.1	0.9	1.4	1.3	1.3	2.5
92–96	2.4	2.6	3.1	1.7	2.4	2.6	1.4	1.7	2.1	1.7	2.6	1.5	2.2
97–01	1.3	0.8	2.5	2.0	1.9	1.1	1.5	2.0	2.2	–0.2	2.2	2.0	1.5
02–06	1.6	1.4	2.8	1.7	1.4	0.2	1.3	1.4	2.6	0.2	2.1	2.0	1.1

overall productivity growth in the euro area was reduced noticeably by remarkably low productivity growth in Italy and in Spain. This may partly reflect the responses of these economies to unanticipated increases in the labour force.[3] Over the same period, labour productivity growth in Finland and Ireland – two euro-area members – was higher than in the USA and in the EU member states outside EMU.

Spain has seen significant increases in employment, which rose by around 30 percentage points more than the euro-area average between 1997 and 2006. This was largely due to an increase in the labour force because of inward migration, but about a third came from reductions in unemployment. Both of these will push the supply of labour down an existing labour demand curve, and hence wages and productivity growth will be lower than they otherwise would have been. Once investment takes place to provide capital for productive use, productivity rises again as the labour demand curve shifts out. However, it is possible that much of the initial capital accumulation after large-scale migration might be in the stock of housing, as in Spain, and hence labour productivity growth might take some time to return to trend.

While productivity growth in the euro area lagged behind the same measure in the USA and in the non-EMU members, levels of productivity present a more nuanced story, as Barrell *et al.* (2008a) discuss. Measured in constant US dollars at 2000 purchasing power parities, productivity per person hour in France has been at or at times slightly higher than in the USA since the mid-1990s. While productivity levels in the euro area as a whole have been declining relative to the USA since the mid-1990s, the overall figure is influenced largely by the developments in Spain. Those countries outside the euro area have not experienced a significant catch-up in productivity levels relative to the USA. Notably, productivity levels in the UK have been remarkably constant relative to the USA for much of the past decade. These differences in the levels of productivity reflect different levels of skills, knowledge and capital endowments, and catching up to the higher levels can take place through the accumulation of any one of these factors.

The comparison of productivity levels is inevitably broad brush, as the levels of the data series may not be comparable across countries, but comparisons of productivity growth rates are less subject to this problem. Using standard growth accounting techniques, labour productivity can be disaggregated into capital deepening and total factor productivity (TFP) (see for example Barrell *et al.*, 2007a), allowing us to determine if the differences in labour productivity growth across countries stem from factors that drive capital accumulation or factors that drive the efficiency of use of factor inputs. We can compare TFP for the whole economy in all EU countries using output at constant basic prices. This output measure removes indirect taxes and subsidies from the volume data, and is available up until the end of 2006 for all countries except Greece.[4] We take estimates of the whole economy capital stock along with employment and hours data and use equation (1) for TFP growth (tfp), where Y_t is constant price output in basic prices, K_t is the constant price value of the whole economy capital stock, E_t is total employment in the economy, and H_t are hours per person in employment. The parameters b_t are the average of the capital share in output for the two most recent years.[5]

$$\text{tfp} = \text{dln}Y_t - [b_t\text{dln}K_t + (1 - b_t)\text{dln}(E_tH_t)] \tag{1}$$

Figure 15.3 presents a comparison of TFP growth in the euro area and the non-EMU EU members. The EU countries outside the euro area experienced faster TFP growth compared to the euro-area members well in advance of the introduction of the common currency. TFP growth in EMU slowed down after the introduction of the euro.

Figure 15.4 illustrates the calculations for TFP growth on a country-by-country basis.[6] TFP growth decelerated between 1997–2001 and 2002–6 in almost all EU countries, both inside and outside of EMU. TFP growth was particularly robust in Finland and Ireland[7] between 1997 and 2001. Productivity growth in the UK and in Sweden was higher in this period than in any of the other euro-area countries, and it remained so between 2002 and 2006. However, TFP growth was only noticeably lower than in the UK in Italy, Spain and Belgium between 1997 and 2001, and in the same countries along with the Netherlands, Austria and Portugal between 2002 and 2006. In both these periods productivity growth in France and Germany was marginally lower than in the UK. Productivity levels actually declined in Spain in the second two subperiods and in Italy in the last sub-period.

Some of the factors affecting TFP growth are discussed in Barrell (2007), Crafts (2007) and McMorrow and Röger (2007). We can decompose them into the skills of the workforce, the level of scientific knowledge and the efficiency with which factors of production are used. Any production function may be written as $Y_t = f(capital_t, labour_t, tech_t)$ where the labour input is in efficiency units and $tech_t$ picks up other forms of technical progress. If we cannot measure labour in efficiency

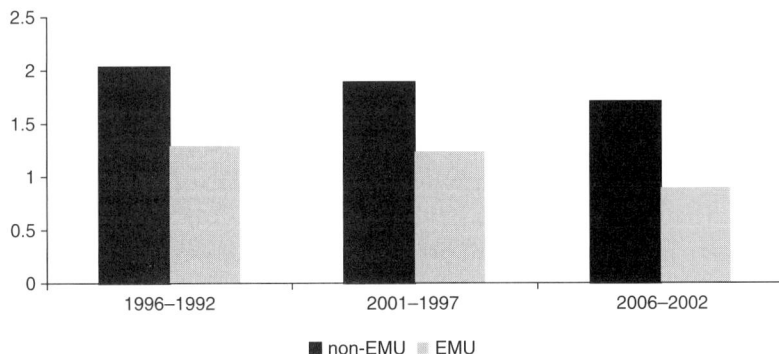

Figure 15.3: Growth of total factor productivity
* The non-EMU aggregate covers the UK, Sweden and Denmark

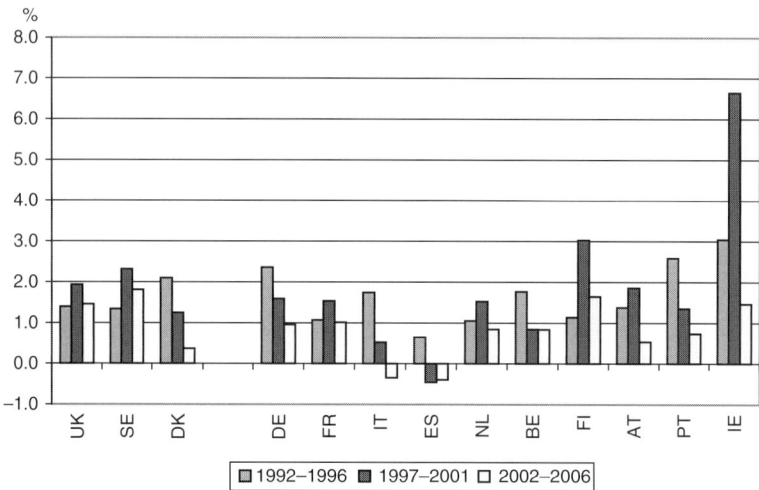

Figure 15.4: TFP growth (basic prices)

units, then the tech term will be a combination of labour skills effects and other technology and productivity effects.

If we were able to measure labour in efficiency units (rather than in person hours), then the resulting tfp calculated from equation (1) above would reflect only the impacts of scientific knowledge and the efficiency of factor use. It is possible to construct an index of efficiency units of labour for each country based on the assumption that wage differentials reflect underlying productivity differentials. A higher value of the index implies a higher level of knowledge embodied in workers, which raises the productivity of labour. The efficiency index uses indicators of relative wages for each of three skill groups to combine the numbers employed in each skill group to give a weighted average skill indicator. We assume that the wage of unskilled workers in the base year 1992 is 1.0 and the skill premium for the other two groups means that medium-skilled workers receive a weight in excess of 1 and skilled workers an even higher weight. These weights are based on the average wage of the higher skill groups relative to that of unskilled workers and are plotted in Figure 15.5. When the number of skilled workers increases then the stock of skills rises in the economy. We assume that a 1 per cent increase in skills raises effective labour input by 1 per cent.

The skills and wages data come from the EU KLEMS[8] database, which contains information on the skill mix of the members of the EU

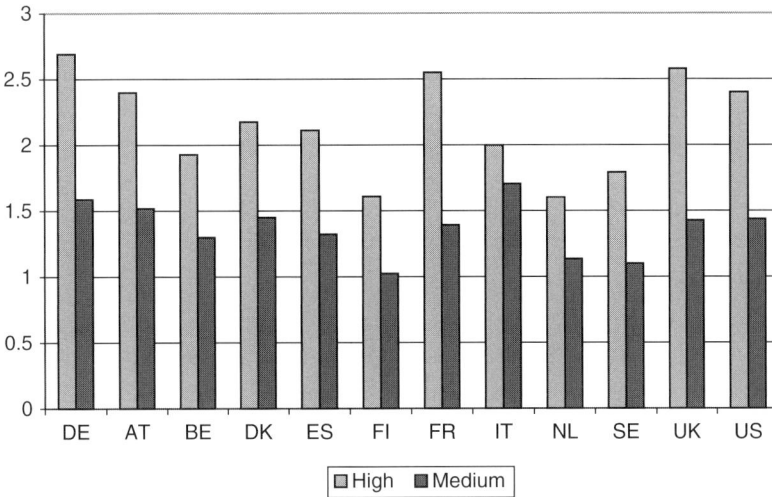

Figure 15.5: Relative wages by skill category (1992 unskilled =1)

and the USA, with proportions of the workforce in low-, medium- and high-skill occupations. There are also data on the relative compensation of these groups over time and therefore it is possible to produce a compound skill indicator if we assume that the skill level of the unskilled is constant and that relative wages reflect relative marginal products.[9] Table 15.4 reports average annual growth of a skills index with fixed weights based on 1992 for each of the countries where we have data. Care has to be taken in the interpretation of these data when making cross-country comparisons at a single point in time, as definitions of skill categories differ between countries, especially amongst the high-skilled groups. Educational systems also differ, with average graduates representing a larger and different group in the USA than in most European countries. However, these differences matter less when we make comparisons over time within a country as definitions and educa-tion systems change much less in this dimension.

The existence of the skills data constrains both the time frame and the country coverage of this study. The data are available from 1980 onwards for most countries, but EU KLEMS data start later for Sweden and the other excluded EU countries. We have extended the Swedish data back-wards using national sources. In other countries, such as Spain, the growth of skilled and semi-skilled occupations has been rapid because of the

Table 15.4: *The growth rate of skills*

Period	BE	DK	FI	FR	DE	IT	NL	AT	SE	ES	UK	US
85–89	0.4	0.5	0.4	0.7	0.4	0.2	0.4	0.5	0.3	0.8	0.7	0.3
90–94	0.8	0.6	0.7	0.8	0.3	0.2	0.3	0.5	0.3	0.8	1.0	0.3
95–99	0.5	0.4	0.2	0.6	0.0	0.2	0.3	0.5	0.2	0.7	0.8	0.3
00–04	0.4	0.3	0.2	0.4	0.2	0.1	0.2	0.3	0.6	0.7	0.6	0.4

Source: Own calculations using EU KLEMS data.

urbanisation and industrialisation catching-up process that the country has undergone, and the meaning of the unskilled group may change over time in such situations, so these data must be used with caution.

Whilst it is difficult to make cross-country comparisons because definitions of skills vary greatly across countries, the relatively slow accumulation of skills in Germany over the past two decades as compared to the UK and France may be one reason for relatively low productivity growth in the euro area's largest economy. Figure 15.6 shows the share of university graduates in total employment. It suggests that the proportion of employees with university education has grown faster in the UK and France compared to Germany over the past several decades. This difference may be one of the main sources of slower skills accumulation in Germany.

We can repeat our growth accounting exercise, taking into account the quality of labour. If we call the stock of skills S_t, we can calculate a skills-adjusted tfp indicator, denoted tfps, as:

$$\text{tfps} = \text{dln}Y_t - [b_t\text{dln}K_t + (1 - b_t)\text{dln}(E_tH_tS_t)] \tag{2}$$

For growth accounting purposes we can use the time period from 1991 for comparison. If we do that, we only lose Greece, Portugal and Ireland from our calculations. Greece is missing the basic price GDP data and skills information, while Portugal and Ireland have no data on skills and relative wages.

Figure 15.7 plots the skills-adjusted TFP growth for the Europeans where we have a sufficiently reliable dataset, and compares the period before the formation of EMU with that afterwards. After skills adjustment, TFP growth was similar in the UK, Germany and the USA over the period

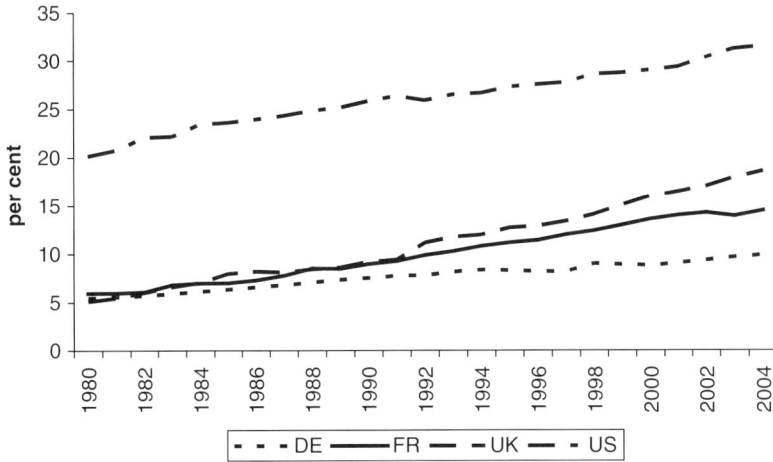

Figure 15.6: Per cent of university graduates in total employment

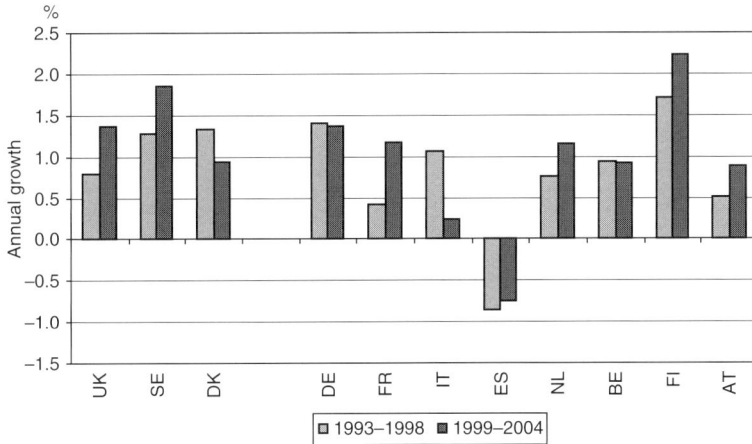

Figure 15.7: Skills-adjusted TFP growth

1999–2004. However, in the euro area as a whole, TFP growth on a skills-adjusted basis averaged less than 1 per cent per annum or about half a percentage point lower than in Germany, the UK and the USA.[10]

Figure 15.8 reports TFP growth before skills adjustment for the same period and countries. It is clear that TFP growth was particularly low in Spain and Italy, especially during the EMU period, but skills adjusted or not, TFP growth rates, especially in Spain, were also weak before the

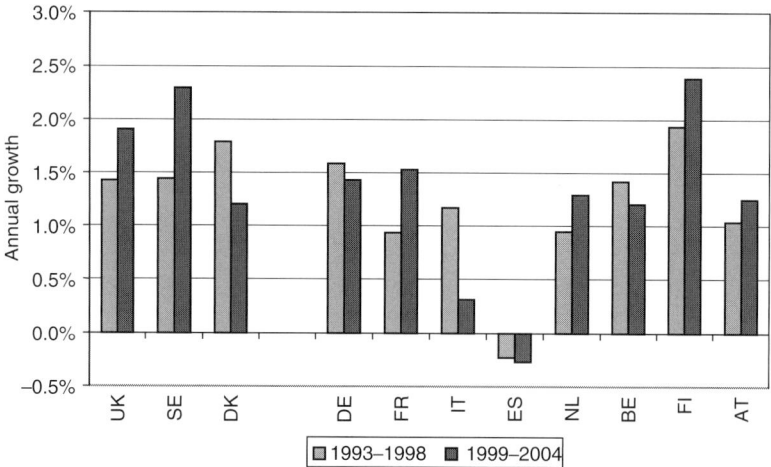

Figure 15.8: Unadjusted TFP growth

formation of EMU. TFP growth was positive and accelerated in the EMU period in France, the Netherlands, Finland and Austria, and only Italy experienced a marked slowdown of skills-adjusted TFP growth in the EMU period.

As with the previous analysis we also lose the USA because it lacks data for constant price output at basic prices, although we can approximate these data for the USA over the same period. These estimates suggest that TFP growth was around 1.7 per cent per annum between 1993 and 2004, and that skills contributed about 0.2 percentage points per annum of this, leaving underlying TFP growth (tfps above) at around 1.5 per cent a year on average over this period. These figures for TFP growth may appear to be lower than those commonly referred to for the USA as they reflect whole economy output and whole economy capital stocks as well as whole economy labour input. Most work on the USA, including that published by the Bureau of Economic Analysis, reports figures for TFP growth in the non-farm business sector and hence misses out the more slowly developing government and agricultural sectors.

We can also plot the contribution of skills to the growth rate of these countries, and we do so in Figure 15.9. The contribution of skills growth in the UK is noticeably greater than that in Germany or Italy, as we might expect from Table 15.4, but the contribution of skills

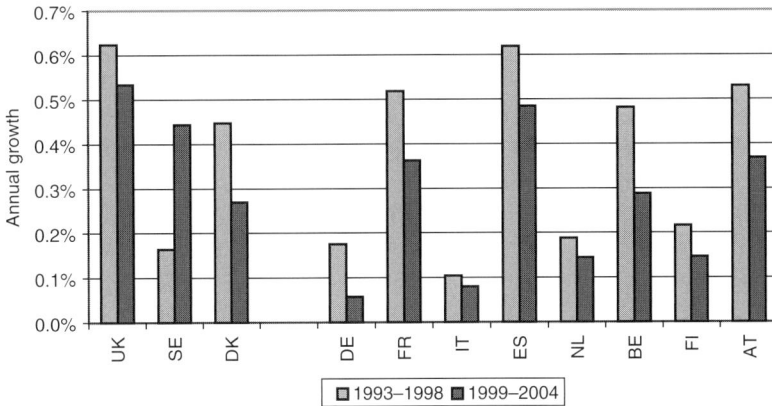

Figure 15.9: Skills component of TFP growth

growth was also quite noticeable in France, Spain, Belgium and Austria. It would not be surprising if it were also rapid in Ireland over this period. It would appear that most of the poor productivity performance of the German economy in the EMU period has been due to slow skills growth and, to a lesser extent, the same is true of France. A low contribution from skills has also been important in Italy, but there are also other factors holding back productivity growth there, as there are in Spain. Productivity growth after factoring out skills has been particularly strong in Sweden and Finland. It would appear that differences in skills growth have contributed about a quarter of a point to the euro-area growth deficit against the UK since 1999, and around a fifth of a percentage point in the period in the run-up to the formation of EMU. Skills growth rates were similar in aggregate to the USA.[11]

Our skills-adjusted TFP growth can result from either increases in the stock of knowledge or changes in the competitive environment that make factor use more efficient. All of the European countries were members of the EU, and hence all will have been influenced by the Single Market Programme, and the only major market efficiency-related initiative that separates them is the EMU process. Knowledge comes from many sources, and that part not embodied in the skills of the workforce depends on access to the knowledge base associated with scientific activity. In practice, the stock of knowledge in an economy is often proxied by the levels of research and development (R&D) activity

Table 15.5: *Stock of FDI as a per cent of GDP*

Period	BE	DK	FI	FR	DE	IE	IT	NL	AT	SE	ES	UK	US
1991	11.2	11.6	8.3	11.4	11.7	10.8	11.1	11.2	9.3	11.8	11.4	12.0	12.9
1996	11.6	11.8	8.9	12.0	11.7	10.8	11.0	11.6	9.7	12.4	11.5	12.1	13.3
2001	12.4	13.3	10.2	12.7	12.6	12.0	11.7	12.6	10.5	13.7	12.2	12.8	14.1
2006	13.0	13.5	10.8	13.2	12.8	11.8	12.2	12.6	10.9	14.2	12.5	13.3	14.4
1991– 2006	1.8	1.9	2.5	1.8	1.1	1.0	1.1	1.4	1.6	2.4	1.1	1.3	1.5

Source: UNCTAD and NIESR calculations. 1991–2006 is the average growth rate.

and access to technology from abroad through imports and foreign direct investment (FDI).

The role of FDI in the growth process has been emphasised by Barrell and Pain (1997) and others. Table 15.5 reports the stock of inward FDI as a share of GDP for many of the countries in this study in selected years. In 2006, the stock of inward FDI in France and the UK was marginally larger relative to GDP than in Germany, but this ratio has not risen very rapidly in any of these countries since 1991. The stock of FDI rose much more rapidly relative to GDP in Finland, Sweden and Denmark over this period, and this may help explain the strong TFP growth recorded in these countries. The growth of FDI stocks between 1991 and 2006, reported in the last row of the table, has a correlation of 0.68 with the growth of skills-adjusted TFP reported in Figure 15.7, and this suggests that there has been some impact from the development of the FDI stocks.

A number of endogenous growth models have been developed where R&D expenditures or the number of researchers drive the growth process, with Aghion and Howitt (1998) and Griffith *et al.* (2004) being amongst the most significant for our purposes. Not only does R&D increase the innovation rate in the technology frontier country, but it also raises the absorptive capacity of an economy to new ideas. Hence we use an estimate of the stock of R&D as an indicator of usable knowledge, based on the accumulation of flows of R&D onto a depreciating stock.[12]

Table 15.6 shows the average growth rates of the R&D stock for all the countries in this study. The stock of R&D grew most rapidly in Finland, Spain and Austria over this sample period. Over the last ten years, the stock of R&D in Germany has risen at about the same rate as

Table 15.6: *Stock of R&D – annual average growth rate*

Period	BE	DK	FI	FR	DE	IT	NL	AT	SE	ES	UK	US
90–94	4.6	5.0	6.9	3.7	3.8	4.0	2.5	6.2	4.9	9.3	1.5	2.8
95–99	4.5	5.6	7.6	2.6	2.9	2.3	2.7	6.1	5.2	6.1	1.3	3.0
00–05	4.0	5.8	7.7	2.4	3.0	2.6	2.1	6.3	5.2	6.8	1.6	3.2

Note: GERD (gross expenditure on R&D) stock, million national currencies, constant prices, 5% depreciation rate.

in the USA, after growing more rapidly in the previous ten-year period. The stock of R&D in France has risen somewhat more slowly than it has in Germany, while the growth of R&D has been particularly slow in the UK. There seems to be no strong pattern emerging from a simple investigation of the table, unlike with FDI, but more careful investigation, allowing for other factors should help us uncover any possible role for R&D in explaining differences in productivity growth.

Both R&D and FDI are potential variables that might explain differences in growth rates. However, a number of other factors have been affecting productivity growth in these countries. Increased openness is often regarded as a factor driving growth; all countries have become more open over time, at least as measured by the ratio of the volumes of exports and imports of goods and services to output. Openness increases in part because the nature of goods changes – they become lighter and more mobile – and import penetration rises. However, it is not clear that such changes increase competition and the efficiency of factor use. Openness can also increase because barriers to trade are removed, as with the European Single Market, the North American Free Trade Agreements and other measures that are designed to increase trade and competition. We include indicators of these agreements in our work.

3. EMU and productivity

Economists generally agree that we may describe output (Y_t) as being produced by capital and labour inputs being mediated by a production function that embeds the current state of technology and efficiency in factor use. Many things change the supply of factors and the efficiency with which they are used. Technology also changes over time. A constant returns to scale production function can be written as:

$$ln\,Y_t = b\ln(labour_t) + (1 - b)\ln(K_t) + Tech_t \tag{3}$$

where *labour$_t$* is person hours input in efficiency terms at time t, K_t is the capital stock (or rather input) at time t, and *Tech$_t$* is an indicator of the level of technical efficiency at time t. The labour input may be decomposed into units of labour, E_t, average hours per unit, H_t and the average skills of the workforce, S_t.

$$Labour_t = E_t H_t S_t \tag{4}$$

Employment and hours data are relatively easily available, but skills per unit of labour are more difficult to derive. It is important to separate out the impacts of skills and we have estimates available for our sample. In order to avoid using low quality capital stock data, and to focus on the role of volatility directly, we substitute out for the capital demand equation, which can be written as:

$$\ln(K_t) = a + \ln(Y_t) - c\ln(user_t + risk_t) \tag{5}$$

where *user$_t$* is the user cost of capital at t and *risk$_t$* is the risk premium at t. We calculate the user cost of capital according to a standard Hall-Jorgensen formula:

$$user_t = \frac{pdk_t}{py_t}\left[c + kdep_t - \Delta\ln\left(\frac{pdk_t}{py_t}\right)^e\right]/(1 - ctaxr_t) \tag{6}$$

where *pdk* is an investment deflator, *py* is the GDP deflator, *c* is the real cost of finance, *kdep* is the depreciation rate, *e* denotes expectations and *ctaxr* is the corporate tax rate. The real cost of finance, *c*, is the weighted average cost of capital, as defined by Brealey and Myers (2005). This weights together the cost of debt finance (r_D) and the cost of equity finance (r_E). The weights are given by the share of capital in the economy that is listed on the stock market. The cost of debt finance is adjusted by the corporate tax rate, reflecting the tax deductibility of borrowing and is calculated as the risk-free long-term real interest rate, plus a measure of corporate spreads. Corporate spreads are calculated as the absolute difference between average corporate bond yields and yields on ten-year government bonds.[13] The cost of equity finance is calculated as the return on equity, which is estimated using price-earnings ratios for a national stock index. While this measure embeds a risk premium into it, our framework allows us to test for the impact of additional risk factors that are not priced into corporate spreads or the return on equity, which do not fully capture expectations.

Substituting our capital equation into our output equation and collecting terms we get:

$$\ln Y_t = \gamma_1 + \ln(labour_t) - \gamma_2 \ln(user_t + risk_t) + \gamma_3 Tech_t \qquad (7)$$

where $\gamma_3 = 1/b$, $\gamma_2 = \gamma_3$ c (1-b) and γ_1 = a (1-b) γ_3. We are interested in explaining output per person hour after factoring out skills, which we assume have a unit elasticity with respect to labour productivity. This is consistent with the construction of the skills data, where relative wages and relative productivity of the skill groups are assumed to remain constant over time. We may rewrite the equation again by taking E_t H_t and S_t to the left-hand side as

$$\ln(Y_t/(EtH_tS_t)) = \gamma_1 - \gamma_2 \ln(user_t + risk_t) + \gamma_3 Tech_t \qquad (8)$$

Output per person hour, after adjusting for skills should in the long run be driven by the user cost of capital, the risk associated with investment and a remaining element we describe as technology, but which covers the general stock of knowledge, the ability to utilise this stock and the efficiency with which factors of production are organised in utilising this stock of knowledge. The factors that impact on the efficiency of factor use may include the openness of the economy, the competitive environment that is constructed through institutions such as laws, regulations and monetary structures, and also social institutions. It is possible that EMU would affect this relationship directly through the competitiveness channel, as it may increase transparency and reduce transactions costs even as compared to having a fixed exchange rate with major trading partners. If we are to find the effects of EMU on output growth, we must factor out all the other dimensions of knowledge and efficiency effects that have been at work in the last decade or so.

There are a number of indicators of knowledge and of the competitive environment that we can utilise. The most obvious are the stocks of research and development (R&D) and foreign direct investment (FDI), which we have discussed above, as these either reflect the creation of knowledge or are channels through which it is absorbed. Openness to trade and investment are also thought to have important effects on productivity growth through both knowledge transfers and their efficiency effects. The ability to trade enables a country to specialise in more efficient production processes, raising the aggregate growth rate temporarily. Endogenous growth models have also pointed to the possibility that contacts with the outside world may potentially raise the growth rate permanently (see, for instance, Coe and Helpman, 1995; and Proudman ands Redding, 1998). There is also evidence that increases in competition brought about by the intentional removal of barriers to trade and investment raise output, and there is a significant literature, discussed in Badinger (2007), on the impacts of the European Single Market Programme (SMP) on productivity. Membership of the EU may also have increased productivity by widening the span of competition. There has also been a significant amount of research on the effect of North American Free Trade Agreements (NAFTAs), much of which is summarised in the symposium edited by Lederman and Serven (2005).

We look at these factors in our countries, following Barrell, *et al.* (2007b) in the construction of our openness and globalisation indicators. The SMP is a variable that starts in the third quarter of 1986 at 0 and rises to 1.0 in 1992.[14] Not all countries were members of the EU at the time; we index the impact of integration using a dummy that increases over the three years until they become full members, and we denote this as EU. In a similar way, we also separately distinguish the impacts of the Canada-US Free Trade Agreement in the 1980s and the subsequent wider NAFTA agreement. In order to pick up other trade and competitiveness-related factors, we have also experimented with openness indicators and have included a measure based on exports plus imports of goods and services divided by GDP (OPEN) in our work. This is the variable that would change if EMU had an impact on trade, as the work surveyed by Baldwin (2006a) suggests it does, but we factor it out separately as well.

If we wish to investigate the impact of EMU after factoring out other influences on productivity, we must include countries which are not members. To that end we include members of the euro area along with the UK, Sweden, Denmark and the USA in order to compare effects between the two groups. Our country choice and timeframe depend on data, and we are in particular constrained by the availability of skills data over long periods; in the EU KLEMS database skills data stop at 2004. Our end date allows us to use simple volatility indicators for risk, based on the work of Blanchard and Simon (2001).

In our work below, we look for the effects of two possible sources of uncertainty for exchange rate volatility and output volatility. We look for a role for the conditional volatility of output, which can be taken as an imperfect indicator of expected volatility. The volatility of output is gauged by the root mean squared deviations (RMSD) of output around a centred 17-quarter moving-average trend. The centred average on which volatility is conditioned uses output data up until the first quarter of 2007 to produce a centred estimate of trend output for the last quarter of 2004, which is the end of our sample period. Barrell *et al.* (2008b) use GARCH techniques to condition the volatility of real exchange rates, which we would expect to influence the equilibrium capital stock. We also test for the effect of real exchange rate volatility in this section by construction of a conditional measure that is equivalent to our output volatility measure. We use a 13-period centred moving-average of real exchange rates as the conditional trend and create the RMSD series for this variable.[15] In both cases these are constructed regressors that give an indication of the variable of interest and as such they are generated regressors that need to be instrumented, as is stressed in Pagan (1984). As these are variables measured with error, which we expect to be closely correlated to the true variable of interest we use Durbin's (1954) method of dealing with errors in variables problems.

We need to find a cointegrating set of variables for each country and then use them to undertake dynamic panel analysis on our dependent variable, output per person hour adjusted for skills (SY). We search across a range of possible sets of driving factors after testing their order of integration, and we look for the smallest cointegrating set in each country, whilst making sure that the contents remain as similar as possible in order that we may undertake panel analysis. If a variable is included in a cointegrating set when it is not needed, that set is not irreducible in the terms of Davidson (1998) and hence we may gain spurious information about the determinants of long-run behaviour.

As increased competition may improve factor efficiency and raise output for given inputs, indicators of competition must be included in our cointegrating set. However, they are not stochastic regressors, but rather intercept shifts, and hence do not need to be included in the choice of cointegration test significance levels. Removal of trade barriers and increases in the scope of markets such as the SMP, EU entry and NAFTA are therefore included in the cointegrating sets. As a common currency may increase transparency and the effective scope of competition, we include an EMU dummy in these sets.

As we wish to look for direct effects from volatility, we separate out the effects of user and volatility ln(user+risk) by noting that ln(a+b) = ln (a*(1+b/a)) = ln(a) +ln(1+b/a). Our basic cointegrating regression is of the form:

$$
\begin{aligned}
\ln(SY_{it}) = {} & c_{i1}\ln(R\,\&\,D_{it}) + c_{i2}\ln(user_{it}) + c_{i3}\ln(1 + volY_{it}/user_{it})) \\
& + c_{i4}\ln(FDI_{it}) + d_{i1}ESM_{it} + d_{i2}EMU_{it} + d_{i3}EU_{it} \\
& + d_{i4}NAFTA_{it}
\end{aligned}
$$

$$(7)$$

but other variables will have been investigated, as we discuss below.

We check data for stationarity by testing for the presence of a unit root. Augmented Dickey-Fuller (ADF) tests are computed with an intercept and a lag length of four using quarterly data. Test results are reported in Table 15.7. Unit root tests indicate that at 5 per cent significance level the null hypothesis for the presence of a unit root cannot be rejected for three out of four variables reported. The stock of R&D has a clear trend over the sample period and was therefore checked for trend stationarity. It can be seen from the table that we cannot reject the hypothesis of trend stationarity in the R&D series. A hypothesis of unit root is rejected when ADF tests are applied to the first differences of logarithms of the remaining three variables. We conclude that the dependent variable, the user cost of capital and one plus volatility of output (from now on referred to as risk) over user cost of capital variables are I (1).

Not all variables are needed in the cointegrating set and in particular, we find that openness does not need to be included, despite the popular debate on the role of EMU in increasing trade. Hence we do not report its order of integration, but find that the logged first difference is I (0). Both stocks of R&D and FDI may drive the efficiency of factor use, but we report only on R&D as it is the preferred variable in all countries except the UK.

It is necessary to check the conditions under which there can be a cointegrating set of variables in the long run. We augment the long-run equation with dummies for trade such as Single Market, NAFTA and EMU and check for the presence of a long-run structure. The residuals from the estimated equations are tested for the existence of a unit root, using t-statistics of Augmented Dickey-Fuller tests by including an

Table 15.7: *Unit root test results*

	Log (dependent variable)		Log (user cost)		Log (R&D)		Log (1+(risk/user cost))	
	Level	Difference	Level	Difference	Level	Level (including trend)	Level	Difference
	Prob.	Prob.	Prob.	Prob.	Prob.	Prob.	Prob.	Prob.
AT	0.513	0.003	0.604	0.002	0.140	0.001	0.067	0.000
BE	0.494	0.000	0.553	0.000	0.000	–	0.465	0.007
DK	0.797	0.000	0.107	0.000	0.417	0.051	0.080	0.000
FI	0.815	0.000	0.788	0.000	0.094	0.002	0.355	0.000
FR	0.498	0.000	0.659	0.000	0.005	–	0.373	0.001
DE	0.577	0.001	0.284	0.006	0.001	–	0.225	0.003
IT	0.121	0.008	0.675	0.001	0.000	–	0.260	0.002
NL	0.423	0.000	0.425	0.000	0.022	–	0.021	–
SE	1.000	0.000	0.277	0.000	0.024	–	0.220	0.001
UK	0.883	0.000	0.095	0.009	0.552	0.001	0.239	0.003
US	0.997	0.000	0.594	0.001	0.334	0.030	0.095	0.011

Note: Data period 1980Q1 2004Q4.

intercept and four lags. The results of the cointegration test for the final set of long-run equations are presented in Table 15.8. All countries pass the cointegration test.

In our final cointegrating set, we have tested for the effects of openness (defined as a sum of exports and imports as a share of GDP) and stock of FDI separately for each country. Adding either openness or FDI raises the critical value for the test but does not raise the test value and, as a result, not all of the countries pass long-run cointegration tests at the 5 percent critical value if they are present. We did not find a systematic role for the openness or FDI in the long-run specification for our list of countries, with the exception of the UK, where FDI was necessary for the existence of the long-run relationship. If we include R&D in the UK equation, but do not include FDI, we do not find cointegration. If we remove R&D from the set including FDI we still find that it cointegrates, and hence the irreducible set for the UK includes FDI but excludes R&D. Openness was not required for cointegration, but the trade and

Table 15.8: *Cointegration of the long run*

t-statistics from the ADF tests for the long run equation

AT	BE	DK	FI	FR	DE	IT	NL	SE	UK	US
–4.27	–3.83	–3.98	–4.45	–4.86	–4.04	–4.61	–4.31	–3.93	–4.25	–6.20

Note: Data period 1980Q1 2004Q4. The appropriate critical values are –3.452, –3.743 and –4.298 at the 10%, 5% and 1% levels, respectively. The exception is the UK where critical values are –3.811, –4.100 and –4.649 at the 10%, 5% and 1% levels.

competition-related variables (ESM and NAFTA) were and they may have driven openness. We return to this issue later.

The level of output responds slowly to its determinants, and hence we specify the equation in equilibrium-correction form. This allows the effects of all the driving factors such as the SMP, EMU and volatility effects to come through gradually. The dynamic equation can be described by:

$$
\begin{aligned}
\mathrm{d}\ln(Y_{it}/(E_{it}H_{it}S_{it})) = {}& \alpha_i + \lambda_i[\ln(Y_{it-1}/(E_{it-1}H_{it-1}S_{it-1})) \\
& - \beta_{i1}\ln(R\&D_{it-1})] - \beta_{i2}\ln(user_{it-1}) \\
& - \beta_{i3}\ln(1 + (vol(Y_{it-1})/user_{it-1}) \\
& - \beta_{i4}\ln(FDI_{it-1}) - \beta_{i5}ESM_{t-1} - \beta_{i6}EMU_{t-1} \\
& - \beta_{i7}EU_{t-1} - .\beta_{i8}NAFTA_{t-1})] \\
& + \gamma_{i1}\mathrm{d}\ln(Y_{it-1}/(E_{it-1}H_{it-1}S_{it-1})) + \varepsilon_{it}
\end{aligned}
$$

$$(8)$$

A panel of eleven countries was constructed and estimated by three-stage least squares. This was used because the volatility of output is a generated regressor measured with an error and we need to instrument it in order to get consistent estimators.[16] We apply a pooled-mean-group (PMG) estimation method as in Pesaran and Smith (1995) to test for common long-run coefficients while allowing for country-specific dynamics. Table 15.9 reports the results from the tests on the coefficient commonality in our panel. We start by checking whether common coefficients for user cost of capital and the one plus ratio of risk over user cost of capital can be imposed across countries. Wald tests for commonalities for both variables cannot be rejected. Common single-market effects were found for Belgium, Denmark, France,

Table 15.9: *Wald test results on commonality*

	Probability
Common user cost	0.602
Common 1+(vol of output/user cost)	0.952
Common ESM	0.061
Common EMU	0.486

Germany, Italy and the Netherlands and we can impose common EMU effects as well in the same set of countries (except for Denmark).

The results from the final estimates are reported in Table 15.10 after common parameters are imposed and insignificant variables are sequentially eliminated. The robustness of deletions and exclusions is discussed below. We consolidate the parameters on the separate US-Canada and NAFTA free trade agreements. Both are significant and we report the net effect. The user cost of capital is significant and has a negative effect on productivity, whilst the impact of the ratio of risk over user cost on productivity is found to be of the same sign. An increase in either user cost of capital or the ratio of risk over user cost of capital reduces the level of productivity per person hour, as we would expect, since it will in the long run reduce the level of the capital stock available to each worker. The single-market effect is significant and positive in six out of ten European countries. Finland, Sweden and Austria were not members of the EU at the time of its implementation, and its insignificance is not surprising. Its absence in the UK may reflect the fact that we need to use FDI as an indicator for knowledge to ensure cointegration. If the SMP led to an increase in FDI to the UK, as Pain and Wakelin (1998) suggest it did, then that variable may well pick up the impact of the Single Market on the UK. The EU entry dummies did not have a significant impact on productivity and were removed from the estimation. The effects of R&D vary across countries, with the highest impact probably being seen in Germany and the lowest in Denmark.

The speed of reaction varies across countries and it is highest in the small open economies of Belgium, Denmark, Finland and the Netherlands. France, Italy and Germany within EMU, and the UK outside it, have slower reactions, with the half-life of adjustment probably coming after five years. The USA adjusts more rapidly than any of the other large economies, despite its size. The EMU effects are positive

Table 15.10: *Final equations*

	Error correction	Log (R&D)	Log (user cost)	Log(1 +risk/user cost)	ESM	EMU	Log (FDI)	Net trade
AT	−0.089	0.235	−0.056	−0.284	–	–	–	–
	(0.041)	(0.000)	(0.000)	(0.008)	–	–	–	–
BE	−0.241	0.190	−0.056	−0.284	0.060	0.021	–	–
	(0.000)	(0.000)	(0.000)	(0.008)	(0.000)	(0.001)	–	–
DK	−0.377	0.150	−0.056	−0.284	0.060	–	–	–
	(0.000)	(0.000)	(0.000)	(0.008)	(0.000)	–	–	–
FI	−0.149	0.294	−0.056	−0.284	–	–	–	–
	(0.009)	(0.000)	(0.000)	(0.008)	–	–	–	–
FR	−0.077	0.267	−0.056	−0.284	0.060	0.021	–	–
	(0.005)	(0.000)	(0.000)	(0.008)	(0.000)	(0.001)	–	–
DE	−0.102	0.459	−0.056	−0.284	0.060	0.021	–	–
	(0.000)	(0.000)	(0.000)	(0.008)	(0.000)	(0.001)	–	–
IT	−0.092	0.324	−0.056	−0.284	0.060	0.021	–	–
	(0.019)	(0.000)	(0.000)	(0.008)	(0.000)	(0.001)	–	–
NL	−0.161	0.301	−0.056	−0.284	0.060	0.021	–	–
	(0.004)	(0.000)	(0.000)	(0.008)	(0.000)	(0.001)	–	–
SE	−0.117	0.237	−0.056	−0.284	–	–	–	–
	(0.011)	(0.000)	(0.000)	(0.008)	–	–	–	–
UK	−0.069	–	−0.056	−0.284	–	–	0.138	–
	(0.029)		(0.000)	(0.008)			(0.000)	
US	−0.147	0.380	−0.056	−0.284	–	–		0.016
	(0.005)	(0.000)	(0.000)	(0.008)				(0.000)

Notes: Probabilities are in parentheses. Data period 1980Q1 to 2004Q4.

and significant in the five core countries, and they indicate that over the longer term output may be raised by 2 per cent or so by membership of EMU. We did not find any significant effect of EMU on other member countries or outsiders. To test the robustness of our conclusions we added back EMU variables into the equations of all countries in the final panel and checked for the significance of the coefficients. The results reported in Table 15.11 show that the effect of EMU is insignificant in all but five core countries. There are no clear negative effects of the existence of EMU on those countries that were outside EMU.

Our result that openness and stock of FDI (except for the UK in the case of the latter variable) are not in the cointegrating set as direct

Table 15.11: Robustness check for EMU effects – adding the dummy back in

Austria	Belgium	Denmark	Finland	France	Germany	Italy	Netherlands	Sweden	UK	US
-0.013	0.019	-0.007	-0.014	0.019	0.019	0.019	0.019	0.014	0.036	0.006
(0.612)	(0.004)	(0.598)	(0.305)	(0.004)	(0.004)	(0.004)	(0.004)	(0.513)	(0.406)	(0.749)

Note: Probabilities in parentheses.

Table 15.12: Openness effects – adding the variables back in

Austria	Belgium	Denmark	Finland	France	Germany	Italy	Netherlands	Sweden	UK	US
-0.216	0.032	-0.026	-0.195	0.302	-0.030	-0.760	-0.061	-0.216	0.442	-0.520
(0.357)	(0.607)	(0.820)	(0.073)	(0.009)	(0.715)	(0.211)	(0.475)	(0.557)	(0.061)	(0.464)

Note: Probabilities in parentheses.

Table 15.13: FDI effects – adding the variables back in

Austria	Belgium	Denmark	Finland	France	Germany	Italy	Netherlands	Sweden	UK	US
-0.052	0.027	-0.011	-0.019	0.064	-0.001	-0.021	-0.031	0.040	–	-0.010
(0.278)	(0.321)	(0.413)	(0.177)	(0.000)	(0.974)	(0.514)	(0.397)	(0.003)	–	(0.545)

Note: Probabilities in parentheses.

determinants of output needs to be tested for robustness, so we undertook further tests. Openness and stock of FDI separately are added back into the final panel specification as a part of the long run, and checked for significance. As demonstrated in Table 15.12 below, openness is insignificant in each country (apart from France) and as a panel variable. The FDI effect reported in Table 15.13 is found be insignificant in most countries as well – the exception being Sweden and again France. It seems that after adding EMU, single market and NAFTA dummies to our equations, there is no direct role left for either openness or FDI stock, except for France where the above effects may still be present.

In this chapter two different indicators of volatility are used, with the conditional volatility of output being included in the cointegrating set. We also use the conditional volatility of real exchange rates and test for the robustness of our results when this variable is added or substituted for the volatility of output. Table 15.14 reports tests where we firstly substitute output volatility in the risk premium term with real exchange rate volatility and second include real exchange rate volatility along with output volatility in the risk premium variable in our final panel set. As real effective exchange rate volatility is a generated regressor, a new instrumental variable is created and used in both cases. We estimate both panels by three-stage least squares. In the first case, where we substitute the volatility measure the new variable is not significant. In the second set, we add the new variable and it is also not significant. In addition the coefficients for the user cost and the output volatility measure are little changed. It appears that there is no role for real exchange rate volatility in our final panel specification.

Our results seem robust to these checks: we can conclude that EMU effects do appear to be present and that there is no statistically significant effect from real exchange rate volatility or from openness on its own in this panel of countries. Hence evidence on the role of monetary union in raising trade, however sound, may not mean that we can trace an effect through to productivity. This is not to say that openness does not matter, but rather that its effects reflect the impact of conscious attempts to increase competition and the efficiency of factor use. The SMP and NAFTA clearly raise the level of output and the level of trade, but the output effects come directly and not just through their impacts on trade. The only open question remains the role of FDI in the European economies. Although it is not needed in the cointegrating

Table 15.14: *Substituting and adding real exchange rate volatility effects*

	Log (user cost)	Log (1 +riskrealx/ user cost)		Log (user cost)	log (risk/ user cost)	Log (1 +riskrealx/ user cost)
Austria	−0.040	−0.015	Austria	−0.057	−0.425	0.0656
	(0.000)	(0.588)		(0.000)	(0.000)	(0.123)
Belgium	−0.040	−0.015	Belgium	−0.057	−0.425	0.066
	(0.000)	(0.588)		(0.000)	(0.000)	(0.123)
Denmark	−0.040	−0.015	Denmark	−0.057	−0.425	0.0656
	(0.000)	(0.588)		(0.000)	(0.000)	(0.123)
Finland	−0.040	−0.015	Finland	−0.057	−0.425	0.0656
	(0.000)	(0.588)		(0.000)	(0.000)	(0.123)
France	−0.040	−0.015	France	−0.057	−0.425	0.0656
	(0.000)	(0.588)		(0.000)	(0.000)	(0.123)
Germany	−0.040	−0.015	Germany	−0.057	−0.425	0.0656
	(0.000)	(0.588)		(0.000)	(0.000)	(0.123)
Italy	−0.040	−0.015	Italy	−0.057	−0.425	0.0656
	(0.000)	(0.588)		(0.000)	(0.000)	(0.123)
Netherlands	−0.040	−0.015	Netherlands	−0.057	−0.425	0.0656
	(0.000)	(0.588)		(0.000)	(0.000)	(0.123)
Sweden	−0.040	−0.015	Sweden	−0.057	−0.425	0.0656
	(0.000)	(0.588)		(0.000)	(0.000)	(0.123)
UK	−0.040	−0.015	UK	−0.057	−0.425	0.0656
	(0.000)	(0.588)		(0.000)	(0.000)	(0.123)
US	−0.040	−0.015	US	−0.057	−0.425	0.0656
	(0.000)	(0.588)		(0.000)	(0.000)	(0.123)

Note: Probabilities in parentheses.

set for France and Sweden, and hence should have no long-run role, it does show up with a positive coefficient in our robustness checks and hence may be having an impact in these countries.

4. Conclusions

To date there has been little evidence about the impact of monetary union in Europe on output and growth. This is in part because the time period between the formation of EMU and the current date is short. It is also because there has been a number of other factors affecting growth that have to be taken into account before evaluating the impact of EMU. Most studies consider either a single driver of growth, or at one of the proximate determinants of growth, and look for EMU impacts on that proximate driver. Trade effects have been the most widely discussed, but it is not clear that, even if EMU has increased trade between members, this will have a major impact on growth. We argue that only a study that takes into account other factors driving growth could uncover the potential effects of EMU on output, and we do that here.

Our analysis of the impact of EMU on output growth suggests that the introduction of the common currency has had a direct positive impact on growth in the core euro-area countries: France, Germany, Italy, Belgium and the Netherlands. Our estimates indicate that EMU will eventually directly raise the output level by around 2 per cent in these countries. This is smaller than the impact of the SMP in the late 1980s and early 1990s, and, like those effects, it will build up only slowly. These findings are robust to the inclusion of other variables that have been driving growth, such as R&D and FDI stocks, and after adjusting the labour force for differences in skills levels across countries. After accounting for EMU, the European Single Market and NAFTA, we found that openness, as measured by a share of total trade in output, had no significant direct role in explaining output or growth in our panel of countries. We were also able to show that the EMU effects were absent from countries such as the UK, the USA, Denmark and Sweden, that are not EMU members. It is not clear that they were present in small economies such as Finland and Austria, which may suggest that EMU has promoted agglomeration in the core of the Union.

The positive impact of EMU on long-term growth is in contrast to the widely discussed relatively slow growth in the euro area. Much of this slower growth is in underlying productivity per person hour, and it reflects the differences in the rate of accumulation of skills across the countries we study. Around a quarter of a percentage point of the difference in growth rates between the UK and the members of the euro area comes from the more rapid accumulation of skills in the UK, both in the run-up to EMU and in the subsequent period. Skills growth was particularly slow in Germany and in Italy, especially in the EMU period, and this alone accounts for half a percentage point difference in the growth rates between these countries and the UK.

Notes

1. We exclude the new member states that joined the EU after the formation of EMU.
2. We use the most commonly quoted measure of output growth, real GDP at market prices in order to compare growth across these countries and construct a consistent euro-area aggregate. This allows comparisons with other studies. Over five-year periods, this should grow at a similar rate to GDP at basic prices, which removes indirect taxes and subsidies.
3. If the labour force increase is anticipated well in advance, then capital can be put in place to match the labour force. This balanced growth path has been common in countries with high natural population growth rates or sustained and anticipated inflows of migrants. Both of these assumptions describe the USA from 1840 to 1920.
4. We do not include the USA in this comparison as it only produces basic price whole economy numbers in current prices. The OECD recalculates these numbers to produce volume figures, but with a delay and hence are not as up to date or at the same stage of revision as other countries. We use data on all other countries up until 2006, while data for the USA stopped in 2005.
5. We have assumed that the self-employed receive the same wage per hour as the employed.
6. Basic price data are not available for Greece and we do not present that country separately. In Figure 15.3 we have made an appropriate but approximate adjustment to the Greek market price data in order to calculate the aggregate for the euro area.
7. Strong growth in Ireland may in part reflect transfer pricing from elsewhere in Europe. In most countries GDP is a good indicator of production and incomes received by domestic residents. Incomes of residents can be scaled by GNI, and as a rule GDP and GNI move together. However, Ireland has been chosen by non-EU firms as a location for declaring profits to ensure that they are remitted at low tax rates. The ratio between GDP and GNI in Ireland was around 1.1 in 1986, and stayed at that level for a decade. When it became clear that Ireland would be in the monetary union, there was a sharp increase in profits-oriented transfer pricing through that country, and between 1996 and 1998 the ratio rose by six percentage points. The allocation of profits to Ireland on this scale will have raised measured output and productivity growth in a spurious way. Over this period, the equivalent ratios in the UK, the USA and Belgium fluctuated around or just below one despite their differing net foreign asset positions.
8. The EU KLEMS database was the result of a large-scale collaborative project between European researchers on productivity, financed by the

European Commission. It was published in March 2007 and is available at www.euklems.net.

9. A skills index can be constructed either by using a Tornquist discrete time version of a Divisia index or it can be constructed with fixed weights. We have experimented with both and marginally prefer the fixed weight index shown in table 15.4. The chain-weighted index introduces a cycle into the quality index that is related to the business cycle, as wage differentials become compressed or expand over the business cycle. If we could choose either similar points on the cycle or calculate cycle average relative wages then we could construct an approximate Tornquist index.

10. In order to calculate this figure we have used our factor price adjustment for Greece and we have assumed that skills in Ireland, Portugal and Greece grew at the same rate as in France, a country that performed well. Changes in these assumptions would only marginally change the results as these three countries represent a small share of euro-area output.

11. The same basic price adjustment and skills assumptions have been made about Greece, Portugal and Ireland, and hence the same caveats hold. Skills growth was probably higher in Ireland and lower in Greece and Portugal than in France and hence our number may be a lower bound.

12. We benchmark the stock in 1974, before the beginning of our data period, as the flow divided by the average growth rate and the depreciation rate, and we cumulate flows onto this stock with a depreciation rate of 5 per cent per annum in line with Coe and Helpman (1995). The data come from the OECD Science and Technology database.

13. These data are available for the euro area, the USA, the UK and Denmark. Sweden is assumed to follow the corporate spreads for Denmark. Prior to 1984, the UK spread is assumed to move in line with the USA; prior to 1994, the spread for Denmark is assumed to move in line with the US and UK average; and prior to 1999, euro-area spreads are assumed to move in line with a proxy measure for Germany.

14. For a detailed description of the Single Market Programme, see European Parliament (2008). The Single European Act (which was signed in February 1986 and came into force on 1 July 1987) was a revision of the Treaty of Rome. Its first objective was the incorporation of the specific concept of the internal market in the Treaty, defining it as 'an area without internal frontiers in which the free movement of goods, persons, services and capital is ensured', and setting a precise deadline for its completion: 31 December 1992. It also wanted to give the completed internal market effective decision-making machinery, by introducing qualified majority voting for most subjects concerned, instead of the

unanimity that had hitherto been required. By the deadline, most of the 1992 targets had been met. Over 90 per cent of the legislative projects listed in the 1985 White Paper had been adopted, largely by using the majority rule. These included full liberalisation of capital movements and total abolition of checks on goods at internal frontiers.

15. The centred window length was chosen in relation to the cyclical properties of the data.

16. We use rank order as an instrument as suggested by Durbin (1954).

Comment 11: Comment on Chapter 15

JÖRG DECRESSIN AND EMIL STAVREV

1. Overview

The topic of the chapter is the impact of EMU on growth and productivity. The authors observe that real GDP growth in the euro area has been weak relative to the United States and other advanced EU countries and attribute this to slumping labor (and total factor) productivity growth. From a broad literature review and an econometric analysis of the drivers of productivity, the authors conclude that EMU had little to do with this slump. On the contrary, they estimate that EMU will ultimately boost productivity and output by about 2 percent.

In many ways, the euro area's performance since EMU has been puzzling. Those who supported EMU believed that it would foster competition, productivity, and employment. Those who questioned the wisdom of a single currency for a group of heterogeneous countries pointed to an apparently dysfunctional labor market, notably low labor mobility, inefficient labor market institutions, and high structural unemployment. The "headline" data have proven both camps wrong. Our main point is that the chapter could usefully have tried to analyze the area's growth and employment performance through the lens of this puzzle.

2. The analytical framework and estimation results

The authors see three key channels through which EMU can affect growth, namely greater macroeconomic stability, increased competition, and more financial market integration. Improved macroeconomic policy frameworks and greater macroeconomic stability – for example, owing to the elimination of intra-area exchange rate variability – promote investment and output growth. The competition channel works through lowering mark-ups, which raises employment, capital stock, and thus output. Financial integration fosters a more efficient allocation of resources, while lowering risk premia, thereby increasing investment and potential growth. From the perspective of these three channels, EMU should have boosted productivity, employment, and total output growth.

The authors find that EMU has a positive effect on economic growth. Using a sample of eleven advanced economies from inside and outside Europe, they estimate an equation that relates labor productivity on the left-hand side to R&D, the user cost of capital, FDI, and various dummies on the right-hand side – specifically, dummies for the onset of EMU, the phasing-in of the Single Market Programme (SMP), EU membership, and NAFTA. While FDI and other openness indicators are insignificant, the SMP and EMU dummies are positive and significant. Based on the estimate of the EMU dummy, the authors conclude that EMU raises productivity and thus output by 2 percent.

The econometric setup is appealing in some ways but raises questions in others. A panel of eleven EMU, EU, and non-European countries is well suited to study the question at hand. However, the cross-sectional variation might be insufficient to reliably estimate some of the effects, for example, those related to SMP, EU, and NAFTA. Furthermore, the specification of the model (equation 8) raises some issues: to what extent could the findings be distorted by cyclical effects? Should differences in the level of productivity and therefore "convergence" effects be considered? What about unanticipated labor supply changes and their effects on productivity? What is the right starting point of EMU: 1999, which the authors chose, or 1992 when the countries pre-committed themselves to the single currency?

The authors identify a positive EMU effect but do not pin down its sources. The question is what lies behind the positive estimate for the EMU dummy, in other words, what explains the EMU dividend? One way to at least partially answer this question would have been to check whether openness and FDI as well as output and exchange rate volatility – the competition and macroeconomic stability channels, respectively – raise productivity once all the dummies (EMU, SMP, NAFTA) are excluded. If the regression results were to suggest that this was not the case, then this would raise further questions about the specification of the econometric model. If, however, the answer was positive, then the authors would need to check whether openness and FDI increased and output and exchange rate volatility fell with EMU.

3. The key puzzle

The results raise an important and difficult question to which the authors devote much space but do not provide a conclusive answer: why has real GDP growth in the euro area been much lower than in the US economy or in other European economies outside EMU? In fact, there is a widespread perception that EMU has delivered stability but not economic growth. Pisani-Ferry *et al.* (2008) conclude that: "The overall economic performance of the euro area economy since the launch of the new currency has been mixed, however. Inflation has been low, but economic growth has been disappointing." A very recent European Commission (2008a) report sums this up as follows: "While the euro is a clear success, so far it has fallen short of some initial expectations. Output and particularly productivity growth have been below those of other developed economies."

The authors, like others, trace the perceived underperformance to productivity, specifically a sharp slowdown in labor productivity. For Spain and Italy, which account for much of the slump, they argue that it may partly reflect unanticipated increases in labor supply. For Germany, and to a lesser extent France and Italy, they identify slow skills accumulation as an important cause. Concurrently, the United States benefited from an ICT-driven surge in productivity and the United Kingdom from a decline in equilibrium unemployment, helped by falling unionization and private sector deregulation. Overall, it is hard to get a clear reading on what lies behind the growth gaps between the euro area and the comparator countries.

1. However, real GDP growth data overstate the euro-area underperformance. The starting point of the growth comparison is somewhat misleading because it fails to consider the lower population growth in the euro area. In per capita terms, euro-area real GDP growth has not lagged US growth during EMU (Table C11.1). True, the United States performed remarkably better during 1993–9. However, the euro area was ahead during 1986–92, driven in large part by an economic boom that was related to the integration of the New Member States and was followed by adjustment, particularly in Germany. Moreover, the euro area has not experienced a widening of external imbalances, unlike the United States and United Kingdom.

Table C11.1: *Euro area, USA, Japan, and UK – key macroeconomic variables (seven-year average, in percent)*

		1992	1999	2007
Per capita GDP growth	Euro area	2.5	1.7	1.3
	US	1.7	2.6	1.3
	Japan	3.6	0.5	1.4
	UK	1.9	2.8	2.1
Real GDP growth	Euro area	2.9	2.0	1.8
	US	2.8	3.7	2.4
	Japan	4.0	0.8	1.5
	UK	2.2	3.1	2.6
Employment growth	Euro area	0.5	0.7	0.9
	US	1.8	1.8	1.4
	Japan	1.3	0.8	0.0
	UK	0.2	0.8	0.7
Employment-population ratio, end of period	Euro area	40.8	41.7	44.4
	US	45.3	47.4	47.8
	Japan	51.7	51.0	50.1
	UK	44.4	46.3	48.0
Current account, end of period	Euro area	-1.1	0.5	-0.2
	US	-0.8	-3.2	-5.3
	Japan	3.0	2.6	4.9
	UK	-2.1	-2.4	-4.9
Inflation	Euro area	3.4	2.1	2.2
	US	3.9	2.5	2.7
	Japan	1.7	0.6	-0.3
	UK	5.6	2.6	2.8

Sources: IFS, WEO, and IMF staff calculations.

If there is reason for disappointment, it is that over the past three decades the euro area has not grown faster than the United States, considering that its per capita income level is noticeably lower, somewhere around 70 percent of the US level. But this is really about long-term trends, which EMU can hardly be expected to change within a decade.

Since a falling utilization of labor has much to do with the euro area's failure to catch up with US per capita income levels, recent trends give grounds for cautious optimism (Figure C11.1). Indeed, a remarkable feature of the euro area has been its strong employment performance

%

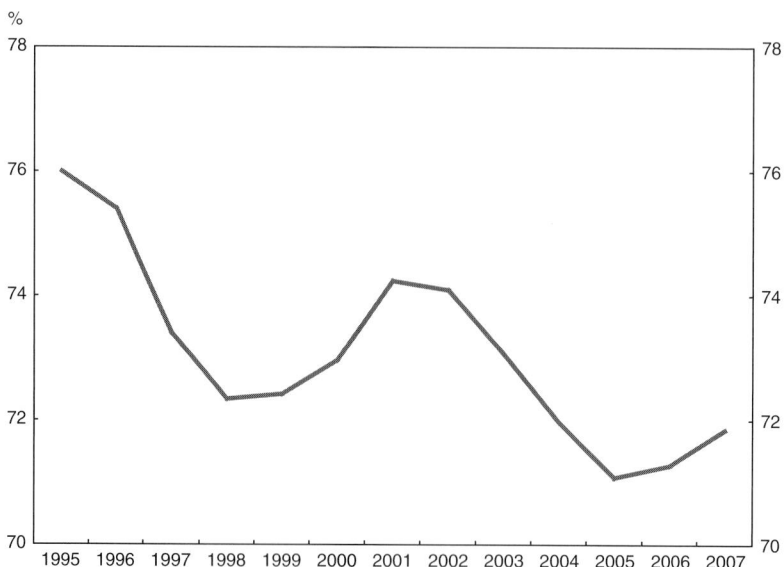

Figure C11.1: Euro-area PPP GDP per capita relative to the United States (in percent)
Sources: OECD and IMF staff calculations.

over the past decade. Specifically, the euro area's employment to (total) population ratio improved by 2.7 percentage points during 2000–7, appreciably outperforming the United States and the United Kingdom in terms of changes and coming closer to them in terms of levels (Table C11.1).

The euro area's strong employment performance may well be related to EMU. It can, for example, be seen as a series of shifts of a Phillips curve (Figure C11.2). Alternatively, a simple Blanchflower-Oswald (1994) type wage-setting equation can be defined and its shifts traced out. This equation essentially relates the real wage (adjusted for TFP growth scaled by the labor share) to the unemployment rate, consistent, for example, with efficiency wage models (Figure C11.3).[1] A downward shift thus indicates that, in equilibrium, a lower unemployment rate is compatible with a given real wage. Overall, this (admittedly superficial) analysis hints at an increase in labor supply that gathered pace during the early 1990s and was sustained after 1999.[2] In this context, EMU was widely perceived as a regime shift, setting off adjustment well ahead of the introduction of the single currency in 1999. For example, potential EMU membership is likely to have featured when the *scala mobile*

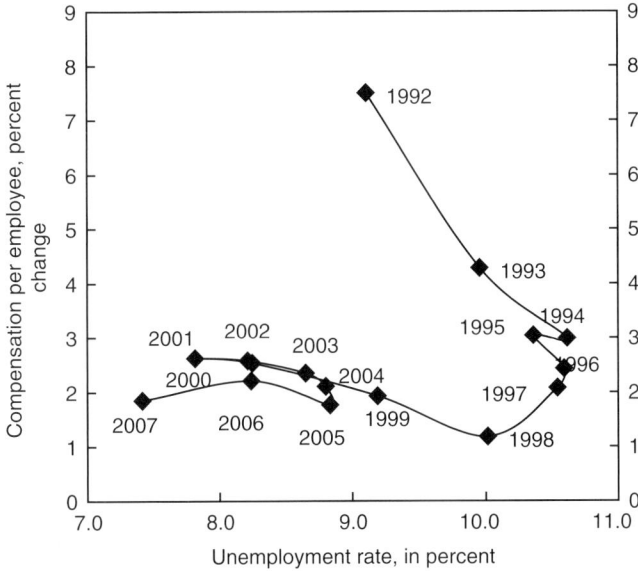

Figure C11.2: Compensation per employee and unemployment
Sources: OECD, ECB, and IMF staff calculations.

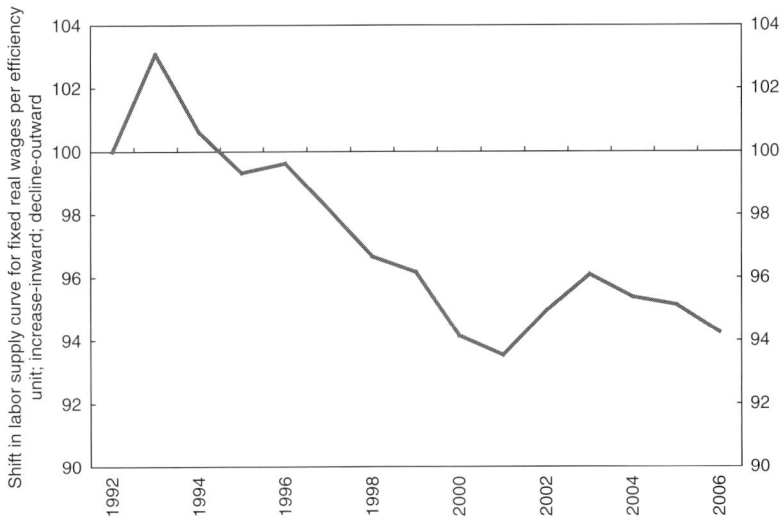

Figure C11.3: Accumulating wage-setting shocks in the euro area[1] (1992 = 100)
[1] For the methodology, see Decressin *et al.* (2001).
Source: EC-AMECO database.

was abolished in Italy in 1993. Today, wage setting in Belgium explicitly orients itself on wages set elsewhere in the euro area. There have been reforms on many fronts in many euro-area countries over the past decade.

Even if, as some argue, the pace of labor market reforms has slowed after EMU, the effect of the introduction of the single currency has likely had important reverberations within labor markets both before and after 1999. Be that as it may, the strong employment performance and its potential relation with EMU would have deserved more analysis.

This leaves another question to be tackled: how can a poor productivity performance be consistent with a remarkable turnaround in the employment performance? One obvious reason is capital-labor substitution in response to reforms that raised labor supply and, possibly, demand (via cuts in payroll taxes). The authors allude to this, but there are also other explanations.[3] For example, the marginal workers might be less productive, because they have lower skills, less work experience, or generally lower ability. This effect could have been amplified by a significant inflow of immigrant workers since the late 1990s. Also, in many countries illegal immigrants were regularized during 2000–7, which may have artificially lowered productivity, notwithstanding efforts to account properly for this by statistical agencies (Codogno, 2008). Another (and related) explanation could be an accelerating structural shift from industry to services. Moreover, as Beaudry and Collard (2002) show, a tradeoff between productivity and employment growth may occur temporarily when countries undergo a major endogenous technological change.

Some of these concerns could be addressed by shifting the focus from labor productivity to TFP. The authors discuss TFP and, like others, find that the euro area has disappointed on this measure too. Neoclassical growth theory postulates that, in principle, labor input should not affect TFP, provided this variable is adequately measured.[4] However, there are significant measurement problems. In particular, the constructed education/skills proxies do not capture fully the differences in ability between insiders and newcomers. The assumption that wage differentials reflect underlying productivity differentials is violated in the presence of labor market imperfections. Also, it is unlikely that the skill level of the unskilled remains constant over time, while as a result of the different degrees of unionization across sectors, relative

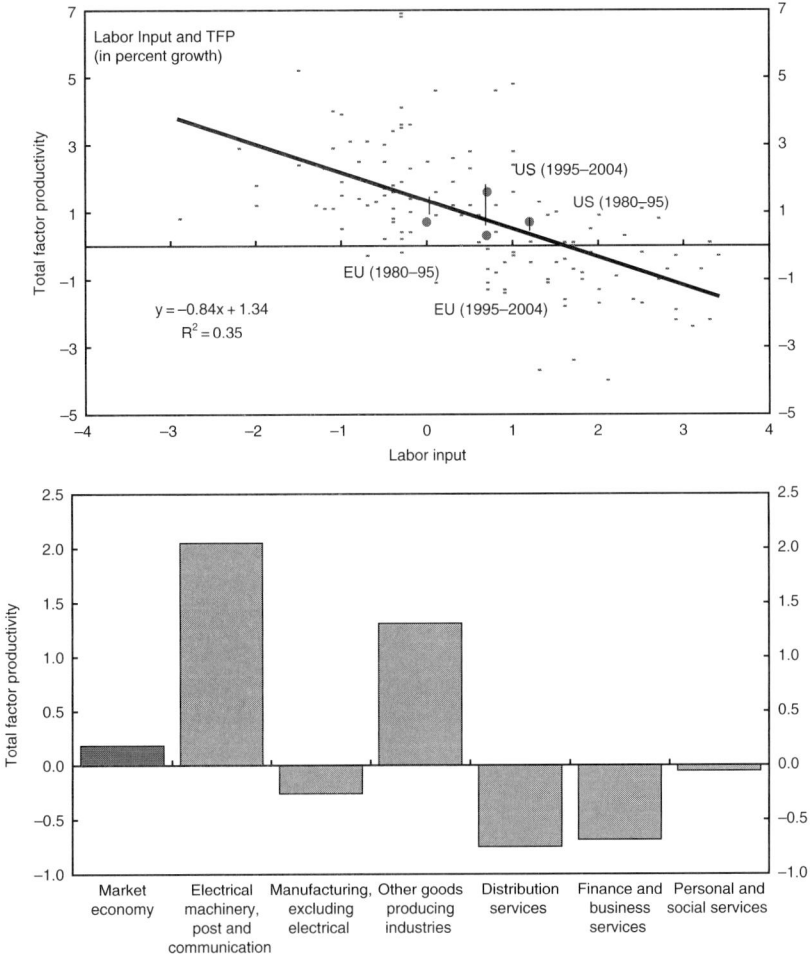

Figure C11.4: Euro area: TFP adjusted for labor input[1] (1995–2004 versus 1980–95; in percentage points)
[1]Negative numbers in the lower panel indicate a deterioration of adjusted TFP performance.
Sources: EU KLEMS database and IMF staff estimates.

wages will be a skewed measure of the relative marginal products.[5] Finally, it is impossible to measure ability and the abilities of marginal workers may be below average. These measurement problems are likely to be worse in times of policy and institutional changes that affect labor input.

Our crude estimates, using the sectoral EU KLEMS database, suggest that there has been a tradeoff between employment and measured TFP. This has been the case during both 1980–95 and 1995–2004, although the significance of the relationship declined in the latter period. We use panel data for six sectors for the EU15 countries excluding Greece, Ireland, and Luxembourg over two subperiods – 1980–95 and 1995–2004 – to estimate the relation between labor input and TFP. Specifically, we regress TFP (y) growth on the labor contribution (x) and find that during 1980–95: $y = -0.83x + 1.29$ (adjusted R2 = 0.43), while during 1995–2004: $y = -0.85x + 1.55$ (adjusted R2 = 0.20).

The results suggest that for a given labor input TFP growth may have accelerated slightly over the past decade relative to the previous one. Specifically, we use the regression results to estimate TFP growth during 1995–2004, controlling for the effect of labor input. Our results suggest that TFP growth would have been modestly higher in 1995–2004 than during 1980–95 (Figure C11.4), if labor input in the former period had been the same as in the latter. As discussed above, because of the low labor input during the 1980s, Europe's measured TFP growth may well have been held up by the fact that only the most productive/able actually worked. This changed since the mid-1990s, as many others were brought into the labor market, and measured TFP growth fell. However, adjusting for the fall in people's inherent "skill/productivity" – assuming that this is correctly measured by the simple regression – the fundamental productivity performance did not worsen but improved modestly. The "headline" data overstate true productivity during 1980–95 and understate it thereafter. Nonetheless, on average, a gap relative to the United States remains.[6]

Overall, the euro area experienced a large increase in employment over the past decade and may well not have experienced a fundamental deterioration in productivity. This is consistent with the authors' finding that EMU should not be blamed for the slowdown in euro-area productivity.

Notes

1. For further details, see Decressin *et al.* (2001).
2. Notice that the shifts in the curves could also reflect improved labor demand.

3. See, among others, Gordon and Dew-Becker (2005), Pichelmann and Röger, (2007), Codogno (2008), and Dew-Becker and Gordon (2008).

4. Note that some theoretical studies using models of equilibrium employment, as in Aghion and Howitt (1994) and Mortensen and Pissarides (1998), find an ambiguous impact of TFP on employment, with the impact being negative when new technology is embodied in new jobs but positive when it is disembodied. Phelps (1994), however, in line with the neoclassical results, argues that the effects are unambiguous but temporary.

5. More generally, there are other measurement errors as a result of which the residually measured TFP does not capture technological change. For example, technological change that results from R&D would not be captured in the TFP, as it is included in labor and capital inputs.

6. Gordon and Dew-Becker (2005) conjectured that the effects of policies and institutions on employment have overstated TFP growth before 1995 and understated it thereafter.

16 | *The impact of the euro on international stability and volatility*

STEFAN GERLACH AND
MATHIAS HOFFMANN

1. Introduction

The establishment of the euro in 1999 was seen by many as perhaps the greatest monetary experiment of all time. While of course currency unification had occurred in the past (as had currency separations),[1] monetary and financial systems have come to play a much greater role in the smooth functioning of the economy, making the introduction of a new currency in an economy as large and as sophisticated as that of the euro area a truly major undertaking.

With a decade having passed, it is an opportune time to assess what the implication of the euro for economic welfare might have been. In this chapter, we investigate the impact of the euro on macroeconomic volatility, broadly defined. The key question we study is straightforward: has the establishment of the euro reduced volatility of macroeconomic aggregates? In addressing this issue, it is essential to note that the *absolute* level of volatility may have changed for reasons unrelated to EMU. Thus, our focus is on investigating whether EMU members have experienced a decline in volatility *relative* to each other and to other countries, in a way we discuss further below.

To preview the results, we find that macroeconomic stability has increased since the inception of EMU. The effect on nominal stability – the volatility of short and long interest rates and of inflation – has been particularly large, but there has also been an increase in the stability of real variables. Much of this decline in volatility has occurred between

We thank Richard Portes for suggesting the topic of this chapter and our discussant, as well as Moreno Bertoldi, Björn Doehring, André Sapir, Heliodoro Temprano and participants at the Commission EMU@10 workshop for their comments and suggestions. Lobsang Tshering provided excellent research assistance. Any errors are our own.

EMU members but also, though to a somewhat lesser extent, between EMU members and non-members. Though our results do not directly allow us to conclude that outsiders' macroeconomies have become more stable as an immediate consequence of EMU, they do – at the least – suggest that there is an important international dimension to the creation of the euro in the sense that the euro area has become a pole of stability in the global economy.

The most important real effect of the euro that we identify is that consumption has become much smoother, a result that we find deserves special emphasis, for two reasons. First, consumption and its volatility directly impact on welfare since – unlike output or income – consumption enters households' utility functions.

Secondly, while consumption volatility could have decreased for a number of reasons, notably better and more synchronised macroeconomic policies – in particular monetary policy – the very pattern of the decline in volatility is informative by itself. The fact that – among real variables – we see increased smoothness mainly in consumption and less so in output or equity returns suggests that the decline in consumption volatility may to a large extent be due to better risk sharing, plausibly brought about through a widening and deepening of financial markets following the inception of EMU. Indeed, we argue that the creation of EMU has been pivotal for the rise in international risk sharing, which has been documented by an emerging literature (e.g. Sørensen *et al.* (2007); Artis and Hoffmann (2007, 2008a, 2008b)). EMU is associated with more risk sharing not only among its members but also between EMU countries and non-members, whereas risk sharing among non-member countries does not seem to have increased very much.

The rest of the chapter is structured as follows. We set the scene by documenting a global decline in macroeconomic volatility in the next section. Since this global decline could have a multitude of causes that are unrelated to the inception of the euro, we focus the discussion on what we call relative volatility – or, specifically, the volatility of relative variables – in Section 3. Section 4 lays out our framework for identifying the internal and international dimension of the impact of EMU on volatility, showing that patterns in relative volatility are indeed closely related to the inception of EMU. Section 5 then focuses on the decline in consumption volatility, singling out improved risk sharing as its main source. Section 6 summarises and concludes.

2. Trends in global volatility

As a first step, we develop some stylised facts with respect to what we call *real* and *nominal* volatility. Real variability is captured by the standard deviations of real GDP growth, real consumption growth and stock market returns as a proxy for the real return to capital. We measure nominal volatility through the standard deviations of changes in short and long interest rates and inflation. All data are quarterly, obtained from the IMF's international financial statistics. There are twenty-five countries in our sample: Australia, Austria, Belgium, Canada, Denmark, Finland, France, Germany, Greece, Iceland, Ireland, Italy, Japan, Korea, Luxembourg, the Netherlands, New Zealand, Norway, Portugal, Singapore, Spain, Sweden, Switzerland, the United Kingdom and the United States.

The reason we limit our sample to industrialised economies is that many emerging market economies have experienced bouts of volatility over our sample period (e.g. the Asian and Russian crises of the late 1990s), for reasons that are unrelated to the creation of the euro. Including such economies in our analysis of the impact of EMU on global volatility might distort our results.

It is well known that volatility declined across the world starting in the mid-1980s, a phenomenon referred to as the Great Moderation (McConnell and Pérez-Quirós (2000), Kose *et al.* (2003), Bordo and Helbling (2004), Stock and Watson (2005)). To avoid having our results unduly affected by this event, we use data starting in 1990 and ending in 2006/7. We break this sample in two subperiods – the ten years before the inception of the euro in January 1999 and the years since then. Our sample ends in the fourth quarter of 2006.

Figure 16.1 provides Artis-Stockman-type cross-plots of these standard deviations for the variables discussed above, for the two subperiods. The top row is for a set of real variables (GDP and consumption growth, stock market returns); the lower row of panels focuses on nominal variables (short and long interest rates and inflation). Points below the 45-degree line indicate that volatility was higher before the establishment of EMU. The figure shows that there is some evidence that the volatility of real GDP growth has generally declined. The volatility of real consumption growth has fallen markedly for all but one of the countries considered. Stock market volatility does not appear to have systematically changed.

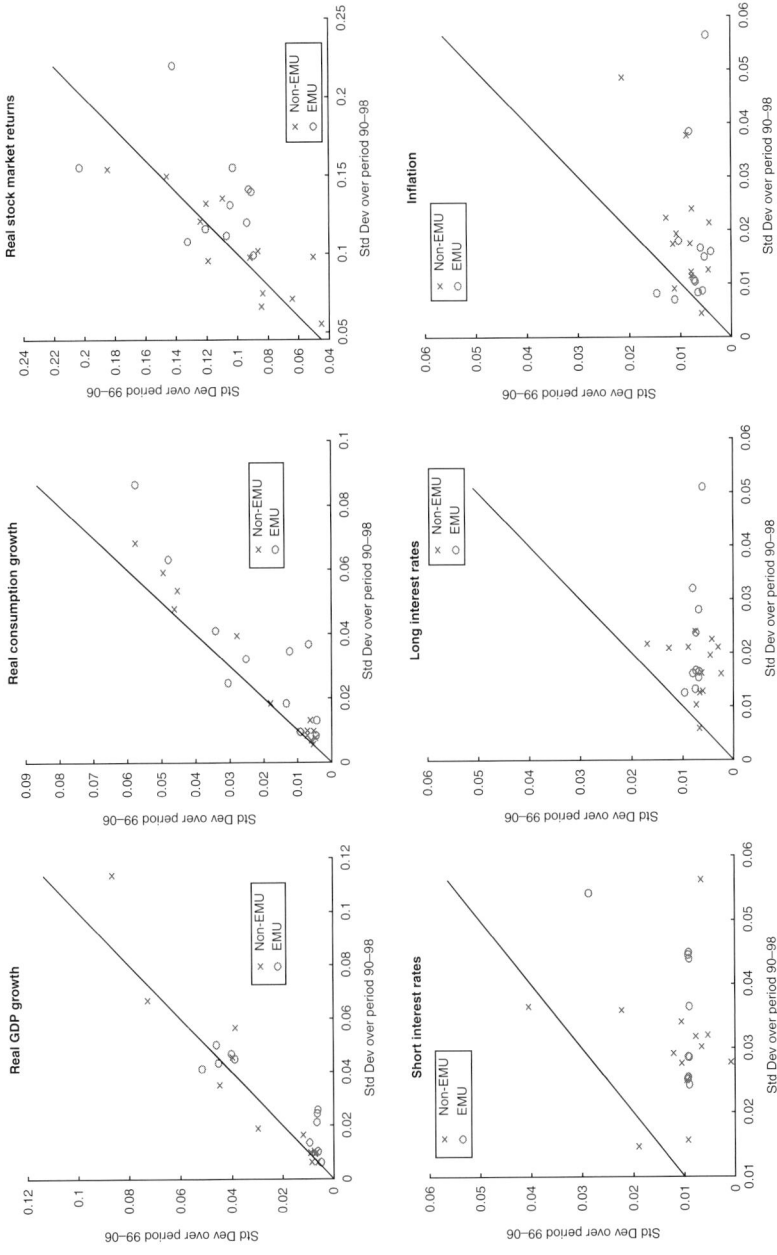

Figure 16.1: Cross-plots of volatilities in the pre-EMU (1990–8) and EMU (1999–2006) periods
Note: For country i these are the standard deviations of x^i where x stands for the growth rate of output, consumption and the stock market index for the real variables and the changes in interest rates and inflation for the nominal variables. Points below the line (45 degrees) indicate lower volatility in the EMU period than before.

Turning to the nominal variables, we see that volatility has declined in almost all countries, reflecting the increased focus by central banks on achieving and maintaining low and stable inflation.

3. Global vs. country-specific volatility

The decline in volatility that is apparent from Figure 16.1 seems to affect EMU and non-EMU countries alike. This suggests that there must be a common, possibly global, factor playing a role. Such a common factor may be unrelated to EMU and may be due to a decline in the volatility of global shocks, lower volatility in financial markets due to financial innovation or increased liquidity, etc. In what follows, we therefore condition on any factor that may have affected all countries by focussing on the volatilities of bilateral differences between consumption and output growth, levels of interest rates, etc. For brevity but with some abuse of language, we refer to the volatility of relative variables as *relative* or as *country-pair-specific* volatility throughout the chapter. This focus on relative volatilities does not preclude us from identifying the international effects of EMU, as we discuss below. Our setup only assumes that the effect of EMU is greater on some industrialised countries than it is on others – a presumption that we deem uncontroversial since only a subset of all industrialised countries in our sample are EMU members.

In fact, looking at relative volatilities directly allows us to study a particularly interesting aspect of the variation in the data. To understand this, note that our dataset comprises n countries and therefore $n(n-1)/2$ independent country pairs. By comparing the results for pairs of EMU members, pairs with one EMU member and pairs with no EMU members, we can get at the important issue of the relative impact of EMU on members and non-members.

Figure 16.2 provides cross-plots of idiosyncratic volatility measures for the two subperiods. Again, the top row is for a set of real variables and the lower row of panels focuses on nominal variables. The figure also allows us to distinguish whether a particular country pair involves one EMU country (dots), two EMU countries (circles) or none at all (x's).

For the nominal variables, there is a generalised decline in idiosyncratic volatility, as is evidenced by the fact that most of the points fall below the 45-degree line. While this effect is apparent for intra-EMU

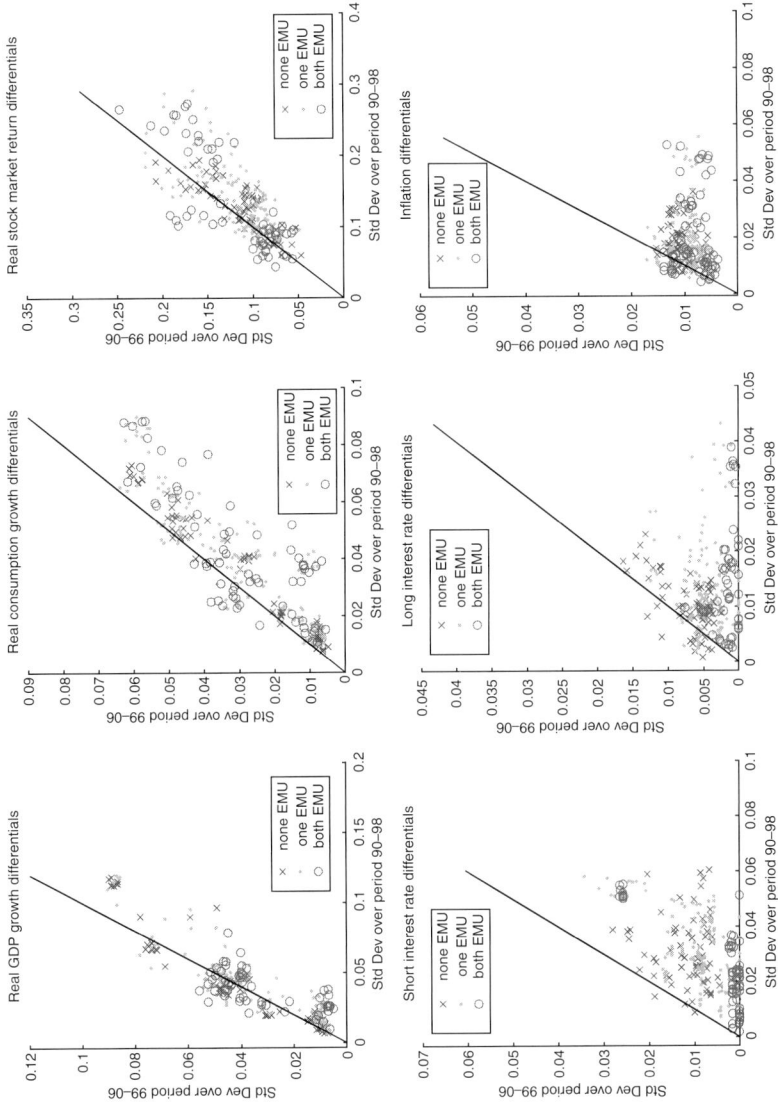

Figure 16.2: Cross-plots of country-pair specific volatilities in the pre-EMU (1990–8) and EMU (1999–2006) periods

Note: For country pair i, j these are the standard deviations of $x^i - x^j$ where x stands for the growth rate of output, consumption and the stock market index for the real variables and the changes in interest rates and inflation for the nominal variables. Points below the line (45 degrees) indicate lower volatility in the EMU period than before.

country pairings, it also seems to be important for pairs that involve only one EMU country.

From Figure 16.2, a general decline in idiosyncratic volatility is less readily apparent for real variables. In particular, the period since the creation of EMU does not appear to be characterised by systematically less volatile GDP growth or stock market return differentials. This is in contrast to the findings for absolute volatility in the previous section and suggests that the continued great moderation in stock markets and in real GDP growth is indeed largely due to a moderation in the volatility of global factors and not so much to a diminishing role of country-specific influences. This finding is in line with those reported in Panetta *et al.* (2006) and Gerlach *et al.* (2006).

Among the real variables, a general decline in relative volatility is clearest for consumption. This is noteworthy because theory holds that consumption enters directly into the utility function of agents and consumption volatility therefore has an important impact on economic welfare. By contrast, theory has less to say about the importance of a decline in the volatility of output or income.

Furthermore, economic theory predicts that financial integration directly affects idiosyncratic volatility of consumption through better risk sharing. The effect of financial globalisation on consumption risk sharing has generally been quite hard to capture empirically (see the survey in Kose *et al.* (2007)). However, recent literature has made some progress along these lines (Artis and Hoffmann (2007, 2008a, 2008b) and Sørensen *et al.* (2007)), showing that consumption risk sharing has indeed increased with the internationalisation of the external invest-ment position of most industrialised economies. Our results are compa-tible with these findings.

Finally, the theoretical case for a decline in the relative volatility of consumption is much more clear-cut than it is for output or stock market volatility. Other things being equal, one would expect financial integration to lead to lower relative volatility of consumption. Conversely, while economic integration might also increase the symme-try of output fluctuations, the theoretical case for economic integration to increase the importance of idiosyncratic influences on output growth can equally well be made. For instance, economic integration may allow regions and countries to exploit patterns of comparative advantage. To the extent that supply shocks are sector specific, this could actually lead to increased asymmetry. This point was prominently suggested by

Krugman (1993b) and the results in Kalemli-Ozcan *et al.* (2001) provide strong support for its empirical relevance. In the same mould, Heathcote and Perri (2004) suggest that output growth in the USA has actually become less synchronised with the rest of the world as financial integration has advanced.

For all these reasons, the decline in the volatility of consumption is significant and we explore its implications further below.

4. Internal and international effects of EMU on volatility

4.1 *EMU and volatility levels*

What is the role of EMU in determining volatility? We investigate this question in Tables 16.1 and 16.2. For the two subperiods, these tables provide regressions of relative volatility on a dummy that takes the value of unity if a country in the pair is an EMU member (the 'international' dummy) and a dummy that takes the value of unity if both countries are EMU members (the 'EMU' dummy). To see how these regressions may shed light on the issues at hand, suppose that EMU has reduced the importance of country-specific shocks. If so, one would expect the volatility of EMU pairs to have fallen quite a bit relative to pairs not involving EMU members. Similarly, the elimination of idiosyncratic policies within EMU could have lowered the volatility of pairs involving only one EMU country, though we would expect this to have declined somewhat less. While it is beyond the scope of this chapter to offer a full taxonomy of the structural causes of the decline in volatility, we provide a further interpretation of our findings related to these two dummies below.

Since other factors, in particular globalisation, could have affected the observed patterns of macroeconomic volatility, in our regressions, we also use a range of control variables that capture trade and financial openness, financial deepening as well as the exposure of countries to terms-of-trade shocks.

Specifically, we use the sum of exports and imports divided by GDP to measure trade openness. Financial openness is gauged by the sum of foreign assets and liabilities relative to GDP and by an indicator for capital account restrictions. We use the ratio of M2 to GDP to proxy for financial deepening and the volatility of the terms of trade to control for the size of external shocks. To capture the exposure of an economy

Table 16.1: *Pre-EMU volatility and the international and internal dimensions*

	GDP	Consumption	SMI	Inflation	Long interest	Short interest
International dummy	**-0.019**	0.009	-0.005	**-0.010**	-0.004	**-0.024**
	(-3.3)	(1.6)	(-0.3)	(-3.9)	(-1.8)	(-7.4)
EMU dummy	**-0.039**	0.014	-0.017	**-0.022**	**-0.010**	**-0.053**
	(-3.8)	(1.4)	(-0.55)	(-4.4)	(-2.3)	(-8.9)
Trade concentration	0.017	0.032	-0.014	**-0.026**	-0.008	0.009
	(0.7)	(1.3)	(-0.2)	(-2.1)	(-0.8)	(0.6)
Trade diversification	-0.009	**0.090**	-0.055	0.017	**0.019**	-0.022
	(-0.04)	(3.9)	(-0.8)	(1.5)	(2)	(-1.6)
Trade openness	**0.045**	**0.048**	**-0.160**	0.008	**-0.032**	0.002
	(4.5)	(4.9)	(-5.2)	(1.6)	(-7.9)	(0.3)
Financial openness	**-0.007**	**-0.015**	**0.015**	-0.000	**0.004**	0.001
	(-3.1)	(-6.8)	(2.3)	(-0.0)	(3.8)	(0.6)
Capital account restr.	**0.047**	**0.027**	**-0.078**	**0.027**	-0.007	**0.029**
	(4.8)	(2.8)	(-2.6)	(5.5)	(-1.9)	(5.0)
Relative income	**0.001**	**0.002**	-0.001	**-0.000**	**-0.001**	**-0.001**
	(2)	(6.9)	(-0.5)	(-2.9)	(-7.4)	(-5.2)
M2/GDP	0.006	**-0.008**	**0.037**	**0.003**	**0.009**	**0.006**
	(1.7)	(-2.4)	(3.8)	(2)	(6.5)	(2.9)
ToT volatility	**-0.560**	**-0.820**	**1.000**	**-0.230**	-0.049	**-0.310**
	(-4.2)	(-6.4)	(2.6)	(-3.6)	(-0.9)	(-4)
Constant	-0.024	**-0.091**	**0.200**	0.016	**0.050**	**0.082**
	(-1.2)	(-4.7)	(3.3)	(1.6)	(6.1)	(6.9)
Adj. R^2	0.55	0.68	0.25	0.47	0.72	0.61
No of Obs.	91	91	91	91	91	91

Notes: For each variable indicated in the column headings, country-pair standard deviations for the pre-EMU (1990–8) period are regressed on EMU (international/internal dimension) dummies and a set of controls. OLS regressions. Parentheses contain t-statistics. Bold coefficients indicate significance at the 5 per cent level.

Table 16.2: EMU-period volatility and the international and internal dimensions

	GDP	Consumption	SMI	Inflation	Long Interest	Short Interest
International dummy	-0.040	-0.031	0.067	0.001	-0.001	0.000
	(-5.2)	(-6.4)	(4.7)	(0.7)	(-0.9)	(0.2)
EMU dummy	-0.077	-0.063	0.130	0.001	-0.002	-0.001
	(-5.5)	(-7.1)	(5.2)	(0.5)	(-1.6)	(-0.3)
Trade concentration	0.074	0.120	-0.059	-0.004	-0.006	-0.01
	(2.2)	(5.6)	(-1.0)	(-0.9)	(-2.3)	(-0.9)
Trade diversification	0.039	0.021	0.300	-0.002	0.003	0.024
	(2.0)	(1.7)	(8.4)	(-0.7)	(1.8)	(3.7)
Trade openness	0.023	0.017	0.013	0.000	-0.000	-0.001
	(5.3)	(6.1)	(1.7)	(0.6)	(-0.2)	(-0.5)
Financial openness	-0.003	-0.003	-0.012	0.000	-0.000	-0.001
	(-3.3)	(-4.5)	(-6.5)	(1.4)	(-4.8)	(-4.1)
Capital account restr.	0.032	0.031	-0.005	-0.001	-0.005	-0.021
	(2.7)	(4.1)	(-0.2)	(-0.7)	(-5.3)	(-5.1)
Relative income	-0.000	-0.000	0.003	-0.000	-0.000	-0.000
	(-1.4)	(-0.71)	(6.1)	(-0.1)	(3.9)	(0.6)
M2/GDP	0.015	0.013	-0.018	-0.000	0.000	-0.000
	(4.3)	(6.1)	(-2.8)	(-0.4)	(1.4)	(-0.1)
ToT volatility	-0.230	-0.200	-0.430	0.030	0.018	0.008
	(-3.7)	(-5.1)	(-3.8)	(3.9)	(3.8)	(0.4)
Constant	-0.022	-0.036	-0.150	0.007	0.0016	0.012
	(-1.0)	(-2.5)	(-3.6)	(2.6)	(0.9)	(1.6)
Adj. R^2	00.41	0.66	0.4	0.27	0.68	0.48
No of Obs.	136	136	136	136	136	136

Notes: For each variable indicated in the column headings, country-pair standard deviations for the EMU (1999–2006) period are regressed on EMU (international/internal dimension) dummies and a set of controls. OLS regressions. Parentheses contain t-statistics. Bold coefficients are significant at the 5 per cent level.

to such shocks, we also include a measure of trade concentration in natural resource or primary sectors and an indicator of trade diversification. Finally, we also control for relative income. With the exception of foreign assets and liabilities, which are obtained from the External Wealth of Nations Mark II dataset by Lane and Milesi-Ferretti (2006), all data are updated from Gerlach (1999) and the sources described there.[2]

As is apparent from Table 16.1, pairs of countries that later joined EMU had consistently lower relative nominal volatility as well as a lower volatility of real GDP already in the period *before* 1999. This reflects the considerable convergence that had been achieved by the EMU candidates before monetary union. Almost the same is true for the 'mixed' pairs, though, as one would expect, the point estimate of the effect of EMU on volatility is somewhat smaller than that for the EMU pairs.

Table 16.2 reports the results for the EMU period. Interestingly, there is no longer a significant effect of EMU on nominal volatility – be it among member or vis-à-vis outsiders. This again can be read as an indication that the bulk of nominal convergence that EMU has fostered took place already in the run-up to 1999. Conversely, Table 16.2 clearly shows that after 1999, EMU has had a pronounced effect on the relative volatility of real variables. While country pairs involving EMU members continue to display lower relative GDP volatility, the relative volatility of stock market returns has increased notably. Most importantly, EMU is now associated with much lower volatility of relative consumption growth rates. All of these effects, again, pertain to both the international and the internal dimension of EMU, with the impact on mixed country pairs being somewhat smaller but still large and significant.

As shown by Tables 16.1 and 16.2, in both subperiods the signs of the control variables – to the extent that they are significant – are generally as expected. Trade openness is associated with higher volatility of GDP and consumption growth, as is the presence of capital controls, while financial openness is negatively related to volatility. This is an important finding since it suggests that international financial trade depresses volatility, an effect that we will return to further below. There is no robust effect across subperiods of the control variables on nominal volatility or on stock market returns.

One notable aspect of these results is that we consistently find the volatility of the terms of trade to be associated with *lower* relative volatility of GDP and consumption growth. If the terms of trade were a truly exogenous source of shocks, we would expect a positive sign: higher terms of trade volatility should be associated with higher consumption and GDP volatility. The fact that we find a negative sign suggests that the terms of trade and the real exchange rate could by themselves act as a shock absorber rather than as a source of shocks. This interpretation is supported by the recent findings of other researchers.

4.2 *EMU and the decline in global volatility*

While our results suggest that EMU has had a significant effect on the level of relative volatility for both member and non-member pairs of countries, the findings reported in Tables 16.1 and 16.2 are not directly informative about the role that EMU may have played in explaining the decline in macroeconomic volatility over time. We turn to this issue next.

To this end, we provide in Table 16.3 regressions of the change in volatility on the EMU and international dummies along with the controls used in the previous sections.[3] As an additional conditioning variable, for each of our three real and nominal variables, we also include the respective lagged (i.e. pre-EMU) volatility variables into the regression. This is motivated by Figure 16.2 which would suggest that – in spite of the general decline in relative volatility – the level of volatility in the period before EMU remains an important determinant of volatility also in the period after 1999.

For each of our three nominal and real variables, we run the regression:

$$\sigma_{EMU}^{ij} - \sigma_{PRE}^{ij} = \alpha_1 \sigma_{PRE}^{ij} + \alpha_2 Inter_{ij} + \alpha_3 EMU_{ij} + \gamma' Z_{PRE}^{ij} + \varepsilon^{ij}$$

where *ij* denotes the pair of countries *i* and *j*, σ is the relative variability of the respective nominal or real variable, *Inter* and *EMU* are our international dimension and EMU dummies, respectively, that take the value of one if one (*Inter*) or both (*EMU*) countries in pair *ij* are EMU members and zero otherwise. The subscripts *PRE* and *EMU* denote variables from the pre-EMU and EMU periods respectively. The vector Z^{ij} stacks the trade and financial openness controls.

The results in Table 16.3 show a highly significant and negative estimate of α_1 for all variables except output growth. This effect is particularly pronounced for the three nominal variables, for which the

Table 16.3: *EMU and the decline in volatility*

	GDP	Consumption	SMI	Inflation	Long interest	Short interest
International dummy	-0.009	-0.011	0.001	-0.004	-0.002	-0.0006
	(-2.41)	(-4.55)	(0.21)	(-3.83)	(-2.91)	(-0.37)
EMU dummy	-0.022	-0.026	0.002	-0.008	-0.004	-0.005
	(-3.17)	(-5.71)	(0.13)	(-4.52)	(-3.95)	(-1.26)
σ^{PRE}	0.092	-0.166	-0.276	-1.038	-1.007	-0.85
	(1.29)	(-3.29)	(-6.21)	(-28.43)	(-37.19)	(-17.93)
Trade concentration	-0.048	-0.013	-0.028	0.002	0.013	0.044
	(-2.93)	(-1.18)	(-0.91)	(0.41)	(5.23)	(6.98)
Trade diversification	0.044	0.011	0.031	-0.01	-0.009	-0.016
	(2.87)	(0.97)	(1.06)	(-2.69)	(-3.69)	(-2.62)
Trade openness	-0.014	-0.015	0.083	0.007	-0.002	-0.003
	(-1.99)	(-2.94)	(5.95)	(4.3)	(-1.41)	(-1.35)
Financial openness	-0.0007	0.002	-0.011	-0.0003	-0.0001	0.0001
	(-0.47)	(1.25)	(-4.05)	(-0.95)	(-0.54)	(0.32)
Capital account restr.	-0.004	-0.013	0.034	0.008	-0.002	-0.004
	(-0.63)	(-2.80)	(2.79)	(4.1)	(-1.65)	(-1.61)
Relative income	-0.0001	-0.0005	0.001	-0.0005	0.0004	0.0004
	(-0.57)	(-3.1)	(2.74)	(-1.16)	(1.24)	(0.55)
M2/GDP	0.0007	0.008	-0.019	0.001	0.001	-0.0001
	(0.33)	(5.2)	(-4.47)	(2.37)	(2.21)	(-0.14)
ToT volatility	-0.338	-0.04	-0.529	0.05	0.067	0.079

	(1)	(2)	(3)	(4)	(5)	(6)
	(−3.61)	(−0.57)	(−3.19)	(2.19)	(5.06)	(2.19)
Constant	0.02	**0.023**	−0.038	0.005	**0.005**	0.008
	(1.57)	(2.33)	(−1.47)	(1.57)	(2.01)	(1.31)
Adj. R^2	0.51	0.61	0.66	0.94	0.99	0.91
No of Obs.	91	91	91	91	91	91

Notes: For each variable given in the column heading, we regress the differences in the country-pair-specific standard deviations between the pre-EMU and EMU periods on the EMU (international/internal dimension) dummies. In addition, the regressions also include our set of controls, including the lagged (i.e. pre-EMU period) volatility σ^{pre} of the respective variable. OLS regressions. Bold coefficients are significant at the 5 per cent level.

estimate of α_1 is close to unity in negative terms. This confirms the impression from Figure 16.2 that relative volatility has fallen almost across the board but that this decline has been far more drastic for nominal variables.

In addition, those country pairs that involve at least one EMU country have generally experienced even more drastic declines in volatility. Among the nominal variables, this is true for both inflation and long interest rates. Among the real variables, EMU has had a strong effect on the decline in relative GDP and consumption growth volatility. Again, for all variables, the intra-EMU effect is stronger than it is vis-à-vis outsiders (by about a factor of two), but still the international dimension is highly significant and sizable.

The order of magnitude of the impact of EMU on the volatility of GDP and consumption is worth noting: EMU membership reduces the relative volatility of GDP growth by 2 percentage points vis-à-vis other members and still by 1 percentage point vis-à-vis outsiders. The effect on relative consumption volatility appears even slightly higher.

4.3 Interpreting the international dimension of EMU

The results in the previous tables suggest that the decline in relative volatility, already apparent from Figure 16.2, is particularly pronounced among EMU members. In addition, we have identified an important international dimension of EMU in the sense that relative volatility also declines more than average if only one of the two countries i or j is an EMU member (though not quite as much as for intra-EMU pairings). To understand these results better, let x^i denote one of the real and nominal variables that we considered in our analysis so far. Assume that x^i is determined by three factors: a global factor that affects all countries in the same way, a European factor that we also allow to affect all countries but to potentially different degrees, and a purely country-specific factor. Then for two countries i and j we can write:

$$x_t^i = g_t + a_i f_t + s_t^i$$
$$x_t^j = g_t + a_j f_t + s_t^j$$

where g_t is the global factor, f_t is the European factor and s_t is the country-specific influence. The factor loadings a_i and a_j capture the exposure of the respective economy to the European factor. Assuming that f_t and s_t are uncorrelated, it is easy to see that the country-pair-specific or relative variance is:

$$\text{var}(x_t^i - x_t^j) = (a_i - a_j)^2 \, \text{var}(f_t) + \text{var}(s_t^i - s_t^j)$$

Note first that the idiosyncratic variance is independent of the global factor, which is one reason why we focus on relative variances. Secondly, note that the European factor affects the relative variance to the extent that the exposure of the two economies to Europe-wide shocks differs. To capture the idea that exposure to the European factor is more similar among pairs of EMU members than between mixed pairs or non-EMU pairs of countries, we assume that the squared difference between the factor loadings $(a_i - a_j)^2$ is generally smaller if both country i and j are EMU members than if only one of the countries is an EMU member.

Then the pattern we observe in the data is compatible with the following explanations: first, $(a_i - a_j)^2$ has declined for all country pairs, but it has declined by more for intra-EMU pairs than for pairs involving only one or no EMU country. Secondly, the purely idiosyncratic variances have declined, possibly due to the elimination of disturbances related to poor fiscal and monetary policy. Third, $\text{var}(f_t)$ could have declined. We do not distinguish between these explanations since there is no reason to believe that they are mutually exclusive.

Before proceeding, we note that the pattern we observe in the data cannot be explained by a decline in $\text{var}(f_t)$ alone, because – under the plausible assumption that the factor loadings, a_i, for EMU countries are on average more similar than those of non-EMU countries – we would expect such a decline to have led to a larger decline in relative volatilities among outsiders than among EMU members. Furthermore, we emphasise that the decline in $\text{var}(x_t^i - x_t^j)$ can have occurred without the absolute level of $\text{var}(x_t^i)$ and $\text{var}(x_t^j)$ changing, which would reflect an increase in the correlation between the two variables.

5. The decline in consumption volatility

Our findings highlight that EMU has been associated with a decline in relative consumption volatility – in so far as both intra-EMU volatility and the international dimension are concerned. At a theoretical level, we could think of this decline in two ways. First, it may reflect a decline in the volatility of other macroeconomic variables. For instance, more synchronised fiscal policy stances as well as the creation of a single monetary policy itself – and the removal of speculative attacks as a source of occasional episodes of sharp interest rate increases – could all have had a direct impact on the volatility of output, interest rates and inflation and this in turn could have affected consumption volatility.

Secondly, consumption may have become more insulated against idiosyncratic macroeconomic shocks due to better international risk sharing: the deepening and widening of financial markets that resulted from EMU may have allowed households to insure better against fluctuations in their consumption (perhaps as a consequence of financial institutions offering a wider range of financial products). According to our results from the previous sections, the volatility of consumption has fallen by somewhat *more* than that of output, which would indeed suggest that better consumption risk sharing is a potentially important factor in the decline of consumption volatility.[4]

To study the extent to which consumption has become better insulated against business cycle volatility, we turn to a by now well-established literature (Asdrubali *et al.* (1996), Sørensen and Yosha (1998), Crucini (1999), Becker and Hoffmann (2006)), which measures risk sharing through panel regressions in the form:

$$\tilde{c}_t^{ij} = \alpha + \beta \widetilde{gdp}_t^{ij} + \mu^{ij} + \tau_t + const + \xi_t^{ij} \tag{1}$$

Here, $\tilde{x}_t^{ij}$ denotes the difference $x^i - x^j$ for countries i and j and c and gdp denote the logarithm of real consumption and GDP respectively. We capture time-specific fixed effects through τ_t and country-pair-specific fixed effects through μ^{ij}. Finally, ξ_t^{ij} is the residual and *const* the regression constant.[5]

Estimates of β are typically between zero and one, which allows us to interpret the coefficient as a measure of risk sharing. Specifically, β tells us the fraction of country-specific volatility in business cycles (i.e. in $\widetilde{gdp}_t^{ij}$) that remains uninsured and that systematically spills over into volatility in consumption. A value of β near zero would therefore imply almost perfect risk sharing, whereas a value near one would indicate no risk sharing. If risk sharing has indeed increased, we would expect that β has fallen over time.

Table 16.4: *EMU and international consumption risk sharing*

	Panel A	
	Pre-EMU period (1990–8)	EMU period (1999–2004)
β	0.6	0.52
	(48.9)	(55.2)
Adj. R^2	0.5	0.67
No of Obs.	2277	1518
	Panel B	
β_0	0.67	0.79
	(26.34)	(23.09)
β_1	-0.04	-0.26
	(-1.35)	(-7.22)
β_2	-0.22	-0.35
	(-6.09)	(-9.23)
Adj.R^2	0.51	0.69
No of Obs.	2277	1518
	Panel C: Risk sharing by country-pair group	
EMU Outsiders	0.67	0.79
EMU and Non-EMU	0.63	0.53*
IntraEMU	0.45	0.44*

Notes: For both the pre-EMU and the EMU periods, the table reports panel regressions of the form:

$$\tilde{c}_t^{ij} = \alpha + \beta_0 \tilde{gdp}_t^{ij} + \mu_{ij} + \tau_t + const + \varepsilon_t^{ij}$$

in panel A and:

$$\tilde{c}_t^{ij} = \alpha + \beta_0 \tilde{gdp}_t^{ij} + \beta_1 \left(Inter_{ij} \times \tilde{gdp}_t^{ij} \right) + \beta_2 \left(EMU_{ij} \times \tilde{gdp}_t^{ij} \right) + \mu^{ij} + \tau_t + \varepsilon_t^{ij}$$

in panel B, where $\tilde{x}_t^{ij} = x^i - x^j$ and x stands for the logarithms of consumption (c) and GDP in turn. t-statistics in parentheses, coefficients significant at the 5 per cent level are in bold. Panel C reports the fraction of unshared risk among the respective country-pair groups, i.e. β_0 for outsiders, $\beta_0 + \beta_1$ for risk sharing between EMU and non-EMU countries and $\beta_0 + \beta_2$ for risk sharing among EMU countries. An asterisk in panel C signals if risk sharing in the respective country-pair group is significantly different (at the 5 per cent level) from the risk sharing achieved among non-EMU members.

We present the results from regressions of the form in Panel A of Table 16.4. As is apparent, risk sharing has indeed increased globally since the inception of EMU. The coefficient β has fallen from about 0.6 to roughly 0.5, suggesting that around 50 per cent of all idiosyncratic

risk was shared among the countries in our sample, up from 40 per cent
in the decade before EMU – a sizeable increase of about one quarter.
There are by now a number of papers that document a statistically
significant link between consumption risk sharing and financial globalisation (Artis and Hoffmann (2007, 2008a, 2008b) and Sørensen *et al.*
(2007)), which show that consumption risk sharing has indeed
increased over the last decade. The results in Panel A are compatible
with these findings. The question we ask here is what role has EMU
played in this global increase in international risk sharing. In order to
address this question, we let β vary across country pairs. Specifically, we
posit the linear relation:

$$\beta_{ij} = \beta_0 + \beta_1 \, Inter_{ij} + \beta_2 EMU_{ij} \tag{2}$$

where *Inter* and *EMU* are again our international and EMU dummies
respectively. A negative value of $\beta_1 (\beta_2)$ would then imply that a country
pair shares more risk if it involves one (two) EMU member(s). The
coefficient β_0 tells us how much risk sharing a country pair outside the
EMU would achieve, whereas $\beta_0 + \beta_1 (\beta_0 + \beta_2)$ indicates the amount of
risk shared by country pairs involving one (two) EMU country(ies).
Once these coefficients have been estimated, we can then also ask what
accounts for the rise in risk sharing. If it is a global phenomenon, then β_0
should have decreased. If it is due to better risk sharing between EMU
and non-EMU members, then β_1 should have decreased, whereas if
international risk sharing has just increased because of better intra-
EMU risk sharing, we should find that β_2 has fallen.

To estimate the coefficients β_0, β_1 and β_2 we use (1) and (2) which
gives us two interaction terms between $\widetilde{gdp}_t^{ij}$ and $Inter_{ij}$ and EMU_{ij}
respectively, so that the regression we estimate becomes:

$$\tilde{c}_t^{ij} = \alpha + \beta_0 \tilde{gdp}_t^{ij} + \beta_1 \left(Inter_{ij} \times \tilde{gdp}_t^{ij} \right) + \beta_2 \left(EMU_{ij} \times \tilde{gdp}_t^{ij} \right) + \mu^{ij}$$
$$+ \tau_t + \varepsilon_t^{ij}$$

Panel B of Table 16.4 provides the estimates. The first column gives the
results for the pre-EMU period, 1990–98, the second for the period
since the beginning of EMU.

The results in Table 16.4 confirm our conjecture that the creation of
EMU plays an important role for international consumption risk sharing: β_2 is significant in the regressions for both subperiods, indicating
that EMU members (or, in the pre-EMU period, candidates that were

eventually to become EMU members) share significantly more risk with each other than does the average non-EMU country pair in our sample.

There is, again, also an important international dimension to the results. The international dummy (β_1) is significantly negative in the second period: since the inception of the euro, outsiders share risk with countries inside EMU more effectively than among themselves. Again, this effect is of the same order of magnitude as the effect of bilateral EMU membership, though generally somewhat weaker: the coefficient β_1 is significantly negative but smaller in absolute value than β_2.

Panel C summarises our results by providing the net extent of risk sharing for non-EMU members (β_0) and along the international $(\beta_0 + \beta_1)$ and internal $(\beta_0 + \beta_2)$ dimensions respectively. This synopsis helps illustrate the pivotal role that the creation of EMU seems to have played in the international rise in risk sharing. In fact, non-EMU members share somewhat *less* risk among themselves than before 1999, as evidenced by the fact that β_0 increases from 0.67 to 0.79. But this seems to be more than substituted for by the significant increase in risk sharing between outsiders and EMU members. The sum $\beta_0 + \beta_1$ decreases from 0.63 to 0.53. Interestingly, the level of risk sharing achieved between members – which was already much higher than among the other two country-pair groups in the period before 1999 – seems to have increased only marginally.[6] Therefore, it seems that better risk sharing of EMU members with outsiders (the international dimension) accounts for most of the global increase in risk sharing that we see from the results in Panel A and that others have already documented.

6. Conclusions

To our knowledge, this chapter constitutes the first systematic exploration of the effect of EMU on the stability and volatility of key macroeconomic variables both within the euro area and internationally. We have documented that, since the inception of the euro, industrialised economies have seen a considerable decline in the volatility of both key nominal and – to a somewhat smaller extent – also real macroeconomic indicators, including inflation, interest rates, GDP, stock markets and, most notably, consumption. While the global decline in volatility is also likely to be due to a more stable international macroeconomic environment, we condition on the impact of global factors by focussing on the role that EMU has played in moderating idiosyncratic volatility among its members and relative to non-members. We find that EMU has hugely increased not only the stability of EMU members relative to each other but also relative to non-members.

While EMU seems to have particularly strongly affected the volatility of nominal variables, such as inflation or interest rates, on the real side, our results concerning the volatility of consumption stand out as particularly important. Not only is the decline in the volatility of consumption more marked and more clearly associated with EMU than it is for other real aggregates but we also find evidence to suggest that this decline is clearly associated with better risk sharing through a widening and deepening of financial markets and that EMU has been pivotal in the recent increase of consumption risk sharing that we and others have documented.

Notes

1. See Bordo and James (this volume), and Eichengreen (this volume).
2. Note that we do not have data on bilateral country characteristics, such as financial and trade flows or capital account openness. We generate such country-pair-specific characteristics as simple arithmetic means of the respective country-specific variables.
3. It would appear that one way to obtain insight into the decline in volatility over time is to look at a version of the regressions in Table 16.1 or 16.2 where the regressors and the dependent variable have been differenced across subperiods. This is, however, not practically feasible, because the regressors do not change at all (EMU membership status) or very little (e.g. relative measures of trade openness change very little).
4. This interpretation is also supported by empirical results in Bekaert *et al.* (2006), who show that consumption volatility tends to fall by more than output volatility after financial liberalisations.
5. In the literature, such regressions have often been estimated in first differences of the idiosyncratic variables. However, Artis and Hoffmann (2008b) caution against this practice by showing that in an environment in which the variability of business cycles may also be declining over time, the coefficient of the differenced regression will fail to pick up improvements in international risk sharing. Since a continued decline in output variability forms the backdrop for our analysis here, we follow Becker and Hoffmann (2006) and Artis and Hoffmann (2007, 2008a) and estimate these regressions in relative (log) levels, a procedure that is less sensitive to changes in the volatility of business cycles by putting more emphasis on the identification of longer-term trends in risk sharing. To facilitate the

identification of these trends further, for this part of our analysis, we also use annual data from the Penn World tables, release 6.2 (Heston *et al.* (2006)). This data ranges until 2004.

6. This finding is compatible with Artis and Hoffmann (2008a), who show that EMU *is* associated with better risk sharing among its members but that much of this increase already occurred before the inception of the euro area.

Comment 12: Comment on Chapter 16

PHILIPP HARTMANN

This is a thought-provoking chapter about the effects that the introduction of a common currency among a number of industrial countries can have on the second moments (variances and/or correlations) of selected major macroeconomic and financial variables. The main hypothesis of interest the authors advance is that the euro has 'exported' macroeconomic stability also to other industrial countries. They argue that this applies particularly to consumption smoothing, which is more directly relevant for economic welfare than the smoothing of national GDPs, stock market returns and short and long interest rates, and that it happened through the greater stability of consumption linkages between countries that joined the euro and those that did not. The authors speculate that this finding may be explained by the widening and deepening of euro-area financial markets, which allow for a better sharing of risk both within the area and with countries outside.

1. Three international roles of currencies

In this discussion I shall look at the chapter from the perspective of the international role of currencies. There are at least three international roles a currency can take on. The first is defined by the extent to which residents from abroad use it for their transactions (as medium of exchange, store of value or unit of account; see for example Kenen, 1983). The second role relates to 'leadership' in monetary policy, in that one central bank leads in setting interest rates and central banks from other countries follow in time. The third role is whether a currency contributes to international stability or even creates instability. These roles are distinct but not independent, since the decision of a country to peg its currency to another (official unit of account) will require it to follow the monetary policy of the other country, while an unstable currency will usually not be used by residents abroad.

Which role did the euro assume after its introduction in 1999? In relation to the first role, its first ten years were characterised by two features. First, by most dimensions of the international use of a currency the euro started at a similar level as the Deutschmark or slightly higher, which made it the second most used currency after the US dollar as of day 1 of EMU, and then started a gradual expansion without fully catching up to the dollar so far (see Hartmann, 1998a; ECB, 2001, 2008b). Second, in terms of the denomination of international bond issues, however, the euro expanded quite quickly, becoming even a challenger to the dollar relatively early on (see McCauley, 1997; Detken and Hartmann, 2000, 2002). Interestingly, this development seemed to be at least partly driven by the demand from euro-area investors for foreign fixed income securities without exchange rate risk (see ECB, 2002).

As regards the second role of an international currency, some expected a relatively significant 'decoupling' between the US and euro-area economies after EMU, so that the traditionally perceived interest rate leadership of the Fed would be diminished or removed. Interestingly, transatlantic interest rate relationships seem to have strengthened in the early years of EMU. Chinn and Frankel's (2005) analysis suggests that Fed monetary policy still leads ECB monetary policy. Belke and Gros (2005) find this only for the period after 2001 and caution that the conventional wisdom may not have held before this time.

The third international role of a currency can be seen as the subject of the chapter by Gerlach and Hoffmann. International relations theories suggest that a stable international economic system requires the presence of a dominant power – a hegemon. Eichengreen (1989) has analysed these 'hegemonic stability theories' economically and came to the conclusion that they may be difficult to reconcile with the evidence on international monetary relations. As for example in the case for the British Empire and the US post-World War II dominance, an economic hegemon often also possesses a dominant international currency. In line with 'hegemonic stability' thinking it has been argued that an international monetary system characterised by two or small number of more rival currencies could be more unstable, for example, as it might give rise to destabilising capital flows between them.[1] The chapter tries to make a somewhat opposite point. The euro may have contributed to greater macroeconomic stability during its first ten years, although it created (or expanded) a second major international currency in addition to the dollar. This is an important hypothesis worth examining more deeply.

In my role as a discussant, I should raise points that might question the authors' results. Future research could then address these open issues to further harden their conclusions. I would like to fulfil my assignment by first discussing some points of an econometric or statistical nature and then comparing some of the authors' findings with related ones from the literature. Second, I would like to suggest ways in which the main explanation of how European financial markets promoted risk sharing could be further substantiated and developed. Finally, I would like to look ahead to see whether the results on consumption risk sharing are likely to be sustained.

2. Has the euro diminished macroeconomic volatility and enhanced consumption smoothing?

The most obvious objection to associating the decline in macroeconomic and financial volatility to EMU is that it could have originated from global developments unrelated to the introduction of the euro. The authors address this point by focusing on 'relative' volatilities, by which they mean the volatilities of the differences in growth rates for the variables of interest between pairs of countries (see start of Section 3). Taking the example of consumption the relative volatility (σ) between consumption growth (c) in countries i and j is given by the following expression:

$$\sigma^{ij} = \sqrt{\operatorname{var}(c^i - c^j)} = \sqrt{\operatorname{var}c^i + \operatorname{var}c^j - \operatorname{cov}(c^i, c^j)}. \tag{1}$$

Therefore, σ^{ij} captures the variability of consumption growth in both countries controlling for their (linear) comovements, including any global factor(s). This is a simple and intuitive approach but it also implies some challenges. First, when judging the 'export' of stability to countries outside the euro area, one cannot directly see from the measure whether lower volatility is originating from country i, say a euro-area country, country j, say a non-euro-area country, or both. In order to draw the conclusion that a lower level of σ^{ij} between a euro-area and a non-euro-area country implies also greater stability in the non-euro-area country, one would have to explicitly check whether the lower 'relative' volatility is not mainly related to $\operatorname{var}(c^i)$ being low. (Non-euro-area consumers would only care about smoothing their own consumption.)

Second, in particular for tracking the 'relative' volatility (1) over time one needs to be aware that it not only moves in response to changes in variances but also in covariances. For example, if the influence of a global or any other joint factor on consumption growth strengthens over time, then σ^{ij} may decline without any reduction in the volatilities of countries i and j. This is an important point for interpreting the authors' results. Their notion of stability cannot distinguish between variance and covariance. And we cannot be sure that the control variables included in Tables 16.1 through 16.3 capture all joint factors increasing cross-border covariances of consumption growth. (To be fair, a short disclaimer at the end of Section 4 acknowledges that their main finding may also result from increased correlations.) Moreover, as regards welfare implications, the covariance does not enter consumers' utility functions in the euro area or abroad.

I am also concerned about correlations in the error terms of the main regressions underlying Tables 16.1 through 16.4. Notice that the explanatory variable is defined by (1) above and therefore each observation relates to two countries. So, some groups of observations share one country and others do not share a country. The regression errors of groups of observations sharing a country are likely to be correlated with one another, which could for example lead to block-wise heteroskedasticity patterns. If the econometric approach does not control for such patterns, then standard errors will be biased and statistical inference potentially misleading. From the information provided, it is not clear whether the authors control for heteroskedasticity, let alone for a block-wise form of it. Hence, statistical significance of the results might not be ensured.

Last, one may have desired some robustness checks with respect to the break points assumed. While 1 January 1999 is a plausible break point, clearly related to the euro, given the convergence period and other interfering events it is not necessarily the only or main break point. There are testing methods that find break points 'endogenously' or one could have experimented with exogenously imposed alternative break points. (The usefulness of such an approach will also be illustrated in the next section of this discussion, when parallel market developments and policy initiatives are considered.)

Readers may also regard it useful if Gerlach and Hoffmann compared their very favourable results for consumption smoothing with other emerging results in the literature. Balli and Sørensen (2006) find that consumption smoothing in the EU has not improved after the introduction of the euro. The differences might be reconciled by considering pre-EMU levels of consumption risk sharing, the various ways in which it can emerge and finer country groups. It would also be helpful if the authors compared their results to a series of related results on income risk sharing in Europe (see Ekinci *et al.*, 2007; Artis and Hoffmann, 2007, and references therein).

3. The development of euro-area financial markets

The authors' main explanation for why consumption risk sharing has increased among euro-area countries and between euro-area and other industrial countries is the 'widening and deepening of financial markets' associated with the inception of EMU. This raises a number of important questions. First, the hypothesis that the EMU process promoted the above financial market developments, which in turn foster consumption risk sharing, is not tested. The EMU dummy (and also the international dummy) is treated as a separate explanatory variable from the financial variables included in the regressions in Tables 16.1 through 16.3. To test the above hypothesis some form of two-stage estimation procedure would have been necessary, in which EMU first explains financial openness, the M2/GDP ratio etc., and second the predicted part of these variables explains the extent of risk sharing.

Second, given that the 'widening and deepening of financial markets' is the main explanation, the variables that capture them in the authors' regressions are relatively crude. Financial openness may be capturing one important aspect of the process of financial integration reasonably well. But it ignores price-based dimensions of integration. Capital account restrictions play only a limited role among most industrial countries, except perhaps for some countries at the very start of the sample. Baele *et al.* (2004) discuss a wide range of financial integration measures and the ECB (2007b, 2008a) and the European Commission (2004b) comprehensively track the process of European financial integration over time. Financial development, however, is hardly captured in the chapter, as the amount of money in circulation (the M2/GDP ratio) is only a sensible measure of it in highly underdeveloped countries. Hartmann *et al.* (2007) have found that total capital market size, defined as the aggregate of loan, corporate bond and stock markets as a share of GDP, is a good summary measure of financial development for industrial countries, such as the countries captured in the Gerlach and Hoffmann chapter. The latest data on total capital market size for all euro-area countries, the euro-area average, the USA, UK, Sweden,

Switzerland and Japan are reproduced in Figure C12.1. It shows that in the aggregate euro-area capital markets have grown to a similar extent as UK or US capital markets over the last two decades, although they remain still smaller relative to the size of the domestic economy. Heterogeneity across the area also remains significant, but less financially developed countries catch up faster than more developed ones. Overall, the process of financial development progressed similarly in most major industrial countries, except for Japan where capital markets contracted. Together with international financial integration this process should have promoted risk sharing both within and across these countries, in line with Gerlach and Hoffmann's findings.

Third, while both financial integration and development have clearly been promoted by the EMU process, there were also other important European policy initiatives, including for example various banking reforms during the 1990s (such as the Second Banking Directive[2]) or the Financial Services Action Plan (European Commission, 1999). These other policy initiatives apply to the European Union as a whole and not only to the euro area. Therefore they may explain more easily part of the greater risk sharing between euro-area and non-euro-area countries. Moreover, there were also specific market developments, such as technical progress and financial innovation. These market developments were global, so they may go even further towards explaining the results by Gerlach and Hoffmann.[3] While undoubtedly EMU plays an important role in further integrating and developing European financial markets, thereby contributing to better risk sharing, these other factors need to be taken into account as well. An explicit and differentiated consideration of them would greatly enhance the understanding of greater consumption risk sharing in the euro area and between euro-area and other industrial countries.

4. Outlook

A last issue is whether favourable consumption risk sharing patterns in the euro area and between the area and outside countries are likely to persist. Major international shocks may have the potential to disrupt the situation. For example, the surge in energy and food prices could have more lasting effects on inflation and inflation variability than is currently expected. Or, the financial market turmoil that started in the summer of 2007 could disturb the processes of financial development

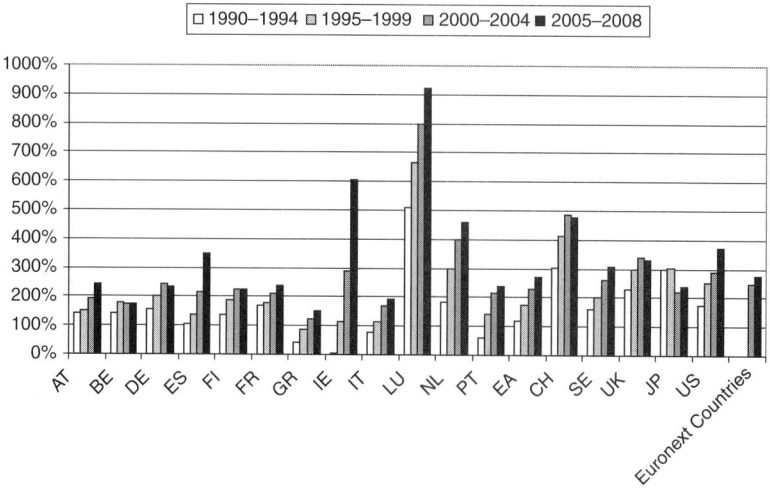

Figure C12.1: Size of capital markets (percentage of GDP)
Notes: Sum of (i) stock market capitalisation, (ii) bank credit to the private sector and (iii) debt securities issued by the private sector divided by GDP. Stock market capitalisation: Data for BE, FR and NL start in 1991; data for IE and PT start in 1995; figures for JP include Tokyo Stock Exchange; figures for USA include AMEX, NYSE and NASDAQ; figures for the euro area (EA) is the sum of the values for Euronext and for countries not included in Euronext; Euronext data start in 1995 and 'Euronext countries' is the sum of the values for countries included in Euronext. Bank credit to the private sector: loans granted to the domestic private sector; euro-area figures are the sum of EA country figures and include cross-border loans between EA countries. Debt securities issued by the private sector: for EA countries data are from the ECB securities database; data for GR start in 1995; for IE BIS data are used for the years 1992 to 2002 for financial institutions and for the years 1992 to 2008 for corporate issuers; for LU BIS data for the years 1992–2008; are used for corporate issuers; for non-EA countries BIS data are used (sum of international and domestic amounts outstanding of bonds issued by corporate issuers and financial institutions).
Sources: BIS, Datastream, ECB, Eurostat, IMF, World Federation of Exchanges and own calculations.

and integration. While a significant impairment of risk sharing through these developments may not be the most likely outcome, only the future will show whether the relatively benign macroeconomic environment of the recent past changes and thereby also adversely affects how consumption is smoothed within and outside the euro area. Macroeconomic and financial policies may have a role to play in containing the likelihood that such a scenario materialises.

Notes

1. Eichengreen (1985) suggests that the Bank of England could prevent destabilisations of the classical gold standard as a result of 'tugs of wars' between central banks for capital flows, as all other central banks had to follow the Bank of England's discount rate policy.
2. Second Council Directive 89/646/EEC of 15 December 1989 on the coordination of laws, regulations and administrative provisions relating to the taking-up and pursuit of the business of credit institutions and amending Directive 77/780/EEC (OJ L 311, 14.11.1997, p. 42).
3. As the recent financial turmoil suggests, however, not all innovative financial products may have been designed in a beneficial way.

17 | *The euro's impact on trade and foreign direct investment*

RICHARD BALDWIN

1. Introduction

The euro was created for political reasons. Economics – especially the trade and investment effects – were a minor issue in the minds of the men and women who launched Europe's monetary union. Of course, they were discussed in the Commission's famous 'One Market, One Money' report (Emerson *et al.*, 1992) and in my 1991 background paper entitled 'On the Microeconomics of the European Monetary Union' (Baldwin, 1991). But the report came out *after* the big political push organised by Helmut Kohl, François Mitterrand and Jacques Delors.

While politics will incessantly swirl around the European monetary union, the big decisions are a *fait accompli*. Economics are what matters most for euro-area enlargement and smooth functioning of the monetary union. The microeconomics especially concern two distinct groups of policy makers: those who must decide whether their countries want to join the monetary union, and those who run the euro area and decide on whether/when to let them in.

The standard way to think about the costs and benefits of the euro is called the Optimal Currency Area, or OCA, logic.[1] This views a currency union as a tradeoff between macroeconomic costs (loss of a national stabilisation tool) and microeconomic gains (closer economic integration). However, the vast majority of the OCA literature focuses on the costs of forgoing monetary policy autonomy. If OCA theorists think about the micro side at all, their thoughts are guided by the classic OCA articles of Mundell (1961, 1973a) and his followers which focus on the reduction of transaction costs – the story being that a common currency reduces transaction costs among nations using it.

Recent research has demonstrated quite clearly that this cannot be the main mechanism by which a monetary union fosters economic integration. This chapter presents the latest advances in our understanding of the euro's impact on trade and foreign direct investment (FDI). The

678

interested reader may refer to a much longer report written by myself and V. DiNino, L. Fontagné, R. A. De Santis and D. Taglioni (henceforth BDFST (2008)).

2. Trade and FDI channels

The standard Mundellian 'transaction cost' approach on the euro's microeconomic effects just cannot be of first-order importance. There are three strands of evidence that argue against it. The first piece concerns the lack of trade diversion. A very robust theoretical prediction of the Mundellian 'transaction cost' mechanism is that intra-euro-area trade creation should be accompanied by extra-euro-area trade diversion. The key is that under the Mundellian 'transaction cost' mechanism, euro-using nations enjoy lower transaction costs on their bilateral trade while non-euro-using nations do not. By lowering the cost of imports from other euro-using nations without altering the bilateral costs from non-euro nations, the reduced transaction costs should raise the relative price of imports from non-euro-using nations. Since imports depend upon relative prices, the euro's trade creation within the euro area should have been accompanied by trade diversion for other nations. Almost all empirical studies of the euro's trade effect fail to find trade diversion, as the extensive literature review in BDFST (2008: Chapter 2) makes clear, so it is unlikely that the Mundellian 'transaction cost' mechanism is important.

The second piece of evidence concerns the price effects. Under the Mundellian 'transaction cost' story, the trade effect operates via prices. That is, some of the lower bilateral transaction costs are passed on to consumers and thus intra-euro-area trade rises because the price of intra-euro-area imports falls. Almost all empirical studies of trade pricing in the euro area reject the hypothesis that the euro has altered trade prices (see BDFST, 2008: Chapter 3), so once again the Mundellian 'transaction cost' mechanism cannot be the main conduit.

The third piece of evidence against the Mundellian 'transaction cost' story concerns sectoral differences in the euro trade effect. If the key channel of trade effects was operating via transaction costs, one would expect to see a positive trade effect on most goods. After all, international trade of all types of goods involves financial transactions, so a reduction in these costs should boost all types of trade. Of course, different goods have different market structures and face different import demand elasticities, so one could anticipate a broad range of positive estimates, but all or most should be positive and significant. Yet, almost all empirical studies of the euro's trade effects find that the euro effect is concentrated in very few sectors – mainly ones marked by product differentiation and imperfect competition (see BDFST, 2008: Chapter 2). The fact that a large number of sectors experience no euro trade effect suggests that the economic mechanism cannot be as broad as the Mundellian 'transaction cost' mechanism. The driving force must be something that is much more sector-specific than transaction costs.

What then are the channels through which the euro affects trade and FDI? I will address these in order, starting with trade.

2.1 Trade channels

The best way to organise a discussion of trade channels is to realise that all trade works through a consumer's or firm's demand function. Demand depends upon the good's relative price and the customer's expenditure on the product category. This tells us that the euro's trade effect must work either via:

- a change in the relative price of the exported good, or
- a change in customers' expenditure shares on the good.[2]

The level of bilateral trade costs as well as the degree and nature of competition in the importing nation are the main determinants of a product's relative price. The euro's trade effect could thus conceivably work via either of these subchannels (bilateral trade-cost effects or competition effects). This reasoning applies to trade of a given product. Aggregate exports, however, consist of the sum of product-level exports, so a third channel comes from:

- a change in the range of products exported.

This third channel is the so-called 'extensive margin', or newly traded goods hypothesis.[3]

The dominant assumption in the literature up until very recently was that the euro's trade effect was coming solely via the relative price channel. This was based on two points. First, people made the reasonable assumption that euro usage per se does not shift the expenditure shares much, so the expenditure-share channel was negligible. Second, the dominant theoretical paradigm – the Helpman and Krugman (1985) synthesis of old and new trade theory – did not allow for changes in the range of traded products; it made assumptions that implied that every good produced was traded. The combination of the two tenets produced the standard, often implicit, assumption that the euro lowered transaction costs and these savings were at least partly passed on to lower trade prices, stimulating trade in the process.

Since the emergence of the new new-trade theory (e.g. Melitz, 2003), the extensive margin channel has gained a great deal of attention. Starting with Baldwin and Taglioni (2004) and Baldwin (2005, 2006a) this 'new goods' hypothesis (or to be more precise, 'newly traded goods' hypothesis) suggested that in addition to the relative-price channel, the euro could boost trade by increasing the number of products exported to the euro-area nations. Specifically, Baldwin and Taglioni (2004) showed theoretically that one can account for all the empirical findings if one presumes that the euro's trade effect operates by stimulating the export of new products rather than simply increasing the volume of already traded varieties. The idea is simple to explain in the new new-trade theory model of Melitz (2003), also called the heterogeneous firm trade (HFT) model.

In the HFT model, firms' decision to export involves a two-step process. First, firms determine what their optimal exports to a given nation would be if they decided to export. Second, they decide whether the resulting profits would be sufficient to cover the cost of establishing a marketing beachhead in the given nation. The model assumes that firms are heterogeneous in terms of their competitiveness. Different firms can thus look at the same two-step problem and come to different conclusions. In equilibrium, big, competitive firms will export; smaller, less competitive firms will not. The threshold level of competitive dividing the two groups is a key variable of adjustment in the HFT model.

Since the threshold is the key to understanding the euro's impact on the range of exported products, we illustrate the basic issues with a diagram. Figure 17.1 shows the basic logic. We arrange firms in order of increasing competitiveness and assume – for simplicity's sake – that each firm makes a single product. We assume a standard market structure (where more competitive firms sell more and make a higher operating profit in any given market) so the firm profit line in the diagram is upward sloped. To account for the beachhead cost (i.e. the fixed cost of entering a particular export market) the firm profit line is shifted downwards by the beachhead cost, namely F_X. In the extreme, a firm with zero competitiveness would

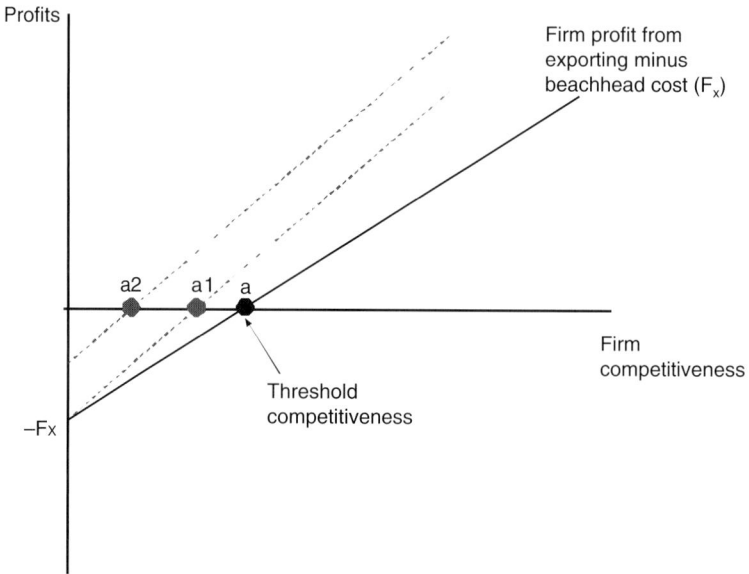

Figure 17.1: Export decision in the HFT model and the newly traded goods hypothesis

sell nothing and thus earn nothing if it entered the export market in question. Its profit would be $-F_X$ as shown by the intercept.

The euro's impact

What happens when the euro is adopted by the origin and destination nations? First, to the extent that the euro lowers *marginal* trade costs, the profit line rotates back towards the origin, as shown by the middle dashed line in Figure 17.1. The reason is simply that with lower marginal trade costs, each firm is more competitive in the export market than it was before the euro. This means that each firm would sell more and earn more from exporting (except of course, the extreme case of a firm with zero competitiveness, i.e. the intercept does not move). Since the trade costs are marginal, firms that sell the most initially – i.e. the most competitive firms – see their sales and profits rise the most. This is why the profit line rotates rather than shifts upwards.

Second, to the extent that the euro lowers beachhead costs – i.e. the *fixed* market entry costs – the profit line shifts up. The topmost dashed line in Figure 17.1 reflects both the marginal and fixed trade-cost effects of the euro.

The fixed trade-cost effect could come from many sources, but the easiest to imagine are those involving the administrative cost of dealing with an extra foreign currency. When the two nations share a currency, the usual finance overhead costs (accounting, hedging, bank accounts, etc.) are reduced. In this simple example we consider only a single export market, but it is trivial and useful to extend it to multiple markets using the euro. Doing so we see that even if the euro did not change the range of products that a particular nation exported, its introduction could expand the list of export destinations due to economies of scope in foreign currency costs. For example, a French firm that previously only found it worth exporting to Belgium might find it worthwhile exporting to the Netherlands since the cost of setting up a euro bank account would already have been sunk.

More formally, we can write the aggregate bilateral exports from origin nation-o to destination nation-d as:

$$V_{od} = \int_{o}^{\bar{i}} v_{od}(i)di \; ; \qquad v_{od}(i) = \left(\frac{p_{od}(i)}{P_d}\right)^{1-\sigma} \alpha_d E_d$$

where V_{od} is the aggregate exports from nation-o to nation-d, $v_{od}(i)$ and $p_{od}(i)$ are the export value and price of product i, with P_d being the sectoral price index in nation-d. σ is the elasticity of substitution among varieties. The products are arranged from zero to $\bar{i}$ in order of decreasing competitiveness, so $\bar{i}$ is the threshold product. Also, α_d is the sectoral expenditure share and E_d is total expenditure in nation-d. Given this, the change in aggregate exports can be decomposed into our three channels by totally differentiating V_{od} with respect to p, α and E. The result is:

$$dV_{od} = (1 - \sigma)V_{od}\frac{d(p_{od}/P_d)}{p_{od}/P_d} \quad + \quad V_{od}\frac{d\alpha_d}{\alpha_d} \quad + \quad v_{od}(\bar{i})d\bar{i} \; ;$$
$$\frac{d(p_{od}/P_d)}{p_{od}/P_d} = \hat{p}_{od} - \hat{P}_d$$

where we have assumed that all products exported from nation-o to nation-d experience the same proportional change in relative price (this is why we can move the term out of the integral).

The first right-hand term is the relative-price channel; it depends on the expenditure elasticity, $1-\sigma$, the initial level of trade, V_{od}, and the proportional change in relative prices. Note that as the last expression shows, the proportional change in relative prices equals the direct impact on p_{od} minus the indirect impact that this price effect will have on the sectoral price index P_d (the $\wedge$ indicates proportional change as usual). More precisely, we can break down the relative price term into the changes in the average mark-up on sales from euro-area nation-o to euro-area destination nation-d:

$$\frac{d(p_{EA,EA}/P_{EA})}{p_{EA,EA}/P_{EA}} = (\hat{\mu}_{EA,EA} + \hat{\tau}_{EA,EA}) - s_{EA}(\hat{\mu}_{EA,EA} + \hat{\tau}_{EA,EA})$$
$$- (1 - s_{EA})(\hat{\mu}_{NEA,EA} + \hat{\tau}_{NEA,EA})$$

where μ is the mark-up, τ are the bilateral trade costs and we use the standard 'from, to' subscript to indicate the direction of trade. Thus s_{EA} is the expenditure share of imports from the euro area in nation-d's price index, and the μ's and τ with EA (euro area) and NEA (non-euro area) subscripts indicate the relevant variables for euro-area and non-euro-area partners. This expression shows that the relative-price channel could be operating via a reduction in bilateral trade costs among euro-area nations, or via a pro-competitive effect of the euro that depressed bilateral mark-ups. Moreover, the expression allows for the fact that euro usage in the importing nation might raise or lower the bilateral cost of exporting for (NEA) nations. It also allows for a distinct pro-competitive effect for NEA to EA exports; for most market structures, however, the equilibrium mark-ups for EA and NEA firms would typically move together. For example, if the euro made competition in the importing market tougher – say due to increased transparency, or easier/safer third-party arbitrage – then we would expect both mark-ups (μ_{EA} and μ_{NEA}) to fall.

The second right-hand term is the expenditure channel and it depends on the extent to which euro usage alters expenditure patterns. Typically, changes in expenditure shares are driven by changes in relative prices, so it is normally difficult to separate this channel from the relative price channel. Most authors ignore this channel by assuming that expenditure shares are fixed.

The third right-hand term is the 'newly traded goods' channel. It depends upon the size of exports by firms with threshold level competitiveness and the size of the change in the threshold.

Trade diversion prediction
If the euro lowered the bilateral trade costs and thus export prices charged by firms based in the euro area, the price index P_d would fall; all the exporting firm's p's are inside P_d as are the prices of locally produced substitutes. If the origin nation-o is not inside the euro area, it

would not benefit from lowering marginal trade costs, but it would still see the drop in P_d. To the extent that the relative-price channel is driven by a euro-related reduction in marginal trade costs – as in the classic transaction cost story – firms outside the euro area should experience a drop in their sales to the euro area due to a P_d-driven increase in their relative price. This is commonly known as trade diversion.

2.2 FDI channels

Mainstream thinking on foreign direct investment (FDI) classifies FDI into two basic types, horizontal and vertical. These are terms of art. They do not exactly correspond to the terminology in the data. 'Horizontal' here means that the firm making the FDI is making exactly the same good in one factory located in the home market and in another factory located in the foreign market: for example, Johnson & Johnson making the same sort of shampoo for the Southern European markets in Spain and for the Northern European markets in Poland. The basic motive is to reduce trade costs by placing manufacturing close to the consumer. This type of FDI is clearly a substitute for trade. Indeed reducing trade is the only benefit from such FDI in the simplest model (e.g. Markusen, 2002).

The term 'vertical' means that the FDI-generating firm is engaged in a process in a facility located at home that is different from the process undertaken in the facility located abroad. This FDI – what might be called unbundling FDI – is clearly a complement to trade. Before the FDI, both processes were bundled spatially at home and only the final output was exported. After FDI, the production process is spatially unbundled and part of it moved abroad, an intermediate good is exported from one factory to another and then the final good is sold to both markets. In other words, unbundling FDI stimulates trade in intermediate goods. Note that in the early versions of this model, e.g. Helpman (1984), the intermediate 'good' was actually intangible headquarter services, so the FDI stimulated trade in what used to be called invisible goods (intellectual property rights, administration, management, marketing, accounting and financial services, etc.).

The latest twist in this approach to FDI has been to add firm heterogeneity. This is not an ideal intellectual exercise since one of the most obvious features of FDI is the role of firm size. While there are always exceptions, FDI is a game played primarily by the largest, most productive firms. (Earlier thinking on the matter ignored firm differences for the most part.) In fact, it is quite easy and instructive to marry the trade effects and FDI effects in a framework where firms have the option of supplying the foreign market via exports, as discussed above, or via local production, i.e. horizontal FDI.

FDI and trade as substitutes: horizontal FDI with heterogeneous firms
Adding in the extra option of local production requires only a minor modification of Figure 17.1. This is done in Figure 17.2. The export profit line is as before, starting from $-F_X$ and rising with firm competitiveness. All firms that are more competitive than the threshold shown will choose to export. The new element is the second solid curve that starts from $-F_H$ and rises faster than the export profit line. Here F_H represents the fixed cost of establishing a second factory to enable local production (H is short for horizontal FDI). It rises faster than the export profit line since local production incurs no bilateral trade costs. (The slope of the FDI profit line is exactly the slope the export profit line would have if bilateral trade costs were zero.) The extra option of local production means that some firms with competitiveness above point 'a' will find it even more profitable to establish a local production facility. The switch-over level is indicated as a_H.

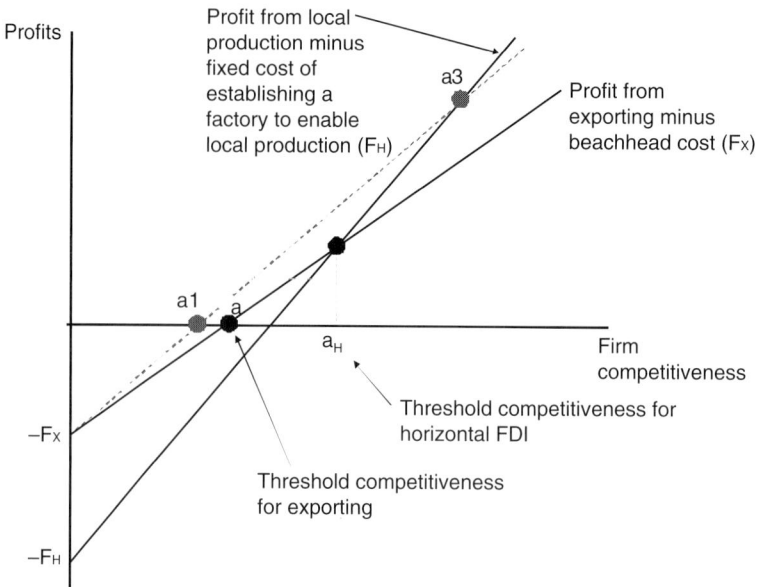

Figure 17.2: Export vs. FDI decision in the HFT model

This equilibrium outcome has many useful contact points with reality. It generates a pattern where small firms sell only in their local market, bigger firms export and the biggest of the big supply the foreign market via horizontal FDI and local production. This is the Helpman *et al.* (2003) framework.

The euro's impact

What happens when the euro is adopted by the origin and destination nations? To keep the diagram simple, consider only the impact of a euro-driven reduction in bilateral marginal trade costs. Nothing happens to the FDI profit line, but the export profit line rotates counter clockwise as before. Interestingly, we see that this moves both the export threshold down and the horizontal FDI threshold up. In other words, the lower trade costs would produce a pro-trade extensive margin effect as more firms found it worthwhile to export, but it would also have an anti-FDI effect since the balance between saving trade costs and sacrificing manufacturing scale tilts towards exporting. More specifically, the euro would not affect the FDI choice of the most competitive firms that already have established production facilities, but it would discourage new firms from setting up new plants aimed at jumping over trade costs. In the terminology of Russ (2007), the euro would be anti-FDI for first-time participants, but less so for veterans.

FDI and trade as complements: vertical FDI with heterogeneous firms (Antras and Helpman, 2007)

The prediction that trade and FDI should be substitutes is extremely unattractive for the job at hand since virtually every empirical investigation over the past two decades has found that they are complements (see BDFST (2008: Chapter 6). Indeed the world pattern of FDI is very close to the world pattern of trade – both in terms of sectoral and geographic patterns. More to the point, the available evidence (see e.g. BDFST, 2008: Chapter 6) suggests that the euro has had a positive effect on FDI, especially within the same manufacturing sector and especially for first-timers. Given the evidence on the euro's pro-trade effect, a model that necessarily predicts a negative correlation between the trade and FDI effects lacks some essential contact points with reality.

As mentioned above the vertical FDI models tend to predict a positive correlation between trade and FDI since the FDI is really just a way of getting parts and components made in foreign nations for less than they can be made locally. To the extent that the euro made this offshoring easier, it stimulates trade in intermediate goods and FDI, while potentially boosting final-good exports as well.

Putting these considerations into a diagram is intrinsically more difficult since we are dealing with a minimum of two types of goods (final and intermediate) and two decisions (the decision to unbundle manufacturing and offshore intermediate good production and the final-good export decision). To deal with this in Figure 17.3, we have to subsume the cost-saving aspects of unbundling FDI (i.e. offshoring) within the firms' overall competitiveness in the final-good market. Thus the thresholds will concern the competitiveness of firms in the final-good market, with the trade implications in intermediate goods pushed behind the scene.

Figure 17.3 is quite similar to Figure 17.2 since the basic economic logic is the same – a tradeoff between high fixed costs and low marginal costs (with FDI), and low fixed but higher marginal costs (with exporting). The difference is in the interpretation of the variables. More importantly, lower trade costs will rotate both curves since both involve trade. Indeed, in the case at hand – where the vertical FDI involves the

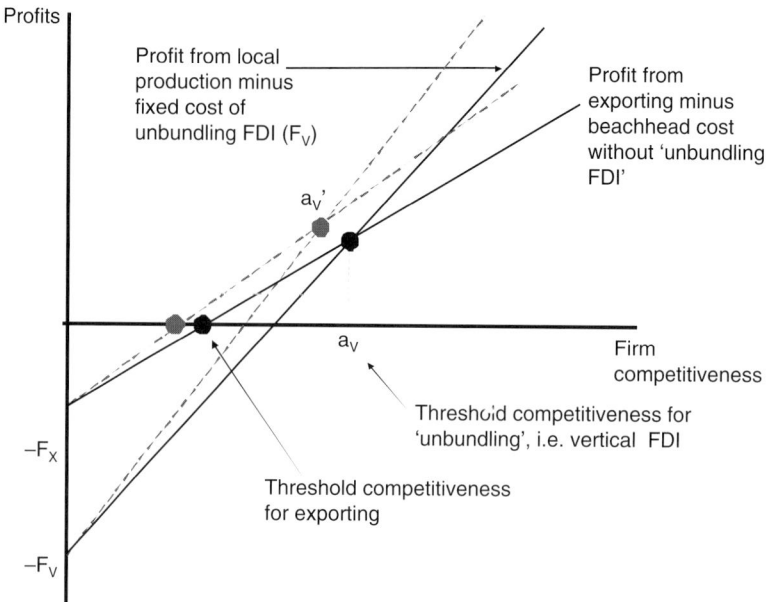

Figure 17.3: Export and unbundling FDI decision in the HFT model

offshored production of a component that is then reimported to the home nation to be incorporated in a final good that is then exported – trade cost changes have a *bigger* impact on the FDI profit line. The reason is simply that this sort of unbundling FDI involves more trade than the bundled production alternative; in both cases, the final good is exported but unbundling FDI creates additional trade in components.

If the euro lowers trade costs, both the export and FDI profit lines rotate counterclockwise for the usual reasons (see above). If, as argued above, the lower trade costs have a bigger impact on the profitability of offshoring FDI (viz. vertical FDI, or unbundling FDI), the new threshold between exporting when production is bundled (i.e. no FDI) and exporting with unbundled production (i.e. FDI) shifts to the left. This means that the euro will raise the level of FDI. Moreover, the impact will be largest on first-timers, i.e. the firms that were competitive enough to export, but not quite large enough to make offshored production profitable. As before, the lower trade costs also boost the range of goods exported (the export threshold shifts left).

3. Evidence on the trade channels

Before turning to the evidence on *how* the euro has affected trade, it is worth reviewing the evidence that it has boosted trade. For most of the last hundred years, the received wisdom of economists and policy makers held that exchange rate volatility and multiple currencies depressed trade. This wisdom derived from causal empiricism – most of it related to the growth of trade during the 'classical gold standard', in the period from 1880 to 1914 (Bordo, 2002). Mundell (1961) used this received wisdom to assert that more trade would be the main microeconomic gain enjoyed when two nations formed a currency union.

Strange as it may seem, this cornerstone of Mundell's famous 'optimal currency area' theory rested on no econometric evidence. Until relatively recently, economists could not find robust empirical evidence that exchange rate volatility had a negative impact on trade flows – despite three decades of increasingly sophisticated empirical methods and larger datasets following the introduction in the 1960s of computers in economic research. Clear results remained elusive, even when empiricists focused on the massive exchange rate turmoil accompanying the break-up of the Bretton Woods system in the 1970s (see, for instance, Wei 1999 or McKenzie 1999).

The situation changed dramatically at the turn of the twenty-first century. Rose (2000) published the startling finding that both exchange rate stability and a common currency were powerful stimulants to trade. More importantly, his estimates seemed to be robust. They withstood an initial barrage of cross-checks and sensitivity analyses (Baldwin 2006a). The pendulum had swung from one extreme to the other.

While it is impossible to fully understand the euro's trade impact without another decade or so of data, the pendulum seems to be coming to rest. The best available estimates of the aggregate trade effect of the euro – the Rose effect – suggest that it is positive, but small (BDFST, 2008: Chapter 2).

3.1 Estimates of the euro's aggregate trade effect

3.1.1 The gravity model

The workhorse in this literature is the gravity model. Taking the GDP of nation-o (Y_o) as a proxy for its production of traded goods, and nation-d's GDP (Y_d) as a proxy for its expenditure on traded goods, and bilateral distance ($dist_{od}$) as a proxy for bilateral trade costs, trade from nation-o to nation-d (V_{od}) can be rewritten to look just like the physical law of gravity:

$$V_{od} = G_{od} \frac{Y_o Y_d}{(dist_{od})^{elasticity-1}}.$$

$$G_{od} \equiv n_{od}\mu_{od}^{1-\sigma} \frac{1}{\Omega_o} \frac{1}{p_d^{1-elasticity}} \quad \text{and} \quad \Omega_o \equiv \sum_j \left(n_{oj}\left(\mu_{oj}\tau_{oj}\right)^{1-\sigma} \frac{E_j}{P_j^{1-\sigma}} \right), ^4$$

where n_{od} stands for the number of nation-o varieties sold in nation-d, μ_{oj} is the bilateral price mark-up, τ_{oj} are the bilateral trade costs, E_d is nation-d expenditure, P_d is nation-d's price index and σ is the elasticity of substitution among varieties.

For panel data, the equation to be estimated is:

$$\ln V_{odt} = (1 - \sigma) \ln(\tau_{odt}) + \ln Y_{ot}E_{dt} - \ln G_{odt}$$

The 'gravitational unconstant' G_{od} is the key to a correct specification of the gravity equation. Since Ω includes E's and P's, it varies over time and over nations. It is important to note that the potential drivers of the euro effect, n_{od}, μ_{od}, and τ_{od} (the number of varieties traded, the price mark-up and bilateral trade costs, respectively), all enter into G_{odt} directly and/or indirectly via P and Ω. Most of the abundant econometric errors in the euro trade literature stem from a failure to properly specify the 'gravitational unconstant' G_{odt}.

Assuming that bilateral trade costs (τ) are related to bilateral distance, common euro usage and other factors (which potentially vary over time and across partners and that we denote as Z_{odt}), the log of τ_{odt} equals $-\beta_1 EZ_{odt} + \beta_2 \ln Dist_{od} + \beta_3 \ln Z_{odt}$. Using the definition of G_{odt}, the model to be estimated is:

$$
\begin{aligned}
\ln V_{odt} = {} & \beta_1(\sigma - 1) EZ_{odt} - \beta_2(\sigma - 1) \ln Dist_{od} + \ln Y_{ot}E_{dt} \\
& + \ln n_{odt} - \beta_3(\sigma - 1) \ln Z_{odt} - (\sigma - 1) \\
& \ln \mu_{odt} - \ln \Omega_{ot} - \ln(P_{dt}^{1-\sigma})
\end{aligned}
\tag{1}
$$

All empirical studies of the euro's trade effects take account of the terms in the first row of the equation; the mistakes arise when they fail to account for the terms in the second row. When these terms are ignored, they show up in the residuals and end up biasing the estimated coefficients for the variables in the first row. The points made above are worth repeating:

- Ω and P are time-varying, so they cannot be controlled by time-invariant country or pair fixed effects – except of course, if one uses cross-section data as in Anderson and van Wincoop (2003); and
- the euro's impact on trade shows up via Z, n and μ as well as EZ; if the second row terms are ignored, the residuals will be correlated with EZ and thus the coefficient for the euro impact on trade will be biased.

Taken at face value, the empirical literature on the boost to trade due to the formation of a monetary and currency union – the so-called Rose effect – is a disaster. Estimates published by eminent professors range from 0 per cent (Berger and Nitsch 2005) to 1,387 per cent (Alesina *et al.*, 2002). Looking beyond the face value, however, the literature is quite cohesive – indeed one can say that a consensus view has emerged. To gain this informed perspective, however, one needs to feel confident about which estimates can be dismissed and why. This requires an investment in understanding the main empirical tool in the field – the gravity equation. While this goes far beyond the scope of this chapter, readers can find an extensive discussion in BDFST (2008) arguing that most estimates of the Rose effect are fatally flawed by misspecification and/or econometric errors. Though those estimates may still be interesting from a history-of-thought perspective, they are useless for today's policymakers.[5]

3.1.2 Improving the estimates

This section summarises the main econometric results from BDFST (2008) which control for two sorts of problems with the existing estimates – econometric flaws and problems with the policy proxies. The first is easily fixed. The second requires some more thinking.

Problems with the naïve euro-area dummy

Almost all of the estimates of the euro's aggregate trade effect proxy for the euro's policy impact with a zero-one dummy that turns on in 1999 or 2002. However, the euro was not a once-and-forever change in the European trading environment. Leaving aside the gradual adjustment of firms to the changes, the actual policy implementation itself was gradual. Most obviously, the euro area was only a monetary union from 1999 to 2001, becoming a full monetary and currency union from January 2002 with the introduction of notes and coins. But there is much more to it. Two major initiatives aimed at facilitating transactions in euro – measures that almost surely affect the cost of intra-euro-area trade and investment – are worth mentioning: the Single Euro Payments Area programme (SEPA), and the Trans-European Automated Real-time Gross settlement Express Transfer system (TARGET).

To counter the problem of costly cross-border electronic payments, the SEPA programme has been championed by the European Commission, the ECB and the European Payments Council (a collection of banks and other interested financial and payments private institutions). The SEPA measures have been gradually implemented since 2001. TARGET is for much larger transfers. It consists of the national real-time gross settlement systems (RTGSs) of the euro-area countries and of the ECB payment mechanism; the RTGSs of Denmark, Poland, Estonia, Slovenia and Britain are connected to provide a uniform platform for the processing of euro payments. The system went live on 4 January 1999, but it has continuously been refined and improved (ECB 2004b).

Single Market measures also pose enormous problems. Since implementation of the Single Market is proceeding in tandem with the introduction of the euro and accompanying policies, it is easy to conflate the Single Market and single currency trade effects. Distinguishing between them requires an accurate proxy for Single Market measures. This is difficult. The Single Market was not a once-and-for-all policy change. Of course, on the face of it, the Single Market started with the Single European Act of 1986 and was completed by December 1992. This reading of history – adopted by many authors in literature (including Baldwin and Taglioni 2007) – hides important initiatives that have happened since and in fact are still ongoing. Many of these 'in process' changes are likely to affect EU trade flows, including those among euro-using nations. This suggests that there is a serious possibility that the existing empirical studies of the Rose effect are conflating unmeasured Single Market integration with euro usage and its amplification by the measures discussed above.

Direct measures of policy changes
In addition to the discussion of policy reforms and the indirect evidence on the economic impact of things that seem to reflect ongoing integration, we have a way of measuring the policy changes – the indices of institutional integration developed by economists following European integration, such as Mongelli *et al.* (2005) shown in Figure 17.4.

Given the facts in the figure, there will be econometric problems when proxying for the currency union with a simple digital dummy that becomes 1 from 1999 for bilateral trade flows among euro-area nations. The same can be said for trying to control for the Single Market's impact with another digital dummy.

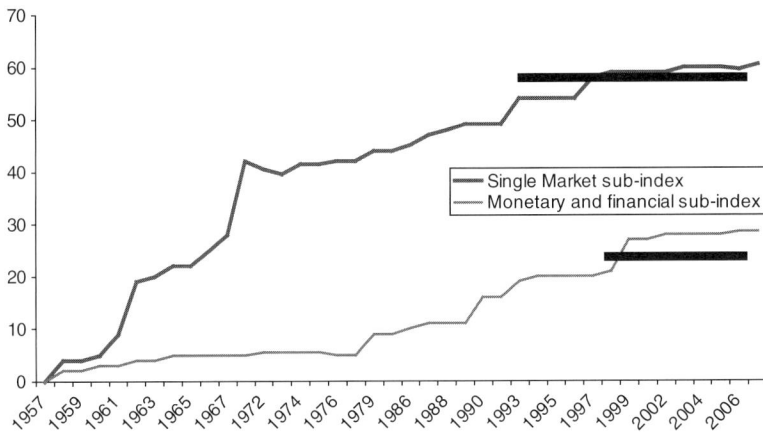

Figure 17.4: The Mongelli-Dorrucci-Agur index of EU integration: Single Market and monetary and financial subindices
Source: Mongelli *et al.* (2005) updated by data provided bilaterally by the authors.

Fixing the estimation problems

A useful strategy is to use the Mongelli-Dorrucci-Agur index to improve the measurement of the two major integration policies operating in the EU over the past fifteen years. Specifically, the estimates use the Single Market index for the whole period to control for the impact of the Single Market and the Monetary and Financial subindex to improve the euro dummy. Specifically, the standard euro dummies $(EA_{11}, EA_{10}, EA_{01})^6$ are interacted with the two Mongelli-Dorrucci-Agur indices. Using data on bilateral goods trade among the EU15 during the period 1995–2006, the new estimates of the euro's trade effects are shown in Table 17.1.

Table 17.1: *OLS on EU15 data, 1995–2006*

	A	B	C	D	E	F
EA_{11}	0.04***	−0.01	0.01	−0.01	0.01***	0.02***
EA_{01}	0.06***	−0.01***	0.00	0.00	0.00	−0.01**
EA_{10}	−0.03***	−0.01*	0.00	−0.02	0.01***	0.03***
ly_o		0.69***			0.2***	
ly_d		0.76***			0.68***	
lry_o	0.71***					
lry_d	0.62***					
Ldistw	−1.22***	−1.12***	−1.18***	−1.27***		
Contig	0.13**	0.1**	0.15***	0.22***		
comlang_off	0.38***	0.42***	0.18***	0.09		
lremot_o	−1.6***	−1.66***			0.00	
lremot_d	3.49***	2.35***			0.00	
landlocked_o	−0.78***	−0.74***			1.49***	
landlocked_d	−0.69***	−0.7***			0.63***	
Lrber	−0.12	0.18***	−0.01	0.39		
lreer_d	0.97**	−1.42***			−0.37**	
smp_o	0.04***	0.01***	−0.01**	−0.04	−0.01***	−0.04***
smp_d	−0.06***	0.01**	0	−0.05*	0.01*	0.02*
_cons	−65.06**	−29.12	30.96***	33.28***	−1.82	21.5***

Dependent variable

Nominal exports = direction-specific value of bilateral exports from country o to country d, current USD (IMF DOT), e.g. for France: $X_\epsilon{}^*$ (USD/EUR)= X_{USD}.

Real exports = value of bilateral exports, CPI deflated IFS and WDI, current USD

Right-hand side variables

EA11 = euro dummy* Index of Monetary and Financial Integration

EA01 = euro importer dummy* Index of Monetary and Financial Integration

EA10 = euro exporter dummy* Index of Monetary and Financial Integration

Table 17.1: (*cont.*)

ly_o = Nominal GDP exporter (source: OECD)

ly_d = Nominal GDP importer (source: OECD)

lry_o = Real GDP exporter, CPI deflated (source: OECD and WDI, current USD)

lry_d = Real GDP exporter, CPI deflated (source: OECD and WDI, current USD)

ldistw = Weighted distance (CEPII)

contig = contiguity

comlang_off = common official language

lremot_o = remoteness exporter (GDP weighted average of distance to all other countries in sample)

lremot_d = remoteness importer (GDP weighted average of distance to all other countries in sample)

landlocked_o

landlocked_d

lrber = real bilateral exchange rate

lreer_d = real effective exchange rate destination country

smp_o = Index measuring EU integration in all fields excluding Monetary and Financial, country of origin

smp_d = Index measuring EU integration in all fields excluding Monetary and Financial, country of destination

Notes: A = OLS in real terms using log-gravity and time dummies; B = OLS in nominal terms using log-gravity and time dummies; C = Importer, exporter and time dummy (i.e. Anderson-Van Wincoop + time dummy) using log-gravity in nominal terms; D = Time-varying importer and exporter using log-gravity in nominal terms; E = Time and pair dummies using log-gravity in nominal terms; F = Time-varying importer and exporter and time invariant pair using log-gravity in nominal terms.
The asterisks (***, ** and *) indicate as usual significance at 1%, 5% and 10% level.

Consider first the correctly specified estimator that takes account of the time-varying aspects of nations' Ω and P in column F. Here the Rose effect is estimated to be positive and highly significant, but small – about 2 per cent. Interestingly, we find some evidence of trade diversion since the EA_{01} measure of the euro's impact (recall that this is now time-varying according to the Mongelli-Dorrucci-Agur subindex) is negative and significant at the 5 per cent level, but very, very small. The impact on the euro area's exports to non-euro users, however, is 3 per cent and highly significant. What this says is that the finding that the euro had no impact or a positive impact on outsiders may have to be revised.

The other estimates, all of which are econometrically flawed (see BDFST, 2008 for further details), tell a similar story. Where the standard gravity controls can be estimated, they are of the expected sign and significance. This is comforting since it shows that our use of the novel proxy for the euro did not introduce major problems with the equation.

It is also noteworthy that our Single Market proxies have some problems in this very short sample: smp_o and smp_d (the dummy variables that switch on when the origin and destination nations are in the Single Market and interact with the Mongelli-Dorrucci-Agur subindex) are estimated to have, respectively, a negative and significant effect and a positive but only borderline significant impact.

In the longer datasets since 1990 (results shown in Table 17.2), where there should be less of a problem with the time-varying policy proxies than

Table 17.2: *OLS on EU15 data, 1990–2006*

	A	B	C	D	E	F
EA11	0.02***	0.01***	0	−0.03	0.01***	0.02***
EA01	0.02***	0	−0.01**	−0.05***	0	0
EA10	−0.01	0	0**	0.01	0**	0.01***
ly_o		0.68***			0.38***	
ly_d		0.75***			0.63***	
lry_o	0.7***					
lry_d	0.59***					
ldistw	−1.21***	−1.11***	−1.15***	−1.14***		
contig	0.18***	0.14***	0.16***	0.24***		
comlang_off	0.39***	0.44***	0.23***	0.18***		
lremot_o	−1.93***	−1.31***			0	
lremot_d	4.35***	2.21***			0	
landlocked_o	−0.82***	−0.76***			−0.81***	
landlocked_d	−0.72***	−0.69***			1.79***	
lrber	−0.25***	0.15***	−0.03	0.2		
lreer_d	−1.6***	−1.06***			−0.44***	
smp_o	0***	0***	0*	0.02***	0*	0.01***
smp_d	0	0***	0	0.02***	0	0
_cons	−81.24***	−36.61**	28.69***	27.46***	−2.91*	20.41***

Notes: A = OLS in real terms using log-gravity and time dummies; B = OLS in nominal terms using log-gravity and time dummies; C = Importer, exporter and time dummy (i.e. Anderson-Van Wincoop + time dummy) using log-gravity in nominal terms; D = Time-varying importer and exporter using log-gravity in nominal terms; E = Time and pair dummies using log-gravity in nominal terms; F = Time-varying importer and exporter and time invariant pair using log-gravity in nominal terms.

there was with the simple digital dummy approach, the Rose effect estimates are found to be remarkably stable, except now the trade diversion result disappears. Still, we find that euro usage seems to promote both trade among euro users and exports from the euro area to non-euro-using nations. The Single Market proxies are also more in line with expectations, although quite small. It would seem that there is still some work to be done on improving our proxy for the Single Market. When we re-do these exercises with the Poisson maximum likelihood estimator, we find qualitatively identical results, which we do not show here for the sake of brevity.

Bottom line: a small 'Rose effect' happened
The bottom line is that some form of 'Rose effect' happened. Trade among euro-using nations is greater than it would have been without the euro. The impact on non-euro-area nations, however, is less clear, apart from the solid fact that it has not led to trade diversion. The cleanest estimates suggest that aggregate trade was boosted by about 2 per cent. Of course, it is a vast oversimplification to talk about 'the' impact of the euro on trade. Much evidence suggests that it is quite different across sectors. Many estimates (see BDFST, 2008: Chapter 2) also suggest that it is different across member states, but there is really not enough data to firmly establish such differences in a credible fashion.

3.2 Relative price channel

Given that it seems clear now that the euro did affect trade, the question arises: how did the euro stimulate trade? Following the analytic framework on the possible channels, we start with evidence on the relative price channel.

The key question is: did the euro's introduction affect trade pricing? Some studies found the price convergence was faster after the euro's introduction but others found the opposite.[7] As far as convergence is concerned, BDFST (2008) presents fresh evidence using the latest data and best econometric techniques. They confirm the negative finding – i.e. prices converged at the same rate before and after the euro – when assuming that there was only one change in the convergence rate and that change occurred in 1999. However, when one estimates year-by-year convergence rates, it is clear that the rate has declined steadily in the euro area, especially since the currency union in January 2002, but has not in the control group of non-euro-area nations. This finding helps explain the lack of consensus in the empirical literature and it leads us to believe that the euro has indeed promoted market integration in terms of pricing.

To test this more carefully, BDFST (2008) provide a theoretically based empirical analysis (inspired by the innovative empirical strategy of Knetter, 1989) that presents more precise evidence on the market integration hypothesis. For all euro-area members, except Ireland, BDFST (2008, Table 12) find that the introduction of the euro reduced export prices by approximately 1–5 per cent. This estimated average export price drop could be due either to a reduction in transaction costs or to changes in market structure that made the market more competitive. Examples of the latter would include the oft-mentioned notion that common pricing in euro increases market transparency and thus makes consumers more price sensitive. In an imperfect competition setting, such heightened price sensitivity translates into lower price-marginal cost mark-ups. However, the export-price drop was observed for only two of the eight non-euro-area nations in the sample.

More specifically, the first bit of evidence on the relative price channel comes from pricing-to-market (PTM) regressions. What the PTM regressions do is to look at the extent to which firms from various euro-area and non-euro-area nations were pricing-to-market before and after the euro. Before the euro the theory tells us that the relation between the export prices of origin nation-o (measured in its own currency) and the bilateral exchange rate for destination nation-d should be:

$$\ln p_{odt} = D_{ot} + D_{od} + \beta \ln e_{odt}.$$

The basic idea is that the first dummy, D_{ot}, captures fluctuations in nation-o's marginal costs that affect the price of its exports to all nations (t); the second dummy, D_{od}, captures pair-specific features like bilateral trade costs and the equilibrium price-cost mark-up in market-d, and finally the last term reflects the pure PTM factor. Here the bilateral exchange rate (e_{od}) is defined as importer currency units per exporter currency unit, so a rise in e_{od} is an appreciation of the exporter's currency. If β is negative, then the exporter is engaging in PTM, since it does not allow the bilateral appreciation to be fully passed through to higher consumer prices in market-d.

The results in BDFST (2008) provide direct evidence that the euro's introduction did change trade pricing inside the euro area. In particular, the euro dummy was negative and significant for all euro-area exporters on their sales to the euro area, with the sole exception of Ireland.

Moreover, when we look at euro-area exports to non-euro-area nations, we do not find this effect. We have eight nations as destinations outside the euro area and we can estimate the change in the level dummy D_{od} (where the nation-o is a euro-area member while the nation-d is not) after 1999, and the change in β. Of the eight possibilities, only one of the level dummies drops (indicating a drop in bilateral trade cost or the equilibrium mark-up). Only one of the PTM coefficients (i.e. β) changes. Using the usual difference in differences interpretation, this suggests that it was the euro area's usage of the euro that was driving down exporter prices within the area rather than, for example, Single Market integration or a general trend towards tougher competition worldwide.

Unfortunately, after the bilateral exchange rate disappears inside the euro area (ln e_{odt} is zero after 1999) we cannot separately identify the change in the level of the mark-up and the change in bilateral trade costs (i.e. the pro-competitive effect and transaction cost savings) from changes in the degree of PTM (reduction in β). There is, nevertheless, indirect evidence that adoption of the euro has led to more unified pricing in the area. This evidence comes from the change in behaviour of outsiders pricing in euro-area nations. The idea behind this deduction is simple. If the euro has made the euro area a more integrated, more competitive market due to, say, greater transparency and cheaper third-party arbitrage, then outsiders should have increased the extent to which they price-to-market in the euro area. In the sample, there are eleven possible destinations in the euro area; Danish firms moved toward pricing-to-market in six of these, Sweden in seven and the UK in ten of them. The USA and Canada moved towards PTM in ten and eleven out of eleven possible markets, respectively. Japanese exporters, by contrast, moved more toward PTM (i.e. the change in β was negative and significant) in only three of the eleven cases.

This indirect evidence is far from perfect since the different exporters send different bundles of goods to the euro area and our estimated changes are an average of the changes in all the markets. Thus, is it conceivable that the market structure changes that clearly affected the export pricing behaviour of the euro area's major trading partners did not affect pricing within the euro area? Given the similarity of the export competition of the UK, Sweden and Denmark to that of the euro area, we believe that this possibility should not be taken too seriously. In short, it seems that the euro changed the pricing behaviour for flows inside the euro area due to changes in market structure as well as changes in bilateral trade costs.

3.3 Lack of trade diversion

While it is not possible to discern the impact of the euro on bilateral trade costs within the euro area (e.g. transaction cost savings), we have indirect evidence that this effect could not have been very large. If the euro stimulated trade by preferentially lowering the transaction cost of nations sharing the euro, we should have witnessed trade diversion at the same time as the trade creation. As BDFST (2008) and other studies it surveys discuss at length, there is no clear evidence that the euro harmed exports from non-euro nations. Indeed some studies show that outsiders' exports to the euro area rose.

Note that the finding that there was a drop in the intra-euro-area export prices after the euro (controlling for other factors) is perfectly consistent with the lack of transaction cost savings. The export price is always the marginal cost of selling to the particular market plus an equilibrium mark-up. Thus what seems to have happened was that the euro's introduction lowered the mark-ups and thus lowered the trade prices of all exporters to the euro area, not just those nations using the euro. To put it differently, the euro's pro-competitive effect impacted prices from all destinations and so did not necessarily lead to trade diversion.

3.4 The newly traded goods channel

The presence of a common currency throughout the euro area is likely to have made it easier for firms to sell products there. One aspect of this may be the lower variable trade cost effect (e.g. transaction cost savings), but as argued above this effect does not seem to have been important. The euro, however, could reduce the fixed cost of entering euro-area markets via economies of scope. For example, instead of having to hold bank accounts in eleven different currencies, arranging hedging for them, making provisions in the company's books; post-1999 an exporter would have only a single currency to deal with. Moreover, if the exporter is located in a euro-using nation, then the forex dimension disappears altogether. Plainly currency-linked fixed costs are not the only market-entry costs – and probably not the most important – but it seems plausible that the euro did lower these beachhead costs.

Lower beachhead costs would stimulate trade in products that firms were already producing and selling in their local markets. This would account for several important empirical facts. First, the euro's trade effect – as extensively documented in BDFST (2008: Chapter 2) – happened rather quickly. Many studies (see BDFST, 2008: Chapter 2) pick up a change in 1998 and almost all see a break by 1999; some find an additional change when the monetary union became a currency union in 2002. If firms were merely selling a wide slice of their product range to foreigners, the pro-trade effect could happen extremely quickly.

Second, the lack of trade diversion is also consistent with the newly traded goods channel. As the discussion of how a common currency would yield economies of scope across markets revealed, the euro's adoption would easily broaden the export range of outsiders as well as that of insiders. This was the story posited in Baldwin (2006a). However, the new evidence presented in BDFST (2008: Chapter 4) based on firm-level data contradicts this. As Figures 17.5 and 17.6 show for euro-outsiders Sweden and Hungary, by comparing the behaviour for euro-area and non-euro-area markets that were in the EU15 (and thus subject to all the Single Market integration schemes), there was very little impact on any of the extensive margins. The number of firms exporting to the two groups of markets tracks extremely closely for the Swedish case. For the Hungarian case, it is the EU15 non-euro-area markets that increase faster.[8] The products-per-firm extensive margin and geographical extensive margin (number of markets per product) move in precisely the same way for the in and out markets, as far as Swedish firms are concerned. The movement is not quite as similar for Hungarian firms, but there is no clear pattern that would suggest that the euro was systematically expanding the range of exported goods for euro-area markets in excess of the effect for non-euro-area markets.

What this leads us to conclude is that the newly traded goods channel operated primarily among euro-area nations. Note that at least for Sweden, the average sale per good per market rose around 1999. We would explain this with the relative price channel as discussed above.

Evidence from trade data for a wider group of nations
Firm-level data is well suited for the task of finding extensive margin changes, but it is currently available only for certain nations. This caveat is what leads us to estimate a quasi-extensive margin using publicly available trade data. The data are based on the harmonised system of trade classification, six-digit level of disaggregation (HS6), the lowest level where worldwide data is available (about 5,000 different product categories). The basic conclusions can be seen in Figure 17.7.

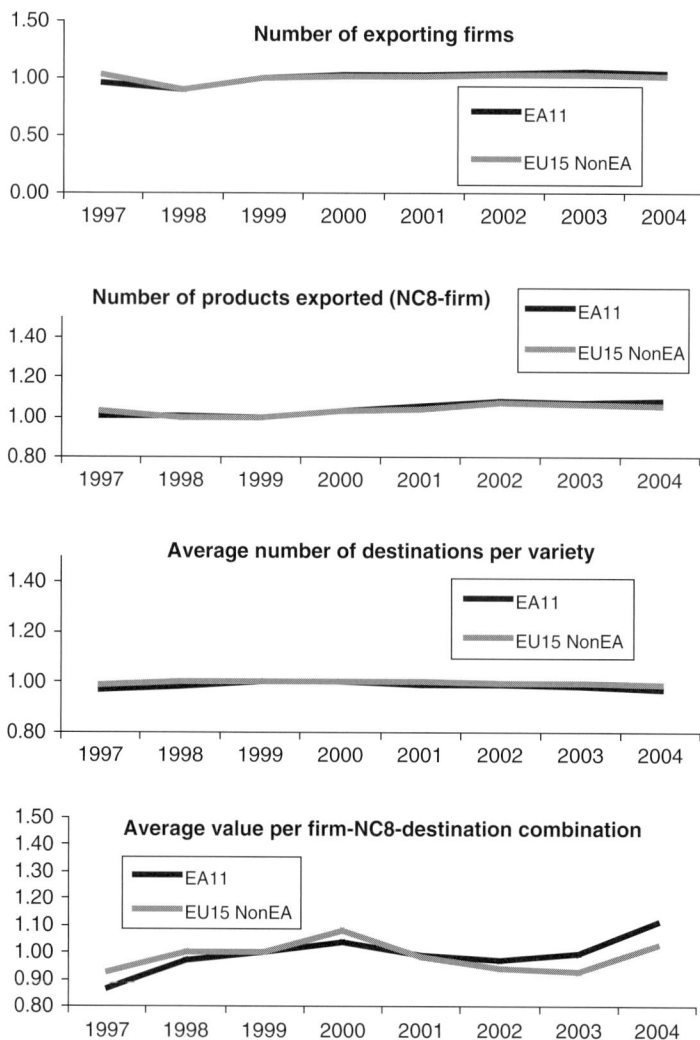

Figure 17.5: Swedish firm-level data, intensive and extensive margins (1999 = 1.0)

Four lines are plotted: the index (1999=1.0) of the number of zeros in trade flows in EA-to-EA trade (EA_{11}), EA-to-non-EA trade (EA_{10}), non EA-to-EA trade (EA_{01}), and non EA-to-non-EA trade (EA_{00}). Since this data is not firm-level, we can only detect a newly exported good when the initial trade flow was zero; this is why we call it the quasi-extensive margin. What we see is that the drop in the number of bilateral zeros

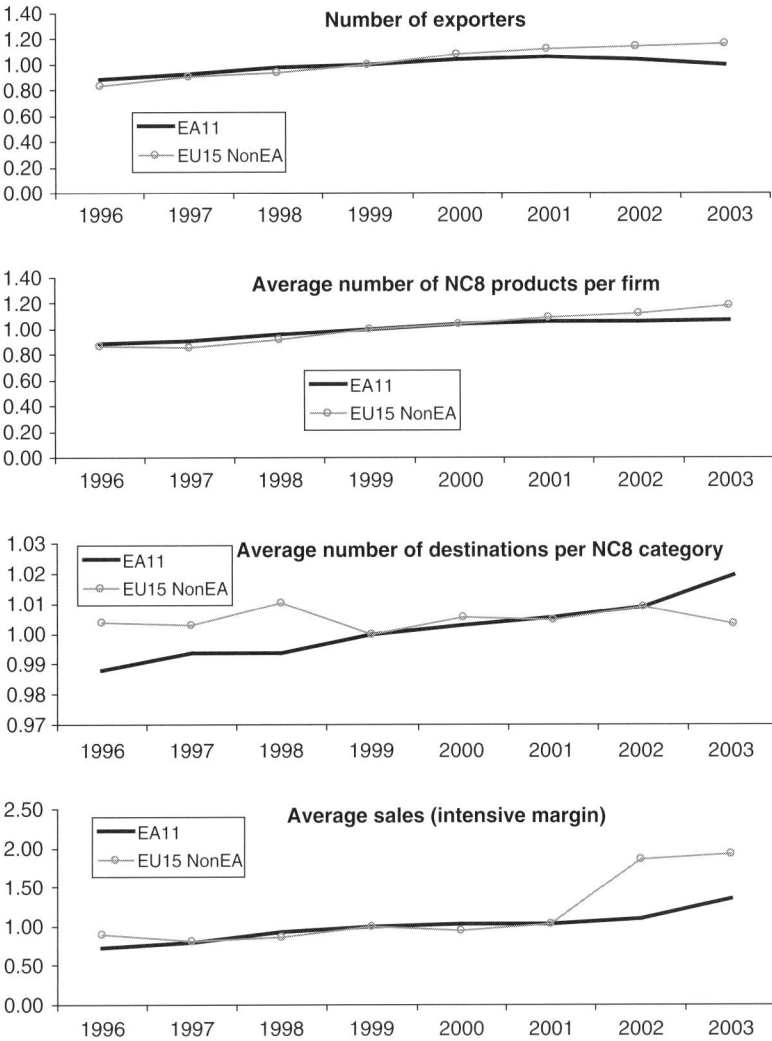

Figure 17.6: Hungarian firm-level data, intensive and extensive margins (1999 = 1.0)

(i.e. the number of HS6 product categories that are not exported from one nation to another) is much more marked for intra-euro-area trade flows (shown as the EA_{11} line) than it is for other flows. Although all of the zeros fall, especially after the physical euro was introduced, the fall is more clear-cut for the intra-EA flows. In particular, we note that

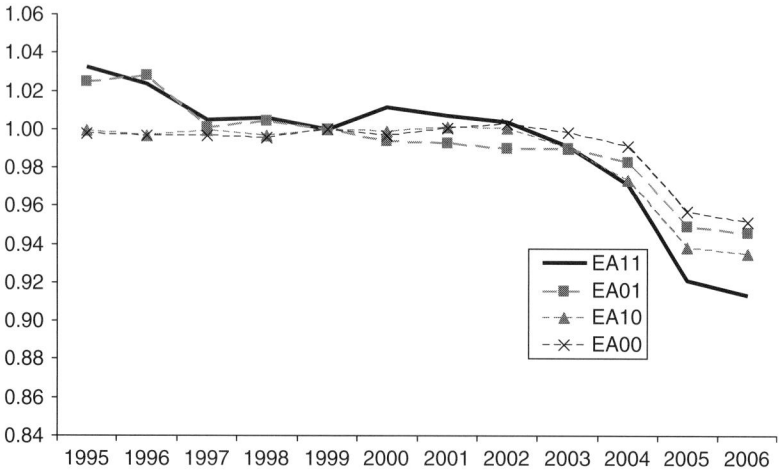

Figure 17.7: Evolution of zeros (prima facie evidence on the newly traded goods hypothesis)

although the flows from the outs to the ins (shown as the EA_{01} line) is below the out-to-out line (shown as EA_{00}), the difference is not great. Therefore, Figure 17.7 provides the basis for believing the econometric results in BDFST (2008), namely that the euro has had an independent impact on the extensive margin of trade.

4. Evidence on the FDI channel

Plainly lower trade costs would make horizontal FDI (where the firm places production in the foreign market in order to avoid the trade cost involved in making the goods at home and shipping it to the foreign market) less attractive so the euro's introduction would be expected to reduce intra-euro-area FDI. Vertical FDI – what we called unbundling FDI – involves a fragmentation of the manufacturing process with each production segment being produced in the nation with the most appropriate cost structure. This geographical dispersion of manufacturing depends upon trade in intermediate goods, and so the euro's pro-trade effects would be expected to stimulate such FDI.

The evidence in the existing literature[9] as well as the new evidence in BDFST (2008: Chapter 6) suggest that overall the euro has been pro-FDI. Various elements seem to suggest that the euro has stimulated vertical FDI. For example, the euro's pro-FDI effect is much larger in manufacturing than it is in services. This fits in perfectly with the unbundling production paradigm as well as with the newly traded goods hypothesis since new vertical FDI would create trade in new intermediate goods. For one thing, while unbundling FDI does go on in services, it is not clear how the euro's adoption would directly affect the desirability of doing so, since little or no trade in goods is involved. It may also be that domestic regulatory barriers in Europe's service sector deter such investments. Moreover, the euro's pro-FDI effect is much larger for deals within sectors than across sectors. Here sectors are very broadly defined (at least compared to the trade data), so this would encompass both pure horizontal FDI, where the firm produces exactly the same good in more than one market, and unbundling FDI that, for example, offshored the production of labour-intensive automobile parts to lower wage nations inside the euro area. The euro has fostered domestic and cross-border M&A activity by both large and small firms, but its effect on small firms is biased towards cross-border activity. Again, this fits right in with the Figure 17.3 analysis. As trade gets easier, more unbundling FDI occurs as firms that were previously indifferent to FDI now engage in it. Since the threshold firms are systematically smaller and less competitive than the firms already engaged in offshoring, we would expect that the euro would have the greatest impact on smaller firms.

When it comes to outsiders investing in the euro area, the evidence (see BDFST, 2008: Chapter 7) points to a clear pro-FDI effect of the euro, but the effect is only about half as strong as the impact within the area. For such countries, the greater integration of the euro-area market might make it more attractive to have a production platform inside the euro area. The conjecture requires further investigation into the nature of the outsiders' investment.

5. Concluding remarks

The introduction of the euro was an immense political and symbolic step towards an integrated Europe. It was also the world's largest economic 'experiment'. This experiment opens the door to a major advance in our understanding of how a common currency affects economic activity, ranging from trade and FDI to wage-setting behaviour and corporate business strategies. A series of studies stretching back to the early years of the decade has begun to piece together a wide range of results. Though the resulting collage is still not fully coherent, BDFST (2008), on which this chapter is based, made a number of coherence-building contributions.

When it comes to the euro's trade effects our first contribution is to refine 'the number'. Using the latest data and best empirical methodology, we confirm the received wisdom that the euro has promoted trade significantly, with the aggregate impact being in the range of 2 per cent or so. Note that this result is obtained after we have made great efforts to separate the euro's impact from the impact of other pro-integration policies that were also being implemented in the 1999–2006 period, notably the Single Market programmes. This effort has tended to shift down the aggregate number but it is necessary to be absolutely sure that it is the euro that has caused the effect.

Our second main contribution is to advance and refine our understanding of exactly *how* the euro is boosting trade. Which economic channels are important and which are not? Logically, there are two main channels to consider, each with a number of subchannels. The first is the relative price channel. Simply put, this argues that the euro has boosted trade inside the euro area since it has lowered the relative price of traded goods coming from the euro area. Since prices depend upon marginal costs and the price-cost mark-ups, the lower relative price could come from two main sources – a reduction in bilateral trade costs among euro-area nations (e.g. lower transaction costs, hedging costs, etc.), or an increase in competition that pushed down trade prices via a pro-competitive effect. The two sources are easily distinguished since the lower trade costs were preferential – affecting only intra-euro-area trade – and should, therefore, have led to trade diversion. They did not, so we can be fairly confident that the transaction cost story is not of first-order importance. Direct evidence from pricing regressions suggests that the euro did indeed have a pro-competitive effect on exporters' prices, for both euro-area and non-euro-area-based exporters. We also found evidence that outsiders were moving towards pricing-to-market strategies, suggesting that they view the euro area as a single market. Indirect evidence on this exact point comes from the heightened convergence of export prices within the euro area.

The second main channel – first posited by Baldwin and Taglioni (2004) and elaborated in Baldwin (2005, 2006a) – is the newly traded goods channel. The basic idea is that the euro induced firms to export a wider range of their products to the euro area. Thus, not only was trade in existing products stimulated, but newly traded goods also contributed to the pro-trade effect. Evidence based on four firm-level datasets seems to confirm the new-goods hypothesis rather resoundingly. Moreover, this new evidence sheds important light on the lack of trade diversion. Earlier studies had suggested that the lack of trade diversion might have been caused by an expansion of the range of goods exported by the 'outs' to the 'ins'. Firm-level trade data from Sweden and Hungary, however, show that this did not happen. In the Swedish case the main rise in its exports to the euro area was due to the so-called intensive margin, namely the old-fashioned way of raising trade – increasing the average sales per product exported. Combining this evidence with our new pricing regressions suggests that the absence of trade diversion was due to the pro-competitive effect of the euro on outsiders' export pricing strategy. That is, as the euro made the euro-using nations more like a single market, boosting pricing transparency and making third-party arbitrage safer, euro-area import customers became more price sensitive and the outsider exporters responded by cutting price-cost margins. This lowered their relative prices and thus stimulated sales. In BDFST (2008) we have also looked at new evidence on this second channel taken from data that is more aggregated than the firm-level data, though still very disaggregated overall and available for all nations. The new evidence confirms the firm-level findings.

Our third main contribution concerns the euro's pro-FDI effects. The empirical work on the FDI effects is much less rich than that on the trade effect. This is not due to a lack of interest; in the world of modern business, cross-border investment is an integral part of firms' (especially large firms') international strategies. Moreover, it is widely thought that FDI brings with it valuable foreign know-how that comes from trade alone. The problem is that both the data and the empirical methodology are much less well developed.

Using the best available data, theory and econometric techniques, one may conclude that both Single Market integration and euro-area membership have pro-FDI effects. The key points are as follows. First, the euro's pro-FDI effect was much larger in manufacturing than in services. It is likely that the level of protection and barriers to entry in the service sector act as a strong deterrent to cross-border mergers and acquisitions (M&As) in services across countries. To the extent that the new 2006 services directive breaks down such barriers, it may trigger a new wave of cross-border M&As within the EU.

Second, the euro's pro-FDI effect has been much larger for deals within sectors than across sectors. Thus the euro has facilitated cross-border M&As within the euro area, which aim to restructure capital within the same sector of activity, rather than boosting the formation of conglomerate activities between sectors.

Third, the euro has fostered domestic and cross-border M&A activity by both large and small firms, but its effect on small firms is biased towards cross-border activity.

Fourth, the euro has promoted FDI from outside the euro area, but this effect is only about half as strong as the impact within the area.

Finally, the 'bottom line' number – the overall pro-FDI effect – is not clear. Most authors find it is positive, but the estimates range from +15% for in-to-in flows and +7.5% for out-to-in, to +200% and +100%, respectively for the in-to-in and out-to-in flows.

5.1 Look forward

Whatever else we have learned about the microeconomics of European monetary union, it is now clear that it did not operate via the standard Mundellian transaction costs story that suggests the microeconomic gains from monetary union are very much like preferential tariff cuts. While the profession is a long way from fully understanding the euro's pro-trade and pro-FDI effects, it is clear that much of the measured impact has come from newly traded goods and much less from price effects. There is, however, much more to learn.

Notes

1. See Mongelli (this volume) for a survey and the link between the OCA theory and the path to monetary union in Europe.
2. Of course if the euro had a growth effect it could boost trade by boosting expenditure, but this is not typically considered part of the euro's trade effect and indeed all empirical work controls directly or indirectly for expenditure, so when the literature (e.g. Rose 2000) speaks of the pro-trade effects of a currency union, it is explicitly ruling out the effect that might occur via a change in the level of expenditure in the importing nation.
3. There are a couple of more exotic possibilities, controlling for relative prices and expenditure. Preferences can change, especially for intermediate goods where preferences reflect production technology rather than

subjective preferences, and this may raise or lower exports at constant relative prices and expenditure. There is also the possibility that customers' information sets change, i.e. they find out about foreign varieties that they did not know about previously. Normally this sort of change heightens trade.

4. In the economic geography literature Ω_o is called the exporting nation's 'market access' or 'market potential'. Wei (1996) calls it nation-o's 'remoteness'

5. Micco et al (2003) is the first published study applying the techniques of Rose (2000) to the euro area. Subsequent work by Gomes *et al.* (2004), Flam and Nordstrom (2003, 2006, 2007), Berger and Nitsch (2005), Barr *et al.* (2003), Bun and Klaassen (2007), Vinhas de Souza (2002), Piscitelli (2003), Baldwin and Taglioni (2004), Baldwin *et al.* (2005), Anderton *et al.* (2005), Mancini-Griffoli and Pauwels (2006), De Nardis and Vicarelli (2003a; 2003b) De Nardis *et al.* (2007), Gil-Pareja *et al.* (2008), and Baldwin and Taglioni (2007).

6. EA stands for euro area and the subscripts indicate whether both origin and destination nations use the euro (11), when the origin nation does not use the euro, while the destination nation does (01), and when the origin nation uses the euro, but the destination nation does not (10).

7. The studies that found that the euro has had a significant effect on price convergence include papers like Allington *et al.* (2005), Imbs *et al.* (2004), Isgut (2004), Matha (2003) and Parsley and Wei (2001). Baye *et al.* (2006), Engel and Rogers (2004), Lutz (2003) and Rogers (2002) are the main papers that find no evidence of faster convergence in pricing behaviour. The conflicting results are accounted for by several factors. Notably, the datasets employed in these studies are not exhaustive; many concentrate on a few goods. Another problem is the lack of consensus on the definition of price dispersion. Some studies use the log average of price difference, the average price volatility or mean squared error, the coefficient of variation, the log of absolute average difference, or the difference between minimum and maximum prices. Some authors use national prices, other use local (city) prices. Some studies are purely cross-sectional while others use panel data and the studies are different along other econometric-techniques dimensions as well.

8. This had to do with a trade offset deal concerning Hungary's purchase of the Swedish Grippen fighter planes.

9. See for example Taylor (2008), Petroulas (2007), Coeurdacier *et al.* (2008), Russ (2007), De Sousa and Lochard (2006) and Schiavo (2007).

Comment 13: Comment on Chapter 17

KARL PICHELMANN

This is a fine summary chapter on refining and retelling the story about the euro's impact on trade and foreign investment (based on a much larger study by Baldwin *et al.* 2008). It makes three main contributions: firstly, it offers a refinement of 'the number' attached to the aggregate pro-trade effect, with its 'best estimate' well below the prevailing consensus figures; secondly, it advances and refines our understanding of exactly how the pro-trade channels are operating, basically rejecting the conventional explanations related to the elimination of transaction costs and exchange rate volatility with the associated currency risk; and thirdly, it aims to contribute to a refined knowledge about the size and nature of the euro's pro-FDI effects.

1. The refined 'number': getting close to zero?

After a brief period of euphoria in some quarters following Rose's (2000) result that a common currency would raise trade by as much as 235 per cent, both economists and policy makers have now arrived at a much more sober assessment of the trade creation effect of adopting a single currency. Indeed, subsequent literature has pointed to a series of technical issues blurring these initial estimates and pointed to at most a 10 per cent trade increase in the case of the euro (Baldwin and Taglioni, 2007), with a prevailing consensus estimate in the range of 5–15 per cent. The present chapter provides new estimates of the 'Rose effect' which attempt to correct for misspecification and/or other econometric flaws; and in particular, the new estimates try to take into account the gradual nature of the change in the European trading environment due to the Single Market Programme and the introduction of the euro. The result of a specification in terms of two processes evolving over time rather than of discrete events at one point in time (replacing the usual simple digital dummies for the impact of the Single Market and the euro by time-varying indices) is to reduce the estimate of the 'Rose effect' even further to only about 2 per cent. Thus, in a statistical sense, the euro appears to have significantly boosted aggregate trade among euro-area members, but the size of the estimated impact has come down to a value which is quite unlikely to impress policy makers. Indeed, if one thinks (wrongly, in my view, but not totally uncommon) in terms of a tradeoff between macroeconomic costs and microeconomic gains such a finding, if taken at face value, should make monetary union, all else being equal, considerably less attractive. However, the downward correction of the 'Rose number' may have gone too far as interacting the standard Single Market and euro dummies with the upward trending time-varying Mongelli indices also leads to implausibly low – and even negative – estimates of the Single Market effect. Therefore, as acknowledged by the author, clearly 'there is still some work to be done to improve our proxy for the Single Market'. In any case, though, separating the euro's impact from the impact of other pro-integration policies, notably the Single Market programmes, will probably always be somewhat artificial, as it may be reasonably argued that 'you cannot have one without the other', interacting in a complex dynamic process.

In line with much of the recent literature – and unsurprisingly, given the small estimated aggregate trade effect – the chapter finds little or no trade diversion effects. In conclusion, it is rightly argued that the transaction cost savings entailed by common euro usage cannot be a major part of the explanation for the pro-trade effect. Additional evidence for this comes from the fact that the impact of the euro on trade varied greatly across sectors and firms, while the conventional currency-linked transaction cost story would suggest that the impact should spread quite evenly over most sectors. Instead, the chapter identifies two other relevant channels, namely (i) a pro-competitive effect pushing down trade prices of all exporters to the euro-zone, not just of those nations using the euro; and (ii) the 'newly traded goods' channel in the form of increased trade in the euro area along the extensive margin (the number of varieties and the number of destinations for each variety within the euro area) due to lower beachhead costs, i.e. the fixed market entry costs. A growing body of literature based on firm-level data does indeed suggest that this mechanism has been at work in the euro area (see for example Berthou and Fontagné (2008) who show that changes in French firms' exports to eurozone markets have been driven more by the extensive margin than the intensive margin), while such effects were not present for outsiders. Obviously, as in all good research, these findings raise a host of new questions, in particular how the working of these channels relates to specific market structures, such as the extent of concentration, ease of entry and scale economies, and to prevailing product market regulations.

As regards the euro's impact on FDI, the chapter concisely summarises the available findings in the literature, suggesting in particular that the pro-FDI effect is coming primarily from investment related to the establishment of international supply chains, so-called unbundling FDI. It is noteworthy that the euro's pro-FDI effect was much larger in manufacturing than it was in services, no doubt due to the much higher degree of integration of goods markets. However, as the chapter admits, given the host of problems with FDI data it is notoriously difficult to pin down a number on the pro-FDI effect in any narrow range.

PART VII

Structural reforms

18 | *Labor markets in EMU: what has changed and what needs to change*

GIUSEPPE BERTOLA

1. Introduction

Labor market policies have desirable and undesirable implications regarding the tradeoffs between employment and unemployment on the one hand, and unemployment benefits, wage levels, and wage inequality on the other. The position and shape of the relevant tradeoffs and respective policy choices depend on both the structural and political characteristics of countries. Economic integration is an important source of change in both respects, and the Economic and Monetary Union (EMU) might influence national labor market policies and outcomes through a variety of channels. Policy making, like markets, is far from perfect, and does not always take into account all of its implications within and across countries. Loss of alternative macroeconomic instruments can overcome resistance to reforms of labor market institutions. In the "there-is-no-alternative" (TINA) view, monetary union would force reform of "bad" policies, as national policy makers would face the consequences of inefficient regulation. Moreover, the closure of devaluation "escape routes" would also foster wage moderation as wage setters would face clearer and sharper employment costs. Loss of monetary policy independence, however, could instead release wage demands that were kept in check by the threat of tough monetary policy reactions at the national level. And resistance to reform may remain strong if labor market policies are perceived to protect household income from uninsurable risk, a goal that may be more important and become more elusive when labor markets are subject to international competitive pressures that introduce new risks and make it difficult for national policy makers to implement policies aimed at correcting market imperfections.

I acknowledge helpful comments on a preliminary draft from Commission staff and remain responsible for any errors and all views expressed.

This chapter brings such theoretical perspectives to bear on empirical policy and outcome patterns before and after EMU. If policy making processes are shaped by sharper disemployment effects and more damaging efficiency losses in more tightly integrated economies, EMU should be associated with labor market deregulation. To the extent that reforms take time and are at least partly unrelated to the changing effects of policies, we also expect labor market policies to have stronger effects on unemployment and employment in more open economies. And if regulation aims at equalizing and smoothing labor income, reforms should be associated with higher inequality and more intense access to private financial markets as well as with lower unemployment and higher employment rates.

Section 2 characterizes the desirable and undesirable aspects of labor market policies and discusses how their effects and objectives may become more or less important with international economic integration. Policies may aim at changing the distribution of income between labor and other factors of production while inefficiently reducing the amount of output produced by available resources, or at correcting market imperfections, improving protection against risks, and fostering incentives to undertake human capital investments. Economic integration changes the position and shape of the relevant tradeoffs in ways that worsen the undesirable side effects of labor market policies. And the ability of policies to target their desirable effects is further weakened by the fact that, as each policy maker only considers costs and benefits within his or her own constituencies, uncoordinated policy choices differ from those that would be chosen by political interactions at the level of the integrated economic area. As a number of opposing tendencies may be at work in theory, Section 3 examines the empirical question of how in practice EMU has affected labor market policies and outcomes. A broad range of formal comparisons of policies and outcomes across groups of EMU, EU, and other countries uncovers evidence of an association of EMU with deregulation and higher employment. The evidence also confirms that economic integration strengthens the negative effects of labor market policies. For example, labor tax rates do appear to depress employment more in the EMU portion of the available sample. If this is what drives reforms, the intended effects of labor market policies should also become less apparent in the data. To see whether any price has to be paid for better employment performance, and whether other concurrent developments also affect outcomes, Section 4 studies the empirical relationship between EMU, inequality, and financial market development. Section 5 concludes, discussing the policy implications of the theoretically plausible pattern of empirical results, focusing in particular on the sustainability of economic integration in the absence of international policy coordination or of access to efficient financial markets for purposes of household consumption smoothing.

2. Labor market policy and economic integration

Many labor market policies reduce employment and increase unemployment but, of course, that is not their primary purpose. When financial markets and/or public redistribution schemes are imperfect, inaccessible, or ineffective, then minimum wages, collective bargaining, unemployment insurance, and employment protection legislation can target income redistribution across individuals and over time. In doing so, they cannot generally avoid loss of productive efficiency: unemployment insurance and employment protection tend to shift labor into unemployment, and to remove individual mobility incentives to allocate labor where it would be most productive. This section discusses how labor market regulation's desirable and undesirable effects depend on an economy's structure and, in particular, on the extent of international economic integration.

2.1 Motivation and effects of labor market policy

Policy interferes with laissez-faire in labor markets for a variety of reasons, and with a variety of microeconomic and macroeconomic effects (see Bertola, 1999, and Arpaia and Mourre, 2005, for reviews of the theoretical and empirical literature). Difficult access to financial markets and limited ownership of non-labor income flows can explain why workers benefit from increased wages and decreased employment even though that decreases total production and other agents' income.

Financial market imperfections can similarly support other types of labor market policies. Much as it would be desirable for households to obtain insurance against job loss, private markets cannot supply it as easily as insurance against earthquakes. Job loss, like serious health problems and other life-shaping events, can result from the individual's own behavior as well as from objective circumstance. To the extent that the former cannot be observed and the latter are hard to verify, an insurance contract specifying the circumstances where a worker would be entitled to compensation when fired would be exceedingly complex to write, and essentially impossible to enforce privately. Workers covered by private insurance contracts would not work as hard, and would be fired so much more promptly than uninsured workers as to make insurance either unprofitable for the issuer, or too costly for purchasers.

Governments have obvious enforcement advantages (and indeed supply law and contract enforcement services to market interactions), and may exploit better information about individual circumstances and interactions across agents. When market interactions cannot exploit sufficiently broad and reliable information, taxation of lucky individuals and payment of subsidies to unlucky ones can potentially fulfill the same need for insurance as missing financial contracts. If it does succeed in serving the same purpose that markets would pursue, redistribution need not decrease productive efficiency, and may well increase it if they encourage risk-taking behavior. For example, unemployment insurance, by allowing risk-averse workers to prolong their search, improves the productivity of the job they eventually accept (Acemoglu and Shimer, 1999).

But policies face tradeoffs, because they could unambiguously improve all aspects of welfare only in very unrealistic circumstances. There is no guarantee that efficiency is the only goal of policy makers, because political decision processes are also shaped by inefficient rent-seeking incentives. And, even more importantly, the information problems that prevent financial markets from providing insurance also imply efficiency losses from imperfect government policies. Workers will not work as hard to avoid job loss and to find new jobs when they are insured against unemployment, and making it difficult for employers to fire redundant workers stabilizes workers' labor income but also slows down labor reallocation towards more productive jobs, thus reducing production and profitability.

The simplest and most familiar illustration of the impact of labor market policies is that shown in Figure 18.1. If workers faced by a downward-sloping labor demand function only care about the aggregate wage bill, they are collectively better off when the wage is set at a level higher than that which equates supply and demand, and employment is correspondingly lowered: working is a matter of indifference at

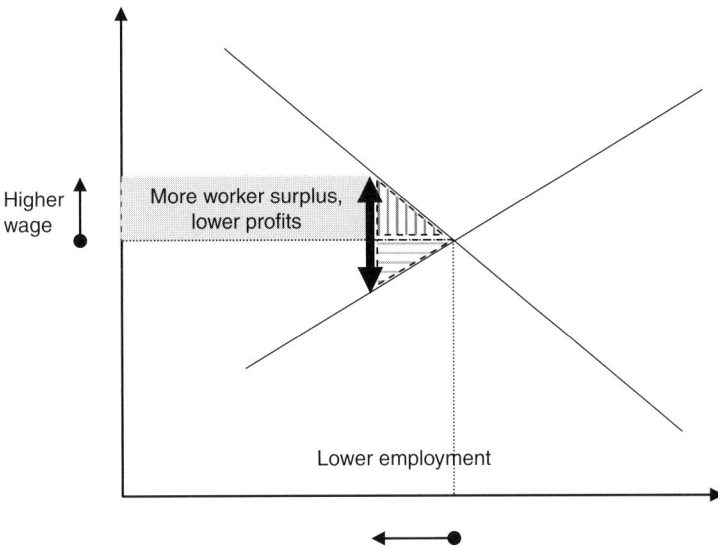

Figure 18.1: The effect of minimum wages or labor taxes that finance subsidies to workers

Notes: Labor's surplus increases (and non-labor income declines) by the area of the shaded rectangle. The triangles near the equilibrium points are a labor surplus loss (horizontal shading), and a further profit loss (vertical shading).

the margin in competitive equilibrium, and as wages become discretely higher (along the demand curve) than the opportunity cost of working (along the supply curve) the lower welfare of workers who fall back on that outside opportunity is more than compensated for by the higher wage earned by the workers who remain employed, up to a point that is reached sooner when labor demand is flatter.

The shape of labor supply is also relevant to the effects of policies. As discussed by Bertola *et al.* (2007), policy wedges between labor demand and labor supply are associated with sharper employment effects but smaller worker-welfare losses when labor supply is flatter. This can explain why labor market regulation tends to cause larger employment declines for worker groups with relatively elastic labor supply, such as women and youth. Of course, a variety of other factors also affect employment rates of different demographic groups, and it will be important to take them into account when analyzing theoretical and empirical implications of economic integration below.

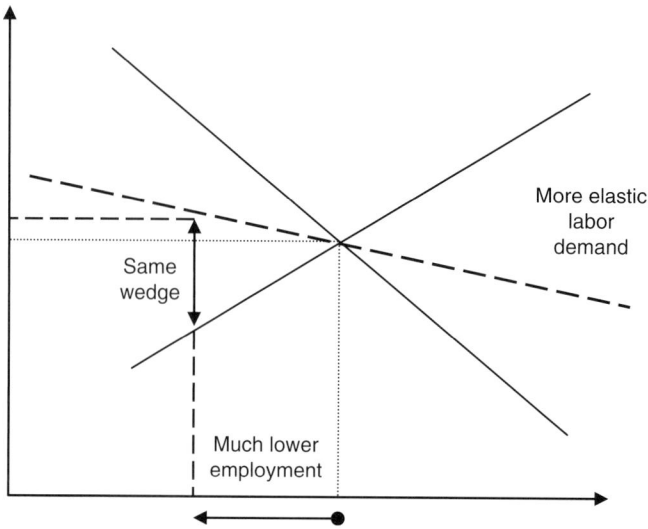

Figure 18.2: Flatter slope of labor demand strengthens the employment and unemployment impact of policy wedges

2.2 *Economic integration and the impact of policies*

A basic implication of international economic integration for the con-figuration and performance of labor markets is simply stated and illu-strated. Trade and factor mobility increase the elasticity of employers' reactions to labor costs. As shown in Figure 18.2, a flatter (more elastic) labor demand relationship implies greater employment losses for any given wedge inserted between labor demand and supply, such as those implied by legal or contractual constraints that prevent the unemployed from underbidding employed workers, or by payroll taxation funding non-employment subsidies, such as pensions or unemployment benefits or other welfare transfers. Lower employment, up to a point, still increases aggregate labor income (to be distributed across workers in the form of transfers within families and over their lifetime as well as of formal unemployment or pension benefits). But the smaller wage gains implied by flatter labor demand reduce the positive (for workers) effects of labor market policies.

Further, efficiency losses from these and other policies are more damaging when production choices can react more promptly and more widely to them. For example, employment protection stabilizes labor incomes at the expense of production efficiency and profits, as it shifts to firms the labor income risk that otherwise would be shared in financial markets or borne by unemployment insurance schemes, while it slows down labor reallocation (Bertola, 2004). The price to pay for labor income stability is higher when lower profits imply capital outflows, or international shocks require more frequent and intense labor reallocation.

Higher elasticity of labor demand is a theoretically and empirically plausible consequence of economic integration (see OECD, 2007b, for empirical evidence). It is not its only consequence, however, and economic integration has broader implications for the desirability and feasibility of labor market policies. Whether and the extent to which economic integration tends to increase the elasticity of labor demand depends on modeling details, on the structure of economic interactions, and on concurrent technological and cultural trends which may also affect the position and shape of labor supply.

While economic integration effects on demand elasticity should be most pronounced in tradeable sectors of the economy, labor market outcomes in nontradeable sectors may be driven by labor supply developments, such as more intense unskilled immigration and increased female labor supply participation. However, deindustrialization trends, foreign direct investment patterns (Scheve and Slaughter, 2004), and new ways to trade service components of traditional production processes (Baldwin, 2006c) blur the traditional distinction between tradeable and nontradeable goods, and make it difficult to assess the interaction between sectoral labor demand patterns and demographic labor supply developments.

As integration tends to foster efficiency of employment, it increases the level as well as the cost sensitivity of labor demand. Hence, wages and employment can both increase even as the optimal collective bargaining mark-up falls (Nicoletti *et al.*, 2001; Andersen and Skaksen, 2007). To the extent that labor market rigidities prevent countries from reaping the fruits of economic integration, their effects on employment and productivity should be all the more negative as technical progress and policy reforms dismantle barriers to international trade and factor mobility. But a higher elasticity of labor demand also implies more volatility of employment and wages in response to product market shocks (Scheve and Slaughter, 2004). This increases the appeal of policies meant to buffer the welfare implications of uninsurable risk.

International economic integration, however, allows market participants not only to pursue efficiency more freely, but also to circumvent
collective regulation. As economic integration makes it difficult or
impossible to enforce policies meant to shape individual choices differently from what would be implied by imperfect market mechanisms, it
increases the desirability of labor market regulation (as long as markets
remain imperfect) at the same time as it decreases its efficacy.

   In practice, the balance of these forces may associate economic integration with more or less pervasive institutional interference with labor
market mechanisms (Agell, 2002). There is evidence in the literature on
the tension between more general government policies and internationalization of economic relationships. While the risks entailed by international trade and specialization may lead more open countries to
engage in more pervasive interference with market-driven income distribution processes, increasing openness may make such interference
moot. Rodrik (1998a) documents a positive association between government size and openness in a short panel of countries; but in a longer
panel, in specifications with country fixed effects, Bertola and Lo Prete
(2008) find that increasing openness is significantly associated with
smaller government size and lower social expenditure, and more
strongly so in countries with better developed financial markets. This
is consistent with the notion that international competition increases the
relevance of cost competitiveness and challenges governments' power
to regulate markets (Sinn, 2003; Bertola, 2007a), and a stronger
tendency for globalization to erode government policies is not surprising in countries where financial markets make it less necessary to rely
on government redistribution in order to smooth consumption. Bertola
and Lo Prete (2008) also report similar (if weaker) evidence of a
negative association between greater openness and labor market
regulation.

2.3 Economic integration, macroeconomics, and policy implications

If economic integration increases the responsiveness of market interactions and heightens the negative implications of interference with
laissez-faire labor markets, one might expect less pervasive and less
distortive policies to be chosen by policy makers (Bertola and Boeri,
2002). But smooth adjustment to changing structural conditions

requires a suitable environment. Centralized wage bargaining can be beneficial when it is "coordinated" (Calmfors and Driffill, 1988), i.e. when it properly takes into account the country-level employment implications of wage demands. Collective bargaining at intermediate levels of centralization, such as sectors or occupations, can instead generate excessive unemployment, even from the union's own point of view, if it leads to uncoordinated wage demands to leap-frog each other in an attempt to grab purchasing power from other sectors. Stronger product market competition (and, in tradeable sectors, international competition) tend to reduce such excessive unemployment tendencies, because wage moderation will be enforced by loss of market share and employment in favour of foreigners (Danthine and Hunt, 1994). But unions, whether nationwide or not, may fail to internalize this mechanism: if bad labor relations imply that wage demands are slow to learn that the changing structure of economic interactions imposes a stronger penalty on high labor costs, then international economic integration and product market deregulation may increase unemployment (Blanchard and Philippon, 2004). Slow adaptation is all the more likely and dangerous if wages and labor costs are shaped by institutional constraints, such as legal minimum wages and tax wedges, that should but need not be reformed when international economic integration increases the elasticity of employment to cost conditions.

There are other interactions between labor market institutions and internationalization of economic activities. Encompassing unions, such as those traditional in Scandinavian countries, can assess the implications of unemployment insurance and other labor market policies from the perspective of the country as a whole: in particular, a transparent link between contributions and benefits at the level of the government's budget reduces wage-setters' inclination to demand high take-home pay (Summers *et al.*, 1993), and puts them in a better position to understand that allowing wage differentiation can serve collective goals when globalization increases the returns of reallocation of labor towards more productive occupations and sectors (Andersen *et al.*, 2008).

Internationalization of economic relationships also has implications for the conduct of monetary policy. To the extent that international competition flattens the Phillips curve relationship between economic activity and wages or prices, globalization reduces time-inconsistent temptations to produce inflationary surprises.[1] Since monetary policy is conducted by the European Central Bank for all member countries of EMU, however, any change in monetary policy's economic impact should be attributed to the new monetary policy environment rather than to tighter economic integration across the member countries.

2.4 Labor markets in a monetary union

Broader and stronger markets shape the effects of labor market policies in any economic integration experience. That mechanism is operative in EMU because a single money strengthens the single market's implications for the competitiveness of markets. The absence of currency risk reduces the extent to which price and wage stickiness may blur relative productivity signals, and assigns a more important role to competitiveness in broader and integrated markets for goods, services, and financial products. Deeper integration fosters efficiency not only by letting market participants make wider-ranging and better informed production and consumption choices, but also by exerting pressure towards efficiency-enhancing reforms, which may also be spurred by the absence of devaluation and other macroeconomic escape routes towards at least temporarily better competitiveness (Belke *et al.*, 2007, review the relevant theoretical channels and evidence).

The European countries that joined EMU are characterized by particularly pervasive and possibly inefficient regulation of labor markets, and EMU's peculiarly strong form of economic integration also fosters political incentives to improve labor market flexibility: since member countries renounce all independence in monetary and trade policy, and much independence in other policies, political processes that might otherwise preserve the institutional status quo of labor markets can be forced into reform. According to the TINA view, EMU countries will be forced to deregulate their labor markets (Bertola and Boeri, 2002, and other references in Bertola, 2006).

Monetary union also has specific implications regarding the character of macroeconomic adjustment. As emphasized by Bean (1998), Bentolila and Saint-Paul (2001), and other speculative studies of EMU's possible labor market impact before its inception, irrevocable fixing of exchange rates has the obvious implication of preventing individual countries from choosing their own monetary policies and, to the extent that the Stability and Growth Pact (SGP) is a binding constraint, fiscal policies as well.

Such labor market features as the structure of collective wage contracting also have macroeconomic implications. If nominal prices and wages are rigid, for example, the absence of currency devaluation options may require sharper activity slowdowns and unemployment increases when competitiveness needs to be restored in the aftermath of negative shocks.

On the other side of the coin, ruling out devaluation options may enforce wage moderation at any given level of unemployment. Before EMU inception, this channel of interaction between labor market and policy attracted much attention. While under poor monetary policy credibility wage negotiations would routinely discount devaluation and imply real wage rigidity, national coordination of wage demands played a key role in allowing Italy and other weak-currency, inflation-prone countries to avoid currency crises, control wage-price spirals, satisfy the Maastricht criteria, and join EMU. Calmfors (2001b) pointed out that nominal wage flexibility should remain important in the absence of exchange rate flexibility, and argued that EMU could continue to foster national coordination of wage demands (and perhaps even transnational coordination of wage bargaining). The macroeconomic pros and cons of centralization and their interaction with monetary policy regimes are not simple, and may change once a country has entered EMU. Before the fact, the threat of a crisis in weak-currency countries could muster a measure of social partner solidarity, and wage moderation. Once in EMU, wage-setting may only be restrained by product market competition. Unions, especially those representing workers in the public or other nontradeable sectors, may therefore coordinate poorly and increase wages at the expense of employment opportunities and, ultimately, of the country's competitiveness.

It is important, however, to take into account that the relevant political-economic interactions occur at different levels of decision-making power, and that other relevant aspects are also affected by economic integration. From the macroeconomic point of view, defusing crises can actually foster a "there is no need" rather than a TINA attitude in political-economic interactions. And while aggregate wage and employment flexibility is certainly important in the absence of exchange rate changes, relative wage and employment flexibility is perhaps even more important across the regions, sectors, and occupations of countries where market integration reduces the relevance of country-level shocks and increases that of specific shocks. Thus, centralized and unavoidably homogeneous wage setting in large countries (let alone euro-area-wide wage bargaining) is less likely to be viable in EMU than outside EMU.

More generally, it is doubtful that national macroeconomic policy and labor market reactions would be able to support favorable income dynamics within an integrated economic area. Activity is still less regionally specialized in Europe than in a fully integrated economy like that of the United States. As economic integration proceeds, however, regions and sectors will typically span national borders. This blunts national monetary and fiscal policies as stabilization tools: when most labor market shocks occur at the regional or industry level, the fiscal policy independence suppressed by EMU would likely be a source rather than a remedy for national economic fluctuations (Darvas *et al.*, 2005). Market adjustment mechanisms, conversely, become more important if a single currency enforces price transparency and promotes macroeconomic stability (in conjunction with SGP constraints on fiscal policy). In an environment of macroeconomic stability, market adjustment mechanisms are very important, because correction of disequilibria cannot be left to devaluation and fiscal escape routes. Relative prices, wages, employment, and production levels should respond more promptly to exogenous shocks, even in the absence of institutional reforms, as it becomes more important for economic agents to exploit margins of adjustment.[2] And as macroeconomic stability and tight market integration calls for wage and employment flexibility in response to sector- and region-level shocks, the coordinated wage bargains that proved useful in order to cope with country-specific adjustments to shocks may hinder the necessary adjustments, as centralization tends to compress wages.

As other adjustment channels are shut down in a single-currency area, flexibility of labor markets may be a priority from the EMU-wide point of view. But labor market policy making remains essentially national, so actual reform patterns are influenced by coordination problems. And many financial and services markets, as well as labor markets themselves, remain segmented and imperfect within each country. Hence, political-economic interactions at the national level also influence the resilience of status quo policy configurations (Bertola 2006, 2007a). It may well be relatively easy for smaller and more homogeneous countries to reap the rewards of enhanced labor market flexibility, while deregulation can be difficult politically and inefficient economically in countries where labor market rigidity addresses more serious redistributive issues, or where underdeveloped financial markets make it important for households to rely on stable jobs and wages in order to smooth consumption patterns. If not accompanied by development of market-based risk-management frameworks, openness to international competition may in fact increase the desirability of labor market and social policies meant to reduce the welfare impact of new sources of sharper labor market shocks. And the increasingly negative efficiency impact of such policies in economically integrated countries may, in the absence of appropriate policy reforms and market developments, challenge the political sustainability of economic integration itself.

3. What has changed

Aiming to assess the relevance and relative strength of the theoretical mechanisms reviewed above, this section examines empirical associations between EMU, labor market policies, and labor market outcomes. The theoretical possibilities reviewed in Section 2 can be empirically relevant along two related dimensions of the data. Theory predicts that the undesirable side effects of labor market rigidities are more pronounced in the more tightly integrated member countries of EMU and that – depending on the character of policy making processes – this may or may not be conducive to labor market reform. Thus, it is interesting to try and see whether in those countries flexibility-oriented reforms were in practice sharper, and/or labor market institutions had more negative outcome implications.

The relevant evidence is not abundant, and not easy to disentangle along these two dimensions. The literature so far has looked for evidence of the first implication, on the basis of the TINA argument, and has not detected significant evidence of an association of EMU with faster or more intense reforms (see Duval and Elmeskov, 2006; European Commission, 2007g; and the discussion below of these and other contributions' approach and results).

In this chapter, empirical exercises are purposely kept simple, and aim at offering suggestive and illustrative evidence of interesting theoretical effects' practical relevance. While unavoidably limited by data scarcity and joint-endogeneity concerns, statistical assessment of empirical patterns certainly helps sharpen theoretical arguments, and can offer useful policy insights.

3.1 Data

The available data of course can offer only limited information, for two reasons. First, EMU is a recent and unprecedented experiment. Second, macroeconomic indicators are unavoidably imperfect indicators of a more complex and nuanced reality. But neither more abundant, nor better information is currently available, and the policy relevance of the phenomena under study is too strong for research to wait until more precise evidence perhaps becomes available.

Empirical investigation of available data can be usefully disciplined by a narrow focus on the experience of euro area and other countries in the period surrounding EMU inception. What follows analyzes the relationship of EMU to the interaction of institutional change and labor market outcomes in data from two standard sources. Relevant outcome indicators are available from Eurostat for all EU countries, as well as, in some cases, for EEA countries, accession candidates, the USA, and Japan. The Bassanini and Duval (2006) dataset, available for years up to 2003 only, collects similar outcome indicators for major OECD countries. The sample includes the EU15 countries (except Greece) as well as other major OECD countries (Australia, Canada, Japan, New Zealand, Norway, Switzerland, and the United States).

The Bassanini-Duval dataset also includes a number of institutional indicators. For the purpose of detecting reform tensions and policy patterns, the yearly indicators of "de facto" configurations drawn from the Bassanini-Duval dataset have advantages and disadvantages vis-à-vis legislation-based information, such as that made available for research by the DeBenedetti Foundation and the European Commission. It has proven somewhat difficult to detect a sharp overall tendency in analysis of count data drawn from those reform sets (European Commission, 2007g), possibly because a degree of arbitrariness is unavoidable when summarizing complex laws in a simple index: consistently with this, it has been possible to detect some interesting results concerning the configuration effects of reforms targeted to groups with low participation rates (European Commission, 2008c). Indicators based on observation of current institutional features are easier to interpret, though they may be driven by endogenous responses of economic phenomena and legal practices. Duval and Elmeskov (2006) define discrete "reforms" according to whether observed changes of OECD institutional indicators are unusually large, in a country and year, relative to the sample. This approach did not detect any evidence of more frequent such reform events in EMU.

Here, the focus will be on comparisons across EMU and non-EMU groups of countries and, over time, on a small number of policy and outcome indicators. The sample is restricted to 1995–2005. Labor tax rates and social expenditure indicators are available only up to 2005 (a recent redefinition of these and other databases makes it very difficult to compare later and future data to those published before 2000). Other institutional indicators are available only up to 2003 in the Bassanini and Duval (2006) database. Some indicators, such as unemployment insurance (UI) replacement rates, are available in raw form for later years. Longer samples, when available, yield very similar results in regressions such as those reported below. The 2008 update of the OECD EPL (employment protection legislation) indicator will make it possible to characterize more fully and reliably EMU policy patterns.

The analysis focuses narrowly on the relationship between employment and the policies that may lead it to move along any given labor demand schedule (as in Figures 18.1 and 18.2). Several potentially interesting aspects cannot be analyzed empirically for lack of information. Collective bargaining has an important role in theory, but the most important institutional characteristic (coverage of the labor force by contracts) is difficult to measure objectively at suitably short frequencies and for recent periods. The sources and extent of wage rigidities are similarly difficult to assess on short time series.[3] Aggregate evidence on unit labor cost convergence is not clear-cut: it is hard to tell whether it is driven by productivity or wage dynamics, i.e. whether employment and wages dynamics reflect shifts of the labor demand curve or movements along it.[4] And while it would be interesting to see whether traded and nontraded sectors in EMU and other economies experience different wage and competitiveness dynamics, it is very hard to do so in practice, both because the definition and measurement of the relevant concepts is too debatable for comparable information to be easily compiled, and because Balassa-Samuelson effects on the relative price of nontraded goods in countries at different levels of development can easily blur the information content of time-series data across the relevant groups of countries and different labor force groups.

It is important to keep in mind, however, that employment opportunities for secondary worker groups may be more plentiful in nontradeables and services as well as more severely affected by labor market rigidities. Thus, empirical patterns may be driven by shifts across trade-able and nontradeable sectors (arguably, albeit increasingly loosely, linked to services and manufacturing productions) as much as by reforms triggered by international competitiveness concerns. The empirical strategy discussed and implemented below will be able to focus on the latter mechanism if the former type of structural change is not more important in EMU member countries. It has to be recognized, however, that reforms enhancing employment opportunities for secondary labor force segments may also have been triggered by fiscal constraints, and that EMU may have made those constraints more binding by limiting deficit spending as much as by weakening taxation powers via international competition pressure.

3.2 *Empirical strategy*

To assess the extent to which differences and developments are accounted for by policy configurations and reforms, it is possible to focus on the methods and insights of existing empirical work on the relationship between labor market institutions and employment/unemployment (Bassanini and Duval, 2006, and its references) and with labor income and overall inequality (Koeniger *et al.*, 2007; Checchi and García Peñalosa, 2008).

Of course, each country has its own problems, different shocks, and different political resistance to reform. But many shocks, such as those originating in global development and integration patterns, or in international financial markets, are common to all European countries. A comparison of labor market policies and performances across EU15 countries and over the period of EMU inception can, to the extent possible, isolate the implications of what some of them have in common, and others do not: membership in EMU. Such an approach has been applied by Bertola (2008) to inequality indicators and social policy expenditure, finding that EMU membership is associated with somewhat higher inequality, and that the empirical patterns of inequality changes are largely explained by those of public social expenditure as a share of GDP. That paper also detects an association of EMU with significantly stronger trade, services, and FDI integration, as well as with higher per capita GDP. Crucially from the present chapter's point of view, there is also significant evidence of a negative association between EMU and unemployment, which in turn appears to be negatively associated with household income inequality.

Since the amount of information about EMU is limited by its recent, local, and unprecedented character, only tightly focused specifications can hope to detect empirical patterns. In the regressions reported and discussed below, a dummy variable captures changes associated with EMU membership. This dummy, denoted EMU in the tables, is equal to unity in 1999 and later years for Austria, Belgium, Germany, Spain, Finland, France, Ireland, Italy, the Netherlands and Portugal, and in 2001 and later years for Greece. It is meant to capture variation associated, for a given country and in comparison to countries that remain out, with adoption of the common currency. A similar summary statistic is the slope of a trend computed across the adoption date which, when allowed to differ across countries that do or do not enter EMU, can also detect more or less gradual changes in the variables of interest.

Simple differences across these estimates, however, cannot disentangle the effects of EMU from those of other synchronous developments. Since most of the countries in the sample ended up adopting the euro during the period considered, regression specifications need to differentiate the association with EMU from that with the time of observation, and that with permanent characteristics of the countries considered (other than those associated with their inclination to join EMU). To control for common developments, it is possible to include year effects. To control for country characteristics, fixed effects specifications allow estimation of country-specific intercept.

The size and character of the comparison group is of course not such as to foster complete confidence in the results: Denmark, Sweden, and the UK when the sample is restricted to the EU15; other industrialized countries when comparable data are available. The results, however, are reassuringly robust across a variety of specifications. The timing of the EMU switch can be altered without changing the message of the regressions, and a very similar message is conveyed by specifications where countries that did and did not adopt the euro are allowed to have different trends: the magnitude and significance of the coefficient of an EMU-specific trend component is always very similar to that of the dummy coefficient, and either may pick up a structural effect of EMU developing slowly over time through anticipation and lagged reactions.

When interpreting the evidence it is important to keep in mind that countries that adopted the euro certainly differ from the others in many relevant respects. They were not forced by an experimenter to join EMU. They chose to do so, and their decision was presumably influenced by their own characteristics as well as by the relationships between observable variables detected in the data. Finding that in EMU member countries labor markets regulation and unemployment decreased, or inequality increased, does not imply that those effects would be observed in any country were it to join the euro area. The observed pattern of institutional and outcome dynamics can be a natural consequence of the fact that many of the first wave of euro-area countries had the most room for unemployment reduction and flexibility-oriented reforms. There is no way of knowing for sure whether countries that joined EMU would have followed a similar path if they had not. In this sense, the evidence can only be descriptive. Analysis of the data, however, can test the practical relevance of the theoretical insight, discussed above, that the desirability and effects of labor market policies are affected by tighter economic integration. The data can neither confirm nor deny that countries in the sample that did not but could join (Denmark, the UK and Sweden) did not want or need to reform, or that countries that did join EMU may have done so also in order to obtain suitable reform incentives. But they can tell us whether the intensity and the (good or bad) effects of country-level policy interference with labor market outcomes are correlated with EMU membership and, to the extent that the effects of labor market institutions are (or are perceived to be) desirable, empirical evidence can detect the extent to which membership in a monetary union requires different policy approaches.

3.3 Evidence

The results are similar in various specifications of the relationships of interest. For brevity and simplicity of interpretation, Sections 3.3.1 and 3.3.2 mostly focus on regressions estimates from the EU15 sample specification that include EMU dummies (capturing the association between the left-hand-side variable's realization and euro-area membership), along with year dummies and country-specific fixed effects. The tables also report estimates on the broader OECD sample (and shorter time period, stopping in 2003) and from specifications detect gradual changes by allowing for separate trends across the samples of countries that do or do not adopt the single currency around 2000; these are discussed only when they deliver different messages. In Section 3.3.3, more complex multivariate specifications aim at detecting plausible structural mechanisms.

3.3.1 Unemployment and employment outcomes

Consider first the evidence regarding employment and unemployment. In theory, the effects of integration on these indicators depend on whether policies are reformed in light of their effects, or reform inertia leads unchanged institutions to have more negative side effects. In practice, as we shall see, the available data strongly suggest that EMU was associated with higher employment and lower unemployment, especially in the "secondary" labor force segments where labor market policies are expected to have stronger disemployment effects (Bertola *et al.*, 2007) and where EMU member countries may have concentrated their reform efforts (possibly because of the political strength of primary workers or "insiders," and with the consequence of increasing the "dualism" of labor markets' institutional structure).

Figure 18.3 displays aggregate and youth unemployment rates in terms of deviations from country means, separately for the EMU and non-EMU

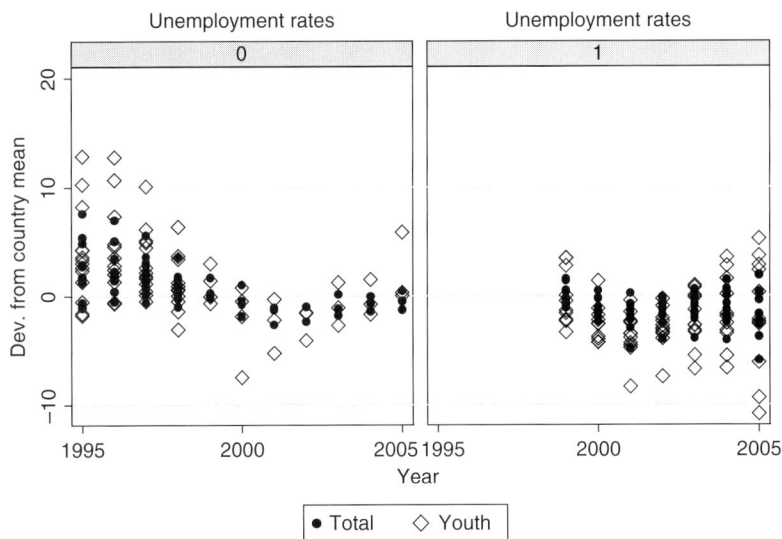

Figure 18.3: Deviations from country means of unemployment rates in the EMU and non-EMU subsamples of the EU15
Definitions and sources: see Data Appendix.

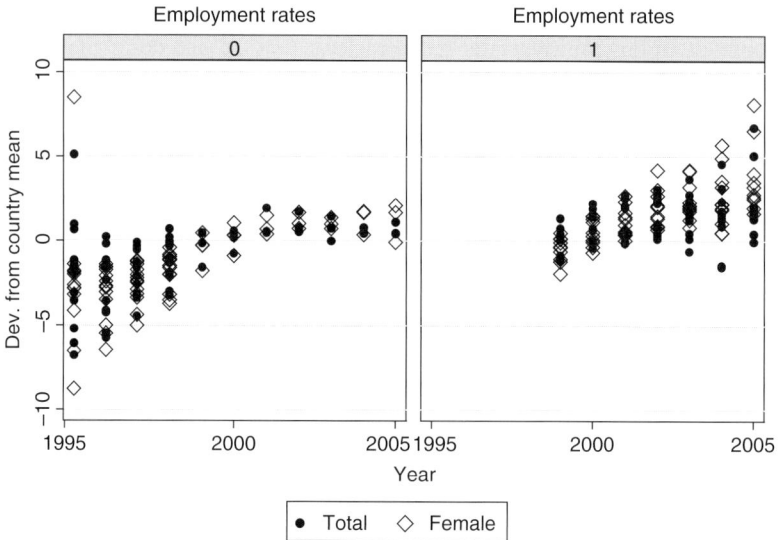

Figure 18.4: Deviations from country means of employment rates in the EMU and non-EMU subsamples of the EU15
Definitions and sources: see Data Appendix.

observations. There is a clear tendency for unemployment to be lower when the EMU dummy equals one, but it is also clearly apparent that this may be driven by cyclical developments. Figure 18.4 conveys a similar impression regarding employment rates, which tend to be higher in the EMU subsample.

The regression evidence in Table 18.1–18.5 confirms this impression and makes it possible to sharpen its interpretation. Table 18.1 reports that labor market outcome indicators are very significantly different across the EMU and non-EMU portions of the sample (in these and all other tables, t statistics are robust and account for clustering at country level), and also detects a significant difference in GDP per capita (driven by higher employment, rather than by labor productivity, which is not significantly different). Of course, however, unemployment and employment rates are affected by many other factors. The presence in the sample of countries that did not adopt the euro (and were not "treated" by EMU) makes it possible to try to detect associations between EMU and labor market outcomes. But since some countries could be less inclined to regulate their labor markets regardless of whether they adopt the single currency at some point during the sample period, and a large proportion of the countries observed

Table 18.1: *Simple mean difference between before and after EMU observations for the sample of countries that did adopt EMU within the 1995–2005 sample period (Austria, Belgium, Germany, Spain, Finland, France, Greece, Ireland, Italy, the Netherlands, Portugal).*

	Unemp. (tot.)	Youth unemp.	Long term un.	Emp. rate(tot.)	Emp.rate (female)	GDP p.c.	Lab. prod.
EMU	–2.9106	–6.1716	–1.7772	3.6855	4.9680	3.3949	4.5174
t	*–3.70*	*–4.30*	*–3.55*	*4.62*	*6.84*	*5.02*	*1.31*
N	121	121	119	121	121	121	121

Table 18.2: *Regressions on EMU dummy (equal to unity in 1999–2005 for Austria, Belgium, Germany, Spain, Finland, France, Ireland, Italy, the Netherlands, Portugal) and year dummies, with country fixed effects. Sample: EU15 (except Greece) and other major OECD countries, 1995–2003.*

	Unemp. (2554)	Youth Unemp.	Emp.rate (prime-age male)	Emp.rate (prime-age female)	GDP p.c.	Lab.prod.
EMU	–1.5295	–3.6367	1.5522	3.3570	–0.0388	–1.2513
t	*–1.71*	*–2.25*	*1.77*	*3.21*	*–0.07*	*–0.27*
N	180	180	180	180	176	187

end up belonging to EMU during the sample period, the regression could mistakenly attribute to EMU the broad trends common to all countries. And since the dummy can only capture EMU's timing, its coefficient can be influenced by the global cycle, by EU enlargement, and by any other event occurring at roughly the same time.

Regressions that control for country and year effects (reported in Table 18.1 and 18.2 for two different samples of countries and different indicators) address these issues. Country dummies can control for relevant permanent characteristics, and if regressions include year effects the coefficient of an EMU dummy picks up the average difference (between countries that do and do not use the single currency) of year-specific means of the left-hand-side variable, which could be influenced by contemporaneous developments only to the extent that they affect euro-area countries differently from others.

Table 18.3: *Regressions on EMU dummy (equal to unity in 1999–2005 for Austria, Belgium, Germany, Spain, Finland, France, Ireland, Italy, the Netherlands, Portugal) and year dummies, with country fixed effects. Sample: EU15, 1995–2005.*

	Unemp. (tot)	Youth unemp.	Long term un.	Emp. rate (tot.)	Emp. rate (female)	GDP p.c.	Lab. prod.
EMU	–0.8328	–3.1229	–0.6547	1.7308	2.0362	–0.0299	1.9127
t	–0.94	–1.86	–1.22	2.13	1.73	–0.05	0.63
N	154	154	152	154	154	154	154

Table 18.4: *Regressions on a trend (1/10 time unit per year) and on an additional trend only for countries that adopt EMU within the sample period, with country fixed effects. Sample: EU15 (except Greece) and other major OECD countries, 1995–2003.*

	Unemp. (2554)	Youth Unemp.	Emp.rate (prime-age male)	Emp.rate (prime-age female)	GDP p.c.	Lab. prod.
trend*EMU0	–3.0307	–7.1991	2.9907	7.1414	–0.4488	–4.3545
t	–4.21	–5.32	3.92	8.52	–1.04	–1.71
trend	–1.9475	–2.1276	0.4445	4.4641	5.1536	7.9636
t	–3.83	–2.22	0.82	7.53	14.38	3.89
N	180	180	180	180	176	187

This specification yields fairly strong evidence of lower unemployment (especially in the more sensitive youth segment of the labor force) and higher employment (again, more strongly so in "secondary" labor force segments, such as the female one) in EMU. There is also evidence of lower long-term unemployment, and no evidence of changes in per capita or per hour production, suggesting that a movement along the labor demand curve was accompanied by an upward shift of labor productivity relative to the control group. The message of specifications modeling EMU effects in trend terms is qualitatively, quantitatively, and statistically similar in Tables 18.4 and 18.5. Thus, at least part of the raw change in labor market outcomes for the sample of countries that did join EMU, shown in Figures 18.3 and 18.4 and in Table 18.1, appears to be associated with EMU itself, rather than with the identity

Table 18.5: *Regressions on a trend (1/10 time unit per year), on an additional trend only for countries that adopt EMU within the sample period, with country fixed effects. Sample: EU15, 1995–2005. Robust standard errors account for clustering at country level.*

	Unemp. (tot)	Youth unemp.	Long term un.	Emp. rate(tot.)	Emp.rate (female)	GDP p.c.	Lab. prod.
trend* EMU0	–0.7314	–4.9333	–0.5240	3.2042	4.6216	–0.5319	1.6970
t	–0.68	–2.27	–0.83	3.12	4.53	–0.98	0.64
trend	–3.2273	–2.6939	–1.7303	1.9859	2.9593	5.2367	1.9121
t	–3.37	–1.40	–3.09	2.18	3.27	10.89	0.81
N	154	154	152	154	154	154	154

of the countries or with the influences of common (to the industrialized countries in the sample) factors captured by year effects.

3.3.2 Policies

From the theoretical perspective outlined in Section 2, unchanged policies should have implied worse disemployment in more tightly integrated countries. Thus, the tendency detected above for EMU to be associated with higher employment and lower unemployment leads us to expect that it should also be associated with less rigidity in labor market policies. Figures 18.5 and 18.6 display available data over the sample of interest for some important policy variables: EPL, for regular and nonstandard contracts, and average and marginal labor tax rates.[5] These are highly heterogeneous across EU15 countries, and much of the policies' heterogeneity of course depends on country-specific characteristics. To highlight the changes associated with EMU membership, the plot shows deviations from country-specific means, separately for the EMU and non-EMU country-year observations.

Both tax rates and EPL appear to decline in EMU. It is also apparent that the dynamics of policy variables are very different across countries. To isolate the EMU-specific component of policy changes and assess their significance, Tables 18.6–18.10 display coefficients of EMU-specific dummies and trends in a variety of regression specifications for these and other policy indicators, along with robust t-statistics testing whether they are different from zero.

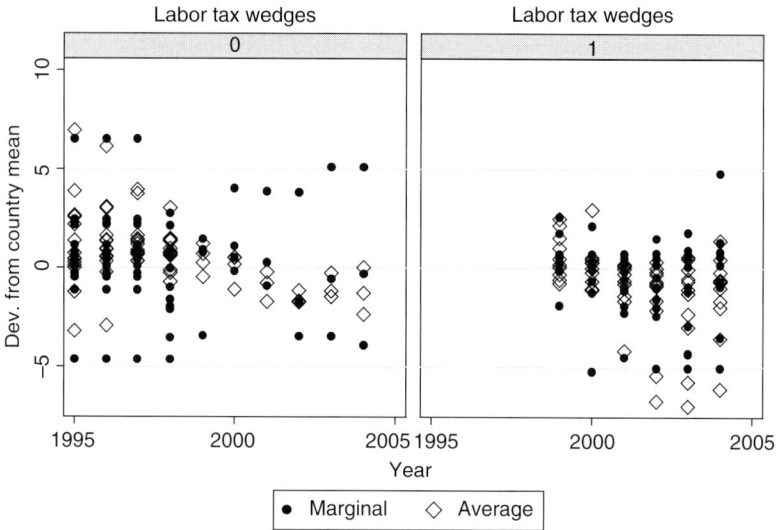

Figure 18.5: Deviations from country means of labor tax rates in the EMU and non-EMU subsamples of the EU15
Definitions and sources: see Data Appendix.

The preferred specification of Table 18.8 offers some evidence of an association between EMU and changes in labor market regulation. Relaxation of nonstandard contract EPL provisions is almost significant, and there is a significant increase in the generosity of unemployment insurance systems as measured by average replacement rates (which increased in EMU countries such as Ireland and Italy, and decreased in control countries such as Sweden and Denmark). The decline in the two measures considered of labor taxation is sizable, but statistically insignificant. However, it is easy to find stronger evidence of regulation with regressions specifications meant to investigate a little deeper the determinants of policy choices. In Table 18.11, controlling for government deficits (Maastricht definition) increases the size and significance of the average labor tax reduction in EMU vis-à-vis the non-EMU portion of the sample: since year and country dummies are included, the significantly negative impact of EMU on labor taxation becomes evident when the relative need to improve government finances is accounted for.

The other specifications aimed at detecting associations between EMU and labor market policy similarly offer intriguing and often significant evidence of laxer EPL, smaller labor taxation, and higher unemployment

Table 18.6: *Simple mean difference between before and after EMU observations for the sample of countries that did adopt EMU within the 1995–2005 sample period (Austria, Belgium, Germany, Spain, Finland, France, Greece, Ireland, Italy, the Netherlands, Portugal).*

	UI rep.rate	Lab.Tax (marg)	Lab.Tax (avg)	EPL(reg)	EPL(tmp)
EMU	2.8348	−0.5801	−1.4582	−0.0332	−0.4722
t	*1.89*	*−0.49*	*−1.34*	*−1.31*	*−2.09*
N	90	110	110	90	90

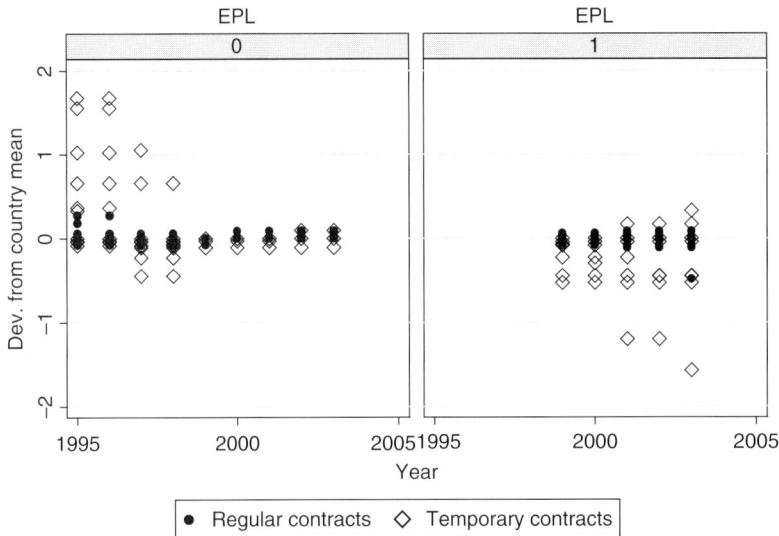

Figure 18.6: Deviations from country means of employment protection indicators in the EMU and non-EMU subsamples of the EU15
Definitions and sources: see Data Appendix.

insurance (UI) replacement rates. This evidence is not as negative as that discussed in European Economic Advisory Group (2008), Duval and Elmeskov (2006), European Commission (2007g). Drastic reform may not have been observed in euro-area countries, but their labor market institutions, relative to non-euro-area ones, have significantly changed over the period when they completed monetary union. A milder, but significant version of the TINA hypothesis does appear to be at work.

An important exception to the tendency towards labor market deregulation is the statistically significant increase of unemployment

Table 18.7: *Regressions on EMU dummy (equal to unity in 1999–2005 for Austria, Belgium, Germany, Spain, Finland, France, Ireland, Italy, the Netherlands, Portugal) and year dummies, with country fixed effects. Sample: EU15 (except Greece) and other major OECD countries, 1995– 2003.*

	UI rep.rate	Lab.Tax (marg)	Lab.Tax (avg)	EPL(reg)	EPL(tmp)
EMU	3.9308	–0.6191	–1.4701	–0.0866	–0.4616
t	*1.96*	*–0.41*	*–1.32*	*–2.09*	*–1.80*
N	180	210	209	180	180

insurance average replacement rate. This is of course only one of an unemployment insurance scheme's relevant characteristics: a higher UI replacement rate can be associated with lower unemployment if it is accompanied by more stringent availability-to-work and other eligibility requirements, and can be consistent with the decline in aggregate and long-term unemployment rates documented above. It is, however, interesting to observe that if any typical pattern can be detected for EMU countries, it is one where UI replacement rates increase as EPL decreases: in Figure 18.7, we see that the trajectories followed by EMU countries in terms of UI and EPL lie along a tradeoff relationship where all of them initially lie except Ireland, which appears to converge towards it (while the UK remains well below that line, and Denmark well at one extreme).

Unemployment insurance and EPL are alternative ways to shift labor market income risk away from workers and their families, towards firms with better access to financial markets (in the case of EPL) or to collective redistribution schemes (in the case of UI). As demands for protection against labor market risk are if anything stronger in more open economies, and need not be addressed by private financial market development, an alternative does need to be found to pure deregulation. The data indicate that UI tends to substitute EPL in more tightly internationally integrated countries, and this can be sensibly interpreted in terms of the two schemes' different implications for competitiveness: when product markets are more competitive and capital can move across borders, it is harder for policy to burden firms with efficiency losses, and collectively administered unemployment insurance schemes may be better ways of addressing workers' protection demands.

Table 18.8: *Regressions on EMU dummy (equal to unity in 1999–2005 for Austria, Belgium, Germany, Spain, Finland, France, Ireland, Italy, the Netherlands, Portugal) and year dummies, with country fixed effects. Sample: EU15, 1995–2005.*

	UI rep.rate	Lab.Tax (marg)	Lab.Tax (avg)	EPL(reg)	EPL(tmp)
EMU	7.3658	–2.0822	–0.2589	–0.0776	–0.4098
t	*2.51*	*–0.75*	*–0.35*	*–1.55*	*–1.58*
N	117	140	140	117	117

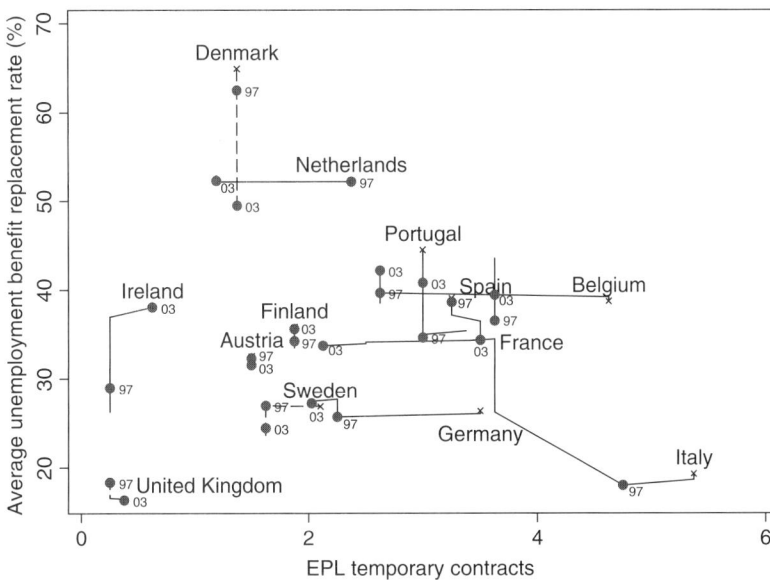

Figure 18.7: Employment protection and unemployment insurance in the EU15, 1995–2003
Definitions and sources: see Data Appendix.

3.3.3 Outcomes, policies, and economic integration

Does economic integration really have the implications discussed in Section 2? In theory, the employment impact of labor market rigidities should be stronger in more open and more competitive economies (and this is the reason why, in the TINA view, deregulation should and to some extent is observed in EMU). To assess the empirical relevance of these insights, one might include economic integration indicators in standard

Table 18.9: *Regressions on a trend (1/10 time unit per year) and on an additional trend only for countries that adopt EMU within the sample period, with country fixed effects. Sample: EU15 (except Greece) and other major OECD countries, 1995–2003.*

	UI rep. rate	Lab.Tax (marg)	Lab.Tax (avg)	EPL (reg)	EPL (tmp)
trend*EMU0	8.0234	−1.2662	−3.0921	−0.2072	−0.9942
t	5.35	−1.04	−3.67	−4.51	−4.70
trend	−2.6987	−1.1693	−0.9138	0.1185	−0.0108
t	−2.54	−1.32	−1.49	3.65	−0.07
N	180	210	209	180	180

Table 18.10: *Regressions on a trend (1/10 time unit per year), on an additional trend only for countries that adopt EMU within the sample period, with country fixed effects. Sample: EU15, 1995–2005.*

	UI rep. rate	Lab.Tax (marg)	Lab.Tax (avg)	EPL (reg)	EPL (tmp)
trend*EMU0	14.9192	−3.7568	−0.7034	−0.1813	−0.8689
t	6.27	−2.23	−0.56	−2.82	−2.37
trend	−9.5945	1.3213	−3.3025	0.0926	−0.1361
t	−4.59	0.89	−2.96	1.64	−0.42
N	117	140	140	117	117

labor-market-oriented empirical work, such as the regressions run by Bassanini and Duval (2006). The European Economic Advisory Group (2008) did not uncover significant evidence of a role for such interactions: in their regressions, openness appears to be associated with better labor market performance, but the impact of various institutions is not significantly affected by openness. The main effect of openness may or may not warrant structural interpretation, but can certainly be consistent with a positive impact of product market competition and higher efficiency on labor demand at given wages, on labor supply through the higher purchasing power of product wages, and on wage moderation. The theoretically sound interaction effects are, not surprisingly, difficult to detect in a specification that, after extensive investigation of the limited information present in a small dataset, leaves little to be explained.[6]

Table 18.11: *Regression of labor tax rates on EMU dummy and year dummies, with country fixed effects, controlling for government deficits. Sample: EU15, 1995–2005, where data available.*

	Lab.Tax (avg)	Lab.Tax (marg)
GovtBudg	0.1344	0.0185
t	*1.30*	*0.13*
EMU	−2.3557	−1.2371
t	*−5.44*	*−2.15*
N	124	124

Table 18.12: *Simple mean difference between openness indicators before and after EMU observations for the sample of countries that did adopt EMU within the 1995–2005 sample period (Austria, Belgium, Germany, Spain, Finland, France, Greece, Ireland, Italy, the Netherlands, Portugal).*

	Openn.(goods)	Openn.(serv.)	Openn.(FDI)
EMU	5.6671	2.8415	2.3158
t	*2.21*	*1.97*	*3.72*
N	114	114	102

The next set of tables implement a simpler approach, trying again to make the best use of the limited information available, and focusing on the most important interaction regressions. The regressions of Tables 18.12–18.14 test whether EMU is associated with stronger market integration. We see in Table 18.12 that goods trade and foreign direct investment flows have become more intense after EMU in participating countries, and that services openness has also increased (more weakly, and unsurprisingly so in light of the overall underdeveloped harmonization of that market's regulation). Tables 18.13 and 18.14, however, show that only for goods is there some evidence of an EMU-related increase in openness when time effects are included in the regressions.

Does closer economic integration have the implications illustrated in Figure 18.2, where labor taxation has sharper negative implications for employment as labor demand becomes more elastic? Figure 18.8 shows employment rate and tax wedge data. The overall association between the two is ambiguously sloped: some countries, such as Sweden, are able to sustain both high employment and high taxes,

Table 18.13: *Regressions on EMU dummy (equal to unity in 1999–2005 for Austria, Belgium, Germany, Spain, Finland, France, Ireland, Italy, the Netherlands, Portugal) and year dummies, with country fixed effects. Sample: EU15 (except Greece) and other major OECD countries, 1995–2003.*

	Openn.(goods)	Openn.(serv.)	Openn.(FDI)
EMU	1.6292	0.4829	0.4507
t	*1.36*	*0.29*	*0.53*
N	180	180	178

Table 18.14: *Regressions on EMU dummy (equal to unity in 1999–2005 for Austria, Belgium, Germany, Spain, Finland, France, Ireland, Italy, the Netherlands, Portugal) and year dummies, with country fixed effects. Sample: EU15, 1995–2005.*

	Openn.(goods)	Openn.(serv.)	Openn.(FDI)
EMU	1.1908	–0.8699	–0.5266
t	*0.83*	*–0.50*	*–0.51*
N	147	147	134

while others, such as Greece, lie low along both dimensions. This presumably reflects specific characteristics of each country's economic and social structure, such as the more or less "encompassing" character of their policy making and wage bargaining processes. But the figure also shows that many countries experienced large shifts in both of these variables over the sample period, and that typical country-specific trajectories are negatively sloped (in the direction of lower taxes and higher employment).

To see whether the data support the association of tighter integration with more negative effects of labor market regulation, it is possible to run regressions of employment rates on labor taxation and its interaction with economic integration. Controlling for country fixed effects, the first two columns of Table 18.15 estimate a very significant and large coefficient of the two available tax measures as explanatory variables of aggregate employment rates in the EU15 sample. The OECD sample interactions, not reported, are very similar, and the effects are even stronger for female employment rates: this is consistent with the

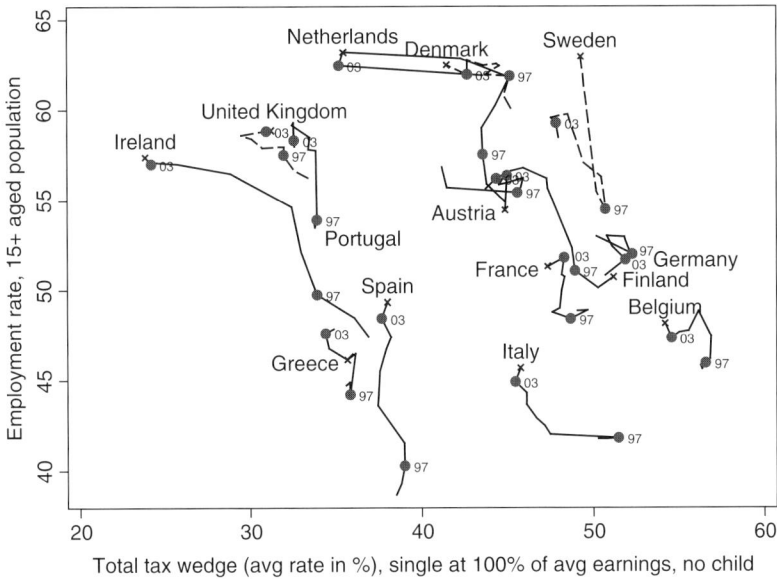

Figure 18.8: Employment and labor tax rates in the EU15, 1995–2005
Definitions and sources: see Data Appendix.

arguments of Bertola *et al.* (2007), but of course female employment may be more strongly affected by cultural differences and trends that have little to do with economic integration.

Among the forces driving tax and employment outcomes along trade-offs such as that illustrated in Figure 18.1, some – such as increasing openness to Far East trade and technological changes – are common across the entire sample. But others may be specific to EMU members and years. The third and fifth columns of Table 18.15 include the EMU dummy and its interaction between with labor tax rates among the explanatory variables, thus allowing the relationship between taxes and employment to differ across the EMU and non-EMU subsamples. Again controlling for country fixed effects, the regressions detect a negative and strongly significant interaction. As shown by the fourth and sixth columns of Table 18.15, there is also a negative (and significant when the regression uses marginal measures of labor taxation) interaction between labor taxes and trade openness.

This evidence is consistent with the mechanisms outlined in Section 2: monetary union fosters market development, and strengthens the negative association between marginal labor tax rates and employment (the

Table 18.15: *Regressions of total employment rate on tax measures and their interactions with EMU dummy (equal to unity in 1999–2005 for Austria, Belgium, Germany, Spain, Finland, France, Ireland, Italy, the Netherlands, Portugal, in 2002–05 for Greece) or openness indicators, with country fixed effects. Sample: EU15, 1995–2004; openness data for Belgium not available in the first seven years.*

	Emp. rate	Emp. rate	Emp. rate	Emp. rate	Emp. rate	Emp. rate
Tax measure	*marginal*	*average*	*marginal*	*marginal*	*average*	*average*
Labor Tax	−0.2957	−0.6777	−0.0789	0.2668	−0.3470	−0.7045
t	−3.83	−9.36	−1.28	1.71	−4.63	−4.07
EMU			9.8128		6.8981	
t			5.35		4.27	
Lab. Tx*EMU			−0.1297		−0.1035	
t			−3.75		−2.89	
Op.(goods)				0.9311		0.2060
t				4.37		1.21
Op.(g.) *EMU				−0.0165		−0.0004
t				−4.11		−0.11
N	140	140	140	133	140	133

evidence is qualitatively similar, but much weaker and mixed as regards average tax rates and economic integration in the services and financial markets). While the limited amount of information available in the data prevents reliable testing and measurement of plausible theoretical mechanisms, the observed patterns of coefficient can help focus attention on mechanisms that are theoretically obvious in terms of their direction and relationships, but may be realized with different intensity in the EMU experience. Average deviations from country means differ across the EMU (sixty-four yearly observations) and non-EMU (seventy-six yearly observations) subsamples of EU15 observations by 2.4 percentage points for employment rates, by -1.1 percentage points for marginal tax rates, and by -1.6 percentage points for average tax rates. The interaction coefficients in the regressions predict that each percentage point of labor tax rates is associated with 0.13 fewer points of employment in the EMU sample, and with 0.10 fewer points in the non-EMU sample. The difference of predicted employment rates (in deviations from country means) can be decomposed as

$Emp_{EMU} - Emp_{NOT}$
$$= \alpha_{EMU} - \beta_{EMU}Tax_{EMU} - (\alpha_{NOT} - \beta_{NOT}Tax_{NOT})$$
$$= \alpha_{EMU} - \alpha_{NOT} - (\beta_{EMU} - \beta_{NOT})Tax_{EMU} - \beta_{NOT}(Tax_{EMU} - Tax_{NOT})$$

The regressions with marginal tax rates indicate that if the slope of the relationship between employment and taxes had remained as steep in EMU as it was outside of it, the change in tax rates would imply a $\beta_{NOT}(Tax_{EMU} - Tax_{NOT}) = 0.08$ percentage point change in employment rates; the average tax rate results yield 0.542. While statistically significant, tax reductions associated with EMU have a modest economic impact in this exercise, confirming that reforms have not been as dramatic as TINA views might have predicted.

But the change in slope illustrated in Figure 18.2 above can be detected in the data, and does have negative implications for employment. The mean average labor tax rate is about 0.43 in EMU observations, and the mean marginal tax rate is about 0.52; taking the regression estimates at face value, the change in slope would imply lower employment, by $(\beta_{EMU} - \beta_{NOT})Tax_{EMU}$, of some 4.4–6.7 percentage points. In the regression results, this effect is more than offset by a large estimate of EMU's main effect on employment rates (between 7 and 10 percent). This may reflect the higher productivity and relative wage moderation effects of economic integration but, of course, could also be generated by spurious associations between EMU membership and, for example, female labor supply developments.

The evidence is similar, albeit weaker, as regards other policies and outcomes. For example, Table 18.16 reports regressions of long-term unemployment rates on a very plausible policy determinant, the indicator of employment protection legislation for temporary contracts. The first column of the Table indeed detects a significantly positive impact of EPL on long-term unemployment. As shown in Section 3.3.1, long-term unemployment is lower in EMU, and Section 3.3.2 reported evidence that this dimension of EPL is significantly less stringent in EMU. The interaction terms in the second and third column of the Table try to see whether the impact of policy on outcomes differs across the two samples. The interaction of EPL and EMU is positive, consistently with the notion

Table 18.16: *Regressions of long-term unemployment rate on an EPL indicator and its interactions with EMU dummy (equal to unity in 1999–2005 for Austria, Belgium, Germany, Spain, Finland, France, Ireland, Italy, the Netherlands, Portugal, in 2001–05 for Greece) or openness indicators, with country fixed effects. Sample: EU15, 1995–2003; openness data for Belgium not available in the first seven years, EPL indicator not available for Greece.*

	Long-term unemployment	Long-term unemployment	Long-term unemployment
EPL(tmp)	0.5826	–0.2611	0.9750
t	*2.38*	*–1.26*	*1.70*
EMU		–2.5391	
t		*–5.16*	
EPL(tmp) * EMU		0.2487	
t		*1.31*	
Openn. (goods)			–0.0687
t			*–1.25*
EPL(tmp) * Op.(g.)			–0.0291
t			*–1.28*
N	115	115	108

that more powerful market forces strengthen the negative side effects of labor market policies: but is not significant, probably also because the sample size is further limited by data availability. The negative interaction of EPL with openness to international trade in goods also fails to support a mechanism associating EMU with stronger market competition.

4. What else may need to change?

The previous sections provide significant evidence that EMU was associated with less unemployment, more employment, less taxation of labor, and sharper negative effects of taxes. This is consistent with TINA views: as market competition becomes more intense, it worsens the tradeoff between income smoothing or redistribution on the one hand, and employment losses on the other hand. Policy makers appear to be sufficiently sensitive to the latter effect to implement flexibility-oriented reforms, and increase employment. Labor market policies, however, are not primarily meant to reduce employment and increase unemployment. As discussed in Section 2, these are unavoidable side effects of policies meant to improve workers' welfare. Thus, as the tradeoffs between their benefits and costs worsens, a price may have to be paid for more favorable employment outcomes in terms of higher risk and less even income distribution.

There is much less, and less reliable, information about inequality than about employment and unemployment rates. No recent earnings inequality information is available from the OECD "Earnings trends" database, and different definitions would anyway make those data difficult to use for cross-country comparative (rather than trend assessment) purposes. The association between disposable household income inequality and EMU is analyzed in Bertola (2008) on the basis of Eurostat quintile ratio statistics. The quality of those indicators is not very high, because of recent changes in definitions and measurement. But in a regression specification that explains inequality by per capita GDP and population, the EMU dummy is positive and significant. Of course integration, while making markets more efficient and powerful and increasing average production, does not benefit everybody equally. But the estimated effects of integration on inequality need not be a reflection of direct effects, because income gains and losses from international trade and factor mobility are not related to income levels in simple ways: if before integration market power or scarcity benefits relatively rich producers, removal of international barriers to trade and factor mobility reduces inequality. As remarked above, however, international competition also reduces national governments' powers to tax and target benefits. In fact, Bertola (2008) finds that controlling for social policy expenditure (a very strong determinant, alongside per capita GDP, of disposable income inequality) the EMU dummy is not significant. This is an indication that economic integration has no strong effect on inequality, but may increase after-tax inequality indirectly through policies. To the extent that redistribution reduces production efficiency, this is another reason why removal of international barriers should increase aggregate welfare. To the extent that financial and other markets are imperfect, however, redistribution can be beneficial, and its retrenchment has negative as well as positive welfare implications.

The analysis of Bertola (2008) focuses on public social expenditure as an indicator of government policy that is empirically very relevant to inequality, but not as directly relevant to the present chapter's focus on labor market phenomena. In the dataset analyzed here, larger social expenditure is empirically associated with higher employment rates, and very significantly so if the specification controls for the negative association of employment with labor tax rates. This may reflect the correlation of social public expenditure with public employment which, as discussed in detail by Algan *et al.* (2002), also influences unemployment, in theory and in the data, depending on the public sector's fields of activity and wage-setting criteria. The different configuration of social and labor market policy "models" within and between the EMU and other country groups would in principle deserve careful analysis, as different policy interventions may be more or less strongly affected by international competition among systems. While the scarce data available make it empirically impossible to detect separate roles for regulation, taxes and subsidies, and public employment, it is important to recognize that policy channels of interaction between economic integration and inequality or risk can also play out in labor markets, where economic integration can foster production efficiency both directly and by making it more difficult for policy to interfere with markets so as to achieve beneficial effects.

The regressions reported in Table 18.17 explore the empirical relevance of tradeoffs and interactions between inequality, unemployment, and EMU. In the country panel data for which comparable measures of inequality are available from Eurostat (restricted to EU15 countries, disregarding the few observations available for some EEA countries), disposable income quintile ratios are strongly negatively related to per capita income. Inequality followed a U-shaped path in the 1995–2005 period, beginning to increase strongly just at the time of EMU inception. While inequality is lower in EMU countries in the second half of the sample, it is important to control for simultaneous developments of other relevant variables in those and other ("control") countries. Per capita income is robustly associated with lower inequality, and using it as a control variable detects a significantly positive association between EMU and inequality in the first column of Table 18.17. This empirical relationship may tell us that integration increases income, and reduces inequality by less than would typically be implied by the overall relationship between these two country-level characteristics.

It is interesting to examine the relationship between inequality and unemployment alongside that between inequality and social policy

Table 18.17: *Regressions of income inequality indicators on unemployment, social policy, and EMU dummy (equal to unity in 1999–2005 for Austria, Belgium, Germany, Spain, Finland, France, Ireland, Italy, the Netherlands, Portugal, in 2001–05 for Greece), all regressions include a constant, all but the first control for inequality definition and measurement method (see Data Appendix). Sample: EU15, 1995–2005 where data available.*

	Inc.ineq.	Inc.ineq.	Inc.ineq.	Inc.ineq.
GDPp.c.	–0.1749	–0.1622	–0.1921	–0.1482
t	–13.98	–10.27	–24.70	–6.96
EMU	0.2901	–0.0021	0.1323	0.0308
t	2.18	–0.02	1.25	0.25
Pub.Soc.Exp.		–0.0765		–0.0815
t		–2.51		–2.49
Unemp.(tot)		–0.0547	–0.0580	
t		–2.24	–2.26	
IneqDef		0.5451	0.4733	0.5762
t		6.06	4.99	5.61
N	154	151	154	151

expenditure analyzed in Bertola (2008). The regression reported in the second column of Table 18.17 includes both unemployment and social public expenditure as explanatory variables for inequality. Both display a negative and significant association with inequality, and together they deprive the EMU indicator of all economic or statistical significance (in regressions not shown, the sharp decline of wages' share of GDP since EMU inception is instead completely unrelated to household income inequality, for reasons discussed in Bertola, 2008). This identifies declines in unemployment, presumably due to the labor market reforms discussed above, as a common and inequality-relevant characteristic of euro-area countries along with social policy expenditure reduction. In the next two columns, each of these indicators remains significant, with a stable coefficient, as the other is excluded from the regression. While the evidence is weaker than other relationships discussed in the paper, a possible interpretation is that in some welfare state models public social expenditure is the prominent inequality-reduction tool, while in others regulation (in the form of collectively bargained minimum wages, employment protection, and within-household redistribution) creates unemployment but also reduces inequality.

In Bertola (2008), changes in social policy were found to absorb all of EMU's association with inequality. Here, higher employment and lower unemployment play a similar role. As discussed in Checchi and García Peñalosa (2008), unemployment is not a risk when induced by rigidity and subsidized. It is instead permanently associated with individuals' labor market position, and correlated to lower wage inequality and household income equalization. For example, generous unemployment benefits increase the disposable income of the unemployed at the same time as they increase their number, and since the unemployed earn less than they would if employed and than other workers earn, higher benefits induce a negative association between income inequality and unemployment. Legal or contractual wage minima, and employment protection for primary breadwinners, also tend to increase their income at the same time as they make it more difficult for other members of their household to find employment.

Lower unemployment (of this intentional type) and higher inequality may be viewed as good news or bad news, depending on whether one views labor market policy as a useful or misguided tool for pursuing goals that markets should in principle but might in practice fail to achieve. Financial market development can indeed fulfill some of the needs addressed by social policy in theory, and a consequence of flexibility-oriented developments in the labor market policies field should be a larger volume of financial market transactions: certainly as demand goes up along a given supply schedule, with negative welfare implications for families forced to purchase expensively from imperfect private providers of credit and insurance what they used to obtain from collective schemes; perhaps, with less negative implications, as supply conditions improve, either as a consequence of technical progress or market development, or fostered by appropriate reforms of the institutional structure of financial markets.

There is little doubt that EMU has led to yield convergence and substantial growth in the volume of financial transactions in the euro area (Jappelli and Pagano, this volume). Financial market integration across the boundaries of countries can decrease the need for employment and wage coordination within each country and ease the impact of labor market shocks at the country level, as savings can buffer some of the consequences of wage and employment fluctuations. To the extent that competition also improves financial market access and decreases transaction costs within each country, households may rely

Table 18.18: *Regressions of private credit/GDP on EMU dummy (equal to unity in 1999–2005 for Austria, Belgium, Germany, Spain, Finland, France, Ireland, Italy, the Netherlands, Portugal, in 2001–05 for Greece), unemployment, social policy. Regressions include a constant when they do not include country or year fixed effects. Sample: see last row.*

	Priv. credit	Priv. credit	Priv. credit	Priv. credit	Priv. credit
Inc. ineq.	7.9252		13.2088		
t	1.29		2.42		
Unemp.(tot)		–4.4948	–4.8482		
t		–5.21	–5.66		
EMU				20.3908	–1.6491
t				2.96	–0.39
Country eff	No	No	No	yes	Yes
Year effects	No	no	no	no	yes
N	116	116	116	94	116
Sample	EU15, 95–05	EU15, 95–05	EU15, 95–05	EMU11, 95–05	EU15, 95–05

on self-insurance and portfolio adjustments rather than on unemployment insurance or employment protection legislation in order to shelter their consumption from labor market shocks. This makes it less necessary for policy to interfere with laissez-faire outcomes, and can address concerns about lack of such policy instruments at the area-wide level.

As shown in the first three columns of Table 18.18, over the whole panel dataset credit is positively associated with income inequality, and negatively associated with unemployment (which again can be viewed as a summary measure of a labor market's degree of institutional rigidity). Thus, the data confirm that credit serves as a substitute for labor market policy as a tool for consumption smoothing in the face of higher labor income inequality or volatility. Financial market development can substitute government policies in some of their risk-management role, and if it accompanied labor market deregulation it would bring Continental European countries closer to the United States and other Anglo-Saxon countries along both dimensions. The fourth column of Table 18.18 shows that private credit did increase strongly in member countries after the inception of EMU. But the next column shows that all of the increase is accounted for by year fixed effects – i.e. that credit increased just as strongly, on average, in EU15 countries that did not adopt the common currency, and did not experience the other effects analyzed in this chapter. Labor market deregulation in the apparent absence of better accessible and more efficient financial markets may significantly affect workers' welfare, justify many European citizens' distrust of the euro, and threaten the sustainability of the EMU experiment.

5. Conclusion and policy implications

This chapter has illustrated interactions between economic integration and labor market policies and outcomes with a suggestive empirical analysis of evidence from the first ten years of EMU. It is important to re-emphasize that the empirical evidence can only speak of associations, not causal effects. Countries were not forced to join EMU, and presumably chose to do so in foreseeing effects of EMU that (aside from expectation errors) should be those we observe ex post. Still, EMU can in theory and does in practice improve performance of labor markets, chiefly through an evolution of member countries' labor markets towards increasingly flexible institutional configurations. This path may have negative welfare effects and could be politically difficult to sustain if labor market institutions still do (or are perceived to) serve useful purposes in the absence of suitable private financial market instruments for consumption smoothing.

The evidence is of course limited by the small amount of information available, and the association between labor market phenomena and economic integration need not warrant causal interpretation. But it does have important policy implications when interpreted in light of labor market policy's potential benefits and possible failures in practice. To the extent that limited financial market access burdens workers with uninsurable risk, correctly configured labor market policy can improve welfare. And if deeper economic integration enhances labor market risk at the same time as it blunts policies meant to control such risk, it needs to be accompanied by suitably coordinated and coherent development not only of labor market institutional structures, but also of financial markets and of policy instruments meant to reconcile production flexibility with consumption security.

Policies meant to address the welfare implications of income volatility are less necessary when private financial and insurance markets are accessible and efficient.[7] Financial exclusion is increasingly recognized as an important dimension of poverty (European Commission, 2008b) and an essential cause and consequence of persistently low welfare. Structural policies aimed at building informational and regulatory infrastructures for European household financial markets would reduce the problems posed by international opt-out opportunities to mandatory social security schemes. And to the extent that collective organization of insurance against life risks remains useful, it would not be necessary to implement such schemes at the European levels as long as a clear, actuarially fair link exists between contributions and benefits in national or occupational schemes. Just like competition among private insurers, competition among collective systems should be appropriately regulated and monitored, so as to ensure that individual participants are adequately informed. EU-level institutions can therefore play an important role in clarifying to citizens the appropriateness and sustainability of the relevant schemes, not only by enforcing budget rules that ensure coherence over time of public finances, but also by certifying that pension, health, and unemployment insurance schemes are consistent with individual choices.

Interactions between markets, policies, and countries are of course much broader than those discussed and empirically analyzed here. The influence of international trade and factor mobility on European labor markets spans beyond the borders of the highly developed EU15 countries, on which this chapter focuses, and also beyond the borders of the EU27 countries. The effects of trade between Europe and other countries on the appropriateness and feasibility of labor market regulation at the European supranational level (such as the stringency of recently revised working-time rules) is qualitatively similar to that discussed above. To the extent that uncoordinated policies loosen labor market regulation in an integrated economic area, economic integration is sustainable only if regulation becomes less necessary, for example because financial and other markets improve, or if it is coordinated at the same level as that of market interactions.

Supranational policies have addressed similar issues in other areas. Establishing a single market in goods required harmonization of policy instruments, such as safety and quality regulations, and a single capital market and fixed exchange rates led to adoption of a common currency. Just as uncoordinated macroeconomic policies were inconsistent with fixed exchange rates and free capital mobility before adoption of a single currency, market integration and subsidiary decision-making powers coexist uneasily in the labor market and social protection area. But harmonization is difficult in the labor market policy field, where heterogeneity within and across countries implies that similar policies have different costs and benefits, while different policies are used to target similar goals. Therefore efforts to foster international coordination run the risk of imposing excessively complex or excessively uniform constraints on economic agents. The theories and data reviewed in this paper – and new data, such as those collected and analyzed in the framework of the Eurosystem's Wage Dynamics Network[8] and the 2008 update of the OECD's employment protection indicators – may help assess the pros and cons of further reforms.

Data Appendix:definitions and sources

Emp.rate (prime-age female)	Prime-age (age 25–54) female employment rate (%). Source: Bassanini and Duval (2006).
Emp.rate (prime-age male)	Prime-age (age 25–54) male employment rate (%). Source: Bassanini and Duval (2006).
Emp.rate (female).	Employment rate, 25+ female. Source: Eurostat.
EPL (reg)	EPL stringency indicator: regular contracts. Source: Bassanini and Duval (2006).
EPL (tmp)	EPL stringency indicator: temporary contracts. Source: Bassanini and Duval (2006).
GDP p.c.	GDP per capita at 1995 prices, thousands of euro. Source: Eurostat.
GovtBudg:	General government deficit(-) /surplus (+), % GDP (Maastricht criteria definition).
Inc.ineq.	$80^{th}/20^{th}$ quantile share ratio, net equivalized household income. Missing values are interpolated. Source: Eurostat.
IneqDef	Dummy, equal to zero for country and periods when Eurostat makes available the ECHP-based inequality measure or data are missing, to one for country and periods when the EU-SILK measure is available.
Lab.prod.	Labor productivity per hour worked, PPS gdp, EU15=100. Source: Eurostat.

Lab.Tax (avg)	Tax on the average production worker: total tax wedge in %, single workers at 100% of average earnings, no child. Source: OECD.
Lab.Tax (marg)	Unweighted average of marginal tax wedges for four family types. Source: Bertola and Lo Prete (2008) computations on OECD data.
Long term un.	Long-term unemployment rate, % of total active population. Source: Eurostat.
Openn.(FDI)	Foreign direct investment flows as % of GDP. Source: Eurostat.
Openn.(goods)	Imports+exports of goods as % of GDP. Source: Eurostat.
Openn.(serv.)	Imports+exports of services as % of GDP. Source: Eurostat.
P.social exp.	Public social public expenditure (except old age and survivor pensions), ratio to GDP. Source: Eurostat.
Priv.credit	Ratio to GDP of consolidated credit to total residents granted by the resident banking sector (monetary financial institutions, or MFIs). Includes MFI loans to residents and MFI holdings of securities issued by residents. Securities comprise shares, other equity and debt securities. Source: Eurostat.
UI rep.rate	Average unemployment benefit replacement rate across several worker and family types. Source: Bassanini and Duval (2006).
Unemp.(tot)	Unemployment rate, age 15 and over (%). Source: Eurostat.
Unemp.(2554)	Unemployment rate, age 25–54 (%). Source: Bassanini and Duval (2006).
Youth Unemp.	Unemployment rate, age 15–24 (%). Source: Bassanini and Duval (2006).

Notes

1. See Rogoff (2006) for an extensive discussion. Sbordone (2007) assesses whether a more competitive economic structure, modeled in terms of market-size-dependent mark-up as in Mélitz and Ottaviano (2008), can imply a flatter inflation/output relationship in response to monetary and

other shocks. In practice the effect is small, because the lower mark-ups implied by more intense international trade are also variable and more sensitive to economic conditions.

2. See Bertola and Boeri (2002), and Nicoletti *et al.* (2001) for empirical evidence from the quasi-monetary union of the so-called D-Mark area in the 1980s and 1990s.

3. European Commission (2007h) contains an extensive discussion of recent developments. Arpaia and Pichelmann (2007) uncover a number of interesting, but difficult-to-interpret differences in wage adjustment mechanisms across European countries.

4. European Commission (2007c, Chapter 3) examines the evidence regarding the tradeoff between productivity and employment implied by movements along labor demand curves, finding that such a relationship explains only a portion of observed labor productivity, and that it is unstable and disturbed by total factor productivity changes.

5. Both average and marginal taxes are theoretically relevant to labor market participation and labor supply choices. See Pissarides (1998) for a discussion of their effects on unemployment.

6. Bassanini and Duval also find only weak and mixed evidence of interactions between various dimensions of labor market regulation. A large and influential body of work argues that comprehensive policy reforms have larger effects than piecemeal ones. Of course, however, labor market institutions reinforce each other's effects along both the undesirable (lower employment) and desirable (higher and more stable labor incomes) dimensions: thus, policy complementarities need to be taken into account when considering how structural change affects the desirability of reforms, but need not imply that comprehensive reforms are "better" than piecemeal ones.

7. Differences across countries in the efficiency of financial markets are both theoretically and empirically relevant to the desirability of redistribution policies. See Bertola and Koeniger (2007) for theory, evidence, and references.

8. www.ecb.int/events/conferences/html/wage_dynamics_network.en.html.

19 How product market reforms lubricate shock adjustment in the euro area

JACQUES PELKMANS,
LOURDES ACEDO MONTOYA AND
ALESSANDRO MARAVALLE

1. Aim and structure

After ten years of experience of the euro, few would dispute that it and the euro area have fared much better than many observers expected (see e.g European Commission, 2008a, for a very detailed account and analysis). However, this does not mean that some policy concerns have not lingered on. One prominent concern on which analysts, defenders, advocates and diehard opponents agree is the fear of a too weak adjustment capacity of the euro area. This chapter deals with one element of adjustment in the absence of national exchange rates and monetary policies, namely, the functioning of product markets when improved by reforms.

One question amongst several which preoccupy policy makers in the euro area is the rather unequal and overall insufficient ability of euro-area countries to adjust to asymmetric shocks, or, to common shocks with asymmetric effects. As is well known, in a monetary union, monetary policy and, by implication, exchange rate policy, are no longer available for individual countries, so that alternative channels of adjustment have to be relied upon. The better these work, the greater the ability to adjust, i.e. the lower the costs of adjustment to such shocks. Such abilities to adjust are a complex function of a range of options, including fiscal responses, temporary financial capital flows and market flexibilities, distinct as to countries and varying over time or case by case. This chapter will focus on the lubrication of adjustment brought about by well-functioning markets. In particular, it deals with the subset of what are called *product market reforms* (comprising goods and services markets) meant to improve market functioning and thereby helping to facilitate adjustment processes in EMU. Other markets matter, too, such as labor, financial,[1] housing, and land markets but these will not be dealt with, except in passing and with some attention for the link (both substitutability and complementarity) with labor markets.

This chapter aims to:

- make the case as to why product market reforms lubricate adjustment processes in EMU and underpin it with empirical evidence;
- substantiate shortcomings in product market functioning in the euro area, based on available empirical evidence e.g. about price stickiness in services markets and a lack of competition hindering resource allocation processes;
- clarify the "fit" of product market reforms in wider euro-area reform strategies, in terms of sequencing, complementarities with other reforms and subsidiarity constraints.

This chapter can neither be a fully fledged survey (given the space available) nor pretend to shift the frontiers of economic analysis in this domain, even if we hope to contribute with some new empirical work in Section 3. It will first (in Section 2) set out what product market reforms are (and distinguish them from structural, microeconomic and regulatory reforms) as well as the main measurement issues, followed by an analysis of how such reforms lubricate adjustment processes in EMU, in particular via the *competitiveness channel*. Attention is paid to the short-run and longer-run aspects of adjustments to shocks and the scant empirical evidence on the role of product markets in adjustment is discussed. In Section 3, we investigate empirically the need for product market reforms in the euro area, based on the EU KLEMS dataset. Two questions are addressed: how likely is it for euro-area countries to experience an asymmetric shock, and what empirical evidence can we deduce about their capacity to adjust to asymmetric shocks? The approach is disaggregated and highlights sectors (especially services) with relatively greater adjustment problems. In Section 4, the record of product market reforms of the euro-area countries is briefly summarized. We show that substantial reforms have been undertaken; however, there is considerable evidence that the eurozone, in particular with respect to services, could significantly intensify product market reforms and thereby augment the net benefits of having a single currency. Subsequently, product market reforms are placed in the context of wider reform efforts (complementarities e.g. with labor and financial markets) as well as in the two-tier institutional structure of the euro area and the EU at large (given cross-border spillovers and the case for coordination) in Section 5. Designing reforms in this euro-area context is briefly discussed. A final section with policy messages concludes.

2. Product market reforms: definition, scope, and significance for adjustment

By definition, countries joining a monetary union lose their monetary and exchange rate policy. Therefore, those countries will need alternative adjustment channels when facing asymmetric shocks or common shocks with asymmetric effects. Such shocks can be cushioned via temporary financial capital flows, by means of national fiscal policy, or via market-based channels in the short and longer run respectively. Disregarding fiscal policy and realizing that capital flows may postpone real adjustment, a country's ability to adjust or its resilience to shocks amounts to the capacity (a) to absorb the shock without increasing the volatility of economic aggregates (growth, unemployment, and/or inflation), while (b) returning to trend performance with relatively high speed.

As the modern *optimal currency area* (OCA) theory suggests (Mongelli, 2008 and this volume), the costs of shocks are minimized if: i) prices and wages are sufficiently flexible; ii) factors are mobile; iii) financial markets are fully integrated; iv) member countries are open to global trade; v) consumption and production risks are amply diversified; vi) fiscal stabilization tools work smoothly; and vii) there are few asymmetries in shocks and their transmission process. The significance of product market reforms is directly related to items (i), (iii), and (iv) and possibly items (v) and (vii). With respect to item (iii), one might wonder why OCA theory has not simply considered "product market integration", rather than the integration of one subset: financial markets. Presumably, a reasonable assumption is that price and wage flexibility is likely to be fostered by the deep market integration the euro area has achieved. A direct route to market integration is found in openness to trade. Mongelli distinguishes four elements making up this item. First, there is the overall openness to world trade. However, in the eurozone, this is predominantly the openness to EU, and especially euro-area, countries, which is actually the second element the author identifies. This is, of course, a direct function of product market integration. Third, there is the share of tradeables versus non-tradeables. What remains "non-tradeable" is largely a matter of the nature of demand (e.g. local) and limits of technology; still, in the margin, deep services integration tends to enlarge the share of tradeables services.[2] All in all, product market integration can certainly be considered as a most useful "reform", contributing to smoother shock adjustment.

This summing up underscores that product market reforms should not be considered in isolation. However, if cross-border and (even intra-country) labor mobility is limited, automatic stabilizers turn out to be constrained by the Stability and Growth Pact (SGP) and shocks are mostly asymmetric, the relative importance of product market reforms in "lubricating" adjustment quickly increases. In the EU's EMU, therefore, reforming product markets matters.

The present section defines and explains the concepts of product market reforms as well as adjustment capacity, and how the former can support the latter in a monetary union. Section 2.1 sets out what product market reforms are in the EU context and briefly refers to some measurement issues. Section 2.2 defines the adjustment problem in a monetary union and explains the role of product market reforms in lubricating adjustment. Section 2.3 then discusses the existing empirical evidence on the matter.

2.1 Product market reforms: concept and measurement

At a general level, product market reforms are changes in market institutions with a view to have goods and services markets functioning better. However, once one becomes interested in measurement and/or the nuts and bolts of policies to accomplish such reforms, we need much greater detail and precision. The literature is not very disciplined in sticking to one clear and well-accepted definition.

Four terms are often used interchangeably or with fuzzy boundaries: product market reforms, regulatory reforms, structural reforms, and microeconomic reforms. The latter two amount to concepts with a very wide scope, including regulatory reforms for all markets (not just goods and services), the degree and nature of state ownership as well as competition policy, but may also include bottleneck infrastructures, education and up-skilling of workers, innovation systems, taxation and public administration including e-government, pension reform, and possibly many other aspects. The present chapter cannot go into

Capital Markets / FDI	Product Market Reforms (narrow)	Labor Market Reforms (narrow)

o golden shares
 	
[some link with state ownership more generally]*
 	
o effective free establishment
 	
IPRs
o national (patent) regulation
 	
[tension with IM & EU competition policy]
[link with knowledge-based economy]**
	o market integration
	  o EU regulation
	    • filling IM gaps
	    • better (EU) regulation
	    public procurement
	    • effect. free movement + MR
	o effective free establishment
	o competition policy
	  • anti-trust + mergers
	  • state-aids
	o national regulation
	  • network industries
	  • professional services
	  • wholesale/retail
	o openness to world economy
		o national labour market regulation
		  • job protection (EPL, etc.)
		  • working hours
		o wage bargaining
		o internal market
		  • free movement of workers
		  • posted workers
		  • EU minimum regulatory requirements (health / safety)
		  • extra-EU immigration
		o labour taxation

PMRs (wider)		LMRs (wider)

o business environment & entrepreneurship
  • start-up conditions
  • improving SME context
    • efficiency legal system
    • cut red tape (regulation)
    • better regulatory quality
    • G2B and G2G e-government
o state ownership[3]
[links with knowledge-based economy, esp. R & D and innovation]
		o unemployment & welfare-related benefits
		o incentives-based employment policy
		  • active labour market policies
		  • intra-EU, interregional, inter sectoral mobility incentives
		o education
		  • systemic responses to future (skill) needs
		  • vocational; up-skilling (on the job)

Figure 19.1: Product market reforms as subsets of microeconomic reforms

the considerable problems of taxonomy and methodology for conceptualizing reforms and their measurement (see Pelkmans, 2008, forthcoming). Product market reforms are only a limited subset of structural reforms (see Figure 19.1) or, for that matter, of microeconomic reforms. It is also not correct to regard regulatory reforms as fully equivalent to product market reforms: in Figure 19.1, under a strict definition of regulatory reforms, only the six aspects in gray would qualify.

Figure 19.1 is designed to clarify for the reader what is meant by product market reforms in an EU (and euro-area) context. The center column in the top part of the figure and the left column in the bottom part together can be seen as product market reforms. Distinguishing the two is merely a function of how broadly or narrowly one defines the concept. In designing Figure 19.1, we based it largely on the MICREF and LABREF datasets of microeconomic reforms in the EU.[4] The figure shows clearly that product market reforms should not be seen in isolation from other (microeconomic or structural) reforms, whether they are in labor markets (again, in a narrow and wider perspective) or in capital markets (including foreign direct investment and the right of establishment) or with respect to patents, for example.

The narrow view of product market reforms is concerned with internal market integration (both effective free movement of goods and services, including mutual recognition, as well as regulatory aspects of the internal market and open and competitive public procurement), EU and national competition policy, national regulation in such markets (such as network industries, professional services and wholesale and retail), and the openness to the world economy (which tends to improve the contestability of markets beyond what the internal market already accomplishes). The wider concept of product market reforms, designed with a view to promote (more) dynamic market conduct and rivalry, is concerned with what is usually called the business environment and (fewer barriers to) entrepreneurship as well as the longer-run impact of the knowledge-based economy, especially R&D and innovation. One may also include state ownership, as indeed the reform literature typically does.[5] Altogether, product market reforms in the EU context can be deep and intrusive so as to engender permanent pro-competitive effects in all relevant goods and services markets in the Union.

Product market reforms in Figure 19.1 are complex and multifaceted. Tracking such reforms for all Member States and/or for the euro-area countries every year as well as over time requires considerable investment in a common methodology, taxonomy, and proper reporting. In the absence of systematic reporting, it would be next to impossible to appreciate their meaning and progress in achieving better functioning markets. Following the experience in the Lisbon Strategy and stimulated by earlier work in the OECD (see Box 19.1), the EU has developed the common LABREF and MICREF taxonomies which will enable objective and transparent comparisons between Member States, also over time. Dependent on an agreed methodology, it will become feasible as well to develop quantitative indicators of progress. Given the importance of smooth adjustment in the euro area, policy makers in the euro area (if not at the EU level more generally, in the framework of the Lisbon Strategy, for example) need a more strategic, rather than lengthy and descriptive, overview. This explains the search for quantitative indicators as proxies for these reforms and their progress over time. By definition, the policy activities referred to in Figure 19.1 are hard to measure exactly. Nevertheless, by ranking measures or interventions in terms of degrees of restrictiveness of competition in markets, considerable progress has been made during the last decade or so in developing indicators in the literature. Box 19.1 provides a summary of the more important indicators, with very brief comments.

Box 19.1: **Indicators measuring product market reform**

In the literature, indicators have been developed in order to dispose of empirical proxies for restrictiveness of regulation and other public and private interventions hindering or distorting competitive processes in goods and services markets. These datasets allow, in principle, comparisons between countries and between different points in time. Changes of indicators over time in the direction of less restrictiveness are usually regarded as empirical evidence of product market reforms (note that this assumes that none of the indicators relate to market failures, so that less restrictiveness would not lead to underregulation). Interested readers are referred to Dierx *et al.* (2007) and the European Commission (2006a: Chapter 4) for recent surveys and to the literature indicated below.

The most important indicators are:

a. The *OECD PMR indicators*: they combine restrictiveness measures in sixteen domains of regulation and other interventions (scaling 0–6, from least to most restrictive), aggregated to three categories: state control, barriers to entrepreneurship, and barriers to trade and investment; single country PMR indicators are found by aggregation via weights. Although the OECD indicators have advantages such as objectivity, transparency, and quantifiability, probably they are no longer deep and targeted enough to identify the relevant pockets of restrictiveness in product markets of euro-area countries having already reformed at EU and national level over a period of two decades or more (Conway *et al.*, 2005).

b. *New, targeted OECD indicators*: OECD economists have published several new, more targeted indicators since 2006. One set refers solely to specific subsets of services such as six network industries (and road transport), plus retail distribution and four professional services (together called the NMR indicators). The idea is that the more important pockets of restrictiveness are nowadays to be found in specific services markets. The data underlying NMRs are far more refined than the (services elements of) PMRs.

Another indicator attempts to measure the strength of competition policies of OECD *countries*, including most euro-area countries. Of course, well-designed and properly enforced competition policies greatly help markets to function better. A significant drawback of this CLP (competition law and policy) indicator is the failure to account for *EU-level* competition policy. A third indicator is the FDI restrictiveness index, measuring the deviations from national treatment[6] (Conway and Nicoletti, 2006; Hoj *et al.*, 2007; Koyama and Golub, 2006).

c. The World Bank's annual *Doing Business* survey focuses on the business environment, with ten indicators relating mainly to entry, transaction costs, and market access. Horizontal aspects such as starting a business, enforcing contracts and getting credit are combined with specific issues such as licensing, trading across borders and employing workers. The indicators do not target specific markets other than the labor market (World Bank, 2007a).

d. The Fraser Institute's (2007) *index of economic freedom* is built up – *inter alia* – from indices on business regulation, on state involvement and on freedom of trade. The data are derived from opinion surveys of business leaders in the World Competitiveness Report (of the World Economic Forum) and are therefore largely subjective; the comparability between countries and over time is to some extent intuitive and hard to verify. Conway and Nicoletti (2006: 48) show that practically all OECD countries in 2003 cluster in the 5–7½ range of Fraser (leaving out state involvement); this means that more targeted indicators are needed for identifying relevant pockets of restrictiveness hindering proper market functioning.

e. The Copenhagen Economics *Market Opening Index*, for seven network industries and based on twelve market opening milestones, ranging from ownership, third-party access, the pricing of third-party access, unbundling, regulation of user prices, etc. Not unlike the OECD (see b. above), a system of weights makes it possible to obtain aggregate indices per country, and for 1993 and 2003 (Copenhagen Economics, 2005).

Further discussion about the merits and shortcomings of product market reform indicators can be found in Pelkmans (2008, forthcoming). Note that MICREF data might enable the Commission to develop a quantitative approach in the near future.

2.2 Adjustment in EMU: *the role of product market reforms*

EMU is a unique economic structure in which monetary policy has been delegated to a single common authority, and members' fiscal policy discretion is constrained in the margin by the SGP rules. Given this macroeconomic context, "there is no alternative" (TINA) but to foster structural reforms, in order to facilitate market-based adjustment to asymmetric shocks.

When regulations and other private and/or public interventions are restrictive, without a proper justification of market failures, such policies, regulations, and other market institutions are likely to engender adverse effects on goods and services markets functioning. This is most clear in the case of protection against external competitors or indeed shelter against domestic ones. Indicators on product market reform mostly refer to what is often denoted as economic regulation – i.e. a direct intervention in markets rarely sustained by an economic rationale for such an intrusive action (the motives could be redistributional or related to vested interests). In such cases product market regulations can impede effective competition, hence increasing firms' market power and their ability to raise prices via higher mark-ups.

Easing product market regulations therefore leads to an increase in competition via sharper pricing by less constricted rivals, be it in the domestic market or via intra-EU or world trade, via higher firm entry (domestic or via FDI) and/or wider consumer choice (which increases demand elasticities and/or product substitutibility).[7] One must also differentiate between the short- and the long-run effects of reforms since they are important for policy design (Schiantarelli, 2005).[8] Thus, price flexibility typically appears as a short-run effect, strengthened by a high degree of market integration and the price transparency effect from using a common currency. The time perspective lengthens when considering the productive efficiency effects of product market reforms. Intra-firm reallocation and market selection processes between firms with different productivity profiles may mean that time is needed to modify firms' entry and exit patterns. A still longer time perspective arises from the dynamics of firm innovation.[9]

In a monetary union, the main functional risks of which are found in asymmetric shocks, the efficiency effects of product market reforms will reinforce members' adjustment capacity in two ways. First, pro-growth reforms will foster real as well as structural convergence by speeding up the catching-up process over the longer run. In other words, product market reforms, by promoting convergence in the long run, reduce the probability of suffering asymmetric shocks and subsequently the need for adjustment. Second, reforms grease short-run adjustment mechanisms when asymmetric shocks occur.

2.2.1 Structural convergence effects of product market reforms

Panel (a) of Figure 19.2 explains the structural convergence effect of product market reforms, which is essentially a long-term effect. There is evidence that product market reforms may reduce structural differences across EMU in the long run through sustained productivity growth rates and gradually converging industrial specialization patterns. Indeed, several empirical studies demonstrate that reforming product markets generates efficiency gains which translate into higher productivity and changes in industrial concentration and specialization (Lane, 2006a). By fostering competition, product reforms favor resource reallocation, lower price mark-ups and facilitate innovation[10] (allocative, productive, and dynamic efficiency gains), increasing in turn growth and employment.

Hence, the market restructuring effects of product market reforms may lead in the long run to changes in industrial concentration and specialization which in turn influence the synchronization of business cycles. Following Krugman (1993b), Dierx *et al.* (2004a) point to a modest decline in industrial concentration for individual Member States while the opposite occurs at EU level. Still, they also consider that, as negative agglomeration economies appear due to increasing concentration in some areas of the EU, one may observe a redispersion of economic activities looking for cheaper production factors. However, these modest effects for industry might be swamped by the more or less constant structures of the activities of much larger services. On specialization, two diverging economic theories have coexisted since the early nineties: Krugman (1993b) on the one hand, who considers that deeper economic integration leads to further spatial specialization, and the European Commission (1990) on the other hand, foreseeing increasing intra-industry trade and a decline in specialization.

The empirical studies testing for both hypotheses on the affiliation of business cycles are numerous and to some extent inconclusive. Some, like Bergman (2004), consider that flexible exchange rate regimes are more favorable to the synchronization of business cycles, so EMU could

Panel (a):Long-run effects of PMRs: Productivity and structural convergence

PMRs

Structural convergence

Productivity

Industrial specialization

Less asymmetric shocks

Panel (b): Adjustment effects of PMRs (short and long run)

PMRs

Competition

Factor reallocation

Lower price mark-ups

Growth and employment

Competitiveness

Ease fiscal policy

Ease monetary policy (Real interest rate)

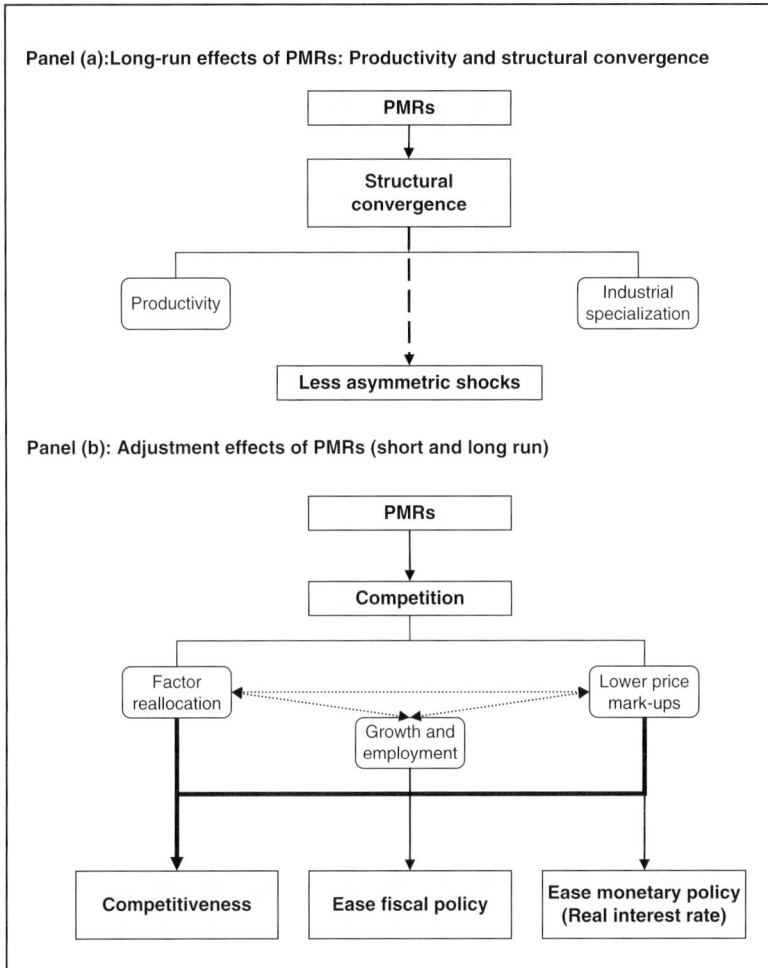

Figure 19.2: Product market reforms for adjustment

lead to further asymmetries. Others like Inklaar *et al.* (2008) consider that business cycles in the euro area have gone through periods of both convergence and divergence. Nonetheless, they find evidence of stronger cyclical affiliations during the run-up to EMU (which is also a period of strong reform intensity) compared with the evolution of cycles in the previous two decades. Gayer (2007) finds some desynchronization around 2003 as a result of different adjustment speeds (which could also be explained to some extent by divergent liberalization efforts).

However, when comparing affiliations among EMU members with the rest of the EU, Gayer (2007) identifies a "eurozonization" of business cycles. This is interpreted as a relative increase in synchronization within the euro area compared to non-EMU countries.[11]

All in all, it is probably fair to say that product market reforms induce flexibility, boosting productivity catching-up (Conway *et al.* 2006) and increasing the synchronization of business cycles, which can be considered as a catch-all property for optimum currency areas.[12] This, in turn, means fewer asymmetric shocks and a better functioning of the common monetary policy.

2.2.2 Adjustment channels: competitiveness, real interest rate, and fiscal policy

As Panel (b) of Figure 19.2 shows, product market reforms carry more weight in the short/medium term when they play a role in lubricating adjustment via three channels: competitiveness, real interest rate, and fiscal policy. However, the *competitiveness channel* is the principal mechanism (the thicker arrow in the picture) to counteract the destabilising effects of an idiosyncratic shock.[13]

A smooth functioning of the *competitiveness channel* implies realignments of the real effective exchange rate via changes in prices and costs reflecting the new cyclical conditions imposed by the asymmetric shock. For instance, if a negative demand shock occurs, prices will decrease more easily as a result of fiercer competition. Thus, a depreciation of the real exchange rate of the country experiencing the slowdown will make its products more attractive for its EMU trading partners, thereby increasing international demand, which may cancel out the initial negative shock and so restoring equilibrium. Conway *et al.* (2006) test empirically the case of a positive supply shock. Their conclusions are consistent with the theory, showing that restrictive product market regulation slows down the adjustment process, hindering cross-border technology diffusion and FDI.

As a result of product market reforms aimed at increasing the number of competitors and facilitating market entry, incumbents will experience a reduction of their monopolistic rents and be forced to set prices closer to marginal costs, thereby reducing mark-ups and relaxing price stickiness downward. Since the euro area is characterized by persistent nominal wage stickiness, which impedes labor adjustments either in terms of hours worked or employment, the burden of adjustment falls on price changes (European Commission, 2006a). It should be noted, however, that stronger product market competition may eventually prompt changes in labor market policies and institutions.[14] This means that, when assessing the total effects of product market reforms, one needs to consider both the direct effect and the effect through induced changes in labor market policies and institutions.

Moreover, the functioning of the price system can be improved by wage changes spurred by labor market reforms. The combined effect of reforming product and labor markets will exceed the sum of individual effects both in terms of growth and employment as well as adjustment capacity. Using consumption smoothing as a sign of adjustment capacity, Ernst *et al.* (2007) find out that improving the functioning of labor and product markets reduces consumption volatility. Thus, households' consumption is less correlated with employment and production shocks, which ensures better resilience to shocks and higher welfare.[15]

Policy complementarities are also found between product market and financial sector reforms. In the euro area, financial liberalization is essential because it helps to cushion shocks by allowing for risk diversification and by stimulating investment. It also has a significant impact on growth and employment (Tressel, 2008; European Commission, 2008a).

In another attempt to highlight empirically the effects of competition on price flexibility, Álvarez and Hernando (2006), using a dataset on pricing behavior for nine euro-area countries, confirm that heavy product market regulation diminishes price flexibility and that more competitive markets are better suited to cope with economic shocks via price adjustments.[16] Moreover, capital and labor will be allocated (within firms and between firms) to the production of the goods and services that consumers value more, so less efficient firms will exit the market, increasing the market shares and profits of the remaining firms. Besides increasing allocative efficiency, productive efficiency gains are reaped through three conduits: i) increased competition facilitates the comparison of performance of different firms, in turn, improving investors' decisions; ii) bankruptcy is more likely in a competitive environment so managers need to enhance their efforts to avoid such failures; and iii) workers and managers have an incentive to reduce costs to capture part of the profits derived from stronger competition (Schiantarelli, 2005 and European Commission, 2006a). In the EMU context, the reallocation effect will be reinforced by the so-called price transparency effect from using a common currency. Greater price transparency also limits the possibility of increasing mark-ups, leading to greater competition and more efficient factor utilization (Gasiorek *et al.* 2004).

Increasing potential growth via product market reforms will also help euro-area members to overcome their current account imbalances via trade or by making the euro area more attractive to real and financial investments (IMF, 2004c). As was previously mentioned, product market reforms also generate dynamic gains from additional innovation efforts. Though the effect of innovation is mainly observed in the long run, there are some types of innovations either in products or processes that take a shorter time to materialize and hence may facilitate adjustment by increasing competitiveness.

Allocative and productive efficiency gains in terms of output can be reaped in the short to medium term since they are normally the consequence of a one-off measure. On the contrary, dynamic gains can be obtained "indefinitely" but they usually take a much longer time to materialize. In terms of adjustment to shocks and its rapidity, the effects on price mark-ups and reallocation will be accomplished more swiftly.

Though it is difficult to identify the effect of product market reforms on adjustment via the *real interest rate* and *fiscal policy channel*, we can derive some indirect positive effects of reforms.

Real interest rates shape investment and consumption decisions in an economy. In the EMU, nominal interest rates are fixed by the ECB on the basis of a common strategy for the whole euro area. However, the common interest rate may have divergent effects according to a country's cyclical position in the euro area (the Walters critique). Thus if the country is in an expansionary cyclical position, inflation is expected to be higher than the average euro-area inflation. In this case, national real interest rates will be lower than the average, hence procyclical. The opposite will happen if the country experiences a downturn compared to the euro area as a whole: again, the real interest remaining too high is procyclical, thereby hardening the recovery. However, differences in the cyclical position are just one of the explanatory variables of inflation differentials (European Commission, 2008a). Indeed, one could also blame structural inefficiencies (heavily regulated product, labor, and financial markets) and misaligned national policies as possible explanations for inflation differentials in EMU. Therefore, competition-enhancing product market reforms are expected to weaken price stickiness, and in turn inflation persistence.

Given the destabilising effects of the *real interest rate* channel, it is important to take the necessary actions to minimize its effects by enhancing the functioning of the *competitiveness* and/or the *fiscal policy* channel. According to recent estimates, the competitiveness channel seems to be powerful enough to compensate for the destabilizing effects of the real interest rate channel (European Commission, 2008a). However, as we shall show later, there is still ample scope for further product market reforms. In an EMU context, these continued reforms can be expected to enhance the competitiveness channel and to reduce inflation differentials, thereby facilitating the conduct of the ECB's monetary policy at a lower sacrifice ratio.[17]

Finally, there is a twofold interaction between product market reforms and fiscal policy. On the one hand, as product market reforms positively affect growth and employment, governments will enjoy healthier public finances, leaving more room to maneuver in the event of a shock and improving the functioning of automatic stabilizers.[18] On the other hand, aggregate demand policies might stimulate product market reforms since they can be used to counteract the temporary negative supply effects of reforms and so reducing political resistance.[19] Moreover, the reformed SGP gives euro-area governments sufficient leeway to confront a negative shock and it also contains special provisions to facilitate the reform of labor and product markets in the event of future disturbances.

EMU implies stronger economic and political links among its members (e.g. common currency, single monetary authority, fiscal commitments, etc). Given this strong interdependence between euro-area members, there is a higher probability that the actions taken by a single country spill over to the others. Hence, beyond the need for smooth adjustment for individual euro-area countries, there is a case for a coordinated and comprehensive approach to reforms when there are significant synergies/complementarities across reform areas and/or countries; there may also be a more powerful incentive for policy learning by spreading good practises. These reasons justify common reform strategies in EMU as a whole (IMF, 2004c; European Commission, 2007d). The practical details of a common euro-area reform strategy would require a separate study, but a good deal of the strategy could and should piggy-back on the Lisbon Strategy. What it means in any event is that euro-area countries, in being explicit about their profound joint interest in national reforms, should aim to be front runners. A common, deep reform commitment (in product markets and beyond) can become manifest and more credible with a publicly known common strategy, with specific commitments, motivated by the joint benefits of smoother adjustment. It is also likely that the recently initiated product market monitoring in the framework of the Single Market Review[20] can help to identify badly functioning product markets in the EU Single market on which euro-area countries could focus with priority.

2.2.3 Reforming product markets for adjustment: empirical evidence

Based on the above theoretical explanations, we conclude that product market reforms (presumably combined with labor and financial market ones) are most desirable in EMU for the sake of adjustment, spillovers, and/or complementarities. Reforming product markets does indeed improve the euro-area resilience to economic shocks, that is to say, the ability to contain the initial effect of the shock and to minimize the time needed to get back to the trend after the shock (European Commission, 2008a).[21] This question has recently been assessed in two empirical papers: Duval *et al.* (2007) and Grenouilleau *et al.* (2007). Though their methodologies differ, their conclusions are essentially the same: product market reforms do improve adjustment capacity.

Duval *et al.* (2007) study the impact of policy and institutional settings on resilience to common shocks.[22] Using a dataset for twenty OECD countries (of which ten are euro-area members), the econometric analysis takes two steps. First, the authors estimate a dynamic panel using output gap as the dependent variable which provides estimations for a country-specific output gap variable and a country-specific reaction to common shocks (amplification mechanism of the shock). Second, these two parameters are regressed against labor and product market regulation (unemployment replacement rates, employment protection legislation, collective bargaining coverage, centralization/coordination of wage bargaining) and an indicator for regulation stringency for seven non-manufacturing industries (mainly network industries, see Box 19.1, item b.). Their results suggest that strict labor and product market regulation may mitigate the initial impact of a common shock while making it more persistent.[23] By including some indicators of financial flexibility in the model, the authors find that these are also relevant in reducing both the time of recovery and the impact of the shock (though with a smaller degree of confidence). A country-disaggregated analysis shows that Continental Europe is the worst performer because of its relatively more stringent product, labor, and financial markets.[24]

Grenouilleau *et al.* (2007) estimate a DSGE model to compare responsiveness to shocks in the euro area and the USA. The model first identifies the structural differences between the euro area and the USA that may explain divergent responsiveness to shocks. They found three main sources of rigidities: i) differences in price adjustment costs (which is also found to be the most relevant); ii) differences in labor adjustment costs; and iii) differences in labor supply elasticity. The impact of these rigidities is assessed against two types of shocks: demand and supply (total factor productivity) shock. Price rigidities are found especially relevant for impeding adjustment to a productivity shock. In fact, fast price reactions could cushion the employment effects and facilitate the technology transmission. A quick price decrease means higher real wages, ergo stronger demand. Price rigidities also delay employment adjustment leading to higher cumulated output losses. These results seem to confirm those of Conway *et al.* (2006).

These empirical studies support the reform motive that more flexible product markets (especially when combined with labor and capital reforms) improve the resilience to economic shocks, mainly via their price effect. Our empirical analysis below complements these findings and provides additional insights into the specific country and sectoral capacity to adjust, an issue that has hardly been treated by the literature.

3. Adjustment capabilities and product market reforms: new empirical evidence

Euro-area countries can no longer count on the nominal exchange rate or the national monetary policy to adjust to country-specific shocks. The burden of the adjustment for them relies principally on changes in the intra-area real effective exchange rate (REER), that is the so-called *competitiveness channel*. However, euro countries also have to face a real interest rate channel that moves against the adjustment. Indeed, if asymmetric shocks are thought to drive the country-specific business cycle away from the euro-area business cycle, then the real interest rate will move procyclically and against the adjustment.

In this section we focus on empirical evidence about the need for product market reforms in the euro area. First, we investigate whether

EMU countries are flexible enough by providing evidence on their capacity to adjust to asymmetric shocks (or to common shocks with asymmetric effects). Second, we investigate the likelihood of a euro-area country experiencing an asymmetric shock since the ability to adjust only matters if asymmetric shocks are probable. In order to provide guidance on which sectors are most in need of reforms, we adopt a sectoral approach (at a fairly high level of aggregation) in which several goods and services sectors are considered. Our analysis tries to highlight empirically which sectors should be reformed in priority.

3.1 Dataset

Both analyses are based on the EU KLEMS dataset which provides sectoral data at annual frequency over the period 1970–2005 for eleven euro countries (Luxembourg excluded). Twelve sectors are taken into account to obtain a finer representation of the good- and services-producing sectors of the economy.[25] In particular, Table 19.1 shows that the first three sectors belong to the goods-producing activities while the remaining nine to the services-producing activities.[26]

Table 19.1: *Sector classification*

N.	Description	Abbreviation
Goods-producing sectors		
1	Agriculture, hunting, forestry and fishing	Agriculture
2	Mining and quarrying	Mining
3	Total manufacturing	Manufacturing
Service-producing sectors		
4	Electricity, gas and water supply	Electricity and gas
5	Construction	Construction
6	Wholesale and retail trade	Trade
7	Hotels and restaurants	Hotels
8	Transport and storage	Transport
9	Post and telecommunications	Post
10	Financial intermediation	Finance
11	Real estate, renting and business activities	Business
12	Community social and personal services	Community services

Source: EU KLEMS dataset.

3.2 Estimating the ability to adjust across sectors and countries in the euro area

The ability of a country to adjust has been evaluated in the literature in two ways. The first approach estimates or calibrates a DSGE model that is used to simulate the economic reaction to the shock of interest (i.e. European Commission 2006a; Grenouilleau *et al.* 2007); the second approach, instead, relies only on the econometric analysis of the data (i.e. Duval *et al.* 2007). While a model-based analysis is more sophisticated, as it allows the taking into account of a specific economic structure and analysis of really detailed research questions, since our goal is to find some general evidence about sectoral divergences in the ability to adjust across euro-area countries, a simple econometric approach is sufficient.

We measure the ability to adjust across countries and sectors by means of a simple bivariate VAR that allows us to measure the impact on inflation and output growth rate of demand and supply shocks. The variables that are considered are the real output growth rate and the inflation rate, both taken at the sectoral level. Following Blanchard and Quah (1989), we identify supply and demand shocks through the long-run restriction that demand shocks have no long-run real effects. The basics of the technical methodology is explained in the Appendix to this chapter.

The ability to adjust to both kind of shocks, or resilience to shocks, is measured through the cumulative output growth loss (only for supply shocks as demand shocks by construction have no long-run effects) and the cumulative inflation change over a period of eight years. The use of cumulative change contains information on both persistence and size of the shocks. The use of a yearly frequency makes it less significant to use measures like the impact effect or the persistence that are usually adopted with quarterly frequency.[27]

3.2.1 Results

In Table 19.2 we report for each sector the average and the standard deviation of the output growth loss after a supply shock.[28]

The average cumulative output growth loss is interpreted as a measure of the sectoral resilience to shock, so that sectors with a lower cumulative supply loss are regarded as those that are more able to absorb the shock. The standard deviation of the cumulative output

Table 19.2: *First measure of the sectoral resilience to supply shocks*

Sector	Average	Sector	Standard Dev.
Agriculture	1.05	Electricity & gas	0.24
Mining	1.25	Agriculture	0.31
Transport	1.29	Mining	0.45
Electricity & gas	1.36	Construction	0.58
Finance	1.48	Finance	0.65
Manufacturing	1.58	Post	0.81
Hotels	1.85	Manufacturing	0.82
Construction	1.92	Transport	0.87
Post	2.19	Hotels	0.91
Business	2.24	Business	1.30
Trade	2.31	Trade	1.72
Community services	3.95	Community services	1.73

growth instead signals how the reaction to the shock varies across euro-area countries. Accordingly, higher standard deviations are interpreted as a signal of a lower degree of market integration in that sector, which in turn might stand for the need for implementation of product market reforms.[29] For both criteria the sectors are ranked increasingly, from the sector showing the lowest average (standard deviation) to the one showing the highest value.[30]

Both criteria deliver a similar ranking. On the one hand, goods-producing sectors and three services-producing sectors (electricity, gas, and water supply; financial intermediation and transportation) are both better equipped to face supply shocks and more integrated in the euro area. On the other hand, the remaining services-producing sectors appear to be both less resilient to shocks and less integrated. In particular, four sectors have an average output growth loss that is at least 40 percent larger than manufacturing: wholesale and retail trade; community, social and personal services; real estate, renting and business activities and post and telecommunications. If manufacturing is considered as a benchmark (it is the most important sector but less flexible than mining and agriculture; so, by adopting it as a benchmark for comparison with the services sector we assume a conservative approach), there is clear evidence that many services-producing sectors lag behind in terms of both resilience and the degree of market integration, signaling a need for product market reforms.

Table 19.3: *Second measure of the sectoral resilience to supply shocks*

Cumulative inflation change – supply shock			
Sector	Average	Sector	Standard Dev.
Mining	0.73	Finance	0.57
Finance	1.38	Mining	0.95
Agriculture	1.46	Transport	1.25
Transport	1.52	Electricity & gas	1.68
Electricity & gas	1.62	Construction	1.85
Construction	1.65	Manufacturing	2.02
Manufacturing	2.13	Agriculture	2.45
Post	2.29	Post	2.48
Hotels	2.61	Business	2.78
Business	3.55	Hotels	2.98
Trade	4.78	Trade	7.53
Community services	13.10	Community services	10.77

Table 19.4: *Measure of the sectoral resilience to demand shocks*

Cumulative inflation change – demand shock			
Sector	Average	Sector	Standard Dev.
Mining	1.81	Mining	0.44
Agriculture	2.40	Electricity & gas	0.98
Electricity & gas	2.43	Finance	1.22
Finance	2.47	Community services	1.26
Manufacturing	3.12	Manufacturing	1.45
Community services	3.70	Agriculture	1.73
Construction	4.05	Construction	1.81
Transport	4.05	Transport	1.89
Post	4.22	Post	2.01
Trade	4.55	Business	2.27
Business	4.91	Trade	3.20
Hotels	5.85	Hotels	3.20

The result that the goods-producing industry tends to be more flexible than most of the services-producing industry also holds when the cumulative inflation change after a supply shock (Table 19.3) and a demand shock (Table 19.4) is taken into account.

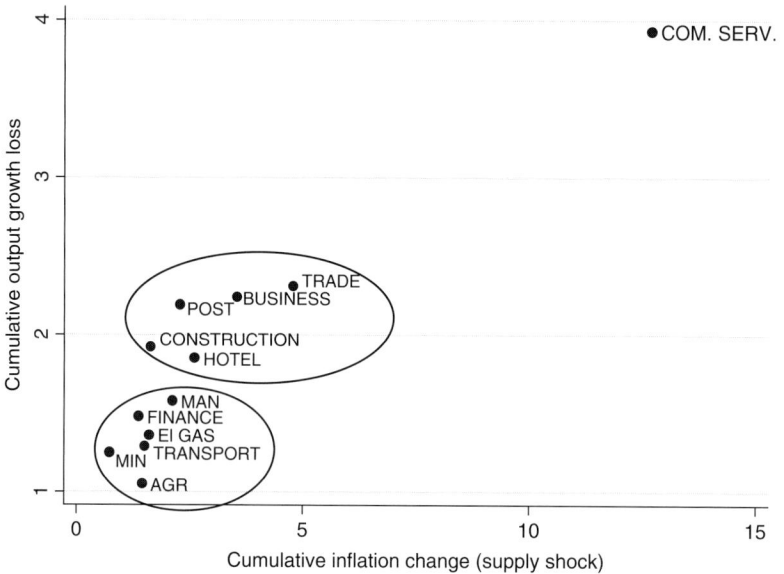

Figure 19.3: Graphical representation of the sectoral resilience to supply shocks

The three goods-producing industries, together with the electricity, gas and water supply, and the financial intermediation sectors, tend to be more flexible than the other services-producing industry for any kind of shock.

Moreover, sectors with a low ability to adjust also show a large standard deviation. This highlights the fact that some countries perform either much better or far worse than the others. A graphical representation allows us to easily compare the different capacities to adjust across sectors along the three dimensions we use to measure flexibility.

More specifically, Figure 19.3 reports on the y axis the cumulative output growth rate loss and on the x axis the cumulative inflation change both induced by a supply shock. The closer a point is to the origin, the better is the ability to adjust to a supply shock of the corresponding sector as measured along the two dimensions.

According to Figure 19.3, we can clearly distinguish two groups. The first group, made up from the three goods-producing sectors plus three services-producing sectors (financial intermediation; electricity, gas, and water supply, and transport), comprises the sectors that are more flexible with respect to a supply shock. The second group, made up

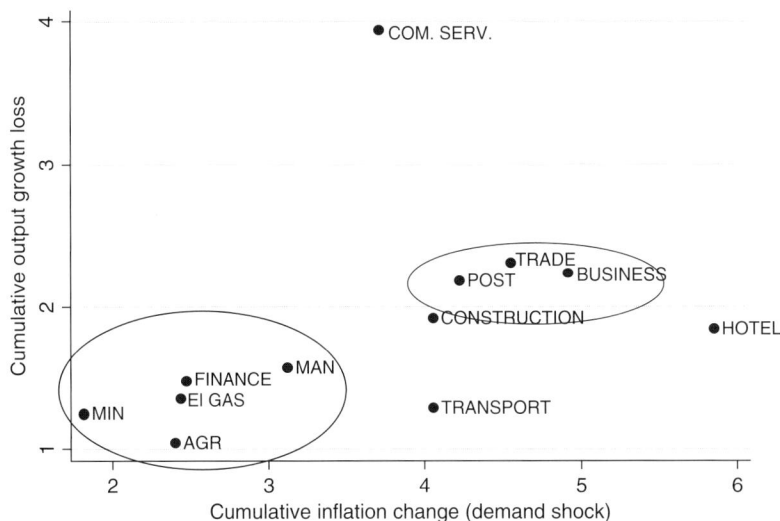

Figure 19.4: Graphical representation of the sectoral resilience to supply and demand shocks

only of services sectors (hotel, trade, business activities, post and tele-communications and construction), instead contains the sectors that are less flexible to supply shocks with respect to both dimensions. Finally, the sector of community, social, and personal services appears as an outlier as it is isolated and far away from the origin, appearing as the less flexible sector with respect to supply shocks.[31]

Figure 19.4 replicates the same analysis but considers on the y axis the cumulative output growth rate loss resulting from a supply shock, and on the x axis the cumulative inflation change induced by a demand shock. Again, with the exception of transportation, those sectors that appear as the most flexible with respect to a supply shock also perform better than the other sectors with respect to demand shocks.

Similarly, construction, post and telecommunications, trade and business services appear quite homogenous and form a second group that is, however, less flexible to demand shocks than the first one. Finally, two sectors appear as outliers, as they show a degree of rigidity much stronger than all the other sectors, though along a different dimension: the sector of hotels and restaurants shows the greatest rigidity with respect to demand shock, while community services shows the greatest rigidity with respect to a supply shock.

Table 19.5: *Relatively rigid sectors in the euro area*

	Sectors		
Country	Supply – cum output growth loss	Supply – cum inflation change	Demand – cum inflation change
Austria	Manufacturing, Community services Manufacturing, Business	Community services	Community services,
Belgium	Community services	Community services, Business	Business, Hotels
Germany	Community services	Community services	Hotels, Post
Finland	Finance, Community services	Community services	Transport, Hotels
France	Community services	Community services	Transport, Trade
Greece	Finance, Community services	Finance	Trade, Finance
Ireland	Construction, Hotels	Hotels	Business, Hotels
Italy	Community services	Community services	Construction, Agriculture, Post
Netherlands	Hotels, Post, Trade	Transport, Trade	Construction
Portugal	Business	Trade, Post	Business
Spain	Business, Construction	Business, Construction	Trade, Business

3.3 Where to reform? A country-by-country and sector-by-sector assessment

In the following tables we analyse, country by country, which sectors appear to be exceptionally rigid (Table 19.5) and, sector by sector, which countries appear to be less resilient to shocks (Table 19.6). In Table 19.5 we report, for each country and along any of the three dimensions with which we measure a country's ability to adjust, the sectors that appear to be relatively rigid.[32] A sector has been considered relatively rigid with respect to any of the three measures of flexibility, if the corresponding cumulative response is larger than the average cumulative response plus one standard deviation.

Table 19.6: *Sector-by-sector list of the most rigid countries in the euro area*

Sector	Country
Agriculture	Portugal, Italy
Mining	Italy
Manufacturing	Austria, Spain
Electricity, gas and water supply	Portugal, France
Construction	Portugal, Spain, the Netherlands
Trade	Spain, the Netherlands
Hotels	Spain, theNetherlands
Transport	The Netherlands
Post and telecommunications	Italy, Portugal
Financial services	Greece
Real business activity	Spain, Portugal, Italy
Community services	Spain, Portugal, Italy

Again, it clearly emerges that for each country the main source of rigidity comes from services-producing sectors, with only two exceptions, Austria (manufacturing) and Italy (agriculture), and in both cases with respect to only one measure of flexibility. Obviously it is not surprising that the sector of community services often represents the main source of rigidity of a country, as it is a sector highly domestically oriented, that is, essentially a nontradeable sector.

In Table 19.6, we consider for each sector which countries are relatively rigid. A country has been considered as relatively rigid if, for at least two out of the three measures with which flexibility is measured, the cumulative response is larger than the average cumulative response plus one standard deviation. From the table it clearly emerges that Mediterranean countries are the most problematic, for almost any sector. In particular Spain and Portugal with six sectors, and Italy with five, signal the high degree of rigidity of their economies, relative to the other euro-area countries.

3.4 Do asymmetric shocks matter at the sectoral level?

In this section we report some results from the investigation about the importance of idiosyncratic shocks across sectors. We estimate for eleven euro-area countries (Luxembourg being omitted) twelve bivariate VARs,

Table 19.7: *Sector-by-sector measure of the relative importance of common shocks*

Average % of the FEVD of country-specific output explained by common shock

Sector / Horizon	1	3	5
Post and telecommunications	39%	61%	67%
Total manufacturing	37%	41%	47%
Transport and storage	27%	32%	35%
Mining and quarrying	19%	22%	27%
Agriculture, hunting, forestry and fishing	19%	20%	25%
Electricity, gas and water supply	18%	26%	30%
Wholesale and retail trade	16%	24%	29%
Financial intermediation	15%	21%	27%
Hotels and restaurants	13%	16%	19%
Real estate, renting and business activities	13%	25%	30%
Construction	11%	18%	22%
Community social and personal services	10%	13%	16%

one for each of the twelve sectors defined above. For each pair of sector and country, the bivariate VAR consists of a euro-area and a country-specific variable: the real output per hour worked at the euro area and the real output per hour worked at the country level. Common and country-specific (idiosyncratic) shocks at the sectoral level are identified following Giannone and Reichlin[33] (2006b). To compare the importance of common to country-specific shocks the forecast error variance decomposition (FEVD) of the real output per hour worked at the country level is computed. Indeed, the contribution of a given shock to the forecast error variance (FEV) of the variable of interest shows the relative importance of the shock in driving the variable.

Table 19.7 reports the percentage of the FEV of the country-specific real output per hour work that is explained by common shocks, and is computed at three different time horizons: one, three, and five years. The higher the average percentage, the less important the idiosyncratic shocks in that sector over the euro area. The table shows that in the euro area two sectors clearly stand out as less affected by idiosyncratic shocks: post and telecommunications, and manufacturing. At the other end, asymmetric shocks are still important for most sectors and at any time horizon, as common shocks often explain less than 30 percent of the forecast error variance.[34]

As manufacturing is by far the most important goods-producing sector, this result again highlights the need for product market reforms for services-producing sectors, though the final picture is somewhat blurred. Indeed, on the one hand, only two sectors (post and telecommunication, and to a lesser extent transportation) stand out as less affected by idiosyncratic shocks (with common shocks explaining more than 30 percent of FEV at almost any horizon). On the other hand, all other sectors perform similarly, with two sectors (community, social, and personal services, and hotel and restaurants) always at the lower end.

4. The euro-area record in product market reforms

In this section we summarize the actual product market reform record of euro-area countries. We are particularly interested in whether these countries have reformed in services, with a view to achieving greater flexibility and in so doing enhancing their adjustment capacity. The findings of Section 3 clearly suggest that product market reforms in the euro area ought to be concentrated in services, and indeed, within services, in the more sheltered sectors. After a reminder of overall product market reform trends in the euro area, we summarize evidence about the relative rigidity of services in the euro area, with immediate consequences for the euro-area inflation rate (in 4.1). In Section 4.2, selective evidence is provided about the restrictiveness of specific domains in services and the product market reforms observed (here defined as reductions of these degrees of restrictiveness over time).[35]

There is little doubt that euro-area countries have been reforming product markets over the last two decades.[36] The relevant questions are principally about the depth and scope of such reforms, the type of markets where reforms have been weak or absent, and the speed of reform. Price controls are almost phased out, state control over business has reduced significantly, ownership barriers have come down and many market access obstacles for third countries have been lowered or removed, to mention some important trends. Competition policy now exists in all euro countries and EU competition policy (including state aids) has been widened and tightened. The EU has gradually but steadily liberalized network markets and these endeavors have not petered out. Therefore, more targeted reform approaches are needed. Nowadays, it is more fruitful to focus on the remaining pockets of restrictiveness hindering market functioning, in particular in services.

Box 19.3: **Comparing sectoral reform needs in different approaches**

Do other approaches trying to identify sectors in need of reform yield results similar to ours? In this box we consider two such approaches: the "Product Market and Sector Monitoring" analysis in the European Commission (2007e, 2007k); as well as the recommendations and "points to watch" in the Commission's annual progress report on the Lisbon Strategy.

In the former approach, the Commission investigates market-based sectors at the two-digit level of the NACE industrial classification and considers a sector as problematic if it fulfills three criteria:

1. economic importance (static and dynamic);
2. contribution to economic adjustment (economic interlinkages, presence of general purpose technology, contribution to the price adjustment);
3. presence of market malfunctioning (consumer survey, TFP, and employment growth rate).

By applying these criteria the following sectors are found to be problematic:

1. three manufacturing sectors;
2. wholesale and retail trade;
3. post and telecommunications;
4. financial intermediation and insurance and pension funding;
5. other business activities (heterogeneous service sector including mainly professional services).

While results for manufacturing are not comparable with ours, given the fact that we kept the manufacturing sector aggregated, the similarity of results with respect to services sectors is striking. In particular, the two approaches, though very different in their methodology, highlight that trade, other business activities and post and telecommunications are among the more problematic sectors.

Also, the country-specific recommendations and "points to watch" found in the Commission's annual progress report on the Lisbon Strategy repeatedly stress that the policy area where reforms need to be tackled with high priority are principally trade and professional services (Germany, Greece, France, Austria, Italy, Spain), and to a lesser extent energy markets (Belgium, Spain, France, Germany) and financial services (Italy, Portugal).

4.1 Why reforms in services lubricate adjustment

The conglomerate of services is large. The exposure to domestic or EU-wide, let alone global, competition varies enormously between sectors within this conglomerate. The present subsection will merely provide indicative (but strong) evidence that services as a whole tend to be a principal source of price stickiness and inflation persistence in the euro area. Insofar as product market reforms can help to increase price flexibility and enhance competitive pressures in these markets, product market reforms can effectively contribute to the lubrication of adjustment processes in EMU. To keep this essay readable and short, we shall focus on some telling results in the recent literature.

A Task Force of the Monetary Policy Committee of the ESCB (2006) has studied competition and pricing behavior in services markets in the euro area. It finds for the period 1996 to 2005 that services contribute most to the aggregate euro-area (HICP) inflation rate, except for energy during short spells. As the Task Force (2006: 26–7) writes, "[W]hile euro area aggregate inflation amounted to 1.9 percent on average during the period considered, average services inflation stood 0.4 p.p. higher at 2.3 percent." Apart from communication services (with the sharp fall in telecoms tariffs), all services contribute to this positive inflation differential.

That a lack of exposure to competition and the property of nontradability of (some) services might well play a role in this phenomenon is well known. Consistent with this explanation, the Task Force shows that inflation differentials between euro countries over a ten-year period are positively correlated with each country's gap between services inflation rates and those of (non-energy) industrial goods (Task Force, 2006: 28).

Behind the somewhat higher services inflation, one suspects a significant determinant to be labor costs. This is confirmed when regressing unit labor cost growth over this period with inflation in the services sector.[37] Another factor is likely to be the presence of administered prices in a range of services, such as refuse and sewerage collection, medical, dental and hospital services, passenger transport by railway and road, postal services, cultural services, education, and social protection.[38] Furthermore, work emerging from the ECB Inflation Persistence Network (see e.g. Angeloni *et al.*, 2006) points to a slower price responsiveness (such as the frequency of price changes) in the services component compared with other inflation components. When prices are changed in services, only two out of ten are price decreases (Dhyne *et al.*, 2005; see also Fabiani *et al.*, 2007).

The importance of services markets reform should not, however, be regarded as a matter for services only. Numerous services are consumed by manufacturing, mining, and agricultural activities as well as other services sectors. For that reason alone, the price rigidities of services inputs will have a knock-on effect. The OECD has recently moved beyond the product market reform indicators to so-called non-manufacturing indicators (NMRs, see Box 19.1, item b.) and has developed estimates of knock-on effects of restrictive services regulation for manufacturing, using input-output tables.[39] These knock-on effects are solely measured on a scale of restrictiveness (from 0 to 1) but the advantage is that, in so doing, they become comparable between countries.

First presented in Conway and Nicoletti (2006: 60), for euro-area countries, the knock-on effects range from a low of 0.1 (the Netherlands and Ireland) up to a high of 0.35 for Austria, and a little higher than 0.25 for Germany, Italy, and Belgium. Even when accepting that these calculations are probably no more than rough proxies, such evidence is a forceful reminder of the intersectoral spillover of these rigidities throughout the economy. It may therefore also negatively affect the working of the competitiveness channel.

4.2 Reforms and remaining restrictiveness in services markets

The present section focuses on specific services sectors for which product market reforms have been undertaken in the euro area. It will not include fully sheltered domestic sectors such as the ones where administered prices may play a role (see 4.1 and note 42), even though these sectors exhibit above-average price stickiness. In these markets, the introduction of competition *in* the market or, at times, *for* the market (via e.g. concessions, etc.) is difficult and generalizations are imprudent. A lot of these activities are intrinsically local as well and the internal market may not play a role or only remotely so. They require separate analysis and reform, with a view to minimizing the inflation persistence and price stickiness.

The first set of specific services which have been and still are subject to product market reforms are network industries. The OECD has developed indicators in this field (see Box 19.1, item b.). This has made it possible to obtain a long-term reform perspective for the EU15 for six network industries in energy, transport, and communication (Conway and Nicoletti, 2006: 43). The movement over two and a half decades is quite compelling: euro-area countries have reformed considerably and mostly just before or since the euro introduction.[40] It takes a detailed analysis to draw any further conclusion. Thus, the annual report by the European Commission on the performance of network industries (European Commission, 2007b) provides a careful and detailed analytical survey for the EU27 but, once this degree of detail is pursued, simple indicators have to give way to lengthy descriptions which are not easily comparable between sectors, between countries (even if the EU element is strong) and over time. However, there is no doubt that the EU has steadily pursued further liberalization in network industries, since 2003, with a mix of liberalization, competition policy, and regulatory interventions at the two levels of governments. A new wave of policy initiatives provides yet another boost to this process. In 2007 there was the recent third generation liberalization of postal services, the proposed gas and electricity package, the electronic communication proposals, the detailed rail freight package of October, and the sharpening of the justification of state aids in broadcasting following the Altmark case. The newest proposals in 2008 to allow secondary trading in slots in congested airports demonstrate that the EU is determined to pursue further network industry liberalization in the internal market, accompanied by the appropriate regulation, competition policy, and adaptations of two-tier institutional setting.

The question is whether, in the context of shock adjustment in the euro area, further reform would contribute to its lubrication. It is interesting to study Table 19.8, comparing the price developments of network industries in the EU and also comparing them with various inflation rates for the period 1996–2006.

Of the six network industries, four have sectoral price developments outpacing the (HICP) inflation rate of the Union, although electricity and postal services only do so by a small margin. The problem is that, in sectors such as gas, the price only depends very partially on the emerging competition in the EU gas sector (that is, on product market reform), and to a significant extent on world oil and gas prices. If one compares the network industries other than gas with the inflation rate of all services in the EU25, however, they all remain below the latter (but all of them remain above the inflation rates of the goods sector, which is typically more exposed).

Table 19.8: *Inflation in EU25 network industries*

	HICP-weight (2006)	1997	1998	1999	2000	2001	2002	2003	2004	2005	2006	January 2006	November 2006
Telecommunications (EU15)	2.3	-3.9	-1.6	-5.1	-2.1	-10.4	-2.0	-0.5	0.0	-0.8	-2.0	74.5	73.8
Electricity	2.1	0.1	0.0	-0.9	1.0	3.3	3.1	3.4	3.3	3.3	4.5	122.9	129.9
Gas	1.5	4.6	2.6	-2.5	4.7	17.3	2.8	1.1	3.0	8.0	14.4	169.8	188.7
Railways	0.5	1.4	3.1	3.0	2.4	2.4	2.3	3.3	2.2	4.5	2.9	131.2	132.9
Air	0.7	1.4	3.9	0.9	-0.1	5.0	-0.3	3.1	-2.3	6.7	2.1	122	124.7
Postal services	0.2	2.4	6.7	0.3	0.9	1.6	1.9	0.9	4.6	1.4	2.9	126.1	128.9
All-Items HICP	100	3.1	2.2	1.4	2.2	2.3	2.6	1.9	1.9	2.0	2.3	124.1	126.8
Goods	59.6	2.6	1.3	0.6	2.0	2.0	2.2	1.1	1.2	1.4	2.2	118.1	120.8
Services	40.4	3.2	2.9	2.4	2.3	2.5	3.3	3.2	2.7	2.8	2.4	131.2	133.7

NB: The last two columns display the price level index (1996=100). Price changes are calculated for January of each year. The telephone and telefax services price index to the EU15 only.

Source: Eurostat.

Even if it is improper from an analytical point of view to draw immediate conclusions from Table 19.8 – the conclusion that product market reforms in network industries would tend to suppress inflation would only be correct if controlled for other influences on prices – the impression one gets from Table 19.8 is consistent with the inference from the careful analysis of Martin *et al.*, (2005), finding that EU network liberalization has tended to reduce prices in the EU at the margin.

A second service sector standing out in terms of public and self-regulation, often held to be (overly) restrictive, is the cluster of professional services. Professional services are credence goods subject to market failures that have to be overcome by regulation. In this case it is particularly difficult to find the balance between (justified) public and self-regulation as the sector specifies e.g. fee setting, entry, and advertising are extremely complex.[41]

For the EU this is of special importance since the internal market for professional services has never worked well (if it ever worked at all!), despite at least four decades of distinct attempts to remove the barriers, where possible in principle. Also, the competition issues are far from simple.[42] This introduction is indispensable before one begins to read, let alone appreciate, product market reform indicators in this field.

Conway and Nicoletti (2006: 56) compare the degree of restrictiveness of regulation of professional services, based on the 1998 and 2003 OECD questionnaires (which are very detailed in this respect). Euro-area countries are spread horizontally all over the range of restrictiveness, from being very modestly regulated in Finland to the most restrictive one, Italy.[43]

Between 1998 and 2003, there is no clear pattern, even if reductions of restrictiveness are slightly more numerous (and Austrian, Spanish, and German liberalization is quite forceful, from high initial levels). The problem is that the market failures in professional services are profound and the idea of merely comparing restrictiveness, without assessing the quality of self-regulation and competition policy, is almost certainly inappropriate. In Garoupa (2004), an attempt is made, based on a very detailed questionnaire, to assess national self-regulation in terms of quality (including aspects such as entry, fees, organizational forms, advertising, and conduct restrictions), whereas the quality criteria are derived from a careful literature survey, in law and economics, of professional services. The analysis is limited to medical doctors and lawyers (the former not in Conway and Nicoletti, 2006) and to a snapshot, largely but not entirely based on Paterson *et al.* (2003). The USA comes out best (in terms of quality) by far, followed by (euro) countries such as Belgium, France, and Spain. Since the professions in Conway and Nicoletti's, and in Garoupa's contributions, are mostly different, one cannot jump to conclusions but it is striking that all four of these (in Garoupa, the best performing) countries find themselves only in the middle range in Conway and Nicoletti. Therefore, it appears imprudent to generalize.[49] Reform efforts should at least aim at improving the functioning of the internal market for professionals by facilitating entry as well as other manifestations of competition, whilst avoiding market failures and ensuring a minimum quality level set up by EU law. Indicators to monitor such reform efforts require deep investment in a sophisticated approach to reforms in this field. If policy makers and citizens can be provided with objective indicators, so much the better, but one should be under no illusion: a profound and careful approach is indispensable.[45] At the level of the euro area (or EU) Member States, reforms are undertaken, as shown in Conway and Nicoletti (2006) but the great diversity in restrictiveness suggests considerable room for further reform.

A third area in services where indicators exist and concerns about restrictiveness have long prevailed is retail. Whereas the retail indicator in the OECD product market reform (see Box 19.1, item a.) is limited and blended with sector-specific administrative burdens (hence, of little use), the detail in the NMR indicators (see Box 19.1, item b.) is far greater and a series of relevant questions on retail competition have been posed. As shown in Conway and Nicoletti (2006: 53), euro-area countries are again spread horizontally over the range of restrictiveness but most of them are on the more restrictive side, with six of the most restrictive seven being euro countries. Interesting it is that, in contrast to frequent assertions about the easy entry and other freedoms in the USA when it comes to retail, the USA finds itself slightly to the right of the middle group. There are, however, several problems with the indicators, such as the local level of regulation, including self-regulation (not reflected in the OECD data) and the *costs* of light regulation in terms of attractiveness for city centers which, in Europe, are typically historic centers and are expected to maintain "ambiance." At the same time, space for large-scale shopping malls or hypermarkets is limited in many parts of the densely populated eurozone. Whether and when restrictiveness is anti-competitive or protectionist for incumbents or small shop-owners and/or expresses preferences for "ambiance" and pleasant shopping streets in centers is exceedingly hard to make out. Without denigrating the latter argument for Europe, it is nevertheless interesting that some euro-area countries with old, historic centers (such as Italy, Portugal, and the Netherlands) find themselves on a less restrictive range compared to the USA. All this suggests that, in retail, there is still room for enhancing competition by means of reforms.

5. Product market reforms in wider euro-area reform strategies

Product market reforms should not be considered in isolation, as Figure 19.1 and Sections 2.2 and 2.3 have already emphasized. The present section briefly addresses the design issue of reforms, in other words, how product market reforms should be embedded in wide reforms at two levels of government within the eurozone. Figure 19.5 can serve as an aid for rationally approaching reform design. It proposes a stepwise approach when product market reforms are integrated in a wider structural reform strategy. Figure 19.5 suggests four steps, starting with the components of microeconomic reforms in the left column – largely in a national framework but with product markets reforms strongly conditioned by the internal market setting – and taking account of the socioeconomic context and (national and eurozone) conditions (indicated at the bottom of Figure 19.5).

The first step consists in identifying those reform areas which yield maximum benefits for the euro area either in terms of growth, employment and/or adjustment capacity. The issue has been widely discussed in the economic literature and most authors point to product, labor, and capital markets as the most relevant for EMU (of course, one also needs to look at different policy options within each area, e.g. services and/or goods for product markets).[46]

Once the main reform areas are defined, policy makers should explore whether there are within- and/or cross-policy complementarities (Step 2). The case of within-policy complementarities in products markets (services vs. goods) has not been well exploited in the euro area despite the fact that services represent 70 percent of the EU economic activity. Section 4 provides evidence that the reform record of euro-area countries in services has been relatively poor. This explains why services appear to be less resilient to economic shocks according to our empirical analysis (Section 3). Boeri *et al.* (2006) show that vested interests are

Step 1	Step 2	Step 3	Step 4
Policies and sub-policies	Complementarities	Type of reform	Coordination under subsidiarity constraints

- Product Markets
  o Services
  o Goods
- Labour Markets
  o Unemployment benefits
  o Employment protection legislation
  o Minimum wages
  o …
- Financial Markets
  o Housing markets
  o Credit constraints
  o …
- Others
	- Across policies
	- Within policies
		- Comprehensive
		  o Unconditional
		  o Sequential
		  o Simultaneous
		- Partial reform
			- Cross-border spillovers
			- Policy complementarities at EU level

Socio-economic conditions/context			

Figure 19.5: Designing market reforms in the euro-area context

deeply anchored in the services sector. National policy makers, should in our view, profit from the EU framework in carrying out their reforms at national level. National policy makers could far more successfully piggy-back on the rolling internal market strategies. There are some success stories at EU level, which could open the way to further initiatives, e.g. air transport, telecommunications and broadcasting. It is not impossible that the Services Directive[47] will boost EU-services trade and establishment (Pelkmans, 2007). National policy complementarities with the goods market have proven to be insufficient to boost services reforms. Therefore, the European framework may be a better anchor.[48]

As far as cross-policy complementarities are concerned – still in Step 2 – they are important for two reasons: enhancing the efficiency and adjustment gains of product market reforms, besides reducing political opposition to reforms. There is considerable evidence in the literature that product market reforms foster labor market liberalization (e.g. Fiori *et al.*, 2008; Duval and Elmeskov, 2006; Boeri, 2005a). Hence, when assessing the total growth and employment effects of product market reforms, one needs to consider both their direct effect and the effect through induced changes in labor market policies and institutions. In terms of the effect of labor and product market regulations on adjustment, Duval *et al.* (2007) show that stringent regulation lengthens the adjustment period. Moreover, the cumulative effects are higher than the sum of the individual effects of rigid labor and product market regulations. There is also evidence that restrictive product market regulation (especially in services markets) may be due, to some extent, to restrictive labor market regulation. Of course, services have a very large wage component[49] and thus the link might not come as a surprise. Altogether, what this means is that there is a two-way relationship between labor and product markets. Reforming labor markets is not only a reform route in and by itself, but also a way of reducing rigidities in the services market (and which is the less resilient sector to economic shocks). Financial liberalization will also improve capital reallocation towards the most productive investment while improving risk diversification. Coupled with product market reforms, financial liberalization is expected to increase growth and employment in the euro area (Tressel, 2008; European Commission, 2008a; Taylor, 2008a).[50]

Step 3 studies the costs and benefits of various policy options as suggested by Berger and Danninger (2005) for labor and product markets reform.[51] Their taxonomy of policy options include:

i) No reform. But as shown, no reform is not an option in the euro area;

ii) Partial reform occurs when the benefits in one market justify reform but reforming the other market leads to high net costs. Section 4 suggests that euro-area countries have adopted this approach by reforming product markets while letting labor markets go largely untouched. The lack of adjustment in some markets, which we report in Section 3, militates against such partiality: a partial reform is neither efficient nor advisable for EMU;

iii) Comprehensive reform that exploits policy synergies and complementarities as the most welfare improving (unconditional, sequential, simultaneous).

If unilateral reforms are optimal in both labor and product markets, Berger and Danninger (2005) conclude that coordinated deregulation becomes self-supporting. Usually however, the upfront costs and political opposition associated with some reforms will make unconditional reform very difficult to implement. Simultaneous reforms are desirable when the benefits of reforming one market suffice to compensate the costs associated with reforming another. Finally, sequential reform is possible when reforming one market is expected to pave the way for reforming the other.[52] In general, the authors conclude that a comprehensive reform package will not only increase economic welfare but also reduce political resistance to reforms.

In a two-tier government structure like EMU, designing a reform strategy is further complicated (Step 4) by two aspects: the size and direction of cross-border spillovers as well as core principles in the EC Treaty constraining EU action to some areas while limiting or blocking others. Leaving aside the discussion on cross-border spillovers' measurement difficulties and the strength of transmission mechanisms (see Box 19.2), product and financial market reforms are usually regarded as engendering strong cross-border spillover effects regardless of the methodology used, while labor markets are typically found to induce small cross-border spillovers (IMF, 2004b; Taylor, 2008a).

Step 4 requires respect for the subsidiarity principle, applied to powers shared between the EU level and the Member States level: the principle helps to define the attribution of competences between Member States and the EU. European action should only be pursued when there is sufficient evidence on sizeable cross-border spillover effects and reform action

Box 19.2: **Spillovers and complementarities: an additional reason to reform**

Spillover effects are cross-border externalities derived from a country's (or group of countries) economic policy. The complex nature of the economic and institutional links between EMU members renders a purely theoretical analysis of spillovers next to impossible. Therefore, the literature has preferred to test empirically for the intensity and the nature of spillovers and the case for reform coordination.[53]

Ultimately, the size of the spillover effect depends on the strength of the transmission channels (trade, FDI or M&A, among others). According to Ilzkovitz *et al.* (2007) intra-EU25 trade of manufactured goods amounts to nearly 40 percent of the GDP, whereas intra-EU25 services trade barely reaches 10 percent. The strength of trade among EU countries (at least for manufactured goods) is expected to facilitate spillovers across the Union. Intra-euro-area exports in manufactures as a percentage of GDP is slightly higher than that of the EU25.

For the next decade, it will be interesting to observe whether trade will further intensify in the gradually enlarging euro area. From the first ten years one can observe that trade integration has barely intensified since the introduction of the euro. From detailed empirical analysis, it follows that the trade effects of the euro would only amount to some 5 percent according to Baldwin *et al.* (2008). Thus, as the euro area expands to the new Member States, some – though modest – additional trade effects of enlargement will be captured by the euro area. Therefore, in a euro area of, say, twenty-plus members the effects of structural policies (e.g. product and labor market reforms) will spread somewhat more easily through the area.[54]

With respect to cross-border spillovers and policy complementarities (e.g between product and labor reforms, as explained in Section 2.2.2), it is worth considering whether the effectiveness of product market reforms can be enhanced by a credible form of cooperation or coordination.[55] While most researchers agree on the benefits in general terms, whilst disagreeing on the costs of such coordination, controversy arises when defining the areas that need to be coordinated at euro-area level as well as the degrees of binding.

Tabellini and Wyplosz (2006) suggest that product and financial market reforms should be coordinated at EMU level, but labor markets should remain in the realm of Member States. In areas of strong spillovers and complementarities, the influence of national governments should be minimized, since they may opt for protectionist measures. A similar conclusion is reached by Pisani-Ferry *et al.* (2008) who consider that cross-border spillovers are not only relatively small but complementarities exist most prominently at the national level. The case for reform is nonetheless more compelling in the euro area. The reasoning goes as follows. A country which implements an inflation-reducing reform is a potential handmaiden for easing the common monetary policy. However, when acting in isolation, the effect may well be too small (or, coming about too slowly over time) for monetary policy to respond. Short-sighted governments or those with tiny majorities in parliament might therefore feel discouraged to go it alone. A coordinated reform effort in the euro area would not only create clear political support from other euro-area countries acting similarly but also facilitate the ECB's decision to accommodate the expected increase in the overall output of the eurozone.[56]

Hughes Hallet *et al.* (2005) call for coordinated and simultaneous reforms in order to make EMU attractive to more flexible economies and avoid "free-riding" by the rigid ones. By increasing the average level of flexibility through the admission of more reformed economies, the incumbent countries in the euro area could transfer some of the cost of their own macroeconomic adjustment problems to those economies. A common reform strategy would avoid this problem, since the adjustment costs would be shared and flexible economies would not "fear" to join the euro area.

Even if structural reforms are primarily beneficial to the country undertaking them, and common strategies can only be based on the two arguments set out above, there are softer routes to persuasion amongst euro-area countries as well. Whereas a coordinated reform approach increases trade in the euro area as a whole (facilitating the absorption of asymmetric shocks), individual reforms will pay, in the long run, in terms of higher competitiveness (lower prices and wages) partly at the expense of other Member States whose structural disadvantages will increase. Similarly, reforming countries will attract financial and direct investment, dampening even more the adjacent economies (European Commission, 2007d). Without necessarily centralizing reforms, this prospect may persuade countries to follow suit with their own reforms. This is typically encouraged in initiatives for policy coordination at EU and EMU level, such as the rolling Single Market strategies[57] and the Lisbon Strategy, even though they differ in their policy coverage, governance structure, and degree of binding. Broadly speaking, one may say that market liberalization measures (goods, services, and capital) are covered by the Single Market strategies while reforms dealing with the countries' economic structure (innovation, education, pension, labor, etc) fall under the Lisbon Strategy. A specific reference to euro-area needs has nonetheless been made under the new Lisbon Strategy since 2005, so as to stimulate a coherent and targeted reform for those areas relevant for the functioning of the monetary union.

Thus, a sensible euro-area reform strategy should combine the national dimension (taking into account structural policies and their specific supply and demand needs) and the common dimension (internalizing cross-border spillovers and policy complementarities).

---

cannot be taken more efficiently at Member State level. A systematic analysis is offered by recent attempts to develop and apply a subsidiarity test, which can equally serve the design process of reform strategies.[58]

Last but not least, an efficient reform strategy should also take account of the socioeconomic context and conditions. For instance, economic conditions may determine the appropriate timing for the reform. Policy makers could profit from buoyant economic conditions to undertake far-reaching reform programs. Reform practice, however, tells otherwise since policy makers have often undertaken reforms when the economy is so deteriorated that reforming is the only viable option. Additional factors such as demography, the state of new technologies, international influences, etc.[59] may also shape a reform strategy.

6. Conclusions

This chapter has shown, theoretically and empirically, that product market reforms do help to lubricate adjustment processes in the euro area. Of course, these reforms should not be pursued in isolation from, for example, labor market reforms and efforts to make financial markets work better. This case for product market reforms in the euro area is additional to that in pursuit of higher economic growth and employment, usually made in the context of the Lisbon Strategy. In other words, for euro-area countries there is a *double dividend* from such reforms. This is the central message of the present chapter. It is crucial that this message is actively communicated, for the sake of obtaining higher net benefits (of having a common currency) as a result of lower cumulative adjustment costs.

Four more specific messages for national and euro area (and EU) policy makers are noteworthy, too. First, the euro area is well served by a common microeconomic reform strategy ensuring that all euro countries undertake significant reform efforts, including product market reforms. Rather than being centralized, such a strategy is best envisaged as a two-way interactive setting. In the Eurogroup, the much needed explicit recognition of the joint interest does not imply a drive for uniformity in national reforms. On the contrary, the local socio-economic context, the national reform efforts in the recent past, and the diversity in reform needs are compelling reasons for targeted reforms at the national level. Nonetheless, all euro-area countries jointly manage and share a common public good and therefore credible deliverables, ultimately facilitating shock adjustment, have to be shown in a transparent manner. At the same time, the national reform efforts have to be much more explicitly and politically associated with the common euro-area interest and embedded in the common strategy.

Second, the record of euro-area countries in reforming services is subject to considerable improvement. Whereas for network industries there continues to be steady – be it gradual – progress, in domains such as retail distribution and retail banking but also in professional services, the scope for deeper reforms rendering market functioning more flexible and responsive remains quite large. Several opportunities currently present themselves to stimulate a deepening of such reforms. The Commission's market monitoring exercise in the framework of the 2007 Single Market Review is capable of identifying badly functioning services markets which ought to be reformed urgently. The current screening of national (and regional and local) services regulation in the framework of the services directive should not be regarded as a mere exercise in notification and consistency with the directive but exploited as a basis for wide-ranging reforms in national services regulation, which is often still restrictive and/or heavy in terms of red tape (hence, constricting entry).

Third, some services, like typical local community services, remain truly sheltered from both domestic and intra-EU competition. Whatever good reasons there might be for this constellation, empirical evidence shows clearly that the absence of competition leads to a higher than average inflation and greater inflation persistence. Although the EU or euro-area level is not qualified to play any role of significance in reforming these services activities, it is in the enlightened self-interest of euro-area countries, their local communities and, in the final analysis, also the euro area, that some form of mainstreaming of reforms is also applied to these activities.

Fourth, in calling for a strategic role of the Eurogroup with respect to product market reforms, which are not the typical expertise of finance ministers anyway, it is crucial to have an appropriate empirical basis to monitor reform progress (over time and between euro-area countries) in a strategic fashion, including the formulation of meaningful beacons or benchmarks. A significant improvement over relatively simplistic Lisbon-related indicators, the MICREF and LABREF datasets seem to have the potential to serve this strategic purpose well. The Eurogroup should request the Commission to support the former's strategic function by focusing in particular on specific services domains where the reform needs can be analytically demonstrated and empirically supported.

Appendix to Section 3 – the Blanchard-Quah methodology

The identification of the supply and demand shocks in any of the sectoral two-variable VAR follows the identification methodology presented by Blanchard and Quah (1989). The vector of endogenous variables, Y_t, contains the rate of growth of real output and the inflation rate. The two variables are assumed to respond to two types of shocks: supply shocks and demand shocks.

Let's consider the vector moving average representation of the structural model: $Y_t = A(L) \, \varepsilon_t$, where $A(L)$ is a polynomial in the lag operator L, Y_t is the vector of endogenous variables (the rate of growth of real output and inflation), and ε_t are orthonormal structural errors ($E(\varepsilon_t\varepsilon_t') = I_2$, $E(\varepsilon_t\varepsilon_{t+s}) = 0$ for all s different from 0.

The structural model cannot be estimated directly, so that the reduced form model is estimated first, that is: $Y_t = B(L) \, u_t$. As B_0 is an identity matrix I_2, the following relation holds between the structural and the reduced form representation: $u_t = A_0\varepsilon_t$. It follows that, to identify the structural errors, it is necessary to recover the two-by-two matrix A_0 from the estimated parameters by setting four restrictions.

The first three restrictions derive from the variance-covariance matrix of the reduced-form errors: $E(u_t u_t') = \Sigma = E[A_0' \varepsilon_t \varepsilon_t' A_0] = A_0 A_0'$. The last restriction is imposed on the matrix of long-term effects of the structural shocks, A_1.

It is possible to show that the following relationship between A_1 and the matrix of long-term effect of reduced-form shocks B_1 exists: $A_1 = B_1 A_0$.

By imposing a triangular structure on A_1, it is possible to assume that demand shocks have no long-term effect on output. In this case A_1 can be derived from a Cholesky decomposition of the known matrix $B_1 \Sigma B_1'$ as $A_1 A_1' = B_1 A_0 A_0' B_1' = B_1 \Sigma B_1'$.

Once A_1 is obtained, it is possible to find A_0 as: $A_0 = B_1^{-1} A_1$. The structural residuals are then easily obtained via: $\varepsilon_t = A_0^{-1} u_t$.

Notes

1. On labor market reforms, see Bertola (this volume); on financial markets, see Jappelli and Pagano (this volume).
2. The fourth element is the marginal propensity to import, likely to be dependent on the other three elements.
3. Not in MICREF (EU law pre-empts any special privilege) but in "markets for corporate control" (see capital markets, left-upper column), state ownership can render takeovers impossible.
4. See the MICREF User Guide and the reference guide of the Economic Policy Committee "Coverage and structure of the LABREF database," December 2005 on: http://ec.europa.eu/economy_finance/indicators/labormarketre forms/documents/guide_en.pdf; note that we have added the item of "state ownership" and adapted the inventory for the present purpose or for clarity.
5. Whereas the EC Treaty says that matters of ownership are a competence of the Member States, for the proper functioning of the internal market the existence of state ownership or private ownership should not make any difference under EU law. State ownership cannot imply any privilege or advantage over privately owned companies in goods and services markets. However, one property of state-owned firms remains: a Member State's government can always prevent (hostile) takeovers – see the column on capital markets in Figure 19.1. For product markets in the EU, it is the competitive environment which should equally discipline privately owned and state-owned companies. One should therefore be cautious about applying the premises about state ownership (and the implications for performance) of the reform literature to the EU of today.

6. Euro-area countries score well, for the simple reason that national treatment is a EC Treaty obligation (Art. 48, TEC).

7. The efficiency effects of product market reforms have been widely studied in the literature. See, *inter alia*, Nicodème and Sauner-Leroy (2007) and Dierx *et al.* (2004a, 2004b). Overall, product market reforms increase competition and this in turn leads to higher productivity via three efficiency channels: allocative efficiency (lower mark-ups, within and across firm factor reallocation), productive efficiency (incentives for workers and managers to work more efficiently and capture some of the new rents and internal restructuring), and dynamic efficiency (incentives to innovate and ease of technology absorption).

8. For instance, an increase in the degree of substitutability between goods only has a short-run effect via lower mark-ups; in the long run, firms will exit the market without any significant output effect. On the other hand, policies aimed at suppressing entry barriers will also have a long run (output and employment) effect (Blanchard and Giavazzi, 2003).

9. The new endogenous growth models rely on two mechanisms by which product market reforms promote innovation. First, innovation allows firms to stay in the market when confronted with strong competition. Second, oligopolistic firms with similar cost structures can diminish costs (and consequently increase their market share and profits) only by taking a technological lead over their rivals. Thus, dynamic efficiency could shift forward the technological frontier and increase total factor productivity (Griffith *et al.*, 2006).

10. There is some controversy on the innovation effect of reforms. While lower mark-ups tend to discourage innovation, competition will stimulate it. Overall, the competition effect tends to prevail (Schiantarelli, 2005).

11. A study of the causes behind this phenomenon falls beyond the scope of this chapter. Yet it seems reasonable to point to product market reforms and extra policy coordination as plausible explanations. It is nonetheless difficult to disentangle the long-run convergence effects of product market reforms from the effects of, *i.a.*, capital markets deepening, labor market reforms, European policy coordination, and common European policies, etc. In most cases, these effects are cumulative.

12. See Mongelli (2008), on the implications of business cycle affiliations for the conduct of monetary policy.

13. See European Commission (2006a, 2008a) for further analysis.

14. See for instance Fiori *et al.* (2008); Duval and Elmeskov (2006); and Boeri (2005a).

15. See also Fiori *et al.* (2008); Amable and Gatti (2004); IMF (2004c); and Griffith *et al.* (2006) on policy complementarities. The reader is also referred to Corsetti (this volume).

16. The Inflation Persistence Network of the ECB has conducted several detailed studies on price setting behavior. For additional information, see for example Altissimo *et al.* (2006).
17. That is, lower loss of output for 1 percent change in inflation.
18. On the growth and employment effects of product market reforms see for instance Fiori *et al.* (2008); Griffith *et al.* (2006); OECD (2007c, 2008).
19. This suggestion, called the two-handed approach, was firstly explored by Blanchard *et al.* (1986).
20. See European Commission (2007e, 2007k).
21. The effects on resilience may vary among policies affecting different types of markets and among institutions.
22. The idea is that a common shock may have an asymmetric effect because of divergent structural policies and institutions affecting the transmission channels.
23. The effects are stronger when considering both (employment protection and product market regulation) as a multiplicative term.
24. The only euro-area country that seems to perform moderately well is the Netherlands. Germany is found to be between both groups.
25. A general limitation of the analysis comes from the use of yearly data. Indeed, over thirty-five years many sectors have undergone changes in their economic structure, and also the extent of change might vary across countries.
26. We consider a one-digit level of the NACE industrial classification. This allows us to focus on the entire economy while distinguishing between goods and services. It is worth noting that for two sectors – that is, manufacturing and community, social and personal services – the level of aggregation is comparatively much higher than in the other sectors. However, a further disaggregation of manufacturing, while delivering a more in-depth analysis, has lower priority since most goods industries are exposed to competition in the internal market as well as worldwide. For services, disaggregation is expected to pay off since exposure to competition differs greatly. On the other hand, community, social and personal services is also a special sector as it comprises non-market-based activities. Please note that it comprises public administration, defense, education, health, social work and other community, social and personal services. Finally, network industries are represented by sectors 4 and 9.
27. By using yearly data rather than higher frequency data it becomes more difficult to highlight differences across sectors in the reaction to shocks when using either the impact effect or the persistence. For example, consider the case in which a persistence measure, such as the number of periods for the shock to half its impact value, is used. In the realistic case

in which the persistence measure ranges between one to eight quarters across sectors, then the use of yearly data would fail to detect sector differentiation as the value for persistence would be the same for any sector.

28. One-standard deviation shock is used in the impulse response to make the size of the supply shock homogeneous across countries and equal to an initial adverse shock of minus 1 percent output growth.

29. The presence of a deep market integration would cause cross-country homogeneity in price and resource allocation in any sector. Thus, an increase in the standard deviation of the measure of the resilience to shocks would reveal a lower degree of market integration. Finally, a potential explanation for the lack of market integration is the need for product market reforms.

30. For each sector and each of the three measures of flexibility, the standard deviation and the average reported are computed by taking out outliers' values. Outliers' values are those that exceed the interval constituted by the average plus four times the standard deviation.

31. Any attempt to divide data into homogenous groups is subject to a certain degree of discretionality, also when adopting cluster analysis. In this case, we opt for simplicity, and decide to have only two groups of similar size, the first grouping the more resilient to shock sectors and the second the less resilient. These two groups are identified by adding up the cumulative output growth loss and the cumulative inflation change (Euclidian measure of distance). Then, the sectors are ranked and the first 5/6 sectors attributed to the first group and the remaining to the second group. The crucial point is whether to consider manufacturing in the first or second group; however, as it can be deduced even graphically, manufacturing appears to be closer to the first group, for the distance from finance (the closest sector in the most resilient to shock group) is much lower than the one from hotels (the closest sector in the less resilient to shock group).

32. This analysis has the purpose of determining which sectors are relatively rigid within a country, but does not allow us to compare across countries.

33. The identification relies on the assumption that country-specific sectoral shocks affect euro-area variables proportionally to the relative importance of the country in the sector of interest.

34. It is worth noticing that in this analysis the importance of *idiosyncratic* shocks appears larger than what is usually reported for similar analyses that are performed at the aggregate level. This is a consequence of taking an average across countries where each country has the same weight. Indeed, the importance of *common* shocks is greater for larger (Germany, France, Italy) rather than smaller countries. Thus, if for each sector the

average took into account the relative importance of the country in the sector, then the importance of common shocks would increase and that of idiosyncratic shocks decrease.

35. In presenting selective empirical evidence on the product market reform record of euro-area countries, it is important to realize that there is a lack of appropriate indicators (see Box 19.1 and Pelkmans, 2008, forthcoming) for authoritative analysis. Readers are cautioned that the empirical evidence, though rich, is subject to considerable improvement.

36. The relevant empirical literature will not be reiterated; the reader is referred to Box 19.1 and the references therein. Other helpful sources include OECD (2007c): Sections 6.4 and 6.5 in the European Commission (2008a), and Section 2.5 in the European Commission (2007j).

37. See Task Force ECSB (2006: 29, Chart 15; R2 = 0.8677).

38. See Luenneman and Mathae (2005). The authors suggest that these services add up to about 7 percent of the EU15 aggregate HICP in 2002. Luenneman and Mathae's findings include: regulated prices generate a higher inflation rate than sectors outside services and, for example, higher inflation persistence than overall inflation.

39. Note that the European Commission (2007e: 16–7) is also incorporating this element in the product market monitoring methodology.

40. This rise in reform intensity in network industries since the early 1990s is very similar to the overall perspective which emerges when employing the Copenhagen Economics' Market Opening Index (see Box 19.1, item e.). See their Figure 2.6, p. 30 in Copenhagen Economics (2005, Part I).

41. See e.g. Andrews (2002); Faure *et al.* (1993); Ogus (1995); and Paterson *et al.* (2003).

42. See European Commission (2004d) and OECD (2000).

43. The OECD has studied accounting, legal, architecture and engineering services.

44. How difficult it is to liberalize this field is illustrated by Garoupa's conclusion that the Netherlands is an example of a good-quality regulatory setup for the legal profession and a poor one for physicians.

45. The EU legislature has adopted Directive 2005/36 on the recognition of professional qualifications (OJ L255, 30.9.2005, p. 22–142) which consolidates the numerous mutual recognition procedures for professional qualifications. This, however, is more like a necessary, far from a sufficient, condition for a genuine internal market, with the appropriate measure of competition. Also, the European Court of Justice has so far remained rather cautious in respecting national differences which can be characterized as restrictive; see e.g. the 2004 Wouters case. A sectoral approach is probably the only way forward.

46. For additional information see i.a. Leiner-Killinger *et al.* (2007). IMF (2004b) also studies tax and trade reforms (for twenty OECD economies). The latter are usually considered in our analysis as part of product market reforms while the former are not considered since they belong to the realm of Member States' fiscal policy discretion which limits the scope of EMU-specific action.

47. Directive 2006/123/EC of the European Parliament and of the Council on services in the internal market (OJ L 376, 27.12.2006, p. 36–68).

48. In contrast, within-policy complementarities in *labor* markets have been widely studied. For a comprehensive review, see Bassanini and Duval (2006).

49. See Task Force ECSB (2006: 27–30), for telling data.

50. On the link between well-functioning financial markets and product and labor market reforms, see Buti *et al.* (2009).

51. Of course, a comprehensive reform strategy should also study complementarities and spillovers with other policy areas but we believe that their analysis is useful to establish general recommendations.

52. The economic literature has traditionally considered that reforms in the product markets ease labor market reforms. Nonetheless, as noted above, this relationship is blurred, or, if one wishes, a two-way one, in some euro-area countries.

53. See Weyerstrass *et al.* (2008) for a theoretical classification of spillovers and Bongardt and Torres (2007); European Commission (2007d); and Lejour and Rojas-Romagosa (2008), among others, for empirical analyses.

54. FDI and M&A can also act as transmission channels. Recent estimates by Baldwin *et al.* (2008) signal an increase of FDI and M&A within the euro area though smaller than for the EU as a whole. But FDI may play a stronger role as the euro area enlarges.

55. Cross-border spillovers only arise at EU level, while policy complementarities can be observed at national and European level.

56. Debrun and Pisani-Ferry (2006) add another argument for coordinated reforms based on political risks for the proper functioning of the monetary union. When there is a domestic crisis of competitiveness in a euro-area country (say, due to a lack of downward wage flexibility) or a sharp rise in local inflation prompted primarily by a lack of competition in the non-tradeables sector (e.g. services) and calling for painful disinflation measures, countries might resort to behavior that could be harmful to euro-area partners (e.g. resist further opening of trade, undue economic nationalism until the European Court of Justice stops them several years later, etc.). Coordinated reforms for all euro-area countries and explicitly in the joint euro-area interest will render it much more difficult to resort to misconduct, while also helping to remove the cause of the problem.

57. There has been a series of internal market strategies in the post-1992 period, including for example two three-year strategies under Commissioner Bolkestein and the recent Single Market Review (European Commission, 2007f).
58. See e.g. Pelkmans (2006), and Ederveen *et al.* (2008).
59. See IMF (2004b) and Hoj *et al.* (2006) for some insights on the framework conditions.

Comment 14: Comment on Chapters 18 and 19

GERT JAN KOOPMAN

Product and labour market reforms in the euro area – evidence from the first ten years and an agenda for the future

1. Introduction

The two chapters by Bertola and Pelkmans and co-authors review the available evidence relating to the effects of EMU membership on the pace of structural reforms from both theoretical and empirical angles. In addition to assessing the evidence, the authors also map out some recommendations for the structural reform agenda – mostly in terms of design and areas that merit particular attention going forward. In a monetary union structural reforms are a crucial complement to budgetary policies and many authors underlined at the inception of EMU that the pace of structural reforms should be stepped up to allow EMU to function properly. Given the theoretical ambiguity of the effects of EMU membership per se, these review chapters are important reference points since they present some new empirical results and review other results found in the literature. Interestingly, both contributions suggest that EMU is associated with stronger structural reforms in the euro area, thereby offering a relatively positive assessment whilst admitting that data limitations dictate caution.

This commentary first recaps the main theoretical considerations underlining the importance of structural reforms for the euro area. On this basis a number of key policy questions are formulated. It then sets out to review the available evidence on the product and labour market reforms in EMU to answer these questions. It subsequently focuses on

The author would like to thank colleagues at the Commission's Directorate General for Economic and Financial Affairs for helpful comments on a previous version of this commentary. This commentary does not necessarily reflect the views of the European Commission.

remaining priorities for reforms and then concludes with some thoughts on the governance of structural reforms in the euro area.

2. Some theoretical considerations

Pelkmans and co-authors set out the three principal reasons why structural reforms in product markets are an important precondition for a well-functioning monetary union. These reasons apply equally to reforms in labour markets. In a monetary union without fiscal transfers such as EMU asymmetric shocks can put severe adjustment pressures on member countries as their relative competitiveness changes. Flexible markets allow rapid and easy adjustment of wages and prices in the face of such shocks leading to corrections in real effective exchange rates. Failing this, prolonged deviations from potential output and large external imbalances would occur. If coupled with widening public deficits this could lead to widening sovereign spreads and raise the cost of capital, which may, in extreme cases, cause financing difficulties. Whilst this mechanism could be considered as exerting a positive disciplining market incentive for structural reforms, it could also, if it overshoots, put significant strain on the functioning of EMU.

The first reason to pursue structural reforms in EMU is, therefore, that by removing rigidities in product and labour markets these reforms can improve the functioning of the competitiveness adjustment channel thereby avoiding the materialisation of significant strains. Faced with an asymmetric negative demand shock flexible wages and prices will restore economic activity through improved external competitiveness.[1] Secondly, structural reforms facilitate the reallocation of resources and thus adjustment. Thirdly, in light of low trade barriers in the euro area, Member States could profit from relatively large benefits from structural reforms through the trade channel.

The mechanisms set out above suggest that countries in monetary union have relatively strong incentives to undertake structural reforms. However, there is a countervailing pressure coming from externalities from structural reforms: in monetary union, the benefits of structural reforms spill over in a relatively significant manner to other members, thereby reducing the incentive to reform in the absence of coordination (European Commission, 2007d).

It should of course be pointed out that these reasons are particular to countries in monetary union and that they are additional to the basic objective of structural reforms which is to increase potential growth through improved allocative and dynamic efficiency. Perversely, this fundamental incentive for reforms may have diminished in many euro-area countries that had weak monetary and fiscal policy frameworks previously and that, upon joining the euro area, benefited from lower real interest rates as a result of the credibility flowing from ECB-led monetary policies and the fiscal discipline imposed by the Stability and Growth Pact (SGP). With sovereign spreads in these countries falling dramatically, there is at least a *prima facie* suggestion that this effect may also have boosted growth temporarily (though, absent structural reforms, not on a sustainable basis).

All in all, a rough summary of the literature would suggest that in the euro area the need for structural reforms increases, but that it is unclear whether the incentives for structural reforms in individual member states increases commensurably. Empirical evidence is needed to address this question.

On this basis, the remainder of this commentary attempts to answer the following policy questions:

(i) Have euro-area member states introduced significant reforms? (ii) To what extent have these reforms benefited from euro-area membership? (iii) Are these reforms sufficient? (iv) If not, what priorities remain? (v) And how can incentives for more robust reforms be strengthened?

3. The evidence

Both chapters reviewed in this contribution recognise that there are severe data limitations hampering the empirical analysis of the effect of euro-area membership on the pace of structural reforms. This is largely due to the fact that the empirical data on product market regulations typically refer to indices constructed on the basis of questionnaires – often for a limited number of years and countries with, inevitably, a degree of arbitrariness in the selection and weighting of the components. Similar difficulties surround indicators of labour market regulation which is an inherently complex concept covering many dimensions. Bertola, therefore, also resorts to assessing the direct correlation of EMU membership with labour market *outcomes*. These factors all imply that the results of econometric tests need to be considered with significant caution. It is useful, therefore, to commence the analysis by considering the stylised facts first. These can be summarised as follows:

1. Both product and labour market regulatory indices (PMI and LMI) have come down significantly in the euro area since 1999, although the OECD has tentatively found that the pace of reform in product markets slowed somewhat since 2003.
2. However, there is considerable evidence suggesting that, at least in EU15 countries, this development occurred from much higher starting points and that – on average – restrictions in the euro area are still stronger than in EU Member States outside the euro area.
3. This in turn suggests that catching-up effects may have played a role. EU-wide legislation opening sectors to competition would, therefore, *ceteris paribus*, have had a bigger impact on euro-area members. Given that a significant part of internal market legislation was introduced through sectoral measures (e.g. in rail, in banking, etc.) a sectoral perspective is essential to disentangle the differentiated effects from harmonisation through EU legislation and from the measures that euro-area Member States may have adopted to go beyond minimum standards. There is a near complete absence of analysis in the literature on this point, rendering the analysis of 'pure' EMU effects very difficult.
4. In terms of results, there is by now a considerable body of evidence suggesting that the labour markets of euro-area Member States have become much more flexible and efficient, with the NAIRU coming down significantly. Real wages have also become more responsive to deviations of unemployment rates from the NAIRU. Employment rates have also increased significantly. However, while product market reforms would be expected to increase total factor productivity (TFP) growth, it is difficult to detect this in the data at the macro level. Moreover, the gap between EU and US TFP levels is not closing. Given the inherent difficulties in measuring TFP, it is worth inspecting other indicators of the dynamic efficiency of markets; but also here the general conclusion must be that progress has been limited (this is notably true for R&D and innovation performance in the euro area). There is a paradox: despite considerable reforms in product markets, the effects at the macro level seem very hard to establish.[2]

5. Very considerable differences in reforms across euro-area Member States can be observed, with countries like Finland, the Netherlands and Ireland scoring much better than average in terms of reforms and outcomes. Considerable deficits in labour market reforms and outcomes characterise the performance of most Mediterranean countries.

6. Importantly, the reform efforts undertaken by the different euro-area countries have not been able to prevent the emergence of very significant macroeconomic imbalances – notably sizable imbalances in external competitiveness as reflected by widening current account surpluses and deficits (European Commission, 2008a). The competitiveness adjustment channel in EMU, therefore, at best works only in a limited way.

3.1 Discussion

There has been considerable reform in financial markets in the euro area as a result of single market policies. Whilst the implementation of the Financial Services Action Plan is only very partly covered by the data, it is plausible that the effects have been largest in euro-area countries given the much more restrictive practices prevailing in these countries than in other EU Member States such as the United Kingdom. By allowing the benefits of structural reforms to be brought forward, more efficient financial markets should have contributed to changing the incentive structure of economic agents and to bringing forward the implementation of the structural reform agenda in the euro area. Buti *et al.* (2009) also demonstrate that such reforms tend to increase the chances of reforming governments to be re-elected, thereby providing a further channel through which financial market reforms should facilitate product and labour market reforms more widely.

As regards the sequencing of structural reforms, it is often suggested that financial and product market reforms should precede labour market reforms since they tend to remove the rents of incumbents. However, the evidence is mixed.[3] Alesina *et al.* (2008), while finding some support that lower rents are associated with a higher intensity of product market reform, also show that product market reforms are more frequent if unemployment benefits are increased and employment protection relaxed. Workers may be more willing to accept reforms that can lead to job losses if they are – at least partly – insured against the financial consequences whilst employers find it easier to reduce the workforce to respond to more competitive pressures. This suggests that in reality product and labour market reforms should be designed in an integrated manner and implemented in tandem since they are mutually reinforcing. In addition, significant emphasis should be placed on the efficiency of financial markets and the social security system.

When assessing product market reforms the picture varies considerably across sectors and countries. Services stand out as an area of concern, although, as Pelkmans and co-authors point out, significant progress has been achieved in network industries. However, large parts of the services sector, pending the implementation of the Services Directive, remain subject to highly restrictive regulations – on entry, prices, advertising, etc. Retail and wholesale trade are particularly noteworthy given their size and importance in terms of inter-linkages with the rest of the economy. In manufacturing, restrictions are generally lower. The differences across countries are also significant, although they seem to be declining with euro-area countries that had very restrictive practices having undertaken the largest reforms. A key issue that needs careful further analysis is the extent to which reforms are triggered through internal market legislation. With euro-area starting positions typically being more restrictive, there is a risk that the relatively strong progress in the euro area would wrongly be attributed to euro-area membership. Analysis by Alesina *et al.* (2008), however, suggests that, in addition to starting positions, there is a clear, albeit modest, euro-area membership effect driving down regulation in EMU.

In assessing the analyses based on indicators of product market regulation, it is important to bear in mind the significant data limitations referred to above. It is, therefore, also useful to explore alternative approaches to assessing the functioning of product markets. Pelkmans and co-authors provide an interesting econometric assessment using a bivariate VAR model evaluating the reaction to sectoral demand and supply shocks at a sectoral level on the basis of cumulative output growth loss and cumulative inflation change. This can be interpreted as a measure of resilience to shocks. Broadly speaking, this approach confirms the general results of PMI-based analysis, suggesting that sectors like trade, post, community, social and personal services, and real estate, renting and business activities are least resilient. Pelkmans and co-authors, however, find considerable variation across countries.

The European Commission launched an in-depth analysis of the functioning of product markets under the heading 'Market Monitoring' as part of its review of the functioning of the Single Market (Ilzkovitz *et al.* (2008) and European Commission (2009b)). Essentially this approach consists of assessing the performance of sectors in the European economy across a number of dimensions (e.g. productivity growth, innovation, competition and integration) compared to a benchmark – for the EU this is often the USA. Whilst the analytical approach is different and some manufacturing sectors are identified as performing poorly as well, essentially the same service sectors are found to show signs of market malfunctioning.

Although the above assessment is necessarily very condensed, it nevertheless summarises the main observations that can be gleaned from the literature. A key problem in all of this is that, given data limitations, econometric techniques only allow simple correlations to be established. Even there, the evidence is very mixed: for example, the chapter by Bertola finds that there has been a correlation between EMU membership and labour market reforms whereas an analysis by Alesina *et al.* (2008) indicates that no such association can be found.[4] This difference may well be due to the relatively limited nature of the two indicators for labour market regulation used by Alesina *et al.* (i.e. an indicator for employment protection legislation and an unemployment benefit replacement rate for low income workers).

Against this background, it is reasonable to suggest in summary that overall EMU has contributed to generating improvements in structural reform performance in euro-area Member States, although the pattern is mixed across countries and policy areas and is not as impressive as the progress that has been achieved with improving public finances, notably under the reformed SGP.

However, as pointed out by the European Commission (2008a), '*there is no alternative*' (TINA) has not been a sufficiently strong driver to allow structural reforms to avoid the emergence of significant macro imbalances which in the longer run could create significant strains within the euro area. All this suggests that stronger coordination of structural reforms in the euro area is necessary.

4. Reform priorities for the next decade

The above analysis shows that despite certain progress with structural reforms having been achieved much remains to be done in the years ahead to ensure a better functioning of product and labour markets in the euro area. Against this background, it is useful to highlight a number of key priorities.

As a general observation, the broad thrust of labour market reforms has begun to pay off in terms of structurally higher employment rates, but a similar effect cannot easily be found in the case of product market reforms and higher total factor productivity growth. This suggests that policy makers should give particular priority to microeconomic reforms designed to improve productivity growth. The impending effects of ageing which are set to reduce the potential output growth of the EU and the euro area by more than 0.5 per cent per year in the next decades (European Commission and EPC (2008)) further underline this necessity.

Whilst significant progress has been achieved with bringing down regulatory barriers in certain product markets, the lack of an increase in productivity growth suggests that the work on remaining individual sectors should be complemented by a more horizontal approach to address obstacles to R&D, innovation and competition across industries. The available evidence suggests that the functioning of the knowledge triangle in the EU deserves particular attention. This raises institutional and regulatory issues – with a considerable variation across Member States (with especially the Nordics performing extremely well) and a rich potential to experiment and learn from best practices within the EU.

In addition, the work on individual product markets should increasingly focus on sectoral deregulation in sectors where barriers remain. While different approaches lead to somewhat varying results in terms of defining sectoral priorities, it is clear that the emphasis should be on retail trade, professional services and post and rail in most Member States.

Many of these services are regulated at the EU level and euro-area members, therefore, have a particular interest in the evolution of EU frameworks. Of particular interest in this context is the transposition and implementation of the Services Directive which holds out the potential of reaping significant gains. A detailed sectoral analysis of the extent to which euro-area Member States go beyond the minimum EU requirements is, therefore, required. Consideration should be given to the establishment of ambitious euro-area benchmarks. For researchers, such analyses would provide interesting evidence complementing the rather generalised available research results based on econometric tests of PMI and LMI. The work on market monitoring launched by the European Commission could usefully be extended to the level of individual Member States to assist such a development. More in general, the aggregate results for sectors of the EU economy should be analysed with regards to country specificities using a variety of analytical approaches as also advocated in Pelkmans and co-authors to arrive at priorities for individual Member States. This will also be of particular importance when addressing the contribution structural reforms can make to unwinding macroeconomic imbalances within the euro area.

Significant progress has been achieved with labour market reforms and the 'flexicurity' concept has provided a broad framework to guide further reforms in the EU. Key challenges that remain, however, concern:

- the need to introduce more flexibility in open-ended employment contracts in many euro-area Member States; also with a view to reversing the segregation between insiders and outsiders on fixed-term employment contracts;
- while marginal tax rates have on the whole come down and unemployment insurance reforms have been undertaken in many Member States, there are still many 'traps' in the labour market inhibiting transitions into employment (European Commission (2009a));
- activation is still not a general feature of labour market policies and more progress here is badly needed in many countries; given the poor labour market results for certain groups (e.g. low skilled, migrants), there is a strong case for having at least a tailored component in these activation policies;
- many countries would benefit from moving towards more adequate and appropriately designed income support measures, conditional on strict work-acceptance rules. The available evidence indicates that this leads to significantly better labour market outcomes than other systems;
- wage formation systems differ strongly across euro-area countries (e.g. in the degree of centralisation and coordination), but further reforms to ensure that wage and productivity growth are better aligned at sectoral, regional and firm level are necessary in many euro-area Member States.

Thus, whilst the differences across euro-area Member States are significant, also in the function of institutional variation, there is a strong case for identifying remaining priorities at the national level with regards to the above challenges.

This points to the more general importance of developing comparable assessment frameworks to identify policy deficits and, thereby, priorities at Member State level. Joint work by the Economic Policy Committee and the European Commission has led to the development of the 'LAF' assessment framework that allows the identification of relatively poorly performing policy areas (e.g. older workers, business environment, or R&D and innovation) compared with a benchmark (European Commission, 2008d). In combination with evidence on growth performance, this helps to identify reform priorities at a national level. This work should be complemented by the assessment of the relative effectiveness of different reforms to assist the design of appropriate policy instruments.[5] Work in this area can provide a more robust basis for assessing priorities and possible results which should also assist with the political economy challenges surrounding structural reforms.

4.1 Policy coordination and governance

This then leaves the question of policy coordination and governance within the euro area. Given the insufficiency of reforms in the past decade, which governance reforms could be contemplated that may help to accelerate reforms? How can incentives for reform be strengthened?

At present, the coordination of structural reforms is based on the Lisbon Strategy and discussions in the Eurogroup. A strengthening of both mechanisms would, therefore, be desirable.

A strengthening of the peer support/pressure element in the Lisbon Strategy through a further development of its evidence base would allow policy recommendations under Article 99 of the EU Treaty to be more specific, explicit and operational. This could be achieved by further pursuing the analytical work on the assessment framework undertaken since the successful relaunch of the Lisbon Strategy in 2005, for example by applying the market monitoring approach at country level. While the benefits would accrue to all EU countries, the explicit inclusion of adjustment needs – e.g. through the competitiveness channel – and corresponding reform requirements for countries in the euro area in this assessment framework would further enhance the relevance of the strategy to the euro area. More generally, a further strengthening of the Lisbon agenda as an economic policy coordination tool will be of the essence when the strategy is reformed after 2010.

In addition, a more active role of the Eurogroup in reviewing structural reforms would be useful; focusing on euro-area specific challenges such as spillovers and competitiveness challenges. In addition, given the greater importance of wage and price adjustment in the euro area generally, this could also lead to the establishment of more ambitious euro-area benchmarks.

Furthermore, as proposed in the Commission's EMU@10 report (European Commission, 2008a), it would be highly beneficial to improve the link between the structural reform agenda and the SGP, by addressing the public finance implications of structural reforms in the context of the assessment of stability and convergence programmes and excessive deficit procedures. This may be of particular importance in the coming decade given the need to re-establish sound public finances after the discretionary expansion under the European Economic Recovery Programme to respond to the financial crisis in 2009 and 2010.

More generally, careful thought should be given to what extent incentives for reforms could be built into Community economic policies – e.g. the structural funds (possibly through Lisbon reforms-related performance reserves) and research policies (idem) – that are directly relevant to the Lisbon Strategy.

5. Conclusion

The available evidence suggests that euro-area Member States have introduced significant structural reforms in the past decade and that euro-area membership has broadly played a positive role in this regard. However, it is equally clear that the reforms have been insufficient to increase the potential rate of growth in the euro area and to avoid the emergence of significant macroeconomic imbalances.

Remedying these twin deficits is the main challenge for the next decade. In essence, a further development of the instruments that have been created over the past years will assist with the identification of reform priorities in product and labour markets. It is to be hoped that a strengthening of the evidence base and, therefore, of the expected benefits of reforms, will in and of itself assist with the more forceful implementation of the structural reform agenda. However, it seems equally clear that stronger incentives and coordination mechanisms will be needed to fully reach this objective. Aligning the policy recommendations under the Lisbon Strategy and the SGP in combination with a stronger role for the Eurogroup – focused on the euro area's specificities – should greatly assist this.

Notes

1. This effect will partly be offset by the real interest rate channel (asymmetric shocks leading to higher real interest rates) but research reported in European Commission (2007c) suggests that the effects through the competitiveness channel outweigh this impact.
2. Of course, one could argue that failing these reforms the results would have been worse, but this would still not explain why the gap with the USA – which arguably reformed less (given its better starting position) is not closing.
3. This conclusion rests on the political economy argument that lower rents reduce the incentives of trade unions to resist labour market reform (Blanchard and Giavazzi, 2003). Spector (2002) suggests that labour market reforms can facilitate product market reform by making them more effective. This is due to the fact that the positive effects of product market deregulation are stronger under the more flexible setup of labour market institutions. Theoretically, the result is thus ambiguous. In a recent empirical paper, Fiori *et al.* (2008) found though that there is some evidence that product market reforms precede labour market reform.
4. Duval and Elmeskov (2006) also found no acceleration of reforms in EMU and Duval (2006) even a slowdown in reforms after the launch of EMU in 1999.
5. To this end the Commission has developed databases for reforms in labour markets (LABREF), product markets (MICREF), tax systems (TAXREF) and is also systematically inventorying reforms undertaken at Member State level under the Lisbon Strategy (LISREF). These databases are, or will be, available on the website of the Commission's Directorate General for Economic and Financial Affairs. The Commission has also developed a database of empirical evidence on the macroeconomic effects of structural reforms to facilitate the design of policy measures.

PART VIII

Enlargement and governance

20 Euro-area enlargement and euro adoption strategies

ZSOLT DARVAS AND GYÖRGY SZAPÁRY

1. Introduction

The twelve new Member States (NMS) which have joined the EU since 2004 do not have an opt-out like Denmark and the United Kingdom and have to adopt the euro under the terms of the Treaty. The timing of the euro adoption depends on satisfying the Maastricht requirements of nominal convergence. The benefits of a currency union, in general, and of the adoption of the euro by the EU Member States, in particular, have been widely discussed in the literature. It will suffice here to recall the main ones. By eliminating exchange rate fluctuations and the associated uncertainty and transaction costs, a currency union promotes trade and financial integration. Furthermore, it enhances price transparency and hence competition. For the NMS, membership of the euro area could also contribute to credibility to the extent that the credibility of the single monetary policy is regarded as greater than the monetary policy of the individual country. Finally, the drive towards euro adoption and the attendant desire to make real and nominal convergence sustainable may promote reforms, for instance in the areas of fiscal institutions and transparency, deregulation, incomes policy, etc. All these benefits can lead to higher growth and better living standards for the society as a whole.

This paper was commissioned by the European Commission as part of the 'EMU@10' project. The authors thank, for discussion and useful comments, Olivier Blanchard, Marco Buti, Attila Csajbók, Zdeněk Čech, Servaas Deroose, Balázs Égert, Jürgen Kröger, Paul Kutos, Jean Pisani-Ferry, Christopher Pissarides, Zoltán Schepp, Massimo Suardi and István Székely, as well as participants in workshops at the European Commission in Brussels, at the Magyar Nemzeti Bank and Corvinus University in Budapest, at the Bank of Estonia in Tallinn, at the University of Münster, at the joint conference of the Banco Central do Brasil and European Commission in São Paulo, and at the Wilfrid Laurier University in Waterloo, Canada. The views expressed are those of the authors and do not necessarily reflect the views of the European Commission.

The aim of this chapter is to discuss the following issues: (i) given the characteristics and initial conditions of the NMS, what are the risks and challenges on the road to the euro and after its adoption; and (ii) what should be the strategy for and the timing of adoption of the euro.

To this end, we investigate the real-nominal convergence nexus during the catching-up process, as it has a bearing on the strategies to adopt, including the choice of exchange rate regime and the timing of euro adoption. We demonstrate that the initial level of development of a country measured by its GDP per capita and the speed of real convergence are the main determinants of the price level convergence and hence of the relative inflation in the long run, which also depends on the exchange rate regime. The countries with the lowest per capita income have the largest initial price level gap to close. The less developed NMS had also the lowest initial level of credit to GDP ratio and hence the greatest potential for credit booms as credit converges toward its equilibrium level. The key issue then is whether, taking into account the initial level of development, the convergence process of the price level can be better managed inside or outside the monetary union and, by implication, whether the transition to the euro can be better managed with a floating or with a fixed exchange rate regime.

What the most appropriate monetary-cum-exchange rate regime is to best manage the catching-up process is a complex issue. We argue in this chapter that the main risks for the NMS with hard pegs is that with no room to let the nominal exchange rate appreciate to accommodate the price level convergence and with little or no risk premia, the real interest rates become excessively low due to higher inflation. This carries the danger of credit booms and can lead to large external account imbalances. Such developments have taken place in the Baltic countries recently.

For the inflation-targeting countries with floating exchange rates, the possibility of letting the nominal exchange rate appreciate provides somewhat more flexibility to control inflation and accommodate price level convergence, but the room for manoeuvre should not be overestimated. This is because owing to the high degree of financial integration of the NMS and euro-area entry expectation-driven capital inflows, the effectiveness of domestic monetary policy is constrained.

An issue related to the real convergence process is whether the Maastricht criteria of inflation and exchange rate stability laid down fifteen years ago or so for a group of countries with less divergent levels of economic development can be reconciled with the lesser degree of real convergence of most of the new members. Or to put it differently, whether these criteria as such will unavoidably keep out of the monetary union countries which will have already reached a stage where they could function normally in the euro area and reap the benefits of membership. We suggest a modification of the Maastricht inflation criterion which as currently defined has lost its economic logic.

It is necessary to mention what this chapter does not study. It does not investigate to what extent the NMS satisfy the optimum currency area (OCA) criteria. Satisfying these criteria is a key condition for joining a monetary union. In a longer version of this chapter (Darvas and Szapáry, 2008), we investigated this issue in detail and concluded that the NMS are not in a worse position – and in some cases are even in a better one – to join the monetary union than the old members were when they adopted the euro.

This chapter was finalised in the spring of 2008, that is, before the spread of the global financial crisis to the NMS. It, therefore, does not examine the possible effects of the crisis on euro-adoption strategies. The crisis has affected to various extents the economies of the NMS through slowing down, and even reversing in some countries, capital flows, credit growth and trade integration. With the sole exception of Poland, the crisis has led to GDP declines in the NMS. However, the crisis does not basically change the long-term challenges and strategies of euro adoption during the catching-up process as analysed in this chapter. Some NMS even converged further in terms of GDP per capita toward the euro area during the crisis as their GDP declined less than in the euro area. It is reasonable to assume that when the world economy recovers, the other NMS will also resume the catching-up process, albeit most likely at a slower pace than before the crisis, due to the heightened recognition by the markets of the risks that we identify in this chapter.

The rest of the paper is organised as follows. Section 2 reviews some of the most relevant economic features of the NMS from the perspective of euro adoption. Section 3 discusses the risks, challenges and the long-term strategies on the road to the euro. In the light of these challenges, Section 4 considers the strategies and timing for euro adoption. Section 5 concludes.[1]

2. Economic features of the NMS from the perspective of euro adoption

2.1 The real-nominal convergence nexus: large differences among the new members

A salient feature of the economic developments of the new members is their catching-up in terms of GDP per capita and the associated price level convergence (Figures 20.1 and 20.2). A well-established fact in economic theory is that richer countries tend to have higher price levels expressed in the same currency and therefore the overall inflation rate in the catching-up countries is higher and/or their nominal exchange rate appreciates as they close the gap.

The key theoretical underpinning of price level convergence is the Balassa-Samuelson (BS) effect. If the higher inflation is due to the BS effect, i.e. to the faster productivity growth in the NMS, then the implied real appreciation of the exchange rate is competitiveness-neutral, an important consideration once a country has adopted the euro. Égert (2007) presents a recent update of the size of the BS effect and finds that *relative to the euro area* the BS effect in the NMS ranges between zero or a negative value and 1.2 per cent. While the BS effect undoubtedly does explain part of the price level convergence between countries with different levels of development, its conventional measurement has a number of weaknesses and there are a number of other factors as well to be considered when assessing the likely influence of the BS effect on price convergence in the years ahead (Darvas and Szapáry, 2008). Furthermore, transitory factors, such as for instance overheating, can also affect the actual speed of price level increases.

Since price level convergence is inherent to the catching-up process, countries experiencing high growth rates, such as most of the NMS, are unlikely to achieve simultaneously a stable nominal exchange rate and a low level of inflation, at least until a certain degree of price level convergence has already been reached.

The five countries with the lowest relative per capita GDP in 1995 were the three Baltic States, Bulgaria and Romania. Even in recent years, these countries recorded the fastest annual rates of growth of GDP, the fastest credit growth, the largest current account deficits and the most rapid wage increases. Four of them had the highest inflation if we disregard Hungary, where inflation has been boosted recently by tax

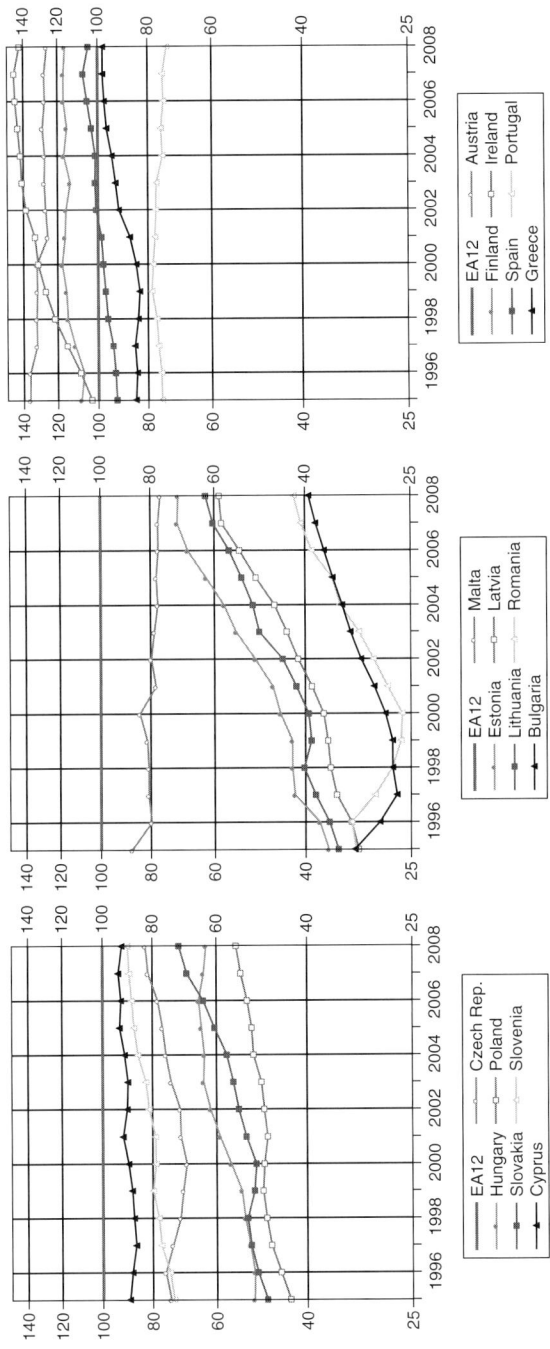

Figure 20.1: GDP per capita in purchasing power standards (EA12 = 100), 1995–2008
Source: Eurostat.

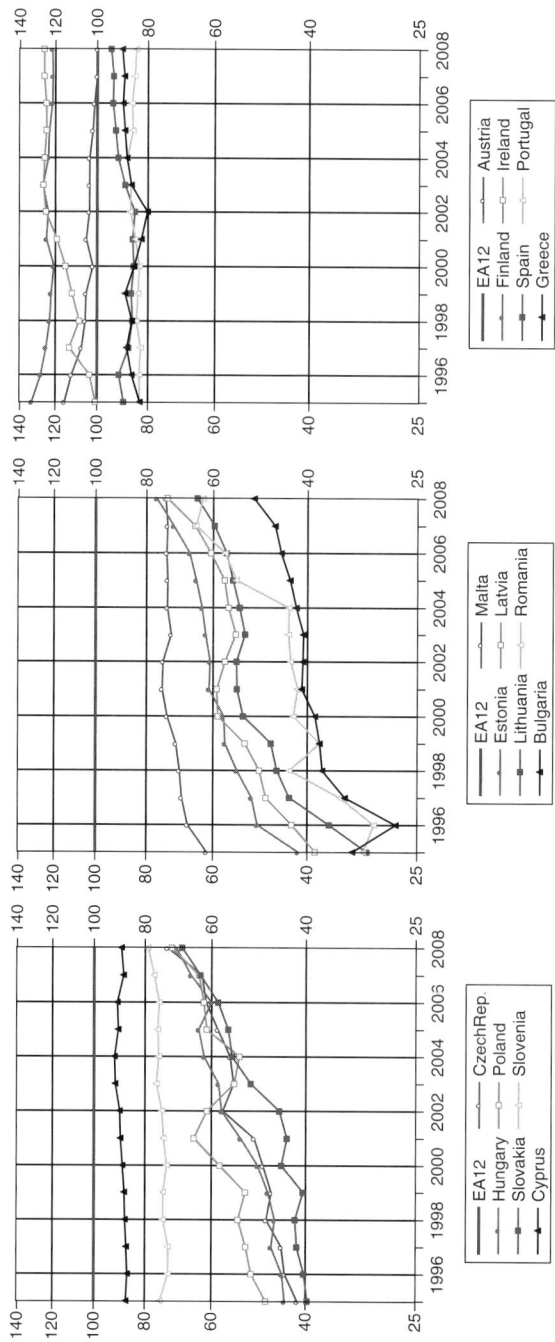

Figure 20.2: Price level of consumption (EA12 = 100), 1995–2008

Sources: Eurostat for 1995–2007; 2008 values were calculated by us using domestic and EA12 inflation and euro exchange rate changes. Note: Values shown correspond to comparative price levels of final consumption by private households including indirect taxes (EA12 = 100)

increases and administrative price adjustments to deal with a runaway fiscal deficit. Those five countries also had the lowest starting price level in the mid-1990s (except Estonia) and the lowest credit/GDP ratios (Figure 20.3). Four of those countries have been operating under fixed exchange rate arrangements, but Romania has had a floating rate.

If we look at the four NMS with the highest relative per capita GDP in 1995, i.e. Cyprus, Malta, the Czech Republic and Slovenia, they recorded lower output growth, slower credit expansion, smaller current account deficits and lower wage growth and inflation in recent years. Two of these countries, Cyprus and Malta, had fixed rates, the Czech Republic had a floating rate and Slovenia was under a tightly managed float, with practically a fixed rate in more recent years. The three countries in the middle of the rankings in terms of GDP per capita (Hungary, Slovakia and Poland) also recorded, compared to the five countries in the bottom of the rankings, slower output growth (except Slovakia), smaller credit expansion, lower current account deficits and lower inflation (except Hungary as noted). All three countries had floating rates.

Looking at the evolution of nominal exchange rates since the mid-1990s of those six countries which had floating rates,[2] we see a mixed picture (Figure 20.4). Only in the Czech Republic and Slovakia has the nominal exchange rate been on a fairly strong appreciating trend since the mid-1990s. These two countries, which had the lowest price levels among the more developed central and eastern European countries (CEEs) in the mid-1990s, are also among the countries which have registered the lowest inflation in recent years.

The economy-wide unit labour cost (ULC)-based real effective exchange rate is another representation of the catching-up phenomenon. The three more developed countries have registered much less appreciation between 1995 and 2007 than the less developed ones, with the ULC-based real exchange rate of Slovenia actually stagnating (Figure 20.5). The largest appreciations took place in Romania (180 per cent) and Lithuania (140 per cent). On the other hand, the appreciation was only 20 per cent in Bulgaria. In the rest of the less developed CEEs, the appreciations ranged between 60 per cent and 90 percent.

This bird's-eye view of the main economic indicators allows us to make a number of observations. First, the low starting level of per capita GDP and the associated low level of prices, as well as the low initial level of credit, are important factors explaining the rapid growth of credit and the high rate of inflation in the countries at the bottom of the

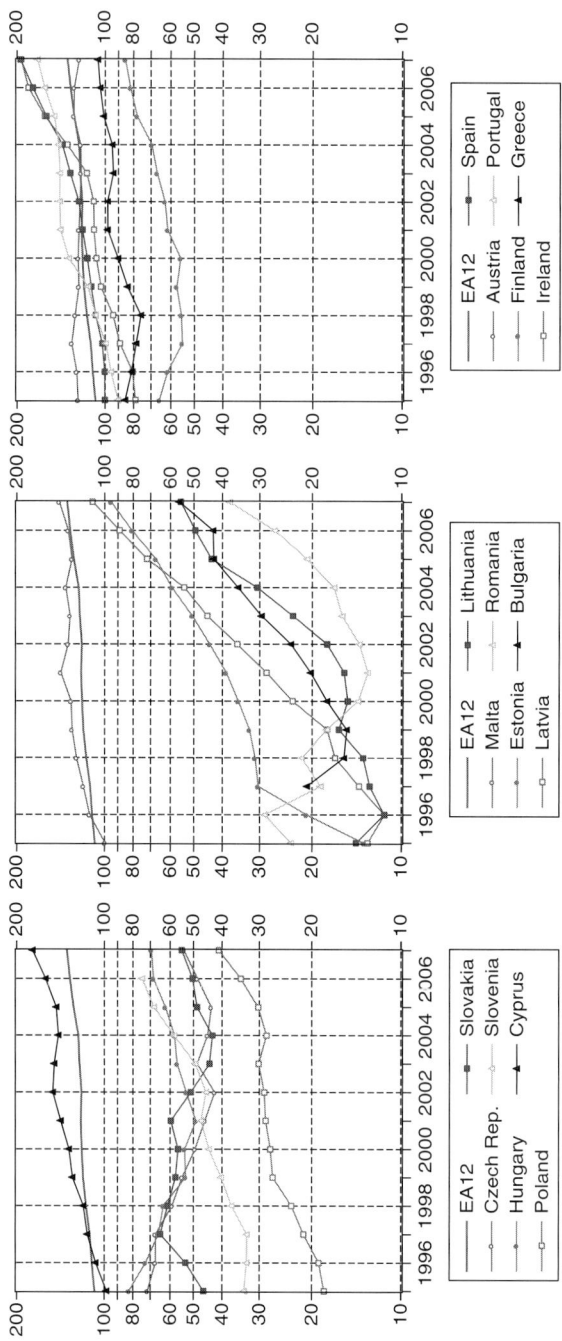

Figure 20.3: Domestic credit (in per cent of GDP), 1995–2007

Source: IMF, IFS. Note: Values for 2007 are projections by us using data of 2007Q3 for most of the countries and 2007Q2 for some of the countries.

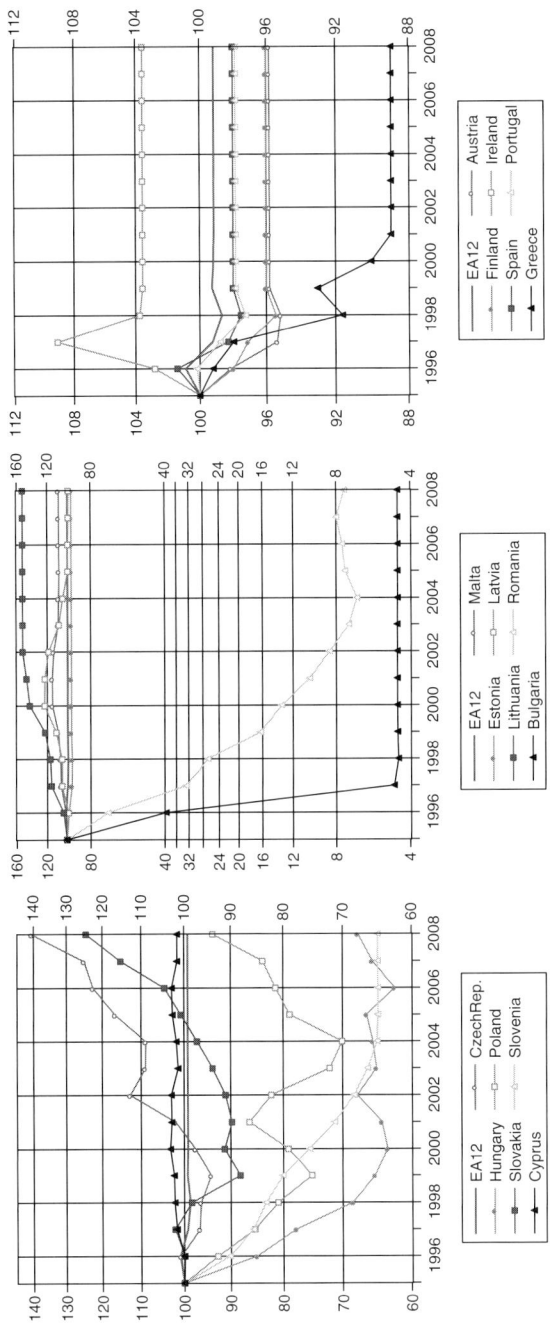

Figure 20.4: Nominal exchange rate against the ECU/EUR (1995 = 100), 1995–2008
Source: Authors' calculation based on data from Eurostat. Values for 2008 assume unchanged exchange rate from August 2008 till the end of the year. Note: a rise in the index means nominal appreciation.

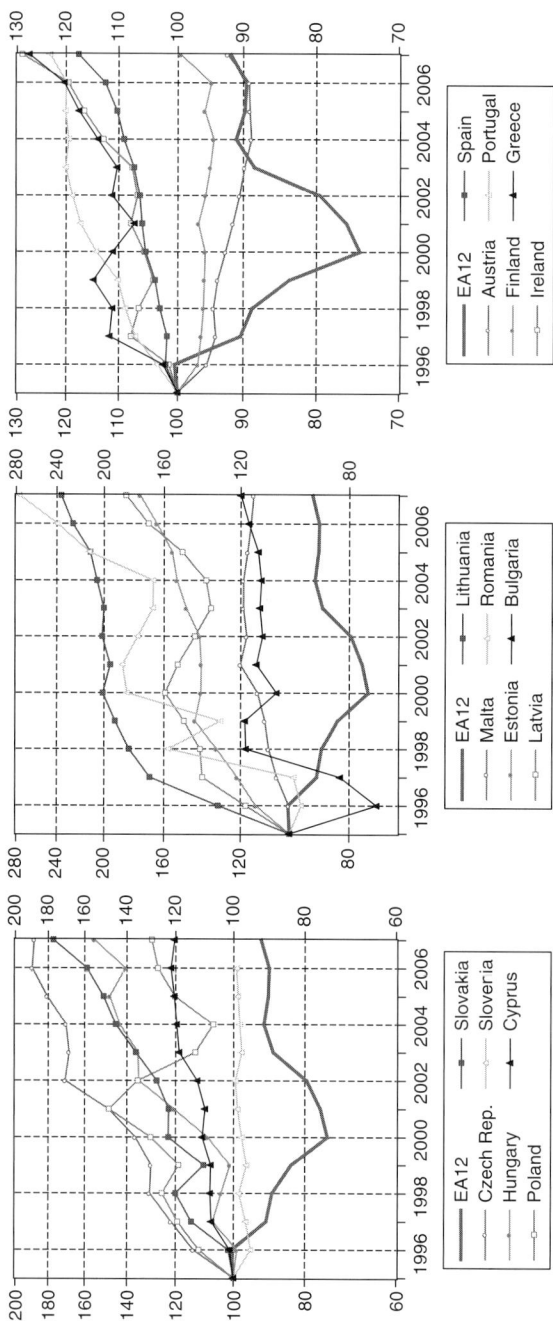

Figure 20.5: Total economy unit labour cost-based real effective exchange rates (2000 = 100), 2000–7
Source: Eurostat. Note: A rise in the index means real appreciation. Values for 2007 are projected using data up to 2007Q3.

rankings. This applies both to the Baltic countries and Bulgaria with fixed exchange rates and to Romania with a floating rate.

To test this hypothesis, we estimated some panel models for the period of 1998–2006 to uncover the determinants of price level convergence in the NMS. The selected specification is the following:[3]

$$
\frac{P_{t,i}}{P_{t,EMU}} = \beta_0 + \frac{\left(Y^{(PPS)}/Y^{(PPS)}POP\right)_{t,i}}{\left(Y^{(PPS)}/Y^{(PPS)}POP\right)_{t,EMU}} + \beta_1 \left(\frac{DD_{t,i}}{Y_{t,i}} - \frac{DD_{t,EMU}}{Y_{t,EMU}}\right)
$$
$$
+ \beta_2 \left(i_{t,i} - i_{t,EMU}\right) + \beta_2 FIXED_i + \varepsilon_{t,i}
$$

where $P_{t,i}$ is the price level of private consumption at time t in country i; $\left(Y^{(PPS)}/POP\right)_{t,i}$ is per capita GDP at purchasing power standards; $DD_{t,i}/Y_{t,i}$ is the share of domestic demand in GDP at current prices; $i_{t,i}$ is the nominal interest rate; $FIXED_i$ is a time-invariant dummy variable for six countries (Bulgaria, Cyprus, Estonia, Latvia, Lithuania, and Malta), and $\varepsilon_{t,i}$ is the error term.

We found – in line with the literature – that per capita income is indeed the key explanatory variable of the price level, and we restricted its parameter to one because we could not reject the null hypothesis that it is equal to one. Domestic demand in excess of GDP is also a significant explanatory factor. To the extent that credit expansion influences domestic demand, and further that the credit expansion is influenced by the initial level of credit, the latter is an important factor determining the price level.

A higher real (and nominal) interest rate compared to the euro-area interest rate, which influences the inflow of interest rate-sensitive capital, is also a factor that has significant positive effects on the price level, since it can appreciate the nominal exchange rate, leading to a rise in the price level relative to the euro area (if the exchange rate passthrough to the overall consumer price level is less than perfect). We also found that the fixity of the nominal exchange rate is an additional explanatory factor of the price level, but that its significance declines over time, in parallel with the convergence of per capita income. This confirms the principle that, under fixed exchange rates, the price level convergence takes place via higher inflation and as the real convergence proceeds, this influence diminishes. However, if the peg contributes to excess domestic demand growth, for instance via lower real interest, as we discuss later, then of course the peg itself has an (indirect) effect on price level increases and inflation, since the parameter of domestic demand is found to be significantly positive.

Under fixed exchange rate conditions, the price level convergence translates into higher domestic inflation. Under floating exchange rates, the price level convergence can be accommodated either by higher inflation or an appreciation of the nominal exchange rate, or by a combination of the two. The results of the model calculations also show that the interest rate-sensitive capital inflows can temporarily appreciate the nominal exchange rate in excess of what would be required by price level convergence implied solely by the catching-up of GDP per capita.

We used the estimated model described above to offer some quantitative prospects of future price level convergence and its effect on inflation. To this end, we assumed various catching-up scenarios in terms of GDP per capita, and assumed that domestic demand and the interest rate converge to EA12 levels as the catching-up process levels out. We further assumed that the catching-up, that is, the excess growth of GDP compared to EA12, is fast when a country has a much lower per capita GDP than the EA12, but that the speed decreases as the catching-up process advances.

The long-run level of per capita GDP was set either at 90 per cent of the EA12 level (roughly the average of Greece, Portugal and Spain) or at 100 per cent. The initial speed of catching up was set equal to actual excess growth in 2000–7. Projections of domestic demand per GDP were derived on the basis of an empirical relationship between excess growth and domestic demand. We assumed that the interest rate differential will be zero by 2015 and declines (increases in the case of the Czech Republic where the interest rate is currently below the euro level) linearly in time until then. For illustrative purposes, Table 20.1 shows the inflationary consequences of the price level convergence under these assumptions. For instance, assuming a price level convergence of 90 per cent in the long run, the excess inflation over EA12 inflation ranges between 1.2 and 3.6 per cent per year during 2008–12. This excess inflation can be also accommodated by a nominal appreciation of the exchange rate of the same magnitude, or by a combination of excess inflation and appreciation.

A second observation is that the significant appreciation of the real effective exchange rates inherent in the catching-up process is not dependent on the exchange rate regime, although the regime can determine the risks of overshooting of the real exchange rate, as will be discussed later.

A third observation is that in the Czech Republic, Slovakia and, more recently, in Poland and Romania, the real exchange rate appreciation has been accompanied by a significant appreciation of the nominal exchange

Table 20.1: *Projected annual average price level convergence*

	Catching-up to 90 per cent of EA12			Catching-up to 100 per cent of EA12		
	2008–12	2013–17	2018–22	2008–12	2013–17	2018–22
Bulgaria	1.2	1.8	1.8	1.2	2.0	2.0
Cyprus	n.a.	n.a.	n.a.	0.4	0.3	0.2
Czech Republic	2.5	0.9	0.3	3.0	1.6	0.8
Estonia	3.3	0.0	–0.3	4.3	0.9	0.0
Hungary	3.2	1.9	1.3	3.3	2.2	1.6
Latvia	2.3	0.5	–0.1	2.6	1.3	0.5
Lithuania	3.4	1.2	0.3	3.8	1.9	0.9
Malta	0.4	0.4	0.3	0.4	0.4	0.4
Poland	1.8	1.5	1.3	1.9	1.6	1.4
Romania	2.7	2.6	2.2	2.8	2.8	2.5
Slovenia	n.a.	n.a.	n.a.	1.6	0.4	0.1
Slovakia	3.6	1.6	0.7	3.8	2.2	1.2

Note: The interpretation of the values shown is the following: either inflation will exceed the EA12 inflation rate by the magnitudes shown, or the nominal exchange rate should appreciate by these same magnitudes, or a combination of these two factors should occur.

rate. The first three countries are also among those which have had the lowest average inflation rates in the more recent period of 2004–7, and Romania has seen its inflation rate decline rapidly. In other words, the price level convergence was accompanied by a lower inflation rate when the nominal exchange rate was allowed to appreciate, a finding which is confirmed by the above-mentioned model calculations.

Fourth, the faster rate of growth in the less developed NMS except Bulgaria has been largely driven by consumption rather than productivity gains which, together with investment growth and despite a rapid increase in exports, has led to large current account deficits. This means that the catching-up of these countries has been largely at the cost of accumulating foreign debt. Fiscal looseness has not been the source of the large current account deficits of these countries, which recorded surpluses or deficits of less than 1 per cent of GDP per year on average during 2004–7. Only Romania had an average deficit of 2 per cent per year in that period.

Finally, the Baltic countries and especially Estonia are fast catching up to the countries in midfield in terms of per capita GDP, but Bulgaria and Romania, which started the catching-up process only around 2000, are still further behind. This suggests that the price level convergence due to the catching up-process should moderate in the Baltics, but that it will still be a significant source of future inflationary pressure in Bulgaria and Romania.

These observations indicate that the starting level and the speed of real convergence, as well as the exchange rate regime, have a bearing on the challenges facing the new members in meeting the *nominal* convergence criteria for euro adoption and, as a consequence, on the choice of strategies to adopt on the road to the euro and on the timing of euro adoption.

2.2 Monetary transmission: limits on the effectiveness of domestic monetary policy

The relevance of the monetary transmission mechanism from the perspective of euro adoption is that when the effects of domestic monetary policy on inflation and output are large and very different from the effects observed in the euro area, then the cost of losing monetary policy independence might be significant. In the opposite case, the loss is less important.

There are characteristics of the NMS that limit the effectiveness of monetary policy in general, and factors that limit the effectiveness of domestic monetary policy in particular.

Two characteristics limit the effectiveness of monetary policy *in general*. First, the ratio of credit to GDP is still low in these countries, ranging from around 41 per cent for Poland to less than 76 per cent for the other CEEs except in Latvia (110 per cent) and Estonia (95 per cent), compared with an average of about 135 per cent in the euro area (Figure 20.3). In the latter two Baltic countries, the credit to GDP ratio has increased very sharply in recent years. Second, stock market capitalisation is low and holdings of financial assets by households is small, both of which weaken the channels through balance sheets and wealth effects.

More relevant from the perspective of euro adoption and the surrender of monetary policy independence are the factors that already constrain the effectiveness of *domestic* monetary policy. The main factor is the large and growing share of foreign currency loans (Table 20.2), which weakens the effectiveness of the domestic interest rate policy. Among the countries with floating exchange rates, the share of foreign currency

Table 20.2: *Share of foreign currency loans (in per cent of total loans),*
2004–6

	Households		Non-financial corporations		Total	
	2004	2006	2004	2006	2004	2006
Bulgaria	12	17	n.a.	n.a.	47	46
Czech Republic	0.3	0.2	18.7	18.6	11.2	10.2
Estonia	64.9	77.8	78.7	75.6	72.1	76.7
Cyprus	n.a.	n.a.	n.a.	n.a.	n.a.	n.a.
Latvia	65.1	77.1	56.3	77.0	59.8	77.0
Lithuania	42.8	43.9	64.8	58.2	58.0	52.3
Hungary	12.9	42.7	43.4	45.7	31.9	44.5
Malta	1.0	1.4	6.7	16.1	4.3	9.4
Poland	27.2	30.9	23.7	22.1	25.4	27.1
Romania	47	40	n.a.	n.a.	61	48
Slovenia	3	43	n.a.	n.a.	32	57
Slovakia	0.6	1.7	33.5	33.5	21.5	20.1

Sources: ECB, World Bank (2007b).
Note: Calculated on the basis of outstanding amounts at the end of the period.

loans reached 45 per cent in Hungary and 48 per cent in Romania in 2006 due to the high positive spreads between the domestic and the relevant foreign interest rates. In the Czech Republic, on the other hand, where the interest rate spreads are negative, the share is only 10 per cent.

The shares are highest in the Baltic States, ranging between 52 per cent in Lithuania and 77 per cent in both Estonia and Latvia. In the latter country, the interest rate spreads have widened recently and 100 per cent of the recent growth of loans has been in euro. In Bulgaria, at 44 per cent, the share is also high. Since these countries have pegged exchange rates, the high share of foreign currency loans no longer adds significantly to the loss of monetary policy independence, but does represent a substantial risk if the exchange rate depreciates for some reason.

Another factor circumventing the domestic monetary policy is the borrowing by firms from their mother companies abroad or from other sources of external lending. According to World Bank (2007b), the foreign debt stock of enterprises exceeds the level of their domestic bank loans in Poland, the Czech Republic, Slovakia, Bulgaria and

Estonia. Since foreign-owned firms have easier access to external sources of lending and since they contribute considerably to output in the NMS, the share of external financing is a significant limiting factor on the effectiveness of domestic monetary policy, which is also one reason why the level of domestic credit is low.

2.3 Financial integration

Financial integration enhances risk pooling and consumption smoothing, improves the effectiveness of the transmission of the common monetary policy and, through the pooling and channelling of resources to investment opportunities, improves the allocation of resources. Hence, it promotes growth and helps adjust to idiosyncratic shocks. Financial integration is usually measured by the integration of money, bond and equity markets, cross-border holdings of financial assets, the cross-border integration of banking systems, and whether the institutional setups ensure a common set of rules and provide equal access and treatment of market participants (Ferrando *et al.*, 2004). By adopting the *acquis communautaire*, the NMS by and large satisfy the institutional requirements.

Regarding the integration of money and bond markets, Figures 20.6 and 20.7 show, respectively, the three-month money market rates and the ten-year bond market interest rates. There has been a substantial convergence of the nominal interest rates in the NMS towards the lower levels prevailing in the euro area. This convergence has been driven in part by the decline in risk premia, reflecting the more stability-oriented macroeconomic policies in the NMS and market expectations that they will adopt the euro following a relatively short period of time after their entry into the EU. In addition, the search for yields in the environment of abundant global liquidity has increased the markets' risk appetite, generating substantial portfolio capital inflows into many of the NMS. The spreads are particularly low in Estonia, Lithuania and Bulgaria, which operate fixed exchange rate regimes. In the Czech Republic, the spreads are actually negative, consistent with the appreciating exchange rate and expectations of further appreciations.

With respect to the cross-border integration of banking systems, it is substantial in the NMS, owing to the very significant share of foreign-owned banks in banks' total assets, except in Slovenia, Cyprus and Malta. In the other countries, it ranges from about 60 per cent in

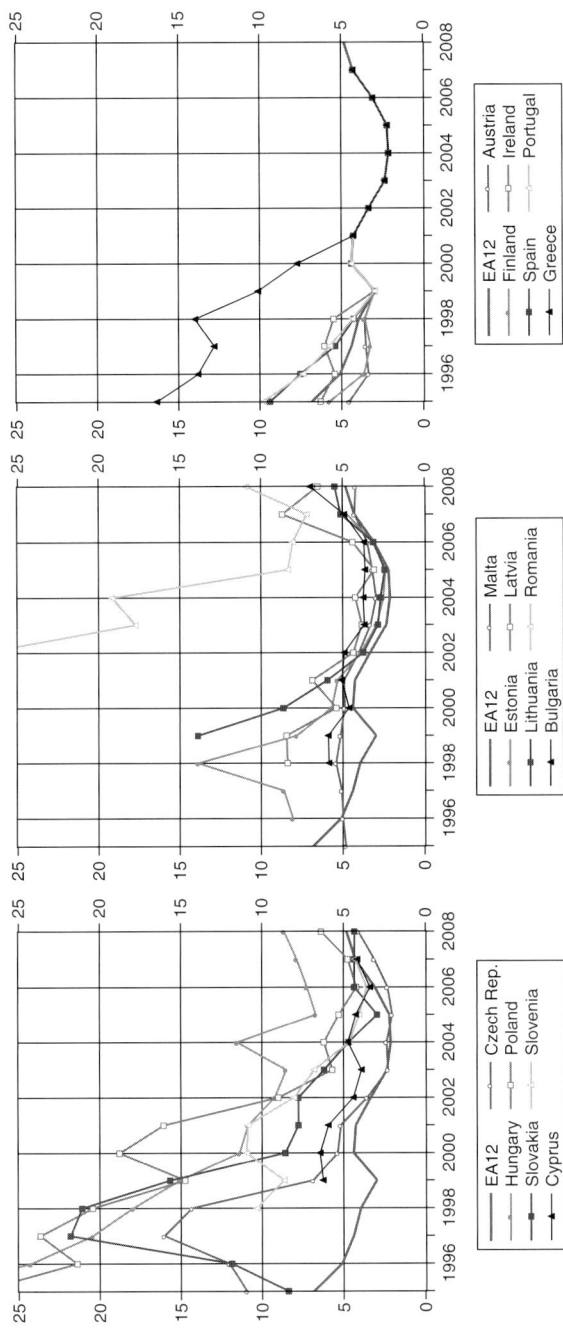

Figure 20.6: Three-month interbank interest rates, 1995–2008

Source: Eurostat. Values for 2008 assume unchanged interest rate from July 2008 until the end of the year.

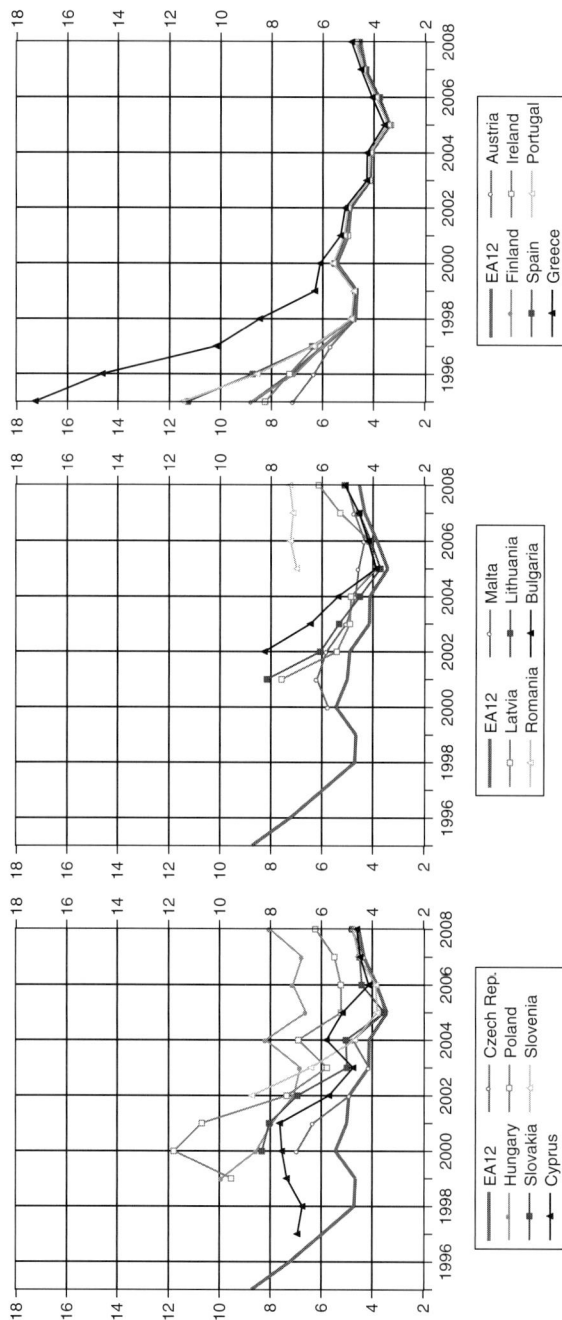

Figure 20.7: Ten-year government bond yields, 1995–2008

Sources: Eurostat and ECB. Values for 2008 assume unchanged interest rate from July 2008 until the end of the year.

Latvia and Romania to over 90 per cent in Estonia, Slovakia and the Czech Republic (World Bank, 2007b). The high shares in the CEEs are a result of the privatisation of banks to strategic foreign investors and of the letting-in of foreign banks to set up new banks. This was a way of infusing capital into the domestic banking system and was seen as transferring management know-how, especially in risk analysis and risk management, as well as bringing in new financial products.

3. Risks, challenges and long-term strategies

3.1 Capital flows: several risks

The NMS have experienced considerable net capital inflows in the form of foreign direct investment (FDI), portfolio capital and capital of other natures. FDI has gone into these countries to exploit profitable investment opportunities. The intensity of FDI has depended on such factors as the pace of privatisation, the evolution of the legal and institutional environment and the absorbtion capacity in the individual NMS. It has been also influenced by the macroeconomic situation and prospects in both the originating and recipient countries. Although at times FDI inflows can experience big swings from one year to another, from a macroeconomic stability point of view these swings constitute less of a risk, since they can mostly be anticipated and thus better handled.

The more serious risks lie in the non-FDI capital flows which are sensitive to risk premia and interest rate differentials. Most NMS have experienced strong non-FDI capital inflows which have been driven by the initially higher domestic nominal interest rates and the expectation of yield convergence ahead of euro adoption, as well as by the favourable growth prospects. In the countries with floating exchange rates, the inflows have been at times reinforced by expectations that policy makers will not fully counteract the nominal appreciation of the exchange rate caused by these very capital inflows because of their concern with inflation. In many NMS, the problem has been compounded by the foreign currency borrowings driven by strong domestic demand for credit. Boosted by such borrowings, the non-FDI net capital inflows have been especially large in countries with fixed exchange rates, representing about 30 per cent of GDP in Latvia, over 15 per cent in Lithuania and about 20 per cent in Estonia in 2006–7. In the Czech Republic, Poland and Slovakia, with floating rates, these inflows have been significantly smaller.

Romania, in contrast, had large yield differentials which boosted capital inflows. In Hungary, where the yield differential has also been large, the non-FDI capital inflows mostly took the form of portfolio investment in government securities.

The danger in such large inflows of capital is that they boost domestic demand and lead to large current account deficits and high inflation. They can also put undue upward pressure on the exchange rates of countries with floating rate regimes, threatening an erosion of competitiveness that might force the authorities to lower interest rates to levels inconsistent with the goal of price stability and/or forcing them to undertake costly interventions.

Another danger of large portfolio capital inflows is that they can have the pervasive effect of making policy makers believe that the willingness of investors to buy and hold domestic financial assets is a vote of confidence, delaying needed reforms and letting the authorities indulge in policies that are clearly unsustainable. A case in point is that of Hungary, where despite fiscal deficits ranging between 6 and 9.2 per cent of GDP and similarly high current account deficits during 2002–6, non-resident holdings of government securities have increased. By virtue of the mere size of the potential portfolio shifts relative to the small size of the capital markets of the NMS, a reversal of capital, due to loss of confidence or contagion, can trigger large destabilising movements in exchange rates and domestic interest rates. Hungary experienced such sudden shifts in 2003 and again in 2006 when doubts arose about the policy intentions of the authorities.

3.2 Danger of credit booms and overheating: the great challenge

The rapid expansion of credit and the consequent danger of overheating and inflation is one of the greatest challenges facing the NMS, irrespective of whether or not they are members of the euro area. Both demand and supply factors combine to boost credit expansion.

On the demand side, the initial low level of credit and of indebtedness, the rapid output growth, the rise in income expectations and the stronger confidence boosted also by EU entry have led to a greater willingness of economic agents to take on debt. This has been particularly true for households. The demand for credit has been fuelled by the sharp decline in real interest rates. The fall in risk premia and the convergence of domestic interest rates toward euro levels, driven by the inflow of convergence capital buoyed by euro-area entry expectation, together with higher inflation owing to the BS effect or other reasons, have produced very low or even negative domestic real interest rates.[4] This environment of low borrowing cost has been compounded in several countries by the use of foreign currency and external loans as mentioned above.

On the supply side, the development of the banking sector after privatisation and the predominance of foreign banks increased the lending capacity of banks. At the same time, rising competition among banks to expand their activity in the household sector once the corporate sector was saturated, together with the narrowing of margins due to the fall in interest rates, have constituted strong incentives for them to lend to households to maintain profitability.

The fastest growing segments of the credit market have been household loans, in particular mortgage loans (Figure 20.8). The latter have also been encouraged by deregulation in the property market and by the rapid rise in property prices and the expectation of further price increases, which have encouraged speculative buying, including by non-residents. Just like total domestic credit, the credit to households has also risen the fastest in the five less developed NMS, i.e. the Baltic countries and Bulgaria and Romania, where the starting levels of credit were the lowest.

Several studies have made estimates of the equilibrium level of credit in the CEEs looking at explanatory variables, such as per capita GDP, real interest rate, inflation, a proxy for financial liberalisation, etc. (Schadler *et al.* 2005; Kiss *et al.*, 2006; Égert *et al.*, 2006; World Bank, 2007b). A common finding of these studies is that credit in the CEEs is generally below equilibrium levels, highlighting the potential for further rapid expansion of credit. However, the *speed* at which the equilibrium level of credit is reached matters for macroeconomic stability.[5] From the perspective of inflationary pressure, it is not the level but the rate of growth of credit that matters.

Several dangers emanating from excessive credit growth must be reckoned with. First, it feeds inflation and wage growth that can erode competitiveness, not only in countries with fixed exchange rates, but also in those with floating rates, if the demand for credit-generated external capital continues to flow in and place upward pressure on the exchange rate. The rates of inflation, after falling in all new members since the mid-1990s, have picked up speed in recent years, in particular in the Baltic States and Bulgaria, and also in Hungary for the specific reasons mentioned earlier (Figure 20.9). In the former four, nominal

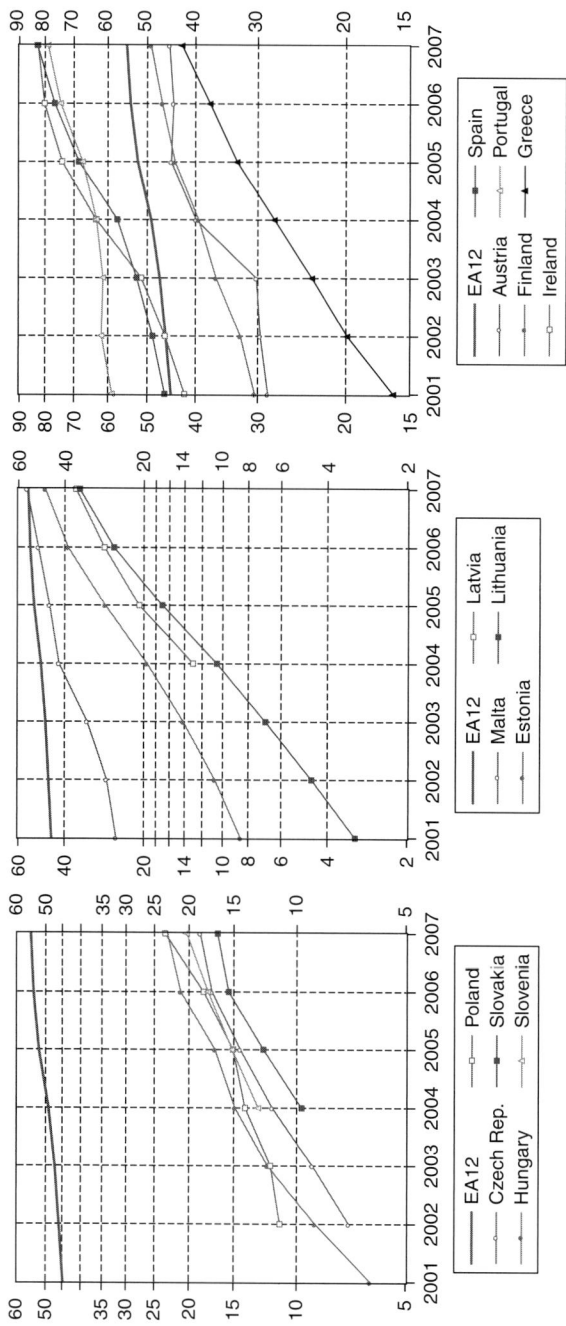

Figure 20.8: Bank loans to the household sector, 2001–7 (in per cent of GDP)

Note: Data is available until June 2007. Values shown for 2007 assume that the growth rate of loans from June to December 2007 is the same as from December 2006 to June 2007.

Source: Eurostat.

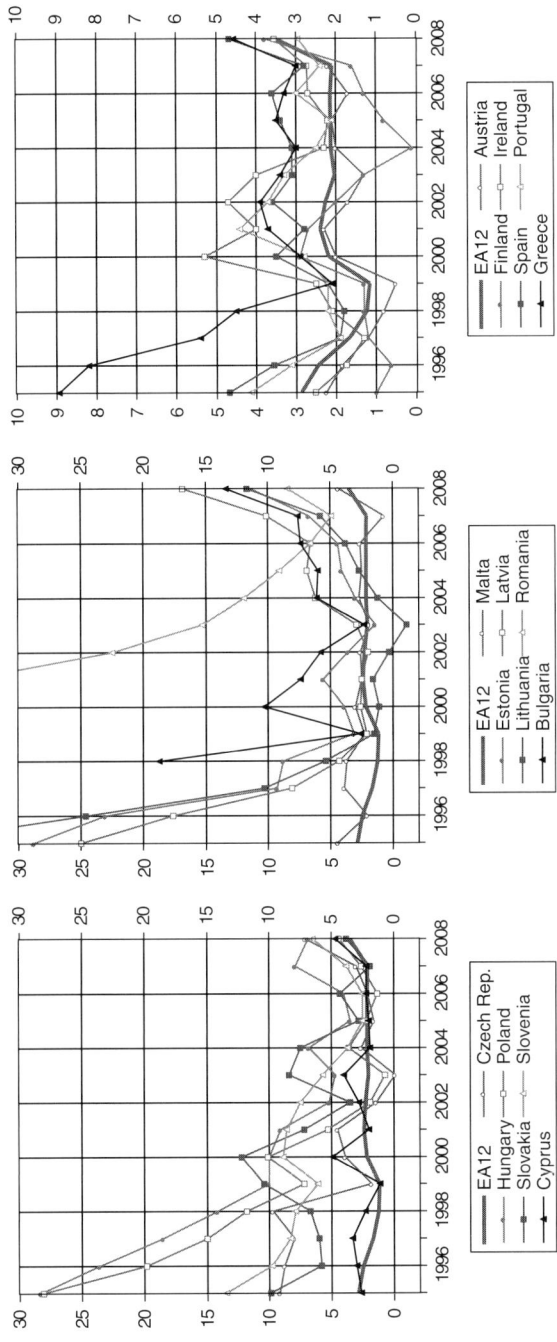

Figure 20.9: Inflation rate (in per cent), 1995–2008

Note: Annual average change in Harmonized Indices of Consumer Prices (HICP) since 1997, CPI for 1995–1996. For Bulgaria, change in HICP is available only since 1998. Values for 2008 are the average of January–July 2008 over the average of January–July 2007.

Sources: Eurostat (HICP) and IMF, IFS (CPI).

wage growth has also risen significantly and unit labour costs, particularly in Latvia, have increased at a very rapid pace in recent years.

A point to emphasise here is that if the risk premium is not rising, either because a hard peg is credible as under currency boards in the Baltics and Bulgaria, or because of the prospect of euro-area entry in the case of floating exchange rates, then the credit boom and the consequent rise in inflation further lower the level of real interest rates. In this way, the interest rate acts in a procyclical fashion, giving further impetus to credit expansion. Since the higher inflation takes place essentially in the nontradeable sector, the lowest real interest rates will prevail in that sector, channelling the resources away from the tradeable sector. This mechanism will continue to apply also once a country has joined the euro area.

Second, the rapid growth in mortgage credit can lead to sharp rises in house prices in real terms. Égert and Mihaljek (2007) report real house price increases of between 20 and 30 per cent per year in Estonia and Lithuania during 2000–6. In the other NMS for which they report data, the house price increases have remained more modest, but if mortgage credit continues to expand at a fast rate, housing price bubbles might well develop. Such bubbles might boost credit expansion further by increasing the value of collateral. During credit booms, the risks generally rise because banks become willing to lend to less creditworthy customers, exposing the banks to heavy losses when the bubbles burst.

Third, the rapid expansion of credit has fuelled consumption. As can be seen from Figure 20.10, the contribution of private consumption to GDP growth has increased in all NMS between 1997–2001 and 2002–6, except in Poland and Slovenia. The problem with the rapid growth of consumption is that it keeps savings low and increases the investment-saving gap. The five less developed NMS, where credit expansion has been the fastest, have recorded very large current account deficits, ranging from about 15 per cent in Estonia to about 24 per cent in Latvia in 2007 (Figure 20.11). In Bulgaria and Romania, a large part of the deficits have been financed by FDI, as these countries have attracted foreign investment with the prospect of EU entry. In contrast, in the Baltic countries, most of the deficits have been financed by debt, principally foreign borrowing by banks and enterprises. External debt levels have increased sharply, especially in Latvia where debt reached over 110 per cent of GDP in 2006. When the counterpart of indebtedness is consumption and housing loans, it means that resources are

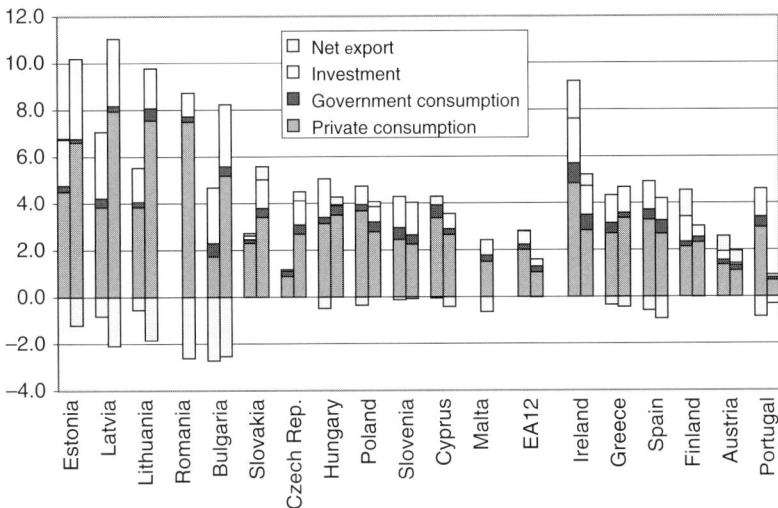

Figure 20.10: Contribution to GDP growth, averages of 1997–2001 and 2002–6 (in percentage points)

Note: there are two columns for each country (except Romania and Malta): the left one refers to 1997–2001 and the right one to 2002–6. Countries are ordered (within both country groups) according to their average GDP growth rates in the 2002–6 period. The average GDP growth rate is the sum of the four components shown.

Source: Authors' calculation based on data from Eurostat.

diverted away from investment in the tradeable sector, which is bound to negatively affect competitiveness and growth down the road.

External competitiveness has become a cause for concern in countries where wages and unit labour costs have risen sharply in recent years and where, as a result, the real effective exchange rates have also increased considerably. Competitiveness could be an issue in Estonia, where the export market share has slightly declined in recent years (Figure 20.12) and the current account deficit has ballooned. In Romania, after very rapid growth between 2000 and 2004, the market share stagnated in 2005–6 and fell temporarily in 2007. In Slovenia, the market share has been stagnating over the past decade, but the country has recorded only modest current account deficits. The fact that export volume growth has been robust and export market shares have increased in most of the NMS would indicate that the main cause of the large current account deficits is excessive domestic demand rather than any significant loss of competitiveness.

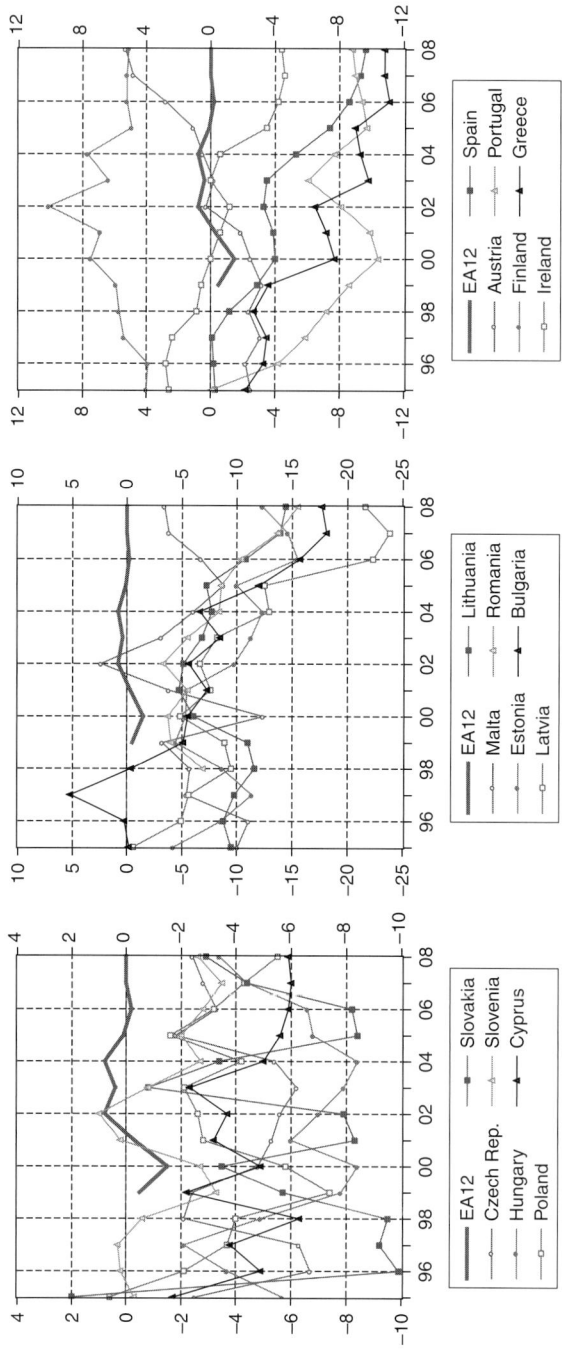

Figure 20.11: Balance of the current account (in per cent of GDP), 1995–2008

Note: the scaling of the vertical axis is different for the three panels.

Sources: 1995–2006 Eurostat, 2007–8 European Commission economic forecast autumn 2007.

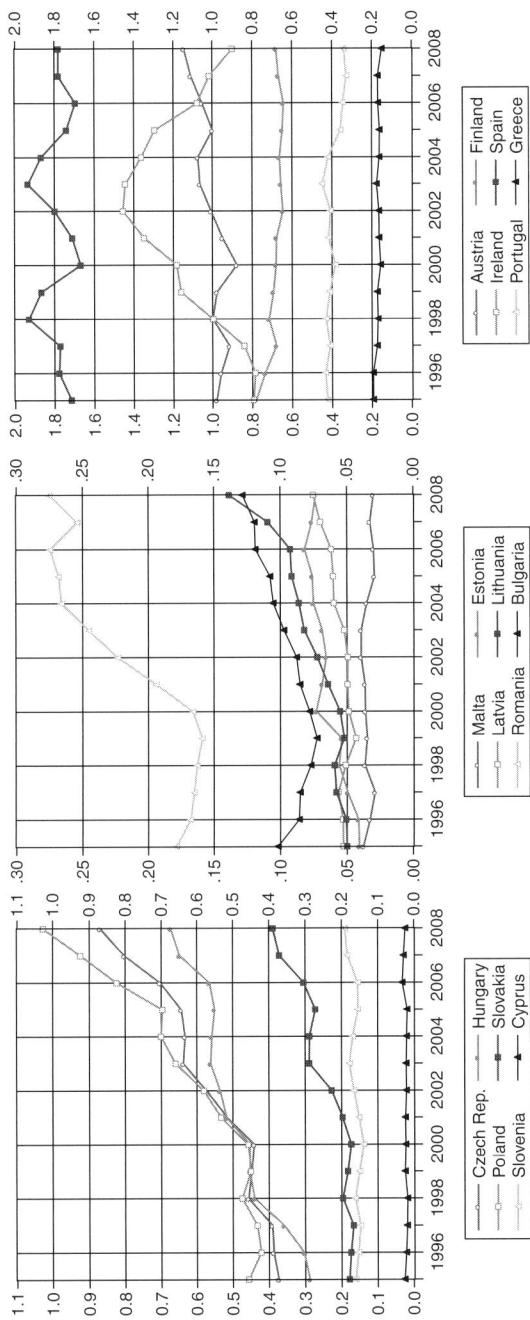

Figure 20.12: Export market shares in total imports of the world (in per cent), 1995–2008

Note: 2008 values refer to January-April 2008.

Source: Authors' calculation based on data from IMF: Direction of Trade Statistics.

It is not known at what level of current account deficit that foreign capital will retrench in the current environment of weakening but still relatively high risk appetite and euro-area entry expectation. Such high deficits clearly increase the exposure of countries to capital flow reversal. EU membership and euro-area entry prospects have so far provided a protective shield, allowing countries to finance current account deficits of a size that would have not been possible without such a shield. Surely there are limits to the indulgence of the markets. Financial crises have often been preceded by rapid credit growth to the private sector, strong real effective exchange rate appreciation and large current account deficits.

The banking sectors in the NMS are in a relatively healthy position currently: non-performing loans (NPLs) are low, capital adequacy ratios are relatively high (World Bank, 2007b) and ownership of local banks by internationally renowned foreign ones is considerable. However, none of these is insurance against a crisis occurring. The low level of NPLs today does not mean that the current loan portfolio will not worsen in the future, particularly in view of the large share of foreign currency loans. If there is a reversal of capital, borrowers in foreign currency will face higher payment obligations due to a depreciation of the domestic currency. While companies producing for exports have a natural hedge, firms producing for the domestic market and households do not possess such a safety net. Local currency borrowers will also face higher payment obligations due to a rise in interest rates. In the household sector, defaults on mortgage loans could occur and consumption would be negatively affected. Through balance sheet effects, banks would tighten credit, having a further negative impact on growth.

For this scenario to happen, the depreciation of the exchange rate would have to be significant and durable, an event that cannot be altogether excluded if there were a shift in global market sentiment. If many defaults occurred, the stability of the banking system could ultimately be affected. Capital adequacy ratios could deteriorate rapidly if there were a significant growth in NPLs, and there is no guarantee that the foreign mother banks would want to inject additional capital, especially if they themselves faced with difficulties back home, such as many do now in the wake of the subprime debacle.

All these militate in favour of reining in the growth of credit and reducing the excessive current account deficits before it is too late. At the same time, the bank regulatory and supervisory structures should be strengthened as much as possible. The NMS have made great progress in this area over the years, but experience shows that vigilance is never enough. In particular, the cooperation between home and host country supervision should be improved and strengthened, for which the EU framework provides a good opportunity.

3.3 *Foreign currency loans: how to deal with them?*

Several old and new EU members have applied administrative and regulatory measures to slow down the growth of credit and to limit unhedged foreign currency loans. World Bank (2007b) provides a list of such measures introduced. Administrative measures may include limits on the growth of foreign currency loans or on the ratio of such loans to the banks' own capital. Regulatory measures typically aim at raising the cost of borrowing by imposing tighter rules on foreign currency loans. These may include special reserve requirements and lower interest rates paid on those reserves, tighter provisioning and assets qualification rules, stricter non-price requirements (e.g. higher down payments, additional collateral), higher capital requirement or other measures applied to foreign currency borrowings.

The problem with such measures is that if they are maintained for a long time, they will distort markets and weaken competition. Furthermore, they can be evaded by switching from domestic to direct borrowing from abroad, a technique made easier in countries where foreign-owned banks play a dominant role. They can also reroute financing from bank to non-bank channels, such as leasing, and can encourage foreign banks to switch from subsidiaries to branches, a channel less supervised by the local authorities. On the whole, the effectiveness of such measures is questionable in the long run and can best serve as a short-term expedient to slow excessive credit expansion when the economy overheats. The authorities may also use moral suasion on banks, although its effectiveness is uncertain.

There are other ways to slow down the growth of household mortgage credit which are less distorting overall because they would be aimed specifically at this fast-expanding market in the NMS. The most effective would be a tax on interest payment on mortgage credit and a comprehensive real estate tax on housing, which could be reinforced by a mandatory reduction in the loan to value ratio. Where it exists, the tax deduction on the interest paid on mortgage debt should be eliminated. Such measures were used successfully in Denmark to slow down a consumption boom in 1986 (World Bank, 2007b).

3.4 Fiscal policy: not a full substitute to deal with the monetary policy shock

In view of the loss of monetary policy autonomy in the NMS under fixed exchange rate arrangements, and the constraints on monetary policy independence in the countries operating under floating rate regimes, fiscal policy plays a key role as a stabiliser during the run-up to the euro and thereafter. There is no uniform yardstick of what the level of budget deficits should be in the new members. From a strictly analytical point of view, fundamentally it is a question of debt sustainability. From that perspective, the new members with very low debt would have more room for manoeuvre. In addition, as catching-up economies, the new members have a higher potential growth rate, which implies that to maintain the long-run stability of public finances, the NMS with very low debt could run higher deficits.

From a short- to medium-term policy perspective, however, these long-term analytical considerations will have to take a back seat in circumstances where fiscal policy needs to be in a position to counteract the demand pressures emanating from the interest rate shock. The appropriate fiscal stance will depend on the intensity of inflationary pressures and the degree of overheating. One must be realistic though about the extent to which fiscal policy can be used to counteract inflationary pressures due to excessive credit expansion and price level convergence. Lags in the impact of fiscal measures,[6] the difficulty of assessing the right timing of policy intervention, the irreversibility of some actions and the reluctance of politicians to cut back on discretionary public spending all inhibit the effectiveness of fiscal policy as a tool to cool overheating. Furthermore, because of the import leakage, large fiscal contractions would be needed in small open economies to get a significant impact on output or inflation.

The situation is compounded in the NMS by the fact that despite higher output volatilities, the cyclical sensitivity of the budgets is lower in the NMS than in the EU15 (European Commission, 2006b). This is because of the smaller share of cycle-sensitive direct taxes and unemployment-related expenditures. The low share of direct taxes is due in part to tax holidays and the low level of corporate taxes which have been used to attract FDI. The relatively large share of the black economy and tax evasion are contributing factors. The smaller share of expenditure on unemployment is generally due to the less generous benefits. This means that these countries would have to rely on even more discretionary changes to affect output and inflation. The same situation will apply after euro-area entry, increasing the burden on other policies.

3.5 Incomes policy: should be part of the arsenal

The factors limiting the use of fiscal policy as a countercyclical policy tool heighten the role of other instruments to control inflation, namely incomes policy. Wage developments have to be supportive of the goal of price stability and consistent with the gains in productivity in order to maintain competitiveness. If real wage growth exceeds productivity gains and a devaluation of the nominal exchange rate is no longer a policy option, the resulting rise in unit labour costs and loss of competitiveness will entail a painful adjustment period.

There are examples of social 'pacts' or social 'consensuses' which have worked well. A good example is Austria where the social consensus has been an important pillar of the hard currency policy adopted in the early 1970s. Many other countries have resorted with more or less success to such pacts in the run-up to the euro (Boeri, 2005b). One should not underestimate, though, the difficulty of reaching such common understandings in the NMS, taking into account the heightened expectations for 'wage convergence' and 'fair wages' accompanying the integration into the EU. What is certain is that governments have a leading role to play in promoting wage moderation by clearly communicating to the public the costs of excessive wage increases and by signalling through their own public sector wage policy the importance they attach to wage moderation. The best solution would be to forge social consensuses around the goal of entering the euro area that could pave the way for a lasting practice after adoption of the euro.

3.6 Structural policies: flanking instruments

Structural reforms are essential in many NMS for achieving lasting fiscal consolidation. One of the most important challenges stems from the ageing of the population in the CEEs, which calls for reforms in the pension and health care systems. It is common wisdom that labour and product market flexibility improves the ability to adjust to shocks. Employment protection tends to be lower in the NMS than in the euro area (OECD, 2004), but demands for greater protection could emerge in the new members, owing to the demonstration effect coming from old members with higher employment protection. Governments would be well advised to resist such demands. Product market flexibility increases the benefits of labour market flexibility and wage moderation. Conway *et al.* (2005) identify the main areas where regulation is high in the 'Visegrád countries' and where improvements should be made. These are different state controls and barriers to entrepreneurship and investment.

There are many other areas where reforms may be needed, such as the provision and financing of education, the downsizing of public employment or measures to reduce the losses of and the budgetary subsidies granted to state enterprises. What reforms are needed and how they should be implemented vary according to countries and there is no uniform recipe.

It does not seem to be indispensable to start, let alone finish all the necessary structural reforms prior to euro adoption, since these reforms take many years to be implemented. However, a country preparing for euro adoption should at least have a clear agenda of reforms and display a strong commitment to carry them out. Reforms in the pension and health care systems need the broad support of the society and mustering such support might be easier prior to entering the euro area if there is support in the society in favour of euro adoption. On the other hand, if there is strong resistance to such reforms, pushing them as a requirement for euro adoption might trigger a backlash against the euro. Each country will have to work out its own approach to reforms in light of its circumstances. It is advisable to at least initiate some of the most important reforms needed prior to euro adoption because once in the euro area, the political will to reform may falter.

4. Strategies and timing for euro adoption

The strategy and timing for euro adoption has to be assessed from two perspectives: (i) what does it take to meet the Maastricht nominal convergence criteria, and (ii) whether the convergence process can be better managed inside or outside the euro area. This has to be then weighed against the well-known benefits of being a member of the monetary union.

4.1 Choice of monetary-cum-exchange rate policy: which way is better?

The globalisation and integration of financial markets, together with euro-area entry expectations, have fundamentally altered the environment in which the catching-up process has to be managed and in which monetary policy can be operated in the new members. This is largely an unprecedented situation. In the initially less developed Western European countries, the catching up proceeded over the years in a less globalised world and a more progressive liberalisation of capital movements, without the impetus to capital flows fed by the anticipation of an early entry into a monetary union. This provided vastly more room for pursuing an independent monetary and exchange rate policy, even as efforts were made to eliminate exchange rate fluctuations by various arrangements (snake, EMS).

A key issue is how best to tackle the inflationary pressures stemming from the combined impact of price level convergence associated with the catching-up process and the strong boost to domestic demand due to the financial integration-cum-interest rate shock. A hard peg exchange regime such as a currency board arrangement can shield against speculative exchange rate fluctuations and provide a more stable environment for small open economies, although the recent experience of Latvia is a warning sign that this is not necessarily the case even within ERM II. But as long as the peg is credible and there is little or no exchange risk premia, low domestic interest rates heighten the danger of credit booms and overheating. Since countries with hard pegs do not have the possibility of letting the nominal exchange rate appreciate to moderate inflation, the price level convergence associated with the catching-up process translates into higher domestic inflation, which pushes real interest rates down to a very low or negative level, further fuelling credit expansion and domestic demand.

The inflation-targeting regime with floating exchange rates provides more flexibility to deal with inflationary pressures, as the risk premia can give some room for manoeuvre and there is the possibility of letting the nominal exchange rate appreciate. But this flexibility should not be overestimated. As seen, the risk premia might be small due to euro-area entry anticipation-driven capital inflows and expectations of exchange rate appreciation. Furthermore, the tightness of domestic monetary policy can be circumvented by the foreign currency loans and the direct external borrowing channels as discussed earlier. Letting the exchange rate appreciate to fight inflation might in any case only give a temporary respite if the credit boom persists. Once within the euro area, appreciation is no longer available and if the underlying inflationary pressures have not been brought under control, inflation will raise its head again.

Furthermore, the risk of capital flow reversal remains significant if strong capital inflows driven by interest rate differential place undue upward pressure on the floating exchange rate. For instance, in Romania, where the current account deficit exceeds 10 per cent of GDP, the capital inflows have strongly appreciated the nominal exchange rate, rendering the country vulnerable to capital flow reversal. In Hungary, when macroeconomic imbalances emerged because of inappropriate policies, the sudden outflow of capital led to a sharp depreciation of the exchange rate and an increase in interest rate spreads in 2003 and 2006.

Among the inflation targeters, the Czech Republic has been quite successful so far in maintaining high growth, modest inflation and a low current account deficit, although inflation has picked up recently. Part of the success may lie in the fact that following the exchange rate crisis in 1997 and the subsequent recession, inflation expectations became anchored at a low level. The appreciation of the nominal exchange rate, which has been driven mostly by FDI inflows since the interest rate spread has been negative, has also helped to keep the level of inflation low. The growth of credit has been moderate despite the low level of interest rates. However, the Czech Republic is also among those countries where the ULC-based real exchange rate has appreciated considerably. In this country, the initial level of prices was low compared to its level of per capita GDP, so that the strong appreciation of the real exchange rate can be regarded in part as a 'correction' of the initial discrepancy. Nevertheless, if the rapid trend appreciation persists, it could undermine competitiveness. In Poland and Slovakia, the real exchange rates have also appreciated considerably. In the latter, both growth and inflation are somewhat higher, while in both the current account deficit is larger than in the Czech Republic. On the whole, these three inflation targeters have managed to record high growth, while keeping inflation and the current account deficit under reasonable control. It remains to be seen if these achievements can be preserved.

It may turn out to be a paradox of history that four out of the five new members with the lowest initial per capita GDP, i.e. the Baltic countries and Bulgaria, which started out with the largest price level gaps to close and the lowest financial depth and hence the greatest potential for credit booms, have opted for a fixed exchange rate arrangement on the road to the euro. These countries do not have the freedom of letting the nominal exchange rate appreciate to moderate inflation and have to manage the price convergence with higher inflation. This is a difficult task when the price gap to close is large, because it feeds inflation expectations and can lead to a rapid loss of competitiveness. In fact, market forces have already triggered adjustments in the Baltic countries, leading to sharp drops in output growth from the high levels of the earlier years. At this point it is still unclear how such boom-bust cycles might negatively affect the long-term convergence process of these countries.

Price level convergence can nevertheless be managed successfully with fixed exchange rates under certain circumstances. The hard currency policy adopted in Austria in the early 1970s, whereby the schilling was fixed to the German mark, is a good example (see Hochreiter and Tavlas, 2004). The price level gap to close back then was about 25 per cent in Austria (Figure 20.13), roughly the gap still to be closed in most of the CEEs, but much less than the gap that had to be closed when the CEEs started their catching-up process in the mid-1990s (Figure 20.2). In Bulgaria, Romania and Latvia, however, the gap to be closed is still 30–50 per cent. The key to success in Austria was a social pact that kept wage growth more or less in line with productivity gains and a fiscal policy that was supportive of the

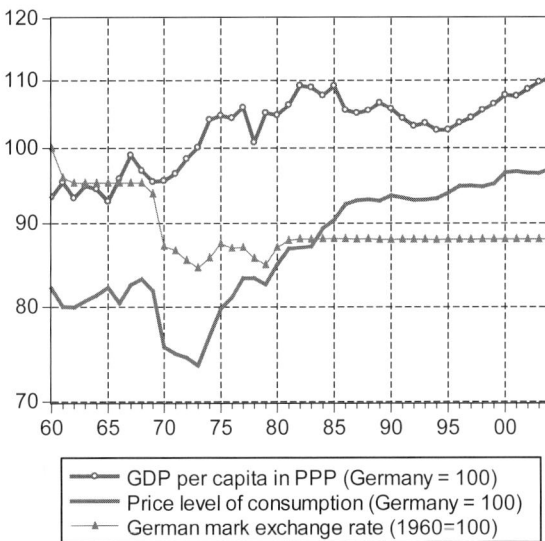

Figure 20.13: Catching-up of Austria to Germany, 1960–2004
Note: Downward movement in the exchange rate indicates nominal depreciation.
Source: Penn World Tables.

hard peg. It is also true that Austria's task was facilitated by the fact that capital liberalisation proceeded more gradually than in the CEEs and it did not therefore experience the kind of capital inflows that have been feeding the credit booms in some of the CEEs. Also, Austria's banking system was more regulated than those in the present-day CEEs.

What conclusions can be drawn from the above discussion regarding the monetary framework best suited to manage the real and nominal convergence on the road to the euro? The most important one in our view is that inflation targeters seem to have a better set of tools at their disposal than peggers to manage the convergence process on an equilibrium path toward euro adoption. The main risk for the targeters is excessive exchange rate fluctuations, but if policies are geared to macroeconomic stability, the likelihood of this happening is reduced. The more likely danger then is rather excessive appreciation of the nominal exchange rate, which can force a country into costly intervention or a lowering of the domestic interest rate, which can fuel credit expansion.

For the peggers, the options are limited. Exiting from the hard peg before euro adoption carries the danger of a loss of confidence and a depreciation of the currency, which could create a deep recession via negative wealth effects on the debt of households and firms in countries where the debt is highly euroised, as in the Baltic States. If the exit is well communicated as a transitional step toward earlier euro adoption, the recession might not occur or would be mild, after which the country would become better positioned to control inflation. The danger here is that the nominal exchange rate appreciation could overshoot and lead to a loss of competitiveness, or exacerbate an already weak competitive position. Therefore, the risks of exiting from the hard peg should be carefully weighed before contemplating such an action. A well-timed and well-prepared step revaluation of the peg could be another option to consider if competitiveness is not at stake. The risks here are the positive wealth effects on the euroised debt which would boost demand precisely at a time when the current accounts are already very large in these countries.

4.2 Maastricht criteria: are they suitable for the new members?

4.2.1 Inflation criterion: why it should be modified

The inflation criterion states that the inflation rate of the country wishing to join the euro area cannot exceed by more than 1.5 percentage points the average inflation of the three best-performing EU Member States in terms of price stability. This criterion will prove hard to meet in the near term, especially for the Baltic countries and Bulgaria which have fixed exchange rates. Countries might be tempted to resort to techniques – such as a freezing of administered prices, a reduction of consumption taxes or a tightening of credit growth by various short-term expedients – to squeeze in under the reference value. Such behaviour would be tantamount to what Szapáry (2000) labelled as the 'weighing-in' syndrome: like the boxer who refrains from eating for hours prior to the weighing-in to satisfy the weight limit only to consume a big meal thereafter, the candidate country would resort to all sorts of techniques in order to squeeze in under the inflation criteria, only to shift gears after it has joined the euro area. This can turn out to be counter-productive if inflation accelerates after euro adoption, due to the relaxation of credit conditions, the unavoidable upward adjustment of administered prices and/or because of a reversal of the reduction in consumption taxes for budgetary reasons. Such a policy would not help the smooth path of convergence.

There are few options available. One is to postpone euro adoption until a greater degree of real and nominal convergence has been achieved. While this might be unavoidable for countries with the largest price level gaps and a pegged exchange rate, it would deprive some others from the benefits of being a member of the monetary union. A way to ease entry into euro area for countries which have already achieved the conditions permitting them to operate normally in the monetary union would be to change the criterion. It is understandable that the inflation criterion was originally defined in terms of the three best performers among the potential candidate countries at the time when a European monetary union did not yet exist. It was also natural that the principle of equal treatment was laid down since it would have been difficult to negotiate an agreement in any other way. Now that the euro area exists, the criterion based on the three best performers including those which are not members of the euro area is more difficult to justify on economic grounds. This is true even though it is the policy to exclude from the three best performers the countries where the low inflation level is due to special factors and is therefore judged as not sustainable (so far only countries with negative inflation have been excluded).

A reasonable solution would be to define the criterion as the euro-area inflation plus 1.5 percentage points. The economic justification to use the euro-area inflation is that this is the relevant indicator that contributes to the imported inflation of the new members whose trade is essentially with the euro area. Furthermore, this is the indicator that the ECB tries to control and it is not logical that the basis for the reference value for the new members should be different. The margin of 1.5 percentage points would constitute the room for accommodating the 'equilibrium' forces of price level convergence. Such modification of the inflation criterion would free decision makers from ruling which best-performer country's inflation is sustainable and which is not, an exercise that is bound to be a source of friction. To discourage 'weighing-in' practices, such modification of the reference value could be accompanied by increasing the period during which the inflation criterion has to be respected from one year to two years. It could be complemented with a stricter interpretation of the allowable exchange rate appreciation within this period, which also corresponds to the compulsory length of stay in ERM II. The close to 25 per cent appreciation of the exchange rate in Slovakia in ERM II may well turn out to be a practice of weighing-in if inflation cannot be kept in check by improvements in productivity after euro adoption. The modifications proposed would also provide a better perspective for judging whether a candidate country can maintain its low level of inflation in a sustainable way when an exchange rate appreciation is no longer available to moderate inflation.

With the enlargement of the European Union, the reference to 'equal treatment' as the rationale for not changing the inflation criterion is also questionable. Between 1970 and 1990, the lowest inflation rates among the members of the EU at that time were recorded by Germany, the Netherlands and Luxembourg. In the early 1990s when the Maastricht criteria were formulated, policy makers presumably wanted the inflation in the other countries to converge to the low level of German inflation, while the decision to take the average inflation rate of the three countries with the lowest inflation was meant to provide some flexibility. Germany was the major trading partner of the then EU members, so that the criterion meant that the other countries' inflation had to converge to the inflation of the major trading partner. This made good sense economically. With enlargement, however, the likelihood that the three lowest inflation countries will be minor trading partners has considerably increased. For March 2008, for instance, the criterion was based on the inflation rates of Malta, the Netherlands and Denmark, which were the three countries recording the lowest inflation during the reference period. The major trading partners were thus left out of the definition of the reference value. Because of this, if the criterion is left unchanged, the chances are that the principle of equal treatment will not be upheld in many cases. Our proposal to take the euro-area inflation as a reference value would eliminate this discrimination.

The impact on the overall inflation of the euro area of the above modification would be limited. The total GDP of the twelve new members represented about 8.8 per cent of the combined GDP of the twelve old euro-area members plus the twelve new members in 2007. With Cyprus, Malta and Slovenia already members of the euro area, the share of the other nine countries represents 7.6 per cent. If in all nine countries the inflation rate were exactly 1.5 percentage points above the euro area HICP, then this would add a mere 0.1 percentage point to the overall inflation of the euro area. This has to be compared to the effect when the current rule is applied, which is around 0.05. The impact of the proposed modification would thus be only an additional 0.05. In fact, the actual impact would be less, since the entry of countries is spread out over time and it is unlikely that all countries will have the maximum 1.5 percentage points of extra inflation. The relative importance of the new members' GDP will rise with the catching-up, but the higher inflation associated with the price level convergence will also diminish. Figure 20.14 illustrates the difference between the current reference value and our suggestion for modification.

4.2.2 Long-term interest rate criterion: not an obstacle

The criterion stipulates that the ten-year interest rate cannot exceed by more than two percentage points the average of such interest rates in the three best-performing countries in terms of price stability. This is meant to test the durability of price stability and its economic rationale is clear. The only point worth making is that with euro-area entry expectation-driven capital inflows, the convergence of the long-term interest rates has been much stronger than the convergence of inflation. For instance, in Bulgaria, Lithuania and Romania, where the inflation exceeds the reference value by wide margins, the interest rate criterion is met.

4.2.3 Exchange rate criterion: timing of entry and length of stay in the ERM II

This criterion stipulates that a candidate country must enter ERM II for at least two years and respect the normal fluctuation bands of +/-15 per cent without severe tensions and without devaluing against the currency of any other Member State. Countries may choose a smaller band or no band at all as a unilateral commitment. This criterion serves as a test of the ability of a country to handle shocks with exchange rate stability.

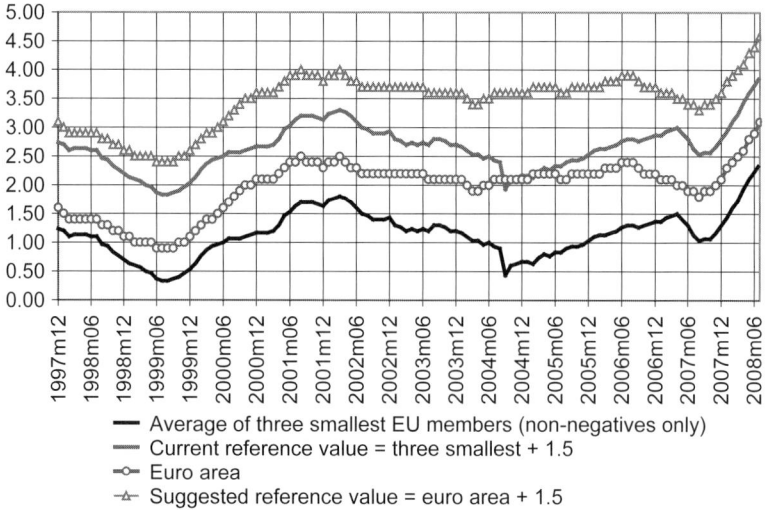

Figure 20.14: Inflation criterion: current and suggested reference values, December 1997 – July 2008
Note: Values shown correspond to '12-month average rate of change' as required by the Treaty for assessing the inflation criterion.
Source: Authors' calculation based on data from Eurostat.

The commonly formulated criticism in respect of this criterion is that it is inconsistent to have both an inflation and an exchange rate target. Theoretically this is a correct view. If the candidate country is committed to sound macroeconomic policies and it meets or is firmly on a path to meet in a sustainable manner the other Maastricht criteria, the most likely scenario is that market forces will push toward an appreciation, as was seen in a number of current euro-area member countries during the run-up to the euro. Some appreciation could be accommodated even with the above-suggested stricter interpretation of the allowable appreciation.

The real issue concerns the choice of the ERM II central rate. Ideally it should be set at an equilibrium level, but model calculations would at best give a very wide range of the equilibrium exchange rate. This rate is a dynamic concept which changes over time, particularly in catching-up economies and, unless the misalignment is clearly unsustainable, countries are able to adjust to temporary misalignments in ways that the equilibrium exchange rate derived from statistical models is not capable of capturing. Given these uncertainties, there are good reasons to set the

ERM II central rate at the prevailing market rate. Setting it at a depreciated level compared to the market rate could jeopardise meeting the inflation target. Such a step should be contemplated only if competitiveness was so weak and the current account deficit so large that devaluation was clearly needed.

Setting the central rate at a stronger level than the market rate might make sense under circumstances where competitiveness is not seen as a problem, since it can ease inflation pressures and also the pressure for appreciation beyond the central rate, if markets expect that there will be no further revaluation. The risk in this strategy is that markets may come to a different conclusion, namely that the central rate was set at an appreciated level to fight inflation and that in order to make sure that the inflation target is met, the authorities will resort to a further revaluation. This then would stimulate capital inflows and require costly sterilisation. Consequently, whether setting an appreciated central rate is the right strategy will depend on where inflation and competitiveness stands at the time of ERM II entry and what the prospects are.

If reasonable macroeconomic stability has been achieved, the best bet is to set the central rate at the prevailing market rate. It is not surprising that all new members which entered ERM II have done so with a central rate set at the rate prevailing at the time of entry.

The timing of entering ERM II must be carefully chosen. A country should join ERM II only if demand management policies are on a firm path toward sustainable price stability and a large degree of nominal convergence – in inflation, interest rate and budget deficit – has already occurred. A main benefit of ERM II participation is that it can anchor inflation expectations so that the latter can work toward stability, relieving the burden on policies. For that to take place, markets have to be convinced that the fundamentals of the economy are strong and that the authorities are committed to maintaining price stability.

There is also the question of the optimal length of stay in ERM II. The strongest argument in favour of not staying longer than the minimum two years required is the risk of an undue upward pressure on the exchange rate owing to inflows of convergence capital when policies are on a credible path toward euro adoption. The risks are that the markets will speculate on an appreciation of the final euro-area entry rate, particularly in view of the precedents of Ireland, Greece and Slovakia where revaluations took place within ERM II. If the appreciation is excessive, it could require costly interventions as was the case for instance in Greece.

A longer stay is sometimes suggested on the grounds that it can serve as a discipline multiplier helping countries to learn to pursue stability-oriented policies and live with exchange rate stability. However, ERM's role of anchoring expectations would only work if a country entered it with strong policies in place, which then obviates the need for a longer stay. Another argument advanced for a longer stay is that it would allow more time for the exchange rate to find its 'equilibrium' level. Under the circumstances of speculative capital inflows driven by expectations of convergence or the lack of it, the prospects that the exchange rate will find its equilibrium level more easily by a longer stay in ERM II are not very promising. Some current ERM II members may well have to stay much longer in it because they will be unable to meet the inflation criterion as fast as they had originally anticipated. This is not a strong reason for choosing at the outset to stay in ERM II longer than required. Rather, it is an indication that the authorities may have misjudged the speed at which they could tame inflation.

4.2.4 Fiscal criteria: the rationale is valid for the new members as well

According to these criteria: (i) the government debt should not exceed 60 per cent of GDP, unless the ratio is sufficiently diminishing and approaching the reference value at a satisfactory pace; and (ii) the government budget deficit should not exceed 3 per cent of GDP, unless the excess over 3 per cent is exceptional, temporary and small. We discussed earlier the considerations that need to be taken into account when assessing the sustainability of the debt. The 60 per cent of GDP debt criterion is hard to argue with. If anything, it is too high if one takes into account the contingent liabilities due to the ageing of populations. Some academics have argued that the 3 per cent of GDP deficit criterion should be relaxed because the stock of public capital is insufficient in the new members and they need to spend more on infrastructure development (see for instance Blanchard and Giavazzi, 2004). Another argument advanced sometimes is that the implementation of structural reforms, such as for instance health care reform, needs to be supported with additional spending.

While it is true that the NMS need to develop their infrastructure and have to undertake structural reforms, they need room to use the fiscal tool to counteract if necessary the overheating coming from strong credit expansion, irrespective of when they adopt the euro. Where the debt is high as in Cyprus, Malta and Hungary, they also have to worry about debt sustainability. Now that EU provides grants to help finance infrastructure investment, and given the constraints on absorption capacities, there seems to be little justification for not meeting the fiscal criterion on the grounds of the need for infrastructure development. Moreover, as catching-up economies, the new members have a higher potential growth rate and do in fact grow faster than the old members, hence the 3 per cent criterion is less stringent for them.

4.3 Timing of euro adoption: push for early date or wait for more real convergence?

Last but not least, the question of optimal timing of euro adoption has to be addressed. The potentially most difficult nominal convergence criterion to satisfy is the inflation one. This is because the catching-up process itself means price level convergence that can be achieved by either higher inflation or exchange rate appreciation. The authorities' control in both of these areas is limited due to the unrestricted flow of capital and the associated constraints on domestic monetary policy.

Giving up the tool of exchange rate policy can present problems. If the catching-up related factors feeding inflation, i.e. the structural price level convergence and the low level of financial deepening that drives the demand for credit, are still forcefully present in an economy, the loss of the exchange rate policy can lead to boom-bust cycles and derail the smooth process of catching up, as the difficulties currently faced by Latvia in cooling down an overheated economy testify. This is because it seems easier to keep the appreciation of the real exchange rate inherent in the catching-up process on a more or less equilibrium path by letting the nominal exchange rate appreciate than by keeping inflation on an equilibrium path after giving up all the flexibility, however limited it is, of an independent monetary policy. If an overheated economy leads to a loss of competitiveness and slow growth, it is difficult to regain it by wage and price disinflation after the surrender of monetary policy independence within the euro area, as the experience of Portugal has shown.[7]

This is not to say that it is easy to keep the nominal exchange rate on an equilibrium appreciating path in the current conditions of free movement of capital and globalised financial markets. As shown in Darvas and Szapáry (2008), for the small open economies of the CEEs, the exchange rate has been more a propagator of shocks than a shock absorber. The issue therefore evolves around a proper assessment of the pros and cons of (i) pushing for an early euro adoption and face the risks of higher inflation and the need to regain competitiveness without the disposal of the exchange rate tool; or (ii) postponing euro-area membership and its benefits and face the risks of exchange rate instability. Based on our analysis, this dilemma can be approached from the perspective of where a country is situated in the catching-up process. If the gaps to close in per capita GDP and price level are still fairly large and the speed of catching-up is fast, a country will have difficulty in controlling inflation once it is in the monetary union. Consequently, it might be advisable to postpone euro adoption until the gaps have narrowed.

5. Conclusions

The objective of this chapter was to assess the risks and challenges facing the new members on the road to the euro and to discuss the strategies for and the timing of euro adoption. The starting level of development measured by the per capita GDP and the speed of real convergence have an important bearing on the challenges faced on the road to the euro and on the strategies to be adopted. They also have a bearing on the choice of the timing of euro adoption. This is because the countries with the lowest per capita income have the largest price level gap to close. They also have the lowest initial credit to GDP ratio and hence the greatest potential for credit booms and overheating as credit converges toward its equilibrium level.

What the optimal level of real convergence is prior to joining the monetary union is hard to judge *ex ante*. To an extent, it will depend on the size of the GDP per capita and price level gaps remaining. If the gaps to close are still fairly large and the speed of catching-up is fast, a country will have difficulty in keeping inflation low once it is within the euro area. Consequently, it might be advisable to postpone euro adoption until the gaps have narrowed. The timing of euro adoption will also depend on how successful the country in question has been in taming the forces driving credit expansion, in implementing structural reforms that help increase productivity and the overall efficiency of the economy, and in consolidating the fiscal position in a sustainable manner.

It follows from the above that inflation targeting with floating rates is better suited than hard pegs to manage the price level convergence for *fast* catching-up economies. This is because in pegged regimes, the price level convergence associated with the catching-up process translates into higher domestic inflation, which pushes the real interest rate into very low or negative territory, fuelling credit expansion and domestic demand and adding to the inflationary pressure. Under a floating exchange rate regime, the real appreciation of the exchange rate inherent in the catching-up process can be accommodated by an appreciation of the nominal exchange rate rather than solely by higher inflation.

The difficulties of managing the convergence process under inflation targeting with a floating exchange rate should not be underestimated either. To keep the nominal appreciation on an equilibrium path is a challenging task, given the euro-area entry expectation-driven convergence capital inflows and the risk of capital flow reversal if there is a shift in market sentiment. The risks are either undue appreciation if confidence is buoyant or excessive exchange rate fluctuations if confidence falters. Furthermore, the room for manoeuvre of monetary policy is constrained by such channels as foreign currency loans and direct borrowing from abroad, which circumvent the effectiveness of domestic monetary policy. These arguments would militate in favour of earlier rather than later euro adoption for countries where the degree of real convergence is more advanced.

Whether under a fixed or a floating exchange rate regime, the need to implement structural reforms which increase the efficiency of the economy as well as those which contribute to the long-term consolidation of the fiscal accounts cannot be emphasised enough. A core challenge is to secure robust productivity growth, which is indispensable for the real convergence to proceed in a sustained way. Measures which increase the flexibility of labour and product markets and increase the ease of doing business are the key ingredients of success.

Social pacts have been used successfully in some countries to keep wage growth in line with productivity gains. The new members could forge such social pacts as a policy to facilitate euro adoption, which could then form the basis of a more permanent feature of policy once inside the monetary union.

The inflation criterion as currently defined has lost its economic logic and may prevent the adoption of the euro by countries which have already satisfied the conditions permitting them to function normally within the monetary union and reap the benefits of euro-area membership. We suggest that the reference value be defined as the euro-level HICP plus 1.5 percentage points to accommodate the equilibrium price level convergence. This could be accompanied by increasing the period during which the inflation criterion has to be respected from one year to two, and could be complemented with a stricter interpretation of the allowable exchange rate appreciation within this period. Such modifications would provide a better perspective for judging whether a candidate country can maintain the low level of inflation in a sustainable way once monetary independence has been surrendered. The impact of the suggested modification on the overall inflation rate of the euro area would be minimal. Furthermore, leaving the inflation criterion unchanged violates the principle of 'equal treatment' in an economic sense, since for the countries that introduced the euro in 1999 the criterion had meant convergence to the inflation rate of the major trading partner, while after enlargement the chance that minor trading partners will define the criterion has increased substantially.

Notes

1. We include among the new member states Cyprus, Malta, Slovenia and Slovakia, which have already joined the euro area. Therefore, when we talk about the euro area, we refer to the twelve old euro-area members (EA12).
2. The NMS have maintained different exchange systems over time and have also changed regimes on occasion. The regimes practiced included currency boards, fixed pegs to a basket, crawling pegs, managed float and free float. Currently, three NMS are members of ERM II: Estonia and Lithuania with a fixed rate as a unilateral commitment, and Latvia with +/–1 per cent fluctuation band as a unilateral commitment. Bulgaria has a currency board arrangement, with the euro being the anchor currency. The Czech Republic, Poland and Romania are under inflation-targeting regimes with free floating exchange rates, while Hungary's inflation targeting was conducted in conjunction with an exchange rate band of +/–15 per cent against the euro until April 2008; since then inflation-targeting has been conducted under free floating. Before joining the euro area, the exchange rate of Cyprus fluctuated within relatively narrow margins, Malta had a fixed rate; Slovenia used to practice a more or less managed float and Slovakia had an inflation-targeting regime under free floating until November 2005 when the country joined ERM II with the standard fluctuation band of +/–15 per cent.
3. For details, see Darvas and Szapáry (2008).
4. Relevant data are provided in Darvas and Szapáry (2008).
5. Égert *et al.* (2006) estimate that credit in Bulgaria, Estonia, Hungary, Latvia and Slovenia have approached the estimated equilibrium level.

6. Deroose *et al.* (2004) find that countercyclical budgetary policy actually disrupts the adjustment process when the policy lag is four quarters.

7. The adjustment experiences of the euro-area countries and the lessons for the NMS to learn from these experiences are analysed in detail in European Commission (2006a). The experience of Portugal is particularly interesting because it has had limited success in adjusting to the interest rate shock. When a country loses competitiveness due to high price and wage inflation, it is difficult to regain it by increases in productivity (see Blanchard, 2006a).

21 | *Economic governance in an enlarged euro area*

IAIN BEGG

1. Background and issues

EMU has to be understood and analysed as a profound regime change, even though it is a change that has been implemented via incremental steps and which does not have a clear *finalité*. A corollary is that the present arrangements for economic governance cannot be regarded as stable. Further evolution of the system may encompass a substantial increase in the number of members of the euro area, the degree of engagement of the EU level in policy formulation and implementation, and the balance between the 'economic' and the 'monetary' in EMU. This characterisation of EMU as a system in flux, in turn, has far-reaching implications for the 'demand' for governance, as well as how it is 'supplied'.

Ten years on from the launch of the euro, therefore, it is timely to ask whether the governance structures put in place in the early 1990s and refined since are suited to the demands of a euro area that, before long, will have doubled its membership. Enlargement of the euro area will pose additional challenges by greatly widening the range of economic conditions that have to be accommodated by a single monetary policy. Awkward questions also arise, for example, about whether soft means of governance will become more problematic and whether the Eurogroup, as presently constituted, with its informality and lack of formal executive capability, can fulfil an effective governance role. As the euro area enlarges calls for some form of European economic government can be expected, although the form remains to be clarified. These and many other debates around how to govern EMU are far from resolved.

I am grateful to Joost Kuhlmann and Jean Pisani-Ferry for constructive comments on earlier drafts. They are, naturally, absolved from any blame for remaining infelicities.

1.1 EMU economic governance, performance and transformations

Since the extensive reforms in 2005 and 2006 of the different components of economic governance, a new architecture of economic policy making has emerged in the EU, embracing structural policies as well as the demand side. These reforms comprised the revisions to the Stability and Growth Pact (SGP), the relaunch of the Lisbon strategy and the settlement of the EU budget for the period 2007–13, as well as recast sustainable development and social policy strategies. These changes have manifestly built on the policy framework put in place by the Treaty on European Union as it evolved from Maastricht to Nice, which provided a clear policy structure for the governance of monetary union, rooted in a stability-orientated approach to macroeconomic policy. More weight is now accorded to policy coordination under the Lisbon strategy. Within reason, 'Lisbon relaunched' is the big umbrella under which all the other economic governance processes now shelter and is manifestly also the core political project of the current Commission. Another intriguing feature of the emerging system is the growing degree of process integration, with connections of various sorts between different strands of economic governance.

Although the headline data for the last decade are not very encouraging about the 'performance' of EMU in terms of growth or unemployment (for a more detailed presentation, see Pisani-Ferry *et al.*, 2008), it has to be recognised that it has had, and continues to have, a transformative effect on economic structures. Certainly, as was stressed by Commissioner Almunia (2007) in his address to the Brussels Economic Forum, the stability that has come from EMU has radically altered the economic environment by bringing in not just low inflation but also low interest rates. For some euro-area members, these changes have resulted in large windfall gains. In addition, significant fiscal consolidation took place during the 1990s, notably while Member States sought to qualify for Stage III of EMU. However, after the launch of EMU, the larger countries, especially, did not consolidate their public finances sufficiently to attain the position of 'close to balance or in surplus' at the heart of the SGP. Then, as the slowdown from 2001 became more prolonged than was generally forecast, the French and German deficits breached the 3 per cent limit, triggering the excessive deficit procedure

(EDP). Concerns have also surfaced in some Member States about the strength of the euro.

The transformations wrought by the euro have nevertheless fed into the dynamics of European integration. Mongelli and Vega (2006), in summing up the evidence on the effects of the euro on its member economies, come to a number of conclusions:

- Trade intensity has increased for euro-area members;[1]
- Financial integration has accelerated and, probably, has been more to the benefit of larger than smaller members, but also shows signs of contributing to risk pooling;[2]
- Structural reform was reasonably rapid during the run-up to the start of the euro, but has been slower since in the larger countries of the euro area;[3]
- There is a high degree of business-cycle synchronisation, but it has not increased and there has been no change in the divergence of growth rates.

1.2 Uncomfortable bed-fellows

Although EMU appears to have a solid constitutional and institutional basis, there is continuing controversy about some of its key features. Indeed, political and policy cleavages that have had a significant bearing on how the governance of the euro area developed have long characterised the EMU project. There have been many strands to these debates, with differing camps such as the economists' versus the monetarists' standpoints in determining how to engineer the transition to the single currency, and presumed disjunctions between the interests of core and periphery, or of large and small members. Other debates have concerned the need for a centralised fiscal stabilisation capacity (included in the Werner blueprint for EMU, but discarded by the late 1980s), the case for more explicit coordination mechanisms or the necessity of an economic counterpart to the powerful, centralised monetary authority. For some, the notion of the ECB on a pedestal at the heart of the governance system is seen as regrettable.

Although the forms of governance that are in place typically owe more to one side than the other, there are many facets of EMU that continue to be uneasy compromises. Thus, it was the 'economists' who won the argument about the transition to the single currency, notably through the imposition of nominal convergence criteria, rather than seeking an optimal combination according to optimal currency area principles. But as Wyplosz (2006) argues, it may have been an incomplete victory insofar as the 'monetarist' view prevailed in the implementation of the rules, with many countries acceding in the first wave, despite not fulfilling the convergence criteria convincingly,[4] and subsequently reneging on their SGP commitments.

A compelling explanation is that the often inadequately acknowledged cleavage at the heart of EMU is between its two most prominent protagonists and core members: France and Germany. Many of the loose ends and shortcomings in governance can be traced directly to the competing French and German visions, and the tensions between them have been an obstacle to more effective governance. France has a long tradition of active exchange rate management, whereas Germany has stressed stable money. The sharing between the Council and the ECB of responsibility for exchange rate policy is a fudge that leaves neither in charge and reflects neither country's predilection. For Puetter (2004) German scepticism about *gouvernement économique* derives from fears that it would compromise the independence of the ECB. The make-up of EMU is a compromise between what Pisani-Ferry (2006a) describes as a German preference for avoidance of excessive deficits and a French insistence on the necessity of coordinated non-monetary economic policies. But he also notes the asymmetry between the loose nature of the latter and the hard rules of the former. The 'S' in SGP is a German preference, whereas the 'G' is a concession to French concerns about more active demand management. In the 2001–3 recession, it seemed that the two countries were more in harmony in promoting a more flexible interpretation of the SGP, but with Germany having consolidated its public finances over the last couple of years, they again appear to be on opposite sides.

1.3 Structure of the chapter

This chapter looks at the governance of EMU and how it may need to evolve as the euro area enlarges. The next section looks in more detail at the meaning of governance, explores the challenges of coordination, and considers their salience for the euro area, while Section 3 assesses the record of EMU's first decade. Section 4 then looks at ways forward for governance, and the last section concludes.

Various themes emerge in the essay. A first is the importance of recognising that EMU has moved a long way in its first decade and that the parameters for governance have, consequently, evolved. A more mature and embedded EMU needs new principles, pointing to a second theme which is that the political dimensions of economic policy making deserve to be made more explicit, while unresolved issues such as divergent visions and preferences have to be confronted and settled. Third, enlargement of the euro area ought to take account of the different circumstances of the potential new members. Looking forward, it is questionable whether a one-size-fits-all system for fiscal and structural policies can be retained, and whether greater differentiation should be contemplated. Similarly, can a system reliant on 'soft' modes of governance be enough in a euro area of twenty or more? Channels for promoting legitimacy warrant fresh thought, given the widespread disquiet about the perceived democratic deficit.

2. Governance

What is meant by economic governance?[5] It combines the philosophy and architecture of economic policy making with the institutions, machinery and practices that shape the evolution of the economy. What has progressively been put in place in the EU is a system that has distinctive characteristics. These can partly be explained by the manner in which integration itself has evolved, partly by reference to the experience gained as the EU has evolved from the customs union to EMU, partly by the manner in which ideas about economic policy making have changed, and partly by how policy actors have 'learned by doing'. Six facets of governance can be distinguished in a framework for appraising the system as a whole.

A first is what might be termed the **policy paradigm**, which can be explained as the theoretical or conceptual basis – or model – for the conduct of policy. While there will often be competing models, at any point there is likely to be a dominant view – or orthodoxy – that sets the parameters within which choices are made and focuses the content of policy discourse, while options rooted in alternative models cannot easily be put forward for consideration. The dominant paradigm will tend to evolve only slowly, though there may be very pronounced shifts from one decade to the next. In EMU today, the term 'stability oriented'[6] captures the dominant model for macroeconomic policy, though the expression 'new Keynesian/neo-classical synthesis' might reflect the academic literature more accurately. Its focus is on identifying and correcting microeconomic market failures and government failures (especially time inconsistency), dealing with them in a quite interventionist/activist manner, with the underlying ambition to strengthen market forces. Key characteristics include a belief in the neutrality of monetary policy and relatively restrictive fiscal policy.

The second dimension of governance can, loosely, be labelled **approach to policy making**, comprising the nature of policy processes (such as the formulation of rules or restrictions on discretion), the degree of legal codification of the policy machinery, whether targets or benchmarks are employed and the character of decision making. Both the EU and EMU today have rather diverse methodologies in different policy domains. Rules are, ostensibly, central to both fiscal and monetary policies – though the experience of the SGP suggests a disjunction between principles and implementation – and even ECB policy in practice often suggests that more discretion is exercised than is commonly assumed. By contrast 'softer' methodologies for policy coordination are more evident in other policy domains, especially those lumped under the Lisbon strategy. A key observation is that economic governance largely eschews political processes at the heart of EMU policy making. In the relaunched Lisbon strategy, especially, it can be argued that a form of hybrid governance has emerged in which methods that can be categorised as the traditional *méthode communautaire* (especially in much of the Community Lisbon Programme which includes internal market measures) function alongside the open method of coordination.

Third is **the institutional mix** which concerns the division among the different tiers of government (EU, national, sub-national), and the split between governmental and other forms of governance, including agencies or forms of self-regulation by private actors. Here, too, the EMU system is very diverse, with dominance of the Member State level of government for fiscal and structural policy; an independent executive agency (the ECB) responsible for monetary policy; shared competence between the Commission and Member State agencies for competition policy, and so on. Although most economic policy measures are supposed to function at the Member State level, coordination of these measures raises awkward questions. A second, key issue is what role the Community level should have and how it is exercised. While the respective roles of Member States and the Community institutions, in partnership, are becoming clearer, the implications of 'hybridity' – in the sense described above – as a model of governance remain to be fleshed out.

A fourth dimension, of a more political character, is **accountability and legitimacy**, embracing not just the mechanisms through which institutions of governance are held to account, but also the different facets of legitimacy. The dichotomy between input and output legitimacy posited by Scharpf (1999) offers one means of analysing the challenges of economic performance by asking whether it is better to have institutions of governance that are not, at first sight, subject to democratic oversight, provided that they deliver better outcomes. Legitimacy cannot be reduced to an exclusively positive assessment as it has many normative dimensions. 'Better' performance as an arithmetic average may hide significant distributive differences and the preferences of the population need to be appraised with subtlety. At issue here is not only whether mechanisms exist, but whether they function effectively in ensuring that economic governance is consistent with political preferences.

Fifth, and related to the fourth category, is the issue of **transparency and communication** which bears on governance from two quite distinct perspectives. The first is provision of information that allows the agency of governance to be held to account and can thus be interpreted politically. The second is communication strategies that inform economic agents subject to the policy area about the stance of policy in a way that is conducive to optimal behaviour. For example, central bank transparency has come to play a pivotal role in the conduct of monetary policy. Communication also encompasses the transmission of information from the governed to the governing agency, including how receptive the latter is prepared to be in responding to emerging signals.

A sixth component of the economic governance framework is the **range and scope of participation by different actors** in policy making. Among the key aspects of this are where effective 'ownership' of the policy area resides, how different constituencies are heard (for example, formal consultation or informal lobbying), whether there are either effective vetoes or provisions for constraining the autonomy of the decision-making body, and the means by which competing positions are reconciled. One of the most forceful criticisms of the Lisbon strategy concerns the lack of ownership. Too often, the European Parliament is inaudible, while the voice of civil society is rarely listened to by decision makers. By contrast, the ECB is often attacked for being too deaf to demands for policy changes emanating either from other public authorities or wider constituencies.

2.1 Policy coordination

The manner in which macroeconomic policy is conducted in the euro area has no real parallel elsewhere. In particular, what distinguishes it is the nature and conduct of policy coordination; indeed many of the most disputed aspects of EMU governance concern the extent and purpose of coordination. In the academic literature, coordination has traditionally been about the scope for orchestrating the thrust of policy (Williamson, 2005), usually in response to perceived disequilibria or common shocks such as the response to the oil price increases in the 1970s, the falling dollar in the mid-1980s or, today, the accumulated effects of imbalances and the fall-out from the subprime crisis. More systematic macroeconomic management at global level has been an aspiration that has not been achieved. By contrast, in the EU, and especially around EMU, policy coordination is intended to be more routine and has taken a variety of forms, embracing both macroeconomic and structural policies.

The virtues of coordination are hotly disputed. Minimalist coordination encourages greater accountability because it means that 'principals' can more easily ascertain whether 'agents' have done what they are supposed to do, whereas attempts at coordination between fiscal and monetary policy in the pursuit of a 'right' policy mix will blur roles and weaken commitments (Alesina *et al.*, 2001; Issing, 2002). The alternative view is that strong coordination is needed to articulate an explicit policy mix, defined here to include not just the traditional combination of fiscal and monetary policy, but also structural policies. Calmfors (2001c) identifies five lessons about policy coordination:

- There need to be significant cross-border spillovers to warrant coordination;
- There has to be evaluation to ensure that commitments are adhered to and that policy coordination is achieving results, otherwise free-riding will be encouraged;
- Even if there are gains from coordination, they can be negated if decision-making is ineffective;

- Policy innovation is inhibited; and
- Country diversity is not given sufficient attention, with coordination aims over-shadowing national preferences or needs.

2.1.1 Coordination in EMU governance

The constitutional position regarding coordination was, largely, established in the Maastricht Treaty and only marginal changes have been incorporated in the Lisbon Treaty. The principal mechanisms today are the SGP, covering fiscal policy, the Lisbon strategy, which now incorporates the Broad Economic Policy Guidelines (BEPGs) – in place since the early 1990s and covering different economic policies – and the Employment Guidelines initially known as the Luxembourg process. What is lacking, however, are explicit mechanisms for coordination between fiscal and monetary policy, or for aggregating Member States' fiscal policies. Two significant reforms have, however, taken place since the original Maastricht criteria were promulgated, despite the fact that the Treaty has been unchanged. These are:

- The adoption of the SGP in 1997, which did not explicitly refer to the debt ratio as a rule (although, obviously, it remained in the Treaty) and created the conjunction of the close-to-balance target for public finances and the 3 per cent deficit limit;
- The reform of the SGP in 2005, with the introduction of more political discretion, a change in the definition of a steep fall in GDP growth, and other corrections.

One of the key challenges of fiscal policy coordination is striking the right balance between what many authors (Buti and Pench, 2004; Annett, 2006) have described as preventive and dissuasive policies. The SGP, manifestly, embraces both, yet has been bedevilled by an enduring ambiguity about where the policy emphasis should lie. Indeed, Pisani-Ferry (2006a: 828) asserts that the institutional provisions for fiscal coordination are 'markedly weaker … than those inspired by the need to safeguard central bank independence and price stability'. Enforceability is seen as a key attribute of a 'good' fiscal rule, but if tested against this attribute, the SGP performs poorly (Buti, Eijffinger and Franco, 2003). The approach to enforcement is a mishmash of hard, soft and informal methods; they are rule-based and discursive; and political as well as technical. The EDP can be criticised as a procedure that ought to be used sparingly, but which (because the

Commission has no choice but to act if Member States breach the rules) over the years has become routine, undermining its credibility.

In the run-up to the 2005 reform of the SGP, there was a cascade of proposals for its revision (for two overviews see Fischer *et al.*, 2007; Verde, 2006). The reforms eventually agreed sought to strengthen the economic rationale behind the Pact while augmenting political discretion, but instead of a simple rule, introduced more complex governance arrangements for fiscal policy. The changes agreed did not go as far as many protagonists hoped in emphasising public debt as the yardstick of sustainability of public finances, yet also cast doubt on whether it would encourage responsible fiscal policy. Three questions then arise:

- Can governance mechanisms be devised that are capable of applying discretion without tending towards a breakdown of fiscal discipline as Member States refer to the 'jurisprudence' of treatment of others?
- In a softer regime, is there any way to contain the propensity of governments to use fiscal policy for electoral reasons? Buti and van den Noord (2004) argue that systems of surveillance are unlikely to be robust enough to deter such opportunistic behaviour by governing parties. Although they find that governments often build up 'war chests' by fiscal austerity in non-election years, few have gone as far as would be implied by the SGP.
- Do the methods employed for assessing fiscal positions provide accurate and unambiguous information? Accounting tricks may have undermined discipline (Buti, Nogueira Martins and Turrini 2007) although the 2005 reforms of the SGP, by stressing debt, will diminish the scope for playing off debt against deficits. However, Balassone *et al.* (2006, 2007) show that neither a debt criterion nor a deficit one, on its own, provides an adequate yardstick of fiscal sustainability. Instead, they argue for consistency cross-checks between the two classes of indicators, observing though that all fiscal indicators are susceptible to distortion. One dimension of fiscal sustainability that does not receive due attention is the net worth of the public sector, both in a conventional balance sheet sense and, considering off balance sheet items, the prospects either for future flows of income (user charges, for example) or of outlays (such as pension obligations). Yet in the final analysis, the problem is less the computation of the ratios so much as the reluctance (or inability) of Member States to abide by the rules.

2.1.2 Bringing in the supply side

As in any polity, in EMU there is a three-way interaction among monetary, fiscal and supply-side policies, and decisions in each will be influenced by what happens in the others. *Ceteris paribus*, the ECB will find it easier to maintain price stability (its primary mandate) if the fiscal authorities maintain a tight fiscal policy. Interdependencies between fiscal and monetary policies are much discussed, but it is in the area of structural reform (including its connections to monetary policy) that, arguably, the rationale for coordination is least well developed. If product market competition and/or labour market flexibility (broadly defined) are enhanced, the likelihood is that inflationary pressures will be muted for a given pressure of demand. This cuts both ways, harking back to the 'two-handed' approach to reform, dating from Blanchard *et al.* (1986), which argues that structural reform is much less likely to take hold if it is not accompanied by demand conditions that are supportive.

In a typical national setting this can then become either an explicit policy mix in which the settings of fiscal, structural and monetary policy are negotiated, or can be the outcome of a tacit recognition by one of the agencies (typically, with central bank independence having become the norm, the monetary authority) that the decision of the other affects its own (given the framework for EMU, the more likely option). As a result, the central bank can also be expected to factor-in to its judgements on monetary policy how the supply side is evolving. The central bank reaction function would, in this logic, include the stance of fiscal and structural policies as an independent variable. The key point is that in a 'normal' polity, the fiscal authority that exercises discipline or the supply-side authority that delivers greater flexibility can expect a 'reward' in the form of lower interest rates. Conversely, loose fiscal policy or supply-side rigidities will be penalised by higher rates.

In the euro area, a notable difference is that fiscal or supply-side actions by Member States will be diluted because they have only a small weight in the overall calculation by the central bank. Even Germany accounts for below a third of euro-area GDP, implying that fiscal consolidation by Germany will only attract a third of the pay-off that it would have compared with the DMark era when the counterparty of the German government was the Bundesbank. The significance of the arithmetic of the linkages is, first, that governments adopting 'virtuous' policies will see less pay-off, thus lowering incentives to play by the rules, and second, governments that do not comply face lower penalties and thus greater temptations to free-ride.

The political economy of structural reform makes the links between monetary, fiscal and structural policies hard to assess. Leiner-Killinger *et al.* (2007), in surveying the literature on the links between structural reform and monetary policy, suggest that, on balance, EMU should encourage structural reform and diminish opposition to it. However, for countries which, on joining a monetary union, benefit from a lower nominal interest rate, monetary union may stimulate the economy in the short to medium term, and mask structural problems. Yet Tabellini and Wyplosz (2006) make a convincing case that supply-side coordination in the EU at present is neither optimal nor well thought-out. Nevertheless coordinated structural reform (Bentolila and Saint-Paul, 2001) deserves attention, although the modalities and focus matter, given that coordination in structural policies works least well in the labour market, but is more promising in other areas.

Solving the problem of lack of national ownership of Lisbon strategy commitments will not be easy and there is an air of unreality to many of the solutions canvassed, however well intended or sensible in principle. For example, Tabellini and Wyplosz (2006) call for national parliaments to be obliged to debate the recommendations of the Council in relation to labour market reform. Yet it is hard to see even the more compliant of national assemblies being receptive to such an obligation, while many would positively bristle at it. Similarly, the criticisms in the Kok group (2004) report of Member State commitments to the Lisbon strategy suggest a lack of credibility. The upshot is that neither macroeconomic constraints nor supply-side reforms have been able to garner sufficient credibility.

A euro-area component to the Lisbon strategy – orchestrated by the Eurogroup – could contribute to better linkages between the demand and supply sides of the economy. This has already been foreshadowed in the Commission's 2006 and 2007 *Annual Progress Reports* on the Lisbon strategy in which there were not only separate 'fiches' for each Member State, but also one for the euro area as a whole. The problem though is that while the fiche contains suggestions for the euro area, it is less clear what institutional machinery there is within the euro area to act on these suggestions, although the Eurogroup is the body that has the potential to be the relevant actor.

Yet manifestly there is a problem where the intensity and content of structural reform differs from one country to another, and where the value of any accompanying demand-side stimulus will be uneven. Moreover, since the degree of any demand-side stimulus cannot easily be tailored to the circumstances of an individual country when the ECB can only set a single monetary policy, the challenge is greater still. Pisani-Ferry (2006b: 3) suggests that 'the ECB should explicitly let it be known that provided there is a common political commitment to reform and without prejudice to price stability, it stands ready to back policies that lower structural unemployment and put the euro area on a higher growth path'.

2.1.3 Track record

The implementation of policy coordination has been mixed. In the fiscal arena, it has arguably had enough of an impact to prevent much resort to discretionary fiscal policy, yet has not been sufficiently potent to bring down debt by pushing countries to respect the 'close to balance' requirement of the SGP. The evidence of relatively disciplined fiscal policy over the first decade of EMU suggests that the SGP *has* constrained governments, though it seems to have done so more via the 'soft' pressures of peer esteem and calling into question of their domestic reputation for competence, than the hard sanctions of the last two stages in the EDP (obliging a Member State to deposit up to 0.5 per cent of GDP, then the conversion of the deposit into a fine) which have never been, nor are likely to be, used. The relationship between the 'hard law' of the SGP and the softer 'recommendations' under the BEPGs (or, now, the macroeconomic elements of the Lisbon Integrated Guidelines) has proved to be an uncomfortable one and there is force in Pisani-Ferry's criticism (2006a: 836) of the BEPGs as having become a 'Brussels talking to Brussels' exercise, with little impact on national policy processes, let alone decisions. Yet it is often the softer elements that have proved most influential (Hodson and Maher, 2004).

In structural policies, the record is less convincing, prompting questions about whether more explicit incentives or procedural changes are needed. Even the relaunched Lisbon strategy is undermined by a lack of hard cash (Pisani-Ferry and Sapir, 2006), despite the Kok group recommendations. In these circumstances, it is unclear what the incentives are for 'good' policies if there are short-term political costs of tough measures. An easy answer to the sheer complexity of coordination is simply not to try it on the grounds that, even if well intentioned, it will make matters worse by blurring incentives and fostering uncertainty. But this would be unduly defeatist and, instead, the imperative should be to find ways of avoiding the pitfalls. One suggestion (Leiner-Killinger *et al.*, 2007: 22) is that the ECB could signal its likely reaction to specified reform measures, thereby contributing 'to reducing the typically large degree of uncertainty surrounding the outcome of reforms'.

The 2006/7 'fiche' for the euro area, annexed to the Commission's *Annual Progress Report*, states that the 'euro area Member States should aim at deepening coordination and strengthening governance, especially in the context of the Eurogroup', a change that, it is claimed, would 'contribute to more effectively address policy challenges'. If the euro area is to improve on how structural policies interact with macroeconomic policies for reasons of good governance of EMU, it is the obvious way forward. The nub of the question, though, is whether a euro-area member would do anything differently because it is part of the euro area, and in this context, three options can be considered. The first would be that a different policy is adopted; and the second, a country might act on a different timetable, either by implementing reforms in a sequence or by doing them sooner. But it is the third that is more intriguing: would a country be more willing to act because it was in a closer coordination process?

2.2 The institutions of euro-area governance

Not surprisingly, the institutional structure of euro-area governance is somewhat messy. EMU is in a curious limbo insofar as its institutional structure very largely presumes that all members of the EU will join the euro area and that non-participation is a derogation (except for Denmark and the UK with their formal opt-out provisions). But with eleven out of twenty-seven Member States not fully in EMU as it passed its tenth anniversary, the temporary character of the transition is open to question. Certainly, anomalies arise in governance: all Member States are subject to surveillance in fiscal policy and are subject to the excessive deficit procedure, yet only the full participants face sanctions under the disciplinary provisions of the SGP.

The division of powers between the ECB, the ECOFIN Council (or the Eurogroup) and the Commission may even give rise to technical complications when there is uncertainty about key variables such as the true output gap or the projected fiscal deficit (Balboni *et al.*, 2007: 4, who show that 'almost universally, the texts adopted by the Council are softer than those put forward by the Commission'). It follows that a governance challenge is how to reconcile conflicting views on the true position of the economy.

2.2.1 The Eurogroup

Since the start of Stage III, the Eurogroup has progressively become the most influential political forum for the governance of the euro area. It came into being for two distinct reasons: first, because the body formally charged with overseeing the economic dimensions of EMU (the ECOFIN Council) has to balance the interests of the euro area and those of its other members; and, second, because the incomplete membership of full EMU created an institutional vacuum in matching the economic and monetary aspects of EMU. The fact that the Eurogroup membership is a qualified majority of the ECOFIN Council is important, because it means that even informally agreed positions can become policy, provided that the caucus remains firm. Equally, if a measure either requires unanimity or is currently blockable, but only pertains to the euro area, any attempt to block it in the ECOFIN Council will engender resentment.

Above all the Eurogroup's activity is debate on economic developments and policy making, not legislative activity. But it is evident that the Eurogroup has become the de facto forum for deciding on breaches of the SGP. The Commission also can use the Eurogroup as a channel to convey messages to Member States, especially about fiscal discipline. In addition, having adopted a more permanent presidency from the start of 2005, a greater degree of continuity has been introduced. The European Parliament has responded to these changes by inviting the president of the Eurogroup to attend a meeting every semester (half as frequently as the ECB, however). What appears to be happening is a kind of creeping institutionalisation of the Eurogroup that has been taken a stage further by new provisions in the Lisbon Treaty. The new chapter 3a provides enabling clauses to enhance euro-area governance, effectively defining the equivalent of Art. 99 coordination for the euro area.

It still, however, represents a compromise insofar as the Eurogroup will remain informal (although a potentially significant development is that any Council votes on budgetary surveillance or economic policy guidelines will be limited to the euro-area members (Art. 114(2)). Similarly, the new Art. 115a provides for common euro-area positions and representation in international financial institutions, though only in enabling rather than prescriptive terms, prompting the question of whether privileged Member States will forgo their existing rights. Art. 116 also sets out a range of areas in which non-members of the euro area will not have decision-making powers, such as in nominating ECB Executive Board members.

The question that arises is whether the informal Eurogroup of the early years of the euro is a creature of its time which will have to emerge from its chrysalis in an altogether different form. Informality, together with the one-plus-one membership has encouraged full and frank debates and the absence of formal record encourages greater candour. Reaching consensus is at the heart of the method. The Eurogroup, according to Puetter (2004), acts as a complement to formal procedures, rather than as a nascent economic government – a crucial distinction. Because of informality, peer pressure can be more effective. The Eurogroup is also reported more recently to have gained in confidence and authority, helped in part by the shift to a more permanent president, but also because it has simply matured enough to have learned by doing.

Despite these new provisions in the Lisbon Treaty, the Eurogroup will not acquire legislative powers, so that although its status will be boosted, it will remain an informal body that lacks the authority to enforce decisions other than through peer pressure. Indeed, it would be open to question whether it would even possess executive/administrative powers other than through the medium of the ECOFIN Council. Yet the accretion of power to the Eurogroup is manifestly a sign of change in governance, despite its unplanned character.

An evident problem is that the Eurogroup is composed of finance ministers, whereas many structural policies engage other ministries, notably those responsible for labour market and employment policy, enterprise, social protection and technology. These other ministries will, to a degree, have different 'client bases' among economic actors. It follows that, by being limited to finance ministries, the Eurogroup's influence over the ministries responsible for structural reform is less clear. Should there then be informal groupings parallel to the Eurogroup for issues normally covered by EPSCO (Employment, Social Policy, Health and Consumer Affairs) and the Competitiveness Council? Alternatively, should a variant on economic government that cuts across sectoral policies be envisaged? On all these matters, the Lisbon Treaty provides no formal proposals, although further informal developments should not be precluded.

The decision of Nicolas Sarkozy in July 2007 to attend the Eurogroup and to make demands on the path of fiscal policy (to the evident dismay of other members and the ECB) highlighted two factors. First, if heads of state or government do become involved, they can be expected to shape the agenda in a manner that might not be congenial to finance ministers and might over-ride them. Second, the cosy but closed nature of the Eurogroup may be weakened and it may have to become more transparent. Nevertheless, the most likely way forward is for the Eurogroup to be the focus of EMU economic policy making, yet progressively to bring in other segments of government, so as to embrace the full range of economic policies at issue. Ultimately, the membership of the Eurogroup might well mutate towards being euro-area ministers with wider economic responsibilities, rather than just finance ministers.

2.2.2 The Commission and other institutions of governance

In the governance of the euro area, the Commission is bound to be a central actor. It has a range of roles, some of which are evident and accepted, while for others there is a pronounced ambivalence about how much power or influence it should have. The accepted roles include the core analysis of EU economic developments, the surveillance of Member State policies, and the procedural elements of the various stages in implementing the SGP, the Lisbon strategy and other coordination processes. However, where the Commission's role comes in for most criticism or appears to be resented by Member States is in the exercise of disciplinary measures and in criticising policy developments.

Since the 2005 relaunch of the Lisbon strategy, the Commission has become more central in economic governance than in the early days of EMU, and has regained (or acquired) greater influence over the direction of policy making. It has done so, first, by being the prime mover in establishing the Integrated Guidelines that Member States are asked to use in formulating NRPs (national reform programmes). Second, the Commission is now very much centre stage in the policy procedures, as the principal orchestrator of the annual Lisbon cycle, as well as being the leading agent for the delivery of the Community Lisbon Programme. In addition, it is evident that the Commission devotes greater collective effort to 'Lisbon', having given it the highest political priority, broadened the range of Directorates-General engaged and established a strong central coordination of its contribution at very senior level.

However, where the Commission appears still to be somewhat tentative is in the degree to which it is openly critical of Member States. In 2005/6, the Commission chose not to issue national recommendations and had already elected not to use overt naming and shaming, despite this being a strong recommendation of the Kok committee (Pisani-Ferry and Sapir, 2006; Begg, 2007). In 2006/7, national recommendations were restored, but have been drafted very guardedly. Although the Commission has been more forceful in bi-lateral discussions with Member States over the content and implementation of NRPs, the fact that it has largely been behind closed doors may have undermined transparency in a way that diminishes the domestic pressures on governments to take full ownership of reform strategies.

The Lisbon Treaty strengthens the Commission by providing, under Art. 99, for the Commission to be able to criticise Member State economic policies and to issue proposals rather than mere recommendations concerning excessive deficits. The protocol on the Eurogroup also provides for the Commission, as well as the finance minister, to prepare meetings – arguably legitimating an activity currently undertaken by the Commission, but open to dispute.

Key roles in the governance of EMU continue to be played by expert committees, especially the Economic and Financial Committee (EFC) which prepares the ECOFIN Council meetings and its working group responsible for preparing Eurogroup meetings, the Eurogroup Working Group (EWG). Both these bodies work very much behind the scenes, do not publicise their activities using a website and rarely produce public reports. Yet they are highly influential, with the EFC often perceived to be first among equals of the various expert committees. The EFC meets in two formations (the full committee, including national central bank (NCB) officials) when discussing the general economic situation, financial stability and IMF topics, and in a restricted formation that excludes NCB officials when discussing other matters.

2.2.3 Scrutiny: the European Parliament and the Committees

Scrutiny of economic policies is shared between the Commission, the European Parliament and various committees, with formal provisions alongside procedures that have evolved as EMU itself has matured. They are subject to two particular sources of tension: first, a degree of balkanisation of scrutiny and, second, disparities in impact. The European Parliament has a comparatively strong role vis-à-vis monetary policy, but a much more diffuse one in relation to structural policies, not least because its committee structure does not map easily into the broad range of areas covered by the Integrated Guidelines. There is a Lisbon coordinating committee in the Parliament, but it is informal and does not have the political clout of sectoral committees.

By all accounts the scrutiny of Member States' 'Lisbon' NRPs by the Economic Policy Committee and the Employment Committee is effective, if rather truncated. These committees do provide peer review, possibly the only real way in which it is exercised. The European Economic and Social Committee contributes to governance through its work on the engagement of social partners and other interests, albeit with limited impact. Overall, what is lacking is a more systematic attempt to pull together the oversight of governance processes (Begg and Larsson, 2007), other than very rapidly at the spring European Councils, and these Councils often have other, more pressing business. The danger, therefore, is that scrutiny, although exercised diligently, does not feed into wider evaluation of national policies.

3. How well has the system functioned?

Governance of the euro area has, in many ways, been more effective than it is often given credit for and it is easy to forget some of the predictions of doom that surrounded the birth of the euro. However, even if the legitimacy of the governance system is assessed in terms of outputs rather than democratic accountability, the fact that the improved economic performance that was expected from EMU has not (yet?) materialised engenders criticisms. These focus on the choice of monetary policy strategy (which some believe to be behind the state of the art – for example, Pisani-Ferry *et al.* (2008), advocate a shift to inflation targeting), the overly rigid application of the SGP and the incoherence of supply-side policies. It would be easy to dismiss the shortcomings in economic performance as the teething troubles of a very ambitious change in policy regime and it is important to distinguish between transitional problems that have undermined economic performance and aspects of the governance of EMU that have proved to be sufficiently dubious to require attention. For example, how can widening divergence, especially in competitiveness, be addressed? Similarly, if different trajectories of structural reform accentuate the differences between Member States, there are likely to be repercussions for transmission mechanisms that complicate or undermine the functioning of monetary policy.

3.1 What worked well up to 2008

There is much to commend in the first decade of EMU. So far, the ECB has, by and large, delivered price stability and the consensus seems to be that the ECB has not been unduly severe in the priority it has given to stability. Thus, Wyplosz (2006) argues that the Eurosystem has been wise in its policy decisions and has not slavishly followed what its own statements indicated it might. To this extent, publicly stated principles and action have diverged. Clearly, too, the EU has seen a strong convergence in inflation rates, both inside and outside the euro area, and the data show that inflation is now low across the EU and exhibits few signs of any resurgence.

Volatility in the real economy declined prior to the onset of crisis in 2008, though towards steadier but lower growth rates. Whether this is because of the governance changes adopted with the aim of assuring stability (and not just in the euro area), the pressures of international competition or behavioural changes in societies that recognise that inflation is ultimately pernicious, is an unresolved research question. However, recent signs suggest that supply-side improvements are now contributing in key countries like Germany.

Some critics argue that the SGP is effectively dead (Calmfors, 2005; Buiter, 2006a), but a conclusion of this essay echoes that of Mark Twain – rumours of its demise have been seriously exaggerated. Adherence to the letter of the Pact has not been perfect, but compared with the excesses of the pre-Maastricht era, fiscal deficits have been surprisingly restrained (Hughes Hallett *et al.*, 2004). The revised SGP has more economics, more scope for (sensible) political discretion and less of a hidebound resort to rules. It also (see Verde, 2006) has more country specificity and is more likely to assure long-run sustainability, though Verde considers that the new flexibility may be excessive. Nor is there any persuasive evidence that the limited breaches of the excessive deficit rules have led to higher interest rates. This may sound like a Panglossian conclusion, considering the SGP's previous problems, but it is important to distinguish between the methods and institutions of governance of the euro area and underlying structural weaknesses. The latter, as Paul de Grauwe has insisted (see, for example, de Grauwe, 2002; and the comments by Nickell on Wyplosz, 2006b: 247–253), pre-date the euro and cannot, consequently, be blamed on it. Fiscal discipline has improved partly because there has been a trend towards greater centralisation (within Member States) in budget setting, and more power to 'delegated' finance ministers, according to Hallerberg *et al.* (2007). It is an open question whether an inference to draw is that centralisation at EU or euro-area level might add to the discipline. Certainly, the willingness of the Eurogroup to discuss timetables and orientations suggests that there is a disposition to go in this direction. Buti (2005) has also advocated a split of the fiscal year into a euro-area semester and a domestic semester.

3.2 What remains unsatisfactory

Although fiscal coordination has worked better than it is often given credit for in maintaining discipline, it has not yet found the answer to two related problems. The first is delivering a coherent euro-area fiscal stance to complement monetary policy. It may be attained implicitly, but the scope for it to lead to unbalanced policy is still considerable. Second, the governance mechanisms have patently failed to fulfil the objective of fiscal consolidation in good times – the close-to-balance rule of the SGP. It may be that the rule is misconceived, but the lack of progress in many euro-area countries in bringing down public debt ratios suggests otherwise. Annett (2006) suggests a number of explanations, including:

- Systematic overestimation of the strength of the economy;
- A disposition to resort to gimmicks or one-off devices to massage statistics; and
- The impact of elections.

Solutions include trying to construct a common means of assessing the economy (which could be via independent forecasts, following Jonung and Larch, 2006) or by having independent institutions to the fore in managing fiscal policy (as advocated by Wyplosz, 2005), rather than government bodies.

A second problem is that the EU economy had exhibited imbalances that contributed to instability once the crisis hit in 2008. Significant divergences emerged between euro-area members, with large trade surpluses in Germany and the Netherlands, and burgeoning deficits in Spain and Portugal. Moreover, despite some improvement since 2005, unemployment remains doggedly high in several Member States. According to Blanchard (2006b) many explanations of EU unemployment struggle to explain differences among countries. What is undeniable is that the EU as whole, despite achieving productivity levels close to those of the USA,[7] lags a long way behind in terms of GDP per head, adjusted for purchasing power. Arithmetically, the principal explanation is the significantly lower hours worked, but there are differing views on whether the explanation is a preference for leisure, the effects of high taxes on labour, an overly generous welfare state or the effects of union power in restricting hours worked. Gordon (2004) finds the first of these explanations to be the most powerful, but also notes that the drift towards flexibility in Europe has reduced some of the gap in recent years.

A third shortcoming is that the link between macroeconomic policy and structural policies is, at best, unsatisfactory. Although the Integrated Guidelines bring together the different strands of policy and call for a single National Reform Programme, these programmes do not often cut across conventional policy boundaries very effectively. Nor has the taking of ownership for structural reform – put forward as a key element of the recast Lisbon strategy – really happened and the aspiration that public and peer group pressures on governments would underpin commitments to reform has not been realised.

3.3 An interim verdict

The EMU governance system has strengths, but a larger euro area will pose new challenges. In term of the six categories of governance set out in Section 2, a verdict is as follows.

Policy model: the core of macroeconomic stability and market-orientated reforms, together with a focus on the knowledge-based economy that can be said to be at the heart of EU economic governance, is well supported. It does not need significant change to cope with enlargement of EMU, although the emphasis between different elements (employment policies, research, education and social cohesion) within structural reform may be worth revisiting. There is also a tendency to gloss over the disagreements between the two largest euro-area members (France and Germany) about some of the broad policy orientations within the stability model.

Policy approach: many of the mechanisms of economic policy governance have been under strain and have the character of unfinished business. Yet there is not an unambiguous direction for change either for the present euro area or for an enlarged one. The Sapir report (Sapir *et al.* 2004) emphasised the need to match governance methods to policy demands, including allowing Member States to choose how to deliver. Equally, the EU (and, by extension, the euro area) needs to have carrots as well as sticks. Hard law and soft law mechanisms work uncomfortably together and it is difficult to work out which is the more effective or dominant. A larger euro area will only accentuate these problems.

The institutional mix has one not inconsiderable virtue which is that it has, up to now, achieved the desired results, at least in the sense of making things happen. Yet in the economic as opposed to the monetary dimension of EMU, it can have the appearance of being almost accidental in character and is likely to need reinforcement to cope with enlargement of the euro area. Some form of economic government is the most likely answer, but given the enduring differences between Member States and different classes of policy makers about the virtues of more formal economic government, it will need extensive consultation to shape it.

Accountability within the policy framework is open to question. Macroeconomic policy making cannot be portrayed as a normative vacuum: policy choices have significant distributive implications, and a system that lacks such choice risks becoming a policy framework that lacks legitimacy (Jabko, 2003). There are established channels for holding the ECB to account, notably through the quarterly meetings with the European Parliament, yet it is a moot point whether the public sees it as sufficiently accountable. The independence accorded to national central banks derives from laws that, as Amtenbrink (2005) argues, legitimate the position of the central bank within the national constitutional order, but it is elected governments that are ultimately responsible to citizens for the conduct of economic policy. Here the governance system is less satisfactory. There is also a challenge to legitimacy in the perceived shadowy nature of powerful committees such as the Economic and Financial Committee (EFC) or the Economic Policy Committee (EPC), even though they are composed of

Member State representatives, while the Eurogroup's very informality and lack of reporting amount to dubious legitimacy. Enlargement of the euro area as such would not necessarily alter this facet of governance, but may afford an opportunity for innovation.

Transparency has been a key development across the world in monetary policy, partly as an instrument of policy in itself, and partly as a means of enhancing accountability, and the ECB has espoused these principles. In economic policy, the record on transparency is less satisfactory, with shortcomings in the visibility of, and explanations for, both fiscal and structural policy that have undermined confidence in governance in many Member States. The point made by Wyplosz (2006) that some of the principles underlying the governance of EMU are outdated is telling, as is his observation that pragmatism in policy making has seen these principles over-ridden where they conflict with economic realities. But it is not a recipe for sound governance. Arguably, the best way to square this particular circle is for policy makers to explain more comprehensively why they have done what they have done.

The imperative of 'ownership' in the revised Lisbon strategy deserves to be stressed insofar as it has to be nurtured by timely provision of information, something governments have shown themselves to be reluctant to espouse. This is likely to be counterproductive, because the time lags in structural reform need more careful explanation. Yet the record suggests that openness about the Lisbon strategy's aims and rationale tend to be stymied by the reluctance of Member States to refer to it in policy making. However, if enlargement leads to a more customised approach to reform policies rather than the one-size-fits-all approach implicit in having common integrated guidelines, an enhancement of policy communication will be desirable. An emphatic conclusion of this chapter is, therefore, that transparency in policy making should be enhanced.

Participation of actors is also patchy. The Commission has seen its role revitalised since 2005, but the limited input, whether in scrutiny or policy innovation, of the European Parliament and, even less so, national parliaments, is problematic. Yet for EMU to build on what has been achieved in its first decade, it will have to engage diverse interests more effectively. Engagement of other stakeholders remains a weakness in governance, exemplified by the shortcomings of ownership in the Lisbon strategy.

3.4 Enlargement and governance mechanisms

Although the Eurosystem has, in general, functioned effectively in terms of decision making and policy approach, there are issues that can be expected to surface as the number of members increases. The cap agreed on the number of members of the ECB Governing Council will, henceforth, bite and it remains to be seen how well the rotation procedure will work. A parallel question is whether the informal arrangement that has, so far, allocated seats on the Executive Board to the four largest Member States can persist. Padoa-Schioppa (2004) has argued that the ECB should be a 'wisdom-based' collegial system, yet 'reserved' seats are surely incompatible with this characterisation (de Grauwe, 2006a). Clearly, as the number of members rises towards twenty, the notion that four of the six executive board seats can be ring-fenced for the four larger founder members cannot be sustained. Yet who will be first to blink?

Even if the 2008/9 crisis had not arisen, financial stability could have been expected to become a more pressing issue as new members join. The rapid increase in private sector borrowing and the likelihood that house prices will accelerate in rapidly growing economies will need greater attention than has been the norm (Begg, 2008), with implications for how the liquidity operations of the Eurosystem are conducted. In addition, the high degree of foreign ownership of financial intermediaries in most of the recently acceded Member States (Slovenia is the exception) will prompt questions about how supervision is conducted and may call for a more extensive engagement of the Eurosystem in such supervision. Article 105(5) is an enabling one, but may now have to be used to assign specific tasks to the ECB as provided for in Article 105(6), despite the obligation stated in Article 58 to respect national provisions on prudential supervision. In addition, thought is needed on the politics of the lender of last resort function, and on where the costs of depositor protection should ultimately fall.

An issue for the future governance of EMU is whether enlargement alters the conditions conducive to successful soft governance. Sheer numbers may well prove to be a problem. In a Eurogroup of eleven, twelve or thirteen, the one-plus-one formula meant that (including Commission, EFC and ECB participation) the number of participants in the meeting is around thirty. If membership reaches twenty-two or twenty-three, the number rises to fifty; a *tour de table* that might have taken half an hour will become twice as long, consuming a much bigger proportion of a two- or three-hour meeting, unless some members forgo the opportunity to speak. If the result is to alter the subtle dynamics of debate, the value of peer pressure risks being diminished.

Many have argued that the external dimension of euro-area governance is also unfinished business (Bini-Smaghi, 2006; Coeuré and Pisani-Ferry, 2007). There is still confusion, for example, despite what is written in the Treaty, about where power ultimately lies, in exchange rate arrangements. It is not obvious that enlargement of the euro area per se alters the picture, yet with the euro area unable to be a formal member of the IMF, coordination of euro-area members' position is likely to become more pressing as the euro consolidates its role as the world's second currency. Yet the idea that the larger euro-area members will readily give up their seats at the IMF in favour of a single euro-area one still seems fanciful.

4. Revising governance arrangements

There are several potential ways forward for the governance of the euro area, turning on a number of strategic choices. These include: the degree of political choice (as opposed to rules) to be exercised in policy making; innovation in, and reinforcement of, capacities to adjust to economic shocks and longer-run trends; and possible institutional development. It is also important to distinguish between what might be desirable economically, what can be done within the constraints of the Lisbon Treaty and what might reasonably be placed on the agenda for future Treaty changes. Largely technical improvements can be separated from those that require difficult compromises.

4.1 *Politicisation*

EMU, to date, has been mainly a 'technical' project that has largely eschewed politicised decision making, a facet of governance that may be unsustainable in the longer term (Padoa-Schioppa, 2004). In contrast, national governments have to contend with heterogeneous backgrounds in terms of unemployment, inflation and wage-bargaining systems, not to mention social policy priorities. Yet, by having very limited channels for political dialogue, debate about policy choices is stifled, as a result of which valid policy choices may not be put on the table. Only the Eurogroup, in practice, provides political input, prompting questions about whether, and if so how, the EMU governance system can be recast to offer more political choice.

There has been some debate about whether the answer lies in the Eurogroup acquiring power to legislate, and thus pre-empting some of what the ECOFIN Council does, but that would require Treaty change and would certainly be highly provocative for 'outs' and 'pre-ins', even if, for the former group, it could be presented as a corollary of remaining 'out'. Enhanced powers for the Eurogroup leading in the direction of *gouvernement économique* would also require a resolution of the French and German differences on how to run EMU. But with EMU close to entering adolescence, it is time for these to be settled.

However, the fact that the Eurogroup is only a finance ministry grouping is limiting. Even for the EU as a whole, the policy areas are balkanised, with the various committees mapping into their respective national ministries: the EFC and the EPC corresponding to the macro and structural elements of finance ministries; the Employment Committee to labour ministries; and the Social Protection Committee to social security ministries. This structure tends to foment opposition between the committees rather than common approaches. A basis for a new approach to governance may, therefore, be to have an overall body at euro-area level – not necessarily composed exclusively of finance ministry representatives, but rather of ministers able to represent all relevant ministries – but to have sectoral euro-area bodies that feed into the top-level committee.

One option would be to resort to an approximation of cabinet-style government in which there is an enhanced Eurogroup which has its agenda prepared by the equivalent of cabinet committees, although an obvious problem would be that already overstretched national ministers would simply lack the time to attend such subcommittees regularly. Widening the range of expert committees (instead of just the finance ministry-dominated EWG) that prepare the policy decision may be another option. National differences in how economic policy portfolios are assigned might present a problem, insofar as some countries have relatively limited mandates for the finance minister, possibly with a concentration on public finances, and give greater powers to an economy minister, while for others the finance ministry is the strategic player. Employment or science may be separated or lumped with either economy or economic development. In national administrations the solution is typically for there to be cabinet committees made up of sectoral ministry representatives to prepare decisions for the full cabinet.

A difficult unresolved issue in economic governance in the EU and the euro area alike is how to align incentives so as to cajole Member States into 'responsible' behaviour. Is peer pressure enough and, even if it has been successful in the euro area so far, can it remain successful as the euro area enlarges? A possible answer would be to bolster peer pressure by enabling public pressure also to become a weapon. At a procedural level, the importance of dialogue in different areas deserves to be stressed. If, as is often suggested, fiscal and structural reforms are either facilitated or rewarded by more benign monetary conditions, it can be difficult to achieve when the strong independence of the ECB – sometimes portrayed as being on a pedestal on its own – appears to preclude 'bargaining' across policy areas. Dialogue in this area may therefore be an important tool and fostering bottom-up pressure may be more effective than an over-reliance on top-down mechanisms.

A further political question is whether (or to what degree) additional forms of governance specific to the euro area are necessary in the EU context; this is something that is bound to be contentious, but that also has a growing air of inevitability about it. Possible areas include prudential supervision, developing a distinctive euro-area agenda for structural reform, or initiatives on the exchange rate. The evident sensitivity of the outs to separate formal structures has to be set against the need to reinforce, where appropriate, the governance arrangements for EMU. A credible way to do so would be to experiment within the confines of the Treaty, using some of the enabling clauses (for example in relation to prudential supervision). Longer term, however, the challenges of governing a euro area that becomes more closely integrated as well as having many more members will need institutional deepening that it is difficult to see happening without further Treaty change. The sherpas and negotiators may cringe at the thought, but so be it.

4.2 Rethinking coordination

Further awkward questions – recasting policy coordination for a more diverse euro area – will have to be considered, as the policy mix will often be harder to optimise. National rules in fiscal policy may help to prevent excessive deficits and the still comparatively small economic weight of the new members still not in EMU means that even if fiscal positions do diverge a bit, the overall compatibility with monetary policy will not be greatly undermined. But it is in the links between structural policy and monetary policy (and, to some degree, fiscal policy), that more imaginative solutions are needed. A fairly stark choice is which of rules, political discretion or independent technical oversight offers the most promising solutions. The answer is linked to the maturity and embeddedness of EMU. In the launch phase, rules played an important part in shaping the behaviour of policy actors, but may since have become less effective because they have been undermined.

Eichengreen (2007) has proposed reform of fiscal institutions so as to assure quality of public finances, with a focus on issues such as unfunded pension liabilities, too many publicly owned enterprises with soft budget constraints or fiscal arrangements at subnational level that invite indiscipline. Another solution, which Wyplosz (2005) concedes could be a serious infringement on parliamentary sovereignty, is national fiscal policy councils with mandates on fiscal policy akin to that of monetary policy committees in independent central banks, with the aim of guaranteeing fiscal (that is public debt) sustainability. He answers the sovereignty concern by suggesting that the proposed committee should concern itself only with the budget balance, not its composition. However, Steve Nickell, in his comment on Wyplosz (2006b) is rather dismissive of the idea on the grounds that politicians will refuse to give up such powers.

Concerning fiscal coordination, the guarded conclusion of this chapter is that because there is likely to be an enduring difference between the fast-growing and rapidly restructuring CEECs and the slower-growing core of the euro area, even the revised SGP will be problematic. Yet customised targets will be hard to manage and may undermine fiscal discipline. In these circumstances, looser rules aligned to some variant on a 'sustainability pact', as advocated by Coeuré and Pisani-Ferry (2005), may be the best solution. To contain politically motivated slippage, especially around elections, Wyplosz's proposal for fiscal policy councils may have merit in bridging the gap between political and more technocratic approaches, perhaps complemented by independent forecasting to avoid gimmickry (Jonung and Larch, 2006). To forestall manipulation of fiscal indicators by national authorities, transparency in fiscal indicators could also be enhanced (for suggestions as to how, see Koen and van den Noord, 2006; and Balassone *et al.*, 2006, 2007).

There are even stronger analytic and political reasons for doubting, if not avoiding, a one-size-fits-all policy framework for structural reform.

Member States have to deal with their own, possibly idiosyncratic, reform imperatives, while concentrating at EU level on structural reforms needed to confront common challenges. This dichotomy can never be clear-cut, but there is an evident difference between, say, reforms associated with countering climate change and action to improve the efficacy of a national employment service. Yet in political economy terms, an attraction of an organised process of coordination such as the Lisbon strategy is that it forces Member States to put policies in place.

4.3 Specific proposals

Numerous other proposals have been canvassed, some of which warrant consideration. There have been regular calls for the ECB to adopt full inflation forecast targeting, regarded by many (at least prior to the 2008/9 crisis) as 'best practice' in monetary policy (for a dissenting view, see Buiter, 2006b) instead of the amended two-pillar approach that it has followed since 2003. Pisani-Ferry *et al.* (2008) identify as a particular attraction that the improved transparency of a precise target would enhance credibility and facilitate communication. However, insofar as markets perceive the ECB already to be targeting 2 per cent HICP it is open to question whether the change would make a great difference.

In monetary policy, a significant change in attitudes towards transparency has occurred over the last two decades, to the extent that a communication strategy is seen as a complementary instrument. In the post-2005 Lisbon strategy, ownership has been highlighted as a key governance aim, yet it is evident that success in promoting it has been limited. Nevertheless, the scope for increased transparency to be an instrument of economic policy in the euro area has not been sufficiently explored. It is, for example, suggested that transparency can help to boost the acceptability of fiscal consolidation and that governments which explain any deviation from a rule will also find it easier to secure public support (Guichard *et al.* 2007).

Rainy day funds have been tried in some Member States and may be a way of systematising a degree of fiscal discretion. The principle is very straightforward: governments build up the funds in good times and draw on them in bad times. But provided the funds in question have a neutral fiscal impact over the cycle, the risk of an incompatibility with monetary policy should be low. Indeed a rainy day fund would help to counter the procyclical effects of the SGP. Other ideas include the proposal to have a market for deficits within an overall euro-area ceiling, allowing members to bid for bigger deficits (Casella, 1999, 2001) and even a fully fledged *European Republic* (Collignon, 2003), the essence of which is that a European government should take responsibility for the governance of European collective goods – defined in the widest sense and including macroeconomic management.

4.4 Concluding comment

Debate on the governance of EMU has been extensive, inconclusive and often divisive. As Pisani-Ferry (2006a: 824) puts it, since the days of the Werner report 'advocates and opponents of economic policy coordination have been exchanging arguments in a never-ending controversy'. There is plainly a need for clarity and, ideally, greater simplicity in governance, as the Sapir report (Sapir *et al.* 2004) noted: 'the picture that emerges is one of confusion and tension – confusion created by the complexity of the system and diversity of the roles performed, tension in the gap between goals and means'. Yet it also has to be recognised that the EU and EMU are always going to be subject to complicated and messy political economy processes.

A summary verdict on the governance of EMU might be 'could do better, and will need to be improved to deal with enlargement of the euro area'.

Notes

1. See Baldwin (this volume).
2. See Jappelli and Pagano (this volume).
3. See Pelkmans *et al.* (this volume).
4. A very benevolent view is required to regard Italian debt as having been converging rapidly to the 60 per cent of GDP threshold.
5. These issues were discussed in European Commission (2004c).
6. Pisani-Ferry *et al.* (2008) note, however, that there are multiple facets of stability, including prices, public finances, financial markets, the real economy and what they term 'agility', defined as the ability to cope with shocks or crises, especially in bad times
7. To the extent that the lower EU employment rate means that the least productive of the working age population are not in the workforce, the relatively favourable productivity figures can exaggerate EU performance (see, for example, Bourlès and Cette, 2007).

Comment 15: Comment on Chapters 20 and 21

JEAN PISANI-FERRY

1. Economics strikes back

The enlargement of the euro area is an issue of major economic and political significance that has unfortunately been addressed in an economically flawed and politically hazardous way. Defining when and on the basis of what criteria it is appropriate for the new member states (NMS) to join the euro is a serious challenge for economic analysis. Decades of discussions on exchange rate strategies have taught us that 'no single currency regime is right for all countries or at all times', as Jeff Frankel (1999) put it, and this applies to Europe too. Euro-area enlargement is also delicate politically, as the existence of a currency zone inside the EU de facto perpetuates a sort of divide between old and new Europe.

Instead of recognising the challenge and taking it up, however, the European Union has relied on an overly legalistic approach that gives priority to equality of treatment in a very formal sense and bases decisions on criteria designed for other countries at other times. The chapter by Zsolt Darvas and György Szapáry rightly does the opposite: it puts economics first and starts from an identification of the tradeoffs involved in the choice of an exchange rate strategy for the NMS. This is a much better approach as it tackles the issue on the basis of an explicit recognition of the specific situation of the NMS.

In my discussion, I will focus on three questions:

(a) How should the NMS be characterised?
(b) What are the implications of their situation for the choice of an exchange rate regime?
(c) How should the entry criteria be amended, if amendment is to be considered?

1.1 How should the NMS be characterised?

There are many potential criteria for assessing whether a country is fit to participate in a monetary union. The Maastricht criteria are a

901

particular set, inspired by the will to ensure that the applicant's commitment to price stability is credible and underpinned by a record of budgetary discipline. The five British tests (HM Treasury, 1997) are another set that puts more emphasis on asymmetries and adjustment. In the same vein, economic research has tried to operationalise Mundell's optimum currency area (OCA) criteria and to provide empirical estimates of the appropriateness of EMU membership for all EU members. The question here is, what are the criteria that are relevant from the point of view of the member states recently admitted into the EU?

Darvas and Szapáry recall that by and large the NMS fulfil all the Maastricht criteria, apart from inflation, and that they rank well according to most of the OCA criteria. They list a number of features that make these countries different from the current euro-area members. But their focus is on one undisputable characteristic of the NMS: that they start from a lower price level that is bound to converge as their real income catches up with the rest of the EU. This is both a simple and profound observation that starts from the very fact that the new members of the EU are less developed than the old ones, and the estimates provided suggest that the corresponding effect is large enough for inflation differentials to be significant.

One can obviously argue about technicalities – how much lower prices are in the NMS, what drives the Balassa-Samuelson effect, how fast they can be expected to converge, whether currently inflation is accounted for by catching-up – but the essential hypothesis that underpins the analysis by Darvas and Szapáry is undisputable. Qualitatively at least, the conclusions they draw from it are not model-dependent.

Darvas and Szapáry mention other characterisations of the NMS, especially the low credit-to-GDP ratio and the high share of foreign currency loans in total credit, which they claim may both reduce the effectiveness of monetary policy. Here I have some doubts. The appropriate criterion for deciding on the effectiveness of the monetary policy transmission channels is not the ratio of credit to GDP, but the impact of the interest rate at the margin on the demand for and the supply of credit. The fact that private agents are still not in debt to the same extent as in Western Europe is not necessarily relevant. As to the composition of credit, the share of foreign currency loans is an ambiguous criterion. A high share of foreign currency loans may limit the effectiveness of *domestic* monetary policy, but this is not an argument for not joining the euro. Think of a country where all credit would be denominated in euro. Would this be a reason for *not* joining?

1.2 What implications for the choice of an exchange rate regime?

Darvas and Szapáry claim that if the catching-up of the price level takes place in a fixed exchange rate regime, this is bound to imply higher inflation along the growth path and therefore result in a lower real interest rate that distorts the allocation of capital and involves the risk of booms and busts. Therefore, they argue that countries starting from a very low price level – the least developed ones among the NMS – are especially likely to suffer from microeconomic distortions and macroeconomic instability because along the path to convergence the appreciation of their real exchange rate is bound to be faster initially. In a floating exchange rate regime, instead, price convergence would take the form of a real appreciation of the currency, leaving inflation under the control of national monetary authorities. This is the reason why they should consider delaying the adoption of the euro.

Again, the argument is very strong, because it does not hinge on any particular assumption that could be disputed. Especially, the higher inflation rate along the path to convergence is an equilibrium phenomenon and it can therefore be anticipated, which means without doubt a lower *ex ante* real interest rate. Too low an interest rate is also without doubt a distortion, the implications of which are a misallocation of capital and risks of macroeconomic and financial instability, as illustrated by the recent experiences of Spain and Ireland. This must be regarded as a cost of participating in EMU – and a potentially significant one for the least developed countries. Finally, this cost was until recently mostly ignored in the analyses and policy discussions on EMU, because the participating countries were, by and large, homogenous in terms of development levels.

This leads to two questions, one of which is addressed in the paper and the other somehow overlooked. The question that is addressed is whether other policy instruments such as fiscal, structural and income policies can be relied on in the context of an excessively low real interest rate. Darvas and Szapáry discuss to what extent each can contribute to offsetting the effects of the interest rate, and they come up with a pessimistic conclusion.

I think pessimism is warranted. For sure, there are temporary remedies to an excessive demand for credit or a real estate boom, but as discussed by the authors the remedies either create other distortions or risk proving unsustainable. This is because the real interest rate is a fundamental price that determines intertemporal choices. Regulatory fixes are likely to be in contradiction with the adoption of the EU economic legislation framework and a prolonged fiscal restraint ultimately leading to the disappearance of the public debt is both an imperfect substitute and unsustainable politically. Even the opening of markets for goods and services to foreign competition, which may help to contain inflationary pressures, is unlikely to be a sufficient response. Of course, it helps in strengthening the so-called competitiveness channel and speeding up the response of prices to an excessive real appreciation. But foreign competition cannot be expected to tame higher inflation as inflation is required to deliver convergence of the real exchange rate towards equilibrium. Therefore, it cannot be expected either to avoid the real interest rate being too low, with potential adverse consequences for capital allocation and macroeconomic instability. Furthermore, the competitiveness channel affects sectors differently depending on their exposure to foreign competition and it is therefore unlikely to be sufficient to tame a boom originating in the nontraded goods sector.

The question that is overlooked is what this implies for the choice of would-be members of EMU. The welfare cost involved in the adoption of too low an interest rate must be weighed against the benefits of adopting the euro. The balance between those costs and benefits is unlikely to be the same for larger, relatively closed countries and for small open economies where the competitiveness channel is stronger and for which the transaction cost benefits of participating in a currency union are larger. Therefore, the choice cannot be analysed without discussing its various dimensions. For all countries, also, the implication of the analysis by Darvas and Szapáry is that there is an optimal time of entry that depends on the characteristics of the country.

1.3 How should the entry criteria be amended?

From a policy standpoint, two uncomfortable conclusions can be derived from the chapter by Davras and Szapáry. One is that EMU is not for the poor. The other is that it is difficult to define appropriate criteria for entry as the optimal time for entry is likely to differ from one country to the next. The question is where these observations lead.

Clearly, income per capita cannot be a valid criterion for deciding whether a country is fit for the euro or not. Inflation, however, comes close to being such a criterion because it is higher along the convergence path for a country that starts from a lower GDP per capita level. De facto, then, the criterion used by the EU discriminates against lower-income countries. As observed by Darvas and Szapáry, the way out for these countries is then to repress inflation temporarily – what they call the boxer's 'weighing in' strategy. The situation is therefore one where the EU puts forward a criterion that is ill-suited to the NMS – and where the NMS cheat.

Economic analysis would suggest starting from a recognition of reality. Instead of insisting that EMU is for all provided its criteria are met, the EU should first accept that euro adoption is a matter for national choice; and that on economic grounds, it may make considerable sense for some EU members to postpone it. In discussions with them, the Commission should aim at establishing a fact-based dialogue about the pros and cons of early entry. This may become less difficult now that the potential costs of macroeconomic instability within monetary union have been made apparent by the experiences of Spain and Ireland.

Second, for those who intend to join the euro, the EU should recognise that the inflation criterion is ill-designed and that insistence on fulfilment is bound to create incentives to repress price rises artificially. Because the economic situation of the EU newcomers is different and because the EU itself has changed as a consequence of EMU, to rely on the same criteria that were used in 1998 for the first wave of euro applicants is simply absurd. The problem here is that the EU's insistence, against all economic evidence, on equality of treatment between the new and the old member states epitomises the system's difficulty in adapting and addressing questions as they appear. The proposal by Darvas and Szapáry to redefine the reference value as euro-area HICP plus 1.5 percentage points and to lengthen the observation period is a sensible one. There are other possible variants of such a redefinition which lead to similar results (Pisani-Ferry *et al.*, 2008). Their relative merits must be assessed from a legal standpoint also, in reference to the Treaty.

Third, the implication of the analysis put forward by Darvas and Szapáry is that decisions should be grounded in a broad-based assessment of the benefits and risks of early entry. The approach they follow provides guidelines for what such an assessment should be. The question is how it should be managed procedurally. The answer is in the Treaty, whose Art. 121 puts emphasis on the achievement of a 'high degree of sustainable convergence' and envisages the four Maastricht criteria as mere instruments for assessing this convergence. The EU should recognise that the spirit of the Treaty matters more than the criteria designed for other countries at other times and that it belongs to the Commission and the ECB to report on whether a given country has achieved a high degree of sustainable convergence. This is bound to involve judgement and admittedly risks of arbitrariness, but what Darvas and Szapáry tell us is precisely that economic judgement matters. The answer to the risk of arbitrariness should be sought in the transparency of the procedure and the open character of the discussion.

2. Can EMU evolve?

The chapter by Iain Begg is a comprehensive, competent and balanced account of the governance of EMU culminating in a cautiously optimistic view of the future. As the author does not plead any particular case, the discussant's role is less straightforward than with a paper advocating a controversial proposal. However, Begg clearly has a view on the governance of EMU, a view that may be termed 'evolutionary': instead of asking whether the solutions in place are optimal, he prefers to assess how the governance of the euro area has evolved over the course of a decade and what further developments are possible and/or desirable.

This is a less down-to-earth approach than it seems at first blush. In fact, EMU was not conceived as an evolving construct at all. It was rather designed on the basis of the policy thinking of the 1980s and its principles were then set in stone in the treaties. To claim that this system now needs to evolve therefore raises a host of challenges.

Rather than taking issue with this or that particular idea put forward by Begg, I would like to focus here on the themes that cut across his analysis and discuss the evolutionary view. I will address three issues in particular: first, the relationship between the economics and the politics of the euro; second, the evolution of EMU governance and the underlying model of a monetary union; third, the consequences of the coming enlargement.

2.1 Economics and politics

Jacques Rueff famously claimed in the 1950s that 'Europe will be built on money or will never be built'. Indeed, monetary union was for a long time seen as much more than the mere pooling of national monetary policies. Because the common currency was (first and foremost in Germany but in other countries too) a political project, the corresponding assumption was that it would almost mechanically lead to political union. Even after the Maastricht Treaty negotiations had failed to deliver tangible political results, the expectations remained that further discussion would result in the strengthening of political institutions (see for example Padoa-Schioppa, 2004). Thus, EMU was meant to trigger an evolution – but in the political institutions rather than the economic ones. The politics would catch up with the economics.

The lessons from two decades of negotiation, from Maastricht to Amsterdam, Nice, Rome and Lisbon,[1] is that this is not happening and is not going to happen in the foreseeable future. Political union – at least in its ambitious version – has been tried, and has failed to elicit consensus. Therefore, the euro is no longer a part of a broader and more ambitious project but is a *sui generis* institutional innovation that is not buttressed by other institutions. It cannot even count on the existence of a political community.

This is not the place for discussing the reasons for this failure, but it is worth noting that both France and Germany were in favour of some sort of political union. Alas, they had very different views of it: a federal structure, or at least a federal community, for Germany and an intergovernmental body – the *gouvernement économique* – for France. Neither of these views prevailed and the euro was left without a strong political counterpart.

This is not what the founding fathers had in mind but it does have profound implications. The hypothesis that the euro will have to survive – and possibly prosper – in an environment of low *affectio societatis* and weak Union institutions can no longer be considered pure fantasy. This would imply less drive towards centralisation, a lesser capacity to enforce common disciplines and a lesser ability to cope with the potential political consequences of economic divergence.

This state of affairs would not necessarily be critical. There is nothing in economic theory or in economic history to claim that monetary integration necessarily implies political unification. On the contrary, monetary union without political union was precisely the setup of the gold standard. But there are implications: a probably more decentralised EMU where countries internalise the economic and budgetary disciplines involved in membership of a monetary union and where they take full responsibility for the potential consequences of any inability to abide by those disciplines.

2.2 Which model of EMU?

Begg puts emphasis on the fact that 'EMU has moved a long way in its first decade and that the parameters for governance have consequently evolved'. The observation is undoubtedly correct and the best example of evolution is probably the Stability and Growth Pact (SGP), whose reform in 2005 amounted to a significant change, not in the goals but in the operation of the arrangement. It was in essence an exercise in pragmatic learning by doing. Furthermore, the EMU@10 report by the European Commission (2008a) indicates an evolution in the institution's policy thinking.

   The question then is where the gradual evolution of the governance of EMU is leading to. The strength of the model which EMU was initially based on is that it was simple yet sufficient to encompass the main policy lessons from the 1970s and the 1980s. However, developments over the last ten years have called into question some of its basic assumptions. To take the most important ones:

a) *Price stability and fiscal rectitude are sufficient to ensure overall stability and the smooth operation of EMU.* What we have learned is that they are both necessary, but hardly sufficient. The rise of financial stability as a matter for common concern and the example of countries like Ireland and Spain, whose budgetary record was impeccable but which have nonetheless experienced damaging instability, is a powerful reminder that not all the problems in EMU are budgetary in origin. It is therefore not sufficient for countries to abide by the provisions of the Pact in order to ensure that EMU works properly – as clearly recognised in the European Commission's (2008a) report.

b) *Budgetary discipline is best guaranteed by rules.* In fact, the 2005 reform of the SGP marked a recognition that a quasi-mechanical rule is not sufficient and that preventive action based on economic

assessment is necessary. This amounts to saying either that governments do not behave rationally, or that they are not able to assess
risks properly, or that they expect to be free to bend the rules in their
favour in the event that they find themselves in excessive deficit.
Whatever the interpretation, the focus on prevention implies a
stronger emphasis on analysis and evidence-based recommendations. It is a significant departure from the assumption of the original
model. It amounts to a move from a policy-by-rules model to a
constrained-discretion model.

c) *EMU includes built-in incentives to structural reform, as governments will rationally anticipate that only structural policies can
help improve growth performance.* In the event, it is now widely
accepted that the euro has not had a strong incentive effect on
structural reforms. Since EMU has removed the threat of exchange
crises, it may even have slowed down the pace of reform, which
implies that there is a case for building a stronger incentive framework for the countries taking part in the euro. This is another theme
of the European Commission's (2008a) EMU@10 report but, again,
action implies departing from the initial approach and considering
EMU as an incentive framework for national policies as much as a
system of rules.

2.3 The consequences of enlargement

Begg expresses concern about the ability of the EMU system to adapt to
its possible enlargement to twenty members or more. This is a very
legitimate concern, for two reasons. The first one is a matter of sheer
size. As Begg observes, EMU governance is not based on delegation, as
the governance of other Union policies is. It relies to a large extent on
governance by committees (the Governing Council of the ECB) and on
coordination (the Eurogroup). Such a model is vulnerable to an increase
in size. This is far from being insurmountable, but the choice of a
complex rotation system to solve the problem at the ECB indicates
that first-best solutions are not easy to agree on.

The second issue is a matter of diversity. EMU was not designed to
include countries whose development levels differ significantly. On the
contrary, the choice of deficit and debt thresholds was based on the
assumption that all countries would have roughly similar growth and
inflation rates (an assumption that was already questionable for Ireland

and Spain – precisely the two countries that, thanks in part to low real interest rates, have experienced real estate booms). Here again, whether or not it makes economic sense to join for countries whose initial conditions differ considerably from those of the euro-area members is a matter for case-by-case decision, and there is nothing in principle that indicates they should not make this choice. But enlargement implies a more tailor-made approach to surveillance and therefore an evolution of the EMU system. A third issue, the most pressing one, would be that of the admission criteria for the new candidate countries that I discussed above by reference to Darvas and Szapáry's contribution.

3. Conclusion

So the question of change has become a major one for the euro, which is about to enter its second decade. The issue is whether the EMU system is capable of evolving and of overcoming two sets of constraints on learning by doing: intellectual constraints, stemming from the need to maintain logical consistency in the underlying model; and institutional constraints, as a consequence of the fact that many of the basic tenets of EMU are laid down in precise terms in the Treaty. The experience so far augurs better than might have been feared for the ability of the EMU system to learn on the job. Nevertheless, the challenge going forward should not be underestimated.

Note

1. At the time of writing, the ratification of the Lisbon Treaty was still pending.

References

Abiad, A., D. Leigh and A. Mody (2007), 'International Finance and Income Convergence: Europe is Different', IMF Working Papers, 07/64.

Acedo Montoya, L. and J. de Haan (2008), 'Regional Business Cycle Synchronization in Europe?', *International Economics and Economic Policy*, 5(1): 123–37.

Acemoglu, D. and R. Shimer (1999), 'Efficient Unemployment Insurance', *Journal of Political Economy*, 107: 893–928.

Adam, K., T. Jappelli, A. Menichini, M. Padula and M. Pagano (2002), 'Analyze, Compare, and Apply Alternative Indicators and Monitoring Methodologies to Measure the Evolution of Capital Market Integration in the European Union', Report for the DG Internal Market and Services (European Commission).

Adão, B., I. Correia and P. Teles (2003), 'Gaps and Triangles', *Review of Economic Studies*, 70(4): 699–713.

Adão, B., I. Correia and P. Teles (2005), 'Monetary Policy with Single Instrument Feedback Rules', CEPR Discussion Papers, 4948.

Adão, B., I. Correia and P. Teles (2006), 'On the Relevance of Exchange Rate Regimes for Stabilization Policy', Banco de Portugal Working Papers, 16.

Adjaouté, K. and J.-P. Danthine (2003), 'European Financial Integration and Equity Returns: A Theory-Based Assessment' in V. Gaspar, P. Hartmann and O. Sleijpen (eds.), *The Transformation of the European Financial System*, Frankfurt am Main: European Central Bank.

Afonso, A., W. Ebert, L. Schuknecht and M. Thöne (2005), 'Quality of Public Finances and Growth', ECB Working Papers, 438.

Agell, J. (2002), 'On the Determinants of Labour Market Institutions: Rent Seeking vs. Social Insurance', *German Economic Review*, 3(2): 107–35.

Aghion, P. and P. Howitt (1994), 'Growth and Unemployment', *Review of Economic Studies*, 61: 477–94.

Aghion, P. and P. Howitt (1998), *Endogenous Growth Theory*, Cambridge, MA: MIT Press.

Aghion, P. and P. Howitt (2006), 'Appropriate Growth Policy: A Unifying Framework', *Journal of the European Economic Association*, 4(2–3).

Aghion, P., T. Fally and S. Scarpetta (2007), 'Credit Constraints as a Barrier to the Entry and Post-Entry Growth of Firms', *Economic Policy*, 22(52): 731–79.

Aghion, P., P. Howitt and D. Mayer-Foulkes (2005), 'The Effect of Financial Development on Convergence: Theory and Evidence', *Quarterly Journal of Economics*, **120**(1): 173–222.

Aghion, P., G. M. Angeletos, A. Banerjee and K. B. Manova (2006), 'Volatility and Growth: Credit Constraints and Productivity-Enhancing Investment', NBER Working Papers, 11349.

Aghion, P., P. Bacchetta, R. Rancière and K. Rogoff (2006), 'Exchange Rate Volatility and Productivity Growth: The Role of Financial Development', NBER Working Papers, 12117.

Ahmed A., A. Levin and B. Wilson (2004), 'Recent U.S. Macroeconomic Stability: Good Luck, Good Policies, or Good Practice?', *Review of Economic and Statistics*, **86**(3): 824–32.

Aizenman, J. and J. Lee (2007), 'International Reserves: Precautionary versus Mercantilist Views, Theory and Evidence', *Open Economies Review*, **18**(2): 191–214.

Aizenman, J. and N. Marion (2003), 'The High Demand for International Reserves in the Far East: What's Going On?', *Journal of the Japanese and International Economies*, **17**(3): 370–400.

Alesina A. and Giavazzi F. (eds.) (2010), *Europe and the Euro*, University of Chicago Press for the NBER.

Alesina A., S. Ardagna and V. Galasso (2008), 'The Euro and Structural Reforms', paper prepared for the NBER conference on Europe and the Euro (17–18 October.)

Alesina, A., R. Barro and S. Tenreyro (2002), 'Optimum Currency Areas', NBER Working Papers, 9072.

Alesina, A., O. Blanchard, J. Galí, F. Giavazzi and H. Uhlig (2001), 'Defining a Macroeconomic Framework for the Euro Area', *Monitoring the European Central Bank*, 3, London: CEPR.

Alfaro, L. and A. Charlton (2007), 'International Financial Integration and Entrepreneurship', NBER Working Papers, 13118.

Algan, Y., P. Cahuc and A. Zylberberg (2002), 'Public Employment and Labour Market Performance', *Economic Policy*, **34**: 9–65.

Alho, K. (2003), 'The Impact of Regionalism on Trade in Europe', Discussion Papers, 843 (The Research Institute of the Finnish Economy).

Allen, F. and D. Gale (2000), 'Financial Contagion', *Journal of Political Economy*, **108**(1): 1–33.

Allen, F. and R. Michaely (2003), 'Payout Policy' in G. Constantinides, M. Harris and R. Stulz (eds.), *Handbooks of the Economics of Finance*, North-Holland.

Allington, N., P. Kattuman and F. Waldmann (2005), 'One Market, One Money, One Price?' *International Journal of Central Banking*, **1**(3): 73–115.

Almunia, J. (2007), 'Making EMU Fit for the 21st Century', speech before the Brussels Economic Forum 2007 – "Global Adjustment and EMU", 31 May.

Alogoskoufis, G. and R. Portes (1991), 'International Costs and Benefits from EMU', in 'The Economics of EMU', *European Economy*, Special Issue, 1: 231–45.

Alogoskoufis, G. and R. Portes (1992), 'European Monetary Union and International Currencies in a Tripolar World' in M. Canzoneri, V. Grilli and P. Masson (eds.), *Establishing a Central Bank: Issues in Europe and Lessons from the U.S.*, Cambridge University Press.

Alogoskoufis, G. and R. Portes (1997), 'The Euro, the Dollar, and the International Monetary System', in P. Masson, T. Krueger and B. Turtelboom (eds.), *EMU and the International Monetary System*, Washington, DC: International Monetary Fund.

Altissimo, F., M. Ehrmann and F. Smets (2006), 'Inflation Persistence and Price-Setting Behaviour in the Euro Area: A Summary of IPN Evidence', ECB Occasional Papers, 46.

Altshuler, R. and T. J. Goodspeed (2002), 'Follow the Leader? Evidence on European and U.S. Tax Competition', Rutgers University Department of Economics Working Papers, 200226.

Altshuler, R. and H. Grubert (2005), 'The Three Parties in the Race to the Bottom: Host Governments, Home Governments and Multinational Corporations', *Florida Tax Review*, 7(3).

Álvarez, L. J. and I. Hernando (2006), 'Competition and Price Adjustment in the Euro Area', Banco de España Documentos de Trabajo, 0629.

Alworth, J. S. (1998), 'Taxation and Integrated Financial Markets: The Challenges of Derivatives and Other Financial Innovations', *International Tax and Public Finance*, 5(4): 507–34.

Amable, B. and D. Gatti (2004), 'Labour and Product Market Reforms: A Case for Policy Complementarity', IZA Discussion Papers, 1190.

Amisano G. and C. Giannini (1997), *Topics in Structural VAR Econometrics*, Berlin: Springer-Verlag.

Amtenbrink, F. (2005), 'The Three Pillars of Central Bank Governance: Towards a Model Central Bank Law or a Code of Good Governance', in *International Monetary Fund, Current Developments in Monetary and Financial Law*, volume 4, Washington, DC: IMF Legal Department.

Andersen, T. and J. R. Skaksen (2007), 'Labour Demand, Wage Mark-ups, and Product Market Integration', *Journal of Economics*, 92(2): 103–35.

Andersen, T., B. Holmström, S. Honkapohja, S. Korkman, H. S. Soderstrom and J. Vartiainen (2008), *The Nordic Model Embracing Globalisation and Sharing Risks*, Helsinki: Taloustieto Oy.

Anderson, J. and E. van Wincoop, (2003), 'Gravity with Gravitas: A Solution to the Border Puzzle', *American Economic Review*, 93(1): 170–92.

Anderton, R., B. H. Baltagi, F. Skudelny and N. Sousa (2005), 'Intra- and Extra-Euro Area Import Demand for Manufacturers', ECB Working Papers, 532.

Andrés, J., R. Doménech and A. Fatás (2007), 'The Stabilizing Role of Government Size', Banco de España Documentos de Trabajo, 0710.

Andrews, P. (2002), 'Self-Regulation by Professions – The Approach under EU and US Competition Rules', *European Competition Law Review*, **23**.

Ang, A., G. Bekaert and M. Wei (2008), 'The Term Structure of Real Rates and Expected Inflation', *Journal of Finance*, **63**(2): 797–849.

Angeloni, I. and M. Ehrmann (2003), 'Monetary Transmission in the Euro Area: Early Evidence', *Economic Policy*, **37**.

Angeloni, I., A. Kashyap, B. Mojon and D. Terlizzese (2003), 'Monetary Transmission in the Euro Area: Where Do We Stand?', in I. Angeloni, A. Kashyap and B. Mojon, *Monetary Policy Transmission in the Euro Area*, Cambridge University Press.

Angeloni I., L. Aucremanne, M. Ehrmann, J. Galí, A. Levin and F. Smets (2006), 'New Evidence on Inflation Persistence and Price Stickiness in the Euro Area: Implications for Macro Modeling', *Journal of the European Economic Association*, **4**(2–3): 562–74.

Annett, A. (2006), 'Enforcement and the Stability and Growth Pact: How Fiscal Policy Did and Did Not Change Under Europe's Fiscal Framework', IMF Working Papers, 06/116.

Antras, P. and E. Helpman (2007), 'Contractual Frictions and Global Sourcing', CEPR Discussion Papers, 6033.

Arachi, G. (2001), 'Efficient Tax Competition with Factor Mobility and Trade: A Note', *International Tax and Public Finance*, **8**(2): 171–88.

Arachi, G. (2007), 'Optimal Origin-based Commodity Taxation in a Small Open Economy', *The B.E. Journal of Economic Analysis & Policy*, **7**(1), Article 59.

Arachi, G. and M. D'Antoni (2004), 'Redistribution as Social Insurance and Capital Market Integration', *International Tax and Public Finance*, **11**(4): 531–47.

Armas, A., E. Levy-Yeyati and A. Ize (eds.) (2006), *Financial Dollarization: The Policy Agenda*, New York: Palgrave Macmillan.

Armstrong, H. W., V. N. Balasubramanyam and M. A. Salisu (1996), 'Domestic Savings, Intra-national and Intra-European Union Capital Flows, 1971–1991', *European Economic Review* **40**(6): 1229–35.

Arnone, M., B. Laurens, J.-F. Segalotto and M. Sommer (2007), 'Central Bank Autonomy: Lessons from Global Trends', IMF Working Papers, 07/88.

Arpaia, A. and G. Carone (2004), 'Do Labour Taxes (and their Composition) Affect Wages in the Short and Long Run?', *European Economy – Economic Papers*, 216 (Economic and Financial Affairs DG, European Commission).

Arpaia, A. and G. Mourre (2005), 'Labour Market Institutions and Labour Market Performance: A Survey of the Literature', *European Economy* – Economic Papers, 238 (Economic and Financial Affairs DG, European Commission).

Arpaia, A. and K. Pichelmann (2007), 'Nominal and Real Wage Flexibility in EMU', *European Economy* – Economic Papers, 281 (Economic and Financial Affairs DG, European Commission).

Artis, M. J. (2003), 'Reflections on the Optimal Currency Area (OCA) Criteria in the Light of EMU', *International Journal of Economics*, 8: 297–307.

Artis, M. J. and M. Hoffmann (2007), 'The Home Bias and Capital Income Flows between Countries and Regions', Institute for Empirical Research in Economics Working Papers, 316.

Artis, M. J. and M. Hoffmann (2008a), 'Declining Home Bias and the Increase in International Risk Sharing: Lessons from European Integration' in L. Jonung, C. Walkner and M. Watson (eds.), *Building the Financial Foundations of the Euro: Experiences and Challenges*, London: Routledge.

Artis, M. J. and M. Hoffmann (2008b), 'Financial Globalization, International Business Cycles and Consumption Risk Sharing', *Scandinavian Journal of Economics*, **110**(3): 447–71.

Artis, M. J. and W. Zhang (1997), 'On Identifying the Core of EMU: An Exploration of Some Empirical Criteria', CEPR Discussion Papers, 1689.

Asdrubali, P., P. E. Sørensen and O. Yosha (1996), 'Channels of Interstate Risk Sharing: United States 1963–90', *Quarterly Journal of Economics*, **111**(4): 1081–110.

Athanasoulis S. and E. van Wincoop (1998), 'Risksharing within the United States: What Have Financial Markets and Fiscal Federalism Accomplished?', Federal Reserve Bank of New York Research Papers, 9808.

Auerbach, A. J. (2006), 'The Future of Capital Income Taxation', *Fiscal Studies*, **27**(4): 399–420.

Aviat, A. and N. Coeurdacier (2007), 'The Geography of Trade in Goods and Assets', *Journal of International Economics*, **71**: 22–51.

Ayuso, J. and R. Blanco (2001), 'Has Financial Market Integration Increased during the Nineties?', *Journal of International Financial Markets, Institutions & Money*, **11**(3): 265–87.

Bacchetta, P. and E. van Wincoop (2005), 'A Theory of the Currency Denomination of International Trade', *Journal of International Economics*, **67**(2): 295–319.

Badinger H. (2007), 'Has the EU's Single Market Programme Fostered Competition? Testing for a Decrease in Mark-up Ratios in EU Industries', *Oxford Bulletin of Economics and Statistics*, **69**(4): 497–519.

Baele, L. (2005), 'Volatility Spillover Effects in European Equity Markets', *Journal of Financial and Quantitative Analysis*, 40(2): 373–401.

Baele, L., A. Ferrando, P. Hördahl, E. Krylova and C. Monnet (2004), 'Measuring Financial Integration in the Euro Area', ECB Occasional Papers, 14.

Bagella, M., L. Becchetti and I. Hasan (2004), 'The Anticipated and Concurring Effects of EMU: Exchange Rate Volatility, Institutions and Growth, *Journal of International Money and Finance*, 23(7–8): 1053–80.

Bailey, W. and K.-H. Bae (2003), 'The Latin Monetary Union: Some Evidence on Europe's Failed Common Currency', Cornell University College of Business Administration Working Paper.

Balassone, F., D. Franco and S. Zotteri (2006), 'EMU Fiscal Indicators: A Misleading Compass', *Empirica*, 33: 63–87.

Balassone, F., D. Franco and S. Zotteri (2009) 'The Reliability of EMU Fiscal Indicators: Risks and Safeguards' in M. Larch and J. Nogueira Martins (eds.), *Fiscal Policy Making in the European Union*, London: Routledge, 153–71.

Balboni, F., M. Buti and M. Larch (2007), 'ECB vs Council vs Commission: Monetary and Fiscal Policy in the EMU when Cyclical Conditions Are Uncertain', *European Economy* – Economic Papers, 277 (Economic and Financial Affairs DG, European Commission).

Baldwin, R. (1991), 'On the Microeconomics of the European Monetary Union', *European Economy*, Special Issue, 1 ('The Economics of EMU – Background Studies for *European Economy*, 44: "One Market, One Money"'): 21–35.

Baldwin, R. (2005), 'Heterogeneous Firms and Trade: Testable and Untestable Properties of the Melitz Model', NBER Working Papers, 11471.

Baldwin, R. (2006a), 'The Euro's Trade Effects', ECB Working Papers, 594 (prepared for the ECB workshop 'What Effects Is EMU Having on the Euro Area and Its Member Countries?', Frankfurt am Main, 16 June 2005).

Baldwin, R. (2006b), *In or Out: Does It Matter? An Evidence-based Analysis of the Euro's Trade Effects*, London: CEPR.

Baldwin, R. (2006c), 'Globalisation: The Great Unbundling(s)', report prepared for the Finnish Prime Minister's Office.

Baldwin, R. and D. Taglioni (2004), 'Positive OCA Criteria: Microfoundations for the Rose Effect', COE/RES Discussion Papers, 34.

Baldwin, R. and D. Taglioni (2007), 'Trade Effects of the Euro: A Comparison of Estimators', *Journal of Economic Integration*, 22(4).

Baldwin, R. and C. Wyplosz (2006), *The Economics of European Integration*, 2nd ed., McGraw-Hill.

Baldwin, R., F. Skudelny and D. Taglioni (2005), 'Trade Effects of the Euro: Evidence from Sectoral Data', ECB Working Papers, 446.

Baldwin, R., V. DiNino, L. Fontagné, R. A. De Santis and D. Taglioni (2008), 'Study on the Impact of the Euro on Trade and Foreign Direct Investment', *European Economy* – Economic Papers, 321 (Economic and Financial Affairs DG, European Commission).

Balli, F. and B. E. Sørensen (2006), 'The Impact of the EMU on Channels of Risk Sharing', mimeo, University of Houston.

Balli, F. and B. E. Sørensen (2007), 'The Role of Capital Gains, Capital Income, Transfers, and Savings on Risk Sharing among OECD Members', paper presented at the Southern Economic Association, 76th Annual Conference, Charleston, South Carolina.

Bańbura, M., D. Giannone, and L. Reichlin (2008), 'Large Bayesian VARs', ECB Working Papers, 966 (*Journal of Applied Econometrics*, forthcoming).

Bank for International Settlements (2007), *Triennial Central Bank Survey: Foreign Exchange and Derivative Market Activity in 2007*, Basel: Bank for International Settlements.

Barr, D., F. Breedon and D. Miles (2003), 'Life on the Outside', *Economic Policy*, 18: 573–613.

Barrell, R. (2007), 'Economic Growth in Europe', *National Institute Economic Review*, 199(1): 65–8.

Barrell, R. and N. Pain (1997), 'Foreign Direct Investment, Technological Change and Economic Growth within Europe', *Economic Journal*, 107: 1770–86.

Barrell, R. and N. Pain (1998), 'Real Exchange Rates, Agglomerations and Irreversibilities: Macroeconomic Policy and FDI in EMU', *Oxford Economic Review of Economic Policy*, 14: 152–67.

Barrell, R. and N. Pain (1999), 'Domestic Institutions, Agglomerations and Foreign Direct Investment in Europe', *European Economic Review*, 43: 925–34.

Barrell, R., C. Guillemineau and D. Holland (2007a), 'Decomposing Growth in France, Germany and the UK Using Growth Accounting and Production Function Approaches', *National Institute Economic Review*, 199(1): 99–113.

Barrell, R., I. Liadze and O. Pomerantz (2007b), 'Import Growth and the Impact of Globalisation', NIESR Discussion Paper, 294.

Barrell, R., S. Gottschalk, D. Holland, E. Khoman, I. Liadze and O. Pomerantz (2008a), 'The Impact of EMU on Growth and Employment', *European Economy* – Economic Papers, 318 (Economic and Financial Affairs DG, European Commission).

Barrell, R., E. P. Davis and O. Pomerantz (2008b) 'The Impact of EMU on Real Exchange Rate Volatility of EU Countries', Brunel University Discussion Paper.

Barro, R. J. (1990), 'Government Spending in a Simple Model of Endogenous Growth', *Journal of Political Economy*, **98**: S103–S125.

Barro, R. J. and D. B. Gordon (1983), 'A Positive Theory of Monetary Policy in a Natural Rate Model', *Journal of Political Economy*, **91**(4): 589–610.

Bassanini, A. and R. Duval (2006), 'Employment Patterns in OECD Countries: Reassessing the Role of Policies and Institutions', OECD Social Employment and Migration Working Papers, 35.

Basso, H. S., O. Calvo-Gonzalez and M. Jurgilas (2007), 'Financial Dollarization: The Role of Banks and Interest Rates', ECB Working Papers, 748.

Baye, M. R., R. Gatti, P. Kattuman and J. Morgan (2006), 'Did the Euro Foster Online Price Competition? Evidence from an International Price Comparison Site', *Economic Inquiry*, **44**(2).

Bayoumi, T. and B. Eichengreen (1993), 'Shocking Aspects of European Monetary Integration', in F. Torres and F. Giavazzi (eds.), *Adjustment and Growth in the European Monetary Union*, Cambridge University Press for CEPR.

Bayoumi, T. and B. Eichengreen (1997), 'Ever Closer to Heaven? An Optimum-Currency-Area Index for European Countries', *European Economic Review*, **41**: 761–70.

Bayoumi, T. and P. Masson (1995), 'Fiscal Flows in the United States and Canada: Lessons for Monetary Union in Europe', *European Economic Review*, **39**: 253–74.

Bayoumi, T., D. Laxton and P. Pesenti (2004), 'Benefits and Spillovers of Greater Competition in Europe: A Macroeconomic Assessment', International Finance Discussion Papers (Board of Governors of the Federal Reserve System), 803.

Bean, C. (1998), 'The Interaction of Aggregate Demand Policies and Labour Market Reform', *Swedish Economic Policy Review*, **5**(2): 353–82.

Beaudry, P. and F. Collard (2002), 'Why Has the Employment-Productivity Tradeoff Among Industrialized Countries Been so Strong?', NBER Working Papers, 8754.

Beck, T., R. Levine and N. Loayza (2000a), 'Financial Intermediation and Growth: Causality and Causes', *Journal of Monetary Economics*, **46**(1): 31–47.

Beck, T., R. Levine and N. Loayza (2000b), 'Finance and the Sources of Growth', *Journal of Financial Economics*, **58**(1–2): 261–300.

Becker, S. O. and M. Hoffmann (2006), 'Intra- and International Risk-Sharing in the Short Run and the Long Run', *European Economic Review*, **50**: 777–806.

Beechey, M., B. Johanssen and A. Levin (2007), 'Are Long-run Inflation Expectations Anchored More Firmly in the Euro Area than in the United States?', mimeo, Board of Governors.

Beetsma, R. and H. Jensen (2005), 'Monetary and Fiscal Policy Interactions in a Micro-Founded Model of a Monetary Union', *Journal of International Economics*, **67**: 320–52.

Beetsma, R., M. Giuliodori and F. Klaassen (2008), 'The Effects of Public Spending Shocks on Trade Balances and Budget Deficits in the European Union', *Journal of the European Economic Association – Papers and Proceedings*, **6**(2–3): 414–23.

Begg, D., P. de Grauwe, F. Giavazzi, H. Uhlig and C. Wyplosz (1998), 'The ECB: Safe at Any Speed?', *Monitoring the European Central Bank*, 1, London: CEPR.

Begg, I. (2002), 'Introduction' in I. Begg (ed.), *Europe Government and Money – Running EMU: the Challenges of Policy Co-ordination*, London: The Federal Trust.

Begg, I. (2007), 'Lisbon II, Two Years On: An Assessment of the Partnership for Growth and Jobs', Special CEPS Paper.

Begg, I. (2008) 'Catch-up, the Transition to Full Participation in EMU and Financial Stability' in L. Jonung, C. Walkner and M. Watson (eds.), *Building the Financial Foundations of the Euro: Experiences and Challenges*, London: Routledge.

Begg, I. and A. Larsson (2007), 'Time for Better Governance of EU "Mega-strategies"?' mimeo.

Bekaert, G., C. R. Harvey and C. T. Lundblad (2006), 'Growth Volatility and Equity Market Liberalization', *Journal of International Money and Finance*, **25**(3): 370–403.

Belke, A. and D. Gross (2005), 'Asymmetries in Transatlantic Monetary Policymaking: Does the ECB Follow the Fed?', *Journal of Common Market Studies*, **43**(5): 921–46.

Belke, A. and D. Gross (2007), 'Instability of the Eurozone? On Monetary Policy, House Prices and Labour Market Reforms', IZA Discussion Papers, 2547.

Belke, A., B. Herz and L. Vogel (2006), 'Are Monetary Rules and Reforms Complements or Substitutes? A Panel Analysis for the World versus OECD Countries, ONB Working Papers, 129.

Belke, A., B. Herz and L. Vogel (2007), 'Reforms, Exchange Rates and Monetary Commitment: A Panel Analysis for OECD Countries', *Open Economies Review*, **18**: 369–88.

Bénassy-Quéré, A., L. Fontagné and A. Lahrèche-Révil (2001), 'Exchange-Rate Strategies in the Competition for Attracting Foreign Direct Investment', *Journal of Japanese and International Economies*, **15**: 178–98.

Benati, L. and P. Surico (2008), 'VAR Analysis and the Great Moderation', ECB Working Papers, 866.

Benigno, P. (2004), 'Optimal Monetary Policy in a Currency Area', *Journal of International Economics'*, **63**(2): 293–320.

Benigno, P. and J. D. López-Salido (2006), 'Inflation Persistence and Optimal Monetary Policy in the Euro Area', *Journal of Money, Credit and Banking*, 38: 587–614.

Benigno, P. and M. Woodford (2006), 'Optimal Taxation in an RBC Model: A Linear Quadratic Approach', *Journal of Economic Dynamics and Control*, 30: 1445–89.

Bentolila, S. and G. Saint-Paul (2001), 'Will EMU Increase Eurosclerosis?', in C. Wyplosz (ed.), *The Impact of EMU on Europe and the Developing Countries*, Oxford University Press.

Berg, J., M. Grande and F. P. Mongelli (2005), *Elements of the Euro Area: Integrating Financial Markets*, Aldershot: Ashgate Publishing.

Berger, H. and S. Danninger (2005), 'Labor and Product Market Deregulation: Partial, Sequential or Simultaneous Reform?', IMF Working Papers, 227.

Berger, H. and V. Nitsch (2005), 'Zooming Out: The Trade Effect of the Euro in Historical Perspective', CESifo Working Papers, 1435.

Berger, H., J. de Haan and J. E. Sturm (2006), 'Does Money Matter in the ECB Strategy? – New Evidence Based on ECB Communication', CESifo Working Papers, 1652.

Bergin, P. and G. Corsetti (2005), 'Towards a Theory of Firm Entry and Stabilization Policy', NBER Working Papers, 11821, CEPR Discussion Papers, 5376.

Bergman, M. (1999), 'Do Monetary Unions Make Economic Sense? Evidence from the Scandinavian Currency Union, 1873–1913', *Scandinavian Journal of Economics*, 101: 363–77.

Bergman, M. (2004), 'How Similar are European Business Cycles?', EPRU (University of Copenhagen) Working Papers, 04–13.

Bergman, M., S. Gerlach and L. Jonung (1993), 'The Rise and Fall of the Scandinavian Currency Union, 1873–1920', *European Economic Review*, 37: 507–17.

Bergsten, F. C. (1997), 'The Dollar and the Euro', *Foreign Affairs*, 76(4): 83–95.

Bernadell, C., P. Cardon, J. Coche, F. X. Diebold and S. Manganelli (eds.) (2004), *Risk Management for Central Bank Foreign Reserves*. Frankfurt am Main: ECB.

Bernanke, B. (2003), '"Constrained Discretion" and Monetary Policy', speech before the Money Marketeers of New York University, New York, 3 February.

Bernanke, B. (2004), 'The Great Moderation', remarks at the meetings of the Eastern Economic Association, Washington, DC, 20 February.

Bernoth, K., L. Schuknecht and J. von Hagen (2004), 'Sovereign Risk Premiums in the European Bond Market', ECB Working Papers, 369.

Berthou, A. and L. Fontagné (2008), 'The Euro and the Extensive and Intensive Margins of Trade. Evidence from French Firm Level Data', CEPII Working Papers, 2008–6.

Bertola, G. (1999), 'Microeconomic Perspectives on Aggregate Labour Markets', in O. Ashenfelter and D. Card (eds.), *Handbook of Labour Economics*, vol. 3, Amsterdam: North-Holland: 2985–3028.

Bertola, G. (2000), 'Labor Markets in the European Union', *Ifo-Studien*, **46**(1): 99–122.

Bertola, G. (2004), 'A Pure Theory of Job Security and Labour Income Risk', *Review of Economic Studies*, **71**(1): 43–61.

Bertola, G. (2006), 'Social and Labour Market Policies in a Growing EU', *Swedish Economic Policy Review*, **13**(1): 189–232.

Bertola, G. (2007a), 'Welfare Policy Integration Inconsistencies' in H. Berger and T. Moutos (eds.), *Designing the New European Union*, Amsterdam: Elsevier: 91–120.

Bertola, G. (2007b), 'Finance and Welfare States in Globalising Markets' in C. Kent and J. Lawson (eds.), *The Structure and Resilience of The Financial System*, Sydney: Federal Reserve Bank of Australia: 167–95.

Bertola, G. (2007c), 'Finance and Welfare States in Globalizing Markets', CEPR Discussion Papers, 6480.

Bertola, G. (2008), 'Economic Integration, Growth, Distribution: Does the Euro Make a Difference?' in L. Jonung and J. Kontulainen (eds.), 'Growth and Income Distribution in an Integrated Europe: Does EMU Make a Difference?', *European Economy* – Economic Papers, 325 (Economic and Financial Affairs DG, European Commission).

Bertola, G. and T. Boeri (2002), 'EMU Labour Markets, Two Years On: Microeconomic Tensions and Institutional Evolution' in M. Buti and A. Sapir (eds.), *EMU and Economic Policy in Europe: The Challenge of the Early Years*, Cheltenham: Edward Elgar: 249–80.

Bertola, G. and T. Boeri (2004), 'Product Market Integration, Institutions and the Labour Markets', mimeo.

Bertola, G. and W. Koeniger (2007), 'Consumption Smoothing and Income Redistribution', *European Economic Review*, **51**(8): 1941–58.

Bertola, G. and A. Lo Prete (2008), 'Openness, Financial Markets, and Policies: Cross-Country and Dynamic Patterns', CCPR Discussion Paper, 7048 (forthcoming in *Annales d'Economie et de Statistique*).

Bertola, G., F. D. Blau and L. M. Kahn (2007), 'Labour Market Institutions and Demographic Employment Patterns', *Journal of Population Economics*, **20**: 833–67.

Bertrand, M., A. Schoar and D. Thesmar (2007), 'Banking Deregulation and Industry Structure: Evidence from the French Banking Reforms of 1985', *Journal of Finance*, **62**(2): 597–628.

Bertuch-Samuels, A. and P. Ramlogan (2007), 'The Euro: Ever More Global', *Finance and Development*, **44**(1): 46–9.

Besley, T. and A. Case (1995), 'Does Political Accountability Affect Economic Policy Choices? Evidence From Gubernatorial Limits', *Quarterly Journal of Economics*, **110**(3): 769–98.

Besley, T., R. Griffith and A. Klemm (2001), 'Empirical Evidence on Fiscal Interdependence in OECD Countries', mimeo, Institute for Fiscal Studies.

Besson, E. (2007), *TVA Sociale*, Paris: Secrétariat d'État chargé de la prospective et de l'évalutation des politiques publiques.

Bettendorf, L., J. Gorter and A. van der Horst (2006), 'Who Benefits from Tax Competition in the European Union?', CPB documents, 125, The Hague: CPB (Netherlands Bureau for Economic Policy Analysis).

Beyer, A., V. Gaspar, C. Geberding and O. Issing (2008), 'Opting Out of the Great Inflation: German Monetary Policy After the Break Down of Bretton Woods', NBER Working Papers, 14596, and CFS Working Papers, 2009/01.

Biais, B., F. Declerck, J. Dow, R. Portes and E.-L. von Thadden (2006), *European Corporate Bond Markets: Transparency, Liquidity, Efficiency*, London: CEPR.

Bill, S. (2004), 'The VAT Strategy' (European Commission, Taxation and Customs Union DG).

Bini-Smaghi, L. (2006), 'IMF Governance and the Political Economy of a Consolidated European Seat' in E. M. Truman (ed.), *Reforming the IMF for the 21st Century*, Washington, DC: Peterson Institute.

Bini-Smaghi, L. (2007), 'The Euro as an International Currency: Implications for Exchange-Rate Policy', address to Euro50 Group meeting, Rome, 2–3 July.

Bini-Smaghi, L., T. Padoa-Schioppa and F. Papadia (1993), 'The Policy History of the Maastricht Treaty: the Transition to the Final Stage of EMU', in *The Monetary Future of Europe*, London: CEPR.

Bjørnland, H. C., T. Ekeli, P. M. Geraats and K. Leitemo (2004), 'Norges Bank Watch 2004: An Independent Review of Monetary Policymaking in Norway', *Norges Bank Watch Report 5*, Centre for Monetary Economics.

Blanchard, O. (2006a), 'Adjustment Within the Euro Area. The Difficult Case of Portugal', *Portuguese Economic Journal*, **6**: 1–21.

Blanchard, O. (2006b), 'European Unemployment: the Evolution of Facts and Ideas', *Economic Policy*, **21**(45): 5–59.

Blanchard, O. (2007), 'Current Account Deficits in Rich Countries', IMF Staff Papers, **54**(2): 191–219.

Blanchard, O. and F. Giavazzi (2002), 'Current Account Deficits in the Euro Area: The End of the Feldstein-Horioka Puzzle?', *Brookings Papers on Economic Activity*, **33**(2): 147–86.

Blanchard, O. and F. Giavazzi (2003), 'Macroeconomic Effects of Regulation and Deregulation in Goods and Labour Markets', *Quarterly Journal of Economics*, **118**(3): 189–213.

Blanchard O. and F. Giavazzi (2004), 'Improving the SGP Through Proper Accounting of Public Investment', CEPR Discussion Paper, 4220.

Blanchard, O. and R. Perotti (2002), 'An Empirical Characterization of the Dynamic Effects of Changes in Government Spending and Taxes on Output', *Quarterly Journal of Economics*, **107**(4): 1329–68.

Blanchard, O. and T. Philippon (2004), 'The Quality of Labour Relations and Unemployment', NBER Working Papers, 10590.

Blanchard, O. and D. Quah (1989), 'The Dynamic Effects of Aggregate Demand and Supply Disturbances', *American Economic Review*, **79**(4): 655–73.

Blanchard, O. and J. Simon (2001), 'The Long and Large Decline in U.S. Output Volatility', *Brookings Papers on Economic Activity*, **32**(1): 135–64.

Blanchard O. and L. Summers (1984), 'Perspective on High World Real Interest Rates', *Brookings Papers on Economic Activity*, **2**: 273–334.

Blanchard, O. and J. Wolfers (2000), 'The Role of Shocks and Institutions in the Rise of European Unemployment: The Aggregate Evidence', *Economic Journal*, **110**: C1–C33.

Blanchard, O., F. Giavazzi and F. G. Sá (2005), 'International Investors, the U.S. Current Account, and the Dollar', *Brookings Papers on Economic Activity*, **36**(1): 1–66.

Blanchard, O., R. Dornbusch, J. Drèze, H. Giersch, H. Layard and M. Monti (1986), 'Employment and Growth in Europe: A Two-handed Approach', in O. Blanchard, R. Dornbusch and R. Layard (eds.), *Restoring Europe's Prosperity*, Cambridge, MA: MIT Press.

Blanchflower, D. and A. Oswald (1994), *The Wage Curve*, Cambridge, MA: MIT Press.

Blinder, A. and R. Solow (1974), 'Analytical Foundations of Fiscal Policy' in *The Economics of Public Finance*, Washington, DC: The Brookings Institution.

Blinder, A., M. Ehrmann, M. Fratzscher, J. De Haan and D. Jansen (2008), 'Central Bank Communication and Monetary Policy: A Survey of Theory and Evidence', *Journal of Economic Literature*, **46**(4): 910–45.

Blonigen, B. (2005), 'A Review of the Empirical Literature on FDI Determinants', *Atlantic Economic Journal*, **33**(4): 383–403.

Bloom, N. and J. van Reenen (2007), 'Measuring and Explaining Management Practices Across Firms and Countries', *Quarterly Journal of Economics*, **122**(4): 1351–408.

Bloomfield, A. (1959), *Monetary Policy under the International Gold Standard*, New York: Federal Reserve Bank of New York.

Bobba, M., G. Della Corte and A. Powell (2007), 'On the Determinants of International Currency Choice: Will the Euro Dominate the World?', Inter-American Development Bank Working Papers, 61.

Bodenhorn, H. (2000), *A History of Banking in Ante-Bellum America*, Cambridge University Press.

Bodenhorn, H. (2002), 'Making the Little Guy Pay: Payments-System Networks, Cross-Subsidization, and the Collapse of the Suffolk System', *Journal of Economic History*, **62**: 147–68.

Bodenhorn, H. and H. Rockoff (1992), 'Regional Interest Rates in Antebellum America' in C. Goldin and H. Rockoff (eds.), *Strategic Factors in Nineteenth Century American Economic History*, University of Chicago Press, 159–88.

Boeri, T. (2005a), 'Reforming Labor and Product Markets: Some Lessons from Two Decades of Experiments in Europe', IMF Working Papers, 05/97.

Boeri, T. (2005b), 'Euro Adoption and the Labor Market' in S. Schadler (ed.), *Euro Adoption in Central and Eastern Europe: Opportunities and Challenges*, Washington, DC: IMF.

Boeri, T., M. Castanheira, R. Faini and V. Galasso (eds.) (2006), *Structural Reforms Without Prejudices*, Oxford University Press.

Bonfiglioli, A. (2007), 'Financial Integration, Productivity and Capital Accumulation', Institute for Economic Analysis', UFAE and IAE Working Papers (Unitat de Fonaments de l'Anàlisi Econòmica and Institut d'Anàlisi Econòmica, Barcelona), 680.07.

Bongardt, A. and F. Torres (2007), 'Institutions, Governance and Economic Growth in the EU: Is There a Role for the Lisbon Strategy?', *Intereconomics: Review of European Economic Policy*, **42**(1): 32–42.

Bordo, M. (2002), 'Gold Standard', *The Concise Encyclopaedia of Economics*.

Bordo, M. (2004), 'The United States as a Monetary Union and the Euro: A Historical Perspective', *Cato Journal*, **24**: 163–70.

Bordo, M. (2007), 'The Crisis of 2007: The Same Old Story, Only the Players Have Changed', remarks prepared for the Federal Reserve Bank of Chicago and International Monetary Fund conference; Globalization and Systemic Risk. Chicago, IL, 28 September.

Bordo, M. and T.F. Helbling (2004), 'Have National Business Cycles Become More Synchronized?' in H. Siebert and R. Langhammer (eds.), *Macroeconomic Policies in the World Economy*, Berlin: Springer Verlag.

Bordo, M. and L. Jonung (1997), 'The History of Monetary Regimes Including Monetary Unions – Some Lessons for Sweden and the EMU', *Swedish Economic Policy Review*, **4**(2): 285–358.

Bordo, M. and L. Jonung (2000), *Lessons for EMU from the History of Monetary Unions*, London: Institute of Economic Affairs.

Bordo, M. and L. Jonung (2003), 'The Future of EMU: What Does the History of Monetary Unions Tell Us?' in F. Capie and G. Woods (eds.), *Monetary Unions. Theory, Hystory, Public Choice*, London: Routledge.

Bordo, M. and F. Kydland (1995), 'The Gold Standard as a Rule: An Essay in Exploration', *Explorations in Economic History*, **32**: 423–64.

Bordo, M. and F. Kydland (1999), 'The Gold Standard as a Commitment Mechanism' in M. D. Bordo, *The Gold Standard and Related Regimes: Collected Essays*, Cambridge University Press.

Bordo, M. and H. Rockoff (1996), 'The Gold Standard as a Good Housekeeping Seal of Approval', *Journal of Economic History*, **56**: 389–428.

Bordo, M., C. Goldin and E. N. White (eds.) (1998), *The Defining Moment: The Great Depression and the American Economy in the Twentieth Century*, University of Chicago Press.

Bordo, M., L. Jonung and A. Markiewicz (2007), 'Does the Euro need a Fiscal Union?', mimeo.

Bordo, M., C. Meissner and A. Redish (2005), 'How Original Sin Was Overcome: The Evolution of External Debt Denominated in Domestic Currencies in the United States and the British Dominions, 1800–2000' in B. Eichengreen and R. Hausmann (eds.), *Other People's Money: Debt Denomination and Financial Instability in Emerging Market Economies*, University of Chicago Press, 122–53.

Bourlès, R. and G. Cette (2007), 'Trends in Structural Productivity Levels in the Major Industrialized Countries', *Economics Letters*, **95**: 151–6.

Bovenberg, L., S. Cnossen and R. de Mooij (2003), 'Introduction: Tax Coordination in the European Union', *International Tax and Public Finance*, **10**: 619–24.

Bowles, C., R. Friz, V. Genre, G. Kenny, A. Meyler and T. Rautanen (2007), 'The ECB Survey of Professional Forecasters (SPF): A Review after Eight Years' Experience', ECB Occasional Papers, 59.

Brakman, S., H. Garretsen and C. van Marrewijk (2006), 'Cross-Border Mergers & Acquisitions: The Facts as a Guide for International Economics', CESifo Working Papers, 1823.

Brandt, N., J.-M. Burniaux and R. Duval (2005), 'Assessing the OECD Jobs Strategy: Past Developments and Reforms', OECD Economics Department Working Papers, 429.

Brealey, R. A. and S. C. Myers (2005), 'Investment and Uncertainty in the G7', *Review of World Economics*, **41**(1): 1–32.

Bris, A., Y. Koskinen and M. Nilsson (2006), 'The Real Effects of the Euro: Evidence from Corporate Investments', *Review of Finance*, **10**(1): 1–37.

Broz, J. L. (1999), 'Origins of the Federal Reserve System: International Incentives and the Domestic Free-Rider Problem', *International Organization*, **53**: 39–70.

Brueckner, J. K. (2003), 'Strategic Interaction Among Governments: An Overview of Empirical Studies', *International Regional Science Review*, **26**(2): 175–88.

Brunila, A., M. Buti and D. Franco (eds.) (2001), *The Stability and Growth Pact. The Architecture of Fiscal Policy in EMU*, Basingstoke: Palgrave.

Buiter, W. H. (1999), 'Alice in Euroland', *Journal of Common Market Studies*, **37**(2): 181–209.

Buiter W. H. (2000), 'Optimal Currency Areas: Why Does the Exchange Rate Regime Matter? With an Application to UK Membership in EMU', *Scottish Journal of Political Economy*, **47**(3): 213–50.

Buiter, W. H. (2006a), 'The "Sense and Nonsense" of Maastricht Revisited: What Have We Learned about Stabilization in EMU?' *Journal of Common Market Studies*, **44**(5): 687–710.

Buiter, W. H. (2006b), 'Rethinking Inflation Targeting and Central Bank Independence', background paper for inaugural lecture, London School of Economics and Political Science, 28 October.

Bun, M. J. G. and F. J. G. M. Klaassen (2002), 'Has the Euro Increased Trade?', Tinbergen Institute Discussion Papers, 02-108/2.

Bun, M. J. G. and F. J. G. M. Klaassen (2007), 'The Euro Effect on Trade is not as Large as Commonly Thought', *Oxford Bulletin of Economics and Statistics*, **69**(4): 473–96.

Burnside, C., M. Eichenbaum and J. D. M. Fisher (2004), 'Fiscal Shocks and Their Consequences,' *Journal of Economic Theory*, **115**(1): 89–117.

Burnside, C., M. Eichenbaum and S. Rebelo (2006), 'Government Finance in the Wake of Currency Crises', *Journal of Monetary Economics*, **53**: 401–40.

Burnside, C., M. Eichenbaum and S. Rebelo (2007), 'The Returns to Currency Speculation in Emerging Markets', *American Economic Review*, **96**: 333–8.

Buti, M. (2005), 'Interactions and Coordination between Monetary and Fiscal Policies in EMU: What Are the Issues?' in M. Buti (ed.), *Monetary and Fiscal Policies in EMU*, Cambridge University Press: 1–28.

Buti, M. (2006), 'Will the New Stability and Growth Pact Succeed? An Economic and Political Perspective' in F. Breuss (ed.), *The Stability and Growth Pact: Experiences and Future Aspects*, Wien: Springer Verlag: 155–82.

Buti, M. and L. R. Pench (2004), 'Why Do Large Countries Flout the Stability Pact? And What Can Be Done About It?', *Journal of Common Market Studies*, **42**(5): 1025–32.

Buti, M. and A. Sapir (eds.) (1998), *Economic Policy in EMU – A Study by the European Commission Services*, Oxford University Press.

Buti, M. and A. Sapir (eds.) (2002), *EMU and Economic Policy in Europe*, Cheltenham: Edward Elgar.

Buti, M. and P. Van den Noord (2004), 'Fiscal Discretion and Elections in the Early Years of EMU', *Journal of Common Market Studies*, **42**(4): 737–56.

Buti, M., S. Eijffinger and D. Franco (2008), 'The Stability Pact Pains: A Forward-looking Assessment of the Reform Debate' in R. Neck and J. E. Sturm (eds.), *Sustainability of Public Debt*, Cambridge, MA: MIT Press: 131–60.

Buti, M., J. Nogueira Martins and A. Turrini (2007) 'From Deficits to Debt and Back: Political Incentives under Numerical Fiscal Rules', *CESifo Economic Studies*, **55**(1): 115–52.

Buti, M., W. Röger and A. Turrini (2007), 'Is Lisbon Far from Maastricht? Trade-offs and Complementarities between Fiscal Discipline and Structural Reforms', *CESifo Economic Studies*, **55**(1): 165–96.

Buti, M., C. Martinez-Mongay, K. Sekkat and P. van den Noord (2003), 'Automatic Stabilisers and Market Flexibility in EMU: Is There a Trade-Off?', *CESifo Economic Studies*, **49**(6): 123–40.

Buti, M., A. Turrini, P. van den Noord and P. Biroli (2009), 'Defying the "Junker Curse": Can Reformist Governments Be Re-elected?', *Empirica*, **36**(1): 65–100.

Buti, M., S. Eijffinger and D. Franco (2003), 'Revisiting the Stability and Growth Pact: Grand Design or Internal Adjustment?', *European Economy* – Economic Papers, 180 (Economic and Financial Affairs DG, European Commission).

Butler, M. (2002), 'Tax-Benefit Linkages in Pension Systems: A Note', *Journal of Public Economic Theory*, **4**(3): 405–15.

Byrne, J. P. and E. P. Davis (2005a), 'The Impact of Short- and Long-run Exchange Rate Uncertainty on Investment: A Panel Study of Industrial Countries', *Oxford Bulletin of Economics and Statistics*, **67**(3): 307–29.

Byrne, J. P. and E. P. Davis (2005b), 'Investment and Uncertainty in the G7', *Review of World Economics*, **41**(1): 1–32.

Caballero, R. (2006), 'On the Macroeconomics of Asset Shortages' in A. Beyer and L. Reichlin (eds.), *The Role of Money – Money and Monetary Policy in the Twenty-First Centrury*, Frankfurt am Main: ECB, 272–83.

Caballero, R. J. and A. Krishnamurthy (2004), 'Exchange Rate Volatility and the Credit Channel in Emerging Markets: A Vertical Perspective', NBER Working Papers, 10517.

Caballero, R. J. and A. Krishnamurthy (2006), 'Flight to Quality and Collective Risk Management', NBER Working Papers, 12136.

Caballero, R., E. Farhi and P.-O. Gourinchas (2008), 'An Equilibrium Model of Global "Imbalances" and Low Interest Rates', *American Economic Review*, **98**(1): 358–93.

Calderón, C. A., N. Loayza and L. Serven (2004), 'Greenfield Foreign Direct Investment and Mergers and Acquisitions: Feedback and Macroeconomic Effects', World Bank Policy Research Working Papers, 3192.

Calmfors, L. (1993), 'Lessons from the Macroeconomic Experience of Sweden', *European Journal of Political Economy*, 9(1): 25–72.

Calmfors, L. (1998), 'Macroeconomic Policy, Wage Setting and Employment – What Difference Does the EMU Make?', *Oxford Review of Economic Policy*, 14(3): 125–51.

Calmfors, L. (2001a), 'Unemployment, Labour Market Reform, and Monetary Union', *Journal of Labour Economics*, 19(2): 265–89.

Calmfors, L. (2001b), 'Wages and Wage-Bargaining Institutions in the EMU – A Survey of the Issues', *Empirica*, 28: 325–51.

Calmfors, L. (2001c), 'Macroeconomic Policy Co-ordination in the EU: How Far Should it Go?', *Swedish Economic Policy Review*, 8: 3–14.

Calmfors, L. (2005), *What Remains of the Stability Pact and What Next?*, Stockholm: Swedish Institute for European Policy Studies.

Calmfors, L. and Driffill, E. J. (1988), 'Bargaining Structure, Corporatism and Macroeconomic Performance, *Economic Policy*, 6: 14–47, reprinted in P. N. Junankar (ed.), *The Economics of Unemployment*, vol. III, Edward Elgar.

Calvo, G. (1983), 'Staggered Contracts in a Utility-Maximising Framework', *Journal of Monetary Economics*, 12(3): 383–98.

Campbell, J. and N. G. Mankiw (1989), 'Consumption, Income and Interest Rates: Reinterpreting the Time Series Evidence', *NBER Macroeconomics Annual*, 185–216.

Campbell, J. Y., K. Serfaty de Medeiros and L. Viceira (2007), 'Global Currency Hedging', NBER Working Papers, 13088.

Canzoneri, M. (2007), 'Coordination of Monetary and Fiscal Policies in a Monetary Union: Policy Issues and Analytical Models', *The Manchester School*, 75(1): 21–43.

Canzoneri, M., R. Cumby and B. Diba (2001), 'Is the Price Level Determined by the Needs of Fiscal Solvency?', *American Economic Review*, 91(10): 1221–38.

Cappiello, L., R. Engle and K. Sheppard, (2006), 'Asymmetric Dynamics in the Correlations of Global Equity and Bond Returns', *Journal of Financial Econometrics*, 4(4): 537–72.

Carlin, W. and C. Mayer (2003), 'Finance, Investment and Growth', *Journal of Financial Economics*, 69(1): 191–226.

Carone, G., G. Nicodème and J. H. Schmidt (2007), 'Tax Revenues in the European Union: Recent Trends and Challenges Ahead', *European Economy* – Economic Papers, 280 (Economic and Financial Affairs DG, European Commission).

Carruth, A., A. Dickerson and A. Henley (2000), 'What Do We Know about Investment under Uncertainty?', *Journal of Economic Surveys*, 14(2): 119–53.

Carstensen, K. and R. Colavecchio (2005), 'The ECB Monetary Policy and Its Taylor-type Reaction Function', paper presented on the 6th IWH Workshop in Macroeconometrics, Halle.

Casella, A. (1999), 'Tradable Deficit Permits: Efficient Implementation of the Stability Pact in the European Monetary Union', *Economic Policy*, **14**(29): 323–61.

Casella, A. (2001), 'Tradable Deficit Permits', in A. Brunila, M. Buti and D. Franco, *The Stability and Growth Pact – The Architecture of Fiscal Policy in EMU*, Basingstoke: Palgrave: 394–413.

Caselli, F. and S. Tenreyro (2006), 'Is Poland the Next Spain?' in R. H. Clarida, J. A. Frankel, F. Giavazzi and K. D. West (eds.), *NBER International Seminar on Macroeconomics 2004*, MIT Press, 459–523.

Cassola, N., C. Holthausen and F. Würtz (2008), 'Liquidity Management under Market Turmoil: the 2007/2008 Experience of the ECB', paper presented at the Federal Reserve Bank of Chicago and European Central Bank conference on The Credit Market Turmoil of 2007–2008: Implications for Public Policy.

Cattoir, P. (2006), 'A History of the "Tax Package": The Principle and Issues Underlying the Community Approach', Taxation Papers, 10 (Taxation and Customs Union DG, European Commission).

Cecchetti, S., A. Flores-Lagunes and S. Krause (2006), 'Financial Development, Consumption Smoothing, and the Reduced Volatility of Real Growth', mimeo.

Chakrabarti, R. and B. Scholnick (2002), 'Exchange Rate Regimes and Foreign Direct Investment Flows', *Weltwirtschaftliches Archiv*, **138**(1): 1–21.

Chari, V. V. and P. J. Kehoe (2004), 'On the Desirability of Fiscal Constraints in a Monetary Union', NBER Working Papers, 10232.

Chawla, M., G. Betcherman and A. Banerji, with A. M. Bakilana, C. Feher, M. Mertaugh, M. L. Sanchez Puerta, A. M. Schwartz, L. Sondergaard and A. Burns (2007), *From Red to Gray: The "Third Transition" of Aging Populations in Eastern Europe and the Former Soviet Union*, Washington, DC: World Bank.

Checchi, D., and C. García Peñalosa (2008), 'Labour Market Institutions and Income Inequality', *Economic Policy*, **23**(56): 601–49.

Chen, Z. and P. J. Knez (1995), 'Measurement of Market Integration and Arbitrage', *Review of Financial Studies*, **8**(2): 287–325.

Chinn, M. and J. Frankel (2005), 'The Euro Area and World Interest Rates', Santa Cruz Center for International Economics Working Papers, 1016.

Chinn, M. and J. Frankel (2007), 'Will the Euro Eventually Surpass the Dollar as Leading International Reserve Currency?' in R. Clarida, *G7 Current Account Imbalances: Sustainability and Adjustment*, University of Chicago Press, 285–323.

Chinn, M. and J. Frankel (2008), 'The Euro May Over the Next 15 Years Surpass the Dollar as Leading International Currency', *International Finance*, **11**(1): 49–73.

Chortareas, G., D. Stasavage and G. Sterne (2002), 'Does it Pay to Be Transparent? International Evidence from Central Bank Forecasts', *Federal Reserve Bank of St. Louis Review*, **84**(4): 99–117.

Chortareas, G., D. Stasavage and G. Sterne (2003), 'Does Monetary Policy Transparency Reduce Disinflation Costs?', *The Manchester School*, **71** (5): 521–40.

Christiano, L., M. Eichenbaum and C. Evans (1999), 'Monetary Policy Shocks: What Have We Learnt and to What End?' in J. Taylor and M. Woodford (eds.), *Handbook of Macroeconomics*, IA, Amsterdam: North-Holland.

Christiano, L., M. Eichenbaum, and C. Evans (2005), 'Nominal Rigidities and the Dynamic Effects of a Shock to Monetary Policy', *Journal of Political Economy*, **113**(1): 1.

Christiano, L., R. Motto and M. Rostagno (2008), 'Shocks, Structures or Monetary Policies: The Euro Area and the US after 2001', *Journal of Economic Dynamics and Control*, **32**(8): 2476–506.

Claessens, S., D. Klingebiel and S. Schmukler (2002a), 'Explaining the Migration of Stocks from Exchanges in Emerging Economies to International Centers', CEPR Discussion Papers, 3301.

Claessens, S., D. Klingebiel and S. Schmukler (2002b), 'The Future of Stock Exchanges in Emerging Markets: Evolution and Prospects' in R. E. Litan and R. Herring (eds.), *Brookings-Wharton Papers on Financial Services 2002*, Washington, DC: The Brookings Institution, 167–212.

Clarida, R., J. Galí and M. Gertler (1999), 'The Science of Monetary Policy: A New Keynesian Perspective', *Journal of Economic Literature*, **37**(4): 1661–707.

Clarida, R., J. Galí, M. Gertler (2000), 'Monetary Policy Rules and Macroeconomic Stability: Evidence and Some Theory', *Quarterly Journal of Economics*, **115**(1), 147–80.

Clausing, C. A. (2007), 'Closer Economic Integration and Corporate Tax Systems', paper presented at the conference on tax havens and tax competition, Università Bocconi, Milan, 18–19 June.

Cnossen, S. (2002), 'Tax Policy in the European Union', CESifo Working Papers, 758.

Cobham, D. (2007), 'Euro versus Dollar: Who Goes with Which?', Heriott-Watt University, mimeo.

Cochrane, J. H. (1991), 'A Simple Test of Consumption Insurance', *Journal of Political Economy*, **99**(5): 957–76.

Codirla, C., G. Siourounis and D. Woo (2006), *'The Barclays Capital FX Optimiser: A User's Manual'*, London: Barclays Capital.

Codogno, L. (2008), 'Two Italian Puzzles: Are Productivity Growth and Competitiveness Really so Depressed?' in M. Buti, *Italy in EMU – The Challenges of Adjustment and Growth*, Basingstoke: Palgrave Macmillan, 87–116.

Codogno, L., C. Favero and A. Missale (2003), 'EMU and Government Bond Spreads', *Economic Policy*, **18**(37): 503–32.

Coe, D. and E. Helpman (1995), 'International R&D Spillovers', *European Economic Review*, **39**(5): 859–87.

Coeurdacier, N. and P. Martin (2007), 'The Geography of Asset Trade and the Euro: Insiders and Outsiders', CEPR Discussion Papers, 6032.

Coeurdacier, N., R. A. De Santis and A. Aviat (2008), 'Cross-border Mergers and Acquisitions: Institutional and Financial Forces', presented at the 47th Economic Policy Panel, Ljubljana.

Coeuré, B. and J. Pisani-Ferry (2005), 'Fiscal Policy in EMU: Towards a Sustainability and Growth Pact?' *Oxford Review of Economic Policy*, **21**(4): 598–617.

Coeuré, B. and J. Pisani-Ferry (2007), 'The Governance of the European Union's International Economic Relations: How Many Voices?' in A. Sapir (ed.), *Fragmented Power: Europe and the Global Economy*, Brussels: Bruegel, 21–60.

Coffinet, J. and S. Gouteron (2007), 'Euro Area Market Reactions to the Monetary Developments Press Release', ECB Working Papers, 792.

Cohen, B. J. (1971), *The Future of Sterling as an International Currency*, London: Macmillan.

Cohen, B. J. (2006), 'The Macrofoundations of Monetary Power' in D. M. Andrews (ed.), *International Monetary Power*, Ithaca, NY: Cornell University Press, 31–50.

Cohen, B. J. (2008), 'The Euro in a Global Context: Challenges and Capacities' in K. Dyson, *The Euro at Ten – Europeanization, Power, and Convergence*, Oxford University Press: 37–53.

Cole, H. L. and M. Obstfeld (1991), 'Commodity Trade and International Risk Sharing: How Much Do Financial Markets Matter?', *Journal of Monetary Economics*, **28**: 3–24.

Collignon, S. (2003), *The European Republic: Reflections on the Political Economy of a Future Constitution*, London: Bertelsmann Foundation.

Committee for the Study of Economic and Monetary Union ('Delors Committee') (1989), *Report on Economic and Monetary Union in the European Community*, Luxembourg: OPOCE.

Conway, P. and G. Nicoletti (2006), 'Product Market Regulation in the Non-manufacturing Sectors of the OECD Countries: Measurement and Highlights', OECD Economics Department Working Papers, 530.

Conway, P., V. Janod, and G. Nicoletti (2005), 'Product Market Regulation in OECD Countries: 1998 to 2003', OECD Economics Department Working Papers, 419.

Conway, P., D. de Rosa, G. Nicoletti and F. Steiner (2006), 'Regulation, Competition and Productivity Convergence', OECD Economics Department Working Papers, 509.

Copenhagen Economics (2005), *Market Opening in Network Industries*, report for the European Commission (DG Internal Market).

Corsetti, G. (2006), 'Openness and the Case for Flexible Exchange Rates', *Research and Economics*, **60**: 1–21.

Corsetti, G. (2008), 'New Open Economy Macroeconomics' in S. Durlauf and L. Blume (eds.), *The New Palgrave Dictionary of Economics*, 2nd edition, Palgrave Macmillan.

Corsetti, G. and L. Dedola (2005), 'A Macroeconomic Model of Price Discrimination', *Journal of International Economics*, **67**(1): 129–56.

Corsetti, G. and G. Müller (2006), 'Twin Deficits: Squaring Theory, Evidence and Common Sense', *Economic Policy*, **48**: 597–638.

Corsetti, G. and P. Pesenti (2005a), 'International Dimensions of Optimal Monetary Policy', *Journal of Monetary Economics*, **52**(2): 281–305.

Corsetti, G. and P. Pesenti (2005b), 'The Simple Geometry of Transmission and Stabilization in Closed and Open Economy', CEPR Discussion Papers 5080, forthcoming in R. Clarida and F. Giavazzi (eds.), *International Seminar of Macroeconomics 2007*, University of Chicago Press.

Corsetti, G., L. Dedola and S. Leduc (2007), 'Optimal Monetary Policy and the Source of Local-Currency Price Stability', CEPR Discussion Papers 6557, forthcoming in J. Galí and M. Gertler (eds.), *International Dimensions of Monetary Policy*, University of Chicago Press.

Corsetti, G., P. Martin and P. Pesenti (2005), 'Productivity Spillovers, Terms of Trade and the "Home Market Effect"', CEPR Discussion Papers, 6492.

Crafts, N. (2007), 'Recent European Economic Growth: Why Can't it Be Like the Golden Age?', *National Institute Economic Review*, **199**(1): 69–81.

Crowe, C. and E. E. Meade (2008), 'Central Bank Independence and Transparency: Evolution and Effectiveness', NBER Working Papers, 13003.

Crowley, P. and J. Lee (2003), 'Exchange Rate Volatility and Foreign Investment: International Evidence', *The International Trade Journal*, **17**(3): 227–52.

Crucini, M. (1999), 'On International and National Dimensions of Risk Sharing', *The Review of Economics and Statistics*, **81**(1): 73–84.

Cushman, D. O. (1985), 'Real Exchange Rate Risk, Expectations and the Level of Direct Investment', *Review of Economics and Statistics*, **67**(2): 297–308.

Cushman, D. O. (1988), 'Exchange Rate Uncertainty and Foreign Direct Investment in the United States', *Weltwirtschaftliches Archiv*, **124**(2): 322–36.

Danthine, J. P, and J. Hunt (1994), 'Wage Bargaining Structure, Employment and Economic Integration', *Economic Journal*, **104**: 528–41.

Danthine, J. P., F. Giavazzi, and E. L. von Thadden (2000), 'European Financial Markets after EMU: A First Assessment', CEPR Discussion Papers, 2413.

Danthine, J. P., K. Adjaouté, L. Botazzi, A. Fischer, R. Hamaui, R. Portes and M. Wickens (2001), *EMU Portfolio Adjustment*, London: CEPR.

Darby, J. and J. Mélitz (2007), 'Labour Market Adjustment, Social Spending and the Automatic Stabilizers in the OECD', CEPR Discussion Papers, 6230.

Darby, J., A. Hughes Hallett, J. Ireland and L. Piscatelli (1999), 'The Impact of Exchange Rate Uncertainty on the Level of Investment, *Economic Journal*, **10**(454): 55–67.

Darvas, Z. and G. Szapáry (2008), 'Euro Area Enlargement and Euro Adoption Strategies', *European Economy* – Economic Papers, 304 (Economic and Financial Affairs DG, European Commission).

Darvas, Z., A. K. Rose and G. Szapáry (2005), 'Fiscal Divergence and Business Cycle Synchronization: Irresponsibility is Idiosyncratic', NBER Working Papers, 11580.

Daveri, F. and G. Tabellini (2000), 'Unemployment, Growth and Taxation in Industrial Countries', *Economic Policy*, **15**(30): 47–104.

Davidson J. (1998), 'Structural Relations, Cointegration and Identification: Some Simple Results and Their Application, *Journal of Econometrics*, **87**(1): 87–113.

Davis, L. (1965), 'The Investment Market, 1870–1914: Evolution of a National Market', *Journal of Economic History*, **25**(3): 355–99.

De Cecco, M. (1992), 'European Monetary and Fiscal Cooperation before the First World War', *Rivista di Storia Economica*, **9**: 55–76.

De Grauwe, P. (2002), 'Challenges for Monetary Policy in Euroland', *Journal of Common Market Studies*, **40**(4), 693–718.

De Grauwe, P. (2005), *Economics of Monetary Union*, Oxford University Press.

De Grauwe, P. (2006a), 'On Monetary and Political Union', mimeo, Catholic University of Leuven.

De Grauwe, P. (2006b), 'Flaws in the design of the Eurosystem?' *International Finance*, **9**(1): 137–44.

De Grauwe, P. and F. P. Mongelli (2005), 'Endogeneities of Optimum Currency Areas: What Brings Countries Sharing a Single Currency Closer Together?', ECB Working Papers, 468.

De Grauwe, P. and W. Vanhaverbeke (1993), 'Is Europe an Optimum Currency Area? Evidence from Regional Data' in P. Masson and M. Taylor, *Policy Issues in the Operation of Currency Unions*, Cambridge University Press.

De la Fuente, A. (1997), 'Fiscal Policy and Growth in the OECD', CEPR Discussion Papers, 1755.

De Mooij, R. and G. Nicodème (2008), 'Corporate Tax Policy and Incorporation in the EU', *International Tax and Public Finance*, 15(4): 478–98.

De Nardis, S. and C. Vicarelli (2003a), 'The Impact of Euro on Trade: the (Early) Effect is not so Large', ISAE Working Papers, 31.

De Nardis, S. and C. Vicarelli (2003b), 'Currency Unions and Trade: The Special Case of EMU', *World Review of Economics*, 139(4): 625–49.

De Nardis, S., R. De Santis and C. Vicarelli (2007), 'The Euro's Effect on Trade on a Dynamic Setting', ISAE Working Papers, 80.

De Nicolò, G. and A. Tieman (2006), 'Economic Integration and Financial Stability: A European Perspective', IMF Working Papers, 06/296.

De Santis, R. A. and B. Gérard (2006), 'Financial Integration, International Portfolio Choice and the European Monetary Union', ECB Working Papers, 1593.

De Sousa, J. and J. Lochard (2006), 'Does the Single Currency Affect FDI? A Gravity-like Aproach', mimeo, University of Paris I.

Debrun, X. and J. Pisani-Ferry (2006), 'Economic Reforms in the Euro Area: Is there a Common Agenda?', Bruegel Policy Contribution, 5.

Decressin, J., H. Faruqée and W. Fonteyne (2007), *Integrating Europe's Financial Markets*, Washington, DC: IMF.

Decressin, J., M. Estevão, P. Gerson and C. Klingen (2001), 'Job-Rich Growth in Europe', IMF Country Report, 01/203.

Delbecque, V. and A. Larèche-Révil (2007), 'Do EU Member States Compete on Social Systems?', presented at the June 2007 Euroframe Conference.

della Paolera, G. and A. M. Taylor (1999), 'Economic Recovery from the Argentine Great Depression: Institutions, Expectations, and the Change of Macroeconomic Regime', *Journal of Economic History*, 59(3): 567–99.

Dellas, H. and C. B. Yoo (1991), 'Reserve Currency Preferences for Central Banks: The Case of Korea', *Journal of International Money and Finance*, 10(1): 406–19.

Delors, J. (1989), 'Regional Implications of Economic and Monetary Integration' in Committee for the Study of Economic and Monetary Union ('Delors Committee'), *Report on Economic and Monetary Union in the European Community*, Luxembourg: OPOCE.

Demertzis, M., A. Hughes and O. Rummel (2000), 'Is the European Union a Natural Currency Area, or is it Held Together by Policy Makers?', *Weltwirtschaftliches Archiv*, 136(4): 657–79.

Demirgüc-Kunt, A. and E. Detragiache (1999), 'Financial Liberalization and Financial Fragility' in B. Pleskovic and J. E. Stiglitz (eds)., *Annual World Bank Conference on Development Economics 1998*, Washington, DC: World Bank, 303–31.

Demirgüç-Kunt, A. and R. Levine (eds.) (2001), *Financial Structure and Economic Growth. A Cross-Country Comparison of Banks, Markets and Development*, Cambridge: MIT Press.

Demirgüç-Kunt, A. and V. Maksimovic (1998), 'Law, Finance, and Firm Growth', *Journal of Finance*, **53**(6): 2107–37.

Deroose, S., S. Langedijk and W. Röger (2004), 'Reviewing Adjustment Dynamics in EMU: from Overheating to Overcooling', *European Economy* – Economic Papers, 198 (Economic and Financial Affairs DG, European Commission).

Deroose, S., M. Larch and A. Schaechter (2008), 'Constricted, Lame and Pro-cyclical? Fiscal Policy in the Euro Area Revisited, *European Economy* – Economic Papers, 353 (Economic and Financial Affairs DG, European Commission).

Desai, M. A. and J. R. Hines Jr. (2005), 'Value-Added Taxes and International Trade: The Evidence', mimeo, University of Michigan.

Dessy, O. (2004), 'Nominal Wage Flexibility and Institutions: Preliminary Micro-evidence from the Europanel', Departmental Working Papers (Department of Economics, University of Milan), 17.

Detken, C. and P. Hartmann (2000), 'The Euro and International Capital Markets', *International Finance*, **3**(1): 53–94.

Detken, C. and P. Hartmann (2002), 'Features of the Euro's Role in International Financial Markets', *Economic Policy*, **35**(2): 555–97.

Devereux, M. B. and C. Engel (2003), 'Monetary Policy in the Open Economy Revisited: Price Setting and Exchange Rate Flexibility', *Review of Economic Studies*, **70**(4): 765–83.

Devereux, M. B., R. Griffith and A. Klemm (2002), 'Corporate Income Tax Reforms and International Tax Competition', *Economic Policy*, **17**(35): 449–95.

Devereux, M. B., B. Lockwood and M. Redoano (2008), 'Do Countries Compete Over Corporate Tax Rates?, *Journal of Public Economics*, **92**(5–6): 1210–35.

Dew-Becker, I. and R. J. Gordon, (2008), 'The Role of Labor Market Changes in the Slowdown of European Productivity Growth', CEPR Discussion Papers, 6722.

Dhyne, E., L. Álvarez, H. Le Bihan, G. Veronese, D. Dias, J. Hoffmann, N. Jonker, P. Lunemman, F. Rumler and J. Vilmunen (2005), 'Price Setting in the Euro Area: Some Stylized Facts from Individual Consumer Price Data', ECB Working Papers, 524.

Dierx, A., F. Ilzkovitz and J. H. Schmidt (2007), 'Competition, Regulatory Cost and Economic Growth' in A. M. Mateus and T. Moreira (eds.), *Competition Law and Economics: Advances in Competition Policy and Antitrust Enforcement*, Kluwer: 163–89.

Dierx, A., F. Ilzkovitz and K. Sekkat (2004a), 'Product Market Integration in the EU: An Overview', in A. Dierx, F. Ilzkovitz and K. Sekkat (eds), *European Integration and the Functioning of Product Markets*, Cheltenham: Edward Elgar: 1–16.

Dierx, A., K. Pichelmann and W. Röger (2004b), 'Product Market Reforms and Macroeconomic Performance in the European Union', in A. Dierx, F. Ilzkovitz and K. Sekkat (eds.), *European Integration and the Functioning of Product Markets*, Cheltenham: Edward Elgar.

Dincer, N. N. and B. Eichengreen (2007), 'Central Bank Transparency: Where, Why, and With What Effects?', NBER Working Papers, 13003.

Disney, R. (2004), 'Are Contributions to Public Pension Programmes a Tax on Employment?', *Economic Policy*, **19**(39): 267–311.

Dixit, A. and L. Lambertini (2001), 'Monetary-Fiscal Policy Interactions and Commitment versus Discretion in a Monetary Union', *European Economic Review*, **45**(4–6): 977–87.

Dixit, A. K. and R. S. Pindyck (1994), *Investment under Uncertainty*, Princeton University Press.

Djankov, S., C. McLiesh and A. Shleifer (2007), 'Private Credit in 129 Countries', *Journal of Financial Economics*, **84**(2): 299–329.

Djankov, S., R. La Porta, F. Lopez-de-Silanes and A. Shleifer (2003), 'Courts', *Quarterly Journal of Economics*, **118**(2): 453–517.

Dominguez, K. (2006), 'The European Central Bank, the Euro, and Global Financial Markets', *Journal of Economic Perspectives*, **20**(4): 67–88.

Donnenfeld S. and A. Haug (2003), 'Currency Invoicing in International Trade: An Empirical Investigation', *Review of International Economics*, **11**(2): 332–45.

Dooley, M. P., D. Folkerts-Landau and P. M. Garber (2003), 'An Essay on the Revived Bretton Woods System', NBER Working Papers, 9971.

Dooley, M. P., F. Folkerts-Landau and P. M. Garber (2005), 'Interest Rates, Exchange Rates and International Adjustment', NBER Working Papers, 11711.

Dooley, M. P., S. Lizondo and D. Mathieson (1989), 'The Currency Composition of Foreign Exchange Reserves', *IMF Staff Papers*, **36**(2): 385–434.

Dornbusch, R. (1992), 'Monetary Problems of Post-Communism: Lessons from the End of the Austro-Hungarian Empire', *Weltwirtschaftliches Archiv*, **128**: 391–424.

Dornbusch, R., C. Favero and F. Giavazzi (1998), 'Immediate Challenges for the European Central Bank', *Economic Policy*, **13**(26): 15–64.

Duarte, M. and M. Obstfeld (2008), 'Monetary Policy in Open Economy Revisited: The Case for Exchange-Rate Flexibility Restored', *Journal of International Money and Finance*, **27**(6), 949–57.

Dullien, S. (2007), 'Improving Economic Stability in Europe: What the Euro Area Can Learn from the United States' Unemployment Insurance', SWP Discussion Papers, FG 1 2007/11 (Stiftung Wissenschaft und Politik).

Dunne, P., M. Moore and R. Portes (2006), *European Government Bond Markets: Transparency, Liquidity, Efficiency*, London: CEPR.

Dunning, J. (1997), 'The European Internal Market Programme and Inbound Foreign Direct Investment', *Journal of Common Market Studies*, 35(1): 1–30.

Durbin, J. (1954), 'Errors in Variables', *Review of International Statistics Institute*, **22**: 23–32.

Duval, R. (2006), 'Fiscal Positions, Fiscal Adjustment and Structural Reforms in Labour and Product Markets' in S. Deroose, E. Flores and A. Turrini (eds.), 'The Budgetary Implications of Structural Reforms', *European Economy* – Economic Papers, 248: 169–206.

Duval, R. and J. Elmeskov (2006), 'The Effects of EMU on Structural Reforms in Labour and Product Markets', ECB Working Papers, 596.

Duval, R., J. Elmeskov and L. Vogel (2007), 'Structural Policies and Economic Resilience to Shocks', OECD Economics Department Working Papers, 567.

Dwane, C., P. Lane and T. McIndoe (2006), 'Currency Unions and Irish External Trade', IIIS Discussion Papers, 189 (Institute for International Integration Studies, Dublin).

Dwyer, G. and J. Lothian (2003), 'The Economics of International Monies', Federal Reserve Bank of Atlanta Working Papers, 2003–37.

Dyson, K. (ed.) (2008), *The Euro at Ten – Europeanization, Power and Convergence*, Oxford University Press.

Edelberg, W. and D. Marshall (1996), 'Monetary Policy Shocks and Long-term Interest Rates', *Economic Perspectives* (Federal Reserve Bank of Chicago), **20**: 2–17.

Edelberg, W., M. Eichenbaum and J. D. M. Fisher (1999), 'Understanding the Effects of a Shock to Government Purchases', *Review of Economics Dynamics*, **2**(1): 166–206.

Ederveen, J., G. Gelauff and J. Pelkmans (2008), 'Assessing Subsidiarity' in G. Gelauff, I. Grilo and A. Lejour (eds.), *Subsidiarity and Economic Reform in Europe*, Berlin and Heidelberg: Springer.

Égert, B. (2007), 'Real Convergence, Price Level Convergence and Inflation Differentials in Europe', CESifo Working Papers, 2127.

Égert, B. and D. Mihaljek (2007), 'Determinants of House Prices in Central and Eastern Europe', BIS Working Papers, 236 (Bank of International Settlements).

Égert, B., P. Backé and T. Zumer (2006), 'Private Sector Credit in Central and Easter Europe: New (Over) Shooting Stars?', *Comparative Economic Studies*, **49**: 201–31.

Ehrmann, M. and M. Fratzscher (2007a), 'Communication and Decision-Making by Central Bank Committees: Different Strategies, Same Effectiveness?', *Journal of Money, Credit and Banking*, **39**(2–3): 509–41.

Ehrmann, M. and M. Fratzscher (2007b), 'Explaining Monetary Policy in Press Conferences', ECB Working Papers, 767.

Ehrmann, M., M. Fratzscher, R. S. Gürkaynak, and E. T. Swanson (2007), 'Convergence and Anchoring of Yield Curves in the Euro Area', ECB Working Papers, 817.

Eichengreen, B. (1984), 'Mortgage Interest Rates in the Populist Era', *American Economic Review*, **74**(5): 995–1015.

Eichengreen, B. (1985), 'Conducting the International Orchestra: Bank of England Leadership under the Classical Gold Standard', *Journal of International Money and Finance*, **6**: 5–29.

Eichengreen, B. (1989), 'Hegemonic Stability Theories of the International Monetary System', NBER Working Papers, 2193.

Eichengreen, B. (1991), 'Is Europe an Optimum Currency Area?', NBER Working Papers, 3579.

Eichengreen, B. (1992), 'Designing a Central Bank for Europe: A Cautionary Tale from the Early Years of the Federal Reserve System' in M. Canzoneri, V. Grilli and P. Masson (eds.), *Establishing a Central Bank: Issues in Europe and Lessons from the U.S.*, Cambridge University Press, 13–40.

Eichengreen, B. (1993). 'Labor Markets and European Monetary Unification' in P. Masson and M. Taylor (eds.), *Policy Issues in the Design of Currency Unions*, Cambridge University Press.

Eichengreen, B. (1996), *Globalizing Capital: A History of the International Monetary System*, Princeton University Press.

Eichengreen, B. (1997a), 'One Money for Europe?' in B. Eichengreen, *European Monetary Unification: Theory, Practice, and Analysis*, Cambridge, MA: MIT Press.

Eichengreen, B. (1997b), 'Is Europe an Optimum Currency Area?' in B. Eichengreen, *European Monetary Unification: Theory, Practice, and Analysis*, Cambridge, MA: MIT Press.

Eichengreen, B. (1998), 'The Euro as a Reserve Currency', *Journal of the Japanese and International Economies*, **12**(4): 483–506.

Eichengreen, B. (2005), 'Sterling's Past, Dollar's Future: Historical Perspectives on Reserve Currency Competition', NBER Working Papers, 11336.

Eichengreen, B. (2007), 'The Break-up of the Euro Area', NBER Working Papers, 13393.

Eichengreen, B. and D. Mathieson (2000), 'The Currency Composition of Foreign Exchange Reserves: Retrospect and Prospect', IMF Working Papers, 131–2000.

Eijffinger, S. C. and P. M. Geraats (2006), 'How Transparent Are Central Banks?', *European Journal of Political Economy*, **22**(1): 1–21.

Einaudi, L. (2001), *Money and Politics: European Monetary Unification and the International Gold Standard (1865–1873)*, Oxford and New York: Oxford University Press.

Ejsing, J., J. A. García and T. Werner (2007), 'The Term Structure of Euro Area Break-Even Inflation Rates: The Impact of Seasonality', ECB Working Papers, 830.

Ekinci, M., S. Kalemli-Ozcan and B. Sørensen (2007), 'Financial Integration within EU Countries: The Role of Institutions, Confidence and Trust', NBER Working Papers 13440, forthcoming in R. Clarida, J. Frankel, F. Giavazzi and K. West (eds.), *NBER International Seminar on Macroeconomics*, Cambridge, MA: MIT Press.

Elmeskov, J., J. P. Martin and S. Scarpetta (1998), 'Key Lessons for Labour Market Reforms: Evidence from OECD Countries' Experiences', *Swedish Economic Policy Review*, **5**: 205–52.

Emerson, M., D. Gros, A. Italianer, J. Pisani-Ferry and H. Reichenbach (1992), *One Market, One Money: An Evaluation of the Potential Benefits and Costs of Forming an Economic and Monetary Union*, Oxford University Press, initially published in 1990 at *European Economy*, 44.

Engel, C. (2002), 'Currency Unions and International Integration', *Journal of Money, Credit, and Banking*, **34**(4): 1067–89.

Engel, C. and J. Rogers (2004), 'European Product Market Integration After the Euro', *Economic Policy*, **19**(39): 347–84.

Erceg, C., D. Henderson, and A. Levin (2000), 'Optimal Monetary Policy with Staggered Wage and Price Contracts', *Journal of Monetary Economics*, **46**(2): 281–313.

Erceg, C., L. Guerrieri and C. Gust (2006), 'Sigma: a New Open Economy Model for Policy Analysis', *International Journal of Central Banking*, **2**: 1–50.

Ernst, E., G. Gong and W. Semmler (2007), 'Resilience, Consumption Smoothing and Structural Reforms', paper prepared for the OECD Workshop 'Structural reforms and economic resilience: evidence and policy implications', Paris, 14 June.

European Central Bank (1998a), 'The Quantitative Reference Value for Monetary Growth', Press Release, 1 December.

European Central Bank (1998b), 'A Stability-Oriented Monetary Policy Strategy for the ESCB', Press Release, 13 October.

European Central Bank (1999), 'The Stability-Oriented Monetary Policy Strategy', *ECB Monthly Bulletin*, January: 39–50.

European Central Bank (2001), *Review of the International Role of the Euro*, Frankfurt am Main: ECB.

European Central Bank (2002), *Review of the International Role of the Euro*, Frankfurt am Main: ECB.

European Central Bank (2003a), 'The ECB's Monetary Policy Strategy' and 'Press Seminar on "The evaluation of the ECB's monetary policy strategy"', Press Releases, 8 May.

European Central Bank (2003b), 'The Outcome of the ECB's Evaluation of its Monetary Policy Strategy', *ECB Monthly Bulletin* (June): 79–92.

European Central Bank (2004a), *The Monetary Policy of the ECB*, Frankfurt am Main: ECB.

European Central Bank (2004b), *TARGET – Annual Report*, Frankfurt am Main: ECB.

European Central Bank (2005), *Review of the International Role of the Euro*, Frankfurt am Main: ECB.

European Central Bank (2008d), *Statistics Pocket Book*, Frankfurt am Main: ECB.

European Central Bank (2006a), 'The EU Arrangements for Financial Crisis Management', *Financial Stability Review* (December): 165–74.

European Central Bank (2006b), 'Measures of Inflation Expectations in the Euro Area', *ECB Monthly Bulletin* (July): 59–68.

European Central Bank (2007a), *Review of the International Role of the Euro*. Frankfurt am Main: ECB.

European Central Bank (2007b), *Financial Integration in Europe*, Frankfurt am Main: ECB.

European Central Bank (2008a), *Financial Integration in Europe*, Frankfurt am Main: ECB.

European Central Bank (2008b), *Review of the International Role of the Euro*, Frankfurt am Main: ECB.

European Central Bank (2008c), '10th Anniversary of the ECB', special edition of the ECB Monthly Bulletin (May), Frankfurt am Main: ECB.

European Central Bank (2009), *The Euro at Ten: Lessons and Challenges*, 5th ECB Central Banking Conference, Frankfurt am Main: ECB.

European Commission (1962), 'Memorandum de la Commission sur le Programme d'Action de la Communauté pendant la Deuxième Étape' (Marjolin Memorandum), 24 October.

European Commission (1977a), 'Report of the Study Group on the Role of Public Finance in European Integration', Vol. I, *Studies: Economic and Financial Series*, A13, Brussels.

European Commission (1977b), 'Report of the Study Group on the Role of Public Finance in European Integration', Vol. II, *Studies: Economic and Financial Series*, B13, Brussels.

European Commission (1990), 'One Market, One Money: An Evaluation of the Potential Benefits and Costs of Forming an Economic and Monetary Union', *European Economy*, 44, reprinted as Emerson *et al.* (1992).

European Commission (1999), 'Financial Services: Implementing the Framework for Financial Services: Action Plan', COM(1999)232, Brussels.

European Commission (2000), 'Public Finances in EMU – 2000', *European Economy*, 3.

European Commission (2002), 'Public Finances in EMU – 2002', *European Economy*, 3.

European Commission (2004a), 'EMU after Five Years', *European Economy*, Special Report 1: 1–260.

European Commission (2004b), 'Financial Integration Monitor – 2004', SEC (2004)559, Brussels and subsequent issues.

European Commission (2004c), 'Ongoing Issues in Economic Surveillance' Chapter 7, *The EU Economy 2004 Review*, Luxembourg: OPOCE.

European Commission (2004d), 'Report on Competition in Professional Services', Communication, COM(2004)83.

European Commission (2005), 'Public Finances in the EMU – 2005', *European Economy*, 3.

European Commission (2006a), 'The EU Economy 2006 Review – Adjustment Dynamics in the Euro Area: Experiences and Challenges', *European Economy*, 6.

European Commission (2006b), 'Public Finances in the EMU – 2006', *European Economy*, 3.

European Commission (2007a), *Quarterly Report on the Euro Area*, 6(4).

European Commission (2007b), 'Evaluation of the Performance of Network Industries Providing Services of General Economic Interests', *European Economy*, 1.

European Commission (2007c), 'Moving Europe's Productivity Frontier – The EU Economy: 2007 Review', *European Economy*, 8.

European Commission (2007d), 'Spillovers and Complementarities in the Context of the Lisbon Growth and Jobs Strategy Including Economic Effects of the Community Lisbon Programme', Staff Working Document, SEC(2007)1689.

European Commission (2007e), 'Guiding Principles for Product Market and Sector Monitoring', *European Economy* – Occasional Papers, 34 (Economic and Financial Affairs DG, European Commission).

European Commission (2007f), 'A Single Market for 21st Century Europe', Commission Communication, COM(2007)724.

European Commission (2007g), 'Labour Market Reforms in the Euro Area', *Quarterly Report on the Euro Area*, **IV**: 29–33.

European Commission (2007h), 'Labour Market and Wage Developments in 2006, with Special Focus on Relative Unit Labour Cost Developments in the Euro Area', *European Economy*, **4**.

European Commission (2007i), 'European Competitiveness Report 2006', Staff Working Document, SEC(2006)1467 (Enterprise and Industry DG).

European Commission (2007j), 'Annual Report on the Euro Area – 2007', *European Economy*, **5**.

European Commission (2007k), 'Implementing the New Methodology for Product Market and Sector Monitoring: Results of a First Sector Screening', Commission Staff Working Document, SEC(2007)1517.

European Commission (2008a), 'EMU@10 – Successes and Challenges of 10 Years of EMU', *European Economy*, **2**.

European Commission (2008b), 'Financial Services Provision and Prevention of Financial Exclusion', report for DG Employment, Social Affairs and Equal Opportunities (European Commission) by L. Anderloni, B. Bayot, P. Błędowski, M. Iwanicz-Drozdowska and E. Kempson.

European Commission (2008c), 'Recent Labour Market Reforms in the Euro Area: Characteristics and Estimated Impact', *Quarterly Report on the Euro Area*, **I**: 18–23.

European Commission (2008d), 'The LIME Assessment Framework (LAF): A Methodological Tool to Compare, in the Context of the Lisbon Strategy, the Performance of EU Member States in Terms of GDP and in Terms of Twenty Policy Areas Affecting Growth', *European Economy* – Occasional Papers, **41**.

European Commission (2009a), 'Recent Reforms of the Tax and Benefit Systems in the Framework of Flexicurity', *European Economy* – Occasional Papers, **43**.

European Commission (2009b), 'Product Market Review 2009', *European Economy*, (forthcoming).

European Commission and Economic Policy Committee (EPC) (2008), 'The 2009 Ageing Report: Underlying Assumptions and Projection Methodologies for the EU-27 Member States (2007–2060)', *European Economy*, **7**.

European Economic Advisory Group (2008), *Europe in a Globalised World – The EEAG Report on the European Economy – 2008*, CESifo.

European Parliament (2008), 'Principles and General Completion of the Internal Market', European Parliament Fact Sheets, 3.1.0.

Eurostat (2007), *Taxation Trends in the European Union – Data for the EU Member States and Norway*, Luxembourg.

Evans, C. L. and D. A. Marshall (1998), 'Monetary Policy and the Term Structure of Nominal Interest Rates: Evidence and Theory', *Carnegie-Rochester Conference Series on Public Policy*, **49**: 53–111.

Evers, M. P. (2006), 'Federal Fiscal Transfers in Monetary Unions: A NOEM Approach', *International Tax and Public Finance*, **13**(4): 463–88.

Fabiani, S., C. Loupias, F. Martins and R. Sabbatini (2007), *Pricing Decisions in the Euro Area – How Firms Set Prices and Why*, Oxford University Press.

Fagan, G., J. Henry and R. Mestre (2001), 'An Area Wide Model (AWM) for the Euro Area', ECB Working Papers, 42.

Fagan, G., F. P. Mongelli and J. Morgan (2003), *Institutions and Wage Formation in the New Europe*, Cheltenham: Edward Elgar.

Fatás, A. (1998), 'Does EMU Need a Fiscal Federation?', *Economic Policy*, **13**(26): 163–203.

Fatás, A. and I. Mihov (2001a), 'Government Size and Automatic Stabilizers: International and Intranational Evidence', *Journal of International Economics* **55**(1): 3–28.

Fatás, A. and I. Mihov (2001b), 'Fiscal Policy and Business Cycles: An Empirical Investigation', *Moneda y Credito*, **212**: 167–210.

Fatás, A. and I. Mihov (2003), 'The Case for Restricting Fiscal Policy Discretion', *Quarterly Journal of Economics*, **118**(4), 1419–47.

Fatás, A. and A. Rose (2001), 'Do Monetary Handcuffs Restrain Leviathan? Fiscal Policy in Extreme Exchange Rate Regimes', CEPR Discussion Papers, 2692.

Faure, M., J. Finsieger, J. Siegers and R. van den Bergh (1993), *Regulation of Professions*, Antwerpen: Maklu.

Faust, J. (1996), 'Whom Can We Trust to Run the Fed?' *Journal of Monetary Economics*, **37**(2): 267–83.

Favero, C. and F. Giavazzi (2007), 'Debt and the Effects of Fiscal Policy', CEPR Discussion Papers, 6092.

Favero, C., F. Giavazzi and L. Spaventa (1998), 'High Yields: The Spread on German Interest Rates', NBER Working Papers, 5408.

Feld, L. P. (2000), 'Tax Competition and Income Redistribution: An Empirical Analysis for Switzerland', *Public Choice*, **105**(1): 125–64.

Feldstein, M. (1997a), 'The Political Economy of the European Economic and Monetary Union: Political Sources of an Economic Liability', *Journal of Economic Perspectives*, **11**(4): 23–42.

Feldstein, M. (1997b), 'EMU and International Conflict', *Foreign Affairs*, **76**(6): 60–73.

Feldstein, M. (1999), 'Self-protection for Emerging Market Economies', NBER Working Papers, 6907.

Feldstein, M. (2005), 'The Euro and the Stability Pact', NBER Working Papers, 11249.

Feldstein, M. (2009), 'Reflections on Americans' Views of the Euro Ex Ante', NBER Working Papers, 14696.

Feldstein, M. and C. Y. Horioka (1980), 'Domestic Savings and International Capital Flows', *Economic Journal*, 90(358): 314–29.

Ferguson, N. and M. Schularick (2006), 'The Empire Effect: The Determinants of Country Risk in the First Age of Globalization, 1880–1913', *Journal of Economic History*, 66(2): 288–312.

Ferguson, N. and M. Schularick (2008), 'The "Thin Film Of Gold": Monetary Rules and Policy Credibility in Developing Countries', NBER Working Papers, 13918.

Ferguson, R. W., P. Hartmann, F. Panetta and R. Portes (2007), *International Financial Stability*, London: CEPR.

Ferrando, A., L. Baele, P. Hördahl, E. Krylova and C. Monnet (2004), 'Measuring Financial Integration in the Euro Area', ECB Occasional Papers, 14.

Ferrero, A. (2007), 'Fiscal and Monetary Rules for a Currency Union', ECB Working Papers, 502.

Fidora, M., M. Fratzscher and C. Thimann (2007), 'Home Bias in Global Bond and Equity Markets: The Role of Real Exchange Rate Volatility', *Journal of International Money and Finance*, 26(4): 631–55.

Fidrmuc, J. (2005), 'The Endogeneity of the Optimum Currency Area Criteria and Intra-industry Trade: Implications for EMU Enlargement', in P. De Grauwe and J. Mélitz (eds.), *Prospects for Monetary Unions after the Euro*, Cambridge, MA: MIT Press.

Fiori, G., G. Nicoletti, S. Scarpetta and F. Schiantarelli (2008), 'Employment Outcomes and the Interaction Between Product and Labour Market Deregulation: Are They Substitutes or Complements?', IZA Discussion Papers, 2770.

Fischer, B., M. Lenza, H. Pill and L. Reichlin (2008), 'Money and Monetary Policy: The ECB Experience 1999–2006' in A. Beyer and L. Reichlin (eds.), *The Role of Money: Money and Monetary Policy in the Twenty-first Century*, Frankfurt am Main: ECB, 102–75.

Fischer, J., L. Jonung and M. Larch (2007), '101 Proposals to Reform the Stability and Growth Pact. Why So Many? A Survey', *Public Finance and Management*, 8(3): 502–60.

Fisher, S. J. and M. C. Lie (2004), 'Asset Allocation for Central Banks: Optimally Combining Liquidity, Duration, Currency and Non-Government Risk' in C. Bernadell, P. Cardon, J. Coche, F. X. Diebold and S. Manganelli (eds.), *Risk Management for Central Bank Foreign Reserves*, Frankfurt am Main: ECB.

Flam, H. and H. Nordström (2003), 'Trade Volume Effects of the Euro: Aggregate and Sector Estimates', Stockholm University, Institute for International Economic Studies, Seminar Papers, 746.

Flam, H. and H. Nordström (2006), 'Euro Effects on the Intensive and Extensive Margins of Trade', CESifo Working Papers, 1881.

Flam, H. and H. Nordström (2007), 'The Euro and Single Market Impact on Trade and FDI', mimeo, Stockholm University.

Flandreau, M. (1997), 'The Gradient of a River: Bimetallism as an Implicit Fluctuation Band', mimeo, Paris: Observatoire français des conjonctures économiques.

Flandreau, M. (2000), 'The Economics and Politics of Monetary Unions: A Reassessment of the Latin Monetary Union, 1865–71', *Financial History Review* 7(1): 25–43.

Flandreau, M. (2006), 'The Logic of Compromise: Monetary Bargaining in Austria-Hungary, 1867–1913', CEPR Discussion Papers 5397.

Flandreau, M. and C. Jobst (2005), 'The Ties That Divide. A Network Analysis of the International Monetary System', CEPR Discussion Papers, 5129.

Flandreau, M. and N. Sussman (2005), 'Old Sins: Exchange Clauses and European Foreign Lending in the Nineteenth Century' in B. Eichengreen and R. Hausmann (eds.), *Other People's Money: Debt Denomination and Financial Instability in Emerging Market Economies*, University of Chicago Press, 154–89.

Flandreau, M., J. le Cacheux and F. Zumer (1998), 'Stability Without a Pact? Lessons from the European Gold Standard 1880–1914', *Economic Policy*, **13**(26): 115–52.

Fleming, J. M. (1971), 'On Exchange Rate Unification', *Economic Journal*, **81**(323): 467–88.

Florio, M. (2004), *The Great Divestiture: Evaluating the Welfare Impact of the British Privatizations 1979–1997*, Cambridge, MA: The MIT Press.

Fogel, R. W. (2007), 'Capitalism and Democracy in 2040: Forecasts and Speculations', NBER Working Papers, 13184.

Folkerts-Landau, D. and P. Garber (1992), 'The ECB: A Central Bank or Monetary Policy Rule?' in M. Canzoneri, V. Grillio and P. Masson (eds.), *Establishing a Central Bank: Issues in Europe and Lessons from the US*, Cambridge University Press, 86–110.

Forlati, C. (2007), 'Optimal Monetary Policy in the EMU: Does Fiscal Policy Coordination Matter?', mimeo, Universitat Pompeu Fabra.

Fraas, A. (1974), 'The Second Bank of the United States: An Instrument for an Interregional Monetary Union', *Journal of Economic History* **34**(2): 447–67.

Frankel, J. (1995), 'Still the Lingua Franca: The Exaggerated Death of the Dollar', *Foreign Affairs*, **74**(4): 9–16.

Frankel, J. (1999), 'No Single Currency Regime is Right for All Countries or at All Times', *Princeton Essays in International Finance*, 215, Princeton.

Frankel, J. (2008), 'The Euro Could Surpass the Dollar Within Ten Years', *Vox*, 18 March.

Frankel, J. and A. Rose (1998), 'The Endogeneity of the Optimum Currency Area Criteria', *Economic Journal*, 108(449): 1009–25.

Frankel, J. and A. Rose (2001), 'Estimating the Effect of Currency Unions on Trade and Output', CEPR Discussion Papers, 2631.

Frankel, J. and S.-J. Wei (2007), 'Assessing China's Exchange Rate Regime', *Economic Policy*, **51**: 575–627.

Franks, J., C. Mayer, and S. Rossi (2003), 'Ownership: Evolution and Regulation', ECGI – Finance Working Papers, 09/2003.

Fraser Institute (2007), *Economic Freedom of the World: 2007 Annual Report*, Vancouver, BC.

Fratianni, M. and F. Spinelli (1997), *A Monetary History of Italy*, Cambridge University Press.

Fratzscher, M. (2002), 'Financial Market Integration in Europe: On the Effects of EMU on Stock Markets', *International Journal of Finance and Economics*, 7(3): 165–93.

Frenkel, J. and A. Razin (1987), *Fiscal Policies and the World Economy*, Cambridge, MA: MIT Press.

Friedman, M. (1953), 'The Case for Flexible Exchange Rates', in *Essays in Positive Economics*, University of Chicago Press, 157–203.

Friedman, M. (1977), 'Nobel Lecture: Inflation and Unemployment', *The Journal of Political Economy*, **85**(3): 451–72.

Friedman, M. and A. Schwartz (1963), *Monetary History of the United States, 1867–1960*, Princeton University Press.

Fuest, C. and A. Weichenrieder (2002), 'Tax Competition and Profit Shifting: On the Relationship between Personal and Corporate Tax Rates', CESifo Working Paper, 781.

Fuhrer, J. and G. Moore (1995), 'Inflation Persistence', *Quarterly Journal of Economics*, **110**(1): 197–230.

Gaiotti, E. and F. Lippi (2005), 'Pricing Behavior and Introduction of the Euro: Evidence from a Panel of Restaurants', CEPR Discussion Papers, 4893.

Galati, G. and K. Tsatsaronis (2003), 'The Impact of the Euro on Europe's Financial Markets', *Financial Markets, Institutions & Instruments*, **12**(3): 165–222.

Galí, J. (1994), 'Government Size and Macroeconomic Stability', *European Economic Review*, **38**(1): 117–32.

Galí, J. (2008), *Monetary Policy, Inflation and the Business Cycle: An Introduction to the New Keynesian Framework*, Princeton University Press.

Galí, J. and M. Gertler (1999), 'Inflation Dynamics: A Structural Econometric Analysis', *Journal of Monetary Economics*, **44**(2): 195–222.

Galí, J. and T. Monacelli (2005), 'Monetary Policy and Exchange Rate Volatility in a Small Open Economy', *Review of Economic Studies*, **72**(3): 707–34.

Galí, J. and T. Monacelli (2008), 'Optimal Monetary and Fiscal Policy in a Currency Union', *Journal of International Economics*, **76**: 116–32.

Galí, J. and R. Perotti (2003), 'Fiscal Policy and Monetary Integration in Europe', *Economic Policy*, **18**(37): 533–72.

Galí, J., D. Lopez-Salido and J. Vallés (2007), 'Understanding the Effects Government Spending Shocks on Consumption', *Journal of the European Economic Association*, **5**: 227–70.

Galí, J., S. Gerlach, J. Rotemberg, H. Uhlig and M. Woodford (2004), 'The Monetary Policy Strategy of the ECB Reconsidered', *Monitoring the European Central Bank*, 5, London: CEPR.

Galindo, A. J., F. Schiantarelli and A. Weiss (2007), 'Does Financial Reform Improve the Allocation of Investment? Micro Evidence From Developing Countries', *Journal of Development Economics*, **83**(2): 562–87.

Gallarotti, G. (1995), *The Anatomy of an International Monetary Regime: The Classical Gold Standard 1880–1913*, Oxford University Press.

Garber, P. and M. Spencer (1994), 'The Dissolution of the Austro-Hungarian Empire: Lessons for Currency Reform', Princeton Essays in International Finance, 191.

García, A. and T. Werner (2008), 'Inflation Risk and Inflation-risk Premia', ECB Working Papers, forthcoming.

García, J. A. (2003), 'An Introduction to the ECB's Survey of Professional Forecasters', ECB Occasional Papers, 8.

García, J. A. and A. Manzanares (2007a), 'Reporting Biases and Survey Results – Evidence from European Professional Forecasters', ECB Working Papers, 836.

García, J. A. and A. Manzanares (2007b), 'What Can Probability Forecasts Tell Us About Inflation Risks?', ECB Working Papers, 825.

García-Herrero, A. and P. Wooldridge (2007), 'Global Financial Integration: Progress in Emerging Markets', *BIS Quarterly Review* (September): 57–70.

Garoupa, N. (2004), 'Regulation of Professions in the US and the EU: A Comparative Analysis', *American Law and Economics Association Annual Meeting*, 42.

Gasiorek, M., R. Davidson, S. Davies, B. Lyons, D. Ulph, R. Vaughan and A. Winters (2004), 'The Impact of a Single Currency in Europe on Product Markets: Theory and Evidence' in A. Dierx, F. Ilzkovitz and K. Sekkat (eds.), *European Integration and the Functioning of Product Markets*, Cheltenham: Edward Elgar, chapter 2.

Gaspar, V. (2003), 'The Conduct of Monetary Policy under Uncertainty' in *Monetary Policy and Uncertainty: Adapting to a Changing Economy*, proceedings of a symposium sponsored by the Federal Reserve Bank of Kansas City, Jackson Hole, Wyoming (28–30 August), 249–64.

Gaspar, V. and F. P. Mongelli (2003), 'Monetary Unification and the Single Market' in G. Tumpell-Gugerell and P. Mooslechner (eds.), *Economic Convergence and Divergence in Europe: Growth and Regional Development in an Enlarged European Union*, Cheltenham: Edward Elgar: 24–52.

Gaspar, V., F. Smets and D. Vestin (2006), 'Adaptive Learning, Persistence, and Optimal Monetary Policy', *Journal of the European Economic Association*, **4**(2–3): 376–85.

Gaspar, V., F. Smets and D. Vestin (2007), 'Is Time Ripe for Price Level Path Stability?', ECB Working Paper, 818 forthcoming, in P. Siklos (ed.), *Frontiers in Monetary Policy*, Cambridge University Press.

Gayer, C. (2007), 'A Fresh Look at Business Cycle Synchronization in the Euro Area', *European Economy* – Economic Papers, 287 (Economic and Financial Affairs DG, European Commission).

Geraats, P. M. (2002), 'Central Bank Transparency', *Economic Journal*, **112** (483), F532–65.

Geraats, P. M. (2005), 'Transparency and Reputation: The Publication of Central Bank Forecasts', *Topics in Macroeconomics* 5(1): 1–26.

Geraats, P. M. (2006), 'Transparency of Monetary Policy: Theory and Practice', *CESifo Economic Studies* 52(1): 111–52.

Geraats, P. M., F. Giavazzi and C. Wyplosz (2008), 'Transparency and Governance', *Monitoring the European Central Bank*, 6, London: CEPR.

Gerdesmeier, D., F. P. Mongelli and B. Roffia (2007), 'The Eurosystem, the US Federal Reserve, and the Bank of Japan: Similarities and Differences', *Journal of Money, Credit, and Banking*, **39**(7): 1785–1820.

Gerlach, S. (1999), 'Who Targets Inflation Explicitly?', *European Economic Review*, **43**(7): 1257–77.

Gerlach, S. (2004), 'Interest Rate Setting by the ECB: Words and Deeds', CEPR Discussion Papers, 4775.

Gerlach, S., S. Ramaswamy and M. Scatigna (2006), '150 Years of Financial Market Volatility', *BIS Quarterly Review* (September): 77–91.

Gerlach-Kristen, P. (2004), 'Is the MPC's Voting Record Informative about Future UK Monetary Policy?', *Scandinavian Journal of Economics*, **106** (2), 299–313.

Gersbach, H. and V. Hahn (2005), 'Voting Transparency in a Monetary Union', CEPR Discussion Papers, 5155.

Geyer, A., S. Kossmeier and S. Pichler (2004), 'Measuring Systematic Risk in EMU Government Yield Spreads', *Review of Finance*, **8**(2): 171–97.

Ghironi, F. and M. Melitz (2005), 'International Trade and Macroeconomics Dynamics with Heterogenous Firms', *Quarterly Journal of Economics*, **120**(3): 865–915.

Giannetti, M. and S. Ongena (2007), 'Financial Integration and Firm Performance: Evidence from Foreign Bank Entry in Emerging Markets', *Review of Finance*, **13**(2): 181–223.

Giannone, D. and M. Lenza (2008), 'Conditional Forecasting With Large Bayesian VARs', mimeo, European Central Bank.

Giannone, D. and L. Reichlin (2006a), 'Does Information Help Recovering Structural Shocks from Past Observations?', *Journal of the European Economic Association*, **4**(2–3): 455–65.

Giannone, D. and L. Reichlin (2006b), 'Trends and Cycles in the Euro Area. How Much Heterogeneity and Should We Worry About It?', ECB Working Papers, 595.

Giannone, D., M. Lenza and L. Reichlin (2008a), 'Explaining the Great Moderation: It Is Not the Shocks', ECB Working Papers, 865.

Giannone, D., M. Lenza, and L. Reichlin (2008b), 'Business Cycles in the Euro Area', in A. Alesina and F. Giavazzi (eds.), *Europe and the Euro*, forthcoming, University of Chicago Press for the NBER.

Giavazzi, F. and M. Pagano (1990), 'Can Severe Fiscal Contractions Be Expansionary? Tales of Two Small European Countries', *NBER Macroeconomics Annual*, **5**: 75–116.

Giavazzi, F., T. Jappelli and M. Pagano (2000), 'Searching for Non-Linear Effects of Fiscal Policy: Evidence from Industrial and Developing Countries', *European Economic Review*, **44**(7): 1259–89.

Gieve, J. (2008), 'Sovereign Wealth Funds and Global Imbalances', *Bank of England Quarterly Bulletin*, **2**: 196–202.

Gil-Pareja, S., R. Llorca-Vivero and J. Martınez-Serrano (2008), 'Trade Effects of Monetary Agreements: Evidence for OECD Countries', *European Economic Review*, **52**(4): 733–55.

Giovannini Group (1997), 'The Impact of the Introduction of the Euro on Capital Markets', *European Economy* – Euro Papers, 3 (Economic and Financial Affairs DG, European Commission).

Giovannini Group (1999), 'The EU Repo Markets: Opportunities for Change', *European Economy* – Euro Papers, 30, (Economic and Financial Affairs DG, European Commission).

Giovannini Group (2000), 'Co-ordinated Public Debt Issuance in the Euro Area', (Economic and Financial Affairs DG, European Commission).

Giovannini Group (2002), 'Cross-Border Clearing and Settlement Arrangements in the European Union,' *European Economy* – Economic Papers, 163 (Economic and Financial Affairs DG, European Commission.

Giovannini, A. (1989), 'How Do Fixed Exchange Rate Regimes Work? Evidence from the Gold Standard, Bretton Woods and the European Monetary System' in M. Miller, B. Eichengreen and R. Portes (eds.), *Blueprints for Exchange Rate Management*, New York: Academic Press, 13–42.

Girouard, N. and C. André (2005), 'Measuring Cyclically-adjusted Budget Balances for OECD Countries', OECD Economics Department Working Paper, 434.

Glick, R. and A. Rose (2002), 'Does a Currency Union Affect Trade? The Time Series Evidence', *European Economic Review*, **46**(6): 1125–51.

Gmuer, E. and G. Cavegn (2003), 'A View from the Swiss National Bank' in R. Pringle and N. Carver (eds.), *How Countries Manage Reserve Assets*, London: Central Banking Publications.

Goerke, L. (1999), 'Value-Added Tax versus Social Security Contributions', IZA Discussion Papers, 55.

Goldberg, L. S. (2005), 'Trade Invoicing in the Accession Countries: Are They Suited to the Euro?', NBER Working Papers, 11653.

Goldberg, L. S. and C. D. Kolstad (1995), 'Foreign Direct Investment, Exchange Rate Variability and Demand Uncertainty', *International Economic Review*, **36**(4): 855–73.

Goldberg, L. S. and C. Tille (2008), 'Vehicle Currency Use in International Trade', *Journal of International Economics*, **76**(2): 177–92.

Goldsmith, R. W. (1969), *Financial Structure and Development*, New Haven, CT: Yale University Press.

Gomes, T., C. Graham, J. Helliwell, T. Kano, J. Murray and L. Schembri (2004), 'The Euro and Trade: Is There a Positive Effect?', mimeo, Bank of Canada.

Goodhart, C. and D. Schoenmaker (2006), 'Burden Sharing in a Banking Crisis in Europe', *Sveriges Riksbank Economic Review*, **2**: 34–57.

Gordon, R. H. and J. R. Hines Jr. (2002), 'International Taxation', NBER Working Papers, 8854.

Gordon, R. J. (2004), 'Two Centuries of Economic Growth: Europe Chasing the American Frontier', CEPR Discussion Papers, 4415.

Gordon, R. J. (2006), 'Issues in the Comparison of Welfare Between Europe and the United States', paper presented to the Venice Summer Institute, July.

Gordon, R. J. and I. Dew-Becker (2005), 'Why Did Europe's Productivity Catch-up Sputter Out? A Tale of Tigers and Tortoises', paper presented at the Federal Reserve Bank/CSIP Conference, San Francisco, 18 November.

Gordon, R. J. and J. Hines (2002), 'International Taxation', NBER Working Papers, 8854.

Gordon, R. J. and J. MacKie-Mason (1994), 'Why Is There Corporate Income Taxation in a Small Open Economy? The Role of Transfer Pricing and

Income Shifting', *Issues in International Taxation*, University of Chicago Press, 67–91.

Görg, H. and K. Wakelin (2002), 'The Impact of Exchange Rate Volatility on US Investment, *Manchester School*, **70**(3): 380–97.

Gortler, J., J. Jacobs and J. de Haan (2007), 'Taylor Rules for the ECB Using Consensus Data', De Nederlandsche Bank Working Papers, 160.

Gourinchas, P.-O. and H. Rey (2007a), 'From World Banker to World Venture Capitalist: US External Adjustment and the Exorbitant Privilege' in R. Clarida (ed.), *G7 Current Account Imbalances: Sustainability and Adjustment*, University of Chicago Press.

Gourinchas, P.-O. and H. Rey (2007b), 'International Financial Adjustment', *Journal of Political Economy*, **115**(4): 665–703.

Gourinchas, P.-O., C. Lopez and H. Rey (2007), 'World Bankers', mimeo, Princeton University and University of California at Berkeley.

Graboyes, R. (1990), 'The EMU: Forerunners and Durability', *Economic Review of the Federal Reserve Bank of Richmond*, **76**(4): 8–17.

Graham, L. and S. Wright (2007), 'Nominal Debt Dynamics, Credit Constraints and Monetary Policy', *Contributions to Macroeconomics*, **7**(1): 1502–23.

Grant, C. (2003), 'Estimating Credit Constraints Among US Households', *Oxford Economic Papers*, **59**(4): 583–605.

Greenspan, A. (2004), 'Remarks by Chairman Alan Greenspan at the European Banking Congress 2004', Frankfurt am Main, 19 November.

Grenouilleau, D., M. Ratto and W. Röger (2007), 'Adjustment to Shocks: A Comparison between the Euro Area and the US Using Estimated DSGE Models', paper prepared for the OECD Workshop 'Structural reforms and economic resilience: evidence and policy implications', Paris, 14 June.

Griffith, R., R. Harrison and H. Simpson (2006), 'The Link Between Product Market Reform, Innovation and EU Macroeconomic Performance', *European Economy* – Economic Papers, 243 (Economic and Financial Affairs DG, European Commission).

Griffith, R., S. Redding, and J. Van Reenen (2004), 'Mapping the Two Faces of R&D: Productivity Growth in a Panel of OECD Industries', *Review of Economics and Statistics*, **86**(54): 883–95.

Gros, D. and N. Thygesen (1992), *European Monetary Integration – From the European Monetary System to Economic and Monetary Union*, London: Longman.

Guichard, S., M. Kennedy, E. Wurzel and C. André (2007), 'What Promotes Fiscal Consolidation: OECD Country Experiences', OECD Working Papers, 553.

Guiso, L., P. Sapienza and L. Zingales (2004), 'Does Local Financial Development Matter?', *The Quarterly Journal of Economics*, **119**(3): 929–69.

Guiso, L., P. Sapienza and L. Zingales (2006), 'Does Culture Affect Economic Outcomes?,' *Journal of Economic Perspectives*, **20**(2): 23–48.

Guiso, L., T. Jappelli, M. Padula and M. Pagano (2004), 'Financial Market Integration and Economic Growth in the EU', *Economic Policy*, **19**(40): 523–77.

Haberler, G. (1970), 'The International Monetary System: Some Recent Developments and Discussions' in G. Halm (ed.), *Approaches to Greater Flexibility in Exchange Rates*, Princeton University Press: 115–23.

Hall, R. E. (1978), 'Stochastic Implications of the Life Cycle-Permanent Income Hypothesis: Theory and Evidence', *Journal of Political Economy*, **86**(6): 971–87.

Hall, R. E. and D. W. Jorgensen (1967), 'Tax Policy and Investment Behavior', *American Economic Review*, **57**: 391–414.

Hallerberg, M., R. Strauch and J. von Hagen (2007), 'The Design of Fiscal Rules and Forms of Governance in European Union Countries', *European Journal of Political Economy*, **23**(2): 338–59.

Hallerberg, M. and J. von Hagen, (1999), 'Electoral Institutions, Cabinet Negotiations, and Budget Deficits in the EU' in J. Poterba and J. von Hagen (eds.), *Fiscal Institutions and Fiscal Performance*, University of Chicago Press.

Halling, M., M. Pagano, O. Randl and J. Zechner (2008), 'Where Is the Market? Evidence From Cross-listings in the U.S.', *Review of Financial Studies*, **21**(2): 725–61.

Hammond, G. and J. von Hagen (1998), 'Regional Insurance Against Asymmetric Shocks – An Empirical Study for the EC', *The Manchester School*, **66**: 331–53.

Hardouvelis, G. A., D. Malliaropulos and R. Priestley (2006), 'EMU and European Stock Market Integration', *The Journal of Business*, **79**: 365–92.

Harrison, G. and R. Krelove (2005), 'VAT Refunds: A Review of Country Experience', IMF Working Papers, 218.

Hartland, P. C. (1949), 'Interregional Payments Compared With International Payments', *Quarterly Journal of Economics*, **63**: 392–407.

Hartmann, P. (1998a), *Currency Competition and Foreign Exchange Markets: the Dollar, the Yen and the euro*, Cambridge University Press.

Hartmann, P. (1998b), 'The Currency Denomination of World Trade After European Monetary Union', *Journal of the Japanese and International Economies*, **12**(4): 424–54.

Hartmann, P., A. Maddaloni and S. Manganelli (2003), 'The Euro-area Financial System: Structure, Integration, and Policy Initiatives', *Oxford Review of Economic Policy*, **19**(1): 180–213.

Hartmann, P., F. Heider, E. Papaioannou and M. Lo Duca (2007), 'The Role of Financial Markets and Innovation in Productivity and Growth in Europe', ECB Occasional Papers, 72.

Hau, H. and H. Rey (2004), 'Can Portfolio Rebalancing Explain the Dynamics of Equity Returns, Equity Flows, and Exchange Rates?', *American Economic Review*, **94**(2): 126–33.

Hau, H. and H. Rey (2006), 'Exchange Rates, Equity Prices and Capital Flows', *Review of Financial Studies*, **19**(1): 273–317.

Hau, H., W. Killeen and M. Moore (2002a), 'Has the Euro Changed the Foreign Exchange Market?', *Economic Policy*, **17**(1): 149–92.

Hau, H., W. Killeen and M. Moore (2002b), 'The Euro as an International Currency: Explaining Puzzling First Evidence from the Foreign Exchange Markets', *Journal of International Money and Finance*, **21**(3): 351–83.

Heathcote, J. and F. Perri (2004), 'Financial Globalization and Real Regionalization', *Journal of Economic Theory*, **119**(1): 207–43.

Heinemann, F. and K. Ullrich (2007), 'Does it Pay to Watch Central Bankers' Lips? The Information Content of ECB Wording', *Swiss Journal of Economics and Statistics*, **143**(2): 155–85.

Helleiner, E. (2003), *The Making of National Money: Territorial Currencies in Historical Perspective*, Ithaca: Cornell University Press.

Helpman, E. (1984), 'A Simple Theory of Trade with Multinational Corporations', *Journal of Political Economy*, **92**: 451–71.

Helpman, E. and P. Krugman (1985), *Market Structure and Foreign Trade: Increasing Returns, Imperfect Competition, and the International Economy*, Cambridge, MA: MIT Press.

Helpman, E., M. Melitz and S. Yeaple (2003), 'Export versus FDI', CEPR Discussion Papers, 3741.

Hendriksen, I. and N. Kaergard (1995), 'The Scandinavian Currency Union 1875–1914' in J. Reis (ed.), *International Monetary Standards in Historical Perspective*, London: Palgrave Macmillan: 91–112.

Henry, P. B. (2007), 'Capital Account Liberalization: Theory, Evidence, and Speculation', *Journal of Economic Literature*, **65**(4): 887–935.

Heston, A., R. Summers and B. Aten (2006), *Penn World Table Version 6.2*, Center for International Comparisons of Production, Income and Prices at the University of Pennsylvania.

Hix, S., A. Noury and G. Roland (2007), *Democratic Politics in the European Parliament*, Cambridge University Press.

HM Treasury (1997), *UK Membership of the Single Currency: An Assessment of the Five Economic Tests*, London.

HM Treasury (2003), *UK Membership of the Single Currency: an Assessment of the Five Economic Tests*, London.

Hnatkovska, V. and M. Evans (2007), 'International Financial Integration, Macroeconomic Volatility and Welfare', *Journal of the European Economic Association*, **5**(2–3), 500–8.

Hochreiter, E. and G. Tavlas (2004), 'On the Road Again: An Essay on the Optimal Path to EMU for the New Members States', *Journal of Policy Modeling*, **26**(7): 793–816.

Hodson, D. and I. Maher (2004), 'Soft Law and Sanctions: Economic Policy Coordination and the Reform of the Stability and Growth Pact', *Journal of European Public Policy*, **11**(5): 806–21.

Hoj, J., V. Galasso, G. Nicoletti and T.-T. Dang (2006), 'The Political Economy of Structural Reforms: Empirical Evidence from OECD Countries', OECD Economics Department Working Papers, 29.

Hoj, J., M. Jimenez, M. Maher, G. Nicoletti and M. Wise (2007), 'Product Market Competition in OECD Countries: Taking Stock and Moving Forward', OECD Economics Department Working Paper, 575.

Holland, D. (2007), 'An Estimation of the Factors Driving the Mark-up of Prices over Costs', mimeo, NIESR.

Holtfrerich, C.-L. (1989), 'The Monetary Unification Process in 19th Century Germany: Relevance and Lessons for Europe Today' in M. de Cecco and A. Giovannini (eds.), *A European Central Bank?*, Cambridge University Press: 216–41.

Hoon, H.T. and E.S. Phelps (1996), 'Payroll Taxes and VAT in a Labor-Turnover Model of the "Natural Rate"', *International Tax and Public Finance*, **3**(3): 369–83.

Hördahl, P., O. Tristani and D. Vestin (2006), 'A Joint Econometric Model of Macroeconomic and Term-structure Dynamics', *Journal of Econometrics*, **131**(1–2): 405–44.

Huber, B. (1999), 'Tax Competition and Tax Coordination in an Optimum Income Tax Model', *Journal of Public Economics*, **71**: 441–58.

Hughes Hallet, A., S.E. Hougaard Jensen and C. Richter (2005), 'The European Economy at the Cross Roads: Structural Reforms, Fiscal Constraints and the Lisbon Agenda', *Research in International Business and Finance*, **19**: 229–50.

Hughes Hallett, A., J. Lewis and J. von Hagen (2004), *Fiscal Policy in Europe 1991–2003: An Evidence-based Analysis*, London: CEPR.

Huizinga, H. and J. Voget (2006), 'International Taxation and the Direction and Volume of Cross-border M&As', CEPR Discussion Papers, 5974.

Huizinga, H., L. Laeven and G. Nicodème (2008), 'Capital Structure and International Debt Shifting', *Journal of Financial Economics*, **88**(1): 80–118.

Ilzkovitz, F., Dierx, A. and N. Sousa, (2008), 'An Analysis of the Possible Causes of Product Market Malfunctioning in the EU: First Results for Manufacturing and Service Sectors', *European Economy* – Economic Papers, 336 (Economic and Financial Affairs DG, European Commission).

Ilzkovitz, F., A. Dierx, V. Kovács and N. Sousa (2007), 'Steps Towards a Deeper Economic Integration: The Internal Market in the 21st

Century. A Contribution to the Single Market Review', *European Economy* – Economic Papers, 271 (Economic and Financial Affairs DG, European Commission).

Imbs, J., H. Mumtaz, M. O. Ravn and H. Rey (2004), 'Price Convergence: What's on TV?', mimeo.

Ingram, J. C. (1959), 'State and Regional Payments Mechanisms', *Quarterly Journal of Economics*, **73**(4): 619–32.

Ingram, J. C. (1962), *Regional Payments Mechanisms: The Case of Puerto Rico*, Raleigh: University of North Carolina Press.

Ingram, J. C. (1973), *The Case for European Monetary Integration*, Princeton Essays in International Finance, 98, Princeton University.

Inklaar, R., R. Jong-a-Pin and J. de Haan (2008), Trade and Business Cycle Synchronization in OECD Countries – A Re-examination, *European Economic Review*, **52**(4): 646–66.

International Monetary Fund (2004a), 'Has Fiscal Behaviour Changed Under EMU?', in Chapter 2 of *World Economic Outlook*, September, Washington, DC: International Monetary Fund.

International Monetary Fund (2004b), 'Fostering Structural Reforms in Industrial Countries', *IMF World Economic Outlook*, Chapter 3.

International Monetary Fund (2004c), 'Euro Area Policies: Selected Issues', IMF Country Report, 04/235.

International Monetary Fund (2005), *Annual Report 2005*, Washington, DC: International Monetary Fund.

International Monetary Fund (2007a), 'The Changing Dynamics of the Global Business Cycle', Chapter 2 of the *World Economic Outlook*, Washington, DC: International Monetary Fund.

International Monetary Fund (2007b), *World Economic Outlook*, Washington, DC: International Monetary Fund.

Isgut, A. E. (2004), 'Common Currencies and Market Integration Across Cities: How Strong Is the Link?' in V. Alexander, G. M. Von Furstenberg and J. Mélitz (eds.), *Monetary Unions and Hard Pegs: Effects on Trade, Financial Development, and Stability*, Oxford University Press: 113–33.

Issing, O. (1996), 'Monetary Policy Strategies' in Deutsche Bundesbank (ed.), *Monetary Policy Strategies in Europe*, Munich: 197–202.

Issing, O. (1999a), 'The Monetary Policy of the ECB in a World of Uncertainty', contribution to the policy panel at the conference on 'Monetary Policy-making under Uncertainty' organised by the European Central Bank and the Center for Financial Studies, 3–4 December, Frankfurt am Main.

Issing, O. (1999b), 'The Eurosystem: Transparent and Accountable, or "Willem in Euroland"', *Journal of Common Market Studies*, **37**(3): 503–19.

Issing, O. (2000), 'Communication Challenges for the ECB', Opening Statement at the CFS Research Conference, Frankfurt, 26 June.

Issing, O. (2002), 'On Macroeconomic Policy Co-ordination in EMU', *Journal of Common Market Studies*, **40**: 345–68.

Issing, O. (2008a), *Der Euro: Geburt-Erfolg-Zukunft*, Munich: C.H. Beck-Vahlen. (English version: *The Birth of the Euro*, Cambridge University Press.)

Issing, O. (2008b), 'The Euro – A Currency without a State', CFS Working Papers, 2008/51 (Center for Financial Studies, Goethe University).

Issing, O., V. Gaspar, I. Angeloni and O. Tristani (2001), *Monetary Policy in the Euro Area: Strategy and Decision-making at the European Central Bank*, Cambridge University Press.

Jabko, N. (2003), 'Democracy in the Age of the Euro', *Journal of European Public Policy*, **10**(5): 710–39.

James, H. (1997), *Monetary and Fiscal Unification in Nineteenth Century Germany; What Can Kohl Learn From Bismarck?*, Princeton Essays in International Finance, 202.

James, J. (1976), 'The Development of the National Money Market', *Journal of Economic History*, **36**: 878–97.

Jappelli, T. and M. Pagano (2002), 'Information Sharing, Lending and Defaults: Cross-Country Evidence', *Journal of Banking and Finance* **26**(10): 2017–45.

Jayaratne, J. and P. E. Strahan (1996), 'The Finance-Growth Nexus: Evidence from Bank Branch Deregulation', *Quarterly Journal of Economics*, **111**(3): 639–70.

Jeanneret, A. (2008), 'Foreign Direct Investment and Exchange Rate Volatility: A Non-Linear Story', SSRN eLibrary, available at http://ssrn.com/abstract=967873.

Jonung, L. (2007), 'The Scandinavian Monetary Union, 1873–1924' in P. Cottrell, G. Notaras and G. Tortella (eds.), *From the Athenian Tetradrachm to the Euro*, London: Ashgate: 73–96.

Jonung, L. and M. Larch (2006), 'Improving Fiscal Policy in the EU: The Case for Independent Forecasts', *Economic Policy*, **21**(47): 491–534.

Kalemli-Ozcan, S., B. Sørensen and O. Yosha (2001), 'Economic Integration, Industrial Specialization, and the Asymmetry of Macroeconomic Fluctuations', *Journal of International Economics*, **55**: 107–37.

Kalemli-Ozcan, S., B. Sørensen and O. Yosha (2003), 'Risk Sharing and Industrial Specialization: Regional and International Evidence', *American Economic Review*, **93**(3): 903–18.

Kalemli-Ozcan, S., B. Sørensen and O. Yosha (2005), 'Asymmetric Shocks and Risk Sharing in a Monetary Union: Updated Evidence and Policy Implications for Europe' in H. Huizinga and L. Jonung (eds.), *The Internationalization of Asset Ownership in Europe*, Cambridge University Press.

Kamps, A. (2006), 'The Euro as Invoicing Currency in International Trade', ECB Working Papers, 665.

Keen, M. and M. Syed (2006), 'Domestic Taxes and International Trade: Some Evidence', IMF Working Paper, 47.

Keen, M., S. Smith, R. E. Baldwin, and V. Christiansen (1996), 'The Future of Value Added Tax in the European Union', *Economic Policy*, **11**(23): 373–420.

Kenen, P. (1969), 'The Theory of Optimum Currency Areas: An Eclectic View' in R. Mundell and A. Swoboda (eds.), *Monetary Problems of the International Economy*, University of Chicago Press: 41–61; reprinted in *Exchange Rates and the Monetary System: Selected Essays of Peter B. Kenen*, Aldershot: Edward Elgar (1994): 3–22.

Kenen, P. (1983), 'The Role of the Dollar as an International Currency', Group of Thirty Occasional Paper, 13.

Kenen, P. (1989), *Exchange Rates and Policy Coordination*, Manchester University Press.

Kenen, P. (2003), 'The Euro and the Dollar: Competitors or Complements?' in M. Dumoulin and G. Duchenne (eds.), *The European Union and the United States*, P.I.E.-Peter Lang: Brussels: 251–74.

Kim, C.-J. and C. R. Nelson (1999), 'Has the U.S. Economy Become More Stable? A Bayesian Approach Based on a Markov-Switching Model of the Business Cycle', *The Review of Economics and Statistics*, **81**(4): 608–16.

Kim, D. and C.-I. Lee (2007), 'Government Size and Intersectoral Income Fluctuations: An International Panel Analysis', IMF Working Papers, WP/07/93.

Kim, S. and N. Roubini (2007), 'Twin Deficit or Twin Divergence? Fiscal Policy, Current Account and Real Exchange Rate in the U.S.', *Journal of International Economics*, **74**: 362–83.

Kimbrough, K. P. (1984), 'The Corporation Income Tax in the Open Economy', *International Economic Review*, **25**(2): 391–407.

Kindleberger, C. P. (1973), *The World in Depression, 1929–1939*, Berkeley: University of California Press.

King, R. G. and R. Levine (1993a), 'Finance and Growth: Schumpeter May Be Right', *Quarterly Journal of Economics*, **108**(3): 713–37.

King, R. G. and R. Levine (1993b), 'Finance, Entrepreneurship and Growth', *Journal of Monetary Economics*, **32**(3): 513–42.

Kipling, R. (1900), *From Sea to Sea*, London: Macmillan.

Kirsanova, T. and S. Wren-Lewis (2008), 'Optimal Fiscal Feedback on Debt in an Economy with Nominal Rigidities', mimeo, University of Exeter.

Kirsanova, T., S. J. Stehn and D. Vines (2005), 'A Simple View of the Interactions Between Fiscal Policy and Monetary Policy', *Oxford Review of Economic Policy*, **21**(4): 532–64.

Kirsanova, T., D. Vines and S. Wren-Lewis (2006), 'Credit Constrained Consumers, Inflation Inertia and Instability under Fixed Exchange Rates', mimeo, University of Exeter.

Kirsanova, T., M. Satchi, D. Vines and S. Wren-Lewis (2007), 'Optimal Fiscal Policy Rules in a Monetary Union', *Journal of Money, Credit and Banking*, **39**(7): 1759–84.

Kiss, G., M. Nagy and B. Vonnák (2006), 'Credit Growth in Central and Eastern Europe: Trend, Cycle or Boom?', MNB Working Papers, 2006/10, National Bank of Hungary.

Kiyota, K. and S. Urata (2004), 'Exchange Rate, Exchange Rate Volatility and Foreign Direct Investment', *The World Economy*, **27**(10): 1501–36.

Klapper, L., L. Laeven and R. Rajan (2006), 'Entry Regulation as a Barrier to Entrepreneurship', *Journal of Financial Economics*, **82**(3): 591–629.

Kletzer, K. and J. von Hagen (2001), 'Monetary Union and Fiscal Federalism' in C. Wyplosz (ed.), *The Impact of EMU on Europe and the Developing Countries*, Oxford University Press.

Knetter, M. (1989), 'Price Discrimination by U.S. and German Exporters', *American Economic Review*, **79**(1): 198–210.

Koen, V. and P. van den Noord (2006), 'Fiscal Gimmickry in Europe – One-off Measures and Creative Accounting' in P. Wierts, S. Deroose, E. Flores and A Turrini (eds.), *Fiscal Policy Surveillance in Europe*, Basingstoke: Palgrave Macmillan.

Koeniger, W., M. Leonardi and L. Nunziata (2007), 'Labour Market Institutions and Wage Inequality', *Industrial and Labour Relations Review*, **60**(3): 340–56.

Kok Group (2004), *Facing the Challenge: The Lisbon Strategy for Growth and Employment*, report from the High Level Group chaired by Wim Kok, Luxembourg: OPOCE.

Kollmann, R. (2008), 'Welfare Maximizing Operational Monetary and Tax Policy Rules', *Macroeconomic Dynamics*, **12**: 112–25.

Kose, A. M, C. Otrok and C. H. Whiteman (2003), 'International Business Cycles: World, Region, and Country-Specific Factors', *American Economic Review*, **93**(4): 1216–39.

Kose, A. M., E. Prasad and M. E. Terronoes (2007), 'How Does Financial Globalization Affect Risk Sharing? Patterns and Channels', IZA Discussion Papers, 2903.

Kose, A. M., E. Prasad, K. Rogoff and S.-J. Wei (2006), 'Financial Globalization: A Reappraisal', IMF Working Papers, 06/189.

Koszerek, D., K. Havik, K. McMorrow, W. Röger and F. Schönborn (2007), 'An Overview of the EU KLEMS Growth and Productivity Accounts', *European Economy* – Economic Papers, 290 (Economic and Financial Affairs DG, European Commission).

Koyama, T. and S. Golub (2006), 'OECD's FDI Regulatory Restrictions Index: Revision and Extension to More Economies', OECD Economic Department Working Papers, 525.

Krogstrup, S. and C. Wyplosz (2006), 'A Common Pool Theory of Deficit Bias Correction', CEPR Discussion Papers, 5866.

Krugman, P. (1980), 'Vehicle Currencies and the Structure of International Exchange', *Journal of Money, Credit and Banking*, **12**(3): 513–26.

Krugman, P. (1986), 'Pricing to Market When the Exchange Rate Changes', NBER Working Papers, 1926.

Krugman, P. (1993a), 'Integration, Specialization and Regional Growth: Notes on 1992' in F. Torres and F. Giavazzi (eds.), *Adjustment and Growth in the European Monetary Union*, Cambridge University Press.

Krugman, P. (1993b), 'Lesson of Massachusetts for EMU' in F. Giavazzi and F. Torres (eds.), *The Transition to Economic and Monetary Union in Europe*, Cambridge University Press: 241–61.

Krugman, P. (2007), 'Will There Be a Dollar Crisis?', *Economic Policy*, **51**: 435–67.

Krugman, P. and M. Feldstein (1989), 'International Trade Effects of Value Added Taxation', NBER Working Papers, 3163.

Kydland, F. E., E. C. Prescott (1977), 'Rules Rather Than Discretion: The Inconsistency of Optimal Plans', *Journal of Political Economy*, **85**(3): 473–91.

La Porta, R., F. Lopez-de-Silanes and A Shleifer (1998), 'Law and Finance', *Journal of Political Economy*, **106**(6): 1113–55.

La Porta, R., F. Lopez-de-Silanes, A. Shleifer and R. Vishny (1997), 'Legal Determinants of External Finance', *Journal of Finance*, **52**(3): 1131–50.

Lane, P. (2006a), 'The Real Effects of European Monetary Union', *Journal of Economic Perspectives*, **20**(4): 47–66.

Lane, P. (2006b), 'Global Bond Portfolios and EMU', *International Journal of Central Banking*, **2**: 1–23.

Lane, P. and G.-M. Milesi-Ferretti (2006), 'The External Wealth of Nations Mark II: Revised and Extended Estimates of Foreign Assets and Liabilities, 1970–2004', IMF Working Papers, 06/69.

Lane, P. and S. Wälti (2007), 'The Euro and Financial Integration' in D. Cobham (ed.), *The Travails of the Eurozone: Economic Policies, Economic Developments*, Basingstoke: Palgrave Macmillan: 208–30.

Larch, M. and A. Turrini (2007), 'Spillovers Revisited: Fiscal Policy and Inflation in the Euro Area', *Quarterly Report on the Euro Area* (European Commission), **6**(2): 23–8.

Lasfer, M. (2007), 'Taxes and Ex-Day Returns: Evidence From Germany and the UK', *National Tax Journal*, forthcoming.

Layard, R., S. Nickell and R. Jackman (2005), *Unemployment: Macroeconomic Performance and the Labour Market*, 2nd ed., Oxford University Press (1st edition of 1991).

Lederman, D. and L. Serven (2005), 'Tracking NAFTA's Shadow 10 Years On: Introduction to the Symposium', *World Bank Economic Review*, **19**(3): 335–44.

Leiner-Killinger, N., V. López Pérez, R. Stiegert and G. Vitale (2007), 'Structural Reforms in EMU and the Role of Monetary Policy: A Survey of the Literature', ECB Occasional Papers, 66.

Leitemo, K. (2003), 'Targeting Inflation by Constant-Interest-Rate-Forecasts', *Journal of Money, Credit and Banking*, **35**(4), 609–26.

Lejour, A. and H. Rojas-Romagosa (2008), 'International Spillovers of Domestic Reforms: The Joint Application of the Lisbon Strategy in the EU', Industrial Policy and Economic Reforms Papers, 8 (Enterprise and Industry DG, European Commission).

Levine, R. and S. Zervos (1998), 'Stock Markets, Banks, and Economic Growth', *American Economic Review*, **88**(3): 537–58.

Levy-Yeyati, E. (2006), 'Financial Dollarization: Evaluating the Consequences', *Economic Policy*, **21**(45): 61–118.

Lewis, K. (1999), 'Trying to Explain Home Bias in Equity and Consumption', *Journal of Economic Literature*, **37**(2): 571–608.

Licht, A. (1997), 'Regional Stock Market Integration in Europe', CAER II Discussion Paper, 15 (Harvard University).

Liljeblom, E. and K. Felixson (2008), 'Evidence on Ex-Dividend Trading by Investor Tax Category', *European Journal of Finance*, **14**: 1–21.

Lim, E.-G. (2006), 'The Euro's Challenge to the Dollar: Different Views From Economists and Evidence from COFER (Currency Composition of Foreign Exchange Reserves) and Other Data', IMF Working Papers, 06/153.

Lindert, P. (1969), *Key Currencies and Gold, 1900–1913*, Princeton Studies in International Finance, 24, Princeton Univeristy Press.

Lockwood, B. (2001), 'Tax Competition and Tax Co-ordination under Destination and Origin Principles: a Synthesis', *Journal of Public Economics*, **81**: 279–319.

Lopez, C. (2002), 'The Argentina Crisis: A Chronology of Events after the Sovereign Default,' Standard & Poors, 12 April.

López-Córdova, J. E. and C. Meissner (2000), 'Exchange-Rate Regimes and International Trade: Evidence from the Classical Gold Standard Era', CIDER-IBER Working Papers, 188 (Department of Economics, Univerity of California Berkeley).

Lovasz, A. and S. White (2007), 'Dollar Slumps to Record Low on China's Plans to Diversify Reserves', Bloomberg Report, 7 November.

Lucas Jr., R. E. (1987), *Models of Business Cycles*. Cambridge: MIT Press.

Lucas Jr., R. E. (2003), 'Macroeconomic Priorities', *American Economic Review*, **93**(1): 1–14.

Luenneman, P. and T. Mathae (2005), 'Regulated Services Prices and Inflation Persistence', ECB Working Papers, 466.

Lutz, M. (2003), 'Price Convergence Under EMU? First Estimates', University of St. Gallen Department of Economics Working Papers, 2003–08.

Lyons, R. (2001), *The Microstructure Approach to Exchange Rates*, Cambridge, MA: MIT Press.

Mace, B. J. (1991), 'Full Insurance in the Presence of Aggregate Uncertainty', *Journal of Political Economy*, **99**(5): 928–56.

Maddison, A. (2006), *The World Economy, Volume 1: A Millennial Perspective, Volume 2: Historical Statistics*, Paris: OECD.

Mancini-Griffoli, T. and L. L. Pauwels (2006), 'Is There a Euro Effect on Trade? An Application of End-of-Sample Structural Break Tests for Panel Data', HEI Working Papers, 04–2006 (Graduate Institute of International Studies, Geneva).

Mankiw, N. G. (2001), 'The Inexorable and Mysterious Tradeoff Between Inflation and Unemployment', *The Economic Journal*, **111**: C45–C61.

Markusen, J. R. (2002), *Multinational Firms and the Theory of International Trade*, Cambridge: MIT Press.

Martin, P. and H. Rey (2005), 'Globalization and Emerging Markets: With or Without Crash?', CEPR Discussion Papers, 5165.

Martin, R., M. Roma and I. Vansteenkiste (2005), 'Reforms in Selected EU Network Industries', ECB Occasional Papers, 28.

Martinez-Mongay, C. (2000), 'ECFIN's Effective Tax Rates – Properties and Comparisons with Other Tax Indicators', *European Economy* – Economic Papers, 146 (Economic and Financial Affairs DG, European Commission).

Martinez-Mongay, C. and K. Sekkat (2005), 'Progressive Taxation, Macroeconomic Stabilization and Efficiency in Europe', *European Economy* – Economic Papers, 233 (Economic and Financial Affairs DG, European Commission).

Masson, P. R. and C. Patillo (2004), *The Monetary Geography of Africa*, Washington, DC: The Brookings Institution.

Masson, P. R. (1996), 'Fiscal Dimensions of EMU', *The Economic Journal*, **106**(437): 996–1004.

Masson, P. R. and M. P. Taylor (1993), *Policy Issues in the Operation of Currency Unions*, Cambridge University Press.

Matha, T. I. (2003), 'What to Expect of the Euro? Analyzing Price Differences of Individual Products in Luxembourg and its Surrounding Regions', mimeo.

Mathis, A. (2004), 'VAT Indicators', Taxation Papers, 2 (Taxation and Customs Union DG, European Commission).

Matsuyama, K., N. Kiyotaki and A. Matsui (1993), 'Toward a Theory of International Currency', *Review of Economic Studies*, **60**(2): 283–307.

McCallum, J. (1995), 'National Borders Matter: Canada – US Regional Trade Patterns', *American Economic Review*, **85**(3): 615–23.

McCauley, R. (1997), 'The Euro and the Dollar', Princeton Essays in International Economics, 205, Princeton University Press.

McConnell, M. M. and G. Pérez-Quirós (2000), 'Output Fluctuations in the United States: What Has Changed Since the Early 1980s?', *American Economic Review*, **90**(5): 1464–76.

McGuire, P. and N. Tarashev (2007), 'International Banking With the Euro', *Bank for International Settlements Quarterly Review*, December: 47–61.

McKenzie, M. D. (1999), 'The Impact of Exchange Rate Volatility on International Trade Flows', *Journal of Economic Surveys*, **13**: 71–106.

McKinnon, R. (1963), 'Optimum Currency Areas', *American Economic Review*, **53**: 717–24.

McKinnon, R. (1979), *Money in International Exchange: The Convertible Currency System*, Oxford University Press.

McKinnon, R. (1980), 'Dollar Stabilization and American Monetary Policy', *American Economic Review*, **70**(2): 382–7.

McKinnon, R. (2004), 'Optimum Currency Areas and Key Currencies: Mundell I versus Mundell II', *Journal of Common Market Studies*, **42**(4): 689–715.

McMorrow, K. and W. Röger (2007), 'An Analysis of EU Growth Trends, With a Particular Focus on Germany, France, Italy and the UK', *National Institute Economic Review*, **199**(1): 82–98.

McNamara, K. and S. Meunier (2002), 'Between National Sovereignty and International Power: What External Voice for the Euro?', *International Affairs*, **78**(4): 849–68.

Meade, J. E. (1956), 'The Belgium-Luxembourg Monetary Union, 1921–1939: Lessons from an Early Experiment', Princeton Essays in International Finance, 25, Princeton University Press.

Meade, J. E. (1978a), *The Structure and Reform of Direct Taxation*, London: George Allen & Unwin.

Meade, J. E. (1978b), 'Movements of Capital and of Persons Between a Country With an Income Tax and a Country With an Expenditure Tax Regime' in P. Oppenheimer (ed.), *Issues in International Taxation*, Stocksfield: Oriel Press.

Mehra, Y. P. (2004), 'The Output Gap, Expected Future Inflation and Inflation Dynamics: Another Look', *Topics in Macroeconomics*, **4**(1).

Meissner, C. (2005), 'A New World Order: Explaining the Emergence of the Classical Gold Standard', *Journal of International Economics*, **66**: 305–406.

Mélitz, J. (2004), 'Risk Sharing and EMU', *Journal of Common Market Studies*, Special Issue, **42**(4): 815–40.

Mélitz, J. (2005), 'Non-Discretionary and Automatic Fiscal Policy in the EU and the OECD' in P. Wierts. S. Deroose, E. Flores and A. Turrini (eds.), *Fiscal Policy Surveillance in Europe*, Basingstoke: Palgrave Macmillan.

Mélitz, J. and F. Zumer (1999), 'Interregional and International Risk-Sharing and Lessons for EMU', *Carnegie-Rochester Conference Series on Public Policy*, **51**: 149–88.

Mélitz, J. and F. Zumer (2002), 'Regional Redistribution and Stabilization by the Center in Canada, France, the United Kingdom and the United States: A Reassessment and New Tests', *Journal of Public Economics*, **86**: 263–86.

Melitz, M. J. (2003), 'The Impact of Trade on Intraindustry Reallocations and Aggregate Industry Productivity', *Econometrica*, **71**: 1695–1725.

Melitz, M. J. and G. I. Ottaviano (2008), 'Market Size, Trade and Productivity, *Review of Economic Studies*, **75**(1): 295–316.

Meltzer, A. H. (2003), *A History of the Federal Reserve, Volume 1: 1913–1951*, University of Chicago Press.

Mendoza, E. G., V. Quadrini and J. V. Rios-Rull (2007), 'Financial Integration, Financial Deepness and Global Imbalances', NBER Working Papers, 12909.

Messere, K., F. Kam, and C. J. Heady (2003), *Tax Policy: Theory and Practice in OECD Countries*, Oxford University Press.

Micco, A., E. Stein and G. Ordoñez (2003), 'The Currency Union Effect on Trade: Early Evidence From EMU', *Economic Policy*, **18**: 315–56.

Migué, J.-L. (1993), 'Federalism and Free Trade', Hobart Paper, 122, London: Institute of Economic Affairs.

Miniane, J. (2004), 'A New Set of Measures on Capital Account Restrictions', *IMF Staff Papers*, **51**(2): 276–308.

Mintz, J., E. Zorotheos and D. Chen (2000), 'Taxing Issues with Privatization: A Checklist', World Bank Policy Research Working Paper, 2348.

Mintz, N. N. (1970), 'Monetary Union and Economic Integration', *The Bulletin*, New York University.

Mishkin, F. S. (2007), 'Inflation Dynamics', NBER Working Papers, 13147.

Mitchener, K. J. (2005), 'Bank Supervision, Regulation and Financial Instability During the Great Depression', *Journal of Economic History*, **65**: 152–85.

Modigliani, F. (1977), 'The Monetarist Controversy, or Should We Forsake Stabilization Policies?', *American Economic Review*, **67**: 1–19.

Mongelli, F. P. (2005), 'What is European Economic and Monetary Union (EMU) Telling Us About the Optimum Currency Area Properties?', *Journal of Common Market Studies*, **43**(3): 607–35.

Mongelli, F. P. (2008), 'European Economic and Monetary Integration and the Optimum Currency Area Theory', *European Economy* – Economic Papers, 302 (Economic and Financial Affairs DG, European Commission).

Mongelli, F. P. and J.-L. Vega (2006), 'What Effects Is EMU Having on the Euro Area and its Member Countries', ECB Working Papers, 599.

Mongelli, F. P., E. Dorrucci and I. Agur (2005), 'What Does European Institutional Integration Tell Us About Trade Integration?', ECB Occasional Papers, 40.

Morris, S. and H. S. Shin (2002), 'Social Value of Public Information', *American Economic Review*, **92**(5), 1521–34.

Morris, S. and H. S. Shin (2005), 'Central Bank Transparency and the Signal Value of Prices', *Brookings Papers on Economic Activity*, **2**, 1–66.

Morris, R., H. Ongena and L. Schuknecht (2006), 'The Reform and Implementation of the Stability and Growth Pact', ECB Occasional Papers, 47.

Mortensen, D. T. and C. A. Pissarides (1998), 'Technological Progress, Job Creation and Job Destruction', *Review of Economic Dynamics*, **1**: 733–53.

Moutot, P., A. Jung and F. P. Mongelli (2007), 'The Working of the Eurosystem: Monetary Policy Preparations and Decision-Making – Selected Issues', ECB Occasional Papers, 79.

Mundell, R. (1961), 'A Theory of Optimum Currency Areas', *American Economic Review*, **51**(3): 657–65, reprinted in M. I. Bléjer, D. W. Cheney, J. A. Frenkel, L. Leiderman and A. Razin (eds.) (1997), *Optimum Currency Areas: New Analytical and Policy Developments*, Washington, DC: IMF: 17–28.

Mundell, R. (1973a), 'Uncommon Arguments for Common Currencies' in H. G. Johnson and A. K. Swoboda (eds.), *The Economics of Common Currencies*, London: George Allen and Unwin: 114–32.

Mundell, R. (1973b), 'A Plan for a European Currency' in H. Johnson and A. Swoboda (eds.), *The Economics of Common Currencies*, London: George Allen and Unwin: 143–73.

Mundell, R. (2000), 'Currency Areas, Volatility and Intervention', *Journal of Policy Modeling*, **22**: 281–99.

Mundschenk, S. and W. Münchau (2007), 'Some Thoughts About the Future of the Euro', Euro-Intelligence.

Musgrave, R. (1959), *The Theory of Public Finance – A Study in Public Economy*, New York: McGraw-Hill.

Mussa, M. (2003), *Argentina and the Fund: From Triumph to Tragedy*, Washington, DC: Institute for International Economics.

Neumann, M. J. M. (2009), 'Internationale Finanzkrise und die Geldpolitik den Europäische Zentralbank', *Perspektiven des Wirtschaftspolitik*, **10**(4): 367–88.

Neumann, M. J. M. and C. Greiber (2004), 'Inflation and Core Money Growth in the Euro Area', Bundesbank Discussion Papers, Series 1, 35.

Nickell, S. J. (1997), 'Unemployment and Labour Market Rigidities: Europe versus North America', *Journal of Economic Perspectives*, **11**(3): 55–74.

Nickell, S. J. (2006a), 'Comments on R. Duval and J. Elmeskov, "The Effects of EMU on Structural Reform in Labour and Product Markets"', ECB Working Papers, 596.

Nickell. S. J. (2006b), 'Discussion (Wyplosz: The Dark Sides of a Major Success)', *Economic Policy*, **46**: 247–53.

Nicodème, G. and J.-B. Sauner-Leroy (2007), 'Product Market Reforms and Productivity: A Review of the Theoretical and Empirical Literature on the Transmission Channels', *Journal of Industry, Competition and Trade*, 7(1): 53–72.

Nicoletti, G., R. C. G. Haffner, S. Nickell, S. Scarpetta and G. Zoega (2001), 'European Integration, Liberalization, and Labour Market Performance' in G. Bertola, T. Boeri and G. Nicoletti (eds.), *Welfare and Employment in a United Europe*, MIT Press: 147–235.

Nicolò, G. de, P. Honohan and A. Ize (2005), 'Dollarization of Bank Deposits: Causes and Consequences', *Journal of Banking and Finance*, **29**(7): 1697–1727.

Nuti, M. (2006), 'Alternative Fiscal Rules for the New EU Member States', Kozminski & TIGER Working Papers, 84 (Kozminski Business School).

Nye, J. (1990), *Bound to Lead: The Changing Nature of American Power*, New York: Basic Books.

Nye, J. (2004), *Soft Power: The Means to Success in World Politics*, New York: Public Affairs.

Oates, W. (1972), *Fiscal Federalism*, New York: Harcourt Brace.

Oates, W. and J. Wallis (1998), 'The Impact of the New Deal on American Federalism' in M. D. Bordo, C. Goldin and E. N. White (eds.), *The Defining Moment: The Great Depression and the American Economy in the Twentieth Century*, University of Chicago Press: 155–180.

Obstfeld, M. (1994), 'Are Industrial-Country Consumption Risks Globally Diversified?' in L. Leiderman and A. Razin (eds.), *Capital Mobility: The Impact on Consumption, Investment and Growth*, Cambridge University Press.

Obstfeld, M. and G. Peri (1998), 'Regional Non-Adjustment and Fiscal Policy', *Economic Policy*, **26**: 205–60.

Obstfeld, M. and K. Rogoff (1995), 'Exchange Rate Dynamics Redux', *Journal of Political Economy*, **103**: 624–60.

Obstfeld, M. and K. Rogoff (1996), *Foundations of International Macroeconomics*, Cambridge, MA: MIT Press.

Obstfeld, M. and K. Rogoff (2002), 'Global Implications of Self-Oriented National Monetary Rules', *Quarterly Journal of Economics*, **117**(2): 503–35.

Obstfeld, M. and K. Rogoff (2005), 'Global Current Account Imbalances and Exchange Rate Adjustments', *Brookings Papers on Economics*, **1**: 67–123.

Obstfeld, M. and K. Rogoff (2007), 'The Unsustainable US Current Account Position Revisited' in R. Clarida (ed.), *G7 Current Account Imbalances: Sustainability and Adjustment*, University of Chicago Press.

OECD (1994), *The OECD Jobs Study – Facts, Analysis, Strategies*, Paris: OECD.

OECD (1999), 'Implementing the OECD Jobs Strategy: Assessing Performance and Policy', Paris: OECD.

OECD (2000), 'Competition in Professional Services', DAFFE/CLP(2000)2.

OECD (2001a), 'Productivity and Firm Dynamics: Evidence from Micro Data', *OECD Economic Outlook*, **69**: 209–23.

OECD (2001b), *Taxing Wages 2000/2001*, Paris: OECD.

OECD (2004), *Employment Outlook*, Paris: OECD.

OECD (2007a), *Taxing Wages 2006/2007*, Paris: OECD.

OECD (2007b), 'OECD Workers in the Global Economy: Increasingly Vulnerable?', in *OECD Employment Outlook*, Paris: OECD.

OECD (2007c), *Going for Growth 2007*, Paris: OECD.

OECD (2008), *Going for Growth 2008*, Paris: OECD.

Ogus, A. (1995), 'Rethinking Self-Regulation', *Oxford Journal of Legal Studies*, **15**: 97–108.

Orphanides, A. (2003), 'Historical Monetary Policy Analysis and the Taylor Rule', *Journal of Monetary Economics*, **50**(5): 983–1022.

Orphanides, A. (2006), 'The Road to Price Stability', *American Economic Review*, **96**(2): 178–81.

Orphanides, A. and J. Williams (2005), 'Imperfect Knowledge, Inflation Expectations and Monetary Policy' in B. Bernanke and M. Woodford (eds.), *The Inflation Targeting Debate*, University of Chicago Press, 201–34.

Orphanides, A. and J. Williams (2008), 'Learning, Expectations Formation, and the Pitfalls of Optimal Control Monetary Policy', *Journal of Monetary Economics*, **55**: S80–96.

Otrok, C. (2001), 'On Measuring the Welfare Cost of Business Cycles', *Journal of Monetary Economics*, **47**(1): 61–92.

Padoa-Schioppa, T. (1982), 'Mobilita'dei Capitali: Perche la Comunita e' Inadempiente?' in T. Padoa-Schioppa, *La Lunga Via Per l'Euro*, Bologna: Il Mulino.

Padoa-Schioppa, T. (2004), *The Euro and its Central Bank: Getting United After the Union*. Cambridge, MA: MIT Press.

Padoa-Schioppa, T. (2007), 'Europe Needs a Single Financial Rulebook', *Financial Times*, 10 December.

Pagan, A. (1984), 'Econometric Issues in the Analysis of Regressions with Generated Regressors', *International Economic Review*, 25(1): 221–47.

Pagano, M. (1993), 'Financial Markets and Growth: An Overview', *European Economic Review*, 37(2–3): 613–22.

Pagano, M. and E.-L. von Thadden (2004), 'The European Bond Markets under EMU', *Oxford Review of Economic Policy*, 20(4): 531–54, reprinted in X. Freixas, P. Hartmann and C. Mayer (eds.) *Handbook of European Financial Markets and Institutions*, Oxford University Press (2008).

Pagano, M., A. A. Röell and J. Zechner (2002), 'The Geography of Equity Listing: Why Do Companies List Abroad?', *Journal of Finance*, 57(6): 2651–94.

Pagano, M., O. Randl, A. A. Röell and J. Zechner (2001), 'What Makes Stock Exchanges Succeed? Evidence From Cross-listing Decisions', *European Economic Review*, 45(4–6): 770–82.

Pain, N. (2002), 'EMU, Investment and Growth: Some Unresolved Issues', *National Institute Economic Review*, 180(1): 96–108.

Pain, N. and K. Wakelin (1998), 'Export Performance and the Role of Foreign Direct Investment', *The Manchester School of Economic and Social Studies*, 66(0): 62–88.

Pain, N. and G. Young (2003), 'The Macroeconomic Impact of UK Withdrawal From the EU, *Economic Modelling*, 21(3): 387–408.

Panetta, F., P. Angelini, G. Grande, A. Levy, R. Perli, P. Yesin, S. Gerlach, S. Ramaswamy and M. Scatigna (2006), 'The Recent Behaviour of Financial Market Volatility', BIS Papers, 29.

Panic, M. (1992), *European Monetary Union: Lessons from the Gold Standard*, London: Macmillan.

Papademos, L. (2003), 'Economic Cycles and Monetary Policy', speech delivered at the International Symposium of the Banque de France on 'Monetary Policy, the Economic Cycle and Financial Dynamics', 7 March.

Papademos, L. (2007), 'The Financial Market Turmoil, the European Economy, and the Role of the European Central Bank', Speech to the European Institute, New York, 27 September.

Papaioannou, E. (2005), 'What Drives International Bank Flows? Politics, Institutions and Other Determinants', ECB Working Papers, 437.

Papaioannou, E., R. Portes and G. Siourounis (2006), 'Optimal Currency Shares in International Reserves: The Impact of the Euro and the Prospects for the Dollar', *Journal of the Japanese and International Economies*, 20(4): 508–47.

Papaioannou, E., R. Portes and G. Siourounis (2008), 'Allocation of International Reserves Across Asset Classes', mimeo, London Business School.

Parsley, D. C. and S.-J. Wei (2001), 'Limiting Currency Volatility to Stimulate Goods Market Integration: A Price Based Approach', NBER Working Papers, 8468.

Paterson, I., M. Fink and A. Ogus (2003), 'Economic Impact of Regulation in the Field of Liberal Professions in Different Member States', study for the European Commission, Vienna: Institute of Advanced Studies.

Pelkmans, J. (2006), 'Testing for Subsidiarity', Bruges European Economic Policy Briefings, 13 (College of Europe).

Pelkmans, J. (2007), 'Deepening Services Market Integration, a Critical Assessment, *Romanian Journal of European Affairs*, 7(4): 5–32.

Pelkmans, J. (2008), 'How to Measure Product Market Reforms – Pitfalls and Progress', Bruges, forthcoming.

Perotti, R. (2005), 'Estimating the Effects of Fiscal Policy in OECD Countries', CEPR Discussion Papers, 4842.

Perotti, R. (2007), 'In Search of the Transmission Mechanism of Fiscal Policy', NBER Working Papers, 13143.

Persson, T. and G. Tabellini (1996a), 'Federal Fiscal Constitutions: Risk Sharing and Moral Hazard', *Econometrica*, 64: 623–46.

Persson, T. and G. Tabellini (1996b), 'Federal Fiscal Constitutions: Risk Sharing and Redistribution', *Journal of Political Economy*, 104: 979–1009.

Pesaran, H. and R. P. Smith (1995), 'Estimating Long-run Relationships from Dynamic Heterogeneous Panels', *Journal of Econometrics*, 68: 79–113.

Petroulas, P. (2007), 'The Effect of the Euro on Foreign Direct Investment', *European Economic Review*, 51(6): 1468–91.

Phelps, E. S. (1994), *Structural Slumps, the Modern Equilibrium Theory of Unemployment, Interest and Assets*, Cambridge MA: Harvard University Press.

Pichelmann, K. and W. Röger (2007), 'Employment and Labour Productivity in the EU: Reconsidering a Potential Trade-off in the Lisbon Strategy', in B. Eichengreen, M. Landesmann and D. Stiefel (eds.) *The European Economy in an American Mirror*, Routledge: 128–42.

Pisani-Ferry, J. (2002), 'Fiscal Discipline and Policy Coordination in the Eurozone: Assessment and Proposals' in *Budgetary Policy in E(M)U, Design and Challenges*, proceedings of a seminar held at the Dutch Ministry of Finance.

Pisani-Ferry, J. (2006a), 'Only One Bed for Two Dreams: A Critical Retrospective on the Debate Over the Economic Governance of the Euro Area', *Journal of Common Market Studies*, 44(4): 823–44.

Pisani-Ferry, J. (2006b), 'Mediocre Growth in the Euro Area: Is Governance Part of the Answer?', Bruegel Policy Contribution, 1.

Pisani-Ferry, J. and A. Sapir (2006), 'Last Exit to Lisbon', Bruegel Policy Briefs, 2006/02.

Pisani-Ferry, J., A. Italianer and R. Lescure (1993), 'Stabilization Properties of Budgetary Systems: A Simulation Analysis', in 'The Economics of Community Public Finance', *European Economy*, 5: 417–55.

Pisani-Ferry, J., P. Aghion, M. Belka, J. von Hagen, L. Heikensten and A. Sapir (rapporteur: A. Ahearne) (2008), *Coming of Age: Report on the Euro Area*, Brussels: Bruegel Blueprint, 4.

Piscitelli, L. (2003), 'EMU and Trade', background study for the HM Treasury's assessment on the euro, mimeo.

Pissarides, C. A. (1998), 'The Impact of Employment Tax Cuts on Unemployment and Wages: The Role of Unemployment Benefits and Tax Structure', *European Economic Review*, 42(1): 155–83.

Portes, R. (2002), 'The euro and the international financial system', in M. Buti and A. Sapir (eds.), *EMU and Economic Policy in Europe: The Challenge of the Early Years*, Edward Elgar, 334–56.

Portes, R. (2007), 'Sovereign Wealth Funds', *Real IR*, September.

Portes, R. (2008), 'ISK or Euro – Not Both!', address to Iceland Chamber of Commerce annual meeting, Reykjavik, 13 February.

Portes, R. and F. Baldursson (2007), *The Internationalisation of Iceland's Financial Sector*, Reykjavik: Iceland Chamber of Commerce.

Portes, R. and H. Rey (1998), 'The Emergence of the Euro as an International Currency', *Economic Policy*, 26(1): 305–43.

Portes, R. and H. Rey (2005), 'The Determinants of Cross-border Equity Flows', *Journal of International Economics*, 65(2): 269–96.

Posen, A. (2007a), 'The Euro', *New Palgrave Dictionary of Economics*, 2nd edn.

Posen, A. (2007b), 'Not Yet for the Euro', Peterson Institute.

Prati, A. and G. Schinasi (1999), 'Financial Stability in European Economic and Monetary Union', Princeton Studies in International Financc, 86.

Pringle, R. and N. Carver (2003), 'How Countries Manage Reserve Assets' in R. Pringle and N. Carver (eds.), *How Countries Manage Reserve Assets*, London: Central Banking Publications.

Pringle, R. and N. Carver (2005), 'Trends in Reserve Management – Survey Results' in R. Pringle and N. Carver (eds.), *Reserve Management Trends*, London: Central Banking Publications.

Pritchett, L. (1997), 'Divergence, Big-Time', *Journal of Economic Perspectives*, 11(3): 3–17.

Proudman, J. and S. Redding (1998), *Openness and Growth*, Bank of England.

Puetter, U. (2004), 'Governing Informally: The Role of the Eurogroup in EMU and the Stability and Growth Pact', *Journal of European Public Policy*, 11: 854–70.

Rajan, R. G. (2005), 'Has Financial Development Made the World Riskier?' NBER Working Papers, 11728.

Rajan, R. G. and L. Zingales (1998), 'Financial Dependence and Growth', *American Economic Review*, **88**(3): 559–87.

Rajan, R. G. and L. Zingales (2003a), 'The Great Reversals: The Politics of Financial Development in the 20th Century', *Journal of Financial Economics*, **69**(1): 5–50.

Rajan, R. G. and L. Zingales (2003b), 'Banks and Markets – The Changing Character of European Finance' in V. Gaspar, P. Hartmann and O. Sleijpen (eds.), *The Transformation of the European Financial System*, Frankfurt am Main: European Central Bank.

Ramey, G. and V. A. Ramey (1995), 'Cross-Country Evidence on the Link Between Volatility and Growth', *American Economic Review*, **85**(5): 1138–51.

Ramey, V. A. (2006), 'Identifying Government Spending Shocks: It's All in the Timing', mimeo, University of California, San Diego.

Ratto, M., W. Röger and J. in 't Veld (2008), 'An Estimated DSGE Model of the Euro Area With Fiscal and Monetary Policy', *European Economy* – Economic Papers, 335 (Economic and Financial Affairs DG – European Commission).

Ravn, M., S. Schmitt-Grohé and M. Uribe (2007), 'Explaining the Effects of Government Spending Shocks on Consumption and the Real Exchange Rate', NBER Working Papers, 13328.

Redish A. (2000), *Bimetallism: An Economic and Historical Analysis*, Cambridge University Press.

Redoano, M. (2007), 'Fiscal Interactions Among European Countries: Does the EU Matter?', CESifo Working Paper Series, 1952.

Reichlin, L. (2006), 'Panel's Remark' in 'Financial Market and the Real Economy in a Low Interest Rate Environment', *Monetary and Economic Studies* (Institute for Monetary and Economic Studies, Bank of Japan), **24** (S-1): 247–52.

Rey, H. (2001), 'International Trade and Currency Exchange', *Review of Economic Studies*, **68**(2): 443–64.

Ricci, L. (1998), 'Uncertainty, Flexible Exchange Rates and Agglomeration', IMF Working Paper, 98/9.

Robson, P. (1987), *The Economics of International Integration*, London: Allen and Unwin.

Rockoff, H. (1974), 'The Free Banking Era: A Reexamination', *Journal of Money, Credit and Banking*, **6**: 141–67.

Rockoff, H. (2003), 'How Long Did It Take the United States to Become an Optimal Currency Area?' in F. Capie (ed.), *Monetary Unions: Theory, History, Public Choice*, London: Routledge: 76–104.

Rodden, J. A. (2004), 'Achieving Fiscal Discipline in Federations: Germany and the EMU', paper prepared for 'Fiscal Policy in EMU: New Issues and Challenges', workshop organised by European Commission, Brussels, 12 November.

Rodden, J. (2006), 'Achieving Fiscal Discipline in Federations: Germany and the EMU' in P. Wierts, S. Deroose, E. Flores and A. Turrini, *Fiscal Policy Surveillance in Europe*, Basingstoke: Palgrave Macmillan, 137–60.

Rodrik, D. (1998a), 'Why Do More Open Economies Have Bigger Governments?', *Journal of Political Economy*, **106**(5): 997–1032.

Rodrik, D. (1998b), 'Who Needs Capital Account Convertibility?', in *Should the IMF Pursue Capital Account Convertibility*, Essays in International Finance, 207, Princeton University.

Rogers, J. H. (2002), 'Monetary Union, Price Level Convergence, and Inflation: How Close Is Europe to the United States?', International Finance Discussion Papers, 740 (Board of Governors of the Federal Reserve System).

Rogoff, K. (2006), 'Impact of Globalization on Monetary Policy' in *The New Economic Geography*, Federal Reserve Bank of Kansas City: 265–305.

Rogoff, K., M. A. Kose, E. S. Prasad and S.-J. Wei (2006), 'Financial Globalization: A Reappraisal', IMF Working Papers, 06/189.

Rolnick, A. and W. Weber (1983), 'New Evidence on the Free Banking Era', *American Economic Review*, **73**: 1080–91.

Rolnick, A., B. Smith and W. Weber (1993), 'In Order to Form a More Perfect Monetary Union', *Federal Reserve Bank of Minneapolis Quarterly Review*, **17**: 2–13.

Romer, C. D. (1999), 'Changes in Business Cycles: Evidence and Explanations', *Journal of Economic Perspectives*, **13**(2): 23–44.

Romer, C. D. and D. H. Romer (2007), 'The Macroeconomic Effects of Tax Changes: Estimates Based on a New Measure of Fiscal Shocks', NBER Working Paper, 13264.

Rosa, C. and G. Verga (2005), 'Is ECB Communication Effective?', CEP Discussion Paper, 682 (Centre for Economic Performance).

Rose, A. (2000), 'One Money, One Market: Estimating the Effect of Common Currencies on Trade', *Economic Policy*, **30**: 9–45.

Rose, A. (2004), 'A Meta-Analysis of the Effect of Common Currencies on International Trade', NBER Working Papers, 10373

Rose, A. (2006), 'A Stable International Monetary System Emerges: Inflation Targeting Is Bretton Woods, Reversed', NBER Woking Papers, 12711.

Rose, A. and T. D. Stanley (2005), 'A Meta-Analysis of the Effects of Common Currencies on International Trade', *Journal of Economic Surveys*, **19**(3): 347–65.

Rotemberg, J. J. and M. Woodford (1997), 'An Optimization Based Econometric Framework for the Evaluation of Monetary Policy' in

B.S. Bernanke and J.J. Rotemberg (eds.), *NBER Macroeconomics Annual 1997*: 297–345.

Roubini, N. (2007), 'The Instability of the Bretton Woods 2 Regime,' *RGE Monitor*, July.

Roubini, N. and B. Setser (2005), 'The US Twin Deficits and External Debt Accumulation: Are They Sustainable?', working paper, Stern School of Business.

Roush, J. (2007), 'The Expectations Theory Works for Monetary Policy Shocks', *Journal of Monetary Economics*, **54**(6): 1631–43.

Royal Bank of Scotland (2003), 'How Countries Manage Reserve Assets' in R. Pringle and N. Carver (eds.), *RBS Reserve Management Trends 2003*, London: Central Banking Publications.

Royal Bank of Scotland (2005), 'Reserve Management Trends Assets' in R. Pringle and N. Carver (eds.), *RBS Reserve Management Trends 2005*, London: Central Banking Publications.

Royal Bank of Scotland (2006), 'Reserve Management Trends Assets' in R. Pringle and N. Carver (eds.), *RBS Reserve Management Trends 2006*, London: Central Banking Publications.

Royal Bank of Scotland (2007), 'Reserve Management Trends Assets' in R. Pringle and N. Carver (eds.), *RBS Reserve Management Trends 2007*, London: Central Banking Publications.

Russ, K.N. (2007), 'Exchange Rate Volatility and First-time Entry by Multinational Firms', NBER Working Papers, 13659.

Sahuc, J.G. and F. Smets (2007), 'Differences in Interest Rate Policy at the ECB and the Fed: An Investigation with a Medium-Scale DSGE Model', *Journal of Money, Credit and Banking*, **40**(2–3), 505–21.

Saint-Paul, G. (2004), 'Why Are European Countries Diverging in Their Unemployment Experience?', *Journal of Economic Perspectives*, **18**(4): 49–68.

Sala-i-Martin, X. and J. Sachs (1992), 'Fiscal Federalism and Optimum Currency Areas: Evidence for Europe From the United States' in M. Canzoneri, V. Grilli and P. Masson (eds.), *Establishing a Central Bank: Issues in Europe and Lessons From the U.S.*, Cambridge University Press.

Samuelson P.A. (1954), 'The Pure Theory of Public Expenditure', *The Review of Economics and Statistics*, **36**(4): 387–9.

Sapir, A. (2006), 'Is the Euro Ready for a Global Role?', *Europe's World*, **2**: 56–61.

Sapir, A. (2007), 'Europe and the Global Economy' in A. Sapir (ed.), *Fragmented Power: Europe and the Global Economy*, Brussels: Bruegel.

Sapir, A., P. Aghion, G. Bertola, M. Hellwig, J. Pisani-Ferry, D. Rosati, J. Viñals and H. Wallace, with M. Buti, M. Nava and P.M. Smith (2004), *An Agenda for a Growing Europe: The Sapir Report*, Oxford University Press.

Sargent, T. and N. Wallace (1981), 'Some Unpleasant Monetarist Arithmetic', *Federal Reserve Bank of Minneapolis Quarterly Review*, **5**(3): 1–17.

Sarno, L. and M. Taylor (2003), *The Economics of Exchange Rates*, Cambridge University Press.

Sauer, S. and J. E. Sturm (2007), 'Using Taylor Rules to Understand European Central Bank Monetary Policy', *German Economic Review*, **8**(3): 375–98.

Sbordone, A. (2007), 'Globalization and Inflation Dynamics: The Impact of Increased Competition', NBER Working Papers, 13556.

Schadler, S., A. Mody, A. Abiad and D. Leigh (2006), 'Growth in the Central and Eastern European Countries of the European Union', IMF Occasional Papers, 252.

Schadler, S., P. Drummond, L. Kuijs, Z. Murgasova and R. van Elkan (2005), 'Euro Adoption in the Accession Countries: Vulnerabilities and Strategies' in S. Schadler (ed.), *Euro Adoption in Central and Eastern Europe: Opportunities and Challenges*, Washington, DC: IMF.

Scharpf, F. W. (1999), *Governing in Europe: Effective and Democratic*, Oxford University Press.

Scheve, K. and M. J. Slaughter (2004), 'Economic Insecurity and the Globalization of Production', *American Journal of Political Science*, **48**(4): 662–74.

Schiantarelli, F. (2005), 'Product Market Regulation and Macroeconomic Performance: A Review of Cross-Country Evidence', *World Bank Policy Research Working Paper*, 3770.

Schiavo S. (2007), 'Common Currencies and FDI flows', *Oxford Economic Papers*, **59**: 536–60.

Schinasi, G. (2007), 'Resolving EU Financial-Stability Challenges: Is a Decentralized Decision-Making Approach Efficient?', mimeo, IMF.

Schinasi, G. and P. G. Teixeira (2006), 'The Lender of Last Resort in the European Single Financial Market', IMF Working Papers, 06/127.

Schmitt-Grohé, S. and M. Uribe (2006), 'Optimal Fiscal and Monetary Policy in a Medium-Scale Macroeconomic Model', *NBER Macroeconomics Annual*, 383–425.

Schuknecht, L. (2005), 'Stability and Growth Pact: Issues and Lessons from Political Economy', *International Economics and Political Economy*, **2**: 65–89.

Sekkat, K. and O. Galgau (2001), 'The Impact of the Single Market on Foreign Direct Investment in the European Union', mimeo, Université Libre de Bruxelles.

Setser, B. (2008), 'What to Do with Over a Half a Trillion a Year? Understanding the Changes in the Management of China's Foreign Assets', *RGE Monitor*, 15 January.

Shiller, R. (1979), 'The Volatility of Long Term Interest Rates and Expectations Models of the Term Structure', *Journal of Political Economy*, **87**: 1190–219.

Silgoner, M. A, G. Reitschuler and J. Crespo-Cuaresma (2003), 'Assessing the Smoothing Impact of Automatic Stabilizers: Evidence from Europe' in G. Tumpel-Gugerell and P. Mooslechner (eds.), *Structural Challenges for Europe*, Cheltenham: Edward Elgar.

Silva, J. A. da (2004), 'Determinants of the Choice of Invoicing Currency: From Dutch Guilders to Euros in Dutch Goods Trade', mimeo, Tilburg University.

Simmons, R. S. (2006), 'Does Recent Empirical Evidence Support the Existence of International Corporate Tax Competition?', *Journal of International Accounting, Auditing and Taxation*, **15**(1): 16–31.

Simonetta, A. (2007), *The Impact of Taxes on Corporate Financial Decisions: An Empirical Analysis of Euro-area Data*, PhD thesis, Universita' Cattolica, Milano.

Sinn, H. W. (1985), 'Why Taxes Matter: Reagan's Accelerated Cost Recovery System and the US Trade Deficit', *Economic Policy*, **1**(1): 240–50.

Sinn, H. W. (2003), *The New Systems Competition*, Oxford: Basil Blackwell.

Slemrod, J. (2004), 'Are Corporate Tax Rates, or Countries, Converging?', *Journal of Public Economics*, **88**(6): 1169–86.

Smets, F. and R. Wouters (2004), 'Forecasting With a Bayesian DSGE Model. An Application to the Euro Area', *Journal of Common Market Studies*, **42**(4): 841–67.

Smets, F. and R. Wouters (2007), 'Shocks and Frictions in US Business Cycles: A Bayesian DSGE Approach', *American Economic Review*, **97**: 586–606.

Smiley, G. (1975), 'Interest Rate Movements in the United States, 1888–1913', *Journal of Economic History*, **35**: 591–620.

Snow, J. (2006), Interview with Bloomberg TV, 13 January.

Snowden, K. (1995a), 'The Evolution of Interregional Mortgage Lending Channels, 1870–1940: The Life Insurance-Mortgage Company Connection' in N. Lanoreaux and D. Raff (eds.), *Coordination and Information: Historical Perspectives on the Organization of Enterprise*, University of Chicago Press: 209–56.

Snowden, K. (1995b), 'Mortgage Securitization in the United States: Twentieth Century Developments in Historical Perspective' in M. Bordo and R. Sylla (eds.), *Anglo-American Financial Systems*, New York: Irwin: 261–98.

Solow, R. M. (2002), 'Is Fiscal Policy Possible? Is It Desirable?', Presidential address to the XIII World Congress of the International Economic Association, Lisbon.

Sørensen, B. E. and O. Yosha (1997), 'Federal Insurance of US States: An Empirical Investigation' in A. Razin and E. Sadka (eds.), *Globalization: Public Economics Policy Perspectives*, Cambridge University Press.

Sørensen, B. E. and O. Yosha (1998), 'International Risk Sharing and European Monetary Unification', *Journal of International Economics*, **45**: 211–38.

Sørensen, B. E. and O. Yosha (2000), 'Is Risk Sharing in the United States a Regional Phenomenon?', *Federal Reserve Bank of Kansas City Economic Review*, **85**: 33–47.

Sørensen, B. E., Y.-T. Wu, O. Yosha and Y. Zhu (2007), 'Home Bias and International Risk Sharing: Twin Puzzles Separated at Birth', *Journal of International Money and Finance*, **26**(4): 587–605.

Sørensen, P. B. (2007), 'Can Capital Income Taxes Survive? And Should They?', *CESifo Economic Studies*, **53**(2): 172–228.

Spector, D. (2002), 'Competition and the Capital-Labour Conflict', CEPREMAP Working Papers, 0207.

Stark, J. (2008a), 'The Adoption of the Euro', Address to Iceland Chamber of Commerce annual meeting, Reykjavik, 13 February.

Stark, J. (2008b), 'Monetary Policy during the Financial Turmoil: What Have we Learned?', speech delivered at 'The ECB and its Watchers' conference, Frankfurt am Main (5 September).

Steinsson, J. (2003), 'Optimal Monetary Policy in an Economy With Inflation Persistence', *Journal of Monetary Economics*, **50**: 1425–56.

Stewart, K. and M. Webb (2006), 'International Competition in Corporate Taxation: Evidence from the OECD Time Series', *Economic Policy*, **21**(45): 153–201.

Stiglitz, J. and A. Weiss (1988), 'Credit Rationing in Markets With Asymmetric Information', *American Economic Review*, **71**: 393–410.

Stock, J. H. and M. Watson (2003), 'Has the Business Cycle Changed? Evidence and Explanations' in *Monetary Policy and Uncertainty: Adapting to a Changing Economy*, a symposium sponsored by the Federal Reserve Bank of Kansas City, Jackson Hole, Wyoming: 9–56.

Stock, J. H. and M. Watson (2005), 'Understanding Changes in International Business Cycle Dynamics', *Journal of the European Economic Association*, **3**(5): 966–1006.

Stockman, A. C. (1998), 'New Evidence Connecting Exchange Rates to Business Cycles', *Economic Quarterly* (Federal Reserve Bank of Richmond), **84**(2): 73–89.

Stulz, R. (1999), 'Globalization of Equity Markets and the Cost of Capital', *Journal of Applied Corporate Finance*, **12**(3): 8–25.

Summers, L., J. Gruber and R. Vergara (1993), 'Taxation and the Structure of Labour Markets: The Case of Corporatism', *Quarterly Journal of Economics*, **108**(2): 385–411.

Sushka, M. E. and B. W. Barrett (1984), 'Banking Structure and the National Capital Market 1869–1914', *Journal of Economic History*, **44**: 463–77.

Sutherland, A. (2004), 'International Monetary Policy Coordination and Financial Market Integration', CEPR Discussion Paper 4251.

Svaleryd, H. and J. Vlachos (2005), 'Financial Markets, the Pattern of Specialization, and Comparative Advantages: Evidence from OECD Countries', *European Economic Review*, **49**(1): 113–44.

Svensson, L. E. O. (2003), 'In the Right Direction, But Not Enough: The Modification of the Monetary-Policy Strategy of the ECB', briefing paper for the Committee on Economic and Monetary Affairs of the European Parliament.

Svensson, L. E. O. and M. Woodford (2005), 'Implementing Optimal Monetary Policy Through Inflation-Forecast Targeting' in B. S. Bernanke and M. Woodford (eds.), *The Inflation Targeting Debate*, University of Chicago Press.

Swanson, E. T. (2006), 'Have Increases in Federal Reserve Transparency Improved Private Sector Interest Rate Forecasts?', *Journal of Money, Credit and Banking* **38**(3), 791–819.

Swoboda, A. (1968), *The Euro-Dollar Market: An Interpretation*, Essays in International Finance, 64, Princeton.

Sylla, R. (1969), 'Federal Policy, Banking Market Structure, and Capital Mobilization in the United States, 1863–1913', *Journal of Economic History*, **29**: 657–86.

Szapáry, G. (2000), 'Maastricht and the Choice of Exchange Rate Regime in Transition Countries During the Run-Up to EMU', Magyar Nemzeti Bank (Central Bank of Hungary) Working Papers, 7.

Tabellini, G. and C. Wyplosz (2006), 'Supply-side Coordination in the European Union', *Swedish Economic Policy Review*, **13**: 101–56.

Tanzi, V. and L. Schuknecht (2000), *Public Spending in the 20th Century*, Cambridge University Press.

Task Force of the Monetary Policy Committee of the ESCB (2006), 'Competition, Productivity and Prices in the Euro Area Services', ECB Occasional Papers, 44.

Tavlas, G. S. (1991), *On the International Use of Currencies: the Case of the Deutsche Mark*, Princeton Studies in International Economics, 181, Princeton University.

Tavlas, G. S. (1993), 'The "New" Theory of Optimum Currency Areas', *The World Economy*, **16**(6): 663–85.

Tavlas, G. S. (1994), 'The Theory of Monetary Integration', *Open Economies Review*, **5**(2): 211–30.

Tavlas, G. S. (1998), 'Was the Monetarist Tradition Invented?', *Journal of Economic Perspectives*, **12**(4): 211–22.

Taylor, A. (2008a), 'Trade and Financial Sector Reforms: Interactions and Spillovers', paper presented at the IMF Conference on the Causes and Consequences of Structural Reforms (Washington, DC, 28–9 February).

Taylor, C. (2008b), 'Foreign Direct Investment and the Euro: The First Five Years', *Cambridge Journal of Economics*, **32**(1): 1–28.

Tesar, L.L. and I.M. Werner (1995), 'Home Bias and High Turnover', *Journal of International Money and Finance*, **14**(4): 467–92.

Tilford, S. (2006), *Will the Euro Zone Crack?*, London: Centre for European Reform.

Toloui, R. (2007), 'Petrodollars, Asset Prices and the Global Financial System', PIMCO Report, January.

Toniolo, G., L. Conte and G. Vecchi (2003), 'Monetary Union, Institutions and Financial Market Integration: Italy 1862–1905', CEPR Discussion Papers, 3684.

Tower, E. and T. Willett (1976), 'The Theory of Optimum Currency Areas and Exchange Rate Flexibility', Special Papers in International Economics, 11, Princeton University.

Townsend, R. (1994), 'Risk and Insurance in Village India', *Econometrica*, **62**(3): 539–91.

Tressel, T. (2008), 'Unbundling the Effects of Reforms', paper presented at the IMF conference on the Causes and Consequences of Structural Reforms (Washington, DC, 28–9 February).

Trichet, J.-C. (2003), 'The ECB's Monetary Policy Strategy after the Evaluation and Clarification of May 2003', speech at the 'Frankfurter Finanzgespräch' organised by the Konrad Adenauer Stiftung, Frankfurt am Main (27 November).

Trichet, J.-C. (2004), 'Issues in Monetary Policy: Views from the ECB', speech delivered at the luncheon organised by the Economic Club of New York, New York (26 April).

Trichet, J.-C. (2008a), 'Risk and the Macro Economy', keynote address at the conference 'The ECB and its Watchers', Frankfurt am Main (5 September).

Trichet, J.-C. (2008b), 'Keynote Speech at the Second Symposium of the ECB-CFS Research network on "Capital Markets and Financial Integration in Europe"', 13 February, Frankfurt am Main: European Central Bank.

Triffin, R. (1960), *Gold and the Dollar Crisis*, Yale University Press.

Truman, E. (2005a), 'Comment on "Will the Euro Eventually Surpass the Dollar as Leading International Reserve Currency?"' in R. Clarida (ed.), *G7 Current Account Imbalances: Sustainability and Adjustment*, University of Chicago Press.

Truman, E. (2005b), 'Postponing Global Adjustment – An Analysis of the Pending Adjustment of Global Imbalances', Institute for International Economics Working Papers, 05–6.

Truman, E. and A. Wong (2006), 'The Case for an International Reserve Diversification Standard', Institute for International Economics Working Papers, 06–2.

Tsenova, T. (2008), 'Are Long-term Inflation Expectations in the Euro Area Well Anchored? Evidence from the Survey of Professional Forecasters', mimeo, European Central Bank.

Uhlig, H. (2002), 'One Money, But Many Fiscal Policies in Europe: What Are the Consequences?', CEPR Discussion Papers, 3296.

Uhlig, H. (2008), 'Monetary Policy in Europe versus the US: What Explains the Difference?' in J. Galí and M. Gertler (eds.), *The International Dimension of Monetary Policy*, University of Chicago Press.

Van den Noord, P. (2002), 'Automatic Stabilizers in the 1990s and Beyond', in M. Buti, J. von Hagen and C. Martinez-Mongay (eds.), *The Behaviour of Fiscal Authorities – Stabilization, Growth and Institutions*, Basingstoke: Palgrave Macmillan.

Van den Noord, P. and B. Cournède (2006), 'Short-term Pain for Long-term Gain: The Impact of Structural Reform on Fiscal Outcomes in EMU', OECD Working Papers, 522.

Van den Noord, P., B. Döhring, S. Langedijk, J. Nogueira Martins, L. Pench, H. Temprano-Arroyo and M. Thiel (2008), 'The Evolution of Economic Governance in EMU', *European Economy* – Economic Papers, 328 (Economic and Financial Affairs DG, European Commission).

Van der Cruijsen, C. and M. Demertzis (2007), 'The Impact of Central Bank Transparency on Inflation Expectations', *European Journal of Political Economy*, **23**(1): 51–66.

Van Wincoop, E. (1994), 'Welfare Gains from International Risk Sharing', *Journal of Monetary Economics*, **34**(2): 75–200.

Van Wincoop, E. (1995), 'Regional Risksharing', *European Economic Review*, **39**: 1545–68.

Verde, A. (2006), 'The Old and the New Stability and Growth Pact, along with the Main Proposals for its Reform: An Assessment', *Transition Economies Review*, **13**: 475–96.

Vinhas de Souza, L. (2002), 'Trade Effects of Monetary Integration in Large, Mature Economies – A Primer on European Monetary Union', Kiel Working Papers, 1137.

Violi, R. (2004), 'Tax Systems, Financial Integration and Efficiency of European Capital Markets', Quaderni di Ricerche, 58 (Ente per gli Studi Monetari, Bancari e Finanziari Luigi Einaudi).

von Hagen, J. (1992), 'Fiscal Arrangements in a Monetary Union – Some Evidence from the US' in D. Fair and C. de Boissieux (eds.), *Fiscal Policy, Taxes, and the Financial System in an Increasingly Integrated Europe*, Deventer: Kluwer Academic Publishers.

von Hagen, J. (2000), 'Fiscal Policy and Intranational Risk Sharing' in G. D. Hess and E. van Wincoop (eds.), *Intranational Macroeconomics*, Cambridge University Press: 272–94.

von Hagen, J. (2007), 'Achieving Economic Stabilization by Risk Sharing Within Countries' in R. Boadway and A. A. Shah (eds.), *Intergovernmental Fiscal Transfers: Principles and Practice*, Washington, DC: World Bank.

von Hagen, J. and S. Mundschenk (2003), 'Fiscal and Monetary Policy Co-ordination in EMU', *International Journal of Finance and Economics*, **8**: 279–95.

von Hagen, J. and M. J. M. Neumann (1994), 'Real Exchange Rates Within and Between Currency Areas: How Far Away Is EMU', *Review of Economics and Statistics*, **76**(2): 236–44.

von Hagen, J. and M. J. M. Neumann (1996), 'A Framework for Monetary Policy under EMU' in Deutsche Bundesbank (ed.), *Monetary Policy Strategies in Europe*, Munich: 141–65.

von Hagen, J. and I. Traistaru-Siedschlag (2006), 'Macroeconomic Adjustment in the New EU Member States', SUERF Studies, 2006/4.

von Peter, G. (2007), 'International Banking Centres: A Network Perspective', *Bank for International Settlements Quarterly Review*: 33–45.

Wei, S.-J. (1996), 'Intra-national Versus International Trade: How Stubborn Are Nations in Global Integration?', NBER Working Papers, 5531.

Wei, S.-J. (1999), 'Currency Hedging and Goods Trade', *European Economic Review*, **43**: 1371–94.

Weichenrieder, A. (1996), 'Anti-Tax Avoidance Provisions and the Size of Foreign Direct Investment', *International Tax and Public Finance*, **3**(1): 67–81.

Weichenrieder, A. (2005), '(Why) Do We Need Corporate Taxation?', CESifo Working Papers, 1495.

Werner, P. (1970), 'Report to the Council and the Commission on the Realisation of Economic and Monetary Union in the Community ("Werner Report")', *Bulletin of the European Communities*, Supplement, 11–1970.

Westaway, P. (2003), 'Modelling Shocks and Adjustment Mechanisms in EMU', *EMU Study*, London: HM Treasury.

Weyerstrass, K., K. Schoors and B. van Aarle (2008), 'Economic Spillovers, Structural Reforms and Policy Coordination in the Euro-area: An Overview', in B. van Aarle and K. Weyerstrass (eds.), *Economic Spillovers, Structural Reforms and Policy Coordination in the Euro Area*, Heidelberg: Physika-Verlag.

Wheelock, D. C. (2000), 'National Monetary Policy by Regional Design: The Evolving Role of the Federal Reserve System Policy', in J. von Hagen and C. Waller (eds.), *Regional Aspects of Monetary Policy in Europe*, Boston: Kluwer.

White, E. N. (1983), *The Regulation and Reform of the American Banking System, 1900–1929*, Princeton University Press.

Wickens, M. R. (2007), 'Is the Euro Sustainable?', CEPR Discussion Papers, 6337.

Wilander, F. (2004), 'An Empirical Analysis of the Currency Denomination in International Trade', mimeo, Stockholm School of Economics.

Wildasin, D. E. (2000), 'Factor Mobility and Fiscal Policy in the EU: Policy Issues and Analytical Approaches', *Economic Policy*, 15(31): 337–78.

Williamson, J. (2005), 'The Potential of International Policy Coordination', Paper for 'Implications for the IMF's Role in Surveillance and Policy Coordination', roundtable on International Economic Cooperation for a Balanced World Economy, Chongqing, China, 12–13 March.

Woodford, M. (2001), 'Fiscal Requirements for Price Stability', *Journal of Money, Credit and Banking*, 33: 669–728.

Woodford, M. (2003), *Interest and Prices: Foundations of a Theory of Monetary Policy*, Princeton University Press.

Woodford, M. (2006), 'How Important Is Money in the Conduct of Monetary Policy?', NBER Working Papers, 13325.

World Bank (2007a), *Doing Business 2007 – How to Reform*, Washington, DC: World Bank.

World Bank (2007b), 'Credit Expansion in Emerging Europe: A Cause for Concern?', *Regular Economic Report*, Part II: Special Topic, January.

Wren-Lewis, S. (2002), 'The Limits of Discretionary Fiscal Stabilisation Policy', *Oxford Review of Economic Policy*, 16: 92–105.

Wren-Lewis, S. (2003), 'Changing the Rules: Why We Should Not Accede to EMU's Current Fiscal Regime', *New Economy*, 10: 73–8.

Wright, G. (1986), *Old South, New South, New York Revolutions in the Southern Economy Since the Civil War*, New York: Norton.

Wright, S. (2004), 'Monetary Stabilisation With Nominal Asymmetries', *Economic Journal*, 114: 196–222.

Wyplosz, C. (1991), 'Monetary Union and Fiscal Policy Discipline', *European Economy*, 1: 165–84.

Wyplosz, C. (2005), 'Fiscal Policy: Institutions Versus Rules', *National Institute Economic Review*, 191: 64–78.

Wyplosz, C. (2006), 'European Monetary Union: The Dark Sides of a Major Success', *Economic Policy*, 46: 207–47.

Zhang, L. H. (2001), 'Did European Integration Attract More Foreign Direct Investment?', mimeo, John Hopkins University.

Zhou, R. (1997), 'Currency Exchange in a Random Search Model', *Review of Economic Studies*, 64: 289–310.

Index